Brief Contents

College Accounting

A Practical Approach

CHAPTERS 1–25

Eleventh Edition

Jeffrey Slater

North Shore Community College
Danvers, Massachusetts

Prentice Hall

Boston   Columbus   Indianapolis   New York   San Francisco   Upper Saddle River
Amsterdam   Cape Town   Dubai   London   Madrid   Milan   Munich   Paris
Montreal   Toronto   Delhi   Mexico City   Sao Paulo   Sydney   Hong Kong   Seoul
Singapore   Taipei   Tokyo

To Nanny Shelley
With Love,
Papa Jeff

Library of Congress Cataloging-in-Publication Data information is available.

VP/Editorial Director: Natalie Anderson
AVP/Executive Editor: Jodi McPherson
Development Editor: Karen Misler
Assistant Editor: Melissa Arlio
Editorial Assistant: Christina Rumbaugh
AVP/Director of Marketing: Kate Valentine
Senior Marketing Manager: Maggie Moylan Leen
Marketing Assistant: Justin Jacob
Senior Managing Editor: Cynthia Zonneveld
Project Manager: Rhonda Aversa
Senior Operations Specialist: Nick Sklitsis
Senior Art Director: Jonathan Boylan
Text and Cover Designer: Kathy Mrozek
Manager, Visual Research: Beth Brenzel

Photo Researcher: Rachel Lucas
Manager, Rights and Permissions: Zina Arabia
Image Permission Coordinator: Joanne Dippel
Manager, Cover Visual Research & Permissions: Karen Sanatar
Cover Art: © Shutterstock ®
AVP/Director of Product Development: Lisa Strite
Media Editors: Ashley Lulling/Allison Longley
Media Project Manager, Production: John Cassar
Full-Service Project Management: GEX Publishing Services
Composition: GEX Publishing Services
Printer/Binder: Courier/Kendallville
Cover Printer: Lehigh-Phoenix Color/Hagerstown
Text Font: Times Roman 10/12

Pearson Education LTD.
Pearson Education Singapore, Pte. Ltd
Pearson Education, Canada, Ltd
Pearson Education–Japan

Pearson Education Australia PTY, Limited
Pearson Education North Asia Ltd
Pearson Educación de Mexico, S.A. de C.V.
Pearson Education Malaysia, Pte. Ltd

Prentice Hall
is an imprint of

www.pearsonhighered.com

10 9 8 7 6 5 4 3 2 1
ISBN 10: 0-13-606380-2
ISBN 13: 978-0-13-606380-3

Contents

A Memo from the Desk of Jeff Slater . . .

I asked: "What do *college accounting* students really need to know?"

You told me: "Less is more . . . . They just need to *get it*."

I said: "Agreed, but tell me more about *it*."

"It" is

- Basic accounting concepts and processes
- Plenty of ways to practice
- Basic overview of accounting in technologically driven 2009 and beyond

I really listened to you and, in this edition of *College Accounting, A Practical Approach 11e,* I give your students three ways to really "get" accounting like they need to. I thought about "less is more" and took out any material that didn't absolutely focus students on learning accounting. Just by quickly flipping through this edition of my book, you'll see crystal-clear graphics, lots of white space, and new, relevant content.

I also thought about you, the instructor, and "less is more." So no more will you need to fill a cart with your instructor resources. Now you'll have an instructor's edition of the text with teaching notes, tips, and solutions . . . all in an easy-to-use, online format. But I'm getting ahead of myself. All the information you really need can be found on the next few pages.

Get "IT" from IN-CHAPTER LEARNING TOOLS

- **Accounting Cycle Tutorial:** Online practice and review of the accounting cycle. Margin logos direct students to the appropriate ACT section and material. The tutorial provides review, application, and practice. Available in Chapters 1–5.
- **Learning Unit Reviews:** Each chapter is organized into small, bite-sized units. Students are introduced to a new concept in the learning unit, and then they can immediately test their understanding in the learning unit review.
- **Need Help?:** This new feature has been added to each self-review quiz at the end of each learning unit for the first five chapters. This feature is like a private tutoring session with the author, as he anticipates students' questions and walks them through the provided solution, step by step. These Need Help? sections are provided for the first five chapters of the book, as they are the key to retention.
- **Chapter Opening Did You Know?:** Each chapter opens with some new and interesting information about a recognizable company. Each opener is accompanied by a matching photo.
- **Margin Notes:** Short, sweet, and to the point. They're not found on every page; instead they're provided only when a study hint is really needed.
- **In-Text Practice Set:** The in-text Sullivan Realty Practice Set (Chapter 5) enables students to complete two cycles of transactions (in your choice of manual or Peachtree/Quickbooks format).

Get "IT" from END-OF-CHAPTER PRACTICE MATERIAL

- **Student Demonstration Problem/Accounting Cycle Review:** Students need practice in order to master the accounting cycle. This problem is designed around the *Steps in the Accounting Cycle* and can be found at the ends of Chapters 1–5.
- **Blueprint:** A visual summary of the chapter. Students can use it as a roadmap to review what they have learned. It stresses when to perform specific activities.
- **Classroom Demonstration Exercises:** Short exercises (A and B sets) that can be assigned or used in class for difficult topics.
- **Learning Objectives:** A learning objective number and the average time to complete each exercise is now included for all end-of-chapter material.
- **Exercises:** Short exercises that can be assigned or used in class to focus on building skills.
- **Group A and Group B Problems:** Approximately 20% of the problems have been updated for this edition.
- **On the Job Applications:** Real-world scenarios that challenge students to think and act like managers.
- **Financial Report Problem:** Students use the annual financial report of Kellogg's Company (found in Appendix A) to apply theory and applications completed in the chapter.
- **Internet Project:** A new feature that directs students to the Web site of the chapter opening company to find more information.
- **Discussion Questions:** Include ethical questions and critical thinking questions.
- **Computerized Accounting:** Selected end-of-chapter problems can be completed with Peachtree or Quickbooks.
- **Continuing Problem (Sanchez Computer Center):** Students follow the activities of a single company and then are asked to apply concepts to solve specific accounting problems for the company. Problems can be found in Chapters 1–13 and can be solved manually or by using Peachtree or Quickbooks.
- **Computer Workshops:** Seven computer workshops (for Peachtree and QuickBooks) have been added with detailed step-by-step instructions on how to take a manual problem from the end of the chapter and computerize it in both types of software.

  Students need to do accounting manually before they can use the computer. These workshops allow the student to see how fast accounting theory and procedures can be done on the computer. They will need these computer skills when applying for jobs in the field.

  These workshops assume no computer knowledge and provide adjunct and full time faculty a step-by-step teaching package. Each step tells the student (or instructor) exactly what to press on the computer along with detailed explanations of what should print out. Initial instructions appear in the textbook itself and then students are led to the computer to do the actual work online.

- **MyAccountingLab:** Give your students the power of practice! *College Accounting* is now available with MyAccountingLab, an online homework and assessment software for accounting that not only gives students more "I Get It" moments, but also gives instructors the flexibility to make technology an integral part of their course, or a supplementary resource for students. MyAccountingLab content is available for Chapters 1–5 of the student textbook, where students need the most practice. All end-of-chapter Demonstration Exercises, Exercises, Problems, and Continuing Problems in Chapters 1–5 are included.

Special Section for Current Users

Thank you for your continued use of Slater's *College Accounting*. To ease your transition, here are highlights of chapter changes for the 11th edition.

Chapter 1 Accounting Concepts and Procedures

- New chapter opener on Best Buy, with Did You Know? information
- New Need Help? sections to explain the solutions to the learning unit quizzes
- New Internet project

Chapter 2 Debits and Credits: Analyzing and Recording Business Transactions

- New chapter opener on Staples, with Did You Know? information
- New Need Help? sections
- New Internet project

Chapter 3 Beginning the Accounting Cycle

- New chapter opener on Continental Airlines, with Did You Know? information
- New Need Help? sections
- New Internet project
- New Computer Workshop follows Chapter 3

Chapter 4 The Accounting Cycle Continued

- New chapter opener on Black & Decker, with Did You Know? information
- New Need Help? sections
- New Internet project
- New Computer Workshop after Chapter 4

Chapter 5 The Accounting Cycle Completed

- New chapter opener on Amazon, with Did You Know? information
- New Need Help? sections
- New Internet project
- Updated 2008 numbers for the Sullivan Realty Mini-Practice set
- New Computer Workshop after Chapter 5

Chapter 6 Banking Procedure and Control of Cash

- New chapter opener on Bankrate, Inc., with Did You Know? information
- Updated information on trends in banking
- New Internet project

Chapter 7 Calculating Pay and Payroll Taxes: The Beginning of the Payroll Process

- New chapter opener on Johnson & Johnson, with Did You Know? information
- Updated figures and tables throughout to include 2008 rates
- Continued focus on integrating role of employee and employer
- New Internet project

Chapter 8 Paying, Recording, and Reporting Payroll and Payroll Taxes: The Conclusion of the Payroll Process

- New chapter opener on Coca-Cola, with Did You Know? information
- Updated figures and tables throughout to include 2008 rates
- New tax forms updated along with streamlined discussion of payroll deposits
- New Internet project
- New Computer Workshop after Chapter 8

Chapter 9 Sales and Cash Receipts

- New chapter opener on Big Lots, with Did You Know? information
- Special journals moved to an appendix at the end of Chapter 10
- New Internet project

Chapter 10 Purchases and Cash Payments

- New chapter opener on Del Monte, with Did You Know? information
- Clarification of periodic versus perpetual methods of inventory
- New Internet project
- Special journal appendix now appears at the end of Chapter 10
- New Computer Workshop after Chapter 10

Chapter 11 Preparing a Worksheet for a Merchandise Company

- New chapter opener on Build-a-Bear, with Did You Know? information
- More detailed explanation of merchandise inventory adjustment
- New Internet project

Chapter 12 Completion of the Accounting Cycle for a Merchandise Company

- New chapter opener on Chiquita, with Did You Know? information
- New Internet project
- New Computer Workshop after Chapter 12

Chapter 13 Accounting for Bad Debts

- New chapter opener on eBay, with Did You Know? information
- New end-of-chapter blueprint
- New Internet project

Chapter 14 Notes Receivable and Notes Payable

- New chapter opener on Aeropostale, with Did You Know? information
- New Internet project

Chapter 15 Accounting for Merchandise Inventory

- New chapter opener on ExxonMobil, with Did You Know? information
- Expanded coverage of calculations for perpetual inventory
- New Internet project
- New Computer Workshop after Chapter 15

Chapter 16 Accounting for Property, Plant, Equipment, and Intangible Assets

- New chapter opener on Wendy's, with Did You Know? information
- Deleted section on sum of years' depreciation method
- New Internet project

Chapter 17 Partnership

- New chapter opener on the IRS, with Did You Know? information
- Clearer explanation of the use of negative signs
- New Internet project

Chapter 18 Corporations: Organizations and Stock

- New chapter opener on Hormel Foods, with Did You Know? information
- Clearer discussion of par value
- New Internet project

Chapter 19 Corporations: Stock Values, Dividends, Treasury Stock, and Retained Earnings

- New chapter opener on Sara Lee, with Did You Know? information
- Updated figures
- New Internet project

Chapter 20 Corporations and Bonds Payable

- New chapter opener on Anheuser-Busch, with Did You Know? information
- New Internet project

Chapter 21 Statement of Cash Flows

- New chapter opener on PepsiCo, with Did You Know? information
- New "big picture" introduction to explain direct versus indirect method
- Many new visuals
- New Internet project

Chapter 22 Analyzing Financial Statements

- New chapter opener on Garmin, with Did You Know? introduction
- Clearer discussion of industrial ratio standards
- New Internet project

Chapter 23 The Voucher System

- New chapter opener on Office Depot, with Did You Know? information
- New Internet project

Chapter 24 Departmental Accounting

- New chapter opener on Federated Department Stores, with Did You Know? information
- New Internet project

Chapter 25 Manufacturing Accounting

- New chapter opener on Revlon, with Did You Know? information
- New Internet project

For Instructors

Instructor's Resource Center (IRC): Register. Redeem. Login.

www.pearsonhighered.com/slater is where instructors can access a variety of print, media, and presentation resources available with this text in downloadable, digital format. For most texts, resources are also available for course management platforms such as Blackboard, WebCT, and Course Compass.

It gets better. Once you register, you will not have additional forms to fill out or multiple usernames and passwords to remember to access new titles and/or editions. As a registered faculty member, you can log in directly to download resource files and receive immediate access and instructions for installing course management content to your campus server.

Need help? Our dedicated technical support team is ready to assist instructors with questions about the media supplements that accompany this text. Visit http://247pearsoned.custhelp.com for answers to frequently asked questions and toll-free user support phone numbers.

The following supplements are available to adopting instructors. For detailed descriptions, please visit: www.pearsonhighered.com/slater.

Instructor's Resource Center (IRC) online: Login at www.pearsonhighered.com/slater.
Instructor's Resource CD-ROM: ISBN: 0-13-6065694
Chapters 1–12 with Study Guide and Working Papers: 0-13-606566X
Study Guide and Working Papers (Chapters 1–12): 0-13-606572-4
Study Guide and Working Papers (Chapters 13–25): 0-13-606571-6
Instructor's Edition with Solutions: Visit the IRC for this supplement.
TestGen Test Generating Software: Visit the IRC for this supplement.

Test Item File: Visit the IRC for this supplement.
Working Papers in Excel format: Visit the IRC for this supplement.
PowerPoint Presentation Slides: Visit the IRC for this supplement.

MyAccountingLab is a Web-based tutorial and assessment software for accounting that not only gives students more "I Get It" moments, but also gives instructors the flexibility to make technology an integral part of their course, or a supplementary resource for students.

MyAccountingLab provides instructors with a rich and flexible set of course materials, along with course-management tools that make it easy to deliver all or a portion of the course online.

- Powerful homework and test manager
- Comprehensive gradebook tracking
- Department-wide solutions

For Students

Textbook Volumes

Textbook Chapters 1–25: ISBN 0-13-606380-2 *Includes payroll and additional blank worksheets
Textbook Chapters 1–12: ISBN 0-13-606566-X *Includes study guide and working papers for Chapters 1–12

Print Study Aids

Study Guide and Working Papers Chapters 1–12: ISBN 0-13-606572-4
Study Guide and Working Papers Chapters 13–25: ISBN 0-13-606571-6

MyAccountingLab provides students with a personalized interactive learning environment where they can learn at their own pace and measure their progress.

Key Student Features:

- Accounting cycle video tutorial
- Interactive tutorial exercises
- Multimedia learning aids including author and topic videos
- Study plan for self-paced learning
- Full e-text and e-study guide
- RSS feeds for ABC News in accounting and finance

Online Resources

www.pearsonhighered.com/slater contains valuable resources for both students and professors. Don't forget to preview the Accounting Cycle Tutorial and additional NEW videos on the Companion Web site.

Who I Listened To

Reviewers

Terry Aime, Delgado Community College
Cornelia Alsheimer, Santa Barbara City College
Julia Angel, North Arkansas College

Julie Armstrong, St. Clair County Community College
Marjorie Ashton, Truckee Meadows Community College

John Babich, Kankakee Community College
Cecil Battiste, Valencia Community College
Donald Benoit, Mitchell College
Peggy A. Berrier, Ivy Technical State College
Michelle Berube, Everest University
Anne Bikofsky, College of Westchester
Michael Bitting, John A. Logan College
David Bland, Cape Fear Community College
Suzanne Bradford, Angelina College
Beverly Bugay, Tyler Junior College
Gary Bumgarner, Mountain Empire Community College
Betsy Crane, Victoria College
Noel Craven, El Camino College
Don Curfman, McHenry County College
John Daugherty, Pitt Community College
Susan Davis, Green River Community College
Michael Discello, Pittsburgh Technical Institute
Sylvia Dorsey, Florence-Darlington Technical College
Sid Downey, Cochise College
Donna Eakman, Great Falls College of Technology
Steven Ernest, Baton Rouge Community College
John Evanson, Williston State College
Marilyn Ewing, Seward County Community College
Nancy Fallon, Albertus Magnus College
Nicole Fife, Bucks County Community College
Brian Fink, Danville Area Community College
Paul Fisher, Rogue Community College
Carolyn Fitzmorris, Hutchinson Community College
Trish Glennon, Central Florida Community College
Nancy Goehring, Monterey Peninsula College
Jane Goforth, North Seattle Community College
Lori Grady, Bucks County Community College
Gretchen Graham, Community College of Allegheny County
Marina Grau, Houston Community College
Mary Jane Green, Des Moines Area Community College
Joyce Griffin, Kansas City Kansas Community College
Becky Hancock, El Paso Community College
Toni Hartley, Laurel Business Institute
Raymond Hartman, Triton Community College
Scott Hays, Central Oregon Community College
Kathy Hebert, Louisiana Technical College
Sueanne Hely, West Kentucky Community & Technical College
Maggie Hilgart, Mid-State Technical College
Michele Hill, Schoolcraft College
Michelle Hoeflich, Elgin Community College
Mary Hollars, Vincennes University

Donna Jacobs, University of New Mexico-Gallup
Judy Jager, Pikes Peak Community College
Jane Jones, Mountain Empire Community College
Jenny Jones, Central Kentucky Technical College
Patrick Jozefowicz, Southwest Wisconsin Technical College
Nancy Kelly, Middlesex Community College
Karen Kettelson, Western Wisconsin Technical College
Elizabeth King, Sacramento City College
Ken Koerber, Bucks County Community College
David Krug, Johnson County Community College
Christy Land, Catawba Valley Community College
Ronald Larner, John Wood Community College
Lee Leksell, Lake Superior College
Lolita Lockett, Florida Community College at Jacksonville
Sue Mardock, Colby Community College
John Masserwick, Five Towns College
Pam Mattson, Tulsa Community College
Bonnie Mayer, Lakeshore Technical College
Sally McMillin, Katharine Gibbs School
John Miller, Metropolitan Community College
Cora Newcomb, Technical College of Lowcountry
Jon Nitschke, Great Falls Technical College
Lorinda Oliver, Vermont Technical College
Barbara Pauer, Gateway Technical College
Nicholas Peppes, St. Louis Community College
Richard Pettit, Mountain View College
Lisa Phillips, City College
Margaret Pollard, American River College
Shirley Powell, Arkansas State University
Claudia Quinn, San Joaquin Delta College
Jerry Rhodes, Daymar College
Ed Richter, Southeast Technical Institute
Alberta Robinson, Indiana Business College
Beth Sanders, Hawaii Community College
Bob Sanner, Central Community College
Debra Schmidt, Cerritos College
Karen Scott, Bates Technical College
Carolyn Seefer, Diablo Valley College
Jeri Spinner, Idaho State University
Alice Steljes, Illinois Valley Community College
Jack Stone, Linn-Benton Community College
Rick Street, Spokane Community College
Domenico Tavella, Pittsburgh Technical Institute
Bill Taylor, Cossatot Community College
Mary J. Tobaben, Collin County Community College
Elaine Tuttle, Bellevue Community College
Ski Vanderlaan, Delta College
Andy Williams, Edmonds Community College
Jack Williams, Tulsa Community College

Supplement Authors and Invaluable Assistance

Instructor's Edition: Marianne Rexer, Wilkes University

Test Item File: Allan Sheets, International Business College, Indianapolis; Michele Hill, Schoolcraft College

PowerPoint Presentations: Tim Samolis, Pittsburgh Technical Institute

Computerized Workshops: Terri Brunsdon

End-of-chapter Peachtree/QuickBooks problems: Toni Hartley, Laurel Business Institute

Who Dun It? Practice Set: Toni Hartley, Laurel Business Institute

Update of Chapters 7, 8, and Corner Dress Shop Practice Set: Rick Street, Spokane Community College

Text Accuracy Checkers: Richard Pettit, Mountain View College; Susan Davis, Green River Community College

Supplement Quality Assurance: Karen Sneary, Northwestern Oklahoma State University; Marina Grau, Houston Community College; Donald Benoit, Mitchell College; Michelle Berube, Everett University; Toni Hartley, Laurel Business Institute; Jonea Shade, Clarence Perkins, Bronx Community College; Richard Pettit, Mountain View College; Michele Hill, Schoolcraft College; Allan Sheets, International Business College; Wanda Edwards, Troy University; Susan Davis, Green River Community College

I Want to Hear from You

How to "get to me": Please e-mail me at jeffslater@aol.com, and I promise to get back to you within 24 hours or less. You are my customer, and I want to provide you with the best service possible.

1

Accounting Concepts and Procedures

DID YOU KNOW? By 2007 Best Buy employed 10,000 geek squad agents, 3,000 home theatre installers, and 3,000 vehicle installers. Revenues and net income are greatest for Best Buy in quarter 4 (the holiday seasons for the United States and Canada). Visit *www.BestBuy.com* to find more information about Best Buy.

LEARNING OBJECTIVES

1. Defining and listing the functions of accounting.

2. Recording transactions in the basic accounting equation.

3. Seeing how revenue, expenses, and withdrawals expand the basic accounting equation.

4. Preparing an income statement, a statement of owner's equity, and a balance sheet.

Companies like Best Buy have to comply with many federal statutes. In 2002 a federal statute called the Sarbanes-Oxley Act was passed to prevent fraud at public companies. This act requires a closer look at the internal controls and the accuracy of the financial results of a company.

Accounting is the language of business; it provides information to managers, owners, investors, government agencies, and others inside and outside the organization. Accounting provides answers and insights to questions like these:

- Should I invest in Best Buy or Wal-Mart stock?
- How will increasing fuel costs affect American Airlines?
- Can United Airlines pay its debt obligations?
- What percentage of Ford's marketing budget is allocated to e-business? How does that percentage compare with the competition? What is the overall financial condition of Ford?

Smaller businesses also need answers to their financial questions:

- At a local Walgreens, did business increase enough over the last year to warrant hiring a new assistant?
- Should Local Auto Detailing Co. spend more money to design, produce, and send out new brochures in an effort to create more business?
- What role should the Internet play in the future of business spending?

Accounting is as important to individuals as it is to businesses; it answers questions like these:

- Should I take out a loan to buy a new Toyota FJ Cruiser or wait until I can afford to pay cash for it?
- Would my money work better in a money market or in the stock market?

The accounting process analyzes, records, classifies, summarizes, reports, and interprets financial information for decision makers—whether individuals, small businesses, large corporations, or governmental agencies—in a timely fashion. It is important that students understand the "whys" of this accounting process. Just knowing the mechanics is not enough.

The three main categories of business organization are (1) sole proprietorships, (2) partnerships, and (3) corporations. Let's define each of them and look at their advantages and disadvantages. This information also appears in Table 1.1.

Sole Proprietorship A **sole proprietorship,** such as Lee's Nail Care, is a business that has one owner. That person is both the owner and the manager of the business. An advantage of a sole proprietorship is that the owner makes all the decisions for the business. A disadvantage is that if the business cannot pay its obligations, the business owner must pay them, which means that the owner could lose some of his or her personal assets (e.g., house or savings).

Sole proprietorships are easy to form. They end if the business closes or when the owner dies.

Partnership A **partnership,** such as Miller and Kaminsky, is a form of business ownership that has at least two owners (partners). Each partner acts as an owner of the company, which is an advantage because the partners can share the decision making and the risks of the business. A disadvantage is that, as in a sole proprietorship, the partners' personal assets could be lost if the partnership cannot meet its obligations.

Partnerships are easy to form. They end when a partner dies or leaves the partnership, or when the partners decide to close the business.

Corporation A **corporation,** such as Best Buy, is a business owned by stockholders. The corporation may have only a few stockholders, or it may have many stockholders. The

TABLE 1.1 **Types of Business Organizations**			
	Sole Proprietorship (Lee's Nail Care)	**Partnership (Miller and Kaminsky)**	**Corporation (Best Buy)**
Ownership	Business owned by one person.	Business owned by more than one person.	Business owned by stockholders.
Formation	Easy to form.	Easy to form.	More difficult to form.
Liability	Owner could lose personal assets to meet obligations of business.	Partners could lose personal assets to meet obligations of partnership.	Limited personal risk. Stockholders' loss is limited to their investment in the company.
Closing	Ends with death of owner or closing of business.	Ends with death of partner or closing of business.	Can continue indefinitely.

stockholders are not personally liable for the corporation's debts, and they usually do not have input into the business decisions.

Corporations are more difficult to form than sole proprietorships or partnerships. Corporations can exist indefinitely.

> Many corporate executives feel that Sarbanes-Oxley is too strict and results in too high of a cost to implement.

Classifying Business Organizations

Whether we are looking at a sole proprietorship, a partnership, or a corporation, the business can be classified by what the business does to earn money. Companies are categorized as service, merchandise, or manufacturing businesses.

A limo service is a good example of a **service company** because it provides a service. The first part of this book focuses on service businesses.

Gap and JCPenney sell products. They are called merchandise companies. **Merchandise companies** can either make their own products or sell products that are made by another supplier. Companies such as Intel and Ford Motor Company that make their own products are called **manufacturers.** (See Table 1.2.)

Definition of Accounting

LO1

Accounting (also called the accounting process) is a system that measures the activities of a business in financial terms. It provides various reports and financial statements that show how the various transactions the business undertook (e.g., buying and selling goods) affected the business. This accounting process performs the following functions:

- **Analyzing:** Looking at what happened and how the business was affected.
- **Recording:** Putting the information into the accounting system.
- **Classifying:** Grouping all the same activities (e.g., all purchases) together.
- **Summarizing:** Totaling the results.
- **Reporting:** Issuing the statements that tell the results of the previous functions.

TABLE 1.2 **Examples of Service, Merchandise, and Manufacturing Businesses**		
Service Businesses	**Merchandise Businesses**	**Manufacturing Businesses**
Lee's Nail Care	Macy's	Anheuser-Busch
eBay	JCPenney	Ford
Dr. Wheeler, M.D.	Amazon.com	Toro
Accountemps	Home Depot	Levi's
Langley Landscaping	Gap	Intel

Appendix A will look at the annual report of Kellogg Company.

- **Interpreting:** Examining the statements to determine how the various pieces of information they contain relate to each other.
- **Communication:** Providing the reports and financial statements to people who are interested in the information, such as the business's decision makers, investors, creditors, and government agencies (e.g., the Internal Revenue Service).

As you can see, a lot of people use these reports. A set of procedures and guidelines were developed to make sure that everyone prepares and interprets them the same way. These guidelines are known as **generally accepted accounting principles (GAAP).**

Now let's look at the difference between bookkeeping and accounting. Keep in mind that we use the terms *accounting* and the *accounting process* interchangeably.

Difference between Bookkeeping and Accounting

Confusion often arises concerning the difference between bookkeeping and accounting. **Bookkeeping** is the recording (record keeping) function of the accounting process; a bookkeeper enters accounting information in the company's books. An accountant takes that information and prepares the financial statements that are used to analyze the company's financial position. Accounting involves many complex activities. Often, it includes the preparation of tax and financial reports, budgeting, and analyses of financial information.

Today, computers are used for routine bookkeeping operations that used to take weeks or months to complete. The text explains how the advantages of the computer can be applied to a manual accounting system by using hands-on knowledge of how accounting works. Basic accounting knowledge is needed even though computers can do routine tasks. QuickBooks, Excel, and Peachtree are popular software packages in use today.

Learning Unit 1-1 The Accounting Equation

Assets, Liabilities, and Equities

Let's begin our study of accounting concepts and procedures by looking at a small business: Mia Wong's law practice. Mia decided to open her practice at the end of August. She consulted her accountant before she made her decision. The accountant told her some important things before she made this decision. First, he told her the new business would be considered a separate business entity whose finances had to be kept separate and distinct from Mia's personal finances. The accountant went on to say that all transactions can be analyzed using the basic accounting equation: Assets = Liabilities + Owner's Equity.

Mia had never heard of the basic accounting equation. She listened carefully as the accountant explained the terms used in the equation and how the equation works.

Assets Cash, land, supplies, office equipment, buildings, and other properties of value *owned* by a firm are called **assets.**

Equities The rights of financial claim to the assets are called **equities.** Equities belong to those who supply the assets. If you are the only person to supply assets to the firm, you have the sole rights or financial claims to them. For example, if you supply the law firm with $6,000 in cash and $8,000 in office equipment, your equity in the firm is $14,000.

Relationship between Assets and Equities The relationship between assets and equities is

Assets = Equities
(Total value of items *owned* by business)   (Total claims against the assets)

The total dollar value of the assets of your law firm will be equal to the total dollar value of the financial claims to those assets, that is, equal to the total dollar value of the equities.

The total dollar value is broken down on the left-hand side of the equation to show the specific items of value owned by the business and on the right-hand side to show the types of claims against the assets owned.

Liabilities A firm may have to borrow money to buy more assets; when it does, it means the firm *buys assets on account* (buy now, pay later). Suppose the law firm purchases a new computer for $3,000 on account from Dell, and the company is willing to wait 10 days for payment. The law firm has created a **liability:** an obligation to pay that comes due in the future. Dell is called the **creditor.** This liability—the amount owed to Dell—gives the store the right, or the financial claim, to $3,000 of the law firm's assets. When Dell is paid, the store's rights to the assets of the law firm will end because the obligation has been paid off.

Basic Accounting Equation To best understand the various claims to a business's assets, accountants divide equities into two parts. The claims of creditors—outside persons or businesses—are labeled *liabilities.* The claim of the business's owner is labeled **owner's equity.** Let's see how the accounting equation looks now.

> Assets − Liabilities = Owner's Equity

$$\text{Assets} = \qquad \textbf{Equities}$$

1. Liabilities: rights of creditors
2. Owner's equity: rights of owner

$$\textbf{Assets} = \textbf{Liabilities} + \textbf{Owner's Equity}$$

The total value of all the assets of a firm equals the combined total value of the financial claims of the creditors (liabilities) and the claims of the owners (owner's equity). This calculation is known as the **basic accounting equation.** The basic accounting equation provides a basis for understanding the conventional accounting system of a business. The equation records business transactions in a logical and orderly way that shows their impact on the company's assets, liabilities, and owner's equity.

LO2

Importance of Creditors Another way of presenting the basic accounting equation is

$$\textbf{Assets} - \textbf{Liabilities} = \textbf{Owner's Equity}$$

This form of the equation stresses the importance of creditors. The owner's rights to the business's assets are determined after the rights of the creditors are subtracted. In other words, creditors have first claim to assets. If a firm has no liabilities—therefore no creditors—the owner has the total rights to assets. Another term for the owner's current investment, or equity, in the business's assets is **capital.**

As Mia Wong's law firm engages in business transactions (paying bills, serving customers, and so on), changes will take place in the assets, liabilities, and owner's equity (capital). Let's analyze some of these transactions.

> In accounting, capital does not mean cash. Capital is the owner's current investment, or equity, in the assets of the business.

Transaction A Aug. 28: Mia invests $6,000 in cash and $200 of office equipment into the business.

On August 28, Mia withdraws $6,000 from her personal bank account and deposits the money in the law firm's newly opened bank account. She also invests $200 of office equipment in the business. She plans to be open for business on September 1. With the help of her accountant, Mia begins to prepare the accounting records for the business. We put this information into the basic accounting equation as follows:

Assets			= Liabilities + Owner's Equity
Cash	+	Office Equipment	=	Mia Wong, Capital
$6,000	+	$200	=	$6,200
		$6,200 = $6,200		

Note that the total value of the assets, cash, and office equipment—$6,200—is equal to the combined total value of liabilities (none, so far) and owner's equity ($6,200). Remember, Mia has supplied all the cash and office equipment, so she has the sole financial claim to the assets. Note how the heading "Mia Wong, Capital" is written under the owner's equity heading. The $6,200 is Mia's investment, or equity, in the firm's assets.

Transaction B Aug. 29: Law practice buys office equipment for cash, $500.

From the initial investment of $6,000 cash, the law firm buys $500 worth of office equipment (such as a computer desk), which lasts a long time, whereas **supplies** (such as pens) tend to be used up relatively quickly.

	Assets			= Liabilities +	Owner's Equity
	Cash	+	Office Equipment	=	Mia Wong, Capital
BEGINNING BALANCE	$6,000	+	$200	=	$6,200
TRANSACTION	−500		+500		
ENDING BALANCE	$5,500	+	$700	=	$6,200

$$\$6,200 = \$6,200$$

Shift in Assets As a result of the last transaction, the law office has less cash but has increased its amount of office equipment. This **shift in assets** indicates that the makeup of the assets has changed, but the total of the assets remains the same.

Suppose you go food shopping at Wal-Mart with $100 and spend $60. Now you have two assets, food and money. The composition of the assets has *shifted*—you have more food and less money than you did—but the *total* of the assets has not increased or decreased. The total value of the food, $60, plus the cash, $40, is still $100. When you borrow money from the bank, on the other hand, you increase cash (an asset) and increase liabilities at the same time. This action results in an increase in assets, not just a shift.

An accounting equation can remain in balance even if only one side is updated. The key point to remember is that the left-hand-side total of assets must always equal the right-hand-side total of liabilities and owner's equity.

Transaction C Aug. 30: Buys additional office equipment on account, $300.

The law firm purchases an additional $300 worth of chairs and desks from Wilmington Company. Instead of demanding cash right away, Wilmington agrees to deliver the equipment and to allow up to 60 days for the law practice to pay the invoice (bill).

This liability, or obligation to pay in the future, has some interesting effects on the basic accounting equation. Wilmington Company accepts as payment a partial claim against the assets of the law practice. This claim exists until the law firm pays off the bill. This unwritten promise to pay the creditor is a liability called **accounts payable.**

	Assets			=	Liabilities	+	Owner's Equity
	Cash	+	Office Equipment	=	Accounts Payable	+	Mia Wong, Capital
BEGINNING BALANCE	$5,500	+	$700	=			$6,200
TRANSACTION			+300		+$300		
ENDING BALANCE	$5,500	+	$1,000	=	$300	+	$6,200

$$\$6,500 = \$6,500$$

When this information is analyzed, we can see that the law practice increased what it owes (accounts payable) as well as what it owns (office equipment) by $300. The law practice gains $300 in an asset but also takes on an obligation to pay Wilmington Company at a future date.

The owner's equity remains unchanged. This transaction results in an increase of total assets from $6,200 to $6,500.

Finally, note that after each transaction the basic accounting equation remains in balance.

LEARNING UNIT 1-1 REVIEW

AT THIS POINT you should be able to

For additional help go to www.pearsonhighered.com/slater

- Define and explain the purpose of the Sarbanes-Oxley Act.
- Define and explain the differences between sole proprietorships, partnerships, and corporations.
- List the functions of accounting.
- Compare and contrast bookkeeping and accounting.
- Explain the role of the computer as an accounting tool.
- State the purpose of the accounting equation.
- Explain the difference between liabilities and owner's equity.
- Define capital.
- Explain the difference between a shift in assets and an increase in assets.

To test your understanding of this material, complete Self-Review Quiz 1-1. The blank forms you need for all Self-Review quizzes and end-of-chapter material throughout the textbook can be found in the *Study Guide and Working Papers*. The solution to the quiz immediately follows here in the text. If you have difficulty doing the problems, review Learning Unit 1-1 and the solution to the quiz along with a detailed explanation from Jeff Slater, your author. Be sure to check the Slater Web site for student study aids.

Keep in mind that learning accounting is like learning to type: The more you practice, the better you become. You will not be an expert in one day. Be patient. It will all come together.

Self-Review Quiz 1-1

Record the following transactions in the basic accounting equation:

1. Gracie Ryan invests $17,000 to begin a real estate office.
2. The real estate office buys $600 of computer equipment from Wal-Mart for cash.
3. The real estate company buys $800 of additional computer equipment on account from Circuit City.

Solution to Self-Review Quiz 1-1

	Assets		=	Liabilities	+	Owner's Equity	
Cash	+	Computer Equipment	= Accounts Payable	+	Gracie Ryan, Capital	
+$17,000					+$17,000	
17,000			=		17,000	**1. BALANCE**
−600		+$600				
16,400	+	600	=		17,000	**2. BALANCE**
		+800		+$800		
$16,400	+	$1,400	=	$800	+	$17,000	**3. ENDING BALANCE**

$$\$17,800 = \$17,800$$

NEED HELP?

Let's review first: The left side of the accounting equation shows what is owned by the business and the right side of the equation shows you who supplied those assets to a business. Now let's look at the transactions in the solution:

Transaction 1: In your head you must say to yourself, "What did the business get and how did it get it?" The business is getting or increasing its cash by $17,000 and that cash is being supplied by Gracie Ryan. Think of Gracie as increasing her rights in the business since she is supplying cash. Keep in mind that capital does not mean cash. Instead it is what the owner supplies to the business. (Gracie may in the future supply other items to the business.)

So the end result is to put $17,000 on the left side of the equation under cash and put $17,000 under Gracie Ryan, Capital on the right side. The sum of the left side must equal the sum on the right side.

Transaction 2: Here we are NOT looking at the personal finances of Gracie. You must focus on the business. What did the business get and who supplied it to the business?

In this transaction the business is getting $600 of computer equipment by using some of its cash. IT IS SHIFTING ITS ASSETS: MORE EQUIPMENT FOR LESS CASH. Note that capital is not affected since Gracie has not supplied anything new to the business. Note that the right side of the equation is not touched, but the equation still remains in the balance. We are just rearranging the composition of the assets.

Transaction 3: Now the business is getting more equipment but is not paying cash. The equipment is being supplied by a creditor called Accounts Payable. Hopefully in the future the business will be able to pay the creditor back the $800 that it owes. The end result is that the business now has $1,400 in equipment. Note that capital is not affected since no new investments were made by Gracie into the business.

Summary: At the end of these three transactions this company is made up of two assets, Cash $16,400 and Computer Equipment $1,400. The total of the assets was supplied by creditors $800 and the owner Gracie Ryan, Capital $17,000. The sum of the left side must equal the sum of the right side.

Learning Unit 1-2 The Balance Sheet

> The balance sheet shows the company's financial position as of a particular date. (In our example, that date is at the end of August.)

In the first learning unit, the transactions for Mia Wong's law firm were recorded in the accounting equation. The transactions we recorded occurred before the law firm opened for business. A statement called a **balance sheet** or **statement of financial position** can show the history of a company before it opened. The balance sheet is a formal statement that presents the information from the ending balances of both sides of the accounting equation. Think of the balance sheet as a snapshot of the business's financial position as of a particular date.

Let's look at the balance sheet of Mia Wong's law practice for August 31, 200X, shown in Figure 1.1. The figures in the balance sheet come from the ending balances of the accounting equation for the law practice as shown in Learning Unit 1-1.

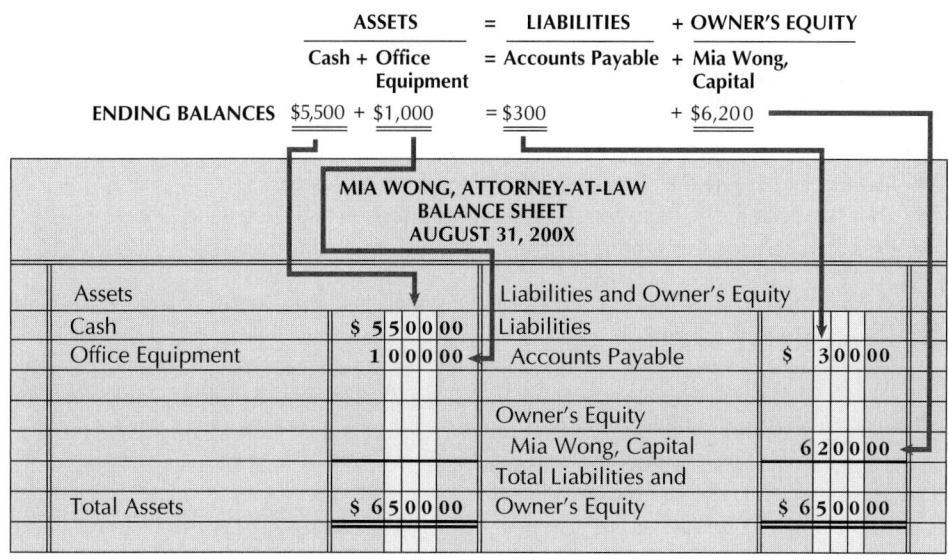

FIGURE 1.1 The Balance Sheet

Note in Figure 1.1 that the assets owned by the law practice appear on the left-hand side and that the liabilities and owner's equity appear on the right-hand side. Both sides equal $6,500. This *balance* between left and right gives the balance sheet its name. In later chapters we look at other ways to set up a balance sheet.

Points to Remember in Preparing a Balance Sheet

The Heading The heading of the balance sheet provides the following information:

- The company name: Mia Wong, Attorney-at-Law
- The name of the statement: Balance Sheet
- The date for which the report is prepared: August 31, 200X

Use of the Dollar Sign Note that the dollar sign is not repeated each time a figure appears. As shown in Figure 1.2, the balance sheet for Mia Wong's law practice, it usually is placed to the left of each column's top figure and to the left of the column's total.

Distinguishing the Total When adding numbers down a column, use a single line before the total and a double line beneath it. A single line means that the numbers above it have been added or subtracted. A double line indicates a total. It is important to align the numbers in the column; many errors occur because these figures are not lined up. These rules are the same for all accounting reports.

The balance sheet gives Mia the information she needs to see the law firm's financial position before it opens for business. This information does not tell her, however, whether the firm will make a profit.

> The three elements that make up a balance sheet are assets, liabilities, and owner's equity.

FIGURE 1.2 Partial Balance Sheet

MIA WONG, ATTORNEY-AT-LAW BALANCE SHEET AUGUST 31, 200X	
Assets	
Cash	$ 5 5 0 0 00
Office Equipment	1 0 0 0 00
Total Assets	$ 6 5 0 0 00

A single line means the numbers above it have been added or subtracted.

A double line indicates a total.

LEARNING UNIT 1-2 REVIEW

AT THIS POINT you should be able to

- Define and state the purpose of a balance sheet.
- Identify and define the elements making up a balance sheet.
- Show the relationship between the accounting equation and the balance sheet.
- Prepare a balance sheet in proper form from information provided.

Self-Review Quiz 1-2

The date is November 30, 200X. Use the following information to prepare in proper form a balance sheet for Janning Company:

Accounts Payable	$40,000
Cash	18,000
A. Janning, Capital	9,000
Office Equipment	31,000

For additional help go to
www.pearsonhighered.com/slater

Solution to Self-Review Quiz 1-2

FIGURE 1.3 Balance Sheet

Accounting Cycle Tutorial

JANNING COMPANY
BALANCE SHEET
NOVEMBER 30, 200X

Assets		Liabilities and Owner's Equity	
Cash	$ 18 0 0 0 00	Liabilities	
Office Equipment	31 0 0 0 00	Accounts Payable	$ 40 0 0 0 00
		Owner's Equity	
		A. Janning, Capital	9 0 0 0 00
		Total Liabilities and	
Total Assets	$ 4 9 0 0 0 00	Owner's Equity	$ 49 0 0 0 00

Capital does not mean cash. The capital amount is the owner's current investment of assets in the business.

NEED HELP?

Let's review first: A photo of your family as of a particular date is like a balance sheet. It gives you a history of your family as of a particular date. The balance sheet is a formal report that lists assets, liabilities, and owner's equity for a business as of a particular date.

Before making the report, identify whether each title is an asset, liability, or owner's equity. Accounts payable is a liability. Hopefully the business will be able to pay. Cash is an asset, or something of value owned by the business. A. Janning, Capital is owner's equity, or what the owner is supplying to the business.

The heading of a balance sheet answers three questions:

Who? Janning Company

What report? Balance Sheet

When? November 30, 200X

The left side of the balance sheet lists out the assets, cash, and office equipment.

The right side lists out who supplies the assets to the business: creditors (accounts payable) or the owner, A. Janning, Capital. Use single rules to add and double rules for totals. The sum of the left side must equal the sum of the right side.

Learning Unit 1-3 The Accounting Equation Expanded: Revenue, Expenses, and Withdrawals

LO3

As soon as Mia Wong's office opened, she began performing legal services for her clients and earning revenue for the business. At the same time, as a part of doing business, she incurred various expenses such as rent.

When Mia asked her accountant how these transactions fit into the accounting equation, she began by defining some terms.

Revenue A service company earns **revenue** when it provides services to its clients. Mia's law firm earned revenue when she provided legal services to her clients for legal fees. When revenue is earned, owner's equity is increased. In effect, revenue is a subdivision of owner's equity.

Assets are increased. The increase is in the form of cash if the client pays right away. If the client promises to pay in the future, the increase is called **accounts receivable.** When revenue is earned, the transaction is recorded as an increase in revenue and an increase in assets (either as cash or as accounts receivable, depending on whether it was paid right away or will be paid in the future).

> *Remember:* Accounts receivable results from earning revenue even when cash is not yet received.
> Record an expense when it is incurred, whether it is paid immediately or is to be paid later.

Expenses A business's **expenses** are the costs the company incurs in carrying on operations in its effort to create revenue. Expenses are also a subdivision of owner's equity; when expenses are incurred, they *decrease* owner's equity. Expenses can be paid for in cash or they can be charged.

Net Income/Net Loss When revenue totals more than expenses, **net income** is the result; when expenses total more than revenue, **net loss** is the result.

Withdrawals At some point Mia Wong may need to withdraw cash or other assets from the business to pay living or other personal expenses that do not relate to the business. We will record these transactions in an account called **withdrawals.** Sometimes this account is called the *owner's drawing account.* Withdrawals is a subdivision of owner's equity that records personal expenses not related to the business. Withdrawals decrease owner's equity (see Fig. 1.4 on the following page).

It is important to remember the difference between expenses and withdrawals. Expenses relate to business operations; withdrawals are the result of personal needs outside the normal operations of the business.

Now let's analyze the September transactions for Mia Wong's law firm using an **expanded accounting equation** that includes withdrawals, revenues, and expenses.

Expanded Accounting Equation

Transaction D Sept. 1–30: Provided legal services for cash, $2,000.

FIGURE 1.4 Owner's Equity

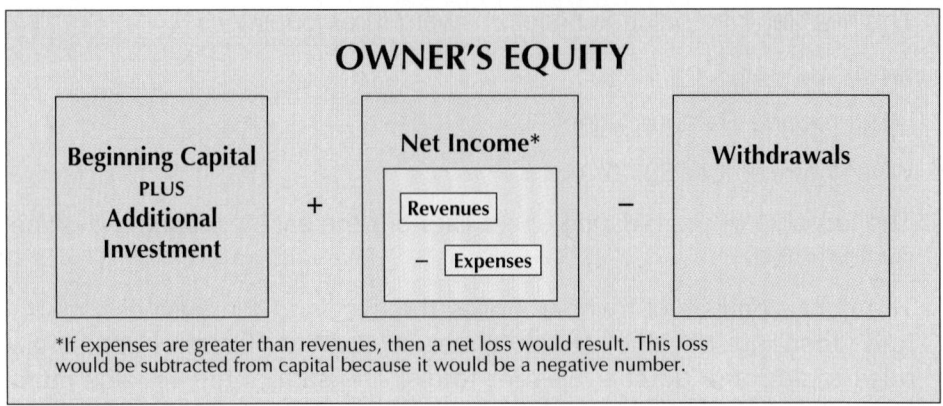

Transactions A, B, and C were discussed earlier, when the law office was being formed in August. See Learning Unit 1.1.

Assets			= Liabilities +				Owner's Equity			
Cash	+ Accts. Rec.	+ Office Equip.	= Accts. Pay.		+ M. Wong, Capital	− M. Wong, Withdr.	+ Revenue	− Expenses
BALANCE FORWARD $5,500		+ $1,000	= $ 300		+ $6,200			
+2,000							+ $2,000	
ENDING BALANCE $7,500		+ $1,000	= $ 300		+ $6,200		+ $2,000	

$8,500 = $8,500

In the law firm's first month of operation, a total of $2,000 in cash was received for legal services performed. In the accounting equation, the asset Cash is increased by $2,000. Revenue is also increased by $2,000, resulting in an increase in owner's equity.

A revenue column was added to the basic accounting equation. Amounts are recorded in the revenue column when they are earned. They are also recorded in the assets column under Cash and/or Accounts Receivable. Do not think of revenue as an asset. It is part of owner's equity. It is the revenue that creates an inward flow of cash and accounts receivable.

Transaction E Sept. 1–30: Provided legal services on account, $3,000.

Assets			= Liabilities +			Owner's Equity			
Cash	+ Accts. Rec.	+ Office Equip.	= Accts. Pay.	+ M. Wong, Capital	− M. Wong, Withdr.	+ Revenue	− Expenses
BAL. FOR. TRANS. $7,500		+ $ 1,000	= $ 300	+ $6,200		+ $2,000	
	+3,000					+ $3,000	
END. BAL. $7,500	+ $3,000	+ $ 1,000	= $ 300	+ $6,200		+ $5,000	

$11,500 = $11,500

Mia's law practice performed legal work on account for $3,000. The firm did not receive the cash for these earned legal fees; it accepted an unwritten promise from these clients that payment would be received in the future.

Transaction F Sept. 1–30: Received $900 cash as partial payment from previous services performed on account.

During September some of Mia's clients who had received services and promised to pay in the future decided to reduce what they owed the practice by making payment of $900. This decision is shown as follows on the expanded accounting equation:

Assets			= Liabilities +		Owner's Equity				
Cash	+ Accts. Rec.	+ Office Equip.	= Accts. Pay.	+ M. Wong, Capital	− M. Wong, Withdr.	+ Revenue	− Expenses		
$7,500	+ $3,000	+ $ 1,000	= $ 300	+ $6,200		+ $5,000			BAL. FOR. TRANS.
+900	−900								
$8,400	+ $2,100	+ $ 1,000	= $ 300	+ $6,200		+ $5,000			END. BAL.

$$\$11,500 = \$11,500$$

The law firm increased the asset Cash by $900 and reduced another asset, Accounts Receivable, by $900. The *total* of assets does not change. The right-hand side of the expanded accounting equation has not been touched because the total on the left-hand side of the equation has not changed. The revenue was recorded when it was earned, and the *same revenue cannot be recorded twice.* This transaction analyzes the situation *after* the revenue has been previously earned and recorded. Transaction F shows a shift in assets resulting in more cash and less accounts receivable.

Transaction G Sept. 1–30: Paid salaries expense, $700.

Assets			= Liabilities +		Owner's Equity				
Cash	+ Accts. Rec.	+ Office Equip.	= Accts. Pay.	+ M. Wong, Capital	− M. Wong, Withdr.	+ Revenue	− Expenses		
$8,400	+ $2,100	+ $ 1,000	= $ 300	+ $6,200		+ $5,000			BAL. FOR. TRANS.
−700							+$700		
$7,700	+ $2,100	+ $ 1,000	= $ 300	+ $6,200		+ $5,000	− $700		END. BAL.

$$\$10,800 = \$10,800$$

As expenses increase, they decrease owner's equity. This incurred expense of $700 reduces the cash by $700. Although the expense was paid, the total of our expenses to date has *increased* by $700. Keep in mind that owner's equity decreases as expenses increase, so the accounting equation remains in balance.

Transaction H Sept. 1–30: Paid rent expense, $400.

Assets			= Liabilities +		Owner's Equity				
Cash	+ Accts. Rec.	+ Office Equip.	= Accts. Pay.	+ M. Wong, Capital	− M. Wong, Withdr.	+ Revenue	− Expenses		
$7,700	+ $2,100	+ $ 1,000	= $ 300	+ $6,200		+ $5,000	− $ 700		BAL. FOR. TRANS.
−400							+400		
$7,300	+ $2,100	+ $ 1,000	= $ 300	+ $6,200		+ $5,000	− $1,100		END. BAL.

$$\$10,400 = \$10,400$$

During September the practice incurred rent expenses of $400. This rent was not paid in advance; it was paid when it came due. The payment of rent reduces the asset Cash by $400 as well as increases the expenses of the firm, resulting in a decrease in owner's equity. The firm's expenses are now $1,100.

Transaction I Sept. 1–30: Incurred advertising expenses of $200, to be paid next month.

	Assets			= Liabilities +		Owner's Equity			
	Cash	+ Accts. Rec.	+ Office Equip.	= Accts. Pay.	+ M. Wong, Capital	− M. Wong, Withdr.	+ Revenue	− Expenses
BAL. FOR. TRANS.	$7,300	+ $2,100	+ $ 1,000	= $ 300	+ $6,200		+ $5,000	− $1,100
				+200				+200
END. BAL.	$7,300	+ $2,100	+ $ 1,000	= $ 500	+ $6,200		+ $5,000	− $1,300

$10,400 = $10,400

Mia ran an ad in the local newspaper and incurred an expense of $200. This increase in expenses caused a corresponding decrease in owner's equity. Because Mia has not paid the newspaper for the advertising yet, she owes $200. Thus her liabilities (Accounts Payable) increase by $200. Eventually, when the bill comes in and is paid, both Cash and Accounts Payable will be decreased.

Transaction J Sept. 1–30: Mia withdrew $100 for personal use.

	Assets			= Liabilities +		Owner's Equity			
	Cash	+ Accts. Rec.	+ Office Equip.	= Accts. Pay.	+ M. Wong, Capital	− M. Wong, Withdr.	+ Revenue	− Expenses
BAL. FOR. TRANS.	$7,300	+ $2,100	+ $ 1,000	= $ 500	+ $6,200		+ $5,000	− $1,300
	−100					+$100		
END. BAL.	$7,200	+ $2,100	+ $ 1,000	= $ 500	+ $6,200	− $100	+ $5,000	− $1,300

$10,300 = $10,300

By taking $100 for personal use, Mia *increased* her withdrawals from the business by $100 and decreased the asset Cash by $100. Note that as withdrawals increase, the owner's equity *decreases.* Keep in mind that a withdrawal is *not* a business expense. It is a subdivision of owner's equity that records money or other assets an owner withdraws from the business for *personal* use.

Subdivision of Owner's Equity Take a moment to review the subdivisions of owner's equity:

- As capital increases, owner's equity increases (see transaction A).
- As withdrawals increase, owner's equity decreases (see transaction J).
- As revenue increases, owner's equity increases (see transaction D).
- As expenses increase, owner's equity decreases (see transaction G).

Mia Wong's Expanded Accounting Equation The following is a summary of the expanded accounting equation for Mia Wong's law firm.

Mia Wong
Attorney-at-Law
Expanded Accounting Equation: A Summary

Assets			= Liabilities +		Owner's Equity				
Cash	+ Accts. Rec.	+ Office Equip.	= Accts. Pay.	+ M. Wong, Capital	− M. Wong, Withdr.	+ Revenue	− Expenses		
$6,000		+$200	=	+$6,200					A.
6,000	+	200	=	6,200					BALANCE
−500		+500							B.
5,500	+	700	=	6,200					BALANCE
		+300	+$300						C.
5,500 +		1,000	= 300 +	6,200					BALANCE
+2,000						+$2,000			D.
7,500	+	1,000	= 300 +	6,200		+ 2,000			BALANCE
	+ $3,000					+3,000			E.
7,500 + 3,000	+	1,000	= 300 +	6,200		+ 5,000			BALANCE
+900	−900								F.
8,400 + 2,100	+	1,000	= 300 +	6,200		+ 5,000			BALANCE
−700							+$700		G.
7,700 + 2,100	+	1,000	= 300 +	6,200		+ 5,000 −	700		BALANCE
−400							+400		H.
7,300 + 2,100	+	1,000	= 300 +	6,200		+ 5,000 −	1,100		BALANCE
			+200				+200		I.
7,300 + 2,100	+	1,000	= 500 +	6,200		+ 5,000 −	1,300		BALANCE
−100					+$100				J.
$7,200 + $2,100	+	$1,000	= $500 +	$6,200	− $100	+ $5,000 −	$1,300		END BALANCE

$10,300 = $10,300

LEARNING UNIT 1-3 REVIEW

AT THIS POINT you should be able to

For additional help go to www.pearsonhighered.com/slater

- Define and explain the difference between revenue and expenses.
- Define and explain the difference between net income and net loss.
- Explain the subdivisions of owner's equity.
- Explain the effects of withdrawals, revenue, and expenses on owner's equity.
- Record transactions in an expanded accounting equation and balance the basic accounting equation as a means of checking the accuracy of your calculations.

Self-Review Quiz 1-3

Record the following transactions into the expanded accounting equation for the Bing Company. Note that all titles have a beginning balance.

1. Received cash revenue, $4,000.
2. Billed customers for services rendered, $6,000.
3. Received a bill for telephone expenses (to be paid next month), $125.

4. Bob Bing withdrew cash for personal use, $500.

5. Received $1,000 from customers in partial payment for services performed in transaction 2.

Solution to Self-Review Quiz 1-3

	Assets			= Liabilities +			Owner's Equity		
	Cash +	Accts. Rec. +	Cleaning = Equip.	Accts. Pay.	+ B. Bing, Capital	− B. Bing, Withdr.	+ Revenue	− Expenses
BEG. BALANCE	$10,000 +	$ 2,500 +	$ 6,500 =	$1,000	+ $11,800	− $ 800	+ $ 9,000	− $2,000
1.	**+4,000**						**+4,000**	
BALANCE	14,000 +	2,500 +	6,500 =	1,000	+ 11,800	− 800	+ 13,000	− 2,000
2.		**+6,000**					**+6,000**	
BALANCE	14,000 +	8,500 +	6,500 =	1,000	+ 11,800	− 800	+ 19,000	− 2,000
3.				**+125**				**+125**
BALANCE	14,000 +	8,500 +	6,500 =	1,125	+ 11,800	− 800	+ 19,000	− 2,125
4.	**−500**					**+500**		
BALANCE	13,500 +	8,500 +	6,500 =	1,125	+ 11,800	− 1,300	+ 19,000	− 2,125
5.	**+1,000**	**−1,000**						
END. BALANCE	$14,500 +	$ 7,500 +	$ 6,500 =	$1,125	+ $11,800	− $1,300	+ $19,000	− $2,125

$28,500 = $28,500

NEED HELP?

Let's review first: You only record revenue when it is earned. What can the business get? Cash and/or promises from customers called Accounts Receivable. Revenue is not an asset but does provide an inward flow of assets into the business. Revenue is part of owner's equity. Think of expenses as always increasing in a business. The end result will be a decrease in owner's equity. Expenses are recorded when they happen and can be paid for by cash or charged as Accounts Payable.

Withdrawals work just like expenses, but they represent personal withdrawals by the owner. Expenses and withdrawals are not recorded together. Each has a separate title.

Transaction 1: The company has done the work. It now records revenue of $4,000 in the revenue column (we only put numbers in this column when we do the work). This time the inward flow from the revenue is all in the form of cash of $4,000.

Transaction 2: This time the company does the work but is not getting the cash. It is receiving promises that it will be paid in the future. You record the $6,000 in the revenue column because you did the work. The inward flow from this revenue is not cash but promises called Accounts Receivable. Thus, the Accounts Receivable column is increased by $6,000.

Transaction 3: An expense has happened and should be recorded whether money is paid or not. The expenses for telephone have

INCREASED by $125, resulting in the total expenses rising to $2,125. As expenses in a business rise, the end result is a reduction in owner's equity.

Since the expense was charged, the $125 is recorded under Accounts Payable because hopefully the expense will be paid in the future. At this point this telephone expense has created a liability. Remember that an expense is not a liability.

Transaction 4: This transaction relates to a personal transaction and does not affect any expenses in the business. Bob Bing takes $500 cash from the business. Think of Bob as gaining the $500, but in reality his owner's rights will be reduced. This is shown by a $500 gain under withdrawals, which now results in a total of $1,300 (a reduction to owner's equity) and a decrease to cash. Note that expenses are not affected since this is a personal transaction.

Transaction 5: No new work is earned, so we do not record any new revenue. Here customers are paying part of what they owe. The result is that company cash increased by $1,000 and Accounts Receivable is reduced by $1,000. This is a shift in assets: more cash, less accounts receivable.

Summary: Note the four subdivisions of owner's equity: Capital, Withdrawals, Revenues, and Expenses. As capital and revenue increases, owner's equity will increase. As expenses and withdrawals increase, owner's equity will decrease. Revenue is not an asset. Rather, it provides assets in the form of cash and/or accounts receivable. Only record revenue when work is done. Only record expenses when they happen, regardless whether cash is received.

Learning Unit 1-4 Preparing Financial Statements   *LO4*

Mia Wong would like to be able to find out whether her firm is making a profit, so she asks her accountant whether he can measure the firm's financial performance on a monthly basis. Her accountant replies that a number of financial statements that he can prepare, such as the income statement, will show Mia how well the law firm has performed over a specific period of time. The accountant can use the information in the income statement to prepare other reports.

The Income Statement

An **income statement** is an accounting statement that shows business results in terms of revenue and expenses. If revenues are greater than expenses, the report shows net income. If expenses are greater than revenues, the report shows net loss. An income statement can cover 1, 3, 6, or 12 months. It cannot cover more than one year. The statement shows the result of all revenues and expenses throughout the entire period and not just as of a specific date. The income statement for Mia Wong's law firm is shown in Figure 1.5 on the following page.

Points to Remember in Preparing an Income Statement

Heading The heading of an income statement tells the same three things as all other accounting statements: the company's name, the name of the statement, and the period of time the statement covers.

The Setup As you can see on the income statement, the inside column of numbers ($700, $400, and $200) is used to subtotal all expenses ($1,300) before subtracting them from revenue ($5,000 − $1,300 = $3,700).

> The income statement is prepared from data found in the revenue and expense columns of the expanded accounting equation. The inside column of numbers ($700, $400, $200) is used to subtotal all expenses ($1,300) before subtracting from revenue.

FIGURE 1.5 The Income
Statement

Software programs may call
this statement a profit and loss
statement or an earnings
statement.

MIA WONG, ATTORNEY-AT-LAW
INCOME STATEMENT
FOR MONTH ENDED SEPTEMBER 30, 200X

Revenue:			
Legal Fees			$ 5 0 0 0 00
Operating Expenses:			
Salaries Expense	$ 7 0 0 00		
Rent Expense	4 0 0 00		
Advertising Expense	2 0 0 00		
Total Operating Expenses		1 3 0 0 00	
Net Income		$ 3 7 0 0 00	

Operating expenses may be listed in alphabetical order, in order of largest amounts to smallest, or in a set order established by the accountant.

The Statement of Owner's Equity

As we said, the income statement is a business statement that shows business results in terms of revenue and expenses, but how does net income or net loss affect owner's equity? To find out, we have to look at a second type of statement, the **statement of owner's equity.**

The statement of owner's equity shows for a certain period of time what changes occurred in Mia Wong, Capital. The statement of owner's equity is shown in Figure 1.6.

The capital of Mia Wong can be

If this statement of owner's
equity is omitted, the information will be included in the
owner's equity section of the
balance sheet.

Increased by: Owner Investment
*   Net Income (Revenue − Expenses) and Revenue Greater Than Expenses*
*   Decreased by: Owner Withdrawals*
*   Net Loss (Revenue − Expenses) and Expenses Greater Than Revenue*

Remember, a withdrawal is *not* a business expense and thus is not involved in the calculation of net income or net loss on the income statement. It appears on the statement of owner's equity. The statement of owner's equity summarizes the effects of all the subdivisions of owner's equity (revenue, expenses, withdrawals) on beginning capital. The ending capital figure ($9,800) will be the beginning figure in the next statement of owner's equity.

Suppose Mia's law firm had operated at a loss in the month of September. Suppose instead of net income, a $400 net loss occurred and an additional investment of $700 was made on September 15. Figure 1.7 shows how the statement would look with this net loss and additional investment.

FIGURE 1.6 Statement of Owner's Equity—Net Income

This state-
ment, called
a statement
of retained
earnings in
Peachtree, is
not available
as a report in
QuickBooks.

MIA WONG, ATTORNEY-AT-LAW
STATEMENT OF OWNER'S EQUITY
FOR MONTH ENDED SEPTEMBER 30, 200X

Mia Wong, Capital, September 1, 200X		$ 6 2 0 0 00
Net Income for September	$ 3 7 0 0 00	
Less Withdrawals for September	1 0 0 00	
Increase in Capital		3 6 0 0 00
Mia Wong, Capital, September 30, 200X		$ 9 8 0 0 00

Comes from
Income
Statement

MIA WONG, ATTORNEY-AT-LAW STATEMENT OF OWNER'S EQUITY FOR MONTH ENDED SEPTEMBER 30, 200X		
Mia Wong, Capital, September 1, 200X		$ 6 2 0 0 00
Additional Investment, September 15, 200X		7 0 0 00
Total Investment for September*		$ 6 9 0 0 00
Less: Net Loss for September	$ 4 0 0 00	
Withdrawals for September	1 0 0 00	
Decrease in Capital		5 0 0 00
Mia Wong, Capital, September 30, 200X		$ 6 4 0 0 00

FIGURE 1.7 Statement of Owner's Equity—Net Loss

*Beginning capital and additional investments.

The Balance Sheet

Now let's look at how to prepare a balance sheet from the expanded accounting equation (see Fig. 1.8). As you can see, the asset accounts (cash, accounts receivable, and office equipment) appear on the left side of the balance sheet.

Accounts payable and Mia Wong, Capital appear on the right side. Notice that the $9,800 of capital can be calculated within the accounting equation or can be read from the statement of owner's equity.

FIGURE 1.8 The Accounting Equation and the Balance Sheet

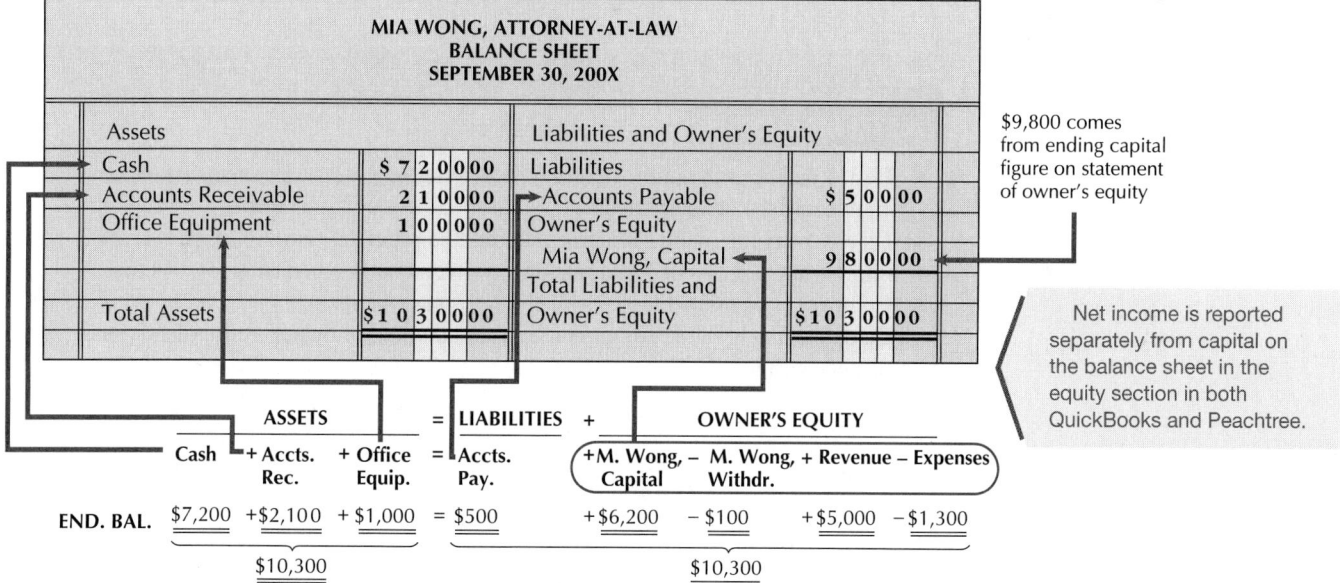

$9,800 comes from ending capital figure on statement of owner's equity

Net income is reported separately from capital on the balance sheet in the equity section in both QuickBooks and Peachtree.

Main Elements of the Income Statement, the Statement of Owner's Equity, and the Balance Sheet

In this chapter we have discussed three financial statements: the income statement, the statement of owner's equity, and the balance sheet. A fourth statement, called the statement of cash flows, will not be covered at this time. Let us review what elements of the expanded accounting equation go into each statement and the usual order in which the statements are prepared. Figure 1.8 presents a diagram of the accounting equation and the balance sheet. Table 1.3 on the following page summarizes the following points:

- The income statement is prepared first; it includes revenues and expenses and shows net income or net loss. This net income or net loss is used to update the next statement, the statement of owner's equity.

TABLE 1.3 What Goes on Each Financial Statement

	Income Statement	Statement of Owner's Equity	Balance Sheet
Assets			X
Liabilities			X
Capital* (beg.)		X	
Capital (end)		X	X
Withdrawals		X	
Revenues	X		
Expenses	X		

*Note: Additional Investments go on the statement of owner's equity.

- The statement of owner's equity is prepared second; it includes beginning capital and any additional investments, the net income or net loss shown on the income statement, withdrawals, and the total, which is the **ending capital.** The balance in Capital comes from the statement of owner's equity.
- The balance sheet is prepared last; it includes the final balances of each of the elements listed in the accounting equation under Assets and Liabilities. The balance in Capital comes from the statement of owner's equity.

LEARNING UNIT 1-4 REVIEW

AT THIS POINT you should be able to

- Define and state the purpose of the income statement, the statement of owner's equity, and the balance sheet.
- Discuss why the income statement should be prepared first.
- Show what happens on a statement of owner's equity when a net loss occurs.
- Compare and contrast these three financial statements.
- Calculate a new figure for capital on the statement of owner's equity and the balance sheet.

For additional help go to
www.pearsonhighered.com/slater

Self-Review Quiz 1-4

From the balances listed next for Rusty Realty prepare the following:

1. Income statement for the month ended November 30, 200X.
2. Statement of owner's equity for the month ended November 30, 200X.
3. Balances as of November 30, 200X.

Cash	$4,000	R. Rusty, Capital	
Accounts Receivable	1,370	November 1, 200X	$5,000
Store Furniture	1,490	R. Rusty, Withdrawals	100
Accounts Payable	900	Commissions Earned	1,500
		Rent Expense	200
		Advertising Expense	150
		Salaries Expense	90

Solution to Self-Review Quiz 1-4

FIGURE 1.9 Financial Reports

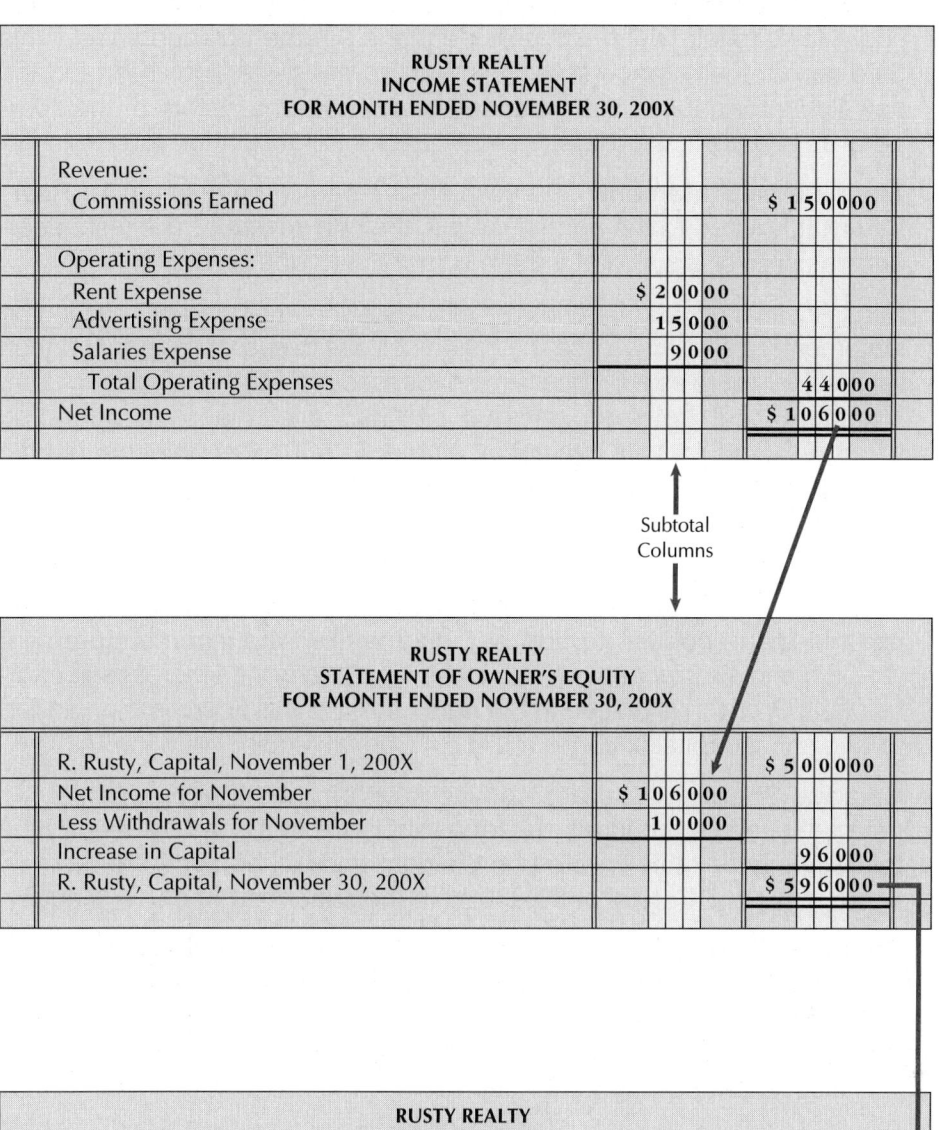

RUSTY REALTY
INCOME STATEMENT
FOR MONTH ENDED NOVEMBER 30, 200X

Revenue:		
Commissions Earned		$ 1 5 0 0 00
Operating Expenses:		
Rent Expense	$ 2 0 0 00	
Advertising Expense	1 5 0 00	
Salaries Expense	9 0 00	
Total Operating Expenses		4 4 0 00
Net Income		$ 1 0 6 0 00

Subtotal
Columns

RUSTY REALTY
STATEMENT OF OWNER'S EQUITY
FOR MONTH ENDED NOVEMBER 30, 200X

R. Rusty, Capital, November 1, 200X		$ 5 0 0 0 00
Net Income for November	$ 1 0 6 0 00	
Less Withdrawals for November	1 0 0 00	
Increase in Capital		9 6 0 00
R. Rusty, Capital, November 30, 200X		$ 5 9 6 0 00

RUSTY REALTY
BALANCE SHEET
NOVEMBER 30, 200X

Assets		Liabilities and Owner's Equity	
Cash	$ 4 0 0 0 00	Liabilities	
Accounts Receivable	1 3 7 0 00	Accounts Payable	$ 9 0 0 00
Store Furniture	1 4 9 0 00		
		Owner's Equity	
		R. Rusty, Capital	5 9 6 0 00
		Total Liabilities and	
Total Assets	$ 6 8 6 0 00	Owner's Equity	$ 6 8 6 0 00

NEED HELP?

Let's review first: The first formal report is the income statement, which is made up of only revenues and expenses. This report shows how a company is performing for a specific period of time. The second report is the statement of the owner's equity. This report shows how capital has changed from its beginning balance. The net income is added to the beginning balance less any personal withdrawals resulting in a new figure for capital, which will also be placed in the balance sheet. This third report, the balance sheet, is made up of assets, liabilities, and the new figure for capital. The balance sheet shows the history of the company as of a particular date.

The Income Statement: Commissions earned is the revenue for Rusty Realty. It is listed to the right since it is the only revenue. The inside column is used for a subtotal if there is more than one revenue.

Rent, Advertising, and Salaries are expenses that are listed on the income statement. Note that we use the inside column to subtotal them and then list the final figure as total operating expenses of $440 in the right column. The difference between revenue ($1,500) and the total operating expenses ($440) results in a net income of $1,060. Keep in mind that net income is not cash. Remember that some revenue may not have resulted in cash and some of the expenses may not have been paid for in cash.

Statement of Owner's Equity: The beginning balance of Rusty, Capital is $5,000. We place this to the right because it is one number. We then use the inside column to add net income from the income statement ($1,060) and subtract any withdrawals ($100) to get an increase in capital of $960, which is placed in the right column. This figure is then added to beginning capital to arrive at Rusty, Capital (ending) of $5,960.

Balance Sheet: All the assets are listed on the left (cash, accounts receivable, and store furniture), for a total of $6,860. The liability of $900 for accounts payable is listed on the right and will be added to the new figure for Rusty, Capital of $5,960 from the statement of owner's equity.

Summary: The income statement lists out revenue and expenses. No withdrawals are found on this report. The statement of owner's equity will show how capital changes by net income, net loss, and/or withdrawals. The balance shows the new history of the company's assets, liabilities, and a new figure for capital.

CHAPTER ASSIGNMENTS

All Classroom Demonstration Exercises, Exercises, Problems, and the Continuing Problem in this chapter can be found within MyAccountingLab, an online homework and practice environment. Your instructor may ask you to complete this material using MyAccountingLab.

DEMONSTRATION PROBLEM

Michael Brown opened his law office on June 1, 200X. During the first month of operations, Michael conducted the following transactions:

1. Invested $6,000 in cash into the law practice.
2. Paid $600 for office equipment.
3. Purchased additional office equipment on account, $1,000.
4. Received cash for performing legal services for clients, $2,000.
5. Paid salaries, $800.
6. Performed legal services for clients on account, $1,000.

7. Paid rent, $1,200.
8. Withdrew $500 from his law practice for personal use.
9. Received $500 from customers in partial payment for legal services performed, transaction 6.

ASSIGNMENT

Record these transactions in the expanded accounting equation.
Prepare the financial statements at June 30 for Michael Brown, Attorney-at-Law.

Solution to Demonstration Problem

	Assets			= Liabilities +		Owner's Equity			
A.	Cash	+ Accts. Rec.	+ Office Equip.	= Accounts Payable	+ M. Brown, Capital	− M. Brown, Withdr.	+ Legal Fees	− Expenses
1.	+$6,000				+$6,000			
BAL.	6,000		=		6,000			
2.	−600		+$600					
BAL.	5,400	+	600 =		6,000			
3.			+1,000	+$1,000				
BAL.	5,400	+	1,600 =	1,000	+ 6,000			
4.	+2,000						+$2,000	
BAL.	7,400	+	1,600 =	1,000	+ 6,000		+ 2,000	
5.	−800							+$800
BAL.	6,600	+	1,600 =	1,000	+ 6,000		+ 2,000 −	800
6.	+$1,000						+1,000	
BAL.	6,600 +	1,000 +	1,600 =	1,000	+ 6,000		+ 3,000 −	800
7.	−1,200							+1,200
BAL.	5,400 +	1,000 +	1,600 =	1,000	+ 6,000		+ 3,000 −	2,000
8.	−500					+$500		
BAL.	4,900 +	1,000 +	1,600 =	1,000	+ 6,000	− 500	+ 3,000 −	2,000
9.	+500	−500						
END. BAL.	$5,400 +	$ 500 +	$1,600 =	$1,000	+ $6,000	− $500	+ $3,000 −	$2,000

$$\$7,500 = \$7,500$$

Solution Tips to Expanded Accounting Equation

- **Transaction 1:** The business increased its Cash by $6,000. Owner's Equity (capital) increased when Michael supplied the cash to the business.
- **Transaction 2:** A shift in assets occurred when the equipment was purchased. The business lowered its Cash by $600, and a new column—Office Equipment—was increased for the $600 of equipment that was bought. The amount of capital is not touched because the owner did not supply any new funds.
- **Transaction 3:** When creditors supply $1,000 of additional equipment, the business Accounts Payable shows the debt. The business had increased what it *owes* the creditors.
- **Transaction 4:** Legal Fees, a subdivision of Owner's Equity, is increased when the law firm provides a service even if no money is received. The service provides an inward flow of $2,000 to Cash, an asset. Remember that Legal Fees are *not* an asset. As Legal Fees increase, Owner's Equity increases.
- **Transaction 5:** The salary paid by Michael shows an $800 increase in Expenses and a corresponding decrease in Owner's Equity as well as a decrease in Cash.

- **Transaction 6:** Michael did the work and earned the $1,000. That $1,000 is recorded as revenue. This time the Legal Fees create an inward flow of assets called Accounts Receivable for $1,000. Remember that Legal Fees are *not* an asset. They are a subdivision of Owner's Equity.
- **Transaction 7:** The $1,200 rent expense reduces Owner's Equity as well as Cash.
- **Transaction 8:** Withdrawals are for personal use. Here the business decreases Cash by $500 while Michael's withdrawals increase $500. Withdrawals decrease the Owner's Equity.
- **Transaction 9:** This transaction does not reflect new revenue in the form of Legal Fees. It is only a shift in assets: more Cash and less Accounts Receivable.

Solution Tips to Financial Statements

B-1. The income statement lists only revenues and expenses for a period of time. The inside column is for subtotaling. Withdrawals are not listed here.

B-2. The statement of owner's equity takes the net income figure of $1,000 and adds it to beginning capital less any withdrawals. This new capital figure of $6,500 will go on the balance sheet. This statement shows changes in capital for a period of time.

B-3. The $5,400, $500, $1,600, and $1,000 came from the totals of the expanded accounting equation. The capital figure of $6,500 came from the statement of owner's equity. This balance sheet reports assets, liabilities, and a new figure for capital at a specific date.

B-1.

MICHAEL BROWN, ATTORNEY-AT-LAW
INCOME STATEMENT
FOR MONTH ENDED JUNE 30, 200X

Revenue:		
Legal Fees		$3,000
Operating Expenses:		
Salaries Expense	$ 800	
Rent Expense	1,200	
Total Operating Expenses		2,000
Net Income		$1,000

B-2.

MICHAEL BROWN, ATTORNEY-AT-LAW
STATEMENT OF OWNER'S EQUITY
FOR MONTH ENDED JUNE 30, 200X

Michael Brown, Capital, June 1, 200X		$6,000
Net income for June	$1,000	
Less withdrawls for June	500	
Increase in Capital		500
Michael Brown, Capital, June 30, 200X		$6,500

B-3.

MICHAEL BROWN, ATTORNEY-AT-LAW
BALANCE SHEET
JUNE 30, 200X

Assets		Liabilities and Owner's Equity	
Cash	$5,400	Liabilities	
Accounts Receivable	500	Accounts Payable	$1,000
Office Equipment	1,600	Owner's Equity	
		M. Brown, Capital	$6,500
Total Assets	$7,500	Total Liabilities and Owner's Equity	$7,500

SUMMARY OF KEY POINTS

LEARNING UNIT 1-1

1. The Sarbanes-Oxley rule helps prevent fraud at trading companies.
2. The functions of accounting involve analyzing, recording, classifying, summarizing, reporting, and interpreting financial information.
3. A sole proprietorship is a business owned by one person. A partnership is a business owned by two or more persons. A corporation is a business owned by stockholders. All forms of business organizations are found in Internet businesses.
4. Bookkeeping is the recording part of accounting.
5. The computer is a tool to use in the accounting process.
6. Assets = Liabilities + Owner's Equity is the basic accounting equation that aids in analyzing business transactions.
7. Liabilities represent amounts owed to creditors, whereas capital represents what is invested by the owner.
8. Capital does not mean cash. Capital is the owner's current investment. The owner could have invested equipment that was purchased before the new business was started.
9. In a shift of assets the composition of assets changes but the total of assets does not change. For example, if a bill is paid by a customer, the firm increases Cash (an asset) but decreases Accounts Receivable (an asset), so no overall increase in assets occurs; total assets remain the same. When you borrow money from a bank, you have an increase in cash (an asset) and an increase in liabilities; overall, assets increase rather than simply shift.

LEARNING UNIT 1-2

1. The balance sheet is a statement written as of a particular date. It lists the assets, liabilities, and owner's equity of a business. The heading of the balance sheet answers the questions *who, what,* and *when* (as of a specific date).
2. The balance sheet is a formal statement of a financial position.

LEARNING UNIT 1-3

1. Revenue generates an inward flow of assets. Expenses generate an outward flow of assets or a potential outward flow. Revenue and expenses are subdivisions of owner's equity. Revenue is not an asset.
2. When revenue totals more than expenses net income is the result; when expenses total more than revenue net loss is the result.
3. Owner's equity can be subdivided into four elements: capital, withdrawals, revenue, and expenses.
4. Withdrawals decrease owner's equity, revenue increases owner's equity, and expenses decrease owner's equity. A withdrawal is not a business expense; it is for personal use.

LEARNING UNIT 1-4

1. The income statement is a statement written for a specific period of time that lists earned revenue and expenses incurred to produce the earned revenue. The net income or net loss will be used in the statement of owner's equity.
2. The statement of owner's equity reveals the causes of a change in capital. This statement lists any investments, net income (or net loss), and withdrawals. The ending figure for capital will be used on the balance sheet.
3. The balance sheet uses the ending balances of assets and liabilities from the accounting equation and the capital from the statement of owner's equity.
4. The income statement should be prepared first because the information on it about net income or net loss is used to prepare the statement of owner's equity, which in turn provides information about capital for the balance sheet. In this way one statement builds upon the next, beginning with the income statement.

KEY TERMS

Accounting   A system that measures the business's activities in financial terms, provides written reports and financial statements about those activities, and communicates these reports to decision makers and others.

Accounts payable   Amounts owed to creditors that result from the purchase of goods or services on account—a liability.

Accounts receivable   An asset that indicates amounts owed by customers.

Assets   Properties (resources) of value owned by a business (cash, supplies, equipment, land).

Balance sheet   A statement, as of a particular date, that shows the amount of assets owned by a business as well as the amount of claims (liabilities and owner's equity) against these assets.

Basic accounting equation   Assets = Liabilities + Owner's Equity.

Bookkeeping   The recording function of the accounting process.

Capital   The owner's investment of equity in the company.

Corporation   A type of business organization that is owned by stockholders. Stockholders usually are not personally liable for the corporation's debts.

Creditor   Someone who has a claim to assets.

Ending capital   Beginning Capital + Additional Investments + Net Income − Withdrawals = Ending Capital. Or: Beginning Capital + Additional Investments − Net Loss − Withdrawals = Ending Capital.

Equities   The interest or financial claim of creditors (liabilities) and owners (owner's equity) who supply the assets to a firm.

Expanded accounting equation   Assets = Liabilities + Capital − Withdrawals + Revenue − Expenses.

Expense   A cost incurred in running a business by consuming goods or services in producing revenue; a subdivision of owner's equity. When expenses increase, there is a decrease in owner's equity.

Generally accepted accounting principles (GAAP)   The procedures and guidelines that must be followed during the accounting process.

Income statement   An accounting statement that details the performance of a firm (revenue minus expenses) for a specific period of time.

Liabilities   Obligations that come due in the future. Liabilities result in increasing the financial rights or claims of creditors to assets.

Manufacturer   Business that makes a product and sells it to its customers.

Merchandise company   Business that buys a product from a manufacturing company to sell to its customers.

Net income   When revenue totals more than expenses, the result is net income.

Net loss   When expenses total more than revenue, the result is net loss.

Owner's equity   Rights or financial claims to the assets of a business (in the accounting equation, assets minus liabilities).

Partnership   A form of business organization that has at least two owners. The partners usually are personally liable for the partnership's debts.

Revenue   An amount earned by performing services for customers or selling goods to customers; it can be in the form of cash or accounts receivable. A subdivision of owner's equity: As revenue increases, owner's equity increases.

Service company   Business that provides a service.

Shift in assets   A shift that occurs when the composition of the assets has changed but the total of the assets remains the same.

Sole proprietorship   A type of business ownership that has one owner. The owner is personally liable for paying the business's debts.

Statement of financial position   Another name for a balance sheet.

Statement of owner's equity   A financial statement that reveals the change in capital. The ending figure for capital is then placed on the balance sheet.

Supplies   One type of asset acquired by a firm; it has a much shorter life than equipment.

Withdrawals   A subdivision of owner's equity that records money or other assets an owner withdraws from a business for personal use.

BLUEPRINT: FINANCIAL STATEMENTS

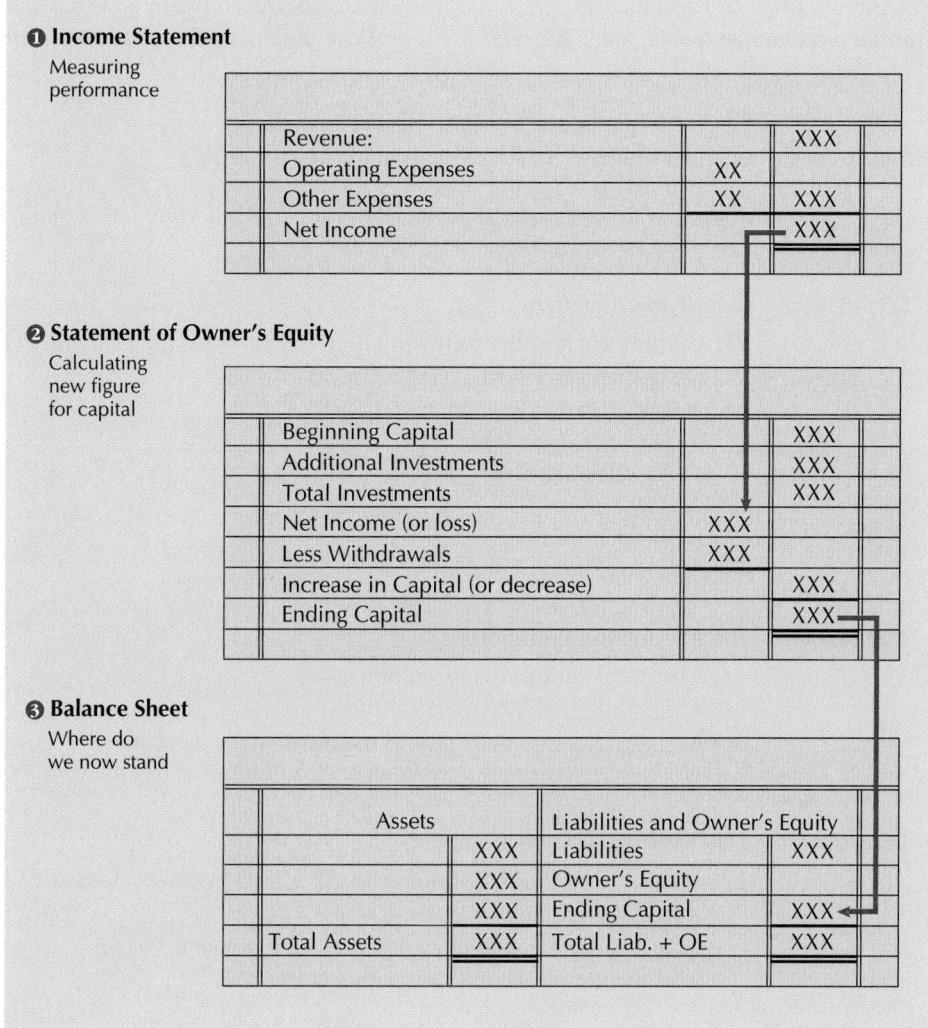

❶ Income Statement
Measuring
performance

Revenue:			XXX
Operating Expenses		XX	
Other Expenses		XX	XXX
Net Income			XXX

❷ Statement of Owner's Equity
Calculating
new figure
for capital

Beginning Capital			XXX
Additional Investments			XXX
Total Investments			XXX
Net Income (or loss)		XXX	
Less Withdrawals		XXX	
Increase in Capital (or decrease)			XXX
Ending Capital			XXX

❸ Balance Sheet
Where do
we now stand

Assets			Liabilities and Owner's Equity	
		XXX	Liabilities	XXX
		XXX	Owner's Equity	
		XXX	Ending Capital	XXX
Total Assets		XXX	Total Liab. + OE	XXX

QUESTIONS, CLASSROOM DEMONSTRATION EXERCISES, EXERCISES, AND PROBLEMS

Discussion and Critical Thinking Questions/Ethical Case

1. What are the functions of accounting?

2. Define, compare, and contrast sole proprietorships, partnerships, and corporations.

3. How are businesses classified?

4. What is the relationship of bookkeeping to accounting?

5. List the three elements of the basic accounting equation.

6. Define capital.

7. The total of the left-hand side of the accounting equation must equal the total of the right-hand side. True or false? Please explain.

8. A balance sheet tells a company where it is going and how well it performs. True or false? Please explain.

9. Revenue is an asset. True or false? Please explain.

10. Owner's equity is subdivided into what categories?

11. A withdrawal is a business expense. True or false? Please explain.

12. As expenses increase they cause owner's equity to increase. Defend or reject.

13. What does an income statement show?

14. The statement of owner's equity only calculates ending withdrawals. True or false? Please explain.

15. Paul Kloss, accountant for Lowe & Co., traveled to New York on company business. His total expenses came to $350. Paul felt that because the trip extended over the weekend he would "pad" his expense account with an additional $100 of expenses. After all, weekends represent his own time, not the company's. What would you do? Write your specific recommendations to Paul.

MyAccountingLab **Classroom Demonstration Exercises**

SET A

LO1 (5 min) **Classifying Accounts**

1. Classify each of the following items as an Asset (A), Liability (L), or part of Owner's Equity (OE).
   a. Apple iPod   _____
   b. Accounts Receivable _____
   c. Accounts Payable   _____
   d. Cash   _____
   e. B. James, Capital   _____
   f. Kodak Digital Camera _____

LO1 (5 min) **The Accounting Equation**

2. Complete the following statements.
   a. _____: rights of the creditors
   b. _____ are total value of items owned by a business.
   c. _____ _____ is an unwritten promise to pay the creditor.

LO1 (5 min) **Shift versus Increase in Assets**

3. Identify which transaction results in a shift in assets (S) and which transaction causes an increase in assets (I).
   a. Staples bought computer equipment on account.
   b. JCPenney bought office equipment for cash.

LO2, 4 (5 min) **The Balance Sheet**

4. From the following, calculate what would be the total of assets on the balance sheet.

B. Fleese, Capital	$18,000
Computer Equipment	4,000
Accounts Payable	6,000
Cash	12,000

LO3 (5 min) **The Accounting Equation Expanded**

5. From the following, which are subdivisions of owner's equity?
   a. Trees   _____
   b. J. Penny, Capital   _____
   c. Accounts Payable   _____
   d. J. Penny, Withdrawals _____
   e. Accounts Receivable _____
   f. Advertising Expense _____
   g. Taxi Fees Earned   _____
   h. Computer Equipment   _____

Identifying Assets   *LO2 (5 min)*

6. Identify which of the following are *not* assets.
   a. DVD Player   _____
   b. Accounts Receivable   _____
   c. Accounts Payable   _____
   d. Grooming Fees Earned _____

The Accounting Equation Expanded   *LO3 (5 min)*

7. Which of the following statements are false?
   a. _____ Revenue provides only outward flows of cash.
   b. _____ Revenue is a subdivision of Assets.
   c. _____ Revenue provides an inward flow of cash or accounts
      receivable.
   d. _____ Expenses are part of Total Assets.

Preparing Financial Statements   *LO4 (5 min)*

8. Indicate whether the following items would appear on the income statement (IS),
   statement of owner's equity (OE), or balance sheet (BS).
   a. _____ Tutoring Fees Earned
   b. _____ Office Equipment
   c. _____ Accounts Receivable
   d. _____ Office Supplies
   e. _____ Legal Fees Earned
   f. _____ Advertising Expenses
   g. _____ J. Earl, Capital (Beg.)
   h. _____ Accounts Payable

Preparing Financial Statements   *LO4 (5 min)*

9. Indicate next to each statement whether it refers to the income statement (IS),
   statement of owner's equity (OE), or balance sheet (BS).
   a. _____ Withdrawals found on it
   b. _____ List total of all assets
   c. _____ Statement that is prepared last
   d. _____ Statement listing net income

SET B

Classifying Accounts   *LO1 (5 min)*

1. Classify each of the following items as an Asset (A), Liability (L), or part of
   Owner's Equity (OE).
   a. Salaries Payable   _____
   b. Accounts Payable   _____
   c. J. Free, Capital   _____
   d. Office Supplies   _____
   e. Cash   _____
   f. Sony Digital Camera   _____

The Accounting Equation   *LO1 (5 min)*

2. Complete the following statements.
   a. A _____ _____ _____ results when the total of the assets remains the
      same but the makeup of the assets has changed.
   b. Assets − _____ = Owner's Equity.
   c. Capital does not mean _____.

LO1 (5 min)   **Shift versus Increase in Assets**

3. Identify which transaction results in a shift in assets (S) and which transaction causes an increase in assets (I).
   a. Office Max bought computer equipment for cash.
   b. The Gap bought office equipment on account.

LO2, 4 (5 min)   **The Balance Sheet**

4. From the following, calculate what would be the total of assets on the balance sheet.

B. Bryan, Capital	$15,000
Word Processing Equipment	2,000
Accounts Payable	8,000
Cash	14,000

LO3 (5 min)   **The Accounting Equation Expanded**

5. From the following, which are subdivisions of owner's equity?
   a. Land   _____
   b. M. Kaminsky, Capital   _____
   c. Accounts Receivable   _____
   d. M. Kaminsky, Withdrawals   _____
   e. Accounts Payable   _____
   f. Rent Expense   _____
   g. Office Equipment   _____
   h. Hair Salon Fees Earned   _____

LO2 (5 min)   **Identifying Assets**

6. Identify which of the following are *not* assets.
   a. Fax Machines
   b. Accounts Payable
   c. Legal Fees Earned
   d. Accounts Receivable

LO3 (5 min)   **The Accounting Equation Expanded**

7. Which of the following statements are false?
   a. _____ Revenue is an asset.
   b. _____ Revenue is a subdivision of Owner's Equity.
   c. _____ Revenue provides an inward flow of cash or accounts receivable.
   d. _____ Withdrawals are part of Total Assets.

LO4 (5 min)   **Preparing Financial Statements**

8. Indicate whether the following items would appear on the income statement (IS), statement of owner's equity (OE), or balance sheet (BS).
   a. _____ B. Clo, Withdrawals
   b. _____ Office Supplies
   c. _____ Accounts Payable
   d. _____ Computer Equipment
   e. _____ Commission Fees Earned
   f. _____ Salaries Expense
   g. _____ B. Clo, Capital (Beg.)
   h. _____ Accounts Receivable

Preparing Financial Statements   *LO4 (5 min)*

9. Indicate next to each statement whether it refers to the income statement (IS), statement of owner's equity (OE), or balance sheet (BS).
   a. _____ Calculate new figure for capital
   b. _____ Prepared as of a particular date
   c. _____ Statement that is prepared first
   d. _____ Statement listing revenues and expenses

Exercises   *MyAccountingLab*

1-1. Complete the following table: *LO2 (5 min)*

Assets = Liabilities + Owner's Equity
   a. $19,000 =   ?   + $4,000
   b.   ?   = $6,000   + $9,000
   c. $10,000 = $4,000   +   ?

1-2. Record the following transactions in the basic accounting equation. Treat each   *LO2 (5 min)*
one separately.

Assets = Liabilities + Owner's Equity
   a. Matty invests $120,000 in company.
   b. Bought equipment for cash, $600.
   c. Bought equipment on account, $900.

1-3. From the following, prepare a balance sheet for Range Co. Cleaners at the end of   *LO2, 4 (10 min)*
November 200X: Cash, $50,000; Equipment, $7,000; Accounts Payable, $14,000; B. Range, Capital.

1-4. Record the following transactions into the expanded accounting equation. The   *LO3 (15 min)*
running balance may be omitted for simplicity.

Assets	= Liabilities +	Owner's Equity

Cash + Accounts + Computer = Accounts + B. Bell, − B. Bell,   + Revenues − Expenses
       Receivable Equipment   Payable   Capital   Withdrawals

   a. Bell invested $60,000 in a computer company.
   b. Bought computer equipment on account, $7,000.
   c. Bell paid personal telephone bill from company checkbook, $200.
   d. Received cash for services rendered, $14,000.
   e. Billed customers for services rendered for month, $30,000.
   f. Paid current rent expense, $4,000.
   g. Paid supplies expense, $1,500.

1-5. From the following account balances, prepare in proper form for June (a) an income   *LO4 (20 min)*
statement, (b) a statement of owner's equity, and (c) a balance sheet for French Realty.

Cash	$3,310	S. French, Withdrawals	$ 40
Accounts Receivable	1,490	Professional Fees	2,900
Office Equipment	6,700	Salaries Expense	500
Accounts Payable	2,000	Utilities Expense	360
S. French, Capital, June 1, 200X	8,000	Rent Expense	500

Group A Problems   *MyAccountingLab*

1A-1. Mia Anabelle decided to open Mia's Nail Spa. Mia completed the following   *LO2 (15 min)*
transactions:
   a. Invested $20,000 cash from her personal bank account into the business.
   b. Bought store equipment for cash, $4,000.

Check Figure:
Cash $15,000

c. Bought additional store equipment on account, $6,000.

d. Paid $1,000 cash to partially reduce what was owed from transaction C.

Based on this information, record these transactions into the basic accounting equation.

LO2, 4 (15 min)

Check Figure:
Total Assets $52,000

1A-2. Bill See is the accountant for See's Internet Service. From the following information, his task is to construct a balance sheet as of September 30, 200X, in proper form. Could you help him?

Building	$20,000	Cash	$18,000
Accounts Payable	15,000	Equipment	14,000
See, Capital	37,000		

LO3 (20 min)

1A-3. At the end of November, Rick Fox decided to open his own typing service. Analyze the following transactions he completed by recording their effects into the expanded accounting equation.
a. Invested $10,000 in his typing service.
b. Bought new office equipment on account, $4,000.
c. Received cash for typing services rendered, $500.
d. Performed typing services on account, $2,100.
e. Paid secretary's salary, $350.
f. Paid office supplies expense for the month, $210.
g. Rent expenses for office due but unpaid, $900.
h. Withdrew cash for personal use, $400.

Check Figure:
Total Assets $15,640

LO4 (30 min)

Check Figure:
Total Assets $3,385

1A-4. Jane West, owner of West Stenciling Service, has requested that you prepare from the following balances (a) an income statement for June 200X, (b) a statement of owner's equity for June, and (c) a balance sheet as of June 30, 200X.

Cash	$2,300	Stenciling Fees	$3,000
Accounts Receivable	400	Advertising Expense	110
Equipment	685	Repair Expense	25
Accounts Payable	310	Travel Expense	250
J. West, Capital, June 1, 200X	1,200	Supplies Expense	190
J. West, Withdrawals	300	Rent Expense	250

LO2, 3, 4 (45 min)

1A-5. John Tobey, a retired army officer, opened Tobey's Catering Service. As his accountant, analyze the transactions listed next and present them in proper form.
a. The analysis of the transactions by using the expanded accounting equation.
b. A balance sheet showing the position of the firm before opening for business on October 31, 200X.
c. An income statement for the month of November.
d. A statement of owner's equity for November.
e. A balance sheet as of November 30, 200X.

Check Figure:
Total Assets,
Nov. 30 $24,060

200X

Oct. 25   John Tobey invested $20,000 in the catering business from his personal savings account.
   27   Bought equipment for cash from Munroe Co., $700.
   28   Bought additional equipment on account from Ryan Co., $1,000.
   29   Paid $600 to Ryan Co. as partial payment of the October 28 transaction.

(You should now prepare your balance sheet as of October 31, 200X.)

Nov. 1   Catered a graduation and immediately collected cash, $2,400.
   5   Paid salaries of employees, $690.
   8   Prepared desserts for customers on account, $300.

10   Received $100 cash as partial payment of November 8 transaction.

15   Paid telephone bill, $60.

17   Paid his home electric bill from the company's checkbook, $90.

20   Catered a wedding and received cash, $1,800.

25   Bought additional equipment on account, $400.

28   Rent expense due but unpaid, $600.

30   Paid supplies expense, $400.

Group B Problems

1B-1. Mia Annabelle began a new business called Mia's Nail Spa. The following transactions resulted:
  a. Mia invested $16,000 cash from her personal bank account into the Nail Spa.
  b. Bought store equipment on account, $1,500.
  c. Paid $800 cash to partially reduce what was owed from transaction B.
  d. Purchased additional store equipment for cash, $3,000.

  Record these transactions into the basic accounting equation.

LO2 (15 min)

Check Figure:
Cash $12,200

1B-2. Bill See, accountant, has asked you to prepare a balance sheet as of September 30, 200X, for See's. Could you assist Bill?

Blues, Capital	$24,000
Accounts Payable	60,000
Equipment	40,000
Building	28,000
Cash	16,000

LO2, 4 (15 min)

Check Figure:
Total Assets $84,000

1B-3. Rick Fox decided to open his own typing service company at the end of November. Analyze the following transactions by recording their effects on the expanded accounting equation:
  a. Rick invested $9,000 in the typing service.
  b. Purchased new office equipment on account, $3,000.
  c. Received cash for typing services rendered, $1,290.
  d. Paid secretary's salary, $310.
  e. Billed customers for typing services rendered, $2,690.
  f. Paid rent expense for the month, $500.
  g. Rick withdrew cash for personal use, $350.
  h. Advertising expense due but unpaid, $100.

LO3 (20 min)

Check Figure:
Total Assets $14,820

1B-4. Jane West, owner of West Stenciling Service, has requested that you prepare from the following balances (a) an income statement for June 200X, (b) a statement of owner's equity for June, and (c) a balance sheet as of June 30, 200X.

LO3 (30 min)

Check Figure:
Total Assets $3,723

Cash	$2,043	Stenciling Fees	$1,098
Accounts Receivable	1,140	Advertising Expense	135
Equipment	540	Repair Expense	45
Accounts Payable	45	Travel Expense	90
J. West, Capital, June 1, 200X	3,720	Supplies Expense	270
J. West, Withdrawals	360	Rent Expense	240

LO2, 3, 4 (45 min)

1B-5. John Tobey, a retired army officer, opened Tobey's Catering Service. As his accountant, analyze the transactions and present the following information in proper form:

a. The analysis of the transactions by using the expanded accounting equation.

b. A balance sheet showing the financial position of the firm before opening on November 1, 200X.

c. An income statement for the month of November.

d. A statement of owner's equity for November.

e. A balance sheet as of November 30, 200X.

200X

Oct.	25	John Tobey invested $17,500 in the catering business.
	27	Bought equipment on account from Munroe Co., $900.
	28	Bought equipment for cash from Ryan Co., $1,500.
	29	Paid $300 to Munroe Co. as partial payment of the October 27 transaction.
Nov.	1	Catered a business luncheon and immediately collected cash, $2,000.
	5	Paid salaries of employees, $350.
	8	Provided catering services to Northwest Community College on account, $4,500.
	10	Received from Northwest Community College $1,000 cash as partial payment of November 8 transaction.
	15	Paid telephone bill, $95.
	17	John paid his home mortgage from the company's checkbook, $650.
	20	Provided catering services and received cash, $1,800.
	25	Bought additional equipment on account, $300.
	28	Rent expense due but unpaid, $750.
	30	Paid supplies expense, $600.

Check Figure:
Total Assets,
Nov. 30 $25,005

ON-THE-JOB TRAINING

LO3, 4 (20 min)

T-1. You have just been hired to prepare, if possible, an income statement for the year ended December 31, 200X, for Roger's Window Washing Company. The problem is that Roger Smith kept only the following records (on the back of a piece of cardboard):

FIGURE 1.10 Financial Records

Dollars in:
My investment .... $ 1,200
Window cleaning 11,376
Loan from brother-in-law 4,000

Dollars out:
Salaries $5,080
Withdrawals 6,200
Supplies expense 1,400

What I owe or they owe me
A. People who work for me but I still owe salaries to $1,800
B. Owe bank interest of $300
C. Work done but clients still owe me $2,900
D. Advertising bill due but not paid $95

Assume that Roger's Window Washing Company records all revenues when earned and all expenses when incurred.

You feel that it is part of your job to tell Roger how to organize his records better. What would you tell him?

T-2. While Jon Lune was on a business trip, he asked Abby Slowe, the bookkeeper for Lune Co., to try to complete a balance sheet for the year ended December 31, 200X. Abby, who had been on the job only two months, submitted the following:

LO2, 4 (30 min)

FIGURE 1.11 Balance Sheet

LUNE CO. FOR THE YEAR ENDED DECEMBER 31, 200X				
Building	$44 6 0 0 00	Accounts Payable	$127 6 0 4 00
Land	72 9 3 5 00	Accounts Receivable	104 3 3 7 00
Notes Payable	75 3 2 8 00	Auto	14 2 6 8 00
Cash	10 0 1 6 00	Desks	6 8 2 5 00
J. Lune, Capital	?	Total Equity	$250 0 3 4 00

1. Could you help Abby fix as well as complete the balance sheet?
2. What written recommendations would you make about the bookkeeper? Should she be retained?
3. Suppose that (a) Jon Lune invested an additional $20,000 in cash as well as additional desks with a value of $8,000, and (b) Lune Co. bought an auto for $6,000 that was originally marked $8,000, paying $2,000 down and issuing a note for the balance. Could you prepare an updated balance sheet?

FINANCIAL REPORT PROBLEM

Reading the Kellogg Annual Report

LO2, 4 (5 min)

Go to the annual report for Kellogg Company in Appendix A. Find the balance sheet and calculate the following: How much did cash increase in 2006 from 2005?

INTERNET PROJECT

Best Buy

Go to the Web and search: Annual Report Best Buy 2008.
Click on Investors Relations.
List out the latest news Best Buy is providing to its investors.
Order a free annual report.

CONTINUING PROBLEM

MyAccountingLab

Sanchez Computer Center

LO3, 4 (45 min)

The following problem continues from one chapter to the next, carrying the balances of each month forward. Each chapter focuses on the learning experience of the chapter and adds information as the business grows.

Assignment

1. Set up an expanded accounting equation spreadsheet using the following accounts:

Assets	Liabilities	Owner's Equity
Cash	Accounts Payable	Freedman, Capital
Supplies		Freedman, Withdrawal
Computer Shop		Service Revenue
Equipment		Expenses (notate type)
Office Equipment		

2. Analyze and record each transaction in the expanded accounting equation.
3. Prepare the financial statements ending July 31 for Sanchez Computer Center.

On July 1, 200X, Tony Freedman decided to begin his own computer service business. He named the business the Sanchez Computer Center. During the first month Tony conducted the following business transactions:

a. Invested $4,500 of his savings into the business.
b. Paid $1,200 (check # 8095) for the computer from Multi Systems, Inc.
c. Paid $600 (check # 8096) for office equipment from Office Furniture, Inc.
d. Set up a new account with Office Depot and purchased $250 in office supplies on credit.
e. Paid July rent, $400 (check # 8097).
f. Repaired a system for a customer and collected $250.
g. Collected $200 for system upgrade labor charge from a customer.
h. Electric bill due but unpaid, $85.
i. Collected $1,200 for services performed on Taylor Golf computers.
j. Withdrew $100 (check # 8098) to take his wife, Carol, out in celebration of opening the new business.

SUBWAY Case

A FRESH START

LO4 (20 min)

"Hey, Stan the man!" a loud voice boomed. "I never thought I'd see you making sandwiches!" Stan Hernandez stopped layering lettuce in a foot-long submarine sandwich and grinned at his old college buddy, Ron.

"Neither did I. But then again," said Stan, "I never thought I'd own a profitable business either."

That night, catching up on their lives over dinner, Stan told Ron how he became the proud owner of a Subway sandwich restaurant.

"After working like crazy at Xellent Media for five years and *finally* making it to marketing manager, then wham . . . I got laid off," said Stan. "That very day I was having my lunch at the local Subway as usual, when. . . . "

"Hmmm, wait a minute! I did notice you've lost quite a bit of weight," Ron interrupted and began to hum the bars of Subway's latest ad featuring Clay Henry, yet another hefty male who lost weight on a diet of Subway sandwiches.

"Right!" Stan quipped, "Not only was I laid off, but I was 'downsizing'! *Anyway,* I was eating a Dijon horseradish melt when I opened up an *Entrepreneur* magazine someone had left on the table—right to the headline 'Subway Named #1 Franchise in All Categories for 11th Time in 15 Years.'"

Well, to make a foot-long submarine sandwich story short, Stan realized his long-time dream of being his own boss by owning a business with a proven product and highly successful business model. When you look at Stan's restaurant, you are really seeing two businesses. Even though Stan is the sole proprietor of his business, he operates under an agreement with Subway of Milford, Connecticut. Subway supplies the business know-how and support (like training at Subway University, national advertising, and gourmet bread recipes). Stan supplies capital (his $12,500 investment) and his food preparation, management, and elbow grease. Subway and Stan operate interdependent businesses, and both rely on accounting information for their success.

Subway, in business since 1965, has grown dramatically over the years and now has more than 18,000 locations in 73 countries. It has even surpassed McDonald's in the number of locations in the United States and Canada. To manage this enormous service business requires careful control of each of its stores. At a Subway regional office, Mariah Washington, a field consultant for Stan's territory, monitors Stan's restaurant closely. In addition to making monthly visits to check whether Stan is complying with Subway's model in everything from décor to uniforms to food quality and safety, she also looks closely at Stan's weekly sales and inventory reports. When Stan's sales go up, Subway's do too, because each Subway franchisee, like Stan, pays Subway, the franchiser, a percentage of sales in the form of royalties.

Why does headquarters require accounting reports? Accounting reports give the information both Stan and the company need to make business decisions in a number of vital areas. For example:

- Before Stan could buy his Subway restaurant, the company needed to know how much cash Stan had and his assets and liabilities (such as credit card debt). Stan prepared a personal balance sheet to give them this information.
- Stan must have the right amount of supplies on hand. If he has too few, he can't make the sandwiches. If he has too many for the amount he expects to sell, items such as sandwich meats and bread dough may spoil. The inventory report tells Mariah what supplies are on hand. In combination with the sales report, it also alerts Mariah to potential red flags: If Stan is reporting that he is using far too much bread dough for the amount of sandwiches he is selling, a problem would be indicated.
- Although Subway does not require its restaurant owners to report operating costs and profit information, Subway gives them the option and most franchisees take it. Information on profitability helps Mariah and Stan make decisions such as whether and when to remodel or buy new equipment.

So that its restaurant owners can make business decisions in a timely manner, Subway requires them to submit the weekly sales and inventory report to headquarters electronically every Thursday by 2:00 P.M. Stan has his latest report in mind as he makes a move to pay the bill for his dinner with Ron. "We had a great week. Let me get this," he says. "Thanks, Stan the Man. I'm going to keep in touch because I may just be ready for a business opportunity of my own!"

Discussion Questions

1. What makes Stan a sole proprietor?
2. Why are Stan and Subway interdependent businesses?
3. Why did Stan have to share his personal balance sheet with Subway? Do you think most interdependent businesses operate this way?
4. What does Subway learn from Stan's weekly sales and inventory reports?

2

Debits and Credits: Analyzing and Recording Business Transactions

DID YOU KNOW? In 2006 20% of sales came from Staples brands. The company plans to increase that number to 30%. Staples has recycled more than 17 million ink and toner cartridges. Visit *www.staples.com* to find more information about Staples.

LEARNING OBJECTIVES

1. Setting up and organizing a chart of accounts.

2. Recording transactions in T accounts according to the rules of debit and credit.

3. Preparing a trial balance.

4. Preparing financial statements from a trial balance.

In Chapter 1 we used the expanded accounting equation to document the financial transactions performed by Mia Wong's law firm. Remember how long it was: The cash column had a long list of pluses and minuses, with no quick system of recording and summarizing the increases and decreases of cash or other items. Can you imagine the problem Staples would have if it used the expanded accounting equation to track the thousands of business transactions it makes each day?

Learning Unit 2-1 The T Account

Let's look at the problem a little more closely. Each business transaction is recorded in the accounting equation under a specific **account.** Different accounts are used for each of the subdivisions of the accounting equation: asset accounts, liabilities accounts, expense accounts, revenue accounts, and so on. What is needed is a way to record the increases and decreases in specific account *categories* and yet keep them together in one place. The answer is the **standard account** form (see Figure 2.1). A standard account is a formal account that includes columns for date, item, posting reference, debit, and credit. Each account has a separate form, and all transactions affecting that account are recorded on the form. All the business's account forms (which often are referred to as *ledger accounts*) are then placed in a **ledger.** Each page of the ledger contains one account. The ledger may be in the form of a bound or a loose-leaf book. If computers are used, the ledger may be part of a computer file. For simplicity's sake, we use the **T account** form. This form got its name because it looks like the letter T. Generally, T accounts are used for demonstration purposes. Each T account contains three basic parts:

1

Title of Account

2 Left side	Right side **3**

All T accounts have this structure.

In accounting, the left side of any T account is called the **debit** side.

Left side Dr. (debit)	

DEBIT DEFINED:
1. The *left* side of any T account.
2. A number entered on the left side of any account is said to be *debited* to an account.

Just as the word *left* has many meanings, the word *debit* for now in accounting means a position, the left side of an account. Do not think of it as good (+) or bad (−).

Amounts entered on the left side of any account are said to be *debited* to an account. The abbreviation for debit, Dr., is from the Latin *debere*.

The right side of any T account is called the **credit** side.

	Right side Cr. (credit)

CREDIT DEFINED:
1. The *right* side of any T account.
2. A number entered on the right side of any account is said to be *credited* to an account.

Amounts entered on the right side of an account are said to be *credited* to an account. The abbreviation for credit, Cr., is from the Latin *credere*.

At this point do not associate the definition of debit and credit with the words *increase* or *decrease*. Think of debit or credit as only indicating a *position* (left or right side) of a T account.

Account Title							Account No.	
Date	Item	PR	Debit	Date	Item	PR	Credit	

FIGURE 2.1 The Standard Account Form Is the Source of the T Account's Shape

Balancing an Account

No matter which individual account is being balanced, the procedure used to balance it is the same.

	Dr.	Cr.
Entries	5,000	400
	600	500
Footings	5,600	900
Balance	4,700	

In the "real" world, the T account would also include the date of the transaction. The date would appear to the left of the entry:

		Dr.		Cr.
4/2		5,000	4/3	400
4/20		600	4/25	500
		5,600		900
	Bal	4,700		

Note that on the debit (left) side the numbers add up to $5,600. On the credit (right) side the numbers add up to $900. The $5,600 and the $900 written in small type are called **footings.** Footings help in calculating the new (or ending) balance. The **ending balance** ($4,700) is placed on the debit or left side, because the balance of the debit side is greater than that of the credit side.

Remember that the ending balance does not tell us anything about increase or decrease. It only tells us that we have an ending balance of $4,700 on the debit side.

> If the balance is greater on the credit side, that is the side the ending balance would be on.

LEARNING UNIT 2-1 REVIEW

AT THIS POINT you should be able to

- Define ledger.
- State the purpose of a T account.
- Identify the three parts of a T account.
- Define debit.
- Define credit.
- Explain footings and calculate the balance of an account.

Self-Review Quiz 2-1

Respond True or False to the following:

1.

	Dr.	Cr.
	3,000	200
	200	600

The balance of the account is $2,400 Cr.

2. A credit always means increase.

3. A debit is the left side of any account.

4. A ledger can be prepared manually or by computer.

5. Footings replace the need for debits and credits.

For additional help go to
www.pearsonhighered.com/slater

Solutions to Self-Review Quiz 2-1

1. False

2. False

3. True

4. True

5. False

NEED HELP?

Let's review first: Debit does not mean good or bad. Instead, it represents a position, the left side of any account. Credit does not mean good or bad either. It represents a position, the right side of any account.

1. It is false because if you add the two debits of 3,000 and 200 you get 3,200 on the debit, or left side. A dr. + dr. = Debit balance. Now if you add the credit side of 200 and 600 you get a balance of 800 on the credit side. A cr. + cr. = Credit balance. To find the ending balance we take 3,200 less the 800 to arrive at a balance that is still larger on the DEBIT side by 2,400.

2. A credit is a position. It is the right side of any account.

3. Yes, the debit is always the left-hand side of any account. It does not mean good or bad.

4. Years ago the ledger, a group of accounts, was prepared manually; however, today most ledgers are updated by computer software.

5. Footings are used to add debits and credits to arrive at a new balance. Think of footings as the totals of a column.

Learning Unit 2-2 Recording Business Transactions: Debits and Credits

Can you get a queen in checkers? In a baseball game, does a runner rounding first base skip second base and run over the pitcher's mound to get to third? No; most of us don't do such things because we follow the rules of the game. Usually we learn the rules first and reflect on the reasons for them afterward. The same is true in accounting.

Instead of first trying to understand all the rules of debit and credit and how they were developed in accounting, it is easier to learn the rules by "playing the game."

T Account Entries for Accounting in the Accounting Equation

Have patience. Learning the rules of debit and credit is like learning to play any game: The more you play, the easier it becomes. Table 2.1 shows the rules for the side on which you enter an increase or a decrease for each of the separate accounts in the accounting equation. For example, an increase is entered on the debit side in the asset account but on the credit side for a liability account.

LO2

TABLE 2.1 **Rules of Debit and Credit**		
Account Category	Increase (Normal Balance)	Decrease
Assets	Debit	Credit
Liabilities	Credit	Debit
Owner's Equity		
Capital	Credit	Debit
Withdrawals	Debit	Credit
Revenue	Credit	Debit
Expenses	Debit	Credit

It might be easier to visualize these rules of debit and credit if we look at them in the T account form, using + to show increase and − to show decrease.

Assets = Liabilities + Owner's Equity

Dr.	Cr.		Dr.	Cr.	+	Capital		−	Withdrawals	+	Revenue		−	Expenses	
+	−		−	+		Dr.	Cr.		Dr.	Cr.	Dr.	Cr.		Dr.	Cr.
						−	+		+	−	−	+		+	−

Rules for Assets Work in the Opposite Direction to Those for Liabilities When you look at the equation you can see that the rules for assets work in the opposite direction to those for liabilities. That is, for assets the increases appear on the debit side and the decreases are shown on the credit side; the opposite is true for liabilities. As for the owner's equity, the rules for withdrawals and expenses, which *decrease* owner's equity, work in the opposite direction to the rules for capital and revenue, which *increase* owner's equity.

Assets		+	Withdrawals		+	Expenses		=	Liabilities		+	Capital		+	Revenue	
Dr.	Cr.		Dr.	Cr.		Dr.	Cr.		Dr.	Cr.		Dr.	Cr.		Dr.	Cr.
+	−		+	−		+	−		−	+		−	+		−	+

This setup may help you visualize how the rules for withdrawals and expenses are just the opposite of those for capital and revenue.

A **normal balance of an account** is the side that increases by the rules of debit and credit. For example, the balance of cash is a debit balance, because an asset is increased by a debit. We discuss normal balances further in Chapter 3.

Balancing the Equation It is important to remember that any amount(s) entered on the debit side of a T account or accounts also must be on the credit side of another T account or accounts. This approach ensures that the total amount added to the debit side will equal the total amount added to the credit side, thereby keeping the accounting equation in balance.

Normal Balance	
Dr.	Cr.
Assets	Liabilities
Withdrawals	Capital
Expenses	Revenue

Chart of Accounts Our job is to analyze Mia Wong's business transactions—the transactions we looked at in Chapter 1—using a system of accounts guided by the rules of debit and credit that will summarize increases and decreases of individual accounts in the ledger. The goal is to prepare an income statement, statement of owner's equity, and balance sheet

LO1

TABLE 2.2 Chart of Accounts for Mia Wong, Attorney-at-Law

Balance Sheet Accounts

Assets		Liabilities
111 Cash		211 Accounts Payable
112 Accounts Receivable		**Owner's Equity**
121 Office Equipment		311 Mia Wong, Capital
		312 Mia Wong, Withdrawals

Income Statement Accounts

Revenue		Expenses
411 Legal Fees		511 Salaries Expense
		512 Rent Expense
		513 Advertising Expense

> The chart of accounts aids in locating and identifying accounts quickly.

for Mia Wong. Sound familiar? If this system works, the rules of debit and credit and the use of accounts will give us the same answers as in Chapter 1, but with greater ease.

Mia's accountant developed what is called a **chart of accounts.** The chart of accounts is a numbered list of all of the business's accounts. It allows accounts to be located quickly. In Mia's business, for example, 100s are assets, 200s are liabilities, and so on. As you see in Table 2.2, each separate asset and liability account has its own number. Note that the chart may be expanded as the business grows.

The Transaction Analysis: Five Steps

We will analyze the transactions in Mia Wong's law firm using a teaching device called a *transaction analysis chart* to record these five steps. (Keep in mind that the transaction analysis chart is not a part of any formal accounting system.) The five steps to analyzing each business transaction include the following:

Step 1 Determine which accounts are affected. Example: Cash, Accounts Payable, Rent Expense. A transaction always affects at least two accounts.

Step 2 Determine which categories the accounts belong to: assets, liabilities, capital, withdrawals, revenue, or expenses. Example: Cash is an asset.

Step 3 Determine whether the accounts increase or decrease. Example: If you receive cash, that account increases.

Step 4 What do the rules of debit and credit say (Table 2.1)?

Step 5 What does the T account look like? Place amounts into accounts either on the left or right side depending on the rules in Table 2.1.

> Remember that the rules of debit and credit only tell us on which side to place information. Whether the debit or credit represents increases or decreases depends on the account category: assets, liabilities, capital, and so on. Think of a business transaction as an exchange: You get something and you give or part with something.

The following chart shows the five-step analysis from another perspective.

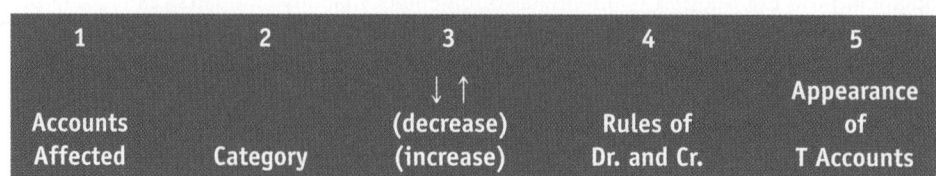

1	2	3	4	5
		↓ ↑		Appearance
Accounts		(decrease)	Rules of	of
Affected	Category	(increase)	Dr. and Cr.	T Accounts

Let us emphasize a major point: *Do not try to debit or credit an account until you go through the first three steps of the transaction analysis.*

Applying the Transaction Analysis to Mia Wong's Law Practice

Transaction A August 28: Mia Wong invests $6,000 cash and $200 of office equipment in the business.

---

1 Accounts Affected	2 Category	3 ↓ ↑	4 Rules of Dr. and Cr.	5 Appearance of T Accounts
Cash	Asset	↑	Dr.	Cash 111 (A) **6,000**
Office Equipment	Asset	↑	Dr.	Office Equipment 121 (A) **200**
Mia Wong, Capital	Capital	↑	Cr.	Mia Wong, Capital 311 **6,200** (A)

> Note in column 3 of the chart that it doesn't matter if both arrows go up, as long as the sum of the debits equals the sum of the credits in the T accounts in column 5.

Note again that every transaction affects at least two T accounts and that the total amount added to the debit side(s) must equal the total amount added to the credit side(s) of the T accounts of each transaction.

Analysis of Transaction A

Step 1 Which accounts are affected? The law firm receives its cash and office equipment, so three accounts are involved: Cash, Office Equipment, and Mia Wong, Capital. These account titles come from the chart of accounts.

Step 2 Which categories do these accounts belong to? Cash and Office Equipment are assets. Mia Wong, Capital, is capital.

Step 3 Are the accounts increasing or decreasing? The Cash and Office Equipment, both assets, are increasing in the business. The rights or claims of Mia Wong, Capital, are also increasing, because she invested money and office equipment in the business.

Step 4 What do the rules say? According to the rules of debit and credit, an increase in assets (Cash and Office Equipment) is a debit. An increase in Capital is a credit. Note that the total dollar amount of debits will equal the total dollar amount of credits when the T accounts are updated in column 5.

Step 5 What does the T account look like? The amount for Cash and Office Equipment is entered on the debit side. The amount for Mia Wong, Capital, goes on the credit side.

A transaction that involves more than one debit or more than one credit is called a **compound entry.** This first transaction of Mia Wong's law firm is a compound entry; it involves a debit of $6,000 to Cash and a debit of $200 to Office Equipment (as well as a credit of $6,200 to Mia Wong, Capital).

> Double-entry bookkeeping system: The total of all debits is equal to the total of all credits.

The name for this double-entry analysis of transactions, where two or more accounts are affected and the total of debits and credits is equal, is **double-entry bookkeeping.** This double-entry system helps in checking the recording of business transactions.

As we continue, the explanations will be brief, but do not forget to apply the five steps in analyzing and recording each business transaction.

Transaction B Aug. 29: Law practice bought office equipment for cash, $500.

1 Accounts Affected	2 Category	3 ↓ ↑	4 Rules of Dr. and Cr.	5 T Account Update
Office Equipment	Asset	↑	Dr.	Office Equipment 121
				(A) 200
				(B) 500
Cash	Asset	↓	Cr.	Cash 111
				(A) 6,000 500 (B)

Analysis of Transaction B

Step 1 The law firm paid $500 cash for the office equipment it received. The accounts involved in the transaction are Cash and Office Equipment.

Step 2 The accounts belong to these categories: Office Equipment is an asset; Cash is an asset.

Step 3 The asset Office Equipment is increasing. The asset Cash is decreasing; it is being reduced to buy the office equipment.

Step 4 An increase in the asset Office Equipment is a debit; a decrease in the asset Cash is a credit.

Step 5 When the amounts are placed in the T accounts, the amount for Office Equipment goes on the debit side and the amount for Cash on the credit side.

Transaction C Aug. 30: Bought more office equipment on account, $300.

1 Accounts Affected	2 Category	3 ↓ ↑	4 Rules of Dr. and Cr.	5 T Account Update
Office Equipment	Asset	↑	Dr.	Office Equipment 121
				(A) 200
				(B) 500
				(C) 300
Accounts Payable	Liability	↑	Cr.	Accounts Payable 211
				300 (C)

Analysis of Transaction C

Step 1 The law firm receives office equipment $300 by promising to pay in the future. An obligation or liability, Accounts Payable, is created.

Step 2 Office Equipment is an asset. Accounts Payable is a liability.

Step 3 The asset Office Equipment is increasing; the liability Accounts Payable is increasing because the law firm is increasing what it owes.

Step 4 An increase in the asset Office Equipment is a debit. An increase in the liability Accounts Payable is a credit.

Step 5 Enter the amount for Office Equipment on the debit side of the T account. The amount for the Accounts Payable goes on the credit side.

Transaction D Sept. 1–30: Provided legal services for cash, $2,000.

1 Accounts Affected	2 Category	3 ↓ ↑	4 Rules of Dr. and Cr.	5 T Account Update
Cash	Asset	↑	Dr.	Cash 111 (A) 6,000 | 500 (B) (D) 2,000 |
Legal Fees	Revenue	↑	Cr.	Legal Fees 411 | 2,000 (D)

Analysis of Transaction D

Step 1 The firm earned revenue from legal services and received $2,000 in cash.

Step 2 Cash is an asset. Legal Fees are revenue.

Step 3 Cash, an asset, is increasing. Legal Fees, or revenue, are also increasing.

Step 4 An increase in Cash, an asset, is debited. An increase in Legal Fees, or revenue, is credited.

Step 5 Enter the amount for Cash on the debit side of the T account. Enter the amount for Legal Fees on the credit side.

Transaction E Sept. 1–30: Provided legal services on account, $3,000.

1 Accounts Affected	2 Category	3 ↓ ↑	4 Rules of Dr. and Cr.	5 T Account Update
Accounts Receivable	Asset	↑	Dr.	Accounts Receivable 112 (E) 3,000 |
Legal Fees	Revenue	↑	Cr.	Legal Fees 411 | 2,000 (D) | 3,000 (E)

Analysis of Transaction E

Step 1 The law practice has earned revenue of $3,000 but has not yet received payment (cash). The amounts owed by these clients are called Accounts Receivable. Revenue is earned at the time the legal services are provided, whether payment is received then or will be received some time in the future.

Step 2 Accounts Receivable is an asset. Legal Fees are revenue.

Step 3 Accounts Receivable is increasing because the law practice increased the amount owed to it for legal fees earned but not yet paid. Legal Fees, or revenue, are increasing.

Step 4 An increase in the asset Accounts Receivable is a debit. An increase in Revenue is a credit.

Step 5 Enter the amount for Accounts Receivable on the debit side of the T account. The amount for Legal Fees goes on the credit side.

Transaction F Sept. 1–30: Received $900 cash from clients for services rendered previously on account.

1 Accounts Affected	2 Category	3 ↓ ↑	4 Rules of Dr. and Cr.	5 T Account Update
Cash	Asset	↑	Dr.	Cash 111
				(A) 6,000 | 500 (B)
				(D) 2,000
				(F) 900
Accounts Receivable	Asset	↓	Cr.	Accounts Receivable 112
				(E) 3,000 | 900 (F)

Analysis of Transaction F

Step 1 The law firm collects $900 in cash from previous revenue earned. Because the revenue is recorded at the time it is earned, and not when the collection is received in this transaction we are concerned only with the collection, which affects the Cash and Accounts Receivable accounts.

Step 2 Cash is an asset. Accounts Receivable is an asset.

Step 3 Because clients are paying what is owed, Cash (asset) is increasing and the amount owed (Accounts Receivable) is decreasing (the total amount owed by clients to Wong is going down). This transaction results in a shift in assets, more Cash for less Accounts Receivable.

Step 4 An increase in Cash, an asset, is a debit. A decrease in Accounts Receivable, an asset, is a credit.

Step 5 Enter the amount for Cash on the debit side of the T account. The amount for Accounts Receivable goes on the credit side.

Transaction G Sept. 1–30: Paid salaries expense, $700.

1 Accounts Affected	2 Category	3 ↓ ↑	4 Rules of Dr. and Cr.	5 T Account Update
Salaries Expense	Expense	↑	Dr.	Salaries Expense 511
				(G) 700 |
Cash	Asset	↓	Cr.	Cash 111
				(A) 6,000 | 500 (B)
				(D) 2,000 | 700 (G)
				(F) 900 |

Analysis of Transaction G

Step 1 The law firm pays $700 of salaries expense by cash.

Step 2 Salaries Expense is an expense. Cash is an asset.

Step 3 The Salaries Expense of the law firm is increasing, which results in a decrease in Cash.

Step 4 An increase in Salaries Expense, an expense, is a debit. A decrease in Cash, an asset, is a credit.

Step 5 Enter the amount for Salaries Expense on the debit side of the T account. The amount for Cash goes on the credit side.

Transaction H Sept. 1–30: Paid rent expense, $400.

---

1 Accounts Affected	2 Category	3 ↓ ↑	4 Rules of Dr. and Cr.	5 T Account Update
Rent Expense	Expense	↑	Dr.	Rent Expense 512
				(H) 400
Cash	Asset	↓	Cr.	Cash 111
				(A) 6,000 | 500 (B)
				(D) 2,000 | 700 (G)
				(F) 900 | 400 (H)

Analysis of Transaction H

Step 1 The law firm's rent expenses of $400 are paid in cash.

Step 2 Rent is an expense. Cash is an asset.

Step 3 The Rent Expense increases the expenses, and the payment for the Rent Expense decreases the cash.

Step 4 An increase in Rent Expense, an expense, is a debit. A decrease in Cash, an asset, is a credit.

Step 5 Enter the amount for Rent Expense on the debit side of the T account. Place the amount for Cash on the credit side.

Transaction I Sept. 1–30: Received a bill for Advertising Expense (to be paid next month), $200.

---

1 Accounts Affected	2 Category	3 ↓ ↑	4 Rules of Dr. and Cr.	5 T Account Update
Advertising Expense	Expense	↑	Dr.	Advertising Expense 513
				(I) 200
Accounts Payable	Liability	↑	Cr.	Accounts Payable 211
				| 300 (C)
				| 200 (I)

Analysis of Transaction I

Step 1 The advertising bill in the amount of $200 has come in and payment is due but has not yet been made. Therefore, the accounts involved here are Advertising Expense and Accounts Payable; the expense has created a liability.

Step 2 Advertising Expense is an expense. Accounts Payable is a liability.

Step 3 Both the expense and the liability are increasing.

Step 4 An increase in an expense is a debit. An increase in a liability is a credit.

Step 5 Enter the amount for Advertising Expense on the debit side of the T account. Enter the amount for Accounts Payable on the credit side.

Transaction J Sept. 1–30: Wong withdrew cash for personal use, $100.

---

1 Accounts Affected	2 Category	3 ↓ ↑	4 Rules of Dr. and Cr.	5 T Account Update
Mia Wong, Withdrawals	Withdrawals	↑	Dr.	Mia Wong, Withdrawals, 312
				(J) 100
Cash	Asset	↓	Cr.	Cash 111
				(A) 6,000 | 500 (B)
				(D) 2,000 | 700 (G)
				(F) 900 | 400 (H)
				| 100 (J)

Analysis of Transaction J

Step 1 Mia Wong withdraws $100 cash from business for *personal* use. This withdrawal is not a business expense.

Step 2 This transaction affects the Withdrawals and Cash accounts.

Step 3 Mia has increased what she has withdrawn from the business for personal use. The business cash decreased.

Step 4 An increase in Withdrawals is a debit. A decrease in Cash is a credit. (*Remember:* Withdrawals go on the statement of owner's equity; expenses go on the income statement.)

> Withdrawals are always increased by debits.

Step 5 Enter the amount for Mia Wong, Withdrawals on the debit side of the T account. The amount for Cash goes on the credit side.

Summary of Transactions for Mia Wong

Assets	=	Liabilities	+			Owner's Equity		
Cash 111	=	Accounts	+	Capital	– Withdrawals	+ Revenue	– Expenses	
(A) 6,000 | 500 (B)		Payable 211		Mia Wong,	Mia Wong,	Legal	Salaries	
(D) 2,000 | 700 (G)	=	| 300 (C)	+	Capital 311	– Withdrawals 312	+ Fees 411	– Expense 511	
(F) 900 | 400 (H)		| 200 (I)		| 6,200 (A)	(J) 100 |	2,000 (D)	(G) 700 |	
| 100 (J)						3,000 (E)		
Accounts							Rent	
Receivable 112							– Expense 512	
(E) 3,000 | 900 (F)							(H) 400 |	
Office							Advertising	
Equipment 121							– Expense 513	
(A) 200 |							(I) 200 |	
(B) 500 |								
(C) 300 |								

LEARNING UNIT 2-2 REVIEW

AT THIS POINT you should be able to

- State the rules of debit and credit.
- List the five steps of a transaction analysis.
- Show how to fill out a transaction analysis chart.
- Explain double-entry bookkeeping.

Accounting Cycle Tutorial

Self-Review Quiz 2-2

King Company uses the following accounts from its chart of accounts: Cash (111), Accounts Receivable (112), Equipment (121), Accounts Payable (211), Jamie King, Capital (311), Jamie King, Withdrawals (312), Professional Fees (411), Utilities Expense (511), and Salaries Expense (512).

Record the following transactions into transaction analysis charts.

a. Jamie King invested in the business $1,000 cash and equipment worth $700 from his personal assets.
b. Billed clients for services rendered, $12,000.
c. Utilities bill due but unpaid, $150.
d. Withdrew cash for personal use, $120.
e. Paid salaries expense, $250.

For additional help go to
www.pearsonhighered.com/slater

Solution to Self-Review Quiz 2-2

a.

1 Accounts Affected	2 Category	3 ↓ ↑	4 Rules of Dr. and Cr.	5 T Account Update
Cash	Asset	↑	Dr.	Cash 111 (A) **1,000**
Equipment	Asset	↑	Dr.	Equipment 121 (A) **700**
Jamie King, Capital	Capital	↑	Cr.	Jamie King, Capital 311 **1,700** (A)

b.

1 Accounts Affected	2 Category	3 ↓ ↑	4 Rules of Dr. and Cr.	5 T Account Update
Accounts Receivable	Asset	↑	Dr.	Accounts Receivable 112 (B) **12,000**
Professional Fees	Revenue	↑	Cr.	Professional Fees 411 **12,000** (B)

c.

1 Accounts Affected	2 Category	3 ↓ ↑	4 Rules of Dr. and Cr.	5 T Account Update
Utilities Expense	Expense	↑	Dr.	Utilities Expense 511 (C)　150 |
Accounts Payable	Liability	↑	Cr.	Accounts Payable 211 | 150　(C)

d.

1 Accounts Affected	2 Category	3 ↓ ↑	4 Rules of Dr. and Cr.	5 T Account Update
Jamie King, Withdrawals	Withdrawals	↑	Dr.	Jamie King, Withdrawals 312 (D)　120 |
Cash	Asset	↓	Cr.	Cash 111 (A)　1,000 | 120　(D)

e.

1 Accounts Affected	2 Category	3 ↓ ↑	4 Rules of Dr. and Cr.	5 T Account Update
Salaries Expense	Expense	↑	Dr.	Salaries Expense 512 (E)　250 |
Cash	Asset	↓	Cr.	Cash 111 (A)　1,000 | 120　(D) | 250　(E)

NEED HELP?

Let's review first: Make up a note card of the rules of debit and credit from Table 2.1. You will notice that assets, withdrawals, and expenses increase when you put amounts on the left, or debit, side of these accounts. The accounting system balances because liabilities, capital, and revenue increase when you put amounts on the right, or credit, side of these accounts. The increase side of any account will represent its normal balance. Think of a chart of accounts as a roadmap to all account titles a company will use. ALL ACCOUNTS AFFECTED MUST COME FROM THE CHART OF ACCOUNTS.

Transaction A: In column 1 all titles must come from the chart of accounts. The order listed does not matter as long as the sum of the left side equals the sum of the right side. In this transaction we see that accounts affected include cash, equipment, and Jamie King, Capital.

Cash and equipment are assets, while capital is categorized as capital. Remember that the six category choices are as follows:

    assets
    liabilities
    capital
    withdrawals
    revenue
    expenses

The cash and equipment in business are increasing (thus arrows up) and because the owner supplied them Jamie King, Capital rights are increasing. Assets are increased by putting amounts on the debit side and capital is increased by putting amounts on the credit side.

Transaction B: Here we do the work but do not get the money. We see from the chart of accounts that revenue is called Professional Fees and customers owing money is called Accounts Receivable. Revenue for King Co. is going up and customers owe the company more money. Increase in an asset is a debit and increase in revenue is a credit.

Transaction C: Here we record utilities expense before it is paid. The expenses have increased for King Co. and it has increased what it owes the utility company. An increase in an expense is a debit and an increase in a liability is a credit. Here an expense has created a liability.

Transaction D: This is not a business expense since this is a personal withdrawal of cash by the owner. King, Withdrawals are increasing since King is taking the withdrawal but the business is lowering its cash from the withdrawal. An increase in withdrawal is a debit and a decrease in cash is a credit. Note the "dr" in the middle of "withdrawal." A withdrawal always increases by a debit.

Transaction E: In this transaction the business has another expense increasing and is paying for it in cash. The end result is that expenses increase on the debit side and cash, which is an asset, decreases on the credit side. Remember that we record expenses when they happen whether they are paid or not. Here they were paid. In transaction C they were not paid.

Summary: The mind process charts are a great way to organize your information before deciding on what to debit or credit. Column 1 must come from the chart of accounts. In the category column you have six choices: assets, liabilities, capital, revenue, withdrawals, and expenses. The arrows tell you if the business accounts are increasing or decreasing. Note in column 5 that if an account is repeated a running summary of all transactions is accumulated in the account.

Learning Unit 2-3 The Trial Balance and Preparation of Financial Statements

Let us look at all the transactions we have discussed, arranged by T accounts and recorded using the rules of debit and credit. This grouping of accounts is much easier to use than the expanded accounting equation because all the transactions that affect a particular account are in one place.

Summary of Transactions of Mia Wong

Assets	=	Liabilities	+				Owner's Equity				

Assets = **Liabilities** + **Owner's Equity**

| Cash 111 | | = | Accounts Payable 211 | + | Capital | − | Withdrawals | + | Revenue | − | Expenses |

Cash 111 = Accounts Payable 211 + Mia Wong, Capital 311 − Mia Wong, Withdrawals 312 + Legal Fees 411 − Salaries Expenses 511

Cash 111:
- (A) 6,000 | 500 (B)
- (D) 2,000 | 700 (G)
- (F) 900 | 400 (H)
- | 100 (J)
- 8,900 | 1,700
- 7,200

Accounts Receivable 112:
- (E) 3,000 | 900 (F)
- 2,100

Office Equipment 121:
- (A) 200
- (B) 500
- (C) 300
- 1,000

Footings
New Balance

Accounts Payable 211:
- | 300 (C)
- | 200 (I)
- | 500

Mia Wong, Capital 311:
- | 6,200 (A)

Mia Wong, Withdrawals 312:
- (J) 100 |

Legal Fees 411:
- | 2,000 (D)
- | 3,000 (E)
- | 5,000

Salaries Expenses 511:
- (G) 700 |

Rent Expense 512:
- (H) 400 |

Advertising Expense 513:
- (I) 200 |

As we saw in Learning Unit 2-2, when all the transactions are recorded in the accounts, the total of all the debits should be equal to the total of all the credits. (If they are not, the accountant must go back and find the error by checking the numbers and adding every column again.)

LO3 ## The Trial Balance

Footings are used to obtain the totals of each side of every T account that has more than one entry. The footings are used to find the ending balance. The ending balances are used to prepare a **trial balance.** The trial balance is not a financial statement, although it is used to prepare financial statements. The trial balance lists all the accounts with their balances in the same order as they appear in the chart of accounts. It proves the accuracy of the ledger. For example, look at the preceding Cash account. The footing for the debit side is $8,900, and the footing for the credit side is $1,700. Because the debit side is larger, we subtract $1,700 from $8,900 to arrive at an *ending debit balance* of $7,200. Now look at the Rent Expense account. It doesn't need a footing because it has only one entry. The amount itself is the ending balance. When the ending balance has been found for every account, we should be able to show that the total of all debits equals the total of all credits.

> As mentioned earlier, the ending balance of Cash, $7,200, is a *normal balance* because it is on the side that increases the asset account.

In the ideal situation, businesses would take a trial balance every day. The large number of transactions most businesses conduct each day makes this impractical. Instead, trial balances are prepared periodically.

Keep in mind that the figure for capital might not be the beginning figure if any additional investment has taken place during the period. You can tell by looking at the capital account in the ledger.

A more detailed discussion of the trial balance is provided in the next chapter. For now, notice the heading, how the accounts are listed, the debits in the left column, the credits in the right, and that the total of debits is equal to the total of credits.

A trial balance of Mia Wong's accounts is shown in Figure 2.2.

FIGURE 2.2 Trial Balance for Mia Wong's Law Firm

MIA WONG, ATTORNEY-AT-LAW
TRIAL BALANCE
SEPTEMBER 30, 200X

	Dr.	Cr.
Cash	7 2 0 0 00	
Accounts Receivable	2 1 0 0 00	
Office Equipment	1 0 0 0 00	
Accounts Payable		5 0 0 00
Mia Wong, Capital		6 2 0 0 00
Mia Wong, Withdrawals	1 0 0 00	
Legal Fees		5 0 0 0 00
Salaries Expense	7 0 0 00	
Rent Expense	4 0 0 00	
Advertising Expense	2 0 0 00	
Totals	11 7 0 0 00	11 7 0 0 00

Because this statement is not a formal one, it doesn't need dollar signs; the single and double lines under subtotals and final totals, however, are still used for clarity.

Preparing Financial Statements

The trial balance is used to prepare the financial statements. The diagram in Figure 2.3 on the following page shows how financial statements can be prepared from a trial balance. Statements do not have debit or credit columns. The left column is used only to subtotal numbers.

LO4

ac
t

Accounting Cycle Tutorial

LEARNING UNIT 2-3 REVIEW

AT THIS POINT / you should be able to

- Explain the role of footings.
- Prepare a trial balance from a set of accounts.
- Prepare financial statements from a trial balance.

In QuickBooks and Peachtree, financial statements are prepared simply by selecting the report you want and changing the date to the current period.

Self-Review Quiz 2-3

As the bookkeeper of Pam's Hair Salon, you are to prepare from the accounts that follow on June 30, 200X (1) a trial balance as of June 30, (2) an income statement for the month ended June 30, (3) a statement of owner's equity for the month ended June 30, and (4) a balance sheet as of June 30, 200X.

For additional help go to www.pearsonhighered.com/slater

Cash 111	
4,500	300
2,000	100
1,000	1,200
300	1,300
	2,600

Accounts Payable 211	
300	700

Salon Fees 411	
	3,500
	1,000

Accounts Receivable 121	
1,000	300

Pam Jay, Capital 311	
	4,000*

Rent Expense 511	
1,200	

Salon Equipment 131	
700	

Pam Jay, Withdrawals 321	
100	

Salon Supplies Expense 521	
1,300	

*No additional investments.

Salaries Expense 531	
2,600	

FIGURE 2.3 Steps in Preparing Financial Statements from a Trial Balance

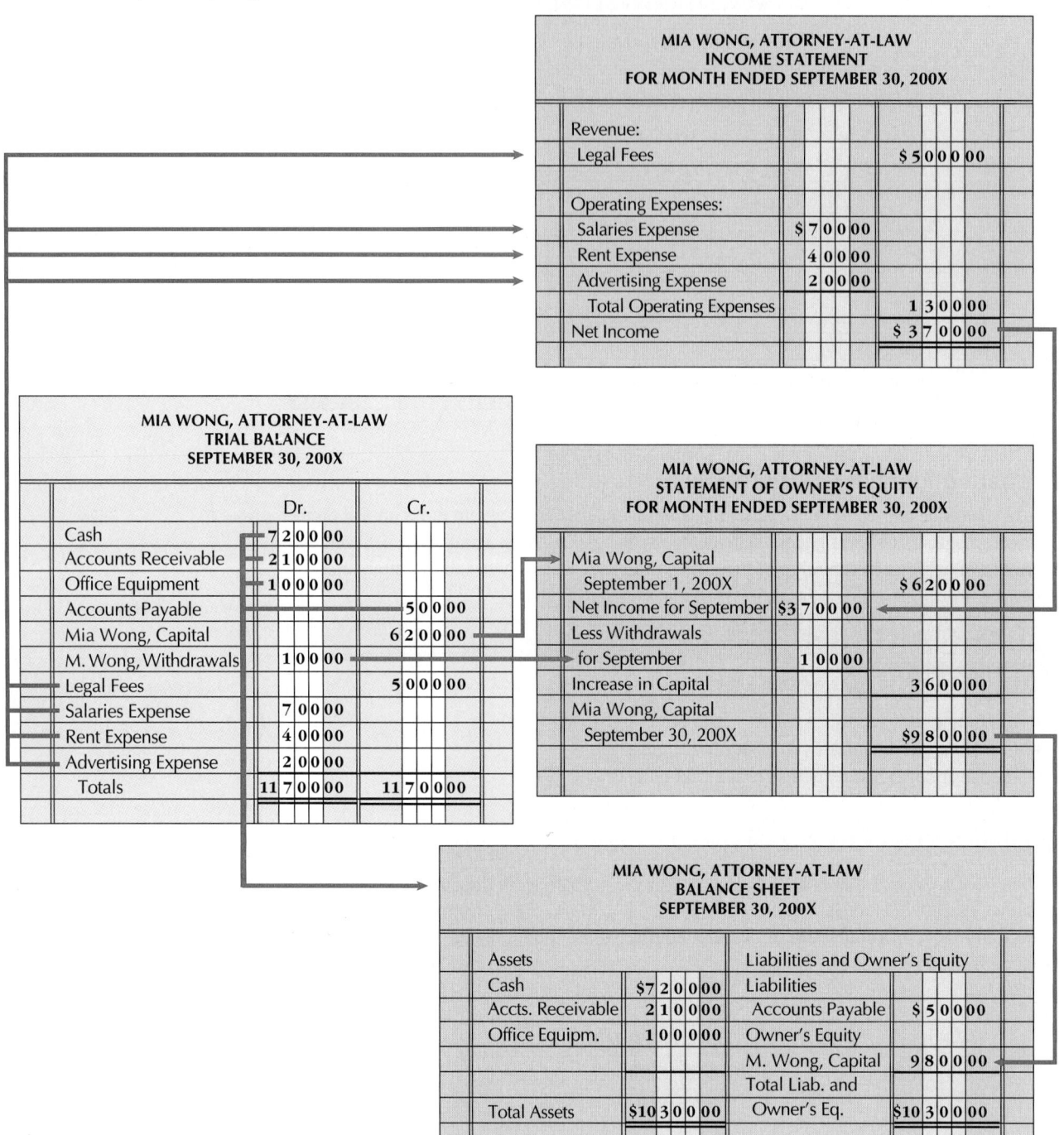

Solution to Self-Review Quiz 2-3

FIGURE 2.4

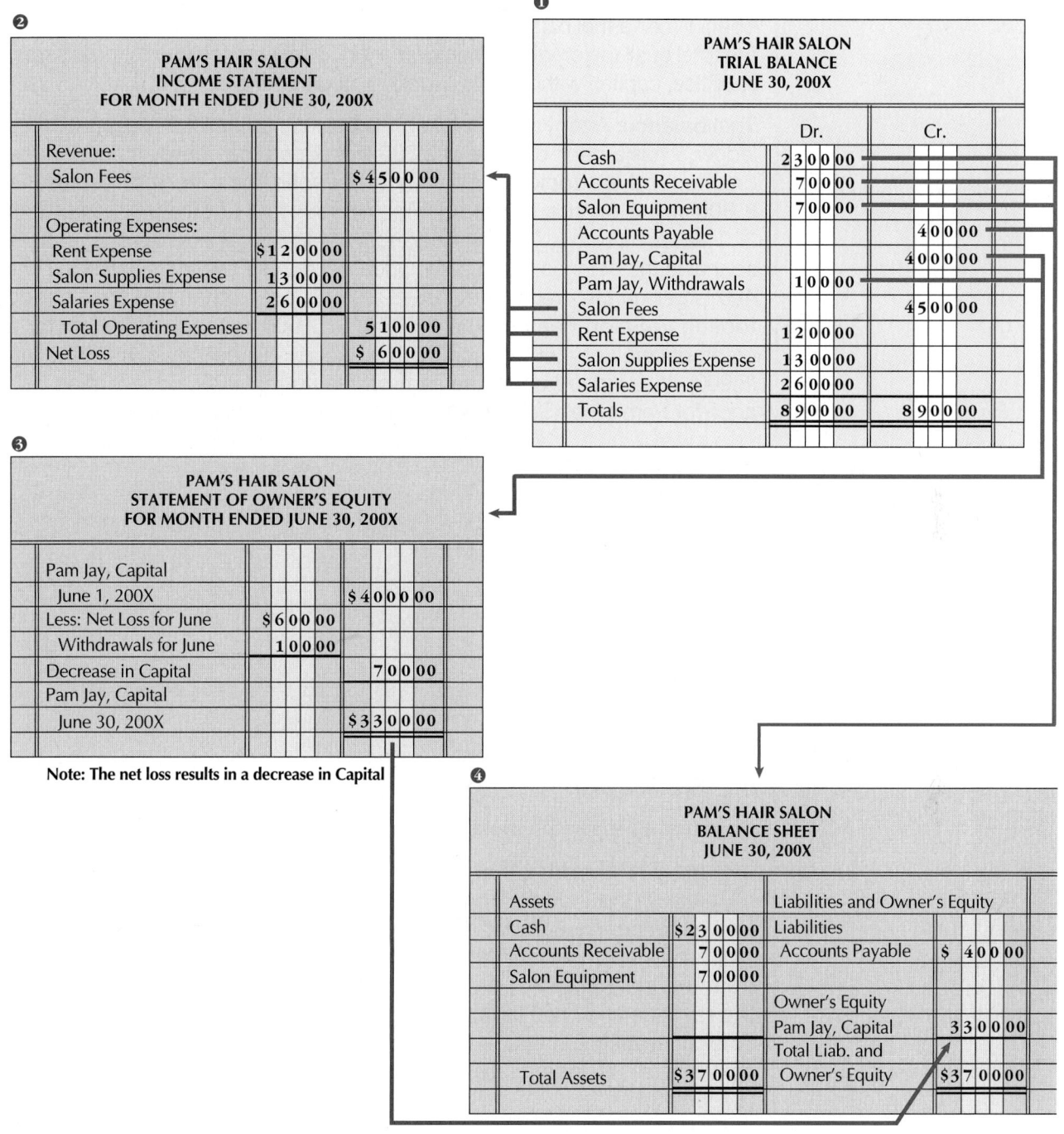

❷

PAM'S HAIR SALON
INCOME STATEMENT
FOR MONTH ENDED JUNE 30, 200X

Revenue:		
Salon Fees		$4 5 0 0 00
Operating Expenses:		
Rent Expense	$1 2 0 0 00	
Salon Supplies Expense	1 3 0 0 00	
Salaries Expense	2 6 0 0 00	
Total Operating Expenses		5 1 0 0 00
Net Loss		$ 6 0 0 00

❶

PAM'S HAIR SALON
TRIAL BALANCE
JUNE 30, 200X

	Dr.	Cr.
Cash	2 3 0 0 00	
Accounts Receivable	7 0 0 00	
Salon Equipment	7 0 0 00	
Accounts Payable		4 0 0 00
Pam Jay, Capital		4 0 0 0 00
Pam Jay, Withdrawals	1 0 0 00	
Salon Fees		4 5 0 0 00
Rent Expense	1 2 0 0 00	
Salon Supplies Expense	1 3 0 0 00	
Salaries Expense	2 6 0 0 00	
Totals	8 9 0 0 00	8 9 0 0 00

❸

PAM'S HAIR SALON
STATEMENT OF OWNER'S EQUITY
FOR MONTH ENDED JUNE 30, 200X

Pam Jay, Capital		
June 1, 200X		$4 0 0 0 00
Less: Net Loss for June	$6 0 0 00	
Withdrawals for June	1 0 0 00	
Decrease in Capital		7 0 0 00
Pam Jay, Capital		
June 30, 200X		$3 3 0 0 00

Note: The net loss results in a decrease in Capital

❹

PAM'S HAIR SALON
BALANCE SHEET
JUNE 30, 200X

Assets		Liabilities and Owner's Equity	
Cash	$2 3 0 0 00	Liabilities	
Accounts Receivable	7 0 0 00	Accounts Payable	$ 4 0 0 00
Salon Equipment	7 0 0 00		
		Owner's Equity	
		Pam Jay, Capital	3 3 0 0 00
		Total Liab. and	
Total Assets	$3 7 0 0 00	Owner's Equity	$3 7 0 0 00

NEED HELP?

Let's review first: The trial balance is a list of accounts and their ending balances. Each account will have either a debit or credit balance (but not both). When a trial balance is complete the total of all the debits must equal the total of all the credits. When preparing a trial balance you list out assets, liabilities, capital, withdrawals, revenue, and expenses.

Trial balance: After you have taken the balance of the Cash account in the ledger, it has a debit balance of 2,300 (we added the debits, we added the credits, and we took the difference between them, which resulted in 2,300 more on the left side). For Accounts Receivable 1,000 less 300 leaves us with a 700 debit balance. Salon Equipment has one number so that is the balance (700 debit). Once Accounts Payable is balanced it is 400 larger on the credit side (700–300). The only other title that needs footing is Salon Fees so the 3,500 and 1,000 are added together for a credit balance of 4,500. Once each balance is listed the sum on the left (8,900) does indeed equal the sum on the right (8,900). Each ending balance for Pam's Hair Salon ends up on the normal balance side.

	Dr.	Cr.
Cash	x	
Acc. Rec.	x	
Salon Equip.	x	
Accounts Pay.		xs
Pam Jay, Cap.		x
Pam Jay, Withd.	x	
Salon Fees		x
Rent Expense	x	
Salon Supp. Exp.	x	
Salaries Exp.	x	

Note that titles on the trial balance are not indented.

Income Statement: Once the trial balance is complete the first report to make is the income statement, which is made up of only revenue and expense. Remember that there are no debits or credits on financial reports. All we are taking are the ending balances of each title from the trial balance. For the income statement, we list salon fees as the revenue and then list the three expense titles in the inside column. Total operating expenses are then subtracted from the salon fees to arrive at a net loss. Here revenue is less than operating expenses ($4,500–$5,100).

Statement of Owner's Equity: The second report to prepare is the statement of owner's equity, which shows how to calculate a new figure for capital. Note that in this case the net loss of $600 is ADDED to the $100 of withdrawals, resulting in a decrease of $700 to capital. The new figure for capital is $3,300 ($4,000–$700).

Balance Sheet: The third report is the balance sheet, which lists out each asset, liability, and the new figure for capital. This report shows that as of June 30 total assets is $3,700 and total liabilities and owner's equity is $3,700. Remember that the ending figure for capital comes from the statement of owner's equity.

Summary: The trial balance is a list of ending balances of ledger accounts. These balances are used to prepare the three financial reports. Financial reports have no debits or credits. The inside columns are used to subtotal numbers. Revenue and expenses go on the income statement. Withdrawals and either net income or net loss go on the statement of owner's equity to calculate a new figure for capital. The balance sheet is a list of assets, liabilities, and the new amount for ending capital. Remember that the trial balance has debit or credits, not the financial reports.

CHAPTER ASSIGNMENTS

All Classroom Demonstration Exercises, Exercises, Problems, and the Continuing Problem in this chapter can be found within MyAccountingLab, an online homework and practice environment. Your instructor may ask you to complete this material using MyAccountingLab.

DEMONSTRATION PROBLEM

The chart of accounts of Mel's Delivery Service includes the following: Cash, 111; Accounts Receivable, 112; Office Equipment, 121; Delivery Trucks, 122; Accounts Payable, 211; Mel Free, Capital, 311; Mel Free, Withdrawals, 312; Delivery Fees Earned, 411; Advertising Expense, 511; Gas Expense, 512; Salaries Expense, 513; and Telephone Expense, 514. The following transactions resulted for Mel's Delivery Service during the month of July:

Transaction A:	Mel invested $10,000 in the business from his personal savings account.
Transaction B:	Bought delivery trucks on account, $17,000.
Transaction C:	Advertising bill received but unpaid, $700.
Transaction D:	Bought office equipment for cash, $1,200.
Transaction E:	Received cash for delivery services rendered, $15,000.
Transaction F:	Paid salaries expense, $3,000.
Transaction G:	Paid gas expense for company trucks, $1,250.
Transaction H:	Billed customers for delivery services rendered, $4,000.
Transaction I:	Paid telephone bill, $300.
Transaction J:	Received $3,000 as partial payment of transaction H.
Transaction K:	Mel paid home telephone bill from company checkbook, $150.

ASSIGNMENT

As Mel's newly employed accountant, you must do the following:
1. Set up T accounts in a ledger.
2. Record transactions in the T accounts. (Place the letter of the transaction next to the entry.)
3. Foot and take the balance of each account where appropriate.
4. Prepare a trial balance at the end of July.
5. Prepare from the trial balance, in proper form, (a) an income statement for the month of July, (b) a statement of owner's equity, and (c) a balance sheet as of July 31, 200X.

Solution to Demonstration Problem

1,2,3.   GENERAL LEDGER

Cash 111			
(A)	10,000	1,200	(D)
(E)	15,000	3,000	(F)
(J)	3,000	1,250	(G)
		300	(I)
		150	(K)
	28,000	5,900	
22,100			

Accts. Payable 211	
	17,000 (B)
	700 (C)
	17,700

Advertising Expense 511	
(C)	700

Accts. Receivable 112			
(H)	4,000	3,000	(J)
	1,000		

Mel Free, Capital 311	
	10,000 (A)

Gas Expense 512	
(G)	1,250

Office Equipment 121	
(D)	1,200

Mel Free, Withdrawals 312	
(K)	150

Salaries Expense 513	
(F)	3,000

Delivery Trucks 122	
(B)	17,000

Delivery Fees Earned 411	
	15,000 (E)
	4,000 (H)
	19,000

Telephone Expense 514	
(I)	300

Solution Tips to Recording Transactions

A. Cash	A	↑	Dr.
Mel Free, Capital	Cap.	↑	Cr.
B. Delivery Trucks	A	↑	Dr.
Accts. Payable	L	↑	Cr.
C. Advertising Expense	Exp.	↑	Dr.
Accts. Payable	L	↑	Cr.
D. Office Equipment	A	↑	Dr.
Cash	A	↓	Cr.
E. Cash	A	↑	Dr.
Del. Fees Earned	Rev.	↑	Cr.
F. Salaries Expense	Exp.	↑	Dr.
Cash	A	↓	Cr.
G. Gas Expense	Exp.	↑	Dr.
Cash	A	↓	Cr.
H. Acc. Receivable	A	↑	Dr.
Del. Fees Earned	Rev.	↑	Cr.
I. Tel. Expense	Exp.	↑	Dr.
Cash	A	↓	Cr.

| **J.** Cash | A | ↑ | Dr. |
| Accts. Receivable | A | ↓ | Cr. |

| **K.** Mel Free, Withd. | Withd. | ↑ | Dr. |
| Cash | A | ↓ | Cr. |

Mel's Delivery Service
Trial Balance
July 31, 200X

	Dr.	Cr.
Cash	22,100	
Accounts Receivable	1,000	
Office Equipment	1,200	
Delivery Trucks	17,000	
Accounts Payable		17,700
Mel Free, Capital		10,000
Mel Free, Withdrawals	150	
Delivery Fees Earned		19,000
Advertising Expense	700	
Gas Expense	1,250	
Salaries Expense	3,000	
Telephone Expense	300	
TOTALS	46,700	46,700

Solution Tips to Taking the Balance of an Account and Preparation of a Trial Balance

3. Footings: Cash   Add left side, $28,000.
Add right side, $5,900.

Take difference, $22,100, and stay on side that is larger.

Accounts Payable   Add $17,000 + $700 and stay on same side.

Total is $17,700.

4. Trial balance is a list of the ledger's ending balances. The list is in the same order as the chart of accounts. Each title has only one number listed either as a debit or credit balance.

FIGURE 2.5 Financial Reports

5a.

MEL'S DELIVERY SERVICE
INCOME STATEMENT
FOR MONTH ENDED JULY 31, 200X

Revenue:		
Delivery Fees Earned		$19 000 00
Operating Expenses:		
Advertising Expense	$ 7 00 00	
Gas Expense	1 2 50 00	
Salaries Expense	3 0 00 00	
Telephone Expense	3 00 00	
Total Operating Expenses		5 2 50 00
Net Income		$13 7 50 00

b.

MEL'S DELIVERY SERVICE
STATEMENT OF OWNER'S EQUITY
FOR MONTH ENDED JULY 31, 200X

Mel Free, Capital		
July 1, 200X		$10 0 00 00
Net Income for July	$13 7 50 00	
Less Withdrawals for July	1 5 00 00	
Increase in Capital		$13 6 00 00
Mel Free, Capital		
July 31, 200X		$23 6 00 00

c.

MEL'S DELIVERY SERVICE
BALANCE SHEET
JULY 31, 200X

Assets		Liabilities and Owner's Equity	
Cash	$22 1 00 00	Liabilities	
Accounts Receivable	1 00 00	Accounts Payable	$17 7 00 00
Office Equipment	1 2 00 00		
Delivery Trucks	17 0 00 00		
		Owner's Equity	
		Mel Free, Capital	23 6 00 00
		Total Liab. and	
Total Assets	$41 3 00 00	Owner's Equity	$41 3 00 00

Solution Tips to Prepare Financial Statements from a Trial Balance

Trial Balance

		Dr.	Cr.
Balance Sheet	Assets	X	
	Liabilities		X
Statement of Equity	Capital		X
	Withdrawals	X	
Income Statement	Revenues		X
	Expenses	X	
		XX	XX

Net income of $13,750 on the income statement goes on the statement of owner's equity.

Ending capital of $23,600 on the statement of owner's equity goes on the balance sheet as the new figure for capital.

Note: Financial statements do not show debits or credits. The inside column is used for subtotaling.

SUMMARY OF KEY POINTS

LEARNING UNIT 2-1

1. A T account is a simplified version of a standard account.
2. A ledger is a group of accounts.
3. A debit is the left-hand position (side) of an account, and a credit is the right-hand position (side) of an account.
4. A footing is the total of one side of an account. The ending balance is the difference between the footings.

LEARNING UNIT 2-2

1. A chart of accounts lists the account titles and their numbers for a company.
2. The transaction analysis chart is a teaching device, not to be confused with standard accounting procedures.
3. A compound entry is a transaction involving more than one debit or credit.

LEARNING UNIT 2-3

1. In double-entry bookkeeping, the recording of each business transaction affects two or more accounts, and the total of debits equals the total of credits.
2. A trial balance is a list of the ending balances of all accounts, listed in the same order as on the chart of accounts.
3. Any additional investments during the period result in the Capital balance on the trial balance not being the beginning figure for the Capital account.
4. *No* debit or credit columns are used in the three financial statements.

KEY TERMS

Account   An accounting device used in bookkeeping to record increases and decreases of business transactions relating to individual assets, liabilities, capital, withdrawals, revenue, expenses, and so on.

Chart of accounts   A numbering system of accounts that lists the account titles and account numbers to be used by a company.

Compound entry   A transaction involving more than one debit or credit.

Credit   The right-hand side of any account. A number entered on the right side of any account is said to be credited to an account.

Debit The left-hand side of any account. A number entered on the left side of any account is said to be debited to an account.

Double-entry bookkeeping An accounting system in which the recording of each transaction affects two or more accounts and the total of the debits is equal to the total of the credits.

Ending balance The difference between footings in a T account.

Footings The totals of each side of a T account.

Ledger A group of accounts that records data from business transactions.

Normal balance of an account The side of an account that increases by the rules of debit and credit.

Standard account A formal account that includes columns for date, explanation, posting reference, debit, and credit.

T account A skeleton version of a standard account, used for demonstration purposes.

Trial balance A list of the ending balances of all the accounts in a ledger. The total of the debits should equal the total of the credits.

BLUEPRINT: PREPARING FINANCIAL STATEMENTS FROM A TRIAL BALANCE

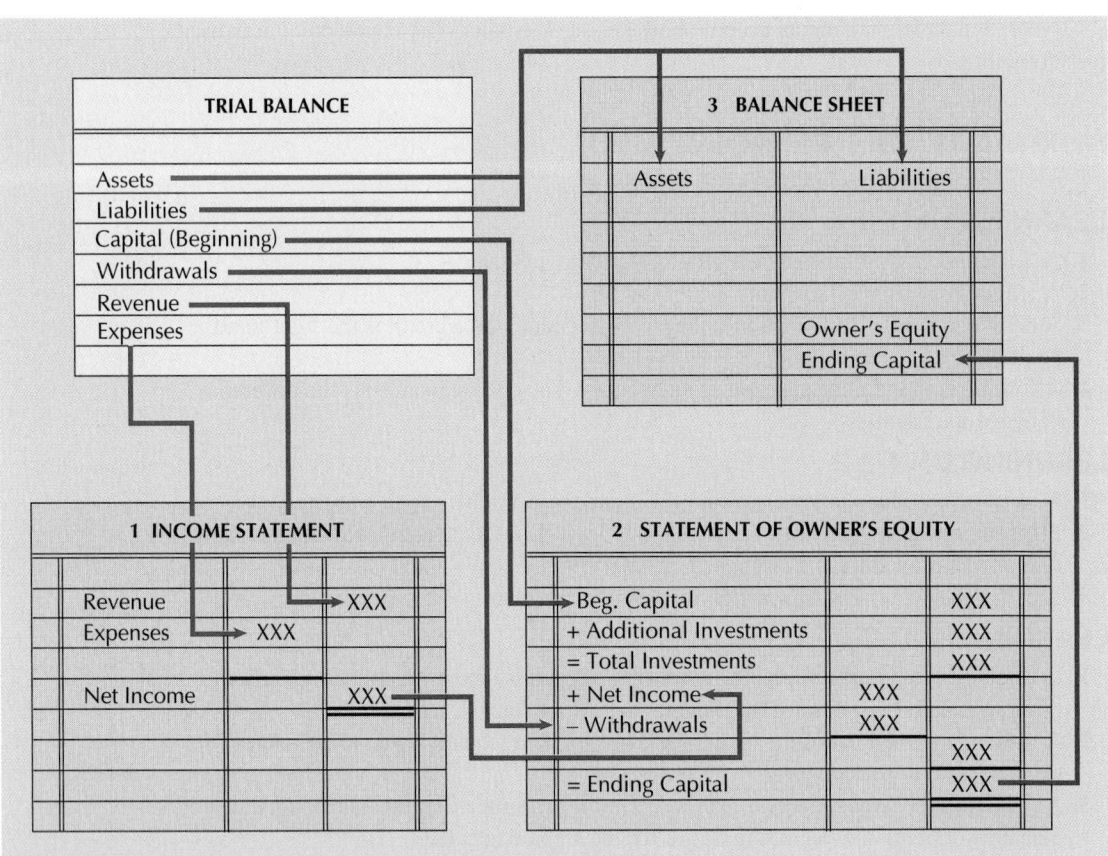

QUESTIONS, CLASSROOM DEMONSTRATION EXERCISES, EXERCISES, AND PROBLEMS

Discussion and Critical Thinking Questions/Ethical Case

1. Define a ledger.
2. Why is the left-hand side of an account called a debit?
3. Footings are used in balancing all accounts. True or false? Please explain.

4. What is the end product of the accounting process?
5. What do we mean when we say that a transaction analysis chart is a teaching device?
6. What are the five steps of the transaction analysis chart?
7. Explain the concept of double-entry bookkeeping.

8. A trial balance is a formal statement. True or false? Please explain.

9. Why are there no debit or credit columns on financial statements?

10. Compare the financial statements prepared from the expanded accounting equation with those prepared from a trial balance.

11. Audrey Flet, the bookkeeper of ALN Co. was scheduled to leave on a three-week vacation at 5:00 on Friday. She couldn't get the company's trial balance to balance. At 4:30, she decided to put in fictitious figures to make it balance. Audrey told herself she would fix it when she got back from her vacation. Was Audrey right or wrong to do this? Why?

Classroom Demonstration Exercises

MyAccountingLab

SET A

The T Account

LO1, 2 (5 min)

1. From the following, foot and balance each account.

Cash 110				Matt Nason, Capital 311		
9/5	12,000	9/7	800		6/9	6,000
9/9	6,000				9/3	4,000
					9/7	1,000

Transaction Analysis

LO2 (5 min)

2. Complete the following:

Account	Category	↑	↓	Normal Balance
A. Accounts Payable				
B. Taxable Fees Earned				
C. Accounts Receivable				
D. M. Blanc, Capital				
E. M. Blanc, Withdrawals				
F. Prepaid Advertising				
G. Rent Expense				

Transaction Analysis

LO2 (5 min)

3. Record the following transaction into the transaction analysis chart: Provided grooming fees for $2,500, receiving $600 cash with the remainder to be paid next month.

Accounts Affected	Category	↓	↑	Rules of Dr. and Cr.	T Accounts

Trial Balance

LO4 (5 min)

4. Rearrange the following titles in the order they would appear on a trial balance:

J. Joy, Withdrawals	Hair Salon Fees Earned
Accounts Receivable	Selling Expense
Cash	Salary Expense
J. Joy, Capital	Advertising Expense
Office Equipment	Accounts Payable

LO3 (10 min) **Trial Balance/Financial Statements**

5. From the following trial balance, identify on which statement each title will appear:
- Income statement (IS)
- Statement of owner's equity (OE)
- Balance sheet (BS)

BERNIE CO.
TRIAL BALANCE
NOV. 30, 200X

		Dr.	Cr.
A. _____	Cash	500	
B. _____	Computer	200	
C. _____	Computer Equipment	600	
D. _____	Accounts Payable		900
E. _____	L. Bean, Capital		240
F. _____	L. Bean, Withdrawals	250	
G. _____	Legal Fees Earned		1,000
H. _____	Consulting Fees Earned		500
I. _____	Wage Expense	300	
J. _____	Supplies Expense	700	
K. _____	Internet Advertising Expense	90	
	TOTALS	2,640	2,640

SET B

LO1, 2 (5 min) **The T Account**

1. From the following, foot and balance each account.

Cash 110				A. Slate, Capital 311		
5/8	3,000	5/11	1,000		4/9	8,000
5/12	9,000				4/12	4,000
					5/2	9,000

LO2 (5 min) **Transaction Analysis**

2. Complete the following:

Account	Category	↑	↓	Normal Balance
A. Digital Cameras				
B. Prepaid Rent				
C. Accounts Payable				
D. A. Sung, Capital				
E. A. Sung, Withdrawals				
F. Legal Fees				
G. Salary Expense				

LO2 (5 min) **Transaction Analysis**

3. Record the following transaction into the transaction analysis chart: Provided legal fees for $4,000, receiving $3,000 cash with the remainder to be collected next month.

Accounts Affected	Category	↓	↑	Rules of Dr. and Cr.	T Accounts

Trial Balance

LO4 (5 min)

4. Rearrange the following titles in the order they would appear on a trial balance:

Selling Expense	Legal Fees
Accounts Receivable	D. Cope, Withdrawals
Accounts Payable	Rent Expense
D. Cope, Capital	Advertising Expense
Computer Equipment	Cash

Trial Balance/Financial Statements

LO5 (10 min)

5. From the following trial balance, identify on which statement each title will appear:
- Income statement (IS)
- Statement of owner's equity (OE)
- Balance sheet (BS)

HEATH CO.
TRIAL BALANCE
SEPT. 30, 200X

		Dr.	Cr.
A. _____	Cash	390	
B. _____	Supplies	100	
C. _____	Office Equipment	200	
D. _____	Accounts Payable		100
E. _____	D. Heath, Capital		450
F. _____	D. Heath, Withdrawals	160	
G. _____	Fees Earned		290
H. _____	Hair Salon Fees		300
I. _____	Salaries Expense	130	
J. _____	Rent Expense	120	
K. _____	Advertising Expense	40	
	TOTALS	1,140	1,140

Exercises

MyAccountingLab

2-1. From the following, prepare a chart of accounts, using the same numbering system used in this chapter.

LO1 (10 min)

Panasonic HD Television	Legal Fees
Salary Expense	L. Jones, Capital
Accounts Payable	Cash
Accounts Receivable	Advertising Expense
Repair Expense	L. Jones, Withdrawals

2-2. Record the following transaction into the transaction analysis chart: Sandy Pointer bought a new piece of computer equipment for $19,000, paying $3,000 down and charging the rest.

LO2 (5 min)

2-3. Complete the following table. For each account listed on the left, fill in what category it belongs to, whether increases and decreases in the account are

LO2 (5 min)

marked on the debit or credit sides, and on which financial statement the account appears. A sample is provided.

Accounts Affected	Category	↑	↓	Appears on Which Financial Statements
Computer Supplies	Asset	Dr.	Cr.	Balance Sheet
Legal Fees Earned				
P. Rey, Withdrawals				
Accounts Payable				
Salaries Expense				
Auto				

LO2 (20 min)

2-4. Given the following accounts, complete the table by inserting appropriate numbers next to the individual transaction to indicate which account is debited and which account is credited.

1. Cash
2. Accounts Receivable
3. Equipment
4. Accounts Payable
5. B. Baker, Capital
6. B. Baker, Withdrawals
7. Plumbing Fees Earned
8. Salaries Expense
9. Advertising Expense
10. Supplies Expenses

Transaction		Rules Dr.	Cr.
Example: **A.**	Paid salaries expense.	**8**	**1**
B.	Bob paid personal utilities bill from the company checkbook.		
C.	Advertising bill received but unpaid.		
D.	Received cash from plumbing fees.		
E.	Paid supplies expense.		
F.	Bob invested in additional equipment for the business.		
G.	Billed customers for plumbing services rendered.		
H.	Received one-half the balance from transaction G.		
I.	Bought equipment on account.		

LO4 (20 min)

2-5. From the trial balance of Hall's Cleaners on the following page (Fig. 2.6), prepare the following:
- Income statement
- Statement of owner's equity
- Balance sheet

MyAccountingLab **Group A Problems**

LO2 (20 min)

2A-1. The following transactions occurred in the opening and operation of Bill's Delivery Service.
   a. Bill O'Brien opened the delivery service by investing $21,000 from his personal savings account.

FIGURE 2.6

HALL'S CLEANERS TRIAL BALANCE JULY 31, 200X		
	Dr.	Cr.
Cash	5 5 0 00	
Equipment	6 9 2 00	
Accounts Payable		4 5 5 00
J. Hall, Capital		8 0 0 00
J. Hall, Withdrawals	1 9 8 00	
Cleaning Fees		4 5 8 00
Salaries Expense	1 6 0 00	
Utilities Expense	1 1 3 00	
Totals	1 7 1 3 00	1 7 1 3 00

b. Purchased used Delivery Trucks on account, $9,000.
c. Rent expense due but unpaid, $900.
d. Received cash for Delivery Fees Earned, $1,400.
e. Billed a client on account, $150.
f. Bill withdrew cash for personal use, $400.

Complete the transaction analysis chart in the *Study Guide and Working Papers.* The chart of accounts includes Cash; Accounts Receivable; Delivery Trucks; Accounts Payable; Bill O'Brien, Capital; Bill O'Brien, Withdrawals; Delivery Fees Earned; and Rent Expense.

Check Figure:
After F:

Cash	
21,000	400
1,400	

2A-2. Bernie Pillows opened a consulting company, and the following transactions resulted:

LO2 (20 min)

a. Bernie invested $20,000 in the consulting agency.
b. Bought office equipment on account, $5,000.
c. Agency received cash for consulting work that it completed for a client, $900.
d. Bernie paid a personal bill from the company checkbook, $90.
e. Paid advertising expense for the month, $400.
f. Rent expense for the month due but unpaid, $1,400.
g. Paid $1,000 as partial payment of what was owed from transaction B.

Check Figure:
After G:

Cash			
(A)	20,000	90	(D)
(C)	900	400	(E)
		1,000	(G)

As Bernie's accountant, analyze and record the transactions in T account form. Set up the T accounts and label each entry with the letter of the transaction.

Chart of Accounts

Assets

Cash 111

Office Equipment 121

Liabilities

Accounts Payable 211

Owner's Equity

Bernie Pillows, Capital 311

Bernie Pillows, Withdrawals 312

Revenue

Consulting Fees Earned 411

Expenses

Advertising Expense 511

Rent Expense 512

2A-3. From the following T accounts of Barry's Cleaning Service, (a) record, foot and take the balances of the accounts in the *Study Guide and Working Papers* where appropriate, and (b) prepare a trial balance in proper form for May 31, 200X.

LO3 (20 min)

Cash 111

(A)	7,000	(D)	200
(G)	3,500	(E)	200
		(F)	400
		(H)	200
		(I)	900

Accounts Payable 211

(D)	200	(C)	1,300

Cleaning Fees Earned 411

(B)	8,000

Accounts Receivable 112

(B)	8,000	(G)	3,500

Barry Joy, Capital 311

(A)	7,000

Rent Expense 511

(F)	400

Office Equipment 121

(C)	1,300
(H)	200

Barry Joy, Withdrawals 312

(I)	900

Utilities Expense 512

(E)	200

LO4 (40 min)

2A-4. From the trial balance of Gracie Lantz, Attorney-at-Law (Fig. 2.7), prepare (a) an income statement for the month of May, (b) a statement of owner's equity for the month ended May 31, and (c) a balance sheet as of May 31, 200X.

FIGURE 2.7

GRACIE LANTZ, ATTORNEY-AT-LAW TRIAL BALANCE MAY 31, 200X	Dr.	Cr.
Cash	5 0 0 00	
Accounts Receivable	6 5 0 00	
Office Equipment	7 5 0 00	
Accounts Payable		4 3 0 0 00
Salaries Payable		6 7 5 00
G. Lantz, Capital		1 2 7 5 00
G. Lantz, Withdrawals	3 0 0 00	
Revenue from Legal Fees		1 3 5 0 00
Utilities Expense	3 0 0 00	
Rent Expense	4 5 0 00	
Salaries Expense	1 5 0 00	
Totals	7 6 0 0 00	7 6 0 0 00

LO2, 3, 4 (60 min)   **2A-5.** The chart of accounts for Angel's Delivery Service is as follows:

Chart of Accounts

Assets	**Revenue**
Cash 111	Delivery Fees Earned 411
Accounts Receivable 112	**Expenses**
Office Equipment 121	Advertising Expense 511
Delivery Trucks 122	Gas Expense 512
Liabilities	Salaries Expense 513
Accounts Payable 211	Telephone Expense 514
Owner's Equity	
Alice Angel, Capital 311	
Alice Angel, Withdrawals 312	

Angel's Delivery Service completed the following transactions during the month of March:

Transaction A:	Alice Angel invested $16,000 in the delivery service from her personal savings account.
Transaction B:	Bought delivery trucks on account, $18,000.
Transaction C:	Bought office equipment for cash, $600.
Transaction D:	Paid advertising expense, $250.
Transaction E:	Collected cash for delivery services rendered, $2,600.
Transaction F:	Paid drivers' salaries, $900.
Transaction G:	Paid gas expense for trucks, $1,200.
Transaction H:	Performed delivery services for a customer on account, $800.
Transaction I:	Telephone expense due but unpaid, $700.
Transaction J:	Received $300 as partial payment of transaction H.
Transaction K:	Alice withdrew cash for personal use, $300.

As Alice's newly employed accountant, you must

1. Set up T accounts in a ledger.
2. Record transactions in the T accounts. (Place the letter of the transaction next to the entry.)
3. Foot and take the balances of the T accounts where appropriate.
4. Prepare a trial balance at the end of March.
5. Prepare from the trial balance, in proper form, (a) an income statement for the month of March, (b) a statement of owner's equity, and (c) a balance sheet as of March 31, 200X.

Group B Problems

MyAccountingLab

2B-1. Bill O'Brien decided to open a delivery service. Record the following transactions into the transaction analysis charts:

LO2 (20 min)

Transaction A:	Bill invested $2,500 in the delivery service from her personal savings account.
Transaction B:	Purchased a used delivery truck on account, $900.
Transaction C:	Rent expense due but unpaid, $250.
Transaction D:	Performed delivery services for cash, $1,200.
Transaction E:	Billed clients for deliveries rendered, $700.
Transaction F:	Bill paid his home heating bill from the company checkbook, $275.

Check Figure:
After F:

	Cash		
(A)	2,500	275	(F)
(D)	1,200		

The chart of accounts for the shop includes Cash; Accounts Receivable; Delivery Truck; Accounts Payable; Bill O'Brien, Capital; Bill O'Brien, Withdrawals; Shuttle Fees Earned; and Rent Expense.

2B-2. Bernie Pillow established a new consulting company. Record the following transactions for Bernie in T account form. Label each entry with the letter of the transaction.

LO2 (20 min)

Transaction A:	Bernie invested $20,000 in the consulting company from his personal bank account.
Transaction B:	Bought office equipment on account, $6,000.
Transaction C:	Company rendered consulting to Jensen Corp. and received cash, $1,200.
Transaction D:	Bernie withdrew cash for personal use, $200.

Transaction E: Paid advertising expense, $600.

Transaction F: Rent expense due but unpaid, $500.

Transaction G: Paid $400 in partial payment of transaction B.

The chart of accounts includes Cash, 111; Office Equipment, 121; Accounts Payable, 211; Bernie Pillows, Capital, 311; Bernie Pillows, Withdrawals, 312; Consulting Fees Earned, 411; Advertising Expense, 511; and Rent Expense, 512.

LO3 (20 min)

2B-3. From the following T accounts of Barry's Cleaning Service, (a) foot and take the balances of the accounts in the *Study Guide and Working Papers* where appropriate and (b) prepare a trial balance for May 31, 200X.

Cash 111				**Accounts Receivable 112**			**Office Equipment 121**	
(A) 10,000	(C)	4,000		(G) 2,000			(B) 2,000	
(F) 4,000	(D)	310					(C) 4,000	
(G) 2,000	(E)	50						
	(H)	600						

Accounts Payable 211		**Barry Joy, Capital 311**		**Barry Joy, Withdrawals 312**	
	(B) 2,000		(A) 10,000	(H) 600	

Cleaning Fees Earned 411		**Rent Expense 511**		**Utilities Expense 512**	
	(F) 4,000	(D) 310		(E) 50	
	(G) 4,000				

LO4 (40 min)

2B-4. From the trial balance of Gracie Lantz, Attorney-at-Law (Fig. 2-8), prepare (a) an income statement for the month of May, (b) a statement of owner's equity for the month ended May 31, and (c) a balance sheet as of May 31, 200X.

FIGURE 2.8

GRACIE LANTZ, ATTORNEY-AT-LAW TRIAL BALANCE MAY 31, 200X		
	Debit	Credit
Cash	6 0 0 0 00	
Accounts Receivable	2 4 0 0 00	
Office Equipment	2 4 0 0 00	
Accounts Payable		2 0 0 00
Salaries Payable		6 0 0 00
G. Lantz, Capital		4 0 0 0 00
G. Lantz, Withdrawals	2 0 0 0 00	
Revenue from Legal Fees		8 8 0 0 00
Utilities Expense	1 0 0 00	
Rent Expense	3 0 0 00	
Salaries Expense	4 0 0 00	
Totals	13 6 0 0 00	13 6 0 0 00

LO2, 3, 4 (60 min)

2B-5. The chart of accounts of Angel's Delivery Service includes the following: Cash, 111; Accounts Receivable, 112; Office Equipment, 121; Delivery Trucks, 122; Accounts Payable, 211; Alice Angel, Capital, 311; Alice Angel, Withdrawals, 312; Delivery Fees Earned, 411; Advertising Expense, 511; Gas Expense, 512; Salaries Expense, 513; and Telephone Expense, 514. The following transactions resulted for Angel's Delivery Service during the month of March:

Check Figure:
Trial Balance Total $84,300

Transaction A:	Alice invested $40,000 in the business from her personal savings account.
Transaction B:	Bought delivery trucks on account, $25,000.
Transaction C:	Advertising bill received but unpaid, $800.
Transaction D:	Bought office equipment for cash, $2,500.
Transaction E:	Received cash for delivery services rendered, $13,000.
Transaction F:	Paid salaries expense, $1,850.
Transaction G:	Paid gas expense for company trucks, $750.
Transaction H:	Billed customers for delivery services rendered, $5,500.
Transaction I:	Paid telephone bill, $400.
Transaction J:	Received $1,600 as partial payment of transaction H.
Transaction K:	Alice paid her home telephone bill from company checkbook, $88.

As Alice's newly employed accountant, you must

1. Set up T accounts in a ledger.
2. Record transactions in the T accounts. (Place the letter of the transaction next to the entry.)
3. Foot the T accounts where appropriate.
4. Prepare a trial balance at the end of March.
5. Prepare from the trial balance, in proper form, (a) an income statement for the month of March, (b) a statement of owner's equity, and (c) a balance sheet as of March 31, 200X.

ON-THE-JOB-TRAINING

T-1. Andy Leaf is a careless bookkeeper. He is having a terrible time getting his trial balance to balance. Andy has asked for your assistance in preparing a correct trial balance. The following is the incorrect trial balance:

LO4 (20 min)

FIGURE 2.9 Incorrect Trial Balance

RANCH COMPANY TRIAL BALANCE JUNE 30, 200X	Dr.	Cr.
Cash	5 1 0 00	
Accounts Receivable		6 3 5 00
Office Equipment	3 6 0 00	
Accounts Payable	1 1 0 00	
Wages Payable	1 0 00	
H. Clo, Capital	6 3 5 00	
H. Clo, Withdrawals	1 4 4 0 00	
Professional Fees		2 2 4 0 00
Rent Expense		2 4 0 00
Advertising Expense	2 5 00	
Totals	3 0 9 0 00	3 1 1 5 00

Facts you have discovered:

- Debits to the Cash account were $2,640; credits to the Cash account were $2,150.
- Amy Hall paid $15 but was not updated in Accounts Receivable.
- A purchase of office equipment for $5 on account was never recorded in the ledger.
- Revenue was understated in the ledger by $180.

Show how these errors affected the ending balances for the accounts involved and explain how the trial balance will indeed balance once they are corrected.

Tell Ranch Company how it can avoid this problem in the future. Write your recommendations.

LO3, 4 (20 min)   **T-2.** Cookie Mejias, owner of Mejias Company, asked her bookkeeper how each of the following situations will affect the totals of the trial balance and individual ledger accounts:

1. An $850 payment for a desk was recorded as a debit to Office Equipment, $85, and a credit to Cash, $85.

2. A payment of $300 to a creditor was recorded as a debit to Accounts Payable, $300, and a credit to Cash, $100.

3. The collection on an Accounts Receivable for $400 was recorded as a debit to Cash, $400, and a credit to C. Mejias, Capital, $400.

4. The payment of a liability for $400 was recorded as a debit to Accounts Payable, $40, and a credit to Supplies, $40.

5. A purchase of equipment of $800 was recorded as a debit to Supplies, $800, and a credit to Cash, $800.

6. A payment of $95 to a creditor was recorded as a debit to Accounts Payable, $95, and a credit to Cash, $59.

What did the bookkeeper tell her? Which accounts were overstated, and which were understated? Which were correct? Explain in writing how mistakes can be avoided in the future.

FINANCIAL REPORT PROBLEM

LO4 (5 min)   ### Reading the Kellogg's Report

Go to Appendix A and find the balance sheet of Kellogg's. Did Kellogg's Accounts Payable go up or down from 2005 to 2006? What does this change mean? Into what category does Accounts Payable fall by rules of debit and credit? Which side of the T account would make it increase?

INTERNET PROJECT

Staples

Go to the Web and search: Annual Report Staples 2008.
Click on Investors Relations.
List out the latest news Staples is providing to its investors.
Order a free annual report.

CONTINUING PROBLEM

MyAccountingLab

Sanchez Computer Center

LO2, 3, 4 (60 min)

The Sanchez Computer Center created its chart of accounts as follows:

Chart of Accounts as of July 1, 200X

Assets		Revenue	
1000	Cash	4000	Service Revenue
1020	Accounts Receivable	**Expenses**	
1030	Supplies	5010	Advertising Expense
1080	Computer Shop Equipment	5020	Rent Expense
1090	Office Equipment	5030	Utilities Expense
Liabilities		5040	Phone Expense
2000	Accounts Payable	5050	Supplies Expense
Owner's Equity		5060	Insurance Expense
3000	Freedman, Capital	5070	Postage Expense
3010	Freedman, Withdrawals		

You will use this chart of accounts to complete the Continuing Problem.

The following problem continues from Chapter 1. The balances as of July 31 have been brought forward in your *Study Guide and Working Papers*.

Assignment

1. Set up T accounts in a ledger.
2. Record transactions k through s in the appropriate T accounts.
3. Foot and take the balances of the T accounts where appropriate.
4. Prepare a trial balance at the end of August.
5. Prepare from the trial balance an income statement, statement of owner's equity, and a balance sheet for the two months ending with August 31, 200X.
   k. Received the phone bill for the month of July, $155.
   l. Paid $150 (check #8099) for insurance for the month.
   m. Paid $200 (check #8100) of the amount due from transaction d in Chapter 1.
   n. Paid advertising expense for the month, $1,400 (check #8101).
   o. Billed a client (Jeannine Sparks) for services rendered, $850.
   p. Collected $900 for services rendered.
   q. Paid the electric bill in full for the month of July (check #8102, transaction h, Chapter 1).
   r. Paid cash (check #8103) for $50 in stamps.
   s. Purchased $200 worth of supplies from Computer Connection on credit.

SUBWAY Case

DEBITS ON THE LEFT . . .

LO2 (20 min)

When Stan took the big leap from being an employee to a Subway owner, the thing that terrified him most was *not* the part about managing people—that was one of his strengths as a marketing manager. Why, at Xellent Media, 40 sales reps reported to him! No, Stan was terrified of having to manage the accounts. Subway restaurant owners have so many accounts to deal with: food costs, payroll, rent, utilities, supplies, advertising, promotion, and, biggest of all, cash. It's critical for them to keep debits and credits straight. If not, both they and Subway could lose a lot of money, quickly.

Even though Stan got some intense training in accounting and bookkeeping at Subway University, he still felt shaky about doing his own books. When he confided his fears to Mariah Washington, his field consultant, she suggested he hire an accountant. "You need to play to your strengths," said Mariah, and she told Stan, "More and more owners are using accountants, and almost all owners of multiple franchises do. In fact, some accountants actually specialize in handling Subway accounts for these multirestaurant owners."

Even though Stan decided to hire his cousin, Lila, to do his accounting, he still needs to feed her the right data so she can calculate his T accounts. Like many small business owners, Stan enters data into an accounting software program such as QuickBooks or Peachtree, which he then uploads to his accountant, who edits it and reviews it for accuracy. Several times in the beginning Stan mistakenly debited both cash and supplies when he paid for orders of paper cups, bread dough, and other supplies.

Lila urged Stan to review the rules for recording debits and credits. She even told him to practice for a while using a paper ledger. "On the computer debits and credits are not as visible as they are with your paper system. Since you only enter the payables, the computer does the other side of the balance sheet. So you have to bone up on debits and credits to ensure that your Peachtree data are correct."

Discussion Questions

1. Why is the cash account so important in Stan's business?
2. Why do you think that most owners of the larger shops use accountants to do their books instead of doing the accounting themselves?
3. Is the difference between debits and credits important to Subway restaurant owners who don't do their own books?

3

Beginning the Accounting Cycle

DID YOU KNOW? In 2006 Property and Equipment represented 55% of the total assets of Continental Airlines. Visit *www.continental.com* to find more information about Continental.

LEARNING OBJECTIVES

1. Journalizing: analyzing and recording business transactions into a journal.

2. Posting: transferring information from a journal to a ledger.

3. Preparing a trial balance.

Companies like Continental have to perform certain accounting procedures. The normal accounting procedures that are performed over a period of time are called the **accounting cycle.** The accounting cycle takes place in a period of time called an **accounting period.** An accounting period is the period of time covered by the income statement. Although it can be any time period up to one year (e.g., one month or three months), most businesses use a one-year accounting period. The year can be either a **calendar year** (January 1 through December 31) or a **fiscal year.**

A fiscal year is an accounting period that runs for any 12 consecutive months, so it can be the same as a calendar year. Big Dollar and Aeropostale, Inc., end their accounting period on January 31. A business can choose any fiscal year that is convenient. For example, some retailers may decide to end their fiscal year when inventories and business activity are at a low point, such as after the Christmas season. This period is called a **natural business year.** Using a natural business year allows the business to count its year-end inventory when it is easiest to do so.

Businesses would not be able to operate successfully if they only prepared financial reports at the end of their calendar or fiscal year. For more timely information, most businesses prepare **interim reports** on a monthly, quarterly, or semiannual basis.

In this chapter, as well as in Chapters 4 and 5, we follow Brenda Clark's new business, Clark's Word Processing Services. We follow the normal accounting procedures that the business performs over a period of time. Clark has chosen to use a fiscal period of January 1 to December 31, which also is the calendar year.

LO1 Learning Unit 3-1 Analyzing and Recording Business Transactions into a Journal: Steps 1 and 2 of the Accounting Cycle

The General Journal

Chapter 2 taught us how to analyze and record business transactions into T accounts, or ledger accounts. Recording a debit in an account on one page of the ledger and recording the corresponding credit on a different page of the ledger, however, can make it difficult to find errors. It would be much easier if all the business's transactions were located in the same place. That is the function of the **journal** or **general journal.** Transactions are entered in the journal in chronological order (January 1, 8, 15, etc.), and then this recorded information is used to update the ledger accounts. In computerized accounting, a journal may be recorded on disk or tape.

> A business uses a journal to record transactions in chronological order. A ledger accumulates information from a journal. The journal and the ledger are in two different books.

We will use a general journal, the simplest form of a journal, to record the transactions of Clark's Word Processing Services. A transaction [debit(s) + credit(s)] that has been analyzed and recorded in a journal is called a **journal entry.** The process of recording the journal entry into the journal is called **journalizing.**

The journal is called the **book of original entry** because it contains the first formal information about the business transactions. The ledger is known as the **book of final entry** because the information the journal contains will be transferred to the ledger. Like the ledger, the journal may be a bound or loose-leaf book. Each of the journal pages looks like the one in Figure 3.1. The pages of the journal are numbered consecutively from page 1. Keep in mind that the journal and the ledger are separate books.

Relationship between the Journal and the Chart of Accounts The accountant must refer to the business's chart of accounts for the account name that is to be used in the journal. Every company has its own "unique" chart of accounts.

The following chart of accounts for Clark's Word Processing Services lists the accounts used in the business. By the end of Chapter 5, we will have discussed each of these accounts.

Note that we will continue to use transaction analysis charts as a teaching aid in the journalizing process.

CLARK'S WORD PROCESSING SERVICES
GENERAL JOURNAL

Page 1

Date	Account Titles and Description	PR	Dr.	Cr.

FIGURE 3.1 The General Journal

Clark's Word Processing Services
Chart of Accounts

Assets (100–199)

111	Cash
112	Accounts Receivable
114	Office Supplies
115	Prepaid Rent
121	Word Processing Equipment
122	Accumulated Depreciation, Word Processing Equipment

Liabilities (200–299)

| 211 | Accounts Payable |
| 212 | Salaries Payable |

Owner's Equity (300–399)

311	Brenda Clark, Capital
312	Brenda Clark, Withdrawals
313	Income Summary

Revenue (400–499)

| 411 | Word Processing Fees |

Expenses (500–599)

511	Office Salaries Expense
512	Advertising Expense
513	Telephone Expense
514	Office Supplies Expense
515	Rent Expense
516	Depreciation Expense, Word Processing Equipment

Journalizing the Transactions of Clark's Word Processing Services Certain formalities must be followed in making journal entries:

- The debit portion of the transaction always is recorded first.
- The credit portion of a transaction is indented a ½ inch and placed below the debit portion.
- The explanation of the journal entry follows immediately after the credit and 1 inch from the date column.
- A one-line space follows each transaction and explanation. This makes the journal easier to read, and there is less chance of mixing transactions.
- Finally, as always, the total amount of debits must equal the total amount of credits. The same format is used for each of the entries in the journal.
- Each transaction must affect at least two different accounts.

MAY 1, 200X: BRENDA CLARK BEGAN THE BUSINESS BY INVESTING $10,000 IN CASH

1 Accounts Affected	2 Category	3 ↓ ↑	4 Rules of Dr. and Cr.
Cash	Asset	↑	Dr.
Brenda Clark, Capital	Capital	↑	Cr.

FIGURE 3.2 Owner Investment

	Date		Account Titles and Description	PR	Dr.	Cr.
			CLARK'S WORD PROCESSING SERVICES			
			GENERAL JOURNAL			
						Page 1
	200X May	1	Cash		10 0 0 0 00	
			Brenda Clark, Capital			10 0 0 0 00
			Initial investment of cash by owner			

> For now the PR (posting reference) column is blank; we discuss it later.

Let's now look at the structure of this journal entry (Fig. 3.2). The entry contains the following information:

1. Year of the journal entry   200X
2. Month of the journal entry   May
3. Day of the journal entry   1
4. Name(s) of accounts debited   Cash
5. Name(s) of accounts credited   Brenda Clark, Capital
6. Explanation of transaction   Investment of cash
7. Amount of debit(s) $10,000
8. Amount of credit(s) $10,000

MAY 1: PURCHASED WORD PROCESSING EQUIPMENT FROM BEN CO. FOR $6,000, PAYING $1,000 AND PROMISING TO PAY THE BALANCE WITHIN 30 DAYS

1 Accounts Affected	2 Category	3 ↓ ↑	4 Rules of Dr. and Cr.
Word Processing Equipment	Asset	↑	Dr.
Cash	Asset	↓	Cr.
Accounts Payable	Liability	↑	Cr.

> Note that in this compound entry we have one debit and two credits, but the total amount of debits equals the total amount of credits.

This transaction affects three accounts. When a journal entry has more than two accounts, it is called a **compound journal entry.**

In this entry, only the day is entered in the date column because the year and month were entered at the top of the page from the first transaction. This information doesn't need to be repeated until a new page is needed or a change of months occurs.

FIGURE 3.3 Purchase of Equipment

		1	Word Processing Equipment		6 0 0 0 00		
			Cash			1 0 0 0 00	
			Accounts Payable			5 0 0 0 00	
			Purchase of equipment from Ben Co.				

MAY 1: RENTED OFFICE SPACE, PAYING $1,200 IN ADVANCE FOR THE FIRST THREE MONTHS			
1 Accounts Affected	**2** Category	**3** ↓ ↑	**4** Rules of Dr. and Cr.
Prepaid Rent	Asset	↑	Dr.
Cash	Asset	↓	Cr.

In this transaction Clark gains an asset called prepaid rent and gives up an asset, cash. The prepaid rent does not become an expense until it expires.

> Rent paid in advance is an asset.

	1	Prepaid Rent		1 2 0 0 00	
		Cash			1 2 0 0 00
		Rent paid in advance—3 mos.			

FIGURE 3.4 Rent Paid in Advance

MAY 3: PURCHASED OFFICE SUPPLIES FROM NORRIS CO. ON ACCOUNT, $600			
1 Accounts Affected	**2** Category	**3** ↓ ↑	**4** Rules of Dr. and Cr.
Office Supplies	Asset	↑	Dr.
Accounts Payable	Liability	↑	Cr.

Remember, supplies are an asset when they are purchased. Once they are used up or consumed in the operation of business, they become an expense.

> Supplies become an expense when used up.

	3	Office Supplies		6 0 0 00	
		Accounts Payable			6 0 0 00
		Purchase of supplies on account			
		from Norris			

FIGURE 3.5 Purchased Supplies on Account

MAY 7: COMPLETED SALES PROMOTION PIECES FOR A CLIENT AND IMMEDIATELY COLLECTED $3,000			
1 Accounts Affected	**2** Category	**3** ↓ ↑	**4** Rules of Dr. and Cr.
Cash	Asset	↑	Dr.
Word Processing Fees	Revenue	↑	Cr.

	7	Cash		3 0 0 0 00	
		Word Processing Fees			3 0 0 0 00
		Cash received for services rendered			

FIGURE 3.6 Services Rendered

MAY 13: PAID OFFICE SALARIES, $650			
1 **Accounts Affected**	**2** **Category**	**3** ↓ ↑	**4** **Rules of Dr. and Cr.**
Office Salaries Expense	Expense	↑	Dr.
Cash	Asset	↓	Cr.

FIGURE 3.7 Paid Salaries

	13	Office Salaries Expense		6 5 0 00	
		Cash			6 5 0 00
		Payment of office salaries			

Remember, expenses are recorded when they are incurred, no matter when they are paid.

MAY 18: ADVERTISING BILL FROM AL'S NEWS CO. COMES IN BUT IS NOT PAID, $250			
1 **Accounts Affected**	**2** **Category**	**3** ↓ ↑	**4** **Rules of Dr. and Cr.**
Advertising Expense	Expense	↑	Dr.
Accounts Payable	Liability	↑	Cr.

FIGURE 3.8 Advertising Bill

	18	Advertising Expense		2 5 0 00	
		Accounts Payable			2 5 0 00
		Bill in but not paid from Al's News			

MAY 20: BRENDA CLARK WROTE A CHECK ON THE BANK ACCOUNT OF THE BUSINESS TO PAY HER HOME MORTGAGE PAYMENT OF $625			
1 **Accounts Affected**	**2** **Category**	**3** ↓ ↑	**4** **Rules of Dr. and Cr.**
Brenda Clark, Withdrawals	Withdrawals	↑	Dr.
Cash	Asset	↓	Cr.

Keep in mind that as withdrawals increase, owner's equity decreases.

FIGURE 3.9 Personal Withdrawal

	20	Brenda Clark, Withdrawals		6 2 5 00	
		Cash			6 2 5 00
		Personal withdrawal of cash			

Reminder: Revenue is recorded when it is earned, no matter when the cash is actually received.

MAY 22: BILLED MORRIS COMPANY FOR A SOPHISTICATED WORD PROCESSING JOB, $5,000			
1 **Accounts Affected**	**2** **Category**	**3** ↓ ↑	**4** **Rules of Dr. and Cr.**
Accounts Receivable	Asset	↑	Dr.
Word Processing Fees	Revenue	↑	Cr.

	22	Accounts Receivable		5 0 0 0 00	
		Word Processing Fees			5 0 0 0 00
		Billed Morris Co. for fees earned			

FIGURE 3.10 Fees Earned

MAY 27: PAID OFFICE SALARIES, $650

1	2	3	4
Accounts Affected	**Category**	↓ ↑	**Rules of Dr. and Cr.**
Office Salaries Expense	Expense	↑	Dr.
Cash	Asset	↓	Cr.

FIGURE 3.11 Paid Salaries

		CLARK'S WORD PROCESSING SERVICES **GENERAL JOURNAL**			
					Page 2
Date		Account Titles and Description	PR	Dr.	Cr.
200X May	27*	Office Salaries Expense		6 5 0 00	
		Cash			6 5 0 00
		Payment of office salaries			

*Note that this is a new page, so the year and month are repeated.

MAY 28: PAID HALF THE AMOUNT OWED FOR WORD PROCESSING EQUIPMENT PURCHASED MAY 1 FROM BEN CO., $2,500

1	2	3	4
Accounts Affected	**Category**	↓ ↑	**Rules of Dr. and Cr.**
Accounts Payable	Liability	↓	Dr.
Cash	Asset	↓	Cr.

FIGURE 3.12 Partial Payment

	28	Accounts Payable		2 5 0 0 00	
		Cash			2 5 0 0 00
		Paid half the amount owed Ben Co.			

MAY 29: RECEIVED AND PAID TELEPHONE BILL, $220

1	2	3	4
Accounts Affected	**Category**	↓ ↑	**Rules of Dr. and Cr.**
Telephone Expense	Expense	↑	Dr.
Cash	Asset	↓	Cr.

FIGURE 3.13 Paid Telephone

	29	Telephone Expense		2 2 0 00	
		Cash			2 2 0 00
		Paid telephone bill			

This concludes the journal transactions of Clark's Word Processing Services.

LEARNING UNIT 3-1 REVIEW

AT THIS POINT you should be able to

- Define an accounting cycle.
- Define and explain the relationship of the accounting period to the income statement.
- Compare and contrast a calendar year to a fiscal year.
- Explain the term *natural business year.*
- Explain the function of interim reports.
- Define and state the purpose of a journal.
- Compare and contrast a book of original entry to a book of final entry.
- Differentiate between a chart of accounts and a journal.
- Journalize a business transaction.
- Explain a compound entry.

Self-Review Quiz 3-1

For additional help go to
www.pearsonhighered.com/slater

The following are the transactions of Lowe's Repair Service. Journalize the transactions in proper form. The chart of accounts includes Cash; Accounts Receivable; Prepaid Rent; Repair Supplies; Repair Equipment; Accounts Payable; A. Lowe, Capital; A. Lowe, Withdrawals; Repair Fees Earned; Salaries Expense; Advertising Expense; and Supplies Expense.

200X

June 1   A. Lowe invested $7,000 cash and $5,000 of repair equipment in the business.

1   Paid two months' rent in advance, $1,200.

4   Bought repair supplies from Melvin Co. on account, $600. (These supplies have not yet been consumed or used up.)

15   Performed repair work, received $600 in cash, and had to bill Doe Co. for remaining balance of $300.

18   A. Lowe paid his home telephone bill, $50, with a check from the company.

20   Advertising bill for $400 from Jones Co. received but payment not due yet. (Advertising has already appeared in the newspaper.)

24   Paid salaries, $1,400.

Solution to Self-Review Quiz 3-1

FIGURE 3.14 Transactions Journalized

LOWE'S REPAIR SERVICE
GENERAL JOURNAL

Page 1

Date			Account Titles and Description	PR	Dr.	Cr.
200X June	1		Cash		7 0 0 0 00	
			Repair Equipment		5 0 0 0 00	
			A. Lowe, Capital			12 0 0 0 00
			Owner investment			
	1		Prepaid Rent		1 2 0 0 00	
			Cash			1 2 0 0 00
			Rent paid in advance—2 mos.			
	4		Repair Supplies		6 0 0 00	
			Accounts Payable			6 0 0 00
			Purchase on account from Melvin Co.			
	15		Cash		6 0 0 00	
			Accounts Receivable		3 0 0 00	
			Repair Fees Earned			9 0 0 00
			Performed repairs for Doe Co.			
	18		A. Lowe, Withdrawals		5 0 00	
			Cash			5 0 00
			Personal withdrawal			
	20		Advertising Expense		4 0 0 00	
			Accounts Payable			4 0 0 00
			Advertising bill from Jones Co.			
	24		Salaries Expense		1 4 0 0 00	
			Cash			1 4 0 0 00
			Paid salaries			

NEED HELP?

Let's review first: When recording transactions into a general journal the debit(s) will be against the date column and the credit(s) will be indented. These titles will come from the chart of accounts. The explanation line will then be indented below the last credit entry. The sum of the left side (Dr.) must equal the sum of the right side (Cr.) for each transaction.

Here are the mind process charts for each transaction. Be sure to remember that the accounts affected come from the chart of accounts. You have six categories: assets, liabilities, capital, withdrawals, revenues, and expenses. You must ask yourself what the company is getting and how it is getting it. Remember to think of expenses and withdrawals as increasing, resulting in a decrease to owner's equity.

June 1	Cash	Asset	↑	Dr.
	Repair Equip.	Asset	↑	Dr.
	A. Lowe, Cap.	Capital	↑	Cr.

Debits are listed first against the date column and credits are indented. This is an investment by the owner. The month is written because the month starts a new page.

| 1 | Prepaid Rent | Asset | ↑ | Dr. |
| | Cash | Asset | ↓ | Cr. |

This is a shift in assets, more rent paid in advance by cash. Note that the month is not repeated.

| 4 | Repair Supplies | Asset | ↑ | Dr. |
| | Accounts Payable | Liability | ↑ | Cr. |

This is an example of buy now and pay later. Supplies will not be an expense until they are used up.

15	Cash	Asset	↑	Dr.
	Acc. Receiv.	Asset	↑	Dr.
	Rep. Fees Earn.	Revenue	↑	Cr.

Here we did the work and got some money as well as some promises that the customer will pay later. Note how the two debits are against the date column and the credit is indented.

| 18 | A. Lowe, Withd. | Withdr. | ↑ | Dr. |
| | Cash | Asset | ↓ | Cr. |

The owner increases her withdrawals for personal use and the end result is that the business has less cash.

| 20 | Advertising Exp. | Expense | ↑ | Dr. |
| | Accounts Pay. | Liability | ↑ | Cr. |

An expense has been incurred but is not paid for. This expense has created a liability. Think of expenses as always increasing.

| 24 | Salaries Exp. | Expense | ↑ | Dr. |
| | Cash | Asset | ↓ | Cr. |

Here the expense is increasing and it is being paid for in cash.

LO2 Learning Unit 3-2 Posting to the Ledger: Step 3 of the Accounting Cycle

The general journal serves a particular purpose: It puts every transaction the business does in one place. It cannot do certain things, though. For example, if you were asked to find the balance of the cash account from the general journal, you would have to go through the entire journal and look for only the cash entries. Then you would have to add up the debits and credits for the Cash account and determine the difference between the two.

What we really need to do to find balances of accounts is to transfer the information from the journal to the ledger. This process is called **posting.** In the ledger we accumulate an ending balance for each account so that we can prepare financial statements.

Accounts Payable				Debit	Credit	Balance Debit	Balance Credit	Account No. 211
	Date	Explanation	Post. Ref.	Debit	Credit	Debit	Credit	
200X May	1		GJ1		5 0 0 0 00		5 0 0 0 00	
	3		GJ1		6 0 0 00		5 6 0 0 00	
	18		GJ1		2 5 0 00		5 8 5 0 00	
	28		GJ2	2 5 0 0 00			3 3 5 0 00	

FIGURE 3.15 Four-Column Account

$5,000 Cr. + $600 Cr. = $5,600 Cr.
Cr. + Cr. = Cr.
Dr. + Dr. = Dr.

In Chapter 2 we used the T account form to make our ledger entries. T accounts are simple, but they are not used in the real business world; they are only used for demonstration purposes. In practice, accountants often use a **four-column account** form that includes a column for the business's running balance. Figure 3.15 shows a standard four-column account. We use this format in the text from now on.

Posting is automatic when using QuickBooks and Peachtree software programs. When you select Save in a transaction, the accounts are immediately updated.

Posting

Now let's look at how to post the transactions of Clark's Word Processing Services from its journal. The diagram in Figure 3.16 shows how to post the cash line from the journal to the ledger. The steps in the posting process are numbered and illustrated in the figure.

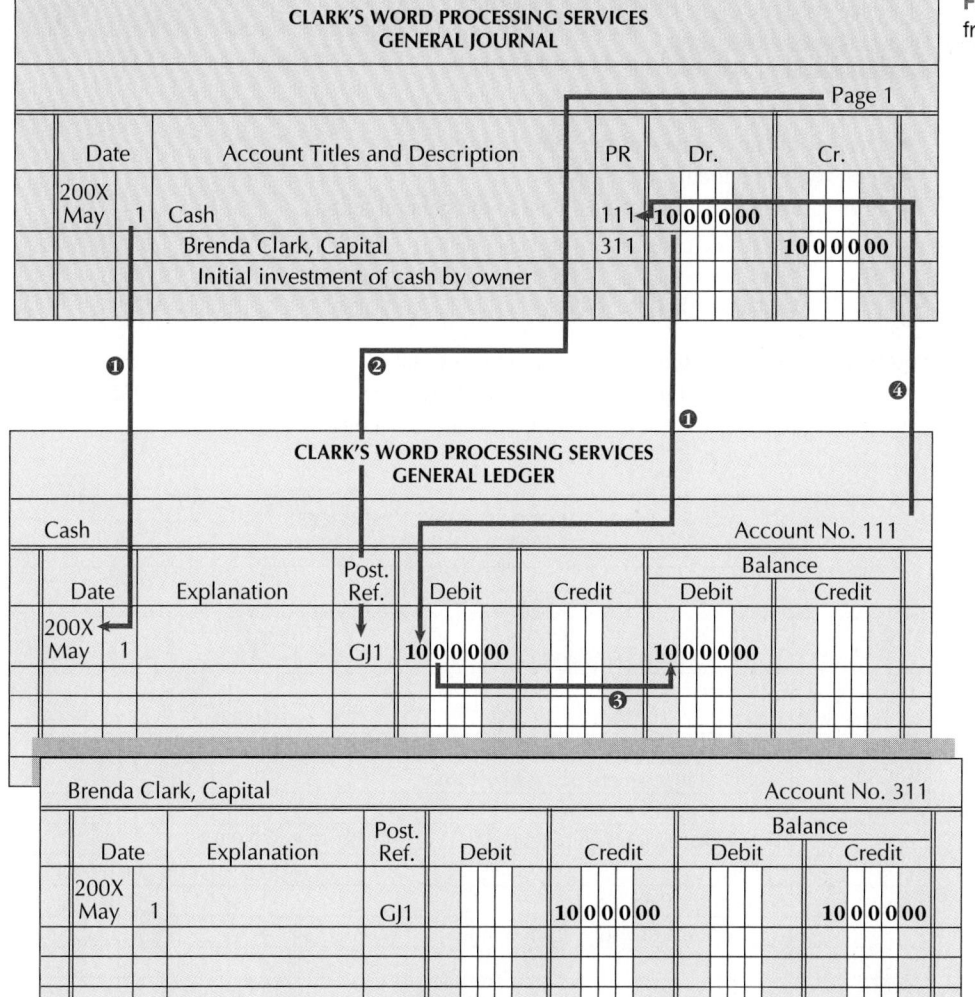

FIGURE 3.16 How to Post from Journal to Ledger

Step 1 In the Cash account in the ledger, record the date (May 1, 200X) and the amount of the entry ($10,000).

Step 2 Record the page number of the journal "GJ1" in the posting reference (PR) column of the Cash account.

Step 3 Calculate the new balance of the account. To keep a running balance in each account, as you would in your personal checkbook, take the present balance in the account on the previous line and add or subtract the transaction as necessary to arrive at your new balance.

Step 4 Record the account number of Cash (111) in the posting reference (PR) column of the journal. This listing is known as **cross-referencing.**

The same sequence of steps occurs for each line in the journal. In a manual system like Clark's, the debits and credits in the journal may be posted in the order they were recorded, or all the debits may be posted first and then all the credits. If Clark's used a computer system, the program menu would post at the press of a button.

Using Posting References The posting references are helpful. In the journal, the PR column tells us which transactions have or have not been posted and also to which accounts they were posted. In the ledger, the posting reference leads us back to the original transaction in its entirety, so we can see why the debit or credit was recorded and what other accounts were affected. (It leads us back to the original transaction by identifying the journal and the page in the journal from which the information came.)

LEARNING UNIT 3-2 REVIEW

AT THIS POINT you should be able to

a$\frac{c}{t}$

Accounting Cycle Tutorial

- State the purpose of posting.
- Discuss the advantages of the four-column account.
- Identify the elements to be posted.
- From journalized transactions, post to the general ledger.

Self-Review Quiz 3-2

Figure 3.17 shows the journalized transactions of Clark's Word Processing Services. Your task is to post information to the ledger. The ledger in your workbook has all the account titles and numbers that were used from the chart of accounts.

FIGURE 3.17 Journalized Entries

	Date		Account Titles and Description	PR	Dr.	Cr.
			CLARK'S WORD PROCESSING SERVICES GENERAL JOURNAL			Page 1
	200X May	1	Cash		10 0 0 0 00	
			Brenda Clark, Capital			10 0 0 0 00
			Initial investment of cash by owner			
		1	Word Processing Equipment		6 0 0 0 00	
			Cash			1 0 0 0 00
			Accounts Payable			5 0 0 0 00
			Purchase of equip. from Ben Co.			
		1	Prepaid Rent		1 2 0 0 00	
			Cash			1 2 0 0 00
			Rent paid in advance (3 months)			

FIGURE 3.17 *(continued)*

CLARK'S WORD PROCESSING SERVICES
GENERAL JOURNAL

Page 1

Date		Account Titles and Description	PR	Dr.	Cr.
	3	Office Supplies		6 0 0 00	
		Accounts Payable			6 0 0 00
		Purchase of supplies on acct. from Norris			
	7	Cash		3 0 0 0 00	
		Word Processing Fees			3 0 0 0 00
		Cash received for services rendered			
	13	Office Salaries Expense		6 5 0 00	
		Cash			6 5 0 00
		Payment of office salaries			
	18	Advertising Expense		2 5 0 00	
		Accounts Payable			2 5 0 00
		Bill received but not paid from Al's News			
	20	Brenda Clark, Withdrawals		6 2 5 00	
		Cash			6 2 5 00
		Personal withdrawal of cash			
	22	Accounts Receivable		5 0 0 0 00	
		Word Processing Fees			5 0 0 0 00
		Billed Morris Co. for fees earned			

FIGURE 3.17 *(continued)*

CLARK'S WORD PROCESSING SERVICES
GENERAL JOURNAL

Page 2

Date			Account Titles and Description	PR	Dr.	Cr.
200X May	27		Office Salaries Expense		6 5 0 00	
			Cash			6 5 0 00
			Payment of office salaries			
	28		Accounts Payable		2 5 0 0 00	
			Cash			2 5 0 0 00
			Paid half the amount owed Ben Co.			
	29		Telephone Expense		2 2 0 00	
			Cash			2 2 0 00
			Paid telephone bill			

Solution to Self-Review Quiz 3-2

FIGURE 3.18 Posting From
Journal to the Ledger Using
PR Columns

CLARK'S WORD PROCESSING SERVICES
GENERAL JOURNAL

Page 1

Date			Account Titles and Description	PR	Dr.	Cr.
200X May	1		Cash	111	10 00 00	
			Brenda Clark, Capital	311		10 00 00
			Initial investment of cash by owner			
	1		Word Processing Equipment	121	6 00 00	
			Cash	111		1 00 00
			Accounts Payable	211		5 00 00
			Purchase of equip. from Ben Co.			
	1		Prepaid Rent	115	1 20 00	
			Cash	111		1 20 00
			Rent paid in advance (3 months)			
	3		Office Supplies	114	6 00 00	
			Accounts Payable	211		6 00 00
			Purchase of supplies on acct. from Norris			
	7		Cash	111	3 00 00	
			Word Processing Fees	411		3 00 00
			Cash received from services rendered			
	13		Office Salaries Expense	511	6 50 00	
			Cash	111		6 50 00
			Payment of office salaries			
	18		Advertising Expense	512	2 50 00	
			Accounts Payable	211		2 50 00
			Bill received but not paid from Al's News			
	20		Brenda Clark, Withdrawals	312	6 25 00	
			Cash	111		6 25 00
			Personal withdrawal of cash			
	22		Accounts Receivable	112	5 00 00	
			Word Processing Fees	411		5 00 00
			Billed Morris Co. for fees earned			

FIGURE 3.18 (*continued*)

CLARK'S WORD PROCESSING SERVICES
GENERAL JOURNAL

Page 2

	Date		Account Titles and Description	PR	Dr.	Cr.
200X	May	27	Office Salaries Expense	511	65000	
			Cash	111		65000
			Payment of office salaries			
		28	Accounts Payable	211	250000	
			Cash	111		250000
			Paid half the amount owed Ben Co.			
		29	Telephone Expense	513	22000	
			Cash	111		22000
			Paid telephone bill			

FIGURE 3.19 Partial General Ledger

CLARK'S WORD PROCESSING SERVICES
PARTIAL GENERAL LEDGER

Cash   Account No. 111

	Date		Explanation	Post. Ref.	Debit	Credit	Balance Debit	Balance Credit
200X	May	1		GJ1	1000000		1000000	
		1		GJ1		100000	900000	
		1		GJ1		120000	780000	
		7		GJ1	300000		1080000	
		13		GJ1		65000	1015000	
		20		GJ1		62500	952500	
		27		GJ2		65000	887500	
		28		GJ2		250000	637500	
		29		GJ2		22000	615500	

Accounts Receivable   Account No. 112

	Date		Explanation	Post. Ref.	Debit	Credit	Balance Debit	Balance Credit
200X	May	22		GJ1	500000		500000	

Office Supplies   Account No. 114

	Date		Explanation	Post. Ref.	Debit	Credit	Balance Debit	Balance Credit
200X	May	3		GJ1	60000		60000	

FIGURE 3.19 (*continued*)

Prepaid Rent — Account No. 115

Date	Explanation	Post. Ref.	Debit	Credit	Balance Debit	Balance Credit
200X May 1		GJ1	1 2 0 0 00		1 2 0 0 00	

Word Processing Equipment — Account No. 121

Date	Explanation	Post. Ref.	Debit	Credit	Balance Debit	Balance Credit
200X May 1		GJ1	6 0 0 0 00		6 0 0 0 00	

Accounts Payable — Account No. 211

Date	Explanation	Post. Ref.	Debit	Credit	Balance Debit	Balance Credit
200X May 1		GJ1		5 0 0 0 00		5 0 0 0 00
3		GJ1		6 0 0 00		5 6 0 0 00
18		GJ1		2 5 0 00		5 8 5 0 00
28		GJ2	2 5 0 0 00			3 3 5 0 00

Brenda Clark, Capital — Account No. 311

Date	Explanation	Post. Ref.	Debit	Credit	Balance Debit	Balance Credit
200X May 1		GJ1		10 0 0 0 00		10 0 0 0 00

Brenda Clark, Withdrawals — Account No. 312

Date	Explanation	Post. Ref.	Debit	Credit	Balance Debit	Balance Credit
200X May 20		GJ1	6 2 5 00		6 2 5 00	

Word Processing Fees — Account No. 411

Date	Explanation	Post. Ref.	Debit	Credit	Balance Debit	Balance Credit
200X May 7		GJ1		3 0 0 0 00		3 0 0 0 00
22		GJ1		5 0 0 0 00		8 0 0 0 00

FIGURE 3.19 *(continued)*

Office Salaries Expense					Account No. 511		
Date	Explanation	Post. Ref.	Debit	Credit	Balance Debit	Balance Credit	
200X May 13		GJ1	650 00		650 00		
27		GJ2	650 00		1300 00		

Advertising Expense					Account No. 512		
Date	Explanation	Post. Ref.	Debit	Credit	Balance Debit	Balance Credit	
200X May 18		GJ1	250 00		250 00		

Telephone Expense					Account No. 513		
Date	Explanation	Post. Ref.	Debit	Credit	Balance Debit	Balance Credit	
200X May 29		GJ2	220 00		220 00		

NEED HELP?

Let's review first: The PR column of the journal will show to which account information has been posting. The PR column in the ledger accounts show from which page of the journal the information came. When updating ledger accounts, two debits added equals a debit balance. Two credits added would be a credit balance. If you have a debit and a credit, take the difference between them; whichever side is larger is the balance (be it a debit or credit).

Partial General Ledger:

Cash: There are nine postings from the journal to the cash account. GJ1 means that posting came from the general journal, page 1. In the second line the credit of 1,000 is subtracted from the debit balance in line 1 (10,000) to show a new balance of 9,000 in line 2. In line 3 the 1,200 credit is then subtracted from the 9,000 debit for a current balance of 7,800. Normally the balance is on the side that causes it to increase. Thus cash is normally a debit balance.

Accounts Payable: In this account the first three postings were credits from the general journal. Note that the month is written only once. Since all three are credits we add each together, arriving at a credit balance of 5,850. On May 28 a debit of 2,500 is posted and we take the difference between a 5,850 credit balance and a 2,500 debit balance to arrive at a 3,350 ending credit balance.

Office Salaries Expense: Note that here we have two debit postings, so they are added together to arrive at a 1,300 debit balance.

> **Summary:** Posting is copying from the journal to the ledger. The ledger will accumulate information in the form of debits and credits. The last line in the balance column will show whether it is a debit or credit balance. The general journal does not show a running balance like the ledger accounts do.

LO3 # Learning Unit 3-3 Preparing the Trial Balance: Step 4 of the Accounting Cycle

Did you note in Quiz 3-2 how each account had a running balance figure? Did you know the normal balance of each account in Clark's ledger? As we discussed in Chapter 2, the list of the individual accounts with their balances taken from the ledger is called a **trial balance.**

The trial balance shown in Figure 3.20 was developed from the ledger accounts of Clark's Word Processing Services that were posted and balanced in Quiz 3-2. If the information is journalized or posted incorrectly, the trial balance will not be correct.

TRIAL BALANCE

Debits	Credits
Assets	*Liabilities*
Expenses	*Revenue*
Withdrawals	*Capital*

The trial balance will not show everything:

- The capital figure on the trial balance may not be the beginning capital figure. For instance, if Brenda Clark had made additional investments during the period, the additional investment would have been journalized and posted to the Capital account. The only way to tell if the capital balance on the trial balance is the original balance is to check the ledger Capital account to see whether any additional investments were made. This confirmation of beginning capital will be important when we make financial reports.

FIGURE 3.20 Trial Balance

CLARK'S WORD PROCESSING SERVICE TRIAL BALANCE MAY 31, 200X		
	Debit	Credit
Cash	6 1 5 5 00	
Accounts Receivable	5 0 0 0 00	
Office Supplies	6 0 0 00	
Prepaid Rent	1 2 0 0 00	
Word Processing Equipment	6 0 0 0 00	
Accounts Payable		3 3 5 0 00
Brenda Clark, Capital		10 0 0 0 00
Brenda Clark, Withdrawals	6 2 5 00	
Word Processing Fees		8 0 0 0 00
Office Salaries Expense	1 3 0 0 00	
Advertising Expense	2 5 0 00	
Telephone Expense	2 2 0 00	
Totals	21 3 5 0 00	21 3 5 0 00

The trial balance lists the accounts in the same order as in the ledger. The $6,155 figure of cash came from the ledger.

- Even careful cross-referencing does not guarantee that transactions have been properly recorded. For example, the following errors would remain undetected: (1) a transaction that may have been omitted in the journalizing process, (2) a transaction incorrectly analyzed and recorded in the journal, and (3) a journal entry journalized or posted twice.

> The totals of a trial balance can balance and yet be incorrect.

What to Do If a Trial Balance Doesn't Balance

The trial balance of Clark's Word Processing Services shows that the total of debits is equal to the total of credits. What happens, however, if the trial balance is in balance but the correct amount is not recorded in each ledger account? Accuracy in the journalizing and posting process will help ensure that no errors are made.

Even if you find an error, the first rule is "don't panic." Everyone makes mistakes, and accepted ways of correcting them are available. Once an entry has been made in ink, correcting an error in it must always show that the entry has been changed and who changed it. Sometimes the change has to be explained.

Some Common Mistakes

If the trial balance does not balance, the cause could be something relatively simple. Here are some common errors and how they can be fixed:

- If the difference (the amount you are off) is 10, 100, 1,000, and so forth, it is probably a mathematical error in addition.
- If the difference is equal to an individual account balance in the ledger, the amount could have been omitted. It is also possible the figure was not posted from the general journal.
- Divide the difference by 2, then check to see whether a debit should have been a credit, or vice versa, in the ledger or trial balance. Example: $150 difference ÷ 2 = $75 means you may have placed $75 as a debit to an account instead of a credit, or vice versa.
- If the difference is evenly divisible by 9, a **slide** or transposition may have occurred. A slide is an error resulting from adding or deleting zeros in writing numbers. For example, $4,175.00 may have been copied as $41.75. A **transposition** is the accidental rearrangement of digits of a number. For example, $4,175 might have been accidentally written as $4,157.
- Compare the balances in the trial balance with the ledger accounts to check for copying errors.
- Recompute balances in each ledger account.
- Trace all postings from journal to ledger.

> Correcting the trial balance: What to do if your trial balance doesn't balance.

If you cannot find the error after taking all these steps, take a coffee break. Then start all over again.

Making a Correction Before Posting

Before posting, error correction is straightforward. Simply draw a line through the incorrect entry, write the correct information above the line, and write your initials near the change. Keep in mind that computer systems use their own methods for making corrections.

Correcting an Error in an Account Title Figure 3.21 shows an error and its correction in an account title:

FIGURE 3.21 Account Error

	1	Word Processing Equipment	6 0 0 0 00			
		Cash		1 0 0 0 00		
		~~Accounts Payable~~ *amp*				
		~~Accounts Receivable~~		5 0 0 0 00		
		Purchase of equipment from Ben Co.				

Correcting a Numerical Error Numbers are handled the same way as account titles, as the next change from 520 to 250 in Figure 3.22 shows:

FIGURE 3.22 Number Error

	18	Advertising Expense		2 5 0 00		
		Accounts Payable			amp 2 5 0 00 5 2 0 00	
		Bill from Al's News				

Correcting an Entry Error If a number has been entered in the wrong column, a straight line is drawn through it. The number is then written in the correct column, as shown in Figure 3.23:

FIGURE 3.23 Correcting Entry

	1	Word Processing Equipment		6 0 0 0 00		
		Cash				1 0 0 0 00
		Accounts Payable		amp 5 0 0 0 00		5 0 0 0 00
		Purchase of equip. from Ben Co.				

Making a Correction After Posting

It is also possible to correct an amount that is correctly entered in the journal but posted incorrectly to the ledger of the proper account. The first step is to draw a line through the error and write the correct figure above it. The next step is changing the running balance to reflect the corrected posting. Here, too, a line is drawn through the balance and the corrected balance is written above it. Both changes must be initialed, as shown in Figure 3.24.

FIGURE 3.24 Correction After Posting

						Balance	
		Word Processing Fees				Account No. 411	
Date		Explanation	Post. Ref.	Debit	Credit	Debit	Credit
200X May	7		GJ1		2 5 0 0 00		2 5 0 0 00
	22		GJ1		4 1 0 0 00 1 0 0 0 00 amp		6 6 0 0 00 2 6 0 0 00 amp

Correcting an Entry Posted to the Wrong Account

Drawing a line through an error and writing the correction above it is possible when a mistake has occurred within the proper account, but when an error involves a posting to the wrong account, the journal must include a correction accompanied by an explanation. In addition, the correct information must be posted to the appropriate ledgers.

Suppose, for example, as a result of tracing postings from journal entries to ledgers you find that a $180 telephone bill was incorrectly debited as an advertising expense. The following illustration shows how this correction is done.

Step 1 The journal entry is corrected and the correction is explained (Fig. 3.25):

		GENERAL JOURNAL			Page 3	
Date		Account Titles and Description	PR	Dr.	Cr.	
200X May	29	Telephone Expense	513	1 8 0 00		
		Advertising Expense	512		1 8 0 00	
		To correct error in which				
		Advertising Exp. was debited				
		for charges to Telephone Exp.				

FIGURE 3.25 Corrected Entry for Telephone

Step 2 The Advertising Expense ledger account is corrected (Fig. 3.26):

				Advertising Expense		Account No. 512		
			Post.			Balance		
Date		Explanation	Ref.	Debit	Credit	Debit	Credit	
200X May	18		GJ1	1 7 5 00		1 7 5 00		
	23		GJ1	1 8 0 00		3 5 5 00		
	29	Correcting entry	GJ3		1 8 0 00	1 7 5 00		

FIGURE 3.26 Ledger Update for Advertising

Step 3 The Telephone Expense ledger is corrected (Fig. 3.27):

				Telephone Expense		Account No. 513		
			Post.			Balance		
Date		Explanation	Ref.	Debit	Credit	Debit	Credit	
200X May	29		GJ3	1 8 0 00		1 8 0 00		

FIGURE 3.27 Ledger Update for Telephone

LEARNING UNIT 3-3 REVIEW

AT THIS POINT you should be able to

- Prepare a trial balance with a ledger, using four-column accounts.
- Analyze and correct a trial balance that doesn't balance.
- Correct journal and posting errors.

Self-Review Quiz 3-3

1.

MEMO

To: *Al Vincent*
From: *Professor Jones*
Re: *Trial Balance*
You have submitted to me an incorrect trial balance (Fig. 3.28). Could you please rework and turn in to me before next Friday?
Note: Individual amounts look OK.

For additional help go to www.pearsonhighered.com/slater

FIGURE 3.28 Incorrect Trial
Balance

A. RICE TRIAL BALANCE OCTOBER 31, 200X	Dr.	Cr.
Cash		8 0 6 0 00
Operating Expenses		1 7 0 0 00
A. Rice, Withdrawals		4 0 0 00
Service Revenue		5 4 0 0 00
Equipment	5 0 0 0 00	
Accounts Receivable	3 5 4 0 00	
Accounts Payable	2 0 0 0 00	
Supplies	3 0 0 00	
A. Rice, Capital		11 6 0 0 00

2. An $8,000 debit to Office Equipment was mistakenly journalized and posted on June 9, 200X, to Office Supplies. Prepare the appropriate journal entry to correct this error.

Solution to Self-Review Quiz 3-3

1.

FIGURE 3.29 Correct Trial
Balance

A. RICE TRIAL BALANCE OCTOBER 31, 200X	Dr.	Cr.
Cash	8 0 6 0 00	
Accounts Receivable	3 5 4 0 00	
Supplies	3 0 0 00	
Equipment	5 0 0 0 00	
Accounts Payable		2 0 0 0 00
A. Rice, Capital		11 6 0 0 00
A. Rice, Withdrawals	4 0 0 00	
Service Revenue		5 4 0 0 00
Operating Expenses	1 7 0 0 00	
Totals	19 0 0 0 00	19 0 0 0 00

2.

FIGURE 3.30 Correcting
Entry

GENERAL JOURNAL				Page 4	
Date	Account Titles and Description	PR	Dr.	Cr.	
200X June 9	Office Equipment		8 0 0 0 00		
	Office Supplies			8 0 0 0 00	
	To correct error in which office supplies				
	had been debited for purchase of				
	office equipment				

NEED HELP?

Let's review first: Items in a trial balance are listed in the same order as in the ledger or chart of accounts. Expect each account to have its normal balance (either a debit or credit). No title in the trial list balance can have both a debit and credit balance.

List the ending balance of each ledger account (last number listed in the balance columns) and list them in the order of the ledger. They should follow this pattern:

Assets	Dr.
Liabilities	Cr.
Capital	Cr.
Withdrawals	Dr.
Revenues	Cr.
Expenses	Dr.

When complete, the total of all debits will equal the total of the credits. In this case the total is 19,000.

Summary: The trial balance lists the accounts in the same order as the ledger. Be sure to refer to the learning unit for what to do if the trial balance does not balance. It could be a posting mistake or just a math error.

CHAPTER ASSIGNMENTS

All Classroom Demonstration Exercises, Exercises, Problems, and the Continuing Problem in this chapter can be found within MyAccountingLab, an online homework and practice environment. Your instructor may ask you to complete this material using MyAccountingLab.

MyAccountingLab

DEMONSTRATION PROBLEM: STEPS 1–4 OF THE ACCOUNTING CYCLE

In March, Abby's Employment Agency had the following transactions:

200X

Mar.	1	Abby Todd invested $5,000 cash in the new employment agency.
	4	Bought equipment for cash, $200.
	5	Earned employment fee commission, $200, but payment from Blue Co. will not be received until June.
	6	Paid wages expense, $300.
	7	Abby paid her home utility bill from the company checkbook, $75.
	9	Placed Rick Wool at VCR Corporation, receiving $1,200 cash.
	15	Paid cash for supplies, $200.
	28	Telephone bill received but not paid, $180.
	29	Advertising bill received but not paid, $400.

The chart of accounts includes Cash, 111; Accounts Receivable, 112; Supplies, 131; Equipment, 141; Accounts Payable, 211; A. Todd, Capital, 311; A. Todd, Withdrawals, 321; Employment Fees Earned, 411; Wage Expense, 511; Telephone Expense, 521; and Advertising Expense, 531.

Your task is to

a. Set up a ledger based on the chart of accounts.

b. Journalize (all page 1) and post transactions.

c. Prepare a trial balance for March 31.

Solution to Demonstration Problem

a.

FIGURE 3.31 General Ledger

Cash   111

Date		PR	Dr.	Cr.	Balance Dr.	Balance Cr.
200X Mar.	1	GJ1	5,000		5,000	
	4	GJ1		200	4,800	
	6	GJ1		300	4,500	
	7	GJ1		75	4,425	
	9	GJ1	1,200		5,625	
	15	GJ1		200	5,425	

Accounts Receivable   112

Date		PR	Dr.	Cr.	Balance Dr.	Balance Cr.
200X Mar.	5	GJ1	200		200	

Supplies   131

Date		PR	Dr.	Cr.	Balance Dr.	Balance Cr.
200X Mar.	15	GJ1	200		200	

Equipment   141

Date		PR	Dr.	Cr.	Balance Dr.	Balance Cr.
200X Mar.	4	GJ1	200		200	

Accounts Payable   211

Date		PR	Dr.	Cr.	Balance Dr.	Balance Cr.
200X Mar.	28	GJ1		180		180
	29	GJ1		400		580

A. Todd, Capital   311

Date		PR	Dr.	Cr.	Balance Dr.	Balance Cr.
200X Mar.	1	GJ1		5,000		5,000

A. Todd, Withdrawals   321

Date		PR	Dr.	Cr.	Balance Dr.	Balance Cr.
200X Mar.	7	GJ1	75		75	

Employment Fees Earned   411

Date		PR	Dr.	Cr.	Balance Dr.	Balance Cr.
200X Mar.	5	GJ1		200		200
	9	GJ1		1,200		1,400

Wage Expense   511

Date		PR	Dr.	Cr.	Balance Dr.	Balance Cr.
200X Mar.	6	GJ1	300		300	

Telephone Expense   521

Date		PR	Dr.	Cr.	Balance Dr.	Balance Cr.
200X Mar.	28	GJ1	180		180	

Advertising Expense   531

Date		PR	Dr.	Cr.	Balance Dr.	Balance Cr.
200X Mar.	29	GJ1	400		400	

b.

FIGURE 3.32 Journal Entries and Post References

	Date		Account Titles and Description	PR	Dr.	Cr.
200X Mar.	1		Cash	111	5 0 0 0 00	
			A. Todd, Capital	311		5 0 0 0 00
			Owner investment			
	4		Equipment	141	2 0 0 00	
			Cash	111		2 0 0 00
			Bought equipment for cash			
	5		Accounts Receivable	112	2 0 0 00	
			Employment Fees Earned	411		2 0 0 00
			Fees on account from Blue Co.			
	6		Wage Expense	511	3 0 0 00	
			Cash	111		3 0 0 00
			Paid wages			
	7		A. Todd, Withdrawals	321	7 5 00	
			Cash	111		7 5 00
			Personal withdrawals			
	9		Cash	111	1 2 0 0 00	
			Employment Fees Earned	411		1 2 0 0 00
			Cash fees			
	15		Supplies	131	2 0 0 00	
			Cash	111		2 0 0 00
			Bought supplies for cash			
	28		Telephone Expense	521	1 8 0 00	
			Accounts Payable	211		1 8 0 00
			Telephone bill owed			
	29		Advertising Expense	531	4 0 0 00	
			Accounts Payable	211		4 0 0 00
			Advertising bill received			

ABBY'S EMPLOYMENT AGENCY — Page 1

Solution Tips to Journalizing

1. When journalizing, the PR column is not filled in.
2. Write the name of the debit against the date column. Indent credits and list them below debits. Be sure total debits for each transaction equal total credits.
3. Skip a line between each transaction.

The Analysis of the Journal Entries

> This analysis is what should be going through your head before determining debit or credit.

March	1	Cash	A	↑	Dr.	$5,000
		A. Todd, Capital	Capital	↑	Cr.	$5,000
	4	Equipment	A	↑	Dr.	$ 200
		Cash	A	↓	Cr.	$ 200
	5	Accts. Receivable	A	↑	Dr.	$ 200
		Empl. Fees Earned	Rev.	↑	Cr.	$ 200
	6	Wage Expense	Exp.	↑	Dr.	$ 300
		Cash	A	↓	Cr.	$ 300
	7	A. Todd, Withdrawals	Withd.	↑	Dr.	$ 75
		Cash	A	↓	Cr.	$ 75
	9	Cash	A	↑	Dr.	$1,200
		Empl. Fees Earned	Rev.	↑	Cr.	$1,200
	15	Supplies	A	↑	Dr.	$ 200
		Cash	A	↓	Cr.	$ 200
	28	Telephone Expense	Exp.	↑	Dr.	$ 180
		Accounts Payable	L	↑	Cr.	$ 180
	28	Advertising Expense	Exp.	↑	Dr.	$ 400
		Accounts Payable	L	↑	Cr.	$ 400

Solution Tips to Posting

The PR column in the ledger cash account tells you from which page journal information came. After the ledger cash account is posted, account number 111 is put in the PR column of the journal for cross-referencing.

Note how we keep a running balance in the cash account. A $5,000 debit balance and a $200 credit entry result in a new debit balance of $4,800.

FIGURE 3.33

ABBY'S EMPLOYMENT AGENCY
TRIAL BALANCE
MARCH 31, 200X

	Dr.	Cr.
Cash	5 4 2 5 00	
Accounts Receivable	2 0 0 00	
Supplies	2 0 0 00	
Equipment	2 0 0 00	
Accounts Payable		5 8 0 00
A. Todd, Capital		5 0 0 0 00
A. Todd, Withdrawals	7 5 00	
Employment Fees Earned		1 4 0 0 00
Wage Expense	3 0 0 00	
Telephone Expense	1 8 0 00	
Advertising Expense	4 0 0 00	
Totals	6 9 8 0 00	6 9 8 0 00

Solution Tip to Trial Balance

The trial balance lists the ending balance of each title in the order in which they appear in the ledger. The total of 6,980 on the left equals 6,980 on the right.

SUMMARY OF KEY POINTS

LEARNING UNIT 3-1

1. The accounting cycle is a sequence of accounting procedures that are usually performed during an accounting period.
2. An accounting period is the time period for which the income statement is prepared. The time period can be any period up to one year.
3. A calendar year is from January 1 to December 31. The fiscal year is any 12-month period. A fiscal year could be a calendar year but does not have to be.
4. Interim statements are statements that are usually prepared for a portion of the business's calendar or fiscal year (e.g., a month or a quarter).
5. A general journal is a book that records transactions in chronological order. Here debits and credits are shown together on one page. It is the book of original entry.
6. The ledger is a collection of accounts where information is accumulated from the postings of the journal. The ledger is the book of final entry.
7. Journalizing is the process of recording journal entries.
8. The chart of accounts provides the specific titles of accounts to be entered in the journal.
9. When journalizing, the post reference (PR) column is left blank.
10. A compound journal entry occurs when more than two accounts are affected in the journalizing process of a business transaction.

LEARNING UNIT 3-2

1. Posting is the process of transferring information from the journal to the ledger.
2. The journal and ledger contain the same information but in a different form.
3. The four-column account aids in keeping a running balance of an account.
4. The normal balance of an account will be located on the side that increases it according to the rules of debit and credit. For example, the normal balances of liabilities occur on the credit side.
5. The mechanical process of posting requires care in transferring to the appropriate account the dates, post references, and amounts.

LEARNING UNIT 3-3

1. A trial balance can balance but be incorrect. For example, an entire journal entry may not have been posted.
2. If a trial balance doesn't balance, check for errors in addition, omission of postings, slides, transpositions, copying errors, and so on.
3. Specific procedures should be followed in making corrections in journals and ledgers.

KEY TERMS

Accounting cycle   For each accounting period, the process that begins with the recording of business transactions or procedures into a journal and ends with the completion of a post-closing trial balance.

Accounting period   The period of time for which an income statement is prepared.

Book of final entry   Book that receives information about business transactions from a book of original entry (a journal). Example: a ledger.

Book of original entry   Book that records the first formal information about business transactions. Example: a journal.

Calendar year   January 1 to December 31.

Compound journal entry   A journal entry that affects more than two accounts.

Cross-referencing   Adding to the PR column of the journal the account number of the ledger account that was updated from the journal.

Fiscal year   The 12-month period a business chooses for its accounting year.

Four-column account   A running balance account that records debits and credits and has a column for an ending balance (debit or credit). It replaces the standard two-column account we used earlier.

General journal   The simplest form of a journal, which records information from transactions in chronological order as they occur. This journal links the debit and credit parts of transactions together.

Interim reports   Financial statements that are prepared for a month, quarter, or some other portion of the fiscal year.

Journal   A listing of business transactions in chronological order. The journal links on one page the debit and credit parts of transactions.

Journal entry   The transaction (debits and credits) that is recorded into a journal once it is analyzed.

Journalizing   The process of recording a transaction entry into the journal.

Natural business year   A business's fiscal year that ends at the same time as a slow seasonal period begins.

Posting   The transferring, copying, or recording of information from a journal to a ledger.

Slide   The error that results in adding or deleting zeros in the writing of a number. Example: 79,200 → 7,920.

Transposition   The accidental rearrangement of digits of a number. Example: 152 → 125.

Trial balance   An informal listing of the ledger accounts and their balances in the ledger to aid in proving the equality of debits and credits.

BLUEPRINT OF FIRST FOUR STEPS OF ACCOUNTING CYCLE

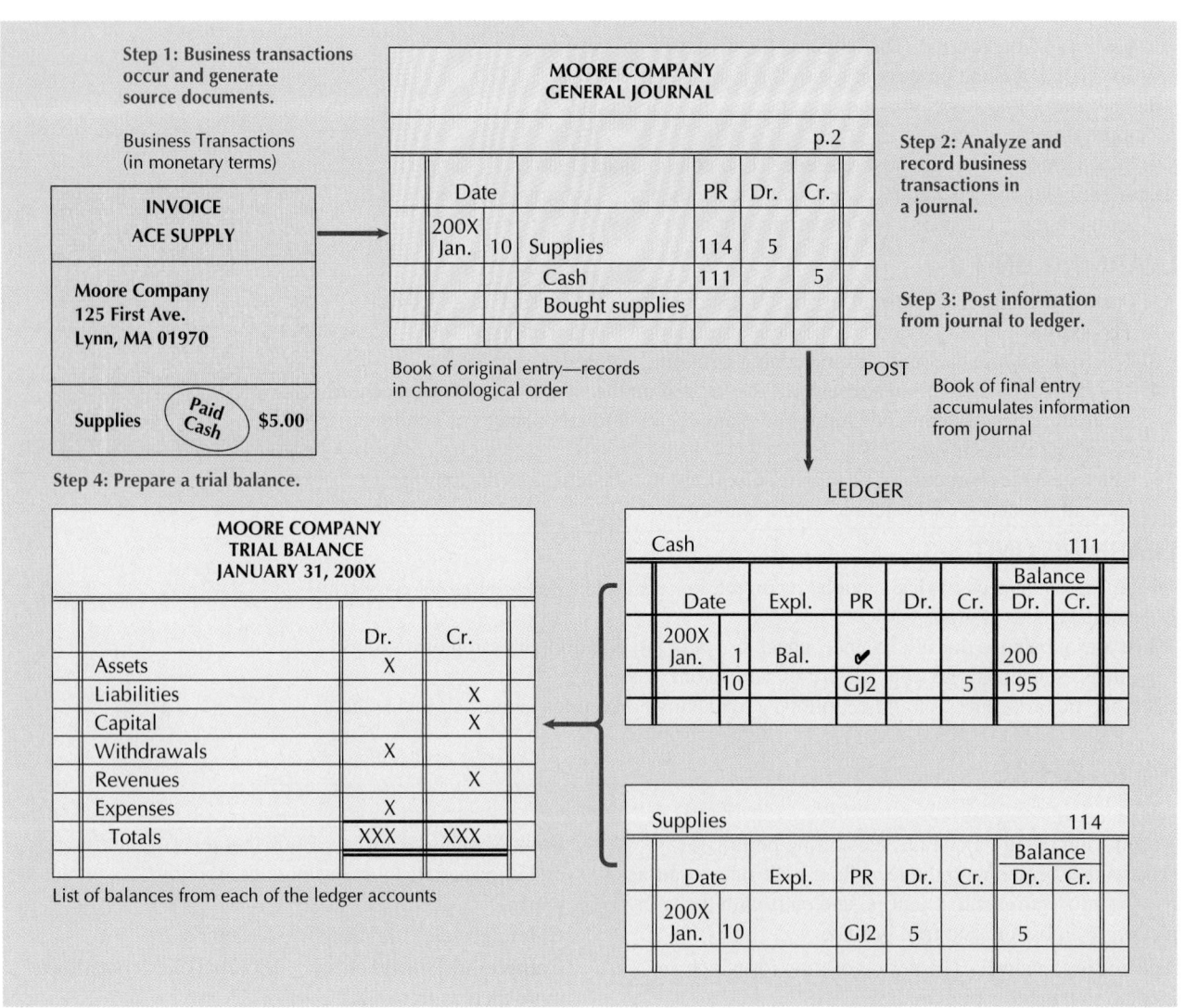

QUESTIONS, CLASSROOM DEMONSTRATION EXERCISES, EXERCISES, AND PROBLEMS

Discussion Questions and Critical Thinking/Ethical Case

1. Explain the concept of the accounting cycle.

2. An accounting period is based on the balance sheet. Agree or disagree?

3. Compare and contrast a calendar year versus a fiscal year.

4. What are interim statements?

5. Why is the ledger called the book of final entry?

6. How do transactions get "linked" in a general journal?

7. What is the relationship of the chart of accounts to the general journal?

8. What is a compound journal entry?

9. Posting means updating the journal. Agree or disagree? Please comment.

10. The side that decreases an account is the normal balance. True or false?

11. The PR column of a general journal is the last item to be filled in during the posting process. Agree or disagree?

12. Discuss the concept of cross-referencing.

13. What is the difference between a transposition and a slide?

14. Jay Simons, the accountant of See Co., would like to buy a new software package for his general ledger. He couldn't do it because all funds were frozen for the rest of the fiscal period. Jay called his friend at Joor Industries and asked whether he could copy its software. Comment on why it is or isn't okay for Jay to make such a request.

Classroom Demonstration Exercises

MyAccountingLab

SET A

General Journal   *LO1 (5 min)*

1. Complete the following from the general journal of Moore Co.:
   a. Year of journal entry _____
   b. Month of journal entry _____
   c. Day of journal entry _____
   d. Name(s) of accounts debited _____
   e. Name(s) of accounts credited _____
   f. Explanation of transaction _____
   g. Amount of debit(s) _____
   h. Amount of credit(s) _____
   i. Page of journal _____

FIGURE 3.34 General Journal

	Date		Account Titles and Descriptions	PR	Dr.	Cr.
	200X Nov.	18	Cash		9 0 0 0 00	
			Equipment		10 0 0 0 00	
			B. Moore, Capital			19 0 0 0 00
			Initial Investment by Owner			

MOORE COMPANY GENERAL JOURNAL — Page 1

LO2 (5 min) **General Journal**

2. Provide the explanation for each of the general journal entries in Figure 3.35.

FIGURE 3.35 Journal Entries

	GENERAL JOURNAL				Page 4
Date	Account Titles and Descriptions	PR	Debit	Credit	
200X June 10	Cash		17 0 0 0 00		
	Computer Equipment		26 0 0 0 00		
	B. Blue, Capital			43 0 0 0 00	
	(A)				
16	Cash		4 0 00		
	Accounts Receivable		7 0 00		
	Legal Fees Earned			1 1 0 00	
	(B)				
18	Salary Expense		4 0 00		
	Accounts Payable			4 0 00	
	(C)				

LO2 (5 min) **Posting and Balancing**

3. Balance this four-column account. What function does the PR column serve? When will Account 111 be used in the journalizing and posting process?

		Cash			Acct. 111 Balance	
Date	Explanation	PR	Dr.	Cr.	Dr.	Cr.
200X						
May 8		GJ 1	19			
16		GJ 1	9			
20		GJ 2		6		
22		GJ 3	2			

LO4 (15 min) **The Trial Balance**

4. The following trial balance (Fig. 3.36) was prepared *incorrectly*.
   a. Rearrange the accounts in proper order.

FIGURE 3.36

LEE CO.
TRIAL BALANCE
OCTOBER 31, 200X

	Dr.	Cr.
D. Lee, Capital	3 0 00	
Equipment	1 1 2 00	
Rent Expense		1 7 00
Advertising Expense		3 00
Accounts Payable		1 0 8 00
Taxi Fees	1 6 00	
Cash	1 7 00	
D. Lee, Withdrawals	—	5 00
Totals	1 7 5 00	1 3 3 00

b. Calculate the total of the trial balance. (Small numbers are used intentionally so that you can do the calculations in your head.) Assume each account has a normal balance.

Correcting Entry   *LO3 (5 min)*

5. On June 1, 2009, a telephone expense for $210 was debited to Repair Expense. On June 10, 2010, this error was found. Prepare the corrected journal entry. When would a correcting entry *not* be needed?

SET B

General Journal   *LO1 (5 min)*

1. Complete the following from the general journal of Ranger Co. (Fig. 3.37):
    a. Year of journal entry   _____
    b. Month of journal entry   _____
    c. Day of journal entry   _____
    d. Name(s) of accounts debited   _____
    e. Name(s) of accounts credited   _____
    f. Explanation of transaction   _____
    g. Amount of debit(s)   _____
    h. Amount of credit(s)   _____
    i. Page of journal   _____

FIGURE 3.37 General Journal

RANGER COMPANY
GENERAL JOURNAL
Page 1

Date		Account Titles and Descriptions	PR	Dr.	Cr.
200X Oct.	15	Cash		6 0 0 0 00	
		Equipment		4 0 0 00	
		L. Swan, Capital			6 4 0 0 00
		Initial Investment by Owner			

General Journal   *LO2 (5 min)*

2. Provide the explanation for each of the general journal entries in Figure 3.38.

FIGURE 3.38 Journal Entries

GENERAL JOURNAL
Page 4

Date		Account Titles and Descriptions	PR	Debit	Credit
200X July	9	Cash		8 0 0 0 00	
		Office Equipment		5 0 0 0 00	
		J. Walsh, Capital			13 0 0 0 00
		(A)			
	15	Cash		3 0 00	
		Accounts Receivable		6 0 00	
		Hair Fees Earned			9 0 00
		(B)			
	20	Advertising Expense		4 0 00	
		Accounts Payable			4 0 00
		(C)			

LO2 (5 min) **Posting and Balancing**

3. Balance this four-column account. What function does the PR column serve? When will Account 111 be used in the journalizing and posting process?

			Cash			Acct. 111 Balance	
Date	Explanation	PR	Dr.	Cr.	Dr.	Cr.
200X						
June 4		GJ 1	15			
5		GJ 1	6			
9		GJ 2		4		
10		GJ 3	1			

LO4 (15 min) **The Trial Balance**

4. The following trial balance (Fig. 3.39) was prepared *incorrectly*.

FIGURE 3.39

LEE CO. TRIAL BALANCE OCTOBER 31, 200X	Dr.	Cr.
D. Lee, Capital	1 7 00	
Equipment	1 2 00	
Rent Expense		4 00
Advertising Expense		3 00
Accounts Payable		8 00
Taxi Fees	1 6 00	
Cash	1 7 00	
D. Lee, Withdrawals	—	5 00
Totals	6 2 00	2 0 00

a. Rearrange the accounts in proper order.
b. Calculate the total of the trial balance. (Small numbers are used intentionally so that you can do the calculations in your head.) Assume each account has a normal balance.

LO3 (5 min) **Correcting Entry**

5. On May 1, 2009, a telephone expense for $210 was debited to Repair Expense. On June 12, 2010, this error was found. Prepare the corrected journal entry. When would a correcting entry *not* be needed?

MyAccountingLab **Exercises**

LO1 (10 min) **3-1.** Prepare journal entries for the following transactions that occurred during October:

200X

Oct. 1 Janet Wills invested $70,000 cash and $6,000 of equipment into her new business.

3 Purchased building for $40,000 on account.

12 Purchased a truck from Lowell Co. for $16,000 cash.

18 Bought supplies from Lee Co. on account, $900.

3-2. Record the following into the general journal of Reggie's Auto Shop.   *LO1 (10 min)*

200X

Jan. 1 Reggie Long invested $16,000 cash in the auto shop.

   5 Paid $7,000 for auto equipment.

   8 Bought from Lowell Co. auto equipment for $6,000 on account.

   14 Received $900 for repair fees earned.

   18 Billed Sullivan Co. $900 for services rendered.

   20 Reggie withdrew $300 for personal use.

3-3. Post the transactions in Figure 3.40 to the ledger of King Company. The partial   *LO2 (10 min)*
ledger of King Company is Cash, 111; Equipment, 121; Accounts Payable, 211;
and A. King, Capital, 311. Please use four-column accounts in the posting process.

FIGURE 3.40 Journal Entries

					Page 4		
Date 200X			PR	Dr.		Cr.	
April	6	Cash		15 0 0 0 00			
		A. King, Capital				15 0 0 0 00	
		Cash investment					
	14	Equipment		9 0 0 0 00			
		Cash				4 0 0 0 00	
		Accounts Payable				5 0 0 0 00	
		Purchase of equipment					

3-4. From the following transactions for Lowe Company for the month of July,   *LO1, 2, 3 (20 min)*
(a) prepare journal entries (assume that it is page 1 of the journal), (b) post
to the ledger (use a four-column account), and (c) prepare a trial balance.

200X

July 1 Joan Lowe invested $6,000 in the business.

   4 Bought from Lax Co. equipment on account, $800.

   15 Billed Friend Co. for services rendered, $4,000.

   18 Received $5,000 cash for services rendered.

   24 Paid salaries expense, $1,800.

   28 Joan withdrew $400 for personal use.

A partial chart of accounts includes Cash, 111; Accounts Receivable, 112;
Equipment, 121; Accounts Payable, 211; J. Lowe, Capital, 311; J. Lowe,
Withdrawals, 312; Fees Earned, 411; and Salaries Expense, 511.

LO3 (15 min)   **3-5.** You have been hired to correct the trial balance in Figure 3.41 that has been recorded improperly from the ledger to the trial balance.

FIGURE 3.41 Incorrect Trial Balance

SUNG CO. TRIAL BALANCE MARCH 31, 200X		
	Dr.	**Cr.**
Accounts Payable	2 0 0 0 00	
A. Sung, Capital		6 5 0 0 00
A. Sung, Withdrawals		3 0 0 00
Services Earned		4 7 0 0 00
Concessions Earned	2 5 0 0 00	
Rent Expense	4 0 0 00	
Salaries Expense	2 5 0 0 00	
Miscellaneous Expense		1 3 0 0 00
Cash	10 0 0 0 00	
Accounts Receivable		1 2 0 0 00
Totals	17 4 0 0 00	14 0 0 0 00

LO3 (10 min)   **3-6.** On February 6, 200X, Mike Sullivan made the journal entry in Figure 3.42 to record the purchase on account of office equipment priced at $1,400. This transaction had not yet been posted when the error was discovered. Make the appropriate correction.

FIGURE 3.42 Recording Error

GENERAL JOURNAL					
Date		Account Titles and Description	PR	Dr.	Cr.
200X Feb.	6	Office Equipment		9 0 0 00	
		Accounts Payable			9 0 0 00
		Purchase of office equip. on account			

MyAccountingLab

Group A Problems

LO1 (30 min)   **3A-1.** Jack Lang operates Jack's Cleaning Service. As the bookkeeper, you have been requested to journalize the following transactions:

200X

Aug.   1   Paid rent for two months in advance, $9,000.

6   Purchased cleaning equipment on account from Ryan's Supply House, $4,000.

12   Purchased cleaning supplies from Lee's Wholesale for $900 cash.

14   Received $1,900 cash from cleaning fees earned.

20   Jack withdrew $900 for his personal use.

21   Advertising bill received from *Salem News* but unpaid, $400.

25   Paid electrical expense, $90.

28   Paid salaries expense, $700.

29   Performed cleaning work for $2,100, but payment will not be received until January.

30   Paid Ryan's Supply House half the amount owed from Nov. 6 transaction.

Check Figure:
Aug 21
Dr. Advertising expense $400
Cr. Accounts Payable $400

Your task is to journalize the preceding transactions. The chart of accounts for Jack's Cleaning Service is as follows:

Chart of Accounts

Assets		Owner's Equity	
111	Cash	311	Jack Lang, Capital
112	Accounts Receivable	312	Jack Lang, Withdrawals
114	Prepaid Rent	**Revenue**	
116	Cleaning Supplies	411	Cleaning Fees Earned
120	Cleaning Equipment	**Expenses**	
121	Office Equipment	511	Advertising Expense
Liabilities		512	Electrical Expense
211	Accounts Payable	514	Salaries Expense

3A-2. On June 1, 200X, Betty Rice opened Betty's Art Studio. The following transactions occurred in June:

LO 1, 2, 3 (45 min)

200X

June	1	Betty Rice invested $12,000 in the art studio.
	1	Paid three months' rent in advance, $1,200.
	3	Purchased $600 of equipment from Aston Co. on account.
	5	Received $900 cash for art-training workshop for teachers.
	8	Purchased $400 of art supplies for cash.
	9	Billed Lester Co. $2,100 for group art lesson for its employees.
	10	Paid salaries of assistants, $600.
	15	Betty withdrew $200 from the business for her personal use.
	28	Paid electrical bill, $140.
	29	Paid telephone bill for June, $210.

Your task is to

    a. Set up the ledger based on the following chart of accounts.
    b. Journalize (journal is page 1) and post the June transactions.
    c. Prepare a trial balance as of June 30, 200X.

> *Check Figure:*
> Trial Balance
> Total $15,600

The chart of accounts for Betty's Art Studio is as follows:

Chart of Accounts

Assets		Owner's Equity	
111	Cash	311	Betty Rice, Capital
112	Accounts Receivable	312	Betty Rice, Withdrawals
114	Prepaid Rent	**Revenue**	
121	Art Supplies	411	Art Fees Earned
131	Equipment	**Expenses**	
Liabilities		511	Electrical Expense
211	Accounts Payable	521	Salaries Expense
		531	Telephone Expense

LO1, 2, 3 (45 min)

3A-3. The following transactions occurred in June 200X for A. French's Placement Agency:

200X

June 1 A. French invested $9,000 cash in the placement agency.

1 Bought equipment on account from Hook Co., $2,000.

3 Earned placement fees of $1,600, but payment will not be received until July.

5 A. French withdrew $100 for his personal use.

7 Paid wages expense, $300.

9 Placed a client on a local TV show, receiving $600 cash.

15 Bought supplies on account from Lyon Co., $500.

28 Paid telephone bill for June, $160.

29 Advertising bill from Shale Co. received but not paid, $900.

Check Figure:
Trial Balance
Total $14,600

The chart of accounts for A. French Placement Agency is as follows:

Chart of Accounts

Assets		Owner's Equity	
111	Cash	311	A. French, Capital
112	Accounts Receivable	312	A. French, Withdrawals
131	Supplies	**Revenue**	
141	Equipment	411	Placement Fees Earned
Liabilities		**Expenses**	
211	Accounts Payable	511	Wage Expense
		521	Telephone Expense
		531	Advertising Expense

Your task is to
   a. Set up the ledger based on the chart of accounts.
   b. Journalize (page 1) and post the June transactions.
   c. Prepare a trial balance as of June 30, 200X.

MyAccountingLab

Group B Problems

LO1 (30 min)

3B-1. In April Jack Lang opened a new cleaning service. Please assist him by journalizing the following business transactions:

200X

Apr. 1 Jack Lang invested $6,000 of cleaning equipment as well as $3,000 cash in the new business.

3 Purchased cleaning supplies on account from Rex Co., $500.

10 Purchased office equipment on account from Ross Stationery, $400.

12 Jack paid his home telephone bill from the company checkbook, $60.

20 Received $600 cash for cleaning services performed.

21 Advertising bill received but not paid, $75.

25 Electrical bill received but not paid, $90.

28 Performed cleaning work for $700, but payment will not be received until May.

29 Paid salaries expense, $400.

30 Paid Ross Stationery half the amount owed from April 10 transaction.

Check Figure:
April 21
Dr. Advertising expense $75
Cr. Accounts payable $75

The chart of accounts for Jack's Cleaning Service includes Cash, 111; Accounts Receivable, 112; Prepaid Rent, 114; Cleaning Supplies, 116; Cleaning Equipment, 120; Office Equipment, 121; Accounts Payable, 211; Jack Lang, Capital, 311; Jack Lang, Withdrawals, 312; Cleaning Fees Earned, 411; Advertising Expense, 511; Electrical Expense, 512; and Salaries Expense, 514.

3B-2. In June the following transactions occurred for Betty's Art Studio:

LO1, 2, 3 (45 min)

200X		
June	1	Betty Rice invested $6,000 in the art studio.
	1	Paid four months rent in advance, $1,200.
	3	Purchased art supplies on account from A.J.K., $700.
	5	Purchased equipment on account from Reese Company, $900.
	8	Received $1,300 cash for art-training program provided to Northwest Junior College.
	9	Billed Long Co. for art lessons provided, $600.
	10	Betty withdrew $400 from the art studio to buy a new chainsaw for her home.
	15	Paid salaries expense, $400.
	28	Paid telephone bill, $118.
	29	Electric bill received but unpaid, $120.

> *Check Figure:*
> Total Trial Balance $9,620

Your task is to

a. Set up a ledger.
b. Journalize (all page 1) and post the June transactions.
c. Prepare a trial balance as of June 30, 200X.

The chart of accounts includes Cash, 111; Accounts Receivable, 112; Prepaid Rent, 114; Art Supplies, 121; Equipment, 131; Accounts Payable, 211; Betty Rice, Capital, 311; Betty Rice, Withdrawals, 312; Art Fees Earned, 411; Electrical Expense, 511; Salaries Expense, 521; and Telephone Expense, 531.

3B-3. In June A. French's Placement Agency had the following transactions:

LO1, 2, 3 (45 min)

200X		
June	1	A. French invested $6,000 in the new placement agency.
	2	Bought equipment for cash, $350.
	3	Earned placement fee commission of $2,100, but payment from Avon Co. will not be received until July.
	5	Paid wages expense, $400.
	7	A. French paid his home utility bill from the company checkbook, $69.
	9	Placed Jay Diamond on a national TV show, receiving $900 cash.
	15	Paid cash for supplies, $350.
	28	Telephone bill received but not paid, $185.
	29	Advertising bill received but not paid, $200.

> *Check Figure:*
> Total Trial Balance $9,385

The chart of accounts includes Cash, 111; Accounts Receivable, 112; Supplies, 131; Equipment, 141; Accounts Payable, 211; A. French, Capital, 311; A. French, Withdrawals, 312; Placement Fees Earned, 411; Wage Expense, 511; Telephone Expense, 521; and Advertising Expense, 531.

Your task is to

a. Set up a ledger based on the chart of accounts.
b. Journalize (all page 1) and post transactions.
c. Prepare a trial balance for June 30, 200X.

ON-THE-JOB TRAINING

LO3 (30 min)

T-1. Paul Regan, bookkeeper of Hampton Co., has been up half the night trying to get his trial balance to balance. Figure 3.43 shows his results.

FIGURE 3.43 Incorrect Trial Balance

HAMPTON CO. TRIAL BALANCE JUNE 30, 200X	Dr.	Cr.
Office Sales		5 7 2 0 00
Cash in Bank	3 2 6 0 00	
Accounts Receivable	5 6 6 0 00	
Office Equipment	8 4 0 0 00	
Accounts Payable		4 1 6 0 00
D. Hole, Capital		11 5 6 0 00
D. Hole, Withdrawals		7 0 0 00
Wage Expense	2 6 0 0 00	
Rent Expense	9 4 0 00	
Utilities Expense	2 6 00	
Office Supplies	1 2 0 00	
Prepaid Rent	1 8 0 00	

Ken Small, the accountant, compared Paul's amounts in the trial balance with those in the ledger, recomputed each account balance, and compared postings. Ken found the following errors:

1. A $200 debit to D. Hole, Withdrawals, was posted as a credit.

2. D. Hole, Withdrawals, was listed on the trial balance as a credit.

3. A Note Payable account with a credit balance of $2,400 was not listed on the trial balance.

4. The pencil footings for Accounts Payable were debits of $5,320 and credits of $8,800.

5. A debit of $180 to Prepaid Rent was not posted.

6. Office Supplies bought for $60 was posted as a credit to Office Supplies.

7. A debit of $120 to Accounts Receivable was not posted.

8. A cash payment of $420 was credited to Cash for $240.

9. The pencil footing of the credits to Cash was overstated by $400.

10. The Utilities Expense of $260 was listed in the trial balance as $26.

Assist Paul Regan by preparing a correct trial balance. What advice could you give Ken about Paul? Can you explain the situation to Paul? Put your answers in writing.

LO 3 (20 min)

T-2. Lauren Oliver, an accountant lab tutor, is having a debate with some of her assistants. They are trying to find out how each of the following five unrelated situations would affect the trial balance:

1. A $5 debit to Cash in the ledger was not posted.

2. A $10 debit to Computer Supplies was debited to Computer Equipment.

3. An $8 debit to Wage Expense was debited twice to the account.

4. A $4 debit to Computer Supplies was debited to Computer Sales.

5. A $35 credit to Accounts Payable was posted as a $53 credit.

Could you indicate to Lauren the effect that each situation will have on the trial balance? If a situation will have no effect, indicate that fact. Put in writing how each of these situations could be avoided in the future.

FINANCIAL REPORT PROBLEM

Reading the Kellogg's Annual Report

LO3 (5 min)

Go to Appendix A and find the statement of earnings. Sales are the revenue for a merchandise company. How much did Kellogg's increase sales from 2005 to 2006? What inward flows could result from these net sales?

INTERNET PROJECT

Continental

Go to the Web and search: Annual Report Continental 2008.
Click on Investors Relations.
List out the latest news Continental is providing to its investors.
Order a free annual report.

CONTINUING PROBLEM

MyAccountingLab

Sanchez Computer Center

LO1, 2, 3 (45 min)

Tony's computer center is picking up in business, so he has decided to expand his bookkeeping system to a general journal/ledger system. The balances from August have been forwarded to the ledger accounts.

Assignment

1. Use the chart of accounts in Chapter 2 to record the following transactions in Figures 3.44 through 3.54.

FIGURE 3.44 Prepaid Rent

Sanchez Computer Center		8104
385 N. Escondido Blvd.		
Escondido CA 92025	*September 1, --200X------*	
Pay		
To the		
Order of—*Capital Management* --- $ *1200.00* -------		
One thousand two hundred and 00/100		
First Union Bank		
322 Glen Ave.		
Escondido, CA 92025		
memo *Prepaid Rent—Aug. Sept. Oct.** --------*Tony Freedman* --------		
0611 062 78 72		

*One check is written for 3 months rent on Sept. 1. That included August rent. For this problem, consider it all prepaid.

FIGURE 3.45 Service Revenue

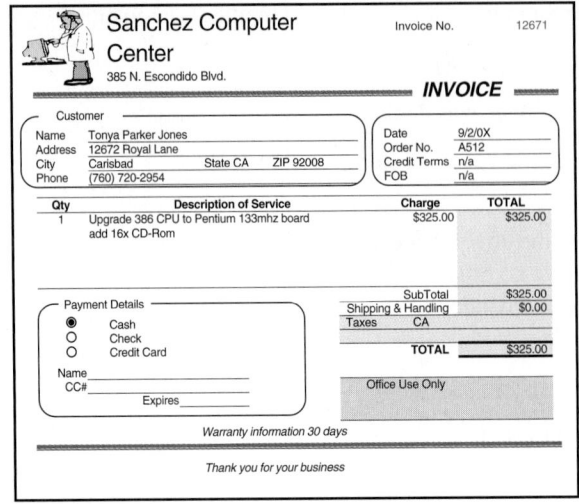

FIGURE 3.46 Service Revenue

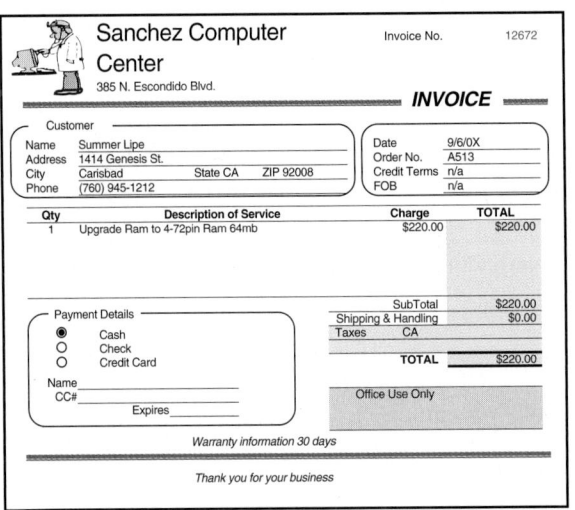

FIGURE 3.47 Phone Bill

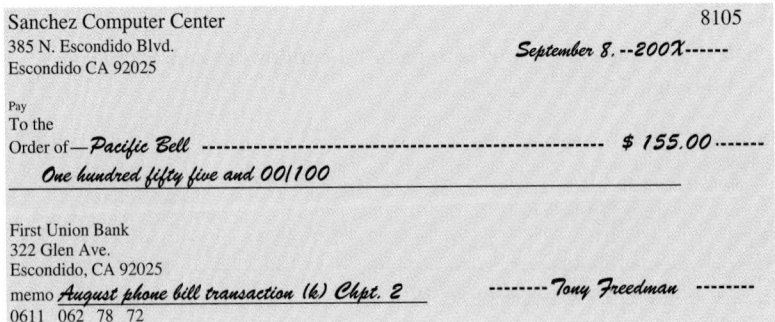

Refer back to Chapter 2, transaction k.

Jeannine Sparks
1919 Sierra St.
Escondido CA 92025

251

September 12, --200X-----

Pay
To the
Order of—*Sanchez Computer Center* ------------------------------- *$ 850.00*------

Eight hundred fifty dollars and 00/100

Bank First
322 Cardiff Ave.
Escondido, CA 92025

memo *Computer Fixed, Transaction (o) Chpt. 2* ------*Jeannine Sparks* -------

0611 062 78 72

FIGURE 3.48 Sparks Collection

Refer back to Chapter 2, transaction o.

Sanchez Computer Center
385 N. Escondido Blvd.
Escondido CA 92025

8106

September 15, --200X-----

Pay
To the
Order of—*Computer Connection* ------------------------------------ *$ 200.00*------

Two hundred dollars and 00/100

First Union Bank
322 Glen Ave.
Escondido, CA 92025

memo *Account due from transaction (s) Chpt. 2* -------*Tony Freedman* -------

0611 062 78 72

FIGURE 3.49 Paid Computer Connection

Refer back to Chapter 2, transaction s.

Sanchez Computer Center
385 N. Escondido Blvd.
Escondido CA 92025

8107

September 17, --200X-----

Pay
To the
Order of—*Multi Systems, Inc* -- *$ 1,200.00*------

Twelve hundred dollars and 00/100

First Union Bank
322 Glen Ave.
Escondido, CA 92025

Purchase order 200

memo *Computer Equipment-Bench Workstations* --------*Tony Freedman* --------

0611 062 78 72

FIGURE 3.50 Purchased Computer Equipment

FIGURE 3.51 Received
Phone Bill

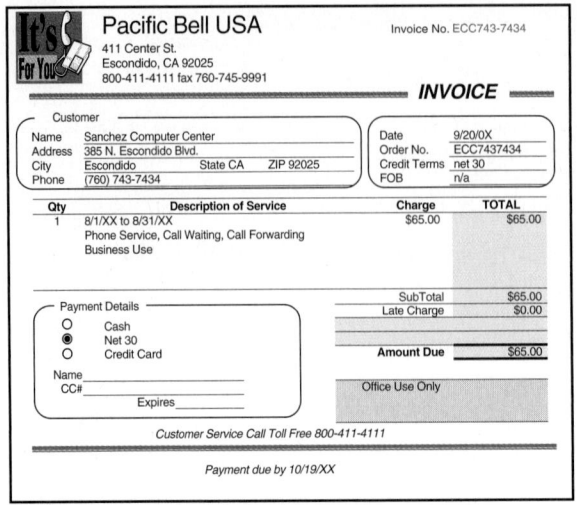

FIGURE 3.52 Received
Electric Bill

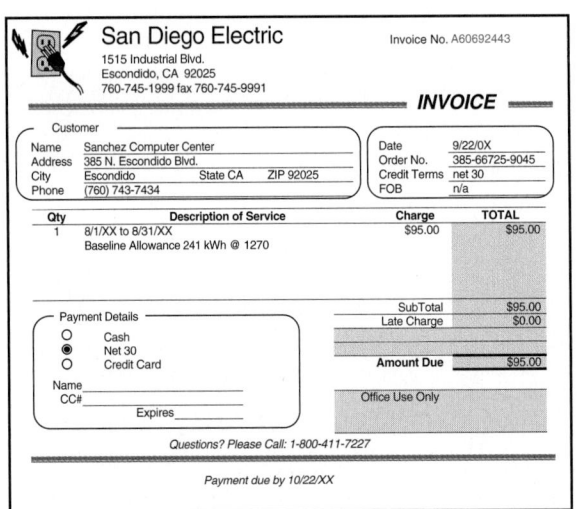

FIGURE 3.53 Service Revenue

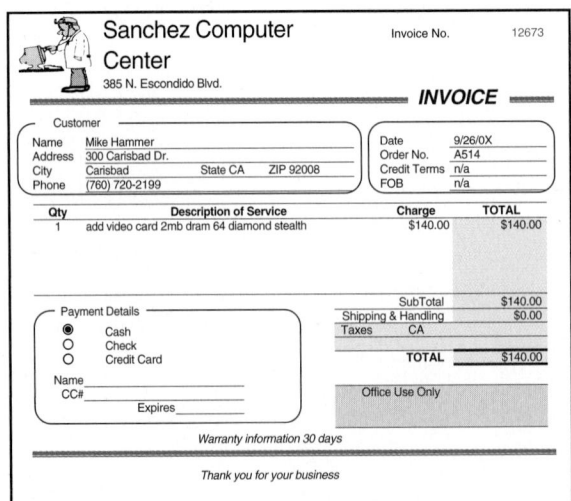

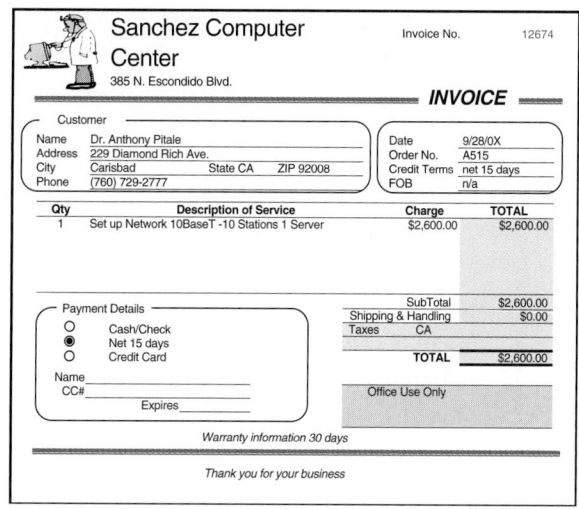

FIGURE 3.54 Service Revenue

2. Post all transactions to the general ledger accounts (the Prepaid Rent Account #1025 has been added to the chart of accounts).
3. Prepare a trial balance for September 30, 200X.
4. Prepare the financial statements for the three months ended September 30, 200X.

PEACHTREE COMPUTER WORKSHOP

COMPUTERIZED ACCOUNTING APPLICATION FOR CHAPTER 3

Preparing to use Peachtree Complete Accounting

Before starting this assignment, visit the multimedia library of the MyAccountingLab Web site and read the following PDF documents for your version of Peachtree.

1. An Introduction to Computerized Accounting
2. Installing Peachtree Complete Accounting and Student Data Files
3. An Introduction to Peachtree Complete Accounting
4. Correcting Peachtree Transactions
5. How to Repeat or Restart a Peachtree Assignment
6. Backing Up and Restoring Your Work in Peachtree

Workshop 1:

Journalizing, Posting, General Ledger, Trial Balance, and Chart of Accounts
In this workshop you enter, post, and edit journal entries for the Atlas Company using Peachtree Complete Accounting. You will also print the general journal report, trial balance, and chart of accounts.

Instructions and data files for completing this assignment are in the multimedia library of the MyAccountingLab Web site. Open the ***Workshop 1 Atlas Company*** PDF document for your version of Peachtree and download the ***Atlas Company*** data file for your version of Peachtree.

QUICKBOOKS COMPUTER WORKSHOP

COMPUTERIZED ACCOUNTING APPLICATION FOR CHAPTER 3

Preparing to use QuickBooks Pro

Before starting this assignment, visit the multimedia library of the MyAccountingLab Web site and read the following PDF documents for your version of QuickBooks.

1. An Introduction to Computerized Accounting
2. Installing QuickBooks Pro and Student Data Files
3. An Introduction to QuickBooks Pro
4. Correcting QuickBooks Transactions
5. How to Repeat or Restart a QuickBooks Assignment
6. Backing Up and Restoring Your Work in QuickBooks

Workshop 1:

Journalizing, Posting, General Ledger, Trial Balance, and Chart of Accounts
In this workshop you enter, post, and edit journal entries for the Atlas Company using QuickBooks Pro. You will also print the general journal report, trial balance, and chart of accounts.

Instructions and data files for completing this assignment are in the multimedia library of the MyAccountingLab Web site. Open the ***Workshop 1 Atlas Company*** PDF document for your version of QuickBooks and download the ***Atlas Company*** data file for your version of QuickBooks.

The Accounting Cycle Continued

DID YOU KNOW? Black & Decker uses the straight-line method to depreciate its property, plant, and equipment.
Building: 10–50 years
Manufacturing equipment: 3–5 years
Visit *www.blackanddecker.com* to find more information about Black & Decker.

LEARNING OBJECTIVES

1. Adjustments: prepaid rent, office supplies, depreciation on equipment, and accrued salaries.

2. Preparing the adjusted trial balance on the worksheet.

3. Preparing the income statement and balance sheet sections of the worksheet.

4. Preparing financial statements from the worksheet.

QuickBooks and Peachtree programs do not use worksheets. Adjustments are made from preparing the trial balance and are recorded in the general journal.

Each year Black & Decker completes an accounting cycle. In Figure 4.1, steps 1–4 show the parts of the manual accounting cycle that were completed for Clark's Word Processing Services in the previous chapter. This chapter continues the cycle with steps 5–6: the preparation of a worksheet and the three financial statements.

Learning Unit 4-1 Step 5 of the Accounting Cycle: Preparing a Worksheet

An accountant uses a **worksheet** to organize and check data before preparing financial statements necessary to complete the accounting cycle. When an accounting software package is used, a worksheet would not be needed. The most important function of the worksheet is to allow the accountant to find and correct errors before financial statements are prepared. In a way, a worksheet acts as the accountant's scratch pad. No one sees the worksheet once the formal reports are prepared. A sample worksheet is shown in Figure 4.2.

The accounts listed on the far left of the worksheet are taken from the ledger. The rest of the worksheet has five sections: the trial balance, adjustments, adjusted trial balance, income statement, and balance sheet. Each of these sections is divided into debit and credit columns.

The Trial Balance Section

We discussed how to prepare a trial balance in Chapter 2. Some companies prepare a separate trial balance; others, such as Clark's Word Processing Services, prepare the trial balance directly on the worksheet. A trial balance is taken on every account listed in the ledger that has a balance. Additional titles from the ledger are added as they are needed. (We will show how to add account titles later.)

FIGURE 4.1

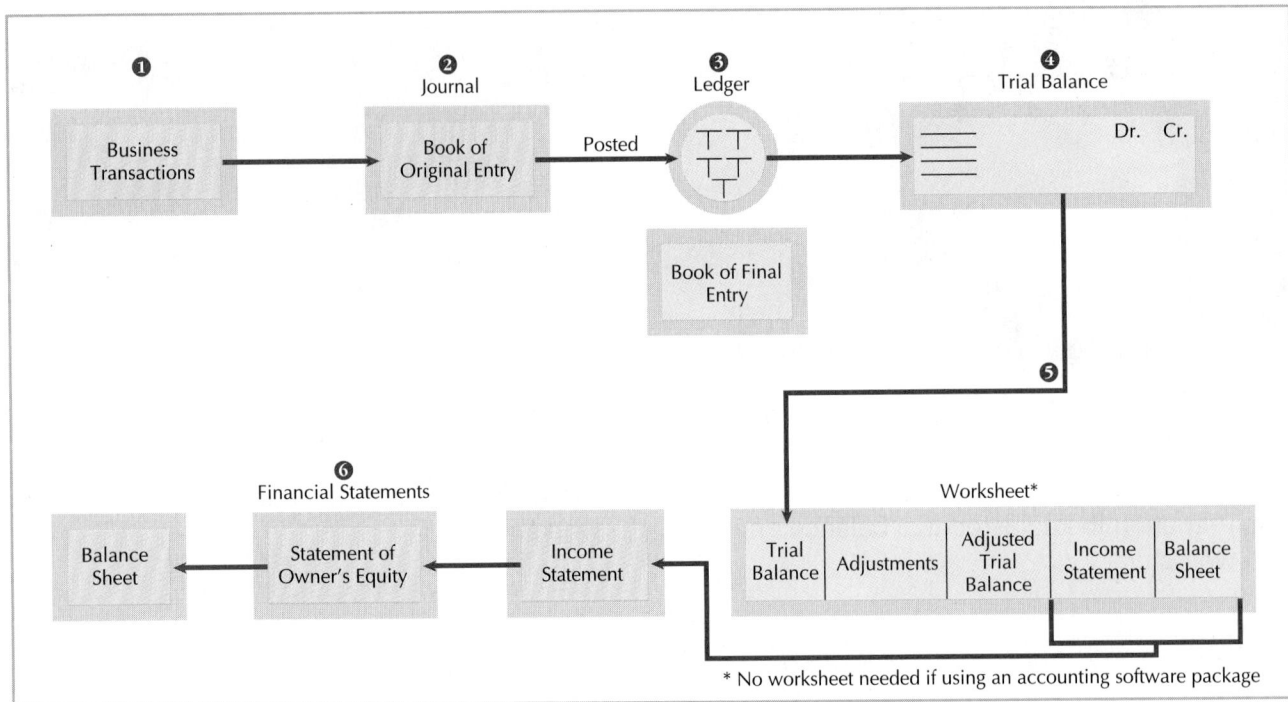

* No worksheet needed if using an accounting software package

FIGURE 4.2 Sample Worksheet

	Trial Balance		Adjustments		Adjusted Trial Balance		Income Statement	
Account Titles	Dr.	Cr.	Dr.	Cr.	Dr.	Cr.	Dr.	Cr.
Cash	6 1 5 5 00							
Accounts Receivable	5 0 0 0 00							
Office Supplies	6 0 0 00							
Prepaid Rent	1 2 0 0 00							
Word Processing Equipment	6 0 0 0 00							
Accounts Payable		3 3 5 0 00						
Brenda Clark, Capital		10 0 0 0 00						
Brenda Clark, Withdrawals	6 2 5 00							
Word Processing Fees		8 0 0 0 00						
Office Salaries Expense	1 3 0 0 00							
Advertising Expense	2 5 0 00							
Telephone Expense	2 2 0 00							
	21 3 5 0 00	21 3 5 0 00						

CLARK'S WORD PROCESSING SERVICES WORKSHEET FOR MONTH ENDING MAY 31, 200X

The Adjustments Section

LO1

Chapters 1–3 discussed transactions that occurred with outside suppliers and companies. In a real business inside transactions also occur during the accounting cycle. These transactions must be recorded, too. At the end of the worksheet process, the accountant will have all of the business's accounts up-to-date and ready to be used to prepare the formal financial reports. The Sarbanes-Oxley Act specifically states the need to have accurate financial reports. By analyzing each of Clark's accounts on the worksheet, the accountant will be able to identify specific accounts that must be **adjusted** to bring them up-to-date. The accountant for Clark's Word Processing Services needs to adjust the following accounts:

> Worksheets can be completed on Excel spreadsheets.

A. Office Supplies
B. Prepaid Rent
C. Word Processing Equipment
D. Office Salaries Expense

Let's look at how to analyze and adjust each of these accounts.

A. Adjusting the Office Supplies Account On May 31, the accountant found out that the company had only $100 worth of office supplies on hand. When the company had originally purchased the $600 of office supplies they were considered an asset. As the supplies were used up, they became an expense.

> The adjustment for supplies deals with the amount of supplies *used up*.

- Office supplies available: $600 on trial balance.
- Office supplies left or on hand as of May 31: $100 will end up on adjusted trial balance.
- Office supplies used up in the operation of the business for the month of May: $500 is shown in the adjustments column.

Office Supplies Exp. 514

500 |

This amount is supplies used up.

Office Supplies 114

600 |**500**

100

↑

This amount is supplies on hand.

As a result, the asset Office Supplies is too high on the trial balance (it should be $100, not $600). At the same time, if we don't show the additional expense of supplies used, the company's *net income* will be too high.

If Clark's accountant does not adjust the trial balance to reflect the change, the company's net income would be too high on the income statement and both sides (Assets and Owner's Equity) of the balance sheet would be too high.

Now let's look at the adjustment for office supplies in terms of the transaction analysis chart.

Will go on income statement

Accounts Affected	Category	↓ ↑	Rules
Office Supplies Expense	Expense	↑	Dr.
Office Supplies	Asset	↓	Cr.

Will go on balance sheet

The Office Supplies Expense account comes from the chart of accounts in Chapter 3. Because it is not listed in the account titles, it must be listed below the trial balance. Let's see how we enter this adjustment on the worksheet in Figure 4.3.

Place $500 in the debit column of the adjustments section on the same line as Office Supplies Expense. Place $500 in the credit column of the adjustments section on the same line as Office Supplies. The numbers in the adjustment column show what is used, *not* what is on hand.

B. Adjusting the Prepaid Rent Account Back on May 1, Clark's Word Processing Services paid three months' rent in advance. The accountant realized that the rent expense would be $400 per month ($1,200 ÷ 3 months = $400).

FIGURE 4.3

Note: Amount "used up" for supplies $500 goes in adjustments column.

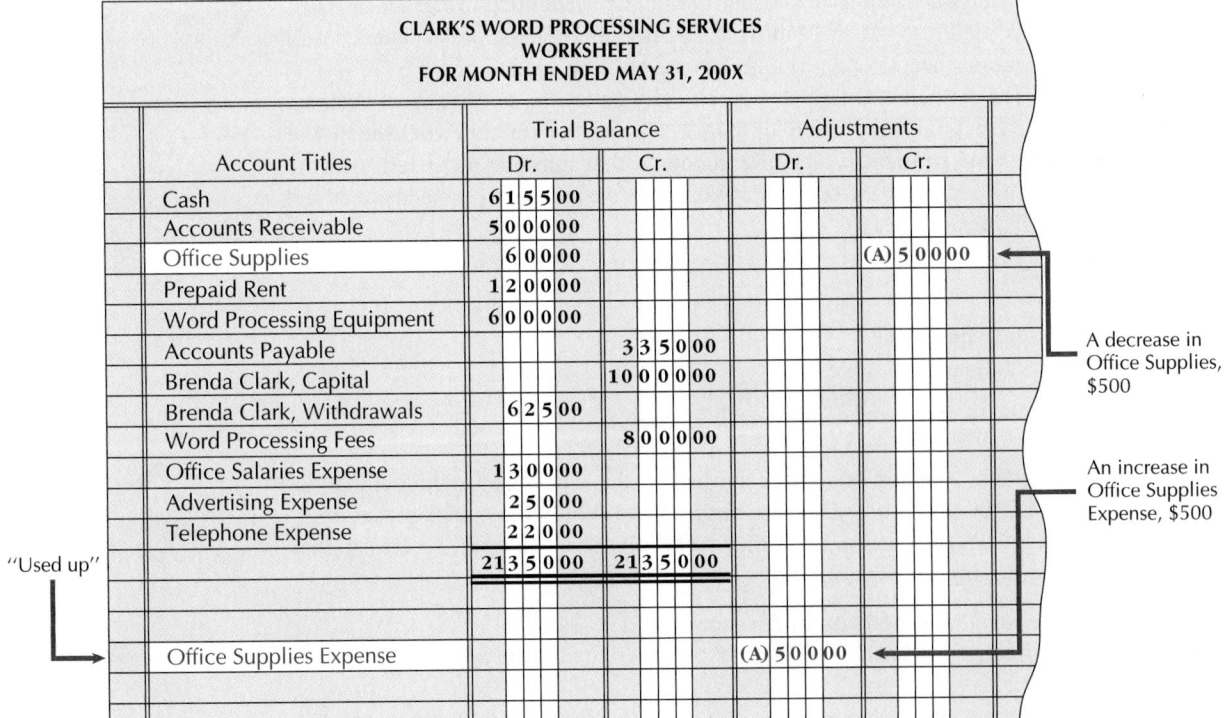

CLARK'S WORD PROCESSING SERVICES
WORKSHEET
FOR MONTH ENDED MAY 31, 200X

Account Titles	Trial Balance Dr.	Trial Balance Cr.	Adjustments Dr.	Adjustments Cr.
Cash	6 1 5 5 00			
Accounts Receivable	5 0 0 0 00			
Office Supplies	6 0 0 00			(A) 5 0 0 00
Prepaid Rent	1 2 0 0 00			
Word Processing Equipment	6 0 0 0 00			
Accounts Payable		3 3 5 0 00		
Brenda Clark, Capital		10 0 0 0 00		
Brenda Clark, Withdrawals	6 2 5 00			
Word Processing Fees		8 0 0 0 00		
Office Salaries Expense	1 3 0 0 00			
Advertising Expense	2 5 0 00			
Telephone Expense	2 2 0 00			
	21 3 5 0 00	21 3 5 0 00		
Office Supplies Expense			(A) 5 0 0 00	

"Used up"

A decrease in Office Supplies, $500

An increase in Office Supplies Expense, $500

Remember, when rent is paid in advance, it is considered an asset called *prepaid rent.* When the asset, prepaid rent, begins to expire or be used up, it becomes an expense. Now it is May 31, and one month's prepaid rent has become an expense.

How is this type of rent handled? Should the account be $1,200, or is only $800 of prepaid rent left as of May 31? What do we need to do to bring Prepaid Rent to the "true" balance? The answer is that we must increase Rent Expense by $400 and decrease Prepaid Rent by $400 (see Fig. 4.4).

Without this adjustment, the expenses for Clark's Word Processing Services for May will be too low, and the asset Prepaid Rent will be too high. If unadjusted amounts were used in the formal reports, the net income shown on the income statement would be too high, and both sides (Assets and Owner's Equity) would be too high on the balance sheet. In terms of our transaction analysis chart, the adjustment would look like this:

Will go on income statement

Accounts Affected	Category	↓ ↑	Rules
Rent Expense	Expense	↑	Dr.
Prepaid Rent	Asset	↓	Cr.

Will go on balance sheet

Rent Expense 515

400 |

Prepaid Rent 115

1200 | **400**
800 |

Like the Office Supplies Expense account, the Rent Expense account comes from the chart of accounts in Chapter 3.

Figure 4.4 shows how to enter an adjustment to Prepaid Rent.

C. Adjusting the Word Processing Equipment Account for Depreciation The life of the asset affects how it is adjusted. The two accounts we just discussed, Office Supplies and Prepaid Rent, involved things that are used up relatively quickly. Equipment—like word processing equipment—is expected to last much longer. Equipment is   *LO2*

FIGURE 4.4

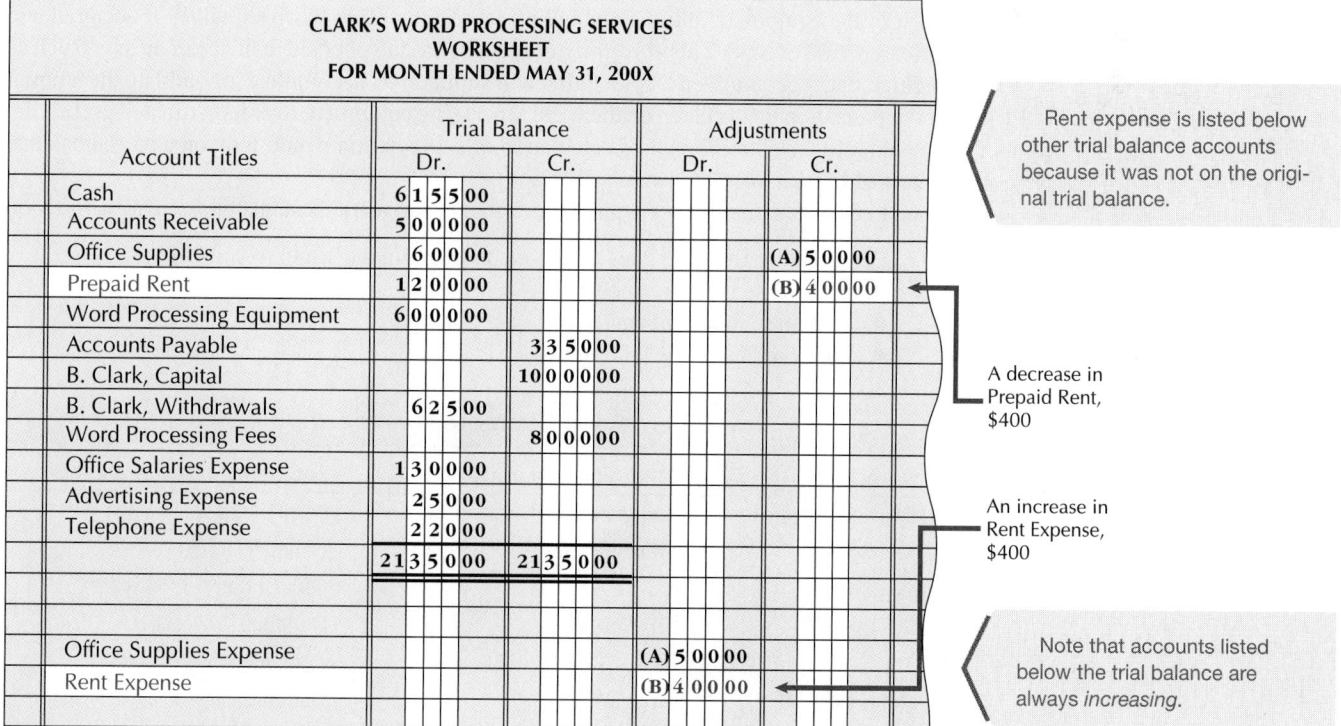

	Trial Balance		Adjustments	
Account Titles	Dr.	Cr.	Dr.	Cr.
Cash	6 1 5 5 00			
Accounts Receivable	5 0 0 0 00			
Office Supplies	6 0 0 00			(A) 5 0 0 00
Prepaid Rent	1 2 0 0 00			(B) 4 0 0 00
Word Processing Equipment	6 0 0 0 00			
Accounts Payable		3 3 5 0 00		
B. Clark, Capital		10 0 0 0 00		
B. Clark, Withdrawals	6 2 5 00			
Word Processing Fees		8 0 0 0 00		
Office Salaries Expense	1 3 0 0 00			
Advertising Expense	2 5 0 00			
Telephone Expense	2 2 0 00			
	21 3 5 0 00	21 3 5 0 00		
Office Supplies Expense			(A) 5 0 0 00	
Rent Expense			(B) 4 0 0 00	

CLARK'S WORD PROCESSING SERVICES
WORKSHEET
FOR MONTH ENDED MAY 31, 200X

Rent expense is listed below other trial balance accounts because it was not on the original trial balance.

A decrease in Prepaid Rent, $400

An increase in Rent Expense, $400

Note that accounts listed below the trial balance are always *increasing.*

expected to help produce revenue over a longer period. For that reason accountants treat it differently. The balance sheet reports the **historical cost,** or original cost, of the equipment. The original cost also is reflected in the ledger. The adjustment shows how the cost of the equipment is allocated (spread) over its expected useful life. This spreading is called **depreciation.** To depreciate the equipment, we have to figure out how much its cost goes down each month. Then we have to keep a running total of how that depreciation mounts up over time. The Internal Revenue Service (IRS) issues guidelines, tables, and formulas that must be used to estimate the amount of depreciation. Different methods can be used to calculate depreciation. We will use the simplest method—straight-line depreciation—to calculate the depreciation of Clark's Word Processing Services' equipment. Under the straight-line method, equal amounts are taken over successive periods of time. Table 4-1 shows how some companies estimate life of equipment using the straight-line method.

> Original cost of $6,000 for word processing equipment remains *unchanged* after adjustments.

The calculation of depreciation for the year for Clark's Word Processing Services is as follows:

$$\frac{\text{Cost of Equipment} - \text{Residual Value}}{\text{Estimated Years of Usefulness}} = (\text{Trade-In or Salvage Value})$$

According to the IRS, word processing equipment has an expected life of five years. At the end of that time, the property's value is called its "residual value." Think of **residual value** as the estimated value of the equipment at the end of the fifth year. For Clark, the equipment has an estimated residual value of $1,200.

$$\frac{\$6,000 - \$1,200}{5 \text{ Years}} = \frac{\$4,800}{5} = \$960 \text{ Depreciation per Year}$$

Our trial balance is for one month, so we must determine the adjustment for that month:

$$\frac{\$960}{12 \text{ Months}} = \$80 \text{ Depreciation per Month}$$

This $80 is known as depreciation expense, which will be shown on the income statement.

Next, we create a new account to keep a running total of the depreciation amount apart from the original cost of the equipment. The "running total" account is called **Accumulated Depreciation.**

> **Accumulated Depreciation**
>
> | Dr. | Cr. |
> |-----|-----|
>
> is a contra-asset account found on the balance sheet.

The Accumulated Depreciation account shows the relationship between the original cost of the equipment and the amount of depreciation that has been taken or accumulated over a period of time. This *contra-asset* account has the opposite balance of an asset such as equipment. Accumulated Depreciation will summarize, accumulate, or build up the amount of depreciation that is taken on the word processing equipment over its estimated useful life.

Figure 4.5 shows how this calculation of depreciation would look on a partial balance sheet of Clark's Word Processing Services.

Let's summarize the key points before going on to mark the adjustment on the worksheet:

1. Depreciation Expense goes on the income statement, which results in
   - an increase in total expenses.
   - a decrease in net income.
   - therefore, less to be paid in taxes.

TABLE 4.1 **How Companies Estimate Useful Life**		
Company	**Method of Depreciation**	**Estimated Life of Equipment**
Claire's Stores	Straight-Line	Furniture: 3–25 years
Merck	Straight-Line	Building: 10–50 years
		Office Equip.: 3–15 years
Big Lots	Straight-Line	Building: 40 years
		Equipment: 3–15 years
Dollar General	Straight-Line	Building: 39–40 years
		Furniture: 3–10 years

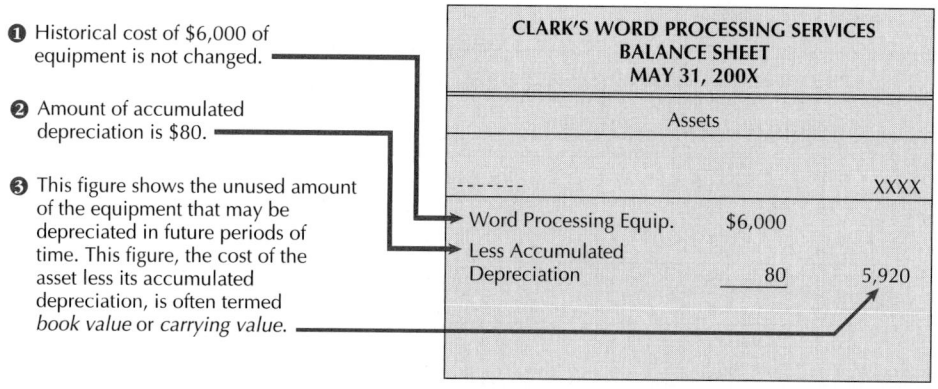

① Historical cost of $6,000 of equipment is not changed.

② Amount of accumulated depreciation is $80.

③ This figure shows the unused amount of the equipment that may be depreciated in future periods of time. This figure, the cost of the asset less its accumulated depreciation, is often termed *book value* or *carrying value*.

CLARK'S WORD PROCESSING SERVICES
BALANCE SHEET
MAY 31, 200X

Assets

-------   XXXX

Word Processing Equip. $6,000
Less Accumulated
Depreciation   80   5,920

FIGURE 4.5

2. Accumulated Depreciation is a contra-asset account found on the balance sheet next to its related equipment account.
3. The original cost of equipment is not reduced; it stays the same until the equipment is sold or removed.
4. Each month the amount in the Accumulated Depreciation account grows larger while the cost of the equipment remains the same.

Now, let's analyze the adjustment on the transaction analysis chart:

Will go on income statement

Accounts Affected	Category	↓ ↑	Rules
Depreciation Expense, Word Processing Equipment	Expense	↑	Dr.
Accumulated Depreciation, Word Processing Equipment	Contra-Asset	↑	Cr.

Will go on balance sheet

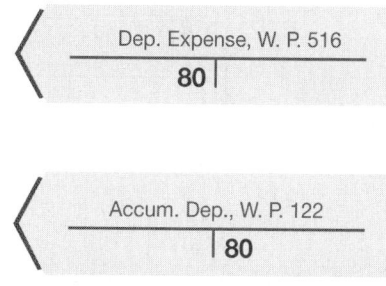

Dep. Expense, W. P. 516
80 |

Accum. Dep., W. P. 122
| 80

Remember, the original cost of the equipment never changes: (1) The Equipment account is not included among the affected accounts because the original cost of equipment remains the same, and (2) the original cost does not change. As the accumulated depreciation increases (as a credit), the equipment's **book value** decreases.

Note that the original cost of the equipment on the worksheet has *not* been changed ($6,000).

Figure 4.6 on the following page shows how we enter the adjustment for depreciation of word processing equipment.

Because it is a new business neither account had a previous balance. Therefore, neither is listed in the account titles of the trial balance. We need to list both accounts below Rent Expense in the account titles section. On the worksheet, put $80 in the debit column of the adjustments section on the same line as Depreciation Expense, W. P. Equipment, and put $80 in the credit column of the adjustments section on the same line as Accumulated Depreciation, W. P. Equipment.

Next month, on June 30, $80 would be entered under Depreciation Expense and Accumulated Depreciation would show a balance of $160. Remember, in May, Clark's was a new company so no previous depreciation had been taken.

Now let's look at the last adjustment for Clark's Word Processing Services.

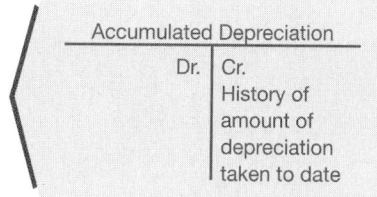

Accumulated Depreciation

Dr.	Cr.
	History of amount of depreciation taken to date

D. Adjusting the Salaries Accrued Account Clark's Word Processing Services paid $1,300 in Office Salaries Expense (see the trial balance of any previous worksheet in this chapter). The last salary checks for the month were paid on May 27. How can we update this account to show the salary expense as of May 31?

John Murray worked for Clark on May 28, 29, 30, and 31 (see Fig. 4.7 on the following page). His next paycheck is not due until June 3. John earned $350 for these four days. Is the $350 an expense to Clark in May when it was earned, or in June when it is due and is paid?

FIGURE 4.6

CLARK'S WORD PROCESSING SERVICES WORKSHEET FOR MONTH ENDED MAY 31, 200X				
Account Titles	Trial Balance		Adjustments	
	Dr.	Cr.	Dr.	Cr.
Cash	6 1 5 5 00			
Accounts Receivable	5 0 0 0 00			
Office Supplies	6 0 0 00			(A) 5 0 0 00
Prepaid Rent	1 2 0 0 00			(B) 4 0 0 00
Word Processing Equipment	6 0 0 0 00			
Accounts Payable		3 3 5 0 00		
B. Clark, Capital		10 0 0 0 00		
B. Clark, Withdrawals	6 2 5 00			
Word Processing Fees		8 0 0 0 00		
Office Salaries Expense	1 3 0 0 00			
Advertising Expense	2 5 0 00			
Telephone Expense	2 2 0 00			
	21 3 5 0 00	21 3 5 0 00		
Office Supplies Expense			(A) 5 0 0 00	
Rent Expense			(B) 4 0 0 00	
Depreciation Exp., W. P. Equip.			(C) 8 0 00	
Accum. Deprec., W. P. Equip.				(C) 8 0 00

An increase in Depreciation Expense, W. P. Equipment.

An increase in Accumulated Depreciation, W. P. Equipment.

> An expense can be incurred without being paid as long as it has helped in creating earned revenue for a period of time.

Think back to Chapter 1, where we first discussed revenue and expenses. We noted then that revenue is recorded when it is earned and expenses are recorded when they are incurred, not when they are actually paid. This principle will be discussed further in a later chapter. For now, it is enough to remember that we record revenue and expenses when they occur because we want to match earned revenue with the expenses that resulted in earning those revenues. In this case, by working those four days, John Murray created some revenue for Clark in May. Therefore, the Office Salaries Expense must be shown in May—the month the revenue was earned.

The results are as follows:

- Office Salaries Expense is increased by $350. This unpaid and unrecorded expense for salaries for which payment is not yet due is called **accrued salaries payable.** In effect, we now show the true expense for salaries ($1,650 instead of $1,300):

Office Salaries Expense

1,300	
350	

FIGURE 4.7

May

Sunday	Monday	Tuesday	Wednesday	Thursday	Friday	Saturday
						1
2	3	4	5	6	7	8
9	10	11	12	13	14	15
16	17	18	19	20	21	22
23	24	25	26	27	28	29
30	31					

● Salaries Payable is also increased by $350. Clark's created a liability called Salaries Payable, which means that the firm owes money for salaries. When the firm pays John Murray, it will reduce its liability Salaries Payable as well as decrease its cash.

In terms of the transaction analysis chart, the following would be done:

Accounts Affected	Category	↓ ↑	Rules
Office Salaries Expense	Expense	↑	Dr.
Salaries Payable	Liability	↑	Cr.

How the adjustment for accrued salaries is entered is shown in Figure 4.8.

> Office Salaries Exp. 511
> 1,300
> **350**

> Salaries Payable 212
> **350**

FIGURE 4.8

CLARK'S WORD PROCESSING SERVICES
WORKSHEET
FOR MONTH ENDED MAY 31, 200X

Account Titles	Trial Balance Dr.	Trial Balance Cr.	Adjustments Dr.	Adjustments Cr.
Cash	6 1 5 5 00			
Accounts Receivable	5 0 0 0 00			
Office Supplies	6 0 0 00			(A) 5 0 0 00
Prepaid Rent	1 2 0 0 00			(B) 4 0 0 00
Word Processing Equipment	6 0 0 0 00			
Accounts Payable		3 3 5 0 00		
B. Clark, Capital		10 0 0 0 00		
B. Clark, Withdrawals	6 2 5 00			
Word Processing Fees		8 0 0 0 00		
Office Salaries Expense	1 3 0 0 00		(D) 3 5 0 00	
Advertising Expense	2 5 0 00			
Telephone Expense	2 2 0 00			
	21 3 5 0 00	21 3 5 0 00		
Office Supplies Expense			(A) 5 0 0 00	
Rent Expense			(B) 4 0 0 00	
Depreciation Exp., W. P. Equip.			(C) 8 0 00	
Accum. Deprec., W. P. Equip.				(C) 8 0 00
Salaries Payable				(D) 3 5 0 00

An increase in Office Salaries Expense, $350

An increase in Salaries Payable, $350

The account Office Salaries Expense is already listed in the account titles, so $350 is placed in the debit column of the adjustments section on the same line as Office Salaries Expense. However, because the Salaries Payable is not listed in the account titles, it is added below the trial balance after Accumulated Depreciation, W. P. Equipment. The amount $350 is also placed in the credit column of the adjustments section on the same line as Salaries Payable.

Now that we have finished all the adjustments that we intended to make we total the adjustments section, as shown in Figure 4.9 on the following page.

The Adjusted Trial Balance Section

The adjusted trial balance is the next section on the worksheet. To fill it out we must summarize the information in the trial balance and adjustments sections, as shown in Figure 4.10.

> Even when using computerized accounting, the user would still prepare an adjusted trial balance.

FIGURE 4.9 The Adjustments
Section of the Worksheet

CLARK'S WORD PROCESSING SERVICES
WORKSHEET
FOR MONTH ENDED MAY 31, 200X

Account Titles	Trial Balance Dr.	Trial Balance Cr.	Adjustments Dr.	Adjustments Cr.
Cash	6 1 5 5 00			
Accounts Receivable	5 0 0 0 00			
Office Supplies	6 0 0 00			(A) 5 0 0 00
Prepaid Rent	1 2 0 0 00			(B) 4 0 0 00
Word Processing Equipment	6 0 0 0 00			
Accounts Payable		3 3 5 0 00		
B. Clark, Capital		10 0 0 0 00		
B. Clark, Withdrawals	6 2 5 00			
Word Processing Fees		8 0 0 0 00		
Office Salaries Expense	1 3 0 0 00		(D) 3 5 0 00	
Advertising Expense	2 5 0 00			
Telephone Expense	2 2 0 00			
	21 3 5 0 00	21 3 5 0 00		
Office Supplies Expense			(A) 5 0 0 00	
Rent Expense			(B) 4 0 0 00	
Depreciation Exp., W. P. Equip.			(C) 8 0 00	
Accum. Deprec.,W. P. Equip.				(C) 8 0 00
Salaries Payable				(D) 3 5 0 00
			1 3 3 0 00	1 3 3 0 00

Note that when the numbers are brought across from the trial balance to the adjusted trial balance, two debits will be added together and two credits will be added together. If the numbers include a debit and a credit, take the difference between the two and place it on the side that is larger.

Now that we have completed the adjustments and adjusted trial balance sections of the worksheet, it is time to move on to the income statement and the balance sheet sections. Before we tackle the statements, look at the chart shown in Table 4.2. This table should be used as a reference to help you in filling out the next two sections of the worksheet.

Keep in mind that the numbers from the adjusted trial balance are carried over to one of the last four columns of the worksheet before the bottom section is completed.

LO3 The Income Statement Section

As shown in Figure 4.11, the income statement section lists only revenue and expenses from the adjusted trial balance. Note that Accumulated Depreciation and Salaries Payable do not go on the income statement. Accumulated Depreciation is a contra-asset found on the balance sheet. Salaries Payable is a liability found on the balance sheet.

The revenue ($8,000) and all the individual expenses are listed in the income statement section. The revenue is placed in the credit column of the income statement section because it has a credit balance. The expenses have debit balances so they are placed in the debit column of the income statement section. The following steps must be taken after the debits and credits are placed in the correct columns:

Step 1 Total the debits and credits.

Step 2 Calculate the balance between the debit and credit columns and place the difference on the smaller side.

Step 3 Total the columns.

The difference between $3,100 Dr. and $8,000 Cr. indicates a Net Income of $4,900. Do not think of the Net Income as a Dr. or Cr. The $4,900 is placed in the debit column to balance both columns to $8,000. Actually, the credit side is larger by $4,900.

CLARK'S WORD PROCESSING SERVICES
WORKSHEET
FOR MONTH ENDED MAY 31, 200X

Account Titles	Trial Balance Dr.	Trial Balance Cr.	Adjustments Dr.	Adjustments Cr.	Adjusted Trial Balance Dr.	Adjusted Trial Balance Cr.
Cash	6155 00				6155 00	
Accounts Receivable	5000 00				5000 00	
Office Supplies	600 00			(A) 500 00	100 00	
Prepaid Rent	1200 00			(B) 400 00	800 00	
Word Processing Equipment	6000 00				6000 00	
Accounts Payable		3350 00				3350 00
Brenda Clark, Capital		10000 00				10000 00
Brenda Clark, Withdrawals	625 00				625 00	
Word Processing Fees		8000 00				8000 00
Office Salaries Expense	1300 00		(D) 350 00		1650 00	
Advertising Expense	250 00				250 00	
Telephone Expense	220 00				220 00	
	21350 00	21350 00				
Office Supplies Expense			(A) 500 00		500 00	
Rent Expense			(B) 400 00		400 00	
Depreciation Exp., W. P. Equip.			(C) 80 00		80 00	
Accum. Deprec., W. P. Equip.				(C) 80 00		80 00
Salaries Payable				(D) 350 00		350 00
			1330 00	1330 00	21780 00	21780 00

If no adjustment is made, just carry over amount from trial balance on same side.

Supplies were $600, but we used up $500, leaving us with a $100 balance (on hand) in Supplies. *Note:* If the account lists both a debit and a credit, take the *difference* between the two and place it on the side that is larger.

Note: Equipment is *not* adjusted here.

Two debits are added together. If there were two credits, they also would have been added together.

Carry these amounts over to adjusted trial balance in the same positions.

Note: The total of the left (debit) must equal the total of the right (credit) ($21,780).

FIGURE 4.10 The Adjusted Trial Balance Section of the Worksheet

TABLE 4.2 Normal Balances and Account Categories

Account Titles	Category	Normal Balance on Adjusted Trial Balance	Income Statement Dr.	Income Statement Cr.	Balance Sheet Dr.	Balance Sheet Cr.
Cash	Asset	Dr.			X	
Accounts Receivable	Asset	Dr.			X	
Office Supplies	Asset	Dr.			X	
Prepaid Rent	Asset	Dr.			X	
Word Proc. Equip.	Asset	Dr.			X	
Accounts Payable	Liability	Cr.				X
Brenda Clark, Capital	Capital	Cr.				X
Brenda Clark, Withdrawals	Withdrawal	Dr.			X	
Word Proc. Fees	Revenue	Cr.		X		
Office Salaries Exp.	Expense	Dr.	X			
Advertising Expense	Expense	Dr.	X			
Telephone Expense	Expense	Dr.	X			
Office Supplies Exp.	Expense	Dr.	X			
Rent Expense	Expense	Dr.	X			
Dep. Exp., W. P. Equip.	Expense	Dr.	X			
Acc. Dep., W. P. Equip.	Contra-Asset	Cr.				X
Salaries Payable	Liability	Cr.				X

FIGURE 4.11 The Income Statement Section of the Worksheet

CLARK'S WORD PROCESSING SERVICES
WORKSHEET
FOR MONTH ENDED MAY 31, 200X

Account Titles	Adjusted Trial Balance Dr.	Adjusted Trial Balance Cr.	Income Statement Dr.	Income Statement Cr.
Cash	6 1 5 5 00			
Accounts Receivable	5 0 0 0 00			
Office Supplies	1 0 0 00			
Prepaid Rent	8 0 0 00			
Word Processing Equipment	6 0 0 0 00			
Accounts Payable		3 3 5 0 00		
B. Clark, Capital		10 0 0 0 00		
B. Clark, Withdrawals	6 2 5 00			
Word Processing Fees		8 0 0 0 00		8 0 0 0 00
Office Salaries Expense	1 6 5 0 00		1 6 5 0 00	
Advertising Expense	2 5 0 00		2 5 0 00	
Telephone Expense	2 2 0 00		2 2 0 00	
Office Supplies Expense	5 0 0 00		5 0 0 00	
Rent Expense	4 0 0 00		4 0 0 00	
Depreciation Exp., W. P. Equip.	8 0 00		8 0 00	
Accum. Deprec., W. P. Equip.		8 0 00		
Salaries Payable		3 5 0 00		
	21 7 8 0 00	21 7 8 0 00	3 1 0 0 00	8 0 0 0 00
Net Income			4 9 0 0 00	
			8 0 0 0 00	8 0 0 0 00

$8,000
−3,100
$4,900

The worksheet in Figure 4.11 shows that the label Net Income is added in the account title column on the same line as $4,900. When the figures result in a net income it will be placed in the debit column of the income statement section of the worksheet. A net loss is placed in the credit column. The $8,000 total indicates that the two columns are in balance.

The Balance Sheet Section

To fill out the balance sheet section of the worksheet the following are carried over from the adjusted trial balance section: assets, contra-assets, liabilities, capital, and withdrawals. Because the beginning figure for Capital* is used on the worksheet, the Net Income is brought over to the credit column of the balance sheet so both columns balance.

> *Remember:* The ending figure for capital is not on the worksheet.

Let's now look at the completed worksheet in Figure 4.12 to see how the balance sheet section is completed. Note how the Net Income of $4,900 is brought over to the credit column of the worksheet. The figure for Capital is also in the credit column while the figure for Withdrawals is in the debit column. By placing the net income in the credit column both sides total $18,680. If a net loss were to occur it would be placed in the debit column of the balance sheet column.

Now that we have completed the worksheet, we can go on to the three financial reports. But first let's summarize our progress.

LEARNING UNIT 4-1 REVIEW

AT THIS POINT / you should be able to

- Define and explain the purpose of a worksheet.
- Explain the need as well as the process for adjustments.
- Explain the concept of depreciation.
- Explain the difference between depreciation expense and accumulated depreciation.
- Prepare a worksheet from a trial balance and adjustment data.

ac
t

Accounting Cycle Tutorial

Self-Review Quiz 4-1

From the accompanying trial balance and adjustment data in Figure 4.13, complete a worksheet for P. Logan Co. for the month ended Dec. 31, 200X. (You can use the blank fold-out worksheet located at the end of the textbook.)

Note: The numbers used on this quiz may seem impossibly small, but we have done that on purpose, so that at this point you don't have to worry about arithmetic, just about preparing the worksheet correctly.

Adjustment Data

a. Depreciation Expense, Store Equipment, $1.
b. Insurance Expired, $2.
c. Supplies on hand, $1.
d. Salaries owed but not paid to employees, $3.

> For additional help go to
> www.pearsonhighered.com/slater

*We assume no additional investments during the period.

CLARK'S WORD PROCESSING SERVICES
WORKSHEET
FOR MONTH ENDED MAY 31, 200X

Account Titles	Trial Balance Dr.	Trial Balance Cr.	Adjustments Dr.	Adjustments Cr.	Adjusted Trial Balance Dr.	Adjusted Trial Balance Cr.	Income Statement Dr.	Income Statement Cr.	Balance Sheet Dr.	Balance Sheet Cr.
Cash	6155 00				6155 00				6155 00	
Accounts Receivable	5000 00				5000 00				5000 00	
Office Supplies	600 00			(A) 500 00	100 00				100 00	
Prepaid Rent	1200 00			(B) 400 00	800 00				800 00	
Word Processing Equipment	6000 00				6000 00				6000 00	
Accounts Payable		3350 00				3350 00				3350 00
B. Clark, Capital		10000 00				10000 00				10000 00
B. Clark, Withdrawals	625 00				625 00				625 00	
Word Processing Fees		8000 00				8000 00		8000 00		
Office Salaries Expense	1300 00		(D) 350 00		1650 00		1650 00			
Advertising Expense	250 00				250 00		250 00			
Telephone Expense	220 00				220 00		220 00			
	21350 00	21350 00								
Office Supplies Expense			(A) 500 00		500 00		500 00			
Rent Expense			(B) 400 00		400 00		400 00			
Depreciation Exp., W. P. Equip.			(C) 80 00		80 00		80 00			
Accum. Deprec., W. P. Equip.				(C) 80 00		80 00				80 00
Salaries Payable				(D) 350 00		350 00				350 00
			1330 00	1330 00	21780 00	21780 00	3100 00	8000 00	18680 00	13780 00
Net Income							4900 00			4900 00
							8000 00	8000 00	18680 00	18680 00

"Used up"

"On hand"

Original cost of $6,000 is not adjusted

contra-asset

FIGURE 4.12

FIGURE 4.13

P. LOGAN COMPANY
TRIAL BALANCE
DECEMBER 31, 200X

	Dr.	Cr.
Cash	1 5 00	
Accounts Receivable	3 00	
Prepaid Insurance	3 00	
Store Supplies	5 00	
Store Equipment	6 00	
Accumulated Depreciation, Store Equipment		4 00
Accounts Payable		2 00
P. Logan, Capital		1 4 00
P. Logan, Withdrawals	3 00	
Revenue from Clients		2 5 00
Rent Expense	2 00	
Salaries Expense	8 00	
	4 5 00	4 5 00

Solution to Self-Review Quiz 4-1

Don't adjust this line! Store Equipment always contains the historical cost.

Note that supplies on hand end up on the adjusted trial balance

Amount used up

P. LOGAN COMPANY
WORKSHEET
FOR MONTH ENDED DECEMBER 31, 200X

Account Titles	Trial Balance Dr.	Trial Balance Cr.	Adjustments Dr.	Adjustments Cr.	Adjusted Trial Balance Dr.	Adjusted Trial Balance Cr.	Income Statement Dr.	Income Statement Cr.	Balance Sheet Dr.	Balance Sheet Cr.
Cash	1500				1500				1500	
Accounts Receivable	300				300				300	
Prepaid Insurance	300			(B) 200	100				100	
Store Supplies	500			(C) 400	100				100	
Store Equipment	600				600				600	
Accum. Depr., Store Equipment		400		(A) 100		500				500
Accounts Payable		200				200				200
P. Logan, Capital		1400				1400				1400
P. Logan, Withdrawals	300				300				300	
Revenue from Clients		2500				2500		2500		
Rent Expense	200				200		200			
Salaries Expense	800		(D) 300		1100		1100			
	4500	4500								
Depr. Exp., Store Equipment			(A) 100		100		100			
Insurance Expense			(B) 200		200		200			
Supplies Expense			(C) 400		400		400			
Salaries Payable				(D) 300		300				300
			1000	1000	4900	4900	2000	2500	2900	2400
Net Income							500			500
							2500	2500	2900	2900

Note that Accumulated Depreciation is listed in trial balance because the company is not new. Store Equipment has already been depreciated $4.00 from an earlier period.

FIGURE 4.14

NEED HELP?

Let's review first: When completing a worksheet we list the original trial balance, add adjustments, complete an adjusted trial balance, and then decide which titles go on the income statement and balance sheet. Since we do not have columns for statement of owner's equity, withdrawals and net income will be placed on the balance sheet columns to arrive at a new figure for capital. Remember, it is the old figure for capital that is placed on the worksheet.

Account title column: Any item not listed on the original trial balance will be listed below the trial balance. This will happen when we make adjustments. Note that when we list each title below the trial balance it will be increasing in value.

Adjustment column:

A. Depreciation:

In this adjustment Accumulated Depreciation is already listed on the trial balance so we only have to add Depreciation Expense below the trial balance. Here is the mind process chart for this adjustment:

Dep. Expense, St. Equip.	Expense	↑	Dr. $1
Acc. Deprec., St. Equip.	Contra-asset	↑	Cr. $1

Note that the original cost of Store Equipment of $6 is not touched.

B. Insurance Expired:

In this adjustment Prepaid Insurance is already listed on the trial balance so we only have to add Insurance Expense below the trial balance. Here is the mind process chart for this adjustment:

Insurance Expense	Expense	↑	Dr. $2
Prepaid Insurance	Asset	↓	Cr. $2

Expired means used up and thus we use the amount of $2.

C. Supplies On Hand:

In this adjustment we have to calculate the amount of supplies used up. We take the beginning amount of supplies of $5 less the amount on hand of $1 to equal the amount used up of $4. This is the amount of the adjustment. Since we have Office Supplies listed on the trial balance we only have to add Supplies Expense below the trial balance. Here is the mind process chart for this adjustment:

Supplies Expense	Expense	↑	Dr. $4
Office Supplies	Asset	↓	Cr. $4

D. Salaries Owed:

In this adjustment we have Salaries Expense already listed on the trial balance. Here we have to add Salaries Expense below the trial balance. The following mind process chart shows the new expense that has been incurred but has not been paid:

Salaries Expense	Expense	↑	Dr. $3
Salaries Payable	Liability	↑	Cr. $3

The sum of all the debits on the adjustments equals the sum of the credits.

Adjusted Trial Balance Columns: Accounts that were not adjusted or added below the trial balance have their balances carried over to the adjusted trial balance. Accounts that were adjusted will have their combined balances carried over to the adjusted trial balance.

For example, Salaries Expense is adjusted by adding the debit balance of $8 and the adjustment of $3 to equal an $11 debit balance on the adjusted trial balance. Every account in the adjusted trial balance will end up on the Income Statement or Balance Sheet columns of the worksheet.

Income Statement Columns: From the adjusted trial balance all revenues and expenses Accounts are listed. Note that when we total the debit and credit columns they do not equal each other until we calculate the difference between revenues and expenses. In this case, the ($5) difference will be added to the debit column of the income statement section so both columns will total $25.

Balance Sheet Columns: From the adjusted trial balance assets and withdrawals will end up in the debit column. The old figures for capital, liabilities, and contra assets are in the credit column. Note that the totals of the columns will not balance until a net income of $5 is placed under the $24. This is done because we use the old figure for capital on the worksheet and there is no column on the worksheet for the statement of owner's equity.

Summary: On the worksheet items accounts listed below the trial balance are increasing. Adjustments for supplies must be used up. The original cost of equipment is never touched in the adjustment process. Capital is the old balance on the worksheet. Net income is the difference between revenue and expenses and is carried over to the credit column of the balance sheet. Net losses would be in opposite columns. Income Statement Columns and Balance Sheet Columns will be out of balance by amount of Net Income.

LO4

Learning Unit 4-2 Step 6 of the Accounting Cycle: Preparing the Financial Statements from the Worksheet

In a computerized system, such as QuickBooks or Peachtree, preparing the financial statements becomes as easy as selecting the statement from the Report menu and setting the date to the correct period.

The formal financial statements can be prepared from the worksheet completed in Learning Unit 4-1. Before beginning, we must check that the entries on the worksheet are correct and in balance. To ensure the accuracy of the figures, we double-check that (1) all entries are recorded in the appropriate column, (2) the correct amounts are entered in the proper places, (3) the addition is correct across the columns (i.e., from the trial balance to the adjusted trial balance to the financial statements), and (4) the columns are added correctly.

Preparing the Income Statement

The first statement to be prepared for Clark's Word Processing Services is the income statement. When preparing the income statement it is important to remember the following:

1. Every figure on the formal statement is on the worksheet. Figure 4.15 on the following page shows where each of these figures goes on the income statement.
2. No debit or credit columns appear on the formal statement.
3. The inside column on financial statements is used for subtotaling.
4. Withdrawals do not go on the income statement; they go on the statement of owner's equity.

Take a moment to look at the income statement in Figure 4.15. Note where items go from the income statement section of the worksheet onto the formal statement.

Preparing the Statement of Owner's Equity

Figure 4.16 is the statement of owner's equity for Clark's. The figure shows where the information comes from on the worksheet. It is important to remember that if additional investments were made, the figure on the worksheet for Capital would not be the beginning figure for Capital. Checking the ledger account for Capital will tell you whether the amount is correct. Note how Net Income and Withdrawals aid in calculating the new figure for Capital.

Preparing the Balance Sheet

In preparing the balance sheet (Fig. 4.17), remember that the balance sheet section totals on the worksheet ($18,680) do *not* match the totals on the formal balance sheet ($17,975). This information is grouped differently on the formal statement. First, in the formal report Accumulated Depreciation ($80) is subtracted from Word Processing Equipment, reducing the balance. Second, Withdrawals ($625) are subtracted from Owner's Equity, reducing the balance further. These two reductions (−$80 − $625 = −$705) represent the difference between the worksheet and the formal version of the balance sheet ($17,975 − $18,680 = −$705). Figure 4.17 shows how to prepare the balance sheet from the worksheet.

LEARNING UNIT 4-2 REVIEW

AT THIS POINT / you should be able to

- Prepare the three financial statements from a worksheet.
- Explain why totals of the formal balance sheet don't match totals of balance sheet columns on the worksheet.

Self-Review Quiz 4-2

From the worksheet for P. Logan, please prepare (1) an income statement for December, (2) a statement of owner's equity, and (3) a balance sheet for December 31, 200X. No additional investments took place during the period.

For additional help go to
www.pearsonhighered.com/slater

Account Titles	Income Statement	
	Dr.	Cr.
Cash		
Accounts Receivable		
Office Supplies		
Prepaid Rent		
Word Processing Equipment		
Accounts Payable		
Brenda Clark, Capital		
Brenda Clark, Withdrawals		
Word Processing Fees		8 0 0 0 00
Office Salaries Expense	1 6 5 0 00	
Advertising Expense	2 5 0 00	
Telephone Expense	2 2 0 00	
Office Supplies Expense	5 0 0 00	
Rent Expense	4 0 0 00	
Depreciation Expense, W. P. Equip.	8 0 00	
Accum. Deprec., W. P. Equip.		
Salaries Payable		
	3 1 0 0 00	8 0 0 0 00
Net Income	4 9 0 0 00	
	8 0 0 0 00	8 0 0 0 00

FIGURE 4.15 From Worksheet to Income Statement

CLARK'S WORD PROCESSING SERVICES
INCOME STATEMENT
FOR MONTH ENDED MAY 31, 200X

Revenue:			
Word Processing Fees			$8 0 0 0 00
Operating Expenses:			
Office Salaries Expense	$1 6 5 0 00		
Advertising Expense	2 5 0 00		
Telephone Expense	2 2 0 00		
Office Supplies Expense	5 0 0 00		
Rent Expense	4 0 0 00		
Depreciation Expense, W. P. Equipment	8 0 00		
Total Operating Expenses			3 1 0 0 00
Net Income			$4 9 0 0 00

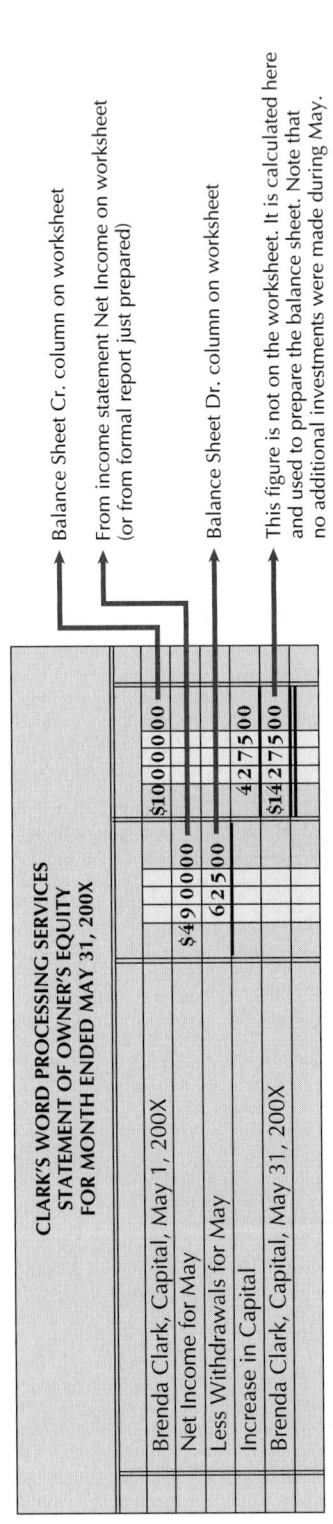

→ Balance Sheet Cr. column on worksheet

→ From income statement Net Income on worksheet (or from formal report just prepared)

→ Balance Sheet Dr. column on worksheet

→ This figure is not on the worksheet. It is calculated here and used to prepare the balance sheet. Note that no additional investments were made during May.

CLARK'S WORD PROCESSING SERVICES
STATEMENT OF OWNER'S EQUITY
FOR MONTH ENDED MAY 31, 200X

Brenda Clark, Capital, May 1, 200X			$10 0 0 0 00
Net Income for May	$4 9 0 0 00		
Less Withdrawals for May	6 2 5 00		
Increase in Capital			4 2 7 5 00
Brenda Clark, Capital, May 31, 200X			$14 2 7 5 00

FIGURE 4.16 Completing a Statement of Owner's Equity

FIGURE 4.17 From Worksheet to Balance Sheet

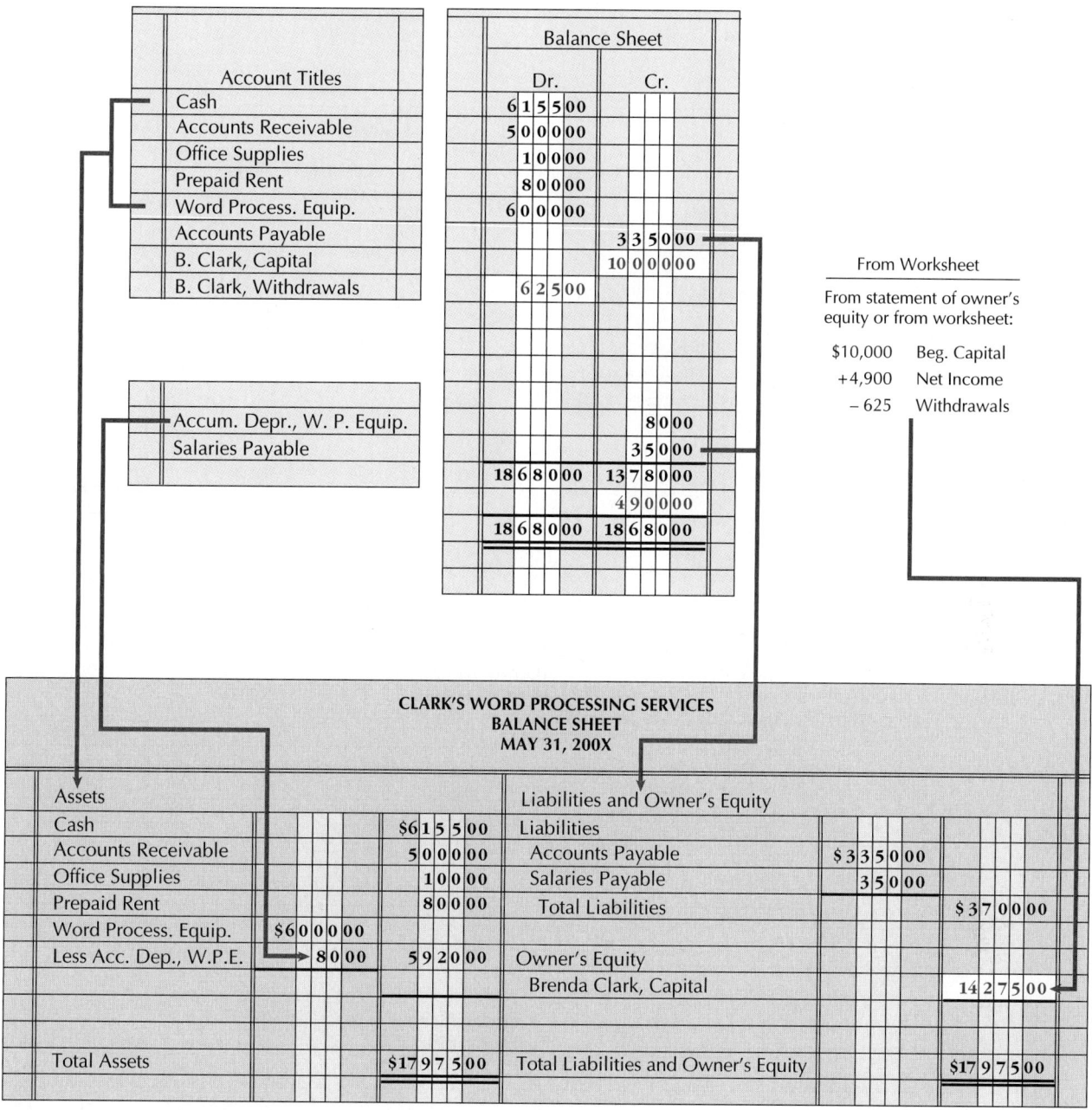

Solution to Self-Review Quiz 4-2

FIGURE 4.18

P. LOGAN COMPANY
INCOME STATEMENT
FOR THE MONTH ENDED DECEMBER 31, 200X

Revenue:			
Revenue from clients			$25 00
Operating Expenses:			
Rent Expense	$2 00		
Salaries Expense	11 00		
Depreciation Expense, Store Equipment	1 00		
Insurance Expense	2 00		
Supplies Expense	4 00		
Total Operating Expenses		20 00	
Net Income		$5 00	

P. LOGAN COMPANY
STATEMENT OF OWNER'S EQUITY
FOR THE MONTH ENDED DECEMBER 31, 200X

P. Logan, Capital, December 1, 200X			$14 00
Net Income for December	$5 00		
Less Withdrawals for December	3 00		
Increase in Capital			2 00
P. Logan, Capital, December 31, 200X			$16 00

P. LOGAN COMPANY
BALANCE SHEET
DECEMBER 31, 200X

Assets			Liabilities and Owner's Equity		
Cash		$15 00	Liabilities		
Accounts Receivable		3 00	Accounts Payable	$2 00	
Prepaid Insurance		1 00	Salaries Payable	3 00	
Store Supplies		1 00	Total Liabilities		$5 00
Store Equipment	$6 00		Owner's Equity		
Less Acc. Dep., St. Eq.	5 00	1 00	P. Logan, Capital		16 00
			Total Liabilities and		
Total Assets		$21 00	Owner's Equity		$21 00

NEED HELP?

Let's review first: There are no debits or credits on the formal financial statements. The three financial statements are made from the last four columns of the worksheet.

Income Statement: The income statement is made up of revenues and expenses. Use the inside column for subtotaling. All numbers found on the income statement are also found on the worksheet.

Statement of Owner's Equity: The net income of $5 is used from the income statement to update the statement of owner's equity. Note that the $14 is the old figure from the worksheet. The increase in capital of $2 is not found on the worksheet. Logan's ending figure of $16 is not found on the worksheet.

Balance Sheet: Logan's ending figure of $16 from the statement of owner's equity is used as the capital figure on the balance sheet. Note under assets how the inside column is used to calculate store equipment less accumulated depreciation. Note that the totals of $21 from the balance sheet are not found on the worksheet. When the financial report is prepared there are no debits or credits.

Summary: The worksheet was prepared in terms of debits and credits, not the formal financial statements. The inside column of the financial statements is for subtotaling. The worksheet used the old figure for Capital while the balance sheet uses the figure from the statement of owner's equity for the new figure of Capital. Many of the numbers on the statement of owner's equity and balance sheet will not be found on the worksheet since there are no debits or credits on formal financial statements.

CHAPTER ASSIGNMENTS

All Classroom Demonstration Exercises, Exercises, Problems, and the Continuing Problem in this chapter can be found within MyAccountingLab, an online homework and practice environment. Your instructor may ask you to complete this material using MyAccountingLab.

MyAccountingLab

DEMONSTRATION PROBLEM: STEPS 5 AND 6 OF THE ACCOUNTING CYCLE

From the following trial balance and additional data complete (1) a worksheet and (2) the three financial statements (numbers are intentionally small so you may concentrate on the theory).

FROST COMPANY
TRIAL BALANCE
DECEMBER 31, 200X

	Dr.	Cr.
Cash	14	
Accounts Receivable	4	
Prepaid Insurance	5	
Plumbing Supplies	3	
Plumbing Equipment	7	
Accumulated Depreciation, Plumbing Equipment		5
Accounts Payable		1
J. Frost, Capital		12
J. Frost, Withdrawals	3	
Plumbing Fees		27
Rent Expense	4	
Salaries Expense	5	
Totals	45	45

Adjustment Data

1. Insurance Expired, $3.
2. Plumbing Supplies on Hand, $1.
3. Depreciation Expense, Plumbing Equipment, $1.
4. Salaries owed but not paid to employees, $2.

Solution Tips to Building a Worksheet

1. Adjustments

a.

Insurance Expense	Expense	↑	Dr.	$3
Prepaid Insurance	Asset	↓	Cr.	$3

Expired means used up

b.

Plumbing Supplies Expense	Expense	↑	Dr.	$2
Plumbing Supplies	Asset	↓	Cr.	$2

$3 − 1 = $2 *used up*

Solution to Worksheet

Original cost not adjusted

"Used up"   "On hand"

FROST COMPANY
WORKSHEET
FOR MONTH ENDED DECEMBER 31, 200X

Account Titles	Trial Balance Dr.	Trial Balance Cr.	Adjustments Dr.	Adjustments Cr.	Adjusted Trial Balance Dr.	Adjusted Trial Balance Cr.	Income Statement Dr.	Income Statement Cr.	Balance Sheet Dr.	Balance Sheet Cr.
Cash	1400				1400				1400	
Accounts Receivable	400				400				400	
Prepaid Insurance	500			(A) 300	200				200	
Plumbing Supplies	300			(B) 200	100				100	
Plumbing Equipment	700				700				700	
Accum. Depr., Plumb. Equip.		500		(C) 100		600				600
Accounts Payable		100				100				100
J. Frost, Capital		1200				1200				1200
J. Frost, Withdrawals	300				300				300	
Plumbing Fees		2700				2700		2700		
Rent Expense	400				400		400			
Salaries Expense	500		(D) 200		700		700			
	4500	4500								
Insurance Expense			(A) 300		300		300			
Plumbing Supplies Expense			(B) 200		200		200			
Depr. Exp. Plumb. Equip.			(C) 100		100		100			
Salaries Payable				(D) 200		200				200
			800	800	4800	4800	1700	2700	3100	2100
Net Income							1000			1000
							2700	2700	3100	3100

FIGURE 4.19

c.

Depreciation Expense, Plumbing Equipment	Expense	↑	Dr.	$1
Contra-Asset Accumulated Depreciation, Plumbing Equipment	Contra-Asset	↑	Cr.	$1

The original cost of equipment of $7 is not "touched."

d.

Salaries Expense	Expense	↑	Dr.	$2
Salaries Payable	Liability	↑	Cr.	$2

2. Last four columns of worksheet prepared from adjusted trial balance.

3. Capital of $12 is the old figure. Net income of $10 (revenue − expenses) is brought over to same side as capital on the balance sheet Cr. column to balance columns.

FROST COMPANY
INCOME STATEMENT
FOR MONTH ENDED DECEMBER 31, 200X

Revenue:		
Plumbing Fees		$27
Operating Expenses:		
Rent Expense	$4	
Salaries Expense	7	
Insurance Expense	3	
Plumbing Supplies Expense	2	
Depreciation Expense, Plumbing Equipment	1	
Total Operating Expenses		17
Net Income		$10

FROST COMPANY
STATEMENT OF OWNER'S EQUITY
FOR MONTH ENDED DECEMBER 31, 200X

J. Frost, Capital, Dec. 1, 200X		$12
Net Income for December	$10	
Less Withdrawals for December	3	
Increase in Capital		7
J. Frost, Capital, Dec. 31, 200X		$19

FROST COMPANY
BALANCE SHEET
DECEMBER 31, 200X

Assets			Liabilities and Owner's Equity		
Cash		$14	Liabilities		
Accounts Receivable		4	Accounts Payable	$1	
Prepaid Insurance		2	Salaries Payable	2	
Plumbing Supplies		1	Total Liabilities		$3
Plumbing Equipment	$7				
Less Accumulated Dep.	6	1	Owner's Equity		
			J. Frost, Capital		19
			Total Liabilities and		
Total Assets		$22	Owner's Equity		$22

Solution Tips for Preparing Financial Statements from a Worksheet

Inside columns of the three financial statements are used for subtotaling. No debits or credits appear on the formal statements.

	Statements
Income Statement	From Income Statement columns of worksheet for revenue and expenses.
Statement of Owner's Equity	Beginning figure for Capital from Balance Sheet worksheet Cr. column. Net Income from Income Statement. Withdrawal figure from Balance Sheet worksheet Dr. column.
Balance Sheet	Assets from Balance Sheet worksheet Dr. column. Liabilities and Accumulated Depreciation from Balance Sheet worksheet Cr. Column. New figure for Capital from statement of owner's equity.

Note how Plumbing Equipment $7 and Accumulated Depreciation $6 are rearranged on the formal balance sheet. The Total Assets of $22 is not on the worksheet. Remember, no debits or credits appear on formal statements.

SUMMARY OF KEY POINTS

LEARNING UNIT 4-1

1. The worksheet is not a formal statement.
2. Adjustments update certain accounts so that they will be up to their latest balance before financial statements are prepared. Adjustments are the result of internal transactions.
3. Adjustments will affect both the income statement and the balance sheet.
4. Accounts listed *below* the account titles on the trial balance of the worksheet are *increasing.*
5. The original cost of a piece of equipment is not adjusted; historical cost is not lost.
6. Depreciation is the process of spreading the original cost of the asset over its expected useful life.
7. Accumulated depreciation is a contra-asset on the balance sheet that summarizes, accumulates, or builds up the amount of depreciation that an asset has accumulated.
8. Book value is the original cost less accumulated depreciation.
9. Accrued salaries are unpaid and unrecorded expenses that are accumulating but for which payment is not yet due.
10. Revenue and expenses go on income statement sections of the worksheet. Assets, contra-assets, liabilities, capital, and withdrawals go on balance sheet sections of the worksheet.

LEARNING UNIT 4-2

1. The formal statements prepared from a worksheet do not have debit or credit columns.
2. Revenue and expenses go on the income statement. Beginning capital plus net income less withdrawals (or, beginning capital minus net loss less withdrawals) go on the statement of owner's equity. Be sure to check the capital account in the ledger to see whether any additional investments took place. Assets, contra-assets, liabilities, and the new figure for capital go on the balance sheet.

KEY TERMS

Accrued salaries payable   Salaries that are earned by employees but unpaid and unrecorded during the period (and thus need to be recorded by an adjustment) and will not come due for payment until the next accounting period.

Accumulated Depreciation   A contra-asset account that summarizes or accumulates the amount of depreciation that has been taken on an asset.

Adjusting   The process of calculating the latest up-to-date balance of each account at the end of an accounting period.

Book value   Cost of equipment less accumulated depreciation.

Depreciation   The allocation (spreading) of the cost of an asset (such as an auto or equipment) over its expected useful life.

Historical cost   The actual cost of an asset at time of purchase.

Residual value   Estimated value of an asset after all the allowable depreciation has been taken.

Worksheet   A columnar device used by accountants to aid them in completing the accounting cycle—often called a spreadsheet. It is not a formal report.

BLUEPRINT OF STEPS 5 AND 6 OF THE ACCOUNTING CYCLE

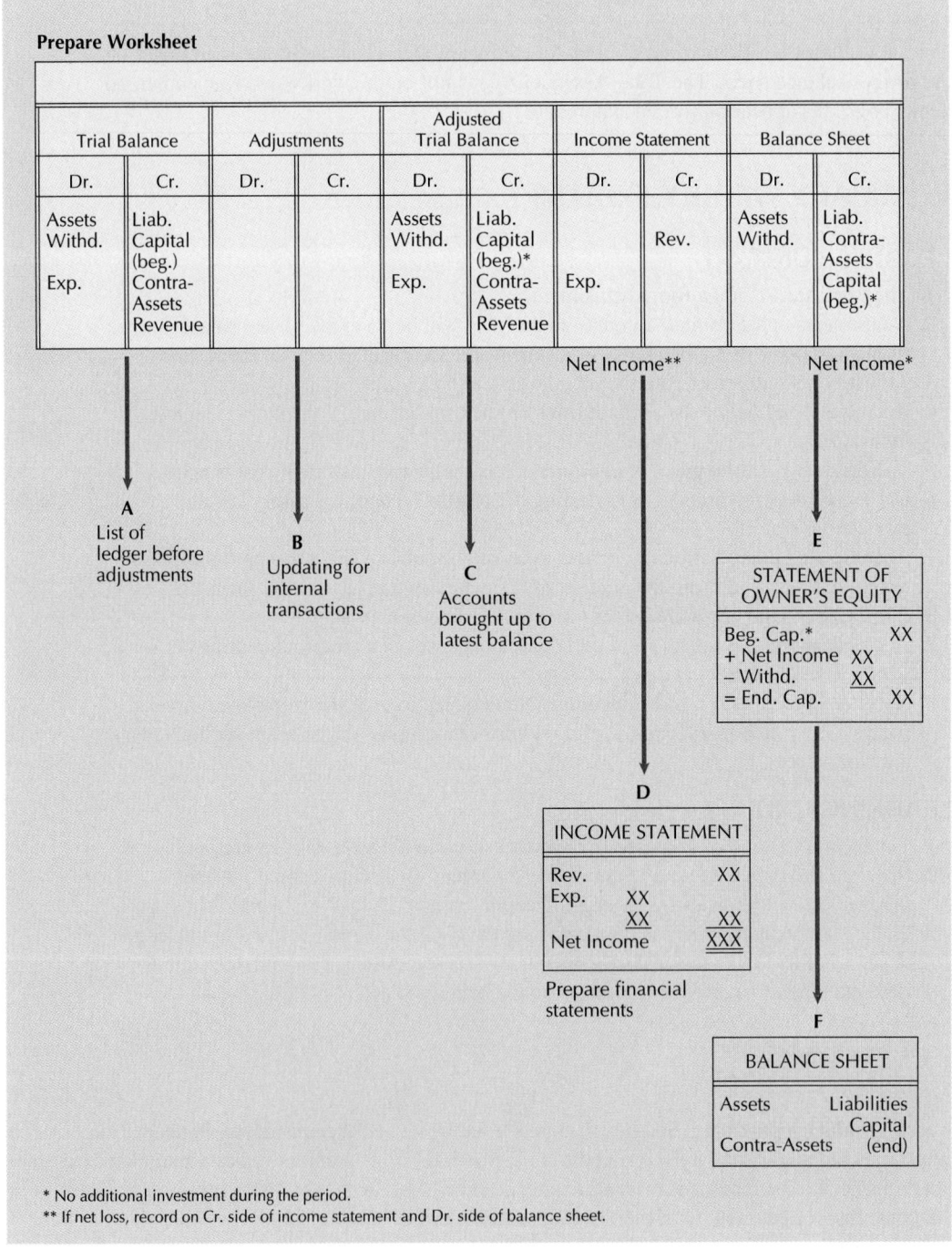

QUESTIONS, CLASSROOM DEMONSTRATION EXERCISES, EXERCISES, AND PROBLEMS

Discussion Questions and Critical Thinking/Ethical Case

1. Worksheets are required in every company's accounting cycle. Please agree or disagree and explain why.

2. What is the purpose of adjusting accounts?

3. What is the relationship of internal transactions to the adjusting process?

4. Explain how an adjustment can affect both the income statement and balance sheet. Please give an example.

5. Why do we need the Accumulated Depreciation account?

6. Depreciation expense goes on the balance sheet. True or false. Why?

7. Each month Accumulated Depreciation grows while Equipment goes up. Agree or disagree? Defend your position.

8. Define the term *accrued salaries*.

9. Why don't the formal financial statements contain debit or credit columns?

10. Explain how the financial statements are prepared from the worksheet.

11. Janet Fox, president of Angel Co., went to a tax seminar. One of the speakers at the seminar advised the audience to put off showing expenses until next year because doing so would allow them to take advantage of a new tax law. When Janet returned to the office, she called in her accountant, Frieda O'Riley. She told Frieda to forget about making any adjustments for salaries in the old year so more expenses could be shown in the new year. Frieda told her that putting off these expenses would not follow generally accepted accounting procedures. Janet said she should do it anyway. You make the call. Write your specific recommendations to Frieda.

Classroom Demonstration Exercises

MyAccountingLab

SET A

Adjustment for Supplies LO1 (5 min)

1. *Before Adjustment*

Office Supplies	Office Supplies Expense
700	

Given: At year end, an inventory of Office Supplies showed $50.
a. How much is the adjustment for Office Supplies?
b. Draw a transaction analysis box for this adjustment.
c. What will the balance of Office Supplies be on the adjusted trial balance?

Adjustment for Prepaid Rent LO1 (10 min)

2. *Before Adjustment*

Prepaid Rent	Rent Expense
1,200	

Given: At year end, rent expired is $700.
a. How much is the adjustment for Prepaid Rent?
b. Draw a transaction analysis box for this adjustment.
c. What will be the balance of Prepaid Rent on the adjusted trial balance?

Adjustment for Depreciation LO1 (10 min)

3. *Before Adjustment*

Equip.	Acc. Dep., Equip.	Dep. Exp., Equip.
9,000	2,000	

Given: At year end, depreciation on Equipment is $2,000.

a. Which of these three T accounts is not affected?

b. Which account is a contra-asset?

c. Draw a transaction analysis box for this adjustment.

d. What will be the balance of these three accounts on the adjusted trial balance?

LO1 (10 min)   **Adjustment for Accrued Salaries**

4. *Before Adjustment*

Salaries Expense		Salaries Payable	
1,400			

Given: Accrued Salaries, $300.

a. Draw a transaction analysis box for this adjustment.

b. What will be the balance of these two accounts on the adjusted trial balance?

LO 2, 3 (15 min)   **Worksheet**

5.   From the following adjusted trial balance titles of a worksheet, identify in which column each account will be listed on the last four columns of the worksheet:

(ID) Income Statement Dr. Column

(IC) Income Statement Cr. Column

(BD) Balance Sheet Dr. Column

(BC) Balance Sheet Cr. Column

	ATB	IS	BS
A. Ex: Legal Fees		IC	
B. Accts. Payable			
C. Cash			
D. Prepaid Advertising			
E. Salaries Payable			
F. Dep. Expense			
G. V., Capital			
H. V., Withdrawals			
I. Computer Supplies			
J. Rent Expense			
K. Supplies Payable			
L. Advertising Expense			
M. Accum. Depreciation			
N. Wages Payable			

LO 4 (15 min)   **6.** From the following balance sheet (which was made from the worksheet and other financial statements), explain why the lettered numbers were not found on the worksheet. *Hint:* No debits or credits appear on the formal financial statements.

LAZE CO. BALANCE SHEET DECEMBER 31, 200X				
Assets			**Liabilities and Owner's Equity**	
Cash		$6	Liabilities	
Acc. Receivable		2	Accounts Payable	$2
Supplies		2	Salaries Payable	1
Equipment	$10		Total Liabilities	$3 (B)
Less Acc. Dep.	4	6 (A)	Owner's Equity	
			J. Laze, Capital	13
			Total Liabilities and	
Total Assets		$16	**Owner's Equity**	$16

SET B

Adjustment for Supplies   *LO1 (5 min)*

1. *Before Adjustment*

Computer Supplies	Computer Supplies Expense
700	

Given: At year end, an inventory of Computer Supplies showed $100.
a. How much is the adjustment for Computer Supplies?
b. Draw a transaction analysis box for this adjustment.
c. What will the balance of Computer Supplies be on the adjusted trial balance?

Adjustment for Prepaid Rent   *LO1 (10 min)*

2. *Before Adjustment*

Prepaid Rent	Rent Expense
700	

Given: At year end, rent expired is $300.
a. How much is the adjustment for Prepaid Rent?
b. Draw a transaction analysis box for this adjustment.
c. What will be the balance of Prepaid Rent on the adjusted trial balance?

Adjustment for Depreciation   *LO1 (10 min)*

3. *Before Adjustment*

Equip.	Acc. Dep., Equip.	Dep. Exp., Equip.
6,000	1,000	

Given: At year end, depreciation on Equipment is $1,000.
a. Which of these three T accounts is not affected?
b. Which account is a contra-asset?
c. Draw a transaction analysis box for this adjustment.
d. What will be the balance of these three accounts on the adjusted trial balance?

Adjustment for Accrued Salaries   *LO1 (10 min)*

4. *Before Adjustment*

Salaries Expense	Salaries Payable
900	

Given: Accrued Salaries, $200.
a. Draw a transaction analysis box for this adjustment.
b. What will be the balance of these two accounts on the adjusted trial balance?

Worksheet   *LO2, 3 (15 min)*

5. From the following adjusted trial balance titles of a worksheet, identify in which column each account will be listed on the last four columns of the worksheet:

(ID) Income Statement Dr. Column

(IC) Income Statement Cr. Column

(BD) Balance Sheet Dr. Column

(BC) Balance Sheet Cr. Column

	ATB	IS	BS
A. Ex: Supplies	~~~	~~~	——	BD
B. Accts. Receivable	~~~	~~~	——	——
C. Cash	~~~	~~~	——	——
D. Prepaid Rent	~~~	~~~	——	——
E. Equipment	~~~	~~~	——	——
F. Acc. Depreciation	~~~	~~~	——	——
G. B., Capital	~~~	~~~	——	——
H. B., Withdrawals	~~~	~~~	——	——
I. Taxi Fees	~~~	~~~	——	——
J. Advertising Expense	~~~	~~~	——	——
K. Off. Supplies Expense	~~~	~~~	——	——
L. Rent Expense	~~~	~~~	——	——
M. Depreciation Expense	~~~	~~~	——	——
N. Salaries Payable	~~~	~~~	——	——

LO2, 3 (15 min)

6. From the following balance sheet (which was made from the worksheet and other financial statements), explain why the lettered numbers were not found on the worksheet. *Hint:* No debits or credits appear on the formal financial statements.

H. WELLS
BALANCE SHEET
DECEMBER 31, 200X

Assets			Liabilities and Owner's Equity		
Cash		$6	Liabilities		
Acc. Receivable		2	Accounts Payable	$2	
Supplies		2	Salaries Payable	1	
Equipment	$10		Total Liabilities		$3
Less Acc. Dep.	4	6	Owner's Equity		
			H. Wells, Capital		13 (B)
			Total Liabilities and		
Total Assets		$16 (A)	**Owner's Equity**		$16

MyAccountingLab

Exercises

LO4 (5 min)

4-1. Complete the following table.

Account	Category	Normal Balance	Which Financial Statement(s) Found
Accounts Payable			
Prepaid Rent			
Office Equipment			
Depreciation Expense			
B. Reel, Capital			
B. Reel, Withdrawals			
Wages Payable			
Accumulated Depreciation			

LO1 (10 min)

4-2. Use transaction analysis charts to analyze the following adjustments:
a. Depreciation on equipment, $600.
b. Rent expired, $400.

4-3. From the following adjustment data, calculate the adjustment amount and record appropriate debits or credits: *LO1 (10 min)*

    a. Supplies purchased, $700.

      Supplies on hand, $200.

    b. Store equipment, $12,000.

      Accumulated depreciation before adjustment, $900.

      Depreciation expense, $200.

4-4. From the following trial balance (Fig. 4.20) and adjustment data, complete a worksheet for J. Trent as of December 31, 200X: *LO3 (20 min)*

    a. Depreciation expense, equipment, $2.00.

    b. Insurance expired, $1.00.

    c. Store supplies on hand, $4.00.

    d. Wages owed, but not paid for (they are an expense in the old year), $5.00.

FIGURE 4.20

J. TRENT
TRIAL BALANCE
DECEMBER 31, 200X

	Dr.	Cr.
Cash	9 00	
Accounts Receivable	2 00	
Prepaid Insurance	7 00	
Store Supplies	6 00	
Store Equipment	7 00	
Accumulated Depreciation, Equipment		2 00
Accounts Payable		4 00
J. Trent, Capital		17 00
J. Trent, Withdrawals	6 00	
Revenue from Clients		24 00
Rent Expense	4 00	
Wage Expense	6 00	
	47 00	47 00

4-5. From the completed worksheet in Exercise 4-4, prepare *LO4 (20 min)*

    a. an income statement for December.

    b. a statement of owner's equity for December.

    c. a balance sheet as of December 31, 200X.

Group A Problems

MyAccountingLab

4A-1. Use the following adjustment data on December 31 to complete a partial worksheet (Fig. 4.21 on the following page) up to the adjusted trial balance. *LO1, 2 (15 min)*

    a. Fitness supplies on hand, $600.

    b. Depreciation taken on fitness equipment, $700.

4A-2. Update the trial balance for Ling's Landscaping Service (Fig. 4.22 on the following page) for December 31, 200X. *LO2, 3 (30 min)*

Adjustment Data to Update the Trial Balance

    a. Rent expired, $600.

    b. Landscaping supplies on hand (remaining), $200.

    c. Depreciation expense, Landscaping equipment, $300.

    d. Wages earned by workers but not paid or due until January, $400.

Your task is to prepare a worksheet for Ling's Landscaping Service for the month of December.

FIGURE 4.21

JILL'S FITNESS CENTER TRIAL BALANCE DECEMBER 31, 200X		
	Debit	Credit
Cash in Bank	10 000 00	
Accounts Receivable	6 000 00	
Fitness Supplies	5 400 00	
Fitness Equipment	9 200 00	
Accumulated Depreciation, Fitness Equipment		7 000 00
J. Walsh, Capital		14 350 00
J. Walsh, Withdrawals	3 000 00	
Fitness Fees		13 300 00
Rent Expense	900 00	
Advertising Expense	150 00	
	34 650 00	34 650 00

Check Figure:
Total of adjusted trial balance
$35,350

FIGURE 4.22

LING'S LANDSCAPING SERVICE TRIAL BALANCE DECEMBER 31, 200X		
	Dr.	Cr.
Cash in Bank	4 000 00	
Accounts Receivable	700 00	
Prepaid Rent	800 00	
Landscaping Supplies	742 00	
Landscaping Equipment	14 000 00	
Accumulated Depreciation, Landscaping Equipment		1 060 00
Accounts Payable		836 00
A. Ling, Capital		3 250 00
Landscaping Revenue		4 356 00
Heat Expense	400 00	
Advertising Expense	200 00	
Wage Expense	1 260 00	
	9 502 00	9 502 00

Check Figure:
Net Income $654

FIGURE 4.23

KEVIN'S MOVING CO. TRIAL BALANCE OCTOBER 31, 200X		
	Dr.	Cr.
Cash	5 000 00	
Prepaid Insurance	2 500 00	
Moving Supplies	1 200 00	
Moving Truck	11 000 00	
Accumulated Depreciation, Moving Truck		9 000 00
Accounts Payable		2 768 00
K. Hoff, Capital		5 442 00
K. Hoff, Withdrawals	1 400 00	
Revenue from Moving		9 000 00
Wage Expense	3 712 00	
Rent Expense	1 080 00	
Advertising Expense	318 00	
	26 210 00	26 210 00

Check Figure:
Net Income $2,140

4A-3. Update the trial balance for Kevin's Moving Co. (Fig. 4.23) for October 31, 200X.   *LO1 (60 min)*

Adjustment Data to Update Trial Balance

   a. Insurance expired, $700.
   b. Moving supplies on hand, $900.
   c. Depreciation on moving truck, $500.
   d. Wages earned but unpaid, $250.

Your task is to
   1. complete a worksheet for Kevin's Moving Co. for the month of October.
   2. prepare an income statement for October, a statement of owner's equity for October, and a balance sheet as of October 31, 200X.

4A-4. The trial balance for Dick's Repair Service appears in Figure 4.24.   *LO2, 3, 4 (60 min)*

FIGURE 4.24

DICK'S REPAIR SERVICE TRIAL BALANCE NOVEMBER 30, 200X		
	Dr.	Cr.
Cash	3 2 0 0 00	
Prepaid Insurance	4 0 0 0 00	
Repair Supplies	4 6 0 0 00	
Repair Equipment	3 0 0 0 00	
Accumulated Depreciation, Repair Equipment		7 0 0 00
Accounts Payable		5 5 7 0 00
D. Horn, Capital		3 8 0 0 00
Revenue from Repairs		7 0 0 0 00
Wages Expense	1 8 0 0 00	
Rent Expense	3 6 0 00	
Advertising Expense	1 1 0 00	
	17 0 7 0 00	17 0 7 0 00

> *Check Figure:*
> Net Income $1,830

Adjustment Data to Update Trial Balance

   a. Insurance expired, $700.
   b. Repair supplies on hand, $3,000.
   c. Depreciation on repair equipment, $200.
   d. Wages earned but unpaid, $400.

Your task is to
   1. complete a worksheet for Dick's Repair Service for the month of November.
   2. prepare an income statement for November, a statement of owner's equity for November, and a balance sheet as of November 30, 200X.

Group B Problems

MyAccountingLab

4B-1. Please complete a partial worksheet (Fig. 4.25 on the following page) up to the adjusted trial balance for Jill's Fitness Center using the following adjustment data: *LO1, 2 (15 min)*
   a. Fitness supplies on hand, $3,000.
   b. Depreciation taken on fitness equipment, $500.

4B-2. Given the trial balance in Figure 4.26 on the following page and adjustment data of Ling's Landscaping Service, your task is to prepare a worksheet for the month of December.

Adjustment Data   *LO2, 3 (30 min)*

   a. Landscaping supplies on hand, $60.
   b. Rent expired, $150.
   c. Depreciation on landscaping equipment, $200.
   d. Wages earned but unpaid, $115.

FIGURE 4.25

JILL'S FITNESS CENTER TRIAL BALANCE DECEMBER 31, 200X		
	Dr.	**Cr.**
Cash	6 0 0 0 00	
Accounts Receivable	2 0 0 0 00	
Fitness Supplies	4 2 0 0 00	
Fitness Equipment	1 1 0 0 0 00	
Accumulated Depreciation, Fitness Equipment		9 7 0 0 00
J. Walsh, Capital		1 1 0 0 0 00
J. Walsh, Withdrawals	1 0 0 0 00	
Fitness Fees		4 4 0 0 00
Rent Expense	8 0 0 00	
Advertising Expense	1 0 0 00	
	25 1 0 0 00	25 1 0 0 00

Check Figure:
Total of Adjusted Trial Balance
$25,600

FIGURE 4.26

LING'S LANDSCAPING SERVICE TRIAL BALANCE DECEMBER 31, 200X		
	Dr.	**Cr.**
Cash in Bank	3 9 6 00	
Accounts Receivable	2 8 4 00	
Prepaid Rent	4 0 0 00	
Landscaping Supplies	3 1 0 00	
Landscaping Equipment	1 0 0 0 00	
Accumulated Depreciation, Landscaping Equipment		2 0 0 00
Accounts Payable		3 4 6 00
A. Ling, Capital		4 5 6 00
Landscaping Revenue		4 6 8 0 00
Heat Expense	6 3 2 00	
Advertising Expense	1 2 0 0 00	
Wage Expense	1 4 6 0 00	
Total	5 6 8 2 00	5 6 8 2 00

Check Figure:
Net Income $673

LO1 (60 min)

4B-3. Using the trial balance in Figure 4.27, and adjustment data of Kevin's Moving Co., prepare
1. a worksheet for the month of October.
2. an income statement for October, a statement of owner's equity for October, and a balance sheet as of October 31, 200X.

Adjustment Data
    a. Insurance expired, $600.
    b. Moving supplies on hand, $310.
    c. Depreciation on moving truck, $580.
    d. Wages earned but unpaid, $410.

LO2, 3, 4 (60 min)

4B-4. As the bookkeeper of Dick's Repair Service, use the information in Figure 4.28, to prepare
1. a worksheet for the month of November.
2. an income statement for November, a statement of owner's equity for November, and a balance sheet as of November 30, 200X.

Adjustment Data
    a. Insurance expired, $300.
    b. Repair supplies on hand, $170.

c. Depreciation on repair equipment, $250.

d. Wages earned but unpaid, $106.

FIGURE 4.27

KEVIN'S MOVING CO. TRIAL BALANCE OCTOBER 31, 200X		
	Dr.	Cr.
Cash	3 9 2 0 00	
Prepaid Insurance	3 2 8 8 00	
Moving Supplies	1 4 0 0 00	
Moving Truck	10 6 5 8 00	
Accumulated Depreciation, Moving Truck		3 6 6 0 00
Accounts Payable		1 3 1 2 00
K. Hoff, Capital		17 4 8 2 00
K. Hoff, Withdrawals	4 2 4 0 00	
Revenue from Moving		8 1 6 2 00
Wages Expense	5 7 1 2 00	
Rent Expense	1 0 8 0 00	
Advertising Expense	3 1 8 00	
	30 6 1 6 00	30 6 1 6 00

Check Figure:
Net Loss $1,628

FIGURE 4.28

DICK'S REPAIR SERVICE TRIAL BALANCE NOVEMBER 30, 200X		
	Dr.	Cr.
Cash	3 2 0 4 00	
Prepaid Insurance	4 0 0 0 00	
Repair Supplies	7 7 0 00	
Repair Equipment	3 1 0 6 00	
Accumulated Depreciation, Repair Equipment		6 5 0 00
Accounts Payable		1 9 0 4 00
D. Horn, Capital		6 2 5 8 00
Revenue from Repairs		5 6 3 4 00
Wages Expense	1 6 0 0 00	
Rent Expense	1 5 6 0 00	
Advertising Expense	2 0 6 00	
	14 4 4 6 00	14 4 4 6 00

Check Figure:
Net Income $1,012

ON-THE-JOB TRAINING

T-1.

LO1 (20 min)

MEMO

To: *Hal Hogan, Bookkeeper*

From: *Pete Tennant, V. P.*

Re: *Adjustments for year ended December 31, 200X*

Hal, here is the information you requested. Please supply me with the adjustments needed ASAP. Also, please put in writing why we need to do these adjustments.

Thanks.

Attached to memo:

a. Insurance data:

Policy No.	Date of Policy Purchase	Policy Length	Cost
100	November 1 of previous year	4 years	$480
200	May 1 of current year	2 years	600
300	September 1 of current year	1 year	240

b. Rent data: Prepaid rent had a $500 balance at the beginning of the year. An additional $400 of rent was paid in advance in June. At year end, $200 of rent had expired.

c. Revenue data: Accrued storage fees of $500 were earned but uncollected and unrecorded at year end.

LO1 (30 min)   **T-2.**

Hint: Unearned Rent is a liability on the balance sheet.

On Friday, Harry Swag's boss asks him to prepare a special report, due on Monday at 8:00 A.M. Harry gathers the following material in his briefcase:

			Dec. 31	
			2009	**2008**
Prepaid Advertising			$300	$600
Interest Payable			150	350
Unearned Rent			500	300
Cash paid for:	Advertising	$1,900		
	Interest	1,500		
Cash received for:	Rent	2,300		

As his best friend, could you help Harry show the amounts that are to be reported on the income statement for (a) Advertising Expense, (b) Interest Expense, and (c) Rent Fees Earned. Please explain in writing why Unearned Rent is considered a liability.

FINANCIAL REPORT PROBLEM

LO1 (20 min)   ### Reading the Kellogg's Annual Report

Go to Appendix A and look at Note 1 under Property. Find out how Kellogg's depreciates its equipment. How is the equipment recorded?

INTERNET PROJECT

Black & Decker

Go to the Web and search: Annual Report Black & Decker 2008.
Click on Investors Relations.
List out the latest news Black & Decker is providing to its investors.
Order a free annual report.

CONTINUING PROBLEM

Sanchez Computer Center

LO2, 3, 4 (45 min)

At the end of September, Tony took a complete inventory of his supplies and found the following:

> 5 dozen ¼″ screws at a cost of $8.00 a dozen
>
> 2 dozen ½″ screws at a cost of $5.00 a dozen
>
> 2 cartons of computer inventory paper at a cost of $14 a carton
>
> 3 feet of coaxial cable at a cost of $4.00 per foot

After speaking to his accountant, he found that a reasonable depreciation amount for each of his long-term assets is as follows:

Computer purchased July 5, 200X	Depreciation $33 a month
Office equipment purchased July 17, 200X	Depreciation $10 a month
Computer workstations purchased Sept. 17, 200X	Depreciation $20 a month

Tony uses the straight-line method of depreciation and declares no salvage value for any of the assets. If any long-term asset is purchased in the first 15 days of the month, he will charge depreciation for the full month. If an asset is purchased on the 16th of the month, or later, he will not charge depreciation in the month it was purchased.

August and September's rent has now expired.

Assignment

Use your trial balance from the completed problem in Chapter 3 and the adjusting information given here to complete the worksheet for the three months ended September 30, 200X. From the worksheets prepare the financial statements.

SUBWAY Case

WHERE THE DOUGH GOES . . .   *LO1, 2, 3 (20 min)*

No matter how harried Stan Hernandez feels as the owner of his own Subway restaurant, the aroma of his fresh-baked gourmet breads *always* perks him up. However, the sales generated by Subway's line of gourmet seasoned breads perks Stan up even more. Subway restaurants introduced freshly baked bread in 1983, a practice that made it stand out from other fast-food chains and helped build its reputation for made-to-order freshness. Since then Subway franchisees have introduced many types of gourmet seasoned breads—such as Hearty Italian or Monterey Cheddar—according to a schedule determined by headquarters.

Stan was one month into the "limited-time promotion" for the chain's new Roasted Garlic seasoned bread when his bake oven started faltering. "The temperature controls just don't seem quite right," said his employee and "sandwich artist," Rashid. "It's taking incrementally longer to bake the bread."

"This couldn't happen at a worse time," moaned Stan. "We're baking enough Roasted Garlic bread to keep a whole town of vampires away, but if we don't get it out of the oven fast enough, we'll keep our customers away!"

That very day Stan called his field consultant, Mariah, to discuss what to do about his bake oven. Mariah reminded Stan that his oven trouble illustrated the flip side of buying an existing store from a retired franchisee—having to repair or replace worn or old equipment. After receiving a rather expensive repair estimate and considering the age of the oven, Stan ultimately decided it would make sense for him to purchase a new one. Mariah concurred, "At the rate your sales are going, Stan, you're going to need that roomier new model."

"Wow, do you realize how much this new bake oven is going to cost me?—$3,000!" Stan exclaimed while meeting with his cousin-turned-Subway-accountant, Lila Hernandez. "Yes, it's a lot to lay out, Stan," said Lila, "but you'll be depreciating the cost over a period of 10 years, which will help you at tax time. Let's do the adjustment on your worksheet, so you can see it."

The two of them were sitting in Stan's small office, behind the Subway kitchen, and they pulled up this month's worksheet on Stan's Peachtree program. Lila laughed, "I'm sure glad you started entering your worksheets on Peachtree again! The figures on those old ones were so doodled over and crossed out that I could barely decipher them! We may need your worksheets at tax time."

"Anything for you, *mi prima*," Stan said. "I may depreciate my bake oven, but my gratitude for your accounting skills only appreciates with time!"

Discussion Questions

1. If you are using a straight-line method of depreciation and Stan's bake oven has a residual value of $1,000, how much depreciation will he account for each year and what would the adjustment be for each month?
2. Where does Lila get the information on the useful life of Stan's bake oven and the estimate for its residual value? Why do you think she gets her information from this particular source?
3. Why is a clear worksheet helpful even after that month's statements have been prepared?

PEACHTREE COMPUTER WORKSHOP

COMPUTERIZED ACCOUNTING APPLICATION FOR CHAPTER 4

Refresher on using Peachtree Complete Accounting

Before starting this assignment, you may want to refresh your memory by reading the following PDF documents found in the multimedia library on the MyAccountingLab Web site. Remember to choose the PDF document for your version of Peachtree.

1. An Introduction to Peachtree Complete Accounting
2. Correcting Peachtree Transactions
3. How to Repeat or Restart a Peachtree Assignment
4. Backing Up and Restoring Your Work in Peachtree

You also should have completed Workshop 1 for the Atlas Company in Chapter 3.

Workshop 2:

Compound Journal Entries, Adjusting Entries, and Financial Reports
In this workshop you will post compound journal entries and adjusting journal entries for Zell Company using Peachtree. You will also print the general journal report, trial balance, income statement, and balance sheet.

Instructions and the data file for completing this assignment are in the multimedia library of the MyAccountingLab Web site. Open the **Workshop 2 Zell Company** PDF document for your version of Peachtree and download the **Zell Company** data file for your version of Peachtree.

QUICKBOOKS COMPUTER WORKSHOP

COMPUTERIZED ACCOUNTING APPLICATION FOR CHAPTER 4

Refresher on using QuickBooks Pro

Before starting this assignment, you may want to refresh your memory by reading the following PDF documents found in the multimedia library on the MyAccountingLab Web site. Remember to choose the PDF document for your version of QuickBooks.

1. An Introduction to Computerized Accounting
2. Installing QuickBooks Pro and Student Data Files
3. An Introduction to QuickBooks Pro
4. Correcting QuickBooks Transactions
5. How to Repeat or Restart a QuickBooks Assignment
6. Backing Up and Restoring Your Work in QuickBooks. You also should have completed Workshop 1 for the Atlas Company in Chapter 3.

Workshop 2:

Compound Journal Entries, Adjusting Entries, and Financial Reports
In this workshop you will post compound journal entries and adjusting journal entries for Zell Company using Quickbooks. You will also print the general journal report, trial balance, income statement, and balance sheet.

Instructions and the data file for completing this assignment are in the multimedia library of the MyAccountingLab Web site. Open the *Workshop 2 Zell Company* PDF document for your version of Quickbooks and download the *Zell Company* data file for your version of Quickbooks.

5

The Accounting Cycle Completed

DID YOU KNOW? Amazon recognizes revenue when delivery has occurred or services have been rendered. Visit *www.amazon.com* to find more information about Amazon.

LEARNING OBJECTIVES

1. Journalizing and posting adjusting entries.

2. Journalizing and posting closing entries.

3. Preparing a post-closing trial balance.

In computerized accounting, this process has been completed. Entries are both journalized and posted at the same time.

Each accounting cycle completed by Amazon will end with the preparation of a post-closing trial balance. In Chapters 3 and 4 we completed these steps of the manual accounting cycle for Clark's Word Processing Services:

Step 1 Business transactions occurred and generated source documents.

Step 2 Business transactions were analyzed and recorded into a journal.

Step 3 Information was posted or transferred from journal to ledger.

Step 4 A trial balance was prepared.

Step 5 A worksheet was completed.

Step 6 Financial statements were prepared.

This chapter covers the following steps to complete Clark's accounting cycle for the month of May:

Step 7 Journalizing and posting adjusting entries.

Step 8 Journalizing and posting closing entries.

Step 9 Preparing a post-closing trial balance.

LO1 Learning Unit 5-1 Journalizing and Posting Adjusting Entries: Step 7 of the Accounting Cycle

Recording Journal Entries from the Worksheet

At this point, many ledger accounts are not up-to-date.

The information in the worksheet is up-to-date. The financial reports prepared from that information can give the business's management and other interested parties a good idea of where the business stands as of a particular date. The problem is that the worksheet is an informal report. The information concerning the adjustments has not been placed into the journal or posted to the ledger accounts, which means that the books are not up-to-date and ready for the next accounting cycle to begin. For example, the ledger shows $1,200 of Prepaid Rent, but the balance sheet we prepared in Chapter 4 shows an $800 balance. Essentially, the worksheet is a tool for preparing financial statements. Now we must use the adjustment columns of the worksheet as a basis for bringing the ledger up-to-date. To update the ledger, we use **adjusting journal entries** (see Figs. 5.1, 5.2). Again, the updating must be done before the next accounting period starts. For Clark's Word Processing Services, the next period begins on June 1.

Figure 5.2 shows the adjusting journal entries for Clark's taken from the adjustments section of the worksheet. Once the adjusting journal entries are posted to the ledger, the accounts making up the financial statements that were prepared from the worksheet will equal the updated ledger. (Keep in mind that we are using the same journal and ledger as in the previous chapters.) Let's look at some simplified T accounts to show how Clark's ledger looked before and after the adjustments (A–D) were posted.

Adjustment (A)

Before Posting:	**Office Supplies 114**	**Office Supplies Expense 514**
	600	
After Posting:	**Office Supplies 114**	**Office Supplies Expense 514**
	600 | 500	500

Account Titles	Trial Balance		Adjustments	
	Dr.	Cr.	Dr.	Cr.
Cash	6 1 5 5 00			
Accounts Receivable	5 0 0 0 00			
Office Supplies	6 0 0 00			(A) 5 0 0 00
Prepaid Rent	1 2 0 0 00			(B) 4 0 0 00
Word Processing Equipment	6 0 0 0 00			
Accounts Payable		3 3 5 0 00		
Brenda Clark, Capital		10 0 0 0 00		
Brenda Clark, Withdrawals	6 2 5 00			
Word Processing Fees		8 0 0 0 00		
Office Salaries Expense	1 3 0 0 00		(D) 3 5 0 00	
Advertising Expense	2 5 0 00			
Telephone Expense	2 2 0 00			
	21 3 5 0 00	21 3 5 0 00		
Office Supplies Expense			(A) 5 0 0 00	
Rent Expense			(B) 4 0 0 00	
Depreciation Exp., W. P. Equip.			(C) 8 0 00	
Accum. Deprec., W. P. Equip.				(C) 8 0 00
Salaries Payable				(D) 3 5 0 00
			1 3 3 0 00	1 3 3 0 00

FIGURE 5.1 Journalizing and Posting Adjustments from the Adjustments Section of the Worksheet

CLARK'S WORD PROCESSING SERVICES
GENERAL JOURNAL

Page 2

Date		Account Titles and Description	PR	Dr.	Cr.
		Adjusting Entries			
May	31	Office Supplies Expense	514	5 0 0 00	
		Office Supplies	114		5 0 0 00
	31	Rent Expense	515	4 0 0 00	
		Prepaid Rent	115		4 0 0 00
	31	Depreciation Expense, W. P. Equip.	516	8 0 00	
		Accumulated Depreciation, W. P. Equip.	122		8 0 00
	31	Office Salaries Expense	511	3 5 0 00	
		Salaries Payable	212		3 5 0 00

FIGURE 5.2 Adjustments A–D in the Adjustments Section of the Worksheet Must Be Recorded in the Journal and Posted to the Ledger

Each adjustment affects both the income statement and balance sheet and never affects cash.

Adjustment (B)

Before Posting:	**Prepaid Rent 115**	**Rent Expense 515**
	1,200	

After Posting:	**Prepaid Rent 115**	**Rent Expense 515**
	1,200 | 400	400

Adjustment (C)

Before Posting:

Word Processing Equipment 121	**Depreciation Expense, W. P. Equipment 516**	**Accumulated Depreciation, W. P. Equipment 122**
6,000		

After Posting:

Word Processing Equipment 121	**Depreciation Expense, W. P. Equipment 516**	**Accumulated Depreciation, W. P. Equipment 122**
6,000	80	| 80

The first adjustment in (C) shows the same balances for Depreciation Expense and Accumulated Depreciation. However, in subsequent adjustments the Accumulated Depreciation balance will keep getting larger, but the debit to Depreciation Expense and the credit to Accumulated Depreciation will be the same. We will see why in a moment.

Adjustment (D)

Before Posting:	**Office Salaries Expense 511**	**Salaries Payable 212**
	650	
	650	

After Posting:	**Office Salaries Expense 511**	**Salaries Payable 212**
	650	350
	650	
	350	

LEARNING UNIT 5-1 REVIEW

AT THIS POINT you should be able to

Accounting Cycle Tutorial

- Define and state the purpose of adjusting entries.
- Journalize adjusting entries from the worksheet.
- Post journalized adjusting entries to the ledger.
- Compare specific ledger accounts before and after posting of the journalized adjusting entries.

Self-Review Quiz 5-1

Turn to the worksheet of P. Logan (Figure 4.14 in Chapter 4) and (1) journalize and post the adjusting entries and (2) compare the adjusted ledger accounts before and after the adjustments are posted. T accounts are provided in your study guide with beginning balances.

Solution to Self-Review Quiz 5-1

Date		Account Titles and Description	PR	Dr.	Cr.
		Adjusting Entries			
Dec.	31	Depreciation Expense, Store Equip.	511	1 00	
		Accumulated Depreciation, Store Equip.	122		1 00
	31	Insurance Expense	516	2 00	
		Prepaid Insurance	116		2 00
	31	Supplies Expense	514	4 00	
		Store Supplies	114		4 00
	31	Salaries Expense	512	3 00	
		Salaries Payable	212		3 00

Page 2

FIGURE 5.3 Journalized Adjusting Entries

> For additional help go to
> www.pearsonhighered.com/slater

Partial Ledger

Before Posting

Depreciation Expense, Store Equipment 511	Accumulated Depreciation Store Equipment 122
	4

Prepaid Insurance 116	Insurance Expense 516
3	

Store Supplies 114	Supplies Expense 514
5	

Salaries Expense 512	Salaries Payable 212
8	

After Posting

Depreciation, Expense, Store Equipment 511	Accumulated Depreciation, Store Equipment 122
1	4
	1

Prepaid Insurance 116	Insurance Expense 516
3 2	2

Store Supplies 114	Supplies Expense 514
5 4	4

Salaries Expense 512	Salaries Payable 212
8	3
3	

NEED HELP?

Let's review first: Once the financial statements are prepared from the worksheet our ledger is still not up-to-date. Information about the adjustments on the worksheet have not been journalized or posted to the ledger.

How to update the ledger with adjustments on the worksheet: Using the worksheet of Logan Company, go to the adjustments column and journalize the four adjusting entries. Once the adjustments are journalized they must be posted to the ledger. When the postings are complete, the titles for depreciation expense, accumulated depreciation, insurance expense, prepaid insurance, supplies expense, store supplies, salaries expense, and salaries payable will have the latest, up-to-date balances.

Summary: The ending balances in the ledger after posting adjustments will be the same amounts that were found on the adjusted trial balance.

LO2 Learning Unit 5-2 Journalizing and Posting Closing Entries: Step 8 of the Accounting Cycle

> Closing is not a necessary step when using Peachtree or QuickBooks. Net income is calculated after each transaction, and financial statements are current.

To make recording of the next period's transactions easier, a mechanical step, called *closing*, is taken by Clark's accountant. Closing is intended to end—or close off—the revenue, expense, and withdrawal accounts at the end of the accounting period. The information needed to complete closing entries will be found in the income statement and balance sheet sections of the worksheet.

To make it easier to understand this process, we will first look at the difference between temporary (nominal) accounts and permanent (real) accounts.

Here is the expanded accounting equation we used in an earlier chapter:

$$\text{Assets} = \text{Liabilities} + \text{Capital} - \text{Withdrawals} + \text{Revenues} - \text{Expenses}$$

> Permanent accounts are found on the balance sheet.

Three of the items in that equation—Assets, Liabilities, and Capital—are known as **real** or **permanent accounts** because their balances are carried over from one accounting period to another. The other three items—Withdrawals, Revenues, and Expenses—are called **nominal** or **temporary accounts** because their balances are not carried over from one accounting period to another. Instead, their "balances" are reset at zero at the beginning of each accounting period by closing their balances at the end of the prior period. This process allows us to accumulate new data about revenue, expenses, and withdrawals in the new accounting period. The process of closing summarizes the effects of the temporary accounts on Capital for that period using **closing journal entries.** When the closing process is complete, the accounting equation will be reduced to

$$\text{Assets} = \text{Liabilities} + \text{Ending Capital}$$

> After all closing entries are journalized and posted to the ledger, all temporary accounts have a zero balance in the ledger. Closing is a step-by-step process.

If you look back to Figure 4.16 in Chapter 4, you will see that we already calculated the new capital on the balance sheet to be $14,275 for Clark's Word Processing Services. Before the mechanical closing procedures are journalized and posted, Clark's Capital account in the ledger is only $10,000 (Chapter 3, Figure 3.19). Let's look now at how to journalize and post closing entries.

How to Journalize Closing Entries

Four steps are needed in journalizing closing entries:

> An Income Summary is a temporary account located in the chart of accounts under Owner's Equity. It does not have a normal balance of a debit or a credit.

Step 1 Clear to zero the revenue balance and transfer it to Income Summary. **Income Summary** is a temporary account in the ledger needed for closing. At the end of the closing process, Income Summary will no longer hold a balance.

$$\text{Revenue} \longrightarrow \text{Income Summary}$$

Step 2 Clear to zero the individual expense balances and transfer them to Income Summary.

$$\text{Expenses} \longrightarrow \text{Income Summary}$$

Step 3 Clear to zero the balance in Income Summary and transfer it to Capital.

$$\text{Income Summary} \longrightarrow \text{Capital}$$

Step 4 Clear to zero the balance in Withdrawals and transfer it to Capital.

$$\text{Withdrawals} \longrightarrow \text{Capital}$$

Figure 5.4 is a visual representation of these four steps. Keep in mind that this information must first be journalized and then posted to the appropriate ledger accounts. The worksheet presented in Figure 5.5 contains all the figures we will need for the closing process.

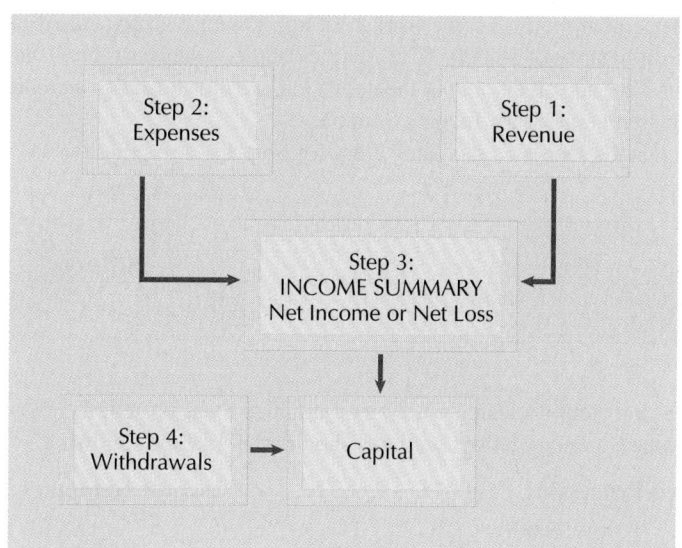

FIGURE 5.4 Four Steps in Journalizing Closing Entries (All numbers can be found on the worksheet in Figure 5.5.)

> *Don't forget two goals of closing:*
> 1. Clear all temporary accounts in ledger.
> 2. Update Capital to a new balance that reflects a summary of all the temporary accounts.

FIGURE 5.5 Closing Figures on the Worksheet

Account Titles	Income Statement Dr.	Income Statement Cr.	Balance Sheet Dr.	Balance Sheet Cr.
Cash			6 1 5 5 00	
Accounts Receivable			5 0 0 0 00	
Office Supplies			1 0 0 00	
Prepaid Rent			8 0 0 00	
Word Processing Equipment			6 0 0 0 00	
Accounts Payable				3 3 5 0 00
B. Clark, Capital		For Step 1		10 0 0 0 00
B. Clark, Withdrawals	For Step 2		6 2 5 00	
Word Processing Fees		8 0 0 0 00		
Office Salaries Expense	1 6 5 0 00		For Step 4	
Advertising Expense	2 5 0 00			
Telephone Expense	2 2 0 00			
Office Supplies Expense	5 0 0 00			
Rent Expense	4 0 0 00			
Depreciation Exp., W. P. Equip.	8 0 00			
Acc. Depreciation, W. P. Equip.		For Step 3		8 0 00
Salaries Payable				3 5 0 00
	3 1 0 0 00	8 0 0 0 00	18 6 8 0 00	13 7 8 0 00
Net Income	4 9 0 0 00			4 9 0 0 00
	8 0 0 0 00	8 0 0 0 00	18 6 8 0 00	18 6 8 0 00

> All numbers used in the closing process can be found on the worksheet. Note that the account Income Summary is not on the worksheet.

Step 1: Clear Revenue Balance and Transfer to Income Summary Here is what is in the ledger before closing entries are journalized and posted:

Word Processing Fees 411	Income Summary 313
8,000	

The income statement section on the worksheet in Figure 5.5 shows that Word Processing Fees has a credit balance of $8,000. To close or clear this balance to zero, a debit of $8,000 is needed. But if we add an amount to the debit side, we must also add a credit—so we add $8,000 on the credit side of the Income Summary.

Figure 5.6 is the journalized closing entry for Step 1:

FIGURE 5.6 Closing Revenue to Income Summary

May	31	Word Processing Fees	411	8 0 0 0 00	
		Income Summary	313		8 0 0 0 00

After the first step of closing entries is journalized and posted, the Word Processing Fees and Income Summary ledger accounts should look like the following:

Word Processing Fees 411		**Income Summary 313**	
8,000	8,000		8,000
Closing	**Revenue**		**Revenue**

Note that the revenue balance is cleared to zero and transferred to Income Summary, a temporary account also located in the ledger.

Step 2: Clear Individual Expense Balances and Transfer the Total to Income Summary
The ledger for each expense account is shown here before closing entries are journalized and posted. Each expense is listed on the worksheet in the debit column of the income statement section in Figure 5.5.

> Remember, the worksheet is a tool. The accountant realizes that the information about the total of the expenses will be transferred to the Income Summary.

Office Salaries Expense 511	**Advertising Expense 512**
650	250
650	
350	

Telephone Expense 513	**Office Supplies Expense 514**
220	500

	Depreciation Expense, W. P. Equipment 516
Rent Expense 515	
400	80

The income statement section of the worksheet lists all the expenses as debits. If we want to reduce each expense to zero, each one must be credited.

Figure 5.7 is the journalized closing entry for Step 2:

FIGURE 5.7 Closing Each Expense to Income Summary

	31	Income Summary	313	3 1 0 0 00	
		Office Salaries Expense	511		1 6 5 0 00
		Advertising Expense	512		2 5 0 00
		Telephone Expense	513		2 2 0 00
		Office Supplies Expense	514		5 0 0 00
		Rent Expense	515		4 0 0 00
		Depreciation Expense, W. P. Equip.	516		8 0 00

> The $3,100 is the total of the expenses on the worksheet.

Individual expenses and Income Summary accounts should look like the following after closing entries are journalized and posted:

Office Salaries Expense 511			
650	Closing	1,650
650		
350		

Advertising Expense 512		
250	Closing	250

Telephone Expense 513		
220	Closing	220

Office Supplies Expense 514		
500	Closing	500

Rent Expense 515		
400	Closing	400

Depreciation Expense, W. P. Equipment 516		
80	Closing	80

Income Summary 313		
Expenses	**Revenue**	
Step 2 3,100	8,000	Step 1

Step 3: Clear Balance in Income Summary (Net Income) and Transfer It to Capital The Income Summary and B. Clark, Capital, accounts look this way before Step 3:

Income Summary 313		**B. Clark, Capital 311**
3,100	8,000	10,000
	4,900	

Note that the balance of Income Summary (Revenues minus Expenses, or $8,000 − $3,100) is $4,900. We must clear that amount from the Income Summary account and transfer to the B. Clark, Capital, account.

In order to transfer the balance of $4,900 from Income Summary (check the bottom debit column of the income statement section on the worksheet in Fig. 5.5) to Capital, it will be necessary to debit Income Summary for $4,900 (the difference between the revenue and expenses) and credit or increase Capital of B. Clark for $4,900.

Figure 5.8 is the journalized closing entry for Step 3:

	31	Income Summary	313	4 9 0 0 00		
		B. Clark, Capital	311			4 9 0 0 00

FIGURE 5.8 Closing Net Income to B. Clark, Capital

The Income Summary and B. Clark, Capital, accounts will look like the following in the ledger after the closing entries of Step 3 are journalized and posted:

	Income Summary 313		**B. Clark, Capital 311**	
Total of Expenses →	3,100	8,000 ← Revenue	10,000	Net
Debit to close account →	4,900	4,900 ← Net Income	4,900 ← Income	

> At the end of these three steps, the Income Summary has a zero balance. If we had a net loss, the end result would be to decrease Capital. The entry would be debit Capital and credit Income Summary for the loss.

Step 4: Clear the Withdrawals Balance and Transfer It to Capital Next, we must close the Withdrawals account. The B. Clark, Withdrawals, and B. Clark, Capital, accounts now look like this:

B. Clark, Withdrawals 312	**B. Clark, Capital 311**
625	10,000
	4,900

To bring the Withdrawals account to a zero balance and summarize its effect on Capital, we must credit Withdrawals and debit Capital.

Remember, withdrawals are a nonbusiness expense and thus are not transferred to Income Summary. The closing entry is journalized as shown in Figure 5.9.

FIGURE 5.9 Closing Withdrawal to B. Clark, Capital

		31	B. Clark, Capital	311	6 2 5 00	
			B. Clark, Withdrawals	312		6 2 5 00

At this point the B. Clark, Withdrawals, and B. Clark, Capital, accounts would look this way in the ledger.

Note that the $10,000 is a beginning balance because no additional investments were made during the period.

B. Clark, Withdrawals 312

625	Closing 625

B. Clark, Capital 311

625	10,000
Withdrawals	Beg. Balance
	4,900
	Net Income

Now let's look at a summary of the closing entries in Figure 5.10.

FIGURE 5.10 Four Closing Entries

			SUMMARY OF CLOSING ENTRIES				
	Date		Account Titles and Description	PR	Dr.	Cr.	
			Closing Entries				
	200X						
	May	31	Word Processing Fees	411	8 0 0 0 00		
			Income Summary	313		8 0 0 0 00	← Step 1
		31	Income Summary	313	3 1 0 0 00		
			Office Salaries Expense	511		1 6 5 0 00	
			Advertising Expense	512		2 5 0 00	
			Telephone Expense	513		2 2 0 00	← Step 2
			Office Supplies Expense	514		5 0 0 00	
			Rent Expense	515		4 0 0 00	
			Depreciation Expense, W. P. Equip.	516		8 0 00	
		31	Income Summary	313	4 9 0 0 00		
			B. Clark, Capital	311		4 9 0 0 00	← Step 3
		31	B. Clark, Capital	311	6 2 5 00		
			B. Clark, Withdrawals	312		6 2 5 00	← Step 4

The following figure shows the complete ledger for Clark's Word Processing Services (see Fig. 5.11). Note how "adjusting" or "closing" is written in the explanation column of individual ledgers, as, for example, in the one for Office Supplies. If the goals of closing have been achieved, only permanent accounts will have balances carried to the next accounting period. All temporary accounts should have zero balances.

FIGURE 5.11 Complete Ledger

CLARK'S WORD PROCESSING SERVICES
GENERAL LEDGER

Cash   Account No. 111

Date	Explanation	Post. Ref.	Debit	Credit	Balance Debit	Balance Credit
200X May 1		GJ1	10 0 0 0 00		10 0 0 0 00	
1		GJ1		1 0 0 0 00	9 0 0 0 00	
1		GJ1		1 2 0 0 00	7 8 0 0 00	
7		GJ1	3 0 0 0 00		10 8 0 0 00	
15		GJ1		6 5 0 00	10 1 5 0 00	
20		GJ1		6 2 5 00	9 5 2 5 00	
27		GJ2		6 5 0 00	8 8 7 5 00	
28		GJ2		2 5 0 0 00	6 3 7 5 00	
29		GJ2		2 2 0 00	6 1 5 5 00	

Accounts Receivable   Account No. 112

Date	Explanation	Post. Ref.	Debit	Credit	Balance Debit	Balance Credit
200X May 22		GJ1	5 0 0 0 00		5 0 0 0 00	

Office Supplies   Account No. 114

Date	Explanation	Post. Ref.	Debit	Credit	Balance Debit	Balance Credit
200X May 3		GJ1	6 0 0 00		6 0 0 00	
31	Adjusting	GJ2		5 0 0 00	1 0 0 00	

(*continued on next page*)

FIGURE 5.11 (*continued*)

Prepaid Rent   Account No. 115

Date		Explanation	Post. Ref.	Debit	Credit	Balance Debit	Balance Credit
200X May	1		GJ1	1 2 0 0 00		1 2 0 0 00	
	31	Adjusting	GJ2		4 0 0 00	8 0 0 00	

Word Processing Equipment   Account No. 121

Date		Explanation	Post. Ref.	Debit	Credit	Balance Debit	Balance Credit
200X May	1		GJ1	6 0 0 0 00		6 0 0 0 00	

Accumulated Depreciation, Word Processing Equipment   Account No. 122

Date		Explanation	Post. Ref.	Debit	Credit	Balance Debit	Balance Credit
200X May	31	Adjusting	GJ2		8 0 00		8 0 00

Accounts Payable   Account No. 211

Date		Explanation	Post. Ref.	Debit	Credit	Balance Debit	Balance Credit
200X May	1		GJ1		5 0 0 0 00		5 0 0 0 00
	3		GJ1		6 0 0 00		5 6 0 0 00
	18		GJ1		2 5 0 00		5 8 5 0 00
	28		GJ2	2 5 0 0 00			3 3 5 0 00

Salaries Payable   Account No. 212

Date		Explanation	Post. Ref.	Debit	Credit	Balance Debit	Balance Credit
200X May	31	Adjusting	GJ2		3 5 0 00		3 5 0 00

Brenda Clark, Capital   Account No. 311

Date		Explanation	Post. Ref.	Debit	Credit	Balance Debit	Balance Credit
200X May	1		GJ1		10 0 0 0 00		10 0 0 0 00
	31	Closing (Net Income)	GJ2		4 9 0 0 00		14 9 0 0 00
	31	Closing (Withdrawals)	GJ2	6 2 5 00			14 2 7 5 00

Note how this amount is same ending balance as Fig 4.15.

FIGURE 5.11 (*continued*)

Brenda Clark, Withdrawals — Account No. 312

Date		Explanation	Post. Ref.	Debit	Credit	Balance Debit	Balance Credit
200X May	20		GJ1	6 2 5 00		6 2 5 00	
	31	Closing	GJ2		6 2 5 00	—	—

Income Summary — Account No. 313

Date		Explanation	Post. Ref.	Debit	Credit	Balance Debit	Balance Credit
200X May	31	Closing (Revenue)	GJ2		8 0 0 0 00		8 0 0 0 00
	31	Closing (Expenses)	GJ2	3 1 0 0 00			4 9 0 0 00
	31	Closing (Net Income)	GJ2	4 9 0 0 00		—	—

Word Processing Fees — Account No. 411

Date		Explanation	Post. Ref.	Debit	Credit	Balance Debit	Balance Credit
200X May	7		GJ1		3 0 0 0 00		3 0 0 0 00
	22		GJ1		5 0 0 0 00		8 0 0 0 00
	31	Closing	GJ2	8 0 0 0 00		—	—

Office Salaries Expense — Account No. 511

Date		Explanation	Post. Ref.	Debit	Credit	Balance Debit	Balance Credit
200X May	13		GJ1	6 5 0 00		6 5 0 00	
	27		GJ2	6 5 0 00		1 3 0 0 00	
	31	Adjusting	GJ2	3 5 0 00		1 6 5 0 00	
	31	Closing	GJ2		1 6 5 0 00	—	—

Advertising Expense — Account No. 512

Date		Explanation	Post. Ref.	Debit	Credit	Balance Debit	Balance Credit
200X May	18		GJ1	2 5 0 00		2 5 0 00	
	31	Closing	GJ2		2 5 0 00	—	—

(*continued on next page*)

FIGURE 5.11 (*continued*)

Telephone Expense						Account No. 513	
		Post. Ref.	Debit	Credit	Balance		
Date	Explanation				Debit	Credit	
200X May 29		GJ2	2 2 0 00		2 2 0 00		
31	Closing	GJ2		2 2 0 00	—	—	

Office Supplies Expense						Account No. 514	
		Post. Ref.	Debit	Credit	Balance		
Date	Explanation				Debit	Credit	
200X May 31	Adjusting	GJ2	5 0 0 00		5 0 0 00		
31	Closing	GJ2		5 0 0 00	—	—	

Note: Accounts 312 to 516 are temporary and are closed to zero.

Rent Expense						Account No. 515	
		Post. Ref.	Debit	Credit	Balance		
Date	Explanation				Debit	Credit	
200X May 31	Adjusting	GJ2	4 0 0 00		4 0 0 00		
31	Closing	GJ2		4 0 0 00	—	—	

Depreciation Expense, Word Processing Equipment						Account No. 516	
		Post. Ref.	Debit	Credit	Balance		
Date	Explanation				Debit	Credit	
200X May 31	Adjusting	GJ2	8 0 00		8 0 00		
31	Closing	GJ2		8 0 00	—	—	

LEARNING UNIT 5-2 REVIEW

AT THIS POINT you should be able to

- Define closing.
- Differentiate between temporary (nominal) and permanent (real) accounts.
- List the four mechanical steps of closing.
- Explain the role of the Income Summary account.
- Explain the role of the worksheet in the closing process.

For additional help go to www.pearsonhighered.com/slater

Self-Review Quiz 5-2

Go to the worksheet for P. Logan in Fig. 4.14 (in Chapter 4). Then (1) journalize and post the closing entries and (2) calculate the new balance for P. Logan, Capital.

Solution to Self-Review Quiz 5-2

FIGURE 5.12 Closing Entries for Logan

		Closing Entries						
Dec.	31	Revenue from Clients	410	2 5 00				
		Income Summary	312			2 5 00		
	31	Income Summary	312	2 0 00				
		Rent Expense	518			2 00		
		Salaries Expense	512			1 1 00		
		Depreciation Expense, Store Equip.	510			1 00		
		Insurance Expense	516			2 00		
		Supplies Expense	514			4 00		
	31	Income Summary	312	5 00				
		P. Logan, Capital	310			5 00		
	31	P. Logan, Capital	310	3 00				
		P. Logan, Withdrawals	311			3 00		

Partial Ledger

P. Logan, Capital 310	Revenue from Clients 410	Supplies Expense 514
3 | 14	25 | 25	4 | 4
5		
16		

P. Logan, Withdrawals 311	Dep. Exp., Store Equip. 510	Insurance Expense 516
3 | 3	1 | 1	2 | 2

Income Summary 312	Salaries Expense 512	Rent Expense 518
20 | 25	11 | 11	2 | 2
5 | 5		

P. Logan, (Beginning) Capital		$14
Net Income	$5	
Less Withdrawals	3	
Increase in Capital		2
P. Logan, Capital (ending)		$16

NEED HELP?

Let's review first: Why are closing entries necessary? In the ledger we need to get the new balance in the Capital account. When financial statements were prepared, the ledger for Capital had only the old balance. Also, to get ready for the next accounting period we must close all temporary accounts to zero so they will be ready to collect new data regarding revenues, expenses, and withdrawals. Without the closing process each year, financial statements would run into the next period and financial analysis would be difficult. Keep in mind that the Income Summary account that will be used in the closing process is a temporary account (I like to call it a storage area for revenues and expenses).

Why use four steps to closing?

The four steps to closing when journalized and posted will do the following:

1. Clear all temporary accounts to zero.
2. Update the Capital account in the ledger to its new balance.

Steps to closing:

1. Close revenue account(s) to Income Summary.
2. Close each INDIVIDUAL expense to Income Summary.
3. Remove the balance in Income Summary (net income or net loss) and transfer it to the Capital account.
4. Close any withdrawals directly to Capital.

All the closing entries can be journalized directly from the last four columns of the worksheet. Each individual expense along with the total of expenses is found on the worksheet. Once these four closing entries are journalized and posted, all temporary accounts have a zero balance and P. Logan, Capital, now has an ending balance of $16. This is same amount of ending capital that was used to make the formal balance sheet.

Summary: If you look at the T-account in the solution you will see four numbers in Income Summary. Can you explain them?

20...this represents the total of all the expenses.

25...this represents the total revenue of all the revenues.

5 on the credit side...this is net income (25–20).

5 on the debit side...this comes from the 3rd closing entry, which transfers the balance in Income Summary to Capital.

LO3 Learning Unit 5-3 The Post-Closing Trial Balance: Step 9 of the Accounting Cycle and the Cycle Reviewed

Preparing a Post-Closing Trial Balance

The post-closing trial balance helps prove the accuracy of the adjusting and closing process. It contains the true ending figure for Capital.

The last step in the accounting cycle is the preparation of a **post-closing trial balance,** which lists only permanent accounts in the ledger and their balances after adjusting and closing entries have been posted. This post-closing trial balance aids in checking whether the ledger is in balance. This checking is important because so many new postings go to the ledger from the adjusting and closing process.

The procedure for taking a post-closing trial balance is the same as for a trial balance, except that, because closing entries have closed all temporary accounts, the post-closing trial balances will contain only permanent accounts (balance sheet). Keep in mind, however, that adjustments have occurred. We will walk through this procedure in the Learning Unit 5-3 quiz coming up after we review the accounting cycle.

The Accounting Cycle Reviewed

Table 5.1 lists the steps we completed in the manual accounting cycle for Clark's Word Processing Services for the month of May.

TABLE 5.1 Steps of the Manual Accounting Cycle

Steps	Explanation
1. Collect source documents from business transactions as they occur.	Cash register tape, sales tickets, bills, checks, payroll cards.
2. Analyze and record business transactions into a journal.	Called journalizing.
3. Post or transfer information from journal to ledger.	Copying the debits and credits of the journal entries into the ledger accounts.
4. Prepare a trial balance.	Summarizing each individual ledger account and listing those accounts to test for mathematical accuracy in recording transactions.
5. Prepare a worksheet.	A multicolumn form that summarizes accounting information to complete the accounting cycle.
6. Prepare financial statements.	Income statement, statement of owner's equity, and balance sheet.
7. Journalize and post adjusting entries.	Use figures in the adjustment columns of worksheet.
8. Journalize and post closing entries.	Use figures in the income statement and balance sheet sections of worksheet.
9. Prepare a post-closing trial balance.	Prove the mathematical accuracy of the adjusting and closing process of the accounting cycle.

> *Remember:* No worksheet is needed in a computerized cycle.

Insight Most companies journalize and post adjusting and closing entries only at the end of their fiscal year. A company that prepares interim statements may complete only the first six steps of the cycle. Worksheets allow the preparation of interim reports without the formal adjusting and closing of the books. In this case, footnotes on the interim report will indicate the extent to which adjusting and closing were completed.

Insight To prepare a financial statement for April, the data needed can be obtained by subtracting the worksheet accumulated totals from the end of March from the worksheet prepared at the end of April. In this chapter we chose a month that would show the completion of an entire cycle for Clark's Word Processing Services.

LEARNING UNIT 5-3 REVIEW

AT THIS POINT you should be able to

- Prepare a post-closing trial balance.
- Explain the relationship of interim statements to the accounting cycle.

a^c_t

Accounting Cycle Tutorial

Self-Review Quiz 5-3

From the ledger in Fig. 5.11, prepare a post-closing trial balance.

> For additional help go to
> www.pearsonhighered.com/slater

Solution to Self-Review Quiz 5-3

FIGURE 5.13 Post-Closing Trial Balance for Clark's Word Processing Services

CLARK'S WORD PROCESSING SERVICES POST-CLOSING TRIAL BALANCE MAY 31, 200X	Dr.	Cr.
Cash	6 1 5 5 00	
Accounts Receivable	5 0 0 0 00	
Office Supplies	1 0 0 00	
Prepaid Rent	8 0 0 00	
Word Processing Equipment	6 0 0 0 00	
Accumulated Depreciation, Word Processing Equip.		8 0 00
Accounts Payable		3 3 5 0 00
Salaries Payable		3 5 0 00
Brenda Clark, Capital		14 2 7 5 00
Totals	18 0 5 5 00	18 0 5 5 00

NEED HELP?

Let's review first: The post-closing trial balance contains only permanent accounts because all temporary accounts have been closed. All temporary accounts are summarized in the Capital account. Remember that Income Summary is a temporary account.

Post-Closing Trial Balance: Once all the closing entries have been journalized and posted we can then prepare a post-closing trial balance. Since only permanent accounts are left after closing, the structure of the post-closing trial balance should look as follows:

Assets ....Dr.

Contra Assets ....Cr.

Liabilities ....Cr.

Ending Capital ......Cr.

Summary: To begin the next accounting cycle only permanent accounts with balances are brought forward. In the new cycle transactions will be journalized and posted. Adjustments will be made and new financial statements will be prepared. By the end of the cycle all temporary accounts will be closed to get a new ending figure for capital in the ledger. The end result will be to prepare a new post-closing trial balance.

CHAPTER ASSIGNMENTS

All Classroom Demonstration Exercises, Exercises, Problems, and the Continuing Problem in this chapter can be found within MyAccountingLab, an online homework and practice environment. Your instructor may ask you to complete this material using MyAccountingLab.

MyAccountingLab

DEMONSTRATION PROBLEM: REVIEWING THE ACCOUNTING CYCLE

From the following transactions for Rolo Co. complete the entire accounting cycle. Use the following chart of accounts:

Assets

111 Cash

112 Accounts Receivable

114 Prepaid Rent

115 Office Supplies

121 Office Equipment

122 Accumulated Depreciation,
    Office Equipment

Liabilities

211 Accounts Payable

212 Salaries Payable

Owner's Equity

311 Rolo Kern, Capital

312 Rolo Kern, Withdrawals

313 Income Summary

Revenue

411 Fees Earned

Expenses

511 Salaries Expense

512 Advertising Expense

513 Rent Expense

514 Office Supplies Expense

515 Depreciation Expense,
    Office Equipment

> *Note:* Accounts 312 to 515 are temporary accounts.

We will use unusually small numbers to simplify calculation and emphasize the theory.

200X

Jan.	1	Rolo Kern invested $1,200 cash and $100 of office equipment to open Rolo Co.
	1	Paid rent for three months in advance, $300
	4	Purchased office equipment on account, $50
	6	Bought office supplies for cash, $40
	8	Collected $400 for services rendered
	12	Rolo paid his home electric bill from the company checkbook, $20
	14	Provided $100 worth of services to clients who will not pay until next month
	16	Paid salaries, $60
	18	Advertising bill received for $70 but will not be paid until next month

Adjustment Data on January 31

    a. Supplies on hand, $6.

    b. Rent expired, $100.

    c. Depreciation, Office Equipment, $20.

    d. Salaries accrued, $50.

Solutions to Demonstration Problem

Journalizing Transactions and Posting to Ledger, Rolo Company

FIGURE 5.14 Journal Entries for Rolo Company

General Journal					Page 1
Date	Account Titles and Description	PR	Dr.	Cr.	
200X Jan 1	Cash	111	1 2 0 0 00		
	Office Equipment	121	1 0 0 00		
	R. Kern, Capital	311		1 3 0 0 00	
	Initial Investment				
1	Prepaid Rent	114	3 0 0 00		
	Cash	111		3 0 0 00	
	Rent Paid in Advance—3 mos.				
4	Office Equipment	121	5 0 00		
	Accounts Payable	211		5 0 00	
	Purchased Equipment on Account				
6	Office Supplies	115	4 0 00		
	Cash	111		4 0 00	
	Supplies purchased for cash				
8	Cash	111	4 0 0 00		
	Fees Earned	411		4 0 0 00	
	Services rendered				
12	R. Kern, Withdrawals	312	2 0 00		
	Cash	111		2 0 00	
	Personal payment of a bill				
14	Accounts Receivable	112	1 0 0 00		
	Fees Earned	411		1 0 0 00	
	Services rendered on account				
16	Salaries Expense	511	6 0 00		
	Cash	111		6 0 00	
	Paid salaries				
18	Advertising Expense	512	7 0 00		
	Accounts Payable	211		7 0 00	
	Advertising bill, but not paid				

Solution Tips to Journalizing and Posting Transactions

Jan 1	Cash	Asset	↑	Dr.	$1,200
	Office Equipment	Asset	↑	Dr.	$ 100
	R. Kern, Capital	Capital	↑	Cr.	$1,300
1	Prepaid Rent	Asset	↑	Dr.	$ 300
	Cash	Asset	↓	Cr.	$ 300

4	Office Equipment	Asset	↑	Dr.	$ 50
	Accounts Payable	Liability	↑	Cr.	$ 50

6	Office Supplies	Asset	↑	Dr.	$ 40
	Cash	Asset	↓	Cr.	$ 40

8	Cash	Asset	↑	Dr.	$ 400
	Fees Earned	Revenue	↑	Cr.	$ 400

12	R. Kern, Withdrawals	Withdrawals	↑	Dr.	$ 20
	Cash	Asset	↓	Cr.	$ 20

14	Accounts Receivable	Asset	↑	Dr.	$ 100
	Fees Earned	Revenue	↑	Cr.	$ 100

16	Salaries Expense	Expense	↑	Dr.	$ 60
	Cash	Asset	↓	Cr.	$ 60

18	Advertising Expense	Expense	↑	Dr.	$ 70
	Accounts Payable	Liability	↑	Cr.	$ 70

Note: All account titles come from the chart of accounts. When journalizing, the PR column of the general journal is blank. It is in the posting process that we update the ledger. The PR column in the ledger accounts tells us from what journal page the information came. After the title in the ledger is posted to, we fill in the PR column of the journal, telling us to what account number the information was transferred.

Completing the Worksheet

See the worksheet in Fig. 5.15 on the following page spread.

Solution Tips to the Trial Balance and Completion of the Worksheet

After the posting process is complete from the journal to the ledger, we take the ending balance in each account and prepare a trial balance on the worksheet (see Fig. 5.15). If a title has no balance, it is not listed on the trial balance. New titles on the worksheet will be added as needed.

Adjustments

Office Supplies Expense	Expense	↑	Dr.	$ 34	($40 − $6)
Office Supplies	Asset	↓	Cr.	$ 34	

Supplies on hand of $6 is not the adjustment. Need to calculate amount used up.

Rent Expense	Expense	↑	Dr.	$100
Prepaid Rent	Asset	↓	Cr.	$100

Do not touch original cost of equipment.	Depr. Exp., Office Equip.	Expense	↑	Dr.	$ 20
	Accum. Dep., Office Equip.	Contra-Asset	↑	Cr.	$ 20

Salaries Expense	Expense	↑	Dr.	$ 50
Salaries Payable	Liability	↑	Cr.	$ 50

Note: This information on the worksheet has *not* been updated in the ledger. (Updating happens when we journalize and post adjustments at the end of the cycle.)

Note that the last four columns of the worksheet come from numbers on the adjusted trial balance.

We move the Net Income of $166 to the Balance Sheet credit column because the Capital figure is the old one on the worksheet.

ROLO CO.
WORKSHEET
FOR MONTH ENDED JANUARY 31, 200X

Account Titles	Trial Balance Dr.	Trial Balance Cr.	Adjustments Dr.	Adjustments Cr.	Adjusted Trial Balance Dr.	Adjusted Trial Balance Cr.	Income Statement Dr.	Income Statement Cr.	Balance Sheet Dr.	Balance Sheet Cr.
Cash	118000				118000				118000	
Accounts Receivable	10000				10000				10000	
Prepaid Rent	30000			(B)10000	20000				20000	
Office Supplies	4000			(A)3400	600				600	
Office Equipment	15000				15000				15000	
Accounts Payable		12000				12000				12000
R. Kern, Capital		130000				130000				130000
R. Kern, Withdrawals	2000				2000				2000	
Fees Earned		50000				50000		50000		
Salaries Expense	6000		(D)5000		11000		11000			
Advertising Expense	7000				7000		7000			
	192000	192000								
Office Supplies Expense			(A)3400		3400		3400			
Rent Expense			(B)10000		10000		10000			
Depr. Exp., Office Equip.			(C)2000		2000		2000			
Acc. Dep., Office Equip.				(C)2000		2000				2000
Salaries Payable				(D)5000		5000				5000
			20400	20400	199000	199000	33400	50000	165600	149000
Net Income							16600			16600
							50000	50000	165600	165600

Supplies used up

Supplies on hand

FIGURE 5.15 Completed Worksheet for Rolo Company

Preparing the Formal Financial Statements

FIGURE 5.16 Income
Statement for Rolo Company

ROLO CO.
INCOME STATEMENT
FOR MONTH ENDED JANUARY 31, 200X

Revenue:		
Fees Earned		$5 0 0 0 0
Operating Expenses		
Salaries Expense	$1 1 0 0 0	
Advertising Expense	7 0 0 0	
Office Supplies Expense	3 4 0 0	
Rent Expense	1 0 0 0 0	
Depreciation Expense, Office Equipment	2 0 0 0	
Total Operating Expenses		3 3 4 0 0
Net Income		$1 6 6 0 0

FIGURE 5.17 Statement of
Owner's Equity for Rolo
Company

ROLO CO.
STATEMENT OF OWNER'S EQUITY
FOR MONTH ENDED JANUARY 31, 200X

R. Kern, Capital, January 1, 200X		$1 3 0 0 0 0
Net Income for January	$1 6 6 0 0	
Less Withdrawals for January	2 0 0 0	
Increase in Capital		1 4 6 0 0
R. Kern, Capital, January 31, 200X		$1 4 4 6 0 0

FIGURE 5.18 Balance Sheet for Rolo Company

ROLO CO.
BALANCE SHEET
JANUARY 31, 200X

Assets			Liabilities & Owner's Equity		
Cash		$1 1 8 0 0 0	Liabilities		
Accounts Receivable		1 0 0 0 0	Accounts Payable	$1 2 0 0 0	
Prepaid Rent		2 0 0 0 0	Salaries Payable	5 0 0 0	
Office Supplies		6 0 0	Total Liabilities		$1 7 0 0 0
Office Equipment	$1 5 0 0 0		Owner's Equity		
Less Accum. Depr.	2 0 0 0	1 3 0 0 0	R. Kern, Capital		1 4 4 6 0 0
			Total Liabilities &		
Total Assets		$1 6 1 6 0 0	Owner's Equity		$1 6 1 6 0 0

Solution Tips to Preparing the Financial Statements

The statements are prepared from the worksheet. (Many of the ledger accounts are not up-to-date.) The income statement (Fig. 5.16) lists revenue and expenses. The Net Income figure of $166 is used to update the statement of owner's equity. The statement of owner's equity (Fig. 5.17) calculates a new figure for Capital, $1,446 (Beginning Capital + Net Income − Withdrawals). This new figure is then listed on the balance sheet (Fig. 5.18) (Assets, Liabilities, and a new figure for Capital).

Journalizing and Posting Adjusting and Closing Entries

See the journal in Figure 5.19.

FIGURE 5.19 Adjusting and Closing Entries Journalized and Posted

General Journal					Page 2
Date	Account Titles and Description	PR	Dr.	Cr.	
	ADJUSTING ENTRIES				
Jan. 31	Office Supplies Expense	514	3 4 00		
	Office Supplies	115		3 4 00	
31	Rent Expense	513	1 0 0 00		
	Prepaid Rent	114		1 0 0 00	
31	Depr. Expense, Office Equipment	515	2 0 00		
	Accum. Depr., Office Equip.	122		2 0 00	
31	Salaries Expense	511	5 0 00		
	Salaries Payable	212		5 0 00	
	CLOSING ENTRIES				
Step 1 → 31	Fees Earned	411	5 0 0 00		
	Income Summary	313		5 0 0 00	
Step 2 → 31	Income Summary	313	3 3 4 00		
	Salaries Expense	511		1 1 0 00	
	Advertising Expense	512		7 0 00	
	Office Supplies Expense	514		3 4 00	
	Rent Expense	513		1 0 0 00	
	Depr. Expense, Office Equip.	515		2 0 00	
Step 3 → 31	Income Summary	313	1 6 6 00		
	R. Kern, Capital	311		1 6 6 00	
Step 4 → 31	R. Kern, Capital	311	2 0 00		
	R. Kern, Withdrawals	312		2 0 00	

Closing { Step 1, Step 2, Step 3, Step 4

Solution Tips to Journalizing and Posting Adjusting and Closing Entries

Adjustments

The adjustments from the worksheet are journalized (same journal) and posted to the ledger. Now ledger accounts will be brought up-to-date. Remember, we have already prepared the financial statements from the worksheet. Our goal now is to get the ledger up-to-date.

Closing

Note that Income Summary is a temporary account located in the ledger.

GOALS

1. Wipe out all temporary accounts in the ledger to zero balances.
2. Get a new figure for Capital in the ledger.

Steps in the Closing Process

Step 1 Close revenue to Income Summary.

Step 2 Close individual expenses to Income Summary.

Step 3 Close balance of Income Summary to Capital. (This amount really is the Net Income figure on the worksheet.)

Step 4 Close balance of Withdrawals to Capital.

All the journal closing entries are posted. (No new calculations are needed because all figures are on the worksheet.) The result in the ledger is that all temporary accounts have a zero balance (Fig. 5.20).

FIGURE 5.20 General Ledger for Rolo Company

GENERAL LEDGER

Cash   111

Date	PR	Dr.	Cr.	Balance Dr.	Balance Cr.
1/1	GJ1	1,200		1,200	
1/1	GJ1		300	900	
1/6	GJ1		40	860	
1/8	GJ1	400		1,260	
1/12	GJ1		20	1,240	
1/16	GJ1		60	1,180	

Accounts Receivable   112

Date	PR	Dr.	Cr.	Balance Dr.	Balance Cr.
1/14	GJ1	100		100	

Accumulated Depreciation, Equipment 122

Date	PR	Dr.	Cr.	Balance Dr.	Balance Cr.
1/31 Adj.	GJ2		20		20

Accounts Payable   211

Date	PR	Dr.	Cr.	Balance Dr.	Balance Cr.
1/4	GJ1		50		50
1/18	GJ1		70		120

Salaries Payable   212

Date	PR	Dr.	Cr.	Balance Dr.	Balance Cr.
1/31 Adj.	GJ2		50		50

FIGURE 5.20 *(continued)*

Prepaid Rent					114
				Balance	
Date	PR	Dr.	Cr.	Dr.	Cr.
1/1	GJ1	300		300	
1/31Adj.	GJ2		100	200	

Rolo Kern, Capital					311
				Balance	
Date	PR	Dr.	Cr.	Dr.	Cr.
1/1	GJ1		1,300		1,300
1/31Clos.	GJ2		166		1,466
1/31Clos.	GJ2	20			1,446

Office Supplies					115
				Balance	
Date	PR	Dr.	Cr.	Dr.	Cr.
1/6	GJ1	40		40	
1/31Adj	GJ2		34	6	

Rolo Kern, Withdrawals					312
				Balance	
Date	PR	Dr.	Cr.	Dr.	Cr.
1/12	GJ1	20		20	
1/31Clos.	GJ2		20	———	

Office Equipment					121
				Balance	
Date	PR	Dr.	Cr.	Dr.	Cr.
1/1	GJ1	100		100	
1/4	GJ1	50		150	

Income Summary					313
				Balance	
Date	PR	Dr.	Cr.	Dr.	Cr.
1/31 Clos.	GJ2		500		500
1/31 Clos.	GJ2	334			166
1/31 Clos.	GJ2	166		———	

Fees Earned					411
				Balance	
Date	PR	Dr.	Cr.	Dr.	Cr.
1/8	GJ1		400		400
1/14	GJ1		100		500
1/31 Clos.	GJ2	500		———	

Rent Expense					513
				Balance	
Date	PR	Dr.	Cr.	Dr.	Cr.
1/31 Adj.	GJ2	100		100	
1/31 Clos.	GJ2		100	———	

Salaries Expense					511
				Balance	
Date	PR	Dr.	Cr.	Dr.	Cr.
1/16	GJ1	60		60	
1/31 Adj.	GJ2	50		110	
1/31 Clos.	GJ2		110	———	

Office Supplies Expense					514
				Balance	
Date	PR	Dr.	Cr.	Dr.	Cr.
1/31 Adj.	GJ2	34		34	
1/31 Clos.	GJ2		34	———	

Advertising Expense					512
				Balance	
Date	PR	Dr.	Cr.	Dr.	Cr.
1/18	GJ1	70		70	
1/31 Clos.	GJ2		70	———	

Depreciation Expenses Office Equipment					515
				Balance	
Date	PR	Dr.	Cr.	Dr.	Cr.
1/31 Adj.	GJ2	20		20	
1/31 Clos.	GJ2		20	———	

Solution Tips for the Post-Closing Trial Balance

The post-closing trial balance is a list of the ledger *after* adjusting and closing entries have been completed. Note that the figure for Capital, $1,446, is the new figure.

FIGURE 5.21 Post-Closing Trial Balance for Rolo Company

	Dr.	Cr.
ROLO CO. POST-CLOSING TRIAL BALANCE JANUARY 31, 200X		
Cash	1 1 8 0 00	
Accounts Receivable	1 0 0 00	
Prepaid Rent	2 0 0 00	
Office Supplies	6 00	
Office Equipment	1 5 0 00	
Accum. Dep., Office Equipment		2 0 00
Accounts Payable		1 2 0 00
Salaries Payable		5 0 00
R. Kern, Capital		1 4 4 6 00
TOTAL	1 6 3 6 00	1 6 3 6 00

The post-closing trial balance contains all permanent accounts.

Accounting Cycle Tutorial
Adjusting & Closing The Books

Beginning Capital	$1,300
+ Net Income	166
− Withdrawals	20
= Ending Capital	$1,446

Next accounting period we will enter new amounts in the Revenues, Expenses, and Withdrawal accounts. For now, the post-closing trial balance is made up of permanent accounts only.

SUMMARY OF KEY POINTS

LEARNING UNIT 5-1

1. After formal financial statements have been prepared, the ledger has still not been brought up-to-date.
2. Information for journalizing adjusting entries comes from the adjustments section of the worksheet.

LEARNING UNIT 5-2

1. Closing is a mechanical process that aids the accountant in recording transactions for the next period.
2. Assets, Liabilities, and Capital are permanent (real) accounts; their balances are carried over from one accounting period to another. Withdrawals, Revenue, and Expenses are temporary (nominal) accounts; their balances are *not* carried over from one accounting period to another.
3. Income Summary is a temporary account in the general ledger and does not have a normal balance. It will summarize revenue and expenses and transfer the balance to Capital. Withdrawals do not go into Income Summary because they are *not* business expenses.
4. All information for closing can be obtained from the worksheet or ledger.
5. When closing is complete, all temporary accounts in the ledger will have a zero balance, and all this information will be updated in the Capital account.
6. Closing entries are usually done only at year-end. Interim reports can be prepared from worksheets that are prepared monthly, quarterly, or some other regular time period.

LEARNING UNIT 5-3

1. The post-closing trial balance is prepared from the ledger accounts after the adjusting and closing entries have been posted.
2. The accounts on the post-closing trial balance are all permanent titles.

KEY TERMS

Adjusting journal entries   Journal entries that are needed in order to update specific ledger accounts to reflect correct balances at the end of an accounting period.

Closing journal entries   Journal entries that are prepared to (a) reduce or clear all temporary accounts to a zero balance or (b) update Capital to a new balance.

Income Summary   A temporary account in the ledger that summarizes revenue and expenses and transfers the balance (net income or net loss) to Capital. This account does not have a normal balance.

Permanent accounts (real)   Accounts whose balances are carried over to the next accounting period. Examples: Assets, Liabilities, Capital.

Post-closing trial balance   The final step in the accounting cycle that lists only permanent accounts in the ledger and their balances after adjusting and closing entries have been posted.

Temporary accounts (nominal)   Accounts whose balances at the end of an accounting period are not carried over to the next accounting period. These accounts—Revenue, Expenses, Withdrawals—help summarize a new or ending figure for Capital to begin the next accounting period. Keep in mind that Income Summary is also a temporary account.

BLUEPRINT OF CLOSING PROCESS FROM THE WORKSHEET

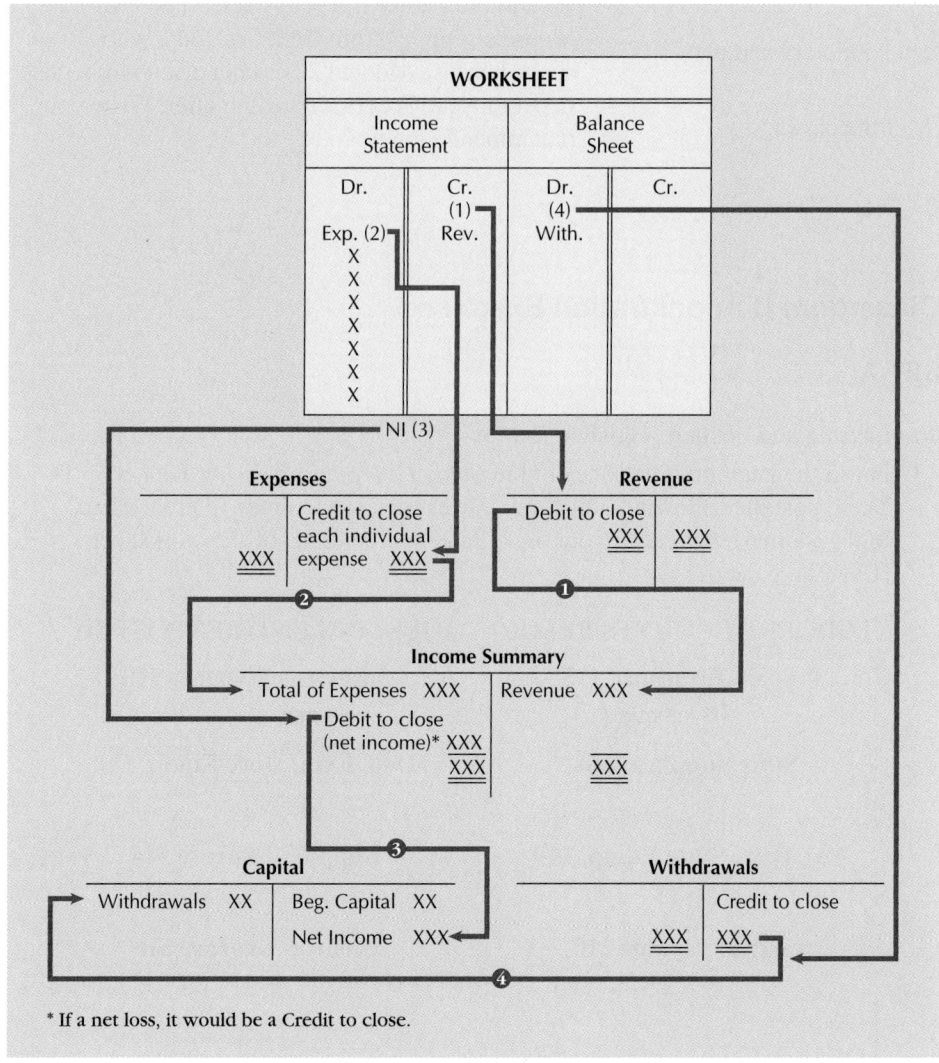

* If a net loss, it would be a Credit to close.

The Closing Steps

1. Close revenue ($) balance to Income Summary.
2. Close each *individual* expense and transfer *total* of all expenses to Income Summary.
3. Transfer balance in Income Summary (net income or net loss) to Capital.
4. Close Withdrawals to Capital.

QUESTIONS, CLASSROOM DEMONSTRATION EXERCISES, EXERCISES, AND PROBLEMS

Discussion and Critical Thinking Questions/Ethical Case

1. When a worksheet is completed, what balances are found in the general ledger?

2. Why must adjusting entries be journalized even though the formal statements have already been prepared?

3. "Closing slows down the recording of next year's transactions." Defend or reject this statement with supporting evidence.

4. What is the difference between temporary and permanent accounts?

5. What are the two major goals of the closing process?

6. List the four steps of closing.

7. What is the purpose of Income Summary and where is it located?

8. How can a worksheet aid the closing process?

9. What accounts are usually listed on a post-closing trial balance?

10. Closing entries are always prepared once a month. Agree or disagree? Why?

11. Todd Silver is the purchasing agent for Moore Co. One of his suppliers, Gem Co., offers Todd a free vacation to France if he buys at least 75% of Moore's supplies from Gem Co. Todd, who is angry because Moore Co. has not given him a raise in over a year, is considering the offer. Write your recommendation to Todd.

MyAccountingLab **Classroom Demonstration Exercises**

SET A

LO1 (5 min) **Journalizing and Posting Adjusting Entries**

1. Put in the beginning balances in the *Study Guide and Working Papers*. Then, post the following adjusting entries (be sure to cross-reference back to the journal) that came from the adjustment columns of the worksheet. (Use Fig. 5.22.)

LEDGER ACCOUNTS BEFORE ADJUSTING ENTRIES POSTED

Prepaid Insurance 115	Insurance Expense 510
18	

Store Supplies 116	Dep. Exp., Store Equip. 512
17	

Acc. Dep., Store Equip. 119	Supplies Expense 514
13	

Salaries Payable 210	Salaries Expense 516
	9

FIGURE 5.22 Journalized Adjusting Entries

Date		Account Titles and Description	PR	Dr.	Cr.
Dec.	31	Insurance Expense		6 00	
		Prepaid Insurance			6 00
	31	Supplies Expense		4 00	
		Store Supplies			4 00
	31	Depr. Exp., Store Equipment		9 00	
		Accum. Depr., Store Equipment			9 00
	31	Salaries Expense		5 00	
		Salaries Payable			5 00

General Journal — Page 3

Steps of Closing and Journalizing Closing Entries

LO2 (10 min)

2. Explain the four steps of the closing process given the following:

Dec. 31 ending balance, before closing

Fees Earned	$200
Rent Expense	100
Advertising Expense	60
J. Rice, Capital	3,000
J. Rice, Withdrawals	15

Journalizing Closing Entries

LO2 (15 min)

3. From the following accounts, journalize the closing entries (assume December 31).

Mel Blanc, Capital 310
	40

Gas Expense 510
8	

Mel Blanc, Withdr. 312
7	

Advertising Exp. 512
12	

Income Summary 314

Dep. Exp., Taxi 516
5	

Taxi Fees 410
	39

Posting to Income Summary

LO2 (10 min)

4. Draw a T account of Income Summary and post to it all entries from Question 3 that affect it. Is Income Summary a temporary or permanent account?

Posting to Capital

LO2 (10 min)

5. Draw a T account for Mel Blanc, Capital, and post to it all entries from Question 3 that affect it. What is the final balance of the Capital account?

SET B

Journalizing and Posting Adjusting Entries

LO1 (5 min)

1. Put in the beginning balances in the *Study Guide and Working Papers.* Then, post the following adjusting entries (be sure to cross-reference back to the journal) that came from the adjustment columns of the worksheet. (Use Fig. 5.23 on the following page.)

LEDGER ACCOUNTS BEFORE ADJUSTING ENTRIES POSTED

Prepaid Insurance 115	Insurance Expense 510
12	

Store Supplies 116	Dep. Exp., Store Equip. 512
15	

Acc. Dep., Store Equip. 119	Supplies Expense 514
12	

Salaries Payable 210	Salaries Expense 516
	7

FIGURE 5.23 Journalized Adjusting Entries

	General Journal				Page 3
Date	Account Titles and Description	PR	Dr.	Cr.	
Dec. 31	Insurance Expense		4 00		
	Prepaid Insurance			4 00	
31	Supplies Expense		3 00		
	Store Supplies			3 00	
31	Depr. Exp., Store Equipment		7 00		
	Accum. Depr., Store Equipment			7 00	
31	Salaries Expense		4 00		
	Salaries Payable			4 00	

LO2 (15 min)   **Steps of Closing and Journalizing Closing Entries**

2. From the worksheet in Figure 5.24, explain the four steps of closing. Keep in mind that each *individual* expense normally would be listed in the closing process.

FIGURE 5.24

	Worksheet		
IS		BS	
Dr.	Cr.	Dr.	Cr.
(2)	Rev. (1)	Withd.	(4)
E			
X			
P			
E			
N			
S			
E			
S			

NI (3)

Goals of Closing

1. Temporary accounts in the ledger should have a zero balance.
2. New figure for Capital in closing.
     Note: All closing can be done from the worksheet. Income Summary is a temporary account in the ledger.

Journalizing Closing Entries   *LO2 (15 min)*

3. From the following accounts, journalize the closing entries (assume December 31).

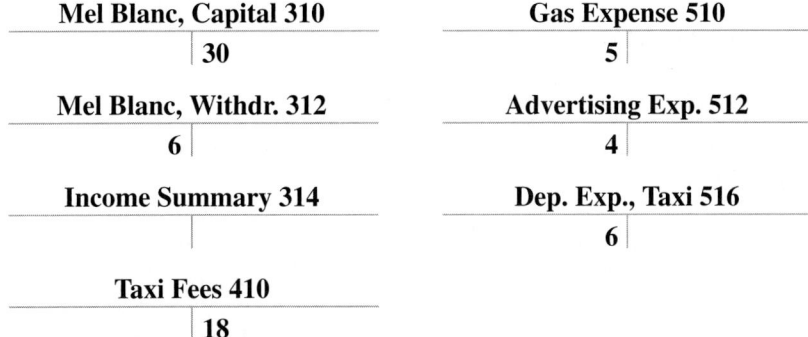

Mel Blanc, Capital 310		Gas Expense 510	
	30	5	

Mel Blanc, Withdr. 312		Advertising Exp. 512	
6		4	

Income Summary 314		Dep. Exp., Taxi 516	
		6	

Taxi Fees 410	
	18

Posting to Income Summary   *LO2 (10 min)*

4. Draw a T account of Income Summary and post to it all entries from Question 3 that affect it. Is Income Summary a temporary or permanent account?

Posting to Capital   *LO2 (10 min)*

5. Draw a T account for Mel Blanc, Capital, and post to it all entries from Question 3 that affect it. What is the final balance of the Capital account?

Exercises   *MyAccountingLab*

5-1. From the adjustments section of a worksheet presented in Figure 5.25, prepare   *LO1 (15 min)*
adjusting journal entries for the end of December.

FIGURE 5.25 Adjustments on Worksheet

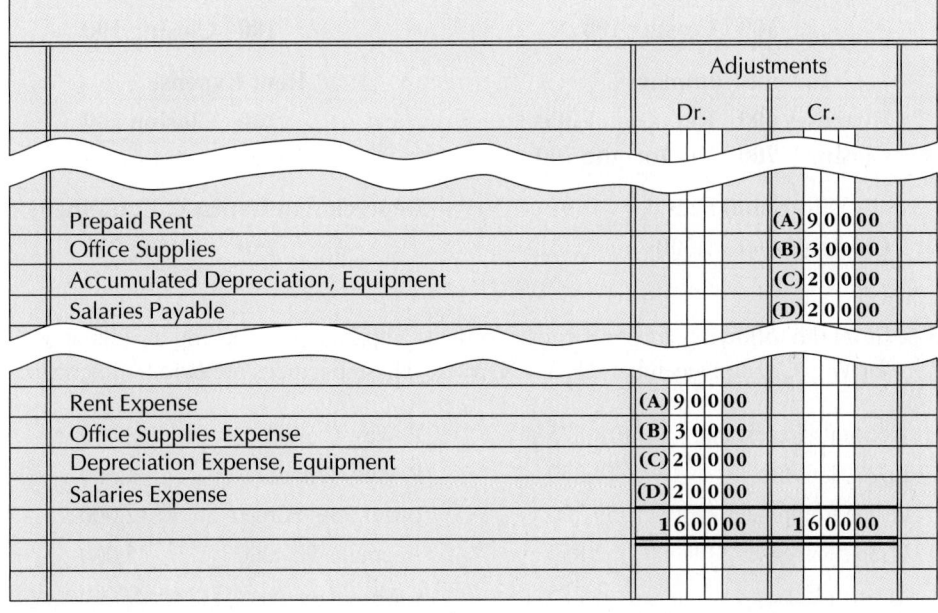

	Adjustments	
	Dr.	Cr.
Prepaid Rent		(A) 9 0 0 00
Office Supplies		(B) 3 0 0 00
Accumulated Depreciation, Equipment		(C) 2 0 0 00
Salaries Payable		(D) 2 0 0 00
Rent Expense	(A) 9 0 0 00	
Office Supplies Expense	(B) 3 0 0 00	
Depreciation Expense, Equipment	(C) 2 0 0 00	
Salaries Expense	(D) 2 0 0 00	
	1 6 0 0 00	1 6 0 0 00

LO1, 2 (10 min)   **5-2.** Complete the following table by placing an X in the correct column.

	Temporary	Permanent	Will Be Closed
Ex. Accounts Receivable		X	
1. Income Summary			
2. Jen Rich, Capital			
3. Salary Expense			
4. Jen Rich, Withdrawals			
5. Fees Earned			
6. Accounts Payable			
7. Cash			

LO2 (15 min)   **5-3.** From the following T accounts, journalize the four closing entries on December 31, 200X.

J. King, Capital
	14,000

J. King, Withdrawals
4,000	

Income Summary

Fees Earned
	33,000

Rent Expense
5,000	

Wage Expense
7,000	

Insurance Expense
1,200	

Dep. Expense, Office Equipment
900	

LO2 (20 min)   **5-4.** From the following posted T accounts, reconstruct the closing journal entries for December 31, 200X.

M. Foster, Capital
Withdrawals 100	2,000 (Dec. 1)
	700 Net income

M. Foster, Withdrawals
100	Closing 100

Income Summary
Expenses 600	Revenue 1,300
Closing 700	Net Income 700

Salon Fees
Closing 1,300	1,300

Insurance Expense
50	Closing 50

Wage Expense
100	Closing 100

Rent Expense
200	Closing 200

Depreciation Expense, Equipment
250	Closing 250

LO3 (20 min)   **5-5.** From the following accounts (not in order), prepare a post-closing trial balance for Wey Co. on December 31, 200X. *Note:* These balances are *before* closing.

Accounts Receivable	$18,875	P. Wey, Capital	63,450
Legal Supplies	14,250	P. Wey, Withdrawals	1,500
Office Equipment	59,700	Legal Fees Earned	12,000
Repair Expense	2,850	Accounts Payable	45,000
Salaries Expense	1,275	Cash	22,000

Group A Problems

5A-1. Given the data in Figure 5.26 for Debbie's Dance Studio:

MyAccounting**Lab**
LO1, 2 (40 min)

FIGURE 5.26 Trial Balance for Debbie's Dance Studio

DEBBIE'S DANCE STUDIO TRIAL BALANCE JUNE 30, 200X	Dr.	Cr.
Cash	40 0 0 0 00	
Accounts Receivable	7 0 0 0 00	
Prepaid Insurance	4 0 0 00	
Dance Supplies	1 5 0 0 00	
Dance Equipment	13 0 0 0 00	
Accumulated Depreciation, Dance Equipment		11 9 0 0 00
Accounts Payable		21 0 0 0 00
D. Dee, Capital		13 2 0 0 00
D. Dee, Withdrawals	8 0 0 00	
Dance Fees Earned		19 8 0 0 00
Salaries Expense	1 6 0 0 00	
Telephone Expense	1 0 0 0 00	
Advertising Expense	6 0 0 00	
	65 9 0 0 00	65 9 0 0 00

Check Figure:
Net Income $14,600

Adjustment Data

a. Insurance expired, $300.
b. Dance supplies on hand, $700.
c. Depreciation on dance equipment, $500.
d. Salaries earned by employees but not to be paid until July, $400.

Your task is to
1. Prepare a worksheet.
2. Journalize adjusting and closing entries.

5A-2. Enter the beginning balance in each account in your working papers from the Trial Balance columns of the worksheet (Fig. 5.27 on the following page). From that worksheet, (1) journalize and post adjusting and closing entries after entering the beginning balance in each account in the ledger, and (2) prepare from the ledger a post-closing trial balance for the month of March.

LO1, 2, 3 (35 min)

Check Figure:
Post-closing trial balance $3,504

5A-3. As the bookkeeper of Pete's Plowing, you have been asked to complete the entire accounting cycle for Pete from the following information.

LO1, 2, 3 (150 min)

200X

Jan. 1   Pete invested $7,000 cash and $6,000 worth of snow equipment into the plowing company.

1   Paid rent for three months in advance for garage space, $2,000.

4   Purchased office equipment on account from Ling Corp., $7,200.

6   Purchased snow supplies for $700 cash.

8   Collected $15,000 from plowing local shopping centers.

12   Pete Mack withdrew $1,000 from the business for his own personal use.

20   Plowed North East Co. parking lots, payment not to be received until March, $5,000.

26   Paid salaries to employees, $1,800.

28   Paid Ling Corp. one-half amount owed for office equipment.

29   Advertising bill received from Bush Co. but will not be paid until March, $900.

30   Paid telephone bill, $210.

(continued on the following page spread)

POTTER CLEANING SERVICE
WORKSHEET
FOR MONTH ENDED MARCH 31, 200X

Account Titles	Trial Balance Dr.	Trial Balance Cr.	Adjustments Dr.	Adjustments Cr.	Adjusted Trial Balance Dr.	Adjusted Trial Balance Cr.	Income Statement Dr.	Income Statement Cr.	Balance Sheet Dr.	Balance Sheet Cr.
Cash	40000				40000				40000	
Prepaid Insurance	52000			(A) 18000	34000				34000	
Cleaning Supplies	14400			(B) 10000	4400				4400	
Auto	272000				272000				272000	
Accum. Depr. Auto		86000		(C) 15000		101000				101000
Accounts Payable		22400				22400				22400
B. Potter, Capital		54000				54000				54000
B. Potter, Withdrawals	46000				46000				46000	
Cleaning Fees		468000				468000		468000		
Salaries Expense	144000		(D) 16000		160000		160000			
Telephone Expense	26400				26400		26400			
Advertising Expense	19600				19600		19600			
Gas Expense	16000				16000		16000			
	630400	630400								
Insurance Expense			(A) 18000		18000		18000			
Cleaning Supplies Expense			(B) 10000		10000		10000			
Depr. Expense Auto			(C) 15000		15000		15000			
Salaries Payable				(D) 16000		16000				16000
			59000	59000	661400	661400	265000	468000	396400	193400
Net Income							203000			203000
							468000	468000	396400	396400

FIGURE 5.27 Worksheet for Potter Cleaning Service

Use the following chart of accounts.

Chart of Accounts

Assets	Owner's Equity
111 Cash	311 Pete Mack, Capital
112 Accounts Receivable	312 Pete Mack, Withdrawals
114 Prepaid Rent	313 Income Summary
115 Snow Supplies	**Revenue**
121 Office Equipment	411 Plowing Fees
122 Accumulated Depreciation,	**Expenses**
Office Equipment	511 Salaries Expense
123 Snow Equipment	512 Advertising Expense
124 Accumulated Depreciation	513 Telephone Expense
Snow Equipment	514 Rent Expense
Liabilities	515 Snow Supplies Expense
211 Accounts Payable	516 Depreciation Expense, Office
212 Salaries Payable	Equipment
	517 Depreciation Expense, Snow Equipment

Adjustment Data

    a. Snow supplies on hand, $400.
    b. Rent expired, $600.
    c. Depreciation on office equipment, $120: ($7,200 ÷ 5 yr. = $1,440/12 mo. = $120).
    d. Depreciation on snow equipment, $100: ($6,000 ÷ 5 yr. = $1,200/12 mo. = $100).
    e. Accrued salaries, $190.

> *Check Figure:*
> Net Income $15,780

Group B Problems

5B-1.

> *MyAccountingLab*
> *LO1, 2 (40 min)*

MEMO

To:	*Matt Kaminsky*
From:	*Abby Ellen*
Re:	*Accounting Needs*

Please prepare ASAP from the following information (Fig. 5.28 on the following page) (1) a worksheet along with (2) journalized adjusting and closing entries.

Adjustment Data

    a. Insurance expired, $100.
    b. Dance supplies on hand, $20.
    c. Depreciation on dance equipment, $200.
    d. Salaries earned by employees but not due to be paid until July, $490.

> *Check Figure:*
> Net Income $3,530

5B-2. Enter the beginning balance in each account in your working papers from the Trial Balance columns of the worksheet (Fig. 5.29). From the worksheet (1) journalize and post adjusting and closing entries after entering beginning balances in each account in the ledger, and (2) prepare from the ledger a post-closing trial balance at the end of March.

> *LO1, 2 (35 min)*

> *Check Figure:*
> Post-closing Trial Balance $3,294

5B-3. From the following transactions as well as additional data, please complete the entire accounting cycle for Pete's Plowing (use the preceeding chart of accounts on this page).

> *LO1, 2, 3 (150 min)*

FIGURE 5.28 Trial Balance for
Debbie's Dance Studio

	Dr.	Cr.
DEBBIE'S DANCE STUDIO TRIAL BALANCE JUNE 30, 200X		
Cash	10 15 0 00	
Accounts Receivable	5 0 0 0 00	
Prepaid Insurance	7 0 0 00	
Dance Supplies	3 0 0 00	
Dance Equipment	12 9 5 0 00	
Accumulated Depreciation, Dance Equipment		4 0 0 0 00
Accounts Payable		5 7 5 0 00
D. Dee, Capital		15 1 5 0 00
D. Dee, Withdrawals	4 0 0 00	
Dance Fees Earned		5 2 0 0 00
Salaries Expense	4 5 0 00	
Telephone Expense	7 0 00	
Advertising Expense	8 0 00	
	30 1 0 0 00	30 1 0 0 00

200X

Jan. 1   To open the business, Pete invested $8,000 cash and $9,600 worth of snow equipment.

     1   Paid rent for five months in advance, $3,000.

     4   Purchased office equipment on account from Russell Co., $6,000.

     6   Bought snow supplies, $350.

     8   Collected $7,000 for plowing during winter storm emergency.

     12   Pete paid his home telephone bill from the company checkbook, $70.

     20   Billed Eastern Freight Co. for plowing fees earned but not to be received until March, $6,500.

     24   Advertising bill received from Jones Co. but will not be paid until next month, $350.

     26   Paid salaries to employees, $1,800.

     28   Paid Russell Co. one-half of amount owed for office equipment.

     29   Paid telephone bill of company, $165.

Check Figure:
Net Income $9,610

Adjustment Data

   a. Snow supplies on hand, $200.

   b. Rent expired, $600.

   c. Depreciation on office equipment, $125: ($6,000/4 yr = $1,500 ÷ 12 = $125).

   d. Depreciation on snow equipment, $400: ($9,600 ÷ 2 = $4,800 ÷ 12 = $400).

   e. Salaries accrued, $300.

ON-THE-JOB TRAINING

LO3 (15 min)

T-1. Carol Miller needs a loan from the Charles Bank to help finance her business. She submitted to the Charles Bank the following unadjusted trial balance. As the loan officer, you will be meeting with Carol tomorrow. Could you make some specific written suggestions to Carol regarding her loan report? What do you think would be the bank loan officer's concerns?

Cash in Bank	770
Accounts Receivable	1,480
Office Supplies	3,310

(continued on following page spread)

POTTER CLEANING SERVICE
WORKSHEET
FOR MONTH ENDED MARCH 31, 200X

Account Titles	Trial Balance Dr.	Trial Balance Cr.	Adjustments Dr.	Adjustments Cr.	Adjusted Trial Balance Dr.	Adjusted Trial Balance Cr.	Income Statement Dr.	Income Statement Cr.	Balance Sheet Dr.	Balance Sheet Cr.
Cash	172400				172400				172400	
Prepaid Insurance	35000			(A) 20000	15000				15000	
Cleaning Supplies	80000			(B) 60000	20000				20000	
Auto	122000				122000				122000	
Accumulated Depreciation, Auto		66000		(C) 15000		81000				81000
Accounts Payable		67400				67400				67400
B. Potter, Capital		248000				248000				248000
B. Potter, Withdrawals	60000				60000				60000	
Cleaning Fees		370000				370000		370000		
Salaries Expense	200000		(D) 17500		217500		217500			
Telephone Expense	28400				28400		28400			
Advertising Expense	27600				27600		27600			
Gas Expense	26000				26000		26000			
	751400	751400								
Insurance Expense			(A) 20000		20000		20000			
Cleaning Supplies Expense			(B) 60000		60000		60000			
Depreciation Expense, Auto			(C) 15000		15000		15000			
Salaries Payable				(D) 17500		17500				17500
			112500	112500	783900	783900	394500	370000	389400	413900
Net Loss								24500	24500	
							394500	394500	413900	413900

FIGURE 5.29 Worksheet for Potter Cleaning Service

Equipment	7,606	
Accounts Payable		684
C. Miller, Capital		8,000
Service Fees		17,350
Salaries	11,240	
Utilities Expense	842	
Rent Expense	360	
Insurance Expense	280	
Advertising Expense	146	
Totals	26,034	26,034

LO2 (15 min) **T-2.** Janet Smother is the new bookkeeper who replaced Dick Burns, owing to his sudden illness. Janet finds on her desk a note requesting that she close the books and supply the ending Capital figure. Janet is upset because she can only find the following:

a. Revenue and expense accounts all were zero balance.

b. Income Summary

    14,360 | 19,300

c. Owner withdrew $8,000.

d. Owner beginning Capital was $34,400.

Could you help Janet accomplish her assignment? What written suggestions should Janet make to her supervisor so that this situation will not happen again?

FINANCIAL REPORT PROBLEM

LO3 (15 min) ### Reading the Kellogg's Annual Report

Go to Appendix A and find Note 1 under Use Estimates in the Accounting Policies section. Why do actual financial reports have different estimates? What is the fiscal year for Kellogg's Company?

INTERNET PROJECT

Amazon

Go to the Web and search: Annual Report Amazon 2008.

Click on Investors Relations.

List out the latest news Amazon is providing to its investors.

Order a free annual report.

MyAccountingLab ## CONTINUING PROBLEM

LO1, 2, 3 (60 min) ### Sanchez Computer Center

Tony decided to end the Sanchez Computer Center's first year as of September 30, 200X. Following is an updated chart of accounts.

Assets	Revenue
1000 Cash	4000 Service Revenue
1020 Accounts Receivable	**Expenses**
1025 Prepaid Rent	5010 Advertising Expense
1030 Supplies	5020 Rent Expense
1080 Computer Shop Equip.	5030 Utilities Expense
1081 Accum. Depr., C.S. Equip.	5040 Phone Expense
1090 Office Equipment	5050 Supplies Expense
1091 Accum. Depr., Office Equip.	5060 Insurance Expense

Liabilities

2000 Accounts Payable

Owner's Equity

3000 T. Freedman, Capital

3010 T. Freedman, Withdrawals

3020 Income Summary

5070 Postage Expense

5080 Depr. Exp., C.S. Equip.

5090 Depr. Exp., Office Equip.

Assignment

1. Journalize the adjusting entries from Chapter 4.
2. Post the adjusting entries to the ledger.
3. Journalize the closing entries.
4. Post the closing entries to the ledger.
5. Prepare a post-closing trial balance.

SUBWAY Case

CLOSING TIME   *LO2, 3 (20 min)*

"You wait and see," Stan told his new sandwich artist Wanda Kurtz. "Everything will fall into place soon." Wanda had a tough time serving customers quickly enough, and Stan was in the middle of giving her a pep talk when the phone rang.

"I'll let the machine pick up," Stan reassured Wanda, as he proceeded to train her in some crucial POS touch-screen maneuvers.

"Stan!" an urgent voice came over the message machine. "I think you've forgotten something!" Stan picked up the phone and said, "Lila, can I get back to you tomorrow? I'm in the middle of an important talk with Wanda." One of Stan's strong points as an employer was his ability to focus 100 percent on his employees' concerns. Yet, Lila simply would not wait.

"Stan," Lila said impatiently, "you absolutely must get me your worksheet by 12 noon tomorrow so I can close your books. Tomorrow's the 31st of March and we close on the last day of the month!"

"*Ay caramba!*" Stan sighed. "Looks like I'm going to be up till the wee hours," he confided to Wanda when he put down the phone.

Although Subway company policy doesn't require a closing every month, closing the books is a key part of their accounting training for all new franchisees. By closing their books, business owners can clearly measure their net profit and loss for each period separate from all other periods. This practice makes activities such as budgeting and comparing performance with similar businesses (or performance over time) possible.

At 9:00 A.M. the next morning, an exhausted Stan opened up the restaurant and e-mailed his worksheet to Lila. He was feeling quite pleased with himself—that is, until he heard Lila's urgent-sounding voice coming over the message machine 10 minutes later.

"I've been over and over this," said Lila after Stan picked up, "and I can't get it to balance. I know it's hard for you to do this during working hours, but I need you to go back over the figures."

Stan opened up Peachtree and pored over his worksheets. Errors are hard to find when closing the books and, unfortunately, the process doesn't offer a set way to detect errors or any set place to start. Stan chose payroll because it is one of the largest expenses and because of the new hire.

At 11:45 he called Lila who sounded both exasperated and relieved to hear from him. "I think I've got it! It looks like I messed up on adjusting the Salaries Expense account. I looked at the payroll register and compared the total to the Salaries Payable account. It didn't match! When I hired Wanda Kurtz on the 26th, I should have increased both the Salaries Expense and the Salaries Payable lines because she has accrued wages."

"Yes," said Lila, "Salaries Expense is a debit and Salaries Payable is a credit, and you skipped the payable. Great! With this adjusting entry in the general journal, the worksheet will balance."

Stan's sigh of relief turned into a big yawn, and they both laughed. "I guess I just find it easier to hire people and train them than to account for them," said Stan.

Discussion Questions

1. How would the adjustment be made if Wanda Kurtz received $7.00 per hour and worked 25 additional hours? Where do you place her accrued wages?
2. Stan bought three new Subway aprons and hats for Wanda Smith for $20 each but forgot to post it to the Uniforms account. How much will the closing balance be off? In what way will it be off?
3. Put yourself in Stan's shoes: What is the value of doing a monthly closing, no matter how much—or little—business you do?

MINI PRACTICE SET

SULLIVAN REALTY

Reviewing the Accounting Cycle Twice

Est Time 5 hours This comprehensive review problem requires you to complete the accounting cycle for Sullivan Realty twice. This practice set allows you to review Chapters 1–5 while reinforcing the relationships between all parts of the accounting cycle. By completing two cycles, you will see how the ending June balances in the ledger are used to accumulate data in July.

First, look at the chart of accounts for Sullivan Realty.

Sullivan Realty
Chart of Accounts

Assets	**Revenue**
111 Cash	411 Commissions Earned
112 Accounts Receivable	**Expenses**
114 Prepaid Rent	511 Rent Expense
115 Office Supplies	512 Salaries Expense
121 Office Equipment	513 Gas Expense
122 Accumulated Depreciation,	514 Repairs Expense
Office Equipment	515 Telephone Expense
123 Automobile	516 Advertising Expense
124 Accumulated Depreciation, Automobile	517 Office Supplies Expense
Liabilities	518 Depreciation Expense,
211 Accounts Payable	Office Equipment
212 Salaries Payable	519 Depreciation Expense, Automobile
Owner's Equity	524 Miscellaneous Expense
311 John Sullivan, Capital	
312 John Sullivan, Withdrawals	
313 Income Summary	

On June 1, 200X, John Sullivan opened a real estate office called Sullivan Realty. The following transactions were completed for the month of June:

200X

June 1   John Sullivan invested $9,000 cash in the real estate agency along with $4,000 of office equipment.

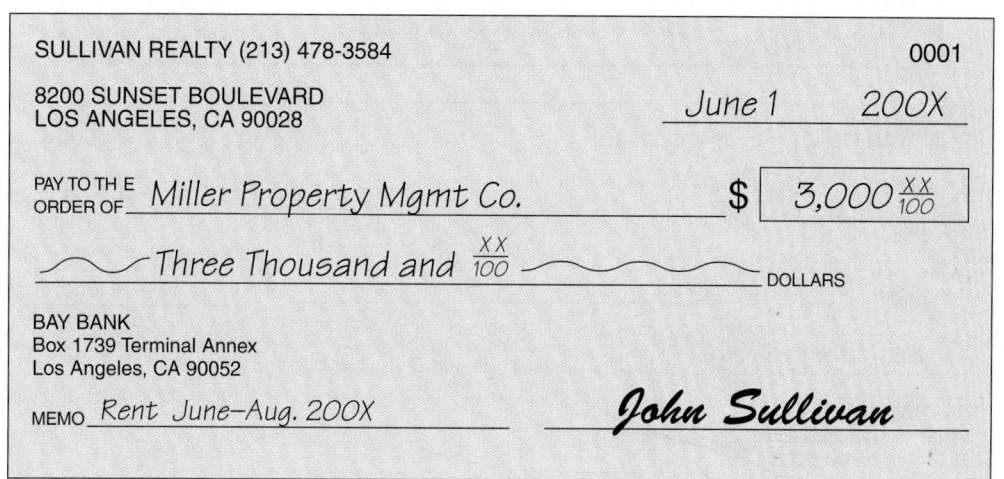

DEPOSIT TICKET

SULLIVAN REALTY (213) 478-3584
8200 SUNSET BOULEVARD
Los Angeles, CA 90028

DATE _____ June 1 _____ 200X _____

SIGN HERE IN PRESENCE OF TELLER FOR CASH RET'D FROM DEP.

BAY BANK
Box 1739 Terminal Annex
Los Angeles, CA 90052

⑈⑈122000661⑈⑈1400⑈03857⑈01362⑈

CASH	CURRENCY	9,000	00
	COIN		
LIST CHECKS SINGLY			
TOTAL FROM OTHER SIDE			
TOTAL		9,000	00
LESS CASH RECEIVED			
NET DEPOSIT		9,000	00

16-66/1220

A hold for uncollected funds may be placed on funds deposited by check or similar instruments. This could delay your ability to withdraw such funds. The delay if any would not exceed the period of time permitted by law.

June 1   Rented and paid three months rent in advance to Miller Property Management $3,000.

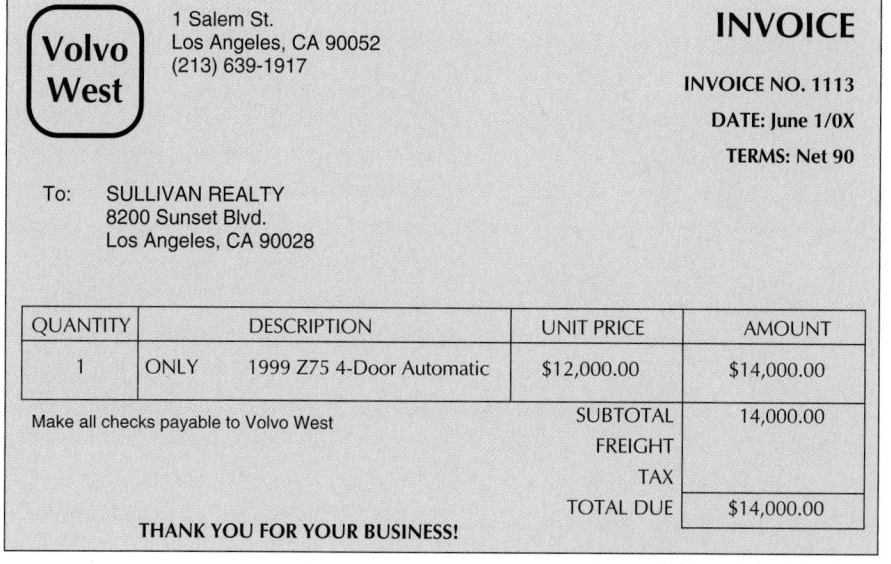

SULLIVAN REALTY (213) 478-3584   0001

8200 SUNSET BOULEVARD
LOS ANGELES, CA 90028   June 1   200X

PAY TO THE
ORDER OF _Miller Property Mgmt Co._____ $ | 3,000 XX/100 |

_____Three Thousand and XX/100_____ DOLLARS

BAY BANK
Box 1739 Terminal Annex
Los Angeles, CA 90052

MEMO _Rent June–Aug. 200X_____   _John Sullivan_

June 1   Bought an automobile on account from Volvo West, $14,000.

Volvo West
1 Salem St.
Los Angeles, CA 90052
(213) 639-1917

INVOICE

INVOICE NO. 1113
DATE: June 1/0X
TERMS: Net 90

To: SULLIVAN REALTY
      8200 Sunset Blvd.
      Los Angeles, CA 90028

QUANTITY	DESCRIPTION	UNIT PRICE	AMOUNT
1	ONLY 1999 Z75 4-Door Automatic	$12,000.00	$14,000.00
Make all checks payable to Volvo West	SUBTOTAL		14,000.00
	FREIGHT		
	TAX		
	TOTAL DUE		$14,000.00

THANK YOU FOR YOUR BUSINESS!

June 4   Purchased office supplies from Office Depot for cash, $300.

Office Depot

INVOICE

1 Ferncroft Rd.
Los Angeles, CA 90052
Phone (213) 631-0288

DATE:	June 4/0X
NUMBER:	D198795
TERMS:	Cash

SOLD TO:	SHIPPED TO:
Sullivan Realty 8200 Sunset Blvd. Los Angeles, CA 90028	Sullivan Realty 8200 Sunset Blvd. Los Angeles, CA 90028

DATE	DESCRIPTION	UNIT PRICE	AMOUNT
Jun 4/0X	Office supplies PAYMENT RECEIVED - - CHK #0002 - THANK YOU		$300.00
		Subtotal	300.00
		Total	$300.00

Business Number: 115555559

THANK YOU FOR YOUR BUSINESS

PLEASE PAY
THE ABOVE

SULLIVAN REALTY (213) 478-3584   0002

8200 SUNSET BOULEVARD
LOS ANGELES, CA 90028   *June 4   200X*

PAY TO THE
ORDER OF *Office Depot* $ *300 XX/100*

Three Hundred and XX/100 ———————————————— DOLLARS

BAY BANK
Box 1739 Terminal Annex
Los Angeles, CA 90052

MEMO *Office supplies*   *John Sullivan*

June 5   Purchased additional office supplies from Office Depot on account, $150.

Office Depot   **INVOICE**

1 Ferncroft Rd.   **DATE:**   June 5/0X
Los Angeles, CA 90052   **NUMBER:**   D198825
Phone (213) 631-0288   **TERMS:**   net 60

SOLD TO:	SHIPPED TO:
Sullivan Realty 8200 Sunset Blvd. Los Angeles, CA 90028	Sullivan Realty 8200 Sunset Blvd. Los Angeles, CA 90028

DATE	DESCRIPTION	UNIT PRICE	AMOUNT
Jun 5/0X	Office supplies		$150.00
		Subtotal	150.00
		Total	$150.00

Business Number: 115555559

THANK YOU FOR YOUR BUSINESS   PLEASE PAY
                                                THE ABOVE

June 6   Sold a house to Bill Barnes and collected a $6,000 commission.

⊢ **DEPOSIT TICKET** ⊢

SULLIVAN REALTY (213)478-3584
8200 SUNSET BOULEVARD
Los Angeles, CA 90028

CASH	CURRENCY		
	COIN		
LIST CHECKS SINGLY 250-99		6,000	00
TOTAL FROM OTHER SIDE			
TOTAL			
LESS CASH RECEIVED			
NET DEPOSIT		6,000	00

16-66/1220

A hold for uncollected funds may be placed on funds deposited by check or similar instruments. This could delay your ability to withdraw such funds. The delay if any would not exceed the period of time permitted by law.

DATE _____ June 6 _____ 200X _____

SIGN HERE IN PRESENCE OF TELLER FOR CASH RET'D FROM DEP.

BAY BANK
Box 1739 Terminal Annex
Los Angeles, CA 90052

⑆12200066⑈1400⁙03857⁙0136 2⑈

SULLIVAN REALTY COMMISSION REPORT			**Date:**	June 6, 200X	
Name:	Bill Barnes				
Date:	**Sales Description**	**Sales No.**	**Commission Amount**		
Jun 6/0X	Home at 66 Sullivan St.	A1001	$6,000.00	Paid in full.	
C001		**Remarks:**			

June 8 Paid gas bill to Petro Petroleum, $22.

SULLIVAN REALTY (213) 478-3584	0003
8200 SUNSET BOULEVARD LOS ANGELES, CA 90028	*June 8* *200X*

PAY TO THE
ORDER OF _Petro Petroleum_ $ 22 XX/100

Twenty-two and XX/100 ———————————————— DOLLARS

BAY BANK
Box 1739 Terminal Annex
Los Angeles, CA 90052

MEMO _Gas Bill – June 6_   *John Sullivan*

June 15 Paid Betty Long, office secretary, $350.

SULLIVAN REALTY (213) 478-3584	0004
8200 SUNSET BOULEVARD LOS ANGELES, CA 90028	*June 15* *200X*

PAY TO THE
ORDER OF _Betty Long_ $ 350 XX/100

Three Hundred fifty and XX/100 ———————————————— DOLLARS

BAY BANK
Box 1739 Terminal Annex
Los Angeles, CA 90052

MEMO _Salary – June 1–15_   *John Sullivan*

June 17 Sold a building lot to West Land Developers and earned a commission, $6,500 payment to be received on July 8.

SULLIVAN REALTY COMMISSION REPORT				*Date:* June 17, 200X	
Name: West Land Developers					
Date:	**Sales Description**	**Sales No.**	**Commission Amount**		
Jun 17/0X	*Lot at 8 Ridge Rd.*	*A1002*	*$6,500.00*		
C002		**Remarks:** Payment due July 8, 200X			

June 20   John Sullivan withdrew $1,000 from the business to pay personal expenses.

SULLIVAN REALTY (213) 478-3584	0005

8200 SUNSET BOULEVARD
LOS ANGELES, CA 90028

June 20   200X

PAY TO THE
ORDER OF _*John Sullivan*_ $ | *1,000 $\frac{XX}{100}$* |

One Thousand and $\frac{XX}{100}$ _____ DOLLARS

BAY BANK
Box 1739 Terminal Annex
Los Angeles, CA 90052

MEMO _*Withdrawal*_   *John Sullivan*

June 21   Sold a house to Laura Harrison and collected a $3,500 commission.

⊣ DEPOSIT TICKET ⊢

SULLIVAN REALTY (213) 478-3584
8200 SUNSET BOULEVARD
Los Angeles, CA 90028

CASH	CURRENCY		
	COIN		
LIST CHECKS SINGLY 270-88		3,500	00
TOTAL FROM OTHER SIDE			
TOTAL			
LESS CASH RECEIVED			
NET DEPOSIT		3,500	00

DATE ___ *June 21   200X* ___

SIGN HERE IN PRESENCE OF TELLER FOR CASH RET'D FROM DEP.

16-66/1220

A hold for uncollected funds may be placed on funds deposited by check or similar instruments. This could delay your ability to withdraw such funds. The delay if any would not exceed the period of time permitted by law.

BAY BANK
Box 1739 Terminal Annex
Los Angeles, CA 90052

⑆122000661⑈1400⑇03857⑈0136 2⑉

SULLIVAN REALTY COMMISSION REPORT			Date:	June 21, 200X	
Name:		Ms. Laura Harrison			
Date:	**Sales Description**		**Sales No.**	**Commission Amount**	
Jun 21/0X	Home at 666 Jersey St.		A1003	$3,500.00	*Paid in full.*
C003			**Remarks:**		

June 22 Paid gas bill, $25, to Petro Petroleum.

SULLIVAN REALTY (213) 478-3584   0006

8200 SUNSET BOULEVARD
LOS ANGELES, CA 90028   *June 22*   *200X*

PAY TO THE
ORDER OF *Petro Petroleum* $ *25 XX/100*

Twenty-five and XX/100 ———————— DOLLARS

BAY BANK
Box 1739 Terminal Annex
Los Angeles, CA 90052

MEMO *Gas Bill–June 22*   *John Sullivan*

June 24 Paid Volvo West $600 to repair automobile.

QUANTITY	DESCRIPTION		UNIT PRICE	AMOUNT
1	ONLY	Z75 Air conditioning repair		$ 600.00

Volvo West
1 Salem St.
Los Angeles, CA 90052
(213) 639-1917

INVOICE

INVOICE NO. 1184
DATE: June 24/0X
TERMS: Cash

To: SULLIVAN REALTY
8200 Sunset Blvd.
Los Angeles, CA 90028

Ship To:
Pickup

Make all checks payable to Volvo West

PAYMENT RECEIVED - Check #0007

SUBTOTAL	600.00
FREIGHT	
TAX	
TOTAL DUE	$ 600.00

THANK YOU FOR YOUR BUSINESS!

SULLIVAN REALTY (213) 478-3584   0007

8200 SUNSET BOULEVARD
LOS ANGELES, CA 90028   *June 24*   *200X*

PAY TO THE
ORDER OF *Volvo West* $ *600 XX/100*

Six Hundred and XX/100 ———————— DOLLARS

BAY BANK
Box 1739 Terminal Annex
Los Angeles, CA 90052

MEMO *Auto Repairs – Inv. 1184*   *John Sullivan*

June   30   Paid Betty Long, office secretary, $350.

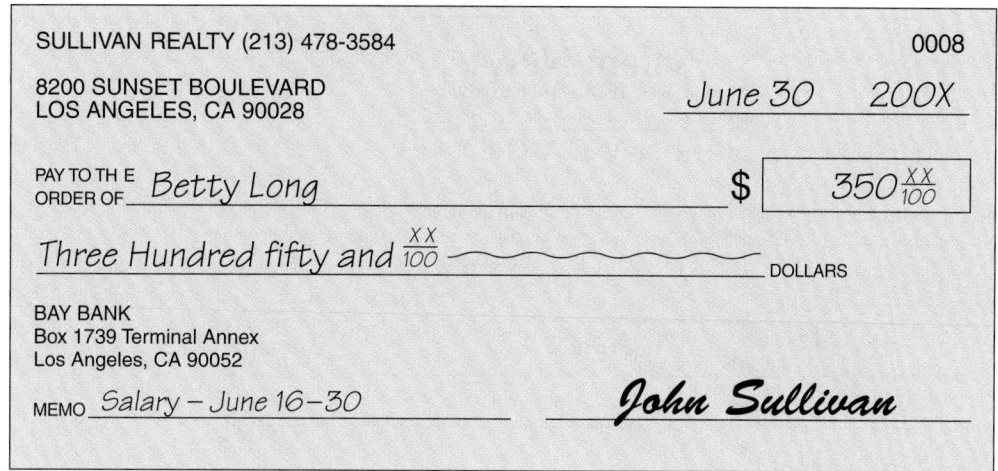

June   30   Paid Verizon June telephone bill, $510.

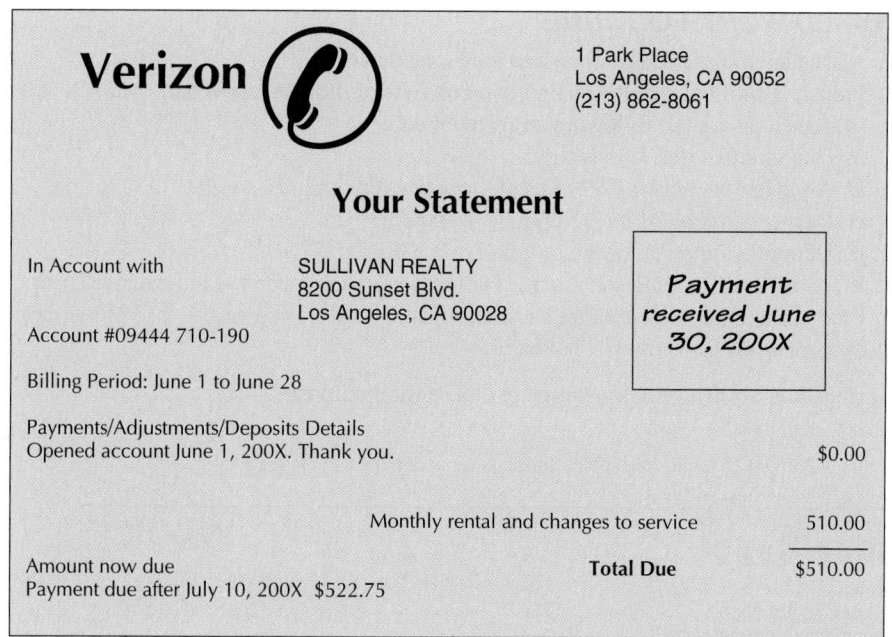

June 30 Received advertising bill for June, $1,200, from *Salem News.* The bill is to be paid on July 2.

Salem News
1 Main St., Los Angeles, CA 90052
(213) 744-1000

I N V O I C E

SOLD TO: Sullivan Realty
8200 Sunset Blvd.
Los Angeles, CA 90028

Invoice No.: 4879
Date: June 30, 200X
Due Date: July 2, 200X

DATE	DESCRIPTION		AMOUNT
June 26/0X	Advertising in Salem News during June 200X		$1,200.00
		SUBTOTAL	1,200.00
Business Number 944122338		TOTAL	$1,200.00

MAKE ALL CHECKS PAYABLE TO SALEM NEWS

REQUIRED WORK FOR JUNE

1. Journalize transactions and post to ledger accounts.
2. Prepare a trial balance in the first two columns of the worksheet and complete the worksheet using the following adjustment data:
   a. One month's rent had expired.
   b. An inventory shows $50 of office supplies remaining.
   c. Depreciation on office equipment, $100.
   d. Depreciation on automobile, $200.
3. Prepare a June income statement, statement of owner's equity, and balance sheet.
4. From the worksheet, journalize and post adjusting and closing entries (p. 3 of journal).
5. Prepare a post-closing trial balance.

During July, Sullivan Realty completed these transactions:

July 1 Purchased additional office supplies on account from Office Depot, $700.

Check Figure:
June post closing trial balance
$38,893

Office Depot

INVOICE

1 Ferncroft Rd.
Los Angeles, CA 90052
Phone (213) 631-0288

DATE: Jul 1/0X
NUMBER: D1996035
TERMS: Net 60

SOLD TO:
Sullivan Realty
8200 Sunset Blvd.
Los Angeles, CA 90028

SHIPPED TO:
Sullivan Realty
8200 Sunset Blvd.
Los Angeles, CA 90028

DATE	DESCRIPTION	UNIT PRICE	AMOUNT
Jul 2/0X	Office supplies		$700.00
		Subtotal	700.00
		Total	$700.00

Business Number: 115555559

PLEASE PAY
THE ABOVE

THANK YOU FOR YOUR BUSINESS

July   2   Paid *Salem News* advertising bill for June.

SULLIVAN REALTY (213) 478-3584	0010
8200 SUNSET BOULEVARD LOS ANGELES, CA 90028	*July 2* *200X*
PAY TO THE ORDER OF ___*Salem News*___	$	*1,200 XX/100*

One Thousand Two Hundred and XX/100 ———————— DOLLARS

BAY BANK
Box 1739 Terminal Annex
Los Angeles, CA 90052

MEMO ___*Invoice # 4879*___   *John Sullivan*

⑂ ⑂2 2000 66 ⑂⑂ ⑂400 ⑄ 03857 ⑄ 0136 2 ⑄ 0010

July   3   Sold a house to Melissa King and collected a commission of $6,600.

SULLIVAN REALTY COMMISSION REPORT				*Date:* July 3, 200X	
Name:	Melissa King				
Date:	*Sales Description*	*Sales No.*	*Commission Amount*		
July 3/0X	Home at 800 Rose Ave.	A1004	$6,600.00	*Paid in full.*	
C004			*Remarks:*		

⊣ DEPOSIT TICKET ⊢					
SULLIVAN REALTY (213)478-3584 8200 SUNSET BOULEVARD Los Angeles, CA 90028	**CASH**	CURRENCY			
		COIN			
	LIST CHECKS SINGLY 278-92		*6,600*	*00*	16-66/1220
					A hold for uncollected funds may be placed on funds deposited by check or similar instruments. This could delay your ability to withdraw such funds. The delay if any would not exceed the period of time permitted by law.
DATE ___*July 3*___ *200X*	TOTAL FROM OTHER SIDE				
	TOTAL				
SIGN HERE IN PRESENCE OF TELLER FOR CASH RET'D FROM DEP.	LESS CASH RECEIVED				
BAY BANK Box 1739 Terminal Annex Los Angeles, CA 90052	**NET DEPOSIT**		*6,600*	*00*	

⑂ ⑂2 2000 66 ⑂⑂ ⑂400 ⑄ 03857 ⑄ 0136 2 ⑄

July   6   Paid gas bill to Petro Petroleum, $29.

SULLIVAN REALTY (213) 478-3584   0011

8200 SUNSET BOULEVARD   July 6   200X
LOS ANGELES, CA 90028

PAY TO THE
ORDER OF   Petro Petroleum $ 29 XX/100

Twenty-nine and XX/100 —————————————— DOLLARS

BAY BANK
Box 1739 Terminal Annex
Los Angeles, CA 90052

MEMO   Gas Bill – July 6   John Sullivan

July   8   Collected commission from West Land Developers for sale of building lot on June 17.

—| DEPOSIT TICKET |—

SULLIVAN REALTY (213)478-3584
8200 SUNSET BOULEVARD
Los Angeles, CA 90028

CASH	CURRENCY		
	COIN		
LIST CHECKS SINGLY 228-114		6,500	00

DATE   July 8   200X

16-66/1220

SIGN HERE IN PRESENCE OF TELLER FOR CASH RET'D FROM DEP.

A hold for uncollected funds may be placed on funds deposited by check or similar instruments. This could delay your ability to withdraw such funds. The delay if any would not exceed the period of time permitted by law.

TOTAL FROM OTHER SIDE		
TOTAL		
LESS CASH RECEIVED		
NET DEPOSIT	6,500	00

BAY BANK
Box 1739 Terminal Annex
Los Angeles, CA 90052

⑆122000661⑈1400‖03857‖0136 2‖

July   12   Paid $300 to Regan Realtors Assoc. to send employees to realtors' workshop.

SULLIVAN REALTY (213) 478-3584   0012

8200 SUNSET BOULEVARD   July 12   200X
LOS ANGELES, CA 90028

PAY TO THE
ORDER OF   Regan Realtors Assoc. $ 300 XX/100

Three Hundred and XX/100 —————————————— DOLLARS

BAY BANK
Box 1739 Terminal Annex
Los Angeles, CA 90052

MEMO   Workshop Registration   John Sullivan

July   15   Paid Betty Long, office secretary, $350.

SULLIVAN REALTY (213) 478-3584	0013

8200 SUNSET BOULEVARD
LOS ANGELES, CA 90028   *July 15   200X*

PAY TO THE ORDER OF *Betty Long* $ 350 $\frac{XX}{100}$

Three Hundred fifty and $\frac{XX}{100}$ —————————— DOLLARS

BAY BANK
Box 1739 Terminal Annex
Los Angeles, CA 90052

MEMO *Salary July 1–15*   *John Sullivan*

July   17   Sold a house to Matt Karminsky and earned a commission of $2,400. Commission to be received on August 10.

SULLIVAN REALTY
COMMISSION REPORT   *Date:*   July 17, 200X

Name: Matt Karminsky

Date:	Sales Description	Sales No.	Commission Amount	
July 17/0X	Home at RR2, Site 3	A1010	$2,400.00	
C005		*Remarks:* Payment due August 10, 200X		

July   18   Sold a building lot to DiBiasi Builders and collected a commission of $7,000.

DEPOSIT TICKET

SULLIVAN REALTY (213)478-3584
8200 SUNSET BOULEVARD
Los Angeles, CA 90028

DATE   *July 18   200X*

SIGN HERE IN PRESENCE OF TELLER FOR CASH RET'D FROM DEP.

BAY BANK
Box 1739 Terminal Annex
Los Angeles, CA 90052

CASH	CURRENCY		
	COIN		
LIST CHECKS SINGLY 269-10		7,000	00
TOTAL FROM OTHER SIDE			
TOTAL			
LESS CASH RECEIVED			
NET DEPOSIT		7,000	00

16-66/1220

A hold for uncollected funds may be placed on funds deposited by check or similar instruments. This could delay your ability to withdraw such funds. The delay if any would not exceed the period of time permitted by law.

⑈122000661⑈1400⑈03857⑈0136 2⑈

SULLIVAN REALTY					
COMMISSION REPORT				**Date:**	July 18, 200X
Name:	DiBiasi Builders				
Date:	**Sales Description**		**Sales No.**	**Commission Amount**	
July 18/0X	Building lot at 5004 King St. E		A1005	$7,000.00	Paid in full.
C006			**Remarks:**		

July 22 Sent a check to Catholic Charities for $40 to help sponsor a local road race to aid the poor. (This amount is not to be considered an advertising expense, but it is a business expense and is posted to Miscellaneous Expense.)

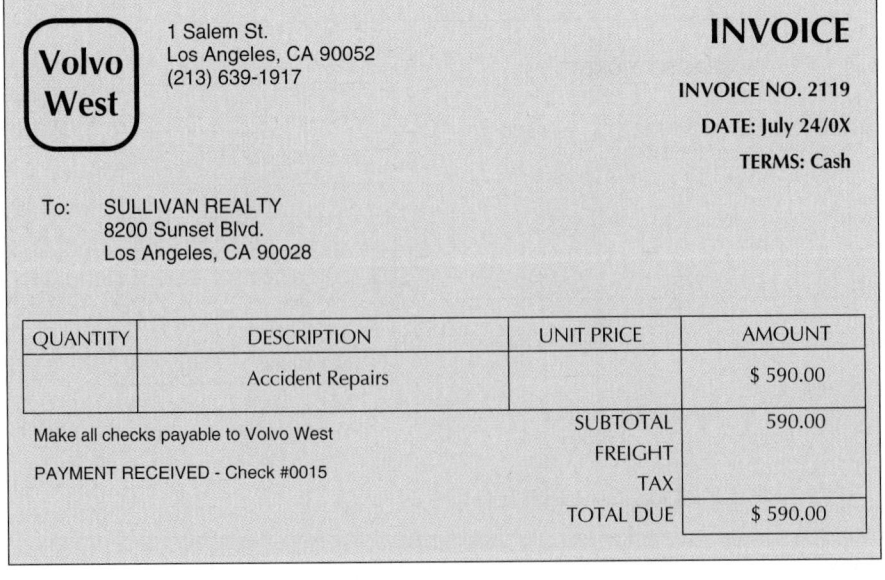

SULLIVAN REALTY (213) 478-3584		0014
8200 SUNSET BOULEVARD LOS ANGELES, CA 90028		July 22 200X
PAY TO THE ORDER OF *Catholic Charities*	$	40 XX/100
Forty and XX/100		DOLLARS
BAY BANK Box 1739 Terminal Annex Los Angeles, CA 90052		
MEMO Aid to Poor		*John Sullivan*

⑆122000661⑆1400 03857 0136 2 0014

July 24 Paid Volvo West $590 for repairs to automobile due to accident.

Volvo West

1 Salem St.
Los Angeles, CA 90052
(213) 639-1917

INVOICE

INVOICE NO. 2119
DATE: July 24/0X
TERMS: Cash

To: SULLIVAN REALTY
8200 Sunset Blvd.
Los Angeles, CA 90028

QUANTITY	DESCRIPTION	UNIT PRICE	AMOUNT
	Accident Repairs		$ 590.00
Make all checks payable to Volvo West		SUBTOTAL	590.00
		FREIGHT	
PAYMENT RECEIVED - Check #0015		TAX	
		TOTAL DUE	$ 590.00

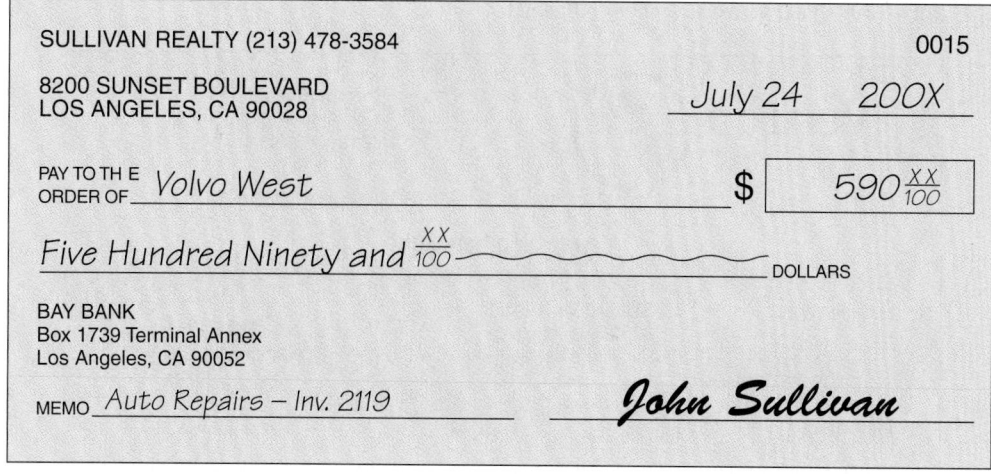

SULLIVAN REALTY (213) 478-3584   0015

8200 SUNSET BOULEVARD
LOS ANGELES, CA 90028   July 24   200X

PAY TO THE ORDER OF _Volvo West_ $ 590 $\frac{XX}{100}$

Five Hundred Ninety and $\frac{XX}{100}$ ———————— DOLLARS

BAY BANK
Box 1739 Terminal Annex
Los Angeles, CA 90052

MEMO _Auto Repairs – Inv. 2119_   *John Sullivan*

July   28   John Sullivan withdrew $1,800 from the business to pay personal expenses.

SULLIVAN REALTY (213) 478-3584   0016

8200 SUNSET BOULEVARD
LOS ANGELES, CA 90028   July 28   200X

PAY TO THE ORDER OF _John Sullivan_ $ 1,800 $\frac{XX}{100}$

One Thousand Eight hundred and $\frac{XX}{100}$ ———————— DOLLARS

BAY BANK
Box 1739 Terminal Annex
Los Angeles, CA 90052

MEMO _Withdrawal_   *John Sullivan*

July   30   Paid Betty Long, office secretary, $350.

SULLIVAN REALTY (213) 478-3584   0017

8200 SUNSET BOULEVARD
LOS ANGELES, CA 90028   July 30   200X

PAY TO THE ORDER OF _Betty Long_ $ 350 $\frac{XX}{100}$

Three Hundred fifty and $\frac{XX}{100}$ ———————— DOLLARS

BAY BANK
Box 1739 Terminal Annex
Los Angeles, CA 90052

MEMO _Salary – July 16–31_   *John Sullivan*

July 30 Paid Verizon telephone bill, $590.

Verizon

1 Park Place
Los Angeles, CA 90052
(213) 862-8061

Your Statement

In Account with

SULLIVAN REALTY
8200 Sunset Blvd.
Los Angeles, CA 90028

Account #09444 710-190

Billing Period: July 1 to July 28

Payment received July 30, 200X

Payments/Adjustments/Deposits Details	$590.00
Payment Received July 2. Thank you.	−590.00
Monthly rental and changes to service	590.00
Amount now due **Total Due**	$590.00

Payment due after August 10, 200X $610.75

SULLIVAN REALTY (213) 478-3584   0018

8200 SUNSET BOULEVARD
LOS ANGELES, CA 90028   *July 30   200X*

PAY TO THE
ORDER OF *Verizon* $ *590 XX/100*

Five Hundred Ninety and XX/100 ———————— DOLLARS

BAY BANK
Box 1739 Terminal Annex
Los Angeles, CA 90052

MEMO *July Phone Bill*   *John Sullivan*

July 30 Advertising bill from *Salem News* for July, $1,400. The bill is to be paid on August 2.

Salem News
1 Main St., Los Angeles, CA 90052
(213) 744-1000

INVOICE

SOLD TO: Sullivan Realty   Invoice No.:   5400
            8200 Sunset Blvd.   Date: July 30, 200X
            Los Angeles, CA 90028   Due Date: August 2, 200X

DATE	DESCRIPTION		AMOUNT
July 30/0X	Advertising in Salem News during July 200X		$1,400.00
		SUBTOTAL	1,400.00
Business Number 944122338		TOTAL	$1,400.00

MAKE ALL CHECKS PAYABLE TO SALEM NEWS

REQUIRED WORK FOR JULY

1. Journalize transactions in a general journal (p. 4) and post to ledger accounts.
2. Prepare a trial balance in the first two columns of a blank, fold-out worksheet located at the end of your textbook and complete the worksheet using the following adjustment data:
   a. One month's rent had expired.
   b. An inventory shows $90 of office supplies remaining.
   c. Depreciation on office equipment, $100.
   d. Depreciation on automobile, $200.
3. Prepare a July income statement, statement of owner's equity, and balance sheet.
4. From the worksheet, journalize and post adjusting and closing entries (p. 6 of journal).
5. Prepare a post-closing trial balance.

PEACHTREE COMPUTER WORKSHOP

COMPUTERIZED ACCOUNTING APPLICATION FOR CHAPTER 5

Refresher on using Peachtree Complete Accounting

Before starting this assignment, you may want to refresh your memory by reading the following PDF documents in the multimedia library of the MyAccountingLab Web site. Remember to choose the PDF document for your version of Peachtree.

1. An Introduction to Peachtree Complete Accounting
2. Correcting Peachtree Transactions
3. How to Repeat or Restart a Peachtree Assignment
4. Backing Up and Restoring Your Work in Peachtree

You also should have completed the following workshops:

1. Workshop 1 Atlas Company from Chapter 3
2. Workshop 2 Zell Company from Chapter 4

Workshop 3:

Accounting Cycle Mini Practice Set

In this workshop you will complete the June and July accounting cycles for Sullivan Realty using Peachtree. Tasks include posting journal entries and adjusting journal entries, printing reports and financial statements, and closing the accounting period.

Instructions and the data file for completing this assignment are in the multimedia library of the MyAccountingLab Web site. Open the **Workshop 3 Sullivan Realty** PDF document for your version of Peachtree and download the **Sullivan Realty** data file for your version of Peachtree.

QUICKBOOKS COMPUTER WORKSHOP

COMPUTERIZED ACCOUNTING APPLICATION FOR CHAPTER 5

Refresher on using QuickBooks Pro

Before starting this assignment, you may want to refresh your memory by reading the following PDF documents in the multimedia library of the MyAccountingLab Web site. Remember to choose the PDF document for your version of QuickBooks.

1. An Introduction to QuickBooks Pro
2. Correcting QuickBooks Transactions
3. How to Repeat or Restart a QuickBooks Assignment
4. Backing Up and Restoring Your Work in QuickBooks

You also should have completed the following workshops:

1. Workshop 1 Atlas Company from Chapter 3
2. Workshop 2 Zell Company from Chapter 4

Workshop 3:

Accounting Cycle Mini Practice Set

In this workshop you will complete the June and July accounting cycles for Sullivan Realty using QuickBooks. Tasks include posting journal entries and adjusting journal entries, printing reports and financial statements, and closing the accounting period.

Instructions and the data file for completing this assignment are in the multimedia library of the MyAccountingLab Web site. Open the ***Workshop 3 Sullivan Realty*** PDF document for your version of QuickBooks and download the ***Sullivan Realty*** data file for your version of QuickBooks.

Banking Procedure and Control of Cash

es | **CD Rates** | **Credit Cards Home Equity Loans Mo**

Help

🔍 Search ⭐ Favorites 🌐 | ✉▾ 🖨 W ▾ 🗋 📖 💬 » ┊ Google

n/

de: **Credit cards** | **CD rates**

Preview Bankrate.com's beta site.

Bankrate.com 〰
omprehensive. Objective. Free.

| News & Advice | Compare Rates | Calculators |

| Mortgage | Home Equity | Auto | CDs & Investments | Retirement | Credit Cards | Checking & Savings | Co Fin |

- advertisement -

Calculate New Payment

Select Your Mortgage ➜

1. 30 Yr Fixed   3. 2/1 ARM   1. Home R
2. 15 Yr Fixed

DID YOU KNOW? In 2006 more than 53 million visited the Bankrate.com Web site. Bankrate continually surveys more than 4,800 financial institutions to keep the bank rates on its Web site up-to-date. Visit *www.Bankrate.com* to find more information about Bankrate.

owerMyBills.com

LEARNING OBJECTIVES

1. Depositing, writing, and endorsing checks for a checking account.

2. Reconciling a bank statement.

3. Establishing and replenishing a petty cash fund; setting up an auxiliary petty cash record.

4. Establishing and replenishing a change fund.

5. Handling transactions involving cash short and over.

Bank Rate, Inc., helps you monitor how interest rates change. Be it in business or personal life, you need to make wise financial decisions. In the first five chapters of this book, we analyzed the accounting cycle for businesses that perform personal services (e.g., word processing or legal services). In this chapter we turn our attention to Becca's Jewelry Store, a merchandising company that earns revenue by selling goods (or merchandise) to customers. When Becca's business began to increase, she became concerned that she was not monitoring the business's cash closely. She understood that a business with good **internal control systems** safeguards cash. Cash is the asset that is most easily stolen, lost, or mishandled. Therefore, it is important to protect all cash receipts and to control cash payments so that payments are made only for authorized business purposes.

> The internal control policies of a company will depend on things such as number of employees, company size, sources of cash, and usage of the Internet.

After studying the situation carefully, Becca began a series of procedures that were to be followed by all company employees. The new company policies that Becca's Jewelry Store would put into place are as follows:

1. Responsibilities and duties of employees will be divided. For example, the person receiving the cash, whether at the register or by opening the mail, will not record this information into the accounting records. The accountant will not be handling the cash receipts.
2. All cash receipts of Becca's Jewelry Store will be deposited into the bank the same day they arrive.
3. All cash payments will be made by check (except petty cash, which is discussed later in this chapter).
4. Employees will be rotated. This change allows workers to become acquainted with the work of others as well as to prepare for a possible changeover of jobs.
5. Becca Baker will sign all checks after receiving authorization to pay from the departments concerned.
6. At time of payment, all supporting invoices or documents will be stamped paid. The stamp will show when the invoice or document is paid as well as the number of the check used.
7. All checks will be prenumbered. Periodically, the number of the checks that were issued and the numbers of the blank check forms remaining should be verified to make sure that all check numbers are accounted for. This change will control the use of checks and make it difficult to use a check fraudulently without its being revealed at some point.
8. Monthly bank statements will be sent to and reconciled by someone other than the employees who handle, record, or deposit the cash.

LO1 Learning Unit 6-1 Bank Procedures, Checking Accounts, and Bank Reconciliation

Becca knew that a checking account is one of the most useful and common banking services available, but she had many questions and decisions to make. She wanted to know about account options, monthly service charges, check printing charges, minimum balance requirements, interest paid on the account, availability of automatic teller machines (ATMs), and debit cards. Before Becca's Jewelry opened on April 1, 200X, she met with the manager at the Sunshine Bank to discuss opening and using a checking account for the company.

Opening a Checking Account

> A signature card is another safeguard.

The bank manager gave Becca a signature card to fill out. The bank uses the **signature card** to verify the authenticity of the signature on all checks. Because Becca would be signing all the checks for her company, she was the only person who needed to sign the card.

After Becca completed the initial paperwork, she received a set of checks and deposit slips. A **deposit slip** is a form that is used when making deposits in a bank or savings and loan association. When filling out a deposit slip, you list the total amount of currency, coins, and checks that you are depositing (see Fig. 6.1). You list each check you are

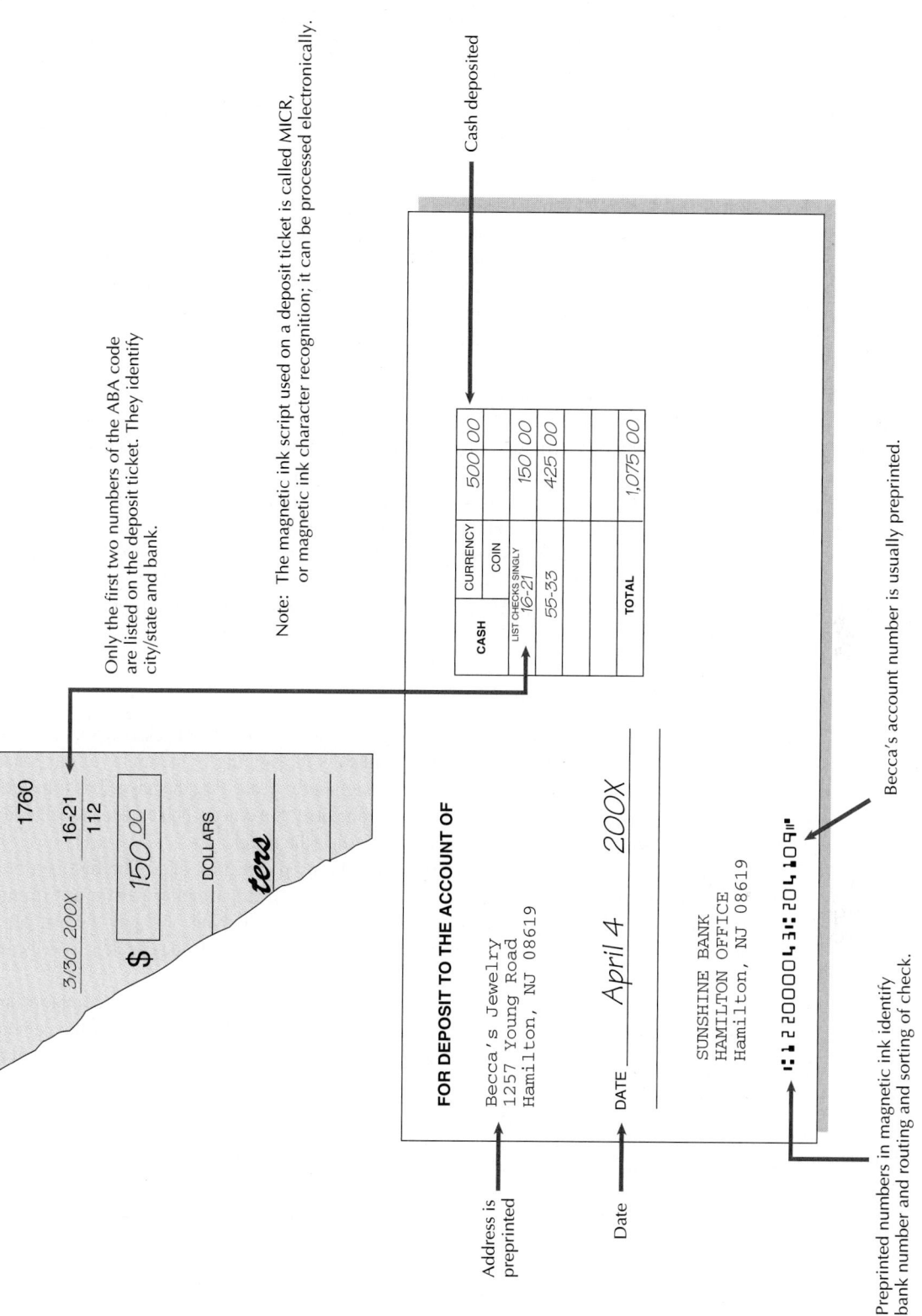

Only the first two numbers of the ABA code are listed on the deposit ticket. They identify city/state and bank.

Note: The magnetic ink script used on a deposit ticket is called MICR, or magnetic ink character recognition; it can be processed electronically.

Cash deposited

1760

16-21
112

3/30 200X

$ 150 00

DOLLARS

ters

CASH	CURRENCY	500	00
	COIN		
LIST CHECKS SINGLY 16-21		150	00
55-33		425	00
TOTAL		1,075	00

FOR DEPOSIT TO THE ACCOUNT OF

Becca's Jewelry
1257 Young Road
Hamilton, NJ 08619

DATE _____ April 4   200X

SUNSHINE BANK
HAMILTON OFFICE
Hamilton, NJ 08619

⑆ ⑈ 2 2 0 0 0 0 4 3 ⑈ 2 0 4 ⑆ 0 9 ⑈

Becca's account number is usually preprinted.

Address is
preprinted

Date

Preprinted numbers in magnetic ink identify
bank number and routing and sorting of check.

FIGURE 6.1 Deposit Ticket

depositing individually. Also, alongside each check you list its American Bankers Association (ABA) code. The ABA code is found in the upper right-corner of each check, below the check number. The 16 identifies the large city or state the bank is located in, and the 21 identifies the bank. The 112 is split into two parts: 1 represents the First Federal Reserve District, and 12 is a routing number used by the Federal Reserve Bank. When completing a deposit slip, only the first two numbers are required.

When a deposit is completed, the depositor receives a copy of the deposit as a receipt or proof of the transaction. The deposit should also be recorded on the current check stub. The bank manager told Becca that she could give the deposits to a bank teller or she could use an automated teller machine (ATM). The ATM could also be used for withdrawing cash, transferring funds, or paying bills. For decades, ATM cards could only be used at ATMs, but in recent years, they took on another function, a debit feature. As a **debit card,** the card carries a VISA or MasterCard logo and can be used anywhere VISA or MasterCard is accepted. The amount of the purchase paid for with a debit card is deducted directly from your checking account.

Often, Becca makes her deposits after business hours when the bank is closed. At those times, she puts the deposit into a locked bag (provided by the bank) and places the bag in the night depository. The bank will credit Becca's account when the deposit is processed. Becca plans to make all business payments by written check (except petty cash) and deposit all money received (cash and checks) in the bank account.

> When a bank credits your account, it is increasing the balance.

Many checking accounts earn interest. For our purposes, however, we assume that the checking account for Becca's Jewelry Store does not pay interest. Also, we must assume that the checking account has a monthly service charge but no individual charge for checks written.

Check Endorsement

Checks have to be *endorsed* (signed) by the person to whom the check is made out before they can be deposited or cashed. **Endorsement** is the signing or stamping of one's name on the back left-hand side of the check. This signature means that the payee has transferred the right to deposit or cash the check to someone else (the bank). The bank can then collect the money from the person or company that issued the check.

> Endorsements can be made by using a rubber stamp instead of a handwritten signature.

Three different types of endorsement can be used (see Fig. 6.2). The first is a *blank endorsement.* A blank endorsement does not specify that a particular person or firm must endorse it. It can be further endorsed by someone else. The bank will pay the last person who signs the check. This type of endorsement is not very safe. If the check is lost, the person who finds it can sign it and get the money.

The second type of endorsement is a *full endorsement.* The person or company signing (or stamping) the back of the check indicates the name of the company or the person to whom the check is to be paid. Only the person or company named in the endorsement can transfer the check to someone else.

> The regulations require the endorsement to be within the top 1½ inches to speed up the check-clearing process.

Restrictive endorsements, the third type of endorsement, are the safest for businesses. Becca's Jewelry Store stamps the back of the check so that it must be deposited in the firm's account. This stamp limits any further use of the check.

The Checkbook

When Becca opened her business's checking account, she received checks. These checks could be used to buy things for the business or to pay bills or salaries.

> Drawer:
> One who writes the check.

A **check** is a written order signed by a **drawer** (the person who writes the check) instructing a **drawee** (the person who pays the check) to pay a specific sum of money to the **payee** (the person to whom the check is payable). Figure 6.3 shows a check issued by Becca's Jewelry Store. Becca Baker is the drawer, Sunshine Bank is the drawee, and Ziegler Wholesalers is the payee.

> Drawee:
> One who pays money to payee.

> Payee:
> One to whom the check is payable.

Look at the check in Figure 6.3. Notice that certain things, such as the company's name and address and the check number, are preprinted. Other things you should notice are (1) the line drawn after $\frac{xx}{100}$ which is to fill up the empty space and ensure that the amount

Types of Check Endorsement

FIGURE 6.2 Types of Check Endorsement

Blank Endorsement

Becca Baker

204109

A signature on the back left side of a check of the person or firm the check is payable to. This check can be *further* endorsed by someone else; the bank will give the money to the last person who signs the check. This type of endorsement is not very safe. If the check is lost, anyone who picks it up can sign it and get the money.

Full Endorsement

Pay to the order of
Sunshine Bank

Becca's Jewelry Store
204109

This type of endorsement is safer than a simple signature, because the person or company signing (or stamping) the back of the check indicates the name of the company or person to whom the check is to be paid. Only the person or company named in the endorsement can transfer the check to someone else.

Restrictive Endorsement

Payable to the order of
Sunshine Bank
for deposit only.

Becca's Jewelry Store
204109

This endorsement is the safest for businesses. Becca's Jewelry Store stamps the back of the check so that it must be deposited in the firm's account. This endorsement limits any further use of the check (it can only be deposited in the specified account).

cannot be changed, and (2) the word *and,* which should be used only to differentiate between dollars and cents.

Figure 6.3 on the following page includes a check stub. The check stub is used to record transactions, and it is kept for future reference. The information found on the stub includes the beginning balance ($3,441), the amount of any deposits ($0), the total amount in the account ($3,441), the amount of the check being written ($580), and the ending balance ($2,861). The check stub should be filled out before the check is written.

If the written amount on the check does not match the amount expressed in figures, Sunshine Bank may pay the amount written in words, return the check unpaid, or contact the drawer to see what was meant.

Many companies use checkwriting machines to type out the information on the check. These machines prevent people from making fraudulent changes on handwritten checks.

During the same time period, in-company records must be kept for all transactions affecting Becca's Jewelry Store's checkbook balance. Figure 6.4 on the following page spread shows these records. Note that the bank deposits ($6,446) minus the checks written ($2,529) give an ending checkbook balance of $3,917.

Banking on the Internet is expanding rapidly.

Monthly Recordkeeping: The Bank's Statement of Account and In-Company Records

Each month, Sunshine Bank will send Becca's Jewelry Store a Statement of Account. This statement reflects all the activity in the account during that period. It begins with the beginning balance of the account at the start of the month, along with the checks the bank has paid and any deposits received (see Fig. 6.5 on the following page spread). Any other charges or additions to the bank balance are indicated by codes found on the statement. All checks that have been paid by the bank are sent back to Becca's Jewelry Store. They are called **cancelled checks** because they have been processed by the bank and are no longer negotiable. The ending balance in Figure 6.5 is $3,592.

Figure 6.5 shows one format for a bank statement. Different banks use different formats.

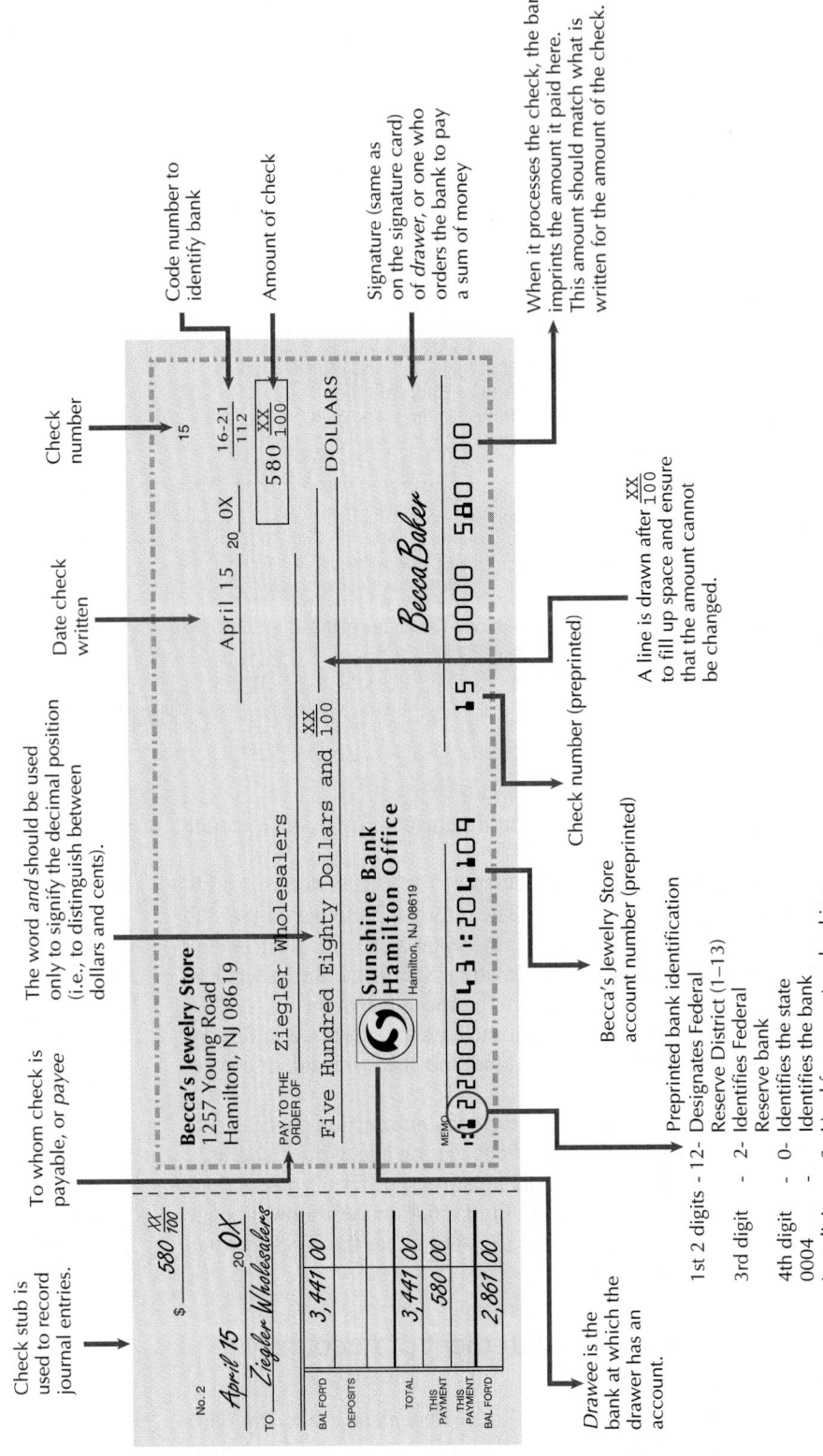

FIGURE 6.3 A Company Check

Bank Deposits Made for April		
Date of Deposit	Amount	Received From
Apr. 1	$5,000	Becca Baker, Capital
4	340	Jennifer Leung
16	89	Mary Figueroa
27	117	Carl Jones
28	900	Cash Sales
Total deposits for month:	$6,446	

Checks Written for the Month of April

Date		Check No.	Payment To	Amount	Description
Apr.	2	10	Quality Insurance	$ 500	Insurance paid in advance
	7	11	ABC Wholesalers	400	Merchandise
	9	12	Payroll	800	Salaries
	10	13	Times Newspaper	100	Advertising
	12	14	Verizon	99	Telephone
	15	15	Ziegler Wholesalers	580	Merchandise
	15		ATM Withdrawal	50	Postage
Total Amount of Checks Written:				$2,529	
Checks Deposited				$6,446	
Checks Paid				−2,529	
Balance in Account				**$3,917**	

FIGURE 6.4 Transactions (In-Company Records) Affecting Checkbook Balance

FIGURE 6.5 A Bank Statement

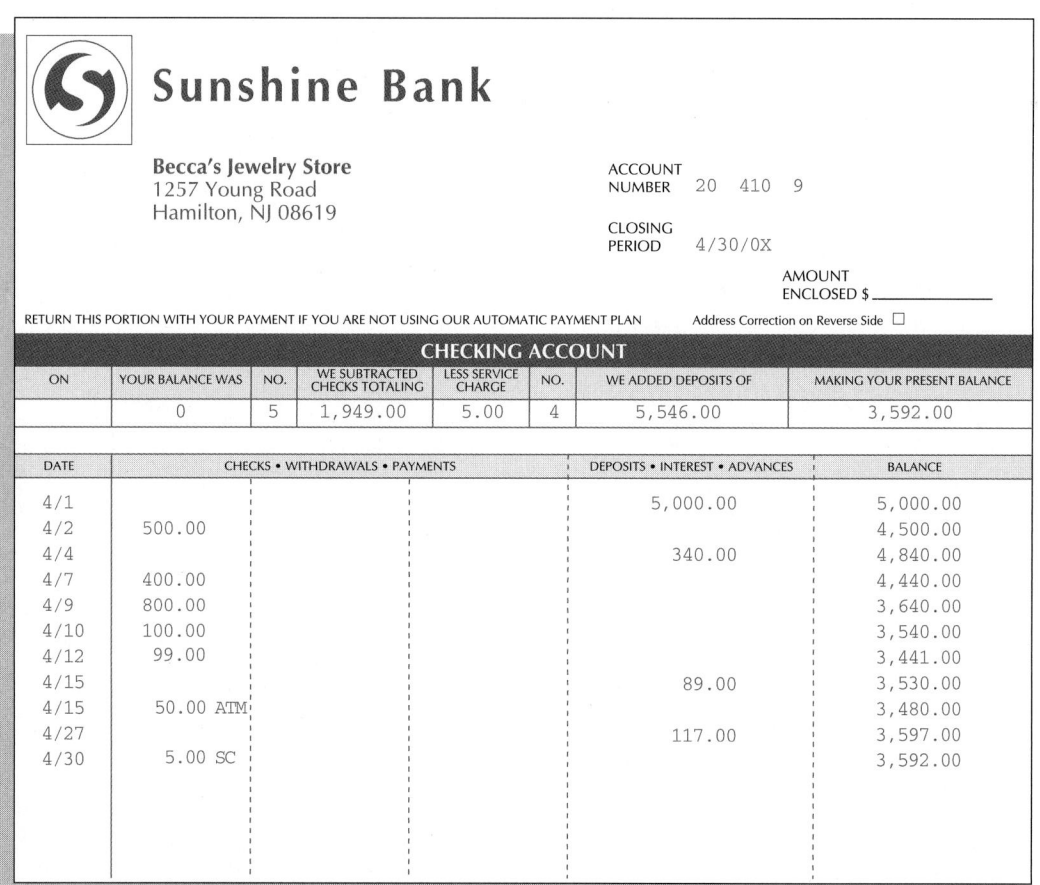

LO2 The Bank Reconciliation Process

The problem is that the ending bank balance of $3,592 does not agree with the amount in Becca's checkbook, $3,917, or the balance in the cash amount in the ledger, $3,917. Such differences are caused partly by the time a bank takes to process a company's transactions. A company records a transaction when it occurs. A bank cannot record a deposit until it receives that deposit, and it cannot pay a check until the check is presented by the payee. In addition, the bank statement will report fees and transactions that the company did not know about.

Becca's accountant has to find out why there is a $325 difference between the balances and how the records can be brought into balance. The process of reconciling the bank balance on the bank statement versus the company's checkbook balance is called a **bank reconciliation.** Bank reconciliations involve several steps, including calculating the deposits in transit and the outstanding checks. The bank reconciliation usually is done on the back of the **bank statement** (see Fig. 6.6). It can also be done by computer software, however.

> Online banking and computer software has made the reconciliation process even easier.

Deposits in Transit In comparing the list of deposits received by the bank with the checkbook, the accountant notices that a deposit made on April 28 for $900 was not on the bank's statement. The accountant realizes that to prepare this statement, the bank only included information about Becca's Jewelry Store up to April 27. This deposit made by Becca was not shown on the monthly bank statement because it arrived at the bank after the statement was printed. Thus, timing becomes a consideration in the reconciliation process. Deposits not yet added to the bank balance are called **deposits in transit.** This deposit needs to be added to the bank balance shown on the bank statement. Becca's checkbook is not affected, because the deposit has already been added to its balance. The bank has no way of knowing that the deposit is coming until it receives it.

> Deposits in transit:
> These unrecorded deposits could result if a deposit were placed in a night depository on the last day of the month.

Outstanding Checks The first thing the accountant does when the bank statement is received is put the checks in numerical order (1, 2, 3, etc.). In doing so, the accountant notices that one payment was not made by the bank and check no. 15 was not returned by the bank.

> Check #15 is outstanding.

FIGURE 6.6 Bank Reconciliation Using the Back of the Bank Statement

CHECKS OUTSTANDING			1. Enter balance shown on this statement	3,592 : 00
NUMBER	AMOUNT			
15	580 : 00		2. If you have made deposits since the date of this statement add them to the above balance.	900 : 00
			3. SUBTOTAL	4,492 : 00
			4. Deduct total of checks outstanding	580 : 00
			5. ADJUSTED BALANCE This should agree with your checkbook.	
TOTAL OF CHECKS OUTSTANDING	580 : 00			3,912 : 00 *

> Keep in mind that both the bank and the depositor can make mistakes that will not be discovered until the reconciliation process.

TO VERIFY YOUR CHECKING BALANCE
1. Sort checks by number or by date issued and compare with your check stubs and prior outstanding list. Make certain all checks paid have been recorded in your checkbook. If any of your checks were not included with this statement, list the numbers and amounts under "CHECKS OUTSTANDING."
2. Deduct the Service Charge as shown on the statement from your checkbook balance.
3. Review copies of charge advices included with this statement and check for proper entry in your checkbook.

IF THE ADJUSTED BALANCE DOES NOT AGREE WITH YOUR CHECKBOOK BALANCE, THE FOLLOWING SUGGESTIONS ARE OFFERED FOR YOUR ASSISTANCE.
- Recheck additions and subtractions in your checkbook and figures to the left.
- Make certain checkbook balances have been carried forward properly.
- Verify deposits recorded on statement against deposits entered in checkbook.
- Compare amount on each checkbook stub.

*Note the $5 service charge is included

Becca's books showed that this check had been deducted from the checkbook balance. The **outstanding check,** however, had not yet been presented to the bank for payment or deducted from the bank balance. When this check does reach the bank, the bank will reduce the amount of the balance.

> Checks outstanding are checks drawn by the depositor but not yet presented to the bank for payment by the payee.

Service Charges Becca's accountant also notices a bank service charge of $5. Becca's book balance will be lowered by $5.

Nonsufficient Funds An **NSF (nonsufficient funds)** check is a check that has been returned because the drawer did not have enough money in its account to pay the check. Accountants are continually on the lookout for NSF (nonsufficient funds) checks. An NSF check means less money in the checking account than was thought. Becca will have to (1) lower the checkbook balance and (2) try to collect the amount from the customer. The bank would notify Becca's Jewelry of an NSF (or other deductions) check by a **debit memorandum.** Think of a <u>d</u>ebit memorandum as a <u>d</u>eduction from the depositor's balance.

> Debit memorandum:
> ↓
> Deducted from balance

If the bank acts as a collecting agent for Becca's Jewelry, say in collecting notes, it will charge Becca a small fee and the net amount collected will be added to Becca's bank balance. The bank will send to Becca a **credit memorandum** verifying the increase in the depositor's balance.

> Credit memorandum:
> Addition to balance.

A journal entry is also needed to bring the ledger accounts of Cash and Service Charge expense up-to-date. Any adjustment to the checkbook balance results in a journal entry. The entry in Figure 6.7 was made to accomplish this step:

Apr.	30	Service Charge Expense			5 00				
		Cash					5 00		
		Bank service charge for April							

FIGURE 6.7 Service Charge Journalized

It is important for Becca to prepare a bank reconciliation when she receives her bank statement every month as part of the cash control procedure. It verifies the amount of cash in her checking account. Another important reason to do a bank reconciliation is that it may uncover irregularities such as employee theft of funds.

Here are step-by-step instructions for preparing a bank reconciliation:

1. **Prepare a list of deposits in transit.** Compare the deposits listed on your bank statement with the bank deposits shown in your checkbook. On your bank reconciliation, list any deposits that have not yet cleared the bank statement. Also, take a look at the bank reconciliation you prepared last month. Did all of last month's deposits in transit clear on this month's bank statement? If not, you should find out what happened.

2. **Prepare a list of outstanding checks.** In your checkbook, mark each check that cleared the bank statement this month. On your bank reconciliation, list all the checks in your checkbook that did not clear. Also, take a look at the bank reconciliation you prepared last month. Did any checks outstanding from last month still not clear the bank? If so, be sure they are on your list of outstanding checks this month. If a check is several months old and still has not cleared the bank, you may want to investigate further.

3. **Record any bank charges or credits.** Take a close look at your bank statement. Are all special charges made by the bank recorded in your books? If not, record them now as if you had just written a check for that amount. By the same token, any credits made to your account by the bank should be recorded as well. Post the entries to your general ledger.

4. **Compute the cash balance per your books.**

5. **Enter bank balance on the reconciliation.** At the top of the bank reconciliation statement, enter the ending balance from the bank statement.
6. **Total the deposits in transit.** Add up the deposits in transit and enter the total on the reconciliation. Add the total deposits in transit to the bank balance to arrive at a subtotal.
7. **Total the outstanding checks.** Add up the outstanding checks, and enter the total on the reconciliation.
8. **Compute the balance per the reconciliation.** Subtract the total outstanding checks from the subtotal in step 6. The result should equal the balance shown in your general ledger.

Before we look at a more comprehensive bank statement, let's look at trends in banking.

Trends in Banking

Adjustments to the checkbook balance must be journalized and posted. These steps keep the depositor's ledger accounts (especially Cash) up-to-date.

This charge could be recorded as a miscellaneous expense.

The Internet is changing how people bank. In the past, banking took place on the main street of your town. The branches were open 9 A.M. to 3 P.M. Monday to Thursday. They were probably open 9 A.M. to 6 P.M. on Friday and possibly 9 A.M. to noon on Saturday. These times were not always convenient for people who worked full time.

Many financial institutions have developed or are developing ways to transfer funds electronically, without the use of paper checks. Such systems are called **electronic funds transfers (EFT).** Most EFTs are established to save money and avoid theft.

Financial institutions use powerful computer networks to automate millions of daily transactions. Today, banks are able to use computer technology to give you the option of bypassing the time-consuming, paper-based aspects of traditional banking so that you can manage your finances more quickly and efficiently.

The first step toward online banking, **automatic teller machines (ATMs),** were first installed into banks about 40 years ago. For the first time, customers could make deposits, withdraw money, and obtain account balances without having to stand in line during the times that the bank was open. Customers are able to use an ATM in banks, supermarkets, malls, and possibly even at your college student center.

Call centers were the next major step forward for banks. Customers could now telephone the center using either a toll-free number or local number and find out information about their accounts without leaving their home.

The latest development in banking is Internet or online banking. Most of the large banks offer fully secure, fully functional online banking for free or for a small fee. Some smaller banks offer limited access; for instance, you may be able to view your account balance and history but may not be able to initiate transactions online. As more banks succeed online and more customers use their sites, fully functional online banking will probably become as common as ATMs.

With a debit card and personal identification number (PIN), you can use an ATM to withdraw cash, make deposits, or transfer funds between accounts. Some ATMs charge a fee if you are not a member of the ATM network or are making a transaction at a remote location.

Retail purchases can also be made with a debit card. You enter your PIN or sign for the purchase. Some banks that issue debit cards are charging customers a fee for a debit card purchase made with a PIN. Although a debit card looks like a credit card, the money for the purchase is transferred from your bank account to the store's account. The purchase will be shown on your bank account statement.

Immediately call the card issuer when you suspect a debit card may be lost or stolen. Most companies have toll-free numbers and a 24-hour service to deal with such emergencies. Although federal law limits your liability for a stolen credit card to $50, your liability for unauthorized use of your ATM or debit card can be much greater—depending on how quickly you report the loss. Also, it is important to remember that when you use a debit card, federal law does not give you the right to stop payment. You must resolve the problem with the seller.

If you don't mind foregoing the teller window and the lobby cookie, a virtual bank or e-bank, such as Virtual Bank or Giant Bank, may save you real money. Virtual banks are banks without bricks. They exist entirely online and offer much of the same range of services and adhere to the same regulations as your corner bank. Virtual banks pass the money that they save on overhead, such as buildings and tellers, along to you in the form of higher yields and lower fees. Banking is available everywhere, all the time. Your finances are at your fingertips.

Advantages of Online Banking Customers who use online banking services enjoy many advantages. They can do almost everything from the comfort of their own homes at convenient times and without standing in long lines.

- *Convenience:* Unlike your corner site, online banks never close. They are available 24 hours a day, seven days a week.
- *Availability:* If you are out of state or even out of the country when a money problem arises, you can log on instantly to your online bank and take care of business, 24/7.
- *Transaction speed:* Online bank sites generally execute and confirm transactions as quickly or even faster than ATM processing speeds.
- *Efficiency:* You can access and manage all of your bank accounts, including IRAs and CDs, from one secure site.
- *Effectiveness:* Many online banking sites now offer sophisticated tools to help you manage all of your assets more effectively. Most of these tools are compatible with money managing programs such as Quicken and Microsoft Money.

Disadvantages of Online Banking Although online banking has many advantages, it also has disadvantages.

- *Start-up may take time:* In order to register for your bank's online program, you will probably have to provide some personal identification and sign a form at a branch bank.
- *Learning curve:* Banking sites can be difficult to navigate at first. Plan to invest time to read the tutorials in order to become comfortable in your virtual lobby.
- *Bank site changes:* Even the largest banks periodically upgrade their online programs, adding new features in unfamiliar places. In some cases, you may need to reenter account information.
- *The trust thing:* For many people, the biggest hurdle to online banking is learning to trust it. Did my transaction go through? Did I push the transfer button once or twice? Best bet: Always print the transaction receipt and keep it with your bank records until it shows up on your personal site or your bank statement.

When problems arise, it is usually much easier to sort them out face to face rather than having to use e-mail or the telephone. Perhaps the biggest problem with online banking is security. It is important to keep passwords safe and to be aware of fake e-mails arriving in your inbox. These e-mails pretend to be from your bank and attempt to obtain information from you. This kind of fraud is called **phishing.**

Fraudulent practices can happen at cash registers when you make a purchase or at restaurants when you pay with a credit card and the waiter is out of your sight. Skimming at ATMs can be much more damaging because of the number of accounts and the amount of money that can be quickly accessed. Card-based purchases—online, debit, and credit— are convenient for consumers. For example, tens of thousands of ATMs are swipe-based. The large number of ATMs contributes to the skimming problem. In a way, we've become victims of the convenience we demand.

Here are some tips to help you avoid becoming a skimming victim.

- Keep your PIN safe. Don't give it to anyone.
- Watch out for people who try to "help" you at an ATM.
- Look at the ATM before using it. If it doesn't look right, don't use it.
- If an ATM has any unusual signage, don't use it. No bank would hang a sign that says, "Swipe your ATM here before inserting it in the card reader" or something to that effect.
- If your card is not returned after the transaction or after pressing cancel, immediately contact the institution that issued the card.
- Check your statement to be sure no unusual withdrawals appear on it.

Check Truncation (Safekeeping) Some banks do not return cancelled checks to the depositor but use a procedure called **check truncation** or **safekeeping.** The bank holds a cancelled check for a specific period of time (usually 90 days) and then keeps a microfilm copy handy and destroys the original check. In Texas, for example, some credit unions and savings and loan institutions do not send back checks. Instead, the check date, number, and amount are listed on the bank statement. If the customer needs a copy of a check, the bank will provide the check or a photocopy for a small fee. (Photocopies are accepted as evidence in Internal Revenue Service tax returns and audits.)

Truncation cuts down on the amount of "paper" that is returned to customers and thus provides substantial cost savings. It is estimated that more than 80 million checks are written each day in the United States.

Example of a More Comprehensive Bank Statement The bank reconciliation of Becca's Jewelry was not as complicated as it is for many companies, even using today's computer technology. Let's look at a reconciliation for Matty's Supermarket (Figs. 6.8 and 6.9), which is based on the following:

Matty's checkbook balance		$13,176.84
Bank balance		23,726.04
Leased space to Subway		8,456.00
Leased space to Dunkin' Donuts		3,616.12
The rental payment is transferred by electronic transfer		
Matty pays a health insurance payment each month by electronic transfer		1,444.00
Deposits in transit 5/30		6,766.52
Checks outstanding		
ck # 738	$1,144.00	
739	1,277.88	
740	332.00	
741	812.56	
742	1,834.12	
Check # 734 was overstated in company's books		1,440.00

Note in Figure 6.9 on the following page spread that each adjustment to Matty's checkbook is the reconciliation process that would result in general journal entries.

FIGURE 6.8 Bank Statement for Matty's Supermarket

Ranger Bank
1 Left St.
Marblehead, MA 01945

ACCOUNT STATEMENT

Matty's Supermarket
20 Sullivan St.
Lynn, MA 01917

Checking Account: 775800061

Checking Account Summary as of 6/30/0X

Beginning Balance	Total Deposits	Total Withdrawals	Service Charge	Ending Balance
$26,224.48	$17,410.56	$19,852.00	$57.00	$23,726.04

Checking Accounts Transactions

Deposits	Date	Amount
Deposit	6/05	4,000.00
Deposit	6/05	448.00
Deposit	6/09	778.40
EFT leasing: Dunkin' Donuts	6/18	3,616.12
EFT leasing: Subway	6/27	8,456.00
Interest	6/30	112.04

Charges	Date	Amount
Service charge: Check printing	6/30	57.00
EFT: Blue Cross/Blue Shield	6/21	1,444.00
NSF	6/21	208.00

Checks

Number	Date	Amount
401	6/07	400.00
733	6/13	12,000.00
734	6/13	600.00
735	6/11	400.00
736	6/18	400.00
737	6/30	4,400.00

Daily Balance

Date	Balance	Date	Balance
5/28	26,224.48	6/18	21,059.00
6/05	30,464.48	6/21	19,615.00
6/07	29,664.48	6/28	28,071.00
6/09	30,442.88	6/30	23,726.04
6/11	30,042.88		
6/13	17,442.88		

LEARNING UNIT 6-1 REVIEW

AT THIS POINT you should be able to

- Define and explain the need for deposit tickets.
- Explain where the American Bankers Association transit number is located on the check and what its purpose is.
- List as well as compare and contrast the three common types of check endorsement.
- Explain the structure of a check.
- Define and state the purpose of a bank statement.
- Explain deposits in transit, checks outstanding, service charge, and NSF.
- Explain the difference between a debit memorandum and a credit memorandum.
- Explain how to do a bank reconciliation.
- Explain electronic funds transfer and check truncation.
- Explain the advantages and disadvantages of online banking.

FIGURE 6.9 Bank Reconciliation for Matty's Supermarket

MATTY'S SUPERMARKET					
Bank Reconciliation as of June 30, 200X					
Checkbook balance			**Bank balance**		
Matty's checkbook balance		$13,176.84	Bank balance		$23,726.04
Add:			Add:		
EFT leasing: Dunkin' Donuts			Deposits in transit, 5/30		6,766.52
	$ 3,616.12				$30,492.56
EFT leasing: Subway					
	8,456.00				
Interest	112.04				
Error: Overstated					
check no. 734	1,440.00	13,624.16			
		$26,801.00			
Deduct:			Deduct:		
Service charge	$ 57.00		Outstanding checks:		
NSF check	208.00		No. 738	$1,144.00	
EFT health insurance			No. 739	1,277.88	
payment	1,444.00	1,709.00	No. 740	332.00	
			No. 741	812.56	
			No. 742	1,834.12	5,400.56
Reconciled balance		$25,092.00	Reconciled balance		$25,092.00

Self-Review Quiz 6-1

Indicate, by placing an X under it, the heading that describes the appropriate action for each of the following situations:

Situation	Add to Bank Balance	Deduct from Bank Balance	Add to Checkbook Balance	Deduct from Checkbook Balance
1. Check printing charge				
2. Deposits in transit				
3. NSF check				
4. A $75 check was written and recorded by the company as $85				
5. Proceeds of a note collected by the bank				
6. Check outstanding				
7. Forgot to record ATM withdrawal				
8. Forgot to record direct deposit of a payroll check				

Solution to Self-Review Quiz 6-1

Situation	Add to Bank Balance	Deduct from Bank Balance	Add to Checkbook Balance	Deduct from Checkbook Balance
1				X
2	X			
3				X

Situation	Add to Bank Balance	Deduct from Bank Balance	Add to Checkbook Balance	Deduct from Checkbook Balance
4			X	
5			X	
6		X		
7				X
8			X	

> Deposits in transit are added to the bank balance, whereas checks outstanding are subtracted from the bank balance.

Learning Unit 6-2 The Establishment of Petty Cash and Change Funds

LO3

> Petty Cash is an asset on the balance sheet.

Becca realized how time-consuming and expensive it would be to write checks for small amounts to pay for postage, small supplies, and so forth, so she set up a **petty cash fund.** Similarly, she established a *change fund* to make cash transactions more convenient. This unit explains how to manage petty cash and change funds.

Setting Up the Petty Cash Fund

> The check for $60 is drawn to the order of the custodian and is cashed, and the proceeds are turned over to John Sullivan, the custodian.

The petty cash fund is an account dedicated to paying small day-to-day expenses. These petty cash expenses are recorded in an auxiliary record and later summarized, journalized, and posted. Becca estimated that the company would need a fund of $60 to cover small expenditures during the month of May. This petty cash was not expected to last longer than one month. She gave one of her employees responsibility for overseeing the fund. This person is called the *custodian.*

Becca named her office manager, John Sullivan, as custodian. In other companies, the cashier or secretary may be in charge of petty cash. Check no. 6 was drawn to the order of the custodian and cashed to establish the fund. John keeps the petty cash fund in a small tin box in the office safe.

Shown here is the transaction analysis chart for the establishment of a $60 petty cash fund, which would be journalized on May 1, 200X, as shown in Figure 6.10.

> Petty Cash is an asset that is established by writing a new check. The Petty Cash account is debited only once unless a greater or lesser amount of petty cash is needed on a regular basis.

Accounts Affected	Category	↑ ↓	Rules
Petty Cash	Asset	↑	Dr.
Cash (checks)	Asset	↓	Cr.

Note that the new asset called Petty Cash, which was created by writing check no. 6, reduced the asset Cash. In reality, the total assets stay the same; what has occurred is a shift from the asset Cash (check no. 6) to a new asset account called Petty Cash.

The Petty Cash account is not debited or credited again if the size of the fund is not changed. If the $60 fund is used up quickly, the fund should be increased. If the fund is too large, the Petty Cash account should be reduced. We take a closer look at this issue when we discuss replenishment of petty cash.

Making Payments from the Petty Cash Fund

John Sullivan has the responsibility for filling out a **petty cash voucher** for each cash payment made from the petty cash fund. The petty cash vouchers are numbered in sequence.

GENERAL JOURNAL				Page 1	
Date	Account Title and Description	PR	Dr.	Cr.	
200X May 1	Petty Cash		60 00		
	Cash			60 00	
	Establishment				

FIGURE 6.10 Establishing Petty Cash

Note that when the voucher (shown in Fig. 6.11) is completed, it will include

- the voucher number (which will be in sequence),
- the date,
- the person or organization to whom the payment was made,
- the amount of payment,
- the reason for payment: in this case, cleaning,
- the signature of the person who approved the payment,
- the signature of the person who received the payment from petty cash, and
- the account to which the expense will be charged.

FIGURE 6.11 Petty Cash Voucher

Petty Cash Voucher No. 1

Date: May 2, 200X   Amount: $3.00
Paid To: Al's Cleaning
For: Cleaning

                              Approved By: *John Sullivan*

                       Payment Received By: *Al Smith*

Debit Account No.: 619

The completed vouchers are placed in the petty cash box. No matter how many vouchers John Sullivan fills out, the total of (1) the vouchers in the box and (2) the cash on hand should equal the original amount of petty cash with which the fund was established ($60).

Assume that at the end of May the following items are documented by petty cash vouchers in the petty cash box as having been paid by John Sullivan:

200X
May   2   Cleaning package, $3.00.

          5   Postage stamps, $9.00.

          8   First-aid supplies, $15.00.

          9   Delivery expense, $6.00.

          14 Delivery expense, $15.00.

          27 Postage stamps, $6.00.

John records this information in the **auxiliary petty cash record** shown in Figure 6.12. It is not a required record but an aid to John, an auxiliary record that is not essential but is quite helpful as part of the petty cash system. You may want to think of the auxiliary petty cash record as an optional worksheet. Let's look at how to replenish the petty cash fund.

How to Replenish the Petty Cash Fund

No postings are done from the auxiliary book because it is not a journal. At some point the summarized information found in the auxiliary petty cash record is used as a basis for a journal entry in the general journal and eventually posted to appropriate ledger accounts to reflect up-to-date balances.

This $54 of expenses (see Fig. 6.12) is recorded in the general journal (Fig. 6.13) and a new check, no. 17, for $54 is cashed and returned to John Sullivan. In replenishment, old expenses are updated in the journal and ledger to show where money has gone. The order is auxiliary before replenishment. The petty cash box now once again reflects $60 cash.

A new check is written in the replenishment process, which is payable to the custodian and is cashed by John, and the cash is placed in the petty cash box.

FIGURE 6.12 Auxiliary Petty Cash Record

Date	Voucher No.	Description	Receipts	Payments	Postage Expense	Delivery Expense	Sundry Account	Sundry Amount
						Category of Payments		
200X May 1		Establishment	60 00					
2	1	Cleaning		3 00			Cleaning	3 00
5	2	Postage		9 00	9 00			
8	3	First Aid		15 00			Misc.	15 00
9	4	Delivery		6 00		6 00		
14	5	Delivery		15 00		15 00		
27	6	Postage		6 00	6 00			
		Total	60 00	54 00	15 00	21 00		18 00

The old vouchers that were used are stamped to indicate that they have been processed and the fund replenished.

Note that in the replenishment process the debits are a summary of the totals (except sundry, because individual items are different) of expenses or other items from the auxiliary petty cash record. Posting these specific expenses will ensure that the expenses will not be understated on the income statement. The credit to Cash allows us to draw a check for $54 to put money back in the petty cash box. The $60 in the box now agrees with the Petty Cash account balance. The end result is that our petty cash box is filled, and we have justified for which accounts the petty cash money was spent. Think of replenishment as a single, summarizing entry.

Remember that if at some point the petty cash fund is to be greater than $60, a check can be written that will increase Petty Cash and decrease Cash. If the Petty Cash account balance is to be reduced, we can credit or reduce Petty Cash. For our present purpose, however, Petty Cash will remain at $60.

FIGURE 6.13 Establishment and Replenishment of Petty Cash Fund

Petty cash is an asset. ➡

	Date	Account Title and Description	PR	Dr.	Cr.
		GENERAL JOURNAL			Page 1
	200X May 1	Petty Cash		60 00	
		Cash			60 00
		Establishment			
	31	Postage Expense		15 00	
		Delivery Expense		21 00	
		Cleaning Expense		3 00	
		Miscellaneous Expense		15 00	
		Cash			54 00
		Replenishment			

Note that the Petty Cash account is not listed in replenishment unless we raise or lower it. To raise it we would debit it; to lower it we would credit it.

The auxiliary petty cash record after replenishment would look as shown in Figure 6.14 (keep in mind no postings are made from the auxiliary). Figure 6.15 may help you put the sequence together.

Before concluding this unit, let's look at how Becca will handle setting up a change fund and problems with cash shortages and overages.

FIGURE 6.14 Auxiliary Petty Cash Record with Replenishment

								Category of Payments		
									Sundry	
Date	Voucher No.	Description	Receipts	Payments	Postage Expense	Delivery Expense	Account	Amount		
200X May 1		Establishment	60 00							
2	1	Cleaning		3 00			Cleaning	3 00		
5	2	Postage		9 00	9 00					
8	3	First Aid		15 00			Misc.	15 00		
9	4	Delivery		6 00		6 00				
14	5	Delivery		15 00		15 00				
27	6	Postage		6 00	6 00					
		Total	60 00	54 00	15 00	21 00		18 00		
		Ending Balance		6 00						
			60 00	60 00						
		Ending Balance	6 00							
31		Replenishment	54 00							
31		Balance (New)	60 00							

LO4 Setting Up a Change Fund and Insight into Cash Short and Over

If a company such as Becca's Jewelry expects to have many cash transactions occurring, it may be a good idea to establish a **change fund.** This fund is placed in the cash register drawer and used to make change for customers who pay cash. Becca decides to put $120 in the change fund, made up of various denominations of bills and coins. Let's look at a transaction analysis chart and the journal entry (Fig. 6.16) for this sort of procedure.

Accounts Affected	Category	↑ ↓	Rules
Change Fund	Asset	↑	Dr.
Cash	Asset	↓	Cr.

At the close of the business day, Becca will place the amount of the change fund back in the safe in the office. She will set up the change fund (the same $120) in the appropriate denominations for the next business day. She will deposit in the bank the *remainder* of the cash taken in for the day.

In the next section, we look at how to record errors that are made in making change, called **cash short and over.**

Beg. change fund
+ Cash register total
= Cash should have on hand
− Counted cash
= Shortage or overage of cash

LO5 Cash Short and Over

In a local pizza shop the total sales for the day did not match the amount of cash on hand. Errors often happen in making change. To record and summarize the differences in cash, an account called *Cash Short and Over* is used. This account

FIGURE 6.15 Which Transactions Involve Petty Cash and How to Record Them

	Date		Description	New Check Written	Petty Cash Voucher Prepared	Recorded in Auxiliary Petty Cash Record	
	200X May	1	Establishment of				Dr. Petty Cash Cr. Cash
			petty cash for $60	X		X	
		2	Paid salaries,				
			$2,000	X			
		10	Paid $10 from petty				
			cash for Band-Aids		X	X	No journal entries
		19	Paid $8 from petty				
			cash for postage		X	X	
		24	Paid light bill,				
			$200	X			
		29	Replenishment of				Dr. individual expenses Cr. Cash
			petty cash to $60	X		X	

Has nothing to do with petty cash (amounts too great)

In this step the old expenses are listed in the general journal and a new check is written to replenish. All old vouchers are removed from the petty cash box.

FIGURE 6.16 Change Fund Established

	Apr.	1	Change Fund			1 2 0 00		
			Cash				1 2 0 00	
			Establish change fund					

records both overages (too much money) and shortages (not enough money). Let's first look at the account (in T account form).

Cash Short and Over

Dr.	Cr.
shortage	overage

All shortages will be recorded as debits and all overages will be recorded as credits. This account is temporary. If the ending balance of the account is a debit (a shortage), it is considered a miscellaneous expense that would be reported on the income statement. If the balance of the account is a credit (an overage), it is considered as other income reported on the income statement. Let's look at how the Cash Short and Over account could be used to record shortages or overages in sales as well as in the petty cash process.

Example 1: Shortages and Overages in Sales On December 5 a pizza shop rang up sales of $560 for the day but only had $530 in cash.

Accounts Affected	Category	↑ ↓	Rules
Cash	Asset	↑	Debit $530
Cash Short and Over	Misc. Exp.	↑	Debit $30
Sales	Revenue	↑	Credit $560

The journal entry would be as shown in Figure 6.17.

FIGURE 6.17 Cash Shortage

Dec.	5	Cash		5 3 0 00			
		Cash Short and Over		3 0 00			
		Sales				5 6 0 00	
		Cash shortage					

Note that the shortage of $30 is a debit and would be recorded on the income statement as a miscellaneous expense.

What would the entry look like if the pizza shop showed a $50 overage?

Accounts Affected	Category	↑ ↓	Rules
Cash	Asset	↑	Debit $610
Cash Short and Over	Other Income	↑	Credit $50
Sales	Revenue	↑	Credit $560

The journal entry would be as shown in Figure 6.18.

FIGURE 6.18 Cash Overage

Dec.	5	Cash		6 1 0 00			
		Cash Short and Over				5 0 00	
		Sales				5 6 0 00	
		Cash overage					

Note that the Cash Short and Over account would be reported as other income on the income statement. Now let's look at how to use this Cash Short and Over account to record petty cash transactions.

Example 2: Cash Short and Over in Petty Cash A local computer company established petty cash for $200. On November 30, the petty cash box had $160 in vouchers as well as $32 in coin and currency. What would be the journal entry to replenish petty cash? Assume the vouchers were made up of $90 for postage and $70 for supplies expense.

If you add up the vouchers and cash in the box, cash is short by $8.

Accounts Affected	Category	↑ ↓	Rules
Postage Expense	Expense	↑	Debit $90
Supplies Expense	Expense	↑	Debit $70
Cash Short and Over	Misc. Expense	↑	Debit $8
Cash	Asset	↓	Credit $168

> **NOTE:**
> The account Petty Cash is not used since the level in petty cash is not raised or lowered.

The journal entry is shown in Figure 6.19.

FIGURE 6.19 Petty Cash Replenished with Shortage

Nov.	30	Postage Expense		9 0 00			
		Supplies Expense		7 0 00			
		Cash Short and Over		8 00			
		Cash				1 6 8 00	

In the case of an overage, the Cash Short and Over would be a credit as other income. The solution to Self-Review Quiz 6-2 shows how a fund shortage would be recorded in the auxiliary record.

LEARNING UNIT 6-2 REVIEW

AT THIS POINT you should be able to

- State the purpose of a petty cash fund.
- Prepare a journal entry to establish a petty cash fund.
- Prepare a petty cash voucher.
- Explain the relationship of the auxiliary petty cash record to the petty cash process.
- Prepare a journal entry to replenish Petty Cash to its original amount.
- Explain why individual expenses are debited in the replenishment process.
- Explain how a change fund is established.
- Explain how Cash Short and Over could be a miscellaneous expense.

Self-Review Quiz 6-2

As the custodian of the petty cash fund, it is your task to prepare entries to establish the fund on October 1 as well as to replenish the fund on October 31. Please keep an auxiliary petty cash record.

200X		
Oct.	1	Establish petty cash fund for $90, check no. 8.
	5	Voucher 11, delivery expense, $21.
	9	Voucher 12, delivery expense, $15.
	10	Voucher 13, office repair expense, $24.
	17	Voucher 14, general expense, $12.
	30	Replenishment of petty cash fund, $78, check no. 108. (Check would be payable to the custodian.)

> How to calculate shortage: $21 + $15 + $24 + $12 = $72 of vouchers. Replenished with $78 check. Thus there was a $6 shortage. Note how cash short and over was entered in the auxiliary petty cash record.

Solution to Self-Review Quiz 6-2

GENERAL JOURNAL				Page 6	
Date	Account Title and Description	PR	Dr.	Cr.	
200X Oct. 1	Petty Cash		90 00		
	Cash			90 00	
	Establishment, Check 8				

31	Delivery Expense		36 00		
	General Expense		12 00		
	Office Repair Expense		24 00		
	Cash Short and Over		6 00		
	Cash			78 00	
	Replenishment, Check 108				

FIGURE 6.20
Establishment and Replenishment of Petty Cash

FIGURE 6.21 Auxiliary Petty Cash Record

						AUXILIARY PETTY CASH RECORD						
							Category of Payments		
						Delivery Expense	General Expense	Sundry	
Date	Voucher No.	Description	Receipts	Payments				Account	Amount
200X Oct. 1		Establishment	90 00						
5	11	Delivery		21 00		21 00			
9	12	Delivery		15 00		15 00			
10	13	Repairs		24 00				Office Repair	24 00
17	14	General		12 00			12 00		
25		Fund Shortage		6 00				Cash Short and Over	6 00
		Totals	90 00	78 00		36 00	12 00		30 00
		Ending Balance		12 00					
				90 00					
30		Ending Balance	12 00						
31		Replenishment	78 00						
Nov. 1		New Balance	90 00						

CHAPTER ASSIGNMENTS

SUMMARY OF KEY POINTS

LEARNING UNIT 6-1

1. Restrictive endorsement limits any further negotiation of a check.
2. Check stubs are filled out before a check is written.
3. The payee is the person to whom the check is payable. The drawer is the one who orders the bank to pay a sum of money. The drawee is the bank with which the drawer has an account.
4. The process of reconciling the bank balance with the company's balance is called the bank reconciliation. The timing of deposits, when the bank statement was issued, and so forth often result in differences between the bank balance and the checkbook balance.
5. Deposits in transit are added to the bank balance.
6. Checks outstanding are subtracted from the bank balance.
7. NSF means that a check has nonsufficient funds to be credited (deposited) to a checking account; therefore, the amount is not included in the bank balance and thus the checking account balance is lowered.
8. When a bank debits your account, it is deducting an amount from your balance. A credit to the account is an increase to your balance.
9. All adjustments to the checkbook balance require journal entries.
10. The Internet has expanded online banking options.

LEARNING UNIT 6-2

1. Petty Cash is an asset found on the balance sheet.
2. The auxiliary petty cash record is an auxiliary book; thus no postings are done from this book. Think of it as an optional worksheet.
3. When a petty cash fund is established, the amount is entered as a debit to Petty Cash and a credit to Cash.
4. At the time of replenishment of the petty cash fund, all expenses are debited (by category) and a credit to Cash (a new check) results. This replenishment, when journalized and posted, updates the ledger from the journal.
5. The only time the Petty Cash account is used is to establish the fund initially or to bring the fund to a higher or lower level. If the petty cash level is deemed sufficient, all replenishments will debit specific expenses and credit Cash (new check written). The asset Petty Cash account balance will remain unchanged.
6. A change fund is an asset that is used to make change for customers.
7. Cash Short and Over is an account that is either a miscellaneous expense or miscellaneous income, depending on whether the ending balance is a shortage or overage.

KEY TERMS

ATM   Automatic teller machine that allow for depositing, withdrawal, and advance banking transactions.

Auxiliary petty cash record   A supplementary record for summarizing petty cash information.

Bank reconciliation   The process of reconciling the checkbook balance with the bank balance given on the bank statement.

Bank statement   A report sent by a bank to a customer indicating the previous balance, individual checks processed, individual deposits received, service charges, and ending bank balance.

Cancelled check   A check that has been processed by a bank and is no longer negotiable.

Cash Short and Over   The account that records cash shortages and overages. If the ending balance is a debit, it is recorded on the income statement as a miscellaneous expense; if it is a credit, it is recorded as other income.

Change fund   Fund made up of various denominations that are used to make change for customers.

Check   A form used to indicate a specific amount of money that is to be paid by the bank to a named person or company.

Check truncation (safekeeping)   Procedure whereby checks are not returned to the drawer with the bank statement but are instead kept at the bank for a certain amount of time before being first transferred to microfilm and then destroyed.

Credit memorandum   Increase in depositor's balance.

Debit card   A card similar to a credit card except that the amount of a purchase is deducted directly from the customer's bank account.

Debit memorandum   Decrease in depositor's balance.

Deposit slip   A form provided by a bank for use in depositing money or checks into a checking account.

Deposits in transit   Deposits that were made by customers of a bank but did not reach, or were not processed by, the bank before the preparation of the bank statement.

Drawee   Bank that drawer has an account with.

Drawer   Person who writes a check.

Electronic funds transfer (EFT)   An electronic system that transfers funds without the use of paper checks.

Endorsement   *Blank:* Could be further endorsed. *Full:* Restricts further endorsement to only the person or company named. *Restrictive:* Restricts any further endorsement.

Internal control system   Procedures and methods to control a firm's assets as well as monitor its operations.

NSF (nonsufficient funds)   Notation indicating that a check has been written on an account that lacks sufficient funds to back it up.

Outstanding checks   Checks written by a company or person that were not received or not processed by the bank before the preparation of the bank statement.

Payee   The person or company to whom the check is payable.

Petty cash fund   Fund (source) that allows payment of small amounts without the writing of checks.

Petty cash voucher   A petty cash form to be completed when money is taken out of petty cash.

Phishing   Fake e-mails that attempt to obtain information about online banking customers.

Signature card   A form signed by a bank customer that the bank uses to verify signature authenticity on all checks.

BLUEPRINT: A BANK RECONCILIATION

Checkbook Balance	Bank Balance
+ EFT (electronic funds transfer)	+ Deposits in transit
+ Interest earned	− Outstanding checks
+ Notes collected	± Bank errors
+ Direct deposits	
− ATM withdrawals	
− Check redeposits	
− NSF check	
− Online fees	
− Automatic withdrawals	
− Overdrafts	
− Service charges	
− Stop payments	
± Book errors*	
CM—adds to balance	
DM—deducts from balance	

* If a $60 check is recorded as $50, we must decrease checkbook balance by $10.

QUESTIONS, CLASSROOM DEMONSTRATION EXERCISES, EXERCISES, AND PROBLEMS

Discussion and Critical Thinking Questions/Ethical Case

1. What is the purpose of internal control?
2. What is the advantage of having preprinted deposit tickets?
3. Explain the difference between a blank endorsement and a restrictive endorsement.
4. Explain the difference between payee, drawer, and drawee.
5. Why should check stubs be filled out first, before the check itself is written?
6. A bank statement is sent twice a month. True or false? Please explain.
7. Explain the end product of a bank reconciliation.
8. Why are checks outstanding subtracted from the bank balance?
9. An NSF check results in a bank issuing the depositor a credit memorandum. Agree or disagree? Please support your response.
10. Why do adjustments to the checkbook balance in the reconciliation process need to be journalized?
11. What is EFT?
12. What are the major advantages and disadvantages of online banking?
13. What is meant by check truncation or safekeeping?
14. Petty cash is a liability. Agree or disagree? Explain.
15. Explain the relationship of the auxiliary petty cash record to the recording of the cash payment.
16. At the time of replenishment, why are the totals of individual expenses debited?
17. Explain the purpose of a change fund.
18. Explain how Cash Short and Over can be a miscellaneous expense.
19. Sean Nah, the bookkeeper of Revell Co., received a bank statement from Lone Bank. Sean noticed a $250 mistake made by the bank in the company's favor. Sean called his supervisor, who said that as long as it benefits the company, he should not tell the bank about the error. You make the call. Write your specific recommendations to Sean.

Classroom Demonstration Exercises

SET A

Bank Reconciliation   *LO2 (10 min)*

1. Indicate what effect each situation will have on the bank reconciliation process.
   1. Add to bank balance.
   2. Deduct from bank balance.
   3. Add to checkbook balance.
   4. Deduct from checkbook balance.
      _____ **a.** Check no. 150 was outstanding for $100.
      _____ **b.** $300 deposit in transit.
      _____ **c.** $162 NSF check.
      _____ **d.** A $15 check was written and recorded as $25.
      _____ **e.** Bank collected a $1,000 note less $50 collection fee.
      _____ **f.** $14 bank service charge.

Journal Entries in Reconciliation Process   *LO2 (5 min)*

2. Which of the transactions in Exercise 1 would require a journal entry?

Bank Reconciliation   *LO2 (10 min)*

3. From the following, construct a bank reconciliation for Ace Co. as of June 30, 200X.

Checkbook balance	$1,869.60
Bank statement balance	1,951.20
Deposits in transit	271.20
Outstanding checks	427.80
Bank service charge	13.80
NSF check	61.20

Petty Cash   *LO3 (10 min)*

4. Indicate what effect each situation will have.
   1. New check written.
   2. Recorded in general journal.
   3. Petty cash voucher prepared.
   4. Recorded in auxiliary petty cash record.
      _____ **a.** Established petty cash.
      _____ **b.** Paid $1,000 bill.
      _____ **c.** Paid $2 for Band-Aids from petty cash.
      _____ **d.** Paid $3 for stamps from petty cash.
      _____ **e.** Paid electric bill, $250.
      _____ **f.** Replenished petty cash.

Replenishment of Petty Cash   *LO3 (15 min)*

5. Petty cash was originally established for $20. During the month, $5 was paid out for Band-Aids and $6 for stamps. During replenishment, the custodian discovered that the balance in petty cash was $8. Record, using a general journal entry, the replenishment of petty cash back to $20.

LO3 (10 min)   **Increasing Petty Cash**

6. In Exercise 5, if the custodian decided to raise the level of petty cash to $30, what would be the journal entry to replenish (use a general journal entry)?

SET B

LO2 (10 min)   **Bank Reconciliation**

1. Indicate what effect each situation will have on the bank reconciliation process.
   1. Add to bank balance.
   2. Deduct from bank balance.
   3. Add to checkbook balance.
   4. Deduct from checkbook balance.
   _____ a. $15 bank service charge.
   _____ b. $725 deposit in transit.
   _____ c. $36 NSF check.
   _____ d. A $78 check was written and recorded as $87.
   _____ e. Bank collected a $5,000 note less $50 collection fee.
   _____ f. Check no. 113 was outstanding for $360.

LO2 (5 min)   2. Which of the transactions in Exercise 1 would require a journal entry?

LO2 (10 min)   3. From the following, construct a bank reconciliation for Ace Co. as of June 30, 200X.

Checkbook balance	$28,724
Bank statement balance	29,840
Outstanding check	3,454
Deposit in transit	1,714
NSF check	600
Bank service charge	24

LO3 (10 min)   4. Indicate what effect each situation will have.
   1. New check written.
   2. Recorded in general journal.
   3. Petty cash voucher prepared.
   4. Recorded in auxiliary petty cash record.
   _____ a. Established petty cash fund for $200.
   _____ b. Paid telephone bill, $135.
   _____ c. Paid $10 to employee A for $10 turnpike tolls from petty cash.
   _____ d. Paid $7.80 for stamps from petty cash.
   _____ e. Replenished petty cash.
   _____ f. Increased original petty cash fund to $300.

LO3 (15 min)   5. Petty cash was original established for $60. During the month, $10 was paid out for parking costs, $15 was paid out for postage, and $25 was paid out for emergency purchase of office supplies. Record, using a general journal entry, the replenishment of the petty cash back to $60.

LO3 (10 min)   6. In Exercise 5, if the custodian decided to raise the level of petty cash to $100, what would be the journal entry to replenish?

Exercises

6-1. From the following information, construct a bank reconciliation for Bing Co. as of July 31, 200X. Then prepare journal entries if needed.

LO2 (15 min)

Checkbook balance	$1,500	Outstanding checks	$678
Bank statement balance	1,200	Bank service charge	40
Deposits (in transit)	900	NSF; Mia Kaminsky's check in payment of account was returned for insufficient funds.	38

6-2. In general journal form, prepare journal entries to establish a petty cash fund on July 1 and replenish it on July 31.

LO3 (15 min)

200X

July 1 A $100 petty cash fund is established.

31 At end of the month, $12 cash plus the following paid vouchers exist: donations expense, $20; postage expense, $18; office supplies expense, $25; miscellaneous expense, $25.

6-3. If in Exercise 6-2 cash on hand is $11, prepare the entry to replenish the petty cash on July 31.

LO3 (15 min)

6-4. If in Exercise 6-2 cash on hand is $13, prepare the entry to replenish the petty cash on July 31.

LO3 (15 min)

6-5. At the end of the day the clerk for Pete's Variety Shop noticed an error in the amount of cash he should have. Total cash sales from the sales tape were $1,200, whereas the total cash in the register was $1,156. Pete keeps a $30 change fund in his shop. Prepare an appropriate general journal entry to record the cash sale as well as reveal the cash shortage.

LO5 (15 min)

Group A Problems

6A-1. Lee.com received a bank statement from Ranch Bank indicating a bank balance of $8,000. Based on Lee.com's check stubs, the ending checkbook balance was $9,000. Your task is to prepare a bank reconciliation for Lee.com as of July 31, 200X, from the following information (journalize entries as needed):

LO2 (20 min)

> *Check Figure:*
> Reconciled Balance $8,690

  a. Checks outstanding: no. 122, $800; no. 130, $710.
  b. Deposits in transit, $2,200.
  c. Lee.com forgot to record a $1,260 equipment purchase made with a debit card.
  d. Bank service charges, $50.
  e. Ranch Bank collected a note for Lee.com, $1010, less a $10 collection fee.

6A-2. From the following bank statement, please (1) complete the bank reconciliation for Rick's Deli found on the reverse of the bank statement on the following page and (2) journalize the appropriate entries as needed.

LO2 (20 min)

> *Check Figure:*
> Reconciled Balance $5,270

  a. A deposit of $2,000 is in transit.
  b. Rick's Deli has an ending checkbook balance of $5,600.
  c. Checks outstanding: no. 111, $600; no. 119, $1,200; no. 121, $330.
  d. Jim Rice's check for $300 bounced due to lack of sufficient funds.

Lowell National Bank
Rio Mean Brand
Bugna, Texas

Rick's Deli
8811 2nd St,
Bugna, Texas

Old Balance	Checks in Order of Payment		Deposits	Date	New Balance
6,000				2/2	6,000
	90.00	210.00		2/3	5,700
	150.00		300.00	2/10	5,850
	600.00		600.00	2/15	5,850
	300.00	NSF	300.00	2/20	5,850
	1,200.00		1,200.00	2/24	5,850
	600.00	30.00 SC	180.00	2/28	5,400

LO3 (30 min)

6A-3. The following transactions occurred in April for Merry Co.:

Check Figure:
Cash Replenishment $76

200X		
April	1	Issued check no. 14 for $100 to establish a petty cash fund.
	5	Paid $15 from petty cash for postage, voucher no. 1.
	8	Paid $20 from petty cash for office supplies, voucher no. 2.
	15	Issued check no. 15 to Reliable Corp. for $200 from past purchases on account.
	17	Paid $18 from petty cash for office supplies, voucher no. 3.
	20	Issued check no. 16 to Roger Corp., $600 for past purchases on account.
	24	Paid $14 from petty cash for postage, voucher no. 4.
	26	Paid $9 from petty cash for local church donation, voucher no. 5 (a miscellaneous payment).
	28	Issued check no. 17 to Roy Kloon to pay for office equipment, $700.
	30	Replenish petty cash, check no. 18.

Your tasks are to

1. Record the appropriate entries in the general journal as well as the auxiliary petty cash record as needed.
2. Be sure to replenish the petty cash fund on April 30 (check no. 18).

LO3, 4, 5 (40 min)

6A-4. From the following, record the transactions into Logan's auxiliary petty cash record and general journal as needed:

Check Figure:
Cash Replenishment $106

200X		
Oct.	1	A check was drawn (no. 444) payable to Roberta Floss, petty cashier, to establish a $150 petty cash fund.
	5	Paid $24 for postage stamps, voucher no. 1.
	9	Paid $12 for delivery charges on goods for resale, voucher no. 2.
	12	Paid $8 for donation to a church (miscellaneous expense), voucher no. 3.
	14	Paid $9 for postage stamp, voucher no. 4.
	17	Paid $18 for delivery charges on goods for resale, voucher no. 5.
	27	Purchased computer supplies from petty cash for $18; voucher no. 6.
	28	Paid $14 for postage, voucher no. 7.
	29	Drew check no. 618 to replenish petty cash and a $3 shortage.

Group B Problems

6B-1. As the bookkeeper of Lee.com, you received the bank statement from Ranch Bank indicating a balance of $9,750. The ending checkbook balance was $10,290. Prepare the bank reconciliation for Lee.com as of July 31, 200X, and prepare journal entries as needed based on the following:

a. Deposits in transit, $2,875.

b. Bank service charges, $25.

c. Checks outstanding: no. 111, $485; no. 115, $1,650.

d. Ranch Bank collected a note for Lee.com, $1,100, plus $110 interest.

e. NSF check $525.

f. Lee.com's records indicate that check no. 107, written on Aug. 15, was issued for $900 to pay the month's rent. However, the cancelled check and the listing on the bank statement shows the actual check was $800.

g. The bank made an error by deducting a check for $560 issued by another business.

LO2 (20 min)

> *Check Figure:*
> Reconciled Balance $11,050

6B-2. Based on the following, please (1) complete the bank reconciliation for Rick's Deli found on the reverse of the bank statement and (2) journalize the appropriate entries as needed.

a. Checks outstanding: no. 110, $80; no. 116, $160; no. 118, $52.

b. A deposit of $416 is in transit.

c. The checkbook balance of Rick's Deli shows an ending balance of $798.

d. Jim Rice's check for $40 bounced due to lack of sufficient funds.

LO2 (20 min)

Lowell National Bank
Rio Mean Brand
Bugna, Texas

Rick's Deli
8811 2nd St,
Bugna, Texas

> *Check Figure:*
> Reconciled Balance $756

Old Balance	Checks in Order of Payment		Deposits	Date	New Balance
718.00				4/2	718.00
	12.00	36.00		4/3	670.00
	20.00		40.00	4/10	690.00
	80.00		80.00	4/15	690.00
	40.00	NSF	40.00	4/20	690.00
	160.00		160.00	4/24	690.00
	80.00	2.00 SC	24.00	4/28	632.00

6B-3. From the following transactions, (1) record the entries as needed in the general journal of Merry Co. as well as the auxiliary petty cash record and (2) replenish the petty cash fund on April 30 (check no. 8).

LO3 (30 min)

200X

Apr. 1 Issued check no. 4 for $60 to establish a petty cash fund.

5 Paid $9 from petty cash for postage, voucher no. 1.

8 Paid $12 from petty cash for office supplies, voucher no. 2.

15 Issued check no. 5 to Reliable Corp. for $400 for past purchases on account.

17 Paid $7 from petty cash for office supplies, voucher no. 3.

20 Issued check no. 6 to Roger Corp. $300 for past purchases on account.

> *Check Figure:*
> Cash Replenishment $46

(continued on next page)

24   Paid $6 from petty cash for postage, voucher no. 4.

26   Paid $12 from petty cash for local church donation, voucher no. 5 (a miscellaneous payment).

28   Issued check no. 7 to Roy Kloon to pay for office equipment, $800.

30   Replenish petty cash, check no. 8.

LO3, 4, 5 (40 min)   **6B-4.** From the following, record the transactions into Logan's auxiliary petty cash record and general journal (p. 2) as needed:

200X
Oct.   1   Roberta Floss, the petty cashier, cashed a check, no. 444, to establish a $90 petty cash fund.

5   Paid $16 for postage stamps, voucher no. 1.

9   Paid $14 for delivery charges on goods for resale, voucher no. 2.

12   Paid $6 for donation to a church (miscellaneous expense), voucher no. 3.

14   Paid $10 for postage stamps, voucher no. 4.

17   Paid $7 for delivery charges on goods for resale, voucher no. 5.

27   Purchased computer supplies from petty cash for $9, voucher no. 6.

28   Paid $3 for postage, voucher no. 7.

29   Drew check no. 618 to replenish petty cash and a $4 shortage.

Check Figure:
Cash Replenishment $69

ON-THE-JOB TRAINING

LO3 (15 min)   **T-1.** Claire Montgomery, the bookkeeper of Angel Co., has appointed Mike Kaminsky as the petty cash custodian. The following transactions occurred in November:

200X
Nov.   25   Check no. 441 was written and cashed to establish a $50 petty cash fund.

27   Paid $8.50 delivery charge for goods purchased for resale.

29   Purchased office supplies for $12 from petty cash.

30   Purchased postage stamps for $15 from petty cash.

Check Figure:
Cash Replenishment $40.50

On December 3, Mike received the following internal memo:

MEMO

To: *Mike Kaminsky*

From: *Claire Montgomery*

Re: *Petty Cash*

Mike, I'll need $5 for postage stamps. By the way, I noticed that our petty cash account seems to be too low. Let's increase its size to $100.

Could you help Mike replenish petty cash on December 3 by providing him with a general journal entry? Support your answer and indicate in writing whether Claire was correct.

LO2 (30 min)   **T-2.** Lee Company has the policy of depositing all receipts and making all payments by check. On receiving the bank statement, Bill Free, a new bookkeeper, is quite upset that the balance in Cash in the ledger is $4,209.50, whereas the ending bank balance is $4,440.50. Bill is convinced the bank has made an error. Based on the following facts, is Bill's concern warranted? What other written suggestions could you offer Bill in the bank reconciliation process?

a. The November 30 cash receipts, $611, had been placed in the bank's night depository after banking hours and consequently did not appear on the bank statement as a deposit.

b. Two debit memorandums and a credit memorandum were included with the returned check. None of the memorandums had been recorded at the time of the reconciliation. The first debit memorandum had a $130 NSF check written by Abby Ellen. The second was a $6.50 debit memorandum for service charges. The credit memorandum was for $494 and represented the proceeds less a $6 collection fee from a $500 non-interest-bearing note collected for Lee Company by the bank.

c. It was also found that checks no. 942 for $71.50 and no. 947 for $206.50, both written and recorded on November 28, were not among the cancelled checks returned.

d. Bill found that check no. 899 was correctly drawn for $1,094, in payment for a new cash register. This check, however, had been recorded as though it were for $1,148.

e. The October bank reconciliation showed two checks outstanding on September 30, no. 621 for $152.50 and no. 630 for $179.30. Check no. 630 was returned with the November bank statement, but check no. 621 was not.

FINANCIAL REPORT PROBLEM

Reading the Kellogg's Annual Report

LO2 (15 min)

Go to Appendix A of the Kellogg's annual report. How do you think Kellogg's reconciles its bank statement? Manually or with computers? Support your position.

INTERNET PROJECT

Bankrate

Go to the Web and search: Annual Report Bankrate 2008.
Click on Investors Relations.
List out the latest news Bankrate is providing to its investors.
Order a free annual report.

CONTINUING PROBLEM

Sanchez Computer Center

LO2, 3, 4 (60 min)

The books have been closed for the first year of business for Sanchez Computer Center. The company ended up with a marginal profit for the first three months in operation. Tony expects faster growth as he enters a busy season.

Following is a list of transactions for the month of October. Petty Cash account #1010 and Miscellaneous Expense account #5100 have been added to the chart of accounts.

Oct.	1	Paid rent for November, December, and January, $1,200 (check no. 8108).
	2	Established a petty cash fund for $100.
	4	Collected $3,600 from a cash customer for building five systems.
	5	Collected $2,600, the amount due from A. Pitale's invoice no. 12674, customer on account.
	6	Purchased $25 worth of stamps using petty cash voucher no. 101.
	7	Withdrew $2,000 (check no. 8109) for personal use.

(continued on next page)

8	Purchased $22 worth of supplies using petty cash voucher no. 102.
12	Paid the newspaper carrier $10 using petty cash voucher no. 103.
16	Paid the amount due on the September phone bill, $65 (check no. 8110).
17	Paid the amount due on the September electric bill, $95 (check no. 8111).
22	Performed computer services for Taylor Golf; billed the client $4,200 (invoice no. 12675).
23	Paid $20 for computer paper using petty cash voucher no. 104.
30	Took $15 out of petty cash for lunch, voucher no. 105.
31	Replenished the petty cash. Coin and currency in drawer total $8.00.

Because Tony was so busy trying to close his books, he forgot to reconcile his last three months of bank statements. A list of all deposits and checks written for the past three months (each entry is identified by chapter, transaction date, or transaction letter) and the bank statements for July through September are provided. The statement for October won't arrive until the first week of November.

Assignment

1. Record the transactions in general journal or petty cash format.
2. Post the transactions to the general ledger accounts.
3. Prepare a trial balance.
4. Compare the Computer Center's deposits and checks with the bank statements and complete a bank reconciliation as of September 30, 200X.

Sanchez Computer Center Summary of Deposits and Checks

Chapter	Transaction	Payor/Payee	Amount
		Deposits	
1	a	Tony Freedman	$4,500
1	f	Cash customer	250
1	i	Taylor Golf	1,200
1	g	Cash customer	200
2	p	Cash customer	900
3	Sept. 2	Tonya Parker Jones	325
3	Sept. 6	Summer Lipe	220
3	Sept. 12	Jeannine Sparks	850
3	Sept. 26	Mike Hammer	140

Chapter	Transaction	Check #	Payor/Payee	Amount
		Checks		
1	b	8095	Multi Systems, Inc.	$1,200
1	c	8096	Office Furniture, Inc.	600
1	e	8097	Capital Management	400
1	j	8098	Tony Freedman	100
2	l	8099	Insurance Protection, Inc.	150
2	m	8100	Office Depot	200
2	n	8101	Computer Edge Magazine	1,400
2	q	8102	San Diego Electric	85
2	r	8103	U.S. Postmaster	50

3	Sept. 1	8104	Capital Management	1,200
3	Sept. 8	8105	Pacific Bell USA	155
3	Sept. 15	8106	Computer Connection	200
3	Sept. 16	8107	Multi Systems, Inc.	1,200

Bank Statement

First Union Bank 322 Glen Ave. Escondido, CA 92025

Sanchez Computer Center   Statement Date: July 22, 200X

Checks Paid:			Deposits and Credits:	
Date paid	Number	Amount	Date received	Amount
7-4	8095	1,200.00	7-1	4,500.00
7-7	8096	600.00	7-10	250.00
7-15	8097	400.00	7-20	1,200.00
			7-21	200.00
Total 3 checks paid for $2,200.00			Total Deposits	$6,150.00

Ending balance on July 22—
$3,950.00

Received statement July 29, 200X.

Bank Statement

First Union Bank 322 Glen Ave. Escondido, CA 92025

Sanchez Computer Center   Statement Date: August 21, 200X

Checks Paid:			Deposits and Credits:	
Date paid	Number	Amount	Date received	Amount
8-2	8098	100.00	8-12	900.00
8-3	8099	150.00		
8-10	8100	200.00		
8-15	8101	1,400.00		
8-20	8102	85.00		
Total 5 checks paid for $1,935.00			Total Deposits	$900.00

Beginning balance on July 22—   Ending balance on August 21—
$3,950.00 $2,915.00

Received statement August 27, 200X.

Bank Statement

First Union Bank 322 Glen Ave. Escondido, CA 92025

Sanchez Computer Center   Statement Date: September 20, 200X

Checks Paid:			Deposits and Credits:	
Date paid	Number	Amount	Date received	Amount
9-2	8103	50.00	9-4	325.00
9-6	8104	1,200.00	9-7	220.00
9-12	8105	155.00	9-14	850.00
Total 3 checks paid for $1,405.00			Total Deposits	$1,395.00

Beginning balance on August 21   Ending balance on September 20
$2,915.00 $2,905.00

Received statement September 29, 200X.

SUBWAY Case

COUNTING DOWN THE CASH
LO1, 2, 3, 4 (20 min)

Subway now requires all of its franchisees to submit their weekly sales and inventory reports electronically using new point-of-sale (POS) touch-screen cash registers. With the new POS registers, clerks use a touch screen to punch in the number and type of items bought. Franchisees can quickly reconfigure prices and products to match new promotions. Not only is this POS method faster than using the old cash registers but it also allows franchisees to view every transaction as it occurs—from their own back office computers or even from home. Also, individual POS terminals within the restaurant are linked, so franchisees are able to see consolidated data quickly.

The transition to electronic reporting and networked POS terminals, however, has not been without bumps, as Stan can testify. About six months before the deadline for all Subway franchisees to "go electronic," Stan attended a heated meeting on the topic at his local chapter of the North American Association of Subway Franchisees (NAASF). The NAASF is an independent organization of franchisees that serves as an advisory council on Subway policies and issues of common concern. Everyone seemed to be talking at once.

"I just don't trust these machines. What am I supposed to do when the system crashes?" complained one man.

"Yeah, and I don't like the idea of a bunch of kids knowing more about how to run the software than I do," said one older franchisee.

"Don't be so quick to assume that our sandwich artists will love POS," said one woman. "I overheard one of my employees say to another, 'POS means **P**eeking **O**ver **S**houlders.' These young kids we hire have more reason to be resistant than we do!"

"I'll say they do!" rejoined Jay Harden, the president of Stan's local NAASF. "Employee theft is one of the largest problems we face as franchisees. I, for one, really welcome the cash control we get with POS."

Stan had to agree with Jay. Training staff to record every sale and record it correctly is a critical component of a cash business such as Subway. In Stan's view, the POS machines would only make that training easier. Cash control is built into the new system, which also provides the owners with information that will help them spot problems—such as employee theft—and track trends. Of course, thought Stan, the chore of counting down the cash at the end of a shift remained. No matter what type of computer program you install, cash still must be counted down and rectified with the register tape at the end of each shift.

As the voices rang louder around him, Stan thought about what had happened that day when Ellen closed out her cash register drawer. He had spent hours figuring out a discrepancy between the cash in the drawer and the register tape. Ellen had forgotten to void a mistaken entry for $99.99. Stan had first suspected that she had made a huge error in counting change.

Thinking of errors in counting brought him back to the topic of the meeting. Stan raised his hand to speak.

"One thing that concerns me is the potential for accounting errors. I still have to key in data from the POS into my Peachtree accounting software. Every time I have to reenter data, the potential for error multiplies."

"That shows some foresight, Stan," said Jay Harden. "We're actually exploring computer programs that will feed the data directly from the POS into our accounting programs." Even some of the technophobes and POS skeptics in the group had to agree it would be a great idea.

Discussion Questions

1. What is an advisory council? Why do you think franchisees need one?
2. Why do you think some small business owners fear computerization?
3. How would Stan catch a discrepancy in the Cash account? How would he record a loss?
4. Why does Subway invest time, money, and effort in investigating new cash handling systems such as its new POS terminals?

7

Calculating Pay and Payroll Taxes: The Beginning of the Payroll Process

DID YOU KNOW? Johnson & Johnson has more than 120,000 employees worldwide. It contributed $158 million dollars to employee savings plans in 2006. Visit *www.jnj.com* to find more information about Johnson & Johnson.

LEARNING OBJECTIVES

1. Calculating gross pay, employee payroll tax deductions for federal income tax withholding, state income tax withholding, FICA (OASDI, Medicare), and net pay.

2. Calculating employer taxes for FICA (OASDI, Medicare), FUTA, SUTA, and workers' compensation insurance.

3. Preparing a payroll register.

4. Maintaining an employee earnings record.

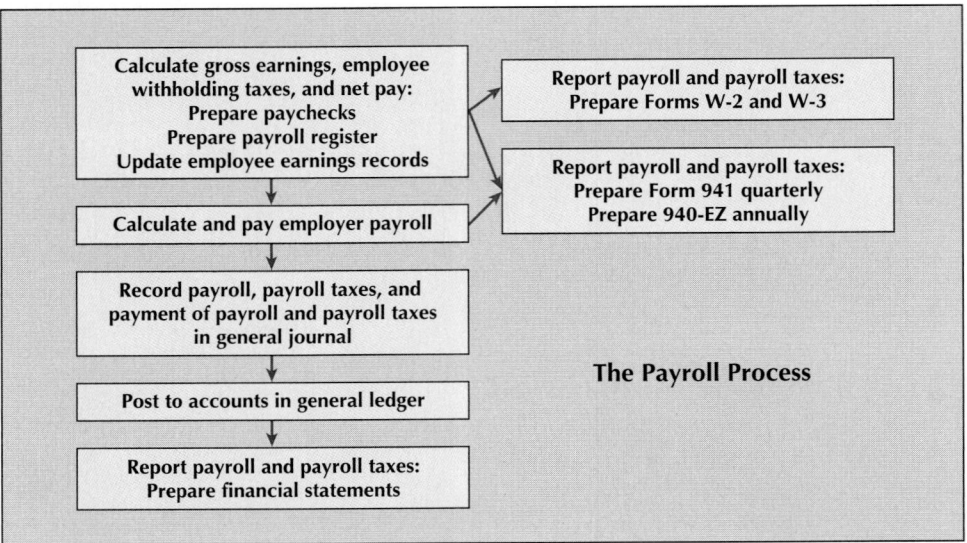

In this chapter we will look at the payroll process for the employer (see above). Use this chart as a reference tool when reading the chapter. Check out the payroll register for Travelwithus.com in Figure 7.3 at the beginning of Learning Unit 7-2. Businesses use this document to calculate employees' pay and the deductions for employee payroll taxes on that pay. In this chapter you will learn how to compute these amounts and prepare a payroll register such as the one shown. You will also learn how to determine the amount of payroll taxes that employers must pay and prepare another payroll report, the employee earnings record.

Most businesses can't run without employees, so hiring and paying employees are pretty typical business events. The accounting for payroll transactions is really the same whether a business is a small, family-owned gardening business in your town or a nationwide retail department store. Either way, it's important to know how to calculate, pay, record, and report payroll and payroll taxes in this payroll process.

Federal, state, and maybe even local laws regulate the payroll process. A business may be fined substantial penalties and interest for failing to follow these laws properly. For example, a business may be fined $50 per statement up to a maximum of $100,000 per year for failing to give its employees their W-2 form, Wage and Tax Statement. Because of this, there are many companies, such as ADP, Paychex, and Ceridian, that will handle payroll for a fee. However, it is often less costly for the business to do these tasks itself.

In this chapter we take a close look at the employees of Travelwithus.com, a new Internet-based company that makes travel arrangements for its customers, to see how a payroll is figured and recorded. Travelwithus.com specializes in two types of travel, cruises and business travel. We look at how its payroll is affected by federal, state, and local taxes and how the accountant at Travelwithus.com handles payroll transactions for the company.

LO1 Learning Unit 7-1 Calculation of Gross Earnings, Employee Withholding Taxes, and Net Pay

Katherine Kurtz is the accountant for Travelwithus.com who calculates and records each payroll for the company. Several parts of Katherine's job are especially important. First, Katherine must be accurate in everything she does, because any mistake she makes in working with the payroll may affect both the employee and the company. Second, Katherine needs to be on time when working on the company's payroll so that employees get their paychecks as expected and governments receive payroll taxes when due. Third, Katherine must at all times obey the appropriate federal, state, and local laws governing payroll matters. Fourth, because processing payroll involves personal employee information such as pay rates and marital status, Katherine always needs to keep payroll data confidential.

Gross Earnings

To begin the payroll process, Katherine must first calculate the earnings for Travelwithus.com employees. To make the correct calculations, Katherine must know how each employee has been classified for payroll purposes. As a rule, a company will classify every employee either as "hourly" or "salaried." If an employee is an hourly employee, that employee only will be paid for the hours he or she worked. Employees classified as salaried employees receive a fixed dollar amount for the hours worked.

Travelwithus.com classified three of its six employees as hourly. For these three employees, Katherine must compute the hours they worked during a specific time period known as a pay period; the number of hours determines how much each has earned. For payroll purposes, **pay periods** are defined as daily, weekly, biweekly (every two weeks), semimonthly (twice each month), monthly, quarterly, or annually. A pay period can start on any day of the week and must end after the specified period of time has passed. Most companies use weekly, biweekly, semimonthly, or monthly pay periods when calculating their payrolls.

Companies can use different pay periods for different groups of employees. Travelwithus.com chose a biweekly pay period for its hourly employees and a monthly pay period for its salaried employees. The biweekly pay period starts on Monday and ends two weeks later on a Sunday. Hourly employees actually receive their paychecks on the following Friday because it takes Katherine a few days to calculate all of the amounts involved in paying an hourly payroll. The monthly pay period starts on the first day of the calendar month and ends on the last day of that month. Salaried employees will be paid on the last day of the month. Because they receive a fixed amount of pay, Katherine is able to calculate these payroll amounts much faster than the hourly ones and can even start these calculations before the month ends.

Now that Katherine knows the pay period for Travelwithus.com's hourly employees, she calculates their total or **gross earnings.** Gross earnings are calculated by adding the regular earnings for an employee for the period to any overtime earnings the employee has earned for that period.

Overtime earnings must be computed according to federal law. The federal law that governs overtime earnings is called the **Fair Labor Standards Act** and is sometimes referred to as the **Federal Wage and Hour Law.** An employer must follow the Fair Labor Standards Act if it is involved in **interstate commerce,** in other words, if it is doing business in more than one state. For most employers, this law says that an hourly employee must be paid at least one and a half times his or her regular pay rate for any hours he or she works over 40 in one workweek. A **workweek,** according to the law, is a seven-day (or 168-hour) period that can start at any time, but once the starting time for the week is determined, it must stay the same for each week.

It is important to know that some states also have payroll laws that need to be followed in determining pay. For example, California requires employers to pay overtime pay to hourly employees who have worked more than 8 hours in any day, even if they work less than 40 hours total for that week. Employers must follow both sets of laws, and in this case, Travelwithus.com would pay overtime if an employee works more than 8 hours in one day and if an employee works more than 40 hours in one week.

Hourly employees of Travelwithus.com have two workweeks in each biweekly pay period. Travelwithus.com's hourly workweek starts on Monday morning at 12:01 A.M. each week and ends seven days later on Sunday evening at 12:00 midnight. Thus, Katherine must calculate overtime pay for any employee who worked more than 40 hours in each week of this two-week period.

Stephanie Higuera is one of the three hourly employees working for Travelwithus.com. Travelwithus.com's most recent biweekly pay period began on Monday, October 16, at 12:01 A.M. and ended on Sunday, October 29 at 12:00 midnight. The first week of this period ended on Sunday, October 22, and during this week Stephanie worked 44 hours. During the second week that ended on October 29, Stephanie worked 38 hours.

How much should she be paid? Katherine will answer this question by first calculating both Stephanie's regular hours and her overtime hours. According to the federal law, Katherine must look at each week separately. Stephanie worked 44 hours during the first week, which means that she worked 40 regular hours and 4 overtime hours. Because she worked fewer than 40 hours in the second week, all of these hours are regular hours.

Week No.	Week Ending	Regular Hours	Overtime Hours	Total Hours
1	October 22	40	4	44
2	October 29	38	0	38
Total		78	4	82

Stephanie earns $11.40 for each hour she works, so Katherine computes Stephanie's pay as follows:

$11.40 regular rate × 1.5 = $17.10 overtime rate
78 regular hours × $11.40 regular rate =   *$889.20 regular earnings*
4 overtime hours × $17.10 overtime rate =   *68.40 overtime earnings*
$889.20 regular earnings + $68.40 overtime earnings = $957.60 gross earnings

Or, Katherine could figure Stephanie's pay this way: | SAME |

$11.40 regular rate × 0.5 = $5.70 extra pay
   for each overtime hour
82 total hours × $11.40 regular rate =   *$934.80 earnings at the regular rate*
4 overtime hours × $5.70 extra pay for each
   overtime hour =   *22.80 extra earnings*
$934.80 earnings at the regular rate + $22.80
   extra earnings =   *$957.60 gross earnings*

Notice that either way, Katherine computed exactly the same amount of gross earnings. The advantage of using the first method is that it clearly shows the amount of extra money that Stephanie earned from working overtime. The advantage of the second is that it shows the effect of being paid at a higher, overtime rate for those extra hours worked.

Julia Regan also works for Travelwithus.com. She, however, is a salaried employee, and earns $4,875 per month. As a salaried (exempt) employee, she is not eligible for overtime pay, and Katherine will list her total earnings for the month of October as $4,875. To be considered a salaried employee, Julia must qualify as a salaried employee according to the specifics of the Fair Labor Standards Act. Thus, Travelwithus.com can't decide to classify employees as salaried just to avoid paying the overtime pay; these employees must be salaried persons according to this law.

Federal Income Tax Withholding

After Katherine determines Stephanie's and Julia's gross earnings, she figures out how much each of them will actually receive in their paychecks after several different taxes have been withheld. These taxes are called payroll taxes, and must be paid by the employees. Employees pay these amounts by having them taken out, or withheld, from their paychecks. Their employer then sends them to the Internal Revenue Service (IRS), state governments, and maybe even local governments so they count against the amount of federal, state, and possible local income taxes that the employees will owe for the year.

In this way, Stephanie and Julia pay their taxes on a "pay as you go basis." In other words, when Stephanie and Julia complete their federal income tax returns at the end of the year, they will deduct the amount of income tax withheld during the year from the total amount owed for the year. How and when Travelwithus.com turns these amounts over to the federal, state, and local governments will be discussed in Chapter 8. Katherine computes the amount of taxes to be withheld based on each employee's gross earnings for the pay period.

Katherine starts figuring out how much to withhold from each employee's pay by looking at the W-4 that he or she completed. The IRS **Form W-4, Employee's Withholding Allowance Certificate,** is completed by every employee and provides information that will be used to determine the amount of **federal income tax (FIT) withholdings** for the period. Figure 7.1 on the following page is Stephanie's W-4 form. Notice that it shows Stephanie's marital status and total number of **allowances** she claims for federal income tax purposes. Usually, an employee may claim one allowance for himself or herself, one for his or her spouse, and one for each of his or her dependents, such as a child. Employees who want more withheld from their paychecks can claim fewer allowances than they really have. However, they are not allowed to claim more allowances than they really have to avoid underpaying taxes owed, which may also result in them owing the government amounts for penalties and interest.

To look up the amount of federal income tax that needs to be withheld from Stephanie's paycheck, Katherine uses Stephanie's marital status and the number of claimed allowances listed on her Form W-4. She also uses Stephanie's gross earnings for the pay period and the length of the pay period. The amount of federal income tax that needs to be withheld is listed in a **wage bracket table** that is in the IRS publication called **Circular E,** *Employer's Tax Guide*, also known as Publication 15. Check out one of the tables from the Circular that's shown in Figure 7.2. Notice from the heading "SINGLE Persons—BIWEEKLY Payroll Period" that this table applies to single persons who are paid biweekly. Wage bracket tables are prepared according to marital status and pay period; Circular E has a similar table for married persons who are paid biweekly, as well as tables for single and married persons who are paid daily, weekly, monthly, semimonthly, monthly, quarterly, and annually. Also notice that the table has rows for different ranges of gross pay, starting from lower amounts of pay in the top rows of the table to higher amounts in the bottom rows.

Katherine determines the amount of federal income taxes that need to be withheld from Stephanie's paycheck by first locating the correct table in Circular E. She finds the table for single persons who are paid biweekly. Then, she locates the row that says "At least $940 but less than $960." Stephanie's gross pay for this pay period is $957.60, so this row applies to her. Katherine traces this row to the column for one withholding allowance, and finds that the amount of withholding tax is $92. Based on Stephanie's gross earnings of $957.60 and her one claimed allowance, Katherine will withhold $92 in federal income taxes from Stephanie's pay.

What if Stephanie had earned $960 instead of 957.60? Would the amount of federal income tax withheld be the same? No, Katherine would have withheld $95. To see this, check out the heading for the columns showing the wages. Notice that it says, "If the wages are—." Katherine will look at the rows of wage ranges, stopping when she sees the line that says, "At least $940 but less than $960." If Stephanie's gross wages are exactly $960—not less than $960—Katherine must go to the next line, which says, "At least $960 but less than $980" and withhold the amount in the column for one withholding allowance, which is $95.

State Income Tax Withholding

Most states also charge their residents an income tax based on the amount of money they earn from their employers. In 2008, only Alaska, Florida, Nevada, South Dakota, Texas, Washington, and Wyoming did not. (Technically, Tennessee also does not have a state income tax; it is only imposed on interest and dividends.) So, in addition to withholding federal income taxes, Katherine may also have to determine amounts for **state income tax (SIT) withholding.** Fortunately for Katherine, the process for withholding state income tax is much the same as it is for withholding federal income tax. In many states, withholding amounts are based on the same information that is listed in the employee's W-4, although some states do have their own versions of this form that are used instead. Employers use

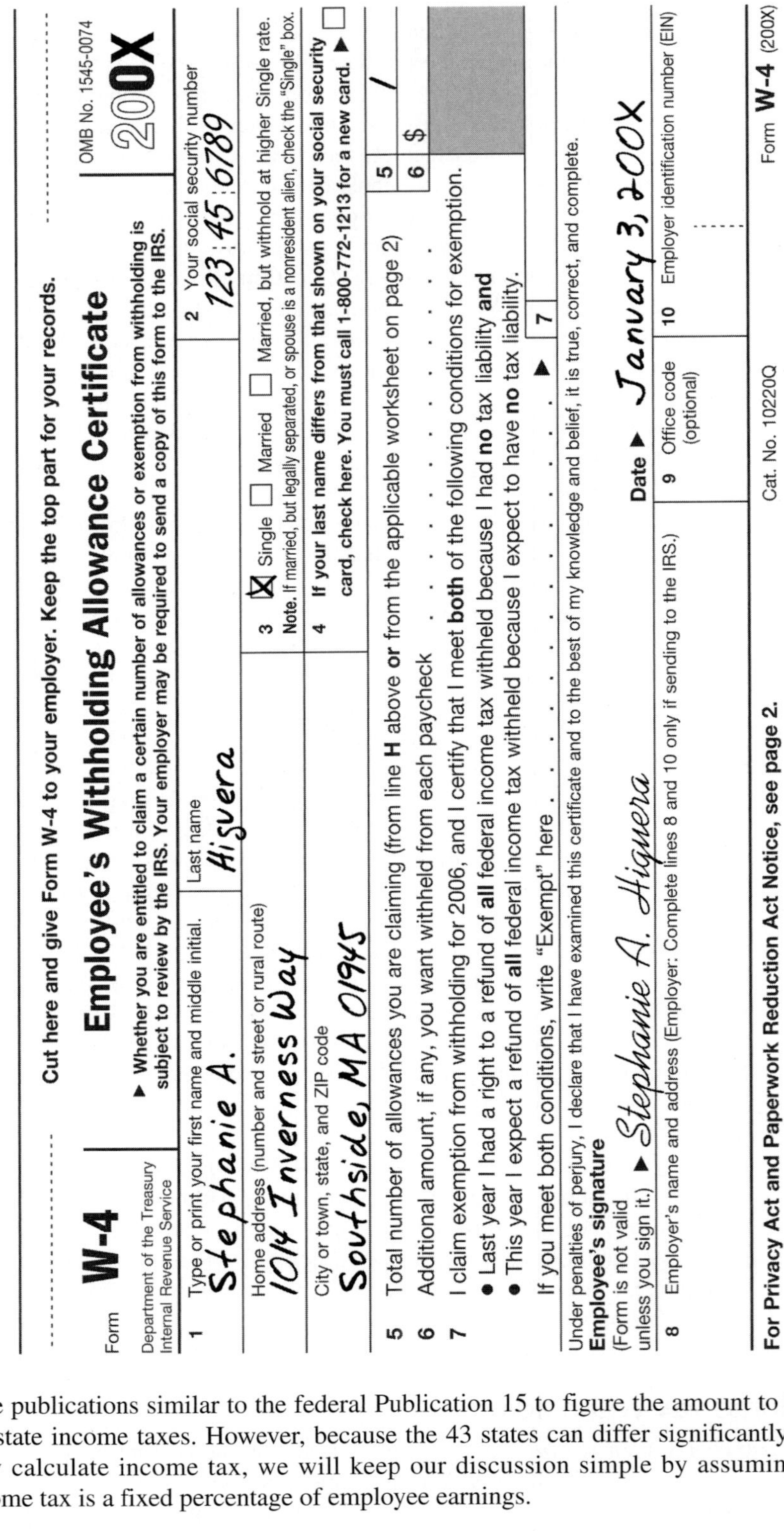

Cut here and give Form W-4 to your employer. Keep the top part for your records.

Form **W-4** | **Employee's Withholding Allowance Certificate** | OMB No. 1545-0074 | **200X**

Department of the Treasury
Internal Revenue Service

▶ **Whether you are entitled to claim a certain number of allowances or exemption from withholding is subject to review by the IRS. Your employer may be required to send a copy of this form to the IRS.**

1 Type or print your first name and middle initial. Stephanie A.	Last name Hisvera	2 Your social security number 123 : 45 : 6789
Home address (number and street or rural route) 1014 Inverness Way	3 ☒ Single ☐ Married ☐ Married, but withhold at higher Single rate. **Note.** If married, but legally separated, or spouse is a nonresident alien, check the "Single" box.	
City or town, state, and ZIP code Southside, MA 01945	4 **If your last name differs from that shown on your social security card, check here. You must call 1-800-772-1213 for a new card.** ▶ ☐	

5 Total number of allowances you are claiming (from line **H** above **or** from the applicable worksheet on page 2) . . . 5 | 1

6 Additional amount, if any, you want withheld from each paycheck . . . 6 | $

7 I claim exemption from withholding for 2006, and I certify that I meet **both** of the following conditions for exemption.
- Last year I had a right to a refund of **all** federal income tax withheld because I had **no** tax liability **and**
- This year I expect a refund of **all** federal income tax withheld because I expect to have **no** tax liability.

If you meet both conditions, write "Exempt" here . . . ▶ 7

Under penalties of perjury, I declare that I have examined this certificate and to the best of my knowledge and belief, it is true, correct, and complete.

Employee's signature
(Form is not valid unless you sign it.) ▶ Stephanie A. Higuera   **Date ▶** January 3, 200X

8 Employer's name and address (Employer: Complete lines 8 and 10 only if sending to the IRS.)	9 Office code (optional)	10 Employer identification number (EIN)

For Privacy Act and Paperwork Reduction Act Notice, see page 2.   Cat. No. 10220Q   Form **W-4** (200X)

FIGURE 7.1 Completed Form W-4

state publications similar to the federal Publication 15 to figure the amount to be withheld for state income taxes. However, because the 43 states can differ significantly in the way they calculate income tax, we will keep our discussion simple by assuming that state income tax is a fixed percentage of employee earnings.

Other Income Tax Withholding

We pointed out previously that employees would have state income taxes withheld from their paychecks if they live in one of the 43 states that charges such a tax. In addition, many cities and counties tax employee earnings. Sometimes the tax will be a percentage of gross earnings much like federal income tax, or it may be a fixed dollar amount that the employer will withhold from every pay period. These cities and counties have their own rules regarding payroll tax deposits and tax reports for this type of withholding tax.

FIGURE 7.2 Wage Bracket Tables: Single Persons—Biweekly Payroll Period

SINGLE Persons—BIWEEKLY Payroll Period
(For Wages Paid in 2008)

If the wages are—		And the number of withholding allowances claimed is—										
At least	But less than	0	1	2	3	4	5	6	7	8	9	10
		The amount of income tax to be withheld is—										
$800	$820	$92	$71	$51	$31	$17	$4	$0	$0	$0	$0	$0
820	840	95	74	54	34	19	6	0	0	0	0	0
840	860	98	77	57	37	21	8	0	0	0	0	0
860	880	101	80	60	40	23	10	0	0	0	0	0
880	900	104	83	63	43	25	12	0	0	0	0	0
900	920	107	86	66	46	27	14	0	0	0	0	0
920	940	110	89	69	49	29	16	2	0	0	0	0
940	960	113	92	72	52	32	18	4	0	0	0	0
960	980	116	95	75	55	35	20	6	0	0	0	0
980	1,000	119	98	78	58	38	22	8	0	0	0	0
1,000	1,020	122	101	81	61	41	24	10	0	0	0	0
1,020	1,040	125	104	84	64	44	26	12	0	0	0	0
1,040	1,060	128	107	87	67	47	28	14	1	0	0	0
1,060	1,080	131	110	90	70	50	30	16	3	0	0	0
1,080	1,100	134	113	93	73	53	33	18	5	0	0	0
1,100	1,120	137	116	96	76	56	36	20	7	0	0	0
1,120	1,140	140	119	99	79	59	39	22	9	0	0	0
1,140	1,160	143	122	102	82	62	42	24	11	0	0	0
1,160	1,180	146	125	105	85	65	45	26	13	0	0	0
1,180	1,200	149	128	108	88	68	48	28	15	1	0	0
1,200	1,220	152	131	111	91	71	51	30	17	3	0	0
1,220	1,240	155	134	114	94	74	54	33	19	5	0	0
1,240	1,260	158	137	117	97	77	57	36	21	7	0	0
1,260	1,280	161	140	120	100	80	60	39	23	9	0	0
1,280	1,300	164	143	123	103	83	63	42	25	11	0	0
1,300	1,320	167	146	126	106	86	66	45	27	13	0	0
1,320	1,340	172	149	129	109	89	69	48	29	15	2	0
1,340	1,360	177	152	132	112	92	72	51	31	17	4	0
1,360	1,380	182	155	135	115	95	75	54	34	19	6	0
1,380	1,400	187	158	138	118	98	78	57	37	21	8	0
1,400	1,420	192	161	141	121	101	81	60	40	23	10	0
1,420	1,440	197	164	144	124	104	84	63	43	25	12	0
1,440	1,460	202	168	147	127	107	87	66	46	27	14	0
1,460	1,480	207	173	150	130	110	90	69	49	29	16	2
1,480	1,500	212	178	153	133	113	93	72	52	32	18	4
1,500	1,520	217	183	156	136	116	96	75	55	35	20	6
1,520	1,540	222	188	159	139	119	99	78	58	38	22	8
1,540	1,560	227	193	162	142	122	102	81	61	41	24	10
1,560	1,580	232	198	165	145	125	105	84	64	44	26	12
1,580	1,600	237	203	170	148	128	108	87	67	47	28	14
1,600	1,620	242	208	175	151	131	111	90	70	50	30	16
1,620	1,640	247	213	180	154	134	114	93	73	53	33	18
1,640	1,660	252	218	185	157	137	117	96	76	56	36	20
1,660	1,680	257	223	190	160	140	120	99	79	59	39	22
1,680	1,700	262	228	195	163	143	123	102	82	62	42	24
1,700	1,720	267	233	200	166	146	126	105	85	65	45	26
1,720	1,740	272	238	205	171	149	129	108	88	68	48	28
1,740	1,760	277	243	210	176	152	132	111	91	71	51	31
1,760	1,780	282	248	215	181	155	135	114	94	74	54	34
1,780	1,800	287	253	220	186	158	138	117	97	77	57	37
1,800	1,820	292	258	225	191	161	141	120	100	80	60	40
1,820	1,840	297	263	230	196	164	144	123	103	83	63	43
1,840	1,860	302	268	235	201	167	147	126	106	86	66	46
1,860	1,880	307	273	240	206	172	150	129	109	89	69	49
1,880	1,900	312	278	245	211	177	153	132	112	92	72	52
1,900	1,920	317	283	250	216	182	156	135	115	95	75	55
1,920	1,940	322	288	255	221	187	159	138	118	98	78	58
1,940	1,960	327	293	260	226	192	162	141	121	101	81	61
1,960	1,980	332	298	265	231	197	165	144	124	104	84	64
1,980	2,000	337	303	270	236	202	169	147	127	107	87	67
2,000	2,020	342	308	275	241	207	174	150	130	110	90	70
2,020	2,040	347	313	280	246	212	179	153	133	113	93	73
2,040	2,060	352	318	285	251	217	184	156	136	116	96	76
2,060	2,080	357	323	290	256	222	189	159	139	119	99	79
2,080	2,100	362	328	295	261	227	194	162	142	122	102	82

$2,100 and over   Use Table 2(a) for a **SINGLE person** on page 38. Also see the instructions on page 36.

Employee Withholding for Social Security Taxes

In addition to withholding federal, and probably, state income tax, Katherine must also compute and withhold Social Security tax from Travelwithus.com employees. Social Security tax is also known as **FICA** because it was created by a 1935 federal law called the **Federal Insurance Contribution Act.** The law became effective in 1937. Ever since then, employers have been required to withhold amounts from employees' pay and turn them over to the federal government. The government then uses these amounts to make the following payments:

- Monthly retirement benefits for persons over 62 years old
- Medical benefits for persons over 65 years old
- Benefits for persons who have become disabled
- Benefits for families of deceased workers who were covered by this law

Before the amount of taxes withheld from employees' pay can be calculated, we need to know a few things about the Social Security (or FICA) tax. First, the tax is really two taxes. One tax is called the old-age, survivor's, and disability insurance (OASDI) tax and the other is known as Medicare (or HI, which stands for health insurance). Usually people talk about the two taxes as though they were one, but it is key to know that they are actually separate because each tax is calculated differently. Also know that OASDI puts a limit on the amount of tax that an employee must pay by setting a maximum dollar amount of earnings that can be taxed, and this amount is called the wage base. The same is not true of Medicare; all wages earned are subject to the Medicare tax. The OASDI and Medicare tax rates and the OASDI wage base amount are all set by the federal government; they can, and typically do, increase a little in each **calendar year.** The amounts for 2008 are as follows:

Tax	2008 Tax Rate	2008 Wage Base*
OASDI	6.2%	$102,000
Medicare	1.45%	None

Katherine begins to calculate the amount of Social Security tax that needs to be withheld from Stephanie's pay by looking at Stephanie's current and year-to-date (YTD) gross earnings. She needs to know the amount of earnings from the current pay period so that she can calculate the current amount of taxes. However, she also needs to know the YTD earnings so that she can see whether Stephanie has reached the maximum amount of OASDI tax yet, or if Stephanie will reach it in this pay period. So far in this calendar year, Stephanie has earned a total of $19,471.20. This amount includes the $957.60 that she has earned for the most recent, biweekly pay period.

Katherine calculates Stephanie's OASDI and Medicare taxes as follows:

$$\$957.60 \text{ gross earnings} \times 6.2\% \text{ OASDI tax rate} = \$59.37 \text{ OASDI tax}$$

$$\$957.60 \text{ gross earnings} \times 1.45\% \text{ Medicare tax rate} = \$13.89 \text{ Medicare tax}$$

Because Stephanie has earned less than the wage base limit of $102,000, all of her earnings for the current pay period are taxable. But what if Stephanie had earned more this year so far? Suppose she had earned $101,340 before this pay period. With her current earnings of $957.60, she would have earned a total of $102,297.60 for the year-to-date, which is more than the wage base limit of $102,000. In that case, Katherine would have calculated the amount of OASDI tax to be withheld from Stephanie's pay by first calculating the amount of taxable earnings for the current period:

Stephanie's YTD earnings before this pay period	$101,340.00
Plus: Stephanie's current earnings	957.60
Stephanie's YTD earnings after this pay period	$102,297.60

* The OASDI wage base in 2009 is $106,800.

Less: 2008 OASDI tax wage base limit	102,000.00
Stephanie's earnings above the limit, and thus, not taxable	$297.60
Stephanie's current earnings	$957.60
Less: Stephanie's earnings above the limit, and thus, not taxable	297.60
Stephanie's current OASDI taxable earnings	$660.00

Now Katherine would calculate the amount of OASDI tax as follows:

$660.00 current taxable earnings × 6.2% OASDI tax rate = $40.92 OASDI tax

Stephanie has now reached the maximum amount of taxable wages (**taxable earnings**), which means she is done paying OASDI tax for the calendar year. What if Stephanie had already earned $102,000 or more before the current pay period? In that case, none of Stephanie's current gross earnings would be subject to OASDI tax. In other words, Stephanie would already have paid her maximum OASDI tax for the year by paying tax on the money she made up to this $102,000 wage base limit. What about next year? Both Social Security taxes are calculated on a calendar year basis, and Stephanie would have to start paying the OASDI tax again until she reaches the maximum for that year.

What about the Medicare tax? Would the current amount tax that Stephanie needs to pay for this tax change too? No, because the Medicare tax does not limit the amount of earnings that can be taxed, all of Stephanie's earnings will be taxable. In other words, even if Stephanie had already earned $102,000 this year, all of her current earnings of $957.60 would be taxable and she would still have $13.89 withheld from her current paycheck for the Medicare tax.

Other Withholdings

Sometimes employees have additional amounts withheld from their paychecks for various reasons. For example, they may choose to buy **medical insurance** for themselves and maybe even their spouse and dependents through an insurance plan offered by their employer. Sometimes the employer pays the premium for this insurance coverage, or at least pays for the part of the premium that covers the employee. Even if the employer pays some of the premium, however, it is common for the employee to pay the rest. The employee pays this premium by having it withheld from his or her pay, just as the employee pays income and Social Security taxes by having these amounts withheld by the employer. Travelwithus.com currently offers this opportunity to its employees, and the cost to the hourly employee is $33 for each pay period.

Net Pay

Katherine's next step in the payroll accounting process is to calculate the amount of pay that Stephanie will actually receive as her paycheck, and this amount is called **net pay.** At this point, Katherine has computed all of the amounts necessary to determine Stephanie's net pay. Now she simply needs to combine them as follows:

Gross earnings for the current, biweekly pay period:		$957.60
Deductions for employee withholding taxes:		
Federal income tax	$92.00	
State income tax	76.61	
OASDI tax	59.37	
Medicare tax	13.89	
Medical insurance	33.00	
Total deductions		274.87
Net pay		$682.73

LEARNING UNIT 7-1 REVIEW

AT THIS POINT you should be able to

- Explain the purpose of the Fair Labor Standards Act (i.e., the Federal Wage and Hour Law).
- Calculate regular, overtime, and total gross pay.
- Complete a W-4 form.
- Discuss the term *claiming an allowance*.
- Use a wage-bracket tax table to determine the amount of federal income tax withholding.
- Define the purpose of the Social Security (FICA) taxes, OASDI, and Medicare.
- Calculate withholdings for OASDI and Medicare taxes.
- Calculate net pay.

Self-Review Quiz 7-1

Tony Kagaragis is an hourly software engineer who is paid biweekly. He earns $23.00 per hour. In the first week of the most recent pay period, he worked 39 hours, and during the second week of the period he worked 46 hours. Please calculate his regular, overtime, and gross earnings.

Solutions to Self-Review Quiz 7-1

1. $23.00 regular rate × 79 regular hours = $1,817.00 regular earnings
2. $23.00 regular rate × 1½ = $34.50 overtime rate × 6 overtime hours = $207.00 overtime earnings
3. $1,817.00 + $207.00 = $2,024.00 gross earnings

LO3 Learning Unit 7-2 Preparing a Payroll Register and Employee Earning Record

At this point, Katherine Kurtz, the accountant for Travelwithus.com, knows how much each of the three hourly employees earned for the most recent biweekly pay period and how many dollars of taxes need to be withheld from their paychecks. She now needs to enter this information into the accounting records for the company. Two primary records are used in accounting systems to keep track of payroll information for a company. The first of these records is a worksheet, known as a payroll register, which shows all information related to an entire pay period. The second record is called the employee earnings record and is used to keep track of an individual employee's payroll history for an entire calendar year.

The Payroll Register

Katherine enters information about the current payroll period for hourly employees in a **payroll register.** The register includes each employee's gross earnings, employee withholding taxes, net pay, taxable earnings, cumulative earnings, and the accounts to be charged for the salary and wage expense for that pay period. Travelwithus.com will actually have two registers, a biweekly one for its hourly employees and a monthly one for its salaried personnel. Figure 7.3 shows the completed, payroll register for the hourly payroll covering the biweekly pay period from October 16 through October 29.

TRAVELWITHUS.COM INC.
HOURLY EMPLOYEE PAYROLL REGISTER
OCTOBER 16–29

Employee / Social Security No.	Allowances and Marital Status	Previous Earnings (YTD)	Regular Hours	Regular Rate	Regular Amount	Overtime Hours	Overtime Rate	Overtime Amount	Gross	Current Earnings (YTD)
Higuera, Stephanie 123-45-6789	S-1	1851360	78	1140	88920	4	1710	6840	95760	1947120
Sui, Annie 123-45-6788	S-0	2122100	80	1515	121200	4	2273	9090	130290	2342390
Taylor, Harold 123-45-6787	S-2	1904370	78	1210	94380	4	1815	7260	101640	2006010
TOTALS					304500			23190	327690	4295520

Marital Status and No. of allowances are from Employee's W-4.
Previous YTD earnings = the employee's total earnings for the year before this pay period.
Regular Hours x Regular Rate = Regular Amount.
Overtime Hours x Overtime Rate = Overtime Amount.
Regular Amount + Overtime Amount = Gross Current Earnings.
Previous YTD Earnings + Gross Current Earnings = Current YTD Earnings.

Taxable Earnings, FUTA/SUTA = Gross Current Earnings < FUTA/SUTA limit of $7,000.
Taxable Earnings, OASDI = GrossCurrent Earnings < OASDI Limit of $102,000.
FIT = FIT from wage Bracket Table in Circular E.
SIT = Gross Current Earnings x 8%.
FICA, OASDI = Taxable Earnings, OASDI x 6.2%.
FICA, Medicare =Gross Current Earnings x 1.45%.
Medical Insurance = $33 per employee.
Net Pay = Gross Current Earnings – FIT – SIT – OASDI – Medicare – Medical Insurance.

TRAVELWITHUS.COM INC.
HOURLY EMPLOYEE PAYROLL REGISTER
OCTOBER 16–29

Employee / Social Security No.	Taxable Earnings FUTA/SUTA	Taxable Earnings OASDI	FIT	SIT	FICA OASDI	FICA Medicare	Medical Insurance	Net Pay	Check No.	Business Scheduling Expense	Cruise Scheduling Expense
Higuera, Stephanie 123-45-6789	—	95760	9200	7661	5937	1389	3300	68273	820	95760	
Sui, Annie 123-45-6788	130290	130290	16700	10423	8078	1889	3300	89900	821		130290
Taylor, Harold 123-45-6787	—	101640	8100	8131	6302	1474	3300	74333	822		101640
TOTALS	130290	327690	34000	26215	20317	4752	9900	232506		95760	231930

FIGURE 7.3 Payroll Register

LO4   ## The Employee Earnings Record

After Katherine prepares the payroll register for the period, and in order to comply with all applicable employment laws and regulations, she also completes a payroll record known as the **individual employee earnings record.** This record provides a summary of each employee's earnings, withholding taxes, net pay, and cumulative earnings during each calendar year, as shown in Figure 7.4. Katherine uses the information summarized in this record to prepare quarterly and annual payroll tax reports. Thus, the employee earnings record is split into calendar quarters, with each quarter being 13 weeks long.

LEARNING UNIT 7-2 REVIEW

AT THIS POINT you should be able to

- Explain and prepare a payroll register.
- Explain the purpose of the taxable earnings columns of the register and explain how they relate to the cumulative earnings column.
- Update an individual employee earnings record.

Self-Review Quiz 7-2

Mike Chen is an hourly employee who is paid biweekly. He is paid overtime at a rate of 1½ times his hourly rate for any hours he works over 40 in a workweek. Mike worked many overtime hours this year to develop a Web site for his employer, and as of December 10 his cumulative earnings total $100,778.06. For the pay period ending on December 24, Mike's gross earnings are $1,940.85. Calculate Mike's net pay based on the following facts:

- Mike is single and claims three withholding allowances per his Form W-4. Use the tax table in Figure 7.2 to find Mike's federal income tax withholding amount.
- The state income tax rate is 8% with no wage base limit.
- The OASDI tax rate is 6.2% with a wage base limit of $102,000 for the year; the Medicare rate is 1.45% with no wage base limit.
- Mike pays $44.00 for medical insurance for the pay period.

Solutions to Self-Review Quiz 7-2

1. Federal income tax = $226.00 (Look at the "At least $1,940" line and trace it into the "3" withholding allowance column.)
2. State income tax is $155.27 ($1,940.85 × .08)
3. FICA OASDI tax is $75.76 ($102,000 − $100,778.06 = $1,221.94 taxable; $1,221.94 × .062)
4. FICA Medicare tax is $28.14 ($1,940.85 × .0145)
5. Mike Chen's net pay is $1,411.68 ($1,940.85 − $226.00 − $155.27 − $75.76 − $28.14 − $44.00)

LO2   # Learning Unit 7-3 Employer Payroll Tax Expense

Employer Withholding for Social Security Taxes

As we discussed, employees pay payroll taxes including federal income tax, Social Security taxes, probably state income tax, and maybe even a city or county income tax. It surprises some employees to find that their employers pay payroll taxes, too. As a matter of fact, employers pay exactly the same amount of Social Security taxes for each employee as the employee pays. In addition to paying Social Security taxes for each employee, employers also pay unemployment taxes that are used to provide unemployed workers with benefits while they are looking for work.

As Travelwithus.com's accountant, Katherine calculates the amount of Social Security taxes that the company must pay as an employer much the same way that she calculated

TRAVELWITHUS.COM INC.
EMPLOYEE EARNINGS RECORD
Stephanie Higuera   Social Security No. 123-45-6789

Pay Period	Hours		Earnings			FIT	SIT	Deductions		Medical Insurance	Net Pay	Check No.	YTD Earnings
	Regular	Overtime	Regular	Overtime	Gross			FICA					
								OASDI	Medicare				
10/2 - 10/15	80	0	912 00	0 00	912 00	86 00	72 96	56 54	13 22	33 00	650 27	806	18513 60
10/16 - 10/29	78	4	889 20	68 40	957 60	92 00	76 61	59 37	13 89	33 00	682 73	820	19471 20
10/30 - 11/12	76	0	866 40	0 00	866 40	80 00	69 31	53 72	12 56	33 00	617 81	825	20337 60
11/13 - 11/26	80	2	912 00	34 20	946 20	92 00	75 70	58 66	13 72	33 00	673 12	839	21283 80
11/27 - 12/10	80	4	912 00	68 40	980 40	98 00	78 43	60 78	14 22	33 00	695 97	844	22264 20
12/11 - 12/24	80	0	912 00	0 00	912 00	86 00	72 96	56 54	13 22	33 00	648 28	858	23176 20
12/25 - 12/31	48	0	547 20	0 00	547 20	32 00	43 78	33 93	7 93	33 00	396 56	863	23723 40
4th Quarter Totals			5950 80	171 00	6121 80	566 00	489 75	379 54	88 76	231 00	4364 74		
YTD Totals			23142 00	581 40	23723 40	2241 86	1897 87	1470 85	343 99	858 00	16910 83		

FIGURE 7.4 Employee Earnings Record

them for each employee. She first determines the amount of current gross earnings for all employees that fall below the wage base limit of $102,000. She looks at the OASDI Taxable Earnings total in the payroll register for the current period. She then multiplies this total by the OASDI tax rate of 6.2% to determine the OASDI tax that Travelwithus.com must pay:

$$\$3{,}276.90 \text{ gross earnings} \times 6.2\% \text{ OASDI tax rate} = \$203.17 \text{ OASDI tax}$$

Katherine then calculates Travelwithus.com's Medicare tax by taking the current gross earnings for all employees and multiplying this total by the Medicare tax rate of 1.45%. Remember that the amount of Medicare tax for each employee is not subject to any limit; every dollar that an employee earns is taxed at the Medicare tax rate of 1.45%.

$$\$3{,}276.90 \text{ gross earnings} \times 1.45\% \text{ Medicare tax rate} = \$47.52 \text{ Medicare tax}$$

The way Katherine computes these taxes differs in only one way compared to how she computed them for each employee. Because Katherine is now calculating Travelwithus.com's share of these taxes, Katherine uses current gross earnings for the company in total instead of using each employee's current gross earnings as she did when she was determining the amount to withhold from each employee's paycheck.

FUTA and SUTA

In addition to paying its employer share of FICA taxes, Travelwithus.com must also pay unemployment taxes. Unemployment tax, or unemployment insurance as it is sometimes called, was created by the same 1935 law that created Social Security. This federal law requires all 50 states, the District of Columbia, and U.S. territories to run unemployment compensation programs that are approved and monitored by the federal government. Unemployment taxes are paid by employers based on wages paid to employees. Federal Unemployment Tax Act (FUTA) taxes pay the costs of administering the federal and state programs, but do not pay benefits to employees. State Unemployment Tax Act (SUTA) taxes pay the benefits to unemployed persons.

Currently, employers pay FUTA tax at a rate of 6.2% on wages earned by each employee up to a wage base limit of $7,000. However, the federal government allows employers to take a tax credit for SUTA tax against this tax, up to a maximum credit of 5.4%.

FUTA tax rate	6.2%
Less: Normal FUTA tax credit	5.4%
Net FUTA tax rate	0.8%

Employers are allowed to take this credit as long as they have paid all amounts that they owe for SUTA taxes, and paid them on time. In other words, the federal law essentially says to employers, "Comply with your state's unemployment tax laws and your total tax will not exceed a maximum of 6.2%: 0.8% to the federal government and a state rate that will vary up to maximum of 5.4%." Remember that employers alone are responsible for paying FUTA tax; it is never withheld from the earnings of employees.

Katherine calculates FUTA tax by referring to the FUTA Taxable Earnings total in the current payroll register. This column tells her how much, in total, Travelwithus.com's employees have earned this period that falls below the FUTA wage base limit of $7,000. She uses this amount to calculate the FUTA tax by multiplying it by the net FUTA tax rate as follows:

$$\$1{,}302.90 \text{ FUTA taxable earnings} \times 0.8\% \text{ FUTA tax rate} = \$10.42 \text{ FUTA tax}$$

Because states run their own unemployment programs, each state may use a different SUTA wage base limit. These amounts are based on the needs of the unemployment funds in each state. In 2005 the wage base limits for states ranged from $7,000 to $34,000. Different states have different SUTA tax rates for the same reason that the wage base limits vary; they are based on the needs of the unemployment funds in each state.

Additionally, the SUTA tax rate can vary from employer to employer within a state. In any state, an employer's SUTA tax rate will be based on how many dollars it contributes to the state unemployment fund and the dollar amount of claims that its employees make against that fund.

In other words, the rate is tied to the employer's employment history. The more frequently an employer lays off its employees, the more unemployment benefits the state will have to pay, and the higher the tax rate for that employer. In other words, employers who rarely lay off their workers will be charged a lower SUTA rate than employers who lay off workers often. In this way, the SUTA tax rate motivates employers to stabilize their workforce.

Travelwithus.com's current SUTA rate is 5.4% and the wage base limit for the state in which it is located is $7,000. Katherine calculates Travelwithus.com's SUTA tax similar to the way she calculated its FUTA tax. She first looks at the SUTA Taxable Earnings total in the current payroll register to see how much, in total, Travelwithus.com's employees earned this period below the SUTA wage base limit of $7,000. She then calculates the SUTA tax by multiplying this amount by the SUTA tax rate as follows:

$$\$1,302.90 \text{ SUTA taxable earnings} \times 5.4\% \text{ SUTA tax rate} = \$70.36$$

Workers' Compensation Insurance

Workers' compensation insurance insures employees against losses they may incur due to accidental injury or death while on the job. Each employer must purchase this insurance either through an insurance broker or state agency. In most states, this tax is paid completely by the employer, not the employee.

Travelwithus.com's premium for this insurance is based on its total estimated gross payroll, and the rate is calculated for each $100 of weekly payroll. By estimating payroll before the beginning of the year, the insurance company can determine the amount of the premium to charge Travelwithus.com. If actual payroll for the year turns out to differ from estimated payroll, then the insurance company will either credit Travelwithus.com for any overpayment or bill it for any underpayment. The rate for Travelwithus.com is based on the type of work that its employees perform as well as the amount and extent of any on-the-job injuries that its employees experience.

Travelwithus.com has two groups of employees: travel schedulers and managers. It estimated that it would have $50,000 of gross payroll for its schedulers in the next year, and its rate is $1.80 for every $100 of this payroll. The company also estimated that it will incur $190,000 of payroll for managers, and its rate for this group is $.22 for every $100 of payroll. Travelwithus.com then calculated its premium as follows:

Workers' compensation premium for		
schedulers:	*$50,000/$100 = 500 × $1.80 =*	*$ 900.00*
Workers' compensation premium for		
managers:	*$190,000/$100 = 1,900 × $.22 =*	*418.00*
Total workers' compensation premium =		*$1,318.00*

Suppose, however, that at the end of the year, Travelwithus.com's scheduler payroll totaled $57,977.14 and its manager payroll totaled $220,648.16. The actual premiums for the year would be calculated in the following manner:

Workers' compensation premium		
for schedulers:	*$57,977.14/$100 = 580 × $1.80 =*	*$1,044.00*
Workers' compensation premium		
for managers:	*$220,648.16/$100 = 2,206 × $.22 =*	*485.32*
Total workers' compensation premium =		*$1,529.32*

Travelwithus.com would then owe an additional amount of premium:

Workers' compensation premium based on actual gross payroll	*$1,529.32*
Workers' compensation premium based on estimated gross payroll	*1,318.00*
Additional workers' compensation premium owed =	*$ 211.32*

LEARNING UNIT 7-3 REVIEW

AT THIS POINT you should be able to

- Explain the use of the taxable earnings column of the payroll register in calculating the employer's payroll tax expense.
- Calculate the employer's payroll taxes of OASDI, Medicare, FUTA, and SUTA.
- Explain the difference between FUTA and SUTA taxes.
- Understand the purpose of workers' compensation insurance.
- Calculate the estimated premium for workers' compensation insurance.

Self-Review Quiz 7-3

Given the following, calculate the employer FICA OASDI, FICA Medicare, FUTA, and SUTA for Farmington Co. for the weekly payroll of July 8. Assume the following:

- FUTA tax is paid at the net rate of 0.8% on the first $7,000 of earnings.
- SUTA tax is paid at a rate of 5.6% on the first $7,000 of earnings.
- FICA tax rate for Social Security is 6.2% on $102,000, and Medicare is 1.45% on all earnings.

Employee	Cumulative Pay Before This Week's Payroll	Gross Pay for Week
Bill Jones	$6,000	$800
Julie Warner	$6,600	$400
Al Brooks	$7,900	$700

Solutions to Self-Review Quiz 7-3

1. FICA OASDI $= \$1,900 \times .062 = \$117.80$
2. FICA Medicare $= \$1,900 \times .0145 = \$27.55$
3. FUTA $= \$1,200 \times .008 = \$9.60$
4. SUTA $= \$1,200 \times .056 = \$67.20$

CHAPTER ASSIGNMENTS

SUMMARY OF KEY POINTS

LEARNING UNIT 7-1

1. The Fair Labor Standards Act states that hourly workers will receive a minimum of one and a half times their regular hourly rate of pay for all hours they work over 40 hours during a workweek.
2. Salaried employees are employees who are classified as salaried according to the provisions of the Fair Labor Standards Act. These employees receive a fixed amount of pay for each pay period.
3. For the rules of the Fair Labor Standards Act to apply to an employer, the employer must be involved in interstate commerce. Most companies today are involved in interstate commerce.
4. Employees and employers pay equal amounts of Social Security tax. Note that Social Security, or FICA tax, is made up of two taxes: OASDI and Medicare. The OASDI tax is based on a tax rate and wage base amount that is set for each calendar year.

The OASDI tax rate for 2008 is 6.2% and the wage base limit for this year is $102,000. Medicare has no wage base limit, so an employee and employer will pay this tax on all of an employee's earnings during the calendar year, at a rate of 1.45% for 2008.

5. Federal income tax withholding amounts are listed in tax tables found in IRS Circular E, *Employer's Tax Guide*, also known as Publication 15.

6. Gross earnings minus deductions equals net pay.

LEARNING UNIT 7-2

1. The two primary accounting records used to keep track of payroll amounts are the payroll register and employee earnings record. The payroll register shows gross earnings, deductions, net pay, and taxable earnings for a payroll period. The employee earnings record shows the gross earnings, deductions, and net pay for an employee for an entire calendar year.

2. The taxable earnings columns of the payroll register do not show the tax. They show the amount of earnings to be taxed for unemployment taxes, OASDI, and Medicare. The individual employee earnings records are updated soon after the payroll register is prepared.

LEARNING UNIT 7-3

1. The payroll tax expense for an employer is made up of FICA OASDI, FICA Medicare, FUTA, and SUTA.

2. The maximum amount of credit given for state unemployment taxes paid against the FUTA tax is 5.4%. This figure is known as the normal FUTA tax credit. The normal FUTA tax credit typically results in employers paying 0.8% for FUTA tax.

3. Employers pay workers' compensation insurance premiums based on estimated payroll. At the end of the year, estimated payroll is compared to actual payroll, and the employer either pays any additional premium or receives a credit for any overpayment of premium.

KEY TERMS

Allowances (also called *exemptions*)   Certain dollar amounts of a person's income tax that will be considered nontaxable for income tax withholding purposes.

Calendar year   A one-year period beginning on January 1 and ending on December 31. Employers must use a calendar year for payroll purposes, even if the employer uses a fiscal year for financial statements and for any other reason.

Circular E   An IRS tax publication of tax tables.

Fair Labor Standards Act (Federal Wage and Hour Law)   A law the majority of employers must follow that contains rules stating the minimum hourly rate of pay and the maximum number of hours a worker will work before being paid time and a half for overtime hours worked. This law also has other rules and regulations that employers must follow for payroll purposes.

Federal income tax (FIT) withholding   Amount of federal income tax withheld by the employer from the employee's gross pay; the amount withheld is determined by the employee's gross pay, the pay period, the number of allowances claimed by the employee on the W-4 form, and the marital status indicated on the W-4 form.

FICA (Federal Insurance Contributions Act)   Part of the Social Security Act of 1935, this law taxes both the employer and employee up to a certain maximum rate and wage base for OASDI tax purposes. It also taxes both the employer and employee for Medicare purposes, but this tax has no wage base maximum.

Form W-4 (Employee's Withholding Allowance Certificate)   A form filled out by employees and used by employers to supply needed information about the number of allowances claimed, marital status, and so forth. The form is used for payroll purposes to determine federal income tax withholding from an employee's paycheck.

Gross earnings (gross pay)   Amount of pay received before any deductions.

Individual employee earnings record   An accounting document that summarizes the total amount of wages paid and the deductions for the calendar year. It aids in preparing governmental reports. A new record is prepared for each employee each year.

Interstate commerce   A test that is applied to determine whether an employer must follow the rules of the Fair Labor Standards Act. If an employer communicates or does business with another business in some other state, it is usually considered to be involved in interstate commerce.

Medical insurance   Health care insurance for which premiums may be paid through a deduction from an employee's paycheck.

Net pay   Gross earnings, less deductions. Net pay, or take-home pay, is what the worker actually takes home.

Pay or payroll period   A length of time used by an employer to calculate the amount of an employee's earnings. Pay periods can be daily, weekly, biweekly (once every two weeks), semimonthly (twice each month), monthly, quarterly, or annual.

Payroll register   A multicolumn form that can be used to record payroll data.

State income tax (SIT) withholding   Amount of state income tax withheld by the employer from the employee's gross pay.

Taxable earnings   Shows amount of earnings subject to a tax. The tax itself is not shown.

Wage bracket table   One of various charts in IRS Circular E that provide information about deductions for federal income tax based on earnings and data supplied on the W-4 form.

Workers' compensation insurance   A benefit plan required by federal regulations in which employers must purchase insurance to protect their employees against losses due to injury or death incurred while on the job.

Workweek   A seven-day (168-hour) period used to determine overtime hours for employees. A workweek can begin on any given day, but must end seven days later.

BLUEPRINT FOR RECORDING TRANSACTIONS IN A PAYROLL REGISTER

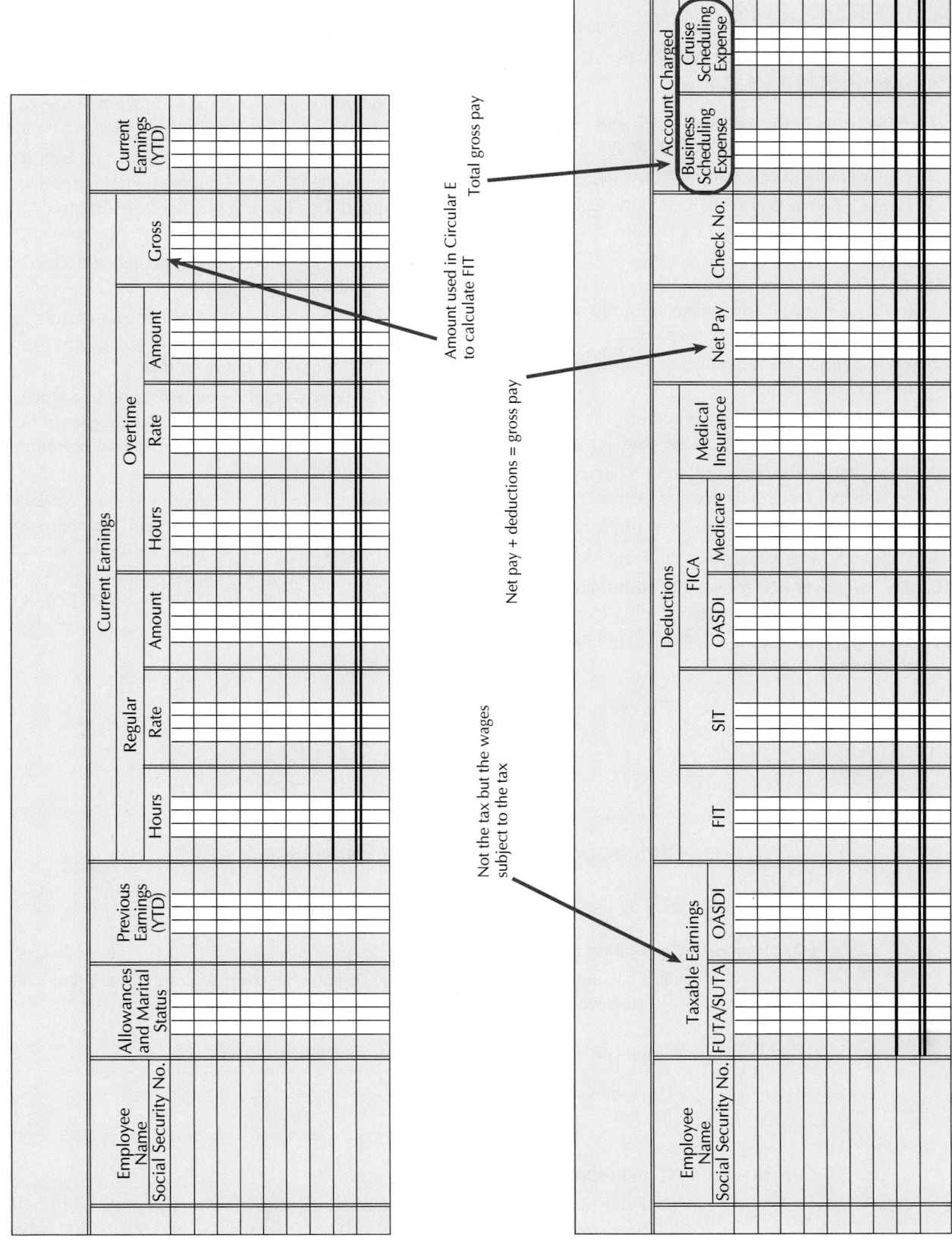

QUESTIONS, CLASSROOM DEMONSTRATION EXERCISES, EXERCISES, AND PROBLEMS

Discussion and Critical Thinking Questions/Ethical Case

1. What is the purpose of the Fair Labor Standards Act (also called the Federal Wage and Hour Law)?

2. Explain how to calculate overtime pay.

3. Explain how a W-4 form, called the Employee's Withholding Allowance Certificate, is used to determine FIT withheld.

4. The more allowances an employee claims on a W-4 form, the more take-home pay the employee gets with each paycheck. Agree or disagree?

5. Explain how federal and state income tax withholdings are determined.

6. Explain why a business should prepare a payroll register before employees are paid.

7. The taxable earnings column of a payroll register records the amount of tax due. Agree or disagree?

8. Define and state the purpose of FICA taxes.

9. Explain how to calculate OASDI and Medicare taxes.

10. The employer doesn't have to contribute to Social Security. Agree or disagree? Please explain.

11. What purpose does the individual employee earnings record serve?

12. Please draw a diagram showing how the following items relate to each other: (a) a weekly payroll, (b) a payroll register, (c) individual employee earnings record, and (d) general journal entries for payroll.

13. If you earned $130,000 this year, you would pay more OASDI and Medicare than your partner who earned $75,000. Do you agree or disagree? Please provide calculations to support your answer.

14. Explain how an employer can receive a credit against the FUTA tax due.

15. Explain what an experience or merit rating is and how it affects the amount paid by an employer for state unemployment insurance.

16. Who pays workers' compensation insurance, the employee or the employer? What types of benefits does this insurance provide? How are premiums calculated?

17. An employee for Repairs to Go, Inc., works different numbers of hours each week depending on the needs of the business. To simplify the accounting, the bookkeeper for Repairs to Go classifies this employee as a salaried person. Is this practice appropriate? Please explain.

Classroom Demonstration Exercises

SET A

LO1 (10 min)   **Calculating Gross Earnings**

1. Calculate the total wages earned (assume an overtime rate of time and a half over 40 hours).

Employee	Hourly Rate	No. of Hours Worked
Dawn Slow	$10	39
Ben Fritz	$12	50

LO1 (15 min)   **FIT and FICA**

2. Peter Martin, single, claiming one exemption, has cumulative earnings before this biweekly pay period of $101,000. If he is paid $2,000 this period, what will his deductions be for FIT and FICA (OASDI and Medicare)? Use the tables and rates in this text.

Net Pay   *LO1 (15 min)*

3. From Exercise 2, calculate Peter's net pay. The state income tax rate is 5% and health insurance is $40.

Payroll Register   *LO3 (10 min)*

4. Match the following:
   1. Total gross pay
   2. A deduction
   3. Net pay
   _____ a. Office Salary Expense
   _____ b. FICA OASDI Payable
   _____ c. FICA Medicare Payable
   _____ d. Federal Income Tax Payable
   _____ e. Medical Insurance Payable
   _____ f. Wages and Salaries Payable

Employer and Employee Taxes   *LO2 (10 min)*

5. Identify which of the following taxes are paid by the employee (EE) and which are paid by the employer (ER):
   _____ a. FICA Medicare
   _____ b. FIT
   _____ c. FUTA
   _____ d. SUTA

SET B

Calculating Gross Earnings   *LO1 (10 min)*

1. Calculate the total wages earned (assume an overtime rate of time and a half over 40 hours).

Employee	Hourly Rate	No. of Hours Worked
Tom Suarez	$14	37
Jim Martin	$12	48

FIT and FICA   *LO1 (10 min)*

2. Cindy Hwang, single, claiming two exemptions, has cumulative earnings before this biweekly pay period of $101,000. If she is paid $1,800 this period, what will her deductions be for FIT and FICA (OASDI and Medicare)? Use the tables and rates in this text.

Net Pay   *LO1 (10 min)*

3. From Exercise 2, calculate Cindy's net pay. The state income tax rate is 6% and health insurance is $30.

Payroll Register   *LO3 (10 min)*

4. Match the following:
   1. Total gross pay
   2. A deduction
   3. Net pay
   _____ a. Store Wage Expense
   _____ b. FICA OASDI Payable
   _____ c. FICA Medicare Payable
   _____ d. State Income Tax Payable
   _____ e. Medical Insurance Payable
   _____ f. Wages and Salaries Payable

LO2 (10 min) **Employer and Employee Taxes**

5. Identify which of the following taxes are paid by the employee (EE) and which are paid by the employer (ER):

_____ **a.** FICA OASDI

_____ **b.** FICA Medicare

_____ **c.** SIT

_____ **d.** SUTA

Exercises

LO1 (15 min) **7-1.** Calculate the total wages earned for each employee assuming an overtime rate of time and a half over 40 hours.

Employee	Hourly Rate	No. of Hours Worked
Carmen Amador	$9	39
Jill West	$12	44
Fred Aster	$14	46

LO1, 3 (20 min) **7-2.** Compute the net pay for each employee using the federal income tax withholding table in Figure 7.2. Assume the FICA OASDI tax is 6.2% on a wage base limit of $102,000; Medicare is 1.45% on all earnings, the payroll is paid biweekly, and no state income tax applies.

Employee	Status	Allowances	Cumulative Pay	This Week's Pay
Alvin Pang	Single	1	$60,000	$1,690
Angelina Potts	Single	0	$64,300	$1,600

LO2 (20 min) **7-3.** From the following information, calculate the payroll tax expense for Baker Company for the payroll of August 9:

Employee	Cumulative Earnings Before Weekly Payroll	Gross Pay for the Week
J. Kline	$3,500	$900
A. Met	6,600	750
D. Ring	7,900	300

The FICA tax rate for OASDI is 6.2% on the first $102,000 earned, and Medicare is 1.45% on all earnings. Federal unemployment tax is 0.8% on the first $7,000 earned by each employee. The experience or merit rating for Baker is 5.6% on the first $7,000 of employee earnings for state unemployment purposes.

LO2 (15 min) **7-4.** Refer to Exercise 7-3 and assume that the state changed Baker's experience/merit rating to 4.9%. What effect would this change have on the total payroll tax expense?

LO2 (15 min) **7-5.** Refer to Exercise 7-3. If D. Ring earned $2,000 for the week instead of $300, what effect would this change have on the total payroll tax expense?

LO2 (20 min) **7-6.** The total wage expense for Howell Co. was $160,000. Of this total, $30,000 was above the OASDI wage base limit and not subject to this tax. All earnings are subject to Medicare tax, and $60,000 was above the federal and state unemployment wage base limits and not subject to unemployment taxes. Please calculate the total payroll tax expense for Howell Co. given the following rates and wage base limits:

   a. FICA tax rate: OASDI, 6.2% with a wage base limit of $102,000; Medicare, 1.45% with no wage base limit

b. State unemployment tax rate: 5.9% with a wage base limit of $7,000

c. Federal unemployment tax rate (after credit): 0.8% with a wage base limit of $7,000

7-7. At the end of the first quarter of 200X, you are asked to determine the FUTA tax liability for Oscar Company. The FUTA tax rate is 0.8% on the first $7,000 each employee earns during the year (assuming 13 weeks).

LO2 (20 min)

Employee	Gross Pay Per Week
J. Kane	$700
A. Ling	800
P. Made	600
C. Slove	500

7-8. From the following data, estimate the annual premium for workers' compensation insurance:

LO4 (10 min)

Type of Work	Estimated Payroll	Rate per $100
Office	$30,000	$ .21
Repairs	84,000	1.70

Group A Problems

7A-1. From the following information, please complete the chart for gross earnings for the week. (Assume an overtime rate of time and a half over 40 hours.)

LO1 (20 min)

Employee	Hourly Rate	No. of Hours Worked	Gross Earnings
Joe Vasquez	$9	45	
Lisa Ferris	$10	40	
Nancy Patt	$12	42	
Dave Johnson	$13	50	

Check Figure:
Dave Johnson: $715 Gross Earnings

7A-2. March Company has five salaried employees. Your task is to use the following information to calculate net pay for each employee:

LO1, 3 (30 min)

Employee	Allowance and Marital Status	Cumulative Earnings Before This Payroll	Biweekly Salary	Department
Dunn, Dylan	S-1	$42,000	$1,100	Customer Service
Fein, Marc	S-1	30,000	900	Office
Kraft, Alison	S-2	59,200	1,300	Office
Mae, Audrey	S-3	101,080	2,090	Customer Service
Zimmer, Lionel	S-0	29,000	810	Customer Service

Assume the following:

1. FICA OASDI is 6.2% on $102,000; FICA Medicare is 1.45% on all earnings.
2. Each employee contributes $30 biweekly for medical insurance.
3. State income tax is 6% of gross pay.
4. FIT is calculated from Figure 7.2.

Check Figure:
Total Net Pay $4,579.73

LO1, 3 (40 min)

7A-3. The bookkeeper of Izumi Co. gathered the following data from individual employee earnings records and daily time cards. Your task is to complete a payroll register on December 12.

Employee	Allowance and Marital Status	Cumulative Earnings Before This Payroll	M	T	W	T	F	Hourly Rate of Pay	FIT
Fine, Pam	M-1	$64,100	5	11	9	8	8	$16	$52
Hale, Don	S-0	15,000	8	10	9	9	4	15	76
Pope, Ria	M-3	66,000	8	10	10	10	10	18	72
Vent, Jane	S-1	19,000	8	8	8	8	8	20	104

Check Figure:
Total Net Pay $2,346.50

Assume the following:

1. FICA OASDI is 6.2% on $102,000; FICA Medicare is 1.45% on all earnings.
2. Federal income tax has been calculated from a weekly table for you.
3. Each employee contributes $30 weekly for health insurance.
4. Overtime is paid at a rate of time and a half over 40 hours.
5. Fine and Pope work in the office; the other employees work in sales.

LO1, 2, 3, 4 (40 min)

7A-4. You gathered the following data from time cards and individual employee earnings records. Your tasks are as follows:

1. On December 5, 200X, prepare a payroll register for this biweekly payroll.
2. Calculate the employer taxes of FICA OASDI, FICA Medicare, FUTA, and SUTA.

Employee	Allowance and Marital Status	Cumulative Earnings Before This Payroll	Biweekly Salary	Check No.	Department
Abers, John	S-3	$37,200	$1,550	30	Production
Gomez, Nicki	S-1	48,000	2,000	31	Office
Moreno, Jeff	S-2	64,800	2,070	32	Production
Sung, Paul	S-1	4,600	800	33	Office

Check Figure:
Total Net Pay $4,748.86

Assume the following:

1. FICA OASDI: 6.2% on $102,000; FICA Medicare: 1.45% on all earnings.
2. Federal income tax is calculated from Figure 7.2.
3. State income tax is 5% of gross pay.
4. Union dues are $12 biweekly.
5. The SUTA rate is 5.4% and the FUTA rate is 0.8% on earnings below $7,000.

Group B Problems

LO1 (20 min)

7B-1. From the following information, please complete the chart for gross earnings for the week. (Assume an overtime rate of time and a half over 40 hours.)

Employee	Hourly Rate	No. of Hours Worked	Gross Earnings
Joe Vasquez	$5	40	
Edna Kane	$10	47	
Dick Wall	$12	36	
Pat Green	$14	55	

Check Figure:
Pat Green: Gross Pay $875

7B-2. March Company employs five salaried employees. Your task is to use the following information to calculate net pay for each employee:

LO1, 3 (30 min)

Employee	Allowance and Marital Status	Cumulative Earnings Before This Payroll	Biweekly Salary	Department
Kool, Alice	S-1	$45,150	$1,290	Sales
Lose, Bob	S-1	22,575	800	Office
Moore, Linda	S-2	59,300	1,240	Office
Relt, Rusty	S-3	101,100	1,300	Sales
Veel, Larry	S-0	21,875	860	Sales

Assume the following:

1. FICA OASDI is 6.2% on $102,000; FICA Medicare: 1.45% on all earnings.
2. Each employee contributes $25 biweekly for union dues.
3. State income tax is 6% of gross pay.
4. FIT is calculated from Figure 7.2.

> **Check Figure:**
> Total Net Pay $4,102.41

7B-3. The bookkeeper of Pearl Co. gathered the following data from individual employee earnings records and daily time cards. Your task is to complete a payroll register on December 12.

LO1, 3 (40 min)

Employee	Allowance and Marital Status	Cumulative Earnings Before This Payroll	M	T	W	T	F	Hourly Rate of Pay	FIT
Boy, Pete	M-1	$64,900	12	11	7	7	7	$16	$62
Heat, Donna	S-0	19,000	8	9	9	9	5	16	82
Pyle, Ray	M-3	102,350	10	10	10	10	5	20	75
Vent, Joan	S-1	13,500	6	8	8	8	8	19	84

(Daily Time columns: M T W T F)

> **Check Figure:**
> Total Net Pay $2,470.73

Assume the following:

1. FICA OASDI is 6.2% on $102,000; FICA Medicare is 1.45% on all earnings.
2. Federal income tax has been calculated from a weekly table for you.
3. Each employee contributes $25 weekly for health insurance.
4. Heat and Vent work in the office; the other employees work in sales.

7B-4. You gathered the following data from time cards and individual employee earnings records. Your tasks are as follows:

LO1, 2, 3, 4 (40 min)

1. On December 5, 200X, prepare a payroll register for this biweekly payroll.
2. Calculate the employer taxes of FICA OASDI, FICA Medicare, FUTA, and SUTA.

Employee	Allowance and Marital Status	Cumulative Earnings Before This Payroll	Biweekly Salary	Check No.	Department
Aulson, Andy	S-3	$30,000	$ 800	30	Factory
Flynn, Jacki	S-1	50,000	1,100	31	Office
Moore, Jeff	S-2	60,000	1,050	32	Factory
Sullivan, Alison	S-1	65,000	1,200	33	Office

Assume the following:

1. FICA OASDI is 6.2% on $102,000; FICA Medicare is 1.45% on all earnings.
2. Federal income tax is calculated from Figure 7.2.
3. State income tax is 5% of gross pay.
4. Union dues are $10 biweekly.
5. The SUTA rate is 5.6%, and the FUTA rate is 0.8% on earnings below $7,000.

ON-THE-JOB TRAINING

LO1, 2, 4 (60 min)   **T-1.** Bert Ryan owns Small Company, a sole proprietorship. During the current pay period, his two employees, Jim Roy and Janice Alter, worked 48 hours and 56 hours, respectively. The reason for these extra hours is that both Jim and Janice worked their regular 40-hour workweek, plus Jim worked 8 extra hours on Sunday and Janice worked 8 extra hours on Saturday and Sunday. Their contract with Small Co. is that they are each paid an hourly rate of $8 per hour with all hours over 40 to be time and a half and double time on Sunday. Bert, the owner, feels he is also entitled to a salary because he works as many hours. He plans to pay himself $425. As the accountant for Small Co., (1) calculate the gross pay for Jim and Janice, and (2) write a letter to Bert Ryan with your recommendations regarding his salary.

LO1, 2, 4 (40 min)   **T-2.** Marcy Moore works for Moose Company during the day and GTA Company at night. Both her employers deduct FICA taxes for OASDI and Medicare. At year-end, Marcy has earned $96,600 at her job at Moose Company and $12,000 at GTA.

At a party she meets Bill Barnes, an accountant, who tells her she has paid too much Social Security tax and that she is entitled to a refund or credit on the tax return she files for the year. Bill suggests that she call the Internal Revenue Service's toll-free number and ask for taxpayer assistance. Assume Social Security of 6.2% on $102,000 and Medicare of 1.45% on all Marcy's earnings during the year.

As Marcy's friend, (1) check to see whether she has actually overpaid any FICA tax, and (2) write a brief note to her and show her your calculations to support your answer.

FINANCIAL REPORT PROBLEM

LO1, 2 (10 min)   ### Reading the Kellogg's Annual Report

Go to Appendix A of the Kellogg's Annual Report and calculate from Note 15 how much Accrued Salaries and Wages has increased from 2005 to 2006.

INTERNET PROJECT

Johnson & Johnson

Go to the Web and Search: Annual Report Johnson & Johnson 2008.
Click on Investors Relations.
List out the latest news Johnson & Johnson is providing to its investors.
Order a free annual report.

CONTINUING PROBLEM

LO1, 2, 3 (60 min)   ### Sanchez Computer Center

In preparing for next year, Tony Freedman hired two hourly employees to assist with some troubleshooting and repair work.

Assignment

1. Record the following transactions in the general journal and post them to the general ledger.

2. Prepare a payroll register for the three pay periods.

3. Prepare a trial balance as of November 30, 200X.

Assume the following transactions:

a. The following accounts have been added to the chart of accounts: Wage Expense #5110, FICA OASDI Payable #2020, FICA Medicare Payable #2030, FIT Payable #2040, State Income Tax Payable #2050, and Wages Payable #2010.

b. Assume FICA OASDI is taxed at 6.2% up to $76,200 in earnings, and Medicare at 1.45% on all earnings. Note that this figure is not the current wage-base limit for Social Security, but will be used for this problem.

c. State income tax is 2% of gross pay.

d. None of the employees has federal income tax taken out of his or her pay.

e. Each employee earns $10 an hour and is paid 1½ times salary for hours worked in excess of 40 weekly.

Nov.	1	Billed Vita Needle Company $6,800, invoice no. 12675, for services rendered.
	3	Billed Accu Pac, Inc., $3,900, invoice no. 12676, for services rendered.
	5	Purchased new shop benches for $1,400 on account from System Design Furniture.
	7	Paid employee wages: Lance Kumm, 38 hours, and Anthony Hall, 42 hours. (This transaction will be recorded as part of the Chapter 8 problem.)
	9	Received the phone bill, $150.
	12	Collected $500 of the amount due from Taylor Golf.
	14	Paid employee wages: Lance Kumm, 25 hours, and Anthony Hall, 36 hours. (This transaction will be recorded as part of the Chapter 8 problem.)
	18	Collected $800 of the amount due from Taylor Golf.
	20	Purchased a fax machine for the office from Multi Systems, Inc., on credit, $450.00.
	21	Paid employee wages: Lance Kumm, 26 hours, and Anthony Hall, 35 hours. (This transaction will be recorded as part of the Chapter 8 problem.)

Note: Transactions on the 7th, 14th, and 21st will be required in the Chapter 8 general journal.

SUBWAY Case

PAYROLL RECORDS: A FULL-TIME JOB?

LO1, 2, 3, 4 (30 min)

Like every Subway restaurant owner, Stan needs to keep a master file of important employee information. This file contains every employee's name, address, phone number, Social Security number, rate of pay, hours worked per week, and W-4 form.

Stan employs two part-time "sandwich artists" and no full-time managers—yet. If his sales continue to be high, he'll need to hire someone to manage operations so that he can spend more time analyzing the financials—with Lila's help—and growing his business. Most restaurants hire primarily part-timers with a core of full-time employees, but the numbers vary from restaurant to restaurant. Benefits vary too. Stan, for instance, plans to offer health and dental benefits when he hires a manager. He knows what a great incentive these benefits are, with health costs so high. He pays his sandwich artists, Rashid and Ellen, the minimum wage because they both have less than a year's experience. However, he's talking to Mariah Washington about creating some incentives to keep them motivated. If Rashid and Ellen are with him for a full year, they'll see a nice raise in their biweekly paychecks. Both the frequency of pay and the tax rates vary by state and sometimes by city or county.

Stan must record all this vital information and report it to the various state, local, and federal authorities. In addition, Stan includes total payroll expenses on the weekly sales and inventory report, which he submits electronically to headquarters from his point-of-sale (POS) screen.

Scheduling workers and keeping payroll records are the bane of Stan's existence. These tasks are so incredibly time-consuming. He was pleased to hear, then, at the last meeting of his local North American Association of Subway Franchisees (NAASF) that the new POS terminals will soon offer an electronic scheduling package.

"Wow! That will really help," said Stan cheerfully to another franchisee. "No more different colors of ink just to keep track of who will work when! Now I can plan around Rashid and Ellen's exam schedules without a hassle. Scheduling might just become my favorite module in the new system."

"Sure," said Javier Gonzalez, another owner. "Now you can concentrate on payroll records. What fun!"

"Ay. Que lata," Stan groaned. What a drag!

Discussion Questions

1. What payroll records does Stan need to keep for his Subway restaurant?
2. What other information might Stan want in order to schedule working hours for each employee?
3. How does the payroll register help Stan prepare the payroll? (Consult the process outlined at the beginning of the chapter.)

Paying, Recording, and Reporting Payroll and Payroll Taxes: The Conclusion of the Payroll Process

DID YOU KNOW? Coca-Cola is more than 120 years old and is still the best-selling beverage brand. A new coolLift delivery system has resulted in a four-day workweek for many employees, along with less manual labor. Visit *www.thecoca-colacompany.com* to find more information about Coca-Cola.

LEARNING OBJECTIVES

1. Recording payroll and payroll taxes.

2. Recording the payroll and the paying of the payroll taxes.

3. Recording employer taxes for FICA OASDI, FICA HI, FUTA, SUTA, and workers' compensation insurance.

4. Paying FUTA, SUTA, and workers' compensation insurance.

5. Preparing Forms W-2, W-3, 941, and 940.

Balance Sheet
ASSETS

Cash 111

XXX |

Cash account used for paying payroll taxes

Payroll Cash 112

XXX |

Cash account used only for writing paychecks

Prepaid WC Insurance 121

XXX |

Account used only for the prepaid workers' compensation insurance premium

LIABILITIES

Wages and Salaries Payable 202

| XXX

Wages and salaries due to employees

FICA OASDI Payable 203

| XXX

Employee and employer's share of FICA OASDI due to the IRS

FICA Medicare Payable 204

| XXX

Employee and employer's share of FICA Medicare due to the IRS

FIT Payable 205

| XXX

Federal income tax withheld and due to the IRS

SIT Payable 206

| XXX

State income tax withheld and due to the state government

FUTA Tax Payable 207

| XXX

Federal unemployment tax due to the IRS

SUTA Tax Payable 208

| XXX

State unemployment tax due to the state government

Medical Insurance Payable 209

| XXX

Medical insurance premium withheld and due to the health insurance carrier

Income Statement
EXPENSES

Business Scheduling Expense 601

XXX |

Wage and salary expense of employees scheduling business travel

Cruise Scheduling Expense 602

XXX |

Wage and salary expense of employees scheduling cruises

Payroll Tax Expense 603

XXX |

Employer's expense for its share of FICA OASDI, its share of FICA Medicare, FUTA, and SUTA

WC Insurance Expense 604

XXX |

Employer's expense for workers' compensation insurance

Coca-Cola has many thousands of employees world wide. With the aid of computers, the accounting department of Coca-Cola must monitor as well as complete in a timely manner its employer tax responsibilities. In Chapter 7 we learned how to calculate gross earnings, employee withholding taxes, net pay, and employer payroll taxes. We now look at how businesses pay, record, and report these amounts. The journal entries necessary to record all of the payroll transactions for Travelwithus.com appear in the next section. Use the preceding T accounts as a reference guide. They will be covered as part of our discussion on completing the payroll process.

Learning Unit 8-1 Recording Payroll and Payroll Tax Expense and Paying the Payroll

At this point in the payroll process, Katherine Kurtz, the accountant for Travelwithus.com, has calculated gross earnings, deductions for employee withholding taxes, and net pay for each of Travelwithus.com's employees. She entered these amounts into two accounting records for Travelwithus.com called the payroll register and the employee earnings record. She also computed the amount of payroll taxes that Travelwithus.com must pay as an employer. At this point, Katherine must record these payroll amounts in the accounts of Travelwithus.com by making journal entries in the general journal and posting these entries to accounts in the general ledger. By entering these amounts into Travelwithus.com's accounting system, Travelwithus.com's financial statements will include these payroll transactions.

Recording Payroll   *LO1*

Before we discuss how payroll transactions are recorded, let's first review the accounts that we will be using and the rules for increasing and decreasing these accounts:

Accounts Affected	Category	↑ ↓	Rules	Financial Statement
Business Scheduling Expense	Expense	↑	Dr.	Income Statement
Cruise Scheduling Expense	Expense	↑	Dr.	Income Statement
Payroll Tax Expense	Expense	↑	Dr.	Income Statement
Workers' Compensation Insurance Expense	Expense	↑	Dr.	Income Statement
Payroll Cash	Asset	↑	Dr.	Balance Sheet
Prepaid Workers' Compensation Insurance	Asset	↑	Dr.	Balance Sheet
FICA OASDI Payable	Liability	↑	Cr.	Balance Sheet
FICA Medicare Payable	Liability	↑	Cr.	Balance Sheet
FIT Payable	Liability	↑	Cr.	Balance Sheet
SIT Payable	Liability	↑	Cr.	Balance Sheet
FUTA Payable	Liability	↑	Cr.	Balance Sheet
SUTA Payable	Liability	↑	Cr.	Balance Sheet
Medical Insurance Payable	Liability	↑	Cr.	Balance Sheet
Wages and Salaries Payable	Liability	↑	Cr.	Balance Sheet

Katherine needs to record the expense of wages and salaries, and the information needed to make these journal entries comes from the hourly and salaried payroll registers. Figure 8.1 on the following page shows the hourly payroll register for the current payroll period. Katherine locates this register and uses totals from it to make the following journal entry:

	Date			PR	Dr.	Cr.
			GENERAL JOURNAL			
	200X					
	Oct.	29	Business Scheduling Expense		9 5 7 60	
			Cruise Scheduling Expense		2 3 1 9 30	
			FIT Payable			3 4 0 00
			SIT Payable			2 6 2 15
			FICA OASDI Payable			2 0 3 17
			FICA Medicare Payable			4 7 52
			Medical Insurance Payable			9 9 00
			Wages and Salaries Payable			2 3 2 5 06
			To record payroll for the pay period			
			ending October 29, 200X			

TRAVELWITHUS.COM INC.
HOURLY EMPLOYEE PAYROLL REGISTER
OCTOBER 16 – 29

Employee / Social Security No.	Allowances and Marital Status	Previous Earnings (YTD)	Current Earnings Regular Hours	Regular Rate	Regular Amount	Overtime Hours	Overtime Rate	Overtime Amount	Gross	Current Earnings (YTD)
Higuera, Stephanie 123-45-6789	S-1	1851360	78	1140	88920	4	1710	6840	95760	1947120
Sui, Annie 123-45-6788	S-0	212100	80	1515	121200	4	22725	9090	130290	342390
Taylor, Harold 123-45-6787	S-2	1904370	78	1210	94380	4	1815	7260	101640	2006010
TOTALS					304500			23190	327690	4295520

TRAVELWITHUS.COM INC.
HOURLY EMPLOYEE PAYROLL REGISTER
OCTOBER 16 – 29

Employee / Social Security No.	Taxable Earnings FUTA/SUTA	Taxable Earnings OASDI	FIT	SIT	FICA OASDI	FICA Medicare	Medical Insurance	Net Pay	Check No.	Account Charged Business Scheduling Expense	Account Charged Cruise Scheduling Expense
Higuera, Stephanie 123-45-6789	—	95760	9200	7661	5937	1389	3300	68273	820	95760	
Sui, Annie 123-45-6788	130290	130290	16700	10423	8078	1889	3300	89900	821		130290
Taylor, Harold 123-45-6787	—	101640	8100	8131	6302	1474	3300	74333	822		101640
TOTALS	130290	327690	34000	26215	203 17	4752	9900	232506		95760	231930

FIGURE 8.1 Payroll Register

A couple things may be surprising about the journal entry. First, notice that the gross earnings, not the net pay, are recorded as expenses for the two different departments that the employees worked in. This total amount of earnings is the real expense to Travelwithus.com. Employees will actually only receive the lower, net pay; the difference relates to deductions that the employees must "pay" to the federal and state governments in the form of withholdings for the different kinds of taxes and insurance.

Also notice that the amounts of taxes withheld are recorded in "Payable" accounts, which means that they are liabilities of Travelwithus.com. How can Travelwithus.com be liable for these taxes if the taxes are paid by employees? The answer is that Travelwithus.com collects these amounts by withholding them from the paychecks of its employees and then turns them over to the federal and, in this case, state governments. In other words, Travelwithus.com is the intermediary in this process. Until it does pay these amounts to the governments, Travelwithus.com owes these taxes to the governments. The same is true of the medical insurance premiums that the employees pay; the company collects them and then pays them to the insurance company.

Recording Payroll Tax Expense

Katherine's next task is to record the employer payroll taxes for Travelwithus.com, and the entry to record the taxes for the current hourly payroll follows:

GENERAL JOURNAL				
Date		PR	Dr.	Cr.
200X				
Oct. 29	Payroll Tax Expense		3 3 1 47	
	FICA OASDI Payable			2 0 3 17
	FICA Medicare Payable			4 7 52
	FUTA Payable			1 0 42
	SUTA Payable			7 0 36
	To record payroll tax expense for the			
	pay period ending October 29, 200X			

Notice that FICA OASDI, FICA Medicare, FUTA, and SUTA were recorded in separate liability accounts because they are different taxes and, except for the FICA taxes, are paid to different government agencies. Also note that the amount of all of these taxes are added together and recorded as one amount for Travelwithus.com's **payroll tax expense**. These amounts are an expense to Travelwithus.com because they represent the cost of the payroll taxes that it must pay as an employer.

Paying the Payroll and Recording the Payment   *LO2*

Katherine next must record the payment of payroll to Travelwithus.com's employees:

GENERAL JOURNAL				
Date		PR	Dr.	Cr.
200X				
Nov. 3	Wages and Salaries Payable		2 3 2 5 06	
	Payroll Cash			2 3 2 5 06
	To record the payment of hourly payroll			
	for the pay period ending October 29,			
	200X			

Travelwithus.com, like most companies, uses a special checking account for paying its payroll. This account is called Payroll Cash and only paychecks are written from this account. A company with a substantial number of employees might want to use an extra account just for payroll for a number of reasons. First, having a separate account just for paychecks provides much better internal control over the funds deposited to pay employees. Also, because only payroll checks are written from this account, it is easier to reconcile it to the bank statement each month and determine whether someone has not cashed his or her paycheck for some reason. Finally, the business can still manage its cash effectively even with this extra bank account; the business simply deposits the total net pay amount in this account and thus has enough money to pay every paycheck without leaving extra in the account that could be used for other purposes.

The paychecks that Travelwithus.com gives to its employees are, like the paychecks of most companies, attached to pay stubs that show the employee's gross earnings, deductions for employee withholding taxes, and net pay. Stephanie Higuera's current paycheck and stub look like this:

Travelwithus.com Inc.

Employee	Social Security	Check	Net Pay	Pay Date	Marital Status	Allowances
Stephanie Higuera	123-45-6789	820	$682.73	11/03/200X	S	1

Earnings	Current			Deductions		
	Pay Rate	Hours	Earnings	Item	Current	YTD
Regular Earnings	11.40	78	889.20	FIT	92.00	2,066.00
Overtime Earnings	17.10	4	68.40	SIT	76.61	1,557.70
Current Gross Earnings			957.60	OASDI	59.37	1,207.21
				Medicare	13.89	282.33
				Medical insurance	33.00	693.00
				Total	274.87	5,806.24

Travelwithus.com Inc.
504 Washington Blvd.
Salem, MA 01970

11-325/1210

No. 820

November 3,   200X

PAY TO THE ORDER OF _Stephanie Higuera_ $682.73

Six hundred eighty two and 73/100 _____ DOLLARS

| BC | Bank of Commerce

MEMO _October 16–29 payroll_   _Julia Regan_

LEARNING UNIT 8-1 REVIEW

AT THIS POINT you should be able to

- Explain how to use the payroll register to record the payroll.
- Journalize the payroll.
- Journalize the employer's payroll tax expense.
- Journalize the payment of a payroll.

Self-Review Quiz 8-1

Given the following information, prepare the general journal entry to record the payroll tax expense for Bill Co. for the weekly payroll of Oct 29. Assume the following:

- SUTA tax is paid at a rate of 5.6% on the first $7,000 of earnings.
- FUTA tax is paid at the net rate of .8% on the first $7,000 of earnings.
- FICA tax rate for OASDI is 6.2% on $102,000, and Medicare is 1.45% on all earnings.

Employee	Cumulative Pay Before This Week's Payroll	Gross Pay for the Week
Bill Jones	$6,000	$800
Julie Warner	$6,600	$400
Al Brooks	$7,900	$700

Solution to Self-Review Quiz 8-1

		GENERAL JOURNAL				
	Date	Account	PR	Dr.	Cr.	
	200X					
	Oct. 29	Payroll Tax Expense		222 15		
		FICA OASDI Payable			117 80	
		FICA Medicare Payable			27 55	
		FUTA Payable			9 60	
		SUTA Payable			67 20	
		To record payroll tax expense for the				
		pay period ending July 8, 200X				

FICA OASDI   = $1,900 × .062 = $117.80

FICA Medicare = $1,900 × .0145 = $ 27.55

FUTA   = $1,200 × .008 = $ 9.60

SUTA   = $1,200 × .056 = $ 67.20

> Remember that OASDI and Medicare are employer payroll taxes even though employees pay these taxes, too.

Learning Unit 8-2 Paying Fit and Fica Taxes and Completing the Employer's Quarterly Federal Tax Return, Form 941

As we discussed in Chapter 7, both employers and employees pay payroll taxes. Employees pay these amounts not by writing checks to the different levels of government, but by having the amounts of these taxes taken out, or withheld, from the amount of pay that they actually receive. Employers withhold these amounts, report them and the related earnings to federal, state, and sometimes local governments, and then turn them over to those levels of government. Let's now discuss how Travelwithus.com carries out these responsibilities.

For Travelwithus.com, the process began when the business opened. When opening a business, every employer must get a federal identification number. This number is also called an **employer identification number (EIN)**, and is like a Social Security number for businesses in the sense that it identifies businesses to the government. To get an EIN, an employer fills out **Form SS-4**, much like individuals fill out Form SS-5 get a Social Security number. Travelwithus.com will use its EIN, 58-1213479, to report employee earnings and payroll taxes.

Travelwithus.com must next determine when its payroll taxes are due to the government, and due dates vary according to the type of tax being paid.

LO3 Paying FIT and FICA Taxes

As required by law, Travelwithus.com withholds federal income tax from employees' paychecks, along with Social Security (OASDI) and Medicare taxes as established by the **Federal Insurance Contribution Act** or **FICA.** As the employer, Travelwithus.com reports and pays these taxes to the federal government. The **Federal Unemployment Tax Act (FUTA)** tax is the unemployment tax that employers pay to the federal government, which is paid and reported separately. To see how Travelwithus.com reports the FIT and FICA taxes to the federal government, let's look at its payroll information for the last **calendar quarter** of the year, which covers October, November, and December.

To comply with federal law, Travelwithus.com must do two things: First, it must determine when FIT and FICA taxes need to be paid to the federal government and make this payment on time. Second, it must report these taxes on **Form 941, the Employer's Quarterly Federal Tax Return.** Figure 8.2 contains a worksheet that Katherine prepared from payroll registers to make sure that these two tasks happen the way they should.

FIGURE 8.2 Form 941 Worksheet

TRAVELWITHUS.COM INC.
Form 941 Taxes
4th Quarter

Payroll Period		Pay Check Date	Earnings	FIT	Taxable FICA Wages for OASDI	Taxable FICA Wages for Medicare	FICA OASDI EE + ER*	FICA Medicare EE + ER	Total Tax	Cumulative Tax
October	2–15	Oct. 20	3 6 8 0 75	3 9 3 84	3 6 8 0 75	3 6 8 0 75	4 5 6 41	1 0 6 74	9 5 6 99	9 5 6 99
October	16–29	Nov. 3	3 2 7 6 90	3 4 0 00	3 2 7 6 90	3 2 7 6 90	4 0 6 34	9 5 04	8 4 1 38	1 7 9 8 37
October	31	Oct. 31	18 3 8 7 33	3 4 9 3 59	18 3 8 7 33	18 3 8 7 33	2 2 8 0 03	5 3 3 23	6 3 0 6 85	8 1 0 5 22
Oct./Nov.	30–12	Nov. 17	3 2 7 6 90	3 5 2 00	3 2 7 6 90	3 2 7 6 90	4 0 6 34	9 5 03	8 5 3 37	8 9 5 8 59
November	13–26	Dec. 1	3 8 7 0 02	4 1 4 09	3 8 7 0 02	3 8 7 0 02	4 7 9 88	1 1 2 23	1 0 0 6 20	9 9 6 4 79
November	30	Nov. 30	18 3 8 7 33	3 4 9 3 59	18 3 8 7 33	18 3 8 7 33	2 2 8 0 03	5 3 3 23	6 3 0 6 85	16 2 7 1 64
Nov./Dec.	27–10	Dec. 15	3 3 4 0 60	3 5 7 44	3 3 4 0 60	3 3 4 0 60	4 1 4 23	9 6 88	8 6 8 55	17 1 4 0 19
December	11–24	Dec. 29	3 2 1 4 50	3 4 3 95	3 2 1 4 50	3 2 1 4 50	3 9 8 60	9 3 22	8 3 5 77	17 9 7 5 96
December	25–31	Dec. 29	1 5 7 8 90	1 6 8 94	1 5 7 8 90	1 5 7 8 90	1 9 5 78	4 5 79	4 1 0 51	18 3 8 6 47
December	31	Dec. 29	18 3 8 7 33	3 4 9 3 59	16 8 8 7 33	18 3 8 7 33	2 0 9 4 03	5 3 3 23	6 1 2 0 85	24 5 0 7 32
4th Quarter Totals			77 4 0 0 56	12 8 5 1 03	75 9 0 0 56	77 4 0 0 56	9 4 1 1 67	2 2 4 4 62	24 5 0 7 32	24 5 0 7 32
			(a)	(b)	(c)	(d)	(e)	(f)	(g)	(h)

*EE stands for employee; ER stands for employer

Notice a few things about this worksheet. First, look at the payroll period dates and see that some cover two-week periods and others show the last day of the month. Remember that the two types of dates relate to the two types of payroll that Travelwithus.com has, hourly and salaried. Next, observe that the quarter is 13 weeks long. By putting 13 weeks into each quarter, companies report all 52 weeks of a calendar year. Also, FIT and FICA are shown in separate columns because the IRS wants those amounts reported separately. Finally, notice that for the December 31 monthly payroll not all of the wages earned are taxable for OASDI because an employee has reached the $102,000 wage base limit by this point in the year.

The total amount of taxes due must be deposited in what is called an authorized depository in Travelwithus.com's area of the country, or in a Federal Reserve Bank. Authorized depositories are banks that have been authorized by the Federal Reserve System to accept payroll deposits from their own checking account customers. A Federal Reserve Bank can accept payroll tax deposits from any business, no matter where the business keeps its checking account.

Types of Payroll Tax Depositors To determine when payroll taxes are due, for payroll tax deposit purposes employers are usually classified as either monthly or semiweekly depositors. Rarely a company will owe less than $2,500 in total taxes, but in this case the taxes may be deposited quarterly. A **monthly depositor** is an employer who only has to deposit **Form 941 taxes** (federal income tax withholdings, OASDI, and Medicare) on the 15th day of every month. **Semiweekly depositors** must deposit their Form 941 taxes once or twice each week, depending on when payroll is paid. These classifications last for an entire calendar year, and employers are reevaluated every year.

Employers are classified according to the dollar amount of the Form 941 taxes that they have paid in the past. The IRS developed a rule known as the **look-back period** rule to determine how to classify an employer for payroll tax deposits. Under this rule, the IRS looks back to a one-year time period that begins on July 1 and ends the following June 30 of the previous year. If during this look-back period an employer paid less than $50,000 of Form 941 taxes, then it is classified as a monthly depositor. Alternately, if the employer paid $50,000 or more during this period, then it is considered a semiweekly depositor. New companies are automatically classified as monthly depositors until they have been in business long enough to have a look-back period that can be used to classify them. Figure 8.3 shows how the look-back period works.

Travelwithus.com is a semiweekly depositor because it made more than $50,000 of FIT and FICA deposits during the most recent look-back period.

Rules for Monthly Depositors If an employer is classified as a monthly depositor, the FIT and both the employee and employer OASDI and Medicare taxes accumulated during any month must be deposited by the 15th day of the next month. If the 15th is a Saturday, Sunday, or bank holiday, then the deposit must be made on the next **banking day.**

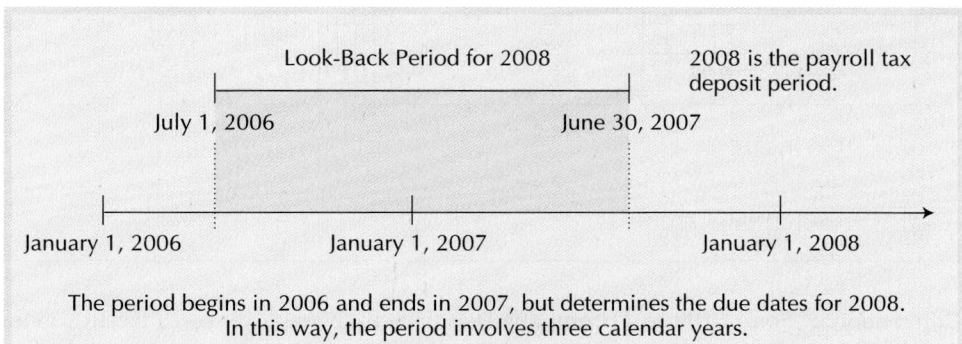

FIGURE 8.3 Look-Back Illustration

Look-Back Period for 2008

2008 is the payroll tax deposit period.

July 1, 2006   June 30, 2007

January 1, 2006   January 1, 2007   January 1, 2008

The period begins in 2006 and ends in 2007, but determines the due dates for 2008. In this way, the period involves three calendar years.

Rules for Semiweekly Depositors   If an employer is classified as a semiweekly depositor, as a general rule it always has three banking days to make its payroll tax deposit. However, semiweekly depositors like Travelwithus.com may have to make up to two payroll tax deposits every week, depending on when they pay their employees. According to the IRS, for this purpose, each week begins on Wednesday and ends on the following Tuesday. This week is broken into two parts, Wednesday through Friday, and Saturday through Tuesday. If the company's payday is a Wednesday, Thursday, or Friday, the payroll tax deposit is due on the following Wednesday. If the company's payday is a Saturday, Sunday, Monday, or Tuesday, the payroll tax deposit is due on the following Friday.

Thus, if an employer pays its employees on a Thursday and a Monday, it must make two payroll tax deposits, one on Wednesday for the Thursday payday, and one on Friday for the Monday payday. If a bank holiday occurs between a payday and the day when the payroll tax deposit is due, the employer gets an extra day to make the deposit. So, a deposit due on a Wednesday will be due on Thursday, or a Friday deposit will be due on the following Monday.

The diagram in Figure 8.4 shows how these rules work:

FIGURE 8.4 Semiweekly Deposit Rules Illustration

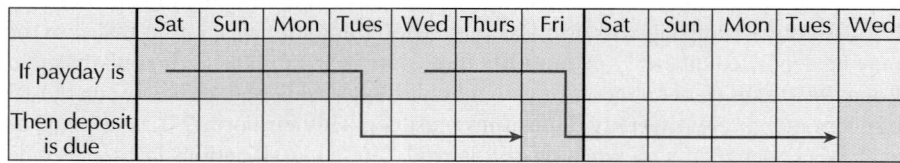

See Figure 8.5 to see how the rules apply to Travelwithus.com. Remember that Travelwithus.com's hourly payroll is always paid on a Friday. Because Travelwithus.com is a semiweekly payroll tax depositor, its Form 941 payroll tax deposits for its hourly payroll are due on the following Wednesday. Because its hourly payroll is paid on a biweekly, or every other week, basis, Travelwithus.com will need to make a deposit every other Wednesday. However, if we look at week 52, the payday for this week is Friday, December 29, which is two days before New Year's Day. Under the law, January 1 is a federal holiday, so Katherine must apply the rule regarding a holiday that falls between a payday and a tax deposit day and will make the Form 941 tax deposit not on Wednesday but on Thursday, January 4, of the next year.

Travelwithus.com also has a salaried payroll, and this payroll is paid on the last day of the month. In October, the last day of the month is a Tuesday, so Travelwithus.com will make its Form 941 tax deposit for this payroll on the following Friday.

FIGURE 8.5 Third Quarter Payroll Calendar for Travelwithus.com

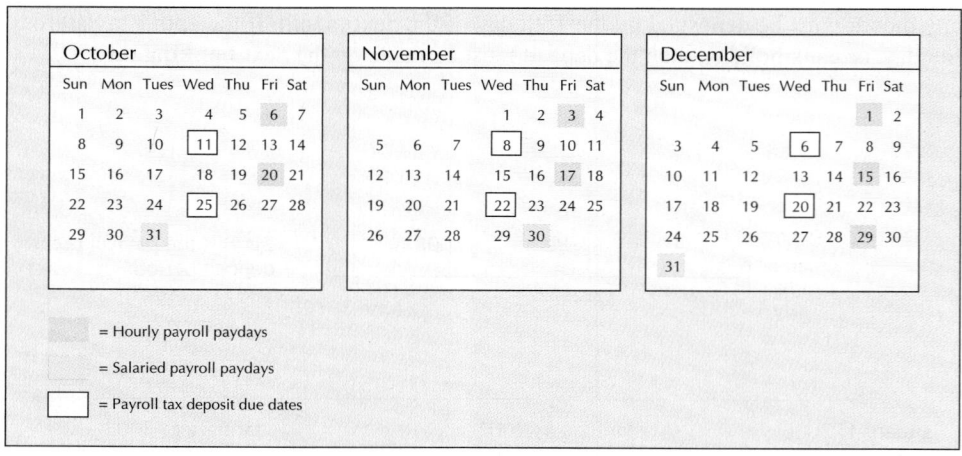

Completion of Form 8109 to Accompany Deposits   If an employer owes the IRS more than $200,000 of deposits in a year in total, then the IRS requires it to pay Form 941 taxes by the Electronic Federal Tax Payment System (EFTPS). If the amount owed is less than

$200,000 as it is for Travelwithus.com, then the IRS allows the employer to pay Form 941 taxes by check. The IRS then also requires employers to use **Form 8109, Federal Tax Deposit Coupon,** to make these deposits. This form is much like a deposit slip used to make deposits into bank accounts, and goes with the check that Travelwithus.com deposits. Remember that by depositing the amount of Form 941 taxes with an authorized financial institution, Travelwithus.com is "paying" these taxes to the IRS.

Katherine received a book of 8109 coupons when she got the EIN for Travelwithus.com. Figure 8.6 on the following page shows a completed Form 8109 for Travelwithus.com. Notice that Katherine completed this coupon for the tax deposit that needed to be made to cover the 941 taxes for the October 16–29 hourly pay period that was paid on November 3. Also notice that the dollar amount at the top of the form, $841.38, is the same as the amount found in the total tax column for the pay period in Figure 8.2. The "941" bubble in the "Type of Tax" section is filled in, as is the "4th Quarter" bubble in the "Tax Period" portion of the coupon. By darkening these bubbles, Travelwithus.com tells the IRS what kind of tax is being reported and to which quarter the deposit applies.

The last task that Katherine must perform is to record the payment of the FIT and FICA taxes. The journal entry that she makes looks like this:

GENERAL JOURNAL				
Date		PR	Dr.	Cr.
200X				
Nov.	8	FICA OASDI Payable		406 34	
		FICA Medicare Payable		95 04	
		FIT Payable		340 00	
		Cash			841 38
		To record payment of FIT and FICA			
		taxes for pay period ending			
		October 29, 200X			

To get a better idea of how payroll tax amounts appear in the accounting system of Travelwithus.com, let's check out its general ledger for the FICA OASDI Payable and FICA Medicare Payable accounts:

FICA OASDI Payable   Account No. 203

Date		PR	Dr.	Cr.	Cr. Bal.
200X					
Oct.	15	GJ28		456 41	456 41
	25	GJ28	456 41		0
	29	GJ29		406 34	406 34
	31	GJ29		2280 03	2686 37
Nov.	3	GJ29	2280 03		406 34
	8	GJ30	406 34		0

FICA Medicare Payable   Account No. 204

Date		PR	Dr.	Cr.	Cr. Bal.
200X					
Oct.	15	GJ28		106 74	106 74
	25	GJ28	106 74		0
	29*	GJ29		95 04	95 04
	31	GJ29		533 23	628 27
Nov.	3	GJ29	533 23		95 04
	8	GJ30	95 04		0

*This represents both the employee and employer deductions.

Notice several things about the ledger accounts. First, the entries on October 29 crediting the FICA OASDI Payable and FICA Medicare Payable accounts came from the general journal entries on this date because the payroll and payroll taxes were recorded on this date. These amounts represent both the employee and employer's shares of OASDI and Medicare. Also notice that the entries on November 8 debiting FICA OASDI for $406.34 and FICA Medicare for $95.04 came from the general journal. They are part of the payment that Travelwithus.com deposited with the Form 941 taxes. To summarize, journal entries crediting these accounts record tax liabilities, and journal entries debiting these accounts record payments of these taxes.

FIGURE 8.6 Completed Form 8109

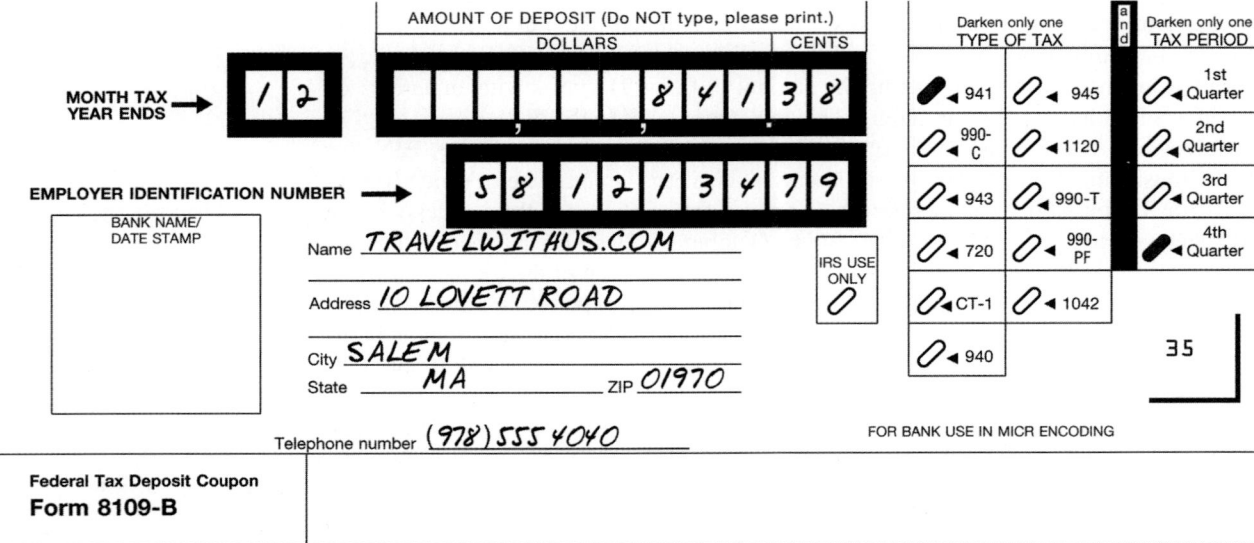

Federal Tax Deposit Coupon
Form 8109-B

↑ **SEPARATE ALONG THIS LINE AND SUBMIT TO DEPOSITARY WITH PAYMENT** ↑ OMB NO. 1545-0257

Note: *Except for the name, address, and telephone number, entries must be made in pencil.* **Use soft lead** *(for example, a #2 pencil) so that the entries can be read more accurately by optical scanning equipment. The name, address, and telephone number may be completed other than by hand.* **You cannot use photocopies of the coupons to make your deposits. Do not** *staple, tape, or fold the coupons.*

Purpose of form. Use Form 8109-B to make a tax deposit **only** in the following two situations:

1. You have not yet received your resupply of preprinted deposit coupons (Form 8109); or

2. You are a new entity and have already been assigned an employer identification number (EIN), but you have not received your initial supply of preprinted deposit coupons (Form 8109). If you have not received your EIN, see **Exceptions** below.

Note: *If you do not receive your resupply of deposit coupons and a deposit is due or you do not receive your initial supply within 5–6 weeks of receipt of your EIN, call 1-800-829-4933.*

How to complete the form. Enter your name as shown on your return or other IRS correspondence, address, and EIN in the spaces provided. **Do not** make a name or address change on this form (see **Form 8822,** Change of Address). If you are required to file a Form 1120, 990-C, 990-PF (with net investment income), 990-T, or 2438, enter the month in which your tax year ends in the MONTH TAX YEAR ENDS boxes. For example, if your tax year ends in January, enter 01; if it ends in December, enter 12. Make your entries for EIN and MONTH TAX YEAR ENDS (if applicable) as shown in **Amount of deposit** below.

    Exceptions. If you have applied for an EIN, have not received it, and a deposit must be made, **do not** use Form 8109-B. Instead, send your payment to the IRS address where you file your return. Make your check or money order payable to the United States Treasury and show on it your name (as shown on **Form SS-4,** Application for Employer Identification Number), address, kind of tax, period covered, and date you applied for an EIN. **Do not** use Form 8109-B to deposit delinquent taxes assessed by the IRS. Pay those taxes directly to the IRS. See **Circular E,** Employer's Tax Guide, for information on depositing by electronic funds transfer.

Amount of deposit. Enter the amount of the deposit in the space provided. Enter the amount legibly, forming the characters as shown below:

Hand print money amounts without using dollar signs, commas, a decimal point, or leading zeros. If the deposit is for whole dollars only, enter "00" in the CENTS boxes. For example, a deposit of $7,635.22 would be entered like this:

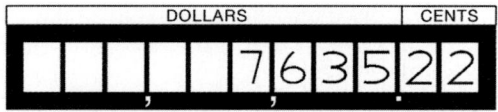

Caution: *Darken one space each in the TYPE OF TAX and TAX PERIOD columns as explained below. Darken the space to the left of the applicable tax form and tax period. Darkening the wrong space may delay proper crediting of your account.*

Types of Tax

Form 941	Employer's Quarterly Federal Tax Return (includes Forms **941-M, 941-PR,** and **941-SS**)
Form 943	Employer's Annual Tax Return for Agricultural Employers
Form 945	Annual Return of Withheld Federal Income Tax
Form 720	Quarterly Federal Excise Tax Return
Form CT-1	Employer's Annual Railroad Retirement Tax Return
Form 940	Employer's Annual Federal Unemployment (FUTA) Tax Return (includes Form **940-PR**)
Form 1120	U.S. Corporation Income Tax Return (includes Form **1120** series of returns and Form **2438**)
Form 990-C	Farmers' Cooperative Association Income Tax Return
Form 990-T	Exempt Organization Business Income Tax Return
Form 990-PF	Return of Private Foundation or Section 4947(a)(1) Nonexempt Charitable Trust Treated as a Private Foundation
Form 1042	Annual Withholding Tax Return for U.S. Source Income of Foreign Persons

Marking the Proper Tax Period

Payroll taxes and withholding. For Forms 941, 940, 943, 945, CT-1, and 1042, if your liability was incurred during:

● January 1 through March 31, darken the 1st quarter space

● April 1 through June 30, darken the 2nd quarter space

● July 1 through September 30, darken the 3rd quarter space

● October 1 through December 31, darken the 4th quarter space

Note: *If the liability was incurred during one quarter and deposited in another quarter, darken the space for the quarter in which the tax liability was incurred. For example, if the liability was incurred in March and deposited in April, darken the 1st quarter space.*

Excise taxes. For Form 720, follow the instructions above for Forms 941, 940, etc. For Form 990-PF, with net investment income, follow the instructions below for Form 1120, 990-C, etc.

Income Taxes (Form 1120, 990-C, 990-T, and 2438). To make an estimated tax deposit for any quarter of the current tax year, **darken only the 1st quarter space.**

    Example 1. If your tax year ends on December 31, 2007, and a deposit for 2007 is being made between January 1 and December 31, 2007, darken the 1st quarter space.

Completing the Employer's Quarterly Federal Tax Return, Form 941

The IRS requires all employers to complete tax returns reporting FICA OASDI, FICA Medicare, and FIT taxes. If these taxes total less than $2,500 for a calendar year, then employers will prepare **Form 944, Employer's Annual Federal Tax Return.** This form is due from employers by January 31 of the following year. Employers will complete this return only if the IRS notifies them that it is the form that they must use. If, however, taxes total more than $2,500 for a calendar year, then employers must instead complete Form 941, Employer's Quarterly Federal Tax Return, and submit it to the IRS for every quarter in a calendar year. Katherine Kurtz, the accountant for Travelwithus.com, used the worksheet in Figure 8.2 to prepare Form 941 for the last quarter of the year because Travelwithus.com's taxes exceeded $2,500.

The top section of Travelwithus.com's fourth quarter Form 941 in Figure 8.7 on the following page identifies the taxpayer, Travelwithus.com, and lists its address, the date that the quarter ended, and its EIN. Refer back to the worksheet in Figure 8.2 and use the letters below the column totals to follow amounts from this worksheet to the Form 941. Line-by-line instructions for completing the Form 941 are as follows:

Part 1: *Answering questions that relate to the current quarter.*

Line 1: This line is used to show how many employees were paid during the quarter.

2: This line is used to report total gross earnings for the quarter, which is $77,400.56 per column (a) of the worksheet.

3: Total income tax withheld is $12,851.03, which comes from column (b).

4: No entry is needed here; this line is only used for special situations.

5a, Column 1: The wages subject to FICA OASDI tax are the total taxable earnings of $75,900.56, which match column (c). The amount on this line is different from the line 2 amount because one employee reached the OASDI wage base limit of $102,000.

5a, Column 2: Katherine multiples the amount on line 5a, Column 1, by 12.4%, which is the 6.2% rate for employees and the 6.2% rate for employers, to get the tax of $9,411.67 entered here. Notice that this amount matches column (e) of the worksheet.

5b: This line is used to report taxable tips that employees might have received. Travelwithus.com employees did not receive any tips, so this line is left blank.

5c, Column 1: The wages subject to Medicare tax are the total taxable earnings of $77,400.56, which match column (d). The amount on this line is the same as the line 2 amount because the Medicare tax has no wage base limit.

5c, Column 2: Katherine multiplies the amount on line 5c, Column 1, by 2.9%, which is the 1.45% rate for employees and the 1.45% rate for employers, to get the tax of $2,244.62 entered here. Notice that this amount matches column (f) of the worksheet.

5d: The total of OASDI tax of $9,411.67 and Medicare tax of $2,244.62 is $11,656.29.

6: This line is used to report the total income tax, OASDI tax, and Medicare tax withheld of $24,507.32. It is the sum of lines 3 and 5d. Notice that it matches column (g).

7a–h: These lines are used to report special tax adjustments. None apply to Travelwithus.com, so these lines are left blank.

8: This line reports total tax after adjustments, so it is the same as line 6.

9: If Travelwithus.com advanced any earned income credit to its employees, it would deduct these amounts on this line.

FIGURE 8.7 Completed Form 941

Form **941 for 200X:** **Employer's Quarterly Federal Tax Return**

9901

(Rev. January 2005)   Department of the Treasury — Internal Revenue Service

OMB No. 1545-0029

Employer identification number   5 8 – 1 2 1 3 4 7 9

Name *(not your trade name)*   TRAVELWITH US.COM

Trade name *(if any)*

Address   10 LOVETT ROAD

Number   Street   Suite or room number

SALEM   MA   01970

City   State   ZIP code

Report for this Quarter ...
(Check one.)

☐ **1:** January, February, March

☐ **2:** April, May, June

☐ **3:** July, August, September

☒ **4:** October, November, December

Read the separate instructions before you fill out this form. Please type or print within the boxes.

Part 1: Answer these questions for this quarter.

1 Number of employees who received wages, tips, or other compensation for the pay period including: *Mar. 12* (Quarter 1), *June 12* (Quarter 2), *Sept. 12* (Quarter 3), *Dec. 12* (Quarter 4)   **1**   6

2 Wages, tips, and other compensation **2**   77400.56

3 Total income tax withheld from wages, tips, and other compensation **3**   12851.03

4 If no wages, tips, and other compensation are subject to social security or Medicare tax . .   ☐ Check and go to line 6.

5 Taxable social security and Medicare wages and tips:

	Column 1		Column 2
5a Taxable social security wages	75900.56	× .124 =	9411.67
5b Taxable social security tips	.	× .124 =	.
5c Taxable Medicare wages & tips	77400.56	× .029 =	2244.62

5d Total social security and Medicare taxes (*Column 2*, lines 5a + 5b + 5c = line 5d) .   **5d**   11656.29

6 Total taxes before adjustments (lines 3 + 5d = line 6) **6**   24507.32

7 Tax adjustments (If your answer is a negative number, write it in brackets.):

7a Current quarter's fractions of cents . . . .

7b Current quarter's sick pay . . . .

7c Current quarter's adjustments for tips and group-term life insurance   .

7d Current year's income tax withholding (Attach Form 941c) . . .   .

7e Prior quarters' social security and Medicare taxes (Attach Form 941c)   .

7f Special additions to federal income tax (reserved use) . . . . .   .

7g Special additions to social security and Medicare (reserved use)   .

7h Total adjustments (Combine all amounts: lines 7a through 7g.) . . . .   **7h**   .

8 Total taxes after adjustments (Combine lines 6 and 7h.) **8**   24507.32

9 Advance earned income credit (EIC) payments made to employees . . . .   **9**   .

10 Total taxes after adjustment for advance EIC (lines 8 – 9 = line 10) **10**   24507.32

11 Total deposits for this quarter, including overpayment applied from a prior quarter . . .   **11**   24507.32

12 **Balance due** (lines 10 – 11 = line 12) Make checks payable to the *United States Treasury* . .   **12**   .

13 **Overpayment** (If line 11 is more than line 10, write the difference here.)   .   Check one ☐ Apply to next return.
☐ Send a refund.

Next ➡

For Privacy Act and Paperwork Reduction Act Notice, see the back of the Payment Voucher.   Cat. No. 17001Z   Form **941** (Rev. 1-2005)

FIGURE 8.7 (*continued*)

9902

Name (not your trade name)	Employer identification number
TRAVELWITHUS.COM	58 - 1213479

Part 2: Tell us about your deposit schedule for this quarter.

If you are unsure about whether you are a monthly schedule depositor or a semiweekly schedule depositor, see *Pub. 15* (*Circular E*), section 11.

14 [M][A] Write the state abbreviation for the state where you made your deposits OR write "MU" if you made your deposits in *multiple* states.

15 Check one: ☐ Line 10 is less than $2,500. Go to Part 3.

☐ You were a monthly schedule depositor for the entire quarter. Fill out your tax liability for each month. Then go to Part 3.

Tax liability: Month 1 [.   ]

Month 2 [.   ]

Month 3 [.   ]

Total [.   ] Total must equal line 10.

☒ You were a semiweekly schedule depositor for any part of this quarter. Fill out *Schedule B (Form 941): Report of Tax Liability for Semiweekly Schedule Depositors,* and attach it to this form.

Part 3: Tell us about your business. If a question does NOT apply to your business, leave it blank.

16 If your business has closed and you do not have to file returns in the future . . . . ☐ Check here, and

enter the final date you paid wages [/   /   ] .

17 If you are a seasonal employer and you do not have to file a return for every quarter of the year . . ☐ Check here.

Part 4: May we contact your third-party designee?

Do you want to allow an employee, a paid tax preparer, or another person to discuss this return with the IRS? See the instructions for details.

☐ Yes. Designee's name [   ]

Phone ( ) – Personal Identification Number (PIN) [ ][ ][ ][ ][ ]

☒ No.

Part 5: Sign here

Under penalties of perjury, I declare that I have examined this return, including accompanying schedules and statements, and to the best of my knowledge and belief, it is true, correct, and complete.

X Sign your name here *Katherine C. Kurtz*

Print name and title KATHERINE C. KURTZ, CONTROLLER

Date 1 / 31 / OX Phone (978) 555 - 4040

Part 6: For paid preparers only (optional)

Preparer's signature	
Firm's name	
Address		EIN	
		ZIP code	
Date / / Phone ( ) –	SSN/PTIN	

☐ Check if you are self-employed.

Form **941** (Rev. 1-2005)

10: This line is the difference between lines 8 and 9.

11: This line shows the total of the Form 941 deposits that Travelwithus.com made for the last quarter; $24,507.32. This amount includes the last deposit that Travelwithus.com made for the quarter on Thursday, January 4, because it applies to the December 31 biweekly and monthly payrolls.

12 and 13: Travelwithus.com's deposits exactly total the Form 941 taxes for the quarter, which means it does not have any balance due, nor has it overpaid its taxes.

Part 2: *Providing information about the deposit schedule.*

Line 14: Katherine indicates the abbreviation of the state in which Travelwithus.com has made its deposits.

Line 15: As a semiweekly depositor, Travelwithus.com checks this box and completes and attaches Schedule B: Report of Tax Liability for Semiweekly Schedule Depositors. By showing each day of the quarter, this schedule requires employers to present tax liability amounts on a day-by-day basis. The IRS requires employers to complete this schedule because, by comparing the dates of the tax liabilities to the dates that the deposits were made, it easily allows them to determine whether deposits were made on time. (Schedule B is not shown here.) The amounts for each day are added together to show the total for each month, and these monthly totals together should equal the total liability on line 10.

Part 3: *Indicating specific situations that relate to the business.*

Lines 16 and 17: If a business has not closed and is not a seasonal employer, these lines do not apply. Katherine leaves them blank.

Part 4: *Indicating whether the business would like to be contacted by the IRS regarding this return.* Katherine checks "No."

Part 5: *Signing the return.* Katherine signs the return on behalf of Travelwithus.com.

LEARNING UNIT 8-2 REVIEW

AT THIS POINT you should be able to

- Explain the purpose of Form SS-4.
- Explain which taxes are reported on Form 941.
- Understand how employers are classified as payroll tax depositors.
- Summarize Form 941 payroll tax deposit rules for monthly depositors.
- Summarize Form 941 payroll tax deposit rules for semiweekly depositors.
- Prepare and explain the purpose of Form 8109.
- Record the general journal entry to pay FIT, FICA OASDI, and FICA Medicare when a payroll tax deposit is made.
- Understand how the general journal entries recording FICA OASDI and FICA Medicare and the payment of these taxes are posted into the general ledger.
- Complete a Form 941, Employer's Quarterly Federal Tax Return, from a worksheet.

Self-Review Quiz 8-2

Carol Ann's Import Chalet is a business that employs five full-time employees and four part-time employees. The accountant for Carol Ann's determined that the business is a monthly depositor. The accountant prepared a worksheet showing the following payroll tax liabilities for the month of October:

Date	OASDI EE + ER	Medicare EE + ER	FIT
10/7	$486.56	$169.05	$829.00
10/14	$632.15	$165.01	$901.00
10/21	$579.43	$131.05	$734.00
10/28	$389.99	$142.24	$765.00
Totals	$2,088.13	$607.35	$3,229.00

1. What is the dollar amount of the Form 941 tax deposit that must be made and when must it be made according to the monthly deposit rule? Use Figure 8.5 for the date.
2. Now assume that Carol Ann is classified as a semiweekly depositor. Please calculate the amount of each Form 941 tax deposit and its due date by completing the following table (use Figure 8.5 for the dates):

Date	Date of Deposit	Amount of Deposit
10/7	?	?
10/14	?	?
10/21	?	?
10/28	?	?

Solutions to Self-Review Quiz 8-2

> The tax for Form 941 is
>   FICA OASDI: employee and employer
>   FICA Medicare: employee and employer
>   FIT: employee only

1. As a monthly depositor, Carol Ann's deposit date is Wednesday, November 15. The total amount of the deposit is $5,924.48 ($2,088.13 + $607.35 + $3,229.00).
2. As a semiweekly depositor, Carol Ann's deposit schedule is completed as follows:

Date	Date of Deposit	Amount of Deposit	
10/7	10/13	$1,484.61	($486.56 + $169.05 + $829.00)
10/14	10/20	$1,698.16	
10/21	10/27	$1,444.48	
10/28	11/3	$1,297.23*	

*Note that this deposit will be made in November according to the calendar dates found in Figure 8.5.

Learning Unit 8-3 Preparing Forms W-2 and W-3, Paying FUTA Tax and Completing the Employer's Annual Unemployment Tax Return, Form 940, and Paying SUTA Tax and Workers' Compensation Insurance

Preparing Form W-2: Wage and Tax Statement

LO5

The Internal Revenue Service requires that employers complete Form W-2, Wage and Tax Statement, a multipart form, each calendar year. The IRS requires Travelwithus.com to give or mail copies of Form W-2 to each person who worked for the company in the past year. These forms must be distributed by January 31 of the following year. Employees use the amount on this form to prepare their income tax returns and calculate the amount of income tax they owe. They must attach one copy of the form to their federal income tax return, and other copies are attached to any state or local income tax returns that they may be required to file.

Figure 8.8 shows the W-2 that Stephanie Higuera received from Travelwithus.com. Travelwithus.com prepares the W-2s by using information from Stephanie's employee earnings record. Note that OASDI wages and taxes are shown separately from the amounts reported for Medicare wages and taxes because of the wage base limit for the OASDI tax that does not apply to the Medicare tax.

If an employee stopped working for Travelwithus.com during the year, he or she may ask for a W-2 before the year ends. Travelwithus.com must provide the W-2 within 30 days of the last paycheck or the date of the request, whichever is later. Travelwithus.com must also give copies of the W-2s for all employees to the Social Security Administration and state and local governments. It will also keep a copy for its own records.

FIGURE 8.8 Completed Form W-2

a Control number	22222	Void ☐	For Official Use Only ▶ OMB No. 1545-0008		
b Employer identification number (EIN) 58-1213479				**1** Wages, tips, other compensation 23 723.40	**2** Federal income tax withheld 2 241.86
c Employer's name, address, and ZIP code TRAVELWITHUS.COM 10 LOVETT ROAD SALEM, MA 01970				**3** Social security wages 23 723.40	**4** Social security tax withheld 1470.85
				5 Medicare wages and tips 23 723.40	**6** Medicare tax withheld 343.99
				7 Social security tips	**8** Allocated tips
d Employee's social security number 123-45-6789				**9** Advance EIC payment	**10** Dependent care benefits
e Employee's first name and initial STEPHANIE A.	Last name HIGUERA		Suff.	**11** Nonqualified plans	**12a** See instructions for box 12
1014 INVERNESS WAY SOUTHSIDE, MA 01945				**13** Statutory employee ☐ Retirement plan ☐ Third-party sick pay ☐	**12b**
				14 Other	**12c**
					12d
f Employee's address and ZIP code					

15 State Employer's state ID number MA 621-8966-4	**16** State wages, tips, etc. 23 723.40	**17** State income tax 1 897.87	**18** Local wages, tips, etc.	**19** Local income tax	**20** Locality name

Form **W-2** Wage and Tax Statement   **200X**   Department of the Treasury—Internal Revenue Service

Copy A For Social Security Administration — Send this entire page with Form W-3 to the Social Security Administration; photocopies are **not** acceptable.

For Privacy Act and Paperwork Reduction Act Notice, see back of Copy D.

Cat. No. 10134D

Do Not Cut, Fold, or Staple Forms on This Page — Do Not Cut, Fold, or Staple Forms on This Page

Preparing Form W-3: Transmittal of Income and Tax Statements

The IRS also requires Travelwithus.com to prepare its **Form W-3, Transmittal of Wage and Tax Statements.** Employers such as Travelwithus.com send this form to the Social Security Administration along with copies of the W-2s for all employees (see Fig. 8.9). Form W-3 reports the total amounts of wages, tips, and compensation paid to employees, the total OASDI and Medicare taxes withheld, and some other information. The information used to complete Form W-3 came from a summary of the individual employee earnings records that Katherine prepared soon after the year ended. (See Fig. 8.10.)

FIGURE 8.9 Completed Form W-3

DO NOT STAPLE

a Control number	33333	For Official Use Only ▶ OMB No. 1545-0008		
b Kind of Payer ▶	941 ☒ Military ☐ 943 ☐ 944 ☐ CT-1 ☐ Hshld. emp. ☐ Medicare govt. emp. ☐ Third-party sick pay ☐	1 Wages, tips, other compensation **286 425.30**		2 Federal income tax withheld **48 063.67**
		3 Social security wages **284 925.30**		4 Social security tax withheld **17655.37**
c Total number of Forms W-2 **6**	d Establishment number	5 Medicare wages and tips **286 425.30**		6 Medicare tax withheld **4 153.17**
e Employer identification number (EIN) **58-1213479**		7 Social security tips		8 Allocated tips
f Employer's name **TRAVELWITHUS.COM**		9 Advance EIC payments		10 Dependent care benefits
		11 Nonqualified plans		12 Deferred compensation
10 LOVETT ROAD **SALEM, MA 01970**		13 For third-party sick pay use only		
g Employer's address and ZIP code		14 Income tax withheld by payer of third-party sick pay		
h Other EIN used this year				
15 State **MA** Employer's state ID number **621-8966-4**		16 State wages, tips, etc. **286 425.30**		17 State income tax **22 914.02**
		18 Local wages, tips, etc.		19 Local income tax
Contact person **KATHERINE C. KURTZ**		Telephone number (**978**) **555 4040**		For Official Use Only
Email address **KKURTZ@TRAVELWITH.US**		Fax number (**978**) **555 4040**		

Under penalties of perjury, I declare that I have examined this return and accompanying documents, and, to the best of my knowledge and belief, they are true, correct, and complete.

Signature ▶ *Katherine C. Kurtz*   Title ▶ **CONTROLLER**   Date ▶ **2/28/200X**

Form **W-3** Transmittal of Wage and Tax Statements   **200X**   Department of the Treasury Internal Revenue Service

Send this entire page with the entire Copy A page of Form(s) W-2 to the Social Security Administration. Photocopies are not acceptable.

Do not send any payment (cash, checks, money orders, etc.) with Forms W-2 and W-3.

Employers send Form W-2 and Form W-3 to the Social Security Administration for FICA tax purposes. The Social Security Administration, under a special agreement with the IRS, makes all information found on individual W-2 forms electronically available to the IRS so that it can check the accuracy of the employer's 941 forms and individual employees' federal income tax returns.

Paying FUTA Tax

LO4

If the total FUTA tax owed for the calendar year is less than $500, an employer must pay the tax to the IRS by the end of January of the next year. If the total amount owed is more than $500, then it is due by the end of the month following the end of the calendar quarter. If the employer is required to make Form 941 tax payments by EFTPS, then it must also deposit FUTA tax by this method; if not, the deposit can be made by check accompanied with Form 8109, Federal Tax Deposit Coupon, at a Federal Reserve Bank or authorized depository.

By the end of the year, all of Travelwithus.com's employees earned more than the $7,000 wage base limit, so its total FUTA tax will be calculated as follows:

6 employees × $7,000 FUTA taxable earnings × 0.8%* FUTA tax rate = $336 FUTA tax

---

*Normal FUTA Tax credit 6.2%–5.4%.

FIGURE 8.10 W-3 Worksheet

Employee	Total Earnings	FICA Taxable Earnings		FICA Tax		FIT
		OASDI	Medicare	OASDI	Medicare	
Goldman, Ernie	103 500 00	102 000 00	103 500 00	6 324 00	1 500 75	20 097 00
Higuera, Stephanie	23 723 40	23 723 40	23 723 40	1 470 85	343 99	2 241 86
Kurtz, Katherine	66 448 16	66 448 16	66 448 16	4 119 79	963 50	12 625 15
Regan, Julia	58 500 00	58 500 00	58 500 00	3 627 00	848 25	9 945 00
Sui, Annie	8 287 14	8 287 14	8 287 14	513 80	120 16	1 077 33
Taylor, Harold	25 966 60	25 966 60	25 966 60	1 609 93	376 52	2 077 33
Total	286 425 30	284 925 30	286 425 30	17 665 37	4 153 17	48 063 67

TRAVELWITHUS.COM INC. — W-3 Amounts — YTD Totals

Because this amount is less than $500, Katherine does not need to make a deposit during the year and will deposit the taxes by the end of January of the following year. She then makes the following journal entry to record the payment of FUTA tax.

	Date			PR	Dr.	Cr.
	200X					
	Jan.	31	FUTA Payable		336 00	
			Cash			336 00
			To record payment of the 200X FUTA			
			tax			

GENERAL JOURNAL

Completing the Employer's Annual Federal Unemployment (FUTA) Tax Return, Form 940

Businesses must complete **Form 940, Employer's Annual Federal Unemployment (FUTA) Tax Return.** Employers must file Form 940 by January 31 of the following year; however, if all taxes owed for the year were deposited by January 31, then the business has until February 10 to file its return.

To make sure that Travelwithus.com makes its FUTA deposits on time, Katherine keeps track of the amount of FUTA tax owed. Katherine prepared the worksheet in Figure 8.11 to determine the amount of FUTA taxes that Travelwithus.com owes for the first quarter of the year. Notice that she calculates the FUTA tax on the total wages because reporting the FUTA tax for each individual employee is not required. Also notice that Annie Sui has no earnings for the first quarter and therefore no earnings that are taxable for FUTA purposes because she was hired after the quarter began. Finally, notice that Ernie Goldman, Katherine Kurtz, and Julia Regan's first quarter earnings are greater than their FUTA taxable earnings because they earned more than $7,000 during the first quarter, and only the first $7,000 of earnings is taxable.

Although Travelwithus.com's other payroll amounts have been shown for the last quarter of the year, showing FUTA tax calculations for this quarter would not be very helpful. Almost all employees will have made more than the $7,000 FUTA limit by the start of the fourth quarter, and Travelwithus.com would only owe FUTA taxes for one employee, Annie Sui, who was hired just before the fourth quarter began.

At the end of the calendar year, Katherine prepares the Form 940 in Figure 8.12. Line-by-line instructions follow:

Part 1:

Line 1a: This line is used to show the state in which payments are made if only one state is involved.

1b is used by employers who pay state unemployment in more than one state.

Part 2:   *Reporting taxable wages and FUTA tax.*

Line 3:   Katherine shows the total wages and salaries paid during the year, $286,425.30, as shown on the W-3 worksheet.

4: This line is used to show any payments that are exempt from FUTA taxes, and does not apply to Travelwithus.com.

5: This line shows the amount of wages and salaries above the $7,000 limit, which is $244,425.30. Because the six employees all reached the $7,000 limit, the total limit is $42,000. Total wages and salaries of $286,425.30 minus taxable wages and salaries of $42,000 equals $244,425.30.

6: Katherine adds the total of lines 4 and 5 and gets $244,425.30.

7: Katherine subtracts line 6 from line 3 to determine the taxable amount of wages and salaries, $42,000.

8: Katherine multiplies line 7, $42,000, by the FUTA tax rate of .008 to get the total FUTA tax of $336.00 for the year.

Part 3 is used to determine adjustments to the FUTA tax calculated in line 8, if any.

Part 4 is used to calculate your FUTA tax.

12: This is the amount of FUTA tax less any adjustments made in Part 3. Travelwithus.com did not have any adjustments.

13: This line shows the amount of FUTA tax that Travelwithus.com paid for the year.

14 and 15: Travelwithus.com paid exactly the right amount of FUTA tax for the year; therefore, no balance is due and no overpayment was made.

Part 5:   *Showing the tax liability by quarter.*

Katherine divides the total FUTA tax for the year into the quarters where the tax liability originated. Notice that the amount of FUTA tax for the first quarter matches the amount that Katherine calculated on the FUTA tax worksheet in Figure 8.11.

FIGURE 8.11 FUTA Worksheet

TRAVELWITHUS.COM INC.
FUTA Taxes
1st Quarter

Employee	1st Quarter Earnings	FUTA Taxable Earnings	FUTA Tax Rate	FUTA Tax
Goldman, Ernie	23 9 2 5 00	7 0 0 0 00		
Higuera, Stephanie	5 9 2 8 00	5 9 2 8 00		
Kurtz, Katherine	16 6 1 2 04	7 0 0 0 00		
Regan, Julia	14 6 2 5 00	7 0 0 0 00		
Sui, Annie				
Taylor, Harold	5 3 2 5 59	5 3 2 5 59		
Total	66 4 1 5 63	32 2 5 3 59	0 008	2 5 8 03

FIGURE 8.12 Completed Form 940

Form **940 for 200X:** **Employer's Annual Federal Unemployment (FUTA) Tax Return**
Department of the Treasury — Internal Revenue Service

850108

OMB No. 1545-0028

(EIN)
Employer identification number 5 8 – 1 2 1 3 4 7 9

Type of Return
(Check all that apply.)

Name *(not your trade name)*

Trade name *(if any)* TRAVEL WITH US . COM

Address 10 LOVETT ROAD
Number   Street   Suite or room number

SALEM   MA   01970
City   State ZIP code

☐ **a.** Amended
☐ **b.** Successor employer
☐ **c.** No payments to employees in 2008
☐ **d.** Final: Business closed or stopped paying wages

Read the separate instructions before you fill out this form. Please type or print within the boxes.

Part 1: Tell us about your return. If any line does NOT apply, leave it blank.

1 If you were required to pay your state unemployment tax in ...

    1a One state only, write the state abbreviation . . . . **1a** m A
    - OR -
    1b More than one state (You are a multi-state employer) . . . . **1b** ☐ Check here. Fill out Schedule A.
                   Skip line 2 for 2008 and go to line 3.
2 If you paid wages in a state that is subject to **CREDIT REDUCTION** . . . . **2** ☐ Check here. Fill out Schedule A (Form 940), Part 2.

Part 2: Determine your FUTA tax before adjustments for 2008. If any line does NOT apply, leave it blank.

3 Total payments to all employees . . . . **3** $ 286,425 . 30

4 Payments exempt from FUTA tax . . . . **4** Ø .

    Check all that apply: **4a** ☐ Fringe benefits   **4c** ☐ Retirement/Pension   **4e** ☐ Other
                    4b ☐ Group-term life insurance   **4d** ☐ Dependent care

5 Total of payments made to each employee in excess of $7,000 . . . . **5** 244,425 . 30

6 Subtotal (line 4 + line 5 = line 6) . . . . **6** 244,425 . 30

7 Total taxable FUTA wages (line 3 – line 6 = line 7) . . . . **7** 42,000 . 00

8 FUTA tax before adjustments (line 7 × .008 = line 8) . . . . **8** 336 . 00

Part 3: Determine your adjustments. If any line does NOT apply, leave it blank.

9 If ALL of the taxable FUTA wages you paid were excluded from state unemployment tax, multiply line 7 by .054 (line 7 × .054 = line 9). Then go to line 12 . . . . **9** Ø .

10 If SOME of the taxable FUTA wages you paid were excluded from state unemployment tax, OR you paid ANY state unemployment tax late (after the due date for filing Form 940), fill out the worksheet in the instructions. Enter the amount from line 7 of the worksheet onto line 10 . **10** Ø .

                  Skip line 11 for 2008 and go to line 12.
11 If credit reduction applies, enter the amount from line 3 of Schedule A (Form 940) . . . . **11** .

Part 4: Determine your FUTA tax and balance due or overpayment for 2008. If any line does NOT apply, leave it blank.

12 Total FUTA tax after adjustments (lines 8 + 9 + 10 + 11 = line 12) . . . . **12** 336 . 00

13 FUTA tax deposited for the year, including any payment applied from a prior year . . . **13** 336 . 00

14 Balance due (If line 12 is more than line 13, enter the difference on line 14.)
    • If line 14 is more than $500, you must deposit your tax.
    • If line 14 is $500 or less, you may pay with this return. For more information on how to pay, see the separate instructions . . . . **14** .

15 Overpayment (If line 13 is more than line 12, enter the difference on line 15 and check a box below.) . . . . **15** .

                              Check one: ☐ Apply to next return.
                                    ☐ Send a refund.

▶ You **MUST** fill out both pages of this form and **SIGN** it.

Next ➡

For Privacy Act and Paperwork Reduction Act Notice, see the back of Form 940-V, Payment Voucher.   Cat. No. 11234O   Form **940** (2008)

FIGURE 8.12 (continued)

Name *(not your trade name)*	Employer identification number (EIN)
	58-1213479

Part 5: Report your FUTA tax liability by quarter only if line 12 is more than $500. If not, go to Part 6.

16   Report the amount of your FUTA tax liability for each quarter; do **NOT** enter the amount you deposited. If you had no liability for a quarter, leave the line blank.

16a   **1st quarter** (January 1 – March 31) **16a**

16b   **2nd quarter** (April 1 – June 30) **16b**

16c   **3rd quarter** (July 1 – September 30) **16c**

16d   **4th quarter** (October 1 – December 31) **16d**

17   **Total tax liability for the year** (lines 16a + 16b + 16c + 16d = line 17) **17**   **Total must equal line 12.**

Part 6: May we speak with your third-party designee?

Do you want to allow an employee, a paid tax preparer, or another person to discuss this return with the IRS? See the instructions for details.

☐   **Yes.**   Designee's name and phone number   (   )   –

Select a 5-digit Personal Identification Number (PIN) to use when talking to IRS

☐   **No.**

Part 7: Sign here. You MUST fill out both pages of this form and SIGN it.

Under penalties of perjury, I declare that I have examined this return, including accompanying schedules and statements, and to the best of my knowledge and belief, it is true, correct, and complete, and that no part of any payment made to a state unemployment fund claimed as a credit was, or is to be, deducted from the payments made to employees. Declaration of preparer (other than taxpayer) is based on all information of which preparer has any knowledge.

✗ Sign your name here   *Katherine C. Kurtz*

Date   2, 10, 200X

Print your name here   KATHERINE C. KURTZ

Print your title here   Controller

Best daytime phone   (   )   –

Paid preparer's use only   Check if you are self-employed . . . . ☐

Preparer's name		Preparer's SSN/PTIN	
Preparer's signature		Date	/ /
Firm's name (or yours if self-employed)		EIN	
Address		Phone	( ) –
City	State	ZIP code	

Paying SUTA Tax

State Unemployment Tax Act (SUTA) taxes are paid to the government of the state in which a business is located and are typically due by the end of the month following each calendar quarter. Employers also usually are required to complete a state unemployment tax report, much like they complete Form 940. Using the first quarter earnings, Katherine calculates the SUTA tax due for the first quarter as follows:

$32,253.59 SUTA taxable earnings × 5.4% SUTA tax rate = $1,741.69

The journal entry to record the payment of SUTA follows:

		GENERAL JOURNAL			
Date			PR	Dr.	Cr.
200X					
April	30	SUTA Payable		1741 69	
		Cash			1741 69
		To record payment of the SUTA			
		tax for the quarter ending March 31,			
		200X			

Paying Workers' Compensation Insurance

Remember from Chapter 7 that the premium for **workers' compensation insurance** is paid at the beginning of the year based on estimated gross payroll for the year, and the journal entry to record this payment is as follows:

		GENERAL JOURNAL			
Date			PR	Dr.	Cr.
200X					
Jan.	5	Prepaid Workers' Compensation Insurance		1318 00	
		Cash			1318 00
		To record payment of the workers'			
		compensation insurance premium			
		for 200X			

Like any prepaid amount, this amount will gradually be transferred from the Prepaid Workers' Compensation Insurance account, an asset, to the Workers' Compensation Insurance Expense account in the month-end adjusting entries for 200X.

At the end of the year, if Travelwithus.com owes an additional premium because actual gross payroll was higher than estimated gross payroll, the payment of the additional premium would be recorded as follows:

		GENERAL JOURNAL			
Date			PR	Dr.	Cr.
200X					
Dec.	31	Workers' Compensation Insurance Expense		211 32	
		Cash			211 32
		To record payment of the additional			
		workers' compensation insurance			
		premium for 200X			

LEARNING UNIT 8-3 REVIEW

AT THIS POINT / you should be able to

- Prepare a Form W-2 and a Form W-3.
- Explain the difference between a Form W-2 and a Form W-3.
- Prepare Form 940.
- Explain when FUTA and SUTA taxes are paid.
- Explain when workers' compensation insurance premiums are paid.
- Record the payment of FUTA, SUTA, and workers' compensation insurance amounts.

Self-Review Quiz 8-3

Are the following statements true or false?

1. Employees must receive W-4s by January 31 of the following year.
2. Form W-3 is sent to the Social Security Administration yearly.
3. A Form 940 can only be prepared by a business that employs workers in only one state.
4. The Employer's Annual Federal Unemployment Tax Return reports the employer's FICA and FIT tax liabilities.
5. A FUTA tax liability of $500 must be paid 10 days after the quarter ends.
6. Premiums for workers' compensation insurance may be adjusted based on actual payroll figures.

Solutions to Self-Review Quiz 8-3

1. False. W-2 forms must be sent to each employee by January 31 of the following year. The W-4 form is filled out by a new employee and is used for calculating federal and state income taxes.
2. True.
3. False. Form 940 can be prepared by a business that employs workers in one or more states.
4. False. The Employee's Annual Federal Unemployment Tax Return, Form 940, reports the FUTA tax liability. Form 941 reports the FICA and FIT tax liabilities.
5. False. A FUTA tax liability of $500 must be paid one month after the quarter ends.
6. True.

> Remember that the employee completes a W-4 when hired. The employer completes a W-2 for the employee at the end of the year.

CHAPTER ASSIGNMENTS

SUMMARY OF KEY POINTS

LEARNING UNIT 8-1

1. The payroll register provides the data for journalizing the payroll in the general journal.
2. Deductions for payroll withholding taxes represent liabilities of the employer until paid.
3. The Accounts Charged columns of the payroll register indicate which accounts will be debited to record the total wages and salaries expense when a journal entry is prepared.
4. The accounts FICA OASDI Payable and FICA Medicare Payable accumulate the tax liabilities of both the employer and the employee for OASDI and Medicare taxes.

5. The payroll tax expense is recorded at the same time that the payroll is recorded.
6. Paying a payroll results in debiting Wages and Salaries Payable and crediting Cash or Payroll Cash.

LEARNING UNIT 8-2

1. Federal Form 941 is prepared and filed no later than one month after the calendar quarter ends. It reports the amount of FIT, OASDI, and Medicare tax withheld from employees and the OASDI and Medicare taxes due from the employer for the calendar quarter.
2. FIT, OASDI, and Medicare taxes are known as Form 941 taxes.
3. The total amount of Form 941 taxes paid by a business during a specific period of time determines how often the business will have to make its payroll tax deposits. This time period is called a look-back period.
4. Businesses will normally make their payroll tax deposits to pay their Form 941 taxes either monthly or semiweekly.
5. Different deposit rules apply to monthly and semiweekly depositors and these rules determine when deposits are due.
6. Form 941 payroll tax deposits must be made using Form 8109, known as the Federal Tax Deposit Coupon, unless they are made by EFTPS.

LEARNING UNIT 8-3

1. Information to prepare W-2 forms can be obtained from the individual employee earnings records.
2. Form W-3 is used by the Social Security Administration in verifying that taxes have been withheld as reported on individual employee W-2 forms.
3. Form 940 is prepared by January 31, after the end of the previous calendar year. This form can be filed by February 10 if all required deposits have been made by January 31.
4. If the amount of FUTA taxes is equal to or more than $500 during any calendar quarter, the deposit must be made no later than one month after the quarter ends. If the amount is less than $500, no deposit is required until the liability reaches the $500 point or until the year ends, when any tax due must be paid by January 31 of the following year.
5. The premium for workers' compensation insurance based on estimated payroll for the year is paid at the beginning of the year by the employer to protect against potential losses to its employees due to accidental death or injury incurred while on the job.

KEY TERMS

Banking day   A banking day is any day that a bank is open to the public for business. Generally, a banking day will end at 2:00 or 3:00 P.M. local time. Banking business transacted after this time is usually considered to be the next day's business. Saturdays, Sundays, and federal holidays are usually not considered banking days.

Calendar quarter   A three-month, 13-week time period. Four calendar quarters occur during a calendar year that runs from January 1 through December 31. The first quarter is January through March, the second is April through June, the third is July through September, and the fourth is October through December.

Employer identification number (EIN)   A number assigned by the IRS that is used by an employer when recording and paying payroll and income taxes.

Federal Insurance Contribution Act (FICA)   Part of the Social Security law that requires employees and employers to pay OASDI taxes and Medicare taxes.

Federal Unemployment Tax Act (FUTA)   A tax paid by employers to the federal government. The current rate is 0.8% on the first $7,000 of earnings of each employee after the normal FUTA tax credit is applied.

Form SS-4   The form filled out by an employer to get an EIN. The form is sent to the IRS, which assigns the number to the business.

Form W-2, Wage and Tax Statement A form completed by the employer at the end of the calendar year to provide a summary of gross earnings and deductions to each employee. At least two copies go to the employee, one copy to the IRS, one copy to any state where employee income taxes have been withheld, one copy to the Social Security Administration, and one copy into the records of the business.

Form W-3, Transmittal of Income and Tax Statement A form completed by the employer to verify the number of W-2s and amounts withheld as shown on them. This form is sent to the Social Security Administration data processing center along with copies of each employee's W-2 forms.

Form 8109, Federal Tax Deposit Coupon A coupon that is completed and sent along with payments of tax deposits relating to Forms 940, 941, or 944. This form can also be used to deposit other types of taxes a business may owe the federal government.

Form 940, Employer's Annual Federal Unemployment Tax Return This form is used by employers at the end of the calendar year to report the amount of unemployment tax due for the year. If more than $500 is cumulatively owed in a quarter, it should be paid quarterly, one month after the end of the quarter. Normally, the report is due January 31 after the calendar year, or February 10 if an employer has already made all deposits.

Form 941, Employer's Quarterly Federal Tax Return A tax report that a business will complete after the end of each calendar quarter indicating the total FICA (OASDI and Medicare) taxes owed plus the amount of FIT withheld from employees' pay for the quarter. If federal tax deposits have been made on time, the total amount deposited should equal the amount due on Form 941. Any difference results in a payment due or a refund.

Form 941 taxes Another term used to describe FIT, OASDI, and Medicare. This name comes from the form used to report these taxes.

Form 944, Employer's Annual Federal Tax Return The new, other version of the form used by employers to report FICA (OASDI and Medicare) taxes owed and the amount of FIT withheld from an employee's pay. This version will be filed by January 31 following the end of the year and can be used by employers who owe $2,500 or less for theses taxes and who have been told by the IRS that they must file this form.

Look-back period A period of time used to determine whether a business should make its Form 941 tax deposits on a monthly or semiweekly basis. The IRS defined this period as July 1 through June 30 of the year prior to the year in which Form 941 tax deposits will be made.

Monthly depositor A business classified as a monthly depositor will make its payroll tax deposits only once each month for the amount of Form 941 taxes due from the prior month.

Payroll tax expense The cost to employers includes the total of the employer's FICA OASDI, FICA Medicare, FUTA, and SUTA taxes.

Semiweekly depositor A business classified as a semiweekly depositor may make its payroll tax deposits up to twice in one week, depending on when payroll is paid.

State Unemployment Tax Act (SUTA) A tax usually paid only by employers to the state for employee unemployment insurance.

Workers' compensation insurance Insurance paid, in advance, by an employer to protect its employees against loss due to accidental death or injury incurred during employment.

BLUEPRINT: FORM 941 TAX DEPOSIT RULES

Ten Frequently Asked Questions and Answers About Depositing OASDI, Medicare, and FIT to the Government

Here is a summary of questions and answers to help you understand the payroll tax deposit rules for Form 941 taxes:

1. **What are Form 941 taxes?** The term *Form 941 taxes* is used to describe the amount of FIT, OASDI, and Medicare paid by employees and the amount of OASDI and Medicare taxes that are matched and paid by an employer. The total of these taxes is known as Form 941 taxes because it is reported on Form 941 each quarter.

2. **When does an employer deposit Form 941 taxes?** How often an employer deposits Form 941 taxes depends on how the employer is classified for this purpose. The IRS usually classifies an employer as either a monthly or semiweekly depositor based on the amount of Form 941 taxes paid during a time period known as a look-back period.

3. **When is a look-back period?** A look-back period is a fiscal year that begins on July 1 and ends on June 30 of the year before the calendar year when the deposits will be made. For example, for the 2008 calendar year, an employer's look-back period will begin on July 1, 2006, and end on June 30, 2007.

4. **What is the dollar amount used to classify an employer for Form 941 tax deposits?** The key dollar amount used to determine whether an employer is a monthly or semiweekly depositor is $50,000 in Form 941 taxes. Two rules apply here:
   a. If the total amount deposited in Form 941 taxes is less than $50,000 during the look-back period, the employer is considered a monthly tax depositor.
   b. If the total amount deposited in Form 941 taxes is $50,000 or more during the look-back period, the employer is considered a semiweekly tax depositor.

5. **How do employers deposit Form 941 taxes?** Unless it makes its deposits by EFTPS, an employer fills out a Form 8109, Federal Tax Deposit Coupon, and gives this form with a check to a bank authorized to receive payroll tax deposits or to a Federal Reserve Bank. Usually, authorized banks will only take checks written from an account maintained at that same bank. Therefore, an employer usually cannot make a Form 941 deposit at Bank A using a check written from an account maintained at Bank B. A Federal Reserve Bank will accept a check from any U.S. bank for payroll tax deposit purposes.

6. **When do monthly depositors make their deposits?** A monthly depositor will figure the total amount of Form 941 taxes owed in a calendar month and then pay this amount by the 15th of the next month. If an employer owes $3,125 in Form 941 taxes for the month of June, it will deposit this same amount no later than July 15 of the same year.

7. **When do semiweekly depositors make their deposits?** The rules for making deposits are a little more complicated for a semiweekly depositor. The depositor may have to make up to two Form 941 deposits each week. When a tax deposit is due depends on when the employees are paid. To keep the rules consistent, the IRS has taken a calendar week and divided it into two payday time periods. It is easiest to think of a two-week period of time when discussing these periods: Wednesday through Friday of week 1, and Saturday of week 1 through Tuesday of week 2.

   Two deposit rules apply to these two time periods. We can call these rules the Wednesday and Friday rules.
   a. Wednesday rule: If employees are paid during the Wednesday through Friday of week 1 period, the tax deposit will be due on Wednesday of week 2.
   b. Friday rule: If employees are paid anytime from Saturday of week 1 through Tuesday of week 2, the tax deposit will be due on Friday of week 2.

   These rules mean that the payroll tax deposit will be due three banking days after the payday time period ends. For the Wednesday rule, the deposit is due three banking days after Friday of week 1, on the following Wednesday in week 2. For the Friday rule, the deposit is due three banking days after Tuesday of week 2, on Friday of week 2. The following illustration shows how this timing works.

	Week 1							Week 2						
	Sun	Mon	Tues	Wed	Thur	Fri	Sat	Sun	Mon	Tues	Wed	Thur	Fri	Sat
If payday is														
Then deposit is due														

8. **What is a banking day?** The term *banking day* refers to any day that a bank is open to the public for business. Saturdays, Sundays, and legal holidays are not banking days.

9. **How do legal holidays affect payroll tax deposits?** If a legal holiday occurs after the last day of a payday time period, the employer will get one extra day to make its Form 941 tax deposit as follows:
   a. For monthly depositors: If the 15th of the month is a Saturday, Sunday, or legal holiday, the deposit will be due and payable on the next banking day.
   b. For semiweekly depositors: A deposit due on Wednesday will be due on Thursday of the same week, and a Friday deposit will be due on Monday of the following week. Remember that the employer will always have three banking days after the last day of either payday time period to make its payroll tax deposit.

10. **What happens if an employer is late with its Form 941 tax deposit?** If a Form 941 tax deposit is not made the day it should be deposited, the employer may be assessed a fine for lateness and may even be charged interest, depending on how late the deposit is.

QUESTIONS, CLASSROOM DEMONSTRATION EXERCISES, EXERCISES, AND PROBLEMS

Discussion and Critical Thinking Questions/Ethical Case

1. What taxes are recorded when recording Payroll Tax Expense?

2. What is a calendar year?

3. An employer must always use a calendar year for payroll purposes. Agree or disagree?

4. Why does payroll information center on 13-week quarters?

5. How is an employer classified as a monthly or semiweekly depositor for Form 941 tax purposes?

6. What is the purpose of Form 8109?

7. How often is Form 941 completed?

8. Under what circumstance(s) does the amount on line 15 of Form 941 match the amount found on line 10?

9. Bill Smith leaves his job on July 9. He requests a copy of his W-2 form when he leaves. His boss tells him to wait until January of next year. Please discuss whether Bill's boss is correct in making this statement.

10. Why would one employer prepare a Form 940 completing Part 1 line 1a, but another would prepare a Form 940 Part 1 line 1 b?

11. Employer A has a FUTA tax liability of $67.49 on March 31 of the current year. When does the employer have to make the deposit for this liability?

12. Employer B has a FUTA tax liability of $553.24 on January 31 of the current year. When does the employer have to make the deposit for this liability?

13. Who completes Form W-4? Form W-2? Form W-3? When is each form completed?

14. Why is the year-end adjusting entry needed for workers' compensation insurance?

15. Happy Carpet Cleaning, Inc., collects FIT, OASDI, and Medicare from its employees by withholding these taxes from its employees' pay. However, Happy does not pay these amounts to the federal government until the end of the calendar year so that it can maximize its cash during the year. Because it will be paying these amounts to the government, it believes that this practice does not affect its employees. Please comment on this practice.

Classroom Demonstration Exercises

SET A

LO1 (10 min)   **Account Classifications**

1. Complete the following table:

Accounts Affected	Category	↑ ↓	Rules
a. Payroll Tax Expense			
b. FICA OASDI Payable			
c. SIT Payable			
d. SUTA Payable			
e. Prepaid Workers' Compensation Insurance			

LO1, 2, 3 (10 min)   **Look-Back Periods**

2. Label the following look-back periods for 200C by months.

A	B	C	D
200A		200B	

LO1, 2, 3 (15 min)   **Monthly versus Semiweekly Depositor**

3. In December 200B, Lin is trying to find out whether she is a monthly or semi-weekly depositor for FICA (OASDI and Medicare) and federal income tax for 200C. Please advise based on the following taxes owed:

200A	Quarter 3	$28,000
	Quarter 4	12,000
200B	Quarter 1	3,000
	Quarter 2	10,000

LO1, 2, 3 (15 min)   **Paying the Tax**

4. Complete the following table:

Depositor	4-Quarter Look-Back Period Tax Liability	Payroll Paid	Tax Paid by
Monthly	$28,000	November	a.
Semiweekly	$66,000	On Wednesday	b.
		On Thursday	c.
		On Friday	d.
		On Saturday	e.
		On Sunday	f.
		On Monday	g.

LO1, 2, 3 (15 min)   **Payroll Account**

5. Indicate which of the following items apply to the following account titles.
   1. An asset
   2. A liability
   3. An expense

4. Appears on the income statement
5. Appears on the balance sheet
_____ **a.** FICA OASDI Payable
_____ **b.** Office Salaries Expense
_____ **c.** Federal Income Tax Payable
_____ **d.** FICA Medicare Payable
_____ **e.** Wages and Salaries Payable

SET B

Account Classifications   *LO1 (10 min)*

   1. Complete the following table:

Accounts Affected	Category	↑ ↓	Rules
a. Store Wage Expense			
b. Federal Income Tax Payable			
c. FICA Medicare Payable			
d. Medical Insurance Payable			
e. Payroll Cash			

Look-Back Periods   *LO1, 2, 3 (10 min)*

   2. Label the following look-back periods for 200E by months.

A	B	C	D
200C		200D	

Monthly versus Semiweekly Depositor   *LO1, 2, 3 (15 min)*

   3. In December 200B, Heather tries to find out whether she is a monthly or semi-weekly depositor for FICA (OASDI and Medicare) and federal income tax for 200C. Please advise based on the following taxes owed:

200A	Quarter 3	$11,000
	Quarter 4	2,000
200B	Quarter 1	3,000
	Quarter 2	10,000

Paying the Tax   *LO1, 2, 3 (15 min)*

   4. Complete the following table:

Depositor	4-Quarter Look-Back Period Tax Liability	Payroll Paid	Tax Paid by
Monthly	$36,000	October	a.
Semiweekly	$56,000	On Wednesday	b.
		On Thursday	c.
		On Friday	d.
		On Saturday	e.
		On Sunday	f.
		On Monday	g.

LO1, 2, 3 (15 min)   **Payroll Account**

5. Indicate which of the following items apply to the following account titles.
   1. An asset
   2. A liability
   3. An expense
   4. Appears on the income statement
   5. Appears on the balance sheet
_____ **a.** FICA OASDI Payable
_____ **b.** Store Wage Expense
_____ **c.** State Income Tax Payable
_____ **d.** FICA Medicare Payable
_____ **e.** Wages and Salaries Payable

Exercises

LO1, 2 (10 min)   **8-1.** Complete the table.

Item	Category	Normal Balance	Account Appears on Which Financial Statements?
Medical Insurance Payable			
Wages and Salaries Payable			
Office Salaries Expense			
Market Wages Expense			
FICA OASDI Payable			
Federal Income Tax Payable			
State Income Tax Payable			

LO1, 2 (20 min)   **8-2.** The following amounts were taken from the weekly payroll register for the Wu Lee Company on October 9, 200X. Using the same account title headings used in this chapter, please prepare the general journal entry to record the payroll for the Wu Lee Company for October 9.

Plant Wages Expense	$7,158.00
Office Salaries Expense	3,194.00
Deduction for FICA OASDI	592.30
Deduction for FICA Medicare	150.10
Deduction for federal income tax	2,225.68
Deduction for state income tax	517.60
Deduction for union dues	960.00

LO1, 2, 3 (20 min)   **8-3.** Use the information from Exercise 8-2 and the following information to prepare the general journal entry to record the payroll tax expense for the weekly payroll of October 9, 200X:

Wages below the FUTA tax wage base limit	$900.00
FUTA tax rate	.8%
Wages below the SUTA tax wage base limit	$900.00
SUTA tax rate	5.4%

LO1, 2, 3 (20 min)   **8-4.** At the end of February 200X, the total amount of OASDI, $590, and Medicare, $210, was withheld as tax deductions from the employees of Wheat Fields Inc. Federal income tax of $2,950 was also deducted from their paychecks. Wheat Fields is classified as a monthly depositor of Form 941 taxes. Indicate when this payroll tax deposit is due and provide a general journal entry to record the payment.

8-5. The following payroll journal entry was prepared by Palmdale Company from its payroll register. Which columns of the payroll register have the data come from? How do the taxable earnings columns of the payroll register relate to this entry?

LO1, 2 (15 min)

		GENERAL JOURNAL			
Date			PR	Dr.	Cr.
200X					
Oct.	15	Customer Service Expense		1 2 5 0 00	
		FIT Payable			1 3 7 50
		SIT Payable			7 5 00
		FICA OASDI Payable			7 7 50
		FICA Medicare Payable			1 8 13
		Payroll Cash			9 4 1 87
		To record payroll			

8-6. Carol's Grocery Store made the following Form 941 payroll tax deposits during the look-back period of July 1, 200A, through June 30, 200B:

LO1, 2, 3 (20 min)

Quarter Ended	Amount Paid in 941 Taxes
September 30, 200A	$15,783.26
December 31, 200A	13,893.22
March 31, 200B	13,601.94
June 30, 200B	14,021.01

Should Carol's Grocery Store make Form 941 tax deposits monthly or semiweekly for 200C?

8-7. If Carol's Grocery Store downsized its operation during the second quarter of 200B and, as a result, paid only $6,121.93 in Form 941 taxes for the quarter that ended on June 30, 200B, should Carol's Grocery make its Form 941 payroll tax deposits monthly or semiweekly for 200C?

LO1, 2, 3 (15 min)

8-8. From the following T accounts, record the following: (a) the July 3 payment for FICA (OASDI and Medicare) and federal income taxes, (b) the July 30 payment of SUTA tax, and (c) the July 30 deposit of any FUTA tax that may be required.

LO1, 2, 3 (15 min)

FICA OASDI Payable 203		FICA Medicare Payable 204	
	June 30 400 (EE)		June 30 100 (EE)
	400 (ER)		100 (ER)

FIT Payable 205		FUTA Tax Payable 206	
	June 30 3,005		June 30 143

SUTA Tax Payable 207	
	June 30 612

Group A Problems

LO1, 2, 3 (30 min)

8A-1. For the biweekly pay period ending on April 10 at Susie's Pet Store, the following partial payroll summary was taken from the individual employee earnings records. Use it to

1. Complete the table. Use the federal income tax withholding table in Figure 7.2 to figure the amount of income tax withheld.
2. Prepare a journal entry to record the payroll tax expense for Susie's. Please show the calculations for FICA taxes.

Check Figure:
Payroll Tax Expense $691.33

| | | | FICA | | |
Employee	Allowance and Marital Status	Gross	OASDI	Medicare	Federal Income Tax
Eddie Janway	S-1	$1,050			
Jan Kunz	S-0	900			
Julia Long	S-2	1,000			
Mike Roald	S-0	1,260			
Tom Valens	S-2	1,580			

Assume the FICA tax rate for OASDI is 6.2% up to $102,000 in earnings (no one earned this much as of April 10), and Medicare is 1.45% on all earnings. The state unemployment tax rate is 5.1% on the first $7,000 of earnings, and the federal unemployment tax rate is .8% of the first $7,000 of earnings. (Only Tom Valens earned more than $7,000 as of April 10.) In cases where the amount of FICA tax calculates to one-half cent, round up to the next cent.

LO1, 2, 3 (50 min)

8A-2. The following is the monthly payroll of White Company, owned by Dean White. Employees are paid on the last day of each month.

JANUARY

| | | | FICA | | |
Employee	Monthly Earnings	YTD Earnings	OASDI	Medicare	Federal Income Tax
Sam Koy	$1,950	$1,950	$120.90	$ 28.28	$ 258.00
Joy Lane	3,200	3,200	198.40	46.40	361.00
Amy Hess	3,800	3,800	235.60	55.10	500.00
	$8,950	$8,950	$554.90	$129.78	$1,119.00

FEBRUARY

| | | | FICA | | |
Employee	Monthly Earnings	YTD Earnings	OASDI	Medicare	Federal Income Tax
Sam Koy	$2,100	$ 4,050	$130.20	$ 30.45	$ 302.00
Joy Lane	3,350	6,550	207.70	48.58	325.00
Amy Hess	3,775	7,575	234.05	54.74	426.00
	$9,225	$18,175	$571.95	$133.77	$1,053.00

MARCH

| | | | FICA | | |
| | | | OASDI | Medicare | Federal Income Tax |
Employee	Monthly Earnings	YTD Earnings	OASDI	Medicare	
Sam Koy	$2,100	$ 6,150	$130.20	$ 30.45	$ 586.00
Joy Lane	2,500	9,050	155.00	36.25	558.00
Amy Hess	4,100	11,675	254.20	59.45	545.00
	$8,700	$26,875	$539.40	$126.15	$1,689.00

Check Figure:
Deposit of SUTA Tax $1,148.55

White Company is located at 2 Square Street, Marblehead, Massachusetts 01945. Its employer identification number is 29-3458822. The FICA tax rate for Social Security is 6.2% up to $102,000 in earnings during the year, and Medicare is 1.45% on all earnings. The SUTA tax rate is 5.7% on the first $7,000. The FUTA tax rate is .8% on the first $7,000 of earnings. White Company is classified as a monthly depositor for Form 941 taxes.

Your tasks are to

1. Journalize the entries to record the employer's payroll tax expense for each pay period in the general journal.
2. Journalize entries for the payment of each tax liability in the general journal.

8A-3. Ed Ward, the accountant for White Company, must complete Form 941 for the first quarter of the current year. Ed gathered the needed data as presented in Problem 8A-2. Suddenly called away to an urgent budget meeting, Ed requested that you assist him by preparing the Form 941 for the first quarter. Please note that the difference in the tax liability, a few cents, should be adjusted on line 7a; this difference is due to the rounding of FICA tax amounts.

LO1, 2, 3 (50 min)

Check Figure:
Total Liability for Quarter
$7,972.90

8A-4. The following is the monthly payroll for the last three months of the year for Henson's Sporting Goods Shop, 2 Boat Road, Lynn, Massachusetts 01945. The shop is a sole proprietorship owned and operated by Bill Henson. The employer ID number for Henson's Sporting Goods is 28-9311893.

LO1, 2, 3 (60 min)

The employees at Henson's are paid once each month on the last day of the month. Pam Adams is the only employee who has contributed the maximum into Social Security. None of the other employees will reach the social security wage-base limit by the end of the year. Assume the rate for social security to be 6.2% with a wage-base maximum of $102,000, and the rate for Medicare to be 1.45% on all earnings. Henson's is classified as a monthly depositor for Form 941 payroll tax deposit purposes.

Check Figure:
Dec. 31 Payroll Tax Expense
$882.37

Your tasks are to

1. Journalize the entries to record the employer's payroll tax expense for each period in the general journal.
2. Journalize the payment of each tax liability in the general journal.
3. Complete Form 941 for the fourth quarter of the current year.

OCTOBER

| | | | FICA | | |
| | | | OASDI | Medicare | Federal Income Tax |
Employee	Monthly Earnings	YTD Earnings	OASDI	Medicare	
Pam Adams	$ 2,850	$ 95,850	$176.70	$ 41.33	$ 530.00
Jim Lee	3,490	40,150	216.38	50.61	427.00
Dave Oswald	3,800	43,900	235.60	55.10	536.00
	$10,140	$179,900	$628.68	$147.04	$1,493.00

NOVEMBER

Employee	Monthly Earnings	YTD Earnings	FICA OASDI	FICA Medicare	Federal Income Tax
Pam Adams	$ 3,030	$ 98,880	$187.86	$ 43.94	$ 597.00
Jim Lee	3,870	44,020	239.94	56.12	468.00
Dave Oswald	3,750	47,650	232.50	54.38	559.00
	$10,650	$190,550	$660.30	$154.44	$1,624.00

DECEMBER

Employee	Monthly Earnings	YTD Earnings	FICA OASDI	FICA Medicare	Federal Income Tax
Pam Adams	$ 4,250	$103,130	$193.44	$ 61.63	$ 867.00
Jim Lee	3,800	47,820	235.60	55.10	479.00
Dave Oswald	4,400	52,050	272.80	63.80	704.00
	$12,450	$203,000	$701.84	$180.53	$2,050.00

LO4, 5 (20 min)

8A-5. Using the information from Problem 8A-4, please complete a Form 940 for Henson's Sporting Goods for the current year. Additional information needed to complete the form is as follows:
a. SUTA rate: 5.7%
b. State reporting number: 025-319-2
c. No FUTA tax deposits were made for this year.
d. Henson's three employees for the year all earned over $7,000.

Check Figure:
Total Exempt Payments $182,000

Group B Problems

LO1, 2, 3 (30 min)

8B-1. For the biweekly pay period ending on April 8 at Kane's Hardware, the following partial payroll summary is taken from the individual employee earnings records. Use it to
1. Complete the table. Use the federal income tax withholding table in Figure 7.2 to figure the amount of income tax withheld.
2. Prepare a journal entry to record the payroll tax expense for Kane's. Please show the calculations for FICA taxes.

Check Figure:
Payroll Tax Expense $536.11

Employee	Allowance and Marital Status	Gross	FICA OASDI	FICA Medicare	Federal Income Tax
Al Jones	S-1	$ 820			
Janice King	S-2	890			
Alice Long	S-0	850			
Jill Reese	S-1	1,100			
Jeff Vatack	S-2	1,340			

Assume the FICA tax rate for OASDI is 6.2% up to $102,000 in earnings (no one has earned this much as of April 8), and Medicare is 1.45% on all earnings. The state unemployment tax rate is 5.2% on the first $7,000 of earnings, and the federal unemployment tax rate is .8% of the first $7,000 of earnings. (Only Jill Reese and Jeff Vatack have earned more than $7,000 as of April 8.) In cases where the amount of FICA tax calculates to one-half cent, round up to the next cent.

8B-2. The following is the monthly payroll of Hogan Company, owned by Dean Hogan. Employees are paid on the last day of each month. Employees are paid on the last day of each month.

LO1, 2, 3 (50 min)

> *Check Figure:*
> Deposit of SUTA tax $1,189.59

JANUARY

Employee	Monthly Earnings	YTD Earnings	FICA OASDI	Medicare	Federal Income Tax
Sam Koy	$1,850	$1,850	$114.70	$ 26.83	$222.00
Joy Lane	3,000	3,000	186.00	43.50	343.00
Amy Hess	3,590	3,590	222.58	52.06	396.00
	$8,440	$8,440	$523.28	$122.39	$961.00

FEBRUARY

Employee	Monthly Earnings	YTD Earnings	FICA OASDI	Medicare	Federal Income Tax
Sam Koy	$2,200	$ 4,050	$136.40	$ 31.90	$ 293.00
Joy Lane	2,900	5,900	179.80	42.05	325.00
Amy Hess	3,775	7,365	234.05	54.74	426.00
	$8,875	$17,315	$550.25	$128.69	$1,044.00

MARCH

Employee	Monthly Earnings	YTD Earnings	FICA OASDI	Medicare	Federal Income Tax
Sam Koy	$ 2,820	$ 6,870	$174.84	$ 40.89	$ 405.00
Joy Lane	4,000	9,900	248.00	58.00	535.00
Amy Hess	4,300	11,665	266.60	62.35	556.00
	$11,120	$28,435	$689.44	$161.24	$1,496.00

Hogan Company is located at 2 Roundy Road, Marblehead, Massachusetts 01945. Its employer identification number is 29-3458821. The FICA tax rate for Social Security is 6.2% up to $102,000 in earnings during the year, and Medicare is 1.45% on all earnings. The SUTA tax rate is 5.7% on the first $7,000. The FUTA tax rate is .8% on the first $7,000 of earnings. Hogan Company is classified as a monthly depositor for Form 941 taxes.

Your tasks are to
1. Journalize the entries to record the employer's payroll tax expense for each pay period in the general journal.
2. Journalize entries for the payment of each tax liability in the general journal.

LO1, 2, 3 (50 min)

8B-3. Ed Ward, the accountant for Hogan Company, must complete Form 941 for the first quarter of the current year. Ed gathered the needed data as presented in Problem 8B-2. Suddenly called away to an urgent budget meeting, Ed requested that you assist him by preparing the Form 941 for the first quarter. Please note that the difference in the tax liability, a few cents, should be adjusted on line 7a; this difference is due to the rounding 319of FICA tax amounts.

Check Figure:
Liability for Quarter $7,851.58

LO1, 2, 3 (60 min)

8B-4. The following is the monthly payroll for the last three months of the year for Henson's Sporting Goods Shop, 1 Roe Road, Lynn, Massachusetts 01945. The shop is a sole proprietorship owned and operated by Bill Henson. The employer ID number for Henson's Sporting Goods is 28-9311892.

The employees at Henson's are paid once each month on the last day of the month. Pete Avery is the only employee who has contributed the maximum into Social Security. None of the other employees will reach the Social Security wage-base limit by the end of the year. Assume the rate for Social Security to be 6.2% with a wage-base maximum of $102,000, and the rate for Medicare to be 1.45% on all earnings. Henson's is classified as a monthly depositor for Form 941 payroll tax deposit purposes.

Your tasks are to
1. Journalize the entries to record the employer's payroll tax expense for each period in the general journal.
2. Journalize the payment of each tax liability in the general journal.
3. Complete Form 941 for the fourth quarter of the current year.

OCTOBER

Employee	Monthly Earnings	YTD Earnings	FICA OASDI	FICA Medicare	Federal Income Tax
Pete Avery	$ 2,950	$ 97,000	$182.90	$ 42.78	$ 530.00
Janet Lee	3,590	41,075	222.58	52.06	427.00
Sue Lyons	3,800	44,000	235.60	55.10	536.00
	$10,340	$182,075	$641.08	$149.94	$1,493.00

NOVEMBER

Employee	Monthly Earnings	YTD Earnings	FICA OASDI	FICA Medicare	Federal Income Tax
Pete Avery	$ 3,000	$100,000	$186.00	$ 43.50	$ 552.00
Janet Lee	3,650	44,725	226.30	52.93	439.00
Sue Lyons	3,710	47,710	230.02	53.80	503.00
	$10,360	$192,435	$642.32	$150.23	$1,494.00

DECEMBER

			FICA		
Employee	Monthly Earnings	YTD Earnings	OASDI	Medicare	Federal Income Tax
Pete Avery	$ 4,250	$104,250	$124.00	$ 61.63	$ 857.00
Janet Lee	3,850	48,575	238.70	55.83	490.00
Sue Lyons	3,900	51,610	241.80	56.55	559.00
	$12,000	$204,435	$604.50	$174.01	$1,906.00

> *Check Figure:*
> Dec. 31 Payroll Tax Expense
> $778.51

8B-5. Using the information from Problem 8B-4, please complete a Form 940 for Henson's Sporting Goods for the current year. Additional information needed to complete the form is as follows:

   a. SUTA rate: 5.7%
   b. State reporting number: 025-319-2
   c. No FUTA tax deposits were made for this year.
   d. Henson's three employees for the year all earned over $7,000.

LO4, 5 (20 min)

> *Check Figure:*
> Line 4 Total Exempt Payments
> $183,435

ON-THE-JOB TRAINING

T-1. Sunshine School Supplies is a leading manufacturer of back-to-school kits and other items used by students in elementary and middle schools. Each summer Sunshine needs additional help to assemble, pack, and ship school items sold in stores around the country. Sunshine's company policy has been to hire 30 additional workers for 12 weeks during the summer. Each employee works 40 hours per week and earns $6.50 per hour. At the end of August these additional workers are laid off.

LO1, 2, 3, 4 (60 min)

    Sunshine's state unemployment rate has risen to 5.4% with no experience/merit rating allowed due to these layoffs in the last few years.

    Miriam Holtz, who is the president of Sunshine, asks for your help to find a way to reduce Sunshine's 5.4% state unemployment rate. When Miriam called the state department of labor and employment, she was told that Sunshine's unemployment rate could drop to 4.1% if it stopped laying off workers.

    Miriam has thought about using temporary employment agency workers during the summer months as a way to obtain the help the company needs and at the same time stop the seasonal layoffs.

    Miriam asks you to evaluate whether this idea would be good for Sunshine. She gives you the following facts to use in analyzing this idea:

1. Five hundred workers who are permanent employees of Sunshine each earn in excess of $7,000 by September of each year.

2. A temporary employment agency told Miriam it would charge Sunshine $7.00 per hour for each worker it supplied during the summer.

3. The current federal unemployment tax rate is .8% up to the first $7,000 each employee earns during a year.

4. The current SUTA wage-base limit is the first $7,000 each employee earns during a year.

5. Sunshine pays a FICA tax rate of 6.2% for social security and 1.45% for Medicare. The Social Security wage-base limit is $102,000; there is no wage-base limit for Medicare.

    Please write a short memo to Miriam Holtz that shows your analysis of two options: (1) continue to hire 30 additional workers for the summer and then lay them off, or (2) have the temporary employment agency provide 30 additional workers for the summer.

In your memo be sure to show the financial effect of both options in terms of the tax calculations on employee earnings for SUTA, FUTA, and FICA. For option 1, be sure to include the SUTA and FUTA tax effects for both the permanent and temporary workers. At the end of your memo please provide Miriam with your conclusion so she can make a good decision for her company.

LO3, 4, 5 (20 min)   **T-2.** Cathy Johnson was recently hired as a bookkeeper for the Pet World Dog Toy Company. She just graduated from the local community college with an associates degree in business. Although she took several accounting courses at school, she was unable to take the school's payroll accounting course.

Cathy is confused about payroll tax forms and their purpose. She wants to learn more about the forms the business must prepare and send in to the government.

You are the accountant for Pet World. Your boss has asked you to help teach Cathy about the forms and why they are used. The boss feels it is best to give Cathy a brief written summary about the following forms:

1. Form 941
2. Form 940
3. Form 8109
4. Form W-2
5. Form W-3

Please write a brief report to Cathy to help her understand the following points about these payroll tax forms:

a. The purpose of each form
b. What is reported on each form
c. When each form is sent to the government
d. Where the amounts found on each form come from in the accounting system

FINANCIAL REPORT PROBLEM

LO4 (20 min)   ### Reading the Kellogg's Annual Report
Go to Appendix A of the Kellogg's Annual Report and find Note 9: Expenses. How much did Kellogg's spend to fund the 401(k) plans and similar saving plans?

INTERNET PROJECT

Coca-Cola
Go to the Web and search: Annual Report Coca-Cola 2008.
Click on Investors Relations.
List out the latest news Coca-Cola is providing to its investors.
Order a free annual report.

CONTINUING PROBLEM

LO1, 2, 3, 4 (40 min)   ### Sanchez Computer Center
As December comes to an end, Tony Freedman wants to take care of his payroll obligations. He will complete Form 941 for the fourth quarter of the current year and Form 940 for federal unemployment taxes. Tony will make the necessary deposits and payments associated with his payroll.

Assignment

1. Using the information in the Chapter 7 problem, record the November payrolls and the payment of the payrolls in the general journal.
2. Using the information in the Chapter 7 problem, record the payroll tax expense for the fourth quarter in the general journal. Use December 31 as the date of the journal entry to record the payroll tax expense for the entire quarter.
3. Record the payment of each tax liability in the general journal. Sanchez Computer Center is classified as a quarterly depositor. The company wishes to pay all payroll taxes on December 31 even if no deposits are required.
4. Prepare Form 941 for the fourth quarter. Sanchez Computer Center's employer identification number is 35-4132588.
5. Complete Form 940 for Sanchez Computer Center. The FUTA tax ceiling is $7,000, and the SUTA tax ceiling is $7,000 in cumulative wages for each employee. The Sanchez Computer Center's FUTA rate is .8% and the SUTA rate is 2.7%. The state reporting number is 025-025-2.

Hint: Sometimes the amount of social security taxes paid by the employee for the quarter will not equal the employee's tax liability because of rounding. Any overage or difference should be reported on line 7a of Form 941.

SUBWAY Case

HOLD THE LETTUCE, WITHHOLD THE TAXES

LO1, 2, 3, 4 (30 min)

"As an employer, Stan, what are your tax responsibilities?" asked Angel Tavarez, president of the Los Palmos Kiwanis club. They were at one of the luncheons sponsored by the club every month, and Stan had been asked to join a discussion on the Role of Small Business in the local economy. Fortunately, Angel had told the panelists the questions in advance, so Stan had his answers ready.

"Well, of course, I pay city, state, and U.S. government taxes myself. I also have to file city, state, and federal withholding taxes for each of my two employees. I have to withhold state unemployment taxes, as well as FICA, which is another name for OASDI and Medicare taxes, for each of them. I pay workers' compensation, too," said Stan.

"That's strange," said a voice from the audience. "My brother-in-law has a Subway restaurant in the southern part of the state, and he doesn't pay any city taxes. What's going on here?"

"Naturally, the situation is slightly different for Subway owners in different cities in our state—and across the country," said Stan confidently. "Not all cities have city income taxes. Different states have different regulations about workers' comp as well."

"Oh, right," said the voice, sounding embarrassed.

"So, Stan, how often do you have to pay taxes?" asked Angel Tavarez, shifting the topic diplomatically.

Stan picked up a piece of chalk and drew four large circles on the blackboard. Then he wrote the word "ASPIRIN" in each of the circles. A murmur of "Huh" and "What" went around the room.

"The average employee working for a company pays taxes once a year on April 15 and has one big tax headache. As an employer," Stan said, "I file tax returns on a quarterly basis, so I have four big tax headaches a year! Rather than filling out the 1040-EZ, I complete the Form 941, the Employer's Quarterly Federal Return, to report and pay payroll taxes to the IRS. Yet, while the form is due quarterly, I actually need to deposit the tax money into a Federal Reserve

Bank once a month. In addition, I have to file the 940 at the end of each year to pay my federal and state unemployment taxes. Then, for each employee...."

"Stan," Angel interrupted, "I'm afraid time is running out for your segment of the panel discussion. We'll move on to Pamela Pudelle, who is going to tell us about advertising her new pet-grooming parlor."

Later, during the reception, Stan tapped Angel on the shoulder, "Sorry I went over my time limit," he said. "You didn't really go over," said Angel, "but you were getting a little too technical for the audience." While Stan was sorry to have let the discussion veer off course, he felt a little burst of pride: Who would have thought a year ago that he would be willing—and able—to expound about the tax burden of a small business owner!

Discussion Questions

1. What are the taxes called "Form 941 taxes"?
2. Why is Stan classified as a monthly depositor of Form 941 taxes?
3. Assume Stan owed $2,069.90 in Form 941 taxes for March. When would it be due? What would happen if that day were a Sunday?

PEACHTREE COMPUTER WORKSHOP

COMPUTERIZED ACCOUNTING APPLICATION FOR CHAPTER 8

Refresher on using Peachtree Complete Accounting

Before starting this assignment, you may want to refresh your memory by reading the following PDF documents in the multimedia library of the MyAccountingLab Web site. Remember to choose the PDF document for your version of Peachtree.

1. An Introduction to Peachtree Complete Accounting
2. Correcting Peachtree Transactions
3. How to Repeat or Restart a Peachtree Assignment
4. Backing Up and Restoring Your Work in Peachtree

You also should have completed the following workshops:

1. Workshop 1 Atlas Company from Chapter 3
2. Workshop 2 Zell Company from Chapter 4
3. Workshop 3 Sullivan Realty from Chapter 5

Workshop 4:

Payroll Mini Practice Set

In this workshop you will prepare January, February, and March payroll for Pete's Market using Peachtree. Tasks include entering payroll data, producing paychecks, and remitting payroll taxes. You will also print payroll reports.

Instructions and the data file for completing this assignment are in the multimedia library of the MyAccountingLab Web site. Open the **Workshop 4 Pete's Market** PDF document for your version of Peachtree and download the **Pete's Market** data file for your version of Peachtree.

QUICKBOOKS COMPUTER WORKSHOP

COMPUTERIZED ACCOUNTING APPLICATION FOR CHAPTER 8

Refresher on using QuickBooks Pro

Before starting this assignment, you may want to refresh your memory by reading the following PDF documents in the multimedia library of the MyAccountingLab Web site. Remember to choose the PDF document for your version of QuickBooks.

1. An Introduction to QuickBooks Pro
2. Correcting QuickBooks Transactions
3. How to Repeat or Restart a QuickBooks Assignment
4. Backing Up and Restoring Your Work in QuickBooks

You also should have completed the following workshops:

1. Workshop 1 Atlas Company from Chapter 3
2. Workshop 2 Zell Company from Chapter 4
3. Workshop 3 Sullivan Realty from Chapter 5

Workshop 4:

Payroll Mini Practice Set

In this workshop you will prepare January, February, and March payroll for Pete's Market using QuickBooks. Tasks include entering payroll data, producing paychecks, and remitting payroll taxes. You will also print payroll reports.

Instructions and the data file for completing this assignment are in the multimedia library of the MyAccountingLab Web site. Open the *Workshop 4 Pete's Market* PDF document for your version of QuickBooks and download the *Pete's Market* data file for your version of QuickBooks.

9

Sales and Cash Receipts

DID YOU KNOW? Rebates, reimbursements for markdowns from vendors, are recognized as a reduction to cost of sales when the inventory is sold. Visit *www.biglots.com* to find more information about Big Lots.

LEARNING OBJECTIVES

1. Recording and posting sales transactions.

2. Preparing, journalizing, and posting a credit memorandum.

3. Recording and posting cash receipts transactions.

4. Recording to the accounts receivable subsidiary ledger.

5. Preparing a schedule of accounts receivable.

When you shop in Big Lots, a merchandise company, you will see a wide variety of products in the store. Let's first look at Chou's Toy Shop to get an overview of merchandise terms and journal entries. After that, we take an in-depth look at how Art's Wholesale Clothing Company keeps its books.

Learning Unit 9-1 Chou's Toy Shop: Seller's View of a Merchandise Company

> Sales are recorded on an invoice (on account) or a receipt (cash) in the Customer module of QuickBooks and Peachtree.

Chou's Toy Shop, owned by Chou Li, is a **retailer.** It buys toys, games, bikes, and similar items from manufacturers and wholesalers and resells these goods (or **merchandise**) to its customers. The shelving, display cases, and so forth are called "fixtures" or "equipment." These items are not for resale.

Gross Sales

Each cash or charge sale made at Chou's Toy Shop is rung up at the register. Suppose the shop had $3,000 in sales on July 18. Of that amount, $1,800 was cash sales and $1,200 was charges. The account that recorded those sales would be

> *Gross sales:*
> Revenue earned from sale of merchandise to customers.

Sales (Gross)

Dr.	Cr.
	3,000

← Revenue account with a credit balance

This account is a revenue account with a credit balance and will be found on the income statement. Figure 9.1 shows the journal entry for the day. *Note:* We talk about sales tax later.

Accounts Affected	Category	↑ ↓	Rules	T Account Update
Cash	Asset	↑	Dr.	**Cash** 1,800 |
Accounts Receivable	Asset	↑	Dr.	**Accounts Receivable** 1,200 |
Sales	Revenue	↑	Cr.	**Sales** | 3,000

Sales Returns and Allowances

It would be great for Chou if all the customers were completely satisfied, but that rarely is the case. On July 19, Michelle Reese brought back a doll she bought on account for $50. She told Chou that the doll was defective and that she wanted either a price reduction or a

FIGURE 9.1 Recording Cash and Charge Sales for the Day

July	18	Cash		1 8 0 0 00		
		Accounts Receivable		1 2 0 0 00		
		Sales			3 0 0 0 00
		Sales for July 18			

new doll. They agreed on a $10 price reduction. Michelle now owes Chou $40. The account called **Sales Returns and Allowances (SRA)** would record this information.

Sales Returns and Allowances

Contra-revenue ——————→ **Dr.** | **Cr.**
account with a   **10**
debit balance

This account is a contra-revenue account with a debit balance. It will be recorded on the income statement. Figure 9.2 shows how the journal entry would look.

Accounts Affected	Category	↑↓	Rules	T Account Update
Sales Returns and Allowances	Contra-revenue	↑	Dr.	**Sales Ret. & Allow.** **Dr.** | **Cr.** **10**
Accounts Receivable, Michelle Reese	Asset	↓	Cr.	**Accounts Receivable** **Dr.** | **Cr.** **1,200** | **10**

Look at how the sales returns and allowances increase.

July	19	Sales Returns and Allowances			1 0 00			
		Accounts Receivable, Michelle Reese	·			1 0 00	
		Issued credit memorandum					

FIGURE 9.2 Issuing a Credit Memorandum in the General Journal

Sales Discount

Chou gives a 2% **sales discount** to customers who pay their bills early. He wants his customers to know about this policy, so he posted the following sign at the cash register:

SALES DISCOUNT POLICY

2/10, n/30   *2% discount is allowed off price of bill if paid within the first 10 days or full amount is due within 30 days.*

n/10, EOM   *No discount. Full amount of bill is due within 10 days after the end of the month.*

Note that the **discount period** is the time when a discount is granted. The discount period is less time than the **credit period,** which is the length of time allowed to pay the amount owed on the bill.

If Michelle pays her $40 bill early, she will get an $.80 discount. This information is recorded in the **Sales Discount account** as follows:

Sales Discount

Contra-revenue ——————→ **Dr.** | **Cr.**
account with a   **.80**
debit balance

> When setting up a new customer in QuickBooks and Peachtree, be sure to include the credit terms. When payment is made the program will calculate the discount if that information is available.

Michelle's discount is calculated as follows:

$$.02 \times \$40 = \$.80$$

Michelle pays her bill on July 24. She is entitled to the discount because she paid her bill within 10 days. Figure 9.3 shows how Chou would record this payment on his books.

Accounts Affected	Category	↑↓	Rules	T Account Update
Cash	Asset	↑	Dr.	**Cash**
				Dr. | Cr.
				39.20 |
Sales Discount	Contra-revenue	↑	Dr.	**Sales Discount**
				Dr. | Cr.
				.80 |
Accounts Receivable	Asset	↓	Cr.	**Accounts Receivable**
				Dr. | Cr.
				1,200 | 40

> Gross Sales
> – Sales discount
> – SRA
> = Net sales

FIGURE 9.3 Recording Sales Discount

	July	24	Cash				3 9 20		
			Sales Discount				80		
			Accounts Receivable, Michelle Reese					4 0 00	
			Payment from Sale on Account						

Although Michelle pays $39.20, her Accounts Receivable is credited for the full amount, $40.

In the examples so far we have not shown any transactions with sales tax. Note that the actual or **net sales** for Chou would be **gross sales** less sales returns and allowances less any sales discounts. Let's look at how Chou would record his monthly sales if sales tax were charged.

Sales Tax Payable

> Sales taxes are special functions in accounting software that usually must be turned on and set up. When set up correctly, the program will automatically calculate the amount of sales tax to be charged or to be returned when issuing a credit memorandum.

None of the preceding examples shows state sales tax. Still, like it or not, Chou must collect that tax from his customers and send it to the state. Sales tax represents a liability to Chou. The amount Chou must pay to the state is recorded in the **Sales Tax Payable account.**

Assume the state Chou's is located in charges a 5% sales tax. Remember that Chou's sales on July 18 were $3,000. Chou must figure out the sales tax on the purchases. For this purpose, let's assume only two sales were made on that date: the cash sale ($1,800) and the charge sale ($1,200).

The sales tax on the cash purchase is calculated as follows:

$$\$1,800 \times .05 = \$90 \text{ Tax}$$
$$\$1,800 + \$90 \text{ tax} = \$1,890 \text{ Cash}$$

Here is how the sales tax on the charge sale is computed:

$$\$1,200 \times .05 = \$60 \text{ Tax} + \$1,200 \text{ Charge} = \$1,260 \text{ Accounts Receivable}$$

It would be recorded as shown in Figure 9.4.

Accounts Affected	Category	↑↓	Rules	T Account Update
Cash	Asset	↑	Dr.	**Cash**
				Dr. Cr.
				1,890
Accounts Receivable	Asset	↑	Dr.	**Accounts Receivable**
				Dr. Cr.
				1,260
Sales Tax Payable	Liability	↑	Cr.	**Sales Tax Payable**
				Dr. Cr.
				90
				60
Sales	Revenue	↑	Cr.	**Sales**
				Dr. Cr.
				3,000

July	18	Cash		1 8 9 0 00		
		Accounts Receivable		1 2 6 0 00		
		Sales Tax Payable			1 5 0 00	
		Sales			3 0 0 0 00	
		July 18 Sales				

FIGURE 9.4 Sales with Sales Tax

In Learning Unit 9-2, we will look in detail at Art's Wholesale Company.

LEARNING UNIT 9-1 REVIEW

AT THIS POINT you should be able to

- Explain the purpose of a contra-revenue account.
- Explain how to calculate net sales.
- Define, journalize, and explain gross sales, sales returns and allowances, and sales discounts.
- Journalize an entry for sales tax payable.

Self-Review Quiz 9-1

Respond true or false to the following:

1. Sales Returns and Allowances is a contra-asset account.
2. Sales Discount has a normal balance of a debit.
3. Sales Tax Payable is a liability.
4. Sales Discount is a contra-asset.
5. Accounts Receivable is a revenue.

Solutions to Self-Review Quiz 9-1

1. False
2. True
3. True
4. False
5. False

Sales: Revenue	↑	Cr.
SRA: Contra-revenue	↑	Dr.
SD: Contra-revenue	↑	Dr.

LO1 ## Learning Unit 9-2* Recording and Posting Sales Transactions on Account for Art's Wholesale Clothing Company: Introduction to Subsidiary Ledgers and Credit Memorandum

Art's Wholesale Clothing Company, as a **wholesaler,** buys merchandise from suppliers and sells the items to retailers, who in turn sell it to individual consumers.

The following transactions occurred in April for Art's Wholesale Clothing Company:

200X

April	3	Sold on account merchandise to Hal's Clothing, $800; terms 2/10, n/30.
	6	Sold on account merchandise to Bevan's Company, $1,600; terms 2/10, n/30.
	12	Credit memo #1 to Bevan's Company for returned merchandise, $600.
	18	Sold on account merchandise to Roe Company, $2,000; terms 2/10, n/30.
	24	Sold on account merchandise to Roe Company, $500; terms 2/10, n/30.
	28	Sold on account merchandise to Mel's Department Store, $900; terms 2/10, n/30.
	29	Sold on account merchandise to Mel's Department Store, $700; terms 2/10, n/30.

Let's look closer at the April 3 transaction of Art selling to Hal's Clothing. Figure 9.5 shows the actual bill on the **sales invoice** for this sale:

April 3   Sold account merchandise to Hal's Clothing, $800. Terms 2/10, n/30.

The Analysis

Accounts Affected	Category	↑ ↓	Rules	Amount
Accounts Receivable, Hal's Clothing	Asset	↑	Dr.	$800
Sales	Revenue	↑	Cr.	$800

The general journal is shown in Figure 9.6.

FIGURE 9.5 Sales Invoice

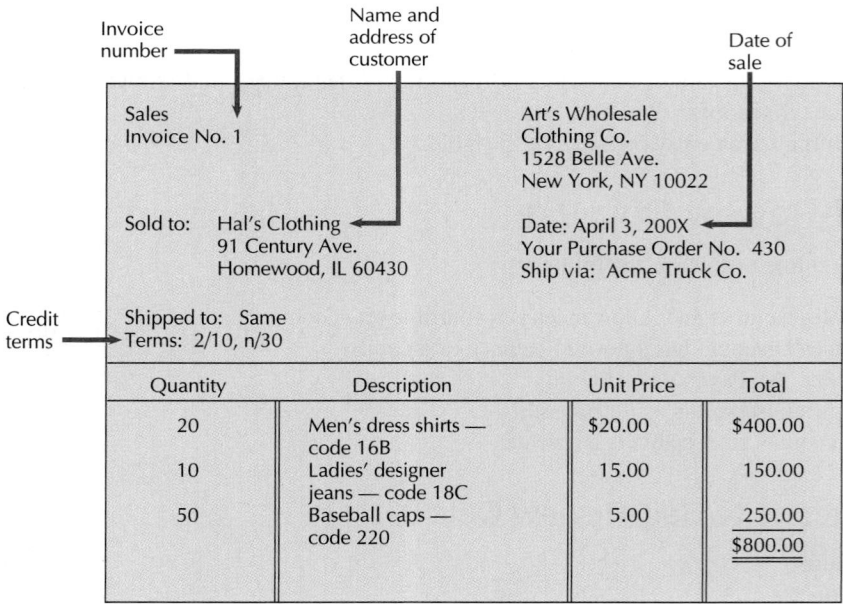

*At the end of Chapter 10, Appendix A shows an alternative method that uses a special journal to record transactions. Your instructor will let you know if this will be covered in your course.

ART'S WHOLESALE CLOTHING COMPANY GENERAL JOURNAL				Page 2		
Date		Account Titles and Description	PR	Dr.	Cr.	
200X						
April	3	Accounts Receivable, Hal's Clothing		80000		
		Sales			80000	
		Sale on account to Hal's				

FIGURE 9.6 Merchandise Sold and Accounts Receivable

Accounts Receivable Subsidiary Ledgers

So far in this text, the only title we have used for recording amounts owed to the seller has been Accounts Receivable. Art could have replaced the Accounts Receivable title in the general ledger with the following list of customers who owe him money:

- Accounts Receivable, Bevans Company
- Accounts Receivable, Hal's Clothing
- Accounts Receivable, Mel's Department Store
- Accounts Receivable, Roe Company

As you can see, this system would not be manageable if Art had 1,000 credit customers. To solve this problem, Art sets up a separate **accounts receivable subsidiary ledger.** Such a special ledger, often simply called a **subsidiary ledger,** contains a single type of account, such as credit customers. An account is opened for each customer, and the accounts are arranged alphabetically.

The diagram in Figure 9.7 shows how the accounts receivable subsidiary ledger fits in with the general ledger. To clarify the difference in updating the general ledger versus the subsidiary ledger, we will *post* to the general ledger and *record* to the subsidiary ledger. The word *post* refers to information that is moved from the journal to the general ledger; the word *record* refers to information that is transferred from the journal into the individual customer's account in the subsidiary ledger.

PARTIAL GENERAL LEDGER

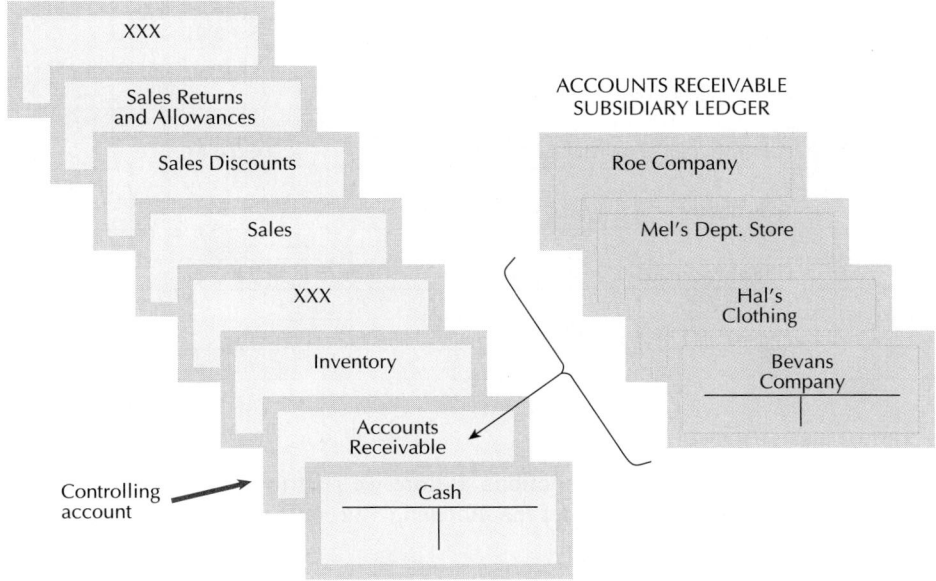

FIGURE 9.7 Partial General Ledger of Art's Wholesale Clothing Company and Accounts Receivable Subsidiary Ledger

Proving: At the end of the month, the sum of the accounts receivable subsidiary ledger will equal the ending balance in accounts receivable, the controlling account in the general ledger.

The general ledger is not in the same book as the accounts receivable subsidiary ledger.

The accounts receivable subsidiary ledger, or any other subsidiary ledger, can be in the form of a card file, a binder notebook, or computer tapes or disks. It will not have page numbers. The accounts receivable subsidiary ledger is organized alphabetically based on customers' names and addresses; new customers can be added and inactive customers deleted.

When using an accounts receivable subsidiary ledger, the account title Accounts Receivable in the general ledger is called the **controlling account—Accounts Receivable** because it summarizes or controls the accounts receivable subsidiary ledger. At the end of the month the total of the individual accounts in the accounts receivable ledger will equal the ending balance in Accounts Receivable in the general ledger.

Figure 9.8 shows how the general journal looks for Art before posting and recording this months sales transactions on account.

FIGURE 9.8 Before Posting and Recording Sales Transactions

		ART'S WHOLESALE CLOTHING COMPANY GENERAL JOURNAL			Page 2
Date		Account Titles and Description	PR	Dr.	Cr.
200X					
Apr.	3	Accounts Receivable, Hal's Clothing		8 0 0 00	
		Sales			8 0 0 00
		Sale on account to Hal's			
	6	Accounts Receivable, Bevan's Company		1 6 0 0 00	
		Sales			1 6 0 0 00
		Sale on account to Bevan's			
	12	Sales Returns and Allowances		6 0 0 00	
		Accounts Receivable, Bevan's Company			6 0 0 00
		Issued credit memo no. 1			
	18	Accounts Receivable, Roe Company		2 0 0 0 00	
		Sales			2 0 0 0 00
		Sale on account to Roe			
	24	Accounts Receivable, Roe Company		5 0 0 00	
		Sales			5 0 0 00
		Sale on account to Roe			
	28	Accounts Receivable, Mel's Dept. Store		9 0 0 00	
		Sales			9 0 0 00
		Sale on account to Mel's			
	29	Accounts Receivable, Mel's Dept. Store		7 0 0 00	
		Sales			7 0 0 00
		Sale on account to Mel's			

Posting and Recording Sales Transactions Before we post to the general ledger and record to the subsidiary ledger, consider the following T accounts, which show what each title would look like.

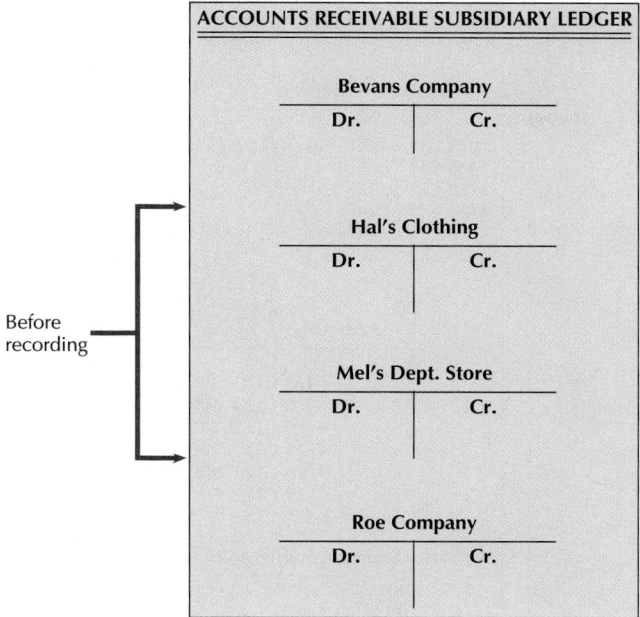

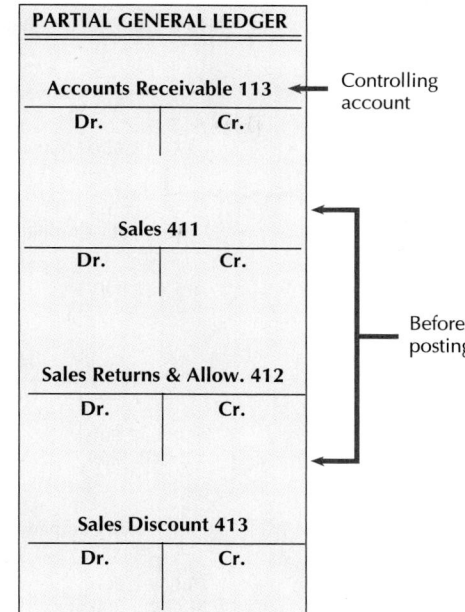

Figure 9.9 shows how the April 3 transaction is posted and recorded.

For this transaction we *post* to the general ledger Accounts Receivable and Sales accounts. Note how the account numbers of 113 and 411 are entered into the PR column of general journal. We must also *record* to Hal's Clothing in the accounts receivable subsidiary ledger. It is placed on the debit side because Hal owed Art the money. When the subsidiary ledger is updated, a (✓) is placed in the PR column of the general journal. The following is how the accounts receivable subsidiary ledger and partial general ledger

FIGURE 9.9 Transaction for April 3 Posted and Recorded

		GENERAL JOURNAL				Page 2	
Date		Account Titles and Description	PR	Dr.		Cr.	
200X							
April	3	Accounts Receivable, Hal's Clothing	113 ✓	8 0 0 00			
		Sales	411			8 0 0 00	
		Sale on account to Hal's					

PARTIAL ACCOUNTS RECEIVABLE SUBSIDIARY LEDGER

Hal's Clothing

Dr.	Cr.
4/3 GJ2 800	

PARTIAL GENERAL LEDGER

Accounts Receivable 113

Dr.	Cr.
4/3 GJ2 800	

Sales 411

Dr.	Cr.
	800 4/3 GJ2

(continued on next page)

FIGURE 9.9
(continued)

Tells us what page of the general journal information comes from

After recording

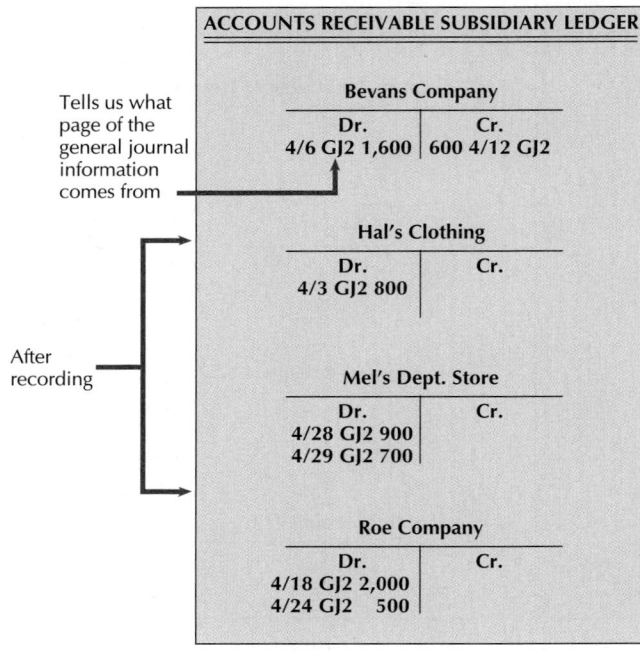

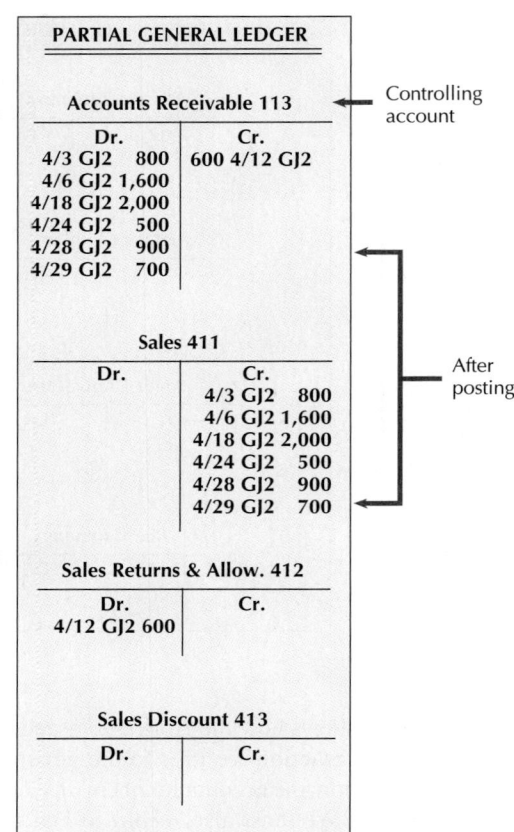

Controlling account

After posting

would look after postings. Before concluding this unit, let's look closely at the April 12 transaction when Art issues a credit memorandum to Bevan. We will analyze the transaction and show how to post and record it.

LO2   The Credit Memorandum

Companies usually handle sales returns and allowances by means of a **credit memorandum.** Credit memoranda inform customers that the amount of the goods returned or the amount allowed for damaged goods has been subtracted (credited) from the customer's ongoing account with the company.

    A sample credit memorandum from Art's Wholesale Clothing Company appears in Figure 9.10. It shows that on April 12, Credit Memorandum No. 1 was issued to Bevans Company for defective merchandise that had been returned.

FIGURE 9.10

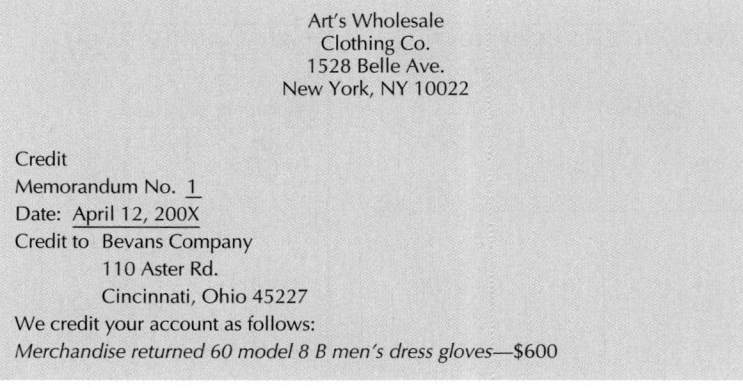

Art's Wholesale
Clothing Co.
1528 Belle Ave.
New York, NY 10022

Credit
Memorandum No. _1_
Date: _April 12, 200X_
Credit to Bevans Company
        110 Aster Rd.
        Cincinnati, Ohio 45227
We credit your account as follows:
Merchandise returned 60 model 8 B men's dress gloves—$600

Let's look at a transaction analysis chart before we journalize, record, and post this transaction.

Accounts Affected	Category	↑↓	Rules
Sales Returns and Allowances	Contra-revenue account	↑	Dr.
Accounts Receivable, Bevans Co.	Asset	↓	Cr.

Journalizing, Recording, and Posting the Credit Memorandum

The credit memorandum results in two postings to the general ledger and one recording to the accounts receivable subsidiary ledger (see Fig. 9.11).

Remember: Sales discounts are not taken on returns.

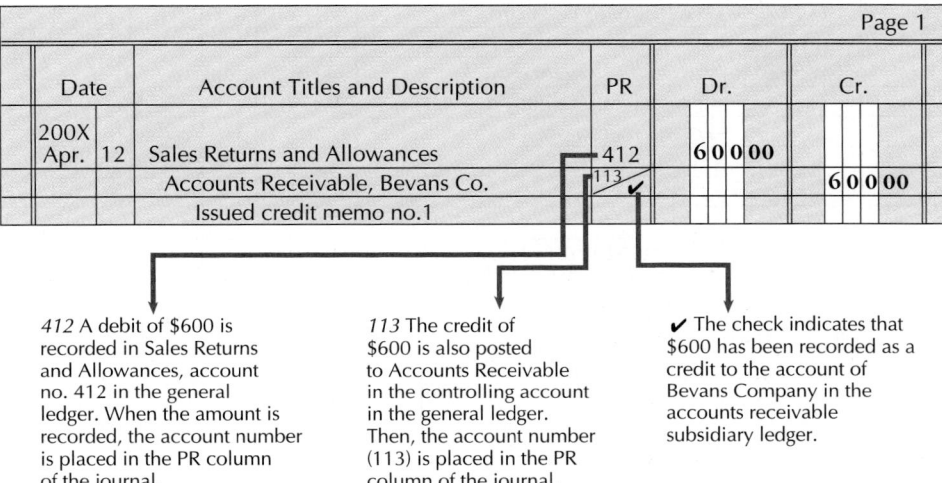

FIGURE 9.11 Postings and Recordings for the Credit Memorandum into the Subsidiary and General Ledgers

412 A debit of $600 is recorded in Sales Returns and Allowances, account no. 412 in the general ledger. When the amount is recorded, the account number is placed in the PR column of the journal.

113 The credit of $600 is also posted to Accounts Receivable in the controlling account in the general ledger. Then, the account number (113) is placed in the PR column of the journal.

✔ The check indicates that $600 has been recorded as a credit to the account of Bevans Company in the accounts receivable subsidiary ledger.

Note in the PR column next to Accounts Receivable, Bevans Co., a diagonal line separates the account number 113 above and a ✔ below. This notation shows that the amount of $600 has been credited to Accounts Receivable in the controlling account in the general ledger *and* credited to the account of Bevans Company in the accounts receivable subsidiary ledger.

LEARNING UNIT 9-2 REVIEW

AT THIS POINT / you should be able to

- Define and state the purposes of the accounts receivable subsidiary ledger.
- Define and state the purpose of the controlling account, Accounts Receivable.
- Journalize, record, or post sales on account to a general journal and its related accounts receivable and general ledgers.
- Explain, journalize, post, and record a credit memorandum.

Self-Review Quiz 9-2

Journalize, post to the general ledger, and record to accounts receivable subsidiary ledger the following transactions of Bernie Company.

200X

May	10	Sold merchandise on account to Ring Company, $600; terms 2/10, n/30.
	18	Sold merchandise on account to Lee Corp., $900; terms 2/10, n/30.
	25	Issued credit memo #1 to Ring Company for returned merchandise, $200.

Solution to Self-Review Quiz 9-2

			BERNIE COMPANY GENERAL JOURNAL			Page 4
	Date		Account Titles and Description	PR	Dr.	Cr.
	200X					
	May	10	Accounts Receivable, Ring Clothing	141 ✔	600 00	
			Sales	310		600 00
			Sale on account to Ring Co.			
		18	Accounts Receivable, Lee Corp.	141 ✔	900 00	
			Sales	310		900 00
			Sale on account to Lee Corp.			
		25	Sales Returns and Allowances	312	200 00	
			Accounts Receivable, Ring Co.	141 ✔		200 00
			Issued credit memo no. 1			

ACCOUNTS RECEIVABLE SUBSIDIARY LEDGER

Lee Corp.

Dr.	Cr.
5/18 GJ4 900	

Ring Co.

Dr.	Cr.
5/10 GJ4 600	200 5/25 GJ4

PARTIAL GENERAL LEDGER

Accounts Receivable 141

Dr.	Cr.
5/10 GJ4 600	200 5/25 GJ4
5/18 GJ4 900	

Sales 310

Dr.	Cr.
	600 5/10 GJ4
	900 5/18 GJ4

Sales Returns & Allow. 312

Dr.	Cr.
5/25 GJ4 200	

LO3 # Learning Unit 9-3 Recording and Posting Cash Receipt Transactions for Art's Wholesale: Schedule of Accounts Receivable

The following cash receipts transactions occurred for Art's Wholesale Clothing in April:

200X

Apr. 1 Art Newner invested $8,000 in the business.

4 Received check from Hal's Clothing for payment of invoice no. 1, less 2% discount.

15 Cash sales for first half of April, $900.

16 Received check from Bevans Company in settlement of invoice no. 2, less returns and 2% discount.

22 Received check from Roe Company for payment of invoice no. 3, less 2% discount.

27 Sold store equipment, $500.

30 Cash sales for second half of April, $1,200.

Figure 9.12 provides a closer look at how the April 4 transaction would be journalized.

Accounts Affected	Category	↑↓	Rules	T Account Update				
Cash	Asset	↑	Dr.	**Cash**				
				Dr.	Cr.			
				784				
Sales Discount	Contra-revenue	↑	Dr.	**Sales Discount**				
				Dr.	Cr.			
				16				
Accounts Receivable, Hal's Clothing	Asset	↓	Cr.	**Acc. Rec.**		**Hal's Clothing**		
				Dr.	Cr.	Dr.	Cr.	
				800	800	800	800	

> Hal's Clothing is located in the accounts receivable subsidiary ledger.

					Dr.		Cr.	
Apr.	4	Cash			7 8 4 00			
		Sales Discount			1 6 00			
		Accounts Receivable, Hal's Clothing					8 0 0 00	

FIGURE 9.12 Recording Sales Discount in General Journal

Figure 9.13 shows the complete set of April cash receipts transactions for Art's Wholesale journalized for the month, followed by a complete posting to the general ledger and recordings to the accounts receivable ledger. (Remember from the past unit that we posted all the sales on account information.)

FIGURE 9.13 Journalized Cash Receipts Transactions

		GENERAL JOURNAL					**Page 2**	
Date		Account Titles and Description	PR	Dr.		Cr.		
200X								
Apr.	1	Cash	111	8 0 0 0 00				
		Art Newner, Capital	311			8 0 0 0 00		
		Owner Investment						
	4	Cash	111	7 8 4 00				
		Sales Discount	413	1 6 00				
		Accounts Receivable, Hal's Clothing	113 ✓			8 0 0 00		
		Hal's paid invoice no. 1						
	15	Cash	111	9 0 0 00				
		Sales	411			9 0 0 00		
		Cash sales for first half of April						
	16	Cash	111	9 8 0 00				
		Sales Discount	413	2 0 00				
		Accounts Receivable, Bevan's Company	113 ✓			1 0 0 0 00		
		Bevan paid invoice no. 2						
	22	Cash	111	1 9 6 0 00				
		Sales Discount	413	4 0 00				
		Accounts Receivable, Roe Co.	113 ✓			2 0 0 0 00		
		Roe paid invoice no. 3						

(continued on next page)

FIGURE 9.13
(continued)

	27	Cash	111	50000			
		Store Equipment	121			50000	
		Sold store equipment					
	30	Cash	111	120000			
		Sales	411			120000	
		Cash sales for second half of April					

LO4

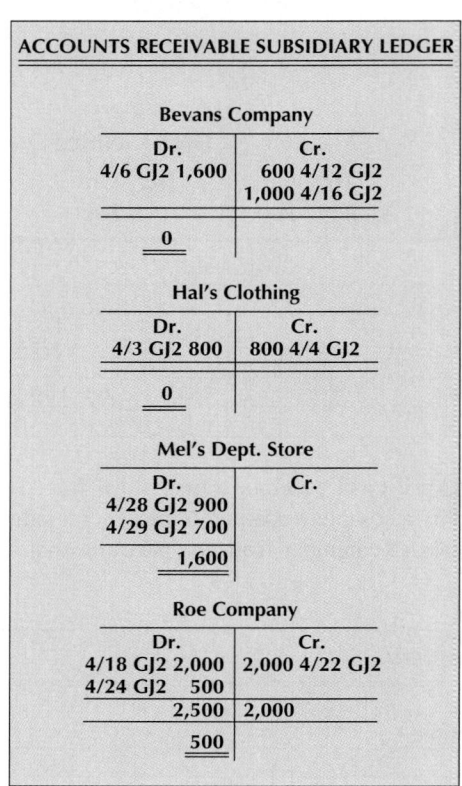

ACCOUNTS RECEIVABLE SUBSIDIARY LEDGER

Bevans Company

Dr.	Cr.
4/6 GJ2 1,600	600 4/12 GJ2
	1,000 4/16 GJ2
0	

Hal's Clothing

Dr.	Cr.
4/3 GJ2 800	800 4/4 GJ2
0	

Mel's Dept. Store

Dr.	Cr.
4/28 GJ2 900	
4/29 GJ2 700	
1,600	

Roe Company

Dr.	Cr.
4/18 GJ2 2,000	2,000 4/22 GJ2
4/24 GJ2 500	
2,500	2,000
500	

PARTIAL GENERAL LEDGER

Cash 111

Dr.	Cr.
4/1 GJ2 8,000	
4/4 GJ2 784	
4/15 GJ2 900	
4/16 GJ2 980	
4/22 GJ2 1,960	
4/27 GJ2 500	
4/30 GJ2 1,200	
14,324	

Accounts Receivable 113 ← Controlling account

Dr.	Cr.
4/3 GJ2 800	800 4/4 GJ2
4/16 GJ2 1,600	600 4/12 GJ2
4/18 GJ2 2,000	1,000 4/16 GJ2
4/24 GJ2 500	2,000 4/22 GJ2
4/28 GJ2 900	4,400
4/29 GJ2 700	
6,500	
Bal. 2,100	

Store Equipment 121

Dr.	Cr.
4/1 Bal. 24,000	500 4/27 GJ2
23,500	

Art Newner, Capital 311

Dr.	Cr.
	8,000 4/1 GJ2
	8,000

Sales 411

Dr.	Cr.
	800 4/3 GJ2
	1,600 4/6 GJ2
	900 4/15 GJ2
	2,000 4/18 GJ2
	500 4/24 GJ2
	900 4/28 GJ2
	700 4/29 GJ2
	1,200 4/30 GJ2
	8,600

Sales Discount 413

Dr.	Cr.
4/4 GJ2 16	
4/16 GJ2 20	
4/22 GJ2 40	
76	

Schedule of Accounts Receivable

The **schedule of accounts receivable** is an alphabetical list of the companies that have an outstanding balance in the accounts receivable subsidiary ledger. This total should be equal to the balance of the Accounts Receivable controlling account in the general ledger at the end of the month.

Let's examine the schedule of accounts receivable for Art's Wholesale Clothing Company in Figure 9.14.

ART'S WHOLESALE CLOTHING COMPANY SCHEDULE OF ACCOUNTS RECEIVABLE APRIL 30, 200X	
Mel's Dept. Store	$1 6 0 0 00
Roe Company	5 0 0 00
Total Accounts Receivable	$2 1 0 0 00

FIGURE 9.14 Schedule of Accounts Receivable

> Schedule is listed in alphabetical order.

The balance of the controlling account, Accounts Receivable ($2,100), in the general ledger does indeed equal the sum of the individual customer balances in the accounts receivable ledger ($2,100) as shown in the schedule of accounts receivable. The schedule of accounts receivable can help forecast potential cash inflows as well as possible credit and collection decisions.

LEARNING UNIT 9-3 REVIEW

AT THIS POINT you should be able to

- Journalize cash receipts transactions.
- Record and post cash receipts transactions to the accounts receivable subsidiary ledger and general ledger.
- Prepare a schedule of accounts receivable.

Self-Review Quiz 9-3

Journalize, post to the general ledger, and record to the accounts receivable subsidiary ledger the following transactions of Mabel Corporation, given the following balances.

Accounts Receivable Subsidiary Ledger

Name	Balance	Invoice No.
Irene Welch	$500	1
Janis Fross	200	2

Partial General Ledger

	Acct. No.	Balance
Cash	110	$600
Accounts Receivable	120	700
Store Equipment	130	600
Sales	410	700
Sales Discount	420	

200X

May	1	Received check from Irene Welch for invoice no. 1, less 2% discount.
	8	Cash sales collected, $200.
	15	Received check from Janis Fross for invoice no. 2, less 2% discount.
	19	Sold store equipment at cost, $300.

Solution to Self-Review Quiz 9-3

MABEL CORPORATION GENERAL JOURNAL					
					Page 3
Date			PR	Dr.	Cr.
200X					
May	1	Cash	110	4 9 0 00	
		Sales Discount	420	1 0 00	
		Accounts Receivable, Irene Welch	120 ✔		5 0 0 00
		Received payment from Irene Welch			
	8	Cash	110	2 0 0 00	
		Sales	410		2 0 0 00
		Cash sale			
	15	Cash	110	1 9 6 00	
		Sales Discount	420	4 00	
		Accounts Receivable, Janis Fross	120 ✔		2 0 0 00
		Received payment from Janis Fross			
	19	Cash	110	3 0 0 00	
		Store Equipment	130		3 0 0 00
		Sold store equipment			

ACCOUNTS RECEIVABLE SUBSIDIARY LEDGER

Janis Fross

Dr.	Cr.
Bal. 200	200

Irene Welch

Dr.	Cr.
Bal. 500	500 5/1 GJ3

PARTIAL GENERAL LEDGER

Cash 110

Dr.	Cr.
Bal. 600	
5/1 GJ3 490	
5/8 GJ3 200	
5/15 GJ3 196	
5/19 GJ3 300	

Accounts Receivable 120

Dr.	Cr.
Bal. 700	500 5/1 GJ3
	200 5/15 GJ3

Store Equipment 130

Dr.	Cr.
Bal. 600	300 5/19 GJ3

Sales 410

Dr.	Cr.
	700 Bal.
	200 5/8 GJ3

Sales Discount 420

Dr.	Cr.
5/1 GJ3 10	
5/15 GJ3 4	

CHAPTER ASSIGNMENTS

SUMMARY OF KEY POINTS

LEARNING UNIT 9-1

1. Sales Returns and Allowances and Sales Discount are contra-revenue accounts.
2. Net Sales = Gross Sales − Sales Returns and Allowances − Sales Discounts.
3. Discounts are not taken on sales tax, freight, or goods returned. The discount period is shorter than the credit period.
4. Sales Tax Payable is a liability account.

LEARNING UNIT 9-2

1. The normal balance of the accounts receivable subsidiary ledger is a debit balance.
2. A (✓) in the PR of the general journal means the subsidiary ledger has been updated.
3. The accounts receivable subsidiary ledger, organized in alphabetical order, is not in the same book as Accounts Receivable, the controlling account in the general journal.
4. When a credit memorandum is issued, the result is that Sales Returns and Allowances increases and Accounts Receivable decreases. When we record this entry into the general journal, we assume all parts of the transaction will be posted to the general ledger and recorded in the subsidiary ledger.

LEARNING UNIT 9-3

1. At the end of the month, the total of all customers' ending balances in the accounts receivable subsidiary ledger should be equal to the ending balance in Accounts Receivable, the controlling account in the general ledger.
2. The schedule of accounts receivable is an alphabetical list of companies with an outstanding balance.

KEY TERMS

Accounts receivable subsidiary ledger   A book or file that contains, in alphabetical order, the individual records of amounts owed by various credit customers.

Controlling account—Accounts Receivable   The Accounts Receivable account in the general ledger, after postings are complete, shows a firm the total amount of money owed to it. This figure is broken down in the accounts receivable ledger, where it indicates specifically who owes the money.

Credit memorandum   A piece of paper sent by the seller to a customer who has returned merchandise previously purchased on credit. The credit memorandum indicates to the customer that the seller is reducing the amount owed by the customer.

Credit period   Length of time allowed for payment of goods sold on account.

Discount period   A period shorter than the credit period when a discount is available to encourage early payment of bills.

Gross sales   The revenue earned from sale of merchandise to customers.

Merchandise   Goods brought into a store for resale to customers.

Net sales   Gross sales less sales returns and allowances less sales discounts.

Retailers   Merchants who buy goods from wholesalers for resale to customers.

Sales discount   Amount a customer is allowed to deduct from bill total for paying a bill during the discount period.

Sales Discount account   A contra-revenue account that records cash discounts granted to customers for payments made within a specific period of time.

Sales invoice   A bill sent to customer(s) reflecting a sale on credit.

Sales Returns and Allowances (SRA) account   A contra-revenue account that records price adjustments and allowances granted on merchandise that is defective and has been returned.

Sales Tax Payable account   An account in the general ledger that accumulates the amount of sales tax owed. It has a credit balance.

Schedule of accounts receivable   A list of the customers, in alphabetical order, that have an outstanding balance in the accounts receivable ledger (or the accounts receivable subsidiary ledger). This total should be equal to the balance of the Accounts Receivable controlling account in the general ledger at the end of the month.

Subsidiary ledger   A ledger that contains accounts of a single type. Example: The accounts receivable subsidiary ledger records all credit customers.

Wholesalers   Merchants who buy goods from suppliers and manufacturers for sale to retailers.

BLUEPRINT: TRANSFERRING INFORMATION FROM THE GENERAL JOURNAL

Post → General Ledger (account #)

Record → Subsidiary Ledger (✓)

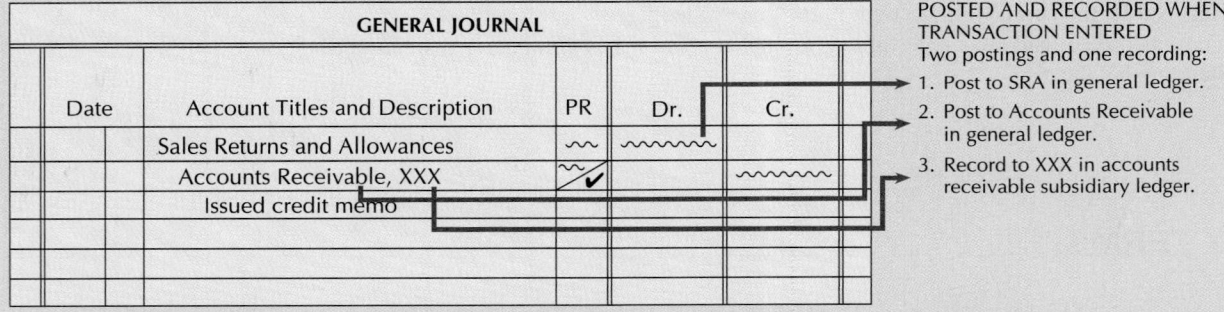

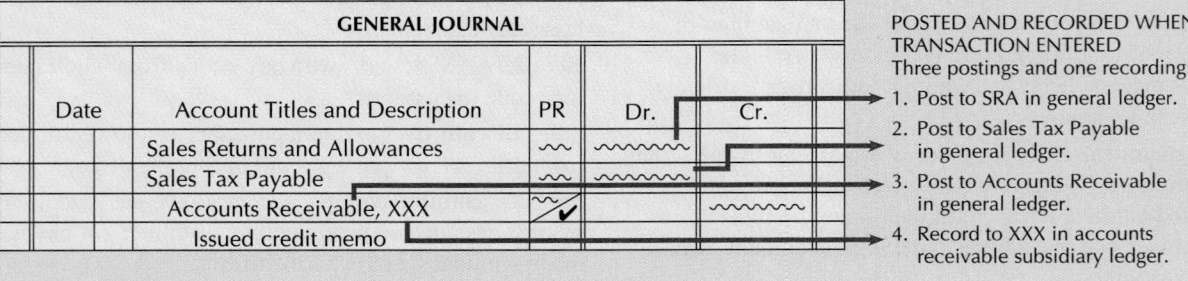

QUESTIONS, CLASSROOM DEMONSTRATION EXERCISES, EXERCISES, AND PROBLEMS

Discussion and Critical Thinking Questions /Ethical Case

1. Explain the purpose of a contra-revenue account.

2. What is the normal balance of Sales Discount?

3. Give two examples of contra-revenue accounts.

4. What is the difference between a discount period and a credit period?

5. Explain the terms:
   a. 2/10, n/30.
   b. n/10, EOM.

6. What category is Sales Discount in?

7. Compare and contrast the Controlling Account— Accounts Receivable to the accounts receivable subsidiary ledger.

8. Why is the accounts receivable subsidiary ledger organized in alphabetical order?

9. When is a (✓) used?

10. What is an invoice? What purpose does it serve?

11. Why is sales tax a liability to the business?

12. Sales discounts are taken on sales tax. Agree or disagree? Explain why.

13. When a seller issues a credit memorandum (assume no sales tax), what accounts will be affected?

14. Amy Jak is the National Sales Manager of Land.com. To get sales up to the projection for the old year, Amy asked the accountant to put the first two weeks' sales in January back into December. Amy told the accountant that this secret would only be between them. Should Amy move the new sales into the old sales year? You make the call. Write down your specific recommendations to Amy.

Classroom Demonstration Exercises

SET A

Overview　　　　　　　　　　　　　　　　　　　　　*LO1 (5 min)*

1. Complete the following table for Sales, Sales Returns and Allowances, and Sales Discounts.

Accounts Affected	Category	↑ ↓	Temporary or Permanent

Calculating Net Sales　　　　　　　　　　　　　　　*LO1 (5 min)*

2. Given the following, calculate net sales:

Gross Sales	$40
Sales Returns and Allowances	9
Sales Discounts	4

General Journal　　　　　　　　　　　　　　　*LO1, 3, 4 (10 min)*

3. Match the following activities to the three journal entries (more than one number can be used).
   1. Record to the accounts receivable subsidiary ledger.
   2. Recorded in the general journal.
   3. Posted to the general ledger.
   a. _____ Sold merchandise on account to Ree Co., invoice no. 1, $50.
   b. _____ Sold merchandise on account to Flynn Co., invoice no. 2, $1,000.
   c. _____ Issued credit memorandum no. 1 to Flynn Co. for defective merchandise, $25.

LO2 (10 min) **Credit Memorandum**

4. Draw a transactional analysis box for the following transaction: Issued credit memorandum to Met.com for defective merchandise, $200.

Journalize Transactions

LO1, 2, 3 (15 min) 5. Journalize the following transactions:
   a. Sold merchandise on account to Ally Co., invoice no. 10, $40.
   b. Received check from Moore Co., $100, less 2% discount.
   c. Cash Sales, $100.
   d. Issued credit memorandum no. 2 to Ally Co. for defective merchandise, $20.

LO5 (15 min) 6. From the following, prepare a schedule of accounts receivable for Blue Co. for May 31, 200X.

Accounts Receivable
Subsidiary Ledger

Bon Co.

	Dr.	Cr.
5/6 GJ1	100	

Peke Co.

	Dr.	Cr.	
5/20 GJ1	30	10	5/27 GJ1

Green Co.

	Dr.	Cr.
5/9 GJ1	10	

General Ledger

Accounts Receivable

	Dr.	Cr.	
5/31 GJ1	140	10	5/31 GJ1

SET B

LO1 (5 min) **Overview**

1. Complete the following table for Accounts Receivable, Sales Tax Payable, and Sales Discounts.

Accounts Affected	Category	↑ ↓	Temporary or Permanent

LO1 (5 min) **Calculating Net Sales**

2. Given the following, calculate net sales:

Gross Sales	$70
Sales Returns and Allowances	15
Sales Discounts	12

LO1, 3, 4 (10 min) **Sales Journal and General Journal**

3. Match the following to the three journal entries (more than one number can be used).
   1. Record to the accounts receivable subsidiary ledger.
   2. Recorded in the general journal.
   3. Posted to the general ledger.
   a. _____ Sold merchandise on account to Ree Co., invoice no. 1, $60.
   b. _____ Sold merchandise on account to Flynn Co., invoice no. 2, $90.
   c. _____ Issued credit memorandum no. 1 to Flynn Co. for defective merchandise, $30.

Credit Memorandum *LO2 (10 min)*

4. Draw a transactional analysis box for the following transaction: Issued credit memorandum to Met.com for defective merchandise, $100.

Sales and Cash Receipts

5. Journalize the following transactions: *LO1, 2, 3 (15 min)*
   a. Sold merchandise on account to Ally Co., invoice no. 10, $30.
   b. Received check from Moore Co., $70, less 20% discount.
   c. Cash Sales, $400.
   d. Issued credit memorandum no. 2 to Ally Co. for defective merchandise, $10.

6. From the following, prepare a schedule of accounts receivable for Blue Co. for May 31, 200X. *LO5 (15 min)*

	Accounts Receivable Subsidiary Ledger			General Ledger	

Accounts Receivable Subsidiary Ledger

Bon Co.

	Dr.	Cr.
5/6 GJ1	90	

Peke Co.

	Dr.	Cr.	
5/20 GJ1	20	10	5/27 GJ1

Green Co.

	Dr.	Cr.
5/9 GJ1	30	

General Ledger

Accounts Receivable

	Dr.	Cr.	
5/31 GJ1	140	10 5/31	GJ1

Exercises

9-1. From the general journal in Figure 9.15 record to the accounts receivable subsidiary ledger and post to the general ledger accounts as appropriate. *LO1, 4 (10 min)*

General Journal					
Date			PR	Dr.	Cr.
200X					
April	18	Accounts Receivable, Amazon.com		600 00	
		Sales			600 00
		Sold merchandise to Amazon			
	19	Accounts Receivable, Bill Valley Co.		900 00	
		Sales			900 00
		Sold merchandise to Bill Valley			

FIGURE 9.15 General Journal, Subsidiary Ledger, and Partial General Ledger

ACCOUNTS RECEIVABLE SUBSIDIARY LEDGER

Amazon.com

Bill Valley Co.

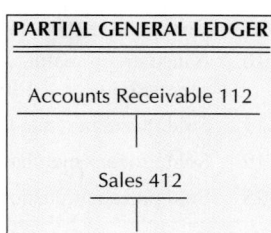

PARTIAL GENERAL LEDGER

Accounts Receivable 112

Sales 412

LO1, 2, 4 (10 min) **9-2.** Journalize, record, and post when appropriate the following transactions into the general journal (all sales carry terms of 2/10, n/30):

200X

May 16 Sold merchandise on account to Ronald Co., invoice no. 1, $1,000.

18 Sold merchandise on account to Bass Co., invoice no. 2, $1,700.

20 Issued credit memorandum no. 1 to Bass Co. for defective merchandise, $700.

Use the following account numbers: Accounts Receivable, 112; Sales, 411; Sales Returns and Allowances, 412.

LO3, 4 (10 min) **9-3.** From Exercise 9-2, journalize the receipt of a check from Ronald Co. for payment of invoice no. 1 on May 24.

LO4, 5 (20 min) **9-4.** From the following transactions for Edna Co., journalize, record, post, and prepare a schedule of accounts receivable when appropriate. You will have to set up your own accounts receivable subsidiary ledger and partial general ledger as needed. All sales terms are 2/10, n/30.

200X

June 1 Edna Cares invested $3,000 in the business.

1 Sold merchandise on account to Boston Co., invoice no. 1, $700.

2 Sold merchandise on account to Gary Co., invoice no. 2, $900.

3 Cash sale, $200.

8 Issued credit memorandum no. 1 to Boston for defective merchandise, $200.

10 Received check from Boston for invoice no. 1, less returns and discount.

15 Cash sale, $400.

18 Sold merchandise on account to Boston Co., invoice no. 3, $600.

LO2 (10 min) **9-5.** From the following facts calculate what Ann Frost paid Blue Co. for the purchase of a dining room set. Sale terms are 2/10, n/30.
a. Sales ticket price before tax, $4,000, dated April 5.
b. Sales tax, 7%.
c. Returned one defective chair for credit of $400 on April 8.
d. Paid bill on April 13.

Group A Problems

LO1, 2, 4, 5 (40 min) **9A-1.** Joan Lunden has opened Pizza and More, a wholesale grocery and pizza company. The following transactions occurred in June:

200X

June 1 Sold grocery merchandise to Cindy Co. on account, $700, invoice no. 1.

4 Sold pizza merchandise to Groom Co. on account, $800, invoice no. 2.

8 Sold grocery merchandise to French Co. on account, $900, invoice no. 3.

10 Issued credit memorandum no. 1 to Cindy Co. for $200 of grocery merchandise returned due to spoilage.

15 Sold pizza merchandise to Groom Co. on account, $300, invoice no. 4.

19 Sold grocery merchandise to French Co. on account, $400, invoice no. 5.

25 Sold pizza merchandise to Cindy Co. on account, $250, invoice no. 6.

Check Figure:
Schedule of accounts
receivable $3,150

Required

    1. Journalize the transactions.

    2. Record to the accounts receivable subsidiary ledger and post to the general ledger as appropriate.

    3. Prepare a schedule of accounts receivable for the end of June.

9A-2. The following transactions of Ted's Auto Supply occurred in November (your working papers have balances as of November 1 for certain general ledger and accounts receivable ledger accounts):

LO1, 2, 4, 5 (50 min)

200X		
Nov.	1	Sold auto parts merchandise to R. Volan on account, $1,000, invoice no. 60, plus 5% sales tax.
	5	Sold auto parts merchandise to J. Seth on account, $800, invoice no. 61, plus 5% sales tax.
	8	Sold auto parts merchandise to Lance Corner on account, $9,000, invoice no. 62, plus 5% sales tax.
	10	Issued credit memorandum no. 12 to R. Volan for $500 for defective auto parts merchandise returned from Nov. 1 transaction. (Be careful to record the reduction in Sales Tax Payable as well.)
	12	Sold auto parts merchandise to J. Seth on account, $600, invoice no. 63, plus 5% sales tax.

Check Figure:
Schedule of accounts
receivable $13,045

Required

    1. Journalize the transactions.

    2. Record to the accounts receivable subsidiary ledger and post to the general ledger as appropriate.

    3. Prepare a schedule of accounts receivable for the end of November.

9A-3. Mark Peaker owns Peaker's Sneaker Shop. (In your working papers balances as of May 1 are provided for the accounts receivable and general ledger accounts.) The following transactions occurred in May:

LO1, 2, 3, 4, 5 (70 min)

200X		
May	1	Mark Peaker invested an additional $12,000 in the sneaker store.
	3	Sold $700 of merchandise on account to B. Dale, sales ticket no. 60; terms 1/10, n/30.
	4	Sold $500 of merchandise on account to Ron Lester, sales ticket no. 61; terms 1/10, n/30.
	9	Sold $200 of merchandise on account to Jim Zon, sales ticket no. 62; terms 1/10, n/30.
	10	Received cash from B. Dale in payment of May 3 transaction, sales ticket no. 60, less discount.
	20	Sold $3,000 of merchandise on account to Pam Pry, sales ticket no. 63; terms 1/10, n/30.
	22	Received cash payment from Ron Lester in payment of May 4 transaction, sales ticket no. 61.
	23	Collected cash sales, $3,000.
	24	Issued credit memorandum no. 1 to Pam Pry for $2,000 of merchandise returned from May 20 sales on account.
	26	Received cash from Pam Pry in payment of May 20, sales ticket no. 63. (Don't forget about the credit memo and discount.)
	28	Collected cash sales, $7,000.
	30	Sold sneaker rack equipment for $300 cash. (Beware.)

Check Figure:
Schedule of accounts
receivable $5,700

(*continued on next page*)

30   Sold merchandise priced at $4,000, on account to Ron Lester, sales ticket no. 64; terms 1/10, n/30.

31   Issued credit memorandum no. 2 to Ron Lester for $700 of merchandise returned from May 30 transaction, sales ticket no. 64.

Required

1. Journalize the transactions.
2. Record to the accounts receivable subsidiary ledger and post to the general ledger as needed.
3. Prepare a schedule of accounts receivable for the end of May.

LO1, 2, 3, 4, 5 (75 min)   **9A-4.** Bill Murray opened Bill's Cosmetic Market on April 1. A 6% sales tax is calculated and added to all cosmetic sales. Bill offers no sales discounts. The following transactions occurred in April:

200X

Apr.   1   Bill Murray invested $8,000 in the Cosmetic Market from his personal savings account.

5   From the cash register tapes, lipstick cash sales were $5,000, plus sales tax.

5   From the cash register tapes, eye shadow cash sales were $2,000, plus sales tax.

8   Sold lipstick on account to Alice Koy Co., $300, sales ticket no. 1, plus sales tax.

9   Sold eye shadow on account to Marika Sanchez Co., $1,000, sales ticket no. 2, plus sales tax.

15   Issued credit memorandum no. 1 to Alice Koy Co. for $150 for lipstick returned. (Be sure to reduce Sales Tax Payable for Bill.)

19   Marika Sanchez Co. paid half the amount owed from sales ticket no. 2, dated April 9.

21   Sold lipstick on account to Jeff Tong Co., $300, sales ticket no. 3, plus sales tax.

24   Sold eye shadow on account to Rusty Neal Co., $800, sales ticket no. 4, plus sales tax.

25   Issued credit memorandum no. 2 to Jeff Tong Co. for $200 for lipstick returned from sales ticket no. 3, dated April 21.

29   Cash sales taken from the cash register tape showed the following:

     1. Lipstick: $1,000 + $60 sales tax collected.

     2. Eye shadow: $3,000 + $180 sales tax collected.

29   Sold lipstick on account to Marika Sanchez Co., $400, sales ticket no. 5, plus sales tax.

30   Received payment from Marika Sanchez Co. of sales ticket no. 5, dated April 29.

Check Figure:
Schedule of accounts receivable $1,643

Required

1. Journalize the transactions.
2. Record to the accounts receivable subsidiary ledger and post to the general ledger when appropriate.
3. Prepare a schedule of accounts receivable for the end of April.

Group B Problems

LO1, 2, 4, 5 (40 min)   **9B-1.** The following transactions occurred for Pizza and More for the month of June:

200X

June   1   Sold grocery merchandise to Cindy Co. on account, $800, invoice no. 1.

4   Sold pizza merchandise to Groom Co. on account, $550, invoice no. 2.

8   Sold grocery merchandise to French Co. on account, $900, invoice no. 3.

10   Issued credit memorandum no. 1 to Cindy Co. for $160 of grocery merchandise returned due to spoilage.

15   Sold pizza merchandise to Groom Co. on account, $700, invoice no. 4.

19   Sold grocery merchandise to French Co. on account, $250, invoice no. 5.

Required

1. Journalize the transactions.

2. Record to the accounts receivable subsidiary ledger and post to the general ledger as appropriate.

3. Prepare a schedule of accounts receivable for the end of June.

Check Figure:
Schedule of accounts receivable $3,040

9B-2. In November the following transactions occurred for Ted's Auto Supply (your working papers have balances as of November 1 for certain general ledger and accounts receivable ledger accounts):

LO1, 2, 4, 5 (50 min)

200X

Nov. 1   Sold merchandise to R. Volan on account, $4,000, invoice no. 70, plus 5% sales tax.

5   Sold merchandise to J. Seth on account, $1,600, invoice no. 71, plus 5% sales tax.

8   Sold merchandise to Lance Corner on account, $15,000, invoice no. 72, plus 5% sales tax.

10   Issued credit memorandum no. 14 to R. Volan for $2,000 for defective merchandise returned from Nov. 1 transaction. (Be sure to record the reduction in Sales Tax Payable as well.)

12   Sold merchandise to J. Seth on account, $1,400, invoice no. 73, plus 5% sales tax.

Required

1. Journalize the transactions.

2. Record to the accounts receivable subsidiary ledger and post to the general ledger as appropriate.

3. Prepare a schedule of accounts receivable for the end of November.

Check Figure:
Schedule of accounts receivable $22,600

9B-3. (In your working papers, all the beginning balances needed are provided for the accounts receivable subsidiary and general ledgers.) The following transactions occurred for Peaker's Sneaker Shop:

LO1, 2, 3, 4, 5 (70 min)

200X

May 1   Mark Peaker invested an additional $14,000 in the sneaker store.

3   Sold $2,000 of merchandise on account to B. Dale, sales ticket no. 60; terms 1/10, n/30.

4   Sold $900 of merchandise on account to Ron Lester, sales ticket no. 61; terms 1/10, n/30.

9   Sold $600 of merchandise on account to Jim Zon, sales ticket no. 62; terms 1/10, n/30.

10   Received cash from B. Dale in payment of May 3 transaction, sales ticket no. 60, less discount.

20   Sold $4,000 of merchandise on account to Pam Pry, sales ticket no. 63; terms 1/10, n/30.

22   Received cash payment from Ron Lester in payment of May 4 transaction, sales ticket no. 61.

(continued on next page)

23   Collected cash sales, $6,000.

24   Issued credit memorandum no. 1 to Pam Pry for $500 of merchandise returned from May 20 sales on account.

26   Received cash from Pam Pry in payment of May 20 sales ticket no. 63. (Don't forget about the credit memo and discount.)

28   Collected cash sales, $12,000.

30   Sold sneaker rack equipment for $200 cash.

30   Sold $6,000 of merchandise on account to Ron Lester, sales ticket no. 64, terms 1/10, n/30.

31   Issued credit memorandum no. 2 to Ron Lester for $800 of merchandise returned from May 30 transaction, sales ticket no. 64.

Check Figure:
Schedule of accounts
receivable $8,000

Required

1. Journalize the transactions.
2. Record and post as appropriate.
3. Prepare a schedule of accounts receivable for the end of May.

LO1, 2, 3, 4, 5 (75 min)

9B-4. Bill's Cosmetic Market began operating in April. A 6% sales tax is calculated and added to all cosmetic sales. Bill offers no discounts. The following transactions occurred in April:

200X

Apr. 1   Bill Murray invested $10,000 in the Cosmetic Market from his personal account.

5   From the cash register tapes, lipstick cash sales were $5,000, plus sales tax.

5   From the cash register tapes, eye shadow cash sales were $3,000, plus sales tax.

8   Sold lipstick on account to Alice Koy Co., $400, sales ticket no. 1, plus sales tax.

9   Sold eye shadow on account to Marika Sanchez Co., $900, sales ticket no. 2, plus sales tax.

15   Issued credit memorandum no. 1 to Alice Koy Co. for lipstick returned, $200. (Be sure to reduce Sales Tax Payable for Bill.)

19   Marika Sanchez Co. paid half the amount owed from sales ticket no. 2, dated April 9.

21   Sold lipstick on account to Jeff Tong Co., $600, sales ticket no. 3, plus sales tax.

24   Sold eye shadow on account to Rusty Neal Co., $1,000, sales ticket no. 4, plus sales tax.

25   Issued credit memorandum no. 2 to Jeff Tong Co. for $300, for lipstick returned from sales ticket no. 3, dated April 21.

29   Cash sales taken from the cash register tape showed the following:

   1. Lipstick: $4,000 + $240 sales tax collected.

   2. Eye shadow: $2,000 + $120 sales tax collected.

29   Sold lipstick on account to Marika Sanchez Co., $700, sales ticket no. 5, plus sales tax.

30   Received payment from Marika Sanchez Co. of sales ticket no. 5, dated April 29.

Check Figure:
Schedule of accounts
receivable $2,067

Required

1. Journalize, record, and post as appropriate.
2. Prepare a schedule of accounts receivable for the end of April.

ON-THE-JOB TRAINING

T-1. Pete O'Brady has been hired by Logan Company to help reconstruct the general journal, which was recently destroyed in a fire. The owner of Logan Company has supplied him with the following data. Please ignore dates, invoice numbers, and so forth and enter the entries into the reconstructed general journal. What written recommendation should Pete make so reconstruction will not be needed in the future?

LO1, 2, 3, 4, 5 (60 min)

ACCOUNTS RECEIVABLE SUBSIDIARY LEDGER

P. Bond

	Dr.	Cr.	
Bal.	100	150	GJ
GJ		150	Entitled to 2% discount

M. Raff

	Dr.	Cr.
Bal.	200	
GJ	100	

J. Smooth

	Dr.	Cr.	
Bal.	300	1,000	GJ
GJ	2,000	1,000	GJ
GJ	1,000	500	GJ
		Entitled to 1% discount

R. Venner

	Dr.	Cr.
Bal.	200	400
GJ	400	

PARTIAL GENERAL LEDGER

Cash

Dr.	Cr.
5,000	
147	
400	
5,000	
1,000	
990	
200	

Accounts Receivable

	Dr.	Cr.	
Bal.	800	1,000	GJ
	150	500	GJ
	100	150	GJ
	400		
	2,000	400	
	1,000	1,000	

Shelving Equipment

	Dr.	Cr.	
Bal.	200	200	GJ

M. Rang, Capital

Dr.	Cr.	
	1,000	Bal.
	5,000	Additional investment this month

(continued on next page)

Sales

Dr.	Cr.	
	800	Bal.
	150	GJ
	100	GJ
	400	GJ
	2,000	GJ
	1,000	GJ
	5,000	Cash Sales

Sales Discount

	Dr.	Cr.
GJ	3	
	10	

Sales Returns and Allowances

	Dr.	Cr.
GJ	1,000	
GJ	500	

LO2, 3, 4, 5 (45 min)

T-2. The bookkeeper of Joy Company records credit sales and returns in a general journal. The bookkeeper did the following:

1. Recorded an $18 credit sale as $180 in the general journal.

2. Correctly recorded a $40 sale in the general journal but posted it to B. Blue's account as $400 in the accounts receivable ledger.

3. Made an additional error in determining the balance of J. B. Window Co. in the accounts receivable ledger.

4. Posted a sales return from B. Katz Co. that was recorded in the general journal to the Sales Returns and Allowance account and the Accounts Receivable account but forgot to record it to the B. Katz Co. subsidiary ledger accounts.

5. Added the total of the general journal incorrectly.

6. Posted a sales return to the Accounts Receivable account but not to the Sales Returns and Allowances account. The Accounts Receivable ledger was recorded correctly.

Could you inform the bookkeeper in writing as to when each error will be discovered?

FINANCIAL REPORT PROBLEM

LO1 (15 min)

Reading the Kellogg's Annual Report

Go to Appendix A, Note 1, Revenue Recognition, and find out what account records the promotional package inserts.

INTERNET PROJECT

Big Lots

Go to the Web and search: Annual Report Big Lots 2008.
Click on Investors Relations.
List out the latest news Big Lots is providing to its investors.
Order a free annual report.

CONTINUING PROBLEM

Sanchez Computer Center

LO1, 2, 3, 4, 5 (60 min)

To assist you in recording these transactions for the month of January, at the end of this problem is the schedule of accounts receivable as of December 31 and an updated chart of accounts with the current balance listed for each account.

Assignment

1. Journalize the transactions.
2. Record in the accounts receivable subsidiary ledger and post to the general ledger as appropriate. A partial general ledger is included in the *Working Papers.*
3. Prepare a schedule of accounts receivable as of January 31, 200X.

The January transactions are as follows:

Jan.	1	Sold $700 worth of merchandise to Taylor Golf on credit, sales invoice no. 5000; terms 2/10, n/30.
	10	Sold $3,000 worth of merchandise on account to Anthony Pitale, sales invoice no. 5001; terms 2/10, n/30.
	11	Received $3,000 from Accu Pac, Inc., toward payment of its balance; no discount allowed.
	12	Collected $2,000 cash sales.
	19	Sold $4,000 worth of merchandise on account to Vita Needle, sales invoice no. 5002; terms 4/10, n/30.
	20	Collected balance in full from invoice no. 5001, Anthony Pitale.
	29	Issued credit memorandum to Taylor Golf for $400 worth of merchandise returned, invoice no. 5000.
	29	Collected full payment from Vita Needle, invoice no. 5002.

Schedule of Accounts Receivable
Sanchez Computer Center
December 31, 200X

Taylor Golf	$ 2,900.00
Vita Needle	6,800.00
Accu Pac	3,900.00
Total Amount Due	$13,600.00

Chart of Accounts and Current Balances as of 12/31/0X

Account #	Account Name	Debit Balance	Credit Balance
1000	Cash	$3,336.65	
1010	Petty Cash	100	
1020	Accounts Receivable	13,600	
1025	Prepaid Rent	1,600	
1030	Supplies	132	
1040	Merchandise Inventory	0	
1080	Computer Shop Equipment	3,800	
1081	Accumulated Dep., C.S. Equip.		$ 99
1090	Office Equipment	1,050	

(continued on next page)

Acct.	Account	Debit	Credit
1091	Accumulated Dep., Office Equip.		20
2000	Accounts Payable		2,050
2010	Wages Payable		0
2020	FICA—Social Security Payable		0
2030	FICA—Medicare Payable		0
2040	FIT Payable		0
2050	SIT Payable		0
2060	FUTA Payable		0
2070	SUTA Payable		0
3000	Freedman, Capital		7,406
3010	Freedman, Withdrawals	2,015	
3020	Income Summary		0
4000	Service Revenue		18,500
4010	Sales		0
4020	Sales Returns and Allowances	0	
4030	Sales Discounts	0	
5010	Advertising Expense	0	
5020	Rent Expense	0	
5030	Utilities Expense	0	
5040	Phone Expense	150	
5050	Supplies Expense	0	
5060	Insurance Expense	0	
5070	Postage Expense	25	
5080	Dep. Exp., C.S. Equipment	0	
5090	Dep. Exp., Office Equipment	0	
5100	Miscellaneous Expense	10	
5110	Wage Expense	2,030	
5120	Payroll Tax Expense	226.35	
5130	Interest Expense	0	
5140	Bad Debt Expense	0	
6000	Purchases	0	
6010	Purchases Returns and Allowances		0
6020	Purchases Discounts		0
6030	Freight In	0	

10

Purchases and Cash Payments

DID YOU KNOW? Trade promotions from companies like Del Monte are amounts paid to retailers for temporary price reductions, circular advertisements, and favorable stock locations. Trade promotions reduce sales and are recorded as accrued liabilities. Visit *www.delmonte.com* to find more information about Del Monte.

LEARNING OBJECTIVES

1. Recording and posting purchase transactions.

2. Recording to accounts payable subsidiary ledger.

3. Preparing, journalizing, and posting a debit memorandum.

4. Recording and posting cash payment transactions.

5. Preparing a schedule of accounts payable.

6. Journalizing transactions for a perpetual accounting system.

LO1 Learning Unit 10-1 Chou's Toy Shop: Buyer's View of a Merchandise Company

Purchases

> Purchases of merchandise on account are recorded on a purchase order in Peachtree and QuickBooks.

When you go into your local supermarket do you ever wonder how a store records all of the merchandise it purchases from a company like Del Monte? First, let's look at Chou's Toy Shop. Chou brings merchandise into his toy store for resale to customers. The account that records the cost of this merchandise is called **Purchases.** Suppose Chou buys $4,000 worth of Barbie dolls on account from Mattel Manufacturing on July 6. The Purchases account records all merchandise bought for resale.

	Purchases	
Purchases is a cost. The rules work the same as an expense.	**Dr.**	**Cr.**
	4,000	

This account has a debit balance and is classified as a cost. Purchases represent costs that are directly related to bringing merchandise into the store for resale to customers. The July 6 entry would be analyzed and journalized as in Figure 10.1.

> If Chou's purchased a new display case for the store, it would not show up in the Purchases account. The case is considered equipment that is not for resale to customers.

Accounts Affected	Category	↑ ↓	Rules	T Account Update	
Purchases	Cost	↑	Dr.	**Purchases**	
				Dr. | Cr.	
				4,000 |	
Accounts Payable, Mattel	Liability	↑	Cr.	**Acc. Payable**	**Mattel**
				Dr. | Cr.	Dr. | Cr.
				| 4,000	| 4,000

FIGURE 10.1 Purchased Merchandise on Account

July	6	Purchases		4 0 0 0 00	
		Accounts Payable, Mattel			4 0 0 0 00
		Purchases on account			

Keep in mind we would have to record to Mattel in the accounts payable subsidiary ledger. We talk about the subsidiary ledger in Learning Unit 10-2.

Purchases Returns and Allowances

Chou noticed that some of the dolls he received were defective, and he notified the manufacturer of the defects. On July 9, Mattel issued a credit memorandum indicating that Chou would get a $500 reduction from the original selling price. Chou then agreed to keep the dolls. The account that records a decrease to a buyer's cost is a contra-cost account called **Purchases Returns and Allowances.** The account lowers the cost of purchases.

Purchases Returns and Allowances	
Dr.	**Cr.**
	500

 ←——— Normal balance is a credit.

Let's analyze this reduction to cost and prepare a general journal entry (Fig. 10.2).

Accounts Affected	Category	↑ ↓	Rules	T Account Update		
Accounts Payable, Mattel	Liability	↓	Dr.	**Acc. Payable**	**Mattel**	
				Dr. | Cr.	Dr. | Cr.	
				500 | 4,000	500 | 4,000	
Purchases Returns and Allowances	Contra-cost	↑	Cr.	**Purchases Ret. & Allow.**		
				Dr. | Cr.		
				| 500		

July	9	Accounts Payable, Mattel			5 0 0 00			
		Purchases Returns and Allowances				5 0 0 00		
		Received credit memorandum						

FIGURE 10.2 Credit Memorandum Received

When posted to general ledger accounts as well as recorded to Mattel in the accounts payable subsidiary ledger, Chou owes $500 less.

Purchases Discount Now let's look at the analysis and journal entry when Chou pays Mattel. Mattel offers a 2% cash discount if the invoice is paid within 10 days. To take advantage of this cash discount, Chou sent a check to Mattel on July 15. The discount is taken after the allowance.

> *Remember:* For Mattel, it is a sales discount, whereas for Chou it is a purchases discount.

$4,000

− 500 allowance

$3,500 × .02 = $70 purchases discount

The account that records this discount is called **Purchases Discount.** It, too, is a contra-cost account because it lowers the cost of purchases.

> *Remember:* Purchases are debits; purchases discounts are credits.

Purchases Discount

Dr. | Cr.   ⟵——— Normal balance is a credit.
     | 70

Let's analyze (on top of next page) and prepare (below) a general journal entry (Fig. 10.3).

July	15	Accounts Payable, Mattel			3 5 0 0 00			
		Purchases Discount				7 0 00		
		Cash				3 4 3 0 00		
		Paid Mattel balance owed						

FIGURE 10.3 Purchase Discount Journalized

Accounts Affected	Category	↑↓	Rules	T Account Update			
Accounts Payable, Mattel	Liability	↓	Dr.	**Acc. Payable**		**Mattel**	
				Dr.	Cr.	Dr.	Cr.
				500	4,000	500	4,000
				3,500		3,500	
Purchases Discount	Contra-cost	↑	Cr.	**Purchases Discount**			
				Dr.	Cr.		
					70		
Cash	Asset	↓	Cr.	**Cash**			
				Dr.	Cr.		
					3,430		

After the journal entry is posted and recorded to Mattel, the result will show that Chou saved $70 and totally reduced what he owed to Mattel. The actual—or net—cost of his purchase is $3,430, calculated as follows:

Purchases	$4,000
− Purchases Returns and Allowances	500
− Purchases Discounts	70
= Net Purchases	$3,430

Freight charges are not taken into consideration in calculating net purchases. Still, they are important. If the seller is responsible for paying the shipping cost until the goods reach their destination, the freight charges are **F.O.B. destination.** (F.O.B. stands for "free on board" the carrier.) For example, if a seller located in Boston sold goods F.O.B. destination to a buyer in New York, the seller would have to pay the cost of shipping the goods to the buyer.

F.O.B. Destination: Seller pays freight to point of destination.

F.O.B. Shipping Point: Buyer pays freight from seller's shipping point.

If the buyer is responsible for paying the shipping costs, the freight charges are **F.O.B. shipping point.** In this situation, the seller will sometimes prepay the freight charges as a matter of convenience and will add it to the invoice of the purchaser, as in the following example:

Bill amount ($800 + $80 prepaid freight)	$880
Less 5% cash discount (.05 × $800)	40
Amount to be paid by buyer	$840

Purchases discounts are not taken on freight. The discount is based on the purchase price.

If the seller ships goods F.O.B. shipping point, legal ownership (title) passes to the buyer *when the goods are shipped.* If goods are shipped by the seller F.O.B. destination, title will change *when goods have reached their destination.* (See Exhibit 10.1 on top of next page.)

LEARNING UNIT 10-1 REVIEW

AT THIS POINT you should be able to

- Explain and calculate purchases, purchases returns and allowances, and purchases discounts.
- Calculate net purchases.
- Explain why purchases discounts are not taken on freight.
- Compare and contrast F.O.B. destination with F.O.B. shipping point.

EXHIBIT 10.1

FOB shipping point	FOB destination

FOB shipping point: title changes hands at the shipping point, and buyer owns the goods while they are in transit. So, the buyer pays the shipping costs.	**FOB destination:** title changes hands at the destination point, and seller owns the goods while they are in transit. So, the seller, not the buyer, pays the shipping costs.

Self-Review Quiz 10-1

Respond true or false to the following:

1. Net purchases = Purchases − Purchases Returns and Allowances − Purchases Discount.
2. Purchases is a contra-cost.
3. F.O.B. destination means the seller covers shipping cost and retains title until goods reach their destination.
4. Purchases discounts are not taken on freight.
5. Purchases Discount is a contra-cost account.

Solutions to Self-Review Quiz 10-1

1. True
2. False
3. True
4. True
5. True

Learning Unit 10-2 Recording and Posting Purchases Transactions on Account for Art's Wholesale Clothing Company: Introduction to Subsidiary Ledgers and Debit Memorandum

200X

April	3	Purchased merchandise on account $5,000 and freight $50 from Abby Blake Co.; terms 2/10, n/60.
	4	Purchased equipment on account $4,000 from Joe Francis Co.
	6	Purchased merchandise on account $800 from Thorpe Co.; terms 1/10, n/30.
	7	Purchased merchandise on account $980 from John Sullivan Co.; terms n/10, EOM.
	9	Art's issued debit memo #1 $200 to Thorpe for defective merchandise.
	12	Purchased merchandise on account $600 from Abby Blake Co.; terms 1/10, n/30.
	25	Purchased $500 of supplies on account from John Sullivan Co.

Let's look at the steps Art's Wholesale Clothing Company took when it ordered goods from Abby Blake Company on April 3.

Step 1: Prepare a Purchase Requisition at Art's Wholesale Clothing Company The inventory clerk notes a low inventory level of ladies' jackets for resale, so the clerk sends a **purchase requisition** to the purchasing department. A duplicate copy is sent to the accounting department. A third copy remains with the department that initiated the request to be used as a check on the purchasing department.

> Authorized personnel initiate purchase requisition.

Step 2: Purchasing Department of Art's Wholesale Clothing Company Prepares a Purchase Order After checking various price lists and suppliers' catalogs, the purchasing department fills out a form called a **purchase order.** This form gives Abby Blake Company the authority to ship the ladies' jackets ordered by Art's Wholesale Clothing Company (see Fig. 10.4).

> Four copies of purchase order: (1) (original) to supplier, (2) to accounting department, (3) to department that initiated purchase requisition, and (4) to file of purchasing department.

Step 3: Sales Invoice Prepared by Abby Blake Company Abby Blake Company receives the purchase order and prepares a sales invoice. The sales invoice for the seller is the **purchase invoice** for the buyer. A sales invoice is shown in Figure 10.5.

The invoice shows that the goods will be shipped **F.O.B.** Englewood Cliffs. Thus, Art's Wholesale Clothing Company is responsible for paying the shipping costs.

The sales invoice also shows a freight charge. Thus, Abby Blake prepaid the shipping costs as a matter of convenience. Art's will repay the freight charges when it pays the invoice.

Step 4: Receiving the Goods When goods are received, Art's Wholesale inspects the shipment and completes a **receiving report.** The receiving report verifies that the exact merchandise that was ordered was received in good condition.

FIGURE 10.4 Purchase Order

PURCHASE ORDER NO. 1
ART'S WHOLESALE CLOTHING COMPANY
1528 BELLE AVE.
NEW YORK, NY 10022

Purchased From:	Abby Blake Company 12 Foster Road Englewood Cliffs, NJ 07632	Date: April 1, 200X Shipped VIA: Freight Truck Terms: 2/10, n/60 FOB: Englewood Cliffs

Quantity	Description	Unit Price	Total
100	Ladies' Jackets Code 14-0	$50	$5,000

Art's Wholesale
By: Bill Joy

Purchase order number must appear on all invoices.

FIGURE 10.5 Sales Invoice

SALES INVOICE NO. 228
ABBY BLAKE COMPANY
12 FOSTER ROAD
ENGLEWOOD, CLIFFS, NJ 07632

Sold To:	Art's Wholesale Clothing Co. 1528 Belle Ave. New York, NY 10022	Date: April 3, 200X Shipped VIA: Freight Truck Terms: 2/10, n/60 Your Order No: 1 FOB: Englewood Cliffs

Quantity	Description	Unit Price	Total
100	Ladies' Jackets Code 14-0 Freight	$50	$5,000 50
			$5,050

TV (to bring it into the store) and that the TV is being returned. On Wal-Mart's books the analysis and journal entry in Figure 10.21 resulted.

Analysis:	Accounts Payable	L	↓	Dr.	$600
	Merchandise Inventory	A	↓	Cr.	$600

Journal Entry:	July	14	Accounts Payable			6 0 0 00							
			Merchandise Inventory						6 0 0 00				
			To record debit memo no. 10										

FIGURE 10.21 Recording a Debit Memorandum

Note that the cost of merchandise inventory has been reduced by $600 due to the return. In the perpetual inventory system there is no purchases, returns, and allowances title. The reduction in cost from the return is recorded *directly* into the Merchandise Inventory account. Let's now look at how Wal-Mart would record any cash discounts it would receive due to payment of the Sony bill within the discount period.

Recording Purchase Discounts Let's assume Wal-Mart pays Sony within the first 10 days. Keep in mind that we take no discounts on returned goods (the $600 return). The amount of purchase discount will be recorded as a reduction to the cost of merchandise inventory. Figure 10.22 shows the analysis and journal entry on July 16. A discount lowers the cost of inventory.

Analysis:	Accounts Payable	L	↓	Dr.	$6,400
	Cash	A	↓	Cr.	$6,272
	Merchandise Inventory	A	↓	Cr.	$ 128

($7,000 – $600 Return)

Journal Entry:	July	14	Accounts Payable			6 4 0 0 00							
			Cash						6 2 7 2 00				
			Merchandise Inventory						1 2 8 00				

2% × $6,400

FIGURE 10.22 Recording a Purchase Discount

Keep in mind that had Wal-Mart missed the discount period it would have debited $6,400 to Accounts Payable and credited Cash for $6,400. Merchandise Inventory would not be reduced.

Recording Cost of Freight The cost of freight ($300) is to be paid by Wal-Mart. When the purchaser is responsible for cost of freight, it is added to the cost of merchandise inventory. If the cost of freight is paid by the seller, it could be recorded in an operating expense account called Freight-Out. Figure 10.23 is the analysis and journal entry for freight on July 10.

Analysis:	Merchandise Inventory	A	↑	Dr.	$300
	Cash	A	↓	Cr.	$300

Freight Cost added to Merchandise Inventory

Journal Entry:	July	10	Merchandise Inventory			3 0 0 00							
			Cash						3 0 0 00				
			Payment of freight										

FIGURE 10.23 Recording Cost of Freight

Wal-Mart: The Seller Now let's look at Wal-Mart as the *seller* of merchandise.

Recording Sales at Wal-Mart Sales revenues are earned at Wal-Mart when the goods are transferred to the buyer. The earned revenue can be for cash and/or credit. Let's look at the following example of the sale of a TV at Wal-Mart for $950 on credit on August 10, which cost Wal-Mart $600. Keep in mind when using the perpetual inventory system that at the time of the earned sale Wal-Mart will

At selling price ⟶ 1. *Record the sales (cash and/or credit).*
At cost ⟶   2. *Record the cost of the inventory sold and the reduction in inventory.*

First, let's analyze the transaction in Figure 10.24. Note that we will have two entries, one to record the sale and one to show a new cost and less inventory on hand.

FIGURE 10.24 Recording Sales and Cost of Goods Sold

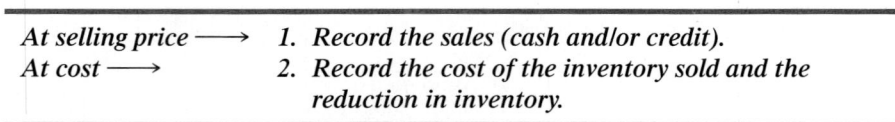

Selling < Price	Accounts Receivable	Asset	↑	Dr.	$950
	Sales	Revenue	↑	Cr.	$950
Cost to < Make sale	Cost of Goods Sold	Cost	↑	Dr.	$600
	Merchandise Inventory	Asset	↓	Cr.	$600

Journal Entries:

Aug.	10	Accounts Receivable		9 5 0 00			
		Sales				9 5 0 00	
		Charge sales					
	10	Cost of Goods Sold		6 0 0 00			
		Merchandise Inventory				6 0 0 00	
		To record cost of					
		merchandise sold on account					

Be sure to go back to steps 1 and 2 of Figure 10.17. These two steps reinforce the preceding journal entries. Remember that if the sale were a cash sale, we would have debited Cash instead of Accounts Receivable. Note also that the Sales account only records sales of goods held for resale.

How Wal-Mart Records Sales Returns Allowances and Sales Discounts Keep in mind that we are now looking at how the *seller* of merchandise records a transaction giving the customer a credit due to an allowance or a return of goods from a previous sale. Usually, the seller will issue a *credit memorandum*, a document informing the customer of the adjustment due to the return or allowance. For example, on August 15, let's look at a customer who returned a $950 TV that had been purchased at Wal-Mart. On Wal-Mart's books, the analysis and journal entry in Figure 10.25 resulted.

The first entry records the return at the original selling price using the contra-revenue account Sales Returns and Allowances. The second entry records putting the inventory back in Wal-Mart's books at cost and reducing its Cost of Goods Sold because the inventory was not sold. Remember that we only record the Cost of Goods Sold when the sale has been earned. Keep in mind that if the customer kept the TV but at a reduced price, no entry affecting Merchandise Inventory and Cost of Goods Sold would be needed.

The Analysis: at Selling Price	Sales Returns and Allowances	Contra-Revenue	↑	Dr.	$950
	Accounts Receivable	Asset	↓	Cr.	$950
At Cost	Merchandise Inventory	Asset	↑	Dr.	$600
	Costs of Goods Sold	Cost	↓	Cr.	$600

FIGURE 10.25 Return of Goods

Journal Entries:

	Aug.	15	Sales Returns and Allowances	9 5 0 00		
			Accounts Receivable*		9 5 0 00	
			Returned goods			
		15	Merchandise Inventory	6 0 0 00		
			Cost of Goods Sold		6 0 0 00	

*If it were a *cash* customer cash would be credited.

Let's assume a customer on August 25 gets a 2% discount for paying for a $950 TV early. The analysis and entry in Figure 10.26 would result on the seller's book:

The Analysis:	Cash	Asset	↑	Dr.	$931
	Sales Discount	Contra-Revenue	↑	Dr.	$ 19
	Accounts Receivable	Asset	↓	Cr.	$950

FIGURE 10.26 Recording Sales Discount

Journal Entry:

	Aug.	25	Cash	9 3 1 00		
			Sales Discount	1 9 00		
			Accounts Receivable		9 5 0 00	

Now let's summarize (Figure 10.27) all the entries for both the buyer and the seller (in this case, Wal-Mart).

FIGURE 10.27

	Wal-Mart the Buyer		Wal-Mart the Seller	

Bought Inventory for Resale on Account	Merchandise Inventory → At
	  Accounts Payable Cost
		Sold Inventory on Account	Accounts Receivable ──→ At
			  Sales Selling Price
			Cost of Goods Sold ──→ At
			  Merchandise Inventory Cost	

Issued a Debit Memo for Merchandise Returned	Accounts Payable ──→ At
	  Merchandise Inventory Cost
		Issued a Credit Memo for Returned Merchandise	Sales Returns and Allowances → At
			  Accounts Receivable Selling Price
			Merchandise Inventory ──→ At
			  Cost of Goods Sold Cost	

Recorded a Purchase Discount	Accounts Payable
	  Cash
	  Merchandise Inventory
		Recorded a Sales Discount	Cash
			Sales Discount
			  Accounts Receivable	

Amount of discount ──┘

Figure 10.28 shows a comparison of Perpetual and Periodic Systems.

FIGURE 10.28 Comparison of Perpetual and Periodic Systems

Transaction	Perpetual System	Periodic System

(A) Sold merchandise that cost $8,000 on account for $20,000.

Perpetual System:

Accts. Receivable	20 0 0 0 00	
Sales		20 0 0 0 00
Cost of Goods Sold	8 0 0 0 00	
Merch. Inventory		8 0 0 0 00

Periodic System:

| Accts. Receivable | 20 0 0 0 00 | |
| Sales | | 20 0 0 0 00 |

(B) Purchased $900 of merchandise on account.

Perpetual System:

| Merch. Inventory | 9 0 0 00 | |
| Accts. Payable | | 9 0 0 00 |

Periodic System:

| Purchases | 9 0 0 00 | |
| Accts. Payable | | 9 0 0 00 |

(C) Paid $50 freight charges.

Perpetual System:

| Merch. Inventory | 5 0 00 | |
| Cash | | 5 0 00 |

Periodic System:

| Freight-In | 5 0 00 | |
| Cash | | 5 0 00 |

(D) Cash customer returned $200 of merchandise. Cost of merchandise was $100.

Perpetual System:

Sales Ret. & Allow.	2 0 0 00	
Cash*		2 0 0 00
Merch. Inventory	1 0 0 00	
Cost of Goods Sold		1 0 0 00

Periodic System:

| Sales Ret. & Allow. | 2 0 0 00 | |
| Cash* | | 2 0 0 00 |

(E) Returned $400 of merchandise previously bought on account due to defects.

Perpetual System:

| Accts. Payable | 4 0 0 00 | |
| Merch. Inventory | | 4 0 0 00 |

Periodic System:

| Accts. Payable | 4 0 0 00 | |
| Pur. Ret. & Allow. | | 4 0 0 00 |

* or accounts receivable if made to charge customers

LEARNING UNIT 10-4 REVIEW

AT THIS POINT you should be able to

- Define the terms *merchandise inventory*, *sales*, and *cost of goods sold*.
- Explain how discounts are recorded in a perpetual inventory system.
- Journalize transactions for a merchandise company using a perpetual system.

Self-Review Quiz 10-4

Pete's Clock Shops completed the following merchandise transactions in the month of June:

200X

June	1	Purchased merchandise on account from Clock Suppliers, $4,000; terms 2/10, n/30.
	3	Sold merchandise on account, $2,000; terms 2/10, n/30. The cost of the merchandise sold was $1,200.
	4	Received credit from Clock Suppliers for merchandise returned, $400.
	10	Received collections in full, less discounts, from June 3 sales.
	11	Paid Clock Suppliers in full, less discount.
	14	Purchased office equipment for cash, $500.
	15	Purchased $2,800 of merchandise from Abe's Distribution for cash.
	16	Received a refund due to defective merchandise from supplier on cash purchase of $400.
	17	Purchased merchandise from Rose Corp., $6,000, free on board shipping point (buyer pays freight); terms 2/10, n/30. Freight to be paid on June 20.
	18	Sold merchandise for $3,000 cash; the cost of the merchandise sold was $1,600.
	20	Paid freight on June 17 purchase, $180.
	25	Purchased merchandise from Lee Co., $1,400, free on board destination (seller pays freight); terms 2/10, n/30.
	26	Paid Rose Corp. in full, less discount.
	27	Made refunds to cash customers for returned clocks, $300. The cost of the defective clocks was $120.

Pete's Clock Shop accounts included the following:

Cash, 101; Accounts Receivable, 112; Merchandise Inventory, 120; Office Equipment, 124; Accounts Payable, 201; P. Rings, Capital, 301; Sales, 401; Sales Discount, 412; Cost of Goods Sold, 501.

Journalize the transactions using a perpetual inventory system.

Solution to Self-Review Quiz 10-4

			GENERAL JOURNAL				Page 2
Date			**Account Titles and Description**	**PR**	**Dr.**	**Cr.**	
200X							
June	1		Merchandise Inventory		4 0 0 0 00		
			Accounts Payable			4 0 0 0 00	
	3		Accounts Receivable		2 0 0 0 00		
			Sales			2 0 0 0 00	
			Cost of Goods Sold		1 2 0 0 00		
			Merchandise Inventory			1 2 0 0 00	
	4		Accounts Payable		4 0 0 00		
			Merchandise Inventory			4 0 0 00	
	10		Cash		1 9 6 0 00		
			Sales Discount		4 0 00		
			Accounts Receivable			2 0 0 0 00	
	11		Accounts Payable		3 6 0 0 00		
			Cash			3 5 2 8 00	
			Merchandise Inventory			7 2 00	
	14		Office Equipment		5 0 0 00		
			Cash			5 0 0 00	
	15		Merchandise Inventory		2 8 0 0 00		
			Cash			2 8 0 0 00	
	16		Cash		4 0 0 00		
			Merchandise Inventory			4 0 0 00	
	17		Merchandise Inventory		6 0 0 0 00		
			Accounts Payable			6 0 0 0 00	
	18		Cash		3 0 0 0 00		
			Sales			3 0 0 0 00	
			Cost of Goods Sold		1 6 0 0 00		
			Merchandise Inventory			1 6 0 0 00	
	20		Merchandise Inventory		1 8 0 00		
			Cash			1 8 0 00	
	25		Merchandise Inventory		1 4 0 0 00		
			Accounts Payable			1 4 0 0 00	
	26		Accounts Payable		6 0 0 0 00		
			Cash			5 8 8 0 00	
			Merchandise Inventory			1 2 0 00	
	27		Sales Returns and Allowances		3 0 0 00		
			Cash*			3 0 0 00	
			Merchandise Inventory		1 2 0 00		
			Cost of Goods Sold			1 2 0 00	

* If this were a charge customer it would have been Accounts Receivable.

CHAPTER ASSIGNMENTS

SUMMARY OF KEY POINTS

LEARNING UNIT 10-1

1. Purchases are merchandise for resale. It is a cost.
2. Purchases Returns and Allowances and Purchases Discount are contra-costs.
3. *F.O.B. shipping point* means that the purchaser of the goods is responsible for covering the shipping costs. If the terms were *F.O.B. destination,* the seller would be responsible for covering the shipping costs until the goods reached the purchaser's destination.
4. Purchases discounts are not taken on freight.

LEARNING UNIT 10-2

1. The steps for buying merchandise from a company may include the following:
   a. The requesting department prepares a purchase requisition.
   b. The purchasing department prepares a purchase order.
   c. Seller receives the order and prepares a sales invoice (a purchase invoice from the buyer).
   d. Buyer receives the goods and prepares a receiving report.
   e. Accounting department verifies and approves the invoice for payment.
2. The general journal records the buying of merchandise or other items on account.
3. The accounts payable subsidiary ledger, organized in alphabetical order, is not in the same book as Accounts Payable, the controlling account in the general ledger.
4. At the end of the month the total of all creditors' ending balances in the accounts payable subsidiary ledger should equal the ending balance in Accounts Payable, the controlling account in the general ledger.
5. A debit memorandum (issued by the buyer) indicates that the amount owed from a previous purchase is being reduced because some goods were defective or not up to a specific standard and thus were returned or an allowance requested. On receiving the debit memorandum, the seller will issue a credit memorandum.

LEARNING UNIT 10-3

1. All payments of cash (check) are recorded in the general journal.
2. At the end of the month, the schedule of accounts payable, a list of ending amounts owed individual creditors, should equal the ending balance in Accounts Payable, the controlling account in the general ledger.

LEARNING UNIT 10-4

1. In a perpetual inventory system, when a sale is recognized the cost of goods sold and merchandise inventory must be updated.
2. Purchases discounts on returns are reflected in the Merchandise Inventory account for a perpetual inventory system.

KEY TERMS

Accounts payable subsidiary ledger A book or file that contains, in alphabetical order, the name of the creditor and amount owed from purchases on account.

Controlling account The account in the general ledger that summarizes or controls a subsidiary ledger. Example: The Accounts Payable account in the general ledger is the controlling account for the accounts payable subsidiary ledger. After postings are complete, it shows the total amount owed from purchases made on account.

Cost of goods sold In a perpetual inventory system, an account that records the cost of merchandise inventory used to make the sale.

Debit memorandum A memo issued by a purchaser to a seller, indicating that some Purchases Returns and Allowances have occurred and therefore the purchaser now owes less money on account.

F.O.B. Free on board, which means without shipping charge either to the buyer or seller up to or from a specified location. In the view of one or the other, the shipment is *free* on board the carrier.

F.O.B. destination *Seller* pays or is responsible for the cost of freight to purchaser's location or destination.

F.O.B. shipping point *Purchaser* pays or is responsible for the shipping costs from seller's shipping point to purchaser's location.

Invoice approval form Used by the accounting department in checking the invoice and finally approving it for recording and payment.

Merchandise Inventory A perpetual inventory system account that records purchases of merchandise. Discounts and returns are recorded in this account for the buyer.

Periodic inventory system An inventory system that, at the *end* of each accounting period, calculates the cost of the unsold goods on hand by taking the cost of each unit times the number of units of each product on hand.

Perpetual inventory system An inventory system that keeps *continual track* of each type of inventory by recording units on hand at beginning, units sold, and the current balance after each sale or purchase.

Purchase invoice The seller's sales invoice, which is sent to the purchaser.

Purchase order A form used in business to place an order for the buying of goods from a seller.

Purchase requisition A form used within a business by the requesting department asking the purchasing department of the business to buy specific goods.

Purchases Merchandise for resale. It is a cost.

Purchases Discount A contra-cost account in the general ledger that records discounts offered by suppliers of merchandise for prompt payment of purchases by buyers.

Purchases Returns and Allowances A contra-cost account in the ledger that records the amount of defective or unacceptable merchandise returned to suppliers and/or price reductions given for defective items.

Receiving report A business form used to notify the appropriate people of the ordered goods received along with the quantities and specific condition of the goods.

BLUEPRINT

Periodic		Perpetual
Purchases	⟶	Merchandise Inventory
Purchase Discounts	⟶	Merchandise Inventory
Sales/Accounts Receivable	⟶	Sales/Accounts Receivable Cost of Goods Sold/Merchandise Inventory
Freight-In	⟶	Merchandise Inventory
Sales Discounts	⟶	Sales Discounts
Sales Returns and Allowances	⟶	Sales Returns and Allowances

QUESTIONS, CLASSROOM DEMONSTRATION EXERCISES, EXERCISES, AND PROBLEMS

Discussion Questions and Critical Thinking/Ethical Case

1. Explain how net purchases is calculated.

2. What is the normal balance of Purchases Discount?

3. What is a contra-cost?

4. Explain the difference between F.O.B. shipping point and F.O.B. destination.

5. F.O.B. destination means that title to the goods will switch to the buyer when goods are shipped. Agree or disagree? Why?

6. What is the normal balance of each creditor in the accounts payable subsidiary ledger?

7. Why could the balance of the controlling account, Accounts Payable, equal the sum of the accounts payable subsidiary ledger during the month?

8. What is the relationship between a purchase requisition and a purchase order?

9. What purpose could a typical invoice approval form serve?

10. Explain the difference between merchandise and equipment.

11. Why would the purchaser issue a debit memorandum?

12. Explain why a trade discount is not a cash discount.

13. What new account is used in a perpetual system compared to the periodic system?

14. What is the normal balance of cost of goods sold?

15. How are discounts recorded in a perpetual system?

16. Spring Co. bought merchandise from All Co. with terms 2/10, n/30. Joanne Ring, the bookkeeper, forgot to pay the bill within the first 10 days. She went to Mel Ryan, the head accountant, who told her to backdate the check so that it looked like the bill was paid within the discount period. Joanne told Mel that she thought they could get away with it. Should Joanne and Mel backdate the check to take advantage of the discount? You make the call. Write down your specific recommendations to Joanne.

Classroom Demonstration Exercises

SET A

Questions 1–6 are based on a periodic inventory system.

Questions 7–10 are based on a perpetual inventory system.

Accounts for Purchase Activities   *LO1, 2, 3 (10 min)*

1. Complete the following table:

To the Seller		To the Buyer
Sales	⟷	a. _____
Sales returns and allowances	⟷	b. _____
Sales discount	⟷	c. _____
Credit memorandum	⟷	d. _____
Schedule of accounts receivable	⟷	e. _____
Accounts receivable subsidiary ledger	⟷	f. _____

LO1 (5 min) **Accounts**

2. Complete the following table:

Account	Category	↑	↓	Temporary or Permanent
Purchases				
Purchases Returns and Allowances				
Purchases Discount				

LO1 (5 min) **Calculating Net Purchases**

3. Calculate Net Purchases from the following: Purchases, $12; Purchases Returns and Allowances, $4; Purchases Discounts, $2.

LO1, 2, 3 (10 min) **Purchases Journal, General Journal, Recording, and Posting**

4. Match the following to the three business transactions (more than one number can be used).
   1. Recorded to the accounts payable subsidiary ledger.
   2. Recorded to the general journal.
   3. Posted to the general ledger.
   _____ a. Bought merchandise on account from Long.com, invoice no. 12, $60.
   _____ b. Bought equipment on account from Lee Co., invoice no. 13, $90.
   _____ c. Issued debit memo no. 1 to Long.com for merchandise returned, $10, from invoice no. 12.

LO1, 5 (15 min) **Journalizing Transactions**

5. Journalize the following transactions:
   a. Issued credit memo no. 2, $40, to Small Co.
   b. Cash sales, $180.
   c. Received check from Blue Co., $50, less 3% discount.
   d. Bought merchandise on account from Mel Co., $35, invoice no. 20; terms 1/10, n/30.
   e. Cash purchase, $15.
   f. Issued debit memo to Mel Co., $15, for merchandise returned from invoice no. 20.

LO5 (10 min) 6. From the following prepare a schedule of Accounts Payable for Web.Com for May 31, 200X:

Accounts Payable Subsidiary Ledger

Rowe Co.

	Dr.	Cr.	
		60	5/7 GJ1

Bloss Co

	Dr.	Cr.	
5/25 GJ1	10	50	5/20 GJ1

General Ledger

Accounts Payable

	Dr.	Cr.	
5/31 GJ1 10		110	5/31 GJ1

LO6 (15 min) 7. Draw a seesaw similar to the one shown in Figure 10.18 and show a sale of $900 that cost the store $400. Be sure to label all the accounts.

8. Bob C. paid $200 to Pete Co. and received a $20 purchases discount.   *LO6 (10 min)*
   Journalize the entry.

9. Pete Morse returned $300 of merchandise to Logan Co. What would be the jour-   *LO6 (10 min)*
   nal entry on the books of both the buyer and seller?

10. Jeans Co. paid the cost of freight, $100. Journalize the transaction.   *LO6 (10 min)*

SET B

Questions 1–6 are based on a periodic inventory system.

Questions 7–10 are based on a perpetual inventory system.

Accounts for Purchase Activities   *LO1, 2, 3 (10 min)*

1. Complete the following table: **Account**
   A cost   a. _____

   A contra-cost   b. _____

   A contra-cost discount   c. _____

   Opposite of accounts receivable ledger   d. _____

   Cost of freight to seller   e. _____

Accounts   *LO1 (5 min)*

2. Complete the following table:

Account	Category	↑	↓	Temporary or Permanent
Sales				
Sales Returns and Allowances				
Sales Discount				

Calculating Net Purchases   *LO1 (5 min)*

3. Calculate Net Purchases from the following: Purchases, $15; Purchases Returns
   and Allowances, $4; Purchases Discounts, $3.

Business Transaction, General Journal, Recording, and Posting   *LO1, 2, 3 (10 min)*

4. Match the following to the three journal entries (more than one number can
   be used).
   1. Recorded to the accounts payable subsidiary ledger.
   2. Recorded in the general journal.
   3. Posted to the general ledger.
      a. Bought merchandise on account from Ace.com, invoice no. 12, $70.
      b. Bought equipment on account from Mabel Co., invoice no. 13, $120.
      c. Issued debit memo no. 1 to Ace.com for merchandise returned, $7, from
         invoice no. 12.

Journalizing Transaction   *LO1, 5 (15 min)*

5. Journalize the following transactions.
   a. Issued credit memo no. 2 to Rose, $50.
   b. Cash sales, $210.
   c. Received check from Lew Co., $90, less 3% discount.

      d. Bought merchandise on account from Mel Co., $50, invoice no. 20; terms 1/10, n/30.

      e. Cash purchase, $25.

      f. Issued debit memo to Ling Co., $15, for merchandise returned from invoice no. 20.

LO5 (10 min)   **6.** From the following, prepare a schedule of accounts payable for Web.Com for May 31, 200X:

<table>
<tr><td colspan="3" align="center">**Accounts Payable Subsidiary Ledger**</td><td colspan="3" align="center">**General Ledger**</td></tr>
<tr><td colspan="3" align="center">**Jones Co.**</td><td colspan="3" align="center">**Accounts Payable**</td></tr>
<tr><td></td><td>**Dr.**</td><td>**Cr.**</td><td></td><td>**Dr.**</td><td>**Cr.**</td></tr>
<tr><td></td><td></td><td>70   5/7 GJ1</td><td>5/31 GJ1</td><td>10</td><td>120   5/31 GJ1</td></tr>
</table>

<table>
<tr><td colspan="3" align="center">**Ring Co.**</td></tr>
<tr><td></td><td>**Dr.**</td><td>**Cr.**</td></tr>
<tr><td>5/25 GJ1</td><td>20</td><td>60   5/20 GJ1</td></tr>
</table>

LO6 (15 min)   **7.** Calculate the gross profit: sales, $50,000; cost of goods sold, $18,000; sales discount, $6,000.

LO6 (10 min)   **8.** Long paid $500 to James Co. and received a $40 purchases discount. Journalize to entry.

LO6 (10 min)   **9.** Lois Long received $400 of merchandise from Blue Co. What would be the journal entry on the books of both the buyer and seller?

LO6 (10 min)   **10.** Jeff Co., the buyer, paid the cost of freight, $60. Journalize the transaction.

Exercises

Exercises 1–6 are based on a periodic inventory system.

    Exercises 7–10 are based on a perpetual inventory system.

LO1 (15 min)   **10-1.** From the general journal in Figure 10.29, record to the accounts payable subsidiary ledger and post to general ledger accounts as appropriate.

FIGURE 10.29

GENERAL JOURNAL				Page 2	
Date		PR	Dr.	Cr.	
200X					
June 3	Purchases		9 0 0 00		
	Accounts Payable, Leese.com			9 0 0 00	
	Purchased merchandise on account				
4	Purchases		6 0 0 00		
	Accounts Payable, Lane.com			6 0 0 00	
	Purchased merchandise on account				
8	Equipment		2 0 0 00		
	Accounts Payable, Sail.com			2 0 0 00	
	Bought equipment on account				

Partial Accounts Payable Subsidiary Ledger

Partial General Ledger

Lee's.com

Dr.	Cr.

Equipment 120

Dr.	Cr.

Lane.com

Dr.	Cr.

Accounts Payable 210

Dr.	Cr.

Sail.com

Dr.	Cr.

Purchases 510

Dr.	Cr.

10-2. On July 10, 200X, Aster Co. issued debit memorandum no. 1 for $400 to Reel Co. for merchandise returned from invoice no. 312. Your task is to journalize, record, and post this transaction as appropriate. **LO3 (15 min)**

10-3. Journalize, record, and post when appropriate the following transactions into the general journal (p. 2) for Morgan's Clothing. All purchases discounts are 2/10, n/30. **LO4, 5 (20 min)**

Accounts Payable Subsidiary Ledger

Name	Balance	Invoice No.
A. James	$1,000	522
B. Foss	400	488
J. Ranch	900	562
B. Swanson	100	821

Partial General Ledger

Account	Balance
Cash 110	$3,000
Accounts Payable 210	2,400
Purchases Discount 511	
Advertising Expense 610	

200X

Apr.	1	Issued check no. 20 to A. James Company in payment of its March 28 invoice no. 522.
	8	Issued check no. 21 to Flott Advertising in payment of its advertising bill, $100, no discount.
	15	Issued check no. 22 to B. Foss in payment of its March 25 invoice no. 488.

10-4. From Exercise 10-3, prepare a schedule of accounts payable and verify that the total of the schedule equals the amount in the controlling account. **LO5 (10 min)**

10-5. Record the following transaction in a transaction analysis chart for the buyer: Bought merchandise for $9,000 on account. Shipping terms were F.O.B. destination. The cost of shipping was $500. **LO1 (10 min)**

10-6. Angie Rase bought merchandise with a list price of $4,000. Angie was entitled to a 30% trade discount as well as a 3% cash discount. What was Angie's actual cost of buying this merchandise after the cash discount? **LO1 (10 min)**

LO6 (15 min)   **10-7.** Journalize the following transactions:

200X		
April	8	Purchased merchandise on account from Jones Supplies, $14,000; terms 2/10, n/30.
	15	Sold merchandise on account, $6,000; terms 2/10, n/30. The cost of merchandise was $4,500.
	20	Received credit from Jones Suppliers for merchandise returned, $150.

LO6 (15 min)   **10-8.** Journalize the following transactions:

200X		
May	4	Sold merchandise for $500 cash. The cost of merchandise was $300.
	9	Purchased merchandise from Ree Co., $3,000, free on board shipping (buyer pays freight); terms 2/10, n/30. Freight to be paid on May 20.
	20	Paid freight on May 9 purchase, $100.

LO6 (15 min)   **10-9.** Journalize the following transactions:

200X		
April	5	Sold merchandise for $1,200 cash. The cost of the merchandise was $900.
	16	Made refunds to cash customers for defective merchandise, $60. The cost of defective merchandise was $20.

LO6 (15 min)   **10-10.** Journalize the following transactions:

200X		
July	8	Sold merchandise on account, $600, Ring; terms 2/10, n/30. Cost of merchandise was $400.
	12	Purchased office equipment on account from Rej Co., $1,000.
	13	Made refunds to cash customers, $200, for defective merchandise. The cost of defective merchandise was $50.

Group A Problems

LO1, 2 (30 min)   **10A-1.** Ron Klay recently opened Ron's Skate Shop. As the bookkeeper of the company, please journalize, record, and post when appropriate the following transactions (account numbers are Store Supplies, 115; Store Equipment, 121; Accounts Payable, 210; Purchases, 510):

200X		
June	4	Bought $900 of merchandise on account from Mail.Com, invoice no. 442, dated June 5; terms 2/10, n/30.
	5	Bought $5,000 of store equipment from Norton Co., invoice no. 502, dated June 6.
	8	Bought $1,600 of merchandise on account from Rolo Co., invoice no. 401, dated June 9; terms 2/10, n/30.
	14	Bought $1,200 of store supplies on account from Mail.Com, invoice no. 419, dated June 14.

Check Figure: Accounts payable ending Bal. $8,700

LO1, 2, 5 (45 min)   **10A-2.** The following transactions occurred for Mabel's Natural Food.

200X		
May	8	Purchased $600 of merchandise on account from Aton Co., invoice no. 400, dated May 9; terms 2/10, n/60.
	10	Purchased $1,200 of merchandise on account from Broward Co., invoice no. 420, dated May 11; terms 2/10, n/60.

12   Purchased $500 of store supplies on account from Midden Co., invoice no. 510, dated May 13.

14   Issued debit memo no. 8 to Aton Co. for merchandise returned, $400, from invoice no. 400.

17   Purchased $560 of office equipment on account from Relar Co., invoice no. 810, dated May 18.

24   Purchased $650 of additional store supplies on account from Midden Co., invoice no. 516, dated May 25; terms 2/10, n/30.

Check Figure: Total schedule of accounts payable $5,810

Your tasks are to
1. Journalize the transactions.
2. Post and record as appropriate.
3. Prepare a schedule of accounts payable.

Accounts Payable Subsidiary Ledger

Name	Balance
Aton Co.	$ 400
Broward Co.	600
Midden Co.	1,200
Relar Co.	500

Partial General Ledger

Account	Number	Balance
Store Supplies	110	$ —
Office Equipment	120	—
Accounts Payable	210	2,700
Purchases	510	16,000
Purchases Returns and Allowances	512	—

Check Figure: Total of schedule of accounts payable $1,900

10A-3. Wendy Jones operates a wholesale computer center. The account balances as of May 1, 200X, are as follows:

LO1, 2, 3, 4, 5 (45 min)

Accounts Payable Subsidiary Ledger

Name	Balance
Alvin Co.	$1,200
Henry Co.	600
Soy Co.	800
Xon Co.	1,400

Partial General Ledger

Account	Number	Balance
Cash	110	$17,000
Delivery Truck	150	—
Accounts Payable	210	4,000
Computer Purchases	510	—
Computer Purchases Discount	511	—
Rent Expense	610	—
Utilities Expense	620	—

Your tasks are to

1. Journalize the following transactions.
2. Record to the accounts payable subsidiary ledger and post to the general ledger as appropriate.
3. Prepare a schedule of accounts payable.

200X

May	1	Paid half the amount owed Henry Co. from previous purchases of appliances on account, less a 2% purchases discount, check no. 21.
	3	Bought a delivery truck for $8,000 cash, check no. 22, payable to Bill Ring Co.
	6	Bought computer merchandise from Lectro Co., check no. 23, $2,900.
	18	Bought additional computer merchandise from Pulse Co., check no. 24, $800.
	24	Paid Xon Co. the amount owed, less a 2% purchases discount, check no. 25.
	28	Paid rent expense to King's Realty Trust, check no. 26, $2,000.
	29	Paid utilities expense to Stone Utility Co., check no. 27, $300.
	30	Paid half the amount owed Soy Co., no discount, check no. 28.

LO1, 2, 3, 4, 5 (130 min)

10A-4. Abby Ellen opened Abby's Toy House. As her newly hired accountant, your tasks are to

1. Journalize the transactions for the month of March.
2. Record to subsidiary ledgers and post to the general ledger as appropriate.
3. Prepare a schedule of accounts receivable and a schedule of accounts payable.

The following is the partial chart of accounts for Abby's Toy House:

Abby's Toy House Chart of Accounts

Assets		**Revenue**	
110	Cash	410	Toy Sales
112	Accounts Receivable	412	Sales Returns and Allowances
114	Prepaid Rent	414	Sales Discounts
121	Delivery Truck	**Cost of Goods**	
Liabilities		510	Toy Purchases
210	Accounts Payable	512	Purchases Returns and Allowances
Owner's Equity		514	Purchases Discount
310	A. Ellen, Capital	**Expenses**	
		610	Salaries Expense
		612	Cleaning Expense

Check Figures: Total of schedule of accounts receivable $7,600. Total of schedule of accounts payable $9,000

200X

Mar.	1	Abby Ellen invested $8,000 in the toy store.
	1	Paid three months' rent in advance, check no. 1, $3,000.
	1	Purchased merchandise from Earl Miller Company on account, $4,000, invoice no. 410, dated March 2; terms 2/10, n/30.
	3	Sold merchandise to Bill Burton on account, $1,000, invoice no. 1; terms 2/10, n/30.
	6	Sold merchandise to Jim Rex on account, $700, invoice no. 2; terms 2/10, n/30.
	8	Purchased merchandise from Earl Miller Co. on account, $1,200, invoice no. 415, dated March 9; terms 2/10, n/30.
	9	Sold merchandise to Bill Burton on account, $600, invoice no. 3; terms 2/10, n/30.
	9	Paid cleaning service, check no. 2, $300.

10	Jim Rex returned merchandise that cost $300 to Abby's Toy House. Abby issued credit memorandum no. 1 to Jim Rex for $300.
10	Purchased merchandise from Minnie Katz on account, $4,000, invoice no. 311, dated March 11; terms 1/15, n/60.
12	Paid Earl Miller Co. invoice no. 410, dated March 2, check no. 3.
13	Sold $1,300 of toy merchandise for cash.
13	Paid salaries, $600, check no. 4.
14	Returned merchandise to Minnie Katz in the amount of $1,000. Abby's Toy House issued debit memorandum no. 1 to Minnie Katz.
15	Sold merchandise for $4,000 cash.
16	Received payment from Jim Rex, invoice no. 2 (less returned merchandise) less discount.
16	Bill Burton paid invoice no. 1.
16	Sold toy merchandise to Amy Rose on account, $4,000, invoice no. 4; terms 2/10, n/30.
20	Purchased delivery truck on account from Sam Katz Garage, $3,000, invoice no. 111, dated March 21 (no discount).
22	Sold to Bill Burton merchandise on account, $900, invoice no. 5; terms 2/10, n/30.
23	Paid Minnie Katz balance owed, check no. 5.
24	Sold toy merchandise on account to Amy Rose, $1,100, invoice no. 6; terms 2/10, n/30.
25	Purchased toy merchandise, $600, check no. 6.
26	Purchased toy merchandise from Woody Smith on account, $4,800, invoice no. 211, dated March 27; terms 2/10, n/30.
28	Bill Burton paid invoice no. 5, dated March 22.
28	Amy Rose paid invoice no. 6, dated March 24.
28	Abby invested an additional $5,000 in the business.
28	Purchased merchandise from Earl Miller Co., $1,400, invoice no. 436, dated March 29; terms 2/10, n/30.
30	Paid Earl Miller Co. invoice no. 436, check no. 7.
30	Sold merchandise to Bonnie Flow Company on account, $3,000, invoice no. 7; terms 2/10, n/30.

10A-5. Jan's Toy Shop completed the following merchandise transactions in the month of April:

LO6 (40 min)

200X

April	2	Purchased merchandise on account to Fred Mills from Lowe Suppliers, $3,000; terms 2/10, n/30.
	4	Sold merchandise on account, $500; terms 2/10, n/30. The cost of the merchandise sold was $300.
	4	Received credit from Lowe Suppliers for merchandise returned, $200.
	10	Received collections in full, less discounts, from April 4 sales.
	11	Paid Lowe Suppliers in full, less discount.
	14	Purchased store equipment for cash, $300.
	15	Purchased $1,000 of merchandise from Leesy Distribution for cash.
	16	Received a refund due to defective merchandise from supplier on cash purchase of $100.
	17	Purchased merchandise from Logan Corp., $4,000, free on board shipping point (buyer pays freight); terms 2/10, n/30. Freight to be paid on April 21.
	18	Sold merchandise for $3,000 cash; the cost of merchandise sold was $1,600.
	21	Paid freight on April 17 purchase, $120.

Check Figure:
Dr. Merchandise inventory 120
Cr. Cash   120

(continued on next page)

	25	Purchased merchandise from Aster Co., $1,200, free on board destination (seller pays freight); terms 2/10, n/30.
	26	Paid Logan Corp. in full, less discount.
	27	Made refunds to cash customers for defective toys, $200. The cost of the defective toys was $140.

Jan's Toy Shop accounts included the following: Cash, 101; Accounts Receivable, 112; Merchandise Inventory, 120; Store Equipment; 124; Accounts Payable, 201; J. Jan, Capital, 301; Sales, 401; Sales Discounts, 412; Sales Returns and Allowances, 414; Cost of Goods Sold, 501.

Assignment
Journalize the transactions using a perpetual inventory system.

Group B Problems

LO1, 2 (30 min)

10B-1. From the following transactions of Ron's Skate Shop, journalize, record, and post as appropriate:

200X

June	4	Bought merchandise on account from Rolo Co., invoice no. 400, dated June 5, $1,800; terms 2/10, n/30.
	5	Bought store equipment from Norton Co., invoice no. 518, dated June 6, $6,000.
	8	Bought merchandise on account from Mail.Com, invoice no. 411, dated June 5, $400; terms 2/10, n/30.
	14	Bought store supplies on account from Mail.Com, invoice no. 415, dated June 13, $1,200.

Check Figure: Accounts payable ending balance $9,400

LO1, 2, 5 (45 min)

10B-2. As the accountant of Mabel's Natural Food Store (1) journalize the following transactions into the general journal (p. 2), (2) record and post as appropriate, and (3) prepare a schedule of accounts payable. Beginning balances are in the *Study Guide and Working Papers.*

200X

May	8	Purchased merchandise on account from Broward Co., invoice no. 420, dated May 9, $500; terms 2/10, n/60.
	10	Purchased merchandise on account from Aton Co., invoice no. 400, dated May 11, $900; terms 2/10, n/60.
	12	Purchased store supplies on account from Midden Co., invoice no. 510, dated May 13, $700.
	14	Issued debit memo no. 7 to Aton Co. for merchandise returned, $400, from invoice no. 400.
	17	Purchased office equipment on account from Relar Co., invoice no. 810, dated May 18, $750.
	24	Purchased additional store supplies on account from Midden Co., invoice no. 516, dated May 25, $850.

Check Figure: Total of schedule of accounts payable $6,000

LO1, 2, 3, 4, 5 (45 min)

10B-3. Wendy Jones has hired you as her bookkeeper to record the following transactions. She would like you to record and post as appropriate and supply her with a schedule of accounts payable. (Beginning balances are in your workbook or Problem 10A-3 in the text.)

200X

May   1   Bought a delivery truck for $8,000 cash, check no. 21, payable to Randy Rosse Co.

        3   Paid half the amount owed Henry Co. from previous purchases of computer merchandise on account, less a 5% purchases discount, check no. 22.

        6   Bought computer merchandise from Jane Co. for $900 cash, check no. 23.

     18   Bought additional computer merchandise from Jane Co., check no. 24, $1,000.

     24   Paid Xon Co. the amount owed, less a 5% purchases discount, check no. 25.

     28   Paid rent expense to Regan Realty Trust, check no. 26, $3,000.

     29   Paid half the amount owed Soy Co., no discount, check no. 27.

     30   Paid utilities expense to French Utility, check no. 28, $425.

> *Check Figure:* Total of schedule of accounts payable $1,900

10B-4. As the new accountant for Abby's Toy House, your tasks are to

    1. Journalize the transactions for the month of March.

    2. Record to subsidiary ledgers and post to the general ledger as appropriate.

    3. Prepare a schedule of accounts receivable and a schedule of accounts payable.

(Use the same chart of accounts as in Problem 10A-4. Your *Study Guide and Working Papers* has all the forms you need to complete this problem.)

LO1, 2, 3, 4, 5 (130 min)

200X

Mar.   1   Abby invested $4,000 in the new toy store.

        1   Paid two months' rent in advance, check no. 1, $1,000.

        1   Purchased merchandise from Earl Miller Company, invoice no. 410, dated March 2, $6,000; terms 2/10, n/30.

        3   Sold merchandise to Bill Burton on account, $1,600, invoice no. 1; terms 2/10, n/30.

        6   Sold merchandise to Jim Rex on account, $800, invoice no. 2; terms 2/10, n/30.

        8   Purchased merchandise from Earl Miller Company, $800, invoice no. 415, dated March 9; terms 2/10, n/30.

        9   Sold merchandise to Bill Burton on account, $700, invoice no. 3; terms 2/10, n/30.

        9   Paid cleaning service, $400, check no. 2.

     10   Jim Rex returned merchandise that cost $200 to Abby. Abby issued credit memorandum no. 1 to Jim Rex for $200.

     10   Purchased merchandise from Minnie Katz, $7,000, invoice no. 311, dated March 11; terms 1/15, n/60.

     12   Paid Earl Miller Co. invoice no. 410, dated March 2, check no. 3.

     13   Sold $1,500 of toy merchandise for cash.

     13   Paid salaries, $700, check no. 4.

     14   Returned merchandise to Minnie Katz in the amount of $500. Abby issued debit memorandum no. 1 to Minnie Katz.

     15   Sold merchandise for cash, $4,800.

     16   Received payment from Jim Rex for invoice no. 2 (less returned merchandise), less discount.

     16   Bill Burton paid invoice no. 1.

     16   Sold toy merchandise to Amy Rose on account, $6,000, invoice no. 4; terms 2/10, n/30.

     20   Purchased delivery truck on account from Sam Katz Garage, $2,500, invoice no. 111, dated March 21 (no discount).

     22   Sold to Bill Burton merchandise on account, $2,000, invoice no. 5; terms 2/10, n/30.

> *Check Figure:* Total of schedule of accounts receivable $9,900. Total of schedule of accounts payable $9,200

(*continued on next page*)

	23	Paid Minnie Katz balance owed, check no. 5.
	24	Sold toy merchandise on account to Amy Rose, $2,000, invoice no. 6; terms 2/10, n/30.
	25	Purchased toy merchandise, $800, check no. 6.
	26	Purchased toy merchandise from Woody Smith on account, $5,900, invoice no. 211, dated March 27; terms 2/10, n/30.
	28	Bill Burton paid invoice no. 5, dated March 22.
	28	Amy Rose paid invoice no. 6, dated March 24.
	28	Abby invested an additional $3,000 in the business.
	28	Purchased merchandise from Earl Miller Co., $4,200, invoice no. 436, dated March 29; terms 2/10, n/30.
	30	Paid Earl Miller Co. invoice no. 436, check no. 7.
	30	Sold merchandise to Bonnie Flow Company on account, $3,200, invoice no. 7; terms 2/10, n/30.

LO1, 2, 3, 4, 5 (40 min)

10B-5. Bob's Sporting Goods Shop completed the following merchandise transactions in the month of August:

200X		
Aug.	1	Purchased merchandise on account from Bob's Suppliers, $6,000; terms 2/10, n/30.
	2	Sold merchandise on account $1,500; terms 2/10, n/30. The cost of the merchandise sold was $800.
	4	Received credit from Bob's Suppliers for merchandise returned, $300.
	10	Received collections in full, less discounts, from August 2 sales.
	11	Paid Bob's Suppliers in full, less discount.
	14	Purchased office equipment for cash, $700.
	15	Purchased $3,000 of merchandise from Abe's Distribution for cash.
	16	Received a refund due for defective merchandise from supplier on cash purchase of $300.
	17	Purchased merchandise from Lee Corp., $5,000, free on board shipping point (buyer pays freight); terms 2/10, n/3. Freight to be paid on August 23.
	18	Sold merchandise for $4,000 cash; the cost of the merchandise sold was $2,700.
	23	Paid freight on August 17 purchase, $180.
	25	Purchased merchandise from Ron Co., $1,300, free on board destination (seller pays freight); terms 2/10, n/30.
	26	Paid Lee Corp., in full, less discount.
	27	Made refunds to cash customers for defective goods, $500. The cost of the defective goods were $350.

Check Figure:
Dr. Merchandise Inventory $180
Cr. Case $180

Bob's Sporting Goods accounts included the following: Cash, 101; Accounts Receivable, 112; Merchandise Inventory, 120; Office Equipment, 124; Accounts Payable, 201; B. Bob, Capital, 301; Sales, 401; Sales Discounts, 412; Sales Returns and Allowances, 414; Cost of Goods Sold, 501.

Assignment

Journalize the transactions using the perpetual inventory system.

ON-THE-JOB TRAINING

T-1. Angie Co. bought merchandise for $1,000 with credit terms of 2/10, n/30. Owing to the bookkeeper's incompetence, the 2% cash discount was missed. The bookkeeper told Pete Angie, the owner, not to get excited. After all, it was a $20 discount that was missed, not hundreds of dollars. Could you please act as Mr. Angie's assistant and show the bookkeeper that his $20 represents a sizable equivalent interest cost? In your calculation assume a 360-day year. Make some written recommendations so that this situation will not happen again.

LO1 (20 min)

FINANCIAL REPORT PROBLEM

Reading the Kellogg's Annual Report

LO1 (15 min)

Go to Appendix A and locate the balance sheet. How much has merchandise inventory increased from 2005 to 2006?

INTERNET PROJECT

Del Monte

Go to the Web and search: Annual Report Del Monte 2008.
Click on Investors Relations.
List out the latest news Del Monte is providing to its investors.
Order a free annual report.

CONTINUING PROBLEM

Sanchez Computer Center

LO1, 2, 3, 4, 5 (60 min)

The following is an updated schedule of accounts payable as of January 31, 200X.

Schedule of Accounts Payable	
Office Depot	$ 50
System Design Furniture	1,400
Pac Bell	150
Multi Systems, Inc.	450
Total Accounts Payable	$ 2,050

Assignment

1. Journalize the transactions.
2. Record in the accounts payable subsidiary ledger and post to the general ledger as appropriate. A partial general ledger is included in the *Study Guide and Working Papers*.
3. Prepare a schedule of accounts payable as of February 28, 200X.

The transactions for the month of February are as follows:

200X		
Feb.	1	Prepaid the rent for the months of February, March, and April, $1,200, check no. 2585.
	4	Bought merchandise on account from Multi Systems, Inc., purchase order no. 4010, $450; terms 3/10, n/30.

(continued on next page)

8 Bought office supplies on account from Office Depot, purchase order no. 4011, $250; terms n/30.

9 Purchased merchandise on account from Computer Connection, purchase order no. 4012, $500; terms 1/30, n/60.

15 Paid purchase order no. 4010 in full to Multi Systems, Inc., check no. 2586.

21 Issued debit memorandum no. 10 to Computer Connection for merchandise returned from purchase order no. 4012, $100.

27 Paid for office supplies, $50, check no. 2587.

PEACHTREE COMPUTER WORKSHOP

COMPUTERIZED ACCOUNTING APPLICATION FOR CHAPTER 10

Refresher on using Peachtree Complete Accounting

Before starting this assignment, you may want to refresh your memory by reading the following PDF documents in the multimedia library of the MyAccountingLab Web site. Remember to choose the PDF document for your version of Peachtree.

1. An Introduction to Peachtree Complete Accounting
2. Correcting Peachtree Transactions
3. How to Repeat or Restart a Peachtree Assignment
4. Backing Up and Restoring Your Work in Peachtree

You also should have completed the following workshops:

1. Workshop 1 Atlas Company from Chapter 3
2. Workshop 2 Zell Company from Chapter 4
3. Workshop 3 Sullivan Realty from Chapter 5
4. Workshop 4 Pete's Market from Chapter 8

Workshop 5:

PART A: Recording Transactions in the Sales, Receipts, Purchases, and Payments Journals

PART B: Accounting Cycle Mini Practice Set with Sales and Purchasing

Part A:

In this part of the workshop you will learn to record customer sales on account, customer credit memos, customer cash receipts, purchases from vendors on account, and payments to vendors for Mars Company using Peachtree. You will also print the aged receivables and aged payables reports and the sales journal, cash receipts journal, purchasing journal, and cash disbursement journals.

Instructions and the data file for completing Part A of the assignment are in the multimedia library of the MyAccountingLab Web site. Open the **Workshop 5 Part A Mars Company** PDF document for your version of Peachtree and download the **Mars Company** data file for your version of Peachtree.

Part B:

In this part of the workshop you will complete a mini practice set of March accounting transactions for Abby's Toy House using Peachtree. Transactions include customer sales on account, customer credit memos, customer cash receipts, purchases from vendors on account, payments to vendors, and general journal entries in Peachtree. You will also print the aged receivables and aged payables reports and the general journal and general ledger reports.

Instructions and the data file for completing Part B of the assignment are in the multimedia library of the MyAccountingLab Web site. Open the **Workshop 5 Part B Abby's Toy House** PDF document for your version of Peachtree and download the **Abby's Toy House** data file for your version of Peachtree.

QUICKBOOKS COMPUTER WORKSHOP

COMPUTERIZED ACCOUNTING APPLICATION FOR CHAPTER 10

Refresher on Using QuickBooks Pro

Before starting this assignment, you may want to refresh your memory by reading the following PDF documents in the multimedia library of the MyAccountingLab Web site. Remember to choose the PDF document for your version of QuickBooks.

1. An Introduction to QuickBooks Pro
2. Correcting QuickBooks Transactions
3. How to Repeat or Restart a QuickBooks Assignment
4. Backing Up and Restoring Your Work in QuickBooks

You also should have completed the following workshops:

1. Workshop 1 Atlas Company from Chapter 3
2. Workshop 2 Zell Company from Chapter 4
3. Workshop 3 Sullivan Realty from Chapter 5
4. Workshop 4 Pete's Market from Chapter 8

Workshop 5:

PART A: Recording Transactions in the Sales, Receipts, Purchases, and Payments Journals

PART B: Accounting Cycle Mini Practice Set with Sales and Purchasing

Part A:

In this part of the workshop you will learn to record customer sales on account, customer credit memos, customer cash receipts, purchases from vendors on account, and payments to vendors for Mars Company using QuickBooks. You will also print the aged receivables and aged payables reports and the sales journal, cash receipts journal, purchasing journal, and cash disbursement journals.

Instructions and the data file for completing Part A of the assignment are in the multimedia library of the MyAccountingLab Web site. Open the *Workshop 5 Part A Mars Company* PDF document for your version of QuickBooks and download the *Mars Company* data file for your version of QuickBooks.

Part B:

In this part of the workshop, you will complete a mini practice set of March accounting transactions for Abby's Toy House using QuickBooks. Transactions include customer sales on account, customer credit memos, customer cash receipts, purchases from vendors on account, payments to vendors, and general journal entries in Peachtree. You will also print the aged receivables and aged payables reports and the general journal and general ledger reports.

Instructions and the data file for completing Part B of the assignment are in the multimedia library of the MyAccountingLab Web site. *Open the Workshop 5 Part B Abby's Toy House* PDF document for your version of QuickBooks and download the *Abby's Toy House* data file for your version of QuickBooks.

APPENDIX A

SPECIAL JOURNALS WITH PROBLEM MATERIAL

Classroom Demonstration Problem: Periodic Method

All credit sales are 2/10, n/30. All merchandise purchased on account has 3/10, n/30 credit terms. Record the following transactions into special or general journals. Record and post as appropriate.

Solution Tips to Journalizing

200X

Mar.	1	J. Ling invested $2,000 into the business.	CRJ
	1	Sold merchandise on account to Balder Co., $500, invoice no. 1.	SJ
	2	Purchased merchandise on account from Case Co., $500.	PJ
	4	Sold $2,000 of merchandise for cash.	CRJ
	6	Paid Case Co. from previous purchases on account, check no. 1.	CPJ
	8	Sold merchandise on account to Lewis Co., $1,000, invoice no. 2.	SJ
	10	Received payment from Balder for invoice no. 1.	CRJ
	12	Issued a credit memorandum to Lewis Co. for $200 for faulty merchandise.	GJ
	14	Received payment from Lewis Co.	CRJ
	16	Purchased merchandise on account from Noone Co., $1,000.	PJ
	17	Purchased equipment on account from Case Co., $300.	PJ
	18	Issued a debit memorandum to Noone Co. for $500 for defective merchandise.	GJ
	20	Paid salaries, $300, check no. 2.	CPJ
	24	Paid Noone balance owed, check no. 3.	CPJ

FIGURE A.1 Sales Journal

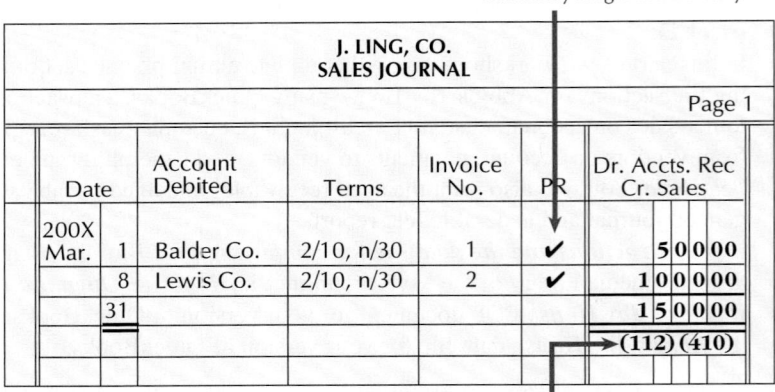

Record accounts receivable subsidiary ledger immediately.

J. LING, CO.
SALES JOURNAL

Page 1

Date		Account Debited	Terms	Invoice No.	PR	Dr. Accts. Rec Cr. Sales
200X Mar.	1	Balder Co.	2/10, n/30	1	✔	500 00
	8	Lewis Co.	2/10, n/30	2	✔	1000 00
	31					1500 00
						(112) (410)

Total posted at end of month to these accounts.

FIGURE A.2 Purchases Journal

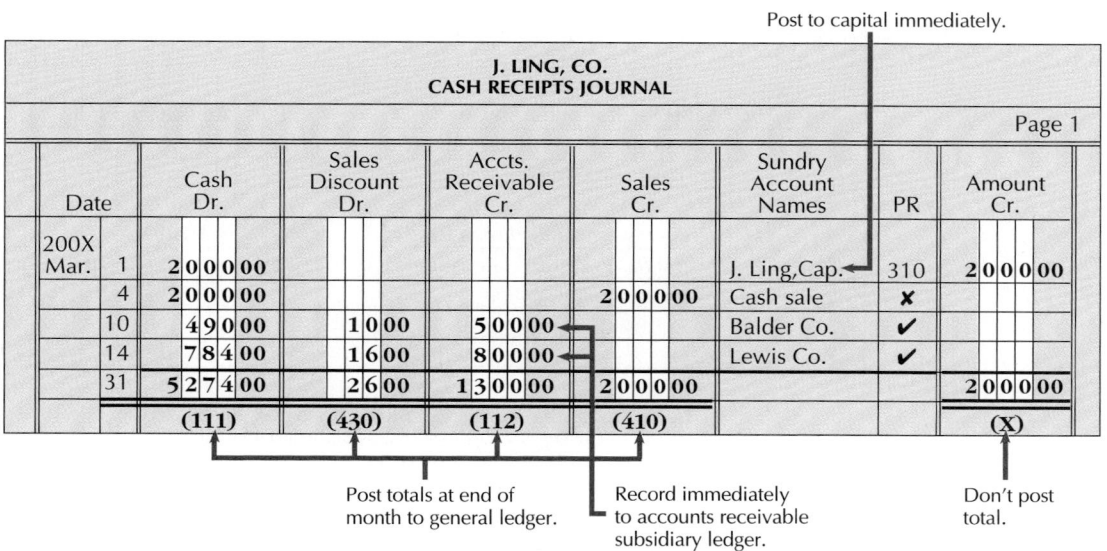

J. LING, CO.
PURCHASES JOURNAL

Page 1

Date		Account Credited	Terms	PR	Accounts Payable Cr.	Purchases Dr.	Sundry–Dr.		
							Acct.	PR	Amount
200X Mar.	2	Case Co.	3/10, n/30	✔	50000	50000			
	16	Noone Co.	3/10, n/30	✔	100000	100000			
	17	Case Co.	3/10, n/30	✔	30000		Equip.	116	30000
	31				180000	150000			30000
					(210)	(510)			(X)

Record to accounts payable subsidiary ledger immediately.

Post totals at end of month to general ledger.

Post immediately to Equipment in general ledger.

Do not post total.

FIGURE A.3 Cash Receipts Journal

Post to capital immediately.

J. LING, CO.
CASH RECEIPTS JOURNAL

Page 1

Date		Cash Dr.	Sales Discount Dr.	Accts. Receivable Cr.	Sales Cr.	Sundry Account Names	PR	Amount Cr.
200X Mar.	1	200000				J. Ling, Cap.	310	200000
	4	200000			200000	Cash sale	✗	
	10	49000	1000	50000		Balder Co.	✔	
	14	78400	1600	80000		Lewis Co.	✔	
	31	527400	2600	130000	200000			200000
		(111)	(430)	(112)	(410)			(X)

Post totals at end of month to general ledger.

Record immediately to accounts receivable subsidiary ledger.

Don't post total.

FIGURE A.4 Cash Payments Journal

Record immediately to accounts payable subsidiary ledger.

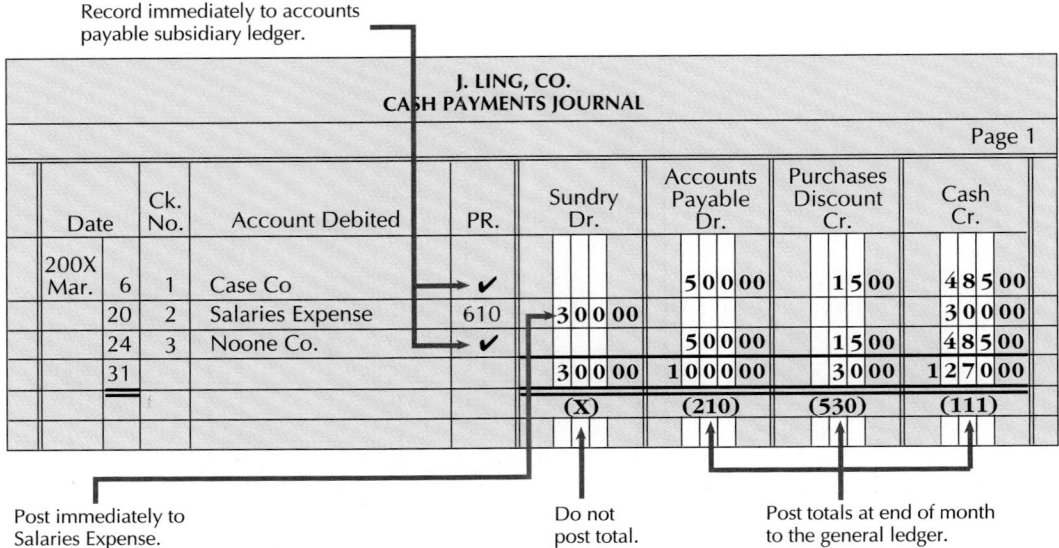

J. LING, CO.
CASH PAYMENTS JOURNAL

Page 1

Date		Ck. No.	Account Debited	PR.	Sundry Dr.	Accounts Payable Dr.	Purchases Discount Cr.	Cash Cr.
200X Mar.	6	1	Case Co	✔		50000	1500	48500
	20	2	Salaries Expense	610	30000			30000
	24	3	Noone Co.	✔		50000	1500	48500
	31				30000	100000	3000	127000
					(X)	(210)	(530)	(111)

Post immediately to Salaries Expense.

Do not post total.

Post totals at end of month to the general ledger.

FIGURE A.5 General Journal

GENERAL JOURNAL

Page 1

Date		Account Titles and Description	PR	Dr.	Cr.
200X Mar.	12	Sales Returns and Allowances	420	20000	
		Accounts Receivable, Lewis Co.	112 ✔		20000
		Issued credit memo			
	18	Accounts Payable, Noone Co.	210 ✔	50000	
		Purchases Returns and Allowances	520		50000
		Issued debit memo			

Record and post immediately to subsidiary and general ledgers.

ACCOUNTS RECEIVABLE SUBSIDIARY LEDGER

Balder Company

Date	PR	Dr.	Cr.	Dr. Bal.
200X 3/1	SJ1	500		500
3/10	CRJ1		500	—

Lewis Company

Date	PR	Dr.	Cr.	Dr. Bal.
200X 3/8	SJ1	1,000		1,000
3/12	GJ1		200	800
3/14	CPJ1		800	—

ACCOUNTS PAYABLE SUBSIDIARY LEDGER

Case Company

Date	PR	Dr.	Cr.	Cr. Bal.
200X 3/2	PJ1		500	500
3/6	CPJ1	500		—
3/17	PJ1		300	300

Noone Company

Date	PR	Dr.	Cr.	Cr. Bal.
200X 3/16	PJ1		1,000	1,000
3/18	GJ1	500		500
3/24	CPJ1	500		—

FIGURE A.6 Subsidiary and General Ledgers

GENERAL LEDGER

Cash 111

3/31 CRJ1 5,274	1,270 3/31 CPJ1
Bal. 4,004	

Accounts Receivable 112

3/31 SJ1 1,500	200 3/12 GJ1
Bal. 0	1,300 3/31 CRJ1

Equipment 116

3/17 PJ1 300	

Accounts Payable 210

3/18 GJ1 500	1,800 3/31 PJ1
3/31 CPJ1 1,000	300 *Bal.*

J. Ling, Capital 310

	2,000 3/1 CRJ1

Sales 410

	1,500 3/31 SJ1
	2,000 3/31 CRJ1
	3,500 *Bal.*

Sales Returns and Allowances 420

3/12 GJ1 200	

Sales Discount 430

3/31 CRJ1 26	

Purchases 510

3/31 PJ1 1,500	

Purchase Returns and Allowances 520

	500 3/18 GJ1

Purchase Discount 530

	30 3/31 CPJ1

Salaries Expense 610

3/20 CPJ1 300	

Summary of Solution Tips

Seller	Buyer
Sales journal	Purchases journal
Cash receipts journal	Cash payments journal
Accounts receivable subsidiary ledger	Accounts payable subsidiary ledger
Sales (Cr.)	Purchases (Dr.)
Sales Returns and Allowances (Dr.)	Purchase Returns and Allowances (Cr.)
Sales Discounts (Dr.)	Purchase Discounts (Cr.)
Accounts Receivable (Dr.)	Accounts Payable (Cr.)
Issue a credit memo	Receive a credit memo
or	or
Receive a debit memo	Issue a debit memo
Schedule of accounts receivable	Schedule of accounts payable

A Step-by-Step Walk-Through of This Classroom Demonstration Problem

Transaction		What to Do Step-by-Step
200X		
Mar.	1	*Money Received:* Record in cash receipts journal. Post immediately to J. Ling, Capital, because it is in sundry.
	1	*Sale on Account:* Record in sales journal. Record immediately to Balder Co. in accounts receivable subsidiary ledger. Place a ✓ in Post. Ref. column of sales journal when subsidiary is updated.
	2	*Buy Merchandise on Account:* Record in purchases journal. Record to Case Co. immediately in the accounts payable subsidiary ledger.
	4	*Money In:* Record in cash receipts journal. No posting needed (put an × in Post. Ref. column).
	6	*Money Out:* Record in cash payments journal. Save $15, which is a Purchases Discount. Record immediately to Case Co. in accounts payable subsidiary ledger (the full amount of $500).
	8	*Sales on Account:* Record in sales journal. Update immediately to Lewis in accounts receivable subsidiary ledger.
	10	*Money In:* Record in cash receipts journal. Because Balder pays within 10 days, it gets a $10 discount. Record the full amount immediately to Balder in the accounts receivable subsidiary ledger.
	12	*Returns:* Record in general journal. Seller issues credit memo resulting in higher sales returns and customers owing less. All postings and recordings are done immediately.
	14	*Money In:* Record in cash receipts journal:

$$\$1,000 - \$200 \text{ returns} = \$800$$
$$\underline{\times\ .02}$$
$$\$\ 16 \text{ discount}$$

Record immediately the $800 to Lewis in the accounts receivable subsidiary ledger.

| | 16 | *Buy Now, Pay Later:* Record in purchases journal. Record immediately to Noone Co. in the accounts payable subsidiary ledger. |
| | 17 | *Buy Now, Pay Later:* Record in purchases journal in Sundry. This item is not merchandise for resale. Record and post immediately. |

18   *Returns:* Record in general ledger. Buyer issues a debit memo reducing the Accounts Payable due to purchases return and allowances. Post and record immediately.

20   *Salaries:* Record in cash payments journal, sundry column. Post immediately to Salaries Expense.

24   *Money Out:* Record in cash payments journal. Save 3% ($15), a purchases discount. Record immediately to accounts payable subsidiary ledger that you reduce Noone by $500.

End of Month Post totals (except sundry) of special journal to the general ledger.

Note: In this problem at the end of the month, (1) Accounts Receivable in the general ledger, the controlling account, has a zero balance, as does each title in the accounts receivable subsidiary ledger; and (2) the balance in Accounts Payable (the controlling account) is $300. In the accounts payable subsidiary ledger, we owe Case $300. The sum of the accounts payable subsidiary ledger does equal the balance in the controlling account at the end of the month.

Appendix A Problems

A-1. Jill Blue opened Food.com, a wholesale grocery and pizza company. The following transactions occurred in June:

200X

June	1	Sold grocery merchandise to Duncan Co. on account, $500, invoice no. 1.
	4	Sold pizza merchandise to Sue Moore Co. on account, $600, invoice no. 2.
	8	Sold grocery merchandise to Long Co. on account, $700, invoice no. 3.
	10	Issued credit memorandum no. 1 to Duncan Co. for $150 of grocery merchandise returned due to spoilage.
	15	Sold pizza merchandise to Sue Moore Co. on account, $160, invoice no. 4.
	19	Sold grocery merchandise to Long Co. on account, $300, invoice no. 5.
	25	Sold pizza merchandise to Duncan Co. on account, $1,200, invoice no. 6.

Required

1. Journalize the transactions in the appropriate journals.
2. Record to the accounts receivable subsidiary ledger and post to the general ledger as appropriate.
3. Prepare a schedule of accounts receivable.

Check Figure: Schedule of accounts receivable $3,310

A-2. The following transactions of Ted's Auto Supply occurred in November (your working papers have balances as of November 1 for certain general ledger and accounts receivable ledger accounts):

200X

Nov.	1	Sold auto parts merchandise to R. Volan on account, $1,000, invoice no. 60, plus 5% sales tax.
	5	Sold auto parts merchandise to J. Seth on account, $800, invoice no. 61, plus 5% sales tax.
	8	Sold auto parts merchandise to Lance Corner on account, $9,000, invoice no. 62, plus 5% sales tax.
	10	Issued credit memorandum no. 12 to R. Volan for $500 for defective auto parts merchandise returned from Nov. 1 transaction. (Be careful to record the reduction in Sales Tax Payable as well.)
	12	Sold auto parts merchandise to J. Seth on account, $600, invoice no. 63, plus 5% sales tax.

Required

1. Journalize the transactions in the appropriate journals.
2. Record to the accounts receivable subsidiary ledger and post to the general ledger as appropriate.
3. Prepare a schedule of accounts receivable.

Check Figure: Schedule of accounts receivable $13,045

A-3. Abby Kim recently opened Skates.com. As the bookkeeper of her company, please journalize, record, and post when appropriate the following transactions (account numbers are Store Supplies, 115; Store Equipment, 121; Accounts Payable, 210; Purchases, 510):

200X		
June	4	Bought $700 of merchandise on account from Mail.com, invoice no. 442, dated June 5; terms 2/10, n/30.
	5	Bought $4,000 of store equipment from Norton Co., invoice no. 502, dated June 6.
	8	Bought $1,400 of merchandise on account from Rolo Co., invoice no. 401, dated June 9; terms 2/10, n/30.
	14	Bought $900 of store supplies on account from Mail.com, invoice no. 419, dated June 14.

Check Figure: Total of purchases column $2,100

A-4. Mabel's Natural Food Store uses a purchases journal and a general journal to record the following transactions (continued from April):

200X		
May	8	Purchased $600 of merchandise on account from Aton Co., invoice no. 400, dated May 9; terms 2/10, n/60.
	10	Purchased $1,200 of merchandise on account from Broward Co., invoice no. 420, dated May 11; terms 2/10, n/60.
	12	Purchased $500 of store supplies on account from Midden Co., invoice no. 510, dated May 13.
	14	Issued debit memo no. 8 to Aton Co., for merchandise returned, $400, from invoice no. 400.
	17	Purchased $560 of office equipment on account from Relar Co., invoice no. 810, dated May 18.
	24	Purchased $650 of additional store supplies on account from Midden Co., invoice no. 516, dated May 25; terms 2/10, n/30.

Check Figure: Total schedule of accounts payable $5,810

The food store decided to keep a separate column for the purchases of supplies in the purchases journal. Your tasks are to

1. Journalize the transactions.
2. Post and record as appropriate.
3. Prepare a schedule of accounts payable.

A-5. Abby Ellen opened Abby's Toy House. As her newly hired accountant, your tasks are to

1. Journalize the transactions for the month of March.
2. Record to subsidiary ledgers and post to the general ledger as appropriate.
3. Total and rule the journals.
4. Prepare a schedule of accounts receivable and a schedule of accounts payable.

The following is the partial chart of accounts for Abby's Toy House:

Abby's Toy House Chart of Accounts

Assets		**Revenue**	
110	Cash	410	Toy Sales
112	Accounts Receivable	412	Sales Returns and Allowances
114	Prepaid Rent	414	Sales Discounts
121	Delivery Truck	**Cost of Goods**	
Liabilities		510	Toy Purchases
210	Accounts Payable	512	Purchases Returns and Allowances
Owner's Equity		514	Purchases Discount
310	A. Ellen, Capital	**Expenses**	
		610	Salaries Expense
		612	Cleaning Expense

Check Figures: Total of schedule of accounts receivable $7,600
    Total of schedule of accounts payable $9,000

200X

Mar. 1   Abby Ellen invested $8,000 in the toy store.

1   Paid three months' rent in advance, check no. 1, $3,000.

1   Purchased merchandise from Earl Miller Company on account, $4,000, invoice no. 410, dated March 2; terms 2/10, n/30.

3   Sold merchandise to Bill Burton on account, $1,000, invoice no. 1; terms 2/10, n/30.

6   Sold merchandise to Jim Rex on account, $700, invoice no. 2; terms 2/10, n/30.

8   Purchased merchandise from Earl Miller Co. on account, $1,200, invoice no. 415, dated March 9; terms 2/10, n/30.

9   Sold merchandise to Bill Burton on account, $600, invoice no. 3; terms 2/10, n/30.

9   Paid cleaning service, check no. 2, $300.

10   Jim Rex returned merchandise that cost $300 to Abby's Toy House. Abby issued credit memorandum no. 1 to Jim Rex for $300.

10   Purchased merchandise from Minnie Katz on account, $4,000, invoice no. 311, dated March 11; terms 1/15, n/60.

12   Paid Earl Miller Co. invoice no. 410, dated March 2, check no. 3.

13   Sold $1,300 of toy merchandise for cash.

13   Paid salaries, $600, check no. 4.

14   Returned merchandise to Minnie Katz in the amount of $1,000. Abby's Toy House issued debit memorandum no. 1 to Minnie Katz.

15   Sold merchandise for $4,000 cash.

16   Received payment from Jim Rex, invoice no. 2 (less returned merchandise) less discount.

16   Bill Burton paid invoice no. 1.

16   Sold toy merchandise to Amy Rose on account, $4,000, invoice no. 4; terms 2/10, n/30.

20   Purchased delivery truck on account from Sam Katz Garage, $3,000, invoice no. 111, dated March 21 (no discount).

22   Sold to Bill Burton merchandise on account, $900, invoice no. 5; terms 2/10, n/30.

23   Paid Minnie Katz balance owed, check no. 5.

24   Sold toy merchandise on account to Amy Rose, $1,100, invoice no. 6; terms 2/10, n/30.

(continued on next page)

25 Purchased toy merchandise, $600, check no. 6.

26 Purchased toy merchandise from Woody Smith on account, $4,800, invoice no. 211, dated March 27; terms 2/10, n/30.

28 Bill Burton paid invoice no. 5, dated March 22.

28 Amy Rose paid invoice no. 6, dated March 24.

28 Abby invested an additional $5,000 in the business.

28 Purchased merchandise from Earl Miller Co., $1,400, invoice no. 436, dated March 29; terms 2/10, n/30.

30 Paid Earl Miller Co. invoice no. 436, check no. 7.

30 Sold merchandise to Bonnie Flow Company on account, $3,000, invoice no. 7; terms 2/10, n/30.

Sales and Cash Receipts Journal in a Perpetual Accounting System for Art's Wholesale Clothing

FIGURE A.7 A Sales Journal Under a Perpetual System

		Account Debited	Terms	Invoice No.	Post. Ref.	Dr. Acc. Rec Cr. Sales	Cost of Goods Sold Dr. Merchandise Inventory Cr.
			ART'S WHOLESALE CLOTHING COMPANY				
			SALES JOURNAL				
							Page 1
200X Apr.	3	Hal's Clothing	2/10, n/30	1	✔	8 0 0 00	5 6 0 00
	6	Bevans Company	2/10, n/30	2	✔	1 6 0 0 00	1 1 2 0 00
	18	Roe Company	2/10, n/30	3	✔	2 0 0 0 00	1 4 0 0 00
	24	Roe Company	2/10, n/30	4	✔	5 0 0 00	3 5 0 00
	28	Mel's Dept. Store	2/10, n/30	5	✔	9 0 0 00	6 3 0 00
	29	Mel's Dept. Store	2/10, n/30	6	✔	7 0 0 00	4 9 0 00
	30						
						6 5 0 0 00	4 5 5 0 00
						(113) (411)	(510) (114)

What's new:

In the journal: New columns for Cost of Goods Sold (Dr.) and Inventory (Cr.). Each time a charge sale is earned, the Cost of Goods Sold increases and the amount of Inventory at cost is reduced.

In the general ledger: New ledger accounts for Inventory and Cost of Goods Sold.

Example: On April 3, Art's Wholesale sold Hal's Clothing $800 of merchandise on account. This sale cost Art's $560 to bring this merchandise into the store.

FIGURE A.8 A Cash Receipts Journal Under a Perpetual System

Date		Cash Dr.	Sales Discount Dr.	Accounts Receivable Cr.	Sales Cr.	Sundry — Account Name	Post. Ref.	Amount Cr.	Costs of Goods Sold Dr. Merchandise Inventory Cr.
ART'S WHOLESALE CLOTHING COMPANY **CASH RECEIPTS JOURNAL**									Page 1
200X Apr.	1	8000 00				Art Newner, Capital	311	8000 00	
	4	784 00	16 00	800 00		Hal's Clothing	✔		
	15	900 00			900 00	Cash Sales	x		630 00
	16	980 00	20 00	1000 00		Bevans Company	✔		
	22	1960 00	40 00	2000 00		Roe Company	✔		
	27	500 00				Store Equipment	121	500 00	
	30	1200 00			1200 00	Cash Sales	x		840 00
		14324 00	76 00	3800 00	2100 00			8500 00	1470 00
		(111)	(413)	(113)	(411)			(X)	(510) (114)

What's new:

  In the journal: New columns for Cost of Goods Sold (Dr.) and Inventory (Cr.). Each
    time a cash sale is earned, the Cost of Goods Sold increases and the amount of
    Inventory at cost is reduced.

Preparing a Worksheet for a Merchandise Company

LEARNING OBJECTIVES

1. Figuring adjustments for merchandise inventory, unearned rent, supplies used, insurance expired, depreciation expense, and salaries accrued.

2. Preparing a worksheet for a merchandise company.

When you build a bear at Build-A-Bear Workshop, do you ever wonder how the workshop controls its inventory? In Chapters 9 and 10 we discussed the subsidiary ledgers as well as entries for a merchandise company. Additional material provided an introduction to perpetual inventory. Now we shift our attention to recording adjustments and completing a worksheet for a merchandise company. Note that the appendix at the end of the chapter shows worksheets for a perpetual system.

Learning Unit 11-1 Adjustments for Merchandise Inventory and Unearned Rent

LO1

The Merchandise Inventory account shows the goods that a merchandise company has available to sell to customers. Companies have several ways to keep track of the **cost of goods sold** (the total cost of the goods sold to customers) and the quantity of inventory on hand. In this chapter we discuss the **periodic inventory system,** in which the balance in inventory is updated only at the end of the accounting period.* This system is used by companies, such as Art's Wholesale Clothing Company, that sell a variety of merchandise with low unit prices.

Assume Art's Wholesale Clothing Company started the year with $19,000 worth of merchandise. This merchandise is called **beginning merchandise inventory** or simply **beginning inventory.** The balance of beginning inventory never changes during the accounting period. Instead, all purchases of merchandise are recorded in the Purchases account. During the accounting period $52,000 worth of such purchases were made and recorded in the Purchases account.

At the end of the period, the company takes a physical count of the merchandise in stock; this amount is called **ending merchandise inventory** or simply **ending inventory.** It is calculated on an inventory sheet as shown in Figure 11.1. This $4,000, which is the ending inventory for this period, will be the beginning inventory for the next period.

When the income statement is prepared, the cost of goods sold section requires two distinct numbers for inventory. The beginning inventory adds to the cost of goods sold, and the ending inventory is subtracted from the cost of goods sold (see margin aids at left). Remember that the two figures for beginning and ending inventory were calculated months apart. Thus, combining these amounts to come up with one inventory figure would not be accurate.

Note that in the calculation (in the margin) of cost of goods sold a title called **Freight-In** is shown. Freight-In is a cost of goods sold account that records the shipping cost to the buyer. Note that net sales (gross sales less sales returns and allowances and sales discounts) less cost of goods sold equals **gross profit.** Subtracting operating expenses from gross profits equals net income.

Net sales
− Cost of goods sold
= Gross profit
− Operating expenses
= Net income

Cost of goods sold
  Beginning inventory
+ Net purchases
+ Freight-in
− Ending inventory
= Cost of goods sold

FIGURE 11.1 Ending Inventory Sheet

ART'S WHOLESALE CLOTHING COMPANY ENDING INVENTORY SHEET AS OF DECEMBER 31, 20X2				
Amount	Explanation	Unit Cost	Total	
20	Ladies' Jackets code 14-0	$50	$1,000	
10	Men's Hats code 327	10	100	
90	Men's Shirts code 423	10	900	
100	Ladies' Blouses code 481	20	2,000	
			$4,000	
Counted by _____ Checked and priced by _____				

*For a discussion of the **perpetual inventory system**, see Learning Unit 10-4.

Adjustment for Merchandise Inventory

Adjusting the Merchandise Inventory account is a two-step process because we must record the beginning inventory and ending inventory amounts separately. The first step deals with beginning merchandise inventory.

Given: Beginning Inventory, $19,000 Our first adjustment removes beginning inventory from the asset account (Merchandise Inventory) and transfers it to Income Summary. We do so by crediting Merchandise Inventory for $19,000 and debiting Income Summary for the same amount. This adjustment is shown in the following T account form and on a transaction analysis chart.

> Note that Income Summary has no normal balance of debit or credit.

Merchandise Inventory 114				Income Summary 313	
Bal.	19,000	Adj.	19,000	Adj.	19,000

(A)

Accounts Affected	Category	↑ ↓	Rules
Income Summary	—	—	Dr.
Merchandise Inventory	Asset	↓	Cr.

(The adjusting entries would be recorded first on the worksheet and then in the general journal.)

The second step is entering the amount of ending inventory ($4,000) in the Merchandise Inventory account. This step is done to record the amount of goods on hand at the end of the period as an asset and to subtract this amount from the cost of goods sold (because we have not sold this inventory yet). To do so, we debit Merchandise Inventory for $4,000 and credit Income Summary for the same amount. This adjustment is shown in the following T account form.

> Second adjustment updates inventory account with a figure for ending inventory.

Merchandise Inventory 114				Income Summary 313			
Bal.	19,000	Adj.	19,000	Adj.	19,000	Adj.	4,000
Adj.	4,000						

(B)

Beginning inventory		$19,000
+ Net cost of purchases*		50,910
= Cost of goods available for sale		$69,910
− Ending inventory		4,000
= Cost of goods sold		$65,910

*$52,000 Purchases − $860 PD − $680 PRA + $450 Freight-In

Let's look at how this process or method of recording merchandise inventory is reflected in the balance sheet and income statement (see Figure 11.2 on following page). Note that the $19,000 of beginning inventory is assumed sold and is shown on the income statement as part of the cost of goods sold. The ending inventory of $4,000 is assumed not to be sold and is subtracted from the cost of goods sold on the income statement. The ending inventory becomes next month's beginning inventory on the balance sheet. When the income statement is prepared, we will need a figure for beginning inventory as well as a figure for ending inventory. The goal of this adjustment is to wipe out the old inventory (a cost) and show the new inventory (not yet a cost).

Adjustment for Unearned Rent

A second new account we have not seen before is a liability called Unearned Rent or Rent Received in Advance. This account records the amount collected for rent before the service (renting the space) has been provided.

Suppose Art's Wholesale Clothing Company is subletting a portion of its space to Jesse Company for $200 per month. Jesse Company sends Art's cash for $600 for three months' rent paid in advance. This unearned rent ($600) is a liability on the balance sheet because Art's Wholesale owes Jesse Company three months' worth of occupancy.

FIGURE 11.2 Recording Inventory on a Partial Balance Sheet and Income Statement

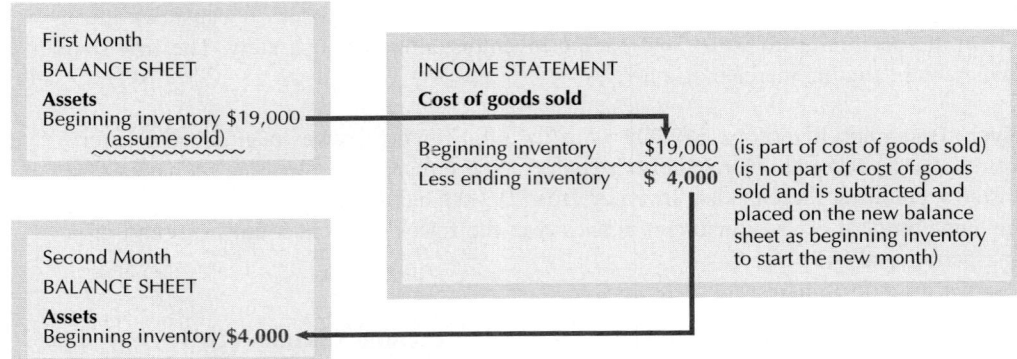

When Art's Wholesale fulfills a portion of the rental agreement—when Jesse Company has been in the space for a period of time—this liability account will be reduced and the Rental Income account will be increased. Rental Income is another type of revenue for Art's Wholesale.

Remember that under accrual accounting, revenue is recognized when it is earned, whether payment is received then or not. Here, Art's Wholesale collected cash in advance for a service that it has not performed as yet. A liability called Unearned Rent is the result. Art's Wholesale may have the cash, but the Rental Income is not recorded until it is earned. Examples of other types of unearned revenue besides unearned rent include subscriptions for magazines, legal fees collected before the work is performed, and insurance.

Received cash for renting space in future:
Cash   Asset   ↑   Dr.
Unearned   Liab.   ↑   Cr.
Rent

The adjustment when rental income is earned:
Unearned   Liab.   ↓   Dr.
Rent
Rental   Rev.   ↑   Cr.
Income

LEARNING UNIT 11-1 REVIEW

AT THIS POINT you should be able to

- Define the periodic method of inventory accounting.
- Explain why beginning and ending inventory are two separate figures in the cost of goods sold section on the income statement.
- Calculate net sales, cost of goods sold, gross profit, and net income.
- Show how to calculate a figure for ending inventory.
- Explain why Unearned Rent is a *liability* account.

Self-Review Quiz 11-1

Given the following, prepare the two *adjusting* entries for Merchandise Inventory on 12/31/0X.

Merchandise Inventory, 1/1/0X	$ 8,000
Purchases	9,000
Purchases Returns and Allowances	3,000
Merchandise Inventory, 12/31/0X	4,000
Cost of Goods Sold	10,000
Unearned Magazine Subscriptions	8,000

Solution to Self-Review Quiz 11-1

Dec.	31	Income Summary	8 0 0 0 00			
		Merchandise Inventory			8 0 0 0 00	
	31	Merchandise Inventory	4 0 0 0 00			
		Income Summary			4 0 0 0 00	

FIGURE 11.3 Merchandise Inventory Adjustments

> Note that Unearned Magazine Subscriptions is a liability and is not involved in the adjustment for Merchandise Inventory.

Learning Unit 11-2 Completing the Worksheet   *LO 2*

In this unit we prepare a worksheet for Art's Wholesale Clothing Company. For convenience, we reproduce the company's chart of accounts in Figure 11.4.

Figure 11.5 on the following page shows the trial balance that was prepared on December 31, 200X, from Art's Wholesale ledger. (Note that it is placed directly in the first two columns of the worksheet.)

In looking at the trial balance, we see many new titles that appeared after we completed a trial balance for a service company in Chapter 5. Let's look specifically at these new titles shown in Table 11.1.

Note the following:

- **Mortgage Payable** is a liability account that records the increases and decreases in the amount of debt owed on a mortgage. We discuss this account more in the next chapter, when financial reports are prepared.

FIGURE 11.4 Art's Wholesale Clothing Company Chart of Accounts

CHART OF ACCOUNTS

Assets 100–199
111   Cash
112   Petty Cash
113   Accounts Receivable
114   Merchandise Inventory
115   Supplies
116   Prepaid Insurance
121   Store Equipment
122   Accum. Depreciation, Store Equipment

Liabilities 200–299
211   Accounts Payable
212   Salaries Payable
213   Federal Income Tax Payable
214   FICA—Social Security Payable
215   FICA—Medicare Payable
216   State Income Tax Payable
217   SUTA Tax Payable
218   FUTA Tax Payable
219   Unearned Rent*
220   Mortgage Payable

Owner's Equity 300–399
311   Art Newner, Capital
312   Art Newner, Withdrawals
313   Income Summary

Revenue 400–499
411   Sales
412   Sales Returns and Allowances
413   Sales Discount
414   Rental Income

Cost of Goods Sold 500–599
511   Purchases
512   Purchases Discount
513   Purchases Returns and Allowances
514   Freight-In

Expenses 600–699
611   Salaries Expense
612   Payroll Tax Expense
613   Depreciation Expense, Store Equipment
614   Supplies Expense
615   Insurance Expense
616   Postage Expense
617   Miscellaneous Expense
618   Interest Expense
619   Cleaning Expense
620   Delivery Expense

*Although Unearned Rent is the only term under Liabilities not using payable, it is a liability.

FIGURE 11.5 Trial Balance Section of the Worksheet

				Trial Balance	
				Dr.	Cr.
		Cash		12 9 2 0 00	
		Petty Cash		1 0 0 00	
		Accounts Receivable		14 5 0 0 00	
		Merchandise Inventory		19 0 0 0 00	
		Supplies		8 0 0 00	
		Prepaid Insurance		9 0 0 00	
		Store Equipment		4 0 0 0 00	
		Acc. Dep., Store Equipment			4 0 0 00
		Accounts Payable			17 9 0 0 00
		Federal Income Tax Payable			8 0 0 00
		FICA—Soc. Sec. Payable			4 5 4 00
		FICA—Medicare Payable			1 0 6 00
		State Income Tax Payable			2 0 0 00
		SUTA Tax Payable			1 0 8 00
		FUTA Tax Payable			3 2 00
		Unearned Rent			6 0 0 00
		Mortgage Payable			2 3 2 0 00
		Art Newner, Capital			7 9 0 5 00
		Art Newner, Withdrawals		8 6 0 0 00	
		Income Summary			
		Sales			95 0 0 0 00
		Sales Returns and Allowances		9 5 0 00	
		Sales Discount		6 7 0 00	
		Purchases		52 0 0 0 00	
		Purchases Discount			8 6 0 00
		Purchases Returns and Allowances			6 8 0 00
		Freight-In		4 5 0 00	
		Salaries Expense		1 1 7 0 0 00	
		Payroll Tax Expense		4 2 0 00	
		Postage Expense		2 5 00	
		Miscellaneous Expense		3 0 00	
		Interest Expense		3 0 0 00	
				127 3 6 5 00	127 3 6 5 00

- **Interest Expense** represents a nonoperating expense for Art's Wholesale and thus is categorized as Other Expense. We look at this expense in the next chapter.
- **Unearned Revenue** is a liability account that records receipt of payment for goods and services in advance of delivery. Unearned Rent is a particular example of this general type of account.

We already discussed the adjustments that make up the two-step process involved in adjusting Merchandise Inventory at the end of the accounting period. Now we show T accounts and transaction analysis charts for other adjustments that need to be made at this point for a merchandise firm, just as they must for a service company.

Adjustment C: Rental Income Earned by Art's Wholesale, $200 A month ago, Cash was increased by $600, as was a liability, Unearned Rent. Art's Wholesale received payment in advance but had not earned the rental income. Now, because $200 has been

TABLE 11.1 Summary of New Account Titles

Title	Category	Report(s) Found on	Normal Balance	Temporary or Permanent
Petty Cash	Asset	Balance Sheet	Dr.	Permanent
Merchandise Inventory* (Beginning)	Asset	Balance Sheet from prior period	Dr.	Permanent
	Cost of Goods Sold	Income Statement of current period		
Federal Income Tax Payable	Liability	Balance Sheet	Cr.	Permanent
FICA—Social Security Payable	Liability	Balance Sheet	Cr.	Permanent
FICA—Medicare Payable	Liability	Balance Sheet	Cr.	Permanent
State Income Tax Payable	Liability	Balance Sheet	Cr.	Permanent
SUTA Tax Payable	Liability	Balance Sheet	Cr.	Permanent
FUTA Tax Payable	Liability	Balance Sheet	Cr.	Permanent
Unearned Rent[†]	Liability	Balance Sheet	Cr.	Permanent
Mortgage Payable	Liability	Balance Sheet	Cr.	Permanent
Sales	Revenue	Income Statement	Cr.	Temporary
Sales Returns and Allowances	Contra-Revenue	Income Statement	Dr.	Temporary
Sales Discount	Contra-Revenue	Income Statement	Dr.	Temporary
Purchases[§]	Cost of Goods Sold	Income Statement	Dr.	Temporary
Purchases Discount	Contra-Cost of Goods Sold	Income Statement	Cr.	Temporary
Purchases Returns and Allowances	Contra-Cost of Goods Sold	Income Statement	Cr.	Temporary
Freight-In	Cost of Goods Sold	Income Statement	Dr.	Temporary
Payroll Tax Expense	Expense	Income Statement	Dr.	Temporary
Postage Expense	Expense	Income Statement	Dr.	Temporary
Interest Expense	Other Expense	Income Statement	Dr.	Temporary

*The ending inventory of current period is a contra-cost of goods sold on the income statement and will be an asset on the balance sheet for the next period.
[†]Referred to as Unearned Revenue.
[§]Note that the categories for Purchases and Freight-In are Cost of Goods Sold, whereas Purchases Discounts and Purchases Returns and Allowances are Contra-Cost of Goods Sold.

earned, the liability is reduced and Rental Income can be recorded for the $200. This step is shown as follows:

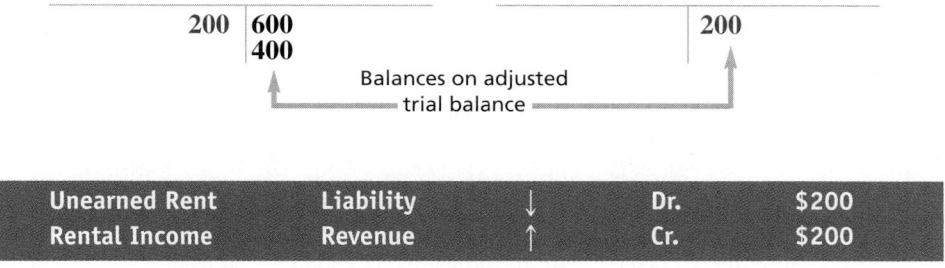

| Unearned Rent | Liability | ↓ | Dr. | $200 |
| Rental Income | Revenue | ↑ | Cr. | $200 |

Adjustment D: Supplies on Hand, $300 Because $500 worth of supplies were used up, Supplies Expense is increased, and the asset Supplies is decreased.

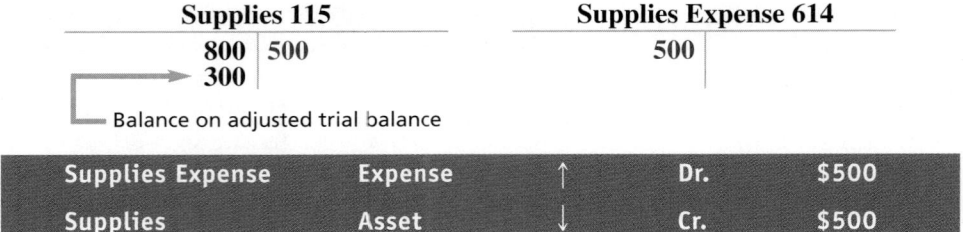

Adjustment E: Insurance Expired, $300 Because insurance has expired by $300, Insurance Expense is increased by $300 and the asset Prepaid Insurance is decreased by $300.

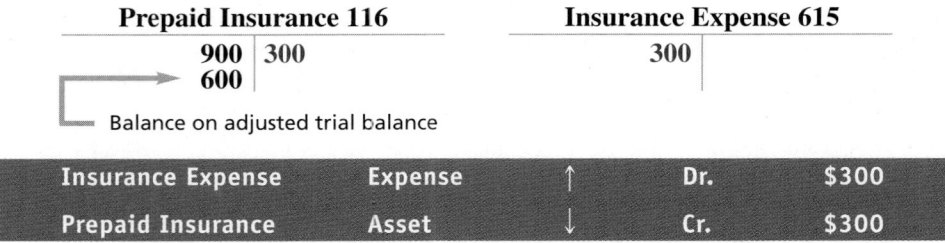

Adjustment F: Depreciation Expense, $50 When depreciation is taken, Depreciation Expense and Accumulated Depreciation are both increased by $50. Note that the cost of the store equipment remains the same.

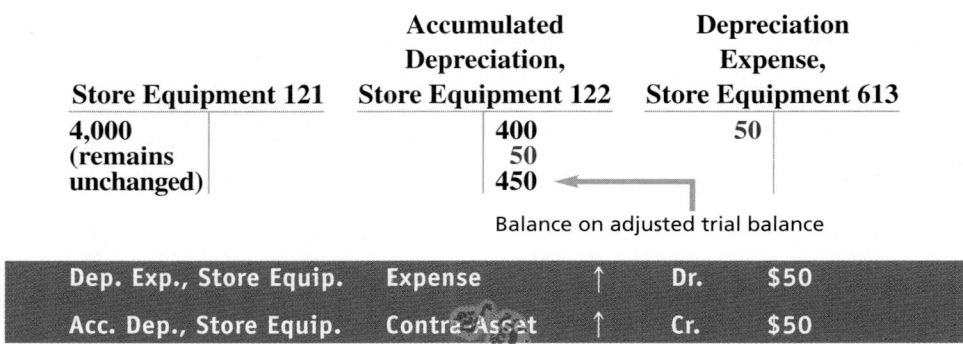

Adjustment G: Salaries Accrued, $600 The $600 in accrued salaries causes an increase in Salaries Expense and Salaries Payable.

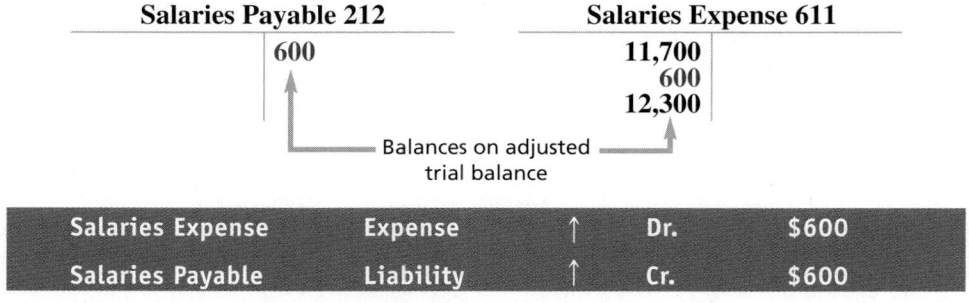

Figure 11.6 shows the worksheet with the adjustments and adjusted trial balance columns filled out. Note that the adjustment numbers in the Income Summary from beginning and ending inventory are also carried over to the adjusted trial balance and are not combined.

The next step in completing the worksheet is to fill out the income statement columns from the adjusted trial balance, as shown in Figure 11.7.

FIGURE 11.6 Worksheet with Three Columns Filled Out

	Trial Balance Dr.	Trial Balance Cr.	Adjustments Dr.	Adjustments Cr.	Adjusted Trial Balance Dr.	Adjusted Trial Balance Cr.
Cash	1292000				1292000	
Petty Cash	10000				10000	
Accounts Receivable	1450000		(B)	(A)	1450000	
Merchandise Inventory	1900000		400000	1900000	400000	
Supplies	80000			(D) 50000	30000	
Prepaid Insurance	90000			(E) 30000	60000	
Store Equipment	400000				400000	
Acc. Dep., Store Equipment		40000		(F) 5000		45000
Accounts Payable		1790000				1790000
Federal Income Tax Payable		80000				80000
FICA—Soc. Sec. Payable		45400				45400
FICA—Medicare Payable		10600				10600
State Income Tax Payable		20000				20000
SUTA Tax Payable		10800				10800
FUTA Tax Payable		3200				3200
Unearned Rent		60000	(C) 20000			40000
Mortgage Payable		232000				232000
Art Newner, Capital		790500				790500
Art Newner, Withdrawals	860000		(A)	(B)	860000	
Income Summary			1900000	400000	1900000	400000
Sales		9500000				9500000
Sales Returns and Allowances	95000				95000	
Sales Discount	67000				67000	
Purchases	5200000				5200000	
Purchases Discount		86000				86000
Purchases Returns and Allowances		68000				68000
Freight-In	45000				45000	
Salaries Expense	1170000		(G) 60000		1230000	
Payroll Tax Expense	42000				42000	
Postage Expense	2500				2500	
Miscellaneous Expense	3000				3000	
Interest Expense	30000				30000	
	12736500	12736500				
Rental Income				(C) 20000		20000
Supplies Expense			(D) 50000		50000	
Insurance Expense			(E) 30000		30000	
Depreciation Expense, Store Equip.			(F) 5000		5000	
Salaries Payable				(G) 60000		60000
			2465000	2465000	13201500	13201500

The next step in completing the worksheet is to fill out the balance sheet columns (Fig. 11.8). Note how ending inventory is carried over to the balance sheet from the adjusted trial balance column. Take time also to look at the placement of the payroll tax liabilities as well as Unearned Rent on the worksheet.

Figure 11.9 is the completed worksheet.

Remember: We do not combine the $19,000 and $4,000 in Income Summary. When we prepare the cost of goods sold section for the formal income statement, we will need both a beginning and an ending figure for inventory.

$19,000 of beginning inventory is assumed sold during the period and thus is part of the cost of goods sold. By placing it in the debit column of Income Summary we increase the cost of goods sold.

$4,000 is the cost of ending inventory at the end of the period. It is assumed to be unsold and therefore is not part of the cost of goods sold. By placing it in the credit column of Income Summary we reduce the cost of goods sold.

$95,000 is the credit balance of Sales. The Sales Returns and Allowances, $950, and Sales Discount, $670, are placed on the debit side, which represents a reduction to total sales:
(Cr.) Sales
(Dr.) Less: Sales Returns and Allowances
(Dr.) Less: Sales Discount

The Purchases account, $52,000, is on the debit side, reflecting an increase in costs due to purchasing additional merchandise. The Purchases Discount, $860, and Purchases Returns and Allowances, $680, are on the credit side, which reduces cost of purchases:
(Dr.) Purchases
(Cr.) Less: Purchases Returns and Allowances
(Cr.) Less: Purchases Discount

Freight-In adds to the cost of goods sold.

Rental Income, which falls under the category "other income" for Art's Wholesale, is increased by $200, because the first month's rental agreement has been fulfilled.

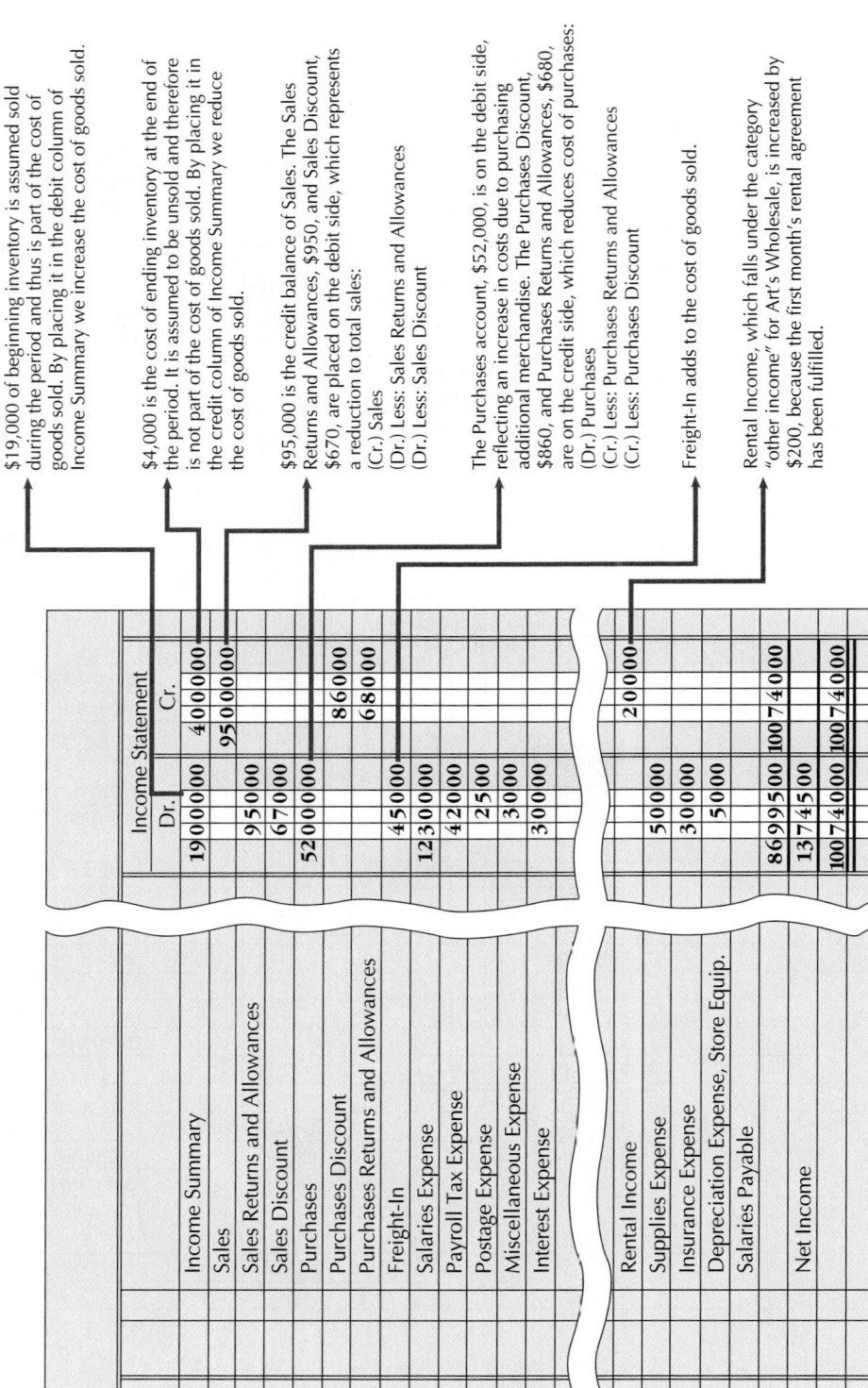

	Income Statement	
	Dr.	Cr.
Income Summary	19 000 00	4 000 00
Sales		95 000 00
Sales Returns and Allowances	9 50 00	
Sales Discount	6 70 00	
Purchases	52 000 00	
Purchases Discount		8 60 00
Purchases Returns and Allowances		6 80 00
Freight-In	4 50 00	
Salaries Expense	12 30 00 0	
Payroll Tax Expense	4 20 00	
Postage Expense	2 5 00	
Miscellaneous Expense	3 0 00	
Interest Expense	3 00 00	
Rental Income		2 00 00
Supplies Expense	5 00 00	
Insurance Expense	3 00 00	
Depreciation Expense, Store Equip.	5 0 00	
Salaries Payable		
	86 995 00	100 740 00
Net Income	13 745 00	
	100 740 00	100 740 00

FIGURE 11.7 Income Statement Section of the Worksheet

FIGURE 11.8 Balance Sheet Section of the Worksheet

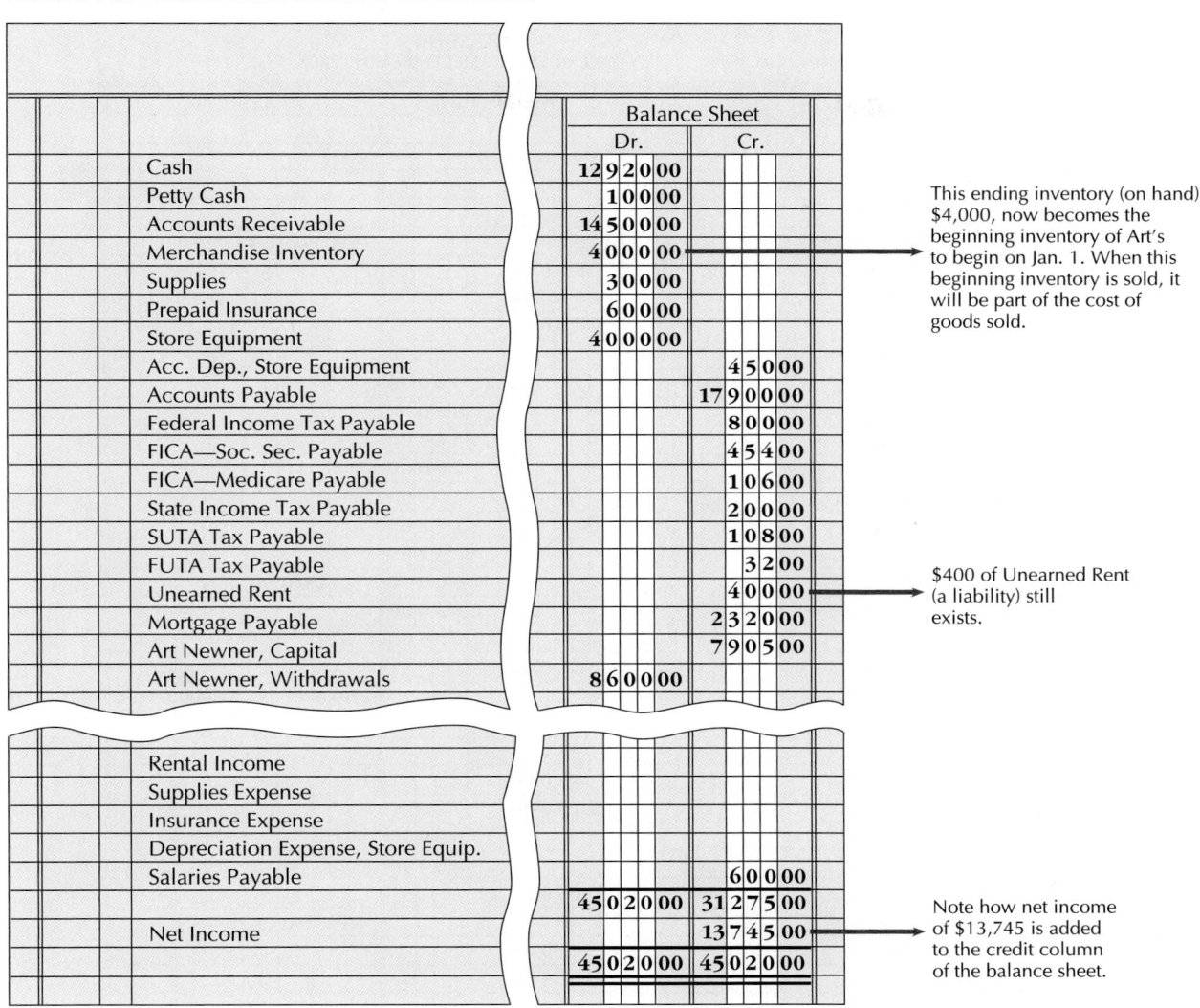

		Balance Sheet	
		Dr.	Cr.
Cash		12 9 2 0 00	
Petty Cash		1 0 0 00	
Accounts Receivable		14 5 0 0 00	
Merchandise Inventory		4 0 0 0 00	
Supplies		3 0 0 00	
Prepaid Insurance		6 0 0 00	
Store Equipment		4 0 0 0 00	
Acc. Dep., Store Equipment			4 5 0 00
Accounts Payable			17 9 0 0 00
Federal Income Tax Payable			8 0 0 00
FICA—Soc. Sec. Payable			4 5 4 00
FICA—Medicare Payable			1 0 6 00
State Income Tax Payable			2 0 0 00
SUTA Tax Payable			1 0 8 00
FUTA Tax Payable			3 2 00
Unearned Rent			4 0 0 00
Mortgage Payable			2 3 2 0 00
Art Newner, Capital			7 9 0 5 00
Art Newner, Withdrawals		8 6 0 0 00	
Rental Income			
Supplies Expense			
Insurance Expense			
Depreciation Expense, Store Equip.			
Salaries Payable			6 0 0 00
		45 0 2 0 00	31 2 7 5 00
Net Income			13 7 4 5 00
		45 0 2 0 00	45 0 2 0 00

This ending inventory (on hand), $4,000, now becomes the beginning inventory of Art's to begin on Jan. 1. When this beginning inventory is sold, it will be part of the cost of goods sold.

$400 of Unearned Rent (a liability) still exists.

Note how net income of $13,745 is added to the credit column of the balance sheet.

FIGURE 11.9 Completed Worksheet

WORKSHEET
FOR YEAR ENDED DECEMBER 31, 200X

	Trial Balance Dr.	Trial Balance Cr.	Adjustments Dr.	Adjustments Cr.
Cash	12 920 00			
Petty Cash	100 00			
Accounts Receivable	14 500 00			
Merchandise Inventory	19 000 00		(B) 4 000 00	(A) 19 000 00
Supplies	800 00			(D) 500 00
Prepaid Insurance	900 00			(E) 300 00
Store Equipment	4 000 00			
Acc. Dep., Store Equipment		400 00		(F) 50 00
Accounts Payable		17 900 00		
Federal Income Tax Payable		800 00		
FICA—Social Security Payable		454 00		
FICA—Medicare Payable		106 00		
State Income Tax Payable		200 00		
SUTA Tax Payable		108 00		
FUTA Tax Payable		32 00		
Unearned Rent		600 00	(C) 200 00	
Mortgage Payable		2 320 00		
Art Newner, Capital		7 905 00		
Art Newner, Withdrawals	8 600 00			
Income Summary			(A) 19 000 00	(B) 4 000 00
Sales		95 000 00		
Sales Returns and Allowances	950 00			
Sales Discount	670 00			
Purchases	52 000 00			
Purchases Discount		860 00		
Purchases Returns and Allowances		680 00		
Freight-In	450 00			
Salaries Expense	11 700 00		(G) 600 00	
Payroll Tax Expense	420 00			
Postage Expense	25 00			
Miscellaneous Expense	30 00			
Interest Expense	300 00			
	127 365 00	127 365 00		
Rental Income				(C) 200 00
Supplies Expense			(D) 500 00	
Insurance Expense			(E) 300 00	
Depreciation Expense, Store Equip.			(F) 50 00	
Salaries Payable				(G) 600 00
			2 465 00	2 465 00
Net Income				

FIGURE 11.9 *(continued)*

Adjusted Trial Bal. Dr.	Adjusted Trial Bal. Cr.	Income Statement Dr.	Income Statement Cr.	Balance Sheet Dr.	Balance Sheet Cr.
12 9 2 0 00				12 9 2 0 00	
1 0 0 00				1 0 0 00	
14 5 0 0 00				14 5 0 0 00	
4 0 0 00				4 0 0 00	
3 0 0 00				3 0 0 00	
6 0 0 00				6 0 0 00	
4 0 0 00				4 0 0 00	
	4 5 0 00				4 5 0 00
	17 9 0 0 00				17 9 0 0 00
	8 0 0 00				8 0 0 00
	4 5 4 00				4 5 4 00
	1 0 6 00				1 0 6 00
	2 0 0 00				2 0 0 00
	1 0 8 00				1 0 8 00
	3 2 00				3 2 00
	4 0 0 00				4 0 0 00
	2 3 2 0 00				2 3 2 0 00
	7 9 0 5 00				7 9 0 5 00
8 6 0 0 00				8 6 0 0 00	
19 0 0 0 00	4 0 0 0 00	19 0 0 0 00	4 0 0 0 00		
	95 0 0 0 00		95 0 0 0 00		
9 5 0 00		9 5 0 00			
6 7 0 00		6 7 0 00			
52 0 0 0 00		52 0 0 0 00			
	8 6 0 00		8 6 0 00		
	6 8 0 00		6 8 0 00		
4 5 0 00		4 5 0 00			
12 3 0 0 00		12 3 0 0 00			
4 2 0 00		4 2 0 00			
2 5 00		2 5 00			
3 0 00		3 0 00			
3 0 0 00		3 0 0 00			
	2 0 0 00		2 0 0 00		
5 0 0 00		5 0 0 00			
3 0 0 00		3 0 0 00			
5 0 00		5 0 00			
	6 0 0 00				6 0 0 00
132 0 1 5 00	132 0 1 5 00	86 9 9 5 00	100 7 4 0 00	45 0 2 0 00	31 2 7 5 00
		13 7 4 5 00			13 7 4 5 00
		100 7 4 0 00	100 7 4 0 00	45 0 2 0 00	45 0 2 0 00

LEARNING UNIT 11-2 REVIEW

AT THIS POINT you should be able to

- Complete adjustments for a merchandise company.
- Complete a worksheet.

Self-Review Quiz 11-2

From the trial balance shown in Figure 11.10, complete a worksheet for Ray Company. Additional data include the following: (A and B) On December 31, 200X, ending inventory was calculated as $200; (C) Storage Fees Earned, $516; (D) Rent Expired, $100; (E) Depreciation Expense, Office Equipment, $60; (F) Salaries Accrued, $200.

FIGURE 11.10 Trial Balance of Ray Company

Account Title	Trial Balance Dr.	Trial Balance Cr.
Cash	2 4 8 6 00	
Merchandise Inventory	8 2 4 00	
Prepaid Rent	1 1 5 2 00	
Prepaid Insurance	6 0 00	
Office Equipment	2 1 6 0 00	
Accumulated Depreciation, Office Equipment		5 6 0 00
Unearned Storage Fees		2 5 1 6 00
Accounts Payable		1 0 0 00
B. Ray, Capital		1 9 3 2 00
Income Summary	—	—
Sales		11 0 4 0 00
Sales Returns and Allowances	5 4 6 00	
Sales Discount	2 1 6 00	
Purchases	5 2 5 6 00	
Purchases Returns and Allowances		1 6 8 00
Purchases Discount		1 0 2 00
Salaries Expense	2 0 1 6 00	
Insurance Expense	1 3 9 2 00	
Utilities Expense	9 6 00	
Plumbing Expense	2 1 4 00	
	16 4 1 8 00	16 4 1 8 00

The ending inventory of $200 becomes next month's beginning inventory.

Solution to Self-Review Quiz 11-2

The solution is shown in Figure 11.11.

RAY COMPANY
WORKSHEET
FOR YEAR ENDED DECEMBER 31, 200X

Account	Trial Balance Dr.	Trial Balance Cr.	Adjustments Dr.	Adjustments Cr.	Adjusted Trial Balance Dr.	Adjusted Trial Balance Cr.	Income Statement Dr.	Income Statement Cr.	Balance Sheet Dr.	Balance Sheet Cr.
Cash	248600				248600				248600	
Merchandise Inventory	82400		(B) 20000	(A) 82400	20000				20000	
Prepaid Rent	115200			(D) 10000	105200				105200	
Prepaid Insurance	6000				6000				6000	
Office Equipment	216000				216000				216000	
Acc. Dep., Office Equipment		56000		(E) 6000		62000				62000
Unearned Storage Fees		251600	(C) 51600			200000				200000
Accounts Payable		10000				10000				10000
B. Ray, Capital		193200				193200				193200
Income Summary			(A) 82400	(B) 20000	82400	20000	82400	20000		
Sales		1104000				1104000		1104000		
Sales Returns and Allowances	54600				54600		54600			
Sales Discount	21600				21600		21600			
Purchases	525600				525600		525600			
Purchases Returns and Allowances		16800				16800		16800		
Purchases Discount		10200				10200		10200		
Salaries Expense	201600		(F) 20000		221600		221600			
Insurance Expense	139200				139200		139200			
Utilities Expense	9600				9600		9600			
Plumbing Expense	21400				21400		21400			
	1641800	1641800								
Storage Fees Earned				(C) 51600		51600		51600		
Rent Expense			(D) 10000		10000		10000			
Depreciation Expense, Equipment			(E) 6000		6000		6000			
Salaries Payable				(F) 20000		20000				20000
			190000	190000	1687800	1687800	1092000	1202600	595800	485200
Net Income							110600			110600
							1202600	1202600	595800	595800

FIGURE 11.11 Worksheet for Ray Company

CHAPTER ASSIGNMENTS

SUMMARY OF KEY POINTS

LEARNING UNIT 11-1

1. The periodic inventory system updates the record of goods on hand only at the *end* of the accounting period. This system is used for companies with a variety of merchandise with low unit prices. With computers today, many companies switch to a perpetual inventory system.
2. In the periodic inventory system, additional purchases of merchandise during the accounting period will be recorded in the Purchases account. The amount in beginning inventory will remain unchanged during the accounting period. At the end of the period, a new figure for ending inventory will be calculated.
3. Beginning inventory at the end of the accounting period is part of the cost of goods sold, whereas ending inventory is a reduction to cost of goods sold.
4. The perpetual inventory system keeps a continuous record of inventory. It is used by companies with high amounts of inventory.
5. Net sales less cost of goods sold equals gross profit. Gross profit less operating expenses equals net income.
6. Unearned Revenue is a liability account that accumulates revenue that has *not* been earned yet, although the cash has been received. It represents a liability to the seller until the service or product is performed or delivered.

LEARNING UNIT 11-2

1. Two important adjustments in the accounting for a merchandise company deal with the Merchandise Inventory account and with the Unearned Revenue account (unearned rent).
2. When a company delivers goods or services for which it has been paid in advance, an adjustment is made to reduce the liability account Unearned Revenue and to increase an earned revenue account.

KEY TERMS

Beginning merchandise inventory (beginning inventory) The cost of goods on hand in a company to *begin* an accounting period.

Cost of goods sold Total cost of goods sold to customers.

Ending merchandise inventory (ending inventory) The cost of goods that remain unsold at the *end* of the accounting period. It is an asset on the new balance sheet.

Freight-In A cost of goods sold account that records the shipping cost to the buyer.

Gross profit Net sales less cost of goods sold.

Interest Expense The cost of borrowing money.

Mortgage Payable A liability account showing amount owed on a mortgage.

Periodic inventory system An inventory system that, at the *end* of each accounting period, calculates the cost of the unsold goods on hand by taking the cost of each unit times the number of units of each product on hand.

Perpetual inventory system An inventory system that keeps *continual track* of each type of inventory by recording units on hand at the beginning, units sold, and the current balance after each sale or purchase.

Unearned Revenue A liability account that records amount owed for goods or services in advance of delivery. The Cash account would record the receipt of cash.

BLUEPRINT: A WORKSHEET FOR A MERCHANDISE COMPANY

Account Titles	Adjustments Dr.	Adjustments Cr.	Adjusted Trial Balance Dr.	Adjusted Trial Balance Cr.	Income Statement Dr.	Income Statement Cr.	Balance Sheet Dr.	Balance Sheet Cr.
Cash			X				X	
Petty Cash			X				X	
Accounts Receivable			X				X	
Merchandise Inventory	X-E	X-B	X-E				X-E	
Supplies			X				X	
Equipment			X				X	
Acc. Dep., Store Equipment				X				X
Accounts Payable				X				X
Federal Income Tax Payable				X				X
FICA—Social Security Payable				X				X
FICA—Medicare Payable				X				X
State Income Tax Payable				X				X
SUTA Tax Payable				X				X
FUTA Tax Payable				X				X
Unearned Sales				X				X
Mortgage Payable				X				X
A. Flynn, Capital				X				X
A. Flynn, Withdrawals			X				X	
Income Summary*	X-B	X-E	X-B	X-E	X-B	X-E		
Sales				X		X		
Sales Returns and Allow.			X		X			
Sales Discount			X		X			
Purchases			X		X			
Purchases Ret. and Allow.				X		X		
Purchases Discount				X		X		
Freight-In			X		X			
Salaries Expense			X		X			
Payroll Tax Expense			X		X			
Insurance Expense			X		X			
Depreciation Expense			X		X			
Salaries Payable				X				X
Rental Income				X		X		

* Note that the figures for beginning (X-B) and ending inventory (X-E) are never combined on the Income Summary line of the worksheet. When the formal income statement is prepared, two distinct figures for inventory will be used to explain and calculate cost of goods sold. Beginning inventory adds to cost of goods sold; ending inventory reduces cost of goods sold.

QUESTIONS, CLASSROOM DEMONSTRATION EXERCISES, EXERCISES, AND PROBLEMS

Discussion and Critical Thinking Questions/Ethical Case

1. What is the function of the Purchases account?

2. Explain why Unearned Revenue is a liability account.

3. In a periodic system of inventory, the balance of beginning inventory will remain unchanged during the period. True or false?

4. What is the purpose of an inventory sheet?

5. Why do many Unearned Revenue accounts have to be adjusted?

6. Explain why figures for beginning and ending inventory are not combined on the Income Summary line of the worksheet.

7. Jim Heary is the custodian of petty cash. Jim, who is short of personal cash, decided to pay his home electrical and phone bill from petty cash. He plans to pay it back next month. Do you feel Jim should do so? You make the call. Write down your specific recommendations to Jim.

Classroom Demonstration Exercises

SET A

LO1 (10 min)   **Adjustment for Merchandise Inventory**

1. Given the following, journalize the adjusting entries for Merchandise Inventory. Note that ending inventory has a balance of $18,000.

Merchandise Inventory 114	Income Summary 313
60,000	

LO1 (15 min)   **Adjustment for Unearned Fees**

2. a. Given the following, journalize the adjusting entry. By December 31, $210 of the unearned dog walking fees were earned.

Unearned Dog Walking Fees 225	Earned Dog Walking Fees 441
900 12/1/XX	5,000 12/1/XX

   b. What is the category of unearned dog walking fees?

LO2 (10 min)   **Worksheet**

3. Match the following:
   1. Located on the Income Statement debit column of the worksheet.
   2. Located on the Income Statement credit column of the worksheet.
   3. Located on the Balance Sheet debit column of the worksheet.
   4. Located on the Balance Sheet credit column of the worksheet.
   _____ a. Beginning Merchandise Inventory
   _____ b. Sales Returns and Allowance
   _____ c. Salaries Payable
   _____ d. Sales
   _____ e. Ending Merchandise Inventory
   _____ f. Accounts Receivable

LO1 (10 min)   **Merchandise Inventory Adjustment**

4. Given beginning merchandise inventory of $2,000 and ending merchandise inventory of $50, what would be the adjusting entries?

LO2 (10 min)   **Income Summary on the Worksheet**

5.

	Adj.		ATB		Income Statement	
	Dr.	Cr.	Dr.	Cr.	Dr.	Cr.
Income Summary	A	B	C	D	E	F

Given a figure of beginning inventory of $400 and a $900 figure for ending inventory, place these numbers on the Income Summary line of this partial worksheet.

SET B

Adjustment for Merchandise Inventory   *LO1 (10 min)*

1. Given the following, journalize the adjusting entries for Merchandise Inventory. Note that ending inventory has a balance of $17,000.

Merchandise Inventory 114		Income Summary 313	
60,000			

Adjustment for Unearned Fees   *LO1 (15 min)*

2. **a.** Given the following, journalize the adjusting entry. By December 31, $300 of the unearned dog walking fees were earned.

Unearned Dog Walking Fees 225		Earned Dog Walking Fees 441	
	650 12/1/XX		4,000 12/1/XX

   b. What is the category of unearned dog walking fees?

Worksheet   *LO2 (10 min)*

3. Match the following:
   1. Located on the Income Statement debit column of the worksheet.
   2. Located on the Income Statement credit column of the worksheet.
   3. Located on the Balance Sheet debit column of the worksheet.
   4. Located on the Balance Sheet credit column of the worksheet.
   _____ **a.**   Ending Merchandise Inventory
   _____ **b.**   Unearned Rent
   _____ **c.**   Sales Discount
   _____ **d.**   Purchases
   _____ **e.**   Rental Income
   _____ **f.**   Petty Cash

Merchandise Inventory Adjustment on Worksheet   *LO1 (10 min)*

4. Adjustment column of a worksheet:

Merchandise Inventory	(A)	(B)
Income Summary	(B)	(A)

   Explain what the letters A and B represent. Why are they never combined?

Income Summary on the Worksheet   *LO2 (10 min)*

5.

	Adj.		ATB		Income Statement	
	Dr.	Cr.	Dr.	Cr.	Dr.	Cr.
Income Summary	A	B	C	D	E	F

Given a figure of beginning inventory of $500 and a $700 figure for ending inventory, place these numbers on the Income Summary line of this partial worksheet.

Exercises

LO1 (10 min) **11-1.** Indicate the normal balance and category of each of the following accounts:
  a. Unearned Revenue
  b. Merchandise Inventory (beginning of period)
  c. Freight-In
  d. Payroll Tax Expense
  e. Purchases Discount
  f. Sales Discount
  g. FICA—Social Security Payable
  h. Purchases Returns and Allowances

LO1 (15 min) **11-2.** From the following, calculate (a) net sales, (b) cost of goods sold, (c) gross profit, and (d) net income: Sales, $22,000; Sales Discount, $500; Sales Returns and Allowances, $250; Beginning Inventory, $650; Net Purchases, $13,200; Ending Inventory, $510; Operating Expenses, $3,600.

LO1 (10 min) **11-3.** Allan Co. had the following balances on December 31, 200X:

Cash		Unearned Janitorial Service
2,100		600

Janitorial Service
7,200

The accountant for Allan has asked you to make an adjustment because $400 of janitorial services has just been performed for customers who had paid for two months. Construct a transaction analysis chart.

LO1, 2 (15 min) **11-4.** Lesan Co. purchased merchandise costing $400,000. Calculate the cost of goods sold under the following different situations:
  a. Beginning inventory $40,000 and no ending inventory
  b. Beginning inventory $50,000 and a $60,000 ending inventory
  c. No beginning inventory and a $30,000 ending inventory

LO2 (20 min) **11-5.** Prepare a worksheet for Moore Co. from the following information using Figure 11.12:
  a/b. Merchandise Inventory, ending   13
    c. Store Supplies on hand   4
    d. Depreciation on Store Equipment   4
    e. Accrued Salaries   2

Group A Problems

You can also use the foldout worksheets at the end of the *Study Guide and Working Papers*.

LO1 (30 min) **11A-1.** Based on the following accounts, calculate
  a. Net sales.
  b. Cost of goods sold.
  c. Gross profit.
  d. Net income.

Check Figure:
Net income $2,125

Accounts Payable	$ 6,000
Operating Expenses	2,000
Bing.com, Capital	19,400
Purchases	1,500
Freight-In	90
Ending Merchandise Inventory, Dec. 31, 200X	65
Sales	6,000

FIGURE 11.12 Trial Balance for Moore Co.

MOORE CO. TRIAL BALANCE DECEMBER 31, 200X	Dr.	Cr.
Cash	8 00	
Accounts Receivable	5 00	
Merchandise Inventory	11 00	
Store Supplies	10 00	
Store Equipment	20 00	
Accumulated Depreciation, Store Equipment		6 00
Accounts Payable		5 00
J. Moore, Capital		34 00
Income Summary		
Sales		64 00
Sales Returns and Allowances	9 00	
Purchases	23 00	
Purchases Discount		3 00
Freight-In	3 00	
Salaries Expense	10 00	
Advertising Expense	13 00	
Totals	112 00	112 00

Accounts Receivable	500
Cash	800
Purchases Discount	50
Sales Returns and Allowances	300
Beg. Merchandise Inventory, Jan. 1, 200X	80
Purchases Returns and Allowances	70
Sales Discount	90

11A-2. From the trial balance in Figure 11.13 on the following page, complete a worksheet for Jim's Hardware. Assume the following:

a/b. Ending inventory on December 31 is calculated at $310.
  c. Insurance expired, $150.
  d. Depreciation on store equipment, $60.
  e. Accrued wages, $90.

LO2 (60 min)

> *Check Figure:*
> Net income $1,984

11A-3. The owner of Waltz Company asked you to prepare a worksheet from the trial balance in Figure 11.14 on the following page.

Additional Data

a/b. Ending merchandise inventory on December 31, $1,805.
  c. Office supplies used up, $210.
  d. Rent expired, $195.
  e. Depreciation expense on office equipment, $550.
  f. Office salaries earned but not paid, $310.

LO2 (60 min)

> *Check Figure:*
> Net income $5,300

11A-4. From the trial balance in Figure 11.15 and additional data, complete the worksheet for Ron's Wholesale Clothing Company.

Additional Data

a/b. Ending merchandise inventory on December 31, $6,000.
  c. Supplies on hand, $400.
  d. Insurance expired, $600.
  e. Depreciation on store equipment, $400.
  f. Storage fees earned, $176.

LO1, 2 (60 min)

> *Check Figure:*
> Net loss $824

FIGURE 11.13 Trial Balance for Jim's Hardware

JIM'S HARDWARE TRIAL BALANCE DECEMBER 31, 200X	Dr.	Cr.
Cash	7 8 6 00	
Accounts Receivable	1 1 5 2 00	
Merchandise Inventory	6 0 0 00	
Prepaid Insurance	6 8 4 00	
Store Equipment	2 1 6 0 00	
Accumulated Depreciation, Store Equipment		6 6 0 00
Accounts Payable		5 1 6 00
Jim Spool, Capital		1 6 3 2 00
Income Summary	—	—
Hardware Sales		1 1 0 4 0 00
Hardware Sales Returns and Allowances	5 4 6 00	
Hardware Sales Discount	2 1 6 00	
Purchases	5 2 5 6 00	
Purchases Discount		1 6 8 00
Purchases Returns and Allowances		1 0 2 00
Wages Expense	1 7 1 6 00	
Rent Expense	7 9 2 00	
Telephone Expense	1 1 4 00	
Miscellaneous Expense	9 6 00	
	1 4 1 1 8 00	1 4 1 1 8 00

FIGURE 11.14 Trial Balance for Waltz Company

WALTZ COMPANY TRIAL BALANCE DECEMBER 31, 200X	Dr.	Cr.
Cash	5 4 0 8 00	
Petty Cash	2 4 0 00	
Accounts Receivable	2 5 1 2 00	
Beginning Merchandise Inventory, Jan. 1	5 0 9 2 00	
Prepaid Rent	6 1 6 00	
Office Supplies	9 4 4 00	
Office Equipment	9 2 8 0 00	
Accumulated Depreciation, Office Equipment		7 6 0 0 00
Accounts Payable		5 9 6 4 00
K. Waltz, Capital		5 4 7 6 00
K. Waltz, Withdrawals	4 8 0 0 00	
Income Summary	—	—
Sales		5 2 4 8 4 00
Sales Returns and Allowances	9 6 00	
Sales Discount	2 4 0 0 00	
Purchases	2 9 3 1 6 00	
Purchases Discount		1 6 00
Purchases Returns and Allowances		3 4 8 00
Office Salaries Expense	7 4 0 8 00	
Insurance Expense	2 4 0 0 00	
Advertising Expense	8 0 0 00	
Utilities Expense	5 7 6 00	
	7 1 8 8 8 00	7 1 8 8 8 00

ED SLOAN, M.D. INCOME STATEMENT FOR YEAR ENDED DECEMBER 31, 20X2				
Professional Fees Earned	50 0 0 0 00			
Expenses	18 0 0 0 00			
Net Income	32 0 0 0 00			

FIGURE 11.19 Income Statement for Ed Sloan, M.D.

FINANCIAL REPORT PROBLEM

Reading the Kellogg's Annual Report

LO1 (10 min)

Go to Appendix A and find the Consolidated Statement of Earnings. What is the cost of goods sold in 2006?

INTERNET PROJECT

Build-A-Bear

Go to the Web and search: Annual Report Build-A-Bear 2008.
Click on Investors Relations.
List out the latest news Build-A-Bear is providing to its investors.
Order a free annual report.

CONTINUING PROBLEM

Sanchez Computer Center

LO1, 2 (60 min)

The first six months of the year have concluded for Sanchez Computer Center, and Tony wants to make the necessary adjustments to his accounts to prepare accurate financial statements.

Assignment

To prepare these adjustments, use the trial balance in Figure 11.20 and the following inventory that Tony took at the end of March:

   10 dozen ¼″ screws at a cost of $10 a dozen

   5 dozen ½″ screws at a cost of $7 a dozen

   2 feet of coaxial cable at a cost of $5 per foot

Merchandise left in stock was valued at $300.

Depreciation of Computer Equipment:

   Computer depreciates at $33 a month; purchased July 5.

   Computer workstations depreciate at $20 per month; purchased September 17.

   Shop benches depreciate at $25 per month; purchased November 5.

Depreciation of Office Equipment:

   Office equipment depreciates at $10 per month; purchased July 17.

   Fax machine depreciates at $10 per month; purchased November 20.

   Six months' worth of rent at a rental rate of $400 per month has expired.

Remember: If any long-term asset is purchased in the first 15 days of the month, Tony will charge depreciation for the full month. If an asset is purchased later than the 15th, he will not charge depreciation in the month it was purchased.

Complete the 10-column worksheet for the six months ended March 31, 200X.

FIGURE 11.20 Trial Balance for Sanchez Computer March 31, 200X

Account Titles	Trial Balance Dr.	Trial Balance Cr.
Cash	12 51 65	
Petty Cash	1 00 00	
Accounts Receivable	11 90 0 00	
Prepaid Rent	2 80 0 00	
Supplies	4 32 00	
Merchandise Inventory		
Computer Shop Equipment	3 80 0 00	
Accumulated Dep., C.S. Equip.		9 9 00
Office Equipment	1 05 0 00	
Accum. Dep., Office Equip.		2 0 00
Accounts Payable		2 84 0 00
T. Freedman, Capital		7 40 6 00
T. Freedman, Withdrawals	2 01 5 00	
Income Summary		
Service Revenue		19 80 0 00
Sales		9 70 0 00
Sales Return and Allowances	4 00 00	
Sales Discounts	2 20 00	
Advertising Expense	8 00 00	
Rent Expense		
Utilities Expense	2 90 00	
Phone Expense	1 50 00	
Supplies Expense		
Insurance Expense	1 00 00	
Postage Expense	1 75 00	
Depreciation Exp., C.S. Equip.		
Depreciation Exp., Office Equip.		
Miscellaneous Expense	1 0 00	
Wage Expense	2 03 0 00	
Payroll Tax Expense	2 26 35	
Purchases	9 50 00	
Purchase Ret. & Allow.		1 00 00
Totals	39 96 5 00	39 96 5 00

APPENDIX

A WORKSHEET FOR ART'S WHOLESALE CLOTHING CO. USING A PERPETUAL INVENTORY SYSTEM

What's New: The Merchandise Inventory account (in Figure A.1 on the following page) does not need to be adjusted. The $4,000 figure for merchandise is the up-to-date balance in the account. The difference between beginning inventory and ending inventory will be part of a new account called *Cost of Goods Sold* on the worksheet.

How the $65,910 of Cost of Goods Sold was calculated from a periodic setup:

	Purchases	$52,000	← **Assumed sold; part of cost**
+	Merchandise Inventory	$15,000	← **Beg. Inv. − Ending Inv.** **$19,000 − $4,000**
−	Purchases Discount	860	→ **Reduces costs**
−	Purchases Returns and Allowances	680	↗
+	Freight-In	450	→ **Adds to cost**
		$65,910	**Cost of Goods Sold**

What's Deleted from the Periodic Worksheet: Account titles for Purchases, Purchases Discounts, Purchases Returns and Allowances, and Freight-In.

Note: Net income is the same on the periodic and the perpetual worksheets.

Problem for Appendix

Using the solution to Self-Review Quiz 11-2 about Ray Company, convert this worksheet to a perpetual inventory system worksheet.

ART'S WHOLESALE CLOTHING CO.
WORKSHEET
FOR YEAR ENDED DECEMBER 31, 200X

Account Titles	Trial Balance Dr.	Trial Balance Cr.	Adjustments Dr.	Adjustments Cr.	Adjusted Trial Balance Dr.	Adjusted Trial Balance Cr.	Income Statement Dr.	Income Statement Cr.	Balance Sheet Dr.	Balance Sheet Cr.
Cash	1292000				1292000				1292000	
Petty Cash	10000				10000				10000	
Accounts Receivable	1450000				1450000				1450000	
Merchandise Inventory	400000				400000				400000	
Supplies	80000			(B)50000	30000				30000	
Prepaid Insurance	90000			(C)30000	60000				60000	
Store Equipment	400000				400000				400000	
Acc. Dep., Store Equip.		40000		(D)5000		45000				45000
Accounts Payable		1790000				1790000				1790000
Federal Income Tax		80000				80000				80000
FICA—Social Security		45400				45400				45400
FICA—Medicare		10600				10600				10600
State Income Tax		20000				20000				20000
SUTA Tax		10800				10800				10800
FUTA Tax Payable		3200				3200				3200
Unearned Rent		60000	(A)20000			40000				40000
Mortgage Payable		232000				232000				232000
Art Newner, Capital		790500				790500				790500
Art Newner, Withdrawal	860000				860000				860000	
Sales		9500000				9500000		9500000		
Sales Returns and Allow.	95000				95000		95000			
Sales Discount	67000				67000		67000			
Cost of Goods Sold	6591000				6591000		6591000			
Salaries Expense	1170000		(E)60000		1230000		1230000			
Payroll Tax Expense	42000				42000		42000			
Postage Expense	2500				2500		2500			
Miscellaneous Expense	3000				3000		3000			
Interest Expense	30000				30000		30000			
	12582500	12582500								
Rental Income				(A)20000		20000		20000		
Supplies Expense			(B)50000		50000		50000			
Insurance Expense			(C)30000		30000		30000			
Dep. Exp., Store Equip.			(D)5000		5000		5000			
Salaries Payable				(E)60000		60000				60000
			165000	165000	12647500	12647500	8145500	9520000	4502000	3127500
Net Income							1374500			1374500
							9520000	9520000	4502000	4502000

FIGURE A.1 Worksheet for Art's Wholesale Clothing Co. Using a Perpetual Inventory System

RAY COMPANY
WORKSHEET
FOR YEAR ENDED DECEMBER 31, 200X

Account Titles	Trial Balance Dr.	Trial Balance Cr.	Adjustments Dr.	Adjustments Cr.	Adjusted Trial Balance Dr.	Adjusted Trial Balance Cr.	Income Statement Dr.	Income Statement Cr.	Balance Sheet Dr.	Balance Sheet Cr.
Cash	248600				248600				248600	
Merchandise Inventory	20000				20000				20000	
Prepaid Rent	115200			(B) 10000	105200				105200	
Prepaid Insurance	6000				6000				6000	
Office Equipment	216000				216000				216000	
Accumulated Dep., Off. Equip.		56000		(C) 6000		62000				62000
Unearned Storage Fees		251600	(A) 51600			200000				200000
Accounts Payable		10000				10000				10000
B. Ray, Capital		193200				193200				193200
Sales		1104000				1104000		1104000		
Sales Returns and Allowances	54600				54600		54600			
Sales Discounts	21600				21600		21600			
COGS*	561000				561000		561000			
Salaries Expense	201600		(D) 20000		221600		221600			
Insurance Expense	139200				139200		139200			
Utilities Expense	9600				9600		9600			
Plumbing Expense	21400				21400		21400			
	1614800	1614800								
Storage Fees Earned				(A) 51600		51600		51600		
Rent Expense			(B) 10000		10000		10000			
Dep. Expense, Equip.			(C) 6000		6000		6000			
Salaries Payable				(D) 20000		20000				20000
			87600	87600	1640800	1640800	1045000	1155600	595800	485200
Net Income							110600			110600
							1155600	1155600	595800	595800

*$624 ($824 − $200) + $5,256 − $168 − $102.

FIGURE A.2 Worksheet for Ray Company Using a Perpetual Inventory System

12

Completion of the Accounting Cycle for a Merchandise Company

DID YOU KNOW? Chiquita now packages single bananas to go that can stay ripe for seven days or more. Any shipping or handling fees are included in net sales as part of cost of sales. Visit *www.chiquita.com* to find more information about Chiquita.

LEARNING OBJECTIVES

1. Preparing financial statements for a merchandise company.

2. Recording adjusting and closing entries.

3. Preparing post-closing trial balance.

4. Completing reversing entries.

When you eat that Chiquita banana just keep in mind all the steps Chiquita must take to complete its accounting cycle. In this chapter we discuss the steps involved in completing the accounting cycle for a merchandise company. These steps include preparing financial reports, journalizing and posting adjusting and closing entries, preparing a post-closing trial balance, and reversing entries.

> When setting up a new entity in QuickBooks or Peachtree, be careful to select the correct type of entity and to select the correct type of Chart of Accounts. Careful selection will ensure that your financial statements will include all of the necessary sections.

Learning Unit 12-1 Preparing Financial Statements

As we discussed in Chapter 5, when we were dealing with a service company rather than a merchandise company, the three financial statements can be prepared from the worksheet. Let's begin by looking at how Art's Wholesale Clothing Company prepares the income statement.

LO1

The Income Statement

Art is interested in knowing how well his shop performed for the year ended December 31, 200X. What were its net sales? What was the level of returns of goods from dissatisfied customers? What was the cost of the goods brought into the store versus the selling price received? How many goods were returned to suppliers? What is the cost of the goods that have not been sold? What was the cost of the Freight-In account? The income statement in Figure 12.1 is prepared from the income statement columns of the worksheet. Note that no debit or credit columns appear on the formal income statement; the inside columns in financial reports are used for subtotaling, not for debit and credit.

The income statement is broken down into several sections. Remembering the sections can help you set it up correctly on your own. The income statement shows the following:

	Net Sales
−	Cost of Goods Sold
=	Gross Profit
−	Operating Expenses
=	Net Income from Operations
+	Other Income
−	Other Expenses
=	Net Income

Let's take these sections one at a time and see where the figures come from on the worksheet.

Revenue Section

> Sales
> − Sales Ret. & Allow.
> − Sales Discount
> = Net Sales

Net Sales   The first major category of the income statement shows net sales. The figure here—$93,380—is not on the worksheet. Instead, the accountant must combine the amounts for gross sales, sales returns and allowances, and sales discount found on the worksheet to arrive at a figure for net sales. Thus these individual amounts are not summarized in a single figure for net sales until the formal income statement is prepared.

> Beg. Inventory
> + Net Cost of Purchases
> − Ending Inventory
> = Cost of Goods Sold

Cost of Goods Sold Section   The figures for Merchandise Inventory are shown separately on the worksheet. The $19,000 represents the beginning inventory of the period, and the $4,000, calculated from an inventory sheet is the ending inventory. Note on the financial report that the cost of goods sold section uses two separate figures for inventory.

> *Remember:* In the periodic inventory system, goods brought in during the accounting period are added to the Purchases account, not to the Merchandise Inventory account.

Note that the following numbers are not found on the worksheet but are shown on the formal income statement (they are combined by the accountant in preparing the income statement):

- Net Purchases: $50,460 (Purchases − Purchases Discount − Purchases Returns and Allowances)
- Net Cost of Purchases: $50,910 (Net Purchases + Freight-In)
- Cost of Goods Available for Sale: $69,910 (Beginning Inventory + Net Cost of Purchases)
- Cost of Goods Sold: $65,910 (Cost of Goods Available for Sale − Ending Inventory)

ART'S WHOLESALE CLOTHING COMPANY
PARTIAL WORKSHEET
FOR YEAR ENDED DECEMBER 31, 200X

	Income Statement	
	Dr.	Cr.
Income Summary	1900000 00	400000 00
Sales		9500000 00
Sales Returns and Allowances	95000 00	
Sales Discount	67000 00	
Purchases	5200000 00	
Purchases Discount		86000 00
Purchases Returns and Allowances		68000 00
Freight-In	45000 00	
Salaries Expense	1230000 00	
Payroll Tax Expense	42000 00	
Postage Expense	2500 00	
Miscellaneous Expense	3000 00	
Interest Expense	30000 00	
Rental Income		20000 00
Supplies Expense	50000 00	
Insurance Expense	30000 00	
Depreciation Expense, Store Equip.	5000 00	
Salaries Payable		
	8699500 00	10074000 00
Net Income	1374500 00	
	10074000 00	10074000 00

ART'S WHOLESALE CLOTHING COMPANY
INCOME STATEMENT
FOR YEAR ENDED DECEMBER 31, 200X

Revenue:			
Gross Sales			$9500000 00
Less: Sales Ret. and Allow.		95000 00	
Sales Discount		67000 00	162000 00
Net Sales			$9338000 00
Cost of Goods Sold:			
Merchandise Inventory, 1/1/0X		$1900000 00	
Purchases	$5200000 00		
Less: Purch. Discount	86000 00		
Purch. Ret. and Allow.	68000 00	154000 00	
Net Purchases		$5046000 00	
Add: Freight-In		45000 00	
Net Cost of Purchases		5091000 00	
Cost of Goods Available for Sale		$6991000 00	
Less: Merch. Inv., 12/31/0X		400000 00	
Cost of Goods Sold			6591000 00
Gross Profit			$2747000 00
Operating Expenses:			
Salaries Expense		$1230000 00	
Payroll Tax Expense		42000 00	
Dep. Exp., Store Equip.		5000 00	
Supplies Expense		50000 00	
Insurance Expense		30000 00	
Postage Expense		2500 00	
Miscellaneous Expense		3000 00	
Total Operating Expenses			1362500 00
Net Income from Operations			$1384500 00
Other Income:			
Rental Income		$20000 00	
Other Expenses:			
Interest Expense		30000 00	10000 00
Net Income			$1374500 00

FIGURE 12.1 Partial Worksheet and Income Statement

Gross Profit Gross profit ($27,470) is calculated by subtracting the cost of goods sold from net sales ($93,380 − $65,910). The amount is not found on the worksheet.

Operating Expenses Section Like the other figures we have discussed, the business's operating expenses do not appear on the worksheet. To get this figure ($13,625), the accountant adds up all the expenses on the worksheet.

Many operating companies break expenses down into those directly related to the selling activity of the company (**selling expenses**) and those related to administrative or office activity (**administrative expenses** or **general expenses**). Here's a sample list broken down into these two categories:

OPERATING EXPENSES

- Selling Expenses:

  Sales Salaries Expense

  Delivery Expense

  Advertising Expense

  Depreciation Expense, Store Equipment

  Insurance Expense

     Total Selling Expenses

- Administrative Expenses:

  Rent Expense

  Office Salaries Expense

  Utilities Expense

  Supplies Expense

  Depreciation Expense, Office Equipment

     Total Administrative Expenses

        Total Operating Expenses

Other Income (or Other Revenue) Section The **other income,** or other revenue, section is used to record any revenue other than revenue from sales. For example, Art's Wholesale makes a profit from subletting a portion of a building. The $200 of rental income the company earns from this is recorded in the other income section.

Other Expenses Section The **other expenses** section is used to record nonoperating expenses, that is, expenses that are not related to the main operating activities of the business. For example, Art's Wholesale owes $300 interest on money it has borrowed. That expense is shown in the other expenses section.

Statement of Owner's Equity

The statement of owner's equity is the same for a merchandise business as for a service firm.

The information used to prepare the statement of owner's equity comes from the balance sheet columns of the worksheet. Keep in mind that the capital account in the ledger should be checked to see whether any additional investments occurred during the period. Figure 12.2 shows how the worksheet aids in this step. The ending figure of $13,050 for Art Newner, Capital, is carried over to the balance sheet, which is the final report we look at in this chapter.

The Balance Sheet

Figure 12.3 (on the next page spread) shows how a worksheet is used to aid in the preparation of a **classified balance sheet.** A classified balance sheet breaks down the assets and liabilities into more detail. Classified balance sheets provide management, owners, creditors, and

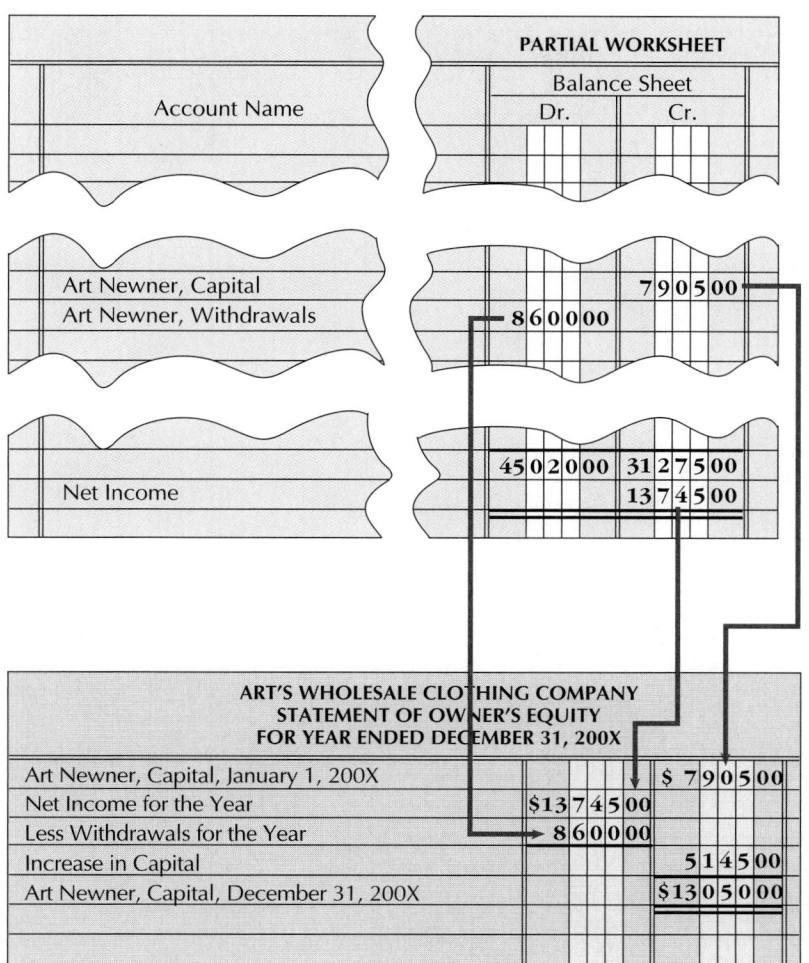

FIGURE 12.2 Preparing Statement of Owner's Equity from the Worksheet

> Any additional investment by the owner would be added to his or her beginning capital amount.

suppliers with more information about the company's ability to pay current and long-term debts. They also provide a more complete financial picture of the firm.

The categories on the classified balance sheet are as follows:

● **Current assets** are defined as cash and assets that will be converted into cash or used up during the normal operating cycle of the company or one year, whichever is longer. (Think of the **operating cycle** as the time period it takes a company to buy and sell merchandise and then collect accounts receivable.)

Accountants list current assets in order of how easily they can be converted into cash (called *liquidity*). In most cases, Accounts Receivable can be turned into cash more quickly than Merchandise Inventory. For example, it can be quite difficult to sell an outdated computer in a computer store or to sell last year's model car this year.

● **Plant and equipment** are long-lived assets that are used in the production or sale of goods or services. Art's Wholesale has only one plant asset, store equipment; other plant assets could include buildings and land. The assets are usually listed in order according to how long they will last; the shortest-lived assets are listed first. Land would always be the last asset listed (and land is never depreciated). Note that we still show the cost of the asset less its accumulated depreciation.

ART'S WHOLESALE CLOTHING COMPANY
CLASSIFIED BALANCE SHEET
FOR YEAR ENDED DECEMBER 31, 200X

Assets

Current Assets:

Cash	$12 9 2 0 00		
Petty Cash	1 0 0 00		
Accounts Receivable	14 5 0 0 00		
Merchandise Inventory	4 0 0 0 00		
Supplies	3 0 0 00		
Prepaid Insurance	6 0 0 00		
Total Current Assets			$32 4 2 0 00

Plant and Equipment:

Store Equipment	$4 0 0 0 00		
Less: Accum. Depreciation	4 5 0 00	3 5 5 0 00	
Total Assets			$35 9 7 0 00

Liabilities

Current Liabilities:

Mortgage Payable (current portion)	$ 3 2 0 00		
Accounts Payable	17 9 0 0 00		
Federal Income Tax Payable	8 0 0 00		
FICA—Social Security Payable	4 5 4 00		
FICA—Medicare Payable	1 0 6 00		
State Income Tax Payable	2 0 0 00		
SUTA Tax Payable	1 0 8 00		
FUTA Tax Payable	3 2 00		
Salaries Payable	6 0 0 00		
Unearned Rent	4 0 0 00		
Total Current Liabilities			$20 9 2 0 00

Long-Term Liabilities:

Mortgage Payable		2 0 0 0 00	
Total Liabilities			$22 9 2 0 00

Owner's Equity

Art Newner, Capital, December 31, 200X			13 0 5 0 00
Total Liabilities and Owner's Equity			$35 9 7 0 00

ART'S WHOLESALE CLOTHING COMPANY
WORKSHEET
FOR YEAR ENDED DECEMBER 31, 200X

	Balance Sheet	
	Dr.	Cr.
Cash	12 9 2 0 00	
Petty Cash	1 0 0 00	
Accounts Receivable	14 5 0 0 00	
Merchandise Inventory	4 0 0 0 00	
Supplies	3 0 0 00	
Prepaid Insurance	6 0 0 00	
Store Equipment	4 0 0 0 00	
Acc. Dep., Store Equipment		4 5 0 00
Accounts Payable		17 9 0 0 00
Federal Income Tax Payable		8 0 0 00
FICA—Social Security Payable		4 5 4 00
FICA—Medicare Payable		1 0 6 00
State Income Tax Payable		2 0 0 00
SUTA Tax Payable		1 0 8 00
FUTA Tax Payable		3 2 00
Unearned Rent		4 0 0 00
Mortgage Payable		2 3 2 0 00
Art Newner, Capital		7 9 0 5 00
Salaries Payable		6 0 0 00
	45 0 2 0 00	31 2 7 5 00
Net Income		13 7 4 5 00
	45 0 2 0 00	45 0 2 0 00

FIGURE 12.3 Partial Worksheet and Classified Balance Sheet

- **Current liabilities** are the debts or obligations of Art's Wholesale that must be paid within one year or one operating cycle. The order of listing accounts in this section is not always the same; many times companies will list their liabilities in the order they expect to pay them off. Note that the current portion of the mortgage, $320 (that portion due within one year), is listed before Accounts Payable.
- **Long-term liabilities** are debts or obligations that are not due and payable for a comparatively long period, usually for more than one year. For Art's Wholesale the only long-term liability is Mortgage Payable. The long-term portion of the mortgage is listed here; the current portion, due within one year, is listed under current liabilities.

> Mortgage Payable:
> $2,320
> − 320 current portion
> ───────────────
> $2,000 long-term liability

LEARNING UNIT 12-1 REVIEW

AT THIS POINT / you should be able to

- Prepare a detailed income statement from the worksheet.
- Explain the difference between selling and administrative expenses.
- Explain which columns of the worksheet are used in preparing a statement of owner's equity.
- Explain as well as compare current assets with plant and equipment.
- Using Mortgage Payable as an example, explain the difference between current and long-term liabilities.
- Prepare a classified balance sheet from a worksheet.

Self-Review Quiz 12-1

Using the worksheet from Self-Review Quiz 11-2 in Chapter 11, prepare in proper form (1) an income statement, (2) a statement of owner's equity, (3) a classified balance sheet for Ray Company.

Solutions to Self-Review Quiz 12-1

1.

FIGURE 12.4 Income Statement for Ray Company

RAY COMPANY INCOME STATEMENT FOR YEAR ENDED DECEMBER 31, 200X				
Revenue:				
Sales				$11 0 4 0 00
Less: Sales Ret. and Allow.			$ 5 4 6 00	
Sales Discount			2 1 6 00	7 6 2 00
Net Sales				$10 2 7 8 00
Cost of Goods Sold:				
Merchandise Inventory, 1/1/0X			$ 8 2 4 00	
Purchases		$5 2 5 6 00		
Less: Pur. Ret. and Allow.	$ 1 6 8 00			
Purchases Discount	1 0 2 00	2 7 0 00		
Net Purchases			4 9 8 6 00	
Cost of Goods Available for Sale			$ 5 8 1 0 00	
Less: Merchandise Inv., 12/31/0X			2 0 0 00	
Cost of Goods Sold				5 6 1 0 00
Gross Profit				$ 4 6 6 8 00
Operating Expenses:				
Salaries Expense		$ 2 2 1 6 00		
Insurance Expense		1 3 9 2 00		
Utilities Expense		9 6 00		
Plumbing Expense		2 1 4 00		
Rent Expense		1 0 0 00		
Depreciation Exp., Equip.		6 0 00		
Total Operating Expenses				4 0 7 8 00
Net Income from Operations				$ 5 9 0 00
Other Income:				
Storage Fees				5 1 6 00
Net Income				$ 1 1 0 6 00

2.

FIGURE 12.5 Statement of Owner's Equity for Ray Company

RAY COMPANY STATEMENT OF OWNER'S EQUITY FOR YEAR ENDED DECEMBER 31, 200X	
B. Ray, Capital, 1/1/0X	$ 1 9 3 2 00
Net Income for the Year	1 1 0 6 00
B. Ray, Capital, 12/31/0X	$ 3 0 3 8 00

3.

RAY COMPANY BALANCE SHEET DECEMBER 31, 200X			
Assets			
Current Assets:			
Cash	$ 2 4 8 6 00		
Merchandise Inventory	2 0 0 00		
Prepaid Rent	1 0 5 2 00		
Prepaid Insurance	6 0 00		
Total Current Assets		$ 3 7 9 8 00	
Plant and Equipment:			
Office Equipment	$ 2 1 6 0 00		
Less: Accumulated Depreciation	6 2 0 00	1 5 4 0 00	
Total Assets		$ 5 3 3 8 00	
Liabilities			
Current Liabilities			
Accounts Payable	$ 1 0 0 00		
Salaries Payable	2 0 0 00		
Unearned Storage Fees	2 0 0 0 00		
Total Liabilities		$ 2 3 0 0 00	
Owner's Equity			
B. Ray, Capital, December 31, 200X		3 0 3 8 00	
Total Liabilities and Owner's Equity		$ 5 3 3 8 00	

FIGURE 12.6 Balance Sheet for Ray Company

Learning Unit 12-2 Journalizing and Posting Adjusting and Closing Entries; Preparing the Post-Closing Trial Balance

LO2

Journalizing and Posting Adjusting Entries

From the worksheet of Art's Wholesale (repeated in Fig. 12.7 on the following page for your convenience), the adjusting entries can be journalized from the adjustments column and posted to the ledger. Keep in mind that the adjustments have been placed only on the worksheet, not in the journal or in the ledger. At this point, the journal does not reflect adjustments and the ledger still contains only unadjusted amounts.

> QuickBooks and Peachtree programs do not use worksheets. Adjustments are made from preparing the trial balance and are recorded in the general journal. Entries are both journalized and posted at the same time when the user selects Save in the General Journal screen.

Partial Ledger

Merchandise Inventory 114		**Income Summary 313**	
Dr.	**Cr.**	**Dr.**	**Cr.**
19,000	19,000	19,000	4,000
4,000			

FIGURE 12.7 Completed Worksheet

ART'S WHOLESALE CLOTHING CO.
WORKSHEET
FOR YEAR ENDED DECEMBER 31, 200X

	Trial Balance Dr.	Trial Balance Cr.	Adjustments Dr.	Adjustments Cr.
Cash	12 9 2 0 00			
Petty Cash	1 0 0 00			
Accounts Receivable	14 5 0 0 00			
Merchandise Inventory	19 0 0 0 00		(B)4 0 0 0 00	(A)19 0 0 0 00
Supplies	8 0 0 00			(D)5 0 0 00
Prepaid Insurance	9 0 0 00			(E)3 0 0 00
Store Equipment	4 0 0 0 00			
Acc. Dep., Store Equipment		4 0 0 00		(F) 5 0 00
Accounts Payable		17 9 0 0 00		
Federal Income Tax Payable		8 0 0 00		
FICA—Social Security Payable		4 5 4 00		
FICA—Medicare Payable		1 0 6 00		
State Income Tax Payable		2 0 0 00		
SUTA Tax Payable		1 0 8 00		
FUTA Tax Payable		3 2 00		
Unearned Rent		6 0 0 00	(C)2 0 0 00	
Mortgage Payable		23 2 0 00		
Art Newner, Capital		79 0 5 00		
Art Newner, Withdrawals	8 6 0 0 00			
Income Summary			(A)19 0 0 0 00	(B)4 0 0 0 00
Sales		95 0 0 0 00		
Sales Returns and Allowances	9 5 0 00			
Sales Discount	6 7 0 00			
Purchases	52 0 0 0 00			
Purchases Discount		8 6 0 00		
Purchases Returns and Allowances		6 8 0 00		
Freight-In	4 5 0 00			
Salaries Expense	11 7 0 0 00		(G)6 0 0 00	
Payroll Tax Expense	4 2 0 00			
Postage Expense	2 5 00			
Miscellaneous Expense	3 0 00			
Interest Expense	3 0 0 00			
	127 3 6 5 00	127 3 6 5 00		
Rental Income				(C)2 0 0 00
Supplies Expense			(D)5 0 0 00	
Insurance Expense			(E)3 0 0 00	
Depreciation Expense, Store Equip.			(F) 5 0 00	
Salaries Payable				(G)6 0 0 00
			24 6 5 0 00	24 6 5 0 00
Net Income				

FIGURE 12.7 *(continued)*

Adjusted Trial Bal. Dr.	Adjusted Trial Bal. Cr.	Income Statement Dr.	Income Statement Cr.	Balance Sheet Dr.	Balance Sheet Cr.
12920 00				12920 00	
100 00				100 00	
14500 00				14500 00	
4000 00				4000 00	
300 00				300 00	
600 00				600 00	
4000 00				4000 00	
	450 00				450 00
	17900 00				17900 00
	800 00				800 00
	454 00				454 00
	106 00				106 00
	200 00				200 00
	108 00				108 00
	32 00				32 00
	400 00				400 00
	2320 00				2320 00
	7905 00				7905 00
8600 00				8600 00	
19000 00	4000 00	19000 00	4000 00		
	95000 00		95000 00		
950 00		950 00			
670 00		670 00			
5200 00		5200 00			
	860 00		860 00		
	680 00		680 00		
450 00		450 00			
12300 00		12300 00			
420 00		420 00			
25 00		25 00			
30 00		30 00			
300 00		300 00			
	200 00		200 00		
500 00		500 00			
300 00		300 00			
50 00		50 00			
	600 00				600 00
132015 00	132015 00	86995 00	100740 00	45020 00	31275 00
		13745 00			13745 00
		100740 00	100740 00	45020 00	45020 00

Supplies 115		Supplies Expense 614	
Dr.	Cr.	Dr.	Cr.
800	500	500	

Prepaid Insurance 116		Insurance Expense 615	
Dr.	Cr.	Dr.	Cr.
900	300	300	

Accum. Dep., Store Equipment 122		Dep. Expense, Store Equip. 613	
Dr.	Cr.	Dr.	Cr.
	400	50	
	50		

Salaries Payable 212		Salaries Exp. 611	
Dr.	Cr.	Dr.	Cr.
	600	11,700	
		600	

Unearned Rent 219		Rental Income 414	
Dr.	Cr.	Dr.	Cr.
200	600		200

The journalized and posted adjusting entries are shown in Figure 12.8. Note that the liability Unearned Rent is reduced by $200 and Rental Income has increased by $200.

Journalizing and Posting Closing Entries

In Chapter 5, we discussed the closing process for a service company. The goals of closing are the same for a merchandise company. These goals are (1) to clear all temporary accounts in the ledger to zero and (2) to update capital in the ledger to its latest balance. The company must use the worksheet and the steps listed here to complete the closing process.

> Closing is not a necessary step when using Peachtree or QuickBooks. Net income is calculated after each transaction, and financial statements are current.

Step 1 Close all balances on the income statement credit column of the worksheet, except Income Summary, by debits.
Then credit the total to the Income Summary account.

Step 2 Close all balances on the income statement debit column of the worksheet, except Income Summary, by credits.
Then debit the total to the Income Summary account.

Step 3 Transfer the balance of the Income Summary account to the Capital account.

Step 4 Transfer the balance of the owner's Withdrawals account to the Capital account.

Let's look now at the journalized closing entries in Figure 12.9. When these entries are posted, all the temporary accounts will have zero balances in the ledger, and the Capital account will be updated with a new balance.

Let's take a moment to look at the Income Summary account in T account form:

	Income Summary 313		
	Dr.	Cr.	
Adj.	19,000	4,000	Adj.
Clos.	67,995	96,740	Clos.
	86,995	100,740	
Net Income → Clos.	13,745		

	Date		Account Titles and Description	PR	Dr.	Cr.
			ART'S WHOLESALE CLOTHING CO. GENERAL JOURNAL			
						Page 2
			Adjusting Entries			
	31		Income Summary	313	1900000	
			Merchandise Inventory	114		1900000
			Transferred beginning inventory			
			to Income Summary			
	31		Merchandise Inventory	114	400000	
			Income Summary	313		400000
			Records cost of ending inventory			
	31		Unearned Rent	219	20000	
			Rental Income	414		20000
			Rental income earned			
	31		Supplies Expense	614	50000	
			Supplies	115		50000
			Supplies consumed			
	31		Insurance Expense	615	30000	
			Prepaid Insurance	116		30000
			Insurance expired			
	31		Dep. Exp., Store Equipment	613	5000	
			Acc. Dep., Store Equipment	122		5000
			Depreciation on equipment			
	31		Salaries Expense	611	60000	
			Salaries Payable	212		60000
			Accrued salaries			

FIGURE 12.8 Journalized and Posted Adjusting Entries

Note that Income Summary before the closing process contains the adjustments for Merchandise Inventory. The end result is that the net income of $13,745 is closed to the Capital account.

The Post-Closing Trial Balance

LO3

The post-closing trial balance shown in Figure 12.10 (on the following page spread) is prepared from the general ledger. Note first that all temporary accounts have been closed and thus are not shown on this post-closing trial balance. Note also that the ending inventory figure of the last accounting period, $4,000, becomes the beginning inventory figure on January 1, 20X3.

FIGURE 12.9 General Journal Closing Entries

	Date	Account Titles and Description	PR	Dr.	Cr.
		Closing Entries			
	31	Sales	411	9500000	
		Rental Income	414	20000	
		Purchases Discount	512	86000	
		Purchases Ret. and Allow.	513	68000	
		Income Summary	313		9674000
		Transfers credit account balances			
		on income statement column of			
		worksheet to Income Summary			
	31	Income Summary	313	6799500	
		Sales Returns and Allowances	412		95000
		Sales Discount	413		67000
		Purchases	511		5200000
		Freight-In	514		45000
		Salaries Expense	611		1230000
		Payroll Tax Expense	612		42000
		Postage Expense	616		2500
		Miscellaneous Expense	617		3000
		Interest Expense	618		30000
		Supplies Expense	614		50000
		Insurance Expense	615		30000
		Depreciation Expense, Store Equip.	613		5000
		Transfers all expenses, and			
		deductions to Sales are			
		closed to Income Summary			
	31	Income Summary	313	1374500	
		A. Newner, Capital	311		1374500
		Transfer of net income to			
		Capital from Income Summary			
	31	A. Newner, Capital	311	860000	
		A. Newner, Withdrawals	312		860000
		Closes withdrawals to			
		Capital Account			

ART'S WHOLESALE CLOTHING CO. GENERAL JOURNAL — Page 2

LEARNING UNIT 12-2 REVIEW

AT THIS POINT you should be able to

- Journalize and post adjusting entries for a merchandise company.
- Explain the relationship of the worksheet to the adjusting and closing process.
- Complete the closing process for a merchandise company.
- Prepare a post-closing trial balance and explain why ending Merchandise Inventory is not a temporary account.

Self-Review Quiz 12-2

Using the worksheet from Self-Review Quiz 11-2 in Chapter 11, journalize the closing entries.

ART'S WHOLESALE CLOTHING COMPANY POSTCLOSING TRIAL BALANCE DECEMBER 31, 200X	Dr.	Cr.
Cash	12 9 2 0 00	
Petty Cash	1 0 0 00	
Accounts Receivable	14 5 0 0 00	
Merchandise Inventory	4 0 0 0 00	
Supplies	3 0 0 00	
Prepaid Insurance	6 0 0 00	
Store Equipment	4 0 0 0 00	
Accum. Depreciation, Store Equipment		4 5 0 00
Accounts Payable		17 9 0 0 00
Federal Income Tax Payable		8 0 0 00
FICA—Social Security Payable		4 5 4 00
FICA—Medicare Payable		1 0 6 00
State Income Tax Payable		2 0 0 00
SUTA Tax Payable		1 0 8 00
FUTA Tax Payable		3 2 00
Salary Payable		6 0 0 00
Unearned Rent		4 0 0 00
Mortgage Payable		2 3 2 0 00
Art Newner, Capital		13 0 5 0 00
	36 4 2 0 00	36 4 2 0 00

FIGURE 12.10 Post-Closing Trial Balance for Art's Wholesale Clothing Company

Solution to Self-Review Quiz 12-2

Date	Account Titles and Description	PR	Dr.	Cr.
	Closing Entries			Page 2
Dec. 31	Sales		11 0 4 0 00	
	Storage Fees Earned		5 1 6 00	
	Purchases Returns and Allowances		1 6 8 00	
	Purchases Discount		1 0 2 00	
	Income Summary			11 8 2 6 00
31	Income Summary		10 0 9 6 00	
	Sales Returns and Allowances			5 4 6 00
	Sales Discount			2 1 6 00
	Purchases			5 2 5 6 00
	Salaries Expense			2 2 1 6 00
	Insurance Expense			1 3 9 2 00
	Utilities Expense			9 6 00
	Plumbing Expense			2 1 4 00
	Rent Expense			1 0 0 00
	Depreciation Exp., Equipment			6 0 00
31	Income Summary		1 1 0 6 00	
	B. Ray, Capital			1 1 0 6 00

FIGURE 12.11 Closing Entries Journalized

LO4 Learning Unit 12-3 Reversing Entries (Optional Section)

The accounting cycle for Art's Wholesale Clothing Company is completed. Now let's look at **reversing entries,** an optional way of handling some adjusting entries. Reversing entries are general journal entries that are the opposite of adjusting entries. Reversing entries help reduce potential errors and simplify the recordkeeping process. If Art's accountant does reversing entries, routine transactions can be done in the usual steps.

> Reversing entries are an option; they are not mandatory.

To help explain the concept of reversing entries, let's look at these two adjustments that could be reversed:

1. When an increase occurs in an asset account (no previous balance).
   Example: Interest Receivable
   Interest Income
   (Interest earned but not collected is covered in later chapters.)
2. When an increase occurs in a liability account (no previous balance).
   Example: Wages Expense
   Wages Payable

With the exception of businesses in their first year of operation, accounts such as Accumulated Depreciation or Inventory cannot be reduced because they have previous balances.

Art's bookkeeper handles an entry without reversing for salaries at the end of the year (see Fig. 12.12). Note that the permanent account, Salaries Payable, carries over to the new accounting period a $600 balance. Remember that the $600 was an expense of the prior year.

FIGURE 12.12 Reversing Entries Not Used

On January 8 of the new year, the payroll to be paid is $2,000. If the optional reversing entry is *not* used, the bookkeeper must make the journal entry in Figure 12.13.

To do so, the bookkeeper has to refer back to the adjustment on December 31 to determine how much of the salary of $2,000 is indeed a new salary expense and what portion was shown in the old year although not paid. It is easy to see how potential errors can result if the bookkeeper pays the payroll but forgets about the adjustment in the previous year. In this way, reversing entries can help avoid potential errors.

Figure 12.14 shows the four steps the bookkeeper would take if reversing entries were used. Note that steps 1 and 2 are the same whether the accountant uses reversing entries or not.

Note that the balance of Salaries Expense is indeed only $1,400, the *true* expense in the new year. Reversing results in switching the adjustment the first day of the new period. Also note that each of the accounts ends up with the same balance no matter which method is chosen. Using a reversing entry for salaries, however, allows the accountant to make the normal entry when it is time to pay salaries.

FIGURE 12.13 Entry When Optional Reversing Entry Is Not Used

Salaries Payable	600 00			
Salaries Expense	1 400 00			
Cash			2 000 00	

Salaries Exp.	Salaries Pay.	Cash
1,400	600 | 600	2,000

FIGURE 12.14 Reversing Entries Used

❶
On December 31, an adjustment for salary was recorded.

Salaries Exp.	Salaries Pay.
11,700	600
600	

❷
Closing entry on December 31.

Salaries Exp.	Salaries Pay.
11,700 | 12,300	600
600 |	

❸
On January 1 (first day of the following fiscal period), a reverse adjusting entry was made for salary on December 31 (a "flipping" adjustment).

Jan.	1	Salaries Payable	600 00		
		Salaries Expense		600 00	

Salaries Exp.	Salaries Pay.
| 600	600 | 600

This way, the liability is reduced to 0. We know it will be paid in this new period, but the Salaries Expense has a credit balance of $600 until the payroll is paid. When the payroll of $2,000 is paid, the following results:

❹
Paid Payroll $2,000.

Jan.	1	Salaries Expense	2 000 00		
		Cash		2 000 00	

Salaries Exp.	Cash
2,000 | 600	2,000

LEARNING UNIT 12-3 REVIEW

AT THIS POINT you should be able to

- Explain the purpose of reversing entries.
- Complete a reversing entry.
- Explain when reversing entries can be used.

Self-Review Quiz 12-3

Explain which of the following situations could be reversed:

1.

Supplies Exp.	Supplies
| 200	800 | 200

2.

Wages Exp.	Wages Payable
3,200 |	| 200
200 |	

3.

Sales	Unearned Sales
| 4,000	50 | 200
| 50	

Solutions to Self-Review Quiz 12-3

1. Not reversed: asset Supplies is decreasing, not increasing.
2. Reversed: liability is increasing and no previous balance exists.
3. Not reversed: liability is decreasing and a previous balance exists.

CHAPTER ASSIGNMENTS

SUMMARY OF KEY POINTS

LEARNING UNIT 12-1

1. The formal income statement can be prepared from the income statement columns of the worksheet.
2. No debit or credit columns are used on the formal income statement.
3. The cost of goods sold section has a figure for beginning inventory and a separate figure for ending inventory.
4. Operating expenses could be broken down into selling and administrative expenses.
5. The ending figure for Capital is not found on the worksheet. It comes from the statement of owner's equity.
6. A classified balance sheet breaks assets into current and plant and equipment. Liabilities are broken down into current and long-term.

LEARNING UNIT 12-2

1. The information for journalizing, adjusting, and closing entries can be obtained from the worksheet.
2. In the closing process all temporary accounts will be zero and the Capital account is brought up to its new balance.
3. Inventory is not a temporary account. The ending inventory, along with other permanent accounts, will be listed in the post-closing trial balance.

LEARNING UNIT 12-3

1. Reversing entries are optional. They can aid in reducing potential errors and simplify the recordkeeping process.
2. The reversing entry "flips" the adjustment on the first day of a new fiscal period. Thus, the bookkeeper need *not* look back at what happened in the old year when recording the current year's transactions.
3. Reversing entries are only used if (a) assets are increasing and have no previous balance or (b) liabilities are increasing and have no previous balance.

KEY TERMS

Administrative expenses (general expenses)   Expenses such as general office expenses that are incurred indirectly in the selling of goods.

Classified balance sheet   A balance sheet that categorizes assets as current or plant and equipment and groups liabilities as current or long-term.

Current assets   Assets that can be converted into cash or used within one year or the normal operating cycle of the business, whichever is longer.

Current liabilities   Obligations that will come due within one year or within the operating cycle, whichever is longer.

Long-term liabilities   Obligations that are not due or payable for a long time, usually for more than a year.

Operating cycle   Average time it takes to buy and sell merchandise and then collect accounts receivable.

Other expenses   Nonoperating expenses that do not relate to the main operating activities of the business; they appear in a separate section on the income statement. One example given in the text is Interest Expense, interest owed on money borrowed by the company.

Other income   Any revenue other than revenue from sales. It appears in a separate section on the income statement. Examples: Rental Income and Storage Fees.

Plant and equipment   Long-lived assets such as buildings or land that are used in the production or sale of goods or services.

Reversing entries   Optional bookkeeping technique in which certain adjusting entries are reversed or switched on the first day of the new accounting period so that transactions in the new period can be recorded without referring back to prior adjusting entries.

Selling expenses   Expenses directly related to the sale of goods.

QUESTIONS, CLASSROOM DEMONSTRATION EXERCISES, EXERCISES, AND PROBLEMS

Discussion and Critical Thinking Questions/Ethical Case

1. Which columns of the worksheet aid in the preparation of the income statement?

2. Explain the components of cost of goods sold.

3. Explain how operating expenses can be broken down into different categories.

4. What is the difference between current assets and plant and equipment?

5. What is an operating cycle?

6. Why journalize adjusting entries *after* the formal reports in a manual system have been prepared?

7. Explain the steps of closing for a merchandise company.

8. Temporary accounts could appear on a post-closing trial balance. Agree or disagree?

9. What is the purpose of using reversing entries? Are they mandatory? When should they be used?

10. Janet Flynn, owner of Reel Company, plans to apply for a bank loan at Petro National Bank. Because the company has a lot of debt on its balance sheet, Janet does not plan to show the loan officer the balance sheet. She plans only to bring the income statement. Do you feel that this move is a sound financial move by Janet? You make the call. Write down your specific recommendations to Janet.

Classroom Demonstration Exercises

SET A

Calculate Net Sales   *LO1 (5 min)*

1. From the following, calculate net sales:

Purchases	$100	Sales Discount	$20
Gross Sales	180	Operating Expenses	50
Sales Returns and Allowances	15		

Calculate Cost of Goods Sold   *LO1 (5 min)*

2. Calculate Cost of Goods Sold:

Freight-In	$ 6	Ending Inventory	$ 4
Beginning Inventory	12	Net Purchases	66

Calculate Gross Profit and Net Income   *LO1 (10 min)*

3. Using Exercises 1 and 2, calculate the following:
   a. Gross profit
   b. Net income or net loss

LO1, 2 (15 min) **Classification of Accounts**

4. Match the following categories to each account listed.
   1. Current Asset
   2. Plant and Equipment
   3. Current Liabilities
   4. Long-Term Liabilities

   _____ a. Petty Cash   _____ f. Mortgage Payable (Current)
   _____ b. Accounts Receivable   _____ g. SUTA Payable
   _____ c. Prepaid Rent   _____ h. Accumulated Depreciation
   _____ d. FICA Payable   _____ i. Computer Equipment
   _____ e. Store Supplies   _____ j. Unearned Rent

LO4 (10 min) **Reversing Entries**

5. a. On January 1, prepare a reversing entry. On January 8, journalize the entry to record the paying of salary expense, $800.
   b. What will be the balance in Salaries Expense on January 8 (after posting)?

December 31:

Salaries Expense		**Salaries Payable**	
Dr.	Cr.	Dr.	Cr.
800	1,200 closing		400 Adj.
Adj. 400			

SET B

LO1 (5 min) **Calculate Net Sales**

1. From the following, calculate net sales:

Purchases	$ 90	Sales Discount	$ 10
Gross Sales	280	Operating Expenses	100
Sales Returns and Allowances	50		

LO1 (5 min) **Calculate Cost of Goods Sold**

2. Calculate Cost of Goods Sold:

Freight-In	$ 5	Ending Inventory	$15
Beginning Inventory	20	Net Purchases	50

LO1 (10 min) **Calculate Gross Profit and Net Income**

3. Using Exercises 1 and 2, calculate the following:
   a. Gross profit
   b. Net income or net loss

BLUEPRINT: FINANCIAL STATEMENTS

(1) INCOME STATEMENT					
Revenue:					
Sales				$ XXX	
Less: Sales Ret. and Allow.			$ XXX		
Sales Discount			XXX	XXX	
Net Sales				$ XXXX	
Cost of Goods Sold:					
Merchandise Inventory, 1/1/0X			$ XXX		
Purchases		$XXX			
Less: Purchases Discount	$XXX				
Purch. Ret. and Allow.	XXX	XXX			
Net Purchases		XXX			
Add: Freight-In		XXX			
Net Cost of Purchases			XXX		
Cost of Goods Avail. for Sale			$XXXX		
Less: Merch. Inv., 12/31/0X			XXX		
Cost of Goods Sold				XXXX	
Gross Profit				$XXXX	
Operating Expenses:					
~~			$XXX		
~~			XXX		
~~			XXX		
Total Operating Expenses				XXX	
Net Income from Operations				$ XXX	
Other Income:					
Rental Income			$ XXX		
Storage Fees Income			XXX		
Total Other Income			$ XXX		
Other Expenses:					
Interest Expenses			XXX	XXX	
Net Income:				$ XXX	

(2) STATEMENT OF OWNER'S EQUITY			
Beginning Capital			$XXX
Additional Investments			XXX
Total Investment			$XXX
Net Income		$XXX	
Less: Withdrawals		XXX	
Increase in Capital			XXX
Ending Capital			$XXX

(3) BALANCE SHEET				
Assets				
Current Assets:				
Cash		$ XXXX		
Acccounts Receivable		XXXX		
Merchandise Inventory		XXXX		
Prepaid Insurance		XXX		
Total Current Assets			$ XXXX	
Plant and Equipment:				
Store Equipment	$XXXX			
Less Accumulated Depreciation	XXXX	$XXXX		
Office Equipment	$XXXX			
Less Accumulated Depreciation	XXX	XXX		
Total Plant and Equipment			XXXX	
Total Assets			$XXXX	
Liabilities				
Current Liabilities:				
Unearned Revenue		$XXX		
Mortgage Payable (current portion)		XXX		
Accounts Payable		XXX		
Salaries Payable		XX		
FICA—Social Security Payable		XX		
FICA—Medicare Payable		XX		
Income Taxes Payable		XX		
Total Current Liabilities			$XXX	
Long-Term Liabilities				
Mortgage Payable			$XXX	
Total Liabilities			$XXXX	
Owner's Equity				
Capital*			XXXX	
Total Liabilities and Owner's Equity			$XXXX	

* From statement of owner's equity

Classification of Accounts   *LO4 (15 min)*

4. Match the following categories to each account listed:

1. Current Asset
2. Plant and Equipment
3. Current Liabilities
4. Long-Term Liabilities

_____ **a.** Merchandise Inventory   _____ **f.** Mortgage Payable (Not Current)
_____ **b.** Unearned Rent   _____ **g.** FUTA Payable
_____ **c.** Prepaid Insurance   _____ **h.** Accumulated Depreciation
_____ **d.** SUTA Payable   _____ **i.** FICA—Social Security Payable
_____ **e.** Store Equipment   _____ **j.** Petty Cash

Reversing Entries   *LO4 (10 min)*

5. a. On January 1, prepare a reversing entry. On January 8, journalize the entry to record the paying of salary expense, $900.
   b. What will be the balance in Salaries Expense on January 8 (after posting)?

December 31:

Salaries Expense		**Salaries Payable**	
Dr.	**Cr.**	**Dr.**	**Cr.**
900	**1,200 closing**		**300 Adj.**
Adj. 300			

Exercises

12-1. From the following accounts, prepare a cost of goods sold section in proper form: Merchandise Inventory, 12/31/X1, $9,000; Purchases Discount, $900; Merchandise Inventory, 12/1/X1, $4,000; Purchases, $58,000; Purchases Returns and Allowances, $1,000; Freight-In, $300.   *LO1 (15 min)*

12-2. Give the category, the classification, and the report(s) on which each of the following appears (for example: Cash—asset, current asset, balance sheet):   *LO1 (10 min)*
   a. Salaries Payable
   b. Accounts Payable
   c. Mortgage Payable
   d. Unearned Legal Fees
   e. SIT Payable
   f. Office Equipment
   g. Land

12-3. From the partial worksheet in Fig. 12.15 on the following page, journalize the closing entries of December 31 for A. Slow Co.   *LO2 (10 min)*

12-4. From the worksheet in Exercise 12-3, prepare the assets section of a classified balance sheet.   *LO1 (15 min)*

12-5. On December 31, 20X1, $300 of salaries has been accrued. (Salaries before the accrued amount totaled $26,000.) The next payroll to be paid will be on February 3, 20X2, for $6,000. Please do the following: *LO2, 4 (30 min)*
   a. Journalize and post the adjusting entry (use T accounts).
   b. Journalize and post the reversing entry on January 1.
   c. Journalize and post the payment of the payroll. Cash has a balance of $15,000 before the payment of payroll on February 3.

FIGURE 12.15
Worksheet for A.
Slow Co.

A. SLOW CO.
WORKSHEET
FOR YEAR ENDED DECEMBER 31, 200X

Account Titles	Income Statement Dr.	Income Statement Cr.	Balance Sheet Dr.	Balance Sheet Cr.
Cash			193 00	
Merchandise Inventory			450 00	
Prepaid Advertising			561 00	
Prepaid Insurance			30 00	
Office Equipment			1080 00	
Accum. Dep., Office Equip.				210 00
Accounts Payable				258 00
A. Slow, Capital				966 00
Income Summary	362 00	450 00		
Sales		5520 00		
Sales Returns and Allowances	223 00			
Sales Discount	108 00			
Purchases	2628 00			
Purchases Returns and Allow.		34 00		
Purchases Discount		51 00		
Salaries Expense	1083 00			
Insurance Expense	696 00			
Utilities Expense	48 00			
Plumbing Expense	57 00			
Advertising Expense	15 00			
Dep. Expenses, Office Equip.	30 00			
Salaries Payable				75 00
	5250 00	6055 00	2314 00	1509 00
Net Income	805 00			805 00
	6055 00	6055 00	2314 00	2314 00

Group A Problems

LO1 (30 min)

Check Figure:
Net Income from operations $761

12A-1. Prepare a formal income statement from the partial worksheet for Ring.com in Figure 12.16.

LO1 (40 min)

Check Figure:
Total Assets $33,340

12A-2. Prepare a statement of owner's equity and a classified balance sheet from the worksheet for James Company in Figure 12.17. (*Note:* Of the Mortgage Payable, $200 is due within one year.)

LO1, 2 (90 min)

Check Figure:
Net Income $4,340

12A-3. **a.** Complete the worksheet for Jay's Supplies in Figure 12.18.
 b. Prepare an income statement, a statement of owner's equity, and a classified balance sheet. (*Note:* The amount of the mortgage due the first year is $800.)
 c. Journalize the adjusting and closing entries.

LO1, 2, 3, 4 (150 min)

Check Figure:
Net Income $4,336

12A-4. Using the ledger balances and additional data shown on the following pages, do the following for Callahan Lumber for the year ended December 31, 200X:
 1. Prepare the worksheet.
 2. Prepare the income statement, statement of owner's equity, and balance sheet.

RING.COM
PARTIAL WORKSHEET
FOR YEAR ENDED DECEMBER 31, 200X

Account Titles	Income Statement	
	Dr.	Cr.
Income Summary	3 7 0 00	2 6 0 00
Sales		2 8 0 0 00
Sales Returns and Allowances	1 1 9 00	
Sales Discount	6 4 00	
Purchases	8 7 0 00	
Purchases Returns and Allow.		1 6 7 00
Purchases Discount		1 2 9 00
Freight-In	1 0 2 00	
Salaries Expense	3 0 0 00	
Insurance Expense	2 0 0 00	
Advertising Expense	1 5 5 00	
Rental Income		2 0 0 00
Rent Expense	2 1 5 00	
Dep. Exp., Store Equip.	2 0 0 00	
Salaries Payable		
	2 5 9 5 00	3 5 5 6 00
Net Income	9 6 1 00	
	3 5 5 6 00	3 5 5 6 00

FIGURE 12.16 Partial Worksheet for Ring.Com

3. Journalize and post adjusting and closing entries. (Be sure to put beginning balances in the ledger first.)
4. Prepare a post-closing trial balance.
5. Journalize the reversing entry for wages accrued.

Account Balances for Callahan Lumber

Acct. No.		
110	Cash	$ 1,340
111	Accounts Receivable	1,300
112	Merchandise Inventory	4,550
113	Lumber Supplies	269
114	Prepaid Insurance	218
121	Lumber Equipment	3,000
122	Accum. Dep., Lumber Equipment	490
220	Accounts Payable	1,160
221	Wages Payable	—
330	J. Callahan, Capital	7,352
331	J. Callahan, Withdrawals	3,000
332	Income Summary	—
440	Sales	22,800
441	Sales Returns and Allowances	200
550	Purchases	14,800
551	Purchases Discount	285
552	Purchases Returns and Allowances	300

(*continued on next page*)

FIGURE 12.17 Partial
Worksheet for James Company

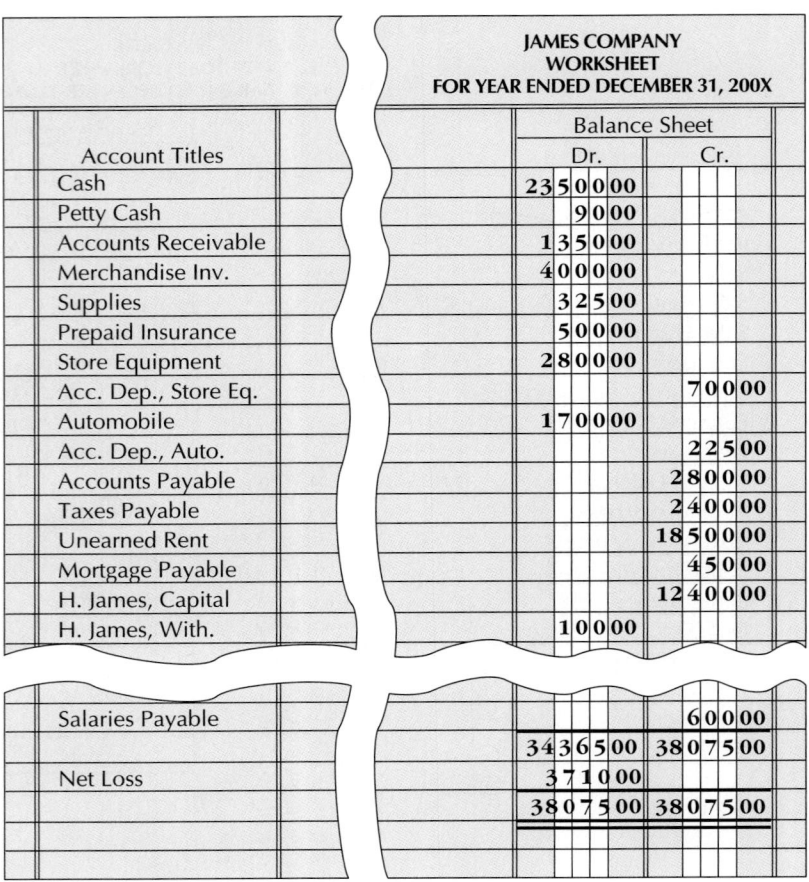

JAMES COMPANY
WORKSHEET
FOR YEAR ENDED DECEMBER 31, 200X

Account Titles	Balance Sheet Dr.	Balance Sheet Cr.
Cash	23 5 0 0 00	
Petty Cash	9 0 00	
Accounts Receivable	1 3 5 0 00	
Merchandise Inv.	4 0 0 0 00	
Supplies	3 2 5 00	
Prepaid Insurance	5 0 0 00	
Store Equipment	2 8 0 0 00	
Acc. Dep., Store Eq.		7 0 0 00
Automobile	1 7 0 0 00	
Acc. Dep., Auto.		2 2 5 00
Accounts Payable		2 8 0 0 00
Taxes Payable		2 4 0 0 00
Unearned Rent		18 5 0 0 00
Mortgage Payable		4 5 0 00
H. James, Capital		12 4 0 0 00
H. James, With.	1 0 0 00	

Salaries Payable		6 0 0 00
	34 3 6 5 00	38 0 7 5 00
Net Loss	3 7 1 0 00	
	38 0 7 5 00	38 0 7 5 00

Account Balances for Callahan Lumber (continued)

660	Wages Expense	2,480
661	Advertising Expense	400
662	Rent Expense	830
663	Dep. Expense, Lumber Equipment	—
664	Lumber Supplies Expense	—
665	Insurance Expense	—

Additional Data

a./b.	Merchandise inventory, December 31	$ 4,900
c.	Lumber supplies on hand, December 31	75
d.	Insurance expired	150
e.	Depreciation for the year	250
f.	Accrued wages on December 31	95

Group B Problems

LO1 (70 min)

12B-1. From the partial worksheet shown in Figure 12.19, prepare a formal income statement.

Check Figure:
Net income from operations $845

FIGURE 12.18
Worksheet for Jay's Supplies

JAY'S SUPPLIES
WORKSHEET
FOR YEAR ENDED DECEMBER 31, 200X

Account Titles	Trial Balance Dr.	Trial Balance Cr.	Adjustments Dr.	Adjustments Cr.
Cash	2 000 00			
Accounts Receivable	3 000 00			
Merch. Inventory, 1/1/XX	11 000 00	(B)	10 400 00	11 000 00 (A)
Prepaid Insurance	1 880 00			500 00 (E)
Equipment	3 400 00			
Accum. Dep., Equipment		1 080 00		400 00 (D)
Accounts Payable		5 080 00		
Unearned Training Fees		2 120 00	(C) 320 00	
Mortgage Payable		1 200 00		
P. Jay, Capital		10 560 00		
P. Jay, Withdrawals	4 280 00			
Income Summary		(A)	11 000 00	10 400 00 (B)
Sales		9 580 00		
Sales Returns and Allowances	3 200 00			
Sales Discount	2 600 00			
Purchases	6 360 00			
Purchases Returns and Allow.		1 360 00		
Purchases Discount		320 00		
Freight-In	2 680 00			
Advertising Expense	1 140 00			
Rent Expense	1 000 00			
Salaries Expense	1 360 00			
	13 264 00	13 264 00		
Training Fees Earned				320 00 (C)
Dep. Exp., Equipment			(D) 400 00	
Insurance Expense			(E) 500 00	
			22 620 00	22 620 00

12B-2. From the worksheet shown in Figure 12.20, complete the following:
  a. Statement of owner's equity
  b. Classified balance sheet
  (*Note:* Of the Mortgage Payable, $3,000 is due within one year.)

LO1 (40 min)

Check Figure:
Total Assets $28,294

12B-3. From the partial worksheet for Jay's Supplies in Figure 12.21, do the following:
  1. Complete the worksheet.
  2. Prepare the income statement, statement of owner's equity, and classified balance sheet. (The amount of the mortgage due the first year is $800.)
  3. Journalize the adjusting and closing entries.

LO1, 2 (90 min)

Check Figure:
Net Loss $12,050

12B-4. From the following ledger balances and additional data shown on the following pages, do the following for Callahan Lumber for the year ended December 31, 200X.
  1. Prepare the worksheet.
  2. Prepare the income statement, statement of owner's equity, and balance sheet.
  3. Journalize and post adjusting and closing entries. (Be sure to put beginning balances in the ledger first.)
  4. Prepare a post-closing trial balance.
  5. Journalize the reversing entry for wages accrued.

LO1, 2, 3, 4 (150 min)

Check Figure:
Net Income $2,730

FIGURE 12.19 Partial Worksheet of Ring.Com

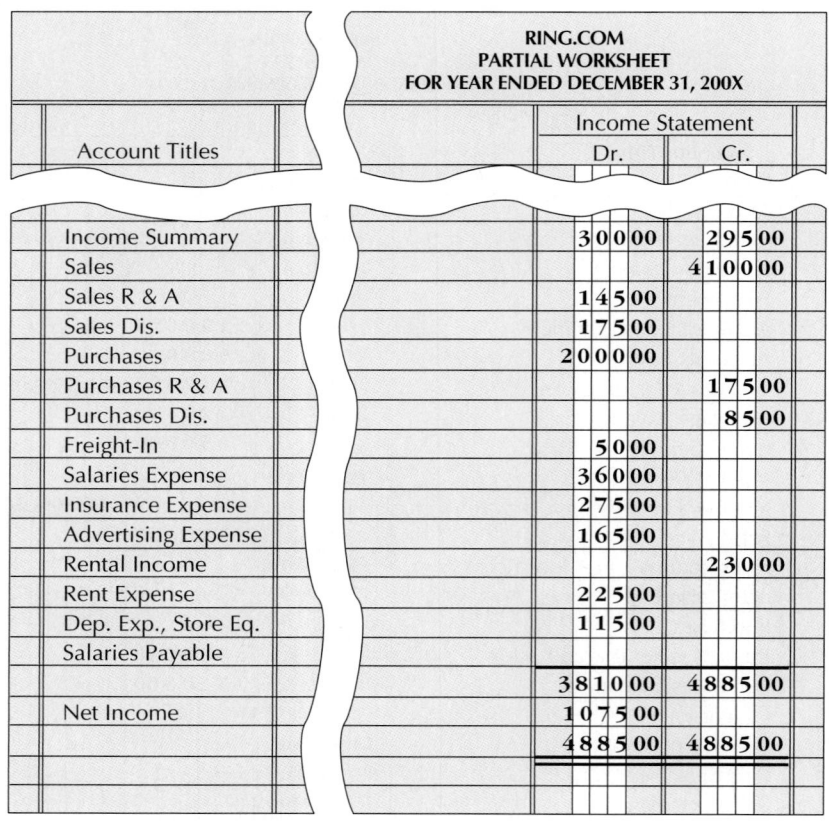

Account Titles	Income Statement	
	Dr.	Cr.
Income Summary	300 00	295 00
Sales		4100 00
Sales R & A	145 00	
Sales Dis.	175 00	
Purchases	2000 00	
Purchases R & A		175 00
Purchases Dis.		85 00
Freight-In	50 00	
Salaries Expense	360 00	
Insurance Expense	275 00	
Advertising Expense	165 00	
Rental Income		230 00
Rent Expense	225 00	
Dep. Exp., Store Eq.	115 00	
Salaries Payable		
	3810 00	4885 00
Net Income	1075 00	
	4885 00	4885 00

RING.COM
PARTIAL WORKSHEET
FOR YEAR ENDED DECEMBER 31, 200X

Account Balances of Callahan Lumber

Acct. No.		
110	Cash	$ 940
111	Accounts Receivable	1,470
112	Merchandise Inventory	5,600
113	Lumber Supplies	260
114	Prepaid Insurance	117
121	Lumber Equipment	2,600
122	Acc. Dep., Lumber Equipment	340
220	Accounts Payable	1,330
221	Wages Payable	
330	J. Callahan, Capital	7,562
331	J. Callahan, Withdrawals	3,500
332	Income Summary	—
440	Sales	23,000
441	Sales Returns and Allowances	400
550	Purchases	14,700
551	Purchases Discount	440
552	Purchases Returns and Allowances	545
660	Wages Expense	2,390
661	Advertising Expense	400
662	Rent Expense	840
663	Dep. Exp., Lumber Equipment	—
664	Lumber Supplies Expense	—
665	Insurance Expense	—

Account Titles			Balance Sheet	
			Dr.	Cr.
Cash			2 5 0 0 00	
Petty Cash			5 0 00	
Accts. Receivable			1 3 0 0 00	
Merch. Inventory			4 2 5 0 00	
Supplies			3 4 4 00	
Prepaid Ins.			6 0 0 00	
Store Equip.			18 0 0 0 00	
Acc. Dep., Store Eq.				7 5 0 00
Automobile			2 5 0 0 00	
Acc. Dep., Auto.				5 0 0 00
Accts. Payable				3 4 5 0 00
Taxes Payable				2 1 0 0 00
Unearned Rent				11 0 0 0 00
Mortgage Payable				8 0 0 0 00
H. James, Capital				10 5 0 0 00
H. James, Withd.			4 0 0 0 00	

JAMES COMPANY
WORKSHEET
FOR YEAR ENDED DECEMBER 31, 200X

Salaries Payable				1 0 0 00
			33 5 4 4 00	36 4 0 0 00
Net Loss			2 8 5 6 00	
			36 4 0 0 00	36 4 0 0 00

FIGURE 12.20 Worksheet for James Company

Additional Data

a./b. Merchandise inventory, December 31 $ 3,900
    c. Lumber supplies on hand, December 31   60
    d. Insurance expired   50
    e. Depreciation for the year   400
    f. Accrued wages on December 31   175

ON-THE-JOB TRAINING

T-1. Chan Company recently had most of its records destroyed in a fire. The information for 20X1 (Fig. 12.22) was discovered by the bookkeeper. Please assist the bookkeeper in reconstructing an income statement for 20X1. *LO1, 2 (60 min)*

T-2. Hope Lang, a junior accountant, has the December 31, 200X, trial balance of Gregot Company sitting on her desk. Attached is a memo from her supervisor requesting that a classified balance sheet be prepared. Hope gathers the following data: *LO1, 2 (60 min)*

1. A physical inventory of merchandise at December 31 showed $80,000 on hand.

2. Office supplies on hand totaled $600.

3. Insurance unexpired was $750.

4. Depreciation (straight-line) is based on a 25-year life.

    Using the trial balance of Gregot Co. in Figure 12.23, please assist Hope with this project. *Hint:* Ending figure for capital is $115,850.

FIGURE 12.21
Worksheet for Jay's
Supplies

JAY'S SUPPLIES
WORKSHEET
FOR YEAR ENDED DECEMBER 31, 200X

Account Titles	Trial Balance Dr.	Trial Balance Cr.	Adjustments Dr.	Adjustments Cr.	
Cash	3 0 0 0 00				
Accounts Receivable	3 0 0 0 00				
Merch. Inventory, 1/1/XX	11 7 0 0 00		(B) 8 0 0 0 00	11 7 0 0 00	(A)
Prepaid Insurance	1 0 0 0 00			3 5 0 00	(E)
Equipment	5 0 0 0 00				
Accum. Dep., Equipment		1 9 0 0 00		5 0 0 00	(D)
Accounts Payable		2 1 0 0 00			
Unearned Training Fees		1 4 5 0 00	(C) 4 0 0 00		
Mortgage Payable		2 4 0 0 00			
P. Jay, Capital		27 7 5 0 00			
P. Jay, Withdrawals	4 0 0 0 00				
Income Summary			(A) 11 7 0 0 00	8 0 0 0 00	(B)
Sales		100 8 0 0 00			
Sales Returns and Allowances	4 1 0 0 00				
Sales Discount	2 8 0 0 00				
Purchases	70 0 0 0 00				
Purchases Returns and Allow.		2 0 0 0 00			
Purchases Discounts		1 4 0 0 00			
Freight-In	2 7 0 0 00				
Advertising Expense	8 0 0 00				
Rent Expense	8 5 0 0 00				
Salaries Expense	16 0 0 0 00				
	139 8 0 0 00	139 8 0 0 00			
Training Fees Earned				4 0 0 00	(C)
Dep. Exp., Equipment			(D) 5 0 0 00		
Insurance Expense			(E) 3 5 0 00		
			20 9 5 0 00	20 9 5 0 00	

FINANCIAL REPORT PROBLEM

LO2, 3 (5 min)

Reading the Kellogg's Annual Report

Go to Appendix A and locate the consolidated statement of earnings. How much has Selling and general administrative expense increased from 2005 to 2006?

INTERNET PROJECT

Chiquita

Go to the Web and search: Annual Report Chiquita 2008.
Click on Investors Relations.
List out the latest news Chiquita is providing to its investors.
Order a free annual report.

FIGURE 12.22 General Journal for Chan Company

CHAN COMPANY
GENERAL JOURNAL

Page 2

20X1 Date		Description	PR	Dr.	Cr.
Dec.	31	Income Summary	312	3 6 3 0 00	
		Sales Returns and Allowances	420		1 4 0 00
		Sales Discount	430		3 0 00
		Purchases	500		2 4 0 0 00
		Delivery Expense	600		9 0 00
		Salaries Expense	610		8 4 0 00
		Rent Expense	620		3 0 00
		Office Supplies Expense	630		5 0 00
		Advertising Expense	640		1 0 00
		Dep. Exp., Store Equipment	650		4 0 00
	31	Sales	410	5 5 4 2 00	
		Purchases Discount	510	1 2 0 00	
		Purchases Returns and Allowances	520	1 0 0 00	
		Income Summary	312		5 7 6 2 00
	31	Income Summary	312	3 7 3 2 00	
		J. Chan, Capital	310		3 7 3 2 00

Beg. Inv. $1,400
End. Inv. 3,000

FIGURE 12.23 Trial Balance for Gregot Company

GREGOT COMPANY
TRIAL BALANCE
DECEMBER 31, 200X

	Dr.	Cr.
Cash	11 0 0 0 00	
Accounts Receivable	38 0 0 0 00	
Merchandise Inventory, Jan. 1	80 0 0 0 00	
Prepaid Insurance	2 0 0 0 00	
Office Supplies	1 0 0 0 00	
Land	17 5 0 0 00	
Building	50 0 0 0 00	
Accumulated Depreciation, Building		10 0 0 0 00
Notes Payable		40 0 0 0 00
Accounts Payable		30 0 0 0 00
G. Gregot, Capital		98 4 0 0 00
G. Gregot, Withdrawals	13 0 0 0 00	
Income Summary		
Retail Sales		329 0 0 0 00
Sales Returns and Allowances	21 0 0 0 00	
Sales Discount	8 0 0 0 00	
Purchases	215 5 0 0 00	
Purchases Returns and Allowances		11 6 0 0 00
Purchases Discount		4 0 0 0 00
Freight-In	5 0 0 0 00	
Advertising Expense	2 5 0 0 00	
Wage Expense	55 0 0 0 00	
Utilities Expense	3 5 0 0 00	
	523 0 0 0 00	523 0 0 0 00

CONTINUING PROBLEM

LO1, 2 (60 min)   ### Sanchez Computer Center

Using the worksheet in Chapter 11 for Sanchez Computer Center, journalize and post the adjusting entries and prepare the financial statements.

MINI PRACTICE SET

THE CORNER DRESS SHOP

Reviewing the Accounting Cycle for a Merchandise Company

This practice set will help you review all the key concepts of a merchandise company, along with the integration of payroll, including the preparation of Form 941.

Because you are the bookkeeper of the Corner Dress Shop, we have gathered the following information for you. It will be your task to complete the accounting cycle for March.

Betty Loeb's dress shop is located at 1 Milgate Rd., Marblehead, MA 01945. Its identification number is 33-4158215.

THE CORNER DRESS SHOP POST-CLOSING TRIAL BALANCE FEBRUARY 28, 200X	1	2
Cash	2 2 3 1 90	
Accounts Receivable	2 2 0 0 00	
Petty Cash	3 5 00	
Merchandise Inventory	5 6 0 0 00	
Prepaid Rent	1 8 0 0 00	
Delivery Truck	6 0 0 0 00	
Accumulated Depreciation, Truck		1 5 0 0 00
Accounts Payable		1 9 0 0 00
FIT Payable		1 0 1 3 00
FICA—OASDI Payable		1 3 3 9 20
FICA—Medicare Payable		3 1 3 20
SIT Payable		7 5 6 00
SUTA Payable		9 7 9 20
FUTA Payable		1 6 3 20
Unearned Rent		8 0 0 00
B. Loeb, Capital		9 1 0 3 10
Total	17 8 6 6 90	17 8 6 6 90

Balances in subsidiary ledgers as of March 1 are as follows:

Accounts Receivable		Accounts Payable	
Bing Co.	$ 2,200	Blew Co.	$ 1,900
Blew Co.	—	Jones Co.	—
Ronald Co.	—	Moe's Garage	—
		Morris Co.	—

Payroll is paid monthly:

FICA rate	OASDI 6.2% on $102,000
	Medicare 1.45% on all earnings
SUTA rate	4.8% on $7,000
FUTA rate	.8% on $7,000
SIT rate	7%
FIT	Use the table provided at the end of this practice set.

The payroll register for January and February is provided. In March, salaries are as follows:

Mel Case	$3,325
Jane Holl	4,120
Jackie Moore	4,760

Your tasks are to do the following:
1. Set up a general ledger, accounts receivable subsidiary ledger and accounts payable subsidiary ledger, auxiliary petty cash record, and payroll register. (Be sure to update ledger accounts based on information given in the post-closing trial balance for February 28 before beginning.)
2. Journalize the transactions, and prepare the payroll register.
3. Update the accounts payable and accounts receivable subsidiary ledgers.
4. Post to the general ledger.
5. Prepare a trial balance on a worksheet and complete the worksheet.
6. Prepare an income statement, statement of owner's equity, and classified balance sheet.
7. Journalize the adjusting and closing entries.
8. Post the adjusting and closing entries to the ledger.
9. Prepare a post-closing trial balance.
10. Complete Form 941 and sign it as of the last day in April.

Chart of Accounts
for the Corner Dress Shop

Assets	**Revenue**
110 Cash	410 Sales
111 Accounts Receivable	412 Sales Returns and Allowances
112 Petty Cash	414 Sales Discount
114 Merchandise Inventory	416 Rental Income
116 Prepaid Rent	
120 Delivery Truck	**Cost of Goods Sold**
121 Accumulated Depreciation, Truck	510 Purchases
	512 Purchases Returns and Allowances
Liabilities	514 Purchases Discount
210 Accounts Payable	
212 Salaries Payable	**Expenses**
214 Federal Income Tax Payable	610 Sales Salaries Expense
216 FICA—OASDI Payable	611 Office Salaries Expense
218 FICA—Medicare Payable	612 Payroll Tax Expense

(*continued on next page*)

220 State Income Tax Payable

222 SUTA Tax Payable

224 FUTA Tax Payable

226 Unearned Rent

Owner's Equity

310 B. Loeb, Capital

320 B. Loeb, Withdrawals

330 Income Summary

614 Cleaning Expense

616 Depreciation Expense, Truck

618 Rent Expense

620 Postage Expense

622 Delivery Expense

624 Miscellaneous Expense

THE CORNER DRESS SHOP
PAYROLL REGISTER
JANUARY AND FEBRUARY 200X

Employees	Allow. and Marital Status	Cum. Earnings	Salary	Earnings Reg.	Earnings O/T	Earnings Gross	Cum. Earnings
Mel Case	M – 2	—	3 300 00	3 300 00		3 300 00	3 300 00
Jane Holl	M – 1	—	3 400 00	3 400 00		3 400 00	3 400 00
Jackie Moore	M – 0	—	4 100 00	4 100 00		4 100 00	4 100 00
Totals for Jan.			10 800 00	10 800 00		10 800 00	10 800 00
Mel Case	M – 2	3 300 00	3 300 00	3 300 00		3 300 00	6 600 00
Jane Holl	M – 1	3 400 00	3 400 00	3 400 00		3 400 00	6 800 00
Jackie Moore	M – 0	4 100 00	4 100 00	4 100 00		4 100 00	8 200 00
Totals for Feb.		10 800 00	10 800 00	10 800 00		10 800 00	21 600 00

PAYROLL REGISTER

Taxable Earnings Unemp.	Taxable Earnings FICA Soc. Sec.	Taxable Earnings FICA Medicare	Deductions FICA OASDI	Deductions FICA Medicare	FIT	SIT	Net Pay	Ck. No.	Distribution Office Salary Expense	Distribution Sales Salary Expense
3 300 00	3 300 00	3 300 00	204 60	47 85	250 00	231 00	2 566 55		3 300 00	
3 400 00	3 400 00	3 400 00	210 80	49 30	310 00	238 00	2 591 90			3 400 00
4 100 00	4 100 00	4 100 00	254 20	59 45	453 00	287 00	3 046 35			4 100 00
10 800 00	10 800 00	10 800 00	669 60	156 60	1 013 00	756 00	8 204 80		3 300 00	7 500 00
3 300 00	3 300 00	3 300 00	204 60	47 85	250 00	231 00	2 566 55		3 300 00	
3 400 00	3 400 00	3 400 00	210 80	49 30	310 00	238 00	2 591 90			3 400 00
4 100 00	4 100 00	4 100 00	254 20	59 45	453 00	287 00	3 046 35			4 100 00
10 800 00	10 800 00	10 800 00	669 60	156 60	1 013 00	756 00	8 204 80		3 300 00	7 500 00

200X

Mar.

1   Bing paid balance owed, no discount.

2   Purchased merchandise from Morris Company on account, $10,000; terms 2/10, n/30.

2   Paid $6 from the petty cash fund for cleaning package, voucher no. 18 (consider it a cleaning expense).

3   Sold merchandise to Ronald Company on account, $7,000, invoice no. 51; terms 2/10, n/30.

5   Paid $3 from the petty cash fund for postage, voucher no. 19.

6   Sold merchandise to Ronald Company on account, $5,000, invoice no. 52; terms 2/10, n/30.

8   Paid $10 from the petty cash fund for first aid emergency, voucher no. 20.

9   Purchased merchandise from Morris Company on account, $5,000; terms 2/10, n/30.

9   Paid $5 for delivery expense from petty cash fund, voucher no. 21.

9   Sold more merchandise to Ronald Company on account, $3,000, invoice no. 53; terms 2/10, n/30.

9   Paid cleaning service, $300, check no. 110.

10   Ronald Company returned merchandise costing $1,000 from invoice no. 52; the Corner Dress shop issued credit memo no. 10 to Ronald Company for $1,000.

11   Purchased merchandise from Jones Company on account, $10,000; terms 1/15, n/60.

12   Paid Morris Company invoice dated March 2, check no. 111.

13   Sold $7,000 of merchandise for cash.

14   Returned merchandise to Jones Company in amount of $2,000; the Corner Dress Shop issued debit memo no. 4 to Jones Company.

14   Paid $5 from the petty cash fund for delivery expense, voucher no. 22.

15   Paid taxes due for FICA (OASDI and Medicare) and FIT for February payroll, check no. 112.

15   Sold Merchandise for $29,000 cash.

15   Betty withdrew $100 for her own personal expenses, check no. 113.

15   Paid state income tax for February payroll, check no. 114.

16   Received payment from Ronald Company for invoice no. 52, less discount.

16   Ronald Company paid invoice no. 51, $7,000.

16   Sold merchandise to Bing Company on account, $3,200, invoice no. 54; terms 2/10, n/30.

21   Purchased delivery truck on account from Moe's Garage, $17,200.

22   Sold merchandise to Ronald Company on account, $4,000, invoice no. 55; terms 2/10, n/30.

23   Paid Jones Company the balance owed, check no. 115.

24   Sold merchandise to Bing Company on account, $2,000, invoice no. 56; terms 2/10, n/30.

25   Purchased merchandise for $1,000 check no. 116.

27   Purchased merchandise from Blew Company on account, $6,000; terms 2/10, n/30.

27   Paid $2 postage from the petty cash fund, voucher no. 23.

28   Ronald Company paid invoice no. 55 dated March 22, less discount.

(continued on next page)

28	Bing Company paid invoice no. 54 dated March 16.
29	Purchased merchandise from Morris Company on account, $9,000; terms 2/10, n/30.
30	Sold merchandise to Blew Company on account, $10,000, invoice no. 57; terms 2/10, n/30.
30	Issued check no. 117 to replenish to the same level the petty cash fund.
30	Recorded payroll in payroll register.
30	Journalized payroll entry (to be paid on 31st).
30	Journalized employer's payroll tax expense.
31	Paid payroll checks no. 118, no. 119, and no. 120.

Additional Data

a./b. Ending merchandise inventory, $13,515.
   c. During March, rent expired, $600.
   d. Truck depreciated, $150.
   e. Rental income earned, $200 (one month's rent from subletting).

MARRIED Persons—MONTHLY Payroll Period
(For Wages Paid in 2008)

If the wages are—		And the number of withholding allowances claimed is—										
At least	But less than	0	1	2	3	4	5	6	7	8	9	10
		The amount of income tax to be withheld is—										
$3,240	$3,280	$324	$280	$237	$193	$149	$114	$84	$55	$26	$0	$0
3,280	3,320	330	286	243	199	155	118	88	59	30	1	0
3,320	3,360	336	292	249	205	161	122	92	63	34	5	0
3,360	3,400	342	298	255	211	167	126	96	67	38	9	0
3,400	3,440	348	304	261	217	173	130	100	71	42	13	0
3,440	3,480	354	310	267	223	179	135	104	75	46	17	0
3,480	3,520	360	316	273	229	185	141	108	79	50	21	0
3,520	3,560	366	322	279	235	191	147	112	83	54	25	0
3,560	3,600	372	328	285	241	197	153	116	87	58	29	0
3,600	3,640	378	334	291	247	203	159	120	91	62	33	4
3,640	3,680	384	340	297	253	209	165	124	95	66	37	8
3,680	3,720	390	346	303	259	215	171	128	99	70	41	12
3,720	3,760	396	352	309	265	221	177	134	103	74	45	16
3,760	3,800	402	358	315	271	227	183	140	107	78	49	20
3,800	3,840	408	364	321	277	233	189	146	111	82	53	24
3,840	3,880	414	370	327	283	239	195	152	115	86	57	28
3,880	3,920	420	376	333	289	245	201	158	119	90	61	32
3,920	3,960	426	382	339	295	251	207	164	123	94	65	36
3,960	4,000	432	388	345	301	257	213	170	127	98	69	40
4,000	4,040	438	394	351	307	263	219	176	132	102	73	44
4,040	4,080	444	400	357	313	269	225	182	138	106	77	48
4,080	4,120	450	406	363	319	275	231	188	144	110	81	52
4,120	4,160	456	412	369	325	281	237	194	150	114	85	56
4,160	4,200	462	418	375	331	287	243	200	156	118	89	60
4,200	4,240	468	424	381	337	293	249	206	162	122	93	64
4,240	4,280	474	430	387	343	299	255	212	168	126	97	68
4,280	4,320	480	436	393	349	305	261	218	174	130	101	72
4,320	4,360	486	442	399	355	311	267	224	180	136	105	76
4,360	4,400	492	448	405	361	317	273	230	186	142	109	80
4,400	4,440	498	454	411	367	323	279	236	192	148	113	84
4,440	4,480	504	460	417	373	329	285	242	198	154	117	88
4,480	4,520	510	466	423	379	335	291	248	204	160	121	92
4,520	4,560	516	472	429	385	341	297	254	210	166	125	96
4,560	4,600	522	478	435	391	347	303	260	216	172	129	100
4,600	4,640	528	484	441	397	353	309	266	222	178	134	104
4,640	4,680	534	490	447	403	359	315	272	228	184	140	108
4,680	4,720	540	496	453	409	365	321	278	234	190	146	112
4,720	4,760	546	502	459	415	371	327	284	240	196	152	116
4,760	4,800	552	508	465	421	377	333	290	246	202	158	120
4,800	4,840	558	514	471	427	383	339	296	252	208	164	124
4,840	4,880	564	520	477	433	389	345	302	258	214	170	128
4,880	4,920	570	526	483	439	395	351	308	264	220	176	133
4,920	4,960	576	532	489	445	401	357	314	270	226	182	139
4,960	5,000	582	538	495	451	407	363	320	276	232	188	145
5,000	5,040	588	544	501	457	413	369	326	282	238	194	151
5,040	5,080	594	550	507	463	419	375	332	288	244	200	157
5,080	5,120	600	556	513	469	425	381	338	294	250	206	163
5,120	5,160	606	562	519	475	431	387	344	300	256	212	169
5,160	5,200	612	568	525	481	437	393	350	306	262	218	175
5,200	5,240	618	574	531	487	443	399	356	312	268	224	181
5,240	5,280	624	580	537	493	449	405	362	318	274	230	187
5,280	5,320	630	586	543	499	455	411	368	324	280	236	193
5,320	5,360	636	592	549	505	461	417	374	330	286	242	199
5,360	5,400	642	598	555	511	467	423	380	336	292	248	205
5,400	5,440	648	604	561	517	473	429	386	342	298	254	211
5,440	5,480	654	610	567	523	479	435	392	348	304	260	217
5,480	5,520	660	616	573	529	485	441	398	354	310	266	223
5,520	5,560	666	622	579	535	491	447	404	360	316	272	229
5,560	5,600	672	628	585	541	497	453	410	366	322	278	235
5,600	5,640	678	634	591	547	503	459	416	372	328	284	241
5,640	5,680	684	640	597	553	509	465	422	378	334	290	247
5,680	5,720	690	646	603	559	515	471	428	384	340	296	253
5,720	5,760	696	652	609	565	521	477	434	390	346	302	259
5,760	5,800	702	658	615	571	527	483	440	396	352	308	265
5,800	5,840	708	664	621	577	533	489	446	402	358	314	271
5,840	5,880	714	670	627	583	539	495	452	408	364	320	277

$5,880 and over — Use Table 4(b) for a MARRIED person on page 38. Also see the instructions on page 36.

PEACHTREE COMPUTER WORKSHOP

COMPUTERIZED ACCOUNTING APPLICATION FOR CHAPTER 12

Refresher on using Peachtree Complete Accounting

Before starting this assignment, you may want to refresh your memory by reading the following PDF documents in the multimedia library of the MyAccountingLab Web site. Remember to choose the PDF document for your version of Peachtree.

1. An Introduction to Peachtree Complete Accounting
2. Correcting Peachtree Transactions
3. How to Repeat or Restart a Peachtree Assignment
4. Backing Up and Restoring Your Work in Peachtree

You also should have completed the following workshops:

1. Workshop 1 Atlas Company from Chapter 3
2. Workshop 2 Zell Company from Chapter 4
3. Workshop 3 Sullivan Realty from Chapter 5
4. Workshop 4 Pete's Market from Chapter 8
5. Workshop 5 Part A Mars Company from Chapter 10
6. Workshop 5 Part B Abby's Toy House from Chapter 10

Workshop 6:

Accounting Cycle for a Merchandising Company

In this workshop you complete an accounting cycle for a merchandising business owned by the Corner Dress Shop using Peachtree. Tasks include maintaining inventory, recording sales on account, merchandise returns, merchandise purchases, vendor payments, and payroll. You will also prepare inventory reports, aged receivables and aged payable reports, general journal and general ledger reports, a trial balance, and financial statements. Finally, you will close the accounting period.

Instructions and the data file for completing this assignment are in the multimedia library of the MyAccountingLab Web site. Open the *Workshop 6 The Corner Dress Shop* PDF document for your version of Peachtree and download *The Corner Dress Shop* data file for your version of Peachtree.

QUICKBOOKS COMPUTER WORKSHOP

COMPUTERIZED ACCOUNTING APPLICATION FOR CHAPTER 12

Refresher on using QuickBooks Pro

Before starting this assignment, you may want to refresh your memory by reading the following PDF documents in the multimedia library of the MyAccountingLab Web site. Remember to choose the PDF document for your version of QuickBooks.

1. An Introduction to QuickBooks Pro
2. Correcting QuickBooks Transactions
3. How to Repeat or Restart a QuickBooks Assignment
4. Backing Up and Restoring Your Work in QuickBooks

You also should have completed the following workshops:

1. Workshop 1 Atlas Company from Chapter 3
2. Workshop 2 Zell Company from Chapter 4
3. Workshop 3 Sullivan Realty from Chapter 5
4. Workshop 4 Pete's Market from Chapter 8
5. Workshop 5 Part A Mars Company from Chapter 10
6. Workshop 5 Part B Abby's Toy House from Chapter 10

Workshop 6:

Accounting Cycle for a Merchandising Company

In this workshop you complete an accounting cycle for a merchandising business owned by the Corner Dress Shop using QuickBooks. Tasks include maintaining inventory, recording sales on account, merchandise returns, merchandise purchases, vendor payments, and payroll. You will also prepare inventory reports, aged receivables and aged payable reports, general journal and general ledger reports, a trial balance, and financial statements. Finally, you will close the accounting period.

Instructions and the data file for completing this assignment are in the multimedia library of the MyAccountingLab Web site. Open the **Workshop 6 The Corner Dress Shop** PDF document for your version of Quickbooks and download the **The Corner Dress Shop** data file for your version of Quickbooks.

13

Accounting for Bad Debts

DID YOU KNOW? Ebay estimates its doubtful accounts at 1% of net revenue. In 2006 1.69% of net revenue turned out to be bad debts. Visit *www.eBay.com* to find more information about eBay.

LEARNING OBJECTIVES

1. Describing how the Bad Debts Expense account and the Allowance for Doubtful Accounts account are used to record bad debts.

2. Using the income statement approach and the balance sheet approach to estimate the amount of Bad Debts Expense.

3. Preparing an aging of Accounts Receivable.

4. Writing off an account using the Allowance for Doubtful Accounts method.

5. Using the direct write-off method.

Did you ever buy something on eBay and the goods were not delivered? Eventually, all companies (Internet-based or not) that sell goods or services on account will come upon customers that do not pay their bills. Today with unemployment rising more and more customers are having trouble paying off their bills. The question of these *bad debts* affects the company's credit policy. If a company extends credit too easily, it may end up with too many uncollectible accounts. On the other hand, if the credit policy is too strict, the company will end up losing customers to other firms with easier credit policies, which could also mean lost profit. For example, Wal-Mart sells for cash and/or credit and would have low bad debt expense.

This chapter looks at how bad debts are recorded in the accrual system of accounting. It also discusses when accounts receivable turn into bad debts (or uncollectible accounts), how and what to charge them to, and how to write them off.

LO1

Learning Unit 13-1 Accrual Accounting and Recording Bad Debts

As discussed in Chapter 2, the accrual system of accounting matches earned revenue with expenses that have been incurred in producing revenue during an accounting period. One expense incurred as a result of sales on credit or on account is a bad debts expense. The problem is that it may take as long as a year for the seller to realize that the debt is uncollectible. What happens in the meantime? How can the books be kept up-to-date?

One way is to estimate at the end of the year what percentage of sales made during that year will turn out to be bad debts. Several approaches can be used to arrive at the percentage. At the moment, let's say Abby Ellen Company estimates that 1.6% of its sales of $100,000 for the year 20X1 will not be collectible; thus, the company expects not to collect $1,600 of the $100,000 owed it from sales. (Other ways to estimate the amount are discussed in Learning Unit 13-2.)

Two accounts that we haven't discussed before, Bad Debts Expense and Allowance for Doubtful Accounts, are needed. **Bad Debts Expense** is an expense account whose normal balance is a debit; it is a temporary account that is closed to Income Summary at year's end. **Allowance for Doubtful Accounts** is a contra-asset account that accumulates the expected amount of bad debts as of a given date; its normal balance is a credit. It is a permanent account that is *not* closed to Income Summary at the end of the year.

In the case of Abby Ellen Company, which expects to be unable to collect $1,600 of the $100,000 owed it from sales, at the end of the year (20X1) an adjustment is made debiting Bad Debts Expense and crediting Allowance for Doubtful Accounts for $1,600. This transaction (Fig. 13.1) is shown with a transaction analysis chart.

> Will go on income statement as an operating expense and eventually be closed to Income Summary.

1 Accounts Affected	2 Category	3 ↑ ↓	4 Rules
Bad Debts Expense	Expense	↑	Dr.
Allowance for Doubtful Accounts	Contra-Asset	↑	Cr.

FIGURE 13.1 Estimating Bad Debts

20X1						
Dec.	31	Bad Debt Expense	1 6 0 0 00		
		Allowance for Doubtful Accounts		1 6 0 0 00
		Record estimate of bad debts		

The allowance account is subtracted from Accounts Receivable, leaving a **net realizable value** of $98,400. Net realizable value is the amount Abby Ellen Company expects to collect. When an account is written off, the net realizable value doesn't change, because both the Accounts Receivable and the Allowance for Doubtful Accounts are reduced (see Fig. 13.2).

ABBY ELLEN COMPANY PARTIAL BALANCE SHEET DECEMBER 31, 20X1			
Assets			
Current Assets:			
Cash			$ 51 4 0 0 00
Accounts Receivable	$100 0 0 0 00		
Less: Allowance for Doubtful Accounts	1 6 0 0 00		98 4 0 0 00
Merchandise Inventory			200 0 0 0 00
Total Current Assets			$349 8 0 0 00

FIGURE 13.2 Partial Balance Sheet

Think of the Allowance for Doubtful Accounts as a reservoir that is filled before bad debts occur. The reservoir is drained when a customer's bill is declared uncollectible. Abby Ellen Company estimates that out of its $100,000 of credit sales, $1,600 will prove to be uncollectible, but it does not know which accounts those will be.

> Accounts Receivable
> – Allowance for Doubtful Accounts
> = Net Realizable Value

Writing Off an Account Deemed Uncollectible

At some point a customer's bill must be written off as uncollectible. Let's look at how Abby Ellen Company would write off the account of Jones Moore on June 5, 20X2. (The $200 sale was made in 20X1.)

Remember, at the end of 20X1, Abby made an adjusting entry increasing Bad Debts Expense (debit) and filling the Allowance for Doubtful Accounts (credit) with the estimate of accounts receivable that will not be collectible. The journal entry shown in Figure 13.3 is recorded to write off this account.

Note that we did *not* debit the account Bad Debts Expense, because the estimate for this account was made on December 31, 20X1 (and applies to that year, not to 20X2). When that estimate was made, we did not know which bills would turn out to be uncollectible. Once the debt is identified as uncollectible, we reduce both the Allowance account and the controlling account, Accounts Receivable, and update the accounts receivable subsidiary ledger. The subsidiary ledger will be credited just as the controlling account is.

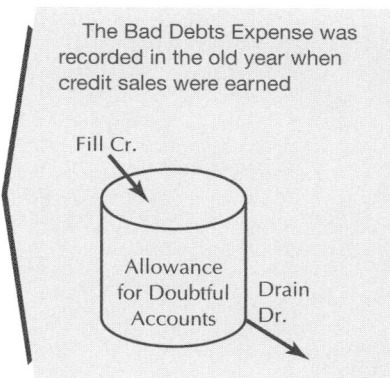

The Bad Debts Expense was recorded in the old year when credit sales were earned

Fill Cr.

Allowance for Doubtful Accounts

Drain Dr.

FIGURE 13.3 Bad Debt Written Off

	20X2					
	June	5	Allowance for Doubtful Accounts	2 0 0 00		
			Accounts Receivable, J. Moore			2 0 0 00
			Writing off J. Moore account			

LEARNING UNIT 13-1 REVIEW

AT THIS POINT / you should be able to

- Define and explain the purpose of Bad Debts Expense and Allowance for Doubtful Accounts.
- Explain why the subsidiary ledger account cannot be updated at the time the Bad Debts Expense is estimated.
- Prepare an adjusting entry for Bad Debts Expense.
- Prepare a partial balance sheet showing the relationship between the Allowance for Doubtful Accounts and Accounts Receivable.

(*continued on next page*)

- Explain net realizable value.
- Prepare a journal entry to write off a customer's debt in a year following the sale.

Self-Review Quiz 13-1

Respond true or false to the following:

> The Allowance account fills with a credit and drains with a debit.

1. The Bad Debts Expense account should be updated only when the customer's debt is declared to be uncollectible.
2. The Allowance for Doubtful Accounts is a contra-asset account on the balance sheet.
3. Bad Debts Expense is part of cost of goods sold.
4. Net realizable value equals Accounts Receivable less Allowance for Doubtful Accounts.
5. When a customer's debt is written off as uncollectible, the account Allowance for Doubtful Accounts is credited.

Solutions to Self-Review Quiz 13-1

1. False
2. True
3. False
4. True
5. False

LO2

Learning Unit 13-2 The Allowance Method: Two Approaches to Estimating the Amount of Bad Debts Expense

> Bad Debts Expense can be based on a percentage of the dollar volume of net credit sales on the income statement.

As mentioned earlier, at the end of each year companies, such as Ford Motor, must estimate what percentage of their sales for that year will turn out to be uncollectible accounts or bad debts. How is this estimate arrived at? In this unit we look at two of the most common ways of arriving at this amount: the income statement approach and the balance sheet approach. The diagram in Figure 13.4 outlines these methods.

The Income Statement Approach

Abby Ellen Company uses the **income statement approach** to calculate how much bad debts expense will be associated with this year's sales. Based on the past several years, the company has averaged bad debts expense of 1% of *net* credit sales. From the following facts, let's prepare an adjusting entry to record the bad debts expense that is based on a percentage of *net* credit sales (see Fig. 13.5).

20X4	Dr.	Cr.
Sales (all credit)		$95,000
Sales Returns and Allowances	$10,000	
Sales Discount	5,000	
Accounts Receivable	7,000	
Allowance for Doubtful Accounts		100

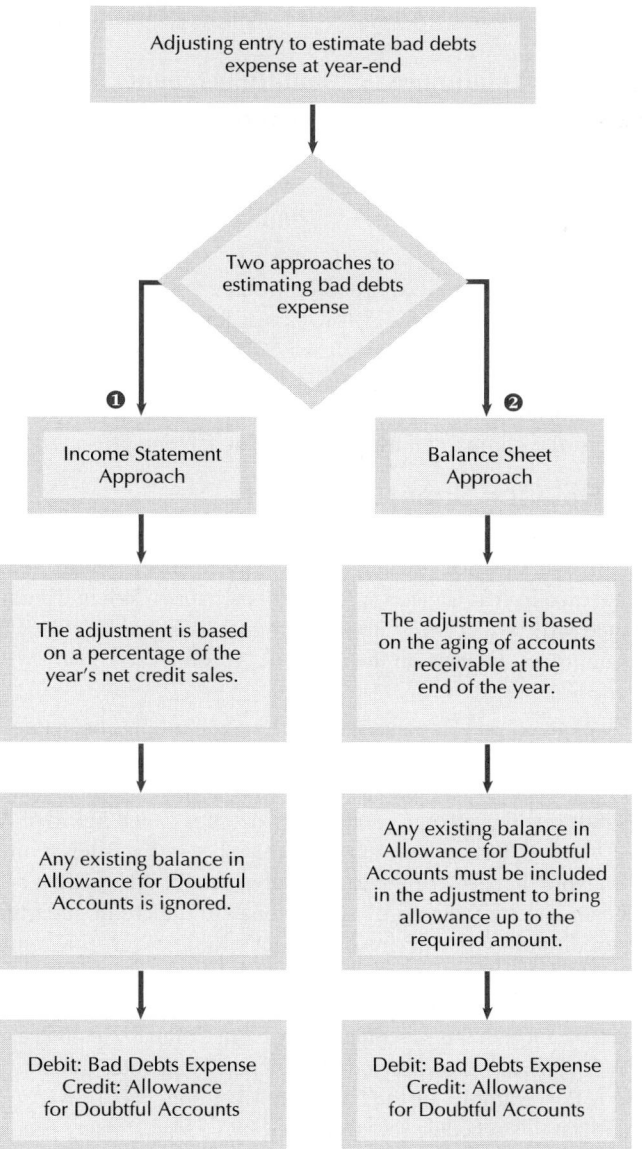

FIGURE 13.4 Two Approaches to Estimating Amount of Bad Debts Expense

1 Accounts Affected	2 Category	3 ↑ ↓	4 Rules
Bad Debts Expense	Expense	↑	Dr.
Allowance for Doubtful Accounts	Contra-Asset	↑	Cr.

	20X4															
	Dec.	31	Bad Debts Expense		8 0 0 00		
			Allowance for Doubtful Accounts			8 0 0 00
			Record estimate of bad debts			
			(.01 × $80,000)			

FIGURE 13.5 Estimating Bad Debts Based on Percentage of Sales

When it is posted, the Allowance account looks like the following:

Allowance for Doubtful Accounts

Dr.	Cr.	
	100 →	Balance *before* adjustment
	800 →	Adjustment
	900 →	New Balance

> Beginning balance in Allowance account represents potential bad debts from previous periods.

The income statement approach emphasizes the matching requirements of the income statement. The $100 in the Allowance account represents a carryover of potential bad debts from *prior* years. Thus, the total of $900 represents total potential uncollectible accounts of several periods of sales. If, over the years, the estimate for Bad Debts Expense has been inaccurate, an adjusting entry can be made in the current year's Bad Debts Expense. If that happens, the company may reevaluate its percentage and use 1½% instead of 1%.

The Balance Sheet Approach

The **balance sheet approach** bases the new total Allowance for Doubtful Accounts on the current Accounts Receivable on the balance sheet. Thus, the adjustment is reduced by the old balance in Allowance for Doubtful Accounts. When the adjustment is credited, the new balance will reflect the state of Accounts Receivable. (See Fig. 13.4 on preceding page.) This approach focuses on the aging of Accounts Receivable.

> Aging classifies uncollected amounts of individual customers according to days past due.

LO3   **Aging of Accounts Receivable**   The longer a bill has been due and not paid, the more likely it is that it is not going to be paid. Therefore, one way of estimating the amount of bad debts for the year just past is to look at Accounts Receivable and analyze it according to how many days past due the accounts are. This process is called **aging of Accounts Receivable.**

> Today, with a computer, an analysis of Accounts Receivable can be completed quickly.

Table 13.1 shows an analysis that the Abby Ellen Company did on December 31, 20X0. Note that 29% of the total receivables for Abby Ellen are past due from 1 to 30 days. (This analysis will also provide feedback to the credit department about how well the current credit policy is working.) Now let's look at how the company will estimate what balance in the Allowance for Doubtful Accounts is required to meet probable bad debts.

> Peachtree and QuickBooks both provide an Aging of Receivables report that can be run at any time and is current after each transaction is recorded.

The schedule shown in Table 13.2 was prepared to assist the company in calculating the needed balance. In this schedule, Abby Ellen Company applied a sliding scale of percentages (3, 4, 10, 20, 50), based on previous experience, to the total amount of receivables due in each time period. For example, of the $3,600 not yet due, 3%, or $108, will probably never be paid. Looking at this schedule reveals that Abby Ellen Company needs $480 to cover estimated bad

TABLE 13.1 Aging of Accounts Receivable

Name of Customer	Total Balance	Not Yet Due	Days Past Due 1–30	Days Past Due 31–60	Days Past Due 61–90	Days Past Due Over 90
Jane Elliot	$ 100	$ 100				
Joshua Harras	30			$ 30		
Alan Kedbury	160	160				
John Sullivan	180				$160	$ 20
Sheri Lissan	80	80				
Others	6,450	3,260	$2,000	840	40	310
Totals	$7,000	$3,600	$2,000	$870	$200	$330
Percent of total (rounded to nearest whole percent)	100%	51%	29%	12%	3%	5%
		$\left(\dfrac{\$3,600}{\$7,000}\right)$	$\left(\dfrac{\$2,000}{\$7,000}\right)$	$\left(\dfrac{\$870}{\$7,000}\right)$	$\left(\dfrac{\$200}{\$7,000}\right)$	$\left(\dfrac{\$330}{\$7,000}\right)$

TABLE 13.2 Balance Required to Meet Probable Bad Debts

	Amount	Estimated Percentage Considered to Be Bad Debts Expense	Amount Needed in Allowance for Doubtful Accounts to Cover Estimated Bad Debts Expense
Not Yet Due	$3,600	3	$108 ($3,600 × .03)
Days Past Due			
1–30	2,000	4	80
31–60	870	10	87
61–90	200	20	40
Over 90	330	50	165
Total Accounts Receivable	$7,000	Total Balance Required in Allowance for Doubtful Accounts	$480
Less current balance			− 100
Adjusting entry			$380

debts. *Currently,* the balance in the Allowance account is $100. Thus, to reach a balance of $480, we must adjust the balance of the account by the adjusting journal entry shown in Figure 13.6.

Bad Debts Expense			Allowance for Doubtful Accounts		
Dr.	Cr.		Dr.	Cr.	
380				100	Beg. Balance
				380	Adj.
				480	New balance in Allowance

> Some companies that feel aging is too time-consuming may estimate bad debts based on a percentage of total Accounts Receivable.

The desired balance of $480 is now reached. If the Allowance had a *debit* balance of $100 before the adjustment, the amount of the adjusting entry would be a $580 credit to the Allowance to arrive at the $480 balance. Once again, the adjustment *must* consider the existing balance in the Allowance account before the adjusting entry is prepared.

> The balance in the Allowance for Doubtful Accounts is not ignored.

20X4						
Dec.	31	Bad Debts Expense		3 8 0 00		
		Allowance for Doubtful Accounts			3 8 0 00	
		Estimate of bad debts				

FIGURE 13.6 Estimating Bad Debts Based on Aging of Receivables

LEARNING UNIT 13-2 REVIEW

AT THIS POINT you should be able to

- Explain the two approaches to estimating Bad Debts Expense.
- Explain why the balance in the Allowance for Doubtful Accounts is ignored when an adjusting entry for bad debts is prepared in the income statement approach.
- Show how to prepare an aging of Accounts Receivable.
- Explain how the aging of Accounts Receivable is used to arrive at the balance required in the Allowance for Doubtful Accounts.

Self-Review Quiz 13-2

From the following, prepare an adjusting journal entry for Bad Debts Expense for (1) the income statement approach and (2) the balance sheet approach.

Allowance for Doubtful Accounts			Income Statement Approach	
			Net Sales	$160,000
Dr.	**Cr.**		1% of Net Sales	
	400			

Balance Sheet Approach		Percent Considered Bad Debts
Not yet due:	$4,000	4
Days past due:		
1–30	3,000	5
31–60	400	10
Over 60	5,000	30

Solution to Self-Review Quiz 13-2

FIGURE 13.7 Estimating Bad Debts

$1,850 is amount required.

Note allowance adjusted:
$1,850 − $400 = $1,450

(1)	Dec.	31	Bad Debts Expense	1 6 0 0 00		
			Allowance for Doubtful Accounts		1 6 0 0 00	
			(.01 × $160,000)			
(2)		31	Bad Debts Expense	1 4 5 0 00		
			Allowance for Doubtful Accounts		1 4 5 0 00	
			$4,000 × .04 = $ 160			
			3,000 × .05 = 150			
			400 × .10 = 40			
			5,000 × .30 = 1,500			
			$1,850			

LO4 Learning Unit 13-3 Writing Off and Recovering Uncollectible Accounts

Writing Off an Account Using the Allowance for Doubtful Accounts

Let's assume that on March 18, 20X7, the Abby Ellen Company determines that the account of Jill Sullivan for $900 is uncollectible. (The sale to Jill Sullivan was back in 20X6.) Thus, this Accounts Receivable amount should no longer be considered an asset and should be written off. The journal entry in Figure 13.8 reduces the Allowance for Doubtful Accounts and reduces the Accounts Receivable controlling account as well as the accounts receivable subsidiary ledger.

FIGURE 13.8 Jill Sullivan Account Written Off

20X7					
Mar.	18	Allowance for Doubtful Accounts	9 0 0 00		
		Accounts Receivable, Jill Sullivan		9 0 0 00	
		Wrote off Sullivan account			

Key Points:

- This journal entry does *not* affect any expenses. Remember that Bad Debts Expense is not affected when an account is finally written off. The estimate for Bad Debts Expense was recorded in the previous year before the bad debt actually occurred.
- If more than one customer is written off, a compound entry can be used, debiting Allowance for the total and crediting each individual account.
- The net realizable value of Accounts Receivable is unchanged. Let's prove it:

Balances Before the Write-Off		Balances After the Write-Off	
Accounts Receivable	$12,000	$900 write-off	$11,100
Less: Allowance for Doubtful Accounts	2,000	$900 drain	1,100
Estimated realizable value	$10,000	No change	$10,000
(what to expect to collect)			

Recording Recovered Debts Using Allowance for Doubtful Accounts What would happen if Jill Sullivan paid all or part of the debt after Abby Ellen Company wrote it off? Consider this situation: Assume that Jill Sullivan is able to pay off half of her debt and send a check to Abby Ellen Company on February 1, 20X8. (Keep in mind that her account was written off on March 18, 20X7, and the original sale was made in 20X6.) To record this payment, Abby Ellen Company reverses in part the entry that was made to write off the account in the amount expected to be recovered and records the amount received from Jill. Figure 13.9 shows the journal entries to record the recovery of $450 out of the original amount of $900.

The reason we record both a debit and a credit to Accounts Receivable is that it provides a clear picture of the transactions involving Jill Sullivan. If the company is considering giving credit again to Jill Sullivan, these previous records could be of assistance in determining how much, if any, credit could be extended. Note how the first entry reinstates the account and the second entry records the cash received.

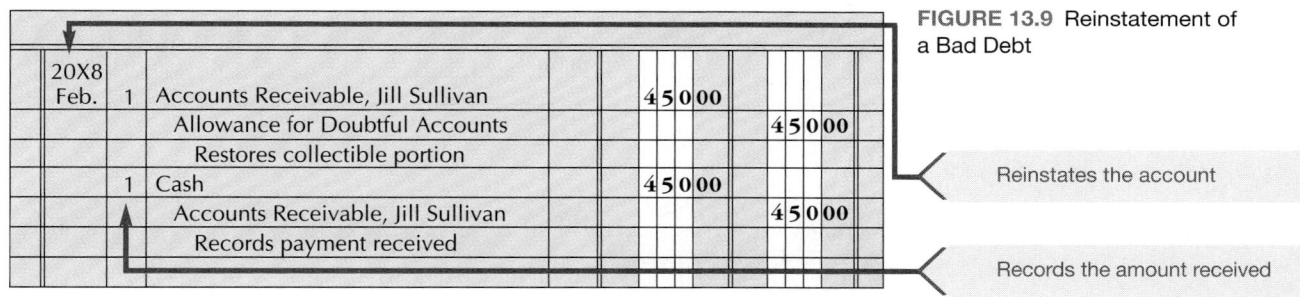

FIGURE 13.9 Reinstatement of a Bad Debt

20X8 Feb.	1	Accounts Receivable, Jill Sullivan	4 5 0 00		
		Allowance for Doubtful Accounts		4 5 0 00	Reinstates the account
		Restores collectible portion			
	1	Cash	4 5 0 00		
		Accounts Receivable, Jill Sullivan		4 5 0 00	Records the amount received
		Records payment received			

The Direct Write-Off Method

LO5

When a company cannot reasonably estimate its Bad Debts Expense, it may use the **direct write-off method.** Using this method, an account that is determined to be uncollectible would be directly written off to this year's Bad Debts Expense account without regard to when the original sale was made. In this method, the Allowance for Doubtful Accounts is not used, because no adjustment is needed at the end of the year to estimate Bad Debts Expense. The journal entry would be a debit to Bad Debts Expense and a credit to Accounts Receivable. (See Figure 13.10 on the following page.)

> The direct write-off method does not fulfill the matching principle but is acceptable for federal income tax reporting.

Recording Recovered Debts Using the Direct Method Let's suppose that Jill Sullivan repays half of her outstanding debt after Abby Ellen Company has written it off. The recovered debt would be accounted for using the direct write-off method as shown in Figure 13.11 on the following page.

FIGURE 13.10 Direct Write-off Method to Record Bad Debt

	20X7												
	Mar.	18	Bad Debts Expense			9	0	0	00				
			Accounts Receivable, Jill Sullivan								9	0	0	00
			Wrote off account											

A new account title, **Bad Debts Recovered,** must be created (Fig. 13.11). Think of this account as a revenue account found in the Other Income section of an income statement.

FIGURE 13.11 Direct Write-Off Method to Record Recovery

	20X8												
	Feb.	1	Acct. Rec., Jill Sullivan			4	5	0	00				
			Bad Debts Recovered								4	5	0	00
			Restores collectible portion											
		1	Cash			4	5	0	00				
			Acct. Rec., Jill Sullivan								4	5	0	00
			Records payment received											

Recovery of half the amount owed by Jill Sullivan on February 1, 20X8. Note that Bad Debts Recovered is used instead of Allowance for Doubtful Accounts.

Bad Debts Recov.	Other Revenue	↑	Cr.

In the direct write-off method, when the amount is written off, no Allowance for Doubtful Accounts is used. Instead, the debit is to Bad Debts Expense. If the debt is recovered later, the direct method credits Bad Debts Recovered (an account in the Other Revenue category). In effect, this method increases the revenue and puts the Accounts Receivable back on the books. If recovery is made the same year (let's say on May 1) as the debt is written off, the entry made to write off the account is reversed (Fig. 13.12).

FIGURE 13.12 Recovery Made in Same Year

	20X7												
	May	1	Accounts Receivable, Jill Sullivan			4	5	0	00				
			Bad Debts Expense								4	5	0	00

LEARNING UNIT 13-3 REVIEW

AT THIS POINT you should be able to

- Write off an account using the Allowance for Doubtful Accounts method.
- Explain why net realizable value is unchanged after a write-off is complete.
- Prepare journal entries to recover entire or partial amounts that were once declared uncollectible.
- Explain the direct write-off method and prepare appropriate journal entries for write-off and recovery.

Self-Review Quiz 13-3

Respond true or false to the following:

1. When an account using the Allowance for Doubtful Accounts method is written off in a period following the sale, the result is a debit to Bad Debts Expense and a credit to Accounts Receivable.
2. The direct write-off method will sometimes use the Allowance for Doubtful Accounts.

3. When an account is written off (using the Allowance for Doubtful Accounts method), net realizable value is unchanged.
4. Bad Debts Recovered is an asset.
5. A debit balance in the Allowance for Doubtful Accounts indicates that the estimate for Bad Debts Expense was too low.

Solutions to Self-Review Quiz 13-3

1. False
2. False
3. True
4. False
5. True

CHAPTER ASSIGNMENTS

SUMMARY OF KEY POINTS

LEARNING UNIT 13-1

1. If accrual accounting is used, Bad Debts Expense should be recognized in the year the sale was earned, even though the actual write-off may not yet have taken place.
2. Bad Debts Expense is an expense found on the income statement.
3. The Allowance for Doubtful Accounts is a contra-asset account found on the balance sheet that accumulates the amount of estimated uncollectibles before they are actually written off.
4. Net realizable value equals Accounts Receivable minus Allowance for Doubtful Accounts.
5. When an account is written off, the Allowance for Doubtful Accounts is debited and Accounts Receivable is credited (along with the subsidiary ledger account).

LEARNING UNIT 13-2

1. The two approaches to estimating Bad Debts Expense are the income statement approach and the balance sheet approach.
2. The income statement approach estimates Bad Debts Expense based on a percentage of net sales. (Some companies use credit sales, some use total sales.) The balance is ignored in the Allowance for Doubtful Accounts when the Bad Debts Expense is estimated from sales of the period.
3. The balance sheet approach estimates the balance required in the Allowance for Doubtful Accounts by aging the Accounts Receivable. The balance in the Allowance account will have to be adjusted based on the aging of the receivables.

LEARNING UNIT 13-3

1. When an account is written off (using the Allowance method) in years following the sale, the result is to debit the Allowance for Doubtful Accounts and credit Accounts Receivable. Do not debit Bad Debts Expense, because it has already been recorded in the year the sale was earned.

> After the write-off, net realizable value is unchanged.

2. When an uncollectible account has been written off and is now recovered, the entry reverses the original write-off by debiting Accounts Receivable and crediting the Allowance for Doubtful Accounts. Then the cash received is debited and the Accounts Receivable is credited.
3. The direct write-off method will recognize the Bad Debts Expense when the customer account is declared uncollectible. The direct method does *not* use the

Allowance for Doubtful Accounts, because no estimate is made for bad debts. This method does not follow the matching principle in the accrual basis of accounting.

4. Bad Debts Recovered is classified as Other Revenue when a customer account is reinstated after being written off in the direct method.

KEY TERMS

Aging of Accounts Receivable The procedure of classifying accounts of individual customers by age group, where age is the number of days elapsed from due date.

Allowance for Doubtful Accounts A contra-asset account that is subtracted from Accounts Receivable. This account accumulates the *expected* amount of uncollectibles as of a given date.

Bad Debts Expense The operating expense account that estimates the amount of credit sales that will probably not be collectible in a given accounting period when the Allowance method is used. For the direct write-off method, this account would be the actual amount written off.

Bad Debts Recovered When an account receivable has been written off and is recovered, this account, which is in the Other Revenue category, is credited in the direct write-off method if the recovery is in a year *following* the write-off.

Balance sheet approach A method used to calculate the amount *required* in the Allowance for Doubtful Accounts

to cover expected uncollectibles. This method is based on the Accounts Receivable amount and the aging process. The adjustment to the Allowance for Doubtful Accounts will bring the new balance of that account to the new required level.

Direct write-off method The method of writing off uncollectibles when they occur and thus *not* using the Allowance for Doubtful Accounts. This method does not fulfill the matching principle of accrual accounting.

Income statement approach A method that estimates the amount of Bad Debts Expense that will result based on a percentage of net credit sales for the period. The amount of the expected bad debt is added to the existing balance of Allowance for Doubtful Accounts.

Net realizable value The amount (Accounts Receivable − Allowance for Doubtful Accounts) that is expected to be collected.

BLUEPRINT

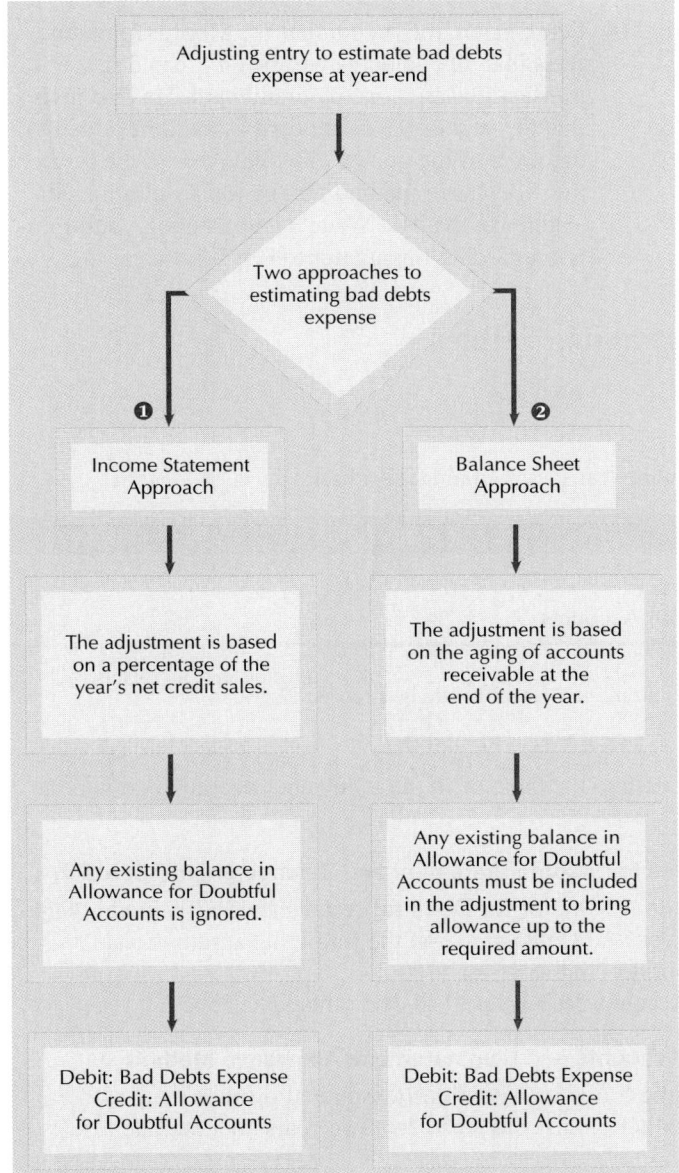

QUESTIONS, CLASSROOM DEMONSTRATION EXERCISES, EXERCISES, AND PROBLEMS

Discussion and Critical Thinking Questions/Ethical Case

1. Explain the matching principle in relationship to recording Bad Debts Expense.

2. What is the purpose of the Allowance for Doubtful Accounts?

3. What is net realizable value?

4. When an account receivable is written off, Bad Debts Expense must be debited. True or false? Please discuss.

5. Explain why the Allowance for Doubtful Accounts is a contra-asset account.

6. Recording Bad Debts Expense is a closing entry. True or false? Defend your position.

7. The income statement approach used to estimate bad debts is based on Accounts Receivable on the balance sheet. Agree or disagree? Why?

8. In which approach is the balance of the Allowance for Doubtful Accounts considered when the estimate of Bad Debts Expense is made? Please explain.

9. Why would a company age its Accounts Receivable?

10. Using the Allowance for Doubtful Accounts method, what journal entries would be made to write off an account as well as later record the recovery of the accounts receivable?

11. Why doesn't net realizable value change when an account is written off in the use of the Allowance account?

12. What is the purpose of using a direct write-off method?

13. Explain the purpose of the Bad Debts Recovered account.

14. Pete Sazich, the accountant for Moore Company, feels that all bad debts will be eliminated if credit transactions are done by credit card. He also feels that the cost of the credit cards should be added to the price of the goods. Pete feels that in the future the Allowance method will be totally eliminated. You make the call. Write a letter stating your opinion regarding this matter to Pete's boss.

Classroom Demonstration Exercises

SET A

LO1 (5 min) **Categorizing Accounts**

1. a. Complete the following transactional analysis chart:

Accounts	Category	↑ ↓	Rules
Bad Debt Expense			
Allowance for Doubtful Accounts			

   b. On which financial statement will each title be recorded?

LO2 (10 min) **Allowance Method**

2. Explain under which method the balance in the Allowance account is ignored. Give an example.

LO2 (15 min) **Journalize Adjusting Entries for Income Statement and Balance Sheet Approach**

3. Given the balance in the Allowance for Doubtful Accounts of $300 credit, prepare adjusting entries for Bad Debts based on the following assumptions:
   a. Bad debts to be 5% of net credit sales or $700.
   b. Based on aging of Accounts Receivable, bad debts should be $600.

LO4 (15 min) **Writing Off Uncollectible Accounts and Reinstatement: Allowance Method**

4. Journalize entries for the following situations (assume allowance method):
   Situation 1: Wrote off Mia Kaminsky as a bad debt two years after the sale for $100.

   Situation 2: Reinstated Mia Kaminsky, who sent in her past due amount.

LO5 (15 min) **Writing Off Uncollectible Accounts and Reinstatement: Direct Write-Off Method**

5. Journalize entries for the following situations (assume direct write-off method).
   Situation 1: Wrote off Mia Kaminsky as a bad debt two years after the sale of $100.

   Situation 2: Reinstated Mia Kaminsky, who sent in her past due amount two years after it had been written off.

SET B

LO1 (5 min) **Categorizing Accounts**

1. a. Complete the following transactional analysis chart:

Accounts	Category	↑ ↓	Rules
Bad Debts Expense			
Accounts Receivable			

b. On which financial statement will each title be recorded?

c. Which account is temporary? Which account is permanent?

Allowance Method

LO2 (15 min)

2. Complete Figure 13.13:

FIGURE 13.13 Two Approaches to Estimating Bad Debts Using Allowance Method

Journalize Adjusting Entries for Income Statement and Balance Sheet Approach

LO2 (15 min)

3. Given the balance in the Allowance for Doubtful Accounts of $200 credit, prepare adjusting entries for Bad Debts based on the following assumptions:

a. Bad debts to be 5% of net credit sales or $600.

b. Based on aging of Accounts Receivable, bad debts should be $500.

Writing Off Uncollectible Accounts and Reinstatement: Allowance Method

LO4 (15 min)

4. Journalize entries for the following situations (assume allowance method):

Situation 1: Wrote off Bill Allen as a bad debt two years after the sale for $50.

Situation 2: Reinstated Bill Allen, who sent in his past due amount.

Writing Off Uncollectible Accounts and Reinstatement: Direct Write-Off Method

LO5 (15 min)

5. Journalize entries for the following situations (assume direct write-off method):

Situation 1: Wrote off Bill Allen as a bad debt two years after the sale of $50.

Situation 2: Reinstated Bill Allen, who sent in his past due amount two years after it had been written off.

Exercises

13-1. Online.com has requested that you prepare a partial balance sheet on December 31, 20XX, from the following: Cash, $120,000; Petty Cash, $70; Accounts Receivable, $70,000; Bad Debts Expense, $50,000; Allowance for Doubtful Accounts, $14,000; Merchandise Inventory, $19,000.

LO1 (20 min)

13-2. The following information is given:

LO2 (20 min)

Accounts Receivable		Sales		Sales Returns and Allowances	
Dr.	Cr.	Dr.	Cr.	Dr.	Cr.
30,000			110,000	500	

Sales Discount		Allowance for Doubtful Accounts	
Dr.	Cr.	Dr.	Cr.
9,500			5,000

Journalize the adjusting entry on December 31, 20XX, for Bad Debts Expense, which is estimated to be 4% of net sales. The income statement approach is used.

LO2 (20 min) **13-3.** Assuming that in Exercise 13-2 the balance sheet approach is used, prepare a journalized adjusting entry for Bad Debts Expense. Based on an aging of Accounts Receivable, an $8,000 balance in the Allowance account will be needed to cover bad debts.

LO2, 4 (20 min) **13-4.** Austin Co., which uses an Allowance for Doubtful Accounts, had the following transactions in 20X5 and 20X6. (Use the income statement approach.)

20X5		
Dec.	31	Recorded Bad Debts Expense of $12,000.
20X6		
Apr.	3	Wrote off Angie Ring account of $4,000 as uncollectible.
June	4	Wrote off Mike Catuc account of $3,000 as uncollectible.
20X7		
Aug.	5	Recovered $500 from Mike Catuc.

a. Journalize the transactions. (The company uses the income statement approach in estimating bad debts.)

b. Journalize how Austin Co. would record the Mike Catuc bad debt situation if the direct write-off method were used.

LO3, 4 (20 min) **13-5.** Rowe Company had credit sales of $200,000 during 20X7. The balance in the Allowance for Doubtful Accounts is a $1,000 debit balance. Journalize the Bad Debts Expense for December 31 using each of the following methods:

a. Bad Debts Expense is estimated at 1.5% of credit sales.

b. The aging of Accounts Receivable indicates that $2,200 will be required in the Allowance account to cover Bad Debts Expense.

Group A Problems

LO1, 2 (25 min) **13A-1.** Logan.com has requested that you prepare journal entries from the following (this company uses the Allowance for Doubtful Accounts method based on the income statement approach):

20X7		
Dec.	31	Recorded Bad Debts Expense of $14,000.
20X8		
Jan.	7	Wrote off Gene Smore's account of $800 as uncollectible.
Mar.	5	Wrote off Paul Jane's account of $600 as uncollectible.
July	8	Recovered $300 from Paul Jane.
Aug.	19	Wrote off Bob Seager's account of $1,300 as uncollectible.
Aug.	24	Wrote off Jill Neuman's account of $750 as uncollectible.
Nov.	19	Recovered $400 from Bob Seager.

> *Check Figure:*
> August 24:
> Dr.: Allowance for Doubtful
> Accounts $750
> Cr.: Accounts Receivable, Jill
> Neuman $750

LO1, 2 (30 min) **13A-2.** Given the information presented in Figure 13.14, do the following:

a. Prepare on December 31, 20X8, the adjusting journal entry for Bad Debts Expense.

b. Prepare a partial balance sheet on December 31, 20X8, showing how net realizable value is calculated.

c. If the balance in the Allowance for Doubtful Accounts were a $300 debit balance, journalize the adjusting entry for Bad Debts Expense on December 31, 20X8.

Balances: Cash, $30,000; Accounts Receivable, $152,000; Allowance for Doubtful Accounts, $300; Inventory, $12,000.

ALVIE CO. DECEMBER 31, 20X8			
	Amount	Estimated Percent Considered to Be Bad Debts Expense	Estimated Amount Needed in Allowance for Doubtful Accounts
Not yet due	$130,000	1%	
0–60	9,000	5%	
61–180	8,000	20%	
Over 6 months	5,000	40%	
	$152,000		

FIGURE 13.14 Aging of Accounts Receivable

Check Figure:
Net realizable value $146,650

13A-3. T. J. Rack Company uses the direct write-off method for recording Bad Debts Expense. At the beginning of 20X8, Accounts Receivable has a $119,000 balance. Journalize the following transactions for T. J. Rack:

LO2, 4 (25 min)

20X8

Mar. 13   Wrote off S. Rose's account for $1,800.

Apr. 14   Wrote off P. Soy's account for $750.

20X9

Nov. 8   P. Soy paid bad debt of $750 that was written off April 14, 20X8.

Dec. 7   Wrote off J. Miller's account as uncollectible, $285.

Dec. 12   Wrote off D. Lovejoy's account for $375 due from sales made on account in 20X7.

Check Figure:
Dec. 7:
Dr.: Bad Debts Expense $285
Cr.: Accts. Rec., J. Miller $285

13A-4. Simon Company completed the following transactions:

LO2, 4 (60 min)

20X8

Jan. 9   Sold merchandise on account to Ray's Supply, $1,500.

Jan. 15   Wrote off the account of Pete Runnels as uncollectible because of his death, $600.

Mar. 17   Received $400 from Roland Co., whose account had been written off in 20X7. The account was reinstated and the collection recorded.

Apr. 9   Received 10% of the $4,000 owed by Lane Drug. The remainder was written off as uncollectible.

June 15   The account of Mel's Garage was reinstated for $1,200. The account was written off three years ago and collected in full today.

Oct. 18   Prepared a compound entry to write the following accounts off as uncollectible: Jane's Diner, $200; Keen Auto, $400; Ralph's Hardware, $600.

Nov. 12   Sold merchandise on account to J. B. Rug, $1,900.

Dec. 31   Based on an aging of Accounts Receivable, it was estimated that $7,000 will be uncollectible out of a total of $160,000 in Accounts Receivable.

Dec. 31   Closed Bad Debts Expense to Income Summary.

From the preceding as well as the following additional data, complete a–c on the following page:

	Acct. No.	Balance
Allowance for Doubtful Accounts	114	$4,100
Income Summary	312	—
Bad Debts Expense	612	—

Check Figure:
Total current asset $272,360

a. Journalize the transactions.

b. Post to Allowance for Doubtful Accounts, Income Summary, and Bad Debts Expense accounts as needed. (Be sure to record the beginning balance in the Allowance account in your *Study Guide and Working Papers.*)

c. Prepare a current assets section of the balance sheet. Ending balances needed: Cash, $13,000; Accounts Receivable, $160,000; Office Supplies, $2,110; Merchandise Inventory, $103,000; Prepaid Rent, $1,250.

Group B Problems

LO1, 2 (25 min)

13B-1. Logan.com has requested that you prepare journal entries from the following (this company uses the Allowance for Doubtful Accounts method based on the income statement approach):

20X7		
Dec.	31	Recorded Bad Debts Expense of $14,800.
20X8		
Jan.	7	Wrote off Woody Tree's account of $1,200 as uncollectible.
Mar.	5	Wrote off Jim Lantz's account of $600 as uncollectible.
July	8	Recovered $600 from Jim Lantz.
Aug.	19	Wrote off Mabel Hest's account of $750 as uncollectible.
Aug.	24	Wrote off Jim O'Reilly's account of $950 as uncollectible.
Nov.	19	Recovered $500 from Mabel Hest.

Check Figure:
Aug. 24:
Dr.: Allow. for D.A. $950
Cr.: Accts. Rec., Jim O'Reilly $950

LO1, 2 (30 min)

13B-2. Given the following information and the information in Figure 13.15, complete a–c: Cash, $42,000; Accounts Receivable, $173,000; Allowance for Doubtful Accounts, $400; Merchandise Inventory, $12,000:

a. Prepare on December 31, 20X8, the adjusting journal entry for Bad Debts Expense.

b. Prepare a partial balance sheet on December 31, 20X8, showing how net realizable value is calculated.

c. If the balance in the Allowance for Doubtful Accounts was a $400 debit balance, journalize the adjusting entry for Bad Debts Expense on December 31, 20X8.

Check Figure:
Net realizable value $166,000

FIGURE 13.15 Aging of Accounts Receivable

	Amount	Estimated Percent Considered to Be Bad Debts Expense	Estimated Amount Needed in Allowance for Doubtful Accounts
ALVIE CO.			
DECEMBER 31, 20X8			
Not yet due	$150,000	2%	
0–60	10,000	6%	
61–180	9,000	20%	
Over six months	4,000	40%	
	$173,000		

LO2, 4 (25 min)

13B-3. T. J. Rack Company uses the direct write-off method for recording Bad Debts Expense. At the beginning of 20X8, Accounts Receivable has an $88,000 balance. Journalize the following transactions for T. J. Rack:

20X8		
Mar.	13	Wrote off Jill Diamond's account for $1,950.
Apr.	14	Wrote off Buffy Hall's account for $900.

20X9

Nov.	8	Buffy Hall paid debt of $900 that was written off April 14, 20X8.
Dec.	7	Wrote off Joe Francis's account as uncollectible, $880.
Dec.	12	Wrote off Joe Martin's account for $410 from sales made on account in 20X7.

Check Figure:
Dec. 7:
Dr.: Bad Debt Expense $880
Cr.: Accts. Rec., Joe Francis $880

13B-4. Simon Company completed the following transactions:

LO2, 4 (60 min)

20X8

Jan.	9	Sold merchandise on account to Lowe's Supply, $1,900.
Jan.	15	Wrote off the account of Kevin Reese as uncollectible because of his death, $700.
Mar.	17	Received $300 from J. James whose account had been written off in 20X7. The account was reinstated and the collection recorded.
Apr.	9	Received 20% of the $5,000 owed by Long Drug. The remainder was written off as uncollectible.
June	15	The account of Morse's Garage was reinstated for $3,100. The account was written off three years ago and collected in full today.
Oct.	18	Prepared a compound entry to write the following accounts off as uncollectible: Sal's Diner, $800; Ring Auto, $1,300; Neel's Hardware, $800.
Nov.	12	Sold merchandise on account to Able Roy, $1,950.
Dec.	31	Based on an aging of Accounts Receivable, it was estimated that $8,000 will be uncollectible out of a total of $170,000 in Accounts Receivable.
Dec.	31	Closed Bad Debts Expense to Income Summary.

Check Figure:
Total current assets $284,200

From these transactions as well as the following additional data, complete a–c:

	Acct. No.	Balance
Allowance for Doubtful Accounts	114	$3,300
Income Summary	312	—
Bad Debts Expense	612	—

a. Journalize the transactions.
b. Post to Allowance for Doubtful Accounts, Income Summary, and Bad Debts Expense accounts as needed.
c. Prepare a current assets section of the balance sheet. Ending balances needed are as follows: Cash, $24,000; Accounts Receivable, $170,000; Office Supplies, $3,000; Merchandise Inventory, $94,000; Prepaid Rent, $1,200.

ON-THE-JOB TRAINING

T-1. Joan Livers, the newly hired bookkeeper of Lyon Company, has until 5:00 P.M. today to prepare an analysis of Accounts Receivable by age on December 31 as well as record the entry for Bad Debts Expense. Please assist Joan, who has found the following invoices and balances scattered on her desk (see Figure 13.16 on the following page). Terms of all sales are n/30. Explain in writing why the allowance method is used.

LO3 (20 min)

T-2.

LO2, 4 (20 min)

MEMO

To: Al Jones
From: Peter Flynn, Pres.
Re: Bad Debts

At a party last night a friend of mine told me that we should not be using the direct write-off method. He told me that it doesn't fulfill the matching principle

(*continued on next page*)

FIGURE 13.16 Invoices and Balances

Jones Co. May 12 $1,500	Ron Co. Aug. 18 $700	Roger Co. Dec. 15 $1,400
Bill Co. Oct. 5 $125	Doe Co. Nov. 1 $ 900 Dec. 18 1,200	Joe Co. Sept. 5 $1,200
Francis Co. July 8 $200 July 15 $400	Balance in Allowance for Doubtful Accounts $350	Not yet due 1% 1–30 3% 31–60 8% 61–90 12% Over 90 30%

of accounting. Check the Tax Reform Act of 1986 in your Research Department to support or reject this information. Please provide me with a written report.

FINANCIAL REPORT PROBLEM

LO2, 4 (10 min)

Reading the Kellogg's Annual Report

Go to Note 15 Supplemental Financial Data and find the balance in Allowance for Doubtful Accounts for 2005 and 2006.

INTERNET PROJECT

eBay

Go to the Web and search: Annual Report eBay 2008.
Click on Investors Relations.
List out the latest news eBay is providing to its investors.
Order a free annual report.

CONTINUING PROBLEM

LO4 (15 min)

Sanchez Computer Center

The Sanchez Computer Center currently has an $11,900 balance in Accounts Receivable. Here is a current schedule of Accounts Receivable:

Sanchez Computer Center
Schedule of Accounts Receivable
March 31, 20XX

Taylor Golf	$ 2,900
Vita Needle	8,100
Accu Pac	900
Total	$11,900

Assignment

Although Accu Pac's account is not 90 days past due, Freedman has determined that it is necessary to write off the entire balance because the business has been foreclosed. Make the necessary journal entry using the direct write-off method.

14

Notes Receivable and Notes Payable

DID YOU KNOW? In 2006 Aeropostale had a 50 million dollar line of credit established with Bank of America. Visit *www.Aeropostale.com* to find more information about Aeropostale.

LEARNING OBJECTIVES

1. Determining interest calculations and maturity dates on notes.

2. Journalizing entries to record renewal of a note, dishonoring of a note, eventual receipt of payment, and note given in exchange for equipment purchased.

3. Discounting an interest-bearing note receivable and recording a discounted note that has been dishonored.

4. Handling adjustments for interest expense and interest income.

When you shop at Aeropostale do you ever wonder how much the inventory in the store is worth? Does Aeropostale own the inventory or did it borrow to bring the goods in? So far the accounts receivable and accounts payable transactions we have been discussing have involved informal promises: Purchase orders and sales receipts are not formal written promises. In this chapter we turn to transactions by buyers and sellers that require promissory notes (or notes), which are *formal written promises*. Notes receivable record amounts owed to a company by others. Notes payable record amounts the company itself owes.

> Notes receivable: asset
> Notes payable: liability

Companies use notes instead of informal promises for many reasons, such as (1) recording sales of high-cost items like farm machinery or construction equipment that have long-term credit periods (usually over 60 days), (2) giving additional time to settle past due accounts, or (3) borrowing money from a bank for a fee. The fee that is charged for the use of one's money over a period of time is called **interest.** In addition, a note gives the seller or lender a stronger legal claim for collecting a past due account because the note acts as formal proof of the transaction.

LO1 # Learning Unit 14-1 Promissory Notes, Interest Calculations, and Determining Maturity Dates

Before looking at recording notes receivable and notes payable, let's discuss the structure of a note and how to determine interest calculations and *maturity dates* (when the note comes due).

A **promissory note** (often called simply a *note*) is a written promise by a borrower to pay a certain sum of money to the lender at a fixed future date. Figure 14.1 is a promissory note that Able Company issued to Green Company. Take a moment to look at the structure of this note. The following explanation is key to the figure:

a. Able Company is borrowing $20,000; this amount is called the **principal.**
b. Money is being borrowed for 60 days.
c. The note is issued on October 2, 20XX.
d. The Green Company is the **payee** to whom the note is payable.
e. The note carries a 6% annual interest rate. (Even though the note is for 60 days, interest is stated as a yearly rate.)
f. The date the note will come due, December 1, 20XX, is called the **maturity date.**
g. Able Company is the **maker,** or the one promising to pay the note plus interest when it comes due.

> The maker is often also called the *payor* or *debtor*.

The maker (Able Company) is the borrower. The borrower calls this obligation a **note payable.** The payee (Green Company) views this note as an asset called a **note receivable.** Able Company's interest expense is interest income for Green Company. Remember that interest expense is classified on the income statement as Other Expenses and interest income is Other Income.

FIGURE 14.1 A Promissory Note

$ 20,000 (A)   Bennington, Vermont *October 2* 20 *XX* (C)

sixty days (B) _____ after date *we* promise to pay

to the order of *Green Company* (D)

Twenty Thousand and 00/100 _____ Dollars

Payable at *National Bank*

Value received *6 %* (E)

No. *115* Due. *December 1, 20XX* (F)

Able Company (G)

Joe Mack

Treasurer

How to Calculate Interest

The formula for calculating the interest on a note is as follows:

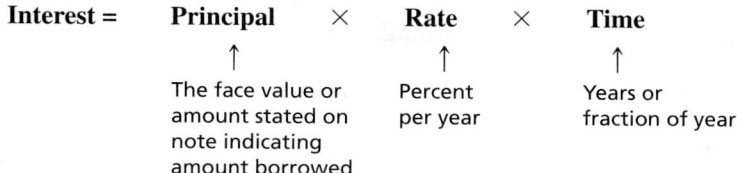

Interest =	**Principal**	×	**Rate**	×	**Time**

The face value or amount stated on note indicating amount borrowed

Percent per year

Years or fraction of year

Let's look at some illustrative situations to show specific interest calculations.

Interest calculated for one year on a $20,000 6% (.06 or 6/100) note:

$$I = P \times R \times T$$
$$= \$20,000 \times .06 \times 1$$
$$= \$1,200$$

Interest calculated for five months on an $8,000 10% note: Time is expressed in twelfths of a year; thus five months is

$$I = P \times R \times T$$
$$= \$8,000 \times .10 \times \tfrac{5}{12}$$
$$= \$333.33$$

Interest calculated for exact number of days based on a 360-day year, 60 days at 6% on a $4,000 note: When the note is given in days, the fraction for time is

$$\frac{\text{Exact Number of Days}}{360}$$

So we have

> Some federal agencies use 365 days, but common business practice is to use 360.

$$I = P \times R \times T$$
$$= \$4,000 \times .06 \times \tfrac{60}{360}$$
$$= \$40$$

How to Determine Maturity Date

Maturity Date Determined by Exact Days To determine the maturity date of a 90-day note dated June 21, the following could be set up (or you could count on a calendar):

Number of days remaining in June (30 − 21)	9
Days in July	31
Days in August	31
Number of days at end of August	71
Days in September to reach 90	19
Term of note	90

> September, April, June, and November have 30 days; all other months have 31, except February, which has 28 (29 during a leap year).

Thus, the maturity date of the note is September 19. Another way to calculate the maturity date is to use a table of days in a year (see Table 14.1 on the following page).

The original note is dated June 21. Look at the top of the table for June and down the left column to day 21. The point of intersection reveals that June 21 is day 172 of the year. If we add 172 and 90 (length of note) we get 262. By searching in the table for 262, we see the date of maturity is September 19.

TABLE 14.1 Days in a Year

Day of Month	Jan.	Feb.*	Mar.	Apr.	May	June	July	Aug.	Sept.	Oct.	Nov.	Dec.	Day of Month
1	1	32	60	91	121	152	182	213	244	274	305	335	1
2	2	33	61	92	122	153	183	214	245	275	306	336	2
3	3	34	62	93	123	154	184	215	246	276	307	337	3
4	4	35	63	94	124	155	185	216	247	277	308	338	4
5	5	36	64	95	125	156	186	217	248	278	309	339	5
6	6	37	65	96	126	157	187	218	249	279	310	340	6
7	7	38	66	97	127	158	188	219	250	280	311	341	7
8	8	39	67	98	128	159	189	220	251	281	312	342	8
9	9	40	68	99	129	160	190	221	252	282	313	343	9
10	10	41	69	100	130	161	191	222	253	283	314	344	10
11	11	42	70	101	131	162	192	223	254	284	315	345	11
12	12	43	71	102	132	163	193	224	255	285	316	346	12
13	13	44	72	103	133	164	194	225	256	286	317	347	13
14	14	45	73	104	134	165	195	226	257	287	318	348	14
15	15	46	74	105	135	166	196	227	258	288	319	349	15
16	16	47	75	106	136	167	197	228	259	289	320	350	16
17	17	48	76	107	137	168	198	229	260	290	321	351	17
18	18	49	77	108	138	169	199	230	261	291	322	352	18
19	19	50	78	109	139	170	200	231	(262)	292	323	353	19
20	20	51	79	110	140	171	201	232	263	293	324	354	20
21	21	52	80	111	141	(172)	202	233	264	294	325	355	21
22	22	53	81	112	142	173	203	234	265	295	326	356	22
23	23	54	82	113	143	174	204	235	266	296	327	357	23
24	24	55	83	114	144	175	205	236	267	297	328	358	24
25	25	56	84	115	145	176	206	237	268	298	329	359	25
26	26	57	85	116	146	177	207	238	269	299	330	360	26
27	27	58	86	117	147	178	208	239	270	300	331	361	27
28	28	59	87	118	148	179	209	240	271	301	332	362	28
29	29		88	119	149	180	210	241	272	302	333	363	29
30	30		89	120	150	181	211	242	273	303	334	364	30
31	31		90		151		212	243		304		365	31

*For leap years, February has 29 days, and the number of each day after February 28 is one greater than the number given in the table.

Maturity Date Determined by Number of Months If the note were expressed in months rather than days, the table or calendar would not be needed. The maturity date could be found by counting the months from the date the note was issued, regardless of the number of days in each month. Here are some examples:

Date of Note	Length of Note	Maturity Date	
March 31	Two months	May 31	
April 30	Three months	July 31	(last day of month)
July 31	Two months	September 30	

LEARNING UNIT 14-1 REVIEW

AT THIS POINT you should be able to

- Explain the advantages of using notes instead of informal promises.
- Define and explain the structure of a promissory note.
- Calculate interest on notes in days, monthly, or yearly.
- Calculate maturity date by days in the month, by special chart, or by months.

Self-Review Quiz 14-1

1. Calculate the interest for the following:
   - **a.** $8,000   4%   1 year
   - **b.** 9,000   13%   7 months
   - **c.** 7,000   10%   80 days
2. Find the maturity date of an 80-day note dated March 3 by (a) days in each month and (b) using a days-in-a-year chart.
3. Find the maturity date of a note dated March 31, due in five months.

Solutions to Self-Review Quiz 14-1

1. a. $8,000 \times .04 \times 1 = \$320.$

   b. $\$9,000 \times .13 \times \frac{7}{12} = \$682.50.$

   c. $\$7,000 \times .10 \times \frac{80}{360} = \$155.56.$

2. a.

Number of days remaining in March (31 − 3)	28
Days in April	30
Number of days at end of April	58
Days in May to reach 80	22
Maturity date—May 22	80

   b. March 3   62   days

   $\quad\quad\quad$ + 80

   $\quad\quad\quad$ 142   May 22

3. March 31, April, May, June, July, August 31

Learning Unit 14-2 Recording Notes   *LO2*

To understand how notes can be used to extend credit periods and to see how a note is paid off, let's look at some illustrative transactions involving Mace Company and Jane Company.

Sale of Merchandise on Account On August 1, 20XX, Mace Company sold $6,000 of merchandise on account to Jane Company (Fig. 14.2 on the following page).

Time Extension with a Note

On September 1, the end of the credit period, Jane Company gave a $6,000, 60-day, 13% note to Mace Company to gain additional time to settle the past due account. The entries in Figure 14.3 on the following page would be made on the books of the buyer and seller.

When this transaction is journalized, both Accounts Receivable and Accounts Payable are reduced. With *notes,* a subsidiary ledger is usually *not* needed, because the file of the notes provides all the information.

Mace might accept this note as an extension because (1) if Jane Company doesn't pay, a formal written promise is in hand, and (2) interest is accumulating on the note.

> We use general journal entries to keep things simple instead of using special journals.

FIGURE 14.2 Sale of Merchandise on Books of Seller and Buyer

		ON BOOKS OF SELLER—MACE COMPANY		
Aug.	1	Accounts Receivable, Jane Co.	6 0 0 0 00	
		Sales		6 0 0 0 00
		Sold merchandise on account		

		ON BOOKS OF BUYER—JANE COMPANY		
Aug.	1	Purchases	6 0 0 0 00	
		Accounts Payable, Mace Co.		6 0 0 0 00
		Purchased merchandise on account		

Seller →	*The end result of this transaction is a shifting of assets of Mace Company from Accounts Receivable to Notes Receivable.*
Buyer →	*For Jane Company, the result is a shift in liabilities from Accounts Payable to Notes Payable.*

Note Due and Paid at Maturity

Now let's look at the journal entries that will be made if Jane Company pays off the note on October 31 (Fig. 14.4). It is important to emphasize that the interest is calculated on the maturity date of the note.

Note Renewed at Maturity

If Jane Company is unable to pay the $6,130 at maturity, it is possible for the company to renew all or part of the note. Let's assume that the company can pay the interest of $130 and give another note for 90 days at 13%. The transaction could be recorded as shown in Figure 14.5 on the books of the buyer and seller.

Note on the seller's books how the interest is received, the old note is canceled, and the new note is put on the books.

FIGURE 14.3 Time Extension of a Note

		SELLER—MACE COMPANY		
Sept.	1	Notes Receivable	6 0 0 0 00	
		Accounts Receivable, Jane Co.		6 0 0 0 00
		Received 60-day, 13% note for		
		extension of past due account		

Notes Receivable is a current asset on the balance sheet.

Notes Payable is a current liability on the balance sheet.

		BUYER—JANE COMPANY		
Sept.	1	Accounts Payable, Mace Co.	6 0 0 0 00	
		Notes Payable		6 0 0 0 00
		Issued 60-day, 13% note for		
		extension of past due account		

FIGURE 14.4 Note Paid at Maturity

SELLER—MACE COMPANY							
Oct.	31	Cash	6 1 3 0 00		
		Notes Receivable		6 0 0 0 00
		Interest Income		1 3 0 00
		Collected Jane Company note		

[$6,000 x .13 x $\frac{60}{360}$ = $130 Interest Income]

BUYER—JANE COMPANY							
Oct.	31	Notes Payable	6 0 0 0 00		
		Interest Expense	1 3 0 00		
		Cash		6 1 3 0 00
		Paid note to Mace Company		

[$6,000 x .13 x $\frac{60}{360}$ = $130 Interest Expense]

FIGURE 14.5 Note Renewed at Maturity

SELLER—MACE COMPANY							
Oct.	31	Cash	1 3 0 00		
		Notes Receivable (new)	6 0 0 0 00		
		Notes Receivable (old)		6 0 0 0 00
		Interest Income		1 3 0 00
		Interest of old note collected and		
		renewal of note for 90 days		

BUYER—JANE COMPANY							
Oct.	31	Notes Payable (old)	6 0 0 0 00		
		Interest Expense	1 3 0 00		
		Notes Payable (new)		6 0 0 0 00
		Cash		1 3 0 00
		Interest of old note paid and		
		renewal of note for 90 days		

Dishonored Note

Mace Company does not have to renew the note if Jane Company fails to pay it at maturity. In this situation the note is said to be a **dishonored note.** Another way to describe this situation is to say that Jane Company has **defaulted** on its note.

On Jane's and Mace's books the amounts in Notes Receivable and Notes Payable will then be removed and transferred back to Accounts Receivable and Accounts Payable, because the note has reached the maturity date. At the same time, whether the note is paid or not, the interest expense is due and payable and should be recorded (for Mace Company this is Interest Income, and for Jane Company it is Interest Expense).

Let's see what entries would look like if Jane Company first defaults and then finally pays the amount owed on December 1 (see Fig. 14.6 on the following page). To keep it simple, no additional charges will be calculated for the extra month Jane Company has taken to pay off the amount owed to Mace Company.

FIGURE 14.6 Note Dishonored and Repaid on Books of Seller and Buyer

			SELLER—MACE COMPANY					
(A) Oct.	31		Accounts Receivable, Jane Co.	6 1 3 0 00				
			Interest Income			1 3 0 00		
			Notes Receivable			6 0 0 0 00		
			Recorded note receivable dishonored					

> Only unmatured notes are in the Notes Receivable account.

			BUYER—JANE COMPANY					
(A) Oct.	31		Notes Payable	6 0 0 0 00				
			Interest Expense	1 3 0 00				
			Accounts Payable, Mace Co.			6 1 3 0 00		
			Recorded note payable dishonored					

			SELLER—MACE COMPANY					
(B) Dec.	1		Cash	6 1 3 0 00				
			Accounts Receivable, Jane Co.			6 1 3 0 00		
			Recorded payment of note					
			receivable dishonored					

			BUYER—JANE COMPANY					
(B) Dec.	1		Accounts Payable, Mace Co.	6 1 3 0 00				
			Cash			6 1 3 0 00		
			Payment of note payable dishonored					

Note Given in Exchange for Equipment Purchased

A note may be given in exchange for an asset that is purchased. For instance, suppose Jane Company decided to buy from Ronald Company some display racks for $7,000. Because the price was high, Jane Company gave a note instead of buying the racks on account. The note issued by Jane Company was a 60-day, 9% interest-bearing note for $7,000. This transaction is recorded on the books of the buyer and seller as shown in Figure 14.7.

When the note is paid at maturity, the same transactions discussed earlier would result.

FIGURE 14.7 Note Exchanged for an Asset

SELLER—RONALD COMPANY

May	9	Notes Receivable	7 0 0 0 00	
		Sales		7 0 0 0 00
		Sold display racks with a		
		60-day, 9% note		

BUYER—JANE COMPANY

May	9	Store Equipment	7 0 0 0 00	
		Notes Payable		7 0 0 0 00
		Purchased display racks with a		
		60-day, 9% note		

LEARNING UNIT 14-2 REVIEW

AT THIS POINT you should be able to

- Journalize entries for buyer and seller to record the extension of a past due account by issuing a note.
- Explain why a subsidiary ledger may not be needed with Notes Payable and Notes Receivable.
- Journalize entries for the buyer and seller to record renewal of a note, dishonoring of a note, eventual receipt of payment, and a note given in exchange for equipment purchased.

Self-Review Quiz 14-2

Journalize the following transactions for Action Company:

a. Action Company sold $8,000 of merchandise on account to Brian Company.
b. Action Company received a 60-day, $8,000, 12% note for a time extension of a past due account of Brian Company.
c. Collected the Brian Company note on the maturity date.
d. Brian Company renewed the note for 90 days and paid interest on the old note. (Alternative to step c.)
e. Assuming that Brian Company defaulted in step c, record the note receivable dishonored.
f. Brian Company paid the note receivable dishonored in step e.

Solution to Self-Review Quiz 14-2

FIGURE 14.8 Journalized Transactions of Action Company

(A)	Accounts Receivable, Brian Co.	8 0 0 0 00		
	Sales		8 0 0 0 00	
	Sold merchandise on account			
(B)	Notes Receivable	8 0 0 0 00		
	Accounts Receivable, Brian Co.		8 0 0 0 00	
	Started note at 12% for 60 days			
(C)	Cash	8 1 6 0 00		
	Interest Income		1 6 0 00	
	Notes Receivable		8 0 0 0 00	
	Collected Brian Co. note			
	($8,000 × .12 × $\frac{60}{360}$ = $160)			
(D)	Cash	1 6 0 00		
	Notes Receivable	8 0 0 0 00		
	Notes Receivable		8 0 0 0 00	
	Interest Income		1 6 0 00	
	Collected interest and renewed note for 90 days			
(E)	Accounts Receivable, Brian Company	8 1 6 0 00		
	Notes Receivable		8 0 0 0 00	
	Interest Income		1 6 0 00	
	Brian Co. defaulted on note			
(F)	Cash	8 1 6 0 00		
	Accounts Receivable, Brian Company		8 1 6 0 00	
	Brian Co. paid dishonored note			

Learning Unit 14-3 How to Discount Customers' Notes

> Think of the bank discount as the cost of cashing in a note before maturity.

Many times a company that accepts notes from customers will not (or cannot) wait to receive its cash until the maturity date. Instead, it goes to a bank and exchanges the note for cash. This process is called **discounting a note.** The company will endorse the note and receive the **maturity value** of the note (principal plus interest) less what the bank charges for holding the note from the date of discounting until the maturity date. The time period during which the bank holds the note (until maturity) is called the **discount period.**

The amount that the bank charges the company is called the **bank discount.** It is the difference between what the company receives from the bank and the maturity value of the note. The actual amount of money the company receives when a note is discounted is called the **proceeds** (maturity value less the bank discount).

Let's see how Marvin Company discounts an interest-bearing note receivable. The best way to understand the process is to take it step by step.

LO3 ## How to Discount an Interest-Bearing Note Receivable

> What Marvin Company will receive from the bank is called the proceeds.

Marvin Company received an $8,000, 90-day, 12% note from Jee Company dated October 1. On October 31 Marvin Company needed cash to finance its inventory, so it discounted the note to Blue Bank, which charges a bank discount rate of 14%. An overview of the process is shown in Figure 14.9.

Step 1 Find the *maturity* value of the note:

$$\text{(a) } \$8,000 \times .12 \times \frac{90}{360} = \$240 \text{ Interest}$$

Issue Date October 1	Date of Discount October 31	Maturity Date
Oct. 31 – Oct. 1 = 30 days	90 days – 30 days = 60 days = Discount Period	
Marvin Company holds note	Bank holds note	

| Face Value: $8,000 | | Maturity Value: $8,240 |

90 days

FIGURE 14.9 Discounting a Note Receivable, $8,000 at 12% for 90 Days

(b) Maturity Value = Principal + Interest
$$= \$8{,}000 + \$240$$
$$= \$8{,}240$$

Step 2 Calculate the *discount* period (number of days from the date of discounting until the maturity date):

90 Days	**Note**
– 30 Days	**Expired before discounting (Oct. 31 – Oct. 1)**
= 60 Days	**That bank holds note until it comes due**

Step 3 Calculate the bank discount (what the bank charges Marvin Company for holding the note until maturity). To do so, we use the following formula:

$$\frac{\textbf{Bank}}{\textbf{Discount}} = \frac{\textbf{Maturity}}{\textbf{Value}} \times \frac{\textbf{Bank Discount}}{\textbf{Rate}} \times \frac{\textbf{No. of Days Bank Holds Note Until Maturity}}{\textbf{360 Days}}$$

$$= \$8{,}240 \times .14 \times \frac{60}{360}$$
$$= \$192.27$$

Note that the bank discount is based on the maturity value, because we are borrowing the maturity value for the number of days in the discount period.

Step 4 Calculate the proceeds (what Marvin Company receives from the bank in the discounting process):

Proceeds = Maturity Value – Bank Discount
$$= \$8{,}240 - \$192.27$$
$$= \$8{,}047.73$$

> Journalizing the discounted note receivable:
> Proceeds $8,047.73
> Face   −8,000.00
> Interest income $ 47.73

If Marvin Company could have waited until the maturity date, it would have received $8,240. By discounting the note the company lost interest of $192.27, or the cost charged by the bank to hold the note until maturity. Let's look at how Marvin Company would record this item on its books (Fig. 14.10; again, for simplicity, we use general journal entries rather than special journals).

Oct.	31	Cash	8 0 4 7 73		
		Notes Receivable		8 0 0 0 00	
		Interest Income		4 7 73	
		Discounted Jee Company's			
		90-day, 12% note at 14%			

FIGURE 14.10 Discounting a Note with Interest Income

This transaction resulted in interest income because the proceeds Marvin Company received were more than the face value of the note ($8,000). In actuality, if the proceeds had been *less* than the $8,000, Marvin Company would have incurred an interest expense. For example, if Marvin Company held the note for only a short period of time and Blue Bank had a bank discount rate much higher than the original note, this would mean an interest expense rather than interest income. Suppose the note was discounted after being held only 2 days, and the bank's discount rate was 18%. The bank discount, or amount the bank charges, would be calculated as follows:

$$\text{Bank Discount} = \overset{\text{Maturity value}}{\overset{\uparrow}{\$8,240}} \times .18 \times \overset{\text{Discount period}}{\overset{\uparrow}{\dfrac{88}{360}}}$$

$$= \$362.56$$

Thus, the proceeds to Marvin Company would be

$$\text{Proceeds} = \$8,240 - \$362.56$$

$$= \$7,877.44$$

Note that here Marvin Company is receiving less than the $8,000 face value of the note. The general journal entry of Marvin Company would thus look as shown in Figure 14.11.

FIGURE 14.11 Discounting a Note with Interest Expense

Oct.	31	Cash	7 8 7 7 44	
		Interest Expense	1 2 2 56	
		Notes Receivable		8 0 0 0 00
		To record discount of note		

Procedure When a Discounted Note Is Dishonored

Note: If Marvin Company endorsed the note without recourse, it would not have any liability. Instead, the bank would have liability if Jee Company did not pay.

Who is liable for the note if Jee Company fails to pay the note at maturity? The answer is Marvin Company.

When Marvin Company endorsed the note to Blue Bank, it agreed to pay the note at maturity if Jee Company defaulted. The potential liability is called a **contingent liability.** Until the note is paid, Marvin Company will state this contingent liability as a footnote on its balance sheet.

At some point before maturity, Jee Company is notified that Blue Bank is holding the note. Let's assume that the maturity date is reached and Jee Company defaults. Blue Bank notifies Marvin Company and charges Marvin Company the full amount of the note, including interest and a $5 protest fee, which is the charge made by Blue Bank for notifying Marvin Company that the note was presented to the maker for payment and was not received. Thus, the bank charges Marvin Company (and Marvin will in turn charge Jee Company) the following:

Note	*$8,000*
Interest	*240*
Protest Fee	*5*
	$8,245

The entry is recorded on Marvin Company's book as shown in Figure 14.12.

FIGURE 14.12 Default of Discounted Note

Dec.	30	Accounts Receivable, Jee Co.	8 2 4 5 00	
		Cash		8 2 4 5 00
		To record default of discounted note		

You can be sure that Marvin Company will try to collect this $8,245 from Jee Company. Marvin Company may charge additional interest for this delay in paying the $8,245. For simplicity, we have left this step out. If the $8,245 becomes uncollectible, the account could be written off as a bad debt using the Allowance for Doubtful Accounts method discussed in Chapter 13.

LEARNING UNIT 14-3 REVIEW

AT THIS POINT you should be able to

- Define and explain discounting, maturity value, discount period, bank discount, and proceeds.
- Explain the four steps required in discounting an interest-bearing note receivable.
- Prepare a journal entry to record the proceeds of a note.
- Define contingent liability and compare it with an endorsement without recourse.
- Journalize the entry to record a discounted note that has been dishonored.

Self-Review Quiz 14-3

Al Gene Company received a $10,000, 60-day, 12% note from Broom Company dated July 5, 20XX. On August 3, Al Gene Company discounted the note to Ryan Bank, which charged a bank discount rate of 15%.

a. Complete the four steps to discount the note.
b. Journalize the entry to record the proceeds.
c. Journalize the entry if a default occurs, assuming a $5 protest fee.

Solution to Self-Review Quiz 14-3

a. Step 1 Maturity value (principal + interest):

$$I = \$10,000 \times .12 \times \frac{60}{360}$$
$$= \$200$$
$$MV = \$10,000 + \$200$$
$$= \$10,200$$

Step 2 Discount period:

July 31	
− 5	
26	**Days Al Gene Held Note in July**
3	**Days Al Gene Held Note in August**
29	**Days Al Gene Held Note**
60	**Days**
− 29	**Days**
31	**Days Bank Holds Note**

Step 3 Bank discount:

$$\frac{\textbf{Bank}}{\textbf{Discount}} = \frac{\textbf{Maturity}}{\textbf{Value}} \times \frac{\textbf{Bank Discount}}{\textbf{Rate}} \times \frac{\textbf{No. of Days Bank Holds Note Until Maturity}}{\textbf{360}}$$

$$= \$10,200 \times .15 \times \frac{31}{360}$$

(Step 1) (Given in facts)

$$= \$131.75$$

(continued on next page)

Step 4 Proceeds:

$$\text{Proceeds} = \text{Maturity Value} - \text{Bank Discount}$$
$$= \$10,200 - \$131.75$$
$$= \$10,068.25$$

FIGURE 14.13 Default of Note

b.	Aug.	3	Cash		10068 25		
			Notes Receivable			1000000	
			Interest Income				6825
			Discounted Broom Company				
			12% note at 15%				
c.	Sept.	3	Accounts Receivable, Broom Company		10205 00		
			Cash			10205 00	
			To record default				

LO4 Learning Unit 14-4 Discounting One's Own Note: Handling Adjustments for Interest Expense and Interest Income

Discounting One's Own Note

In the last unit we looked at how a note of a customer was discounted. Now our attention shifts to Jones Company, which is borrowing $10,000 by giving Alvin Bank its own 12%, 60-day note on December 16, 20XX. In this case, Alvin Bank deducts the interest in advance. The following is the formula to calculate the bank discount (cost of borrowing) and the proceeds (what Jones Company gets):

> Note that maturity value here is the same as the original principal because interest is deducted in advance.

$$\text{Bank Discount} = (\text{Maturity Value}) \times (\text{Interest Rate}) \times \frac{\text{Discount Period}}{360}$$
$$= \$10,000 \quad \times \quad .12 \quad \times \quad \frac{60}{360}$$
$$= \$200$$
$$\text{Proceeds} = \text{Maturity Value} - \text{Discount}$$
$$= \$10,000 - \$200$$
$$= \$9,800$$

> Discount on Notes Payable is a contra-liability.

Thus, Jones Company receives $9,800 and at the time of maturity will pay back $10,000. The $200 of interest is recorded in a new account called **Discount on Notes Payable.** This account is a contra-liability account that is subtracted from Notes Payable on the balance sheet, where it looks like the following:

Current Liabilities

Notes Payable	$10,000
Less: Discount on Notes Payable	200
	$9,800

Later in this unit, when we talk about adjustments, we see that as the note matures, the discount will be reduced and then charged to Interest Expense. For now, however, let's record the journal entry for Jones Company as it discounts its own note with interest deducted in advance (Fig. 14.14).

Dec.	16	Cash	9 8 0 0 00		
		Discount on Notes Payable	2 0 0 00		
		Notes Payable		1 0 0 0 0 00	
		Discounted own note at 12% for 60 days			

FIGURE 14.14 Discounted Note with Interest Deducted in Advance

Accounts Affected	Category	↑ ↓		Rules
Cash	Asset	↑	Dr.	$9,800
Discount on Notes Payable	Contra-Liability	↑	Dr.	$200
Notes Payable	Liability	↑	Cr.	$10,000

When the note is paid, the accountant will debit Notes Payable for $10,000 and credit Cash for $10,000.

Note: Although the bank interest rate is stated at 12%, the truth is that Jones Company really has the use of only $9,800. To calculate the true interest rate, which is called the **effective interest rate,** the following formula applies:

$$\text{Effective Interest Rate} = \frac{(\text{Maturity Value of Note}) \times (\text{Bank Interest Rate})}{\text{Amount of Cash Proceeds Received from Note}}$$

$$= \frac{\$10,000 \times .12}{\$9,800}$$

$$= 12.24\%$$

> Effective interest rate: The cost of borrowing the $10,000 is not 12% but really almost 12¼%.

Now let's look at how adjustments will be handled for some of the transactions presented in this chapter.

Interest: The Need for Adjustments

Because interest-bearing notes are often taken out and then paid off in different accounting periods, it is necessary to adjust or bring up-to-date Interest Income and Interest Expense. The following diagram shows why we need to adjust as well as who does the adjusting:

ACCRUED INTEREST INCOME	**ACCRUED INTEREST EXPENSE**
Must adjust for income that has been earned during the period but has not been received or recorded because payment is not yet due.	*Must adjust for interest that has been incurred during the period but has not been paid or recorded because payment is not yet due.*
↓	↓
Notes Receivable *(payee)*	(A) Note Payable *(maker)*
	(B) Company's own discounted note

> The payee is the seller and the maker is the buyer.

Let's look at how to record adjustments for Interest Income and Interest Expense from the following: Bog Company receives a $24,000, 60-day, 10% note on December 16, 200X, from Jan Company (see Fig. 14.15 on the following page).

Step 1 Calculate interest on the note:

$$\text{Interest} = \$24,000 \times .10 \times \frac{60}{360}$$

$$= \$400$$

FIGURE 14.15 Adjusting for Interest Accrued

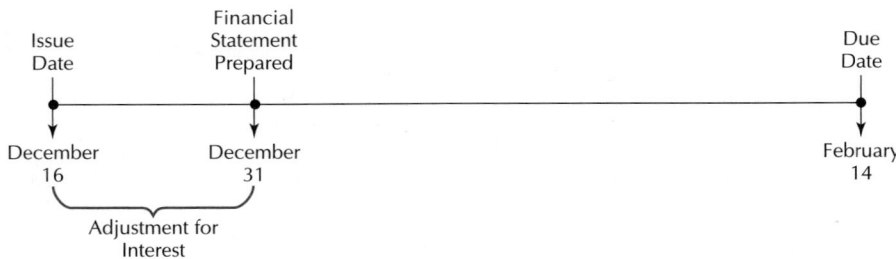

Step 2 Calculate the number of days the note has already run before the end of the current period (see Table 14.1):

Dec. 31	(end of period)
− Dec. 16	(starting date of note)
15	Days

Step 3 Calculate interest incurred for this period:

$$\text{Length of note} \rightarrow \frac{15 \text{ Days}}{60 \text{ Days}} = \frac{1}{4} \times \$400$$
$$= \$100$$

Another way to calculate the interest is

$$\$24,000 \times .10 \times \frac{15}{360} = \$100$$

Step 4 Prepare the adjusting journal entries (Fig. 14.16).

FIGURE 14.16 Adjustment for Interest on Note

On Books of *Seller* (Holder of Note)

Dec.	31	Interest Receivable	1 0 0 00	
		Interest Income		1 0 0 00
		Adj. for int.		
		for 15 days		

On Books of *Buyer* (Debtor)

Dec.	31	Interest Expense	1 0 0 00	
		Interest Payable		1 0 0 00
		Adj. for int.		
		for 15 days		

Interest Receivable

Dr.	Cr.
100	
Current Asset on balance sheet	

Interest Expense

Dr.	Cr.
100	
Other Expense on income statement	

Interest Income

Dr.	Cr.
	100
	Other Income on income statement

Interest Payable

Dr.	Cr.
	100
	Current Liability on balance sheet

When the note is paid off on February 14, the first two entries are made, assuming that no reversing entry is used, as shown in Figure 14.17.

Seller

	Feb.	14	Cash	24 4 0 0 00		
			Interest Receivable			1 0 0 00
			Notes Receivable			24 0 0 0 00
			Interest Income			3 0 0 00
			Received payment of note			

FIGURE 14.17 No Reversing Entry

Buyer

	Feb.	14	Notes Payable	24 0 0 0 00		
			Interest Expense	3 0 0 00		
			Interest Payable	1 0 0 00		
			Cash		24 4 0 0 00	
			Paid off note			

Note that by not using reversing entries, the bookkeepers of the buyer and seller had to look up the amount of accrued interest that was recorded in the *old* year so that this year's interest expense or income would not be overstated.

If a reversing entry (which is optional) is used, the entries shown in Figure 14.18 are made.

Seller

	Feb.	14	Cash	24 4 0 0 00		
			Notes Receivable			24 0 0 0 00
			Interest Income			4 0 0 00
			Received payment of note			

FIGURE 14.18 Reversing Entry Made

Buyer

	Feb.	14	Notes Payable	24 0 0 0 00		
			Interest Expense	4 0 0 00		
			Cash		24 4 0 0 00	
			Paid off note			

The last adjustment deals with a firm discounting its own note. At the beginning of this unit, we saw Jones Company discounting its own note on December 16 for $10,000 for 60 days at 12% interest. Jones Company actually received $9,800 and recorded the $200 interest deducted in advance by the bank in a contra-liability account called *Discount on Notes Payable.*

Discount on Notes Payable		**Interest Expense**	
Dr.	**Cr.**	**Dr.**	**Cr.**
200			

At the end of December, 15 out of the 60 days have passed. Thus, fifteen days' worth of interest on this note should be recorded in the old year. To record this interest, we reduce the amount in the Discount on Notes Payable by $50 ($10,000 × .12 × 15/360). The journal entry shown in Figure 14.19 on the following page is made.

FIGURE 14.19 Recording Interest and Reducing Balance of Discount on Notes Payable

Dec.	31	Interest Expense		50 00			
		Discount on Notes Payable				50 00	
		Recognition of expense incurred					

Accounts Affected	Category	↑ ↓	Rules	
Interest Expense	Other Expense	↑	Dr.	$50
Discount on Notes Payable	Contra-Liability	↓	Cr.	$50

The current liability on the balance sheet will look as follows:

$10,000 × 12% × 45 days remaining in the new year

> **Current Liabilities**
> **Notes Payable**   **$10,000**
> **Less: Discount on Notes Payable**   150
>   **$9,850**

When the note is paid, the journal entry shown in Figure 14.20 will result.

FIGURE 14.20 Note Paid Off

Feb.	14	Notes Payable	10 0 0 0 00			
		Interest Expense	1 50 00			
		Discount on Notes Payable			1 50 00	
		Cash			10 0 0 0 00	
		Note paid				

LEARNING UNIT 14-4 REVIEW

AT THIS POINT you should be able to

- Explain the purpose of the Discount on Notes Payable account.
- Calculate the effective interest rate.
- Make adjustments for interest income and interest expense at the end of the period.
- Adjust the Discount on Notes Payable account.

Self-Review Quiz 14-4

Respond true or false to the following:

1. No bank deducts interest in advance.
2. Discount on Notes Payable is a contra-liability account.
3. When Discount on Notes Payable is reduced, Interest Expense results.
4. The effective rate of interest is lower than the stated rate.
5. Reversing entries are never used to adjust interest at the end of a period of time.

Solutions to Self-Review Quiz 14-4

1. False   2. True   3. True   4. False   5. False

CHAPTER ASSIGNMENTS

SUMMARY OF KEY POINTS

LEARNING UNIT 14-1

1. A promissory note is a written promise by a borrower to pay a certain sum of money to a lender at a fixed future date. The note may be interest-bearing or non-interest-bearing.
2. The payee is the party to whom the note is payable.
3. The maker is the one who will pay the promissory note.
4. Maturity date is the time when the note comes due.
5. $\text{Interest} = \text{Principal} \times \text{Rate} \times \dfrac{\text{Number of Days}}{360}$

LEARNING UNIT 14-2

1. Notes Payable is a current liability on the balance sheet.
2. Notes do not need subsidiary ledgers.
3. Interest Income for the payee is Interest Expense for the maker.
4. A note that is not paid at maturity is said to be dishonored.
5. Notes may be renewed as well as issued to buy assets.

LEARNING UNIT 14-3

1. Maturity Value = Principal + Interest.
2. Discount period is equal to the number of days from date of discounting until the maturity date.
3. The bank discount is what the bank charges for holding a note until the maturity date, as shown in the formula:

$$\begin{matrix} \text{Bank} \\ \text{Discount} \end{matrix} = \begin{matrix} \text{Maturity} \\ \text{Value} \end{matrix} \times \begin{matrix} \text{Bank Discount} \\ \text{Rate} \end{matrix} \times \dfrac{\text{No. of Days Bank Holds Note Until Maturity}}{360 \text{ Days}}$$

4. Proceeds are what one receives from the bank in the discounting process (the maturity value minus the bank discount).
5. If a discounted note is dishonored, the original holder of the note may be liable for payment unless the note was endorsed without recourse. This liability is called *contingent liability.*

LEARNING UNIT 14-4

1. In discounting one's own note, the interest is deducted in advance.
2. The interest that is deducted in advance is recorded in a contra-liability account called Discount on Notes Payable.
3. The effective interest rate is higher than the stated rate.
4. At the end of the period, adjustments are made for Interest Income and Interest Expense that have accrued or built up. These entries can be reversed on the first day starting the next period to simplify recording when interest is paid or received in the new period.
5. The interest in the Discount on Notes Payable account is adjusted by reducing the Discount on Notes Payable and recording it as Interest Expense.

KEY TERMS

Bank discount What the bank charges to hold a note until maturity (Maturity Value − Proceeds).

Contingent liability Liability on the part of one who discounts a note if the maker of the note defaults at maturity date.

Default Failure of maker to pay the maturity value of a note when due.

Discounting a note The process or act of transferring the note to a bank before the maturity date.

Discount on Notes Payable The amount of interest deducted in advance by the lender. This account reduces Notes Payable.

Discount period The amount of time the bank holds a note that was discounted until the maturity date.

Dishonored note A note that was not paid at maturity by the maker.

Effective interest rate The true rate of simple interest.

Interest The cost of using money for a period of time.

Maker One promising to pay a note.

Maturity date Due date of the promissory note.

Maturity value The amount of the note that is due on the date of maturity (Principal + Interest).

Note payable A promissory note from the maker's point of view.

Note receivable A promissory note from the payee's point of view.

Payee One to whom a note is payable.

Principal The face amount of the note.

Proceeds Maturity value less bank discount.

Promissory note A formal written promise by a borrower to pay a certain sum at a fixed future date.

QUESTIONS, CLASSROOM DEMONSTRATION EXERCISES, EXERCISES, AND PROBLEMS

Discussion and Critical Thinking Questions/Ethical Case

1. List three reasons why a company may use Notes Payable instead of Accounts Payable and whether the company is the maker or payee.

2. Explain the parts of a promissory note.

3. What is the difference between finding a maturity date by (a) days or (b) months?

4. Notes Receivable is a current liability on the balance sheet. Accept or reject. Why?

5. Why is a subsidiary ledger not needed for notes?

6. Only matured notes are listed in the Notes Receivable account. Agree or disagree? Please discuss.

7. Explain what will happen if a maker defaults on a note. (Assume the note has not been discounted.)

8. List the four steps to arrive at proceeds in the process of discounting a note.

9. What is meant by a contingent liability?

10. When could interest be deducted in advance by a lender?

11. What is the normal balance of the Discount on Notes Payable account?

12. How is the effective interest rate calculated?

13. How could Discount on Notes Payable be adjusted?

14. Kevin Hoffaman works as a teller in Victory Bank. Yesterday, he looked up confidential information about promissory notes concerning several friends. Kevin told his girlfriend all about the confidential information. Do you think Kevin acted appropriately? You make the call. Write down your recommendations to Kevin.

BLUEPRINT: NOTES PAYABLE AND NOTES RECEIVABLE

	Seller (Payee)	**Buyer (Maker)**
Sales of merchandise on account	Accounts Receivable, XXX 　Sales 　Sold on account	Purchases 　Accounts Payable, XXX 　Bought on account
Time extension with a note	Notes Receivable 　Accounts Receivable, XXX 　Transferred to Note Rec.	Accounts Payable, XXX 　Notes Payable 　Transferred to Note Pay.
Note due and paid	Cash 　Interest Income 　Notes Receivable 　Received payment	Notes Payable Interest Expense 　Cash 　Paid off note
Note renewed at maturity	Cash Notes Receivable (new) 　Notes Receivable (old) 　Interest Income 　Renewed note	Notes Payable Interest Expense 　Notes Payable (new) 　Cash 　Renewed note
Note given in exchange for equipment purchased	Notes Receivable 　Sales 　Sold on Note Rec.	Store Equipment 　Notes Payable 　Bought equip. for note

BLUEPRINT: NOTES PAYABLE AND NOTES RECEIVABLE (CONTINUED)

Situations Affecting Seller Only

Discounting a note— receiving more than face value

Cash		
Interest Income		
Notes Receivable		
Discounted note at the bank		

Discounting a note— receiving less than face value

Cash		
Interest Expense		
Notes Receivable		
Discounted note at the bank		

Discounted note dishonored

Accounts Receivable, XXX		
Cash		
Discounted customer note		

Situation Borrowing from Bank

Discounting one's own note

Cash		
Discount on Notes Payable		
Notes Payable		
Borrowed with a discount		

BLUEPRINT: NOTES PAYABLE AND NOTES RECEIVABLE (CONTINUED)

Adjustments	Seller	Buyer

Adjust interest	20X1 Dec. 31 Interest Receivable
	    Interest Income
	       Interest adj.
		20X1 Dec. 31 Interest Expense
		    Interest Payable
		       Interest adj.

Note paid
(no reversing entry
was made)
	20X2 Feb. 1 Cash
	    Interest Receivable
	    Interest Income
	    Notes Receivable
	       Received cash from note
		20X2 Feb. 1 Interest Expense
		Interest Payable
		Notes Payable
		    Cash
		       Paid cash for note

Note paid
(reversing entry
was made)
	Feb. 1 Cash
	    Interest Income
	    Notes Receivable
	       Received cash from note
		Feb. 1 Interest Expense
		Notes Payable
		    Cash
		       Paid cash for note

Recognizing interest
from Discount on
Notes Payable
	Dec. 31 Interest Expense
	    Discount on Notes Payable
	       Adjustment for interest	

Classroom Demonstration Exercises

SET A

LO1 (10 min) **Determining Maturity Date**

1. Find the maturity date of the following:
   a. 120-day note dated May 8.
   b. 90-day note dated November 9.

LO1 (15 min) **Calculate Maturity Value**

2. Find the maturity value of the following:
   a. $9,000   4%   8 months
   b. $12,000   6%   80 days

LO2 (15 min) **Recording Notes for Buyer and Seller**

3. For each of the following transactions for Bloe Co. (the seller), journalize what the entry would be for the buyer (Lee Co.).

a. Accounts Receivable, Lee Co.	8,000	
Sales		8,000
Sold on account to Lee Co.		
b. Notes Receivable	8,000	
Accounts Receivable, Lee Co.		8,000
Transferred to Notes Rec.		
c. Cash	8,110	
Notes Receivable		8,000
Interest Income		110
Note paid by Lee Co. on due date		

LO3 (20 min) **Discounting a Note**

4. Jill Jay discounted a $10,000, 7%, 90-day note at Friend Bank. She recorded the following entry:

Cash	10,100	
Notes Receivable		10,000
Interest Income		100

How much interest did Jill Jay lose by discounting the note?

LO3 (20 min) **Four Steps in the Discounting Process**

5. Lou Co. received a $2,000, 5%, 60-day note from You Co. dated August 6. On August 30 Lou discounted the note at Reel Bank, which charged a discount rate of 7%. Calculate the following:
   a. Maturity value
   b. Discount period
   c. Bank discount
   d. Proceeds

LO3 (15 min) **Journal Entry for Discounting**

6. Journalize the discounted note for Lou from Exercise 5.

LO3 (15 min) **Defaulting**

7. If You Co. defaults on the note from Exercise 5, what would be the journal entry for Lou Co., assuming a $5 protest fee?

Discounting One's Own Note   *LO3 (10 min)*

8. Range Co. discounts its own note at a bank. This $6,000 note results in the bank deducting $400 interest in advance. Draw a transactional analysis box for this situation.

Adjusting the Discount   *LO4 (10 min)*

9. If in Exercise 8 $50 of the discount needs to be adjusted at year-end, what would be the journalized adjusting entry?

SET B

Determining Maturity Date   *LO1 (10 min)*

1. Find the maturity date of the following:
   a. 120-day note dated July 8.
   b. 90-day note dated October 8.

Calculate Maturity Value   *LO1 (15 min)*

2. Find the maturity value of the following:
   a. $6,000   6%   9 months
   b. $8,000   7%   70 days

Recording Notes for Buyer and Seller   *LO2 (15 min)*

3. For each of the following transactions for Frank Co. (the seller), journalize what the entry would be for the buyer (Bore Co.).

   a. Accounts Receivable, Bore Co.   7,000
          Sales   7,000
              Sold on account
   b. Notes Receivable   7,000
          Accounts Receivable, Bore Co.   7,000
              Transferred to Notes Rec.
   c. Cash   7,140
          Notes Receivable   7,000
          Interest Income   140

Discounting a Note   *LO3 (20 min)*

4. Pete Jones discounted a $9,000, 8%, 90-day note at Friend Bank. He recorded the following entry:

   Cash   9,100
          Notes Receivable   9,000
          Interest Income   100

   How much interest did Pete Jones lose by discounting the note?

Four Steps in the Discounting Process   *LO3 (20 min)*

5. Blue Co. received a $1,000, 6%, 60-day note from Aluin Co. dated August 10. On August 30 Blue Co. discounted the note at Reel Bank, which charged a discount rate of 8%. Calculate the following:
   a. Maturity value
   b. Discount period
   c. Bank discount
   d. Proceeds

Journal Entry for Discounting   *LO3 (15 min)*

6. Journalize the discounted note for Blue Co. from Exercise 5.

LO3 (15 min)   **Defaulting**

   7. If Aluin defaults on the note from Exercise 5, what would be the journal entry for Blue Co., assuming a $5 protest fee?

LO3 (10 min)   **Discounting One's Own Note**

   8. Aster Co. discounts its own note at a bank. This $5,000 note results in the bank deducting $300 interest in advance. Draw a transactional analysis box for this situation.

LO4 (10 min)   **Adjusting the Discount**

   9. If in Exercise 8 $100 of the discount needs to be adjusted at year-end, what would be the journalized adjusting entry?

Exercises

LO1 (15 min)   **14-1.** Calculate the interest for the following:

   a. $15,000   3%   1 year
   b. $20,000   10%   7 months
   c. $ 9,000   12%   80 days

LO1 (15 min)   **14-2.** Determine the maturity date for each of the following without the use of tables:

Note Issued	Length of Time
a. January 17, 20X4	30 days
b. July 14, 20X4	90 days
c. May 31, 20X4	4 months
d. June 25, 20X4	75 days

LO1 (15 min)   **14-3.** Use the table in the text to prove your answers for Exercise 14-2.

LO2 (15 min)   **14-4.** On May 15, 20X4, Ralph Co. gave Blue Co. a 180-day, $9,000, 8% note. On July 21, Blue Co. discounted the note at 9%.

   a. Journalize the entry for Blue to record the proceeds.
   b. Record the entry for Blue if Ralph fails to pay at maturity.

LO2 (15 min)   **14-5.** Jamie Slater negotiated a bank loan for $30,000 for 120 days at a bank rate of 10%. Assuming the interest is deducted in advance, prepare the entry for Jamie to record the bank loan.

Group A Problems

LO2 (30 min)   **14A-1.** Journalize the following entries for (1) the buyer and (2) the seller. Record all entries for the buyer first.

20X9		
June	11	Lee Company sold $8,000 of merchandise on account to Rover Company.
July	11	Lee Company received a 90-day, $5,000, 8% note for a time extension of a past due account of Rover Company.
Oct.	9	Collected the Rover Company note on the maturity date.
Oct.	9	Assume Rover Company defaulted on its July 11 note and record the dishonored note.
Oct.	15	Rover Company paid the note receivable that was dishonored on October 9 (no additional interest is charged).

Check Figure:
Oct. 9 Interest Income and
Interest Expense $100

LO3 (35 min)   **14A-2.** On May 1, 20X4, Apples Company received a $30,000, 90-day, 9% note from Fletcher Company dated May 1. On June 20, 20X4, Apples discounted the note at Run Bank at a discount rate of 10%.

1. Calculate the following:
   a. Maturity value of the note
   b. Number of days the bank will hold the note until maturity date
   c. Bank discount
   d. Proceeds
2. Journalize the entry to record the proceeds.

> **Check Figure:**
> Proceeds $30,334.17

14A-3. Journalize the following transactions for Joye Company:

LO3, 4 (25 min)

20X1		
June	18	Joye discounted its own $40,000, 90-day note at National Bank at 10%.
Sept.	16	Paid the amount due on the note of June 18. (Be sure to record interest expense from Discount on Notes Payable.)
Nov.	2	Joye discounted its own $20,000, 120-day note at National Bank at 11%.
Dec.	31	Record the adjusting entry for interest expense.

> **Check Figure:**
> Nov. 2 Discount on Notes
> Payable $733.33

14A-4. Journalize the following transactions for Rochester Company:

LO1, 2, 3, 4 (60 min)

20XX		
Apr.	18	Received a $15,000, 80-day, 11% note from Mark Castle in payment of account past due.
May	9	Wrote off the Hal Balmer account as uncollectible for $600. (Rochester uses the Allowance method to record bad debts.)
July	7	Mark Castle paid Rochester the note in full.
Nov.	11	Gave Reech Company a $9,000, 30-day, 12% note as a time extension of account now past due.
Nov.	15	Hal Balmer paid Rochester amount previously written off on May 9.
Dec.	3	Discounted its own $5,000, 90-day note at Tree Bank at 10%.
Dec.	5	Received a $10,000, 60-day, 12% note dated December 5 from Beverly Fields in payment of account past due.
Dec.	11	Paid principal and interest due on note issued to Reech Company from November 11 note.
Dec.	16	Received a $20,000, 60-day, 11% note from Larry Company in payment of account past due.
Dec.	28	Discounted the Beverly Fields note to Realty Bank at 13%.
Dec.	31	Recorded adjusting entries as appropriate.

> **Check Figure:**
> Dec. 31 Interest Expense
> $38.89

Group B Problems

14B-1. Journalize the following entries for (1) the buyer and (2) the seller.

LO2 (30 min)

20X9		
July	10	Lee Company sold $8,000 of merchandise on account to Connors Company.
Aug.	10	Lee Company received a 90-day, $6,000, 9% note for a time extension of past due account of Rover Company.
Nov.	8	Collected the Rover Company note on the maturity date.
Nov.	8	Assuming Rover Company defaulted on November 8, record the dishonored note.
Nov.	16	Rover Company paid the note receivable that was dishonored on November 8 (no additional interest is charged).

> **Check Figure:**
> Nov. 8 Interest Expense and
> Interest Income $135

LO3 (35 min)

14B-2. On June 2, 20X4, Apples Company received a $40,000, 90-day, 11% note from Fletcher Company dated June 2. On July 16, 20X4, Apples discounted the note at Run Bank at a discount rate of 12%.

1. Calculate the following:
   a. Maturity value of the note
   b. Number of days the bank will hold the note until maturity date
   c. Bank discount
   d. Proceeds
2. Journalize the entry to record the proceeds.

Check Figure:
Proceeds $40,469.80

LO3, 4 (25 min)

14B-3. As the bookkeeper of Joye Company, record in the general journal the following transactions:

20X2		
May	9	Joye Company discounted its own $25,000, 90-day note at National Bank at 10%.
Aug.	7	Paid the amount due on the note of May 9. (Be sure to record interest expense from Discount on Notes Payable.)
Oct.	7	Joye Company discounted its own $18,000, 120-day note at National Bank at 11%.
Dec.	31	Record the adjusting entry for Interest Expense.

Check Figure:
Dec. 31 Interest Expense
$467.50

LO1, 2, 3, 4 (60 min)

14B-4. Record the following entries into the general journal of Rochester Company:

20XX		
May	12	Received $13,000, 90-day, 9% note from Mark Castle in payment of account past due.
June	15	Wrote off the Hal Balmer account as uncollectible for $900 using the Allowance method.
Aug.	10	Mark Castle paid Rochester the note in full.
Nov.	2	Gave Reech Company a $20,000, 30-day, 8% note as a time extension of account now past due.
Nov.	18	Hal Balmer paid Rochester amount previously written off on June 15.
Dec.	2	Discounted its own $10,000, 90-day note at Tree Bank at 9%.
Dec.	2	Received a $6,000, 60-day, 11% note dated December 3 from Beverly Fields in payment of account past due.
Dec.	2	Paid principal and interest due on note issued to Reech Company from November 2 note.
Dec.	16	Received a $2,000, 60-day, 11% note from Larry Company in payment of account past due.
Dec.	28	Discounted the Beverly Fields note to Realty Bank at 12%.
Dec.	31	Recorded adjusting entries as appropriate.

Check Figure:
Dec. 31 Interest Income $9.17

ON-THE-JOB TRAINING

LO3 (40 min)

T-1. Abby Scale, the bookkeeper of Roland Company, is having difficulty calculating the amount that is due Agent Company on March 19. Based on the following information, prepare a detailed calculation of the amount due Agent Company.

Roland issued Agent Company a $2,000, 60-day, 12% note dated December 19, 20X1. Roland was notified by Alvin Bank that the note had been discounted by Agent Company and that the note would be payable to Alvin Bank. On February 18, the bookkeeper of Roland became ill and the note wasn't paid. Alvin Bank notified Agent Company and charged it an additional $9 protest fee. On March 19, Abby decided to pay Agent Company the amount owed. Agent Company indicated it was charging the maturity value of the note, the protest fee, and interest on *both* for 30 days beyond maturity at 14%. Do you think these charges are fair? Make your recommendation in writing.

T-2. Moe Ring has left the following notes on your desk. As the new bookkeeper of Ryan Company, you realize that no adjusting entries were made in 20X1.   *LO4 (20 min)*

Notes Receivable	
11/25/X1	$20,000
12%	150 days

Notes Payable	
12/16/X1	$33,600
15%	30 days

a. Please prepare the appropriate adjusting entries.

b. Moe would like to know whether reversing entries are needed. Prepare a set of T accounts to show what would result on the books in the year 20X2 when the notes are paid (1) if no reversing entries are made and (2) if reversing entries are made. Provide Moe with a written justification for the use of reversing entries.

FINANCIAL REPORT PROBLEM

Reading the Kellogg's Annual Report   *LO1 (15 min)*

Go to Appendix A and find the Consolidated Statement of Earnings. What was interest expense in 2005 and 2006?

INTERNET PROJECT

Aeropostale

Go to the Web and search: Annual Report Aeropostale 2008.
Click on Investors Relations.
List out the latest news Aeropostale is providing to its investors.
Order a free annual report.

CONTINUING PROBLEM

Sanchez Computer Center   *LO1 (20 min)*

Several banks have offered loans to the Sanchez Computer Center for its expansion. However, Freedman wants to weigh each option to determine the best financial situation for the company. Currently, the Sanchez Computer Center is trying to collect from its customers to strengthen the cash flow of the business.

Assignment

Using the information provided by each bank, determine the due date and interest amount for each.

Bank of America	A 90-day note dated April 15 for $20,000 at a 6% interest rate
Bank One	A 120-day note dated April 10 for $40,000 at a 5% interest rate
Capital One Bank	A 75-day note dated April 5 for $30,000 at a 4% interest rate

SUBWAY Case

SIGNS OF THE TIMES

LO 1, 2, 3 (25 min)

"Perfecto!" Stan shouted up to his friends Javier and Miguel. The two men had just launched their own handyman service, and Stan had given them their first job: installing his new Subway "face" sign—the sign with the Subway logo that goes on the front of the restaurant.

Six months ago, Subway had notified all franchisees that they would be required to install signs with the new logo.

"To tell you the truth, Stan," said Rashid, "I can't see that there's much difference between the old sign and the new one."

"Well, it's a rather subtle change—the Subway lettering is closer together, less curvy, and slants to the right rather than straight up and down," said Stan. "But there's nothing subtle about the cost," he laughed. "Five grand!"

"Whew." Rashid's jaw dropped. "All that for a new slant?"

"As it happens," said Stan, "Subway did mounds of marketing research and found that customers perceive the slanting letters to mean speedier service. Anyway, now that there's a new logo, any stores that have the old one immediately look out-of-date."

The $5,000, Stan mused later, was nothing compared to what he would have to spend to remodel his entire restaurant in the next year or two. Subway Restaurants had recently announced the first complete interior and exterior revamp in the company's history. Called "Tuscany Décor," the new design includes earth tones, wood finishing, brass rails, tiled flooring, and brick textured walls. Stan was impressed when it was unveiled at the last franchisee convention; not only would the new décor be a better match for the chain's commitment to healthy, fresh food, but it would also attract the more upscale customers moving into the area. Still, how to pay for it?

Stan was in a position not uncommon for businesses of all sizes: the need to spend money to make more money. After spending $3,000 on his new bake oven, Stan didn't have the capital to spend $5,000 on a new sign—not to mention the thousands that he would have to spend to redo the interior with the new Tuscany décor. He checked the interest rates at his bank and calculated what it would cost him to repay a note with a principal of $5,000, an interest rate of 9%, and a time of 120 days.

$$\$5{,}000 \times .09 \times \frac{120}{360} = \$150$$

"150 bucks," thought Stan. "That's steep. I wonder if I could do better at another bank?" Stan then checked with Country Bank. It offered him $5,000, an interest rate of 8¾%, and a time of 90 days.

$$\$5{,}000 \times .0875 \times \frac{90}{360} = \$109.38$$

"Just a little over $100 is more like it," thought Stan, "but how can I pay it back in only three months? That really puts the pressure on. Is it worth the $41 difference to pay back the loan so fast? It's 30 days less or $41 less. In either case I can deduct the interest from my taxes as a business expense. But, what about when I take out a loan for the remodel? The difference will be in hundreds of dollars. Hmmm. Time to call Lila!"

Discussion Questions

1. Which loan would you take if you were in Stan's place? Why?
2. Assume Stan wanted the loan on October 1. What is the maturity date for the 90-day loan? The 120-day loan?
3. Why do some loans use 360 days and other loans 365? Which would be better for Stan?

15

Accounting for Merchandise Inventory

DID YOU KNOW? ExxonMobil uses LIFO to determine the cost of crude oil products and merchandise. Visit *www.exxonmobil.com* to find more information about ExxonMobil.

LEARNING OBJECTIVES

1. Understanding and journalizing transactions using the perpetual inventory system and explaining the difference between perpetual and periodic inventory systems.

2. Maintaining a subsidiary ledger for inventory; calculating cost of ending inventory for perpetual inventory.

3. Understanding periodic methods of determining the value of the ending inventory.

4. Estimating ending inventory using the retail method and gross profit method and understanding how the ending inventory amount affects financial reports.

With the high price of oil ExxonMobil must continually monitor its inventory as well as research development costs.

In Chapter 11 we discussed the periodic inventory system. A major weakness of the periodic system is that inventory is checked and counted only at the end of the accounting period and therefore managers do not know the actual amount of inventory on hand nor the actual cost of goods sold until the end of the accounting period. Today, with computers in so many businesses, the trend is toward perpetual inventory. Managers need to have *current* information about how much of their capital is tied up in inventory, and they need to have *current* information about the profitability of their sales of merchandise. The *perpetual* system of accounting for merchandise inventory provides this information on a transaction-by-transaction basis. Managers can know the balance of inventory and the profitability of sales as soon as each sale is completed. The perpetual system requires extra time and effort to gain these benefits, but, fortunately, computers can handle much of the detail. In this chapter we look at how the perpetual inventory system can be used in a merchandising business. We also compare the perpetual system to the periodic system.

In the last part of the chapter we discuss how to assign costs to inventory using the *periodic inventory system,* because many businesses with small inventories still use this system.

> QuickBooks and Peachtree have inventory modules available to keep track of inventory (perpetual system); however, the key to getting useful information is to maintain and keep the inventory system through the use of purchase orders, sales invoices, and fully entering all data on new merchandise.

LO1 Learning Unit 15-1 Perpetual Inventory System

In the **perpetual inventory system*** we have two key accounts: Merchandise Inventory and Cost of Goods Sold.

The Merchandise Inventory account is an asset account that will reveal the current balance of inventory at all times (perpetually). This account is the same one used in the previous discussion of the periodic inventory system, but in the periodic system the balance of the Merchandise Inventory was correct *only* at the end of each accounting period. In the perpetual system entries will be recorded to the Merchandise Inventory account each time the store purchases new merchandise and each time the store sells merchandise to a customer.

The other key account is the Cost of Goods Sold account. As merchandise is sold to customers, an entry will be recorded that will remove the cost of the merchandise from the Merchandise Inventory account and transfer that cost to the Cost of Goods Sold account. Thus, the Merchandise Inventory account will show the correct cost for the inventory on hand, and the Cost of Goods Sold account will show the cumulative total cost of all merchandise that has been sold to customers during the accounting period.

With the perpetual inventory system the key accounts, Merchandise Inventory and Cost of Goods Sold, will always provide current information to managers about their investment in inventory and the cost of the merchandise sold to customers.

Accounts Affected	Category	↑ ↓	Rules
Merchandise Inventory	Asset	↑	Dr.
Cost of Goods Sold	Cost of Goods Sold	↑	Dr.

You have been hired to work for a software retail business called Painless Bytes. A best seller for Painless Bytes is an accounting software package called A-I-B, (<u>A</u>lways <u>I</u>n <u>B</u>alance). Let's record some transactions relating to buying and selling A-I-B software. Because most businesses buy their merchandise inventory on account, we use Accounts Payable in the transactions.

---

*Learning Unit 10-4 in Chapter 10 covered perpetual inventory systems.

20XX
June   2   Purchased 10 packages of A-I-B software at a cost of $25 per package for a total of $250.

Note that the asset account, Merchandise Inventory, has been increased by the cost of the new merchandise we have purchased (Fig. 15.1).

June	2	Merchandise Inventory		2 5 0 00		
		Accounts Payable			2 5 0 00	
		To record the purchase of inventory				

FIGURE 15.1 Purchase of Inventory in Perpetual System

Now let's look at a sales transaction.

20XX
June   3   Sold three software packages for cash to a customer at $50 each for a total of $150.

Note that in the perpetual inventory system we record both the retail value of the sale (three units at $50) in the Sales Revenue account and the cost of the sale (three units at $25) in the Cost of Goods Sold account with two related transactions (Fig. 15.2).

June	3	Cash		1 5 0 00		
		Sales Revenue			1 5 0 00	
		To record sale of three packages of A-I-B				
June	3	Cost of Goods Sold		7 5 00		
		Merchandise Inventory			7 5 00	
		To record the cost of goods sold				

FIGURE 15.2 Matching Sales to Cost of Goods Sold

What if the customer returns one of the packages? Assuming that the returned package is still in new condition, here is what we would record:

20XX
June   5   Allowed the customer to return one package for a cash refund, $50.

In this transaction (Fig. 15.3) we must record the reduction in revenue of $50 and we must also record that we now have returned one package of software to our inventory by adding the $25 cost of that unit back to the Merchandise Inventory account.

June	5	Sales Returns and Allowances		5 0 00		
		Cash			5 0 00	
		To record the return of one				
		package of A-I-B				

FIGURE 15.3 Sales Return to Seller

June	5	Merchandise Inventory		2 5 00		
		Cost of Goods Sold			2 5 00	
		To record return of one package of				
		A-I-B at cost				

20XX

June   6   Returned one damaged A-I-B software package from the June 2 purchase.

Once in a while a business may have to return some inventory that came in damaged or for some other reason. Painless Bytes would prepare a debit memo. Let's see how this transaction is handled in a perpetual inventory system.

This transaction (Fig. 15.4) reduced what is owed the vendor by $25, the cost of the package, and we reduced the Asset account—Merchandise Inventory—because we returned the item to the vendor. *Note:* We do not use a Purchases Returns and Allowances account when we are recording in a perpetual inventory system. The Asset account Merchandise Inventory is directly reduced by the amount we returned to our vendor.

FIGURE 15.4 Return by Buyer of Merchandise

June	6	Accounts Payable		2 5 00		
		Merchandise Inventory				2 5 00
		To record return of damaged A-I-B				
		package to vendor				

Now let's look at how these transactions relate to the accounts and to the financial statements. In the T accounts in Figure 15.5 you can see that the Merchandise Inventory account shows the correct balance for the seven software packages remaining in inventory and that the Cost of Goods Sold account shows the correct amount for the cost of the two software packages actually sold. Asset accounts such as Merchandise Inventory are shown on the balance sheet, and the Sales and Cost of Goods Sold accounts appear on the income statement. Remember that we calculate Gross Profit when we subtract Cost of Goods Sold from Sales. In fact, we know the gross profit on each sale just as soon as the sale is completed.

FIGURE 15.5 General Ledger Accounts

GENERAL LEDGER ACCOUNTS

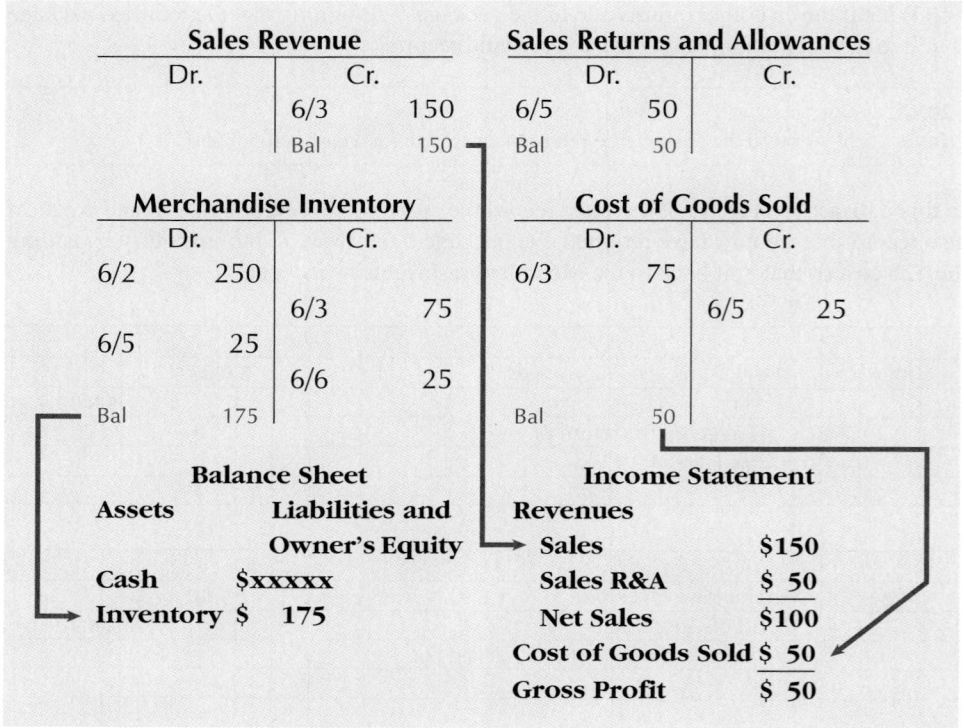

Comparison of the Perpetual and Periodic Inventory Systems

In our discussion of the perpetual inventory system, the primary benefit from this system is that the value of merchandise inventory is known after every purchase and sale. The cost of goods sold is known after every sale. The Merchandise Inventory account becomes an active account. The cost of goods sold is now an account in the general ledger rather than just an item on the income statement. The *periodic inventory system* does not give accurate or up-to-date information about merchandise inventory or cost of goods sold until after an ending inventory is taken.

The taking of a physical inventory at least once a year is not eliminated by a business that uses the perpetual inventory system. An inventory must be taken at least once a year to detect any inventory recording errors, shoplifting, or damages to the merchandise inventory.

The comparisons of the recording of transactions in the two systems are revealed in Figure 15.6. The chart shows that in a perpetual inventory system, the Purchases, Purchases Returns and Allowances, and Freight accounts *do not* exist. Inventory and Cost of Goods Sold are updated immediately.

FIGURE 15.6 Comparison of Perpetual and Periodic Systems

Transaction	Perpetual System			Periodic System		
(A) Sold merchandise that cost $8,000 on account for $20,000.	Accts. Receivable	20 000 00		Accts. Receivable	20 000 00	
	Sales		20 000 00	Sales		20 000 00
	Cost of Goods Sold	8 000 00				
	Merch. Inventory		8 000 00			
(B) Purchased $900 of merchandise on account.	Merch. Inventory	9 00 00		Purchases	9 00 00	
	Accts. Payable		9 00 00	Accts. Payable		9 00 00
(C) Paid $50 freight charges.	Merch. Inventory	5 0 00		Freight-In	5 0 00	
	Cash		5 0 00	Cash		5 0 00
(D) Customer returned $200 of merchandise. Cost of merchandise was $100.	Sales Ret. & Allow.	2 0 0 00		Sales Ret. & Allow.	2 0 0 00	
	Accts. Receivable		2 0 0 00	Accts. Receivable		2 0 0 00
	Merch. Inventory	1 0 0 00				
	Cost of Goods Sold		1 0 0 00			
(E) Returned $400 of merchandise previously bought on account due to defects.	Accts. Payable	4 0 0 00		Accts. Payable	4 0 0 00	
	Merch. Inventory		4 0 0 00	Pur. Ret. & Allow.		4 0 0 00

LEARNING UNIT 15-1 REVIEW

AT THIS POINT / you should be able to

- Explain the perpetual inventory system.
- Journalize transactions for a perpetual inventory system.
- Explain the difference between the perpetual and periodic inventory systems.

Self-Review Quiz 15-1

Journalize the following transactions for a firm that uses a perpetual inventory system:

a. Bought $200 of merchandise on account.
b. Sold $100 of merchandise on account that cost $50.
c. Allowed a customer to return for cash $30 worth of inventory. Our cost was $15.
d. We got permission from our vendor to return $30 worth of inventory.

Solutions to Self-Review Quiz 15-1

FIGURE 15.7 Journalized Entries in a Perpetual System

a.

Merchandise Inventory	200 00	
Accounts Payable		200 00

b.

Accounts Receivable	100 00	
Sales		100 00

Cost of Goods Sold	50 00	
Merchandise Inventory		50 00

c.

Sales Returns and Allowances	30 00	
Cash		30 00

Merchandise Inventory	15 00	
Cost of Goods Sold		15 00

d.

Accounts Payable	30 00	
Merchandise Inventory		30 00

Learning Unit 15-2 Using a Subsidiary Ledger for Inventory; Calculating Cost of Ending Inventory Using a Perpetual System

Suppose the business Painless Bytes sells many different kinds of software packages. How can Painless Bytes keep track of the cost and balances of a variety of inventory items? How do stores such as Wal-Mart keep track of the thousands of items that they keep in inventory? The answer is found in the use of a subsidiary ledger for inventory and the use of computers to maintain the subsidiary ledger.

Do you recall from Chapters 9 and 10 that when we had a large number of Account Receivable or Account Payable accounts, we used subsidiary ledgers to maintain the details for each customer or vendor? This same accounting procedure can be used to keep track of inventory. Our Merchandise Inventory account becomes a control account keeping track of the total balance of inventory, while the details are kept in separate inventory records in a subsidiary ledger for inventory. Let's first show our existing inventory account with a subsidiary ledger and with the transactions from Learning Unit 15-1. On the left is our inventory account in T form, and on the right is an inventory record form for our A-I-B product.

General Ledger Account

Merchandise Inventory

	Dr.	Cr.	
6/2	250		
		6/3	75
6/5	25		
		6/6	25
Bal	175		

Subsidiary Ledger Records

A-I-B Software

Date	Purchased	Sold	Balance
6/2	10 @ $25		$250
6/3		3 @ $25	$175
6/5		(1) @ $25	$200
6/6	(1) @ $25		$175

Notice that the inventory subsidiary ledger record form on the right contains the detail about the quantity and per unit cost for the transactions posted to the general ledger account on the left. Notice too that the return of 6/5 is recorded in the inventory record as a negative sale and that the ending balances agree. The debit memo transaction of 6/6 is entered as a negative purchase and again the ending balances agree. Try using your calculator to see whether you can also calculate the running balance shown in the inventory record.

In this next transaction Painless Bytes adds R&C (<u>R</u>ows and <u>C</u>olumns), a spreadsheet software package, to the line of software it sells.

June   6   Purchased 7 packages of R&C software on account at a cost of $225 per package and a total of $1,575.

Note in Figure 15.8 that the Merchandise Inventory account has again been increased by the cost of the new merchandise we have purchased. Because we now have two products in inventory, our inventory ledger will have a new inventory record form for the R&C product. Check out the way our inventory records relate to the Merchandise Inventory account.

				Dr.		Cr.	
June	6	Merchandise Inventory		1 5 7 5 00			
		Accounts Payable				1 5 7 5 00	
		To record the purchase of inventory					

FIGURE 15.8 Purchase of Inventory in Perpetual System

General Ledger Account

Merchandise Inventory

	Dr.	Cr.	
6/2	250		
		6/3	75
6/5	25		
6/6	1,575	6/6	25
Bal	1,750		

Subsidiary Ledger Records

Product #1:   A-I-B Software

Date	Purchased	Sold	Balance
6/2	10@ $25		$ 250
6/3		3 @ $25	$ 175
6/5		(1) @ $25	$ 200
6/6	(1) @ $25		$ 175

Product #2:   R&C Software

Date	Purchased	Sold	Balance
6/6	7 @ $225		$1,575

Does the total of the balances of the two inventory records agree with the Merchandise Inventory account?

Now let's try another sales transaction.

20XX
June 9 Sold two A-I-B packages at $50 each and three R&C packages at $295 each for a total of $985.

FIGURE 15.9 Matching Sales and Cost of Goods Sold

June	9	Cash				9 8 5 00				
		Sales Revenue						9 8 5 00		
		Sold 2 A-I-B and 3 R&C								
June	3	Cost of Goods Sold				7 2 5 00				
		Merchandise Inventory						7 2 5 00		
		To record the cost of goods sold								

Again, we record both the total sales price of the transaction and the cost of the merchandise sold (Figure 15.9). Do you know how we arrived at the cost of goods sold figure of $725? A quick look at the inventory record forms will show us how we know the cost of goods sold.

General Ledger Account

Merchandise Inventory

	Dr.	Cr.	
6/2	250		
		6/3	75
6/4	25		
6/5	1,575	6/6	25
		6/9	725
Bal	**1,025**		

Subsidiary Ledger Records

Product #1:   A-I-B Software

Date	Purchased	Sold	Balance
6/2	10 @ $25		$ 250
6/3		3 @ $25	$ 175
6/5		(1) @ $25	$ 200
6/6	(1) @ $25		$ 175
6/9		2 @ $25	$ 125

Product #2:   R&C Software

Date	Purchased		Balance
6/6	7 @ $225		$1,575
6/9		3 @ $225	$ 900
		Total	$ 1025

We obtained the cost of goods sold total when we posted the quantities sold to each of the inventory records. Two units of A-I-B at $25 each plus three units of R&C at $225 each equals a total cost of $725. Notice that the ending balances of the two products will total to the same amount as the balance shown in the Merchandise Inventory account.

In summary, a business with a variety of products in inventory will use an inventory subsidiary ledger with an individual record for each different product. These records will contain the details about the quantity and cost of inventory on hand and will allow calculation of the cost of goods sold on each sale.

Computerized accounting systems can handle a perpetual inventory system with ease. You have no doubt seen such systems in operation when the clerk at your local store used a laser scanner or a bar code to enter your purchases into the cash register. The transaction put into the cash register will record the sale and update the cost of goods sold and inventory. Computerized systems keep track of inventory by many different methods. When figuring the value of the inventory, they could use average cost; first-in, first-out (FIFO); or last-in, first-out (LIFO). The examples in Figure 15.10a and Figure 15.10b use the FIFO and LIFO methods in determining the cost of the merchandise for each sale of digital clocks. Keep in mind that in FIFO old inventory is sold first and in LIFO new inventory is sold first.

Note in Figure 15.10a that on January 19 the old inventory (12 at $50) is assumed sold in FIFO. On January 25 when 8 clocks are sold they are taken from the 12 at $50 inventory

FIGURE 15.10a An Inventory Record Using FIFO

Inventory Control

Item VX113

Description Digital Clock

Location Storeroom 1

Maximum 22

Reorder Level 12

Reorder Quantity 10

	Received			Sold			Balance		
Date	Units	Cost per Unit	Total	Units	Cost per Unit	Total	Units	Cost per Unit	Total
20XX Jan. 1	Balance		FWD				14	50	$ 700
12				2	50	100	12	50	600
19	10	60	600	Old Sold First			12	50	
							10	60	1,200
25				8	50	400	4	50	
							10	60	800

Cost of ending inventory in a perpetual inventory system using FIFO

leaving 4 left at $50 along with the 10 at $60. This gives a cost of ending inventory of $800. Note in Figure 15-11 under LIFO that when the 8 units are sold on January 25 they are taken from the 10 units at $60. This leaves 2 left at $60 and the oldest inventory of 12 at $50. The cost of ending inventory is $720. Remember that under LIFO we assume newest inventory is sold first. Under FIFO the oldest inventory is sold first.

FIGURE 15.10b An Inventory Record Using LIFO

Inventory Control

Item VX113

Description Digital Clock

Location Storeroom 1

Maximum 22

Reorder Level 12

Reorder Quantity 10

	Received			Sold			Balance		
Date	Units	Cost per Unit	Total	Units	Cost per Unit	Total	Units	Cost per Unit	Total
20XX Jan. 1	Balance		FWD				14	50	$ 700
12				2	50	100	12	50	600
19	10	60	600	New Sold First			12	50	
							10	60	1,200
25				8	50	400	12	50	
							2	60	720

Cost of ending inventory in a perpetual inventory system using LIFO

LEARNING UNIT 15-2 REVIEW

AT THIS POINT you should be able to

- Understand how a subsidiary ledger for inventory works with a controlling account for inventory and calculate the cost of ending inventory for a perpetual system.
- Journalize and post transactions that affect the general ledger Merchandise Inventory account as well as the individual inventory records in the Merchandise Inventory subsidiary ledger.

Self-Review Quiz 15-2

Journalize and post the following transactions for a firm that uses a subsidiary ledger for Merchandise Inventory. Only post to the accounts that you have.

a. Bought three X-Products at $3 each on account.
b. Sold one of the X-Products we purchased above for cash, $6.
c. Bought four more X-Products at $3 and five Z-Products at $10 on account.
d. Sold for cash two more X-Products at $6 each and three Z-Products at $20 each.

Solutions to Self-Review Quiz 15-2

FIGURE 15.11 Inventory Account in General and Subsidiary Ledgers

a.

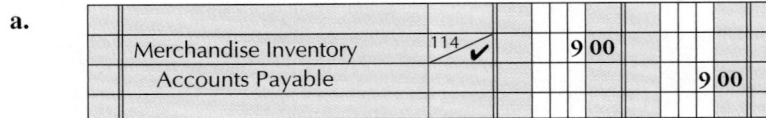

| Merchandise Inventory | 114 ✓ | 9 00 | |
| Accounts Payable | | | 9 00 |

b.

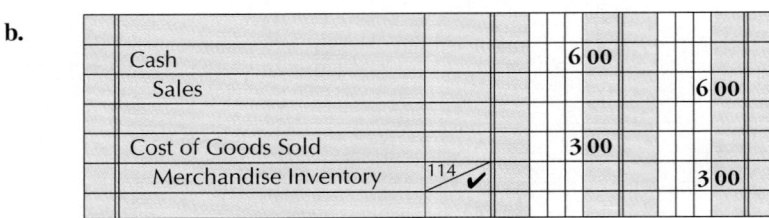

Cash		6 00	
Sales			6 00
Cost of Goods Sold		3 00	
Merchandise Inventory	114 ✓		3 00

c.

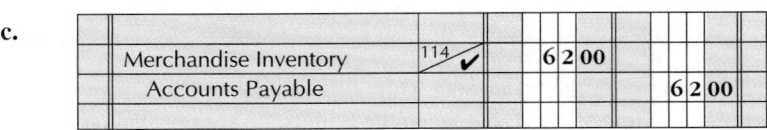

| Merchandise Inventory | 114 ✓ | 6 2 00 | |
| Accounts Payable | | | 6 2 00 |

d.

Cash		7 2 00	
Sales			7 2 00
Cost of Goods Sold		3 6 00	
Merchandise Inventory	114 ✓		3 6 00

General Ledger Account

Merchandise Inventory

	Dr.	Cr.	
a.	9	**b.**	3
c.	62	**d.**	36
Bal	32		

Subsidiary Ledger Records

Product #1:   X-Product

Date	Purchased	Sold	Balance
a.	3 @ $3		9
b.		1 @ $3	6
c.	4 @ $3		18
d.		2 @ $3	12

Product #2:   Z-Product

Date	Purchased	Sold	Balance
c.	5 @ $10		50
d.		3 @ $10	20

LO3
Learning Unit 15-3 Methods of Determining the Value of the Ending Inventory When Using the Periodic Inventory System

For a small business or any business using the **periodic inventory system,*** the method used to assign costs to ending inventory will have a direct effect on the company's cost of goods sold and gross profit. Note in the following table how the ending inventory does in fact have an effect on the gross profit.

---

*This is true for a perpetual system as well.

	Situation A		Situation B		Situation C		Situation D	
Net Sales		$50,000		$50,000		$50,000		$50,000
Beginning Inventory	$ 4,000		$ 4,000		$ 4,000		$ 4,000	
Net Purchases	20,000		20,000		20,000		20,000	
Cost of Goods								
Available for Sale	24,000		24,000		24,000		24,000	
Ending Inventory	5,000		6,000		7,000		8,000	
Cost of Goods Sold		19,000		18,000		17,000		16,000
Gross Profit		$31,000		$32,000		$33,000		$34,000

If all inventory brought into a store had the same cost, it would be simple to calculate the ending inventory, and we would not have to have this discussion. Unfortunately, things are not that easy; often the same products are purchased and brought into the store at different costs during the same accounting period. Over the years, four generally accepted methods have been developed to assign a cost to ending inventory. The reason these methods are needed is that often inventory is brought in at different times. The result is that the inventory is made up of many past purchases at *different* prices. Think of the inventory methods as ways of tracing costs. These methods are (1) specific invoice (identification); (2) first-in, first-out; (3) last-in, first-out; and (4) weighted average. Each is based on an assumed flow of costs, not on the actual physical movement of goods sold in a store.

We now look at how the four inventory cost assumptions are applied within the periodic inventory system. The following situation occurred at Jones Hardware. Jones Hardware sells rakes. The job before us is to come up with the value of the ending inventory and cost of goods sold using the four methods we have listed. The following table provides us with all the information needed to accomplish our task.

> QuickBooks uses the weighted-average method for valuing inventory. Peachtree gives the user the option to choose from FIFO, LIFO, or Average for any inventory item.

Goods Available for Sale

		Units	Cost		Total
January 1	Beginning Inventory	10	@$10	=	$100
March 15	Purchases	9	@ 12	=	108
August 18	Purchases	20	@ 13	=	260
November 15	Purchases	5	@ 15	=	75
		44			$543

Actual inventory on December 31 revealed that 12 rakes remained in stock.

Specific Invoice Method

In the **specific invoice method,** the cost of ending inventory is assigned by identifying each item in that inventory by a specific purchase price and invoice number, and maybe even by serial number.

For our example of this method, let's assume that Jones Hardware knew that six of the rakes not sold were from the March 15 invoice and the other six were from the August 18 purchase. Thus, $150 was assigned as the actual cost of ending inventory. If the total cost of goods available for sale is $543 and we subtract the actual cost of ending inventory ($150), this method provides a figure of $393 for cost of goods sold.

Specific Invoice Method

	Goods Available for Sale			Calculating Cost of Ending Inventory		
	Units	Cost	Total	Units	Cost	Total
January 1 Beg. Inventory	10	@ $10 =	$100			
March 15 Purchased	9	@ 12 =	108	6	@ $12	$ 72
August 18 Purchased	20	@ 13 =	260	6	@ 13	78
November 15 Purchased	5	@ 15 =	75			
	44		$543	12		$150

Cost of Goods Available for Sale $543
Less: Cost of Ending Inventory =   150
Cost of Goods Sold $393

Let's look at the pros and cons of this method.

Specific Invoice Method: A Reference Guide

Pros	Cons
1. Simple to use if company has small amount of high-cost goods, such as autos, jewels, boats, or antiques.	1. Difficult to use for goods with large unit volume and small unit prices such as nails at a hardware store or packages of toothpaste at a drug store.
2. Flow of goods and flow of cost are the same.	2. Difficult to use for decision-making purposes; ordinarily an impractical approach because companies usually deal with high-cost unique items.
3. Costs are matched with the sales they helped to produce.	

First-In, First-Out Method (FIFO)

In the **FIFO method,** we assume that the oldest goods are sold first. Therefore, the items in the ending inventory will be valued at the costs shown on the most recent invoices.

FIFO Method

	Goods Available for Sale			Calculating Cost of Ending Inventory		
	Units	Cost	Total	Units	Cost	Total
January 1 Beg. Inventory	10	@ $10	$100			
March 15 Purchased	9	@ 12 =	108			
August 18 Purchased	20	@ 13 =	260	7	@ $13 =	$ 91
November 15 Purchased	5	@ 15 =	75	5	@ 15 =	75
	44		$543	12		$166

Cost of Goods Available for Sale $543
Less: Cost of Ending Inventory =   166
Cost of Goods Sold $377

In our Jones Hardware example the ending inventory of 12 rakes on hand is assigned a cost from the last two purchase invoices of rakes (purchases made on November 15 and part of the purchases made on August 18), totaling $166. Think of the inventory as being taken from the bottom layer first, then the next one up. If our ending inventory is valued at $166, our cost of goods sold must be $377.

Following are the pros and cons of this method.

FIFO Method: A Reference Guide

Pros	Cons
1. The cost flow tends to follow the physical flow; most businesses try to sell the old goods first (perishables such as fruit or vegetables). 2. The figure for ending inventory is made up of current costs on the balance sheet (because inventory left over is assumed to be from goods last brought into the store).	1. During periods of inflation this method will produce higher income on the income statement and thus more taxes to be paid (discussed later in the chapter). 2. Recent costs are not matched with recent sales, because we assume *old* goods are sold first.

Last-In, First-Out Method (LIFO)

Under the **LIFO method,** it is assumed that the goods *most recently acquired* are sold first. Therefore, the items in the ending inventory will be valued at the invoice costs shown from the top of the list down.

For Jones Hardware this assumption means that the 12 rakes not sold were assigned costs from the 10 listed in beginning inventory and 2 from the March 15 invoice. The ending inventory totals $124 and the cost of goods sold would be $419.

LIFO Method

	Goods Available for Sale			Calculating Cost of Ending Inventory		
	Units	Cost	Total	Units	Cost	Total
January 1 Beg. Inventory	10 @	$10 =	$100	10 @	$10 =	$100
March 15 Purchased	9 @	12 =	108	2 @	12 =	24
August 18 Purchased	20 @	13 =	260			
November 15 Purchased	5 @	15 =	75			
	44		$543	12		$124

Cost of Goods Available for Sale → $543
Less: Cost of Ending Inventory = 124
Cost of Goods Sold $419

The pros and cons of this method are as follows:

> The United Kingdom and Australia do not permit the use of LIFO.

LIFO Method: A Reference Guide

Pros	Cons
1. Cost of goods sold is recorded at or near current costs, because costs of *latest* goods acquired are used. 2. Matches current costs with current selling prices. 3. During periods of inflation this method produces the lowest net income, which is a tax advantage. (The lower cost of ending inventory means a higher cost of goods sold; with a higher cost of goods sold, gross profit and ultimately net income are smaller and thus taxes are lower.)	1. Ending inventory is valued at very old prices. 2. Doesn't match physical flow of goods (but can still be used to calculate flow of costs).

Weighted-Average Method

The **weighted-average method** calculates an average unit cost by dividing the *total cost* of goods available for sale by the *total units* of goods available for sale. In this example the total cost of goods available for sale was $543, and the total units available for sale were 44. Taking the $543 and dividing that number by the 44 total units for the period gives a $12.34 weighted average per unit.

Weighted-Average Method

	Goods Available for Sale		
	Units	Cost	Total
January 1 Beg. Inventory	10 @	$10 =	$100
March 15 Purchased	9 @	12 =	108
August 18 Purchased	20 @	13 =	260
November 15 Purchased	5 @	15 =	75
	44		$543

$$\frac{\$543}{44} = \$12.34 \text{ weighted-average cost per unit}$$

12 rakes × $12.34 = $148.08

Cost of Goods Available for Sale	$543.00
Less: Cost of Ending Inventory =	148.08
Cost of Goods Sold	$394.92

The pros and cons of this method are as follows:

Weighted-Average Method: A Reference Guide

Pros	Cons
1. Weighted average takes into account the number of units purchased at each amount, not a simple average cost. Good for products sold in large volume, such as grains and fuels.	1. Current prices have no more significance than prices of goods bought a month earlier.
2. Accountant assigns an equal unit cost to each unit of inventory; thus when the income statement is prepared, net income will not fluctuate as much as with other methods	2. Compared with other methods, the most recent costs are *not* matched with current sales. This fact is important in financial reporting so as to provide an accurate picture of the company.
	3. Cost of ending inventory is not as up-to-date as it could be using another method.

In this illustration Jones Hardware assumes that the 12 units left on hand are *average* units and therefore assigns an *average* cost figure of $12.34 to each of the 12 rakes left in inventory. Thus, we have a fair approximation of the cost of the ending inventory at $148.08 and of the amount of cost of goods sold, $394.92.

Remember that all four methods are acceptable accounting procedures. Management needs to select the method best suited to its business and be consistent in the application of that method.

When Can an Inventory Method Be Changed?

In accounting, the principle of **consistency** means that once a business selects a particular accounting method, it should follow it consistently from one year to the next without switching to another method. In the previous part of this chapter, we saw four methods of inventory valuations causing four different results for a business in terms of cost of goods sold and, ultimately, net income. Therefore, if a company kept switching from LIFO to FIFO each year, significant changes would result in the profit it reported. The financial reports would become undependable. Keeping with the same method allows readers of the financial reports to make meaningful comparisons of the cost of ending inventory, cost of goods sold, and so forth from year to year.

The principle of consistency doesn't mean that a company can *never* change from one method of inventory valuation to another. If a change is decided upon, however, the company should fully disclose the change, the effects of the change on profit and inventory valuation, and the justification for change in a footnote on the financial report. This principle is called the **full disclosure principle** in accounting.

Items That Should Be Included in the Cost of Inventory

Goods in Transit On the date inventory is taken, goods in transit should be added to inventory if the ownership of the inventory has been transferred to the buyer. For example, if the merchandise was purchased *F.O.B. shipping point,* the buyer becomes the owner of the merchandise when the merchandise is placed on the carrier at the shipping point. On the other hand, if the buyer purchases the merchandise *F.O.B. destination,* the seller has ownership of the merchandise until the merchandise reaches the destination, and it should not be included in the cost of the buyer's inventory.

Merchandise on Consignment **Consignment** means that a business (the **consignor**) is selling its merchandise through an agent (the **consignee**) who doesn't own the merchandise but who has possession of it. Consigned merchandise belongs to the consignor and should not be included in the consignee's inventory cost.

Damaged or Obsolete Merchandise If the merchandise is not saleable, it should *not* be added to the cost of the inventory. For merchandise that is saleable but at a lower cost, the value of that inventory should be estimated at a conservative figure and added to the cost of the inventory.

LEARNING UNIT 15-3 REVIEW

AT THIS POINT / you should be able to

- Calculate cost of ending inventory and cost of goods sold by specific invoice; first-in, first-out; last-in, first-out; and weighted-average method.
- Explain the pros and cons of each method used to calculate cost of ending inventory and cost of goods sold.
- Explain the principles of consistency and full disclosure.
- Explain how merchandise in transit, merchandise on consignment, and damaged or obsolete merchandise are counted in calculating inventory.

Self-Review Quiz 15-3

1. From the information given on the following page, calculate the cost of inventory as well as the cost of goods sold using the (a) specific invoice, (b) weighted-average, (c) first-in, first-out, and (d) last-in, first-out methods.

	Goods Available for Sale			Additional Fact: Inventory Not Sold
	Units	Cost	Total	
January 1 Beg. Inventory	40	@ $ 8 =	$ 320	40 from January 1
April 1 Purchased	20	@ 9 =	180	
May 1 Purchased	20	@ 10 =	200	4 from May 1
October 1 Purchased	20	@ 12 =	240	4 from October 1
December 1 Purchased	20	@ 13 =	260	
	120		$1,200	

2. Respond true or false to the following:
   a. It is possible for a company to change from LIFO to FIFO if the company follows specific guidelines.
   b. Goods in transit (shipped F.O.B. shipping point) will not be included as part of the inventory for the purchaser.
   c. Damaged goods are always added to the cost of inventory.

Solutions to Self-Review Quiz 15-3

1. a. Total cost of goods available for sale $1,200
   Less ending inventory based on specific invoices:

40 units from Jan. 1 purchased at $8	$320
4 units from May 1 purchased at $10	40
4 units from Oct. 1 purchased at $12	48

   48 units in ending inventory   408
   Cost of goods sold $ 792

b. $1,200 ÷ 120 units = $10 weighted-average cost per unit.
   Total cost of goods available for sale $1,200
   Less ending inventory priced at weighted-
      average basis: 48 units at $10.00   480
   Cost of goods sold $ 720

c. Total cost of goods available for sale $1,200
   Less ending inventory priced on FIFO:

20 units from Dec. 1 at $13	$260
20 units from Oct. 1 at $12	240
8 units from May 1 at $10	80

   48 units in ending inventory   580
   Cost of goods sold $ 620

d. Total cost of goods available for sale $1,200
   Less ending inventory priced on LIFO:

40 units from Jan. 1 at $8	$320
8 units from April 1 purchased at $9	72

   48 units in ending inventory   392
   Cost of goods sold $ 808

2. a. True
   b. False
   c. False

Learning Unit 15-4 Estimating Ending Inventory

The actual taking of a physical inventory is time-consuming and expensive. Because of the time and expense involved, most businesses take a physical inventory only once a year. For the business using the periodic inventory system, the need to have an inventory cost figure more often may become necessary, especially when a business makes interim financial reports. This business may find that estimating the inventory rather than taking a physical inventory is accurate enough. Another reason to estimate the ending inventory is in case of a fire when the inventory may be destroyed. The business would need an inventory cost figure when it submits a claim of loss to the insurance company.

Two common and recognized ways to estimate ending inventory are the **retail method**   **LO4** and the **gross profit method.**

Retail Method

To use the retail method, a business must have the following information available:

1. Beginning inventory at cost and at retail (selling price)
2. Cost of net purchases at both cost and at retail
3. The net sales at retail

Let's look at the following diagram to see how French Company estimates ending inventory at cost by the retail method.

French completed the following steps to arrive at an ending inventory cost of $3,600.

Step 1 Calculate cost of merchandise available for sale at cost and retail.

Step 2 Calculate the cost ratio (cost of goods available for sale at cost divided by cost of goods available for sale at retail). It cost French Company .60, or 60 cents, for each $1 of sales for the merchandise.

Step 3 Deduct net sales from retail value of merchandise available for sale to arrive at an estimated ending inventory at retail.

Step 4 Multiply cost ratio (.60 in this case) by ending inventory at retail to arrive at ending inventory at cost of $3,600.

Keep in mind that at year-end French will take a physical inventory.

The Retail Inventory Method

			Cost	Retail
	Goods Available for Sale:			
	Beginning Inventory		$ 4,100	$ 6,900
	Net Purchases		7,900	13,100
Step 1 →	Cost of Goods Available for Sale		$12,000	$20,000
Step 2 →	Cost Ratio (relationship	$\dfrac{\$12,000}{\$20,000} = 60\%$		
	between cost and retail)			
Step 3 →	Net Sales at Retail			14,000
⌐→	Inventory at Retail			$ 6,000
Step 4 →	Ending Inventory at Cost,			
	$ 6,000 × .60		$ 3,600	

Gross Profit Method

Another method of estimating ending inventory without taking a physical count is the gross profit method. This method develops a relationship among sales, cost of goods sold, and gross profit in estimating the cost of ending inventory.

To use this method a company would have to keep track of the following:

1. Average gross profit rate
2. Net sales, beginning inventory, and net purchases

The steps Moose Company takes to estimate its ending inventory are shown in the diagram on the following page. We assume a normal gross profit rate of 30% of net sales. If 30 cents on a dollar is profit, 70 cents on a dollar is cost.

> Freight, if any, would be added to the cost of net purchases.

The Gross Profit Method

	Goods Available for Sale:		
	Inventory, January 1, 20XX		$10,000
	Net Purchases		4,000
Step 1 →	Cost of Goods Available for Sale		$14,000
	Less: Estimated Cost of Goods Sold:		
	Net Sales at Retail	$6,000	
Step 2 →	Cost percentage (100% − 30%)	.70	
	Estimated Cost of Goods Sold		4,200
Step 3 →	Estimated Inventory, January 31, 20XX		$ 9,800

Step 1 Moose determines cost of goods available for sale (beginning inventory plus net purchases).

Step 2 Moose estimates cost of goods sold by multiplying cost percentage (70%) times net sales.

Step 3 Moose subtracts cost of goods sold from cost of goods available for sale to arrive at an estimated inventory of $9,800.

This method, besides helping prepare financial statements, can help determine the amount of inventory on hand at the time of a fire or can verify at year's end the accuracy of the physical inventory.

Before concluding this unit, let's look at how an error made in calculating ending inventory will affect financial statements.

How Incorrect Calculation of Ending Inventory Affects Financial Statements As we stated before, assigning costs to ending inventory can have an effect on cost of goods sold, gross profit, net income, and current assets as well as owner's capital. Let's look at a diagram to see—if a mistake is in fact made—what items on the income statement will be affected and what the mistake's impact will be over time.

	Correct				Incorrect			
	20X1		20X2		20X1		20X2	
Sales		$200		$300		$200		$300
Cost of Goods Sold:		correct				incorrect		
Beginning Inventory	$ 30		$ 70		$ 30		$ 60	
Purchases	95		85		95		85	
Goods Available for Sale	125		155		125		145	
Ending Inventory	−70	55	−100	55	−60	65	−100	45
Gross Profit		$145		$245		$135		$255

SUMMARY:

	Correct	Incorrect	Difference
Year X1, Gross Profit	$145	$135	− $10
Year X2, Gross Profit	245	255	+ 10
Total effect of mistake after two periods			0

Note that when the incorrect figure of $60 is used for ending inventory in 20X1, it causes cost of goods sold to be $65 instead of $55 and profit to be $135 instead of $145. In other words, when ending inventory is understated ($60 instead of $70), cost of goods sold is overstated and profit is understated.

As we look next at 20X2, we see that the ending incorrect inventory of 20X1 is carried as the beginning inventory of 20X2. The understatement of beginning inventory in 20X2 of $60 (instead of $70) causes cost of goods sold to be understated and gross profit to be overstated. Thus, at the end of 20X2, the error will be self-correcting.

To review, look at the following diagram and prove it to yourself by going back over the previous explanation.

If the Item Is	Overstated	Understated
Beginning Inventory	Profit is understated	Profit is overstated
Ending Inventory	Profit is overstated	Profit is understated

> Ending inventory works in the same direction as profit. Beginning inventory is inversely related.

Keep in mind that, because ending inventory is recorded as a current asset on the balance sheet, any mistake will cause the assets to be under- or overstated. The statement of owner's equity will also be affected, with net income over- and understated.

LEARNING UNIT 15-4 REVIEW

AT THIS POINT you should be able to

- Calculate ending inventory by the retail method.
- Calculate ending inventory by the gross profit method.
- Explain how understating or overstating ending inventory will affect financial reports.

Self-Review Quiz 15-4

1. Alon Company needs to estimate its month-end inventory. From the following, estimate the cost of ending inventory on September 30 by the retail method.

	Cost	Retail
Beginning Inventory	$ 8,000	$10,000
Net Purchases	40,000	60,000
Net Sales		30,000

(Carry out the cost ratio to the nearest hundredth percent.)

2. Respond true or false to the following:
   a. The retail inventory method is an estimate.
   b. The cost ratio in the gross profit method represents only sales, not costs.
   c. The first step in the gross profit method is to determine cost of goods available for sale.
   d. If ending inventory is overstated, net income will be overstated.
   e. If beginning inventory is overstated, net income will be overstated.

Solutions to Self-Review Quiz 15-4

	Cost	Retail
1. Beginning Inventory	$ 8,000	$10,000
Net Purchases	40,000	60,000
Cost of Goods Available for Sale	$48,000	70,000
Cost Ratio, $48,000/$70,000 = 68.57%		
Net Sales at Retail		30,000
Inventory at Retail		$40,000
Ending Inventory at Cost, $40,000 × .6857	$27,428	

2. a. True   **b.** False   **c.** True   **d.** True   **e.** False

CHAPTER ASSIGNMENTS

SUMMARY OF KEY POINTS

LEARNING UNIT 15-1

1. In the perpetual inventory method, two key accounts are kept up-to-date at all times. These accounts are Merchandise Inventory and Cost of Goods Sold.
2. Each purchase of merchandise is recorded by a debit to the Merchandise Inventory account.
3. Each sale requires two entries. One entry records the revenue or selling price of the merchandise, and the other entry transfers the cost of the items sold from the Merchandise Inventory account to the Cost of Goods Sold account.
4. Sales returns also require two entries. One entry is to record the reduction in revenue in a Sales Returns and Allowance account, and the other entry is to move the cost of the items returned back to the Merchandise Inventory account from the Cost of Goods Sold account.
5. When the business returns merchandise to the vendor because of damage or some other reason, the Merchandise Inventory account is credited because the merchandise is no longer available to sell.
6. The comparison of the perpetual inventory system and the periodic inventory system reveals that the Purchases, Purchases Returns and Allowances, and Freight accounts do not exist in the perpetual inventory system. The accounts Merchandise Inventory and Cost of Goods Sold become active accounts in the perpetual inventory system.

LEARNING UNIT 15-2

1. If an inventory includes many items, a subsidiary inventory ledger will be used to keep track of the details of quantities and cost for each item in inventory.
2. An inventory record form will be used for each item in the inventory. This form has columns for recording the quantities and cost of units purchased and units sold, and it provides a running balance of inventory on hand.
3. When selling an item, the inventory record form provides the cost information for the debit to Cost of Goods sold and the credit to Merchandise Inventory.
4. The total cost represented by all the inventory record forms will equal the balance of the Merchandise Inventory account in the general ledger.

LEARNING UNIT 15-3

1. In assigning a cost to ending inventory, the flow of goods may *not* follow the actual flow of costs.
2. The specific invoice method identifies each item in inventory with a specific invoice in assigning a cost of ending inventory. It matches costs exactly with revenues.
3. FIFO assumes the old goods are sold first. Because ending inventory is valued at most recent costs, FIFO provides the most realistic figure for ending merchandise inventory.
4. LIFO assumes the newest goods are sold first. It provides the most realistic figure for cost of goods sold. LIFO may also reduce income taxes.
5. The weighted-average method provides an average unit cost of all inventory. Weighted-average inventory value generally falls somewhere between LIFO and FIFO.
6. Accounting principles require consistency in the use of the inventory method that is adopted.

7. Goods in transit should be added to the value of the inventory if they are shipped FOB Shipping Point. Merchandise on consignment and damaged or obsolete merchandise should not be included in the value of the inventory.

LEARNING UNIT 15-4

1. Taking a physical inventory is costly and time-consuming.
2. If a business needs to take an inventory more often than once a year, the retail method or gross profit method may be used to prepare interim financial statements or to submit a claim for insurance purposes.
3. The ending inventory amount has an effect on the financial reports, and a mistake will cause the assets to be understated or overstated. Net income will also be understated or overstated by this mistake.

KEY TERMS

Consignee A company or person to whom merchandise is consigned but who doesn't have ownership.

Consignment Sales of goods through an agent who has possession but not ownership.

Consignor The one who consigns merchandise to the consignee.

Consistency The accounting principle that requires companies to follow the same accounting methods or procedures from period to period.

FIFO (first-in, first-out) method Valuing of inventory assuming that the company sells the first goods received in the store.

Full disclosure principle The accounting principle that requires companies to fully disclose on their financial reports changes in accounting procedures and methods along with effects of the change as well as justification for change.

Gross profit method A method used to determine the value of the ending inventory using a predetermined gross profit rate. This method can be used to determine value of ending inventory if a loss from fire occurs.

LIFO (last-in, first-out) method Valuing of inventory with the assumption the last goods received in the store are the first to be sold.

Periodic inventory system An inventory system that does not keep continuous inventory of merchandise on hand.

Perpetual inventory system The inventory system of a company that keeps a continuous (perpetual) record of inventory on hand and of the cost of goods sold.

Retail method A method used to determine the value of the ending inventory using a cost-to-retail ratio. Often used for interim financial reports.

Specific invoice method Valuing of inventory where each item is identified with a specific invoice.

Weighted-average method Valuing of inventory where each item is assigned the same unit cost. This unit cost is found by dividing cost of goods available for sale by the total number of units for sale.

QUESTIONS, CLASSROOM DEMONSTRATION EXERCISES, EXERCISES, AND PROBLEMS

Discussion and Critical Thinking Questions/Ethical Case

1. Why would a manager prefer the perpetual inventory system over the periodic system of inventory?
2. What are the two key accounts in the perpetual inventory system?
3. In the perpetual system, what account is debited to record the cost of merchandise purchased?
4. Why are there two entries required to record each sale in the perpetual inventory system?
5. Explain the relationship between the Merchandise Inventory account and the subsidiary inventory ledger.
6. Must the flow of cost in inventory match the physical movement of merchandise? Please explain.
7. What are the four methods of inventory valuation? Explain each.
8. During inflation, which inventory method will provide the lowest income on the income statement?

9. Which inventory method provides the most current valuation of inventory on the balance sheet? Please explain.

10. Explain why goods in transit (F.O.B. shipping point) to buyer and goods issued on consignment are added to inventory valuations.

11. When ending inventory is understated, what effect will it have on cost of goods sold and net income?

12. Why would a company use the retail method to determine the value of the ending inventory? Why would it use the gross profit method?

13. Lyon Co. has used a perpetual inventory system for six months. The president of the company issued a memo stating that the new computer system failed to deliver acceptable standards in servicing the customers and too many goods are out of stock. Fran, Lyon's accountant, blames the computer department and tells the president to fire the head of that department. The president wants to return immediately to a periodic inventory system. You make the call. Write down your recommendations to the president.

BLUEPRINT: METHODS OF ESTIMATING INVENTORY

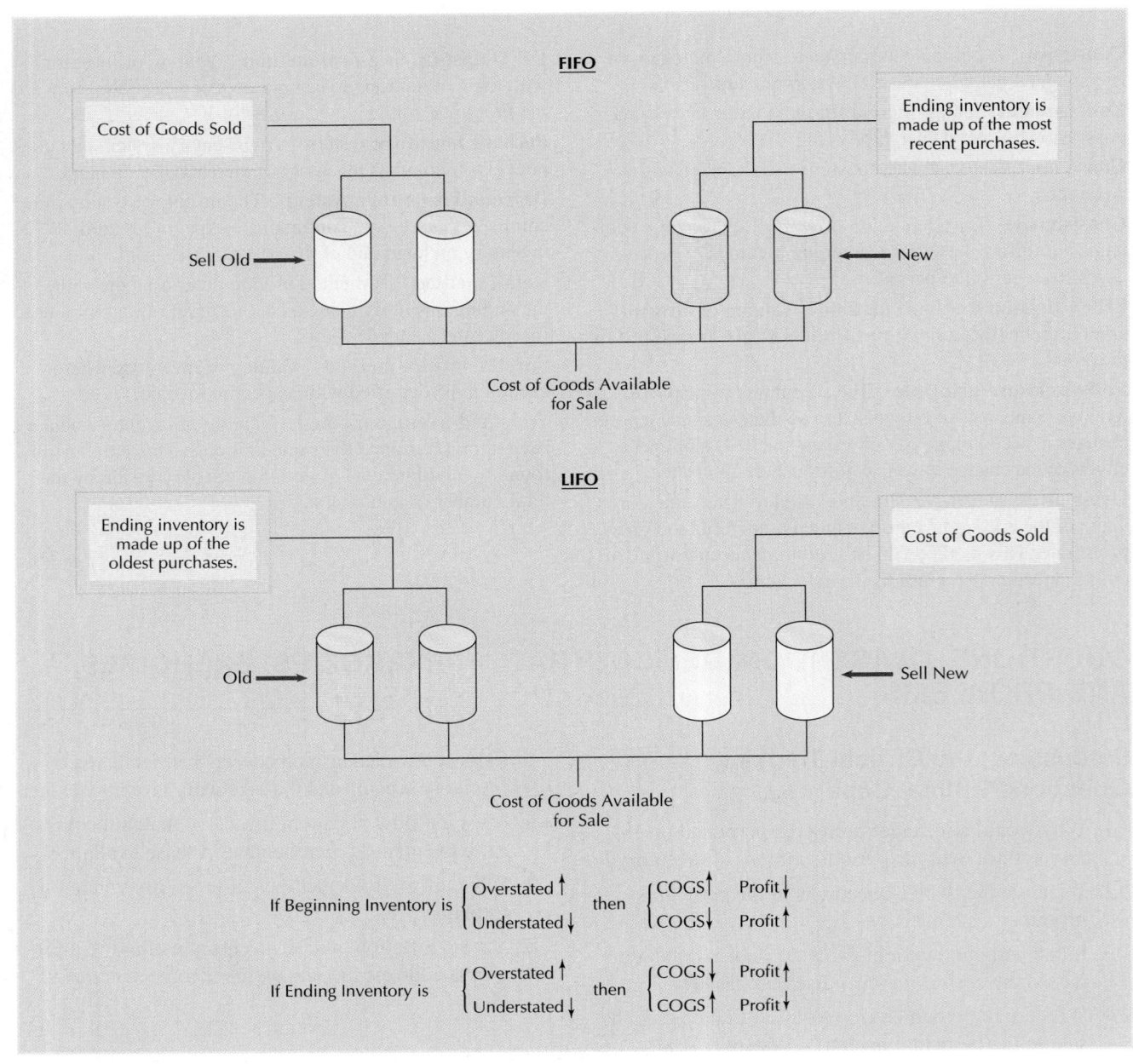

BLUEPRINT: METHODS OF ESTIMATING INVENTORY (*CONTINUED*)

Summary of Pros and Cons of Inventory and Valuation Methods

Pros	Cons	
1. Simple to use if company has small amount of high-cost goods, such as autos, jewels, boats, or antiques. 2. Flow of goods and flow of cost are the same. 3. Costs are matched with the sales they helped to produce.	1. Difficult to use for goods with large unit volume and small unit prices, such as nails at a hardware store or packages of toothpaste at a drug store. 2. Difficult to use for decision-making purposes; ordinarily it is an impractical approach.	**Specific Invoice**

Pros	Cons	
1. The cost flow tends to follow the physical flow; most businesses try to sell the old goods first (perishables such as fruit or vegetables). 2. The figure for ending inventory is made up of current costs on the balance sheet (because inventory left over is assumed to be from goods last brought into the store).	1. During inflation, this method will produce higher income on the income statement and thus more taxes to be paid. 2. Recent costs are not matched with recent sales, because it assumes *old* goods are sold first.	**FIFO**

Pros	Cons	
1. Cost of goods sold is stated at or near current costs, because costs of *latest* goods acquired are used. 2. Matches current costs with current selling prices. 3. During inflation, this method produces the lowest net income, which is a tax advantage. (The lower cost of ending inventory means a higher cost of goods sold; with a higher cost of goods sold, gross profit and ultimately net income are smaller and thus taxes are lower.)	1. Ending inventory is valued at very old prices. 2. Doesn't match physical flow of goods, but can still be used to calculate the flow of costs.	**LIFO**

Pros	Cons	
1. Weighted-average takes into account the number of units purchased at each amount, not a simple average cost. Good for products sold in large volume, such as grains and fuels. 2. Accountant assigns an equal unit cost to each unit of inventory; thus when the income statement is prepared, net income will not fluctuate as much as with other methods.	1. Current prices have no more significance than prices of goods bought months earlier. 2. Compared with other methods, the most recent costs are *not* matched with current sales. 3. Cost of ending inventory is not as up-to-date as it could be using another method.	**Weighted-Average Method**

Classroom Demonstration Exercises

SET A

LO1 (5 min) **Transaction Analysis**

1. What four titles along with their classification are involved in the sale of goods in a perpetual system?

LO1 (10 min) **Journal Entries**

Use the perpetual inventory system.

2. Journalize the following transaction in correct form:

20XX		
April	1	Sold merchandise on account, $1,200. The merchandise cost $700.

LO1 (10 min) 3. Journalize the following transaction in correct form:

20XX		
Mar.	15	A customer returned merchandise for a cash refund of $210. The item cost the seller $75.

LO1 (10 min) 4. Journalize the following transaction in correct form:

20XX		
Mar.	20	The business returned to the vendor a damaged inventory item that cost $400.

LO3, 4 (30 min) **Estimating Inventory Value**

5. From the following information calculate the cost of ending inventory and cost of goods sold using the (a) FIFO, (b) LIFO, and (c) weighted-average methods.

		Units	Cost
January 1	Beginning Inventory	6	$3
March 6	Purchased	4	4
August 9	Purchased	3	5
December 10	Purchased	5	6

The ending inventory reveals seven items unsold.

LO4 (30 min) **Retail Inventory Method**

6. Complete the following using the retail inventory method. (Round cost ratio to the nearest whole percent.)

	Cost	Retail
Goods Available for Sale		
Beginning Inventory	$60	$110
Net Purchases	30	70
Cost of Goods Available for Sale	A	B
Cost Ratio	C	
Net Sales at Retail		130
Inventory at Retail		D
Ending Inventory	E	

Gross Profit Method

LO4 (30 min)

7. Complete the following using the gross profit method. Assume a normal gross profit rate of 30% of net sales.

Goods Available for Sale		
Inventory January 1, 20XX		$70
Net Purchases		20
Cost of Goods Available for Sale		A
Less: Estimated Cost of Goods Sold:		
Net Sales at Retail	$50	
Cost percentage	B	
Estimated Cost of Goods Sold		C
Estimated Inventory Jan. 31, 20XX		D

SET B

Transaction Analysis

LO1 (5 min)

1. Complete the following transaction analysis:

Accounts Affected	Category	↑ ↓	Rules
Merchandise Inventory		↓	
Cost of Goods Sold		↑	

Journal Entries

LO1 (10 min)

Use the perpetual inventory system.

2. Journalize the following transaction in correct form:

20XX
Mar.   1   Sold merchandise on account, $500. The merchandise cost $300.

3. Journalize the following transaction in correct form:

LO1 (10 min)

20XX
Mar.   15   A customer returned merchandise for a cash refund of $250. The item cost the seller $125.

4. Journalize the following transaction in correct form:

LO1 (10 min)

20XX
Mar.   20   The business returned to the vendor a damaged inventory item that cost $150.

Estimating Inventory Value

LO3, 4 (30 min)

5. From the following information calculate the cost of ending inventory and cost of goods sold using the (a) FIFO, (b) LIFO, and (c) weighted-average methods.

		Units	Cost
January 1	Beginning Inventory	5	$1
March 6	Purchased	3	2
August 9	Purchased	2	3
December 10	Purchased	4	4

The ending inventory reveals six items unsold.

LO4 (30 min) **Retail Inventory Method**

6. Complete the following using the retail inventory method. (Round cost ratio to nearest whole percent.)

	Cost	Retail
Goods Available for Sale		
Beginning Inventory	$50	$100
Net Purchases	70	90
Cost of Goods Available for Sale	A	B
Cost Ratio	C	
Net Sales at Retail		140
Inventory at Retail		D
Ending Inventory	E	

LO4 (30 min) **Gross Profit Method**

7. Complete the following using the gross profit method. Assume a normal gross profit rate of 40% of net sales.

Goods Available for Sale		
Inventory January 1, 20XX		$50
Net Purchases		10
Cost of Goods Available for Sale		A
Less: Estimated Cost of Goods Sold:		
Net Sales at Retail	$40	
Cost percentage	B	
Estimated Cost of Goods Sold		C
Estimated Inventory Jan. 31, 20XX		D

Exercises

LO1 (20 min) **15-1.** The Jones Electric Company uses the perpetual inventory system. Record these transactions in a two-column journal.

20XX
Feb. 3 Purchased 10 model 77DX light fixtures on account from Dealer's Electric at total cost of $400; terms n/30.

5 Sold 3 model U67 light fixtures for cash for $84 total. The cost of these 3 fixtures amounted to $54.

6 Our customer returned 1 model U67 light fixture. We gave the customer a $28 cash refund.

10 We issued a debit memo for $40 to Dealer's Electric for 1 model 77DX light fixture that came in damaged in the shipment of February 3.

LO1, 2 (20 min) **15-2.** The RJM Company uses the perpetual inventory system with a subsidiary ledger for inventory. Enter the following information into the inventory balance for product U47. Be sure to keep the balance on hand up-to-date.

20XX
Nov. 5 Purchased 5 units at a cost of $10 each. (Inventory on hand prior to this purchase was zero units.)

6 Sold 3 units for $16 each. (*Hint:* The inventory record form only contains information about the cost of a product, not the selling price!)

7 Sold 1 unit for $15.50.

10 Purchased 12 additional units at a cost of $10 each.

15-3. Journalize and post the preceding transactions using a two-column journal.

15-4. CVR Sales uses the FIFO method with the perpetual inventory system. Enter the following information into the inventory record form for product 44BX. Be sure to keep the balance on hand up-to-date.

LO1, 2 (20 min)
LO3 (20 min)

20XX

Oct.	1	Balance on hand: 3 units at a cost of $21 each.
	2	Purchased 5 units at a cost of $23 each.
	5	Sold 2 units for $31 each. (Remember to use cost and not selling price in the inventory record.)
	6	Sold 5 units for $31 each.
	8	Purchased 6 units at a cost of $24 each.

15-5. The Loyola Company uses the periodic inventory system. Calculate the cost of ending inventory and cost of goods sold using the (a) FIFO, (b) LIFO, and (c) weighted-average methods. Loyola sells only one product, called SM57.

LO3 (20 min)

		Units	Cost per Unit
January 1	Beginning inventory	50	$ 9
March 18	Purchased	12	10
August 19	Purchased	40	12
November 8	Purchased	48	13

Ending inventory is 52 units.

15-6. From the following facts, calculate the correct cost of inventory for Ray Company.

LO3 (20 min)

- Cost of inventory on shelf, $4,000, which includes $300 of goods received on consignment.
- Goods in transit en route to Ray Company shipped F.O.B. shipping point, $22,000.
- Goods in transit en route to Ray shipped F.O.B. destination, $300.
- Ray Company has $600 worth of goods on consignment in Alice's Dress Shop.

15-7. Miles Company's May 1 inventory had a cost of $58,000 and a retail value of $72,000. During May, net purchases cost $255,000 with a retail value of $405,000. Net sales at retail for Miles Company during May were $225,000. Calculate the ending inventory at cost using the retail inventory method. (Round the cost ratio to the nearest hundredth percent.)

LO4 (15 min)

15-8. Amy Company on January 1, 20XX, had inventory costing $30,000 and during January had net purchases of $67,000. Over recent years, Amy Company's gross profit averaged 40% on sales. Given that the company has net sales of $106,000, calculate an estimated cost of ending inventory using the gross profit method.

LO4 (15 min)

Group A Problems

15A-1. The Ajax Company uses the perpetual inventory system. Record these transactions in a two-column journal. All credit sales are n/30.

LO1 (20 min)

20XX

Mar.	5	Purchased merchandise on account totaling $2,000; terms n/30.
	6	Sold merchandise on account to Tommy Dorsey for $85. This merchandise cost $63.

(continued on next page)

8   Returned $100 of defective merchandise purchased March 5.

9   Sold $125 of merchandise for cash. This merchandise cost $98.

9   Allowed a return for credit of $7 of merchandise sold on March 6. The cost of the returned merchandise was $5. (*Hint:* Don't forget to return the cost of the merchandise to the Merchandise Inventory account.)

10   Purchased $800 of merchandise on account from BG Supply; terms n/30.

12   Received payment from Tommy Dorsey for the March 6 sale less the return.

13   Sold $380 of merchandise for cash. The cost was $290.

Check Figure:
Mar. 13
Dr. Cost of Goods Sold $290
Cr. Merch. Inventory $290

LO1, 2 (40 min)   **15A-2.** Sunset Electronics, an electronics supply company, uses the perpetual inventory system with a subsidiary inventory ledger to maintain control over an inventory of thousands of electronic parts. The quantities and costs for three of the parts in inventory follow:

Part No.	Quantity on Hand	Cost per Unit
KT88	3	$17.50
EL34	22	16.40
12AX7	5	8.70

Check Figure:
KT88 Ending balance $192.50

Your job is to do the following:
1. Enter the preceding beginning balances in the inventory record forms; beginning inventory is $456.80.
2. Journalize and post the following transactions.

20XX
Oct.   10   Purchased the following on account:

Part No.	Quantity	Cost per Unit
KT88	24	$17.50
12AX7	36	8.70

(*Hint:* Be sure to update each inventory record.)

11   Sold 4 number KT88 units for cash at a selling price of $27.50 each. (*Hint:* Remember to record both the revenue and the cost. The cost data will be found in the inventory record form for this part number. Don't forget to update the form.)

13   Sold the following for cash:

Part No.	Quantity	Sales Price per Unit
KT88	12	$27.50
EL34	8	25.00
12AX7	14	12.90

15   A customer brought back 1 of KT88 bought two days ago because it did not work.

16   Sunset Electronics sent back to the vendor the faulty KT88 that the customer brought back.

LO1, 2 (30 min)   **15A-3.** Agree Company uses a perpetual inventory system. From the following information, prepare an inventory record form (a) assuming that the FIFO method is in use and (b) assuming that the LIFO method is in use. Assume on January 1, 20XX, a beginning inventory of 800 units at a cost of $8 each.

	Received			Sold	
Date	Quantity	Cost per Unit	Date	Quantity	
Apr. 15	220	$ 7	Mar. 8	500	
Nov. 12	800	9	Oct. 5	350	
Dec. 31	700	10	Nov. 30	400	

Check Figure:
Ending balance (b) $11,960

15A-4. Ashley Company, using the periodic inventory system, began the year with 250 units of product B in inventory with a unit cost of $35. The following additional purchases of the product were made:

LO3 (30 min)

Apr. 1	300 units @ $40 each
July 5	400 units @ 50 each
Aug. 15	500 units @ 60 each
Nov. 20	150 units @ 70 each

At end of year, Ashley Company had 500 units of its product unsold. Calculate cost of ending inventory as well as cost of goods sold by the (a) FIFO, (b) LIFO, and (c) weighted-average methods. (Round the weighted average to the nearest cent.)

Check Figure:
(b) LIFO Cost of Goods Sold
$62,500

15A-5. Marge Company uses the retail method to estimate cost of ending inventory for its monthly interim reports. From the following facts, estimate Marge's ending inventory at cost for the end of January. (Round the cost ratio to the nearest tenth percent.)

LO4 (20 min)

January 1 inventory at cost	$ 16,500
January 1 inventory at retail	32,000
Net purchases at cost	110,800
Net purchases at retail	195,000
Net sales at retail	191,000

Check Figure:
$20,196   Ending
Inventory at cost

15A-6. Over the past four years the gross profit rate for Hall Company was 30%. Last week a fire destroyed all Hall's inventory. Luckily, all the records for Hall were in a fireproof safe and indicated the following facts:

LO4 (20 min)

Inventory (January 1, 20XX)	$ 39,000
Sales	128,500
Sales Returns	3,200
Purchases	78,000
Purchases Returns and Allowances	3,000

Check Figure:
$26,290   Estimated Inventory

Please estimate the cost of inventory that was destroyed in the fire.

Group B Problems

15B-1. The Wren Company uses the perpetual inventory system. Record the transactions on the following page in a two-column journal. All credit sales are n/30.

LO 1 (20 min)

20XX

Mar. 15 Purchased merchandise on account totaling $1,800; terms n/30.

16 Sold merchandise on account to Bobby Hackett for $92. This merchandise cost $71.

18 Returned $120 of defective merchandise purchased March 15.

19 Sold $230 of merchandise for cash. This merchandise cost $175.

19 Allowed a return for credit of $14 of merchandise sold on March 16. The cost of the returned merchandise was $11. (*Hint:* Don't forget to return the cost of the merchandise to the Merchandise Inventory account.)

20 Purchased $900 of merchandise on account from JT Supply; terms n/30.

22 Received payment from Bobby Hackett for the March 16 sale less the return.

23 Sold $410 of merchandise for cash. The cost was $320.

Check Figure:
Mar. 23
Dr. Cost of Goods Sold $320
Cr. Merch. Inventory $320

LO1, 2 (40 min)   **15B-2.** Joy Elder owns an electronics supply company called Sunset Electronics. The company uses the perpetual inventory system with a subsidiary inventory ledger to maintain control over an inventory of thousands of electronic parts. Here are the quantities and costs for three of the parts in inventory:

Part No.	Quantity on Hand	Cost per Unit
6L6	4	$12.50
EL84	18	9.40
12AU7	3	7.80

Check Figure:
12AU7 Ending balance $117

Your job is to do the following:

1. Enter the beginning balances in the inventory record forms; beginning inventory is $242.60.
2. Journalize and post the following transactions:

20XX

Oct. 10 Purchased the following on account:

Part No.	Quantity	Cost per Unit
6L6	18	$12.50
12AU7	28	7.80

(*Hint:* Be sure to update each inventory record.)

11 Sold 4 number 12AU7 units for cash at a selling price of $18.50 each. (*Hint:* Remember to record both the revenue and the cost. The cost data will be found in the inventory record form for this part number. Don't forget to update the form.)

13 Sold the following for cash:

Part No.	Quantity	Sales Price per Unit
6L6	10	$18.50
EL84	9	14.00
12AU7	12	11.80

15 A customer brought back 1 6L6 that was bought two days ago because it did not work.

16 Sunset Electronics returned to the vendor the faulty part that was returned yesterday.

15B-3. Agree Company uses a perpetual inventory system. From the following information, prepare an inventory record form (a) assuming that the FIFO method is in use and (b) assuming that the LIFO method is in use. Assume on January 1, 20XX, a beginning inventory of 500 units at a cost of $7 each.

LO1, 2 (30 min)

Received			Sold	
Date	Quantity	Cost per Unit	Date	Quantity
Apr. 15	200	$ 8	Mar. 8	400
Nov. 12	300	9	Oct. 5	300
Dec. 31	600	10	Nov. 30	200

Check Figure:
$6,900

15B-4. On January 1, 20XX, Ashley Company, a company that uses the periodic inventory system, began with 150 units of product B in inventory with a unit cost of $20. The following additional purchases of the product were made:

LO3 (30 min)

Apr. 1	210 units @ $30 each
Jul. 5	500 units @ 40 each
Aug. 15	450 units @ 50 each
Nov. 20	200 units @ 60 each

At end of year, Ashley Company had 400 units of its product unsold. Calculate cost of ending inventory as well as cost of goods sold by the (a) FIFO, (b) LIFO, and (c) weighted-average methods. (Round the weighted average to the nearest cent.)

Check Figure:
LIFO $52,900 Cost of Goods Sold

15B-5. Marge Company uses the retail method to estimate cost of ending inventory for its monthly interim reports. From the following facts, estimate Marge's ending inventory at cost for the end of January. (Round the cost ratio to the nearest hundredth percent.)

LO4 (20 min)

January 1 inventory at cost	$ 17,000
January 1 inventory at retail	35,000
Net purchases at cost	119,000
Net purchases at retail	204,000
Net sales at retail	189,000

Check Figure:
$28,450 Ending inventory

15B-6. Over the past four years the gross profit rate for Hall Company was 35%. Last week a fire destroyed all of Hall's inventory. Luckily, all the records for Hall were in a fireproof safe and indicated the following facts:

LO4 (20 min)

Inventory (January 1, 20XX)	$ 5,400
Sales	127,000
Sales Returns	3,250
Purchases	94,900
Purchases Returns and Allowances	4,100

Check Figure:
$15,762.50 Estimated inventory

Using the gross profit method, estimate the cost of inventory that was destroyed in the fire.

ON-THE-JOB TRAINING

LO1 (20 min)

T-1. The following inventory errors were discovered during an internal audit:

  a. The beginning inventory was overstated by $200.
  b. The ending inventory was understated by $300.
  c. $900 of purchases were unrecorded.
  d. A sales return of $1,500 was not recorded.

Indicate what effect these mistakes (treat each one separately) will have on (1) the cost of goods sold, (2) the gross profit, and (3) the owner's equity. Please provide a written explanation.

FINANCIAL REPORT PROBLEM

LO3 (10 min)

Reading the Kellogg's Annual Report

Go to Appendix A and find out how inventories are valued. How much inventory did Kellogg's have in 2006?

INTERNET PROJECT

ExxonMobil

Go to the Web and search: Annual Report ExxonMobil 2008.
Click on Investors Relations.
List out the latest news ExxonMobil is providing to its investors.
Order a free annual report.

CONTINUING PROBLEM

LO3 (45 min)

Sanchez Computer Center

The Sanchez Computer Center had 300 pieces of merchandise inventory as of March 31, 20XX. The inventory was purchased with prices as follows:

Lot	Price Each Piece	Number of Pieces	Total Cost
First lot	$1.00	100	$100
Second lot	$1.75	100	$175
Third lot	$2.00	80	$160
Fourth lot	$2.50	100	$250
Fifth lot	$1.65	100	$165

Lot numbers represent oldest to newest.

Assignment

Using the FIFO, LIFO, and weighted-average methods, calculate the dollar value of the Sanchez Computer Center's ending inventory.

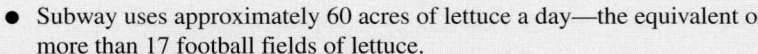

Case

HOW NOT TO SAY "OOPS, WE'RE OUT OF THAT!"

LO3 (40 min)

- Subway uses approximately 60 acres of lettuce a day—the equivalent of more than 17 football fields of lettuce.
- If you take all the cheese that is produced for Subway restaurants in a year and place each slice end to end, they will reach half way to the moon.
- The manufacturing of Subway cookie dough requires 14.4 million eggs a year and the service of 46,602 busy hens.

With his sales climbing higher and higher, Stan Hernandez does his part to layer football fields with lettuce, send cheese ropes to the moon, and ensure the full employment of 46,602 hens. Yet, just how do Stan and his fellow Subway franchisees manage the flow of so many perishable goods in and out of their restaurants every day? By physically counting the goods.

"Not again," Wanda moaned, when Rashid asked her to begin taking inventory of the stockroom. "We did that last week."

"You bet," countered Rashid, "and we do it every week, as you remember."

"But my sister works at Wal-Mart and they only take inventory once a year."

Stan couldn't help overhearing their conversation as he sat crunching numbers at his back office computer and came out from behind his desk.

"Wanda, as I explained to you during training," Stan said patiently, "Subway requires all of its restaurants to do a physical count of their inventory once a week. We're in a very different business than Wal-Mart. We have to make sure that we have enough cheese, lettuce, bread dough, chicken, tuna, tomatoes . . . you name it, but not too much or it will spoil. And I sure don't want to run out of our special sauce for these new sweet onion chicken teriyaki sandwiches."

"It seems like every other sandwich I make is a sweet onion chicken teriyaki," said Wanda. "It's my favorite, too, so I sure don't want us to run out of it." She got out her clipboard of inventory report forms and immediately began taking stock.

The need to keep a steady supply of goods, such as its teriyaki sandwich sauce, on hand is just one of the reasons that Subway requires its franchisees to take a physical inventory every week. Physically counting the goods also serves as a control mechanism to prevent or spot employee theft and to prevent restaurant owners from underreporting sales and, hence, paying fewer royalties to Subway.

In terms of physical flow, perishable inventory must be FIFO; the first inventory in is the first used, so that nothing is allowed to get stale or spoiled. If a Subway restaurant owner uses the FIFO method for accounting, the cost follows the physical flow. Although every Subway shop owner uses the FIFO method for physical flow, not every owner chooses this method of accounting. Some prefer LIFO for financial accounting because, with this method, the cost of goods sold is matched to current selling prices. In a time of inflation, when prices rise quickly, LIFO saves taxes because it lowers net income.

Subway currently uses a periodic inventory system. Perhaps, with widespread use of the POS cash registers, Subway will create a perpetual inventory system one day. However, Wanda, Rashid, Ellen, and their fellow sandwich artists and Subway managers will still do a weekly physical count of inventory because spoilage, shrinkage, and theft are always possible.

Discussion Questions

1. Learning Unit 15-4 discusses the retail inventory method. Why does Subway insist on a physical count?
2. The case discussed the different benefits LIFO and FIFO offer Stan. Why might Stan choose a weighted-average method of accounting for inventory costs?

3. The price of tomatoes, lettuce, peppers, and onions is subject to change, depending on growing conditions in Florida, California, Mexico, and other parts of the United States and the world. What effect might this changeability have on the method of financial accounting a Subway restaurant owner chooses?

PEACHTREE COMPUTER WORKSHOP

COMPUTERIZED ACCOUNTING APPLICATION FOR CHAPTER 15

Refresher on using Peachtree Complete Accounting

Before starting this assignment, you may want to refresh your memory by reading the following PDF documents in the multimedia library of the MyAccountingLab Web site. Remember to choose the PDF document for your version of Peachtree.

1. An Introduction to Peachtree Complete Accounting
2. Correcting Peachtree Transactions
3. How to Repeat or Restart a Peachtree Assignment
4. Backing Up and Restoring Your Work in Peachtree

You also should have completed the following workshops:

1. Workshop 1 Atlas Company from Chapter 3
2. Workshop 2 Zell Company from Chapter 4
3. Workshop 3 Sullivan Realty from Chapter 5
4. Workshop 4 Pete's Market from Chapter 8
5. Workshop 5 Part A Mars Company from Chapter 10
6. Workshop 5 Part B Abby's Toy House from Chapter 10
7. Workshop 6 The Corner Dress Shop from Chapter 12

Workshop 7:

Perpetual Inventory System

In this workshop you focus on maintaining inventory for The Paint Place using Peachtree's perpetual inventory system. Tasks include creating inventory records, reviewing costing systems, and recording sales and purchases of inventory. You will also prepare inventory reports, aged receivables and aged payable reports, general journal and general ledger reports, a trial balance, and financial statements.

Instructions and the data file for completing this assignment are in the multimedia library of the MyAccountingLab Web site. Open the **Workshop 7 The Paint Place** PDF document for your version of Peachtree and download **The Paint Place** data file for your version of Peachtree.

QUICKBOOKS COMPUTER WORKSHOP

COMPUTERIZED ACCOUNTING APPLICATION FOR CHAPTER 15

Refresher on using QuickBooks Pro

Before starting this assignment, you may want to refresh your memory by reading the following PDF documents in the multimedia library of the MyAccountingLab Web site. Remember to choose the PDF document for your version of QuickBooks.

1. An Introduction to QuickBooks Pro
2. Correcting QuickBooks Transactions
3. How to Repeat or Restart a QuickBooks Assignment
4. Backing Up and Restoring Your Work in QuickBooks

You also should have completed the following workshops:

1. Workshop 1 Atlas Company from Chapter 3
2. Workshop 2 Zell Company from Chapter 4
3. Workshop 3 Sullivan Realty from Chapter 5
4. Workshop 4 Pete's Market from Chapter 8
5. Workshop 5 Part A Mars Company from Chapter 10
6. Workshop 5 Part B Abby's Toy House from Chapter 10
7. Workshop 6 The Corner Dress Shop from Chapter 12

Workshop 7:

Perpetual Inventory System

In this workshop you focus on maintaining inventory for The Paint Place using QuickBooks' perpetual inventory system. Tasks include creating inventory records, reviewing costing systems, and recording sales and purchases of inventory. You will also prepare inventory reports, aged receivables and aged payable reports, general journal and general ledger reports, a trial balance, and financial statements.

Instructions and the data file for completing this assignment are in the multimedia library of the MyAccountingLab Web site. Open the *Workshop 7 The Paint Place* PDF document for your version of QuickBooks and download *The Paint Place* data file for your version of QuickBooks.

16

Accounting for Property, Plant, Equipment, and Intangible Assets

DID YOU KNOW? Depreciation is not included in the calculations of Wendy's restaurant margins. Visit *www.wendys.com* to find more information about Wendy's.

LEARNING OBJECTIVES

1. Calculating the cost of an asset.

2. Calculating depreciation using one of three methods: straight line, double declining balance, and units of production.

3. Calculating depreciation for tax purposes using the Modified Accelerated Cost Recovery System.

4. Explaining the difference between capital expenditures and revenue expenditures.

5. Journalizing entries for discarding, selling, or exchanging plant assets.

6. Explaining amortization and how it applies to intangible assets.

When you sit in a Wendy's restaurant do you ever think about how the equipment and building are depreciated? In Chapter 12 we classified assets as either current or plant and equipment. Current assets are used up in a company's operations or converted into cash within one year or one accounting cycle, whichever is longer. Long-term assets, such as plant and equipment, provide benefits to a company for more than one year or one accounting cycle. Types of long-term assets include property (such as land), plant (such as buildings), and equipment (such as trucks and tools). Another classification of assets is called **intangible assets.** These assets are rights owned by a business that do not involve a *physical* object. Examples are patents or franchises. Intangible assets are also considered long-term assets.

In this chapter we look at how to calculate a long-term asset's overall cost and its depreciation (depreciation being the allocation of the cost of the asset over its lifetime). We also show how to record expenditures involved in improving or repairing an asset and how to account for the disposal of these assets.

LO1

Learning Unit 16-1 Cost of Property, Plant, and Equipment

The cost of property, plant, and equipment is not just the price one pays to buy it. One must also include the cost involved in getting it into position and in condition for use in the company. Thus, the cost of a machine includes freight, assembly, and all other costs that are needed to get the machine up and ready to run.

For example, Smith ordered a machine with a list price of $20,000 with terms of 3/10, n/30. A freight charge of $1,500 covered transportation to the railroad station. Smith paid $250 to transport the machine from the railroad station to corporate headquarters. Total costs of assembling and installation amounted to $700. In addition, Smith purchased a special concrete foundation for $900 to keep the machine from tilting when operational. The life of the machine is expected to be 15 years.

How Smith Calculates Cost of the Machine

List price	$20,000
Less: Cash discount (.03 × $20,000)	600
Net purchase price	19,400
Freight	1,500
Transportation from railroad station	250
Assembly and installation	700
Special foundation	900
Total cost of machine	$22,750

> Note that cash discount is deducted in arriving at total cost of the machine. If sales tax were involved, it too would be added to the cost of the asset.

Entries to record freight, assembly, installation, and so forth would be made as a debit to the Machinery account and as a credit to Cash.

> Cost of the machine will be matched with revenue.

The $22,750 cost of the asset will be spread over the years the machine helps Smith produce revenue. This example is one of the matching principle. Notice, however, that all these additional costs were reasonable and necessary to get the machine *ready for use.* If the buyer causes negligence, illegal acts, or gross inefficiencies to occur, these acts would be charged to an expense and not to the cost of the asset.

Let's look now at how to record the cost of land.

Land and Land Improvements

When land (which has unlimited useful life) is purchased, many incidental costs are usually considered part of the *cost* of the land. These costs include surveying, commissions to attorneys and real estate brokers, title searches, grading, draining, and clearing the property. Any special one-time assessment made for paving a street or installing sewers should be charged to cost of land, because it adds "permanent value" to the land.

Now let's look at some items related to land that will not be added to cost of land. **Land Improvements** is an asset account that records improvements to land that have a *limited* useful life. Some examples are driveways, fences, shrubbery, paving of parking lots, and sprinkler systems. These improvements are subject to depreciation, and thus we need an account that is kept separate from the Land account, which does *not* depreciate.

> Land does not depreciate, because it has an unlimited life.

Buildings

The cost of buying a building would include the purchase price and all the cost of repairs and other expenses to get the building *ready for use.* For construction of a new building, the cost would include all reasonable and necessary payments for labor, insurance, building permits, architect's fees, legal fees, and so on to get the building ready for use.

If a building and land are purchased for one lump-sum payment, the cost must be separated (allocated) for each, because land will not depreciate, but buildings will.

LEARNING UNIT 16-1 REVIEW

AT THIS POINT / you should be able to

- Explain how to classify property, plant, and equipment.
- Calculate the cost of an asset.
- Explain the difference between land and land improvements.

Self-Review Quiz 16-1

Respond true or false to the following:

1. Land does not depreciate.
2. Total cost of acquiring an asset cannot include cost of freight.
3. Land improvements are not subject to depreciation.
4. A cash discount is added to list price.
5. Sales tax is added to cost of an asset.

Solutions to Self-Review Quiz 16-1

1. True
2. False
3. False
4. False
5. True

Learning Unit 16-2 Depreciation Methods

LO2

Now that you know which long-term assets are depreciable, let's look at different methods for computing depreciation. If you want to check any of the concepts of depreciation we discussed in Chapter 4, take a moment to refer back to the chapter.

When a company calculates its periodic depreciation expense, different methods will produce significantly different results. Thus, the method of depreciation chosen will affect the net income for current as well as future periods and the **book value** (cost of asset less accumulated depreciation) of the asset on the balance sheet.

Let's assume that Melvin Company purchased a truck on January 1, 20XX, for $20,000, with a **residual (salvage) value** of $2,000 and an estimated life of five years. The following are the three common depreciation methods that Melvin Company could use:

1. Straight-line method
2. Units-of-production method
3. Double declining-balance method

> *Think*
> 1. Determine cost.
> 2. Determine life (years, units).
> 3. Determine residual value.
> 4. Choose a method.

Straight-Line Method

The **straight-line method** is simple to use because it allocates the cost of the asset (less residual value) evenly over its estimated useful life. (At the time an asset is acquired, an estimate is made of its usefulness or **useful life** in terms of number of years it would last, amount of output expected, and so forth.) Let's look at how Melvin Company calculates its depreciation expense for each of the estimated five years of usefulness using the straight-line method. Take a moment to read the key points in the parentheses in the accompanying table.

The formula is

$$\frac{\text{Cost} - \text{Residual Value}}{\text{Service Useful Life in Years}} = \frac{\$20,000 - \$2,000}{5} = \$3,600$$

End of Year	Cost of Delivery Truck	Yearly Depreciation Expense*	Accumulated Depreciation, End of Year	Book Value, End of Year (Cost − Accum. Dep.)
1	$20,000	$3,600	$ 3,600	$16,400
2	20,000	3,600	7,200	12,800
3	20,000	3,600	10,800	9,200
4	20,000	3,600	14,400	5,600
5	20,000	3,600	18,000	2,000
	↑	↑	↑	↑
	(Cost of the machine doesn't change.)	(Note that depreciation expense is the same each year.)	(Accumulated depreciation increases by $3,600 each year.)	(Book value each year is lowered by $3,600 until residual value of $2,000 is reached.)

*The depreciation rate is 100% ÷ 5 years = 20%. The 20% is then multiplied times the cost minus the residual value.

Units-of-Production Method

> Depreciation expense is directly related to use, not to passage of time.

With the **units-of-production method** it is assumed that *passage of time* does not determine the amount of depreciation taken. Depreciation expense is based on *use*, be it total estimated miles, tons hauled, or estimated units of production (e.g., the number of shoes a machine could produce in its expected useful life). The accompanying table shows the calculations that Melvin Company makes for its truck using the units-of-production method. (*Note:* For this example the truck is assumed to have an estimated life of 90,000 miles.)

The formula is

$$\frac{\text{Cost} - \text{Residual Value}}{\text{Estimated Units of Production}} = \frac{\$20,000 - \$2,000}{90,000 \text{ Miles}} = \$.20 \text{ per Mile}$$

$$(\$.20) \times (\text{Number of Miles Driven}) = \text{Depreciation Expense for Period}$$

End of Year	Cost of Delivery Truck	Miles Driven in Year	Yearly Depreciation, Expense	Accumulated Depreciation, End of Year	Book Value, End of Year (Cost − Accum. Dep.)
1	$20,000	30,000	$6,000	$ 6,000	$14,000
2	20,000	21,000	4,200	10,200	9,800
3	20,000	15,000	3,000	13,200	6,800

(*continued on next page*)

End of Year	Cost of Delivery Truck	Miles Driven in Year	Yearly Depreciation, Expense	Accumulated Depreciation, End of Year	Book Value, End of Year (Cost − Accum. Dep.)
4	20,000	5,000	1,000	14,200	5,800
5	20,000	19,000	3,800	18,000	2,000
		↑	↑		↑
		(After 5 years, truck has been driven 90,000 miles.)	(Depreciation expense is directly related to number of miles driven.)		(Residual value of $2,000 is reached.)

Double Declining-Balance Method

The **double declining-balance method** is an accelerated method in which a larger depreciation expense is taken in earlier years and smaller amounts in later years. For this reason it is called an **accelerated depreciation method.** This method depreciates at twice the straight-line rate, which is why it is called the *double* declining-balance method.

A key point in this method is that *residual value* is *not* deducted from cost in the calculations, and the asset cannot be depreciated below its residual value. To calculate depreciation, use the following steps:

1. Calculate the straight-line rate and double it:

$$\frac{100\%}{\text{Useful Life}} \times 2$$

2. At the *end of each year* multiply the rate times the book value of the asset at the beginning of the year.

Let's look at how Melvin Company calculates the depreciation on its truck using this method. Be sure to note the $592 in year 5 of depreciation expense. We could not take more than the $592 or we would have depreciated the asset below the residual value.

Note that the rate of .40 is not changed (20% × 2).

End of Year	Cost	Accumulated Depreciation, Beg. of Year	Book Value Beg. of Year (Cost − Acc. Dep.)	Dep. Exp. (Book Value Beg. of Year × Rate)	Accumulated Depreciation, End of Year	Book Value, End of Year (Cost − Acc. Dep.)
1	$20,000		$20,000	$8,000 ($20,000 × .40)	$ 8,000	$12,000 (20,000 − 8,000)
2	20,000	$ 8,000	12,000	4,800 (12,000 × .40)	12,800 (8,000 + 4,800)	7,200
3	20,000	12,800	7,200	2,880 (7,200 × .40)	15,680	4,320
4	20,000	15,680	4,320	1,728 (4,320 × .40)	17,408	2,592
5	20,000	17,408	2,592	592	18,000	2,000
	↑ (Original cost remains the same.)			↑ (Depreciation is limited to $592, because the asset cannot depreciate below the residual value.)		↑ (The book value now equals the residual value.)

Depreciation for Partial Years

When depreciating for partial years, we assume that for any asset purchased before the 15th of the month, depreciation is calculated for a full month. After the 15th of the month, the depreciation is disregarded for the month.

Straight-Line Method For Melvin Company, if the truck was purchased on May 4, depreciation expense would be calculated as follows:

$$\frac{\$20,000 - \$2,000}{5 \text{ Years}} \times \frac{8}{12} = \$2,400$$

We use 8 because the truck was bought on May 4. Do not count the first four months of the year in the calculation of depreciation. The following year the full yearly depreciation would be taken.

Units-of-Production Method The units-of-production method would not be affected, because depreciation is based on usage, not passage of time.

Double Declining-Balance Method Because Melvin has the benefit of the truck for eight months, his depreciation on year 1 would be as follows:

$$(\$20,000 \times .40) \times \tfrac{8}{12}$$

In year 2 and in future years the annual rate of 40% is multiplied times the *current* book value.

LO3

Depreciation for Tax Purposes: Modified Accelerated Cost Recovery System (MACRS), Including the Tax Act of 1989

General Motors and Home Depot keep two sets of depreciation records, one for financial records and one for tax reporting.

The 1986 tax act generally overhauled the depreciation setup of property placed in service after December 31, 1986. This **Modified Accelerated Cost Recovery System** is known as MACRS.* Previous methods we have discussed have been for financial reporting, not for tax purposes. This tax law requires a business to depreciate assets placed in service after December 31, 1986. To do so, two factors must be known:

1. Recovery classification
2. MACRS depreciation rates

> Note that the auto is now a 5–year class.

Look for a moment at Figure 16.1. According to the 1986 act, classes 3, 5, 7, and 10 use 200% declining balance, switching to straight line, whereas classes 15 and 20 use 150% declining balance, switching to straight line. Both residential and nonresidential real property must use straight line. Note that the recovery period is 27½ years for residential property and 31½ years for nonresidential property.

Let's use Table 16.1 to calculate depreciation on the purchase of a nonluxury car for $5,000 on March 19, 1990.

When we use Table 16.1, we do not have to decide which year we should switch from the declining-balance to the straight-line method.

The Tax Act of 1989

In 1989 the Omnibus Budget Reconciliation Act was passed. One section of the act dealt with depreciation of cellular phones and similar equipment under MACRS. Because cellular phones are subject to personal use, the tax act now treats them as listed property. Thus, unless business use is greater than 50%, the straight-line method of depreciation is required.

---

*MACRS has been renamed the General Depreciation System (GDS). The one-half year depreciation convention is not covered. See the latest IRS publication as Congress is likely to pass new business incentives due to the poor economy. At the time of writing of this text, no new tax bill has been approved.

The following classes use a 200% declining balance, switching to straight line:

🐾 3 year: Race horses more than 2 years old or any horse other than a race horse that is more than 12 years old at time placed into service; special tools of certain industries

🐾 5 year: Automobiles (not luxury); taxis; light general-purpose trucks; semiconductor manufacturing equipment; computer-based telephone central office switching equipment; qualified technological equipment; property used in connection with research and experimentation

🐾 7 year: Railroad track; single-purpose agricultural (pigpens) or horticultural structure; fixtures, equipment, and furniture

🐾 10 year: The 1986 law doesn't add any specific property under this class.

The following classes use a 150% declining balance, switching to straight line:

🐾 15 year: Municipal wastewater treatment plants; telephone distribution plants and comparable equipment used for two-way exchange of voice and data communications

🐾 20 year: Municipal sewers

The following classes use straight line:

🐾 24.5 year: Only residential rental property
🐾 31.5 year: Only residential real property

FIGURE 16.1 Summary of Classes for the Tax Reform Act of 1986

TABLE 16.1 Annual Recovery (Percent of Original Depreciable Basis)

Recovery Year	3-Year Class (200% Depreciable Basis)	5-Year Class (200% Depreciable Basis)	7-Year Class (200% Depreciable Basis)	10-Year Class (200% Depreciable Basis)	15-Year Class (150% Depreciable Basis)	20-Year Class (150% Depreciable Basis)
1	33.00	20.00	14.28	10.00	5.00	3.75
2	45.00	32.00	24.49	18.00	9.50	7.22
3	15.00*	19.20	17.49	14.40	8.55	6.68
4	7.00	11.52*	12.49	11.52	7.69	6.18
5		11.52	8.93*	9.22	6.93	5.71
6		5.76	8.93	7.37	6.23	5.28
7			8.93	6.55*	5.90*	4.89
8			4.46	6.55	5.90	4.52
9				6.55	5.90	4.46*
10				6.55	5.90	4.46
11				3.29	5.90	4.46
12					5.90	4.46
13					5.90	4.46
14					5.90	4.46
15					5.90	4.46
16					3.00	4.46
17						

*Identifies when the switch is made to the straight-line method.

Year	Depreciation
1	.20 × $5,000 = $1,000
2	.32 × $5,000 = 1,600
3	.1920 × $5,000 = 960
4	.1152 × $5,000 = 576
5	.1152 × $5,000 = 576
6	.0576 × $5,000 = 288

LEARNING UNIT 16-2 REVIEW

AT THIS POINT you should be able to

- Explain and calculate the three methods of depreciation.
- Calculate depreciation for partial years.
- Explain and calculate depreciation for MACRS.

Self-Review Quiz 16-2

From the following facts complete depreciation schedules for the (a) straight-line, (b) units-of-production, and (c) declining-balance methods.

Cost of equipment	$40,000
Residual value	7,000
Service life	5 years
Estimated units of output	20,000
Units produced in year 1:	8,000
2:	2,000
3:	5,000
4:	2,800
5:	2,200

> *Remember:* Residual value is not subtracted in the declining-balance method, although the equipment cannot be depreciated below residual value.

Solutions to Self-Review Quiz 16-2

a.

End of Year	Cost of Equipment	Yearly Depreciation Expense	Accumulated Depreciation, End of Year	Book Value, End of Year (Cost − Acc. Dep.)
1	$40,000	$6,600	$ 6,600	$33,400 ($40,000 − $6,600)
2	40,000	6,600	13,200	26,800
3	40,000	6,600	19,800	20,200
4	40,000	6,600	26,400	13,600
5	40,000	6,600	33,000	7,000 ← Book value now equals residual value.

b.

End of Year	Cost of Equipment	Units of Output in Year	Yearly Depreciation Expense	Accumulated Depreciation, End of Year	Book Value, End of Year
$$\frac{\$40,000 - \$7,000}{20,000 \text{ units}} = \$1.65$$					
1	$40,000	8,000	$13,200 (8,000 × $1.65)	$13,200	$26,800
2	40,000	2,000	3,300	16,500	23,500
3	40,000	5,000	8,250	24,750	15,250
4	40,000	2,800	4,620	29,370	10,630
5	40,000	2,200	3,630	33,000	7,000

c.

End of Year	Cost	Accumulated Depreciation, Beg. of Year	Book Value Beg. of Year (Cost − Acc. Dep.)	Dep. Exp. (B.V. Beg. of Year × Rate)	Acc. Dep., End of Year	Book Value, End of Year (Cost − Acc. Dep.)
1	$40,000	—	$40,000	$16,000 ($40,000 × .40)	$16,000	$24,000 ($40,000 − $16,000)
2	40,000	$16,000	24,000	9,600 ($24,000 × .40)	25,600	14,400 ($40,000 − $25,600)
3	40,000	25,600	14,400	5,760	31,360	8,640
4	40,000	31,360	8,640	1,640	33,000	7,000

Rate is 40%

$$\frac{100\%}{5 \text{ Years}} = \frac{1.00}{5}$$
$$= .20 = 20\%$$
$$2 \times 20\% = 40\%$$

Only $1,640 could be taken so that book value would not go below residual value.

Learning Unit 16-3 Capital and Revenue Expenditures and Disposal of Plant Assets

LO4

Now that we have seen depreciation calculations, let's look at capital and revenue expenditures and the disposal of plant assets.

Capital Expenditures

Capital expenditures include the original cost of an asset as well as payments that improve on or enlarge existing assets. Capital expenditures may be broken down into three categories: additions or enlargements, extraordinary repairs, and betterments. The differences among these three categories are based on whether the change will add to the value of the asset, extend the life of the asset, or only improve its efficiency. For example, adding a new wing to a school building will increase the value of the asset, so it is categorized as an **addition or enlargement.** Overhauling an aircraft engine definitely extends the life of the asset, so it is categorized as an **extraordinary repair.** Adding a CB radio to a fleet of delivery trucks improves the efficiency of the asset but does not extend its life, so it is categorized as a **betterment.** These three categories are shown in the chart in Figure 16.2 on the following page.

> Additions or enlargements and betterments are charged to the asset account.

It may be a little difficult at first to see the difference between betterments and extraordinary repairs. Betterments do not extend the life of the asset; the cost of a betterment is debited to the asset account. Extraordinary repairs do extend the life of the asset. The result of the extraordinary repair is to cancel some of the past depreciation.

The following is an example of how to analyze and record an extraordinary repair to a machine that has a cost of $20,000, has no residual value, and has an estimated life of 10 years.

Machine			**Accumulated Depreciation, Machine**	
Dr.	**Cr.**		**Dr.**	**Cr.**
20,000				16,000 (after 8 years)

Note that after eight years the book value of the machine is $4,000 ($20,000 − $16,000). On March 30, a major overhaul of the machine is completed for $3,000. It is believed that this overhaul will extend the machine's life by three years. Thus, the journal entry to record this extraordinary repair is as shown in Figure 16.3 on the following page.

FIGURE 16.2 Three Categories of Capital Expenditures

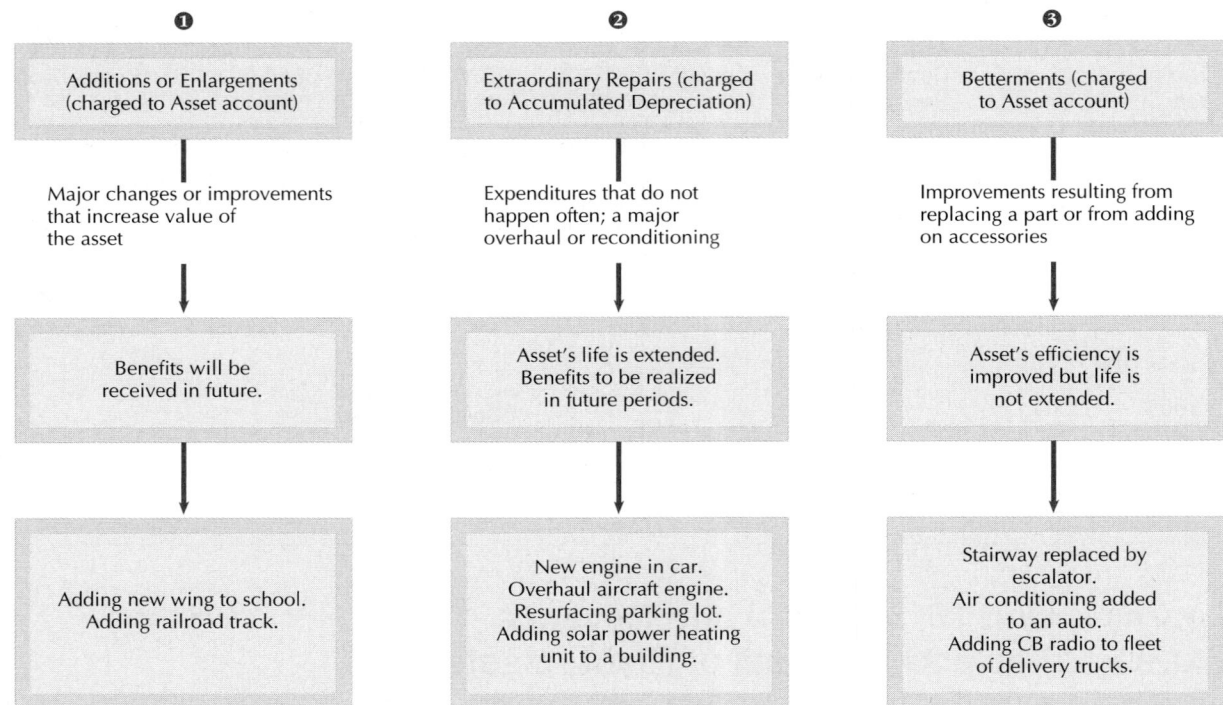

Because the machine's life is extended by three years, the owner can now take five years of depreciation. The new annual depreciation of $1,400 (instead of $2,000) is calculated as follows:

Book value before extraordinary repair	$4,000
Extraordinary repair	3,000
New book value	$7,000 ÷ 5 years = $1,400 per year

If the machine had an estimated residual value, it would be subtracted from the new book value.

FIGURE 16.3 Overhaul Extends Asset's Life

Mar.	30	Accumulated Depreciation, Machine		3 0 0 0 00		
		Cash			3 0 0 0 00	
		To record extraordinary repair				

Revenue Expenditures

Another type of expenditure occurs after an asset has been acquired. **Revenue expenditures** are payments made for ordinary maintenance of an asset or unnecessary or unreasonable situations. These expenditures occur on a regular basis and are recorded as expenses. Examples include changing oil and greasing a car, replacing window panes, changing tires on a truck, repainting a car and adding a sun roof. When an expenditure is treated as a revenue expenditure, it is recorded on the income statement as an expense and thus reduces net income in the period in which it occurred. Now let's turn our attention to the disposal of certain plant assets.

Disposal of Plant Assets

LO5

We now move on to the basic accounting procedures followed when disposing of plant assets in the following ways:

a. Discarding plant assets
b. Selling plant assets
c. Exchanging for similar plant assets

We present a different example for each category (a, b, or c). It is important to remember that depreciation is recorded up until the date a plant asset is disposed of. Take time to compare journal entries to T accounts in each example.

A. Disposal by Discarding Plant Assets A company discards a plant asset when it is no longer operational (e.g., machinery or a truck that no longer works). That also means that no other company is willing to buy or exchange something for the asset.

Situation 1: No Gain or Loss Boulder Company is disposing of a $7,000 truck with no residual value that has been fully depreciated (remember that it is possible to keep using a fully depreciated asset, but in this case the asset—the truck—is no longer in working order). Because the asset has been fully depreciated, it is not necessary to bring any depreciation up-to-date before getting rid of it.

The journal entry shown in Figure 16.4 is made after disposing of the truck.

Accumulated Depreciation, Truck		7 0 0 0 00	
Truck			7 0 0 0 00

FIGURE 16.4 Disposing the Fully Depreciated Truck

Here is how the ledger for these accounts would look after posting:

Truck		**Accumulated Depreciation, Truck**	
Dr.	**Cr.**	**Dr.**	**Cr.**
7,000	7,000	7,000	7,000

Therefore, the truck and the accumulated depreciation associated with it are off the books. Note that no gain or loss occurs here.

Situation 2: Loss on Disposal Moore Company disposed of a partially depreciated truck. The truck, costing $6,000, was considered worthless (depreciation of $5,000 to date). Because nothing is received for this asset that has a book value of $1,000, the difference between the cost of the truck and the accumulated depreciation is a loss. The Loss on Disposal account is categorized as Other Expense on the income statement. Let's look at the journal entry for this loss on disposal (Fig. 16.5) and see how the ledger would look after posting.

Loss on Disposal of Plant Asset		1 0 0 0 00	
Accumulated Depreciation, Truck		5 0 0 0 00	
Truck			6 0 0 0 00

FIGURE 16.5 Loss on Disposal of Truck

Truck		**Accumulated Depreciation, Truck**		**Loss on Disposal of Plant Asset**	
Dr.	**Cr.**	**Dr.**	**Cr.**	**Dr.**	**Cr.**
6,000	6,000	5,000	5,000	1,000	

Situation 3: Loss from Fire Missan Company received a check for $500 from an insurance company, settling a claim on a machine costing $1,500 that was damaged by fire before the end of its useful life. The balance in Accumulated Depreciation was $900. Figure 16.6 shows the journal entry Missan Company records when it receives the $500 check:

FIGURE 16.6 Loss from Fire

Cash		5 0 0 00		
Loss from Fire		1 0 0 00		
Accumulated Depreciation, Machinery		9 0 0 00		
Machinery			1 5 0 0 00	

A loss from the fire amounts to $100; the book value of the machine was $600 ($1,500 − $900), and the amount received from the insurance company was $500.

Here is how the ledger would look after posting:

Machinery			Accumulated Depreciation, Machinery			Loss from Fire	
Dr.	**Cr.**		**Dr.**	**Cr.**		**Dr.**	**Cr.**
1,500	1,500		900	900		100	

Now our attention turns to situations when assets could be sold rather than discarded.

B. Disposal by Selling Plant Assets

Situation 4: Gain on Sale Mason Company sold a truck costing $7,000 for $1,500 cash. The balance in Accumulated Depreciation is $6,000.

To see whether this sale results in a gain or loss, Mason Company must calculate whether the amount of cash received is greater or less than the book value of the truck. If the amount received is greater than the book value, the company realizes a gain. A gain on the sale of a plant asset is categorized as Other Income on the income statement. Let's look at the calculation:

Cost of truck	$7,000	Amount received	$1,500
Less accumulated depreciation	6,000	Less book value	1,000
Book value	$1,000	Gain on sale	$ 500

Because the sale results in a gain, the journal entry in Figure 16.7 is made.

FIGURE 16.7 Gain on Sale of Truck

Cash		1 5 0 0 00		
Accumulated Depreciation, Truck		6 0 0 0 00		
Truck			7 0 0 0 00	
Gain on Sale of Plant Asset			5 0 0 00	

Here is what the ledger would look like after posting:

Truck			Accumulated Depreciation, Truck	
Dr.	**Cr.**		**Dr.**	**Cr.**
7,000	7,000		6,000	6,000

Gain on Sale of Plant Asset	
Dr.	**Cr.**
	500

Situation 5: Loss on Sale Let's assume that in the previous situation Mason Company receives only $900 cash for the truck.

Now let's look at the calculation Mason Company does to see whether the sale results in a loss or gain:

Cost of truck	$7,000
Less accumulated depreciation	− 6,000
Book value	1,000
Amount received	− 900
Loss on sale	$ 100

When price is less than book value, the company realizes a loss. Because Mason's truck has a book value of $1,000 and the cash received is $900, the end result is a loss of $100 on the sale of the plant asset. This entry is categorized as Other Expense on the income statement. Figure 16.8 shows the journal entry prepared by Mason to record this loss.

	Dr.	Cr.
Cash	900 00	
Accumulated Depreciation, Truck	6000 00	
Loss on Sale of Plant Asset	100 00	
Truck		7000 00

FIGURE 16.8 Loss on Sale of Truck

Here is what the ledger would look like after posting:

Truck			Accumulated Depreciation, Truck	
Dr.	**Cr.**		**Dr.**	**Cr.**
7,000	7,000		6,000	6,000

Loss on Sale of Plant Asset	
Dr.	**Cr.**
100	

The final category of disposal is exchanging a plant asset rather than discarding or selling.

C. Disposal by Exchanging for Similar Plant Assets
Situation 6: Loss on Exchange VTR Company trades its old machine costing $19,000 for a new one with a cash price of $22,000 less a trade-in allowance of $2,000. Accumulated Depreciation of the old machine has a balance of $16,000. A **trade-in allowance** is given

when you are buying a new car, for example, and trade in your old one for a sum of money that is applied to the price of the new car. A loss on exchange will result if the book value of the old machine is greater than what is received for the trade-in allowance. Let's look at how VTR calculates its loss on this machine exchange.

Step 1 Calculate the book value of the old machine:

Cost	$19,000
− Accumulated depreciation	16,000
Book value	$ 3,000

Step 2 Compare the book value of the old machine with the trade-in:

$3,000	Book value of old
2,000	Trade-in
$1,000	Loss

Because the book value of the old machine is $3,000 and VTR receives only a $2,000 trade-in, the result is a $1,000 loss. Figure 16.9 shows the journal entry prepared by VTR.

FIGURE 16.9 Loss on Exchange of Machinery

	Dr.	Cr.
Machinery	22000 00	
Loss on Exchange of Machinery	1000 00	
Accumulated Depreciation, Machinery	16000 00	
Machinery		19000 00
Cash		20000 00

The entry puts on the books the cost of the new machine as well as records the loss on the exchange and the removal of the old machine and the related accumulated depreciation. Note that cash is reduced by $20,000 (cash price less trade-in). Here is what the ledger would look like after posting:

Machinery (Old)			**Accumulated Depreciation, Machinery**	
Dr.	**Cr.**		**Dr.**	**Cr.**
19,000	19,000		16,000	16,000

Machinery (New)			**Loss on Exchange of Machinery**	
Dr.	**Cr.**		**Dr.**	**Cr.**
22,000			1,000	

Situation 7: Gain Is Absorbed into Cost of New Machine The Accounting Principles Board ruled that when a gain exists on an exchange of a similar asset it should not be recorded as a gain, but the new asset should be equal to the book value of the old asset plus cash given in the exchange. In other words, no account called Gain is used, but the actual gain is absorbed into the cost of the new machine. The reason behind this decision was that an exchange of similar assets is not the result of an earnings process. In this situation we assume that VTR (situation 6) will receive a $5,000 trade-in allowance (instead of the $2,000) for trading in an old machine for a new machine for a cash price of $22,000. VTR will complete the following steps to calculate the new cost of the machine (assuming a gain). Remember that a gain would be absorbed into the cost of the new machine for exchanges of similar assets.

1. Calculate the book value of the old machine.
2. Identify the cash paid (cash price less trade-in).
3. Calculate the value of the new machine as it will show up on the books. (This value is called the *cash basis* of the machine.) This step is done by adding steps 1 and 2.

Let's now look at VTR's actual calculation of these steps.

Step 1 Calculate the book value of the old machine:

$$\begin{array}{r} \$19,000 \\ -\ 16,000 \\ \hline = \$3,000 \end{array}$$

Step 2 Identify cash paid:

$$\$17,000\ (\$22,000 - \$5,000)$$

Step 3 New cash basis (step 1 + step 2):

$$\$20,000\ (\$3,000 + \$17,000)$$

Note that the cash basis is $20,000, not $22,000 as stated as the original cost of the new equipment. Note also that the new machine shows up on the books at the value of the things that were given up for it: an old machine with a book value of $3,000 and cash of $17,000.

Now let's look at how VTR records this exchange on its books (Fig. 16.10).

FIGURE 16.10 Gain Absorbed in Cost of New Machine

Machinery	20 0 0 0 00	
Accumulated Depreciation, Machinery	16 0 0 0 00	
Machinery		19 0 0 0 00
Cash		17 0 0 0 00

Note that no account records the gain. The gain is absorbed into the cost of the new asset. Remember that a gain results in *less* depreciation in the future, because the cost of the machine has a value of $20,000, not $22,000. The ledger, when posted, would look as follows:

Machinery (Old)			**Accumulated Depreciation, Machinery**	
Dr.	**Cr.**		**Dr.**	**Cr.**
19,000	19,000		16,000	16,000

Machinery (New)	
Dr.	**Cr.**
20,000	

Income tax rules agree with accountants regarding nonrecognition of gains and absorbing them into the cost of the new asset (situation 7). The Internal Revenue Service also believes losses should not be recognized and thus should be absorbed into the cost of new assets.* Often two sets of records are kept. Situation 6 followed guidelines of the Accounting Principles Board. Situation 8 follows tax rules of the Internal Revenue Service. Compare the two.

Situation 8: Loss Is Absorbed in Cost of New Asset Let's assume that VTR receives only a $2,000 trade-in allowance instead of $5,000 (situation 7) when the old machine is traded in for the new machine for a cash price of $22,000. VTR calculates the cost basis of the new machine (assuming it uses the **income tax method** of absorbing losses into the cost of the new machine) as follows:

Cost of old machine	$19,000
− Accumulated depreciation	16,000
= Book value	3,000
+ Cash paid	20,000
($22,000 − $2,000)	
= Cost basis of new machine	$23,000

---

*Accountants will absorb the loss into the asset cost only if the loss is considered to be immaterial.

This loss of $1,000 (VTR having received $1,000 less than the book value) is *added on* to the cost of the new machine, resulting in a cost basis of $23,000. VTR records the exchange in the journal as shown in Figure 16.11.

FIGURE 16.11 Loss Absorbed into Cost of Machine

Machinery	23 00 0 00		
Accumulated Depreciation, Machinery	16 00 0 00		
Machinery		19 00 0 00	
Cash		20 00 0 00	

Note that no Loss account is used. The loss is absorbed into the cost of the equipment, the result being that more depreciation will be taken in future periods ($23,000 versus $22,000), because the cost of the new equipment is $1,000 higher.

Here is what the ledger would look like after posting:

Machinery (Old)			Accumulated Depreciation, Machinery	
Dr.	**Cr.**		**Dr.**	**Cr.**
19,000	19,000		16,000	16,000

Machinery (New)	
Dr.	**Cr.**
23,000	

LEARNING UNIT 16-3 REVIEW

AT THIS POINT you should be able to

- Compare and contrast capital and revenue expenditures.
- Prepare journal entries to record discarding, selling, or exchanging plant assets.
- Compare and contrast Internal Revenue procedures with those of the Financial Accounting Principles Board regarding gains and losses that result from exchanges of plant assets.

Self-Review Quiz 16-3

Respond true or false to the following:

1. In selling a plant asset, a gain results if cash received is greater than the book value of the asset sold.
2. A loss on exchange of equipment can result if the book value of the old equipment is less than the trade-in allowance.
3. The Financial Accounting Principles Board does not recognize gains on exchange of similar assets.
4. Internal Revenue Service rules are consistent with the Financial Accounting Principles Board in recognizing losses when assets are exchanged.
5. When a loss is absorbed into the cost of an asset, it allows for more depreciation in future periods.
6. Revenue expenditures extend the useful life of an asset.
7. Putting an air conditioner in a truck is an example of a betterment.

Solutions to Self-Review Quiz 16-3

1. True
2. False
3. True
4. False
5. True
6. False
7. True

Learning Unit 16-4 Natural Resources and Intangible Assets

Another type of long-term asset is natural resources. Natural resources consist of natural assets such as oil, coal, or timber. The acquisition of oil wells or timber is recorded at cost, and as the oil or timber or coal is extracted from the earth, the allocation of that cost occurs through a process known as **depletion.** Depletion is similar to the units-of-production method of depreciation, discussed earlier in the chapter, and is listed as an operating expense on the income statement.

Let's take the example of a coal deposit. If a coal deposit has 200,000 tons available and was purchased for $200,000, the depletion per ton is $1. Thus, if 91,000 tons were removed from the deposit in 20X1, the depletion charge that year would be recorded as shown in Figure 16.12.

20X1					
Dec.	31	Depletion of Coal Deposit	91 0 0 0 00		
		Accumulated Depletion, Coal		91 0 0 0 00	

FIGURE 16.12 Depletion of Long-Term Asset

Coal Deposit	
Dr.	**Cr.**
200,000	
(on balance sheet)	

Accumulated Depletion, Coal	
Dr.	**Cr.**
	91,000
	(on balance sheet)

Depletion of Coal Deposit	
Dr.	**Cr.**
91,000	
(on income statement)	

> Accumulated Depletion is a contra-asset on the balance sheet.

Intangible Assets and the Concept of Impairment

LO6

Intangible assets are long-lived assets that have no physical existence but do represent valuable legal rights and monetary relationships that benefit a company. (In fact, Prepaid Insurance, Notes, and Accounts Receivable are intangible, but they are classified as *current* assets.) We are looking at intangible assets classified in the *long-term* asset section. Examples include patents, copyrights, franchises, and goodwill. Intangible assets are recorded at cost on the balance sheet and usually have no contra-accounts.

The process of allocating the cost of an intangible asset over all the periods it provides benefits is called *amortization.* The expense incurred in acquiring these assets is **amortized;** that means it is written off over a fixed number of years. **Amortization expense** is an operating expense on the income statement.

> A patent is good for 20 years but is amortized for a shorter period.

Patents A **patent** is an exclusive right to the owner to sell or produce his or her discovery or invention. Let's assume that on January 1, 20XX, a patent costing $100,000 is amortized over 10 years. The adjusting entry shown in Figure 16.13 is made.

FIGURE 16.13 Amortizing a Patent

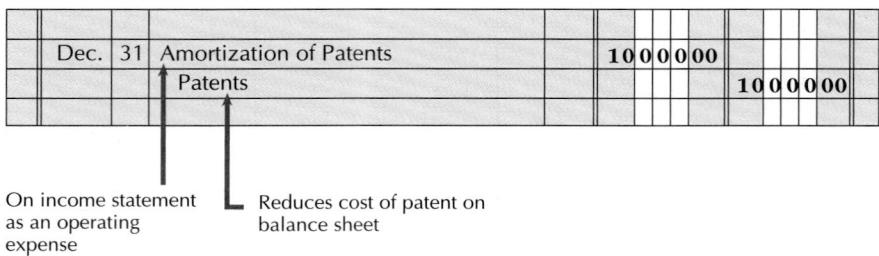

Dec.	31	Amortization of Patents		10 0 0 0 00	
		Patents			10 0 0 0 00

On income statement as an operating expense

Reduces cost of patent on balance sheet

Copyrights **Copyrights** are exclusive rights granted to owners by the federal government to publish artistic, literary, or musical work. In the United States a copyright is granted for the life of the creator and for 50 years thereafter. The cost of the copyright is recorded as a cost and amortized over its expected useful life in an account called Amortization Expense, Copyrights, because the useful life of a copyright is short.

Franchises A **franchise** is the result of someone purchasing an exclusive privilege or right to sell a manufacturer's product or a service in a specifically defined geographical location. Holiday Inns, for example, are franchises. The useful life of many franchises are indefinite and thus not amortized.

> Cost of assets purchased
> − Value of assets identified
> = Goodwill

Goodwill When all or part of a business is purchased, the difference between the price paid and the value of the identifiable assets is called **goodwill.** Goodwill occurs when the expected rate of future earnings is greater than the rate of earnings for the industry standard. Some considerations that may cause goodwill could include brand names, business location, and service. It is not easy to pinpoint the exact amount of goodwill in each accounting period. Thus, in the accounting profession it is agreed not to put a cost on goodwill until a company is bought or sold. According to generally accepted accounting principles (GAAP), goodwill is not amortized because the goodwill of companies increases in value.

Accounting for the Impairment of an Intangible Asset Some intangible assets have definite lives and therefore are not subject to amortization. If the intangible asset experiences some type of **impairment,** or loses value, you may write down the amount of goodwill by a debit to Loss on Goodwill and a credit to Goodwill.

LEARNING UNIT 16-4 REVIEW

AT THIS POINT you should be able to

- Define depletion and accumulated depletion and indicate their normal balances and on which financial reports they are located.
- Explain amortization.
- Discuss how a patent is amortized.
- Explain the life of a copyright.
- Define and explain how goodwill is calculated.

Self-Review Quiz 16-4

Respond true or false to the following:

1. Intangible assets are depleted, not amortized.
2. The life of a patent is 12 years.
3. A copyright lasts for 25 years.
4. The cost of a franchise must be amortized over 40 years.
5. Goodwill represents excess earning power for a company.

Solutions to Self-Review Quiz 16-4

1. False   **2.** False   **3.** False   **4.** False   **5.** True

CHAPTER ASSIGNMENTS

SUMMARY OF KEY POINTS

LEARNING UNIT 16-1

1. The total cost of an asset includes all expenditures that are reasonable and necessary in acquiring it and getting it into position and in condition for use in the company.
2. Cash discounts are deducted from the cost of an asset.
3. Incidental costs related to the purchase of land and special costs that add a permanent value are added to the cost of land.
4. The Land Improvements account records improvements to land that have a limited useful life (such as driveways or fences). This account is subject to depreciation.
5. The cost of buying a building would include purchase price and all cost of repairs and other expenses to get the building ready for use. When constructing a new building, the cost would include all payments necessary to get the building ready for use.

LEARNING UNIT 16-2

In this unit we look at three different depreciation methods.

1. Straight-line method:
   a. Depreciation expense is the same each year.
   b. Book value each year is lowered until residual value is reached.
2. Units-of-production method:
   a. Depreciation expense is directly related to output or usage of asset.
   b. Assets cannot be depreciated below residual value.
3. Double declining-balance method:
   a. Residual value is not deducted from cost.
   b. Depreciation expense is book value at beginning of year times rate.
   c. Asset cannot depreciate below book value.
4. Depreciation can be taken for partial years. If an asset is purchased in the first 15 days of the month, the whole month is considered in the depreciation calculation.
5. MACRS are for tax reporting, whereas the other four depreciation methods are used for financial reports.

LEARNING UNIT 16-3

1. Capital expenditures include the original cost of an asset and three categories of additional payments:
   a. Additions or enlargements are major changes or improvements that increase the value of an asset.
   b. Extraordinary repairs extend the life of the asset.

c. Betterments are improvements that increase efficiency but do not extend the life of an asset.

Additions or enlargements and betterments are charged to the asset account; extraordinary repairs are charged to Accumulated Depreciation.

2. After an asset is acquired, the expenditures for ordinary maintenance and unnecessary or unreasonable situations that do not try to extend useful life are treated as expenses of the current period and are called *revenue expenditures.*

3. A plant asset can be disposed of by discarding, selling, or exchanging it.

4. The Loss on Disposal account appears as Other Expense on the income statement.

5. A gain on sale of an asset occurs if the cash received is greater than the book value of the asset. Such a gain appears as Other Income on the income statement.

6. When a plant asset is exchanged, loss occurs when the trade-in allowance is less than the book value of the asset.

7. In an exchange of similar assets, the Financial Accounting Principles Board ruled that gains are to be absorbed into the cost of the new asset.

8. Income tax rules require that gains *and losses* on exchange of assets be absorbed into the cost of the new asset. This requirement is inconsistent with the Financial Accounting Principles Board's ruling on losses.

LEARNING UNIT 16-4

1. Natural resources, such as oil, coal, or timber, will deplete over a period of time as resources are extracted. Depletion expense is listed as an operating expense on the income statement.

2. Accumulated depletion is a contra-asset on the balance sheet.

3. Intangible assets, such as patents, copyrights, franchises, and goodwill, are also used up over a period of years. Amortization is the process of estimating and recording the charges as these intangible assets are used up.

4. Amortization expenses are operating expenses on the income statement.

5. A patent is good for 20 years; a copyright is granted for the life of the creator and 50 years thereafter.

6. The cost of obtaining a franchise is amortized over its life or 40 years, whichever is shorter.

7. Because it is not easy to put a price on goodwill in each accounting period, it is not until a company is bought or sold that a cost is placed on goodwill. Goodwill is not amortized but impairment could result if a loss in value is incurred.

KEY TERMS

Accelerated depreciation method   More depreciation taken in early years of an asset's life, decreasing amounts in later years.

Additions or enlargements   Major changes or improvements that increase the value of an asset (such as adding a new wing to a school).

Amortization expense   An operating expense on the income statement relating to intangible assets.

Amortize   To charge a portion of an expenditure over a fixed number of years. Those assets with indefinite lives are not subject to amortization.

Betterments   Improvements that increase the efficiency of an asset by adding accessories or replacing parts.

Book value   Cost of asset less accumulated depreciation.

Capital expenditures   Original cost of an asset as well as additions or enlargements, extraordinary repairs, and betterments.

Copyright   The exclusive right that is granted by the federal government to sell and reproduce literary, musical, or artistic works for a period of time.

Depletion   Amount of natural resources that has been exhausted by mining, pumping, and so forth for a period of time.

Double declining-balance method   An accelerated depreciation method that uses up to twice the straight-line rate times book value of asset to calculate depreciation expense. Residual value is not subtracted from the cost of an asset in determining depreciation.

Extraordinary repairs   Infrequent expenditures that extend an asset's life (such as a new engine in a car).

Franchise   A right granted by business or government to produce or sell goods in a specific geographic region. Examples are a Burger King and Holiday Inn.

Goodwill   When a business is purchased, the difference between the price paid and the value of the identifiable assets is goodwill. Goodwill may depend on brand names, business location, service, or other elements; it is a valuable asset that plays an important part in the expected rate of future earnings of a business.

Impairment   Value of an intangible asset that decreases and is written off or taken.

Income tax method   When plant assets are exchanged, tax law says the gain or loss must be absorbed into the cost of the new asset.

Intangible assets   Assets having no physical substance (such as patents or franchises).

Land Improvements   An asset account that records improvements made to land; such improvements have a limited life and are subject to depreciation (an example is a driveway or fences).

Modified Accelerated Cost Recovery System (MACRS)   A system for businesses to calculate depreciation for tax purposes based on the Tax Laws of 1986 and 1989, also known as the General Depreciation System (GDS).

Patent   An exclusive right to sell or produce one's discovery or invention. A patent is good for 20 years.

Residual (salvage) value   The amount of the asset's cost that will be recovered when the asset is sold, traded in, or scrapped.

Revenue Expenditures   Payments made for ordinary maintenance of an asset or unnecessary or unreasonable situations.

Straight-line method   Method that allocates an equal amount of depreciation over an asset's period of usefulness.

Trade-in allowance   A value received when one asset is traded in on the purchase of another asset. For example, when you buy a new car you may trade in your old car for an amount of money that is applied toward the purchase of the new car.

Units-of-production method   A depreciation method that is based on usage and not on time. An example of units of production is the numbers of shoes a machine could produce in its expected useful life.

Useful life   At the time an asset is acquired, an estimate is made of its usefulness in terms of years, output, and so forth.

BLUEPRINT: KEY ACCOUNTS

Review of Key Accounts				
Account	Category*	↑	Normal Balance	Financial Report Found on
Equipment	Plant Asset	Dr.	Dr.	Balance Sheet
Buildings	Plant Asset	Dr.	Dr.	Balance Sheet
Land	Plant Asset	Dr.	Dr.	Balance Sheet
Loss on Disposal of Plant Asset	Other Expense	Dr.	Dr.	Income Statement
Loss from Fire	Other Expense	Dr.	Dr.	Income Statement
Gain on Sale of Plant Asset	Other Income	Cr.	Cr.	Income Statement
Loss on Exchange of Machinery	Other Expense	Dr.	Dr.	Income Statement
Depletion of Coal Deposit	Operating Expense	Dr.	Dr.	Income Statement
Accumulated Depletion	Contra-Asset	Cr.	Cr.	Balance Sheet
Coal Deposit	Natural Resource	Dr.	Dr.	Balance Sheet
Patents	Intangible Asset	Dr.	Dr.	Balance Sheet
Amortization Expense Statement	Operating Expense	Dr.	Dr.	Income
Copyrights, Franchises, or Goodwill	Intangible Assets	Dr.	Dr.	Balance Sheet
Loss of Goodwill	Other Expense	Dr.	Dr.	Income Statement

*We use Plant Assets to represent property, plant, and equipment.

QUESTIONS, CLASSROOM DISCUSSION EXERCISES, EXERCISES, AND PROBLEMS

Discussion and Critical Thinking Questions/Ethical Case

1. What types of payment are considered "reasonable and necessary" when determining the cost of an asset?

2. What is the purpose of the Land Improvements account?

3. What is the difference between revenue and capital expenditures?

4. What are three methods of calculating depreciation? Briefly explain the key points of each.

5. What is the purpose of the Modified Accelerated Cost Recovery System?

6. A betterment is a revenue expenditure. True or false? Please explain.

7. Which method of depreciation does *not* deduct residual value in its calculation?

8. When a plant asset is sold, a loss results if the cash received is greater than book value. Agree or disagree? Please explain.

9. A loss on an exchange of plant assets occurs when the book value of the old machine is more than the trade-in allowance. True or false?

10. Explain how the income tax method differs from the Accounting Principles Board ruling with regard to the recording of exchanges of plant assets that result in a loss.

11. What is the purpose of the Accumulated Depletion account?

12. List and describe three intangible assets.

13. Pete went to an auto dealer to buy a new Jeep. The salesperson told Pete that cars really appreciate in value. He cited antique cars as a perfect example. The dealer went on to tell Pete that buying a car represents some great tax savings. He told Pete that leasing is getting less and less popular. Should Pete buy a new car? You make the call. Write down your recommendations to Pete.

Classroom Demonstration Exercises

SET A

LO1 (5 min) **Cost of Property, Plant, and Equipment**

1. Calculate the total cost of the machine given the following:

List price	$3,000
Cash discount	6%
Freight	$ 60
Assembly	200
Special foundation	60

LO2 (10 min) **Straight-Line Method**

2. Lee Ring depreciates his truck by the straight-line method. Calculate the yearly depreciation expense given the following:

Cost	$7,000
Residual value	$2,000
Service of useful life	5 years

LO2 (10 min) **Book Value**

3. If a machine had a cost of $6,000 with an accumulated depreciation of $500, what would be its book value?

LO2 (10 min) **Units-of-Production Method**

4. If Lee Ring (Exercise 2) depreciated his truck by the units-of-production method, calculate the first year's depreciation based on the following: cost

$7,000; residual value $2,000. Estimated mileage is 50,000. The truck was driven 7,000 miles in year 1.

Double Declining-Balance Method

LO2 (10 min)

5. If Lee Ring (Exercise 2) depreciated his truck by the double declining-balance method, calculate the depreciation expense for year 1.

Capital and Revenue Expenditures

LO4 (5 min)

6. Identify each situation as a capital expenditure or revenue expenditure.

Situation	Capital Expenditure		Revenue Expenditure
	Addition	Betterment/ Extraordinary Repair	
a. New car engine replaced			
b. New air-conditioning filters			
c. New roof			
d. New addition on prep school			

Loss and Gains

LO5 (5 min)

7. Complete the following:

	Account	Category	Financial Statement Found on
a. Gain on Sale of Plant Assets			
b. Accumulated Depletion			
c. Loss on Disposal of Plant Assets			

Exchange with Loss

LO5 (15 min)

8. Lee Co. traded in an old machine costing $20,000 for a new machine for a cash price of $19,000 with a trade-in allowance of $6,000. Accumulated Depreciation on the old machine was $11,000.
a. What is the book value of the old machine? What is the loss?
b. Provide a journal entry to record the exchange.

Exchange with Gain

LO5 (15 min)

9. Assume in Exercise 8 the trade-in value was $10,000. Prepare a journal entry to record the exchange.

Income Tax Method

LO5 (15 min)

10. If in Exercise 8 the income tax method was used, prepare the journal entry to record the exchange.

SET B

Cost of Property, Plant, and Equipment

LO2 (10 min)

1. Calculate the total cost of the machine given the following:

List price	$2,000
Cash discount	5%
Freight	$ 50
Assembly	150
Special foundation	50

LO2 (10 min) **Straight-Line Method**

2. Mel Jones depreciates his truck by the straight-line method. Calculate the yearly depreciation expense given the following:

Cost	$6,000
Residual value	$1,000
Service of useful life	10 years

LO2 (10 min) **Book Value**

3. If a machine had a cost of $4,000 with an accumulated depreciation of $1,000, what would be its book value?

LO2 (10 min) **Units-of-Production Method**

4. If Mel Jones (Exercise 2) depreciated his truck by the units-of-production method, calculate the first year's depreciation based on the following: cost $6,000; residual value $1,000. Estimated mileage is 100,000. The truck was driven 8,000 miles in year 1.

LO2 (10 min) **Double Declining-Balance Method**

5. If Mel Jones (Exercise 2) depreciated his truck by the double declining-balance method, calculate the depreciation expense for year 1.

LO4 (5 min) **Capital and Revenue Expenditures**

6. Identify each situation as a capital expenditure or revenue expenditure.

Situation	Capital Expenditure		Revenue Expenditure
	Addition	Betterment/ Extraordinary Repair	
a. New tires			
b. New air conditioning for a car			
c. New car engine			
d. New addition on school			

LO5 (5 min) **Loss and Gains**

7. Complete the following:

	Account	Category	Financial Statement Found on
a. Accumulated Depletion			
b. Loss on Disposal of Plant Assets			
c. Gain on Sale of Plant Assets			

LO5 (15 min) **Exchange with Loss**

8. Pete Co. traded in an old machine costing $10,000 for a new machine for a cash price of $13,000 with a trade-in allowance of $3,000. Accumulated Depreciation on the old machine was $6,000.
   a. What is the book value of the old machine? What is the loss?
   b. Provide a journal entry to record the exchange.

LO5 (15 min) **Exchange with Gain**

9. Assume in Exercise 8 the trade-in value was $5,000. Prepare a journal entry to record the exchange.

Income Tax Method   *LO5 (15 min)*

10. If in Exercise 8 the income tax method was used, prepare the journal entry to record the exchange.

Exercises

16-1. Mack Company incurred the following expenditures to buy a new machine: *LO1 (15 min)*
- Invoice, $30,000 less 10% cash discount.
- Freight charges, $500.
- Assembly charges, $1,400.
- Special base to support machine, $505.
- Machine dropped and repaired, $350.

What is the actual cost of the machine?

16-2. From the following, prepare depreciation schedules for the first two years for   *LO2 (30 min)*
(a) straight-line, (b) units-of-production, and (c) double declining-balance at twice the straight-line rate methods.
- Machine purchased on January 1, $1,440.
- Residual value, $240.
- Estimated useful life, five years.
- Total estimated output, 600 units.
- Output year 1, 100 units.
- Output year 2, 200 units.

16-3. Larson Co., whose accounting period ends on December 31, purchased a   *LO2 (30 min)*
machine for $6,800 on January 1 with an estimated residual value of $800 and an estimated useful life of 10 years. Prepare depreciation schedules for the current as well as the following year using (a) straight-line, and (b) double declining-balance at twice the straight-line rate methods.

16-4. A machine that cost $9,000 with $3,900 of accumulated depreciation was   *LO4 (30 min)*
traded in for a similar machine having a $5,800 cash price. An $800 trade-in was offered by the seller.
- **a.** Calculate the book value of the old machine.
- **b.** Calculate the loss on the exchange.
- **c.** Prepare the journal entry for the exchange.
- **d.** Calculate the cost basis of the new equipment if the income tax method is used and prepare a journal entry.

16-5. On May 1, 20X1, Osgood Company bought a patent at a cost of $5,000. It is   *LO5 (10 min)*
estimated that the patent will give Osgood a competitive advantage for 10 years. Record in general journal form amortization for 20X1 and 20X2. (Assume December 31 is the end of the accounting period for Osgood.)

16-6. Pultzer Company bought a light general-purpose truck for $9,000 on March 8,   *LO3 (10 min)*
1991. Calculate the yearly depreciation using the MACRS method.

Group A Problems

16A-1. Record the following transactions into the general journal of Orange Company: *LO1, 4 (30 min)*

20XX

Feb.   5   Purchased land for $90,000. The $90,000 included attorney's fees of $6,000.

   18   Orange Company decided to pave the parking lot for $5,400.

Mar. 24   Purchased a building for $90,000, putting down 30% and mortgaging the remainder.

   29   Bought equipment for $32,000. Freight and assembly were an additional $4,000.

May 10   Added a new wing for $175,000 to building that was purchased on March 24.

Check Figure:
Feb. 18
Dr. Land Improvement $5,400
Cr. Cash $5,400

(continued on next page)

June	15	Performed ordinary repair work on equipment purchased March 29, $750, to maintain its normal operations.
July	1	Bought a truck for $14,000.
Oct.	15	Added a hydraulic loader to truck, $2,200.
Nov.	30	Truck purchased in July was brought in for grease and oil, $33.
Dec.	30	Overhauled truck's motor for $900, extending its life by more than one year.
Dec.	31	Changed tires on truck, $325.

LO2 (60 min)

16A-2. On January 1, 20X1, a machine was installed at Lavy Factory at a cost of $58,000. Its estimated residual value at the end of its estimated life of four years is $18,000. The machine is expected to produce 80,000 units with the following production schedule:
- 20X1: 12,000 units
- 20X2: 27,000 units
- 20X3: 15,000 units
- 20X4: 26,000 units

Complete depreciation schedules for (a) straight-line, (b) units-of-production, and (c) double declining-balance at twice the straight-line rate methods.

Check Figure:
(b) Book value end of year 20X4
$18,000

LO2 (60 min)

16A-3. On June 13, 20X1, Cook Company bought equipment for $4,080. Its estimated life is four years with a residual value of $240. Prepare depreciation schedules for 20X1, 20X2, and 20X3 for (a) straight-line, and (b) double declining-balance at twice the straight-line rate methods.

Check Figure:
(b) Book value end of year 20X3
$722.50

LO5 (60 min)

16A-4. Journalize the following transactions for the Robe Company and below each entry show all calculations:

20XX		
Jan.	1	Sold a truck for $1,250 that cost $6,750 and had accumulated depreciation of $6,100.
Feb.	10	A machine costing $3,200 with accumulated depreciation of $2,450 was destroyed in a fire. The insurance company settled the claim for $300.
May	1	Traded in a machine costing $19,400 with $16,500 of accumulated depreciation for a new machine costing $25,100 with a trade-in allowance of $2,700. Note that depreciation is up-to-date. The loss is to be recognized.
July	8	Traded in a machine costing $40,000 with $34,000 of accumulated depreciation (which is up-to-date) for a new machine for a cash price of $45,000 and a trade-in allowance of $8,000.
Aug.	9	Journalize the May 1 transaction using the income tax method.
Sept.	12	A truck costing $7,000 and fully depreciated was disposed of.

Check Figure:
May:
Loss on exchange
$200 Dr.

Group B Problems

LO1, 4 (30 min)

16B-1. Journalize the following transactions for Orange Company.

20XX		
Apr.	1	Purchased a machine for $89,500 along with an additional charge for freight and assembly of $1,500.
	8	Purchased land at a cost of $22,000. The $22,000 included attorney's fees of $2,500.
	15	Purchased a building for $90,000, putting down 10% and mortgaging the remainder.
	29	At a cost of $1,900, cleared and graded the land purchased on April 8 (the additional cost considered as part of the cost of land).

May	1	Performed regular maintenance work on machinery, $160, to maintain its normal operations.
	8	Painted the building purchased on April 15, $2,900. Painting was necessary to have the building ready for proper use.
	30	Purchased a second airplane for company business, $65,000.
June	30	Installed a hydraulic loader on a truck at a cost of $2,900.
July	30	First airplane's engine was overhauled for $7,900.
Sept.	30	Building is completely renovated at a cost of $30,000, which will extend its life by 10 years.

Check Figure:
May 8:
Dr. Building $2,900
Cr. Cash $2,900

16B-2. On January 1, 20X1, Lavy Factory installed a new machine at a cost of $117,000. Its estimated residual value at the end of its estimated life of four years is $9,000. The machine is expected to produce 90,000 units with the following production schedule:
- 20X1: 11,000 units
- 20X2: 9,000 units
- 20X3: 11,000 units
- 20X4: 59,000 units

Complete depreciation schedules for (a) straight-line, (b) units-of-production, and (c) double declining-balance at twice the straight-line rate methods.

LO2 (60 min)

Check Figure:
(b) Book value end of year 20X4
$9,000

16B-3. On April 5, 20X1, Cook Company bought equipment for $6,200. Its estimated life is five years with a residual value of $200. Prepare depreciation schedules for 20X1, 20X2, and 20X3 for (a) straight-line, and (b) double declining-balance at twice the straight-line rate methods.

LO2 (60 min)

Check Figure:
(b) Book value end of year 20X3
$1,562.40

16B-4. Journalize the following transactions for the Robe Company and below each entry show all calculations:

20XX

Jan.	1	Sold a truck for $3,600 that cost $12,800 and had accumulated depreciation of $10,900.
Feb.	8	A machine costing $4,000 with accumulated depreciation of $3,390 was destroyed in a fire. The insurance company settled the claim for $150.
May	9	Traded in a machine costing $18,500 with $15,750 of accumulated depreciation (which is up-to-date) for a new machine costing $26,200 with a trade-in allowance of $2,600. The loss is to be recognized.
July	10	Traded in a machine costing $39,500 with $35,700 of accumulated depreciation (depreciation is up-to-date) for a new machine for a cash price of $44,000 and a trade-in allowance of $11,500.
Aug.	19	Journalize the May 9 transaction using the income tax method.
Sept.	12	A truck costing $11,000 and fully depreciated was disposed of.

LO5 (60 min)

Check Figure:
May:
Loss on Exchange $150 Dr.

ON-THE-JOB TRAINING

T-1. On August 1, 20X1, Hope Co. purchased a customized light truck for $96,000 cash. On August 3, special shelving was added to the truck for $6,000. The truck has a useful life of six years with a trade-in value of $12,000 and is depreciated by the straight-line method. On January 1, 20X4, Hope Co. was trying to decide whether to overhaul the truck at a cost of $15,000 or buy a new truck for $100,000 and depreciate it by MACRS. Overhauling the truck would increase its useful life by two years, and residual value would remain at $12,000.

LO2 (30 min)

As the accountant of Hope Co., you have been called into a meeting with Mr. Reynolds, the vice president, to further discuss this matter. Bring all your data with you, along with a written recommendation.

LO2 (20 min) **T-2.**

MEMO

To: Hal Owen

FROM: Pete Sanchez

RE: Decision on general-purpose truck

We need your assistance on which depreciation method would be best for us to use. I'm thinking that we should use MACRS instead of the straight-line method for both financial and tax purposes. We could save lots of dollars! Could you verify my decision (or not) and work up the numbers for me based on the following:

Cost:	$20,000
Life:	5 years
Residual:	$5,000

FINANCIAL REPORT PROBLEM

LO4 (20 min) ### Reading the Kellogg's Annual Report

Go to Appendix A and explain what the term *impairment* means.

INTERNET PROJECT

Wendy's

Go to the Web and search: Annual Report Wendy's 2008.

Click on Investors Relations.

List out the latest news Wendy's is providing to its investors.

Order a free annual report.

17

Partnership

UNITED STATES

Internal Revenue Service Building

DID YOU KNOW? The IRS considers partners to be self-employed and does not consider them to be employees of a partnership. Visit *www.irs.gov* to find more information about the IRS.

LEARNING OBJECTIVES

1. Journalizing the entry for formation of a partnership.

2. Calculating a partner's share of net income based on fractional ratio, beginning capital investment, and salary and interest allowances.

3. Preparing a statement of partners' equity.

4. Journalizing entries to record admitting a new partner, withdrawal of a partner, and bonuses to partners.

5. Journalizing entries involved in the liquidation process and preparing a statement of liquidation.

Up to this point we have been using the sole proprietorship form of business organization in discussing the accounting process. We are now ready to look at another form of business organization, the **partnership.**

A partnership, as defined by the **Uniform Partnership Act,** is "an association of two or more persons to carry on as co-owners of a business for profit." Examples of partnerships include service businesses and professional practitioners, such as physicians, dentists, attorneys, and accountants. Many small wholesale as well as retail companies are formed as partnerships. Your local conveni ence store may be a partnership.

The recording of business transactions involving assets, liabilities, revenue, and expenses is handled the same for both a sole proprietorship and a partnership. The major difference in recording business transactions for these two forms of organization lies in the equity account(s). A sole proprietorship has only one capital and withdrawals account, whereas in a partnership each partner has his or her own separate capital and withdrawals account. First we look at the characteristics of a partnership and how it is formed.

> When using an accounting software package, be careful to select the correct entity type. This information allows for the correct equity structure and aids in tax form preparation.

Learning Unit 17-1 Partnership Characteristics and Formation of Partnerships

It is quite easy to form a partnership. When two or more people agree orally or in writing to be partners, a contract results. Although the oral agreement is binding, it makes more sense to seek legal advice and have a formal written agreement prepared. Putting agreements in writing may minimize conflicts in the future. This written agreement, which formalizes the partners' relationship, is called the **articles of partnership.**

Some things that should be included in the written articles of partnership are the following:

1. Name and address of each partner, along with the date of agreement
2. Rights and responsibilities of each partner
3. Amount that each partner is investing
4. Specific manner in which partners' profits or losses will be shared
5. Provisions for one or more partners quitting the partnership
6. How new partners will be admitted
7. How assets will be distributed if the business is completely terminated
8. How accounting records will be maintained

> The more partners a partnership has, (1) the easier it may be to finance the business with the partners' investments and (2) the more unique abilities may result from the different backgrounds of the partners.

Characteristics of Partnerships

Limited Life A partnership has a **limited life.** An advantage is that it does have more flexibility than some other forms of ownership to react to the marketplace, because legal restrictions are minimal. When a change takes place in the membership of a partnership—when someone new joins or when someone leaves—the partnership is dissolved, however. Dissolution can occur if a partner dies, becomes incapacitated, goes bankrupt, or withdraws. Admission of a new partner or expiration of the life of the partnership as stated in the articles of partnership could also result in the partnership being dissolved. If a partnership is dissolved, a new partnership can be formed and the business can continue to operate without any interruptions.

Mutual Agency **Mutual agency** means that the actions of one partner are binding on all the other partners. For example, Jill Joy, who is a partner in a merchandise business, enters into a contract with Flynn Company to lease a building. This contract is binding on all Jill's partners because the transaction was within the scope of the business. If Jill, on the other hand, entered into a contract to provide *legal* work to another company, it would not be binding on the partners, because legal work is not in the normal scope of a merchandise company.

Mutual agency allows each partner to act for the partnership as a whole, because all the partners are agents for the business. Poor judgment on the part of one partner, however, could, through mutual agency, result in heavy losses to all partners. An advantage of a partnership is that a credit rating is usually higher because more than one partner is responsible for the company's debt. So the mutual agency characteristic of a partnership can be both an advantage and a disadvantage.

Unlimited Liability **Unlimited liability** means that if a partnership is unable to pay its obligations, all **general partners** are individually liable to cover with their *personal* assets the obligations the partnership cannot meet. Think of a general partner as one who risks not only the personal investment in the partnership but also personal assets. If the personal assets of some of the partners are exhausted, the other partners have the responsibility for covering the debts outstanding. Note that a few exceptions apply to this rule. First, a partner just entering an existing partnership is not held liable for past obligations before joining the partnership. Second, in some states some members of a partnership have liability only up to the amount they invested in the partnership. These people are called **limited partners.**

Co-ownership of Property **Co-ownership of property** means that all partners share all the assets of the partnership. For example, if Bill Boyd invests cash and Joyce Regan invests a building in their partnership, the assets become the property of the partnership. Joyce no longer has a specific claim to the building. Ownership is now shared by Bill and Joyce.

Taxation The partnership itself does not pay taxes, but the partners pay taxes on the share of net income that has been allocated to each of them. (Note that the tax is on the net income and not on the amount that a partner has withdrawn from the partnership.) Remember that in a sole proprietorship, like a partnership, owners are not paid salaries. They take withdrawals from the company.

Formation of a Partnership

LO1

Let's look now at the journal entries that are needed when a partnership is formed. The important point is that when partners invest in a business, the assets should be recorded at their current fair value. This value is established by having the assets appraised. Partners have to agree on the amounts assigned to the noncash assets. These costs now represent the true acquisition cost to the partnership. Appraising of assets at their current fair value avoids inequities in the balances of the capital accounts of the partners.

Let's look at the following situation: On June 1, 20XX, Jane Reedy and Bill Burr enter into a partnership. Reedy invests from her old business $9,000 cash and store equipment worth $25,000 with accumulated depreciation of $5,000. The current appraised value of the equipment is $28,000. Also on the books is Accounts Receivable of $2,000 with an Allowance for Doubtful Accounts of $500. The partnership will take on the responsibility for a $6,000 note issued by Reedy. Burr invests $20,000 cash in the partnership. The journal entries in Figure 17.1 record this information.

	20XX																		
	June	1	Cash		9	0	0	0	00										
			Accounts Receivable		2	0	0	0	00										
			Store Equipment		28	0	0	0	00										
			Allowances for Doubtful Accounts									5	0	0	00				
			Notes Payable								6	0	0	0	00				
			J. Reedy, Capital								32	5	0	0	00				
		1	Cash		20	0	0	0	00										
			B. Burr, Capital								20	0	0	0	00				

FIGURE 17.1 Investing into a Partnership

These entries could be recorded in the cash receipts journal. Note that the $32,500 is the assets minus the liabilities.

Note that the store equipment has no accumulated depreciation associated with it, because the appraised value is now the new book value. If the old book value was used, Reedy's capital would be understated. Reedy should not be penalized because the value of her equipment has increased. Any additional investments made by the partners will result in a journal entry that debits Cash and credits the partners' capital accounts.

LEARNING UNIT 17-1 REVIEW

AT THIS POINT you should be able to

- Define a partnership and compare its equity section with that of a sole proprietorship.
- List the characteristics of a partnership.
- Journalize the formation of a partnership, recording assets at current fair value.

Self-Review Quiz 17-1

Respond true or false to the following:

1. Articles of partnership are required in forming a partnership.
2. Limited life means that when a partnership is dissolved, the business ceases operations.
3. Unlimited liability could result from mutual agency.
4. Co-ownership of property means each asset belongs to the person who invested it.
5. Assets invested in the formation of a partnership are recorded at current fair value.

Solutions to Self-Review Quiz 17-1

1. False
2. False
3. True
4. False
5. True

LO2 Learning Unit 17-2 Division of Net Income and Net Loss Among Partners

Partners work so as to gain a share of the net income of their partnership; they do not earn salaries as their employees do. As a matter of fact, they cannot legally hire themselves and pay themselves a salary. Net income and net loss can be divided among partners in several ways based on partners' differing talents and abilities, time spent working for the partnership, and amount of investment in the partnership.

We need to introduce two terms to help describe how net income is divided among partners. One way is through a **salary allowance.** A salary allowance is not the same thing as the Salary Expense involved in paying employees, and it is not in fact a salary at all; it is just a way to divide net income. It is usually used to account for unequal service contributions among partners, such as if one partner worked full time for the business and the other put in only 20 hours a week. In such a case, the partners might agree to pay $1,000 per week to the first partner and $500 per week to the other. This amount would come out of the net income earned by the partnership.

Another way to divide net income among partners is through **interest allowance.** This method is usually used when partners have put different amounts into the partnership as an initial investment. Let's say that one has invested $5,000 and the other has invested $10,000. At the end of the accounting period, they would each get 10% interest on their investment: The first would get $500 ($5,000 × .10) and the second would get $1,000 ($10,000 × .10). This method is used because it would be unfair to give half of net income to the first partner when that partner invested only one-third of the capital.

Now let's look at several different situations to see how a partnership might divide its net income or net loss. These situations will be based on the following facts. Dot Alexander, John Sullivan, and Sheldon Brown invested $8,000, $6,000, and $4,000, respectively, in a partnership. The partnership in the first year had a net income of $24,300.

Situation 1 Partners could not agree on how to share net income of $24,300. The law states that if an agreement is not reached on how partners share earnings, they will be divided equally.

$$\$24,300 \div 3 = \$8,100 \text{ to each partner}$$

The journal entry at closing to allocate net income will look like the one in Figure 17.2. Note that the closing process now divides the net income into the *three* capital accounts. In a sole proprietorship, the net income was closed to the one capital account. If this situation involved net loss instead of net income, each capital account would be debited and the credit would be to Income Summary.

20XX						
Dec.	31	Income Summary		24 3 0 0 00		
		Dot Alexander, Capital			8 1 0 0 00	
		John Sullivan, Capital			8 1 0 0 00	
		Sheldon Brown, Capital			8 1 0 0 00	

FIGURE 17.2 Share Net Income Equally

> The journal entry at closing to allocate net income looks like this one.

Situation 2 Partners share net income of $24,300 in the ratio of their beginning capital investments.

Step 1 Find the total capital invested:

Alexander	$ 8,000
Sullivan	6,000
Brown	4,000
	$18,000

Step 2 Set up a ratio (fraction) of each partner's investment to the total of capital invested ($18,000):

Alexander	Sullivan	Brown
$\dfrac{\$8,000}{\$18,000}$	$\dfrac{\$6,000}{\$18,000}$	$\dfrac{\$4,000}{\$18,000}$

Step 3 Multiply the ratio in step 2 by the amount of income to be distributed.

Alexander: $\dfrac{\$8,000}{\$18,000} \times \$24,300 = \$10,800$

Sullivan: $\dfrac{\$6,000}{\$18,000} \times \$24,300 = \$8,100$

Brown: $\dfrac{\$4,000}{\$18.000} \times \$24,300 = \$5,400$

The journal entry at closing to allocate net income will look like the one in Figure 17.3.

FIGURE 17.3 Share Net Income Based on Ratio of Investments

	20XX												
	Dec.	31	Income Summary		24 3 0 0 00						
			Dot Alexander, Capital					10 8 0 0 00	
			John Sullivan, Capital					8 1 0 0 00	
			Sheldon Brown, Capital					5 4 0 0 00	

The ratio in step 2 may be used if the net income of the company is related only to the amount the partners have invested. Alexander has invested the most ($8,000) and thus receives the largest portion of the earnings ($10,800).

Alternative to Ratio Based on Investment Only Some partnerships share net income according to an agreed-upon ratio. If a ratio is 3:2:1, it means that 3/6 of net income goes to one partner, 2/6 to the next, and 1/6 to the last. Such a fractional ratio could be based on service as well as capital investment. Such ratios are called **profit and loss ratios.**

Situation 3 Partners' services and capital contributions are unequal, but net income does cover salary and interest allowance. The salary allowance is used to compensate for the partners' unequal service contributions, and the interest allowance is used to compensate for their unequal investments. One way to share net income in this situation is as follows:

a. Annual salary allowance of $6,000 to Alexander, $6,000 to Sullivan, and $9,000 to Brown.
b. Ten percent interest on each partner's capital investment.
c. Remaining net income or net loss shared equally.

		Alexander		Sullivan		Brown		Total
a. Salary Allowance		$6,000	+	$6,000	+	$9,000	=	$21,000
b. Interest on Capital Investments								
.10 × $8,000		800						
.10 × $6,000			+	600				
.10 × $4,000					+	400		
Total Interest Allowance							=	1,800
Total Salary and Interest Allowances		$6,800	+	$6,600	+	$9,400	=	$22,800
c. Net Income	$24,300							
Less: Salary and Interest	22,800							
Income to be distributed equally	$ 1,500	500		500		500		1,500
Share of Net Income to Partners		$7,300	+	$7,100	+	$9,900	=	$24,300

The journal entry at closing to allocate net income will look like Figure 17.4.

FIGURE 17.4 Net Income Left After Salary and Interest Allowance

	20XX												
	Dec.	31	Income Summary		24 3 0 0 00						
			D. Alexander, Capital					7 3 0 0 00	
			J. Sullivan, Capital					7 1 0 0 00	
			S. Brown, Capital					9 9 0 0 00	

Note that in this case, some net income remained after salary and interest allowances. In the next situation we see that net income doesn't always cover all the salary and interest allowance.

Situation 4 Partners' services and capital contributions are unequal, but net income does not cover salary and interest allowance. Assume (1) net income is $20,700 and (2) salary and interest allowance are the same as in Situation 3.

Whether net income covers the salaries and interest makes *no difference* in calculating the salary or interest allowance. As shown in the accompanying calculation, the total of salaries and allowances is $22,800. Net income is only $20,700; thus the partners must all share by $700 each in a reduction of the profits allocated to them. Remember that items (a) and (b) are calculated first *before* we consider the difference between net income and the amount that is needed to cover salary and interest allowance. It is not necessary to think of the $700 **deficit** (negative reduction to each partner) as a loss; think of it as a reduction in the share of profits, because all the interest and salary allowance was not covered.

	Alexander		Sullivan		Brown		Total
a. *Salary Allowance*	$6,000	+	$6,000	+	$9,000	=	$21,000
b. *Interest on Capital Investments:*							
.10 × $8,000	800						
.10 × $6,000		+	600				
.10 × $4,000				+	400		
Total Interest Allowance						=	1,800
Total Salary and Interest Allowance	$6,800	+	$6,600	+	$9,400	=	$22,800
c. *Net Income*	$ 20,700						
Less: Salary and Interest	22,800						
Deficit to be shared equally	($ 2,100)	(700)		(700)		(700)		(2,100)
Share of Net Income to Partners	$6,100	+	$5,900	+	$8,700	=	$20,700

The journal entry at closing to allocate the deficit will look like Figure 17.5.

20XX							
Dec.	31	Income Summary	20 70 0 00		
		D. Alexander, Capital		6 10 0 00
		J. Sullivan, Capital		5 90 0 00
		S. Brown, Capital		8 70 0 00

FIGURE 17.5 Deficit to Be Shared Equally by All Partners

Partnership Financial Statement

LO3

Just as we had a statement of owner's equity for a sole proprietorship, we can prepare a statement of partners' equity. The statement in Figure 17.6 was prepared from Situation 3.

ALEXANDER, SULLIVAN, AND BROWN
STATEMENT OF PARTNERS' EQUITY
FOR YEAR ENDED DECEMBER 31, 20XX

	Alexander	Sullivan	Brown
Capital Balances, January 1, 20XX	$ 8 00 0 00	$ 6 00 0 00	$ 4 00 0 00
Add: Net Income for 20XX	7 30 0 00	7 10 0 00	9 90 0 00
Totals	$15 30 0 00	$13 10 0 00	$13 90 0 00
Less: Withdrawals	4 00 0 00	5 00 0 00	8 00 0 00
Capital Balances, December 31, 20XX	$11 30 0 00	$ 8 10 0 00	$ 5 90 0 00

FIGURE 17.6 Statement of Partners' Equity

On their personal tax returns, partners are taxed on their net income in the partnership, whether they withdraw it or not. For example, Alexander would pay taxes on $7,300, even though she withdrew only $4,000.

The ending balances for each partner would then be reported on the balance sheet. Think of the statement of partners' equity as a supporting document to arrive at a new figure for each capital account on the balance sheet.

LEARNING UNIT 17-2 REVIEW

AT THIS POINT you should be able to

- Explain why salary and interest allowances are not expenses when used to divide up earnings of a partnership.
- Calculate partners' earnings if shared (a) equally, (b) by ratio of beginning capital or fractional ratio, and (c) by salary and interest allowances.
- Prepare a statement of partners' equity.

Self-Review Quiz 17-2

From the following information, calculate the partners' share of net income. J. French and J. Small receive salary allowances of $60,000 and $48,000, respectively. The interest allowance is 12% of their beginning balances of $160,000 and $120,000, respectively. The remainder of the net income will be divided evenly. Net income for the year was $150,000.

Solution to Self-Review Quiz 17-2

		French		Small	=	Total
Salary Allowance		$60,000	+	$48,000	=	$108,000
Interest on Capital Investments:						
.12 × $160,000		19,200				
.12 × $120,000			+	14,400		
Total Interest Allowance					=	33,600
Total Salary and Interest Allowance		$79,200	+	$62,400	=	$141,600
Net Income	$150,000					
Less: Salary and Interest	141,600					
Income to be distributed equally	$8,400	4,200		4,200		8,400
Share of Net Income to Partners		$83,400	+	$66,600	=	$150,000

LO4

Learning Unit 17-3 Recording Admissions and Withdrawals of Partners

This unit looks at how the capital structure of a partnership may change due to (1) admission of a new partner or (2) withdrawal of a partner.

Admission of a New Partner

Joining a partnership can happen in two ways:

1. **Purchase of an equity interest** from one or more of the existing partners.
2. Make an investment in the business.

No matter what approach is taken, the admission of a new partner will technically dissolve the old partnership. Let's look at how Peter Mix bought into the partnership of Jones and Ryan.

Buying an Equity Interest from an Original Partner The partners' balance sheet of Jones and Ryan looked as shown in Figure 17.7 before Peter Mix purchased an interest in the company (there are no liabilities).

JONES AND RYAN				
Assets		**Partners' Equity**		
Cash	$ 5000 00	Jones, Capital	$ 6000 00	
Other Assets	7000 00	Ryan, Capital	6000 00	
Total Assets	$12000 00	Total Equities	$12000 00	

FIGURE 17.7 Balances Before Mix Bought an Equity Interest

On April 3 Ryan sold Peter Mix his equity in the company for $9,000. The entry is recorded on the books of the partnership as shown in Figure 17.8.

Apr.	3	Ryan, Capital	6000 00	
		Mix, Capital		6000 00

FIGURE 17.8 Sale of Equity to Peter Mix

The end result of this transaction is to transfer the $6,000 capital account of Ryan to Mix. Note that the difference in the selling price of $3,000 ($9,000 − $6,000) doesn't affect the books of the partnership, because the cash is paid directly to Ryan and not to the business. Think of it as a side transaction. All this transaction does is transfer the equity amounts. Any personal profit the former partner makes is of a personal nature and is not reflected in the accounts of the business.

Keep in mind also that Jones must agree to the equity exchange by Ryan if Mix is to become a partner. If Jones agrees, a new partnership contract is formed along with new profit or loss ratios. If Jones doesn't accept Mix as a partner, Mix still has the right to share in Ryan's profits and losses, but he will have no voice in the running of the company until he is admitted as a partner.

> Ryan cannot force Jones to accept Mix as a partner.

Investing in an Existing Partnership As an alternative to buying equity from an existing partner, one may simply invest assets in the partnership on one's own. For example, assume Roger Foss wants to invest cash in a business on July 8 so that he will have a one-third interest in the partnership. Before Roger makes his investment, the partners' equity is as follows:

> Having a one-third interest doesn't mean Roger has rights to one-third of the net income. The partners must agree on how to share profit and loss.

Partners' Equity	
B. Blee, Capital	$3,000
A. Jarvis, Capital	1,000

Roger wants one-third interest, and the $4,000 ($3,000 + $1,000) represents two-thirds interest. One-third interest is $2,000 and, therefore, Roger will have to contribute $2,000

$2,000	Roger's Contribution
$6,000	Total Capital with Roger's Contribution

to gain the one-third interest. The entry to record the admission of Roger Foss would be as shown in Figure 17.9.

> $\dfrac{\$4,000}{2 \text{ parts}} = \$2,000$ per part
>
> OR
>
> $\dfrac{\$4,000}{X} = \dfrac{2}{3}$
>
> $2X = \$12,000$
> $X = \$6,000$
>
> (where x is the total capital after Roger's contribution)

July	8	Cash	2000 00	
		R. Foss, Capital		2000 00

FIGURE 17.9 Admission of a Partner

Recording a Bonus to the Old Partners When Admitting a New Partner When the equity of a partnership in reality is worth more than the amounts recorded in its accounting records, the partners may require an incoming partner to pay an additional amount or **bonus** that will increase old partners' equity. This situation could result if a company had an outstanding earnings record with even higher expectations in the future compared with other companies in the industry. Let's see how it would work from the previous example of Roger Foss, assuming the partners Blee and Jarvis on July 8 require a payment of $3,500 (instead of $2,000) to give Foss a one-third interest.

$$\frac{\$7,500}{3 \text{ parts}} = \$2,500 \text{ per part}$$

Blee and Jarvis, Capital	$4,000	Foss only needed to invest $2,000
Investment of Foss	3,500	to gain a one-third interest, but the
Capital of New Partnership	$7,500	old partners required $3,500.
$\frac{1}{3}$ interest of Foss ($\frac{1}{3} \times \$7,500$)	$2,500	

Note that the $1,000 ($3,500 − $2,500) difference represents the bonus the old partners will share. The old partners share all losses and gains equally. Thus, the journal entry to admit Foss is as shown in Figure 17.10.

FIGURE 17.10 Admission of a Partner Resulting in a Bonus to the Old Partners

July	8	Cash	3 5 0 0 00		
		B. Blee, Capital		5 0 0 00	
		A. Jarvis, Capital		5 0 0 00	
		R. Foss, Capital		2 5 0 0 00	

Recording a Bonus to a New Partner A firm often is anxious to bring into the company a new partner who has special skills, business contacts, or abilities. The old partners then must accept a reduction in their capital balances to make up the difference in what the new partner invests compared with the new partner's capital balance. Let's play back the previous example by looking at how "anxious" Blee and Jarvis are to obtain the managerial talents of Roger Foss. Now the old partners have required Foss on July 8 to invest only $1,400 to have a one-third interest in the business.

$$\frac{\$5,400}{3 \text{ parts}} = \$1,800 \text{ per part}$$

Blee and Jarvis, Capital	$4,000
Investment of Foss	1,400
Capital of New Partnership	$5,400
$\frac{1}{3}$ interest of Foss ($\frac{1}{3} \times \$5,400$)	$1,800

Note that Foss invested only $1,400, while in reality he needed to invest $1,800. Thus, the old partners are absorbing equally the bonus of $400 ($1,800 − $1,400) by reducing their capital balance. The journal entry to record the admitting of Foss to the partnership is as shown in Figure 17.11.

FIGURE 17.11 Journalizing Bonus to Partners

July	8	Cash	1 4 0 0 00		
		B. Blee, Capital	2 0 0 00		
		A. Jarvis, Capital	2 0 0 00		
		R. Foss, Capital		1 8 0 0 00	

Recording Permanent Withdrawal of a Partner

When a partnership contract is drawn up, it usually states the procedures to be followed when a partner withdraws. Often the procedures include an audit of the accounting records and the adjustment of the assets to their current fair market value. These steps are done so that the capital of the retiring partner does indeed reflect the current value of his or her equity. Let's look at (1) the balance sheet before revaluation of Ring, Rotter, and Freeze; (2) the entry made to record revaluation; (3) the new, revalued balance sheet; and (4) withdrawal of J. Freeze (assume no liabilities). Partners of Ring, Rotter, and Freeze have a profit and loss ratio of ½, ¼, and ¼, respectively.

1. The balance sheet before revaluation is shown in Figure 17.12.

FIGURE 17.12 Balance Sheet Before Revaluation

RING, ROTTER, AND FREEZE					
Assets			**Partners' Equity**		
Cash		$ 2 2 0 0 00	A. Ring, Capital		$ 4 4 0 0 00
Merchandise Inventory		3 2 0 0 00	B. Rotter, Capital		2 0 0 0 00
Store Equipment	$ 4 0 0 0 00		J. Freeze, Capital		2 0 0 0 00
Less Acc. Dep.	1 0 0 0 00	3 0 0 0 00			
Total Assets		$ 8 4 0 0 00	Total Equities		$ 8 4 0 0 00

2. When the accountant completes the audit, it is reported that inventory, owing to market conditions, is overvalued by $400. The journal entry to record the revaluation is shown in Figure 17.13.

Nov.	30	A. Ring, Capital		2 0 0 00			
		B. Rotter, Capital		1 0 0 00			
		J. Freeze, Capital		1 0 0 00			
		Merchandise Inventory				4 0 0 00	

FIGURE 17.13 Journal Entry to Record Revaluation

$$Ring = \tfrac{1}{2} \times \$400$$
$$= \$200$$
$$Rotter = \tfrac{1}{4} \times \$400$$
$$= \$100$$
$$Freeze = \tfrac{1}{4} \times \$400$$
$$= \$100$$

3. Here is the new, revalued balance sheet (Fig. 17.14).

FIGURE 17.14 New Revalued Balance Sheet

RING, ROTTER, AND FREEZE					
Assets			**Partners' Equity**		
Cash		$ 2 2 0 0 00	A. Ring, Capital		$ 4 2 0 0 00
Merchandise Inventory		2 8 0 0 00	B. Rotter, Capital		1 9 0 0 00
Store Equipment	$ 4 0 0 0 00		J. Freeze, Capital		1 9 0 0 00
Less Acc. Dep.	1 0 0 0 00	3 0 0 0 00			
Total Assets		$ 8 0 0 0 00	Total Equities		$ 8 0 0 0 00

4. The entry to record the withdrawal of Freeze from the partnership is shown in Figure 17.15 on the following page.

FIGURE 17.15 Withdrawal of Partner

Nov.	30	J. Freeze, Capital		1 9 0 0 00		
		Cash				1 9 0 0 00

The withdrawal means a new partnership and a new profit and loss ratio for Ring and Rotter.

Recording Permanent Withdrawal When a Partner Takes Assets of Less Value Than Book Equity

In the last situation Freeze received the revalued amount of his capital by taking out $1,900 in cash. Often, when a partner retires, the assets may not be revalued. In this case the partners have to agree whether the assets are overvalued and whether the withdrawing partner should settle for less than the book value of his or her equity. For example, let's look at the balance sheet for Joll, Smoot, and Jangles (Fig. 17.16) to see what will happen if Smoot settles for less than his book value on July 31 (assume a profit and loss ratio of 2:2:1).

FIGURE 17.16 Balance Sheet Before Settlement

JOLL, SMOOT, AND JANGLES					
Assets			Partners' Equity		
Cash		$25 0 0 0 00	R. Joll, Capital		$28 0 0 0 00
Merchandise Inventory		29 0 0 0 00	A. Smoot, Capital		18 0 0 0 00
			B. Jangles, Capital		8 0 0 0 00
Total Assets		$54 0 0 0 00	Total Equities		$54 0 0 0 00

2:1

2/3 for Joll
1/3 for Jangles

R. Joll = $\frac{2}{3} \times \$6,000$
= $4,000

B. Jangles = $\frac{1}{3} \times \$6,000$
= $2,000

Smoot is extremely anxious to withdraw from the partnership and is willing to accept a cash settlement of $12,000. Joll and Jangles will share the $6,000 ($18,000 − $12,000) of capital that Smoot does not take with him in the ratio of 2:1. The journal entry to record the withdrawal of Smoot is shown in Figure 17.17.

FIGURE 17.17 Withdrawal of Smoot When Smoot Settles for Less Than His Book Equity

July	31	A. Smoot, Capital		18 0 0 0 00		
		Cash				12 0 0 0 00
		R. Joll, Capital				4 0 0 0 00
		B. Jangles, Capital				2 0 0 0 00

Now let's look at what could happen if Smoot withdrew assets valued at *more* than his book equity.

Recording Permanent Withdrawal When a Partner Takes Assets of Greater Value Than Book Equity

Using the previous example, Smoot might withdraw assets valued at *more* than book equity if

1. Partnership assets are undervalued, and
2. Joll and Jangles are anxious to have him retire.

Assume the assets are undervalued by $12,000 and the owners want to leave them this way. Thus, Smoot's capital would be increased by $4,800 ($\frac{2}{5} \times \$12,000$), and the other partners' equity would be reduced to cover this $4,800 increase to Smoot's capital. The entry in Figure 17.18 would be recorded when Smoot leaves the partnership.

July	31	A. Smoot, Capital		1	8	0	0	0	00						
		R. Joll, Capital			3	2	0	0	00						
		B. Jangles, Capital			1	6	0	0	00						
		Cash									22	8	0	00	00

FIGURE 17.18 Smoot Settles For More Than His Book Equity

Note that Smoot receives in cash the $18,000 value of his capital plus the $4,800 to reflect the capital of $22,800 agreed upon by the other partners. Note also how the capital of Joll and Jangles was reduced according to their profit and loss ratio.

Remember that when a partner dies, the partnership ends, and the estate is entitled to receive the proper value of the capital account of the deceased after an audit and revaluation of the assets. Journal entries for the death of a partner are similar to those for other situations when a partner leaves. To have enough cash to pay the full value of the deceased partner's capital account, partnerships often carry life insurance policies on partners.

$$\text{R. Joll} = \tfrac{2}{3} \times \$4,800$$
$$= \$3,200$$
$$\text{B. Jangles} = \tfrac{1}{3} \times \$4,800$$
$$= \$1,600$$

LEARNING UNIT 17-3 REVIEW

AT THIS POINT you should be able to

- Explain how a new partner can be admitted in a partnership.
- Journalize the entry to record the admitting of a new partner.
- Explain why a one-third interest doesn't mean that the net income is split three ways.
- Calculate as well as journalize a bonus to old partners when a new partner is admitted.
- Calculate as well as journalize a bonus to a new partner.
- Explain how assets might be revalued when a partner withdraws.
- Calculate as well as journalize entries to record withdrawal of a partner taking assets for less or more than book equity if assets are not revalued.

Self-Review Quiz 17-3

Respond true or false to the following:

1. When new partner Cohen buys an equity of existing partner Lee-Ying the cash account is always increased in the business.
2. The profit and loss ratio must be based on the capital balances of the partners.
3. A bonus to old partners is based on their profit and loss ratio.
4. A bonus to a new partner could result if the old partners are anxious to recruit the new partner.
5. Any loss or gain when assets are revalued is shared in the partners' profit and loss ratio.
6. Assets of a partnership cannot be revalued.
7. A partner, Jaworski, can never withdraw assets that are valued at less than his book equity.
8. A partner who withdraws assets of greater value than book equity causes the capital of the remaining partners to decrease when assets are not revalued.

Solutions to Self-Review Quiz 17-3

1. False   **2.** False   **3.** True   **4.** True   **5.** True   **6.** False   **7.** False   **8.** True

LO5 # Learning Unit 17-4 The Liquidation of a Partnership

Up to this point we have looked at the admission and withdrawal of partners. Each time this happens, a new partnership is formed and any losses or gains are shared in an agreed-upon ratio. The operations of the business continue, of course, even when the new partnership is formed. In this unit we look at three situations in which a partnership is liquidated. **Liquidation** occurs when the business is completely ended by converting assets into cash and paying off obligations and equity. The following steps complete a liquidation:

1. Assets are sold for cash with any loss or gain recognized.
2. Any loss or gain is divided among the partners based on their profit or loss ratio.
3. Creditors are paid off.
4. Remaining cash is distributed to the partners based on their capital balances.

We will look at three different situations based on the following information. Peters, French, and Smith are liquidating their business on May 31, 20XX. The partners have a profit and loss ratio of 3:2:1. Figure 17.19 shows the updated balance sheet at the end of May. Note that at this point we've closed out the temporary accounts.

FIGURE 17.19 Balance Sheet Before Liquidation

PETERS, FRENCH, AND SMITH BALANCE SHEET MAY 31, 20XX	
Assets	
Cash	$ 7 0 0 0 00
Other Assets	138 0 0 0 00
Total Assets	$145 0 0 0 00
Liabilities and Partners' Equity	
Liabilities	$ 25 0 0 0 00
J. Peters, Capital	30 0 0 0 00
J. French, Capital	70 0 0 0 00
A. Smith, Capital	20 0 0 0 00
Total Liabilities and Partners' Equity	$145 0 0 0 00

Using this information, let's look at three different situations in which liquidation occurs.

Situation 1 Selling assets at a gain (assets sold for $144,000).

THE LIQUIDATION PROCESS

Step 1 Record sale of assets along with any loss or gain from **realization*** (gain = $144,000 − $138,000) on June 7 (Fig. 17.20).

FIGURE 17.20 Selling Assets at a Gain

June	7	Cash	144 0 0 0 00		
		Other Assets		138 0 0 0 00	
		Loss or Gain from Realization		6 0 0 0 00	

---

*Realization means the conversion of noncash assets into cash as part of the liquidation process. It can result in either gain or loss. The account Loss or Gain from Realization is similar to the Cash Short and Over account discussed in Chapter 7. The account will be closed separately, because closing entries take place before liquidation. In using this account think of loss as a debit and gain as a credit.

Step 2 Loss or gain from realization is allocated to each partner in ratio of 3:2:1
(Fig. 17.21).

June	7	Loss or Gain from Realization	6 0 0 0	00	
		J. Peters, Capital		3 0 0 0	00
		J. French, Capital		2 0 0 0	00
		A. Smith, Capital		1 0 0 0	00

FIGURE 17.21 Allocation of Gain to Partners' Capital Accounts

Peters: $\frac{3}{6}$ × $6,000

French: $\frac{2}{6}$ × $6,000

Smith: $\frac{1}{6}$ × $6,000

Step 3 Pay claims of the creditors on June 15 (Fig. 17.22).

June	15	Liabilities	25 0 0 0	00	
		Cash		25 0 0 0	00

FIGURE 17.22 Payment to Creditors

The Ledger Before Step 4

J. Peters, Capital	J. French, Capital	A. Smith, Capital	Cash	
30,000	70,000	20,000	7,000	25,000
3,000	2,000	1,000	144,000	
		Bal:	126,000	

Step 4 Distribute cash that is left to partners based on their capital balance
(Fig. 17.23). *No* profit and loss ratios are used in this step.

June	30	J. Peters, Capital	33 0 0 0	00	
		J. French, Capital	72 0 0 0	00	
		A. Smith, Capital	21 0 0 0	00	
		Cash		126 0 0 0	00

FIGURE 17.23 Cash Paid to Partners

The accompanying statement of liquidation gives a comprehensive report of the liquidation process involved in Situation 1. Keep in mind that the liquidation process takes time to complete; it isn't done overnight.

					Capital		
	Cash	+ Other Assets	= Liabilities +	Peters	+ French	+ Smith
Balances before realization	$7,000 +	$138,000	= $25,000 +	$30,000 +	$70,000 +	$20,000
Recording gain from sales of assets	+$144,000 −	$138,000		+3,000	+2,000	+1,000
Balances updated	$151,000		= $25,000 +	$33,000 +	$72,000 +	$21,000
Paying of liabilities	−$25,000		−$25,000			
Balances updated	$126,000		=	+$33,000 +	$72,000 +	$21,000
Distribution of cash to partners	−$126,000		=	−$33,000 −	$72,000 −	$21,000

Peters, French, and Smith
Statement of Liquidation
For Month of June 20XX

Now let's look at what would happen if the assets were sold at a loss.

Situation 2 Selling assets at a loss (assets sold for $126,000).

THE LIQUIDATION PROCESS

Step 1 Record sale of assets with loss or gain from realization (loss = $138,000 − $126,000) on June 7 (Fig. 17.24).

FIGURE 17.24 Selling Assets at a Loss

June	7	Cash	126 0 0 0 00		
		Loss or Gain from Realization	12 0 0 0 00		
		Other Assets		138 0 0 0 00	

Step 2 Loss or gain from realization is allocated to each partner in ratio of 3:2:1 (Fig. 17.25).

FIGURE 17.25 Loss Allocated to Partners

June	7	J. Peters, Capital	6 0 0 0 00		
		J. French, Capital	4 0 0 0 00		
		A. Smith, Capital	2 0 0 0 00		
		Loss or Gain from Realization		12 0 0 0 00	

Step 3 Pay claims of creditors (Fig. 17.26).

FIGURE 17.26 Payment to Creditors

June	15	Liabilities	25 0 0 0 00		
		Cash		25 0 0 0 00	

The Ledger Before Step 4

J. Peters, Capital		J. French, Capital		A. Smith, Capital		Cash	
6,000	30,000	4,000	70,000	2,000	20,000	7,000	25,000
						126,000	
						Bal: 108,000	

No profit and loss ratios are used in this step.

Step 4 Distribute cash that is left to partners based on their capital balances on June 30 (Fig. 17.27).

FIGURE 17.27 Payment to Partners

June	30	J. Peters, Capital	24 0 0 0 00		
		J. French, Capital	66 0 0 0 00		
		A. Smith, Capital	18 0 0 0 00		
		Cash		108 0 0 0 00	

The accompanying statement of liquidation provides a comprehensive report of this liquidation process.

Peters, French, and Smith
Statement of Liquidation
For Month of June 20XX

	Cash	+	Other Assets	=	Liabilities	+	Peters	+	French	+	Smith
								Capital			
Balances before realization	$7,000	+	$138,000	=	$25,000	+	$30,000	+	$70,000	+	$20,000
Recording loss from sales of assets	+$126,000	−	$138,000				−6,000		−4,000		−2,000
Balances updated	$133,000			=	$25,000	+	$24,000	+	$66,000	+	$18,000
Paying of liabilities	−$25,000				−$25,000						
Balances updated	$108,000			=			$24,000	+	$66,000	+	$18,000
Distribution of cash to partners	−$108,000			=			−$24,000	−	$66,000	−	$18,000

In the final situation, the partners are unable to cover a deficit from the sale of assets.

Situation 3 Selling assets at a loss, with some partner's capital not being enough to cover the deficit (assets sold for $42,000).

THE LIQUIDATION PROCESS

Step 1 Record sale of assets along with any loss or gain from realization (loss = $138,000 − $42,000) on June 7 (Fig. 17.28).

				Debit	Credit
June	7	Cash		42 000 00	
		Loss or Gain from Realization		96 000 00	
		Other Assets			138 000 00

FIGURE 17.28 Loss from Realization

Step 2 Loss or gain from realization is allocated to each partner in ratio 3:2:1 (Fig. 17.29).

				Debit	Credit
June	7	J. Peters, Capital		48 000 00	
		J. French, Capital		32 000 00	
		A. Smith, Capital		16 000 00	
		Loss or Gain from Realization			96 000 00

FIGURE 17.29 Loss Allocated to Each Partner

Peters: $\frac{3}{6} \times \$96{,}000$

French: $\frac{2}{6} \times \$96{,}000$

Smith: $\frac{1}{6} \times \$96{,}000$

When the loss exceeds the capital balance of a partner and the partner cannot make up the deficit, the other partners have unlimited liability to make up the deficit.

Peters, Capital		**French, Capital**		**Smith, Capital**	
48,000	30,000	32,000	70,000	16,000	20,000

Note that Peters has a deficit of $18,000 ($48,000 – $30,000). The other partners must share this deficit in their profit and loss ratio of 2:1 (Fig. 17.30).

FIGURE 17.30 Sharing of Deficit by Partners

French: $\frac{2}{3} \times \$18,000$

Smith: $\frac{1}{3} \times \$18,000$

June	7	J. French, Capital	12000 00			
		A. Smith, Capital	6000 00			
		J. Peters, Capital			18000 00	

Peters, Capital		French, Capital		Smith, Capital	
48,000	30,000	32,000	70,000	16,000	20,000
	18,000	12,000		6,000	

Note that now *Smith* has a $2,000 deficit. French is the only partner left with a capital balance and thus is liable for this deficit (Fig. 17.31).

FIGURE 17.31 French Only Partner Left with a Balance

June	7	J. French, Capital	2000 00			
		A. Smith, Capital			2000 00	

Step 3 Pay claims of creditors on June 15 (Fig. 17.32).

FIGURE 17.32 Pay Creditors

June	15	Liabilities	25000 00			
		Cash			25000 00	

Step 4 Distribute remaining cash on June 30 (Fig. 17.33).

FIGURE 17.33 Pay Cash to Partner

June	30	J. French, Capital	24000 00			
		Cash			24000 00	

French, Capital	
32,000	70,000
12,000	
2,000	

The accompanying statement of liquidation provides a comprehensive report of this liquidation process.

								Capital			
	Cash	+	Other Assets	=	Liabilities	+	Peters	+	French	+	Smith

Peters, French, and Smith
Statement of Liquidation
For Month of June 20XX

	Cash		Other Assets		Liabilities		Peters		French		Smith
Balances before realization	$7,000	+	$138,000	=	$25,000	+	$30,000	+	$70,000	+	$20,000
Recording loss from sale of assets	+$42,000	−	$138,000	=		−	48,000	−	32,000	−	16,000
Balances updated	$49,000				$25,000	−	$18,000	+	$38,000	+	$4,000
Deficit of Peters covered by partners in ratio 2:1						+	$18,000	−	$12,000	−	6,000
Balances updated	$49,000			=	$25,000			+	$26,000	−	$2,000
Deficit of Smith covered by French								−	$2,000	+	$2,000
Balances updated	$49,000			=	$25,000			+	$24,000		
Paying of liabilities	−$25,000				$25,000						
Balances updated	$24,000			=					$24,000		
Distribution of cash to French	−$24,000							−	$24,000		

LEARNING UNIT 17-4 REVIEW

AT THIS POINT you should be able to

- Explain the steps of the liquidation process.
- Explain why the profit and loss ratio is not used to pay off the partners in the liquidation process.
- Prepare a liquidation statement.

Self-Review Quiz 17-4

From the information given here, journalize the (A) sale of assets, (B) loss or gain from realization, (C) payment of liabilities, and (D) distribution of remaining cash to the partners.

1. Cash, $4,000; Other Assets, $13,000; Liabilities, $2,000; Jay, Capital, $3,000; Joger, Capital, $5,000; and Ynet, Capital, $7,000.
2. Partners share losses or gains in a 3:1:1 ratio.
3. Assets sold for $16,000.

Solution to Self-Review Quiz 17-4

FIGURE 17.34 Sale, Distribution, and Payment to Creditors and Owners

Jay: $\frac{3}{5} \times \$3,000$

Joger: $\frac{1}{5} \times \$3,000$

Ynet: $\frac{1}{5} \times \$3,000$

			Debit	Credit
(A)	Cash		1 6 0 0 0 00	
	Other Assets			1 3 0 0 0 00
	Loss or Gain from Realization			3 0 0 0 00
(B)	Loss or Gain from Realization		3 0 0 0 00	
	Jay, Capital			1 8 0 0 00
	Joger, Capital			6 0 0 00
	Ynet, Capital			6 0 0 00
(C)	Liabilities		2 0 0 0 00	
	Cash			2 0 0 0 00
(D)	Jay, Capital		4 8 0 0 00	
	Joger, Capital		5 6 0 0 00	
	Ynet, Capital		7 6 0 0 00	
	Cash			1 8 0 0 0 00

CHAPTER ASSIGNMENTS

SUMMARY OF KEY POINTS

LEARNING UNIT 17-1

1. Forming a partnership is quite easy and can be agreed upon in writing or orally. Having a written articles of partnership clearly spells out the "specifics" of the partnership.
2. Although the life of a partnership is limited, dissolving a partnership does not mean that the business will cease operations.
3. Mutual agency means that in most cases all partners are bound by the acts of one partner who enters into a contract as an agent of the company.
4. In the formation of a partnership, one records assets at their current fair value.

LEARNING UNIT 17-2

1. Salary and interest allowances are not expenses but mechanisms used to divide net income or net loss among partners. Salary is based on personal service; interest is based on a percentage of each partner's capital balance.
2. Whether net income covers the salary and interest allowances makes no difference in calculating them; they are allocated, and *then* one looks to see the effect on partners' equity.
3. The statement of partners' equity is a supporting document that calculates the ending capital balance found on the balance sheet for each partner.

LEARNING UNIT 17-3

1. When a new partner buys an equity interest from an existing partner, any personal profit belongs to the existing partner and is not recorded in the partnership. All that results on the partnership's books is a change of equity.

2. One partner cannot force other partners to accept a new partner.

3. A one-quarter equity interest doesn't necessarily mean a one-quarter share of all earnings; it would depend on the profit and loss ratio agreed upon by the partners.

4. A bonus is given to old partners if a new partner contributes more than his or her equity interest. On the other hand, a bonus is given to a new partner if he or she invests less than equity interest. The bonus is shared based on the profit and loss ratio.

5. At the time a partner leaves, a partnership may be audited and assets adjusted to their current fair market value. Revaluations are shared between the partners based on the profit and loss ratio.

6. A partner may withdraw for less than or more than book equity. The difference is then shared by the other partners based on the profit and loss ratio. If assets are not revalued, partners must agree on whether assets are overstated, and then the equity change of the partner who is leaving is shared in profit and loss ratio by the other partners.

LEARNING UNIT 17-4

1. Liquidation is the winding-up process involved in ending a business.

2. Liquidation includes the following steps:
   a. Selling assets for cash
   b. Dividing loss or gain for realization among partners
   c. Paying creditors
   d. Paying remaining cash to partners based on capital balances

KEY TERMS

Articles of partnership   The written contract that spells out the details of the agreement among the partners.

Bonus   When a new partner is admitted, he or she may pay more or less than equity interest. If the new partner pays more, the old partners share a bonus in the profit and loss ratio. Of course, the opposite could result, and the new partner could receive a bonus if he or she invests less than equity interest.

Co-ownership of property   Each partner owns a share of the assets.

Deficit   Amount by which net income falls short of salary and interest allowance. Also an abnormal, or debit, balance in a partner's capital account.

General partner   A partner who has unlimited liability.

Interest allowance   A mechanism for dividing earnings of a partnership based on a percentage of capital balances of the partners (not an expense).

Limited life   Partnership is dissolved by admission, withdrawal, or death of a partner. Although the partnership is dissolved, the operations of the business continue.

Limited partner   The partner's liability is limited to the amount of investment in the partnership.

Liquidation   Occurs when a business is terminated, the assets are sold, and liabilities and partners are paid off.

Mutual agency   Act of a single partner is binding on all members of the partnership.

Partnership   The association of two or more persons who act as co-owners of a business.

Profit and loss ratio   An agreed-upon ratio used to divide earnings or losses of a partnership.

Purchase of an equity interest   Transfer of ownership between an existing partner and a new partner.

Realization   The conversion of noncash assets into cash in the liquidation process.

Salary allowance   A mechanism for dividing earnings of a partnership based on personal services provided by the partners (not an expense).

Uniform Partnership Act   Laws enacted in most states that govern how a partnership is formed, operated, and liquidated.

Unlimited liability   Partners may be personally liable for debts of the partnership.

BLUEPRINT: ADVANTAGES AND DISADVANTAGES OF A PARTNERSHIP

Advantages	Disadvantages
1. Ease of formation; legal status under Uniform Partnership Act.	1. Limited life expectancy; any changes in membership dissolve the partnership.
2. Ability to raise more capital than a sole proprietorship.	2. Mutual agency; action by one partner binds all other partners.
3. Pooled resource of talents.	3. Unlimited liability; each partner must cover partnership debts with personal assets.
4. Flexibility to react to the marketplace, because legal restrictions are minimal.	4. Cannot admit a new partner without agreement of all other partners; a partner cannot withdraw without agreement of all other partners.
5. Credit rating usually higher, because more than one partner is responsible for company's debts.	

QUESTIONS, CLASSROOM DEMONSTRATION EXERCISES, EXERCISES, AND PROBLEMS

Discussion and Critical Thinking Questions/Ethical Case

1. How is the equity of a partnership different from that of a sole proprietorship?

2. List five characteristics of a partnership.

3. What is the function of the articles of partnership?

4. Explain how a company could operate even when being dissolved.

5. Mutual agency could create unlimited liability. Agree or disagree? Defend your position.

6. Explain why salary and interest allowances are not expenses for a partnership.

7. Give an example of a fractional ratio.

8. The statement of partners' capital is a required report. Agree or disagree? Defend your position.

9. What is meant by a "side transaction" when a new partner is admitted by an existing partner's selling the new partner equity?

10. What is meant by a "bonus" when a partner is admitted?

11. When a partner withdraws, why would a partnership revalue its assets?

12. Why would a partner who is withdrawing take more or less than book equity?

13. What are the four steps of the liquidation process?

14. Jee Jones is in a partnership with Alvin Scott and Morry Flynn. Jee signed a long-term contract with a supplier without telling either partner. When Alvin heard about it, he hit the roof. He told Jee the partnership could not afford this contract and he would have nothing to do with it. Do you think Alvin should be upset? You make the call. Write down your recommendations to Alvin.

Classroom Demonstration Exercises

SET A

LO1 (10 min) **Forming a Partnership**

1. Bernie Pillow and Ralf Lee enter into a partnership. On July 1, 200X, Bernie invests $7,000 cash in the partnership. Ralf invests $4,000 cash and store equipment worth $6,000 with accumulated depreciation of $2,000. The equipment

has a current appraised value of $9,000. Prepare a journal entry to record this transaction.

Division of Net Income   *LO2 (10 min)*

2. James Slater, Scupper Ring, and Molly Flynn invested $3,000, $5,000, and $7,000, respectively. At the end of the first year, the company's net income was $30,000. Assuming no agreement was reached on how to share net income, prepare a journal entry at closing to allocate net income.

Division of Net Income Based on Beginning Capital Balances   *LO2 (10 min)*

3. If the partners in Exercise 2 share net income based on their beginning capital investments, what would be the journal entry at closing to allocate net income?

Calculating Total Salary and Interest Allowance   *LO2 (15 min)*

4. If the partners in Exercise 2 have the following agreement, please calculate the total salary and interest allowance:
  a. *Salary Allowance:* Slater, $8,000; Ring, $7,000; and Flynn, $5,000.
  b. 10% interest on capital investments.

Share of Net Income to Partners; Deficit Sharing   *LO2 (15 min)*

5. Using your answer in Exercise 4, how much more income is to be distributed to the partners (assume each shares equally) after the salary and interest allowance? If net income was $16,000, how much would the partners share in the deficit?

Admission of a New Partner   *LO4 (10 min)*

6. On March 8, Alan Oll sold his equity in the partnership to B. Mills for $5,000. Alan's capital account had a $4,000 balance. Record the journal entry.

Investing into an Existing Partnership   *LO2 (15 min)*

7. Pete Raul wants to have a one-third interest in a law practice that has two partners with capital balances as follows:
  R. Seel, Capital $5,000
  A. Pool, Capital   2,000
  How much must Pete invest into the partnership?

Calculating Profit and Loss Ratio   *LO2 (15 min)*

8. From the following capital balances, calculate the profit and loss ratio for each account:
  B. Bool, Capital $ 200
  A. Jones, Capital   1,000
  T. Pool, Capital   800

Liquidation   *LO4 (15 min)*

9. From the following, journalize the (a) sale of assets and (b) loss or gain from liquidation realization. Given:
  Cash $ 3,150
  Other Assets   16,000
  Liabilities   4,000
  Moxie, Capital   5,000
  Carol, Capital   7,000
  Earl, Capital   8,000
  Partners agreed to share losses or gains in a 4:1:2 ratio and sold assets for $19,500.

SET B

LO1 (10 min)   **Forming a Partnership**

     1. Alice Hall and Jim Brown enter into a partnership. On July 1, 200X, Alice invests $5,000 cash in the partnership. Jim invests $2,000 cash and store equipment worth $6,000 with accumulated depreciation of $2,000. The equipment has a current appraised value of $7,000. Prepare a journal entry to record this transaction.

LO2 (10 min)   **Division of Net Income**

     2. James Slater, Scupper Ring, and Molly Flynn invested $2,000, $4,000, and $6,000, respectively. At the end of the first year, the company's net income was $21,000. Assuming no agreement was reached on how to share net income, prepare a journal entry at closing to allocate net income.

LO2 (10 min)   **Division of Net Income Based on Beginning Capital Balances**

     3. If the partners in Exercise 2 share net income based on their beginning capital investments, what would be the journal entry at closing to allocate net income?

LO2 (10 min)   **Calculating Total Salary and Interest Allowance**

     4. If the partners in Exercise 2 have the following agreement, please calculate the total salary and interest allowance:
       a. *Salary Allowance:* Slater, $7,000; Ring, $6,000; and Flynn, $4,000.
       b. 10% interest on capital investments.

LO2 (15 min)   **Share of Net Income to Partners; Deficit Sharing**

     5. Using your answer in Exercise 4, how much more income is to be distributed to the partners (assume each shares equally) after the salary and interest allowance? If net income was $17,990, how much would the partners share in the deficit?

LO4 (10 min)   **Admission of a New Partner**

     6. On March 8, Alan Oll sold his equity in the partnership to B. Mills for $4,000. Alan's capital account had a $3,000 balance. Record the journal entry.

LO2 (15 min)   **Investing into an Existing Partnership**

     7. Pete Raul wants to have a one-third interest in a law practice that has two partners with capital balances as follows:

     R. Seel, Capital $4,000

     A. Pool, Capital   1,000

     How much must Pete invest into the partnership?

LO2 (15 min)   **Calculating Profit and Loss Ratio**

     8. From the following capital balances, calculate the profit and loss ratio for each account:

     B. Bool, Capital $100

     A. Jones, Capital   500

     T. Pool, Capital   400

LO4 (15 min)   **Liquidation**

     9. From the following, journalize the (a) sale of assets and (b) loss or gain from liquidation realization:

     Cash $ 3,000

     Other Assets   15,000

Liabilities	3,000
Moxie, Capital	4,000
Carol, Capital	6,000
Earl, Capital	5,000

Partners agreed to share losses or gains in a 4:1:2 ratio and sold assets for $19,200.

Exercises

17-1. Earl Munroe and Carol Rogers form a partnership on May 1, 20XX. Munroe contributes $40,000. Rogers contributes $28,000 cash and land costing $18,000 with a current fair value of $29,000. A $30,000 note payable due Rogers is assumed by the new partnership. Please prepare the journal entries to record Munroe's and Rogers's investment in the partnership.

LO1 (20 min)

17-2. A. Lot and B. Stall have decided their partnership earnings will be shared as follows: (a) 10% interest allowance on capital balances at beginning of year, (b) remainder to be shared equally. Capital balances of A. Lot and B. Stall at the beginning of the year are $80,000 and $30,000, respectively. Net income is $16,000 for the year. Record the journal entry to update the capital balances of A. Lot and B. Stall on December 31.

LO2 (20 min)

17-3. Julie Elliott, Tami DiVito, and Abby Ellen are partners who share losses and gains in a ratio of 2:2:1. Their capital balances are $5,000, $6,000, and $4,000, respectively. The partners are anxious to have Tami retire and have paid her $12,000. Give the journal entry to record the payment to Tami along with the absorption of the amount over book equity by Julie and Abby on July 31, 20XX.

LO4 (20 min)

17-4. L. White, V. Slye, and E. Rothe are partners with capital balances of $90,000, $80,000, and $70,000, respectively. Rothe sells his interest in the company for $88,000 to P. Smith. White and Slye have consented to the new partner. Record the journal entry for the admission of Smith on April 8.

LO4 (20 min)

17-5. Sullivan, Roe, and Hinch have capital balances before liquidation of $12,000, $24,000, and $32,000, respectively. Cash balance is $48,000, and the partners share losses and gains in a 3:2:1 ratio. All noncash assets are sold, for a gain on realization of $24,000. In your calculations assume that no liabilities are a factor. What will each partner receive in cash in the liquidation process?

LO4 (20 min)

Group A Problems

17A-1. a. The partnership of Mia and Matt began with the partners investing $4,000 and $2,400, respectively. At the end of the first year, the partnership earned net income of $8,200. Under each of the following independent situations, calculate how much of the $8,200 each is entitled to:

LO2 (30 min)

Check Figure:
(b) Deficit to be shared
equally $1,840

Situation 1:   No agreement on how income was to be shared.

Situation 2:   Mia and Matt share income based on the beginning-of-year investment ratio.

Situation 3:   Salary allowance of $2,800 to Mia and $2,400 to Matt. Ten percent interest on beginning year's investment. Remainder split equally.

b. In Situation 3, what would the earnings to each partner be if net income were $4,000?

LO4 (30 min)

17A-2. Bob Kerne and Whitney Blak are partners with capital balances of $1,600 and $800, respectively. They share all profits and losses equally. From the following independent situations, journalize the admission of the new partner, Jack Ray:

Situation 1:   Ray purchased Blak's interest for $6,000, paying it personally to Blak.

Situation 2:   Ray invested an amount exactly equal to one-third interest in the partnership.

Situation 3:   Ray invested $1,800 for a one-third interest. Kerne and Blak share the bonus.

Situation 4:   Ray invested $600 for a one-third interest. Bonus is credited to Ray's account.

Check Figure:
Sit. 3: $400 bonus to old partners

LO4 (30 min)   **17A-3.** Lane, Right, and Von are partners. On July 30, 20XX, the balance sheet was as follows:

Cash	$12,000	Lane, Capital	$ 7,500
Inventory	5,000	Right, Capital	12,500
Other Assets	8,000	Von, Capital	5,000
Total Assets	$25,000	Total Liab. + Equity	$25,000

Check Figure:
Sit. 1:
Dr. Von, Capital $5,000
Cr. Jones, Capital $5,000

The partners agree to share all losses and gains in a 2:2:1 ratio. Von is withdrawing from the partnership. From the following independent situations, journalize the withdrawal of Von:

Situation 1:   Von sells his equity to Jones for $18,000. Partners agree to admission of Jones.

Situation 2:   On withdrawal of Von, inventory is determined to be overvalued by $1,000. (Before withdrawal, assets are revalued to current fair market value.) Be sure to record entry to revalue inventory as well as the withdrawal of Von.

Situation 3:   Von is paid $3,000 out of the assets of the partnership. Because the assets are overvalued, the partners do not want to decrease the recorded asset values.

Situation 4:   Von is paid $8,500 out of the assets of the partnership. Because the assets are undervalued, the partners do not want to increase the recorded asset values.

LO4 (30 min)   **17A-4.** The partnership of Jones, Reston, and Sullivan is being liquidated. All gains and losses are shared in a 3:2:1 ratio. Before liquidation, their balance sheet looks as follows:

Cash	$22,500	Liabilities	$ 6,300
Other Assets	14,700	A. Jones, Capital	11,100
		C. Reston, Capital	18,000
		J. Sullivan, Capital	1,800
Total Assets	$37,200	Total Liab. + Equity	$37,200

Journalize the entries needed in the liquidation process under the following independent situations and assume a date of October 1, 20XX, for sale of assets and October 15 for paying off liabilities and distributing cash to partners:

Situation 1:   Sold other assets for $32,700.

Situation 2:   Sold other assets for $5,700.

Situation 3:   Sold other assets for $2,100. Sullivan cannot cover his deficit.

Group B Problems

17B-1. a. Mia and Matt began a partnership by investing $4,800 and $3,200, respectively. At the end of the first year, the partnership earned net income of $7,600. Under each of the following independent situations, calculate how much of the $7,600 each is entitled to:

LO2 (30 min)

Situation 1:   No agreement on how income was to be shared.

Situation 2:   Mia and Matt share income based on the beginning-of-year investment ratio.

Situation 3:   Salary allowance of $2,480 to Mia and $2,800 to Matt. Twelve percent interest on beginning year's investment. Remainder split equally.

> *Check Figure:*
> (b) Deficit to be shared
> equally $640

b. In Situation 3 what would the earnings to each partner be if net income were $5,600?

17B-2. Bob Kerne and Whitney Blak are partners with capital balances of $3,000 and $1,000, respectively. They share all profits and losses equally. From the following independent situations, journalize the admission of the new partner, Jack Ray:

LO4 (30 min)

Situation 1:   Ray purchases Blak's interest for $6,000, paying it personally to Blak.

Situation 2:   Ray invested an amount exactly equal to one-fifth interest in the partnership.

Situation 3:   Ray invested $2,000 for a one-fifth interest. Kerne and Blak share the bonus.

> *Check Figure:*
> Sit. 3: $800 bonus to
> old partners

Situation 4:   Ray invested $300 for a one-fifth interest. Bonus is credited to Ray's account.

17B-3. Lane, Right, and Von are partners of LRV Repairs Service. On July 31, 20XX, the balance sheet was as follows:

LO4 (30 min)

Cash	$50,000	Lane, Capital	$30,000
Inventory	20,000	Right, Capital	15,000
Other Assets	10,000	Von, Capital	35,000
Total Assets	$80,000	Total Liab. + Equity	$80,000

The partners agree to share all losses and gains in a 2:1:2 ratio. Von is withdrawing from the partnership. From the following independent situations, journalize the withdrawal of Von:

Situation 1:   Von sells his equity to Jones for $120,000. Partners agree to admission of Jones.

> *Check Figure:*
> Sit. 1:
> Dr. Von, Capital
> $35,000
> Cr. Jones, Capital
> $35,000

(*continued on next page*)

Situation 2: On withdrawal of Von, inventory is determined to be overvalued by $6,000. (Before withdrawal, assets are revalued to current fair market value.)

Situation 3: Von is paid $32,000 out of the assets of the partnership. Although the assets are overvalued, the partners do not want to decrease the recorded asset values.

Situation 4: Von is paid $44,000 out of the assets of the partnership. Because the assets are undervalued, partners do not want to increase the recorded asset values.

LO4 (30 min) **17B-4.** Jones, Reston, and Sullivan are liquidating their partnership. All losses and gains are shared in a 4:2:1 ratio (not based on investment). Before liquidation their balance sheet looked as follows:

Cash	$ 800	Liabilities	$ 6,000
Other Assets	19,200	A. Jones, Capital	4,000
		C. Reston, Capital	8,000
		J. Sullivan, Capital	2,000
Total Assets	$20,000	Total Liab. + Equity	$20,000

Journalize the entries needed in the liquidation process under the following independent situations (assume a date of July 1, 20XX, for sale of assets and a date of July 15 to pay off liabilities and distribute cash that is left to the partners):

Situation 1: Sold other assets for $26,200.

Situation 2: Sold other assets for $17,800.

Situation 3: Sold other assets for $10,800; Jones cannot cover his deficit. (For simplicity, round any calculations to the nearest dollar.)

Check Figure:
Sit. 2: Loss or gain from realization $1,400 Dr.

ON-THE-JOB TRAINING

LO2 (30 min) **T-1.** Al Ring and Marvin Smoy are partners who are extremely worried about the financial condition of their company. As of December 31, 20XX, their balance sheet revealed the following:

Assets		Liabilities and Owner's Equity	
Cash	$ 30,000	Liabilities	$ 60,000
Noncash Assets	400,000	A. Ring, Capital	200,000
		M. Smoy, Capital	170,000
Total Assets	$430,000	Total Liab. + Equity	$430,000

A pending lawsuit could result in a settlement of more than $400,000 against the company for negligence. Al wants out of the partnership before the case is settled. Marvin claims they are both in this together. As the accountant, could you explain in writing to Al how the situation looks? All losses and gains are shared in a 2:1 ratio.

LO4 (30 min) **T-2.** On May 15 Peter Rig and Joan Fess formed a partnership in the catering business. Peter invested $30,000 in cash and $8,000 in equipment. Joan invested land worth $15,000, a building worth $24,000, and merchandise worth $8,000.

The partners decided that they would insure the building and its contents beginning June 1. On May 28 a fire broke out and destroyed half of the merchandise, the building, and the equipment. That night Rig and Fess decided to liquidate the business.

Rig told Fess that he would take his cash (which was in a fireproof safe) and Fess would take the land. Fess argued that in a partnership Rig couldn't do that. Could you settle this dispute? Make your recommendations in writing.

FINANCIAL REPORT PROBLEM

Reading the Kellogg's Annual Report   *LO1 (15 min)*

Go to Appendix A and explain why Kellogg's is not classified as a partnership.

INTERNET PROJECT

IRS

Go to the Web and search: Annual Report IRS 2008.
List out the latest news the IRS is providing.
Order a free report on partnerships.

18

Corporations: Organizations and Stock

DID YOU KNOW? Hormel Foods has more than $850 million in sales from new products introduced since 2000 and has about 34,000 shareholders. Did you know the corporation makes Spam products? Visit *www.hormelfoods.com* to find more information about Hormel Foods.

LEARNING OBJECTIVES

1. Defining a corporation; establishing a corporation; listing the advantages and disadvantages of a corporation.

2. Journalizing entries for issuing par value stock, no-par stock, and no-par with stated value stock.

3. Calculating dividends on preferred and common stock.

4. Recording capital stock transactions under a stock subscription plan.

So far we've learned about sole proprietorships and partnerships; now we're going to learn about corporations. A **corporation** such as Hormel Foods is a separate legal entity. We first look at how a corporation is formed, along with its main characteristics.

LO1
Learning Unit 18-1 Forming a Corporation; Characteristics of the Corporate Structure

Four steps are involved in forming a corporation.

Step 1 The **incorporators,** those wishing to form the corporation, apply to a state for a charter. They do so by submitting **articles of incorporation** drawn up by an attorney, together with a fee. The articles of incorporation consist of the following information:

1. Name of the corporation and incorporation date
2. Purpose of business
3. Organizational structure
4. Expected life (usually "forever")
5. Primary location of business
6. Types of stock to be offered (Stock is what owners purchase to gain ownership rights in the company. We look at stock in detail in a few moments.)

Step 2 The Office of the Secretary of State reviews the application and, if deemed in order, a **charter** (often called a **certificate of incorporation**) is issued to the incorporators. Copies of the charter and the articles of incorporation are placed on file for public record.

> When the charter is issued, the corporation's legal entity is established.

Step 3 The stock is issued by the corporation to the owners (called **stockholders**).

Step 4 The stockholders meet to elect a board of **directors** and adopt the bylaws of the corporation. Often in a new corporation the stockholders become the directors. As the company grows, people are appointed to the board who are not stockholders. Records of meetings of the board of directors and stockholders are kept in a **minute book,** as directed by law. The board of directors appoints the officers to run the company; it is the board's job to oversee the overall management of the corporation, whereas the officers follow the policies set up by the board.

Advantages of the Corporate Form of Organization

1. Limited Liability/Separate Legal Entity Stockholders have **limited liability;** they are not personally liable for the obligations of the corporation, because a corporation is a separate and distinct legal entity. The corporation enters into contracts, buys or sells property, and sues or is sued in its own name. Thus, the only amount the stockholders can lose is the amount of their investment in the business. Of course, stockholders can still be held liable for any fraudulent or negligent actions they perform in connection with the corporation.

2. Unlimited Life A corporation's life is perpetual (goes on forever) except in the case of bankruptcy, mergers, or vote of the stockholders.

3. Ease of Transferring Ownership Interest When an owner invests in a corporation, each share of ownership is represented by one or more formal documents called **stock certificates.** The stockholder can sell or transfer shares of some corporations through *brokerage firms,* companies that act as intermediaries in the trading of stock. This trading occurs at various marketplaces called *stock exchanges.* On the back of the certificate is a form that the seller endorses. A key point is that when the shares of stock are sold by the stockholder, the sale has *no* effect on the company's assets and liabilities. What happens is really a *shift* in the ownership.

4. No Mutual Agency A corporation is not subject to mutual agency the way a partnership is. For example, if John Jones is a stockholder of Passon Corporation and enters into a contract with the city of Lynn, this action by John cannot bind the corporation to complete the contract with the city of Lynn.

5. Ease of Raising Capital With no mutual agency, with limited liability, and with the ease of transferring ownership interest, the investment in a corporation becomes attractive to many people. As a result, the corporation can raise large amounts of capital by assembling investment groups of stockholders.

Disadvantages of the Corporate Structure

1. Difficulties in Forming a Corporation/Government Regulations Because of the steps involved, a corporation is more difficult to form than a sole proprietorship or a partnership. Incorporators must complete the articles of incorporation and pay an incorporation fee. The complexity of forming a corporation also usually means hiring a lawyer to deal with legal aspects. When granted a certificate of incorporation, corporations are required to fulfill many state and federal regulations and to file many governmental reports.

2. Corporate Taxation Because the corporation is a separate legal entity, its income is taxed by the federal government. The corporation may also be taxed at the state and local levels. At the same time, any income that is distributed to the stockholders is taxable to the stockholders. Thus, a corporation's earnings face double taxation.*

LEARNING UNIT 18-1 REVIEW

AT THIS POINT you should be able to

- Explain the steps in forming a corporation.
- List as well as explain the advantages and disadvantages of the corporate form of organization.

Self-Review Quiz 18-1

Respond true or false to the following:

1. The articles of incorporation document is quite easy to fill out.
2. A corporation is a separate legal entity.
3. The officers of a corporation always elect the board of directors.
4. Stocks can be transferred by stockholders without affecting the operations of a corporation.
5. Double taxation does exist in a corporate structure.

Solutions to Self-Review Quiz 18-1

1. False
2. True
3. False
4. True
5. True

Learning Unit 18-2 Stockholders' Equity: Retained Earnings and Capital Stock

The equity section of a balance sheet of a corporation differs from that of a sole proprietorship or a partnership. In the sole proprietorship, we have simply a capital account and a withdrawals account. In the partnership, a separate capital and withdrawals account is

---

*Note S corporations have less than 100 stockholders, are not publicly traded, and are only taxed at the stockholder level, similar to a partnership.

kept for each partner. With the corporation, the stockholders' equity section is broken down into two major parts:

1. **Paid-In Capital** is the amount that stockholders have invested in the business. It is equal to the values of the assets (usually cash) that have been contributed to the business.
2. **Retained earnings** are accumulated profits that are retained or kept in the corporation. Retained earnings does not mean cash; cash is an *asset,* whereas retained earnings is part of stockholders' *equity.*

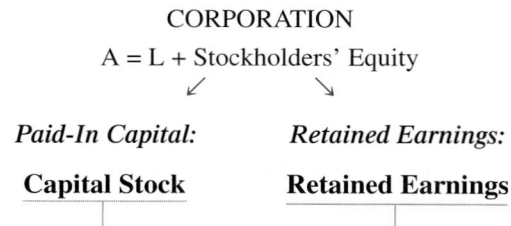

CORPORATION

A = L + Stockholders' Equity

Paid-In Capital: *Retained Earnings:*

Capital Stock   **Retained Earnings**

Let's look more closely at the term *capital stock.*

Capital Stock

In return for their investment in the corporation, stockholders are issued shares of **capital stock.** Think of ownership of a corporation as being represented by shares of stock. The two classes of capital stock are common and preferred. The charter of the corporation indicates the maximum amount of shares of each class of capital stock that a company can legally issue, but the company does not have to issue all of it. **Authorized capital stock** is the amount listed in the charter, **issued capital stock** refers to the shares sold to the stockholders, and **outstanding capital stock** means shares sold and in the stockholders' possession. Let's look at the two classes of capital stock, beginning with common stock.

> In Chapter 19, we look at the difference between issued and outstanding stock.

Characteristics of Common Stock

The most prevalent type of capital stock is called **common stock.** When a corporation has only one kind of capital stock, it will be common stock. When the stock is issued, the owners receive certain rights from the corporation. These rights include the following:

1. The right to vote at stockholders' meetings.
2. The right to share in profits by receiving dividends.
3. The right to dispose of or sell their stock.
4. The right to maintain their proportionate ownership interest in the company. This right is called **preemptive right.** For example, if Jill Evans owns 15% of the common stock of the corporation, she would have the chance to also purchase 15% of any *additional* common stock that is issued, before it is offered to the public at large.
5. The right, when a company is liquidated, to share in assets after creditors and others with prior claims are paid off.

Characteristics of Preferred Stock

Another type of capital stock some corporations may issue is called **preferred stock.** This stock provides stockholders with prior claim to a corporation's profits and assets over holders of common stock. Corporations watch current market conditions and try to offer preferred stock that will be attractive to investors. Holders of preferred stock often give up some of the rights that go with common stock—such as voting rights, preemptive rights, or even some earnings potential—in return for their more stable earnings that come from preferred stock. In many ways preferred stock is a less risky investment than common stock.

Dividends on Common and Preferred Stock

Dividends are paid to stockholders as their share of the corporation's profits. A dividend must be voted by the board of directors, and if it has been a bad year for profits, the board may refuse to vote a dividend. Keep in mind a company may decide against a dividend in a good year, feeling it may be wise to invest money in some aspect of the company's business, such as research and development.

As mentioned, preferred stock gives its stockholders a prior claim to a corporation's profits over holders of common stock. This preferential treatment can happen in several ways:

1. If a stock is **cumulative preferred stock,** the holders have a right to a certain dividend every year. If in some years the board does not issue a dividend, the amount payable will accumulate until the earnings justify the payout. At this time the preferred stockholders will get dividends for all past years as well as the current year before the holders of noncumulative preferred stock and common stock get any dividend.

   For example, Moore Company has 3,000 shares of cumulative preferred stock that are entitled to a dividend of $3 per share. In 20X7, owing to financial problems, Moore Company decided to pay no dividend. Thus, the company has **dividends in arrears** of $9,000. No dividends can be paid to noncumulative preferred stockholders and common stockholders until the preferred dividends are paid off in full: the amount in arrears plus the current year's dividend. Because financial conditions improved in 20X8, Moore paid the $9,000 of dividends in arrears (3,000 shares × $3) to holders of preferred stock plus the current year's dividend of $9,000.

2. If a stock is **noncumulative preferred stock,** holders have a right to the current year's dividend, but without any holdovers from past years in which dividends were not declared.

3. If a stock is **nonparticipating preferred stock,** each year the holders of preferred stock receive a certain percentage as dividend and the remainder goes to common stock. Thus, if a company declared a dividend of $50,000, the preferred stockholders would get their usual percentage and the common stockholders would get all the rest, even if it was a greater percentage dividend than preferred got.

4. If a stock is **participating preferred stock,** preferred stockholders get their yearly dividend and can get a percentage of what's left over, splitting it in various ways with common stockholders.

Stock Value (for Capital Stock)

When a corporation is created, it issues a certain number of shares of stock, which are then sold to stockholders. At the time that the corporation receives its charter, the board of directors may assign a **par value** to the stock, something like $25 or $50 a share. This value is entirely arbitrary; no one can say that the stock is really worth that much. It is a way of dividing up ownership of the corporation into a number of units and putting a value on each unit. Many companies have par values of 5 or 10 cents per share. The key point about par value is that it is a value assigned arbitrarily. It is stated on the stock certificate. Figure 18.1 on the following page can be used as a summary as you read the rest of the chapter.

In most states the assigning of par value per share times the number of shares issued for a corporation represents the **legal capital,** an amount that a corporation must retain in the business for protection of creditors. Because the concept of par value can be quite misleading, some corporations will issue **no-par stock,** stock with no par value. Thus, the *entire* proceeds from selling this issue represents the legal capital (number of shares issued times amount investors paid for each share).

Most states permit (or some require) that the directors of a company set a **stated value** on the shares. This value also is arbitrary but can be changed by the board of directors. Stated value, which has the same purpose as par value, may be less confusing to investors, because it is not printed on the stock certificates.

Whether a stock is issued at par value, no-par value with no stated value, or no-par value with stated value, the capital stock account can be recorded with entries that indicate whether investors paid more or less than par value or stated value. We look at specific examples of recording capital stock in the next unit.

FIGURE 18.1 Par, No-Par, and Stated Value

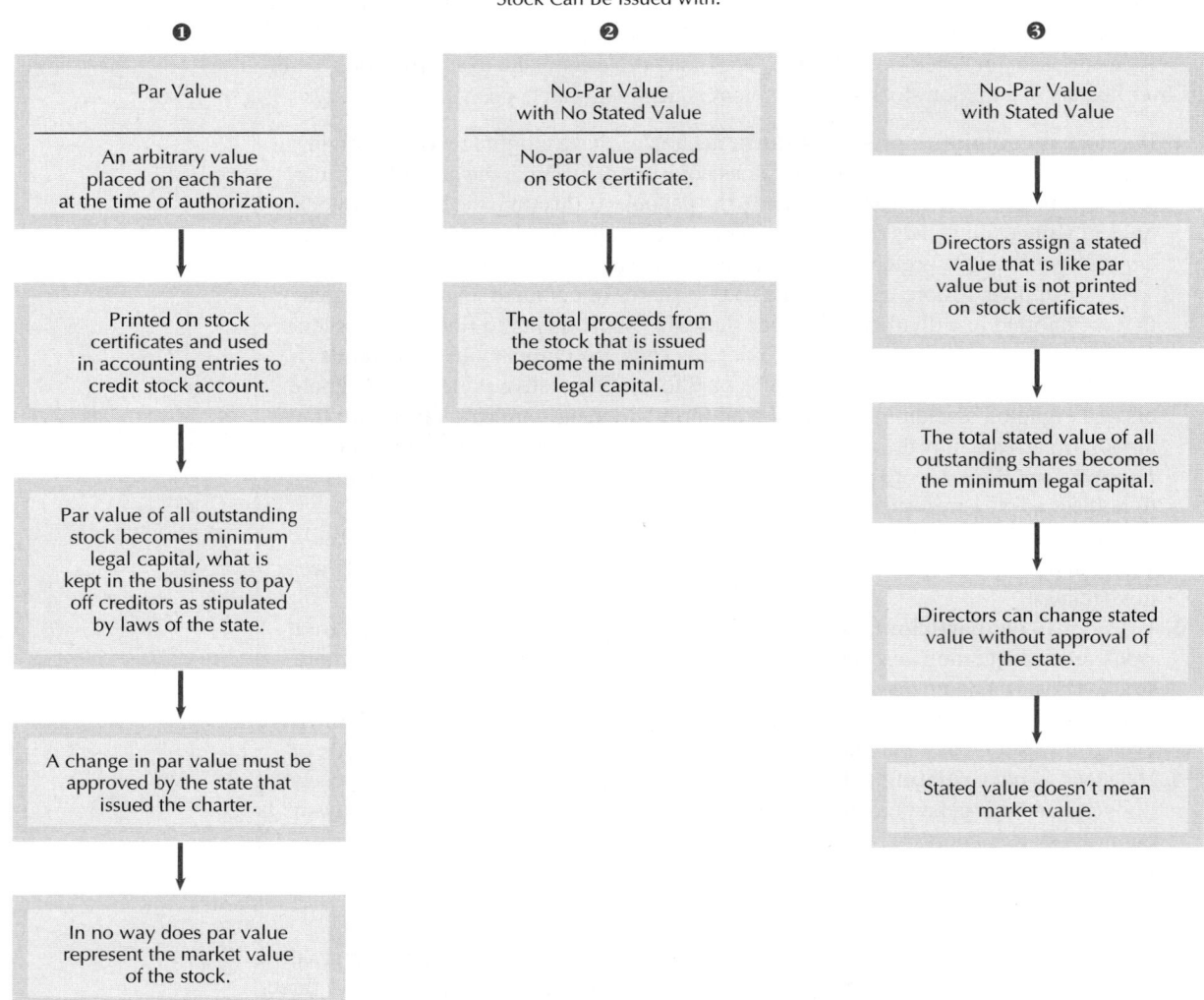

LEARNING UNIT 18-2 REVIEW

AT THIS POINT you should be able to

- Explain the difference between authorized and issued stock.
- List the characteristics of common and preferred stock.
- Define and explain cumulative, noncumulative, participating, and nonparticipating preferred stock.
- Define and explain par value, legal capital, no-par stock, and stated value.

Self-Review Quiz 18-2

Respond true or false to the following:

1. Retained Earnings is part of Paid-In Capital.
2. Preferred stock is the most prevalent type of capital stock.
3. Preemptive right allows one to maintain one's proportionate ownership interest in a company.

4. Preferred stock that is cumulative is entitled to dividends in arrears.

5. Par value doesn't represent the market value of the stock.

6. Stock cannot be issued at par value.

Solutions to Self-Review Quiz 18-2

1. False

2. False

3. True

4. True

5. True

6. False

Learning Unit 18-3 Recording Capital Stock Transactions and Calculating Dividends

LO2

In this unit we look at how to record the issuing of stock that has (1) par value, (2) no-par value, and (3) no-par value with stated value. We also see how to record transactions in which stock is exchanged for noncash assets. We then look at how to calculate dividends for preferred and common stock.

Recording the Sale of Stock That Has Par Value

Situation 1: Selling Common Stock at Par Roger Company sells 200 shares of a $10 par value common stock at $10 per share on February 3, 20XX.

Here is an analysis of the transaction:

Accounts Affected	Category	↑↓	Rules	
Cash	Asset	↑	Dr. $2,000	$10 par
				× 200 shares
Common Stock	SE	↑	Cr. $2,000	= $2,000

Common stock is recorded at number of shares times par value. That value represents the legal capital. The journal entry would be as shown in Figure 18.2.

	20XX						
	Feb.	3	Cash		2 0 0 00		
			Common Stock			2 0 0 00	

FIGURE 18.2 Selling Stock at Par

Situation 2: Selling Preferred Stock at Par Roger Co. sells 300 shares of $50 par value preferred stock at $50 on March 18, 20XX.

Once again, here is an analysis of the transaction:

Accounts Affected	Category	↑↓	Rules	
Cash	Asset	↑	Dr. $15,000	300 shares
				× $50 par
Preferred Stock	SE	↑	Cr. $15,000	= $15,000

Preferred Stock is recorded at number of shares times par value. The journal entry would be as shown in Figure 18.3.

FIGURE 18.3 Selling Preferred Stock at Par

	20XX Mar.	18	Cash		15 00 00 0				
			Preferred Stock				15 00 00 0		

Situation 3: Selling Common Stock at a Premium (More Than Par Value) Roger Co. sells 50 shares of $10 par value common stock at $15 on June 8, 20XX.

The Analysis The common stock is recorded at par value. Because this stock is sold at a **premium** (more than par value), the excess of the par value will be recorded in a new account called **Paid-In Capital in Excess of Par Value—Common.** Note in the transactional analysis that follows that this account is part of stockholders' equity. On the balance sheet it will be listed below Common Stock in the Paid-In Capital section of stockholders' equity.

Accounts Affected	Category	↑ ↓	Rules	
Cash	Asset	↑	Dr. $750	→ 50 shares × $15
Common Stock	SE	↑	Cr. $500	→ 50 shares × $10 par
Paid-In Capital in Excess of Par Value—Common	SE	↑	Cr. $250	→ 50 shares × $5 excess per share over par

The journal entry will be as shown in Figure 18.4.

FIGURE 18.4 Selling Common Stock at a Premium

	20XX June	8	Cash		7 50 00				
			Common Stock				5 00 00		
			Paid-In Capital in						
			Excess of Par Value—Common				2 50 00		

Situation 4: Selling Common Stock at a Discount (Below Par)* Roger Co. sells 100 shares of $10 par value common stock at $8 on July 3, 20XX.

The Analysis When a stock is sold below par, a **discount on stock** results. An account called Discount on Common Stock records the discount. It is a contra-stockholders' equity account that will reduce the Common Stock account it is related to. Some states do not allow stock to be sold at a discount.

Accounts Affected	Category	↑ ↓	Rules	
Cash	Asset	↑	Dr. $800	→ 100 shares × $8
Discount on Common Stock	Contra SE	↑	Dr. $200	→ 100 shares × $2 ($10 par − $8)
Common Stock	SE	↑	Cr. $1,000	→ 100 shares × $10 par

---

*This situation does not occur often and it makes the purchaser liable for the discount amount in the future if there is a bankruptcy.

The journal entry will be as shown in Figure 18.5.

20XX July	3	Cash			8 0 0 0 00								
		Discount on Common Stock			2 0 0 00								
		Common Stock					1 0 0 0 00				

FIGURE 18.5 Selling Common Stock at a Discount

Now let's look at how to record the sale of stock with no-par value, with or without stated value.

Recording Sale of Stock with No-Par Value and Stated Value

Situation 5: Selling No-Par Common Stock with No Stated Value Moss Co. sells 300 shares of no-par common stock for $20 per share on July 19, 20XX.

The transaction analysis chart shows the following:

Note: Corporations cannot legally sell stock at less than the stated value.

Accounts Affected	Category	↑ ↓	Rules	
Cash	Asset	↑	Dr. $6,000	} 300 shares × $20
Common Stock	SE	↑	Cr. $6,000	

The journal entry will be as shown in Figure 18.6.

20XX July	19	Cash			6 0 0 0 00						
		Common Stock					6 0 0 0 00				

FIGURE 18.6 Selling No-Par Common Stock with No Stated Value

Situation 6: Selling No-Par Common Stock with a Stated Value Reese Co. sells 200 shares of no-par common stock with a stated value of $40 for $50 per share on June 19, 20XX.

The Analysis An excess over the stated value will be recorded in a stockholders' equity account called **Paid-In Capital in Excess of Stated Value—Common.**

Accounts Affected	Category	↑ ↓	Rules	
Cash	Asset	↑	Dr. $10,000	→ 200 shares × $50
Common Stock	SE	↑	Cr. $8,000	→ 200 shares × $40
Paid-In Capital in Excess of Stated Value—Common	SE	↑	Cr. $2,000	→ 200 shares × $10 ($50 − $40)

The journal entry will be as shown in Figure 18.7.

20XX July	19	Cash		1 0 0 0 0 00							
		Common Stock				8 0 0 0 00				
		Paid-In Capital in Excess of								
		Stated Value—Common				2 0 0 0 00				

FIGURE 18.7 Selling No-Par Common Stock with Stated Value

Recording Transactions in Which Stock Is Exchanged for Noncash Assets

Situation 7: Exchanging Stock for Noncash Assets On July 8, Moss Corporation exchanged 3,000 shares of $10 par value common stock for machinery, buildings, and land. The assets had fair market values of $5,000, $10,000, and $20,000, respectively.

The Analysis Assets are recorded at fair market value; common stock is recorded at par value. If fair market value is not available for assets, one can try to find the market (not par) value of the stock. In this chapter we assume fair market value of assets is available. The difference between fair market value and par is recorded in the account Paid-In Capital in Excess of Par. Par value is never used to measure the selling price of the assets.

Accounts Affected	Category	↑↓	Rules	
Machinery	Asset	↑	Dr. $5,000	⎤
Buildings	Asset	↑	Dr. $10,000	⎬ Fair market value
Land	Asset	↑	Dr. $20,000	⎦
Common Stock	SE	↑	Cr. $30,000	→ 300 shares × $10 par
Paid-In Capital in Excess of Par— Common	SE	↑	Cr. $5,000	→ ($35,000 − $30,000)

The journal entry will be as shown in Figure 18.8.

FIGURE 18.8 Exchanging Stock for Noncash Assets

20XX July	8	Machinery		5 0 0 0 00		
		Buildings		1 0 0 0 0 00		
		Land		2 0 0 0 0 00		
		Common Stock			3 0 0 0 0 00	
		Paid-In Capital in Excess of Par—Common			5 0 0 0 00	

Situation 8:* Issuing Stock to Organizers of a Business for Services Performed On June 8, Rose Corporation issued 2,000 shares of $10 par common stock to the organizers of the business for services performed.

The Analysis Organization cost in the formation of a corporation (legal fees, printing of stock certificates, etc.) is an intangible asset on the balance sheet. It is usually amortized over 5 years (can be up to 40 years) because that life is used for income tax returns.

Accounts Affected	Category	↑↓	Rules
Organization Cost	Asset*	↑	Dr. $20,000
Common Stock	SE	↑	Cr. $20,000

*Now being expensed

The journal entry will be as shown in Figure 18.9.

---

*At the time of writing, amortization cost is now expensed (by accounts, timing, etc.) rather than an asset. For our discussion, it is an asset that will be amortized.

20XX June	8	Organization Cost	2 0 0 0 0 0			
		Common Stock		2 0 0 0 0 0		

FIGURE 18.9 Organization Costs

How to Calculate Dividends

LO3

Table 18.1 summarizes the process of calculating dividends, which is divided into four steps. For our calculation, we use these basic facts:

- $150,000 dividend declared.
- Preferred stock is 6% and fully participating.
- Preferred stock: 1,000 shares, $200 par.
- Common stock: 6,000 shares, $100 par.

TABLE 18.1 Four-Step Procedure for Calculating Dividends

The Formula	The Calculation	Preferred Stock	Common Stock	Total Dividends
Step 1: Dividend for preferred	1,000 shares × $200 × .06 = $12,000	$12,000		$12,000
Number of Shares × Par Value per Share × Rate of Dividend				
Step 2: Dividend for common	6,000 shares × $100 × .06 = $36,000		$ 36,000	36,000
Number of Shares × Par Value per Share × Rate of Dividend				
Step 3: Find total par value				
Number of Shares × Par Value per Share (Preferred) *plus*	1,000 shares × $200 = $200,000			
Number of Shares × Par Value per Share (Common)	6,000 shares × $100 = 600,000			
	Total par = $800,000			
Step 4: Allocate remainder of dividend based on par value				
$Preferred = \dfrac{\text{Par Value of Preferred}}{\text{Total Par Value}}$ × Remainder of Dividend	$\dfrac{\$200,000}{\$800,000} \times \$102,000* = \$25,500$	25,500		25,500
$Common = \dfrac{\text{Par Value of Common}}{\text{Total Par Value}}$ × Remainder of Dividend	$\dfrac{\$600,000}{\$800,000} \times \$102,000* = \$76,500$		76,500	76,500
		$37,500	$112,500	$150,000

*$150,000 − $48,000 = $102,000.

Step 1 To calculate preferred dividends, you multiply the number of shares (1,000) times the par value ($200) per share times the rate of dividend (6%). The result is a $12,000 dividend to preferred.

Step 2 To calculate the common stock dividend, you multiply the number of shares (6,000) times the par value per share ($100) times the same rate of dividend (6%). The result is a dividend of $36,000.

Step 3 At this point $48,000 of the $150,000 of dividends has been apportioned. Because the preferred is participating—which means it can share in additional dividends beyond the 6% dividend—the next step is to find the total par value and allocate the remainder of the dividend based on the total par.

Note in step 3 how the number of shares of preferred is multiplied by the $200 par and the number of common shares is multiplied by the $100 par. Thus, total par is $800,000.

Step 4 Because preferred is one-fourth of the total par, preferred is allocated $25,500 ($\frac{1}{4} \times$ $102,000) and common is allocated three-fourths of the $102,000, or $76,500.

We can see that both were paid the same percentage on par by the following calculations:

Preferred:
$$\frac{\text{Total Dividends}}{\text{Total Par Value of Preferred}} = \frac{\$37,500}{\$200,000} = 18.75\%$$

Common:
$$\frac{\text{Total Dividends}}{\text{Total Par Value of Common}} = \frac{\$112,500}{\$600,000} = 18.75\%$$

The end result is that the dividends were equally divided in terms of percentage, because preferred was fully participating.

LEARNING UNIT 18-3 REVIEW

AT THIS POINT you should be able to

- Record transactions that issue stock with or without par value.
- Explain the account called Paid-In Capital in Excess of Par Value.
- Tell what the normal balance is for the account Discount on Common Stock.
- Explain when the account Paid-In Capital in Excess of Stated Value is used.
- Calculate Capital in Excess of Par Value when stock is exchanged for noncash assets.
- Explain when one uses the account called Organization Cost.
- Calculate dividends on common and preferred stock.

Self-Review Quiz 18-3

1. Journalize the following transactions:

20XX		
July	5	Boston Company sells 200 shares of $20 par value common stock at $20.
Aug.	8	Jess Company sells 100 shares of $10 par value common stock at $25.
Oct.	9	Mellisa Company sells 300 shares of no-par common stock with a stated value of $30 for $50 per share.
Nov.	12	Moss Company issued 1,000 shares of $25 par value common stock to the organizers of the firm for services rendered costing $30,000.

2. From the following, calculate the dividends for common and preferred stock.

- Fourteen percent fully participating preferred stock.
- Board declared a $210,000 dividend.
- Preferred stock: 3,000 shares, $100 par.
- Common stock: 7,000 shares, $100 par.

Solutions to Self-Review Quiz 18-3

1.

	20XX													
	July	5	Cash	4 0 0 0 00			
			Common Stock		4 0 0 0 00	
	Aug.	8	Cash	2 5 0 0 00		
			Common Stock		1 0 0 0 00	
			Paid-In Capital in Excess of			
			Par Value—Common		1 5 0 0 00	
	Oct.	9	Cash	15 0 0 0 00		
			Common Stock		9 0 0 0 00	
			Paid-In Capital in Excess of			
			Stated Value—Common		6 0 0 0 00	
	Nov.	12	Organization Cost	3 0 0 0 0 00		
			Common Stock		2 5 0 0 0 00	
			Paid-In Capital in Excess of			
			Par Value—Common		5 0 0 0 00	

FIGURE 18.10 Journalizing Issuances of Stock

2.

	Preferred	Common
Dividends for preferred:		
(3,000 shares × $100 par) × .14 =	$42,000	
Dividends for common:		
(7,000 shares × $100 par) × .14 =		$98,000

Amount to be divided based on total par value:
($210,000 − $140,000) = $70,000

Total Par:

Preferred: 3,000 shares × $100 par =	$ 300,000
Common: 7,000 shares × $100 par =	700,000
Total	$1,000,000

Preferred: $\dfrac{\$300,000}{\$1,000,000} \times \$70,000 = \$21,000$ 21,000

Common: $\dfrac{\$700,000}{\$1,000,000} \times \$70,000 = \$49,000$ 49,000

Totals $63,000 $147,000

Proof:

Preferred: $\dfrac{\$63,000}{\$300,000} = 21\%$ Common: $\dfrac{\$147,000}{\$700,000} = 21\%$

Learning Unit 18-4 Recording Capital Stock Transactions Under a Stock Subscription Plan

LO4

In the last unit we assumed that stocks were immediately issued and full payment of cash or other assets was received. In this unit we examine stock transactions under **stock subscription** plans. Under such plans, buyers pledge to buy certain stocks but pay in installments or in a later lump sum. In most cases companies will not issue the actual stock certificates to these buyers until payment is complete.

Let's look at how Krump Corporation receives subscriptions for 1,000 shares of $100 par value common stock at $160 per share on April 1, 20XX. Two equal installments will be paid on August 1 and November 1 by the buyer.

April 1: Accepted Subscription for 1,000 Shares at $160 per Share Because the stock certificates will not be issued until paid in full, Krump Corporation records the ownership at par value in a temporary stockholders' equity account called **Common Stock Subscribed.** This account is shown in the Paid-In Capital section below the issue of the Common Stock. The amount due is recorded in an account called **Subscriptions Receivable—Common Stock.** The difference between the par value and the issue price is accumulated in a permanent account called Paid-In Capital in Excess of Par Value—Common.

Here is an analysis of the transaction:

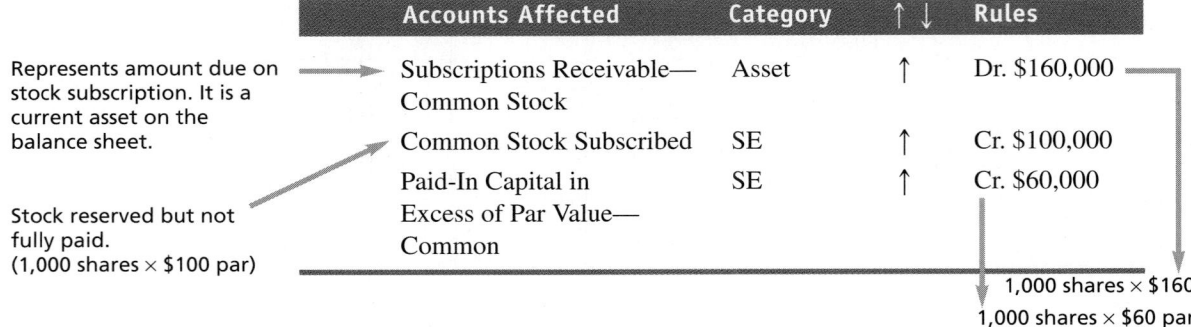

Represents amount due on stock subscription. It is a current asset on the balance sheet.

Accounts Affected	Category	↑ ↓	Rules
Subscriptions Receivable—Common Stock	Asset	↑	Dr. $160,000
Common Stock Subscribed	SE	↑	Cr. $100,000
Paid-In Capital in Excess of Par Value—Common	SE	↑	Cr. $60,000

Stock reserved but not fully paid.
(1,000 shares × $100 par)

1,000 shares × $160
1,000 shares × $60 par

The journal entry will be as shown in Figure 18.11.

FIGURE 18.11 Accepted Subscriptions in Excess of Par

	20XX					
	Apr.	1	Subscriptions Receivable—Common Stock	160 00 0 00		
			Common Stock Subscribed		100 0 0 0 00	
			Paid-In Capital in Excess of Par		60 0 0 0 00	

August 1: Received First Installment on Common Stock Subscription

Accounts Affected	Category	↑ ↓	Rules
Cash	Asset	↑	Dr. $80,000
Subscriptions Receivable—Common Stock	Asset	↓	Cr. $80,000

The journal entry will be as shown in Figure 18.12.

FIGURE 18.12 Received Installment from Stock Subscription

	20XX					
	Aug.	1	Cash	80 0 0 0 00		
			Subscriptions Receivable—			
			Common Stock		80 0 0 0 00	

November 1: Received Final Installment on Common Stock Subscription

Accounts Affected	Category	↑↓	Rules
Cash	Asset	↑	Dr. $80,000
Subscriptions Receivable—Common Stock	Asset	↓	Cr. $80,000

The journal entry will be as shown in Figure 18.13.

20XX					
Nov.	1	Cash	80 0 0 0 00		
		Subscriptions Receivable—			
		Common Stock		80 0 0 0 00	

FIGURE 18.13 Received Final Installment from Stock Subscription

November 1: Issued 1,000 Shares of Fully Paid Common Stock

Accounts Affected	Category	↑↓	Rules
Common Stock Subscribed	SE	↓	Dr. $100,000
Common Stock	SE	↑	Cr. $100,000

The journal entry will be as shown in Figure 18.14.

20XX				
Nov.	1	Common Stock Subscribed	100 0 0 0 00	
		Common Stock		100 0 0 0 00

FIGURE 18.14 Issued Fully Paid Common Stock

Remember that stock is recorded at par value. At this point the Common Stock Subscribed account in the ledger (when posted) is reduced to a zero balance, and the Common Stock account records the issued stock (which has been paid for).

FIGURE 18.15 Stockholders' Equity Section of Balance Sheet

Stockholders' Equity		
Paid-In Capital:		
Common Stock, $100 par value; authorized		
10,000 shares, 7,000 issued and outstanding	$ 700 0 0 0 00	
Common Stock Subscribed, 2,000 shares at par	200 0 0 0 00	
Paid-In Capital in Excess of Par Value—Common	300 0 0 0 00	
Total Paid-In Capital	$1200 0 0 0 00	
Retained Earnings	400 0 0 0 00	
Total Stockholders' Equity	$1600 0 0 0 00	

Stockholders' Equity

Before concluding this chapter, let's take a moment to set up a simplified stockholders' equity section of a balance sheet. The numbers in Figure 18.15 on the previous page are not related to the previous situations. The goal here is to show you the structure of Paid-In Capital and Retained Earnings. In the Blueprint, the complete layout of stockholders' equity is illustrated by the **source-of-capital approach,** which lists classes of stockholders first. An alternative way, called the **legal capital approach,** lists all legal capital first and is illustrated in the next chapter. Both approaches are acceptable.

> The names and addresses of each stockholder are kept in a subsidiary ledger. The Stock account is the controlling account.

LEARNING UNIT 18-4 REVIEW

AT THIS POINT you should be able to

- Journalize the entries in a stock subscription plan.
- Explain the purpose of Common Stock Subscribed.
- Prepare a simplified stockholders' section.

Self-Review Quiz 18-4

Journalize the entries to record the stock subscription plan for Moose Corp. On October 1 Moose Corp. received subscriptions for 500 shares of $50 par value common stock at $80 per share. The buyer will pay two equal installments on December 31 and March 31.

Solutions to Self-Review Quiz 18-4

FIGURE 18.16 Stock Subscriptions and Installments Received

Oct.	1	Subscriptions Receivable—			
		Common Stock	40 000 00		
		Common Stock Subscribed		25 000 00	
		Paid-In Capital in Excess of Par			
		Value—Common		15 000 00	
Dec.	31	Cash	20 000 00		
		Subscriptions Receivable—			
		Common Stock		20 000 00	
Mar.	31	Cash	20 000 00		
		Subscriptions Receivable—			
		Common Stock		20 000 00	
	31	Common Stock Subscribed	25 000 00		
		Common Stock		25 000 00	

CHAPTER ASSIGNMENTS

SUMMARY OF KEY POINTS

LEARNING UNIT 18-1

1. The articles of incorporation are submitted to the state when one wants to form a corporation. It contains all the specifics of the proposed corporation. If approved, a charter (certificate of incorporation) is issued to incorporators.
2. Advantages of a corporation include limited liability, a separate legal entity, unlimited life, ease of transferring ownership interest, no mutual agency, and ease in raising capital. Disadvantages include difficulties in forming a corporation, government regulations, and double taxation.

LEARNING UNIT 18-2

1. Stockholders' equity is broken down in Paid-In Capital and Retained Earnings.
2. Retained Earnings records the accumulated profits that are retained or kept in the corporation.
3. Authorized stock represents the total amount of stock that can be legally issued. Outstanding stock represents the amount of stock issued.
4. Common stockholders have the right to vote, share in profits, sell their ownership, and receive assets at liquidation, if available; they also have preemptive rights (the right to maintain their proportionate ownership interest in the company).
5. Buyers of preferred stock, to gain stability of earnings, may give up voting rights, preemptive rights, and so forth. Preferred stock can be cumulative, noncumulative, participating, nonparticipating, or a combination.
6. Par value is an arbitrary value. It doesn't mean market value. Stocks may have a par value, no-par, or no-par with a stated value.
7. Legal capital is the amount that a corporation must retain in the business for the protection of the creditors. It may be based on par value, no-par value, or stated value.

LEARNING UNIT 18-3

1. Common stock or preferred stock with par value is recorded by number of shares times par value. If stock is sold for more than par, the difference is recorded in a stockholders' equity account called Paid-In Capital in Excess of Par Value. If a stock is sold below par, the difference is recorded in a contra-stockholders' equity account called Discount on Common Stock.
2. If no-par stock with a stated value is sold at a price higher than stated value, the difference is recorded in a stockholders' equity account called Paid-In Capital in Excess of Stated Value.
3. Assets are recorded at fair market value when exchanged for stock. Any difference between par value of stock and fair market value is recorded in a stockholders' equity account called Capital in Excess of Par.
4. Organization Cost is an intangible asset on the balance sheet. Today, it is being expensed.
5. The calculation for a dividend to common or preferred with par value is (Number of Shares × Par) × Rate. If preferred is fully participating, the allocation of the remainder is based on par value of each class of stock over the total par value. This fraction is multiplied times remainder of dividend.

LEARNING UNIT 18-4

1. The source-of-capital approach will present the paid-in capital component of stockholders' equity by classes of stockholders. It does not attempt to list legal capital first.
2. Subscriptions Receivable is an asset representing amounts due on stock that has been subscribed to. It is a current asset on the balance sheet.
3. Common Stock Subscribed is a stockholders' equity account that acts as a temporary account until a subscription is paid for. When paid, the Common Stock Subscribed account is reduced and the Common Stock account is increased.

KEY TERMS

Articles of incorporation Document submitted by incorporators when applying for a charter.

Authorized capital stock As stated in its charter, the number of shares of capital stock (common and preferred) that a corporation can sell.

Capital stock Classes of stock that represent the fractional elements of ownership of a corporation.

Certificate of incorporation Document granted by the state authorizing the creation of a corporation.

Charter Document issued to a corporation by the state that includes certificate of incorporation along with articles of incorporation.

Common stock Part of paid-in capital representing the basic ownership equity of the corporation. If the corporation has only one class of stock, it will be common stock.

Common Stock Subscribed Temporary stockholders' equity account that records at par value stock that has been subscribed to but not fully paid for.

Corporation Business organization that is both a legal and accounting entity.

Cumulative preferred stock Stock that entitles its holders to any undeclared dividends that have accumulated before common stockholders receive their dividends.

Directors Officers elected by stockholders to represent the company and establish policies for the company.

Discount on stock The difference between the par value of the stock and an amount less than the par value that the stockholders have contributed. Discounts do not happen often.

Dividend Cash, other assets, or shares of stock that a corporation issues to the stockholders.

Dividends in arrears Dividends owed to cumulative preferred stockholders that must be paid before common stockholders can receive their dividends.

Incorporators Persons responsible for getting the corporation formed.

Issued capital stock Stock that the corporation issues for assets or services contributed by the stockholders.

Legal capital Minimum amount of capital that a corporation must leave in the company (cannot be withdrawn by stockholders) for protection of the creditors.

Legal capital approach Method of preparing Paid-In Capital by listing the legal section first. (See Blueprint at end of Chapter 19.)

Limited liability Freedom of stockholders from *personal* liability for the debts of the corporation.

Minute book Book that records meetings of the board of directors or stockholders.

Noncumulative preferred stock Preferred stock that does not entitle its holders to a dividend for any year in which a dividend is not declared.

Nonparticipating preferred stock Preferred stock that entitles its holders only to a certain percentage of dividend, the remainder going to holders of common stock.

No-par stock Stock with no par value. A stated value could be placed on it.

Organization cost An intangible asset that records the initial cost of forming the corporation, such as legal and incorporating fees. Today, it is now being expensed.

Outstanding capital stock Stock that is held and owned by stockholders.

Paid-In Capital Section of stockholders' equity representing what stockholders have invested into the corporation.

Paid-In Capital in Excess of Par Value—Common Difference between what stockholders invest and par value. This amount is not credited to the Stock account.

Paid-In Capital in Excess of Stated Value—Common Difference between what stockholders invest and the stated value placed on stock by the board of directors. This amount is not credited to the Stock account.

Participating preferred stock Stock that entitles its holders not only to a fixed dividend but also to an opportunity to share in additional dividends with common stockholders.

Par value An arbitrary value that is placed on each share of stock. Par value represents legal capital and not market value.

Preemptive right The right of the stockholder to purchase additional shares of stock to maintain a proportionate interest when the corporation issues additional stock.

Preferred stock Class of capital stock that has preference to a corporation's profits and assets.

Premium A term that records the sale of stock at more than par value. In this book we use the account Paid-In Capital in Excess of Par to record the premium received.

Retained earnings Accumulated profits of a corporation that have been kept in the business and not paid out as dividends. Retained Earnings is part of stockholders' equity.

Source-of-capital approach Method of preparing Paid-In Capital by listing classes of stockholder sources of capital.

Stated value Arbitrary value placed by the board of directors on each share of no-par stock to fulfill legal capital requirements.

Stock certificate Formal document issued to investors in a corporation that shows the number of shares purchased.

Stockholders Owners of the stock of the corporation.

Stock subscription A contractual agreement to buy a certain number of shares of stock from a corporation at a specific price.

Subscriptions Receivable—Common Stock Current asset on balance sheet that represents amount due on stock subscriptions.

BLUEPRINT: SOURCE-OF-CAPITAL APPROACH

VALLEY CO. PARTIAL BALANCE SHEET

Assets

Current Assets:			
Subscriptions Receivable, Common 8%			
Stock	XXX		
Intangible Assets:			
Organization Cost		XXX	
Total Assets			XXX

Liabilities

Stockholders' Equity

Paid-In Capital:			
Preferred 12% stock, $10 par value,			
authorized 20,000 shares, 8,000 shares			
issued	XXX		
Paid-In Capital in Excess of Par			
Value—Preferred	XXX		
Total Paid-In Capital by preferred			
stockholders		XXX	
Common Stock, no-par value, stated			
value $10 per share, authorized			
100,000 shares, 30,000 issued and			
outstanding	XXX		
Common Stock Subscribed, 1,000 shares			
at par	XXX		
Paid-In Capital in Excess of Stated			
Value—Common	XXX		
Total Paid-In Capital by common			
stockholders		XXX	
Total Paid-In Capital		XXX	
Retained Earnings		XXX	
Total Stockholders' Equity			XXX

Note that preferred stock is listed before common stock.

QUESTIONS, CLASSROOM DEMONSTRATION EXERCISES, EXERCISES, AND PROBLEMS

Discussion and Critical Thinking Questions/Ethical Case

1. What is the difference between the articles of incorporation and a charter?

2. Who elects the board of directors?

3. List the advantages of the corporate form of organization.

4. Explain the difference between paid-in capital and retained earnings.

5. Why can't a company issue more stock than is authorized?

6. What does *preemptive right* mean?

7. Distinguish among legal capital, par value, no-par value, and no-par value with a stated value.

8. Preferred stock can never be cumulative *and* non-participating. True or false? Support your answer.

9. What is the normal balance and the category of the account Discount on Common Stock?

10. How does one calculate Paid-In Capital in Excess of Par Value or Stated Value?

11. Explain the account Paid-In Capital in Excess of Par Value as it relates to exchange of stock for non-cash assets.

12. What is the purpose of the account Organization Costs?

13. In stock subscriptions, why does one credit Common Stock Subscribed?

14. Avan Corporation just published its financial statements. The president of Avan told the accountants not to include in the annual report any information about a pending lawsuit. The president thought it would only worry the stockholders. Do you think the president is correct in not including any information about the pending lawsuit in the annual report? You make the call. Write down your recommendations to the president.

Classroom Demonstration Exercises

SET A

LO1 (15 min)   **Stockholders' Equity**

1. Lang Corporation has capital stock of $7,000. Its Retained Earnings account has a $14,000 balance. Cash has a balance of $9,000. What is the total of stockholders' equity for Lang Corporation?

LO3 (15 min)   **Cumulative Preferred**

2. Jay Co. owed $14,000 each year for three years to holders of cumulative preferred stock. This year Jay pays out $140,000 in dividends to preferred and common. How much did each class of stock receive?

LO2 (20 min)   **Journalizing Sales of Stock**

3. Journalize the following:

July	8	Pete Co. sells 400 shares of $20 par value common stock at $20.
Oct.	15	Jon Co. sells 100 shares of $10 par value common stock at $16.
Nov.	28	Angel Co. sells 100 shares of no-par common stock with a stated value of $18 for $30 per share.
Dec.	30	Lowe Co. issues 600 shares of $5 par value common stock to organizers of the firm for services rendered costing $4,500.

LO3 (20 min)   **Cumulative and Participating Preferred**

4. From the following calculate the dividends for common and preferred stock:
   - 8% fully participating preferred stock.
   - The board declared a $170,000 dividend.
   - Preferred stock 3,000 shares, $50 par value; common stock 9,000 shares, $50 par.

Stock Subscriptions   *LO4 (20 min)*

5. Journalize the entries to record the stock subscription plan for Blue Co. On October 1, Blue received subscriptions for 300 shares of $25 par value common stock at $42 per share. The buyer will pay two equal installments on December 31 and March 31.

SET B

Stockholders' Equity   *LO1 (15 min)*

1. Alan Corporation has capital stock of $8,000. Its Retained Earnings account has a $15,000 balance. Cash has a balance of $12,000. What is the total of stockholders' equity for Alan Corporation?

Cumulative Preferred   *LO3 (15 min)*

2. Lee Co. owed $15,000 each year for three years to holders of cumulative preferred stock. This year Lee pays out $120,000 in dividends to preferred and common. How much did each class of stock receive?

Journalizing Sales of Stock   *LO2 (20 min)*

3. Journalize the following:

20XX		
July	8	Pete Co. sells 300 shares of $10 par value common stock at $10.
Oct.	15	Jon Co. sells 200 shares of $10 par value common stock at $15.
Nov.	28	Angel Co. sells 200 shares of no-par common stock with a stated value of $20 for $30 per share.
Dec.	30	Lowe Co. issues 500 shares of $10 par value common stock to organizers of the firm for services rendered costing $7,500.

Cumulative and Participating Preferred   *LO3 (20 min)*

4. From the following calculate the dividends for common and preferred stock:
- 7% fully participating preferred stock.
- The board declared a $150,000 dividend.
- Preferred stock 2,000 shares, $100 par value; common stock 8,000 shares, $100 par.

Stock Subscriptions   *LO4 (20 min)*

5. Journalize the entries to record the stock subscription plan for Blue Co. On October 1, Blue received subscriptions for 200 shares of $25 par value common stock at $40 per share. The buyer will pay two equal installments on December 31 and March 31.

Exercises

18-1. Val Corporation was authorized to issue 30,000 shares of common stock.   *LO2 (20 min)*
Record the journal entry for each of the following independent situations, assuming Val issues 6,000 shares at $11 on July 20, 20XX:
a. Common stock has a $10 par value.
b. Common stock has no-par and no stated value.
c. Common stock is no-par stock with a stated value of $8.

18-2. On July 10, 20XX, Zeron Corporation issued 3,000 shares of common stock   *LO2 (20 min)*
with a par value of $100 in exchange for equipment with a fair market value of $320,000. Journalize the appropriate entry.

18-3. Vetco Corporation in its first three years of operation paid out the following   *LO3 (30 min)*
dividends:
- Year 1: 0
- Year 2: $30,000
- Year 3: $90,000

Given that Vetco has 3,000 shares of $100 par 9% cumulative, nonparticipating preferred stock and 15,000 shares of $25 par value common stock, what would be the total dividends paid each year to holders of common and preferred?

LO4 (30 min)

18-4. On January 1, 20XX, Lavrel Corporation issued on a subscription basis 1,000 shares of $50 par value common stock at $90 per share. Two equal installments were to be made on July 1 and December 31. Prepare the appropriate journal entries on January 1, July 1, and December 31 to record this stock subscription for Lavrel Corporation.

LO2 (30 min)

18-5. Scupper Corporation began its business on January 1, 20XX. It sold at $30 per share 6,000 shares of no-par common stock with a stated value of $20 per share. The charter of Scupper indicated 40,000 shares were authorized. Retained earnings were $60,000 on December 31. Prepare the stockholders' equity section for Scupper on December 31, 20XX, using the Blueprint example as a guide.

LO1,2 (50 min)

Group A Problems

18A-1. The following is the Paid-In Capital section of stockholders' equity for the Gracie Corporation on June 1, 20XX:

Paid-In Capital:	
Preferred Stock, $100 par, authorized 20,000 shares, 4,000 shares issued	$ 400,000
Paid-In Capital in Excess of Par Value—Preferred Stock	120,000
Common Stock, $25 par, authorized 50,000 shares, 20,000 shares issued	500,000
Paid-In Capital in Excess of Par Value—Common Stock	160,000
Total Paid-In Capital	$1,180,000

Check Figure:
(2) Paid-In Capital $2,732,000

The following transactions occurred in the months of June and July:

20XX		
June	1	Issued 3,000 shares of preferred stock at $102 per share.
	2	Issued 7,000 shares of common stock at $40 per share.
	15	Issued 8,000 shares of common stock at $42 per share.
July	2	Issued 5,000 shares of preferred stock at $104 per share.
	18	Issued 2,000 shares of common stock in exchange for building and land with fair market value of $60,000 and $50,000, respectively.

1. Journalize the preceding entries and update the stockholders' equity ledger. Accounts are provided in the workbook.
2. Prepare a new Paid-In Capital section of stockholders' equity as of July 31, 20XX.

LO3 (50 min)

18A-2. Katie Corporation has 20,000 shares outstanding of $10 par value 8% preferred stock and 40,000 shares outstanding of $10 par value common stock. In its first five years of operation, the company paid the following dividends: 20X1, 0; 20X2, $16,000; 20X3, $48,000; 20X4, 0; 20X5, $82,000. Calculate the dividends paid to preferred and common stockholders under the following three independent situations:

Check Figure:
(b) Pref: $16,000   20X2
*   32,000   20X3*
*   32,000   20X5*

a. Preferred stock is noncumulative and nonparticipating.
b. Preferred stock is cumulative and nonparticipating.
c. Preferred stock is cumulative and fully participating.

18A-3. From the following partial mixed list, select the appropriate titles and prepare a stockholders' equity section using the source-of-capital approach as shown in the Blueprint example for Xenon Corporation on July 31, 20XX:

LO1, 2 (40 min)

Office Equipment	$100,000
Land	200,000
Paid-In Capital in Excess of Par Value—Preferred Stock	100,000
Building	80,000
Accounts Receivable	120,000
Notes Receivable	40,000
Organization Costs	10,000
Common Stock, $10 par value (60,000 shares issued and outstanding; 80,000 shares authorized)	600,000
Retained Earnings	200,000
Subscriptions Receivable—Common Stock	80,000
Patents	10,000
Preferred 14% Stock, $50 Par (6,000 shares issued; 7,000 shares authorized)	300,000
Common Stock Subscribed at Par	225,000
Paid-In Capital in Excess of Par Value—Common Stock	20,000

> **Check Figure:**
> Stockholders' Equity $1,445,000

18A-4. Joilet Corporation was just issued a charter by the state of New York. This charter gives Joilet the authority to issue 400,000 shares of $10 par value common stock. From the following transactions,

LO1, 2 (40 min)

1. Prepare journal entries to record the transactions of Joilet Corp. for the month of August.
2. Prepare the Paid-In Capital section of Joilet's balance sheet at the end of the month.

20XX

Aug. 11 Issued 1,800 shares of stock for land and building with fair market value of $13,000 and $17,500, respectively.

16 Accepted subscriptions to 20,000 shares of stock for $250,000 to be paid in two equal installments.

22 Collected first installment on 10,000 shares of the common stock subscribed on August 16.

28 Sold 7,000 shares of stock for $88,000.

30 Collected last installment on 10,000 shares of the common stock subscribed on August 16 and issued the shares.

> **Check Figure:**
> Total Paid-In Capital $368,500

Group B Problems

18B-1. The following is the Paid-In Capital section of stockholders' equity for the Gracie Corporation on June 1, 20XX:

LO1, 2 (50 min)

Paid-In Capital:	
Preferred Stock, $25, par, authorized 20,000 shares, 5,000 shares issued	$125,000
Paid-In Capital in Excess of Par Value—Preferred Stock	37,500

(continued on next page)

Common Stock, $10 par, authorized 100,000 shares, 20,000 shares issued	200,000
Paid-In Capital in Excess of Par Value—Common Stock	45,000
Total Paid-In Capital	$407,500

The following transactions occurred in the months of June and July:

20XX

June	1	Issued 2,000 shares of preferred stock at $28 per share.
	4	Issued 4,000 shares of common stock at $13 per share.
	15	Issued 5,000 shares of common stock at $16 per share.
July	2	Issued 1,000 shares of preferred stock at $29 per share.
	18	Issued 2,000 shares of common stock in exchange for building and land with fair market value of $25,000 and $29,000, respectively.

Check Figure:
Total Paid-In Capital $678,500

1. Journalize and post the preceding entries and update the stockholders' equity ledger accounts provided in the workbook.
2. Prepare a new Paid-In Capital section of stockholders' equity as of July 31, 20XX.

LO3 (50 min)   **18B-2.** Katie Corporation has 10,000 shares outstanding of $20 par value 10% preferred stock and 120,000 shares outstanding of $5 par value common stock. In its first five years of operation, the company paid the following dividends: 20X1, 0; 20X2, $16,000; 20X3, $80,000; 20X4, $84,000; 20X5, $120,000. Calculate the dividends paid to preferred and common stockholders under the following three independent situations:

a. Preferred stock is noncumulative and nonparticipating.
b. Preferred stock is cumulative and nonparticipating.
c. Preferred stock is cumulative and fully participating.

Check Figure:
(b) Pref: 20X2 $16,000
         20X5 $20,000

LO1, 2 (40 min)   **18B-3.** From the following partial mixed list, select the appropriate titles and prepare a stockholders' equity section using the source-of-capital approach as shown in the Blueprint example for Xenon Corporation on July 31, 20XX.

Paid-In Capital in Excess of Par Value—Common Stock	$ 1,400
Common Stock Subscribed at Par	8,800
Paid-In Capital in Excess of Par Value—Preferred Stock	12,000
Land	15,000
Office Equipment	7,600
Preferred 14% Stock, $50 Par (400 shares issued; 8,000 shares authorized)	20,000
Patents	1,600
Subscriptions Receivable—Common Stock	12,000
Retained Earnings	28,000
Common Stock $10 par value (8,000 shares issued and outstanding; 50,000 shares authorized)	80,000
Organization Costs	1,200
Notes Receivable	5,000
Accounts Receivable	18,000
Building	5,000

Check Figure:
Total Stockholders' Equity
$150,200

18B-4. The state of New York issued a charter to Joilet Corporation with the authorization to issue 10,000 shares of $100 par value common stock. From the following transactions,

1. Journalize the transactions for Joilet for the month of September.

2. Prepare the Paid-In Capital section of Joilet Corporation's balance sheet at the end of the month.

LO1, 2 (40 min)

Check Figure:
Total Paid-In Capital $151,000

20XX

Sept.	8	Issued 500 shares of stock for land and building with fair market value of $29,000 and $24,000, respectively.
	14	Accepted subscriptions to 300 shares of its stock for $39,000 to be paid in two equal installments.
	22	Collected first installment on 150 shares of the common stock subscribed on September 14.
	24	Sold 500 shares of stock for $59,000.
	30	Collected last installment on 150 shares of the common stock subscribed on September 14 and issued the shares.

ON-THE-JOB TRAINING

T-1. The partial balance sheet of Freedom Corporation, as of July 31, 20XX, showed the following balances:

LO2, 4 (30 min)

Preferred Stock, $10 Par	$ 95,000
Paid-In Capital in Excess of Par—Preferred	65,000
Common Stock, $100 par	180,000
Paid-In Capital in Excess of Par—Common	220,000
Common Stock Subscribed	10,000
Retained Earnings	520,000
Subscriptions Receivable	60,000
Bonds Payable	300,000

The bookkeeper, Alice Fall, is quite concerned that the company has not kept enough legal capital in the business. She wants the board of directors to immediately change the par value, because the market value of the stock has increased. She believes it is only fair to protect the rights of the creditors. Support or rebut Alice Fall's position in writing.

T-2. Bill Murray and Jim Smith, full-time high school teachers, had worked together as overnight camping guides for years. They both felt it was time to start their own overnight camp. Bill estimated he would be able to invest $30,000 and Jim could invest $2,000. Both agreed that they would need at least $200,000 to finance the purchase of land as well as the building of bunks and administrative offices.

LO1 (30 min)

Jim felt that forming a corporation was too involved and wanted to form a partnership. Bill, on the other hand, who trusted no one, felt that the corporate structure was best.

Jim and Bill have come to you to recommend what form of organization is best for them and how they can or should raise the money. Please write a recommendation to them.

FINANCIAL REPORT PROBLEM

LO1, 2 (20 min)

Reading the Kellogg's Annual Report

Go to Appendix A to the consolidated balance sheet. What is the amount of retained earnings in 2006? What is the par value of the stock?

INTERNET PROJECT

Hormel Foods

Go to the Web and search: Annual Report Hormel Foods 2008.
Click on Investors Relations.
List out the last news Hormel Foods is providing to its investors.
Order a free annual report.

IN GOOD COMPANY

LO1 (15 min)

The waitress set down a plate of nachos and two pints of beer in front of Stan and his old college buddy, Ron Ebbers. Ever since they'd run into each other at Stan's Subway restaurant, the two had rekindled their friendship over beer and nachos at a local restaurant.

"Sales still on the up and up?" Ron asked Stan.

"Yep. It just doesn't seem to matter how weak the economy is," said Stan. "People will always want a sandwich that's healthy, great tasting, and a good value. And now," Stan lifted a glass, "*salud*—a toast—because as of today I'm a corporation!"

"Cheers, Stan the Man!" exclaimed Ron and clinked Stan's beer mug. "But doesn't incorporating cost you more money, in legal fees and taxes?"

"Well, that may be true, but if I don't incorporate and anything goes wrong or some wacko sues me, it could cost me my shirt! Now I have limited liability, but I still pay wages to my employees, send in my royalty fees to Subway, and *muchos* profits still go to me."

"Maybe *I* should buy stock in Subway," Ron interrupted. "I've been dabbling in the market lately and Subway seems like a good bet!"

"Unfortunately, you can't buy stock in Subway," said Stan. "Doctor's Associates, the corporation that owns the Subway brand, is privately owned by the founders Fred DeLuca and Dr. Peter Buck."

"Doctor's Associates?!" Stan exclaimed. "That's strange. I know the food has helped people lose weight and eat healthy, but is Subway run by a health care outfit?"

"No, it's actually kind of interesting. In 1965 Fred DeLuca was just a teenager who wanted to go to college and become a doctor, but he didn't have enough money. Then his family friend Peter Buck loaned him the money to start a submarine sandwich joint. DeLuca, of course, never did become a doctor, but Peter Buck holds a Ph.D. in nuclear physics, so they called themselves Doctor's Associates—they're the 'doctors' and we franchisees are the 'associates.'"

"I guess we all have dreams that we don't carry out," Ron mused.

"Hey, don't look so *triste*, amigo. I know you're stuck in a dead-end job now, but maybe now is the time to think about new opportunities."

"Whaddaya mean?" Ron asked.

"There's a great space on Alameda Avenue on the other side of Los Palmos—near that fancy new apartment complex. I've been thinking of eventually opening up another store, but I don't want to go it alone. However, I might consider going into a partnership with you to own Subway number 2."

"Well, given the liability risks you just mentioned—which I assume apply to partnerships as well as sole proprietorships, what about a corporation?" said Ron eagerly. "You could be the majority shareholder and I could have a smaller interest in the restaurant until I learn the ropes and eventually buy you out."

"Whoa there. Let's not talk about buying anyone out just yet," laughed Stan. "Before you do anything—if you're serious about being a Subway owner—you'll need to go to Subway University."

Ron raised his glass, "Salute."

"No man, *salud,*" corrected Stan. "A toast. To *opportunidades del futuro y amistad.* To future opportunities and friendship."

Discussion Questions

1. What are all the advantages and disadvantages of forming a corporation?
2. What do you think is the best way for Stan and Ron to own a Subway restaurant jointly? Partnership or corporation? Why?

19

Corporations: Stock Values, Dividends, Treasury Stocks, and Retained Earnings

DID YOU KNOW? Sara Lee has paid out 245 consecutive quarterly dividends. The Kiwi shoe care brand is marketed by Sara Lee in 180 countries. It is number one in market share. Visit *www.saralee.com* to find more information about Sara Lee.

LEARNING OBJECTIVES

1. Calculating the book value of preferred and common stock.

2. Journalizing entries to record issuance of a cash dividend and a stock dividend.

3. Journalizing the purchase and sale of treasury stock.

4. Preparing a statement of retained earnings.

Sara Lee, when making dividend decisions, must take many things into account, including how the company is performing, along with its responsibility to stockholders. In this chapter we continue the study of aspects of corporate equity that we began in the last chapter. We discuss a number of topics, including stock values, how and why dividends are declared and paid, why a corporation buys back its own stock, and the restrictions on retained earnings.

In Chapter 18 we discussed two types of stock value: par value and stated value. In Learning Unit 19-1 we turn our attention to other stock values.

Learning Unit 19-1 Understanding Stock Values: Redemption, Market, and Book Value

Redemption Value

When a corporation issues preferred stock, it often reserves the right to retire or redeem that stock for a specific price. At the time the stock is issued, this price per share, called **redemption value,** is determined, and people buy the stock knowing that the corporation can redeem it at this price.

> Stock prices are traded in decimals today. They used to be traded in fractional amounts.

Market Value

The price at which shares of capital stock are bought and sold in the open market is called the **market value.** Economic conditions, a company's earnings, and investors' expectations all play a factor in determining the market price.

LO1 Book Value per Share

Book value per share is, in general, the total of stockholders' equity (assets minus liabilities) divided by the number of shares issued. Why is book value used? For several reasons:

1. When a company seeks a loan, banks may specify a minimum book value for a loan to be approved.
2. If a merger is being negotiated, book value may be used as a factor in setting an exchange ratio of stock. For example, based on book value, one share of Octon Co. stock could fairly be issued for three shares of Xeron Co. stock, if the book value of Octon stock is $30 and the book value of Xeron stock is $10.
3. Book value may be used when contracts are made. For example, an individual may receive in the future an option to buy or sell stock based on future book value. (That value is *not* market value, which is based on current prices.)

It is important to emphasize that book value doesn't represent what an owner might receive if the assets of a company were *liquidated.* At the time of liquidation the assets may be sold at prices quite different from the values on the books, which are based on cost and not current market prices.

Calculating Book Value with Only One Class of Stock

When a corporation has only common stock, book value is calculated using the following equation:

$$\text{Book Value per Share} = \frac{\text{Total Stockholders' Equity}}{\text{Total Shares Outstanding}}$$

As an example, we use the stockholders' equity shown in Figure 19.1 for Jones Corporation and calculate book value per share of common stock.

The book value is $45 per share ($450,000/10,000 shares). Thus, for each share of stock owned, $45 would be received *if* the corporation were liquidated without any losses from disposing of assets. By the time assets are disposed of, the owner might get much less than book value.

JONES CORPORATION STOCKHOLDERS' EQUITY		
Paid-In Capital:		
Common Stock, $25 par value; 10,000 shares		
authorized, issued, and outstanding		$250 000 00
Paid-In Capital in Excess of Par Value—Common		110 000 00
Total Paid-In Capital		$360 000 00
Retained Earnings		90 000 00
Total Stockholders' Equity		$450 000 00

FIGURE 19.1 Stockholders' Equity

Calculating Book Value with Both Preferred and Common Stock

When a company has two classes of stock, before book value can be calculated, the stockholders' equity must be allocated (divided up) for each class of stock. First, for preferred stock, a corporation assigns the redemption value (or par value if the stock has no redemption value) of the stock along with any dividends in arrears (any dividends that are owed to holders of preferred stock but have not yet been paid out). This total of redemption value plus dividends in arrears is divided by the number of preferred shares outstanding. The *remainder* of stockholders' equity is assigned to the common stockholders, and the book value of the common stock is calculated by that amount divided by the number of common stock shares outstanding. Book value can be shown in the following formulas:

$$\text{Book Value Preferred} = \frac{\text{Redemption Value} + \text{Dividends in Arrears}}{\text{Number of Shares of Preferred Stock Outstanding}}$$

$$\text{Book Value Common} = \frac{\text{Stockholders' Equity} - \text{Amount Assigned to Preferred}}{\text{Number of Shares of Common Stock Outstanding}}$$

Let's illustrate this situation by looking at the stockholders' equity of Ryan Corporation (Fig. 19.2 on the following page) and performing the necessary calculations.

Given: Redemption value of preferred is $103; there are $14,000 worth of dividends in arrears.

Thus,

$$\text{Book Value Preferred} = \frac{\$206,000 + \$14,000}{2,000 \text{ Shares}}$$

$$= \frac{\$220,000}{2,000 \text{ Shares}} = \$110 \text{ per Share}$$

and

$$\text{Book Value Common} = \frac{\$894,000 - \$220,000}{10,000 \text{ Shares}}$$

$$= \frac{\$674,000}{10,000 \text{ Shares}} = \$67.40 \text{ per Share}$$

Note: When preferred stock is redeemed, the paid-in capital in excess of par is *not* returned and thus is *not* included as part of the preferred equity in the book-value calculation.

LEARNING UNIT 19-1 REVIEW

AT THIS POINT you should be able to

- List and define other stock values besides par value.
- Explain the purpose of book value.
- Calculate the book value of preferred and common stock.

FIGURE 19.2 Calculating Book Value from Stockholders' Equity

RYAN CORPORATION STOCKHOLDERS' EQUITY			
Paid-In Capital:			
Preferred 7% Stock, $100 per value, authorized			
3,000 shares cumulative and nonparticipating,			
2,000 shares issued and outstanding	$200 000 00		
Paid-In Capital in Excess of Par Value—Preferred	10 000 00		
Total Paid-In Capital by Preferred Stockholders		$210 000 00	
Common Stock, $50 par value, authorized 12,000			
shares, 10,000 shares issued and outstanding	500 000 00		
Paid-In Capital in Excess of Par Value—Common	20 000 00		
Total Paid-In Capital by Common Stockholders		520 000 00	
Total Paid-In Capital		$730 000 00	
Retained Earnings		164 000 00	
Total Stockholders' Equity		$894 000 00	

Redemption value
$103 × 2,000 shares

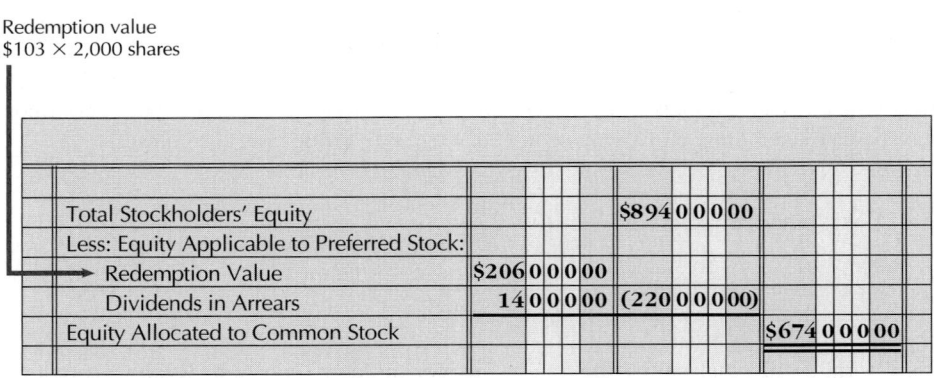

Total Stockholders' Equity		$894 000 00	
Less: Equity Applicable to Preferred Stock:			
Redemption Value	$206 000 00		
Dividends in Arrears	14 000 00	(220 000 00)	
Equity Allocated to Common Stock			$674 000 00

Self-Review Quiz 19-1

From the following information calculate the book value for preferred and common stock:

(4,000 shares issued) Preferred Stock	Paid-In Capital in Excess of Par—Preferred	(3,000 shares issued) Common Stock
300,000	20,000	600,000

Paid-In Capital in Excess of Par—Common	Retained Earnings
30,000	25,000

Dividends in arrears amount to $15,000. Assume a redemption value on preferred stock of $90 per share.

Solution to Self-Review Quiz 19-1

$90 per share × 4,000
shares redemption value

FIGURE 19.3 Book Value for
Preferred and Common Stock

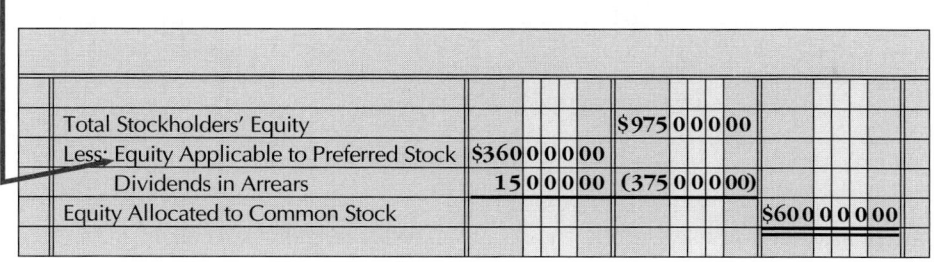

Total Stockholders' Equity		$975 00 00	
Less: Equity Applicable to Preferred Stock	$360 00 00		
Dividends in Arrears	15 00 00	(375 00 00)	
Equity Allocated to Common Stock			$600 00 00

PREFERRED STOCK	COMMON STOCK
Book Value per Share	Book Value per Share
$\dfrac{\$375{,}000}{4{,}000 \text{ shares}} = \$93.75$	$\dfrac{\$600{,}000}{3{,}000 \text{ shares}} = \$200$

Learning Unit 19-2 Dividends

LO2

In this unit we discuss the distribution of cash, stock, or other assets that the board of directors declares as dividends. **Dividends,** as we have seen, are the distribution of earnings of the corporation. It is important to realize that only the board of directors of a corporation has the authority to determine whether a dividend is to be paid, how much it will be, who receives it, and when and how it will be paid.

Three important dates are associated with the dividend process.

1. **Date of declaration:** The day the board of directors announces its decision to pay a dividend. This date creates a liability to the company called **Dividend Payable.**
2. **Date of record:** The date established by the board of directors that determines which stockholders will receive the dividend. These stockholders can be identified in the corporation's subsidiary stockholders' ledger at this date of record.
3. **Date of payment:** The date that the dividend is actually paid to stockholders of record.

> The board of directors declares the dividend.

> Date of record is usually two to four weeks after date of declaration.

Cash Dividends

The distribution of earnings of a corporation in the form of cash to its stockholders is called a **cash dividend.** For example, on March 8, 20XX, the board of directors of Tell Corporation declares a $2 cash dividend per share on the 5,000 shares issued and outstanding. The dividend will be paid on April 16, 20XX, to stockholders of record on March 25, 20XX. Let's look at how to analyze as well as record this cash dividend.

> A sufficient balance in retained earnings (and cash) is necessary to pay the dividend.

Date of Declaration: March 8, 20XX The following chart analyzes this transaction.

Declaration of dividends reduces Retained Earnings. A legally declared dividend is a current liability on the balance sheet.

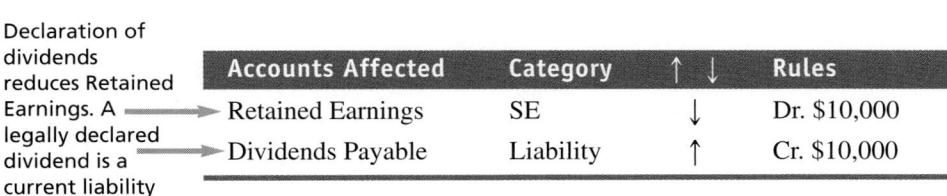

Accounts Affected	Category	↑ ↓	Rules
Retained Earnings	SE	↓	Dr. $10,000
Dividends Payable	Liability	↑	Cr. $10,000

The journal entry will look like Figure 19.4.

FIGURE 19.4 Declaring a Cash Dividend

Mar.	8	Retained Earnings	10 0 0 0 00			
		Dividends Payable			10 0 0 0 00	
		Dividends declared of $2 to stockholders				
		of record Mar. 25, 20XX: payable on				
		Apr. 16, 20XX, as declared by board				
		of directors				

> Note that no entry is made at the date of record.

Date of Payment: April 16, 20XX Here is an analysis of the dividend payment.

Accounts Affected	Category	↑ ↓	Rules
Dividends Payable	Liability	↓	Dr. $10,000
Cash	Asset	↓	Cr. $10,000

The journal entry will look like Figure 19.5.

FIGURE 19.5 Payment of Cash Dividend

Apr.	16	Dividends Payable	10 0 0 0 00			
		Cash			10 0 0 0 00	
		Payment of dividend to stockholders of				
		record on Mar. 25, 20XX				

The end result of these transactions is to reduce Cash and Retained Earnings. (*Remember:* Retained Earnings doesn't mean Cash. Cash is an asset, whereas Retained Earnings is part of stockholders' equity.) In effect, the company is distributing part of its accumulated income to stockholders.

The Stock Dividend

> A stock dividend doesn't reduce cash or the total of stockholders' equity.

A **stock dividend** occurs when a corporation issues its own stock instead of a distribution of assets to its stockholders. A company may declare a stock dividend instead of a cash dividend for a number of reasons:

1. To satisfy stockholders' expectations. The corporation doesn't have enough cash to pay a cash dividend and offers the stock dividend instead. The stockholders make no new investment to receive this type of dividend.
2. To increase permanent capital in the business (because more stock is issued).
3. To reduce the market value of the stock, because the price may be too high in the trading on the open market. When more stock is supplied with no demand for it, stock prices go down.
4. Because income tax is avoided until the stock received is sold.

Recording a Stock Dividend

A stock dividend will *not* reduce total stockholders' equity the way a cash dividend does. The end result of a stock dividend is to transfer an amount based on market value from Retained Earnings to Paid-In Capital.* After a stock dividend a stockholder will own a

---

*For larger stock dividends (over 25% of the outstanding stock) the amount is based on par.

larger number of shares, but the *total* ownership equity stays the same. Let's look at Jesse Corporation to illustrate recording a stock dividend.

On December 27, 20XX, Jesse Corporation declared a 10% stock dividend distributable January 27 to stockholders of record on January 13. Figure 19.6 shows the stockholders' equity of Jesse Corporation before the dividend was declared. The current fair market value of the stock is $30 per share.

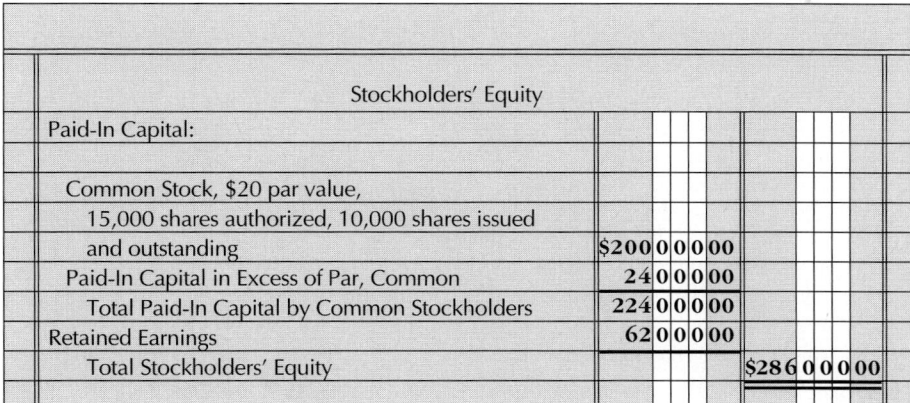

Stockholders' Equity		
Paid-In Capital:		
Common Stock, $20 par value,		
15,000 shares authorized, 10,000 shares issued		
and outstanding	$200 000 00	
Paid-In Capital in Excess of Par, Common	24 000 00	
Total Paid-In Capital by Common Stockholders	224 000 00	
Retained Earnings	62 000 00	
Total Stockholders' Equity		$286 000 00

FIGURE 19.6 Stockholders' Equity

Recording the Declaration of the Dividend The following chart is an analysis of this transaction.

Accounts Affected	Category	↑ ↓	Rules
Retained Earnings	SE	↓	Dr. $30,000
Common Stock Dividend Distributable	SE	↑	Cr. $20,000
Paid-In Capital in Excess of Par Value—Stock Dividend	SE	↑	Cr. $10,000

Retained Earnings is decreased by $30,000. To arrive at that figure we multiply the market value of the stock ($30) times the number of shares issued in the dividend (1,000). The number of shares issued in the dividend is the number of shares issued and outstanding (10,000) times the percent of dividend declared (10%). The Common Stock Dividend Distributable is 1,000 shares times the par value of the common stock ($20).

The journal entry will look like Figure 19.7.

20XX					
Dec.	27	Retained Earnings	3 000 00		
		Common Stock Dividend Distributable		2 000 00	
		Paid-In Capital in Excess of Par			
		Value—Stock Dividend		1 000 00	
		Records declaration of a 10% stock			
		dividend to stockholders of record			
		as of Jan. 13; payable Jan. 27 as			
		declared by the board of directors			

FIGURE 19.7 Declaration of Stock Dividend

Note that the **Common Stock Dividend Distributable** account, which records the par value of the stock, is *not* a liability; it is not payable with assets. It is part of stockholders' equity. When the stock is issued, this account will be reduced and transferred into Common Stock.

Let's first see what the stockholders' equity would look like if it were prepared between the declaration and the payment date. Note in Figure 19.8 that the stocks are listed first, followed by all the additional paid-in capital. This type of layout is called the *legal capital approach;* earlier we showed the *source-of-capital* approach. Both ways are acceptable.

FIGURE 19.8 Legal Capital Approach

Stockholders' Equity		
Paid-In Capital:		
Common Stock, $20 par value, 15,000 shares authorized, 10,000 shares issued and outstanding	$200 000 00	
Common Stock Dividend Distributable, 1,000 shares	20 000 00	
Total Common Stock issued and to be issued		$220 000 00
Additional Paid-In Capital:		
Paid-In Capital in Excess of Par Value—Common	24 000 00	
Paid-In Capital in Excess of Par Value—Stock Dividend	10 000 00	
Total Additional Paid-In Capital		34 000 00
Total Paid-In Capital		$254 000 00
Retained Earnings		32 000 00
Total Stockholders' Equity		$286 000 00

Recording the Issuance of the Stock Dividend Let us first analyze the legal capital approach.

Accounts Affected	Category	↑ ↓	Rules
Common Stock Dividend Distributable	SE	↓	Dr. $20,000
Common Stock	SE	↑	Cr. $20,000

Then the journal entry would look like Figure 19.9.

FIGURE 19.9 Issuance of Stock Dividend

Jan.	27	Common Stock Dividend Distributable	20 000 00		
		Common Stock		20 000 00	
		Issuance of stock dividend declared			
		on Dec. 27 to stockholders of record			
		as of Jan. 13			

The Stock Split A **stock split** is the issuance by a corporation of additional stock to cause a large drop in the market price of the outstanding stock; no assets are received in return. The corporation reduces the par value or stated value of the authorized stock with an increase in the number of shares authorized, issued, and outstanding. The stock split, however, doesn't change the Retained Earnings account as a stock dividend did. To repeat, the stock split will do the following:

1. Increase the number of shares outstanding.
2. Reduce the par or stated value in proportion.

For example, a two-for-one split on 10,000 shares of $20 par would result in 20,000 shares with a $10 par value. The total equity remains the same. Because the stock split doesn't change the balance of any ledger account, only a *memorandum notation** in the journal, as well as in the Stock account, would be needed to update the accounting record. The number of shares in this transaction doubled, but the corporation total equity did not change; thus the market price of $80 per share drops to approximately $40. If Jay Owen owned 100 shares before the split, he would own 200 now, but his market value would be the same.

BEFORE	AFTER
100 shares × $80 = $8,000	200 shares × $40 = $8,000

Jay will benefit from the stock split if

1. The stock price rises on the market.
2. Dividends per share are increased.

LEARNING UNIT 19-2 REVIEW

AT THIS POINT / you should be able to

- List as well as explain the three important dates associated with the dividend process.
- Journalize the appropriate entries for a cash dividend.
- List possible reasons for a stock dividend.
- Journalize appropriate entries for a stock dividend.
- Compare and contrast a stock split to a stock dividend.

Self-Review Quiz 19-2

Journalize the appropriate entries from the following facts. On September 24, 20XX, the directors of Movy Co. declared a 5% stock dividend to be issued on November 8 to stock-holders of record on October 10. There are 20,000 shares outstanding. The stock has a par value of $10 and a current market value of $15 per share.

Solution to Self-Review Quiz 19-2

($15 × 1,000 shares)
($10 par × 1,000 shares)

FIGURE 19.10 Stock Dividend Declared

20XX					
Sept.	24	Retained Earnings	1 5 0 0 0 00		
		Common Stock Dividend Distributable		1 0 0 0 0 00	
		Paid-In Capital in Excess of Par			
		Value—Stock Dividend		5 0 0 0 00	
Nov.	8	Common Stock Dividend Distributable	1 0 0 0 0 00		
		Common Stock		1 0 0 0 0 00	

*An example of such a notation is, "Called in the outstanding $20 par-value 10,000 shares of common stock and issued 20,000 shares of $10 par-value common stock for old shares previously outstanding."

LO3 Learning Unit 19-3 Treasury Stock

Previously issued preferred or common stock that has been reacquired by the corporation (or given as a gift to the corporation) is known as **treasury stock.** Why would a corporation reacquire previously issued stock? Some reasons include the following:

1. A need to issue more stock for stock option plans or for use in acquiring other corporations.
2. A desire to reduce the number of shares of stock outstanding, which might be done to create a favorable market for the sale of the stock.
3. Anticipation of an opportunity at a later date to reissue stock at a higher price.

The following are some of the characteristics of treasury stock:

1. The purchase of treasury stock does not change the amount of issued stock.
2. The purchase of treasury stock does reduce outstanding stock. Remember that stock can be issued but not outstanding.
3. Treasury stock does not have rights to dividends or voting situations (because it is not outstanding).
4. Treasury stock is a contra-stockholders' equity account.
5. When treasury stock is bought, it is recorded at the purchase price. This purchase of treasury stock does not reduce the balance in the Retained Earnings account.
6. Many state laws will restrict the amount of retained earnings available for dividends if treasury stock exists, because the purchase of treasury stock reduces assets and stockholders' equity (like a cash dividend). This restriction is commonly shown in a footnote on the balance sheet.

Let's look now at how to record the purchase of treasury stock.

Purchase of Treasury Stock

On June 1, 20XX, Ashly Corporation has 5,000 shares of $10 par-value common stock and 2,000 shares of preferred stock outstanding. The corporation on June 1 purchases 1,000 shares of its own common stock at a price of $12 per share. The following is the analysis as well as journal entry to record the purchase:

Accounts Affected	Category	↑ ↓	Rules
Treasury Stock— Common	Contra SE	↑	Dr. $12,000
Cash	Asset	↓	Cr. $12,000

(1,000 shares × $12) ⟶ Common

Record treasury stock at the purchase price of $12 (Fig. 19.11). Note that the par value of common is not affected. Think of an *increase* in treasury stock as a reduction to stockholders' equity.

FIGURE 19.11 Purchase of Treasury Stock

June	1	Treasury Stock—Common	1 2 0 0 0 0		
		Cash		1 2 0 0 0 0	
		Purchase at $12 per share of			
		1,000 shares of previously			
		issued stock			

Sale of Treasury Stock

Treasury stock can be reissued at a price above or below the cost of reacquiring the stock. Let's look at how Ashly Company could on July 8 sell 100 shares of the treasury stock at $15 per share that was reacquired on June 1 for $12 per share.

The following chart analyzes the transaction:

	Accounts Affected	Category	↑ ↓	Rules
(100 shares × $15) →	Cash	Asset	↑	Dr. $1,500
(100 shares × $12) →	Treasury Stock—Common	Contra-SE	↓	Cr. $1,200
(100 shares × $3) →	Paid-In Capital from Treasury Stock	SE	↑	Cr. $300

Think of a *decrease* in treasury stock resulting in an increase to stockholders' equity.
The journal entry looks like Figure 19.12.

July	8	Cash		1 5 0 0 00	
		Treasury Stock—Common			1 2 0 0 00
		Paid-In Capital from Treasury Stock			3 0 0 00
		Sold 100 shares of Treasury Stock			
		purchased at $12			

FIGURE 19.12 Sale of Treasury Stock

The Treasury Stock account is decreased by the number of shares reissued times the *cost* when the stock was reacquired by the company. The credit to **Paid-In Capital from Treasury Stock** represents the amount over what was paid for acquiring the treasury stock.

If a corporation sells treasury stock for less than cost, the result is a decrease in stockholders' equity that is recorded in Paid-In Capital from Treasury Stock until the balance of the account is 0. Any further decrease in this account will directly reduce Retained Earnings, because Paid-In Capital from Treasury Stock cannot be a negative balance.

Example of Stockholders' Equity with Treasury Stock

Now let's see what stockholders' equity will look like with the accounts Treasury Stock and Paid-In Capital from Treasury Stock (Fig. 19.13).

FIGURE 19.13 Stockholders' Equity

Paid-In Capital:				
Preferred 14% Stock, $100 par value, authorized 6,000 shares, 2,000 shares issued and outstanding			$200 0 0 0 00	
Common Stock $10 par, authorized 9,000 shares, 5,000 shares issued and 4,100 outstanding, 900 shares in treasury			5 0 0 0 0 00*	
Additional Paid-In Capital:				
Paid-In Capital in Excess of Par Value—Preferred		1 0 0 0 0 00		
Paid-In Capital in Excess of Par Value—Common		3 0 0 0 0 00		
Paid-In Capital from Treasury Stock		3 0 0 00		
Total Additional Paid-In Capital			4 0 3 0 0 00	
Total Paid-In Capital			$290 3 0 0 00	
Retained Earnings			6 0 0 0 0 00	
			$350 3 0 0 00	
Deduct: Treasury Stock—Common (900 shares at cost)			1 0 8 0 0 00	
Total Stockholders' Equity			$339 5 0 0 00	

> The 900 shares of treasury stock don't reduce the number of shares issued; they reduce the number of shares outstanding.

*$50,000 = shares issued (5,000) x Par ($10)

LEARNING UNIT 19-3 REVIEW

AT THIS POINT you should be able to

- Define and explain the characteristics of treasury stock.
- Journalize the purchase as well as sale of treasury stock.
- Explain why treasury stock is a contra-stockholders' equity account.

Self-Review Quiz 19-3

Record the following transactions in general journal form (no explanation needed):

1. Also the Company acquired 100 shares of its own $10 par common stock at $15 per share.
2. Fifty of the treasury shares are reissued at $18 per share.
3. Forty of the treasury shares are reissued at $6 per share.

Solution to Self-Review Quiz 19-3

FIGURE 19.14 Purchase and Sale of Treasury Stock

❶	Treasury Stock (100 × $15)	1 5 0 0 00	
	Cash		1 5 0 0 00
❷	Cash ($18 × 50)	9 0 0 00	
	Treasury Stock (50 × $15)		7 5 0 00
❸	Paid-In Capital from Treasury		
	Stock (50 × $3)		1 5 0 00
	Cash ($6 × 40)	2 4 0 00	
	Paid-In Capital from Treasury Stock	1 5 0 00	
	Retained Earnings	2 1 0 00	
	Treasury Stock (40 × $15)		6 0 0 00

Note that Retained Earnings is reduced by $210, because Paid-In Capital is down to a zero balance:

$$\begin{array}{ll} \$\ 150 & (50 \times \$3) \\ \underline{-\ 360} & (40 \times \$9) \\ \$ <210> & \end{array}$$

Learning Unit 19-4 Appropriation of Retained Earnings and the Statement of Retained Earnings

In the first three units of this chapter we saw that cash dividends as well as stock dividends reduce the amount of retained earnings. Now we look at how companies indicate to those reading their financial reports that some of the retained earnings are not available for declaration of dividends; they are **appropriated (restricted) retained earnings.**

This *appropriating* of retained earnings could be either voluntary or contractual. For example, the board of directors could voluntarily decide that a portion of earnings should be used for plant expansion instead of for dividends. If a company enters into a loan with a bank, the bank may require the company to keep a minimum balance in Retained Earnings to protect its rights until the loan is repaid. Companies in many states are required to keep

> Restrictions on retained earnings limit the amount that is available to declare dividends.

a minimum in the Retained Earnings account at the level of legal capital. We saw in the last unit that treasury stock could result in retained earnings being restricted to the cost of the treasury stock.

In years past these special appropriations were recorded by transferring portions of the Retained Earnings account to accounts such as Retained Earnings Appropriated for Plant Expansion or Retained Earnings Appropriated for Contra Obligations. In reality, these appropriations didn't reduce total Retained Earnings; they just *shifted* a portion into an account that revealed its special purpose. For example, an entry to restrict $20,000 for plant expansion would be as shown in Figure 19.15.

> No actual cash is involved in the appropriation of retained earnings.

Retained Earnings		20 0 0 0 00	
Appropriation for Plant Expansion			20 0 0 0 00

FIGURE 19.15 Plant Expansion Restriction

After the appropriation or restriction has passed (e.g., the loan has been paid off), the balance is transferred back to the Retained Earnings account. No cash is involved in the appropriation.

Today, to make things clear to investors, most companies report restrictions by using a footnote to the Retained Earnings account. Restrictions on retained earnings do not have to be updated in the ledger; thus the use of a footnote is a common practice. (It is good practice to write a memo in the Retained Earnings account to identify each appropriation.) A footnote to announce such restrictions would look like the following:

> *The loan agreement with Jones Bank contains a restriction on the payment of cash dividends. Approximately $600,000 of retained earnings was free of such a restriction as of June 30, 20XX.*

Preparing the Statement of Retained Earnings

LO4

In past chapters we discussed the income statement, balance sheet, statement of owner's equity, and statement of partners' equity. We now turn our attention to a **statement of retained earnings** that will reveal the changes in retained earnings over a period of time. The changes in retained earnings result from the following:

1. Net income or loss
2. Dividends declared
3. Effects of prior period adjustments

Often an error in a financial report of a company from a prior period may not be discovered until a later period. If the error is considered *material*, a **prior period adjustment** should be made to the beginning balance of Retained Earnings. Let's look at a specific example.

Eight months after the close of its books Ralston Company discovered that depreciation was understated by $12,000, which meant in the old period that Depreciation Expense was understated by $12,000 and Net Income was overstated by $12,000. If Net Income was overstated, Retained Earnings also was overstated, because Net Income is closed into Retained Earnings. Thus, the entry shown in Figure 19.16 is recorded in the *new* year to adjust the prior period error (we ignore tax effect here).

Retained Earnings		12 0 0 0 00	
Accumulated Depreciation, Equipment			12 0 0 0 00

FIGURE 19.16 Adjustment of Prior Period Error

A statement of retained earnings for the Ralston Company would look like Figure 19.17.

FIGURE 19.17 Statement of Retained Earnings

RALSTON COMPANY STATEMENT OF RETAINED EARNINGS YEAR ENDED DECEMBER 31, 20X2	
Retained Earnings, Jan. 1, 20X2	$350 0 0 0 00
Less: Prior Period Adjustment:	
Correction of 20X1 error	12 0 0 0 00
Retained Earnings, Jan. 20X2, corrected	$338 0 0 0 00
Add: Net Income for 20X2	40 0 0 0 00
Total	$378 0 0 0 00
Deduct: Dividends declared in 20X2	28 0 0 0 00
Retained Earnings, Dec. 31, 20X2	$350 0 0 0 00

The statement of retained earnings is a formal report.

This ending figure of $350,000, as shown in the statement of retained earnings in Figure 19.17, will appear in the stockholders' equity section of the balance sheet.

Accounting Cycle for a Corporation

Before we conclude our discussion of corporations, Figure 19.18 provides a simplified sample of a worksheet for a corporation. This worksheet will give you a better idea of what titles such as Subscriptions Receivable, Common Stock, Paid-In Capital, and Retained Earnings look like when all are combined on one worksheet.

The cycle is then to prepare financial reports as well as journalize and post the adjusting and closing entries. We use Retained Earnings instead of Capital in the closing process. Also in the adjusting process we adjust the income tax owed. The Income Tax account is closed to Income Summary. The steps are quite similar to those discussed for a merchandise company.

A key point is that the net income shown on the income statement could be substantially different from that reported for tax purposes; certain deductions on the tax return will differ from the expenses on the corporation's books.

FIGURE 19.18 Worksheet for Jane Corporation

JANE CORPORATION
WORKSHEET
FOR YEAR ENDED DECEMBER 31, 20X3

Account Name	Trial Balance Dr.	Trial Balance Cr.	Adjustments Dr.	Adjustments Cr.	Adjusted Trial Balance Dr.	Adjusted Trial Balance Cr.	Income Statement Dr.	Income Statement Cr.	Balance Sheet Dr.	Balance Sheet Cr.
Cash	X				X				X	
Notes Receivable	X				X				X	
Accounts Receivable	X				X				X	
Subscriptions Rec., Com. Stock	X				X				X	
Merchandise Inventory	X		O	X	O				O	
Prepaid Rent	X			X	X				X	
Office Equipment	X				X				X	
Acc. Dep., Office Equip.		X		X		X				X
Organization Costs	X				X				X	
Notes Payable		X				X				X
Accounts Payable		X				X				X
Dividends Payable, Com.		X				X				X
Common Stock		X				X				X
Common Stock Div. Dist.		X				X				X
Paid-In Capital in Excess of Par—Common Stock		X				X				X
Common Stock Subscribed		X				X				X
Paid-In Capital from Treasury Stock		X				X				X
Retained Earnings		X				X				X
Income Summary			X	O	X	O	X	O		
Sales (totals)		X				X		X		
Purchases	X				X		X			
Purch. Ret. & Allow.		X				X		X		
Expenses (totals)	X									
Expenses (adjusted)			X		X		X			
Income Tax	X		X		X		X			
Income Tax Payable				X		X				X

O = Ending inventory

LEARNING UNIT 19-4 REVIEW

AT THIS POINT you should be able to

- Explain what could lead to appropriations of Retained Earnings.
- Explain why footnotes are used on financial reports instead of appropriation accounts to report restrictions to Retained Earnings.
- Prepare a statement of retained earnings.

Self-Review Quiz 19-4

From the following data prepare a statement of retained earnings for Janet Corporation for the year ended December 31, 20X3:

- Retained Earnings, January 1, 20X3, $650,000
- Dividends, 20X3, $50,000
- Correction of error from 20X1, $50,000 for Net Income that was discovered to be understated
- Net Income, 20X3, $80,000

Solution to Self-Review Quiz 19-4

FIGURE 19.19 Statement of Retained Earnings

JANET CORPORATION STATEMENT OF RETAINED EARNINGS YEAR ENDED DECEMBER 31, 20X3	
Retained Earnings, Jan. 1, 20X3	$650 0 0 0 00
Add: Prior Period Adjustment,	
Correction of 20X1 error	50 0 0 0 00
Retained Earnings, Jan. 20X3, corrected	$700 0 0 0 00
Add: Net Income for 20X3	80 0 0 0 00
Total	$780 0 0 0 00
Deduct: Dividends declared in 20X3	50 0 0 0 00
Retained Earnings, Dec. 31, 20X3	$730 0 0 0 00

CHAPTER ASSIGNMENTS

SUMMARY OF KEY POINTS

LEARNING UNIT 19-1

1. Redemption value is the price per share a corporation pays to holders of preferred stock when the stock is retired or redeemed.
2. Market value represents the open-market price of stock bought and sold. Market value doesn't mean the same thing as book value.
3. Book value per share is the amount or value of net assets on a company's books for each share of stockholders' stock in the equity of the corporation. Book value is calculated for preferred and common separately.

LEARNING UNIT 19-2

1. Dividends represent cash, stock, or other assets distributed to stockholders. The board of directors has the authority to declare dividends.
2. Three important dates associated with the dividend process are date of declaration, date of record, and date of payment.

3. A cash dividend results in a reduction of Retained Earnings and an eventual reduction in Cash.
4. Retained earnings doesn't mean cash.
5. A stock dividend will not reduce stockholders' equity like a cash dividend will. The end result is a transfer of retained earnings to Paid-In Capital.
6. Common Stock Dividend Distributable is a stockholders' equity account that is recorded at par value. It is not a liability account.
7. A stock split has no effect on Retained Earnings or any other ledger account. It increases the number of shares outstanding as well as reduces par or stated value.

LEARNING UNIT 19-3

1. Treasury Stock is a contra-stockholders' equity account that is recorded at cost. It represents stock that was previously issued and is now reacquired or received as a gift by a corporation.
2. Treasury stock is recognized as issued but not outstanding for dividends or voting situations.
3. Paid-In Capital from Treasury Stock can never have a negative balance. Any additional "loss" is reduced in Retained Earnings.

LEARNING UNIT 19-4

1. Appropriations of retained earnings can be contractual or voluntary.
2. Appropriations restrict the amount of retained earnings available for dividends.
3. Common practice today is to use footnotes on the balance sheet to reveal any appropriations of retained earnings.
4. The statement of retained earnings is made up of (1) beginning balance, (2) corrections of prior periods, (3) net income, and (4) dividends.

KEY TERMS

Appropriated (restricted) retained earnings   That portion of Retained Earnings that is not available for dividends.

Book value per share   Amount of net assets that a stockholder would receive on a per-share basis, assuming no gain or loss on the sale of the assets.

Cash dividend   Dividend that is paid in cash.

Common Stock Dividend Distributable   Stockholders' equity account that accumulates a stock dividend that has been declared but not yet issued and distributed.

Date of declaration   The date upon which the board of directors of a corporation formally declares a dividend.

Date of payment   The date the dividend is paid.

Date of record   The date of ownership that determines which stockholders will receive the dividend.

Dividend   Cash or other assets that a corporation distributes as earnings to stockholders.

Dividend Payable   Liability showing amount of cash dividend owed.

Market value   The price that a buyer pays to purchase shares of capital stock in the open market. Of course, for every buyer there is a seller.

Paid-In Capital from Treasury Stock   Stockholders' equity account that records amounts more or less than par value of treasury stock sold. The balance of this account can never be negative.

Prior period adjustment   Correction made in the current year of a mistake made in previous years. The adjustment is updated on the statement of retained earnings.

Redemption value   The price per share a corporation pays to redeem or retire capital stock.

Statement of retained earnings   A financial report that reveals the changes in retained earnings for a particular period of time.

Stock dividend   Stock that is distributed to stockholders instead of cash or other assets.

Stock split   Issuing of additional shares of stock to stockholders; total par or stated value remains the same.

Treasury stock   Stock that has been issued but has been bought back by the corporation or received as a gift.

BLUEPRINT: LEGAL CAPITAL APPROACH

MOOSE COMPANY
PARTIAL BALANCE SHEET

Stockholders' Equity

Paid-In Capital:			
Preferred 12% Stock, $10 par value, authorized 30,000 shares, 9,000 shares issued and outstanding		XX	
Common Stock, $10 par value, authorized 100,000 shares, 40,000 shares issued and 29,000 shares outstanding, 11,000 shares in treasury	XX		
Common Stock Dividend Distributable	XX	XX	
Additional Paid-In Capital:			
Paid-In Capital in Excess of Par Value—Preferred	XX		
Paid-In Capital in Excess of Par Value—Common	XX		
Paid-In Capital in Excess of Par Value—Stock Dividend	XX		
Paid-In Capital from Treasury Stock	XX		
Total Additional Paid-In Capital		XX	
Total Paid-In Capital		XX	
Retained Earnings		XX	
Deduct: Treasury Stock		XX	
Total Stockholders' Equity			XX

Note that legal capital is listed first. Both approaches are acceptable, and in the real world both are used. See the Blueprint in Chapter 18 for an example of the source-of-capital approach.

QUESTIONS, CLASSROOM DEMONSTRATION EXERCISES, EXERCISES, AND PROBLEMS

Discussion and Critical Thinking Questions/Ethical Case

1. What is the difference between market value and book value?

2. List the three important dates that are associated with the dividend process.

3. Why is no journal entry needed at the date of record?

4. Explain some possible reasons a company may declare a stock dividend instead of a cash dividend.

5. Explain why stock dividends will not reduce total stockholders' equity.

6. Common Stock Dividend Distributable is a liability. Agree or disagree? Defend your position.

7. Explain the difference between a stock dividend and a stock split.

8. Treasury stock is really an asset. Defend or reject. Support your argument.

9. All treasury stock is recognized as issued and outstanding for dividends. True or false? Please explain.

10. Explain the purpose of the account Paid-In Capital from Treasury Stock.

11. Appropriation of retained earnings is always done for a contractual reason. Agree or disagree? Defend your position.

12. Restrictions on retained earnings have to be updated in the ledger. Agree or disagree? Why?

13. What elements make up the statement of retained earnings?

14. Alan Homes serves on the board of directors of Flynn Company. The president of Flynn told him that in three weeks the corporation would announce a 25% increase in dividends. Alan called his neighbor to tell him to buy some stock. The neighbor told his friend about the stock and the friend told him that Alan was acting unethically. The neighbor called Alan back and Alan told him that no one will know the difference, that in business this happens all the time, and that he shouldn't be left out. Do you think Alan's behavior is appropriate? You make the call. Write down your recommendation to Alan's neighbor.

Classroom Demonstration Exercises

SET A

Book Value per Share for Preferred and Common

1. Given the following, prepare the book value per share for preferred and common stock:
   - Preferred Stock $90,000; 1,000 shares issued.
   - Common Stock $160,000; 800 shares issued.
   - Retained Earnings, $9,000.
   - Dividend in Arrears, $5,000.
   - Paid-in capital in excess of par: preferred, $6,000.
   - Paid-in capital in excess of par: common, $7,000.
   - Redemption value on preferred stock, $17.

LO1 (15 min)

Cash Dividend

2. On March 20, 20XX, the board of directors of Lance Corporation declared $3 cash dividend per share on the 8,000 shares issued and outstanding. The dividend will be paid on April 28, 20XX, to stockholders of record on March 22, 20XX. Record journal entries for date of declaration and date of payment.

LO3 (15 min)

Stock Dividend

3. On December 24, 20XX, Fress Corporation declared a 3% stock dividend distributable January 18 to stockholders of record on January 8. Currently Fress has 6,000 shares of common stock issued and outstanding. The stock has a par value of $15. The current fair market value of the stock is $30. Journalize (a) the declaration of the dividend and (b) the issuance of the stock dividend.

LO3 (15 min)

Treasury Stock

4. Journalize the following transactions:
   a. Janson Co. acquired 100 shares of its own $4 par-value common stock at $12 per share.
   b. Twenty-five of the treasury shares are reissued at $15 per share.
   c. Twenty of the treasury shares are reissued at $6 per share.

LO4 (20 min)

Prior Period Adjustment

5. Seven months after its closing, Brooks Co. discovered that depreciation was understated by $9,000. Provide the journal entry to adjust the prior period error (ignore any tax effects).

LO4 (15 min)

SET B

LO1 (15 min) **Book Value per Share for Preferred and Common**

1. Given the following, prepare the book value per share for preferred and common stock:
   - Preferred Stock $80,000; 1,000 shares issued.
   - Common Stock $150,000; 800 shares issued.
   - Retained Earnings, $8,500.
   - Dividend in Arrears, $4,000.
   - Paid-in capital in excess of par: preferred, $5,000.
   - Paid-in capital in excess of par: common, $6,000.
   - Redemption value on preferred stock, $16.

LO3 (15 min) **Cash Dividend**

2. On March 15, 20XX, the board of directors of Vision Corporation declared $3 cash dividend per share on the 6,000 shares issued and outstanding. The dividend will be paid on April 18, 20XX, to stockholders of record on March 19, 20XX. Record journal entries for date of declaration and date of payment.

LO3 (15 min) **Stock Dividend**

3. On December 24, 20XX, Fress Corporation declared a 5% stock dividend distributable January 18 to stockholders of record on January 8. Currently Fress has 5,000 shares of common stock issued and outstanding. The stock has a par value of $20. The current fair market value of the stock is $35. Journalize (a) the declaration of the dividend and (b) the issuance of the stock dividend.

LO4 (20 min) **Treasury Stock**

4. Journalize the following transactions:
   a. Janson Co. acquired 50 shares of its own $5 par-value common stock at $10 per share.
   b. Twenty-five of the treasury shares are reissued at $13 per share.
   c. Twenty of the treasury shares are reissued at $4 per share.

LO4 (20 min) **Prior Period Adjustment**

5. Seven months after its closing, Brooks Co. discovered that depreciation was understated by $8,000. Provide the journal entry to adjust the prior period error (ignore any tax effects).

Exercises

LO1 (20 min) **19-1.** From the following information determine the book value for preferred and common stocks assuming $15,000 of dividends are in arrears on the preferred stock.

Stockholders' Equity

Preferred 12% Stock cumulative and nonparticipating, $20 par value, $17 redemption value, 10,000 shares issued and outstanding	$200,000
Common Stock, $10 par value, 40,000 shares issued and outstanding	400,000
Retained Earnings	80,000
Total Stockholders' Equity	$680,000

LO2 (20 min) **19-2.** Poole Corporation has 300,000 shares of common stock issued and outstanding. On June 9, 20X6, the board of directors declared a $.50 per share dividend, payable on July 16, 20X6, to stockholders of record on June 29, 20X6. Record the appropriate journal entries on June 9 and July 16.

19-3. On July 31, 20X1, Harvey Corporation had the following stockholders' equity: *LO3 (20 min)*

Common Stock, $10 par value, authorized 90,000 shares,	
60,000 shares issued and outstanding	$600,000
Retained Earnings	200,000
Total Stockholders' Equity	$800,000

On August 5, 20X1, the board of directors declared a 10% stock dividend to be issued on September 6, 20X1, to the stockholders of record on August 19, 20X1. At time of declaration the market price was $17 per share. Prepare the appropriate journal entries for this stock dividend.

19-4. Given the following stockholders' equity: *LO3 (20 min)*

Common Stock, $7 par value, authorized 100,000 shares,	
80,000 shares issued and outstanding	$ 560,000
Retained Earnings	500,000
Total Stockholders' Equity	$1,060,000

Journalize the following entries:

20XX

Apr.	3	Issued 5,000 shares at $12 per share.
	9	Reacquired 200 shares at $8 per share.
	15	Reissued 100 shares of treasury stock at $10 per share.
	17	Reissued 50 shares of treasury stock at $7 per share.

19-5. From the following, prepare in proper form a statement of retained earnings for Williams Company for the year ended December 31, 20X4.   *LO4 (20 min)*

Retained Earnings,		Prior period adjustment increase in recording expense for Land in	
January 20X4	$40,000	20X2 (disregard taxes)	$14,000
Net Income, 20X4	$60,000	Dividends Paid, 20X4	$20,000

Group A Problems

19A-1. The stockholders' equity of Geygo Company is as follows: *LO1 (30 min)*

STOCKHOLDERS' EQUITY

Paid-In Capital:		
Preferred 10% Stock, $100 par value, authorized 5,000 shares, cumulative and nonparticipating, 4,000 shares issued and outstanding	$400,000	
Paid-In Capital in Excess of Par Value—Preferred	50,000	
Total Preferred Paid-In Capital by Preferred Stockholders		$450,000
Common Stock, $50 par value, authorized 15,000 shares, 6,000 shares issued and outstanding	$300,000	
Paid-In Capital in Excess of Par Value— Common	60,000	

(*continued on next page*)

Total Paid-In Capital by Common Stockholders	360,000
Total Paid-In Capital	$810,000
Retained Earnings	160,000
Total Stockholders' Equity	$970,000

Check Figure:
Book value preferred $108

Given a redemption value of $108, calculate the book value of preferred and common stock, assuming

a. No dividends in arrears.

b. Two years' dividends in arrears.

LO2 (30 min)   **19A-2.** Rolo Corporation has 400,000 shares of $7 par-value common stock issued and outstanding. Record the following entries into the general journal for Rolo:

Check Figure:
Aug. 4 Paid-In Capital in Excess
of Par Value—Stock Dividend
$80,000 Cr.

20XX		
July	2	Declared a cash dividend of $.60 per share.
Aug.	1	Paid the $.60 cash dividend to the stockholders.
Aug.	4	Declared a 4% stock dividend. The current market price is $12 per share.
Sept.	12	Issued the stock dividend declared on August 4.
Oct.	1	Declared an 8% stock dividend. The current market price is $17 per share.
Nov.	2	Issued the stock dividend on October 1.

LO2, 3, 4 (50 min)   **19A-3.** At the beginning of January 20XX, the stockholders' equity of Long View Corporation consisted of the following:

Paid-In Capital:		
Common Stock, $25 par value, authorized		
50,000 shares, 13,000 shares issued		
and outstanding	$325,000	
Paid-In Capital in Excess of Par Value—		
Common	70,000	
Total Paid-In Capital by Common		
Stockholders	$395,000	
Retained Earnings	160,000	
Total Stockholders' Equity		$555,000

Check Figure:
Total Stockholders' Equity
$614,300

1. Record the following transactions in general journal form.

2. Prepare the stockholders' equity section at year-end using the Blueprint as a guide.

3. Prepare a statement of retained earnings at December 31, 20XX.

Accounts are provided in the *Study Guide and Working Papers.* Be sure to put in the beginning balances.

20XX		
June	4	Long View Corporation purchased 1,000 shares of treasury stock at $28.
	20	The board of directors voted a $.20 per share cash dividend payable on July 15 to stockholders of record on July 2.
July	15	Cash dividend declared on June 20 is paid.
Sept.	5	Sold 300 shares of the treasury stock at $36 per share.
	29	Sold 700 shares of the treasury stock at $27 per share.

| Oct. | 10 | The board of directors declared a 6% stock dividend distributable on January 2 to stockholders of record on November 2. The market value of the stock is currently $38 per share. |
| Dec. | 31 | Closed the net income of $60,000 in the Income Summary account to Retained Earnings. |

19A-4. The following is the stockholders' equity of Piersal Corporation on October 1, 20XX:

LO2, 3, 4 (60 min)

> Check Figure:
> Total Stockholders' Equity
> $419,500

Paid-In Capital:		
Preferred 14% Stock, $10 par value, authorized 6,000 shares, 3,000 shares issued and outstanding		$ 30,000
Common Stock, $10 par value, authorized 20,000 shares, 10,000 shares issued and outstanding		100,000
Additional Paid-In Capital:		
Paid-In Capital in Excess of Par Value—Preferred	$10,000	
Paid-In Capital in Excess of Par Value—Common	5,000	
Paid-In Capital in Excess of Par Value—Stock Dividend	4,000	
Total Additional Paid-In Capital		19,000
Total Paid-In Capital		$149,000
Retained Earnings		200,000
Total Stockholders' Equity		$349,000

1. Journalize the following transactions in general journal form.
2. Prepare the stockholders' equity section of the balance sheet using the legal capital approach as of December 31, 20XX.

Your *Study Guide and Working Papers* has accounts to update ledger balances. Be sure to put in the beginning balances. Use the Blueprint as a guide to the setup of stockholders' equity.

20XX

Oct.	3	Declared a $.40 per share dividend on the common stock and a $1.20 per share dividend on the preferred. (The Dividends Payable account will record amounts for both common and preferred, although companies could set up Common Dividend Payable and Preferred Dividend Payable accounts.)
Nov.	15	Dividends were paid that were declared on October 3.
	18	Purchased 300 shares of its own common stock at $13 per share.
	25	Reissued 50 shares at $16 per share.
	26	Declared a 20% stock dividend on common. Market value of stock is $40 per share.
Dec.	29	Distributed stock dividend declared on November 26.
	30	Reissued 100 shares of treasury stock at $12 per share.
	31	Closed the Income Summary account, which had net income of $80,000, to Retained Earnings.

Group B Problems

LO1 (30 min)

19B-1. Given a redemption value of $105, calculate the book value of preferred and common stock, assuming (1) no dividends in arrears and (2) two years' dividends in arrears from the following stockholders' equity of Geygo Company:

Check Figure:
Book value preferred $105

Stockholders' Equity

Paid-In Capital:		
Preferred 12% Stock, $100 par value,		
authorized 3,000 shares, cumulative and		
nonparticipating, 1,000 shares issued		
and outstanding	$100,000	
Paid-In Capital in Excess of Par Value—		
Preferred	80,000	
Total Paid-In Capital by Preferred		
Stockholders		$ 180,000
Common Stock, $75 par value,		
authorized 12,000 shares, 8,000 shares		
issued and outstanding	$600,000	
Paid-In Capital in Excess of Par Value—		
Common	70,000	
Total Paid-In Capital by Common Stockholders		670,000
Total Paid-In Capital		$ 850,000
Retained Earnings		300,000
Total Stockholders' Equity		$1,150,000

LO2 (30 min)

19B-2. Rolo Corporation has 200,000 shares of $10 par value common stock issued and outstanding. Record the following entries into the general journal for Rolo:

20XX		
Aug.	3	Declared a cash dividend of $.30 per share.
Sept.	4	Paid the $.30 cash dividend to the stockholders.
	6	Declared a 5% stock dividend. The current market price is $14 per share.
	29	Issued the stock dividend declared on September 6.
Nov.	1	Declared a 10% stock dividend. The current market price is $17 per share.
	29	Issued the stock dividend declared on November 1.

Check Figure:
Sept. 6 Paid-In Capital in
Excess of Par Value—Stock
Dividend $40,000 Cr.

LO2, 3, 4 (50 min)

19B-3. At the beginning of January 20XX, the stockholders' equity of Long View Corporation consisted of the following:

Paid-In Capital:	
Common Stock, $30 par value, authorized	
70,000 shares, 15,000 shares issued and outstanding	$450,000
Paid-In Capital in Excess of Par Value—Common	60,000
Total Paid-In Capital by Common Stockholders	510,000
Retained Earnings	300,000
Total Stockholders' Equity	$810,000

Check Figure:
Total Stockholders' Equity
$817,300

1. Record the following transactions in general journal form.
2. Prepare a stockholders' equity section, using the Blueprint as a guide.
3. Prepare a statement of retained earnings at December 31, 20XX.

Accounts are provided in the *Study Guide and Working Papers*. Be sure to put in the beginning balances.

20XX

May	3	Long View Corporation purchased 2,000 shares of treasury stock at $40.
	15	The board of directors voted a $.70 per share cash dividend payable on July 9 to stockholders of record on June 13.
July	9	Cash dividend declared on May 15 is paid.
Sept.	15	Sold 200 shares of treasury stock at $50 per share.
Oct.	10	Sold 300 shares of treasury stock at $38 per share.
Nov.	1	The board of directors declared a 20% stock dividend distributable on January 2 to stockholders of record on November 17. The market value of the stock is $60 per share.
Dec.	31	Closed the net income of $75,000 in the Income Summary account to Retained Earnings.

19B-4. The following is the stockholders' equity of Piersal Corporation on November 1, 20XX:

LO2, 3, 4 (60 min)

Paid-In Capital:		
Preferred 12% Stock, $10 par value, authorized 8,000 shares,		
2,000 shares issued and outstanding		$ 20,000
Common Stock, $10 par value, authorized 15,000 shares, 10,000 shares issued and outstanding		100,000
Additional Paid-In Capital:		
Paid-In Capital in Excess of Par Value— Preferred	$30,000	
Paid-In Capital in Excess of Par Value— Common	10,000	
Paid-In Capital in Excess of Par Value— Stock Dividend	7,000	
Total Additional Paid-In Capital		47,000
Total Paid-In Capital		$167,000
Retained Earnings		86,000
Total Stockholders' Equity		$253,000

Check Figure:
Total Stockholders' Equity
$218,600

1. Journalize the following transactions in general journal form.
2. Prepare the stockholders' equity section of the balance sheet using the legal capital approach (see the Blueprint) as of December 31, 20XX.

Your *Study Guide and Working Papers* has accounts to update ledger balances. Be sure to put in beginning balances.

20XX

Nov.	3	Due to increased sales, the board of directors of Piersal declared a $3 per share dividend on the common stock and a $1.50 per share dividend on the preferred. (The Dividends Payable account records both common and preferred.)
	8	Purchased 500 shares of its own common stock at $16 per share.
	15	Reissued 200 shares at $18 per share.
	16	Declared a 10% stock dividend on common. Market value is $25 per share.
Dec.	15	Dividends were paid that were declared on November 3.
	28	Distributed stock dividend declared on November 16.
	30	Reissued 200 shares at $15 per share.
	31	Closed the Income Summary account, which had net income of $55,000, to Retained Earnings.

ON-THE-JOB TRAINING

LO2 (30 min) **T-1.** Moose Corporation has the following stockholders' equity prepared by Jesse Ross, head bookkeeper:

Paid-In Capital:	
Common Stock, $5 par, 3000 shares authorized, 1,600 shares issued, of which 900 shares are in the treasury	$ 4,500
Paid-In Capital in Excess of Par Value—Common	2,000
Total Paid-In Capital	5,500
Retained Earnings	2,000
Total	7,500
Add: Cost of Treasury Stock	7,000
Total Stockholders' Equity	$14,500

Explain what error(s) Jesse made in the preparation of stockholders' equity. Also, Moose Corporation wants to declare a cash dividend of $3 per share. Is it feasible? Show your calculations along with a written explanation.

LO2 (20 min) **T-2.** Margaret Jones owns 100 shares of Johnson Corporation. She receives in the mail a notice that a two-for-one stock split is being declared. Currently, the stock is trading on the open market at $120 per share. After the split 600,000 shares will be outstanding. Margaret is worried that this split will reduce her book value, resulting in a loss of market value. She feels her preemptive right has been ignored. She believes that a stock dividend is the best way for the corporation to go. Respond in writing specifically to Margaret's concerns.

FINANCIAL REPORT PROBLEM

LO3 (10 min) ### Reading the Kellogg's Annual Report

Go to Appendix A and find the consolidated balance sheet. What is the cost of treasury stock for Kellogg's in 2006 and 2005?

INTERNET PROJECT

Sara Lee

Go to the Web and search: Annual Report Sara Lee 2008.
Click on Investors Relations.
List out the latest news Sara Lee is providing to its investors.
Order a free annual report.

SUBWAY Case

BUCKING TRADITION

LO1, 2, 3 (20 min)

"A convenience store?" asked Stan, incredulous.

"Yep, a convenience store," replied Carrie Zabrinsky, "or, as they say in the business, a c-store."

Stan had arranged a meeting with his Subway development agent, Carrie, to discuss expansion of his Subway franchise to another location. His future partner, Ron, was almost through with his training program at Subway University, and Stan had just promoted his Sandwich Artist, Rashid, to manager. By leaving a lot of the day-to-day operations in Rashid's hands, Stan planned to help Ron open the new Subway. Everything seemed to be going according to plan, yet he hadn't bargained on the new location being in a Pitt's Stop convenience store!

"Stan, just hear me out," Carrie insisted. "That site you have your eye on is extremely expensive. Also, with nothing around it but that new luxury apartment complex and some very upscale shops, it won't generate the foot traffic you need. This c-store, however, is in a prime high-traffic location."

"But the square footage is so small," Stan protested, pointing to the floor plan in front of him.

"Listen, Stan, in the fast-food industry, Subway leads the pack in opening nontraditional units. We have more than 3,700 Subway restaurants in c-stores, airports, gas stations, schools, grocery stores, and even in hospitals. Headquarters wouldn't encourage these arrangements if they weren't highly lucrative. Sure, these smaller units typically generate less revenue than a full-size restaurant, but they're also cheaper to build and maintain. Look at the figures: Opening in a c-store typically costs as little as $30,000 to develop, while the traditional venue is more like $66,000."

"And you've got a captive audience, I guess," admitted Stan, "particularly in hospitals and schools. What I would've given to eat a sweet onion chicken teriyaki sandwich instead of that stuff that passed for food in high school!"

"Now you're getting the picture," Carrie smiled. "Just imagine. You go into the c-store at 10:00 P.M. to buy a quart of milk or some batteries and then you smell fresh-baked gourmet bread. Your stomach growls and you buy a Subway 6-inch."

"Okay, okay," Stan said. "Once I get some figures for the lease and find out more about this Pitt's Stop's business and its management, I'll run it by Ron. I'm not sure it is what he had in mind when he quit his job to own a Subway."

"Well, he had profits in mind, didn't he?" asked Carrie.

Discussion Questions

1. How might opening a Subway in a convenience store reduce expenses?
2. How might this arrangement increase sales? Suppose you're Stan's development agent and you want him to open a Subway in a gas station. How would you sell him on this arrangement?
3. Like all corporations, Doctor's Associates Inc.'s goal is to increase earnings per share. How does expansion into nontraditional sites help achieve this goal?

20

Corporations and Bonds Payable

DID YOU KNOW? Anheuser-Busch has 90% debt at a fixed rate. The average maturity of debt is 15 years. Visit *www.anheuser-busch.com* to find more information about Anheuser-Busch.

LEARNING OBJECTIVES

1. Journalizing the recording of bonds as well as interest payments.

2. Amortizing bond discounts and bond premiums by the straight-line method and by the interest method.

3. Journalizing year-end adjusting entries for bonds.

4. Journalizing entries related to retirement of bonds and to sinking funds.

A corporation like Anheuser-Busch can raise funds by issuing stock or long-term notes payable. Notes or stock are good sources of funds when a company borrows from only one bank or other type of lending institution, but they may not provide the total amount of funds needed. In the last two chapters we saw how companies issue stock. Now our attention shifts to notes. After all, businesses such as Dell and General Motors may need to borrow millions of dollars. This chapter looks at how corporations can raise large amounts of money from groups of lenders by issuing a type of long-term interest-bearing note payable called a **bond.**

Learning Unit 20-1 Structure and Characteristics of a Bond

Each **bond certificate,** usually issued in denominations of $1,000, contains the following:

1. **Face value** (principal) is the amount that the corporation must repay to the lender at the maturity date.
2. **Contract rate** (stated interest rate) is the annual interest rate, which is based on face value. Usually this interest is paid *semi*annually. The dates of interest payment are also printed on the certificate.

For example, if Joe Rosse owns a $1,000, 12%, 20-year bond that is issued by Von Corporation, it means the following:

1. At the end of 20 years Joe will receive the $1,000.
2. Every six months Joe will receive an interest check for $60 ($1,000 $\times$ .12 $\times \frac{6}{12}$).

Another way to calculate semiannual interest is as follows:

$$\frac{12\%}{2} = \text{Semiannual Rate of 6\%}$$
$$.06 \times \$1,000 = \$60$$

The information on the bond certificate is written by the corporation into a more formal agreement called the **bond indenture.** This agreement is usually monitored by a **trustee** (often a bank), who represents the group of bondholders.

> A trustee (usually a bank) monitors bondholders' interest as stipulated in the bond indenture.

If, before the 20 years have passed, Joe wants to cash in the bond, he can sell it on the securities exchange (like the stock exchange, but dealing in the buying and selling of bonds rather than stock). Bonds are negotiable and generally transferable. Let's assume Joe calls his broker, who indicates that the current market price of the bond is quoted at 94, a percentage (94%) of the bond's face value. This price can be higher or lower than the face amount (100, or 100%), depending on current rates of interest as well as other market factors. If market interest rates are high compared with the current bond's interest rate, the percentage would be lower. Why? The reason is that the bond's interest is not as attractive as current rates. The 94 means that a buyer is willing to pay $940 (.94 $\times$ $1,000) for the bond. If the quote were 104, then Joe could receive $1,040 (1.04 $\times$ $1,000) for the bond.

> A bond quote of 70 would mean that a bond with a face value of $1,000 is selling for $700 (.70 $\times$ $1,000).

The following is a list of different types of bonds. Keep in mind that each bond issue may have special arrangements besides the customary repayment plans. Don't memorize this list; use it as a reference.

Types of Bonds

Corporations can offer many types of bonds. The following are some examples.

Secured Bonds: The corporation issuing the bonds pledges specific assets such as equipment or property as security for meeting the terms of the bond agreement.

Debenture Bonds: The issuing corporation pledges no specific assets as collateral; thus the bonds are unsecured. Risk is higher than with secured bonds; these bonds will generally require a higher rate of interest to make them attractive to the investor.

Serial Bonds: These bonds are made up of a series, each having its own maturity date. For example, a bond issue of $2,000,000 could be made up of a series of 20 $100,000 bonds, one series maturing at the end of each year for a period of 20 years.

Registered Bonds: Owners of bonds are registered with the issuing company, and interest is mailed to the owners of record.

Callable Bonds: These bonds have a provision stating that they can be called in by a corporation after a certain date. When a bond issue is called in, the corporation usually has to pay a price above the face value of the bond.

Convertible Bonds: The bondholder may be allowed to convert bonds into shares of stock. For this right, bondholders give up fixed interest payments for what they hope will be higher dividends and/or stock prices.

Stocks versus Bonds

Why would a corporation prefer to raise money by selling bonds rather than by issuing and selling stock? Let's look at an example. Should Rojer Corporation obtain long-term funds by selling $500,000 worth of 12% bonds, or issue 12% preferred stock for $500,000? Rojer Corporation wants to make the most of its tax savings as well as earnings per share (EPS) of common stock:

$$EPS = \frac{\text{After-Tax Earnings} - \text{Dividends for Preferred}}{\text{Number of Shares of Common Stock Outstanding}}$$

EPS = Earnings per Share of Stock

We are assuming Rojer Corporation has earnings of $700,000 and we assume a tax rate of 40%. Table 20.1 is a worked-out solution to this problem by the corporation's accountant.

TABLE 20.1 Stocks versus Bonds (Stock Dividends versus Bond Interest)		
	$500,000 12% **Preferred Stock Issued**	**$500,000 12%** **Bonds (10-Year) Issued**
Earnings before Taxes or Finance Costs	$700,000	$700,000
Less: Bond Interest	—0—	60,000 (.12 × $500,000)
Earnings Subject to Income Tax	$700,000	$640,000
Less: Income Tax (40%)	280,000	256,000
Net Income	420,000	384,000
Less: Preferred Dividend	60,000 (.12 × $500,000)	—0—
Earnings Available to Common Stockholders	360,000	384,000
Number of Common Stock Shares Outstanding	80,000	80,000
Earnings per Share	$ 4.50 $\left(\dfrac{\$360,000}{80,000}\right)$	$ 4.80 $\left(\dfrac{\$384,000}{80,000}\right)$

Looking just at the numbers, Rojer Corporation would be better off issuing *bonds,* because the $60,000 of bond interest that the corporation would pay to bondholders would serve to reduce earnings on which the corporation would have to pay tax. On the other hand, *dividends* paid to stockholders would not reduce earnings on which the corporation would pay taxes (the dividend for preferred stock is not an expense, as bond interest is, but a distribution of net income *after* tax). With bonds, the common stockholders have an earnings per share of $4.80 versus $4.50.

Note: Bond interest of $60,000 lowers earnings subject to tax. Bond interest is deductible for federal income tax purposes.

Other factors, however, should be considered when deciding whether to issue stocks or bonds to raise money, such as how interest rates are moving in the economy or whether the corporation can meet the bond interest payments each period for 10 years. If interest rates are high, it may be that the bond issue should be delayed to get more favorable interest rates.

For a comparison of stocks and bonds, see the Blueprint at the end of the chapter.

Before concluding this unit, let's see how Rojer Corporation would record the sale and pay interest on the 12%, $500,000 bonds.

LO1   On January 1, Rojer Corporation issued its bonds (Fig. 20.1).

FIGURE 20.1 Issuance of Bonds

> Bonds Payable is a long-term liability on the balance sheet.

Jan.	1	Cash	500 00 0 00		
		Bonds Payable		500 00 0 00	
		Records issuance of bonds			

It then made semiannual interest payments to its bondholders (Fig. 20.2).

FIGURE 20.2 Semiannual Interest Paid

> $500,000 \times .12 \times \frac{6}{12} = \$30,000$,
> or 12%/2 = .06
> $\times \$500,000 = \$30,000$.

June	30	Bond Interest Expense	30 00 0 00		
		Cash		30 00 0 00	
		Paid semiannual interest expense			

This entry will be recorded twice a year for 10 years. At the end of 10 years, Rojer will record the bond maturity.

On the year of retirement, the journal entry would look like Figure 20.3.

FIGURE 20.3 Bonds Retired

Dec.	31	Bonds Payable	500 00 0 00		
		Cash		500 00 0 00	
		Retired bonds			

The face value of the bond, $500,000 has been repaid on maturity date.

Bonds Sold between Interest Dates

What would happen if Rojer Corporation issued the bonds on January 1 but did not actually sell them until March 1? Interest will be paid for all six months from January through June, even though the bonds weren't sold until March 1. How is that handled? And what happens if a person buys a bond that was issued in August, but the person buys it in November? As stated earlier, bond issuers only pay interest every six months. So, when a buyer purchases a bond between the six-month interest dates, the buyer pays the purchase price of the bond *plus* the interest that has built up since the last interest payment date. Keep in mind interest is being paid only twice a year. Think of it as an adjustment as the interest accrues. On the next payment, the buyer will receive the full interest payment for the six-month period. Let's show this situation by seeing how Rojer Corporation records the sale of bonds on March 1 that were issued on January 1 (Fig. 20.4).

FIGURE 20.4 Bonds Issued with Accrued Interest

> Accrued Interest
> ($500,000 \times .12 \times \frac{2}{12} = \$10,000$)
>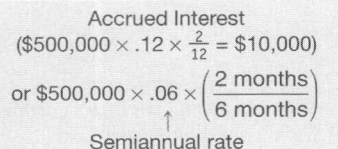
> or $\$500,000 \times .06 \times \left(\dfrac{2 \text{ months}}{6 \text{ months}} \right)$
> Semiannual rate

Mar.	1	Cash	510 00 0 00		
		Bonds Payable		500 00 0 00	
		Bond Interest Payable		10 00 0 00	
		Bond issue plus 2 months' accrued interest			

Note that the buyer pays $510,000 instead of $500,000, because $10,000 of the accrued interest has been accumulated. On June 30, the $10,000 is repaid along with interest earned for four months (Fig. 20.5).

FIGURE 20.5 Semiannual Interest Paid

> ($500,000 \times .12 \times \frac{4}{12} = \$20,000$)
> or $\$500,000 \times .06 \times \left(\dfrac{4 \text{ months}}{6 \text{ months}} \right)$
> Semiannual rate

June	30	Bond Interest Payable	10 00 0 00		
		Bond Interest Expense	20 00 0 00		
		Cash		30 00 0 00	
		Record semiannual interest payment			

In the next unit we look at how to record bond issues when the selling price is less or more than the face value.

LEARNING UNIT 20-1 REVIEW

AT THIS POINT you should be able to

- Explain face value and contract interest rate.
- Calculate the cost of a bond from a bond quote.
- Explain the different classifications of bonds.
- Explain the pros and cons of financing with preferred stock versus bonds.
- Record accounting entries to record issuing of bonds at par as well as the semiannual interest payment.
- Explain and record an accounting entry for accrued bond interest.

Self-Review Quiz 20-1

Prepare general journal entries to record the following (treat items 4 and 5 as a separate situation from items 1 through 3):

1. Issued 20, $10,000, 12%, bonds that mature in 10 years at face value on January 1.
2. Paid semiannual interest on June 30.
3. Bonds retired at end of 10th year.
4. Bonds sold on May 1 instead of January 1 due to poor market conditions.
5. Paid semiannual interest on June 30 from bonds issued on May 1.

Solution to Self-Review Quiz 20-1

FIGURE 20.6 Bond Transactions

		Debit	Credit
❶	Cash	200 000 00	
	Bonds Payable		200 000 00
❷	Bond Interest Expense	12 000 00	
	Cash		12 000 00
	(Interest = $200,000 × .12 × $\frac{6}{12}$		
	or $200,000 × .06 semiannual rate)		
❸	Bonds Payable	200 000 00	
	Cash		200 000 00
❹	Cash	208 000 00	
	Bonds Payable		200 000 00
	Bond Interest Payable		8 000 00
	(Accrued interest = $200,000 × .12 × $\frac{4}{12}$		
	or $200,000 × .06 × $\frac{4}{6}$ = $8,000)		
❺	Bond Interest Payable	8 000 00	
	Bond Interest Expense	4 000 00	
	Cash		12 000 00
	(Bond interest expense = $200,000 × .12 × $\frac{2}{12}$		
	or $200,000 × .06 × $\frac{2}{6}$ = $4,000)		

Learning Unit 20-2 Bonds Issued at a Discount or Premium; Amortization by the Straight-Line Method

LO2

When a corporation issues bonds, it must

1. Receive approval from the board of directors of the corporation as well as from a governmental regulatory agency, the Securities and Exchange Commission.

> On a given day the market rate for bond interest will vary from corporation to corporation: "supply versus demand."

(*continued on next page*)

2. Print the bonds.

3. Advertise the bond issue.

The problem is that by the time these steps have been done, the rate of interest stated on the bond, the *contract* rate, may be lower or higher than the current *market* rate of interest. Investors may require higher rates of interest if the bond issue appears to be different from others offered by companies that may have had fewer financial difficulties.

> Investor willingness to pay more than face value means a premium for the corporation. Such willingness could result from the bond interest rate being more attractive than the market rate.

For example, let's assume that Jossy Corporation is attempting to sell its 12% bond issue. The current market rate is 13%. To make its bonds more attractive (investors are looking for the best return on their investment), Jossy decides to sell the bonds for less than face value (91, or 91% of the face value of $1,000). The bondholder will still receive yearly interest of $120 per bond (.12 × $1,000) but will only pay $910 (.91 × $1,000) per bond. Thus, investors' annual or **effective rate** of interest is 13.2% ($120/$910). The difference between the *issue price* ($910) and the face value ($1,000) is called the *discount*.

Conversely, if Jossy Corporation sells the bond for *more* than the face value (if its contract rate is higher than the market rate), the difference between issue price and face value is called a *premium*.

Recording and Amortizing Bonds Issued at a Discount

> .97 × $1,000 = $970 paid for each bond

To illustrate how to record a bond discount, let's look at the Ronson Corporation, which on January 1, 20XX, issued 200, 12%, $1,000, 10-year bonds at 97 (97% of face value). The discount is used because the current market rate is 12.4%, and Ronson has to be competitive to make its bond attractive to investors. Bondholders will receive yearly bond interest of $120, with an effective rate of 12.4% ($120/$970). The accounts that will make up the journal entry include the following:

Cash	Asset	↑	Dr. $194,000	.97 × $200,000
Discount on Bonds Payable	Contra-Liability	↑	Dr. $ 6,000	($200,000 − $ 194,000)
Bonds Payable	Liability	↑	Cr. $200,000	Face value

The journal entry will look like Figure 20.7.

> **FIGURE 20.7** Bond Issued at a Discount

Jan.	1	Cash		194 0 0 0 00		
		Discount on Bonds Payable		6 0 0 0 00		
		Bonds Payable			200 0 0 0 00	
		Record bond issue				

Let's look at how the Discount on Bonds Payable would look on the balance sheet.

Long-Term Liabilities:		
12% Bonds Payable	$200,000	
Less: Discount on Bonds Payable	6,000	$194,000

> Carrying Value = Face Value − Discount on Bonds Payable

For bonds sold at a discount, the **carrying value** (also called **book value**) of $194,000 is the face value of $200,000 minus the discount on bonds payable of $6,000. At maturity (after 10 years), the carrying value will be the same as face value ($200,000).

When each interest payment is made, a portion of the **Discount on Bonds Payable** is transferred to increase Interest Expense. This portion is called **amortization of discount on bonds payable.** Bond discount causes the total interest expense to increase, because the bond is sold for less than face value, resulting in higher costs of borrowing.

Before looking at how to amortize the discount, let's prove that the interest expense will be more than the contract amount of interest of $240,000 (.12 × $200,000 × 10 years) for 10 years.

Total amount to be paid to bondholder	$440,000	($200,000 bonds +
		$240,000 interest)
Total amount to be received from sale of bond	−$194,000	
Interest to be paid over life of bond	$246,000	
Average interest expense per year	$ 24,600	($246,000 ÷ 10 years)
Semiannual interest expense	$ 12,300	

If no discount has been made, the semiannual interest expense would be $12,000 ($200,000 × .12 × $\frac{6}{12}$ or $200,000 × .06). Now the discount results in an additional $300 of interest expense *each* semiannual payment ($6,000 ÷ 20 periods).

The journal entry for each semiannual payment and amortization of discount will be as shown in Figure 20.8.

June	30	Bond Interest Expense	12300 00		
		Discount on Bonds Payable		300 00	
		Cash		12000 00	
		Semiannual interest and amortization of			
		discount			

FIGURE 20.8 Semiannual Payment and Amortization of Discount by Straight-Line Method

After posting, the ledger would look as follows:

Discount on Bonds Payable		Bond Interest Expense	
6,000	300	12,300	
5,700			

After this amortization the carrying value (book value) of the bond increased from $194,000 to $194,300. By the end of 10 years the carrying value will be back to $200,000, or the amount due at maturity.

In this unit we calculate amortization of the bond's discount by the **straight-line method;** in the next unit we use the *interest* method. The straight-line method transfers an equal amount of bond discount to interest expense over equal periods of time.

Table 20.2 on the following page shows the straight-line method of amortizing a bond discount over the life of the bond for each semiannual period. At the end of the life of the bond, the Discount on Bonds Payable shows a zero balance, with the original $6,000 transferred to Interest Expense. At this point, the book value or carrying value of a bond ($200,000) is the same amount as paid at maturity.

> $200,000 Face value of bond
> − 5,700 Bond discount
> $194,300 New carrying value
>
> After 10 years, the balance on Discount on Bonds Payable will be zero.

Year-End Adjusting Entry: Accrued Interest and Amortization of Discount on Bonds Payable Let's consider what would happen if the semiannual interest payment were on April 1 and October 1. On December 31, $6,000, three months' interest, would be accrued ($12,000 × $\frac{3}{6}$). The amount of discount to be amortized would be $150 ($300 × $\frac{3}{6}$). The journal entry would be recorded as shown in Figure 20.9.

LO3

Dec.	31	Bond Interest Expense	6150 00		
		Discount on Bonds Payable		150 00	
		Bond Interest Payable		6000 00	
		Accrued interest and amortization			

FIGURE 20.9 Discount to Be Amortized by Straight-Line Method

> Bond Interest Expense:
> $12,300 × $\frac{3}{6}$ = $6,150

TABLE 20.2 Amortization Schedule for Bond Discount Using the Straight-Line Method for Each Semiannual Period

Period	Carrying Value, Beg. of Period	Total Interest Expense	Interest Paid to Bondholders (.06 × Face Value)*	Amortized Discount Transferred to Increase Interest Expense	Carrying Value, End of Period
1	$194,000	$12,300	$12,000	$300	$194,300
	(200,000 − 6,000)		(200,000 × .06)	(6,000 ÷ 20 periods)	(194,000 + 300)
2	194,300	12,300	12,000	300	194,600
3	194,600	12,300	12,000	300	194,900
4	194,900	12,300	12,000	300	195,200
19	199,400	12,300	12,000	300	199,700
20	199,700	12,300	12,000	300	200,000

The balance in the Discount on Bonds Payable account will be equal to zero at the end of the 20 periods.

*Half of annual rate of 12% = 6% semiannual rate.

Note that the Discount on Bonds Payable does indeed increase total bond interest expense from $6,000 to $6,150. This adjusting entry would then be reversed on January 1, as shown in Figure 20.10.

FIGURE 20.10 Reversing Entry

Jan.	1	Bond Interest Payable	6 0 0 0 00	
		Discount on Bonds Payable	1 5 0 00	
		Bond Interest Expense		6 1 5 0 00
		Reversing entry		

The regular payment made on April 1 would look like Figure 20.11.

FIGURE 20.11 Paid Semiannual Interest and Amortized Discount

Apr.	1	Bond Interest Expense	12 3 0 0 00	
		Discount on Bonds Payable		3 0 0 00
		Cash		12 0 0 0 00
		Semiannual interest and amortizaton of		
		discount		

Recording and Amortizing Bonds Issued at a Premium

To illustrate bonds issued at a premium, let's look at Ronson Corporation again, but assume on January 1 it issued its 200, 12% bonds at 102 (102% of face value). This premium occurred because the current market rate was 11.8% and Ronson's bonds were thus attractive to investors. The bondholders would receive per bond the yearly interest payment of $120 (.12 × $1,000 bond) with an effective rate of 11.8% ($120/$1,020). The accounts that will make up the journal entry include the following:

> The Premium on Bonds Payable is added to the face value of the bond.

Cash	Asset	↑	Dr. $204,000	1.02 × $200,000
Premium on Bonds Payable	Liability	↑	Cr. $ 4,000	($204,000 − $200,000)
Bonds Payable	Liability	↑	Cr. $200,000	Face value

The journal entry will look like Figure 20.12.

Jan.	1	Cash	204 00 0 00		
		Premium on Bonds Payable		4 00 0 00	
		Bonds Payable		200 00 0 00	
		Issued bond at premium			

FIGURE 20.12 Bond Issued at a Premium

Let's see how the Premium on Bonds Payable would look on the balance sheet:

Long-Term Liabilities:		
12% Bonds Payable	$200,000	
Add: Premium on Bonds Payable	4,000	$204,000

Note: The Premium on Bonds Payable is added to Bonds Payable to arrive at the carrying value of $204,000.

When each interest payment is made, a portion of the **Premium on Bonds Payable** is transferred to *reduce* Interest Expense. This portion is called **amortization of premium on bonds payable.** Let's prove that the interest expense will be less than the contractual amount of $240,000 for 10 years.

Total amount to be paid to bondholders	$440,000	($200,000 bonds + $240,000 interest)
Total amount to be received from sale of bonds	− 204,000	
Interest to be paid over life of bond	$236,000	
Average interest expense per year	$ 23,600	($236,000 ÷ 10 years)
Semiannual interest expense	$ 11,800	

With no discount or premium, the semiannual interest/expense would be $12,000.

If no premium were paid, the semiannual interest expense would be $12,000 ($200,000 × 12 × $\frac{6}{12}$ or $200,000 × .06). Now the premium results in *reducing* the interest expense for each semiannual payment by $200 ($4,000 premium ÷ 20 periods).

The journal entry for semiannual payment will look like Figure 20.13.

June	30	Bond Interest Expense	11 80 0 00		
		Premium on Bonds Payable	2 0 0 00		
		Cash		12 00 0 00	
		Semiannual payment and premium			
		amortization			

FIGURE 20.13 Paid Semiannual Payment and Amortized Premium

After posting, the ledger will look like the following:

Premium on Bonds Payable		**Bond Interest Expense**	
200	4,000	11,800	
	3,800		

We're using the straight-line method of amortizing the bond premium over the life of the bond for each semiannual period. This method is shown in Table 20.3 on the following page. Note that at the end of the schedule, the carrying value is reduced to $200,000 and the balance in the Premium account is zero.

TABLE 20.3 Amortization Schedule for Bond Premium Using the Straight-Line Method for Each Semiannual Period

Period	Carrying Value, Beg. of Period	Total Interest Expense	Interest Paid to Bondholder (.06 × Face Value)	Amortized Premium to Decrease Interest Expense	Carrying Value, End of Period
1	$204,000	$11,800	$12,000	$200	$203,800
	(200,000 + 4,000)		(.06 × 200,000)		(204,000 − 200)
2	203,800	11,800	12,000	200	203,600
3	203,600	11,800	12,000	200	203,400
4	203,400	11,800	12,000	200	203,200
19	200,400	11,800	12,000	200	200,200
20	200,200	11,800	12,000	200	200,000

The balance in the Premium on Bonds Payable account should be equal to zero at the end of the 20 periods.

LEARNING UNIT 20-2 REVIEW

AT THIS POINT you should be able to

- Calculate the effective rate.
- Explain why a bond will sell at a discount or premium.
- Define and explain Discount on Bonds Payable.
- Explain why a discount will increase interest expense when semiannual interest is paid.
- Journalize the recording of bonds issued at a discount.
- Journalize year-end adjusting entries.
- Prepare an amortization schedule of a bond discount by the straight-line method.
- Define and explain Premium on Bonds Payable.
- Explain why a premium on bonds payable will decrease interest expense when semi-annual interest is paid.
- Journalize the recording of bonds issued at a premium.
- Prepare an amortization schedule of a bond premium by the straight-line method.

Self-Review Quiz 20-2

Prepare a partial amortization schedule using the straight-line method for the first three semiannual periods based on the following facts: 100, 14%, 10-year bonds issued at 98. Each bond has a $1,000 face value.

Solution to Self-Review Quiz 20-2

Period	Carrying Value, Beg. of Period	Total Interest Expense	Interest Paid to Bondholders (.07 × Face Value)	Amortized Discount Transferred to Increase Interest Expense	Carrying Value, End of Period
1	$98,000	$7,100	$7,000	$100	$98,100
			(2,000 ÷ 20 periods)	(98,000 + 100)	
2	98,100	7,100	7,000	100	98,200
3	98,200	7,100	7,000	100	98,300

Learning Unit 20-3 Amortization of Bond Discounts and Premiums by the Interest Method

In the last unit we amortized the discount or premium by the straight-line method. The problem with this method is that it recognizes an equal amount of interest expense each period, even though the bond's carrying value changes. Accountants think it is inconsistent for interest expense to stay the same while the amount owed changes. They think interest should be a *constant percentage of the carrying value.* For this reason, another method, called the *interest method,* is used in amortizing bond discounts and premiums. The Accounting Principles Board has ruled that the straight-line method may be used only if the results do not materially differ from those of the interest method.

Amortizing the Bond Discount by the Interest Method

The **interest method of amortization** makes interest expense a constant percentage of the bond carrying value.

The goal of the interest method is to calculate the interest expense to be recorded each year as a constant percentage of the carrying value of the bonds. The interest amount will thus not be the same each period. Two formulas provide the calculations necessary to reach this goal:

1. Carrying Value of Bonds at Beginning of Period × Market Interest Rate = Interest Expense to Be Recorded
2. Face Value × Contract Rate = Interest Expense to Bondholders

The discount to be amortized is the difference between (1) and (2).

To illustrate this method, let's assume Yang Corporation is issuing $200,000 of 12%, 10-year bonds on April 1. Interest is to be paid on October 1 and April 1. The selling price of the bonds is $178,808. The market rate is 14%.

Look at the amortization schedule shown in Table 20.4. Note that the discount amount to be amortized is not constant, as it is in the straight-line method. As a matter of fact, to prove that the interest expense is a constant percentage of the carrying value, let's look at semiannual periods 2 and 19.

> Discount on bond: $200,000 − $178,808 = $21,192

$$\text{Period 2: } \frac{\$12,553}{\$179,325} = .07 \qquad \text{Period 19: } \frac{\$13,746}{\$196,373} = .07$$

TABLE 20.4 **Amortization Schedule for Bond Discount for Each Semiannual Period Using the Interest Method**

Period	(1) Carrying Value, Beginning of Period	(2) Interest Paid to Bondholders (.06 × Face Value)*	(3) Interest Expense Recorded (.07 × Carrying Value)	(4) Discount to Be Amortized	(5) Carrying Value, End of Period
1	$178,808	$12,000	$12,517	$ 517	$179,325
	(200,000 − 21,192)		(.07 × 178,808)		(178,808 + 517)
2	179,325	12,000	12,553	553	179,878
3	179,878	12,000	12,591	591	180,469
19	196,373	12,000	13,746	1,746	198,119
20	198,119	12,000	13,881	1,881	200,000

Adjusted for rounding

*Use 6%, because 12% is for the whole year and the calculations are made semiannually.

Note: Column 4 is the difference between columns 2 and 3.

On October 1, the date of the first semiannual interest payment, the entry in Figure 20.14 would occur.

FIGURE 20.14 Paid Semiannual Payment and Amortized Discount by Interest Method

Oct.	1	Bond Interest Expense	12 5 1 7 00		
		Discount on Bonds Payable		5 1 7 00	
		Cash		12 0 0 0 00	
		Semiannual payment and amortization			

Year-End Adjustment

On December 31, three months' interest of $6,000 ($\frac{3}{6} \times$ $12,000$) has accrued, as well as $276.50 ($\frac{3}{6}$ of 553), the second-period discount shown on the amortization schedule. The adjusting year-end entry in Figure 20.15 is prepared.

FIGURE 20.15 Year-End Adjustment

Dec.	31	Bond Interest Expense	6 2 7 6 50		
		Discount on Bonds Payable		2 7 6 50	
		Bond Interest Payable		6 0 0 0 00	
		Year-end adjustment			

> Bond Interest Expense:
> $12,553 \times \frac{3}{6} = $6,276.50$

> Bond Interest Payable:
> $12,000 \times \frac{3}{6} = 6,000$

The reversing entry on January 1 and the entry to record payment of interest on April 1 would look like Figure 20.16.

FIGURE 20.16 Reversing Entry and Payment of Interest

Jan.	1	Bond Interest Payable	6 0 0 0 00		
		Discount on Bonds Payable	2 7 6 50		
		Bond Interest Expense		6 2 7 6 50	
		Reversing entry			
Apr.	1	Bond Interest Expense	12 5 5 3 00		
		Discount on Bonds Payable		5 5 3 00	
		Cash		12 0 0 0 00	
		Semiannual interest and amortization of			
		discount			

Amortizing the Bond Premium by the Interest Method

Yang Corporation issues on April 1 $200,000 of 12%, 10-year bonds with interest paid on October 1 and April 1. The selling price of the bonds is $224,926. The market interest rate is 10%. The amortization schedule is shown in Table 20.5. On October 1 the entry in Figure 20.17 records the semiannual payment.

FIGURE 20.17 Paid Interest and Amortized Premium by Interest Method

Oct.	1	Bond Interest Expense	11 2 4 6 00		
		Premium on Bonds Payable	7 5 4 00		
		Cash		12 0 0 0 00	
		Semiannual interest and premium			
		amortization			

TABLE 20.5	Amortization Schedule for Bond Premium for Each Semiannual Period Using the Interest Method				
Period	(1) Carrying Value, Beg. of Period	(2) Interest Paid to Bondholder (.06 × Face Value)	(3) Interest Expense Recorded (.05 × Carrying Value)	(4) Premium to Be Amortized	(5) Carrying Value, End of Period
1	$224,926	$12,000	$11,246	$ 754	$224,172 ($224,926 − $754)
2	224,172	12,000	11,209	791	223,381
19	203,726	12,000	10,186	1,814	201,912
20	201,912	12,000	10,088	1,912	200,000

Note: Column 4 is the difference between columns 2 and 3. Column 5 is column 1 minus column 4.

Year-End Adjustment

It should be noted that on December 31, three months' interest has accrued as well as the need to amortize half the premium (for the second period). The journal entry in Figure 20.18 records this year-end adjustment.

Dec.	31	Bond Interest Expense	5 6 0 4 50		
		Premium on Bonds Payable	3 9 5 50		
		Bond Interest Payable		6 0 0 0 00	
		Year-end adjustment			

FIGURE 20.18 Year-End Adjustment

Bond Interest Expense: $\frac{3}{6}$ × $11,209 = $5,604.50
Premium on Bonds Payable: $\frac{3}{6}$ × $791 = $395.50
Bond Interest Payable: $\frac{3}{6}$ × $12,000 = $6,000

The reversing entry on January 1 and the payment of interest in April would look like Figure 20.19.

Jan.	1	Bond Interest Payable	6 0 0 0 00		
		Premium on Bonds Payable		3 9 5 50	
		Bond Interest Expense		5 6 0 4 50	
		Reversing entry			
Apr.	1	Bond Interest Expense	11 2 0 9 00		
		Premium on Bonds Payable	7 9 1 00		
		Cash		12 0 0 0 00	
		Semiannual interest and amortization of			
		premium			

FIGURE 20.19 Reversing Entry and Payment of Interest

LEARNING UNIT 20-3 REVIEW

AT THIS POINT / you should be able to

- Prepare an amortization schedule for bond discounts using the interest method.
- Prepare an amortization schedule for bond premiums using the interest method.
- Journalize year-end adjustments.

Self-Review Quiz 20-3

Prepare a partial amortization schedule like the preceding one using the interest method for the first three periods based on the following facts: 100, 12%, 10-year, $1,000 bonds issued at a selling price of $89,404. Assume a market rate of 14%.

Solution to Self-Review Quiz 20-3

Period	(1) Carrying Amount, Beg. of Period	(2) Interest Paid to Bondholders (.06 × Face Value)	(3) Interest Expense Recorded (.07 × Carrying Value)	(4) Discount to Be Amortized	(5) Carrying Amount, End of Period
1	$89,404	$6,000	$6,258	$258	$89,662
2	89,662	6,000	6,276	276	89,938
3	89,938	6,000	6,296	296	90,234

LO4 Learning Unit 20-4 Retirement of Bonds and Bond Sinking Funds

In the first unit of this chapter we mentioned callable bonds, which permit the corporation to reacquire bonds at a price based on a percentage of face value. Some corporations retire them and issue new bonds (called *bond refunding*) to take their place, paying a lower rate of interest. If this call provision doesn't exist, a company can repurchase its bonds in the open market and then retire them. By retiring bonds, companies can decrease the amount of debt they owe. If interest rates are high, the retirement of bonds could result in substantial cash savings, even if new bonds are issued at lower rates.

When the bonds are retired before they reach maturity, the following points must be recognized:

1. Any amortization of discount or premium must be brought up-to-date at the time of retirement.
2. The premium or discount as well as the bond liability account must be removed.
3. Any gain or loss is recognized on the retirement of the bonds as an extraordinary item that will be shown on the income statement.

Let's use Roberts Corporation as an example. On June 30 the corporation retired a $500,000, 10% bond issue that had an unamortized premium of $19,000. The bonds were called in at 105 (105% of face value). All journal entries relating to interest payments and premium amortization were completed before the bonds' retirement. The entry to record the retirement of the bonds by Roberts Corporation would look like Figure 20.20.

FIGURE 20.20 Retirement of Bond

Bonds Payable	500 00 0 00	
Premium on Bonds Payable	19 00 0 00	
Loss on Bond Retirement	6 00 0 00	
Cash		525 00 0 00
Retirement of bond		

Note that the difference between the bond carrying value of $519,000 ($500,000 + $19,000) and actual cash paid results in the loss of $6,000. Of course, if the carrying value were greater than the cash paid, a gain would be realized.

The Bond Sinking Fund

Often a corporation will agree to establish a fund that will accumulate assets over the life of the bond so as to pay off the bondholders at maturity. In fact, such a fund is often a requirement stated in the bond indentures. This fund is called a **sinking fund.**

For example, Morrel Corporation issued 8%, 15-year bonds for $80,000, agreeing to deposit $2,946.40 at the end of the year so that by the end of the 15th year the fund would contain $80,000 to pay off bondholders. Sinking fund tables are available that make these periodic deposits easy to calculate. For example, Morrel's accountant would go to a sinking fund table and look up 8% for 15 periods and find a table factor of .0368295. By multiplying $80,000 × .0368295, one comes up with a yearly deposit of $2,946.40, which, at this rate of interest compounded annually, will at the end of 15 years bring a total of $80,000.

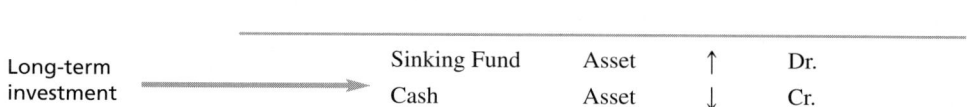

| Long-term investment | Sinking Fund | Asset | ↑ | Dr. |
| | Cash | Asset | ↓ | Cr. |

The journal entries for Morrel Corporation for establishing the sinking fund appear in Figure 20.21.

Sinking Fund		2 9 4 6 40	
Cash			2 9 4 6 40
Establishing sinking fund			

FIGURE 20.21 Sinking Fund Established

When interest is earned on the balance in the sinking fund, the **Sinking Fund Interest Earned** account is credited and the following entry results (Fig. 20.22):

Sinking Fund	Asset	↑	Dr.
Sinking Fund Interest Earned	Other Revenue	↑	Cr.

Sinking Fund		2 3 5 71	
Sinking Fund Interest Earned			
($2,946.40 x .08)			2 3 5 71
Interest earned			

FIGURE 20.22 Interest Earned on Sinking Fund

When the bonds are paid off, a little more or less cash than is needed may be in the sinking fund. The entry to record the payment of the bonds by Morrel is shown in Figure 20.23 (assume $50 extra in the sinking fund).

Cash		5 0 00	
Bonds Payable	80 0 0 00		
Bond Sinking Fund			80 0 5 0 00
Payment of bonds			

FIGURE 20.23 Payoff of Bonds

Keep in mind that the money in the sinking fund cannot be used to meet other current expenses or liabilities. Thus, the sinking fund is recorded in the long-term investment section of the balance sheet. Any cash left over is returned to the Cash account.

LEARNING UNIT 20-4 REVIEW

AT THIS POINT you should be able to

- Journalize the gain or loss on the retirement of bonds.
- Explain as well as journalize entries relating to sinking funds.

Self-Review Quiz 20-4

Journalize the following transactions:

    a. Retired $300,000 of bonds that had a $20,000 premium for 106.
    b. Set up a sinking fund account with an initial deposit of $3,000.
    c. Earned $325 interest on the sinking fund balance.
    d. Sinking fund of $90,000 was used to retire bondholders' amount of $90,000.

Solution to Self-Review Quiz 20-4

FIGURE 20.24 Bond Transactions

(a)	Bonds Payable	300 0 0 0 00		
	Premium on Bonds	20 0 0 0 00		
	Cash		318 0 0 0 00	
	Gain on Retirement		2 0 0 0 00	
(b)	Sinking Fund	3 0 0 0 00		
	Cash		3 0 0 0 00	
(c)	Sinking Fund	3 2 5 00		
	Sinking Fund Interest Earned		3 2 5 00	
(d)	Bonds Payable	9 0 0 0 0 00		
	Sinking Fund		9 0 0 0 0 00	

CHAPTER ASSIGNMENTS

SUMMARY OF KEY POINTS

LEARNING UNIT 20-1

1. Bond certificates state face value and contract rate of interest.
2. A bond indenture is a formal agreement that spells out specifics of the bond issue. The trustee, usually a bank, makes sure the bond indenture is fulfilled.
3. Bonds are negotiable and are quoted in the market as a percentage of the face value. For example, 95 means 95% of a $1,000 bond, or $950.
4. Many types of bonds are issued. In this chapter we discuss secured, debenture, serial, registered, callable, and convertible bonds.
5. To a corporation trying to decide whether to issue stocks or bonds to raise money, an important difference between stocks and bonds is that stock dividends are a distribution of net income *after* tax, whereas bond interest expense is deductible from earnings *before* tax.
6. If bonds are sold between interest dates, the buyer pays the price of the bond plus accrued interest. This accrued interest is paid back when the semiannual interest payment is made.

LEARNING UNIT 20-2

1. By the time a bond is actually issued, the contract rate of interest may be lower or higher than the effective or actual market rate.
2. A bond discount means that the issue price of bonds is less than the face value.
3. A bond premium means that the issue price of bonds is greater than the face value.
4. Discount on Notes Payable is a contra-liability found on the balance sheet. It is not an immediate expense. It will be amortized at the time of the interest payment and thus will increase the total interest expense.
5. The straight-line method of amortizing bond discounts transfers an equal amount of bond discount to interest expense over equal periods of time.
6. Premium on Bonds Payable is a liability found on the balance sheet. It will be amortized at each semiannual payment to decrease interest expense over the life of the bond.

LEARNING UNIT 20-3

1. In the interest method of amortizing a bond discount or premium, interest expense is a constant *percentage* of the carrying value of the bonds. Thus, interest amount will *not* be constant each period.
2. The amortization of the period is the difference between interest expense to be recorded and interest expense paid to bondholders.

LEARNING UNIT 20-4

1. When bonds are retired before their maturity date
   a. amortization of the bond discount or premium must be up-to-date.
   b. the bond liability and either the discount or the premium must be removed.
   c. a gain or loss is recognized as an extraordinary item on the income statement.
2. A bond sinking fund is set up by a corporation to pay bondholders at maturity.
3. The sinking fund is an asset on the balance sheet under long-term investments.

KEY TERMS

Amortization of discount on bonds payable, amortization of premium on bonds payable Writing off the bond premium or discount as a decrease or increase to interest expense for each interest period.

Bond An interest-bearing note payable usually in $1,000 denominations issued by a corporation to a large group of lenders.

Bond certificate A piece of paper held by bondholder showing evidence of a bond(s) issued by a corporation to be payable on a specified date for a specific sum to the order of the person named in the bond certificate or to the bearer.

Bond indenture A contract that spells out the provisions of the contract between the corporation and bondholder.

Callable bond Bond with a provision that it can be called in by a corporation after a certain date.

Carrying value (book value) Face value of bond less bond discount or plus bond premium.

Contract rate Rate of interest (based on face value) stated on bond certificate and bond indenture.

Convertible bond Bondholders have the option of converting bonds into stock at a specified exchange rate.

Debenture bonds Bonds that are unsecured and are issued only on the general credit of a corporation.

Discount on Bonds Payable Account used when bonds are issued below face value; indicates market rate of interest is higher than contract rate. This account is a contra-liability account.

Effective rate The real or actual rate of interest to the borrowing corporation.

Face value The amount the corporation must repay to the bondholder at the maturity date.

Interest method of amortization This method amortizes the premium or discount to *record* interest expense, being equal to the carrying value of the bond times the market rate times the time period. The interest expense is a constant percentage of the carrying value. The discount or premium to be amortized is the difference between the interest to be recorded and the interest paid to bondholders.

Premium on Bonds Payable Account used when bonds are issued above face value; it indicates that market rate is below contract rate. This account is a liability account.

Registered bond Bondholders of record are registered with the corporation, and interest checks are sent directly to them.

Secured bond Bond issued by a corporation that pledges specific assets as security to meet the terms of the bond agreement.

Serial bonds Bonds issued in a series, each one of which has a different maturity date and thus comes due at a different time.

Sinking fund A fund that accumulates cash to pay off bonds when they are retired.

Sinking Fund Earned Other revenue account used to record earnings on sinking fund balance.

Straight-line method A method recognizing equal amounts of interest expense for each period when amortizing a bond discount or premium.

Trustee Organization (usually a bank) or person who monitors a bond indenture for the protection of bondholders.

BLUEPRINT: STOCKS VS. BONDS

Stocks	Bonds
1. Stockholders are the owners of the corporation.	1. Bondholders are creditors to a corporation.
2. Stockholders are paid off in liquidation only after claims of creditors are satisfied.	2. Bondholders, in liquidation, have claims on assets (along with other creditors) before stockholders.
3. Dividends are paid only if earnings are sufficient; no fixed charge is associated with stocks as with bond interest. Preferred stock has a fixed dividend rate. Dividends are not an expense; they are a distribution of income.	3. Interest expense is a fixed charge. Failure to pay could result in creditors bringing bankruptcy proceedings against the corporation.
4. Stockholders have voting rights except with preferred stock.	4. Bondholders have no voting rights.
5. Dividends are deducted *after* tax on earnings.	5. Interest is deductible from earnings *before* tax.
6. Stockholders continue to receive dividends; they are not "paid off."	6. Bondholders are eventually repaid the principal.

QUESTIONS, CLASSROOM DEMONSTRATION EXERCISES, EXERCISES, AND PROBLEMS

Discussion and Critical Thinking Questions/Ethical Case

1. Explain the selling price of a bond quoted at 99.

2. What is the difference between a secured bond and a debenture bond?

3. Dividends reduce earnings before taxes. True or false? Explain.

4. Accrued interest results in the seller paying extra for bonds. True or false? Explain.

5. Explain why a bond may sell at a premium.

6. Why isn't Discount on Bonds Payable an immediate expense?

7. Premium on Bonds Payable will cause total interest expense to be reduced. True or false?

8. The straight-line method of amortizing a bond discount or premium will result in an uneven amount of discount or premium that increases or decreases expense each period. Agree or disagree? Why?

9. What is the carrying value of a bond?

10. Why does the interest method of amortizing a discount or premium use the market rate in calculating interest expense to be recorded?

11. Explain how a gain or loss on retirement of bonds before the maturity date is recorded.

12. What is the purpose of a bond sinking fund?

13. Alice wants to buy bonds, but her husband, Pete, thinks stocks would be a better deal. Pete was watching a finance show on TV that said stocks would be going up and that now is the time to buy stock. He called Alice over and said, "I told you so." Alice told her husband that it was no time to take a risk with their money. Do you think Pete is correct in his thinking? You make the call. Write down your recommendations to Alice and her husband.

Classroom Demonstration Exercises

SET A

Bond Journal Entries *LO1 (15 min)*

1. Journalize the following transactions:
  a. Issued six $30,000, 4% bonds that mature in 20 years at face value on January 1.
  b. Paid semiannual interest on June 30.
  c. Bonds retired at end of 20 years.

Bond Issued at a Discount *LO1 (10 min)*

2. On January 1, Borg Co. issued ten $2,000, 6%, 10-year bonds at 96. Record the journal entry.

Interest and Amortization of Discount *LO2 (10 min)*

3. From Exercise 2, record on June 30 the semiannual payment and amortization of the discount.

Bond Issued at Premium *LO1 (15 min)*

4. Redo Exercise 2 with the straight-line method assuming the bond sells for 106.

Interest and Amortization of Premium with Straight-Line Method *LO2 (15 min)*

5. From Exercise 4, record on June 30 the semiannual payment and amortization of premium on bonds payable.

Amortization of Bond Discount by Interest Method *LO2 (20 min)*

6. *Facts:* Bond issue: $100,000, 5%, 10-year bonds; selling price of bonds $80,000. Market rate 9%. Calculate the following:
  a. Carrying value beginning of period
  b. Interest paid to bondholders every six months
  c. Interest expense each six-month period to be recorded
  d. Discount to be amortized
  e. Carrying value end of period

Journalizing the Semiannual Payment of Amortization of Discount *LO2 (10 min)*

7. From Exercise 6, record a journal entry for the first semiannual interest payment on October 1.

Amortization of Bond Premium by Interest Method *LO2 (20 min)*

8. *Facts:* Bond issue: $100,000, 5%, 10-year bonds; selling price of bonds $115,000. Market rate 4%. Calculate the following:
  a. Carrying value beginning of period
  b. Interest paid to bondholders each six months
  c. Interest expense each six-month period
  d. Premium to be amortized
  e. Carrying value at end of period

Journalizing the Semiannual Payment and Amortization of Bond Premium *LO2 (10 min)*

9. From Exercise 8, record the journal entry for the first semiannual interest payment on October 1.

Sinking Fund *LO4 (10 min)*

10. Journalize the following transactions:
  a. Set up a sinking fund with an initial deposit of $6,000.
  b. Earned $150 interest on sinking fund balance.
  c. Sinking fund of $20,000 was used to pay off bondholders in the amount of $20,000.

SET B

LO1 (15 min)   **Bond Journal Entries**

1. Journalize the following transactions:
   a. Issued five $10,000, 6% bonds that mature in 20 years at face value on January 1.
   b. Paid semiannual interest on June 30.
   c. Bonds retired at end of 20 years.

LO1 (10 min)   **Bond Issued at a Discount**

2. On January 1, Borg Co. issued ten $1,000, 6%, 10-year bonds at 96. Record the journal entry.

LO2 (10 min)   **Interest and Amortization of Discount**

3. From Exercise 2, record on June 30 the semiannual payment and amortization of the discount.

LO1 (15 min)   **Bond Issued at Premium**

4. Redo Exercise 2 with the straight-line method assuming the bond sells for 105.

LO2 (15 min)   **Interest and Amortization of Premium with Straight-Line Method**

5. From Exercise 4, record on June 30 the semiannual payment and amortization of premium on bonds payable.

LO2 (10 min)   **Amortization of Bond Discount by Interest Method**

6. *Facts:* Bond issue: $100,000, 6%, 10-year bonds; selling price of bonds $78,000. Market rate 8%. Calculate the following:
   a. Carrying value beginning of period
   b. Interest paid to bondholders every six months
   c. Interest expense each six-month period to be recorded
   d. Discount to be amortized
   e. Carrying value end of period

LO2 (10 min)   **Journalizing the Semiannual Payment of Amortization of Discount**

7. From Exercise 6, record a journal entry for the first semiannual interest payment on October 1.

LO2 (20 min)   **Amortization of Bond Premium by Interest Method**

8. *Facts:* Bond issue: $100,000, 6%, 10-year bonds; selling price of bonds $120,000. Market rate 4%. Calculate the following:
   a. Carrying value beginning of period
   b. Interest paid to bondholders each six months
   c. Interest expense each six-month period
   d. Premium to be amortized
   e. Carrying value at end of period

LO2 (10 min)   **Journalizing the Semiannual Payment and Amortization of Bond Premium**

9. From Exercise 8, record the journal entry for the first semiannual interest payment on October 1.

LO4 (10 min)   **Sinking Fund**

10. Journalize the following transactions:
    a. Set up a sinking fund with an initial deposit of $5,000.
    b. Earned $110 interest on sinking fund balance.
    c. Sinking fund of $15,000 was used to pay off bondholders in the amount of $15,000.

Exercises

20-1. Ryan Corporation and Hayes Corporation have both earned $100,000 before bond interest and taxes. The companies have the same number of outstanding shares but different capital structures. Calculate the earnings per share of common stock for both companies from the following:

LO1 (30 min)

	Ryan	Hayes
10% bond payable	200,000	— 0 —
10% preferred stock	— 0 —	200,000
Common stock $10 par, 30,000 shares outstanding	300,000	300,000
Operating income before interest and income taxes (assume a 30% tax rate)	100,000	100,000

20-2. On January 1, 20XX, Alpha Corporation issued $800,000 of 10%, 30-year bonds to lenders at par (100). Interest is to be paid semiannually on July 1 and January 1. Journalize the following entries:
  a. Issued the bonds.
  b. Paid semiannual interest payment.
  c. Retirement of bonds, assuming interest expense is up-to-date.

LO1 (30 min)

20-3. Quick Corporation issued $300,000 of 10%, 10-year bonds at 98 on May 1, 20XX, with semiannual interest payable on May 1 and November 1. Amortization of discount is by the straight-line method. Record the journal entries for the following:
  a. Issuance of bonds.
  b. Semiannual interest payment on November 1 and amortization of discount.
  c. Retirement of bonds at maturity.

LO1, 2 (50 min)

20-4. Redo the journal entries for Exercise 20-3 assuming bonds sold at 102.

LO1, 2 (50 min)

20-5. On July 1 Jonald Corporation issued 10%, 10-year bonds with a face value of $100,000 for $90,000, because the current market rate is 12%. Record the following entries, assuming the *interest method* is used to amortize the discount on bonds. Round discount to nearest dollar.
  a. Issuance of bonds.
  b. Semiannual interest payment on December 31 and amortization of discount.
  c. Semiannual interest payment on June 30 and amortization of discount.

LO1, 2 (50 min)

20-6. On January 1 Last Corporation sold $350,000 of 10-year sinking fund bonds. The corporation expects to earn 10% on the sinking fund balance and is required to deposit $23,609 at the end of each year with the trustee. Record the following entries:
  a. The first deposit.
  b. Earnings of $2,361 at end of first period.
  c. Payment of bondholders with sinking fund having a balance of $350,500.

LO4 (35 min)

20-7. From the following prepare the long-term liabilities section of a balance sheet:
  a. Sinking fund $300,000
  b. Premium on 10% bonds   3,000
  c. Discount on 12% bonds   5,000
  d. 10% Bonds Payable   500,000
  e. 12% Bonds Payable   200,000

LO4 (30 min)

Group A Problems

LO1, 2 (60 min)

20A-1. On January 1, 20X5, Lester Corporation sold $400,000 of 8%, 10-year bonds at 97. Interest is to be paid on June 30 and December 31. The straight-line method of amortizing the discount is used. Prepare (1) an amortization schedule for the first three semiannual periods and (2) journal entries to record the following:

    a. Bond issue on January 1.

    b. Semiannual interest payments on June 30 and December 31 for interest and amortization of discount.

    c. If the bonds were issued on March 1 and interest was paid on September 1 and March 1, what would be the year-end adjusting entry on December 31 to record accrued interest and amortization of discount?

Check Figure:
Amortized discount each
period = $600

LO1, 2 (60 min)

20A-2. On May 1, 20X5, Deever Corporation issued $500,000 of 10%, 20-year bonds at 102. The interest is payable on November 1 and May 1. The premium is amortized by the straight-line method. Prepare an amortization schedule for the first three semiannual periods and journalize the following transactions:

Check Figure:
Amortized premium $250

20X5		
May	1	Bonds issued.
Nov.	1	Paid semiannual interest and amortized premium.
Dec.	31	Accrued bond interest and amortized premium.

LO1, 2, 3 (70 min)

20A-3. On January 1, 20X7, Vex Corporation issued $300,000 of 10%, 10-year bonds for $257,616, yielding a market rate of 12%. Interest is paid on July 1 and December 31. Vex uses the interest method to amortize the discount.

    1. Prepare an amortization schedule for the first three semiannual periods.

    2. Prepare journal entries to record:

        a. Bond issuance on January 1.

        b. Semiannual interest payments on July 1 and December 31 as well as amortization of discount.

    3. If the bond were issued on March 1 and interest was paid on September 1 and March 1, what would be the year-end adjusting entry on December 31, 20X7, to record accrued interest and amortization of discount?

Check Figure:
Discount to be amortized
Period 1 $456.96

LO1, 2, 3 (70 min)

20A-4. On April 1, 20X6, Potter Corporation issued $200,000 of 10%, 5-year bonds for $204,100, yielding a market rate of 9%. Interest is paid on October 1 and April 1. Potter Corporation uses the interest method to amortize the premium.

    1. Prepare an amortization schedule for the first three semiannual periods.

    2. Prepare journal entries to record the following:

        a. Bond issuance on April 1.

        b. Semiannual interest payment and amortization of premium on October 1.

        c. The year-end adjusting entry to record expense and premium amortization.

Check Figure:
Premium to be amortized
period 1 $815.50

Group B Problems

LO1, 2 (60 min)

20B-1. On January 1, 20X6, Lester Corporation sold $300,000 of 12%, 10-year bonds at 92. Interest is to be paid on June 30 and December 31. The straight-line method of amortizing the discount is used. Prepare (1) an amortization schedule for the first three semiannual periods and (2) journal entries to record (a) the bond issue on January 1 and (b) semiannual interest payments on June 30 and December 31 for interest and amortization of discount. (c) If the bonds were issued on March 1 and interest was paid on September 1 and March 1, what would be the year-end adjusting entry on December 31 to record interest payment and amortization of discount?

20B-2. On April 1, 20X6, Deever Corporation issued $600,000 of 6%, 10-year bonds at 104. The interest is payable on October 1 and April 1. The premium is amortized by the straight-line method. Prepare an amortization schedule for the first three semiannual periods and journalize the following transactions:

LO1, 2 (60 min)

20X6		
Apr.	1	Bonds issued
Oct.	1	Paid semiannual interest and amortization of premium.
Dec.	31	Accrued bond interest and amortization premium.

Check Figure:
Amortized discount $1,200

Check Figure:
Amortized premium $1,200

20B-3. On January 1, 20X8, Vex Corporation issued $400,000 of 12%, 10-year bonds for $350,937, yielding a market rate of 14%. Interest is paid on July 1 and December 31. Vex uses the interest method to amortize the discount. Prepare an amortization schedule for the first three semiannual periods and prepare journal entries to record the following:

LO1, 2, 3 (70 min)

a. Bond issuance on January 1.

b. Semiannual interest payment on July 1 and December 31 as well as amortization of discount.

Check Figure:
Discount to be amortized $565.59 (b)

If the bonds were issued on March 1 and interest was paid on September 1 and March 1, what would be the year-end adjusting entry on December 31, 20X8, to record accrued interest and amortization of discount?

20B-4. On March 1, 20X8, Potter Corporation issued $100,000 of 12%, 10-year bonds for $104,408, yielding a market rate of 10%. Interest is paid on September 1 and March 1. Potter Corporation uses the interest method to amortize the premium.

LO1, 2, 3 (70 min)

1. Prepare an amortization schedule for the first three semiannual periods.

2. Prepare journal entries to record the following:

a. Bond issuance on March 1.

b. Semiannual interest payment and amortization of premium on September 1.

c. The year-end adjusting entry to record interest expense and premium amortization.

Check Figure:
Premium to be amortized
Period 1 $779.60 (b)

ON-THE-JOB TRAINING

T-1. Ryan Small, president of Janis Corporation, hired you as a financial consultant to analyze three proposals made by the board of directors to raise additional funds of $3,000,000.

LO1, 2, 3 (60 min)

The Plans

1. Issued 12% preferred stock.

2. Issued additional common stock at $10 par.

3. Issue 14%, 20-year bonds.

Given

● Tax rate, 48%.

● Estimated corporation earnings, $1,800,000 annually before bond interest and taxes.

Assume

● Before plan, 300,000 shares of $10 par common stock outstanding. All new stock would be issued at par.

Please submit a written recommendation with supporting data to Mr. Small as soon as possible.

LO1, 2 (60 min) **T-2.** The board of directors of French Corporation is planning to announce a new 10-year bond issue of $300,000. The contract rate of the bonds is 12%. Owing to several delays, the bonds in the marketplace are now 14%.

The directors think this bond issue has to raise at least $280,000 in cash to meet its financial needs. As the company's financial consultant, calculate the actual selling price of the bonds and make appropriate written recommendations to the board of directors of French regarding the pros and cons of the bond issue.

Given

1. Present value of $1.00 at compound interest for 20 periods at 7% equals .2584.

2. Present value of $1.00 received periodically for 20 periods at 7% equals 10.5940.

FINANCIAL REPORT PROBLEM

LO1 (10 min) ## Reading the Kellogg's Annual Report

Go to Appendix A and find note 7 for Debt. What is Kellogg's scheduled repayment in long-term debt in 2006 (in millions)?

INTERNET PROJECT

Anheuser-Busch

Go to the Web and search: Annual Report Anheuser-Busch 2008.
Click on Investors Relations.
List out the latest news the Anheuser-Busch is providing to its investors.
Order a free annual report.

21

Statement of Cash Flows

DID YOU KNOW? Seasonality affects PepsiCo cash from operating activities. In 2006 cash flow from operations was 6.1 billion dollars. Products the company produces include Lay's potato chips, Quaker Oats, and Cap'n Crunch cereal. Visit *www.pepsico.com* to find more information about PepsiCo.

LEARNING OBJECTIVES

1. Understanding the purpose of a statement of cash flows.

2. Preparing the operating activities section of the statement of cash flows using the indirect method.

3. Preparing the operating activities section of the statement of cash flows using the direct method.

4. Preparing a statement of cash flows.

In preceding chapters we analyzed as well as prepared three financial statements. Let's quickly review the purposes of each statement.

- Income statement: Shows the results of the company's operations for a given period. The net income or loss results in an increase or decrease to retained earnings.
- Statement of retained earnings: Summarizes the changes in retained earnings of a company during a period of time.
- Balance sheet: Shows the end-of-period financial position of a company at a particular date.

LO1

In this chapter we turn our attention to a fourth major financial statement that is used to better understand the operating, investing, and financing activities of a company like PepsiCo. It is called the **statement of cash flows,** and it summarizes the sources and uses of cash by a company during an accounting period. It is easy to compute the change in cash balance by looking at the comparative balance sheet, but just the change in total cash tells us nothing about specific cash transactions. The statement of cash flows not only shows in detail the sources and uses of cash; it also gives readers of the financial statements a good basis for judging the possible future cash flows. Internal users of the financial statements (such as management) can also benefit by understanding how to read the statement of cash flows.

> Peachtree and QuickBooks recalculate each account as the transaction is recorded and saved. This features allows any financial statement, including the statement of cash flows, to be prepared at any point in time.

The Big Picture: Usefulness and Layout

Keep in mind that cash does not just refer to the amount of money a company has in the bank or on hand. Cash may include the following types of liquid assets that can be quickly turned into cash:

1. Money market accounts
2. Investment in government securities

Table 21.1 previews the parts of a cash flows statement that we will be looking at. In Learning Units 21-1 and 21-2 we will look at specifics. Use this table as a road map as you progress through the chapter.

TABLE 21.1

LAYOUT OF A CASH FLOWS STATEMENT

1. OPERATING ACTIVITIES (DAY-TO-DAY OPERATIONS OF A BUSINESS):
   - CASH INFLOWS:
     - sales of good and services
     - interest and dividends recieved
   - CASH OUTFLOWS:
     - payment of interest and expenses
     - payment of supplies for inventory, taxes, interest, and other expenses
2. INVESTING ACTIVITIES:
   - CASH INFLOWS:
     - sales of plant, property, and equipment
     - collecting loans and/or interest
     - selling debt and stocks of other companies
   - CASH OUTFLOWS:
     - buying plant, property, and equipment
     - making loans and/or interest
     - buying debt and stocks of other companies
3. FINANCING ACTIVITIES:
   - CASH INFLOWS:
     - issuing bonds and notes
     - selling common stock

TABLE 21.1 **(continued)**

LAYOUT OF A CASH FLOWS STATEMENT

CASH OUTFLOWS:

      paying dividends

      buying back own stock

      redeeming long-term debt

Let's now look at two different ways we will prepare the operating activities. In Learning Unit 21-1 we will look at the indirect method and in Learning Unit 21-2 we will look at the direct method. Table 21.2 presents the big picture of both approaches.

TABLE 21.2	
INDIRECT METHOD	**DIRECT METHOD**
Reconciles net income to cash that is provided by operations	Will show all the cash receipts and payments from operating activities

BOTTOM LINE FOR BOTH METHODS

EACH METHOD WILL GIVE THE SAME AMOUNT OF CASH FROM OPERATIONS.

EACH METHOD HAS NO EFFECT ON INVESTING OR FINANCING ACTIVITIES.

Now let's look at Learning Unit 21-1.

Learning Unit 21-1 Statement of Cash Flows: Indirect Method

We use as our example in this chapter the Zabel Company, which sells soccer equipment and supplies. To prepare a statement of cash flows, we need to obtain information from the other financial statements prepared for the company: the income statement, the statement of retained earnings, and the balance sheet. These statements are shown in Figures 21.1, 21.2, and 21.3 on the following pages. Note that the balance sheet shown in Figure 21.3 is slightly different from the ones we have shown in the past. This one is a **comparative balance sheet,** which shows figures from two separate years side by side. We discuss this type of statement in more detail in Chapter 22.

    The statement of cash flows consists of three main sections: (1) net cash flows from operating activities, (2) net cash flows from investing activities, and (3) net cash flows from financing activities. Some of the complexities of this statement are beyond the scope of this text, but the following paragraphs contain a few examples of transactions reported in each of the three sections.

    Operating activities include selling products or services to customers. **Cash inflows** from operating activities include cash collected from customers. **Cash outflows** from operating activities include paying for merchandise inventory, salaries, rent, and other such expenses.

> Transactions with customers, vendors, and employees are *operating activities*.

    Investing activities include such things as purchase or sale of plant and equipment, buying stocks and bonds (of other companies), and making loans to other businesses or individuals.

> Transactions involving the purchase or sale of plant assets are *investing activities*.

    Financing activities include raising money by issuing stocks and bonds, repurchasing of the company's stock, and paying cash dividends to the stockholders.

    A fourth classification reported on the statement of cash flows is called **noncash investing and financing activities,** which includes such transactions as issuing shares of stock in exchange for assets such as land and buildings. Although cash is not involved, the event is reported because no other financial statement specifically discloses the transaction. If the stock was issued for cash (financing activity, a cash increase) and if we used the cash proceeds to purchase land and a building (investing activity, a cash decrease), the event would be disclosed on the statement of cash flows in two separate sections. Because our example is a noncash transaction, it can be reported on the statement of cash flows as a footnote or on a separate schedule listing such transactions.

FIGURE 21.1 Financial
Statement of Zabel

ZABEL COMPANY INCOME STATEMENT FOR YEAR ENDED DECEMBER 31, 2009			
Sales			$190 0 0 00
Cost of Goods Sold			106 0 0 00
Gross Profit			$ 84 0 0 00
Operating Expenses:			
Salary Expense	$ 51 0 4 0 00		
Insurance Expense	7 2 0 0 00		
Rent Expense	3 6 0 0 00		
Depreciation Expense	11 0 0 0 00		
Miscellaneous Expense	1 2 0 0 00		
Total Operating Expenses			74 0 4 0 00
Net Income			$ 9 9 6 0 00

FIGURE 21.2 Financial
Statement of Zabel

ZABEL COMPANY STATEMENT OF RETAINED EARNINGS FOR YEAR ENDED DECEMBER 31, 2009			
Retained Earnings, January 1, 2009			$ 38 1 4 0 00
Net Income for the Year	$ 9 9 6 0 00		
Less: Cash Dividends	8 0 0 0 00		
Increase in Retained Earnings			1 9 6 0 00
Retained Earnings, December 31, 2009			$ 40 1 0 0 00

LO2 Cash Flows from Operating Activities: Indirect Method

A business needs a positive cash flow to survive. A company's ability to raise money from financing activities (issuing stocks, bonds, or long-term notes) is often tied to its success in generating cash flow from its operations. The operating activities section of the statement of cash flows is therefore of great importance to potential investors and creditors.

This section introduces a procedure known as the **indirect method** of reporting cash flows from operating activities. Note that the distinction between the indirect method and the direct method (discussed in the next learning unit) only applies to the operating activities section of the statement of cash flows.

In the indirect method we are converting the net income on the income statement from the accrual basis to the cash basis. As we have been learning throughout this text, businesses normally report their net income on the accrual basis, which places the primary emphasis on *when* the revenues are earned and *when* the expenses are incurred.

The indirect method's name comes from the way we view the income statement. We begin with the bottom line of the income statement and work backward until we have computed net cash flow from operating activities. We begin the operating activities section with the net income as reported on the income statement (see Figure 21.4) and convert it from the accrual basis to the cash basis. Figure 21.4 shows how the net cash flows from operating activities are computed for the Zabel Company using the indirect method.

In this example, the first item to be added to the net income is Depreciation Expense. The depreciation is *added back* to net income because it was subtracted out as an expense on the income statement to derive the $9,960 net income. You will recall that when depreciation is recorded, the entry involves a debit to Depreciation Expense and a credit to Accumulated Depreciation. Neither of these accounts involves cash. Because depreciation is therefore a "noncash" expense, it is added back to net income when using the indirect method. Next, each of the current assets and current liabilities is examined to determine its effect on cash flow.

FIGURE 21.3 Comparative Balance Sheet for Zabel

ZABEL COMPANY COMPARATIVE BALANCE SHEET AS OF DECEMBER 31, 2008, AND DECEMBER 31, 2009			
Assets	2009	2008	Increase (Decrease)
Current Assets:			
Cash	$ 2 900 00	$ 2 480 00	$ 42 000
Accounts Receivable	19 560 00	14 720 00	4 840 00
Merchandise Inventory	30 000 00	32 000 00	(2 000 00)
Prepaid Insurance	600 00	400 00	200 00
Total Current Assets	$ 53 060 00	$ 49 600 00	$ 3 460 00
Plant and Equipment:			
Office Equipment	$ 96 000 00	$ 66 000 00	$ 30 000 00
Accum. Dep., Office Equipment	(37 200 00)	(26 200 00)	(11 000 00)
Total Plant and Equipment	$ 58 800 00	$ 39 800 00	$ 19 000 00
Total Assets	$111 860 00	$ 89 400 00	$ 22 460 00
Liabilities			
Current Liabilities:			
Notes Payable—Short Term (used to purchase inventory)	$ 17 400 00	$ 14 800 00	$ 2 600 00
Accounts Payable	360 00	460 00	(100 00)
Total Current Liabilities	$ 17 760 00	$ 15 260 00	$ 2 500 00
Long-Term Liabilities:			
Long-Term Note Payable	$ 28 000 00	$ 20 000 00	$ 8 000 00
Total Liabilities	$ 45 760 00	$ 35 260 00	$ 10 500 00
Stockholders' Equity			
Common Stock, $10 par	$ 11 000 00	$ 10 000 00	$ 1 000 00
Paid-In Capital in Excess of Par	15 000 00	6 000 00	9 000 00
Retained Earnings	40 100 00	38 140 00	1 960 00
Total Stockholders' Equity	$ 66 100 00	54 140 00	$ 11 960 00
Total Liabilities and Stockholders' Equity	$111 860 00	$ 89 400 00	$ 22 460 00

FIGURE 21.4 Statement of Cash Flows—Indirect Method

ZABEL COMPANY STATEMENT OF CASH FLOWS (INDIRECT METHOD) FOR YEAR ENDED DECEMBER 31, 2009		
Cash Flows from Operating Activities:		
Net Income from Operations	$ 9 960 00	
Add (deduct) Items to Convert Net Income from		
Accrual Basis to Cash Basis:		
Depreciation Expense	11 000 00	
Increase in Accounts Receivable	(4 840 00)	
Decrease in Merchandise Inventory	2 000 00	
Increase in Prepaid Insurance	(200 00)	
Increase in Notes Payable (Short Term)	2 600 00	
Decrease in Accounts Payable	(100 00)	
Net Cash Provided by Operating Activities		$ 20 420 00

The aid sheet shown in Figure 21.5 is useful for remembering whether to add or subtract a given item on the statement of cash flows. Alternatively, some instructors prefer the simple opposite effect/same effect approach. For current assets, cash flow has the *opposite effect,* whereas for current liabilities, the cash flow has the *same effect.* For example, the increase in Accounts Receivable (a current asset) must be subtracted, whereas the increase in Short-Term Notes Payable (a current liability) would be added.

FIGURE 21.5 Aid Sheet for Converting from Accrual Basis to Cash Basis

	Add to Net Income If This Account Has:	Deduct from Net Income If This Account Has:
Current Assets	DECREASED	INCREASED
Current Liabilities	INCREASED	DECREASED

After each of the items is listed with its proper sign, the entire list is combined with net income to compute the net cash provided by operating activities of $20,420. The term *net cash provided* by operating activities is commonly used if the result is positive, whereas *net cash used* in operating activities indicates that the result is negative. As you might imagine, the goal is to have a strong positive cash flow from operating activities. A negative operating cash flow cannot be tolerated for long. Investors and creditors would hesitate to provide funds to a firm that cannot generate a positive cash flow from its operating activities.

Cash Flows from Investing Activities

The cash flows from investing activities section of the statement of cash flows includes (1) the purchase and sale of other companies' stocks and bonds, (2) the buying and disposal of plant assets, and (3) making loans to other parties. We analyze the noncurrent accounts to find these activities. For example, the following transactions would be recorded in this section:

1. Sale or purchase of equipment
2. Sale or purchase of land
3. Cash spent to invest in other companies' stocks and bonds
4. Cash received from sales of stock or bond investments
5. Loaning cash to borrowers

On the balance sheet for Zabel Company, we see an increase in plant and equipment from 2006 to 2007 of $30,000. Thus, the cash outflow for equipment would be reported as shown in Figure 21.6.

FIGURE 21.6 Cash Outflow for Equipment

Cash Flows from Investing Activities		
Purchase of Plant Asset	$(30 0 0 0 00)	
Net Cash Flows Used in Investing Activities		$(30 0 0 0 00)

Cash Flows from Financing Activities

The cash flows from financing activities section of the statement of cash flows records transactions such as the following:

1. Issuance of long-term notes and bonds
2. Issuance of common stock
3. Purchasing and reissuing treasury stock
4. Payment of cash dividends
5. Retirement of bonds

From the comparative balance sheet for Zabel Company, we see that the Long-Term Notes Payable account increased by $8,000. This increase is shown as a source (increase) of cash, because an increase in Long-Term Notes Payable means that more cash has been borrowed and therefore has been received by the business. Also, note that the issuance of $10,000 of common stock has *increased* the cash flows, whereas the payment of $8,000 in dividends results in a *decrease* in cash flows. The end result is that net cash provided by financing activities has increased by $10,000, as shown in Figure 21.7.

Cash Flows from Financing Activities		
Issuance of Long-Term Note	$ 8 0 0 0 00	
Issuance of Common Stock	10 0 0 0 00	
Payment of Dividends	(8 0 0 0 00)	
Net Cash Flows Provided by Financing Activities		$ 10 0 0 0 00

FIGURE 21.7 Net Cash Flows Provided by Financing Activities

To arrive at net change in cash for the overall statement, we perform the following calculation:

Net Cash Provided by Operating Activities	$ 20,420
− Cash Flow Used by Investing Activities	$(30,000)
+ Net Cash Provided by Financing Activities	10,000
= Net Increase in Cash	$ 420

Figure 21.8 shows all three sections together in the statement of cash flows.

Note that at the bottom of the statement of cash flows the cash has increased by $420 (just as is shown for cash on the comparative balance sheet), but this report gives us a complete breakdown of just what caused the cash to increase by $420.

The statement of cash flows is helpful in evaluating, comparing, and predicting future cash flows. By dividing this report into three sections, creditors as well as investors can judge how cash flows from operations compared with those from investing or financing activities. For example, in the case of Zabel Company, an investor or a creditor can see a substantial reduction in cash in one area (investing) that is offset by an increase in cash from the other areas (operating and financing).

FIGURE 21.8 Statement of Cash Flows—Indirect Method

ZABEL COMPANY
STATEMENT OF CASH FLOWS (INDIRECT METHOD)
FOR YEAR ENDED DECEMBER 31, 2009

Net Cash Flows from Operating Activities		
Net Income	$ 9 9 6 0 00	
Add (Deduct) Items to Convert Net Income		
from Accrual Basis to Cash Basis:		
Depreciation Expense	11 0 0 0 00	
Increase in Accounts Receivable	(4 8 4 0 00)	
Decrease in Merchandise Inventory	2 0 0 0 00	
Increase in Prepaid Insurance	(2 0 0 00)	
Increase in Short-Term Notes Payable	2 6 0 0 00	
Decrease in Accounts Payable	(1 0 0 00)	
Net Cash Flows from Operating Activities		$ 20 4 2 0 00
Cash Flows from Investing Activities		
Purchase of Plant Asset	$(30 0 0 0 00)	
Net Cash Flows Used by Investing Activities		(30 0 0 0 00)
Cash Flows from Financing Activities		
Issuance of Long-Term Note	$ 8 0 0 0 00	
Issuance of Common Stock	10 0 0 0 00	
Payment of Dividends	(8 0 0 0 00)	
Net Cash Provided by Financing Activities		10 0 0 0 00
Net Increase in Cash		$ 4 2 0 00
Beginning Balance of Cash		2 4 8 0 00
Ending Balance of Cash		$ 2 9 0 0 00

A second approach, known as the direct method, gives a more useful presentation of cash flows from operating activities. Although this method gives more understandable data, many firms think it much easier to use the indirect method to prepare the reports. Regardless of the method used, the cash flows from operating activities will be the same. The direct method is illustrated in Learning Unit 21-2.

LEARNING UNIT 21-1 REVIEW

AT THIS POINT you should be able to

- Explain the components of a statement of cash flows.
- Calculate net cash flows from operating activities using the indirect method.
- Calculate net cash flows from investing activities.
- Calculate net cash flows from financing activities.
- Prepare a complete statement of cash flows using the indirect method.

Self Review Quiz 21-1

From Figure 21.9, calculate net cash flows from operating activities.

FIGURE 21.9 Income Statement for Johnson Company

JOHNSON COMPANY INCOME STATEMENT FOR YEAR ENDED DECEMBER 31, 2009		
Sales		$150 000 00
Cost of Goods Sold		90 000 00
Gross Profit		$ 60 000 00
Operating Expenses:		
Salary Expense	$40 000 00	
Depreciation Expense	3 000 00	
Advertising Expense	8 000 00	
Total Operating Expenses:		51 000 00
Net Income		$ 9 000 00

Additional Data	2001	2000
Accounts Receivable	$ 10 600 00	$ 4 000 00
Merchandise Inventory	10 000 00	12 000 00
Prepaid Advertising	1 400 00	3 000 00
Accounts Payable	18 000 00	15 000 00
Salaries Payable	1 800 00	1 900 00

Solution to Self-Review Quiz 21-1

FIGURE 21.10 Net Cash Flows from Operating Activities

Net Cash Flows from Operating Activities:	
Net Income	
Add (deduct) Items to Convert Net Income to Cash	$ 9 000 00
Basis from the Accrual Basis:	
Depreciation Expense	3 000 00
Increase in Accounts Receivable	(6 600 00)
Decrease in Merchandise Inventory	2 000 00
Decrease in Prepaid Advertising	$ 1 600 00
Increase in Accounts Payable	3 000 00
Decrease in Salaries Payable	(1 00 00)
Net Cash Flow from Operating Activities:	$ 11 900 00

Learning Unit 21-2 Statement of Cash Flows: Direct Method

LO3, 4

As indicated in Learning Unit 21-1, cash flows from operating activities include the cash effects of transactions such as selling goods or services to customers and paying for merchandise inventory and operating expenses. Many accountants prefer the **direct method** of reporting the cash flows from operating activities. This approach provides useful information and is easily understood by the users of the financial statements.

The direct method requires listing major groups of operating cash receipts and cash payments. We first compute cash receipts from customers. Because most firms sell products or services on account as well as for cash, the sales figure on the income statement is not the same as total cash received. We analyze Accounts Receivable and combine its change (increase or decrease) with the sales figure from the income statement. An *increase* in Accounts Receivable results in a negative impact on cash, so the amount of the increase is *subtracted* from sales. A *decrease* in Accounts Receivable results in a positive effect on cash, so the amount of the decrease is *added* to sales. Thus, for computing cash received from customers, we can treat Accounts Receivable as we did in the indirect method by using the *opposite effect*.

The same reasoning applies to cash payments, except that because these payments are outflows of cash, any change with a *positive* cash effect is *subtracted* (because a positive effect means less cash to pay out). Any change with a *negative* cash effect is *added* (because a negative effect means more cash to pay out).

Our first example of an operating cash outflow is cash paid for merchandise inventory. We begin the computation with Cost of Goods Sold and then adjust by the change in the Merchandise Inventory account. A further adjustment is necessary to account for changes in Accounts Payable and Short-Term Notes Payable (if notes were used to pay for inventory, as in our example). Specifically, an *increase* in the balance of Merchandise Inventory means a *negative* cash effect that would be *added* in the computation of cash paid for merchandise. A *decrease* in Merchandise Inventory results in a *positive* cash effect that is *subtracted* to compute cash paid for merchandise. After adjusting for inventory changes, if Accounts Payable increased, the cash effect is positive and thus would be subtracted from the computation. If Accounts Payable decreased, the cash effect is negative and thus would be added to the calculation. The changes in Short-Term Notes Payable (assuming notes were used to pay for inventory) would be analyzed in the same way as Accounts Payable.

Cash paid for operating expenses is handled in much the same way as cash paid for merchandise inventory. Cash paid for salaries, for instance, is computed by combining the change in Salaries Payable with the amount of Salary Expense from the income statement. If Salaries Payable increased (positive cash effect), the amount of increase would be subtracted from Salary Expense. If this account decreased (negative cash effect), the amount of the decrease would be added to the Salary Expense.

For expenses involving a prepayment (such as Prepaid Insurance), the insurance expense balance would be combined with the change in Prepaid Insurance. If Prepaid Insurance increased (negative cash effect), the amount of the change would be added to insurance expense to compute cash paid for insurance. If Prepaid Insurance had decreased (positive cash effect), the amount of the change would be subtracted from insurance expense.

We now look at an example of the computation of net cash flow from operating activities. The Zabel Company computes cash received from customers by combining the sales figure from the income statement with the change in Accounts Receivable from the comparative balance sheet (see Figures 21.1 and 21.3). Sales is $190,000, and Accounts Receivable *increased* by $4,840. Because the increase in Accounts Receivable means a negative cash effect (more of our money is currently in the pockets of our customers!), it is *subtracted* from sales to arrive at the cash collected from customers figure of $185,160. This computation is illustrated in Figure 21.11 on the following page.

A second computation in Figure 21.11 shows cash paid for inventory. The Cost of Goods Sold figure is adjusted for changes in Merchandise Inventory, Accounts Payable, and Short-Term Notes Payable (if such notes are used to finance inventory). In our example, Cost of Goods Sold of $106,000 is adjusted by subtracting the decrease in Inventory ($2,000), subtracting the increase in Short-Term Notes Payable ($2,600), and adding the decrease in Accounts Payable ($100) to arrive at the Cash Paid for Inventory figure of $101,500.

Current Asset Increase: Negative effect on cash because more of our cash has been spent on that asset compared with the previous balance sheet date. Example: Inventory increasing means that more of our dollars are tied up in the inventory.

Current Asset Decrease: Positive effect on cash because less of our cash has been spent on that asset compared with the previous balance sheet date. Example: Inventory decreasing means that fewer of our dollars are tied up in the inventory.

Current Liability Increase: Positive effect on cash because compared with a year ago, less of the liability has been paid off (leaving more cash in our pockets).

Current Liability Decrease: Negative effect on cash because although we do not owe as much as we did a year ago, we have paid more of it off (and have less cash still in our pockets).

To summarize, we can still use the "same effect/opposite effect" reasoning mentioned in the previous learning unit. Current asset cash effects are always the opposite effect, whereas current liability cash effects are always the same effect.

FIGURE 21.11 Computations for Zabel Company's Net Cash Flows from Operating Activities

Cash Received from Customers = Sales $\begin{cases} + \text{Decrease in Accounts Receivable} \\ - \text{Increase in Accounts Receivable} \end{cases}$

$= \$190,000.00 \quad - \$4,840.00$

$= \$185,160.00$

Cash Paid for Inventory = COGS $\begin{cases} + \text{Increase in Inventory} \\ - \text{Decrease in Inventory} \end{cases}$ $\begin{cases} + \text{Decrease in Payables} \\ - \text{Increase in Payables} \end{cases}$

$= \$106,000.00 \quad - \$2,000.00 \qquad\qquad - \$2,600.00 + \$100.00$

$= \$101,500.00$

Cash Paid for Insurance = Insurance Expense $\begin{cases} + \text{Increase in Prepaid Insurance} \\ - \text{Decrease in Prepaid Insurance} \end{cases}$

$= \$7,200.00 \quad + \$200.00$

$= \$7,400.00$

Note: The other items on Zabel's net cash flows from operating activities section do not require any adjustment, because no changes occurred in current assets or current liabilities on the income statement figures for such items as salaries, rent, and miscellaneous expenses.

Cash Paid for Insurance is also illustrated in Figure 21.11 by adding the decrease in Prepaid Insurance to the Insurance Expense to yield $7,400 for Cash Paid for Insurance.

Figure 21.12 shows the complete statement of cash flows for the Zabel Company using the direct method. Note that the investing activities and financing activities sections are the same as in Figure 21.8, because the distinction between the indirect and direct methods only applies to the cash flows from operating activities section.

FIGURE 21.12 Statement of Cash Flows—Direct Method

ZABEL COMPANY STATEMENT OF CASH FLOWS—DIRECT METHOD FOR YEAR ENDED DECEMBER 31, 2009			
Net Cash Flows from Operating Activities			
Cash Received from Customers			$185 160 00
Cash Paid for Merchandise Inventory	$(101 500 00)		
Cash Paid for Salaries	(51 040 00)		
Cash Paid for Insurance	(7 400 00)		
Cash Paid for Rent	(3 600 00)		
Cash Paid for Miscellaneous Expenses	(1 200 00)		
Total Cash Paid for Operating Activities			(164 740 00)
Net Cash Flows from Operating Activities			$ 20 420 00
Cash Flows from Investing Activities			
Purchase of Plant Asset	$(30 000 00)		
Net Cash Used by Investing Activities			(30 000 00)
Cash Flows from Financing Activities			
Issuance of Long-Term Note	$ 8 000 00		
Issuance of Common Stock	10 000 00		
Payment of Dividends	(8 000 00)		
Net Cash Provided by Financing Activities			10 000 00
Net Increase in Cash			$ 420 00
Beginning Balance of Cash			2 480 00
Ending Balance of Cash			$ 2 900 00

LEARNING UNIT 21-2 REVIEW

AT THIS POINT / you should be able to

- Explain the difference between the direct method and the indirect method.
- Compute the net cash flows from operating activities section of the statement of cash flows.

Self-Review Quiz 21-2

Using the data from Self-Review Quiz 21-1, show in good form the cash flows from the operating activities section of the statement of cash flows for the Johnson Company using the direct method.

Solution to Self-Review Quiz 21-2

Net Cash Flows from Operating Activities:		
Cash Received from Customers		$143 4 0 0 00
Cash Paid for Merchandise Inventory	$ 85 0 0 0 00	
Cash Paid for Salaries	40 1 0 0 00	
Cash Paid for Advertising	6 4 0 0 00	
Total Cash Paid for Operating Activities		131 5 0 0 00
Net Cash Flows from Operating Activities:		$ 11 9 0 0 00

Explanations of computations:

Cash from Customers = Sales − Increase in Accounts Receivable
Cash Paid for Inventory = COGS − Decrease in Inventory − Increase in Accounts Payable
Cash Paid for Salaries = Salary Expense + Decrease in Salaries Payable
Cash Paid for Advertising = Advertising Expense − Decrease in Prepaid Advertising

FIGURE 21.13 Net Cash Flows from Operating Activities

CHAPTER ASSIGNMENTS

SUMMARY OF KEY POINTS

LEARNING UNIT 21-1

1. In the statement of cash flows, net change in cash equals net cash from operating activities plus or minus cash from investing activities plus or minus cash from financing activities.
2. In figuring the net cash from operating activities section of the statement, it is necessary to convert the net income from the income statement from the accrual basis to the cash basis. This change affects the following accounts: Depreciation Expense, Accounts Receivable, Inventory, Prepaid Expenses, Accounts Payable, and Short-Term Notes Payable. Note that we are analyzing current assets and current liabilities

to see their effect on net income. This approach to computing cash flows from operating activities is known as the indirect method.

3. Cash flows from investing activities include such things as purchase and sale of stocks and bonds (of other companies), buying and selling plant assets, and lending money to other parties.

4. Cash flows from financing activities include such things as issuing and repaying long-term notes and bonds, issuing common stock, buying back common stock (treasury stock), and paying dividends.

LEARNING UNIT 21-2

1. An alternative way of preparing the net cash from operating activities section of the statement is called the direct method.

2. The direct method requires listing separately the major categories of cash inflows and outflows. The major cash inflow for most firms is the cash received from customers, which is computed by adjusting the sales figure by the change in Accounts Receivable.

3. Cash outflows under the operating activities section include cash paid for inventory, cash paid for salaries, and cash paid for other operating expenses. In each case, the appropriate income statement figure is adjusted by the changes in one or more current asset or current liability accounts.

4. Regardless of the method selected, the net cash from operating activities will be the same. Also, the distinction between the direct and indirect methods only applies to net cash from operating activities. The investing and financing sections remain the same.

KEY TERMS

Cash inflow   Any increase in cash is called a cash inflow or a source of cash. When listing the total for a major section of the statement of cash flows, if cash is increased, the figure is often described as "cash provided" by operating activities (or by investing activities or financing activities).

Cash outflow   A decrease in cash is called a cash outflow or a use of cash. When listing a total for a major section of the statement of cash flows, if cash has decreased, the figure is often described as "cash used" in operating activities (or in investing activities or financing activities).

Comparative balance sheet   A balance sheet listing financial condition for two or more years in a side-by-side manner. This format allows the reader to make quick comparisons between the two balance sheet dates.

Direct method   One of two methods of preparing the net cash flow from operating activities section of the statement of cash flows. Each of the major areas of sources and uses of cash for operations is detailed separately.

Financing activities   Activities relating to raising money from investors and creditors such as the issuance of stocks and bonds and long-term notes; also, repurchase of outstanding stock and retiring bonds and notes as well as paying dividends.

Indirect method   One of two methods of preparing the net cash flow from the operating activities section of the statement of cash flows. Involves converting the accrual basis net income figure from the income statement to the cash basis net income.

Investing activities   Activities such as purchase and sale of plant and equipment and placing excess cash in stocks, bonds, and notes of other companies.

Noncash investing and financing activities   Transactions such as the issuance of stock in exchange for land would be listed in a footnote or a separate schedule to the statement of cash flows, because such transactions would not be reported separately on any other financial statement.

Operating activities   Those activities most closely related to conducting the business for which the enterprise was established. Activities such as selling merchandise and services to customers and paying salaries and other expenses needed to continue earning the operating revenue are classified as operating activities.

Statement of cash flows   A financial report that provides a detailed breakdown of the specific increases and decreases in cash during an accounting period. It helps readers of the statement evaluate past performance as well as predict future cash flows of the business.

BLUEPRINT: STATEMENT OF CASH FLOWS

Indirect Method

Net Cash Flows from Operating Activities		
Net Income		XXX
Add (Deduct) Items to Convert Net		
Income to Cash Basis:		
Depreciation Expense		XX
Increase in Accounts Receivable		(XX)
Decrease in Inventory		XX
Increase in Prepaid Expenses		(XX)
Increase in Accounts Payable		XX
Decrease in Salaries Payable		(XX)
Net Cash Flows from Operating Activities		XXX
Cash Flows from Investing Activities		
Purchase of Investment Securities	(XXX)	
Purchase of Equipment	(XXX)	
Sale of Land	XXX	
Cash Used by Investing Activities		(XXX)
Cash Flows from Financing Activities		
Issuance of Common Stock	XX	
Payment of Dividends	(X)	
Cash Provided by Financing Activities		XX
Net Increase in Cash		XXX
Beginning Balance of Cash		XXX
Ending Balance of Cash		XXX

Direct Method

Net Cash Flows from Operating Activities		
Cash Received from Customers		XXX
Cash Paid for Inventory	XXX	
Cash Paid for Salaries	XX	
Cash Paid for Insurance	X	
Cash Paid for Rent	X	
Cash Paid for Other Expenses	XX	
Total Cash Paid for Operations		XX
Net Cash Flows from Operating Activities		XXX

QUESTIONS, CLASSROOM DEMONSTRATION EXERCISES, EXERCISES, AND PROBLEMS

Discussion and Critical Thinking Questions/Ethical Case

1. List the three main sections of the statement of cash flows.

2. Explain how net cash flows from operating activities is calculated using the indirect method.

3. Explain how net cash flows from operating activities is calculated using the direct method.

4. The issuance of stock is an investing activity. Agree or disagree? Why?

5. Explain how a creditor might analyze a statement of cash flows.

6. Explain what is meant by financing activities.

7. Explain why depreciation is *added* to net income when using the indirect method.

8. Risch Company each year prepares an income statement and balance sheet. Tom Martin, the controller, issued a memo to Debbie Kreiger, vice president, that the company should prepare a statement of cash flows. Debbie called the controller and told him that she would not let a cash flows statement be published, that this type of information is for internal purposes only, and that the public has no right to these data. She said that the competition would kill them if they got this information. Do you agree with Debbie's position or with Tom's? Write your recommendation to Dave Risch, the chief executive officer.

Classroom Demonstration Exercises

SET A

LO1, 2 (15 min)   **Calculating Net Cash Flows from Operating Activities: Indirect Method**

1. The following accounts showed an increase or a decrease from the comparative balance sheet. Explain which account will be added to net income and which will be subtracted in calculating net cash flows for operating activities.
   a. Accounts Receivable: Decrease
   b. Inventory: Increase
   c. Short-Term Notes Payable: Decrease
   d. Accounts Payable: Increase

LO2 (20 min)   2. From the following, calculate the net cash flow from operating activities using the indirect method:

	2006	2007
Merchandise Inventory	$3,000	$3,500
Accounts Receivable	600	800
Prepaid Insurance	500	300
Accounts Payable	1,000	800
Salaries Payable	600	800
For the year ended 2007:		
Net Income		$2,100
Depreciation Expense		600

LO3 (30 min)   **Calculating Net Cash Flows from Operating Activities: Direct Method**

3. Using the data from Exercise 2 plus the additional information in Figure 21.14, compute net cash flows from operating activities using the direct method.

Sales				$ 7 9 0 0 00
Cost of Goods Sold				2 3 0 0 00
Gross Profit				$ 5 6 0 0 00
Expenses:				
Depreciation Expense	$ 6 0 0 00			
Salary Expense	2 2 0 0 00			
Insurance Expense	4 0 0 00			
Miscellaneous Expense	3 0 0 00			
Total Expenses			3 5 0 0 00	
Net Income			$ 2 1 0 0 00	

FIGURE 21.14 Income Statement

Calculating Cash Flows from Financing Activities

LO4 (15 min)

4. From the following, calculate net cash flows from financing activities:

Payments of dividends	$ 7,000
Issuance of common stock	2,500
Issuance of long-term note	16,000

Calculating Change in Cash

LO4 (15 min)

5. Given the following, calculate net change in cash:

Net cash flows from operating activities	$4,000
Net cash used by investing activities	(2,500)
Net cash provided by financing activities	900

SET B

Calculating Net Cash Flows from Operating Activities: Indirect Method

LO1, 2 (15 min)

1. The following accounts showed an increase or a decrease from the comparative balance sheet. Explain which account will be added to net income and which will be subtracted in calculating net cash flows for operating activities.
   a. Accounts Receivable: Increase
   b. Inventory: Decrease
   c. Short-Term Notes Payable: Increase
   d. Accounts Payable: Decrease

2. From the following, calculate the net cash flow from operating activities using the indirect method:

LO2 (20 min)

	2006	2007
Merchandise Inventory	$2,000	$2,500
Accounts Receivable	500	700
Prepaid Insurance	400	300
Accounts Payable	1,000	600
Salaries Payable	500	700

For the year ended 2007:

Net Income	$1,900
Depreciation Expense	500

LO3 (30 min)   **Calculating Net Cash Flows from Operating Activities: Direct Method**

3. Using the data from Exercise 2 plus the additional information in Figure 21.15, compute net cash flows from operating activities using the direct method.

FIGURE 21.15 Income Statement

Sales			$ 800000
Cost of Goods Sold			240000
Gross Profit			$ 560000
Expenses:			
Depreciation Expense	$ 50000		
Salary Expense	220000		
Insurance Expense	70000		
Miscellaneous Expense	30000		
Total Expenses		370000	
Net Income		$ 190000	

LO4 (15 min)   **Calculating Cash Flows from Financing Activities**

4. From the following, calculate net cash flows from financing activities:

Payments of dividends	$ 6,000
Issuance of common stock	2,000
Issuance of long-term note	14,000

LO4 (15 min)   **Calculating Change in Cash**

5. Given the following, calculate net change in cash:

Net cash flows from operating activities	$3,000
Net cash used by investing activities	(1,000)
Net cash provided by financing activities	600

Exercises

LO2 (45 min)   **21-1.** Complete the following chart regarding the indirect method.

	Add to Cash Flow	Subtract from Cash Flow
?	Decrease	Increase
?	Increase	Decrease

LO2 (45 min)   **21-2.** From the following, calculate the net cash flows from operating activities (use the indirect method):

	2006	2007
Accounts Receivable	$5,900	$7,900
Prepaid Insurance	900	850
Accounts Payable	4,000	4,600
Salaries Payable	1,200	2,200
For the year ended 2007:		
Net Income	$17,000	
Depreciation Expense	4,000	

21-3. From the following, calculate the net cash flows from operating activities (use the direct method):   **LO3 (45 min)**

Sales	$9,000
Cost of Goods Sold	4,400
Salary Expense	1,600
Insurance Expense	800
Other Expenses (all cash)	1,000

Changes in current assets and liabilities:

Accounts Receivable increased by $600.

Inventory increased by $500.

Accounts Payable increased by $100.

Salaries Payable decreased by $200.

Prepaid Insurance decreased by $150.

21-4. For each of the following transactions, identify the appropriate section of the statement of cash flows (OA = Operating, IA = Investing, FA = Financing, and NC = Noncash).   **LO4 (10 min)**

_____ **a.** Sold merchandise to customers.
_____ **b.** Purchase equipment.
_____ **c.** Buy stocks of another corporation.
_____ **d.** Pay dividends to stockholders.
_____ **e.** Paid salaries to employees.
_____ **f.** Issue stock in exchange for equipment.

Group A Problems

21A-1. From the following income statement (Fig. 21.16), balance sheet (Fig. 21.17 on the following page), and additional data for Dent Company, prepare a statement of cash flows using the indirect method.   **LO1, 2 (60 min)**

Additional Data:

1. All Plant and Equipment was purchased in cash.
2. Sold additional 2,500 shares of stock for cash at par.
3. A $1,400 dividend was declared and paid.
4. Short-term notes used to finance inventory.

FIGURE 21.16 Income Statement for Dent

DENT COMPANY INCOME STATEMENT FOR THE YEAR ENDED DECEMBER 31, 2009		
Sales		$96 5 0 0 0 0
Cost of Goods Sold		69 1 0 0 0 0
Gross Profit		$27 4 0 0 0 0
Operating Expenses:		
Rent Expense	$ 7 5 0 0 0 0	
Depreciation Expense	7 0 0 0 0 0	
Salary Expense	6 6 0 0 0 0	
Miscellaneous Expense	3 2 0 0 0 0	
Total Operating Expenses		24 3 0 0 0 0
Net Income		$ 3 1 0 0 0 0

FIGURE 21.17 Balance Sheet for Dent

DENT COMPANY BALANCE SHEET DECEMBER 31, 2009		
Assets	2007	2006
Current Assets:		
Cash	$ 3 400 00	$ 2 600 00
Accounts Receivable, Net	5 600 00	4 500 00
Merchandise Inventory	2 200 00	2 000 00
Prepaid Rent	1 000 00	1 200 00
Total Current Assets	$ 12 200 00	$ 10 300 00
Plant and Equipment:		
Store Equipment	$ 58 000 00	$ 50 000 00
Accum. Dep., Store Equipment	(12 000 00)	(5 000 00)
Total Plant and Equipment	$ 46 000 00	$ 45 000 00
Total Assets	$ 58 200 00	$ 55 300 00
Liabilities		
Current Liabilities:		
Notes Payable—Short Term	$ 6 800 00	$ 5 200 00
Accounts Payable	4 400 00	4 800 00
Total Current Liabilities	$ 11 200 00	$ 10 000 00
Long-Term Liabilities:		
Bonds Payable	$ 12 500 00	$ 15 000 00
Total Liabilities	$ 23 700 00	$ 25 000 00
Stockholders' Equity		
Common Stock, $1 par	$ 22 500 00	$ 20 000 00
Retained Earnings	12 000 00	10 300 00
Total Stockholders' Equity	$ 34 500 00	$ 30 300 00
Total Liabilities and Stockholders' Equity	$ 58 200 00	$ 55 300 00

LO1, 3 (60 min) 21A-2. From the financial statements and additional information provided in Problem 21A-1 for the Dent Company, prepare a statement of cash flows using the direct method.

Group B Problems

LO1, 2 (60 min)

21B-1. From the income statement (Fig. 21.18) and balance sheet (Fig. 21.19) on the following page, along with the additional data for Blumer Company, prepare a statement of cash flows using the indirect method.

Additional Data

1. All increases in Plant and Equipment were paid for in cash.
2. No dividend was declared in 2007.
3. Sold 2,000 shares of stock for cash at par value.
   Hint: Office Equipment and Machinery are recorded at *net* on the balance sheet. Be sure to add back depreciation expense to the cost of the assets in 2007 to compute the actual cost of the additional assets purchased.

FIGURE 21.18 Income Statement for Blumer

BLUMER COMPANY INCOME STATEMENT FOR THE YEAR ENDED DECEMBER 31, 2009			
Sales			$ 36 0 0 0 00
Cost of Goods Sold			25 0 0 0 00
Gross Profit			$ 11 0 0 0 00
Operating Expenses:			
Depreciation Expense, Equipment	$	8 0 0 00	
Depreciation Expense, Machinery		5 0 0 00	
Advertising Expense		6 6 0 00	
Salary Expense		1 8 0 0 00	
Miscellaneous Expense		3 6 0 0 00	
Total Operating Expenses			7 3 6 0 00
Net Income			$ 3 6 4 0 00

FIGURE 21.19 Balance Sheet for Blumer

BLUMER COMPANY BALANCE SHEET DECEMBER 31, 2009		
Assets	2009	2008
Current Assets:		
Cash	$ 2 0 4 0 00	$ 5 4 0 00
Accounts Receivable, Net	2 6 8 0 00	2 9 1 0 00
Merchandise Inventory	3 2 0 0 00	2 4 3 0 00
Total Current Assets	$ 7 9 2 0 00	$ 5 8 8 0 00
Plant and Equipment:		
Office Equipment, Net	$ 6 0 3 0 00	$ 4 5 3 0 00
Machinery, Net	4 8 3 0 00	3 0 3 0 00
Land	1 1 8 0 00	4 8 0 00
Total Plant and Equipment	$ 12 0 4 0 00	$ 8 0 4 0 00
Total Assets	$ 19 9 6 0 00	$ 13 9 2 0 00
Liabilities		
Current Liabilities:		
Notes Payable—Short Term	$ 2 0 8 0 00	$ 1 9 8 0 00
Accounts Payable	1 0 0 00	1 5 0 00
Total Current Liabilities	$ 2 1 8 0 00	$ 2 1 3 0 00
Long-Term Liabilities:		
Mortgage Payable	$ 2 1 2 0 00	$ 1 7 7 0 00
Total Liabilities	$ 4 3 0 0 00	$ 3 9 0 0 00
Stockholders' Equity		
Common Stock, $1 par	$ 9 5 3 0 00	$ 7 5 3 0 00
Retained Earnings	6 1 3 0 00	2 4 9 0 00
Total Stockholders' Equity	$ 15 6 6 0 00	$ 10 0 2 0 00
Total Liabilities and Stockholders' Equity	$ 19 9 6 0 00	$ 13 9 2 0 00

LO1, 2 (60 min)   **21B-2.** From the financial statements and additional information provided in Problem 21B-1 for the Blumer Company, prepare a statement of cash flows using the direct method.

ON-THE-JOB TRAINING

LO1, 2, 3, 4 (60 min)   **T-1.** Diane Clubb is trying to convert income statement items from an accrual basis to a cash basis. Accounts Receivable at the beginning of the year totaled $205,000. At the end of the year Accounts Receivable amounted to $240,000. On the income statement using accrual accounting, sales were $360,000. Depreciation Expense is $18,000 on the accrual income statement.

Diane calculates her cash received from customers to be $305,000. Do you accept her calculation? What written recommendations could you suggest to Diane? How would she calculate the amount of cash paid for advertising if Advertising Expense was listed as $6,000 and the Prepaid Advertising account showed a decrease of $400?

LO4 (50 min)   **T-2.** Pat Kinne is trying to calculate how much cash is being paid to suppliers of her firm's inventory during 2009. Cost of Goods Sold was reported at $190,500. Pat thinks she needs more data than are provided. From the following facts, could you show Pat how to calculate cash paid to suppliers as well as explain whether this method of computation is a part of the direct method or the indirect method?

	12/31/2009	12/31/2008
Accounts Receivable	$39,000	$37,000
Merchandise Inventory	50,400	53,000
Accounts Payable	28,500	30,700
Notes Payable (used to buy Merchandise Inventory)	17,000	15,000
Salaries Payable	11,000	11,200

FINANCIAL REPORT PROBLEM

LO1 (20 min)   ### Reading the Kellogg's Annual Report

Go to Appendix A and find the Statement of Cash Flows for Kellogg's. What is net cash provided by operations?

INTERNET PROJECT

PepsiCo

Go to the Web and search: Annual Report PepsiCo 2008.
Click on Investors Relations.
List out the latest news PepsiCo is providing to its investors.
Order a free annual report.

22

Analyzing Financial Statements

DID YOU KNOW? Garmin's average sales days for accounts receivable is between 35 and 62 days since 2001. Toyota recommended Garmin specifically in the 2008 brochure for its FJ Cruiser. Visit *www.garmin.com* to find more information about Garmin.

LEARNING OBJECTIVES

1. Preparing comparative balance sheets.

2. Using horizontal and vertical analysis techniques.

3. Calculating the four different types of ratios: liquidity ratios, asset management ratios, debt management ratios, and profitability ratios.

When you drive your car and look at your GPS do you ever wonder how companies like Garmin keep track of all their financial data? Financial reports are used by investors, creditors, and management to assist in making business decisions. Typical business decisions might involve such questions as the following:

- *For investors:* How profitable is the company when compared with competing companies? Will dividends be paid? Can the company expand with adequate financing?
- *For creditors:* Does the company have enough cash to pay back periodic interest payments as well as the balance on maturity?
- *For management:* Is the company, like Garmin, operating as efficiently as possible? How can we do better?

The four financial statements that we have discussed in earlier chapters—the balance sheet, the income statement, the statement of retained earnings, and the statement of cash flows—help provide the answers to these questions. In this chapter we discuss how to analyze the numbers that appear on these statements.

> In both QuickBooks and Peachtree, users have the option of exporting financial statements into a Microsoft® Excel spreadsheet to perform horizontal and vertical analysis.

Numbers on a financial statement may not have meaning in and of themselves; they must be placed in a context. This context may be a comparison with last year's figures, a comparison with other companies in the same industry, or even a comparison with other figures on the same report.

In the following units we look at what the numbers mean as well as how to apply that meaning toward making useful business decisions.

LO1 ## Learning Unit 22-1 Horizontal and Vertical Analysis of Balance Sheets

In the **comparative balance sheet,** a statement showing data from two or more periods side by side, shown in Figure 22.1, the accountant has placed the current year's balance sheet figures next to figures from the preceding year's balance sheet. The third column shows the amount of increase or decrease in the 20X8 figures over the 20X7 figures, and the last column shows the percentage of decrease or increase of 20X8 over 20X7. This type of analysis, in which each item on the report is compared with the same item in other periods, is called **horizontal analysis.**

Horizontal Analysis of the Balance Sheet

Let's perform a sample horizontal analysis on one of the items on Scrupper Supply Company's comparative balance sheet. Look at the entry for Cash in Figure 22.1. In 20X8 it is $3,040 and in 20X7 it was $4,080, for a decrease of $1,040. This decrease is placed in parentheses on the report to show that it is a decrease and not an increase. To figure the percentage that this decrease represents, you use the equation

$$\text{Percent} = \frac{\text{Amount of Change}}{\text{Base (Old Year)}}$$

In this case it would be

$$\frac{\$1,040}{\$4,080} = 25.5\%$$

This type of analysis is called horizontal analysis because in each case you are comparing two figures across columns, from one period to another, rather than comparing figures within a column. Although cash decreased by 25.5%, Scrupper's retained earnings increased by 23.1%. You can see that the percentages in the last column in Figure 22.1 cannot be added down the column to total 100%; each figure relates only to the figures for the same item across the other columns. These percentages provide us with a quick way of monitoring specific accounts.

Vertical Analysis of the Balance Sheet

In **vertical analysis,** each item on a report is shown as a percentage of a total base. The base will be either total assets or total liabilities and stockholders' equity on a balance sheet, and it can be total sales on an income statement. Look at the comparative

SCRUPPER SUPPLY COMPANY COMPARATIVE BALANCE SHEET AS OF DECEMBER 31, 20X8, AND DECEMBER 31, 20X7				
Note: Most recent year is shown first. Assets	December 31		Amount of Increase or Decrease During 20X8	Percent Increase or Decrease During 20X8
	20X8	20X7		
Current Assets:				
Cash	$ 3 040 00	$ 4 080 00	$ (1 040 00)	(25.5)
Accounts Receivable, Net	20 000 00	16 000 00	4 000 00	25
Merchandise Inventory	24 160 00	26 120 00	(1 960 00)	(7.5)
Prepaid Expenses	800 00	600 00	200 00	33.3
Total Current Assets	$ 48 000 00	$ 46 800 00	$ 1 200 00	2.6
Plant and Equipment:				
Office Equipment, Net	$125 200 00	$116 800 00	$ 8 400 00	7.2
Total Assets	$173 200 00	$163 600 00	$ 9 600 00	5.9
Liabilities				
Current Liabilities:				
Notes Payable	$ 20 960 00	$ 17 320 00	$ 3 640 00	21
Accounts Payable	240 00	280 00	(40 00)	(14.3)
Total Current Liabilities	$ 21 200 00	$ 17 600 00	$ 3 600 00	20.5
Long-Term Liabilities:				
Mortgage Payable	60 000 00	60 000 00	–0–	–0–
Total Liabilities	$ 81 200 00	$ 77 600 00	$ 3 600 00	4.6
Stockholders' Equity				
Common Stock, $10 par value	$ 60 000 00	$ 60 000 00	–0–	–0–
Retained Earnings	32 000 00	26 000 00	6 000 00	23.1
Total Stockholders' Equity	$ 92 000 00	$ 86 000 00	$ 6 000 00	7.0
Total Liabilities and Stockholders' Equity	$173 200 00	$163 600 00	$ 9 600 00	5.9

FIGURE 22.1 Comparative Balance Sheet

balance sheet in Figure 22.2 on the following page. Each item is listed for 20X8, and next to it is a percentage, which is that item's percentage of total assets or total liabilities and stockholders' equity. In the next column each item is listed for the preceding year, 20X7, and then the item is listed as a percentage of total assets or total liabilities and stockholders' equity.

Take the item Cash as an example again. In 20X8, Cash is $3,040 and total assets $173,200; thus Cash represents 1.8% of total assets for this year. In 20X7, Cash was $4,080 and total assets $163,600; thus Cash was 2.5% of total assets in that year.

Note how in this type of analysis you do add down the columns to total 100%, unlike horizontal analysis. Keep in mind that vertical analysis provides us with *another* way of analyzing financial reports that contain data for two or more successive accounting periods.

FIGURE 22.2 Vertical Analysis of a Comparative Balance Sheet

SCRUPPER SUPPLY COMPANY COMPARATIVE BALANCE SHEET DECEMBER 31, 20X8, AND DECEMBER 31, 20X7				
Assets	20X8		20X7	
Current Assets:				
Cash	$ 3 0 4 0 00	1.8%	$ 4 0 8 0 00	2.5%
Accounts Receivable, Net	20 0 0 0 00	11.5	16 0 0 0 00	9.8
Merchandise Inventory	24 1 6 0 00	13.9	26 1 2 0 00	16.0
Prepaid Expenses	8 0 0 00	.5	6 0 0 00	.4
Total Current Assets	$ 48 0 0 0 00	27.7%	$ 46 8 0 0 00	28.7%
Plant and Equipment:				
Office Equipment, Net	125 2 0 0 00	72.3%	116 8 0 0 00	71.4%
Total Assets	$173 2 0 0 00	100.0%	$163 6 0 0 00	100.0%*
Liabilities				
Current Liabilities:				
Notes Payable	$ 20 9 6 0 00	12.1%	$ 17 3 2 0 00	10.6%
Accounts Payable	2 4 0 00	.1	2 8 0 00	.2
Total Current Liabilities	$ 21 2 0 0 00	12.2%	$ 17 6 0 0 00	10.8%
Long-Term Liabilities:				
Mortgage Payable	60 0 0 0 00	34.6%	60 0 0 0 00	36.7%
Total Liabilities	$ 81 2 0 0 00	46.8%	$ 77 6 0 0 00	47.5%
Stockholders' Equity				
Common Stock, $10 par value	$ 60 0 0 0 00	34.6%	$ 60 0 0 0 00	36.7%
Retained Earnings	32 0 0 0 00	18.5	26 0 0 0 00	15.9
Total Stockholders' Equity	$ 92 0 0 0 00	53.1%	$ 86 0 0 0 00	52.6%
Total Liabilities and Stockholders' Equity	$173 2 0 0 00	100.0%*	$163 6 0 0 00	100.0%*

* Total equals 100% due to rounding.

A shorter version of this report in Figure 22.3 lists only the percentages of the two columns that have been analyzed. Such a report in general is called a **common-size statement;** this particular one is a common-size comparative balance sheet.

The common-size statement makes it easy to see, for example, that from 20X7 to 20X8 the level of inventory dropped (from 16% to 13.9% as a percentage of total assets) and accounts receivable increased (from 9.8% to 11.5%). In a comparison of companies of different sizes, common-size statements prevent the dollar amounts from getting in the way and make it easier to see each item as a percentage of the base in each company.

SCRUPPER SUPPLY COMPANY COMMON-SIZE COMPARATIVE BALANCE SHEET DECEMBER 31, 20X8, AND DECEMBER 31, 20X7	December 31	
Assets	20X8	20X7
Current Assets:		
Cash	1.8%	2.5%
Accounts Receivable, Net	11.5	9.8
Merchandise Inventory	13.9	16.0
Prepaid Expenses	.5	.4
Total Current Assets	27.7%	28.7%
Plant and Equipment:		
Office Equipment, Net	72.3%	71.4%
Total Assets	100.0%	100.0%*
Liabilities		
Current Liabilities:		
Notes Payable	12.1%	10.6%
Accounts Payable	.1	.2
Total Current Liabilities	12.2%	10.8%
Long-Term Liabilities:		
Mortgage Payable	34.6%	36.7%
Total Liabilities	46.8%	47.5%
Stockholders' Equity		
Common Stock, $10 par value	34.6%	36.7%
Retained Earnings	18.5	15.9
Total Stockholders' Equity	53.1%	52.6%
Total Liabilities and Stockholders' Equity	100.0%*	100.0%*

FIGURE 22.3 Common-Size Comparative Balance Sheet

* Total equals 100% due to rounding.

LEARNING UNIT 22-1 REVIEW

AT THIS POINT you should be able to

- Explain the items that make up a comparative balance sheet.
- Compare and contrast vertical and horizontal analysis.
- Explain the advantage of a common-size statement.

Self-Review Quiz 22-1

Complete the comparative balance sheet in Figure 22.4.

FIGURE 22.4 Comparative Balance Sheet

Assets	December 31 20X5	December 31 20X4	Amount of Increase or Decrease During 20X5	Percent Increase or Decrease During 20X5
Current Assets:				
Cash	$ 5 0 0 0 00	$ 4 0 0 0 00		
Accounts Receivable, Net	4 0 0 0 00	2 5 0 0 00		
Merchandise Inventory	6 0 0 0 00	5 6 0 0 00		
Prepaid Expenses	2 0 0 0 00	4 0 0 00		
Total Current Assets				
Plant and Equipment:				
Store Equipment, Net	146 0 0 0 00	125 0 0 0 00		
Total Assets				

Solution to Self-Review Quiz 22-1

FIGURE 22.5 Completed Comparative Balance Sheet

Assets	December 31 20X5	December 31 20X4	Amount of Increase or Decrease During 20X5	Percent Increase or Decrease During 20X5
Current Assets:				
Cash	$ 5 0 0 0 00	$ 4 0 0 0 00	$ 1 0 0 0 00	$25 $\left(\frac{\$1,000}{\$4,000}\right)$
Accounts Receivable, Net	4 0 0 0 00	2 5 0 0 00	1 5 0 0 00	60
Merchandise Inventory	6 0 0 0 00	5 6 0 0 00	4 0 0 00	7.1
Prepaid Expenses	2 0 0 0 00	4 0 0 00	1 6 0 0 00	400
Total Current Assets	$ 17 0 0 0 00	$ 12 5 0 0 00	$ 4 5 0 0 00	36
Plant and Equipment:				
Store Equipment, Net	146 0 0 0 00	125 0 0 0 00	21 0 0 0 00	16.8
Total Assets	$163 0 0 0 00	$137 5 0 0 00	$ 25 5 0 0 00	18.5

LO2 Learning Unit 22-2 Horizontal and Vertical Analysis of Income Statements; Trend Analysis

In the last unit we showed how to perform a horizontal and a vertical analysis of the balance sheet for Scrupper Supply Company. We now show how to perform the same two types of analysis on the income statement for Scrupper Supply Company.

Horizontal Analysis of the Income Statement

Figure 22.6 shows a comparative income statement for Scrupper Supply Company using horizontal analysis. As in horizontal analysis for the balance sheet, each item on the income statement is compared with the same item for the preceding year; the amount of increase or decrease is recorded and then shown as a percentage. For net sales, the amount

	SCRUPPER SUPPLY COMPANY COMPARATIVE INCOME STATEMENT FOR YEARS ENDED DECEMBER 31, 20X8, AND 20X7		Amount of Increase or Decrease During 20X8	Percent of Increase or Decrease During 20X8
	December 31			
	20X8	20X7		
Net Sales	$317 600 00	$302 000 00	$ 15 600 00	5.2
Cost of Goods Sold	198 000 00	194 000 00	4 000 00	2.1
Gross Profit from Sales	$119 600 00	108 000 00	11 600 00	10.7
Operating Expenses:				
Selling	$ 63 600 00	$ 55 000 00	8 600 00	15.6
General and Administrative	20 000 00	26 000 00	(6 000 00)	(23.1)
Total Operating Expenses	$ 83 600 00	$ 81 000 00	$ 2 600 00	3.2
Operating Income	$ 36 000 00	$ 27 000 00	9 000 00	33.3
Less Interest Expense	4 200 00	4 300 00	(1 00 00)	(2.3)
Income Before Taxes	$ 31 800 00	$ 22 700 00	$ 9 100 00	40.1
Income Taxes	15 900 00	11 350 00	4 550 00	40.1
Net Income	$ 15 900 00	$ 11 350 00	$ 4 550 00	40.1

FIGURE 22.6 Horizontal Analysis of a Comparative Income Statement

was $302,000 in 20X7 compared with $317,600 in 20X8; that is an increase of $15,600, which comes out to a 5.2% increase ($15,600/$302,000). The percent increase or decrease is the amount of increase or decrease divided by the figure for the base year of 20X7.

Vertical Analysis of the Income Statement

Figure 22.7 shows the vertical analysis of a comparative income statement for Scrupper Supply Company. In the case of an income statement, the base used is net sales. (On a balance sheet, it is assets or total liabilities and stockholders' equity.) Thus, on the vertical analysis of an income statement, each item is calculated as a percentage of net sales.

From such an analysis of a comparative income statement we can easily see that cost of goods sold decreased (from 64.2% to 62.3%) from 20X7 to 20X8, selling expenses increased (from 18.2% to 20.0%), and profit before tax was up (7.5% to 10.0%). If we had listed just the percentages (each item as percentage of net sales) and left out the dollar amounts, we would have produced a common-size comparative income statement.

SCRUPPER SUPPLY COMPANY COMPARATIVE INCOME STATEMENT FOR YEARS ENDED DECEMBER 31, 20X8, AND DECEMBER 31, 20X7				
Assets	20X8		20X7	
Net Sales*	$317 600 00	100 %	$302 000 00	100 %
Cost of Goods Sold	198 000 00	62.3	194 000 00	64.2
Gross Profit from Sales	$119 600 00	37.7%	108 000 00	35.8%
Operating Expenses:				
Selling	$ 63 600 00	20.0%	$ 55 000 00	18.2 %
General and Administrative	20 000 00	6.3	26 000 00	8.6
Total Operating Expenses	$ 83 600 00	26.3%	$ 81 000 00	26.8 %
Operating Income	$ 36 000 00	11.3%	27 000 00	8.9
Less Interest Expense	4 200 00	1.3	4 300 00	1.4
Income Before Taxes	$ 31 800 00	10.0%	$ 22 700 00	7.5 %
Income Taxes	15 900 00	5.0%	11 350 00	3.75
Net Income	$ 15 900 00	5.0%	$ 11 350 00	3.75%

*Net sales is 100% or the base.

FIGURE 22.7 Vertical Analysis of a Comparative Income Statement

Trend Analysis

A special type of horizontal analysis, called **trend analysis,** deals with the percentage of changes in a certain item over several years. For example, if we want to understand why sales in 20X8 are 118% of 20X5 of Scrupper Supply Company, we have to look at figures for several years. The following figures list sales, cost of goods sold, and gross profit for 20X5 to 20X8:

	20X8	20X7	20X6	20X5
Sales	$317,600	$302,000	$290,000	$270,000
Cost of Goods Sold	198,000	194,000	184,000	142,000
Gross Profit	$119,600	$108,000	$106,000	$128,000

When the trend analysis is developed, a base year is chosen. We will choose 20X5 (the base year is usually the earliest year listed). For each of the following years, each item is stated as a percentage of the amount of the base year. For example, sales in 20X8 as a percentage of the base year equal 118%. The calculation is as follows:

$$\textbf{BASE} \longrightarrow \frac{\$317,600}{\$270,000} = 118\%$$

Thus sales in 20X8 have increased by 18% since 20X5. Over a period of years these percentages are analyzed in relation to a company's history as well as to industry averages that are supplied by companies like Robert Morse Associates and Dun & Bradstreet.

The following is the trend analysis for Scrupper Supply Company for sales, cost of goods sold, and gross profit.

	20X8	20X7	20X6	20X5
Sales	118%	112%	107%	100%
Cost of Goods Sold	139	137	130	100
Gross Profit	93	84	83	100

Note that in 20X6, sales increased 7% from 20X5, but cost of goods sold was up 30%, resulting in gross profit being down 17%. Such analysis can reveal internal problems in Scrupper Supply Company or industrywide problems in a certain year. For example, Scrupper might want to investigate why cost of goods sold rose 39% in the last three years.

LEARNING UNIT 22-2 REVIEW

AT THIS POINT you should be able to

- Analyze income statement items by vertical and horizontal analysis.
- Prepare a trend analysis.

Self-Review Quiz 22-2

From the following prepare a trend analysis (round to nearest whole percent using 20X3 as the base year).

	20X6	20X5	20X4	20X3
Sales	$189,000	$165,000	$142,000	$130,000
Cost of Goods Sold	85,000	124,000	99,000	88,000
Gross Profit	$104,000	$ 41,000	$ 43,000	$ 42,000

Solution to Self-Review Quiz 22-2

	20X6	20X5	20X4	20X3
Sales	145%	127%	109%*	100%
Cost of Goods Sold	97	141	113	100
Gross Profit	248	98	102	100

Learning Unit 22-3 Ratio Analysis   *LO3*

Another method for understanding the numbers on the financial statement is the use of **ratio** analysis. A ratio is the relationship of two quantities or numbers, one divided by the other. **Ratio analysis** looks at the relationship of figures on the financial statement. For example, if Broome Company's net income is $10,000 and sales are $100,000, the ratio of sales to net income may be expressed as follows:

> In both QuickBooks and Peachtree, users have the option of exporting financial statements into a Microsoft Excel spreadsheet to perform ratio analysis.

  a. Net income is $\frac{1}{10}$ or 10% of sales ($10,000 / $100,000 = .1 = \frac{1}{10} = 10\%$).
  b. Ratio of sales to net income is 10 to 1 or 10 times net income (10:1).
  c. For every $10 of sales, Broome Company earns $1.00 of net income.

   In this unit we look at a number of different ratios that are used to analyze different aspects of a business. To be meaningful, ratios are often compared with other standards, such as past company ratios or industrywide ratios. The ratios we discuss fall into four general categories:

  ● **Liquidity ratios** measure a company's ability to meet short-term obligations.
  ● **Asset management ratios** measure how effectively a company is using its assets.
  ● **Debt management ratios** measure how well a company is using debt versus its equity position.
  ● **Profitability ratios** measure a company's ability to earn profits.

   Let's now do the calculations as well as provide an explanation of each ratio. All calculations for the ratios come from the financial reports of Scrupper Supply Company presented in the last two units.

Liquidity Ratios

Current Ratio The **current ratio** expresses the relationship of Scrupper's current assets to its current liabilities, as follows:

  20X8
    Total Current Assets = $48,000
    Total Current Liabilities = $21,200

$$\text{Current Ratio} = \frac{\text{Current Assets}}{\text{Current Liabilities}} = \frac{\$48,000}{\$21,200} = 2.26:11$$

Thus, for each $1 of debt, Scrupper has $2.26 of current assets to meet its short-term debt obligations.

   It is important to note that this ratio should be evaluated in terms of (1) the type of business Scrupper is in, (2) the composition of current assets, and (3) the type of credit terms Scrupper extends. Ratios can also be compared from year to year to spot trends in a company or in an industry. For example, in 20X7 the current ratio for Scrupper Supply Company was 2.66 ($46,800/$17,600). This year's current ratio is 2.26, which means that

---

*$142,000/$130,000.

Scrupper's ability to pay off short-term debts has decreased from last year to this year. The ratio is something creditors and investors, as well as the management of Scrupper Corporation, will be interested in.

Depending on the inventory or prepaid expenses, the current assets might not be worth what is shown on the balance sheet. For example, if Scrupper Supply Company has overstocked amounts of inventory, a high current ratio could occur. If Scrupper has a large amount of prepaid insurance or rent, it will not be possible to convert these assets into cash because they have already been paid for. Thus current ratio is not a very rigorous test of Scrupper's ability to pay its short-term debts. The next ratio we discuss shows that more clearly.

Acid Test Ratio (Quick Ratio) The **acid test ratio** divides those assets that are most easily converted into cash (called **quick assets**) by the current liabilities. To determine quick assets, we subtract Merchandise Inventory and Prepaid Expenses from current assets (which usually leaves Cash, Notes Receivable, and Accounts Receivable). Thus, the acid test ratio would look like this equation:

$$\text{Acid Test Ratio} = \frac{\text{Current Assets} - \text{Merchandise Inventory} - \text{Prepaid Expenses}}{\text{Current Liabilities}}$$

$$= \frac{\$23,040}{\$21,200} = 1.09 : 1$$

Thus, for each $1 of short-term debt, Scrupper has $1.09 of current or quick assets to meet them. This ratio should be at least 1:1 to pass the acid test or be acceptable. If you compare this 1.09:1 ratio with the current ratio figure of 2.26:1, you will see what a difference the inclusion of Merchandise Inventory and Prepaid Expenses makes.

Asset Management Ratios

Accounts Receivable Turnover The **accounts receivable turnover ratio** shows how many times in a year Scrupper is able to convert its accounts receivables into cash. Usually, the higher the turnover, the better, because a company does not want its money tied up in something that is not yielding any revenue. The turnover rate depends on the length of the credit period Scrupper gives its customers (for Scrupper, all sales are on credit).

$$\text{Accounts Receivable Turnover} = \frac{\text{Net Credit Sales}}{\text{Average Accounts Receivable}}$$

At the end of 20X7 Accounts Receivable was $16,000; at the end of 20X8 it was $20,000. We thus take $18,000 as a figure for *average* accounts receivable.

$$\text{Accounts Receivable Turnover} = \frac{\$317,600}{\$18,0000} = 17.6$$

Thus, Scrupper is able to turn over its accounts receivable 17.6 times a year. Of course, this turnover rate has to be compared with industry standards and must be seen in the context of how aggressive Scrupper is in its attempts to collect the accounts receivable. The next ratio breaks these steps into the number of days per collection period for accounts receivable.

Average Collection Period In 20X8, Scrupper Supply Company turns its accounts receivable into cash every 20.7 days:

$$\text{Average Collection Period} = \frac{365 \text{ days}}{\text{Accounts Receivable Turnover}} = \frac{365}{17.6}$$

$$= 20.7$$

Rate of Return on Common Stockholders' Equity The **return on common stockholders' equity ratio** aids Scrupper in evaluating how well it is earning profit for its common stockholders. The rate of return on common stockholders' equity is calculated as follows:

$$\begin{pmatrix} \text{Rate of Return} \\ \text{on Common} \\ \text{Stockholders'} \\ \text{Equity} \end{pmatrix} = \frac{(\text{Net Income Before Taxes}) - (\text{Preferred Dividends})}{(\text{Common Stockholders' Equity})}$$

$$= \frac{\$31,800 - 0}{\$92,000} = 34.6\%$$

Scrupper compares this return with its competitors' returns. If its rate is higher than the industry standards, Scrupper is using debt financing wisely.

LEARNING UNIT 22-3 REVIEW

AT THIS POINT / you should be able to

- Define, compare, and contrast the following four types of ratios: liquidity ratios, asset management ratios, debt management ratios, and profitability ratios.
- Explain and show the calculations for the following: current ratio, acid test ratio, accounts receivable turnover, average collection period, inventory turnover, asset turnover, debt to total assets, debt to stockholders' equity, times interest earned, gross profit rate, return on sales, rate of return on total assets, and rate of return on common stockholders' equity.

Self-Review Quiz 22-3

From Scrupper's balance sheet and income statement, calculate the 13 ratios presented in this unit for 20X7. Assume the following: Accounts Receivable at the end of 20X6 was $18,000; Merchandise Inventory at the end of 20X6 was $26,000.

Solution to Self-Review Quiz 22-3

1. Current ratio:

$$\frac{\text{Current Assets}}{\text{Current Liabilities}} = \frac{\$46,800}{\$17,600} = 2.66$$

2. Acid test:

$$\frac{\text{Current Assets} - \text{Merchandise Inv.} - \text{Prepaid Expenses}}{\text{Current Liabilities}}$$

$$= \frac{\$20,080}{\$17,600} = 1.14$$

3. Accounts receivable turnover:

$$\frac{\text{Net Credit Sales}}{\text{Average Accounts Receivable}} = \frac{\$302,000}{\$17,000} = 17.8$$

4. Average collection period:

$$\frac{365 \text{ Days}}{\text{Accounts Receivable Turnover}} = \frac{365}{17.8} = 20.5 \text{ Days}$$

5. Inventory turnover:

$$\frac{\text{Cost of Goods Sold}}{\text{Average Inventory}} = \frac{\$194,000}{\$26,060} = 7.4$$

6. Asset turnover:

$$\frac{\text{Net Sales}}{\text{Total Assets}} = \frac{\$302,000}{\$163,600} = 1.8 \text{ Times}$$

7. Debt to total assets:

$$\frac{\text{Total Liabilities}}{\text{Total Assets}} = \frac{\$77,600}{\$163,600} = 47.4\%$$

8. Debt to stockholders' equity:

$$\frac{\text{Total Liabilities}}{\text{Stockholders' Equity}} = \frac{\$77,600}{\$86,000} = 90.2\%$$

9. Times interest earned:

$$\frac{\text{Income Before Taxes and Interest Expense}}{\text{Interest Expense}} = \frac{\$27,000}{\$4,300} = 6.3 \text{ Times}$$

10. Gross profit rate:

$$\frac{\text{Gross Profit}}{\text{Net Sales}} = \frac{\$108,000}{\$302,000} = 36\%$$

11. Return on sales:

$$\frac{\text{Net Income Before Taxes}}{\text{Net Sales}} = \frac{\$22,700}{\$302,000} = 7.5\%$$

12. Rate of return on total assets:

$$\frac{\text{Net Income Before Interest and Taxes}}{\text{Total Assets}} = \frac{\$27,000}{\$163,600} = 16.5\%$$

13. Rate of return on common stockholders' equity:

$$\frac{\text{Net Income Before Taxes} - \text{Preferred Dividends}}{\text{Common Stockholders' Equity}} = \frac{\$22,700 - 0}{\$86,000}$$
$$= 26.4\%$$

CHAPTER ASSIGNMENTS

SUMMARY OF KEY POINTS

LEARNING UNIT 22-1

1. Investors, creditors, and management need to analyze financial statements.
2. Horizontal analysis compares each item in a financial statement with the same item from another period.

3. Vertical analysis compares each item in a financial statement as a percentage of a certain base (usually net sales on an income statement and total assets or total liabilities and stockholders' equity on the balance sheet).

4. A common-size statement shows two or more vertically analyzed columns, usually with the dollar figures deleted and replaced by percentages.

LEARNING UNIT 22-2

1. Vertical and horizontal analysis can be used to analyze income statements as well as balance sheets.

2. In a vertical analysis of an income statement, items are given as a percentage of net sales (as the base).

3. Trend analysis provides a financial picture of how accounts change over the years.

LEARNING UNIT 22-3

1. Ratio analysis shows relationships between two figures, such as ratio of sales to net income or of current assets to current liabilities. These ratios can then be compared with ratios from other years, other companies, or industry standards as a means of analysis.

2. Liquidity ratios measure the ability of a company to meet its short-term obligations.

3. Asset management ratios measure how effectively a company is using its assets.

4. Debt management ratios measure whether the company is using an appropriate mix of debt versus equity financing.

5. Profitability ratios measure the company's ability to earn profits.

6. All ratios should be analyzed in relation to industry standards as well as economic conditions prevailing in the marketplace.

KEY TERMS

Accounts receivable turnover ratio A ratio that indicates the number of times accounts receivables are converted to cash within a given period and the effectiveness of a company's credit policy.

Acid test ratio A liquidity ratio; those assets that are most easily converted to cash are divided by current liabilities to indicate ability to pay off short-term debt. Also called *quick ratio.*

Asset management ratios Those ratios—accounts receivable turnover, average collection period, inventory turnover, and asset turnover—that measure how effectively a company uses its assets.

Asset turnover ratio A ratio that indicates how efficiently a company uses its assets to generate sales and thus helps measure the overall efficiency of the company.

Average collection period A ratio that shows how quickly moneys owed are received from customers and thereby measures how effectively a company collects its accounts receivables.

Common-size statements Comparative reports in which each item is expressed as a percentage of a base amount without dollar amounts.

Comparative balance sheets Current and past financial reports covering two or more successive periods that place data in single columns side by side.

Current ratio A liquidity ratio; current assets are divided by current liabilities to indicate a company's ability to pay its short-term debt. This ratio does not provide as much certainty as the acid test ratio.

Debt management ratios Those ratios—debt to total assets, debt to stockholders' equity, and times interest earned—that measure a company's mix of debt and equity financing.

Debt to stockholders' equity ratio A ratio in which total liabilities are divided by the amount of stock that is owned to measure the risk creditors run in comparison with stockholders.

Debt to total assets ratio A ratio that shows how much of a company's assets are financed by creditors.

Gross profit rate A profitability ratio that indicates how well net sales cover administrative and selling expenses.

Horizontal analysis Amounts of items compared on the same line of comparative financial reports. Horizontal analysis can also be in the form of a trend analysis.

Inventory turnover ratio An asset management ratio that indicates how quickly inventory moves off the shelf and therefore how well a company sells its product.

Liquidity ratios The two ratios—current ratio and acid test ratio—that measure a company's ability to pay off short-term debts.

Profitability ratios Those ratios—gross profit rate, return on sales, return on total assets, and return on common stockholders' equity—that measure a company's ability to earn a profit.

Quick assets Those assets—mainly cash, accounts receivable, and notes receivable—that can be easily turned into money.

Ratio A relationship of two quantities or numbers, one divided by the other. See the Blueprint on this and the following pages.

Ratio analysis An examination of the relationship between two numbers or sets of numbers on financial reports. Analyses of ratios, especially over time, can give a fairly clear picture of how well a company conducts its business.

Return on common stockholders' equity ratio A profitability ratio that indicates how well a company is managing debt financing to earn a profit for holders of common stock.

Return on sales ratio A profitability ratio that shows the relationship of net income before taxes to net sales and thereby the effectiveness of a company's pricing policy.

Return on total assets ratio A profitability ratio that measures how wisely a company has invested in and managed its assets. This ratio can be arrived at in two ways: (1) net income before interest and taxes divided by total assets and (2) return on sales multiplied by asset turnover.

Times interest earned ratio A debt management ratio indicating the degree of risk to lenders that a company will default on its interest payments. Also called *interest coverage ratio*.

Trend analysis A type of horizontal analysis that deals with percentage changes in items on the financial reports for several years. This analysis uses a base year to calculate the percentage change of each item.

Vertical analysis Comparing items in a financial report by expressing each item as a percentage of a certain base total.

BLUEPRINT: RATIOS

Ratio	Formula	What Calculation Says	Key Points
1. Current ratio	$$\frac{\text{Current Assets}}{\text{Current Liabilities}}$$	For each $1 of current liabilities, how many dollars of current assets are available to meet the current debt.	The ratio should be evaluated based on the type of business credit terms, along with the composition of the current assets.
2. Acid test ratio	$$\frac{\text{Current Assets} - \text{Merchandise Inventory} - \text{Prepaid Expenses}}{\text{Current Liabilities}}$$	For each $1 of current liabilities, how many dollars of cash and near-cash assets are available to meet the current debt.	Because inventory and prepaid expenses may not be easily converted into cash, they are not used in the calculation.
3. Accounts receivable turnover	$$\frac{\text{Net Credit Sales}}{\text{Average Accounts Receivable}}$$	How many times accounts receivable are collected and turned into cash.	Cash sales are not included in the calculation. High turnover is often the best unless the credit terms cause a reduction in sales.
4. Average collection period	$$\frac{365 \text{ Days}}{\text{Accounts Receivable Turnover}}$$	The number of days that it takes a business to collect its accounts receivable.	If the average collection period goes up and the credit terms remain the same, increased collection attempts should be emphasized.
5. Inventory turnover	$$\frac{\text{Cost of Goods Sold}}{\text{Average Inventory}}$$	The time period it takes from the purchase of inventory until its sale.	High turnover indicates low amounts of inventory. Care must be taken if frequent stockouts occur.

6. Asset turnover	$\dfrac{\text{Net Sales}}{\text{Total Assets}}$	How effectively the company is using its assets to generate sales.	A low turnover could mean excessive investment in assets or that the sales volume is too low.
7. Debt to total assets	$\dfrac{\text{Total Liabilities}}{\text{Total Assets}}$	Amount of assets financed by the creditors.	A low percentage reduces creditors' risk if liquidation occurs. The higher the percentage, the more coverage a company is using.
8. Debt to stockholders' equity	$\dfrac{\text{Total Liabilities}}{\text{Stockholders' Equity}}$	Amount of debt in relation to total stockholders' equity.	The higher the percentage, the more interest cost results for stockholders.
9. Times interest earned	$\dfrac{\text{Income Before Taxes and Interest Expense}}{\text{Interest Expense}}$	Degree of risk to creditors if a company defaults on interest payments.	A high times interest earned means a company can have declines in earnings but have the ability to meet its annual interest obligations.
10. Gross profit rate	$\dfrac{\text{Gross Profit}}{\text{Net Sales}}$	Profit from a sales dollar that will be used to cover expenses (general, selling, etc.).	This rate could drop if stiff competition results in price cuts.
11. Return on sales	$\dfrac{\text{Net Income Before Taxes}}{\text{Net Sales}}$	How much a company earns on each sales dollar.	A company with a low inventory turnover rate usually prices goods for a high return on sales.
12. Rate of return on total assets	$\dfrac{\text{Net Income Before Interest and Taxes}}{\text{Total Assets}}$	Without looking at how assets are financed, this ratio measures how productively total assets have been used.	The rate of return can be increased by controlling costs and expenses as well as increasing asset turnover.
13. Rate of return on common stockholders' equity	$\dfrac{\text{Net Income Before Taxes} - \text{Preferred Dividends}}{\text{Common Stockholders' Equity}}$	Measures a company's ability to earn profits for the common stockholder.	If this rate is higher than a return on total assets, the company is using financial leverage to its benefit.

QUESTIONS, CLASSROOM DEMONSTRATION EXERCISES, EXERCISES, AND PROBLEMS

Discussion and Critical Thinking Questions/Ethical Case

1. Compare and contrast the needs of investors, creditors, and management as they relate to financial statement analysis.

2. Horizontal analysis cannot be presented on comparative financial statements. Agree or disagree? Please explain.

3. What is meant by vertical analysis?

4. Common-size statements use horizontal analysis. Agree or disagree? Please explain.

5. Why is a base year chosen in trend analysis?

6. How can ratios be expressed?

7. Explain the following types of ratios:
   a. Liquidity
   b. Asset management
   c. Debt management
   d. Profitability

8. What current asset accounts are deleted in the calculation of the acid test ratio? Why?

9. What could a low accounts receivable turnover rate indicate?

10. Stockouts could easily result if inventory is higher than it should be. Agree or disagree? Please explain.

11. What does possible liquidation have to do with the ratio of debt to total assets?

12. Rate of return on assets is affected by return on sales and asset turnover. Agree or disagree?

13. Jill Land, president of Loon Co., is happy to report to the company's stockholders that the company increased its cash position by 20% from last year. Its average collection period decreased by 12 days. Jill knows some customers are unhappy about the new credit terms but believes that you cannot please everyone; that's part of business. Do you think Loon Co. is on the right track? One shareholder is quite upset to learn that the company is holding so much cash. Do you agree with the company's belief that increasing the cash position by 20% is sound? You make the call. Write down your recommendation to Jill.

Classroom Demonstration Exercises

SET A

LO2 (10 min)   **Horizontal Analysis Balance Sheet**

1. Calculate the amount of increase or decrease as well as the percentage of increase or decrease. (Round to the nearest tenth of a percent as needed.)

	20X8	20X7	Amount	%
a. Accounts Receivable	$700	$500		
b. Accounts Payable	500	700		

LO2 (15 min)   **Vertical Analysis Balance Sheet**

2. Complete a vertical analysis of the assets. (Round to the nearest tenth of a percent as needed.)
   - **a.** Cash $ 600
   - **b.** Accounts Receivable   700
   - **c.** Merchandise Inventory   800
   - **d.** Office Equipment   2,000
   -     Total Assets $4,100

LO1, 2 (15 min)   **Common-Size Income Statement**

3. Prepare a common-size income statement from the following (use net sales as 100%):

Net Sales	$600
Cost of Goods Sold	200
Gross Profit from Sales	400
Operating Expenses	150
Net Income	$250

Trend Analysis

LO2 (15 min)

4. Complete a trend analysis from the following data of Blue Corporation using 20X5 as the base year. (Round to the nearest percent.)

	20X8	20X7	20X6	20X5
Sales	$900	$600	$500	$400
Gross Profit	400	300	400	200
Net Income	200	90	60	60

Ratios

LO3 (15 min)

5. From the data given calculate the following. (Round to the nearest hundredth or hundredth of a percent as needed.)
   a. Current ratio
   b. Acid test ratio
   c. Asset turnover ratio
   d. Gross profit rate

Net Sales	$250,000
Current Assets	51,000
Gross Profit	106,000
Current Liabilities	19,000
Total Assets	151,000
Merchandise Inventory	6,000
Prepaid Expenses	4,000

SET B

LO2 (10 min)

Horizontal Analysis Balance Sheet

1. Calculate the amount of increase or decrease as well as the percentage of increase or decrease. (Round to the nearest tenth of a percent.)

	20X8	20X7	Amount	%
a. Accounts Receivable	$600	$500		
b. Accounts Payable	400	600		

Vertical Analysis Balance Sheet

LO2 (15 min)

2. Complete a vertical analysis of the assets. (Round to the nearest tenth of a percent as needed.)
   a. Cash $ 500
   b. Accounts Receivable   600
   c. Merchandise Inventory   900
   d. Office Equipment   1,000
           Total Assets $3,000

LO1, 2 (15 min)   **Common-Size Income Statement**

3. Prepare a common-size income statement from the following (use net sales as 100%):

Net Sales	$500
Cost of Goods Sold	300
Gross Profit from Sales	200
Operating Expenses	60
Net Income	$140

LO2 (15 min)   **Trend Analysis**

4. Complete a trend analysis from the following data of Blue Corporation using 20X5 as the base year. (Round to the nearest percent.)

	20X8	20X7	20X6	20X5
Sales	$800	$700	$600	$500
Gross Profit	600	200	500	300
Net Income	100	60	25	50

LO3 (15 min)   **Ratios**

5. From the data given calculate the following. (Round to the nearest hundredth or hundredth of a percent as needed.)
   a. Current ratio
   b. Acid test ratio
   c. Asset turnover ratio
   d. Gross profit rate

Net Sales	$300,000
Current Assets	42,000
Gross Profit	104,000
Current Liabilities	17,000
Total Assets	149,000
Merchandise Inventory	5,000
Prepaid Expenses	3,000

Exercises

LO1 (30 min)   **22-1.**   From the following, complete a comparative income statement for Auster Co. for December 31, 20X8, and December 31, 20X9. (Round to the nearest hundredth of a percent as needed.)

	20X9	20X8
Net Sales	$70,000	$40,000
Cost of Goods Sold	30,000	20,000
Operating Expenses	17,000	12,000
Interest Expense	5,000	4,000
Net Income (loss)	18,000	4,000

22-2. From the following, prepare a common-size income statement for Ted Co. by converting the dollar amounts into percentages. (Round to the nearest tenth of a percent.) Use net sales as 100%.

LO1, 2 (30 min)

	20X9	20X8
Net Sales	$500,000	$400,000
Cost of Goods Sold	400,000	355,000
Gross Profit from Sales	100,000	45,000
Operating Expenses	60,000	30,000
Net Income	$ 40,000	$ 15,000

22-3. From the following comparative balance sheet of Hoster Co., prepare a common-size comparative balance sheet. (Round all percentages to the nearest tenth of a percent.)

LO1, 2 (50 min)

	December	
	20X9	20X8
Current Assets	$ 90,000	$ 50,000
Plant and Equipment	450,000	310,000
Total Assets	$540,000	$360,000
Current Liabilities	$ 10,000	$ 30,000
Long-Term Liabilities	30,000	100,000
Common Stock	300,000	200,000
Retained Earnings	200,000	30,000
Total Liabilities and Stockholders' Equity	$540,000	$360,000

22-4. Complete a trend analysis from the following data of Band Corporation using 20X5 as the base year. (Round to the nearest percent.)

LO1, 2 (30 min)

	20X8	20X7	20X6	20X5
Sales	$600,000	$500,000	$400,000	$300,000
Gross Profit	166,000	141,000	112,000	124,000
Net Income	48,000	41,000	22,000	38,000

22-5. From the given income statement of Canry Co. as well as from the additional data on the following page, compute the following:
a. Asset turnover for 20X7
b. Inventory turnover for 20X7
c. Accounts receivable turnover for 20X7

LO3 (30 min)

	20X7	20X6
Net Sales	$800,000	$700,000
Cost of Goods Sold	710,000	490,000
Gross Profit	$ 90,000	$210,000
Operating Expenses (includes taxes)	70,000	160,000
Net Income	$ 20,000	$ 50,000

	Additional Data	
	20X7	20X6
Year-End Accounts Receivable	$ 60,000	$ 50,000
Year-End Inventory	90,000	70,000
All sales were on credit		
Total Assets	230,000	160,000

Group A Problems

LO1, 2 (60 min)

22A-1. From the comparative balance sheet of Hesler Corporation in Figure 22.8:
(a) prepare a horizontal analysis of each item for the amount of increase or decrease as well as the percent increase or decrease (to the nearest tenth of a percent); (b) vertically analyze the 20X8 column of the balance sheet (to the nearest tenth of a percent).

FIGURE 22.8 Comparative Balance Sheet of Hesler Corp.

Check Figure:
Cash increase 5.4%

HESLER CORPORATION
COMPARATIVE BALANCE SHEET
DECEMBER 31, 20X8, AND DECEMBER 31, 20X7

	December 31	
Assets	20X8	20X7
Current Assets:		
Cash	$ 39 000 00	$ 37 000 00
Accounts Receivable, Net	28 000 00	16 100 00
Merchandise Inventory	47 000 00	15 000 00
Prepaid Expenses	1 600 00	1 300 00
Total Current Assets	$ 80 500 00	$ 36 100 00
Plant and Equipment:		
Office Equipment, Net	$115 000 00	$110 000 00
Total Assets	$195 500 00	$146 100 00
Liabilities		
Current Liabilities:		
Notes Payable	$ 20 000 00	$ 26 000 00
Accounts Payable	21 200 00	24 000 00
Total Current Liabilities	$ 41 200 00	$ 50 000 00
Long-Term Liabilities:		
Mortgage Payable	$ 50 000 00	$ 40 000 00
Total Liabilities	91 200 00	90 000 00
Stockholders' Equity		
Common Stock, $10 par value	$ 50 000 00	$ 30 000 00
Retained Earnings	54 300 00	26 100 00
Total Stockholders' Equity	$104 300 00	$ 56 100 00
Total Liabilities and Stockholders' Equity	$195 500 00	$146 100 00

22A-2. From the comparative income statement of Oper Company in Figure 22.9, do the following:

a. Prepare a horizontal analysis with the amount of increase or decrease during 20X8 along with the percent increase or decrease during 20X7 (to the nearest tenth of a percent).

b. Vertically analyze the 20X8 column of the income statement (to the nearest tenth of a percent).

c. Prepare a common-size comparative income statement (to the nearest tenth of a percent).

LO2 (60 min)

> *Check Figure:*
> Cost of goods sold
> increase 15.9%

FIGURE 22.9 Comparative Income Statement for Oper Co.

OPER COMPANY COMPARATIVE INCOME STATEMENT FOR YEARS ENDED DECEMBER 31, 20X8, AND DECEMBER 31, 20X7	December 31	
	20X8	20X7
Net Credit Sales	$288 000 00	$275 000 00
Cost of Goods Sold	197 000 00	170 000 00
Gross Profit from Sales	$ 91 000 00	$105 000 00
Operating Expenses:		
Selling	$ 50 000 00	$ 51 000 00
General and Administrative	21 000 00	23 000 00
Total Operating Expenses	$ 71 000 00	$ 74 000 00
Operating Income	$ 20 000 00	$ 31 000 00
Less Interest Expense	6 000 00	8 000 00
Income Before Taxes	14 000 00	23 000 00
Income Taxes	5 600 00	9 200 00
Net Income	$ 8 400 00	$ 13 800 00

22A-3. From the income statement (Fig. 22.10) and balance sheet (Fig. 22.11 on the following page) of Austin Company, compute the following for 20X8: (a) current ratio, (b) acid test ratio, (c) accounts receivable turnover, (d) average collection period, (e) inventory turnover, (f) asset turnover, (g) debt to total assets, (h) debt to stockholders'

LO3 (60 min)

> *Check Figure:*
> Current ratio 2.22

FIGURE 22.10 Comparative Income Statement for Austin Co.

AUSTIN COMPANY COMPARATIVE INCOME STATEMENT FOR YEARS ENDED DECEMBER 31, 20X8, AND 20X7	December 31	
	20X8	20X7
Net Credit Sales	$430 000 00	$376 000 00
Cost of Goods Sold	238 000 00	221 000 00
Gross Profit from Sales	$192 000 00	$155 000 00
Operating Expenses:		
Selling	$ 120 400 00	$110 000 00
General and Administrative	21 600 00	22 400 00
Total Operating Expenses	$ 142 000 00	$132 400 00
Operating Income	$ 50 000 00	$ 22 600 00
Less Interest Expense	8 200 00	8 600 00
Income Before Taxes	$ 41 800 00	$ 14 000 00
Income Taxes	12 540 00	5 600 00
Net Income	$ 29 260 00	$ 8 400 00

FIGURE 22.11 Comparative Balance Sheet for Austin Co.

AUSTIN COMPANY COMPARATIVE BALANCE SHEET DECEMBER 31, 20X8, AND DECEMBER 31, 20X7		
	December 31	
Assets	20X8	20X7
Current Assets:		
Cash	$ 11 00 0 00	$ 24 40 0 00
Accounts Receivable, Net	416 00 00	362 00 00
Merchandise Inventory	612 00 00	624 00 00
Prepaid Expenses	5 60 0 00	3 20 0 00
Total Current Assets	$1194 00 0 00	$126 2 0 0 00
Plant and Equipment:		
Office Equipment, Net	$ 656 00 00	$63 00 0 00
Total Assets	$185 0 0 0 00	$189 2 0 0 00
Liabilities		
Current Liabilities:		
Notes Payable	$ 36 80 0 00	$ 35 20 0 00
Accounts Payable	170 00 00	158 00 00
Total Current Liabilities	$ 538 00 00	$ 510 00 00
Long-Term Liabilities:		
Mortgage Payable	$ 396 00 00	$ 30 00 0 00
Total Liabilities	$ 934 00 00	$ 81 00 0 00
Stockholders' Equity		
Common Stock, $10 par value	$ 56 00 0 00	$51 00 0 00
Retained Earnings	356 00 00	57 2 0 0 00
Total Stockholders' Equity	$ 916 00 00	$108 2 0 0 00
Total Liabilities and Stockholders' Equity	$185 0 0 0 00	$189 2 0 0 00

equity, (i) times interest earned, (j) gross profit rate, (k) return on sales, (l) return on total assets, and (m) return on common stockholders' equity.

LO3 (30 min)   **22A-4.** From the information about Vargo Corporation in Figures 22.12 and 22.13, do the following:

    a. For each year calculate its current ratio and acid test ratio.

    b. For each year prepare the income statement in common-size percentages. (Round to the nearest tenth of a percent.)

    c. Prepare a trend analysis of the balance sheet using 20X6 as the base year. (Round to the nearest percent.)

Check Figure:
20X8 Current assets 72%

Group B Problems

LO1, 2 (60 min)   **22B-1.** From the comparative balance sheet of Hesler Corporation in Figure 22.14 on the following page spread, do the following:

    a. Prepare a horizontal analysis of each item for the amount of increase or decrease as well as the percent increase or decrease (to the nearest tenth of a percent).

    b. Vertically analyze the 20X8 column of the balance sheet (to the nearest tenth of a percent).

Check Figure:
Cash 3.3%

FIGURE 22.12 Comparative Income Statement for Vargo Corp.

VARGO CORPORATION COMPARATIVE INCOME STATEMENT FOR YEARS ENDED DECEMBER 31, 20X8, 20X7, 20X6	20X8	20X7	20X6
Net Sales	$ 32 000 00	$ 28 000 00	$ 24 400 00
Cost of Goods Sold	23 450 00	19 600 00	17 200 00
Gross Profit from Sales	$ 8 550 00	$ 8 400 00	$ 7 200 00
Operating Expenses:			
Selling	$ 4 600 00	$ 4 820 00	$ 3 456 00
General and Administrative	2 400 00	2 280 00	2 482 00
Total Operating Expenses	$ 7 000 00	$ 7 100 00	$ 5 938 00
Operating Income Before Taxes	$ 1 550 00	$ 1 300 00	$ 1 262 00
Income Taxes	620 00	520 00	504 00
Net Income	$ 930 00	$ 780 00	$ 758 00

FIGURE 22.13 Comparative Balance Sheet for Vargo Corp.

VARGO CORPORATION COMPARATIVE BALANCE SHEET FOR YEARS ENDED DECEMBER 31, 20X8, 20X7, 20X6			
Assets	20X8	20X7	20X6
Current Assets*	$ 2 046 00	$ 1 782 00	$ 2 842 00
Plant and Equipment	10 000 00	9 000 00	8 400 00
Total Assets	$ 12 046 00	$ 10 782 00	$ 11 242 00
Liabilities and Stockholders' Equity			
Current Liabilities	$ 1 000 00	$ 960 00	$ 920 00
Common Stock	7 000 00	6 200 00	6 400 00
Retained Earnings	4 046 00	3 622 00	3 922 00
Total Liabilities and Stockholders' Equity	$ 12 046 00	$ 10 782 00	$ 11 242 00

* 20X8 Inventory, $484; 20X7, $310; 20X6, $600.

22B-2. From the comparative income statement of Oper Company in Figure 22.15 on the next page, do the following:

   a. Prepare a horizontal analysis with the amount of increase or decrease during 20X8 along with the percent increase or decrease during 20X7 (to the nearest tenth of a percent).

   b. Vertically analyze the 20X8 column of the income statement (to the nearest tenth of a percent).

   c. Prepare a common-size comparative income statement (to the nearest tenth of a percent).

22B-3. From the income statement and balance sheet of Austin Company (Figs. 22.16 and 22.17 on the following pages), compute the following for 20X8: (a) current ratio, (b) acid test ratio, (c) accounts receivable turnover, (d) average collection period, (e) inventory turnover, (f) asset turnover, (g) debt to total assets, (h) debt to stockholders' equity, (i) times interest earned, (j) gross profit rate, (k) return on sales, (l) return on total assets, and (m) return on stockholders' equity.

LO2 (60 min)

Check Figure:
20X8 Net sales increase 38%

LO3 (60 min)

Check Figure:
Current ratio 2.12

FIGURE 22.14 Comparative
Balance Sheet for Hesler Corp.

HESLER CORPORATION COMPARATIVE BALANCE SHEET DECEMBER 31, 20X8, AND DECEMBER 31, 20X7		
	December 31	
Assets	20X8	20X7
Current Assets:		
Cash	$ 16 50 0 00	$ 12 30 0 00
Accounts Receivable, Net	525 0 0 00	44 70 0 00
Merchandise Inventory	660 0 0 00	78 0 0 0 00
Prepaid Expenses	9 30 0 00	5 70 0 00
Total Current Assets	$1443 0 0 00	$1407 0 0 00
Plant and Equipment:		
Office Equipment, Net	$3516 0 0 00	$330 0 0 0 00
Total Assets	$495 90 0 00	$470 70 0 00
Liabilities		
Current Liabilities:		
Notes Payable	$ 72 0 0 00	$ 54 0 0 00
Accounts Payable	45 0 0 00	28 50 0 00
Total Current Liabilities	$117 0 0 00	$ 82 50 0 00
Stockholders' Equity		
Common Stock, $10 par value	$300 0 0 0 00	$300 0 0 0 00
Retained Earnings	78 90 0 00	88 20 0 00
Total Stockholders' Equity	$378 90 0 00	$388 20 0 00
Total Liabilities and Stockholders' Equity	$495 90 0 00	$470 70 0 00

FIGURE 22.15 Comparative
Income Statement for Oper Co.

OPER COMPANY COMPARATIVE INCOME STATEMENT FOR YEARS ENDED DECEMBER 31, 20X8, AND DECEMBER 31, 20X7		
	December 31	
	20X8	20X7
Net Sales	$ 12 25 0 00	$ 8 88 0 00
Cost of Goods Sold	6 05 0 00	4 24 0 00
Gross Profit from Sales	6 20 0 00	4 64 0 00
Operating Expenses:		
Selling	2 70 0 00	1 92 0 00
General and Administrative	1 05 0 00	96 0 00
Total Operating Expenses	3 75 0 00	2 88 0 00
Operating Income	2 45 0 00	1 76 0 00
Less Interest Expense	2 25 00	2 20 00
Income Before Taxes	2 22 5 00	1 54 0 00
Income Taxes	8 90 00	6 16 00
Net Income	$ 1 33 5 00	$ 9 24 00

FIGURE 22.16 Comparative Income Statement for Austin Co.

AUSTIN COMPANY COMPARATIVE INCOME STATEMENT FOR YEARS ENDED DECEMBER 31, 20X8, AND DECEMBER 31, 20X7		
	December 31	
	20X8	**20X7**
Net Sales	$ 99 0 0 0 00	$ 89 2 5 0 00
Cost of Goods Sold	50 5 0 0 00	55 0 0 0 00
Gross Profit from Sales	48 5 0 0 00	34 2 5 0 00
Operating Expenses:		
Selling	27 0 5 0 00	25 9 0 0 00
General and Administrative	3 5 5 0 00	4 0 0 0 00
Total Operating Expenses	30 6 0 0 00	29 9 0 0 00
Operating Income	17 9 0 0 00	4 3 5 0 00
Less Interest Expense	4 5 5 0 00	2 2 5 0 00
Income Before Taxes	13 3 5 0 00	2 1 0 0 00
Income Taxes	5 3 4 0 00	8 4 0 00
Net Income	$ 8 0 1 0 00	$ 1 2 6 0 00

22B-4. From the information about Vargo Corporation in Figures 22.18 and 22.19 on the following pages, do the following:

LO3 (30 min)

a. For each year calculate its current and acid test ratios.

Check Figure:
20X8 Current assets 136%

b. For each year prepare the income statement in common-size percentages. (Round to the nearest tenth of a percent.)

c. Prepare a trend analysis of the balance sheet using 20X6 as the base year. (Round to the nearest percent.)

ON-THE-JOB TRAINING

T-1. You have been hired as a consultant to determine which of the two following companies is in better shape overall. From the accompanying information, prepare a schedule of ratio calculations that can be derived from the facts along with your recommendations. Both companies are in the same industry.

LO1, 2, 3 (60 min)

	Joyne Co.	Smokey Co.
Cash	$ 17,000	$ 28,000
Accounts Receivable, Net	18,000	55,000
Inventory	80,000	96,000
Plant and Equipment, Net	90,000	170,000
	$205,000	$349,000
Current Liabilities	$ 58,000	$ 89,000
Mortgage Payable	40,000	60,000
Common Stock	79,000	175,000
Retained Earnings	28,000	25,000
	$205,000	$349,000
Sales (all credit)	$230,000	$380,000
Cost of Goods Sold	160,000	275,000
Interest Expense	8,000	12,000
Income Taxes	10,000	16,000
Net Income	24,000	40,000

FIGURE 22.17 Comparative Balance Sheet for Austin Co.

AUSTIN COMPANY COMPARATIVE BALANCE SHEET DECEMBER 31, 20X8, AND DECEMBER 31, 20X7		
	December 31	
Assets	20X8	20X7
Current Assets:		
Cash	$ 3 400 00	$ 5 400 00
Accounts Receivable, Net	9 750 00	8 700 00
Merchandise Inventory	14 500 00	14 900 00
Prepaid Expenses	1 200 00	850 00
Total Current Assets	$ 28 850 00	$29 850 00
Plant and Equipment:		
Office Equipment, Net	$ 14 900 00	$ 11 000 00
Total Assets	$ 43 750 00	$40 850 00
Liabilities		
Current Liabilities:		
Notes Payable	$ 9 750 00	$ 9 050 00
Accounts Payable	3 850 00	3 400 00
Total Current Liabilities	$ 13 600 00	$ 12 450 00
Long-Term Liabilities:		
Mortgage Payable	$ 10 000 00	$ 7 500 00
Total Liabilities	$ 23 600 00	$19 950 00
Stockholders' Equity		
Common Stock, $10 par value	$ 14 050 00	$12 000 00
Retained Earnings	6 100 00	8 900 00
Total Stockholders' Equity	$ 20 150 00	$20 900 00
Total Liabilities and Stockholders' Equity	$ 43 750 00	$40 850 00

FIGURE 22.18 Comparative Income Statement for Vargo Corp.

VARGO CORPORATION COMPARATIVE INCOME STATEMENT FOR YEARS ENDED DECEMBER 31, 20X8, 20X7, 20X6			
	20X8	20X7	20X6
Net Sales	$ 55 500 00	$ 50 400 00	$ 38 700 00
Cost of Goods Sold	40 200 00	37 200 00	23 700 00
Gross Profit from Sales	$ 15 300 00	$ 13 200 00	$ 15 000 00
Operating Expenses:			
Selling	$ 7 200 00	$ 4 800 00	$ 5 400 00
General and Administrative	5 700 00	2 730 00	3 750 00
Total Operating Expenses	$ 12 900 00	$ 7 530 00	$ 9 150 00
Operating Income Before Taxes	2 400 00	5 670 00	5 850 00
Income Taxes	960 00	2 268 00	2 340 00
Net Income	$ 1 440 00	$ 3 402 00	$ 3 510 00

FIGURE 22.19 Comparative
Balance Sheet for Vargo Corp.

VARGO CORPORATION COMPARATIVE BALANCE SHEET DECEMBER 31, 20X8, 20X7, 20X6			
Assets	20X8	20X7	20X6
Current Assets*	$ 6720 00	$ 5550 00	$ 4950 00
Plant and Equipment	18000 00	12000 00	10500 00
Total Assets	$ 24720 00	$ 17550 00	$ 15450 00
Liabilities and Stockholders' Equity			
Current Liabilities	$ 2400 00	$ 1800 00	$ 1560 00
Common Stock	11700 00	10800 00	7500 00
Retained Earnings	10620 00	4950 00	6390 00
Total Liabilities and Stockholders' Equity	$ 24720 00	$ 17550 00	$ 15450 00

*Inventory: 20X8, $1,350; 20X7, $1,800; 20X6, $1,200.

T-2. The bookkeeper of Blue Co. is trying to determine (a) the amount of average inventory, (b) the accounts receivable average balance, and (c) the balance of cash from the following information:

LO3 (30 min)

Prepaid Rent	$16,000
Accounts Receivable Turnover	9 times
Cost of Goods Sold	$270,000
Inventory Turnover	27
Current Liabilities	$90,000
Credit Sales	$270,000

The bookkeeper's assistant thinks there is not enough information available to complete the calculations. Accept or reject the assistant's remarks. Please provide a written response.

FINANCIAL REPORT PROBLEM

Reading the Kellogg's Annual Report

LO1, 2, 3 (20 min)

Go to Appendix A and find the Consolidated Balance Sheet. Calculate for Kellogg's the current ratio for 2005 and 2006.

INTERNET PROJECT

Garmin

Go to the Web and search: Annual Report Garmin 2008.
Click on Investors Relations.
List out the latest news Garmin is providing to its investors.
Order a free annual report.

SUBWAY Case

"AND THE WINNER IS . . . "

LO1, 2, 3 (20 min)

"And the Number 1 for sales this month is . . . " Carrie Zabrinsky smiled broadly and paused to add a little suspense to the announcement. As a development agent for Subway, she had decided to give the franchisees in her region a little push by spurring some healthy rivalry among them. Every month for the next year she was holding a contest to see which franchisee had the highest sales.

" . . . Stan Hernandez for his Subway of Los Palmos!" announced Carrie. "Stan, come up here and get your award." Stan bounded up to the stage, still in a state of shock. Carrie handed him a handsome framed certificate as well as a travel voucher for two nights—all expenses paid—in the Sunset Sands resort.

"Wow!" was all Stan could say at first, but he quickly gained his composure and even delivered a short speech. Stan thanked Subway for providing a wonderful business concept and product. He thanked his wonderful, hardworking employees, his junior partner Ron, and also his accountant Lila. "While it's true that we rang up the sales, Lila Hernandez crunched those numbers," Stan told Carrie, "and gave me a crash course in accounting!"

Carrie's new contest requires the franchisees in her region to send her a lot of accounting information—information that not only enables her to see which restaurant has the highest sales, but also allows her to do some troubleshooting. Stan e-mails a monthly management report to Carrie that includes an income statement. He does the balance sheet quarterly, and Carrie then does a horizontal analysis of Stan's balance sheet, comparing each line to its budget and to last year. That information tells her whether Stan is on target and points up any weak areas in the business. Then she does a vertical analysis of Stan's balance sheet to arrive at percentages of the totals.

Carrie compares Stan's results (in percentages) with each of the other restaurants in his region, using a common-size statement. This exercise is useful because, although each shop is different in size, a common-size statement deals only in percentages. This comparison quickly points up exceptions, which may be good or bad. In either case, Carrie Zabrinsky then has the clues she needs to discover a strength other shops can copy or a weakness Stan can fix.

"So, Stan the Man," said Ron Ebbers after the award ceremony, "are you going to take me to the Sunset Sands to celebrate? As your junior partner, I feel I should share in your success."

"We'll just wait until our c-store is number 1 in sales!" said Stan. "In the meantime, I think it's the perfect time for Ana and me to take our first trip together." Stan Hernandez had a lot to celebrate—a budding love relationship, a thriving business, and a renewed friendship with Ron that had turned into a promising partnership. "In fact," said Stan, getting out his cell phone, "I'm going to call Ana right now to tell her the good news!"

Discussion Questions

1. Why does the development agent use a common-size statement to compare restaurants in her region?
2. Why does she use both horizontal and vertical analyses of the balance sheets for the restaurants in her region?

23

The Voucher System

DID YOU KNOW? The voucher system is still preferred in Office Depot's internal control system. Visit *www.officedepot.com* to find more information about Office Depot.

LEARNING OBJECTIVES

1. Preparing vouchers, recording them in a voucher register, and recording payment of vouchers in a check register.

2. Recording revised vouchers to handle non-routine transactions in a voucher system.

3. Using the net amount method to record invoices and payment.

In small companies owners may be able to do or look at every step of their business themselves. However, as such companies grow larger and as the sheer number of business transactions multiplies, like at Office Depot, that individual control becomes impossible. How, then, do owners or managers keep control over the activities of a company? If they don't sign every check themselves or approve every purchase themselves, how do they know whether money is being spent in approved ways, or even where it's going? Some rules must be formulated for employees to impose order; such rules and procedures are referred to as *internal control.* One type of system used to implement this internal control is called a *voucher system.*

In Chapter 10 we discussed the steps taken when a company purchases goods. You might take a moment to look back at those pages because we use these steps in this chapter to explain how a voucher system works. The steps include the following:

1. Preparing a purchase requisition and getting it authorized.
2. Preparing a purchase order, which specifies details such as company, number of items, and so forth, and getting it authorized.
3. The company receiving the purchase order preparing a sales invoice specifying number and type of goods and price.
4. The company receiving the goods inspecting the shipment, checking it against the purchase order and the sales invoice, and completing a receiving report.
5. Someone in the accounting department verifying the numbers (checking the purchase order, the invoice, and the receiving report to make sure the numbers are in agreement and no steps are left out). This person then issuing a voucher for payment, which is authorized.
6. Issuing payment in the form of a check.

These steps show internal control, in the form of a voucher system, at work. Other procedures discussed in other chapters of this text also are part of internal control, including banking procedures and petty cash and change funds.

What is a voucher? A **voucher** is a written authorization form that is used for every cash payment the company makes. It contains all the details of the transaction in question along with the signatures of appropriate employees as authorization. A **voucher system,** then, is a system in which no payment is made without an approved voucher.

Characteristics of a Voucher System

A number of principles of internal control are embedded in the voucher system. Perhaps the most important is the separation of duties. In a voucher system no one person in a company is in control of all transactions or of everything to do with one transaction. The person who approves purchase and payment is different from the person who makes the accounting entries related to these functions, and that person is different from the person who signs and mails the checks. In this way no one can do anything without other people supplying approval.

A second important principle, perhaps the backbone of a voucher system, is the rule that no purchases are made without an approved voucher backed up by documentation. Several layers of documentation and authorization begin with a purchase requisition, move on to a purchase order, and end up with actual payment by a check. At every layer and step the appropriate documents are presented, checked, and approved before going further.

A lot of cross-referencing and cross-checking takes place in a voucher system. Every document is numbered; transactions are recorded in different places by different people and backed up by reference to numbers of other documents. In this way it is always possible to trace one transaction all the way through the system. After a purchase is made and paid for, the documents and forms are kept on file for a certain period of time to allow such checks to be made.

In the next two learning units we show how a voucher system works in a specific company and then how certain transactions are handled that don't fit into the voucher system.

> Generally vouchers are not used with accounting software programs such as Peachtree and QuickBooks. The user would compare open purchase orders with the invoice received from the vendor and then receive the items into the inventory system.

Learning Unit 23-1 Handling Transactions in a Voucher System

Jones Supply Company is a medium-sized merchandise business that believes in strong internal control practices and procedures. It uses the voucher system to control all cash payments except payments out of the petty cash fund. Company rules state that all invoices must be compared with purchase requisitions, purchase orders, and receiving reports before payment and that all payments must, of course, be supported by appropriate documents and authorizations.

Jones Supply Company's voucher system is made up of the following elements:

1. Vouchers
2. Voucher register
3. Unpaid voucher file
4. Check register
5. Paid voucher file

To see this system in action, let's follow one transaction all the way through. To begin with, Jones Company decides to buy $4,500 worth of merchandise from Beam Enterprise. The purchase order is shown in Figure 23.1. When the merchandise is received, along with an invoice (Fig. 23.2), a special serially numbered form called a *voucher* is prepared (Fig. 23.3).

The Voucher

In preparing the voucher, the accountant responsible for vouchers compares the invoice from Beam Enterprise with the purchase requisition, purchase order, and receiving report to be sure that it matches the specific requirements and prices of the order. For example, the information in Figure 23.1, the purchase order, does indeed match the information on the invoice shown in Figure 23.2 on the following page. The original supporting documents (purchase orders, etc.) are attached to the voucher (Fig. 23.3 on the following page spread), which contains information on its front and back sides. The front side indicates the voucher number, invoice number and date, purchase order number, to whom the amount will be paid, and verification steps. For Jones Supply Company, all supporting documents are attached to the front of the voucher and folded. The back side shows the account distribution along with space to complete the payment summary and final approvals as needed.

FIGURE 23.1 Purchase Order

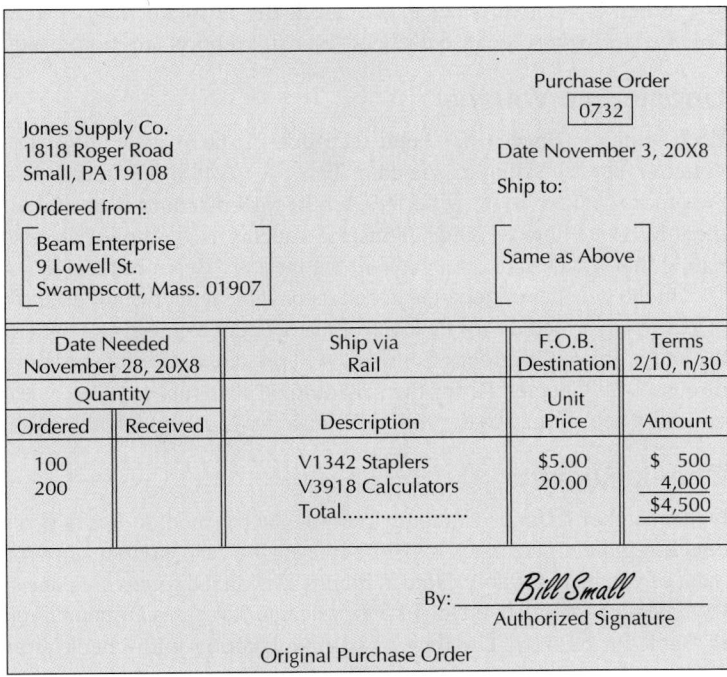

FIGURE 23.2 Invoice

The Voucher Register

Using the approved account distributions, the voucher is recorded in a special journal called the **voucher register** (Fig. 23.4 on the following page spread). This journal replaces the purchases journal. Note that the vouchers are entered in the voucher register in numerical order at the time the liability is *incurred.* For Jones, the **Vouchers Payable** credit column records the amount due on each voucher (before any discounts) for purchases of merchandise, services, or other assets. Special debit columns have been set up for Jones's accountant based on how often they're used. The sundry column, as in other special journals, records amounts that do not have special columns set up. The posting rules are the same as we covered in the past for special journals. Keep in mind that the columns for date of payment and check number are *not* filled in until *time of payment.*

When a balance sheet is prepared, the term *Accounts Payable* is used instead of *Vouchers Payable,* because users of financial reports are more used to that wording.

Unpaid File Voucher

> The voucher remains in the unpaid file until paid.

Each voucher, once it has been recorded in the voucher register, is filed in an **unpaid voucher file** according to due date. This file is often referred to as a **tickler file.** Although the amount owed Beam is $4,500, a $90 cash discount is available if Beam receives payment by December 8, 20X8. Thus the voucher is filed on a *December 5 due date,* anticipating that it will take three days in the mail for Beam to receive it.

> Payment requires notation in three places:
> 1. Check register
> 2. Voucher register payment column
> 3. Back of voucher

In the voucher system, the accounts payable ledger is not used; for Jones, the unpaid file is its subsidiary ledger for the controlling account Vouchers Payable in the general ledger. At the end of the month, Jones Company will prepare a schedule of vouchers payable, just as we discussed in Chapter 10 for the schedule of accounts payable, with the total of all unpaid vouchers being equal to the ending balance in Vouchers Payable in the general ledger.

Check Register

On December 5, Jones Company records the payment to Beam in a special journal called a **check register.** The check register replaces the cash payments journal in recording the payment of vouchers payable. Note in Figure 23.5 on the following page spread that the Vouchers Payable account is debited for $4,500, whereas Purchases Discount is credited for $90 and Cash in Bank for $4,410. The date of payment, along with check number, is updated in the

FIGURE 23.3 Voucher

(front)

VOUCHER

Jones Supply Co.
1818 Roger Road
Small, PA 19108

Voucher No. 23

Date check needed:
December 5, 20X8

Invoice
Number and Date:
B20 November 28, 20X8

Payable to: Beam Enterprise
9 Lowell St.
Swampscott, MA 01907

Purchase
Order Number: 0732

Invoice Amount	$4,500
Less: Discount	90
Net Amount Due	$4,410

Verification Steps:	Approved by:	Date
(1) Invoice compared with purchase requisition and purchase order	JS	12/1/X8
(2) Invoice compared with receiving report	BM	12/1/X8
(3) Extensions and footings done	BJ	12/1/X8
(4) Approved for payment	PS	12/3/X8

(back)

Account Distributory		Voucher No. 23
Debit	Amount	Date check needed: 12/5/X8
Purchases	$4,500	Payable to:
Supplies		
Salaries Expense		Beam Enterprise
Repair Expense		9 Lowell St.
Sundry		Swampscott, MA 01907

Summary of Voucher

Invoice Amount	$4,500
Less: Discount	90
Net Amount Due	$4,410

Payment Summary of Voucher

Date: 12/5/X8
Amount: $4,410
Check No.: 55

Recorded in Voucher
Register by: _____PM_____

Credit Vouchers
Payable for Total $4,500

Distribution approved by: _____JS_____
(Accounting Department)

voucher register. Posting of the check register follows the same rules as other journals. (*Note:* Once the voucher has been paid, it should be marked "Paid" so as to avoid duplication of payments.)

Paid Voucher File

After Beam's voucher is paid, it is filed by Jones in a **paid voucher file.** The voucher is filed in sequential order according to the voucher numbers. Some companies will file the voucher alphabetically based on the creditor's name. Jones keeps all paid vouchers for six years. This amount of time will vary from company to company.

VOUCHER REGISTER

Date	Voucher Number	Payable to	Date of Payment	Check Number	Voucher Payable Cr.	Purchases Dr.	Supplies Dr.	Repair Expense Dr.	Sundry Accounts Account	PR	Dr.	Cr.
20X8 Dec.												
2	22	Petty Cash	12/4	53	5000				Petty Cash	114	5000	
3	23	Beam Enterprise	12/5	55	450000	450000						
3	24	Ron Co.	12/4	54	42500		42500					
7	25	Rose Co.	12/9	56	2800			2800				
9	26	Blew Co.	12/30	67	100000				Equip.	121	100000	
15	27	Security Bank	12/27	58	515000				Note Payable	211	500000	
									Int. Exp.	531	15000	
28	42	Internal Revenue Service	12/28	65	90000				FICA Tax* Payable	212	25000	
									FIT Tax Payable	216	65000	
29	43	Payroll	12/29	66	400000				Salary and Wages Payable	210	400000	
					2066500	795000	600000	1015500			1110000	
					(212)	(513)	(116)	(562)			(X)	

*Includes Medicare and Social Security.

FIGURE 23.4 Voucher Register

FIGURE 23.5 Check Register

		Check Number	Payable to	Voucher Number	Vouchers Payable Dr.	Purchases Discount Cr.	Cash in Bank Cr.	Bank Deposits	Bank Bal.	
20X8 Dec.	1	49	Broom Co.	21	4 6 0 00		4 6 0 00		1 2 0 0 00	
									7 4 0 00	
	2	50	Moore Co.	22	6 0 0 00	1 2 00	5 8 8 00	4 0 0 00	5 5 2 00	
	4	54	Ron Co.	24	4 2 5 00		4 2 5 00	1 0 0 0 00	1 1 2 7 00	
	5	55	Beam Ent.	23	4 5 0 0 00	9 0 00	4 4 1 0 00	4 0 0 0 00	7 1 7 00	
	28	65	Internal Revenue	42	9 0 0 00		9 0 0 00		8 2 0 0 00	
	29	66	Payroll	43	4 0 0 0 00		4 0 0 0 00		4 2 0 0 00	
					(212)	(514)	(111)			

LEARNING UNIT 23-1 REVIEW

AT THIS POINT you should be able to

- List and define the components of a voucher system.
- Explain the steps to record and pay a voucher.
- Discuss why the unpaid voucher file is recorded by due dates.

Self-Review Quiz 23-1

Respond true or false to the following:

1. All companies use the same voucher system.
2. Supporting documents are attached to a voucher.
3. The account distribution is used to record the voucher in the voucher register.
4. Vouchers are recorded in the voucher register in alphabetical order.
5. A schedule of vouchers payable can be prepared from the unpaid voucher file at the end of the month.

Solutions to Self-Review Quiz 23-1

1. False   **2.** True   **3.** True   **4.** False   **5.** True

Learning Unit 23-2 Recording Additional Transactions in Jones's Voucher System

LO2

Situation 1: Purchases Returns and Allowances after Voucher Has Been Recorded

On December 26, Jones Company prepared voucher no. 32 for merchandise that was bought from Booth Company for $400. The accountant records the voucher in the voucher register as a debit to Purchases and a credit to Vouchers Payable for $400. On December 28, $100 of the merchandise is found to be defective and is returned to Booth Company. The procedure that Jones Company uses is to cancel the original voucher and prepare a new voucher for $300. Figure 23.6 shows how Jones Company records the cancellation of voucher no. 32 and the recording of the revised voucher no. 39. The end result is a debit to Purchases of $400, a credit of $300 to Vouchers Payable, and a credit to Purchases Returns and Allowances of $100. Another way of handling this transaction is to modify the original voucher and make a *general journal* entry that debits Vouchers Payable $100 and credits Purchases Returns and Allowances $100.

Situation 2: Partial Payments Planned after Voucher Prepared for Full Amount

On January 18, voucher no. 64 was prepared by Jones Company on the assumption it would pay Ron Co. $15,000 for office equipment in one payment. The top section of Figure 23.7 shows a debit to Office Equipment and a credit to Vouchers Payable for $15,000.

Owing to a cash shortage, on January 29 it was decided by Jones Company to pay Ron Company in three equal installments on February 8, 19, and 21. Thus, the original voucher on January 18 is canceled and a *new* voucher is prepared for each installment. Note in Figure 23.7 how the old voucher is canceled and the new vouchers are prepared. In the date of payment column, the January 18 line shows the cancellation along with the new date recording the new voucher (1/29). The check number column indicates which new vouchers are replacing the canceled voucher. Note in the sundry column how Vouchers Payable is debited three times to cancel the original voucher.

LO3
Recording Purchases at Net Amount

In this chapter Jones Company recorded all invoices at the gross amount, although the check register did show a Purchases Discount column. Many companies, on the other hand, record purchases at net. When a discount is missed using the net approach, a title called Discount Lost is shown in the payment column of the voucher register. Let's look at journal entries showing the same purchase recorded at gross and at net.

> The net approach means that a Purchases Discount account is not needed.

(a) Mill Company buys merchandise on account from Ryan Company for $8,000. Terms are 2/10, n/30. Mill Company issues voucher no. 299.

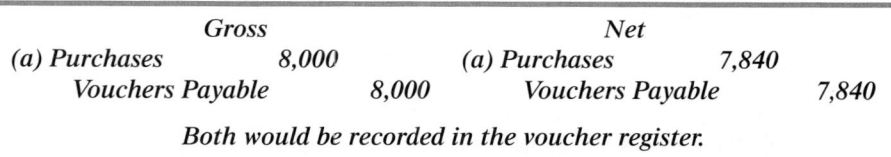

	Gross			Net		
(a) Purchases	8,000		(a) Purchases	7,840	
Vouchers Payable		8,000	Vouchers Payable		7,840

Both would be recorded in the voucher register.

If Discount Is Taken on Time (b) Mill Company issues check no. 531 in payment of voucher no. 299 less the cash discount.

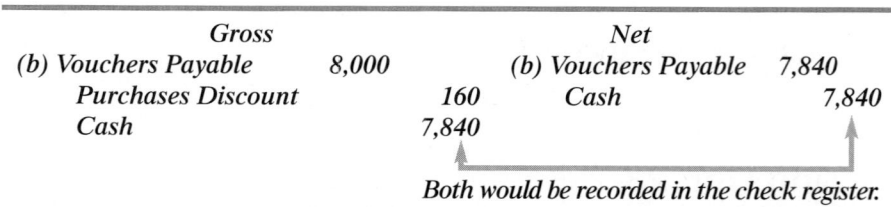

	Gross			Net	
(b) Vouchers Payable	8,000		(b) Vouchers Payable	7,840
Purchases Discount		160	Cash	7,840
Cash		7,840		

Both would be recorded in the check register.

If Discount Is Missed (c) Mill Company issues check no. 531 in payment of voucher no. 299. The discount date has passed.

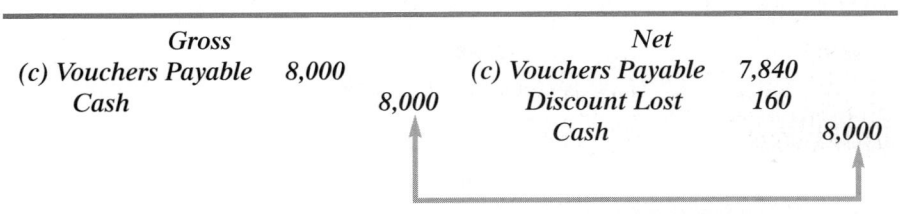

Gross				*Net*		
(c) Vouchers Payable	*8,000*		*(c) Vouchers Payable*	*7,840*	
Cash		*8,000*	Discount Lost	*160*	
			Cash		*8,000*

VOUCHER REGISTER

Date	Voucher Number	Payable to	Date of Payment	Check Number	Voucher Payable Cr.	Purchases Dr.	Account	Sundry Accounts PR	Sundry Accounts Dr.	Sundry Accounts Cr.
Dec. 26	32	Booth Co.	Canceled Voucher	See no. 39	400 00	400 00				
28	39	Booth Co.			300 00		Voucher Payable	212	400 00	
							Purchases Returns and Allowances	515		100 00

FIGURE 23.6 Voucher Register with Purchases Returns and Allowances

VOUCHER REGISTER

Date	Voucher Number	Payable to	Date of Payment	Check Number	Vouchers Payable Cr.	Account	Sundry Accounts PR	Sundry Accounts Dr.	Sundry Accounts Cr.
Jan. 18	64	Ron Co.	Canceled 1/29	V69-71	1500 00 00	Office Equip.	121	1500 00 00	
29	69	Ron Co.			500 00 00	Vouchers Payable	212	500 00 00	
29	70	Ron Co.			500 00 00	Vouchers Payable	212	500 00 00	
29	71	Ron Co.			500 00 00	Vouchers Payable	212	500 00 00	

FIGURE 23.7 Voucher Register with Partial Payments

Note that when the discount is missed in the net method, the Purchases Discount Lost account is used. (The end-of-chapter problems and exercises record all vouchers at gross unless otherwise stated.)

LEARNING UNIT 23-2 REVIEW

AT THIS POINT / you should be able to

- Record transactions in a voucher system involving purchases returns and allowances and/or partial payments.
- Explain how the Discount Lost account could be used in a voucher system.

Self-Review Quiz 23-2

Record the following entries in the voucher register for Joe Corporation:

20X8

Oct.	10	Prepared voucher no. 82 for purchase of merchandise for $3,000 from Rose Co.
Oct.	15	Returned $400 of the merchandise purchased from Rose Co. on October 10 due to poor workmanship. Joe Corp. canceled voucher no. 82 and replaced it with voucher no. 95.

(Solutions on next page)

CHAPTER ASSIGNMENTS

SUMMARY OF KEY POINTS

LEARNING UNIT 23-1

1. In a voucher system, no payment is made without an approved form called a *voucher.* The voucher system consists of these elements: vouchers, voucher register, unpaid voucher file, check register, and paid voucher file.
2. Supporting documents are attached to a voucher.
3. When approved, the distribution of accounts is the basis for the entry into the voucher register.
4. The voucher register, a special journal, replaces the purchases journal.
5. Cash discounts can be taken advantage of by filing vouchers in an unpaid voucher file (tickler file) by due dates.
6. A schedule of vouchers payable can be prepared at the end of the month. The accounts payable subsidiary ledger in a voucher system is eliminated.
7. The check register is a special journal that replaces the cash payments journal.

LEARNING UNIT 23-2

1. After a voucher is recorded, a purchases return can be recorded by canceling the original voucher and debiting Vouchers Payable and crediting Vouchers Payable and Purchases Returns and Allowances.
2. For partial payments after a voucher has been prepared, the old voucher is canceled and a new voucher is prepared for each installment.
3. Companies recording invoices at the net amount would record any discounts missed in the Discount Lost account.

Solution to Self-Review Quiz 23-2

VOUCHER REGISTER

Date	Voucher Number	Payable to	Date of Payment	Check Number	Voucher Payable Cr.	Purchases Dr.	Account	Sundry Accounts PR	Sundry Accounts Dr.	Sundry Accounts Cr.
20X8 Oct. 10	82	Rose Co.	Canceled Voucher	See no. 95	3 000 00	3 000 00	Vouchers Payable		3 000 00	
15	95	Rose Co.			2 600 00		Purchases Returns and Allowances			400 00

FIGURE 23.8 Voucher Register

KEY TERMS

Check register   A special journal that replaces the cash payments journal in recording payments of vouchers.

Paid voucher file   Holds paid vouchers filed either in sequential order by voucher number or alphabetically by creditor's name.

Unpaid voucher file (tickler file)   The file containing unpaid vouchers arranged by due dates to take advantage of cash discounts.

Voucher   A written authorization form containing data about a transaction along with proper authorizations for payment, account distributions, and so forth.

Voucher register   A special journal replacing the purchases journal; it records prenumbered vouchers at the time the liabilities are incurred.

Voucher system   An internal control system designed to control a company's cash payments.

Vouchers Payable   A liability account in the general ledger that represents the controlling account for the sum of individual vouchers.

QUESTIONS, CLASSROOM DEMONSTRATION EXERCISES, EXERCISES, AND PROBLEMS

Discussion and Critical Thinking Questions/Ethical Case

1. What is the structure of a voucher?
2. List the five components of a voucher system.
3. What source documents are attached to a voucher?
4. Compare a voucher register to a purchases journal.
5. Why are vouchers filed by due dates?
6. Posting to a voucher register is quite different from posting to other special journals. Agree or disagree? Why?
7. Why is an accounts payable ledger eliminated in the voucher system?
8. Once a voucher is recorded, it cannot be canceled. Agree or disagree? Why?
9. Explain how partial payments would be recorded in the voucher register.
10. Most companies use the voucher system. Due to poor profitability, several employees in the accounting office were let go. Joe Rose, who handled the verification of the vouchers in the voucher register, was now given the responsibility of writing the checks from the check register. The head of accounting thought Joe was the most honest person in the company and that all would be fine. Do you agree with this move? What would you recommend? You make the call. Write down your recommendation to Jay Flynn, head of accounting.

Classroom Demonstration Exercises

SET A

LO1 (10 min)   **Journal Entries to Record and Pay Vouchers**

1. Record the following transactions in the general journal:

20XX		
July	9	Voucher no. 8 was prepared for the purchase of $800 of merchandise from Reel Co.; terms 2/10, n/30.
	12	Voucher no. 9 was prepared for $2,000 of equipment; terms 2/10, n/30.
	16	Check no. 15 was issued in payment of voucher no. 8.

LO1 (10 min)   **Petty Cash**

2. Record the following transactions into the general journal. The company uses a voucher system along with a petty cash fund.

20XX		
Sept.	9	Voucher no. 18 was prepared to establish petty cash for $120.
	28	Voucher no. 42 was prepared to replenish the petty cash fund from the following receipts: supplies, $25; delivery, $29.

LO2 (10 min)   **Purchases Returns and Allowances**

3. On November 15, Pete Co. prepared a voucher for $400 for merchandise purchased from Pool Co. On November 19, Pete Co. decided to return merchandise valued at $100 due to poor workmanship. Record the general journal entries.

BLUEPRINT: STEPS TO RECORD AND PAY A LIABILITY USING THE VOUCHER SYSTEM

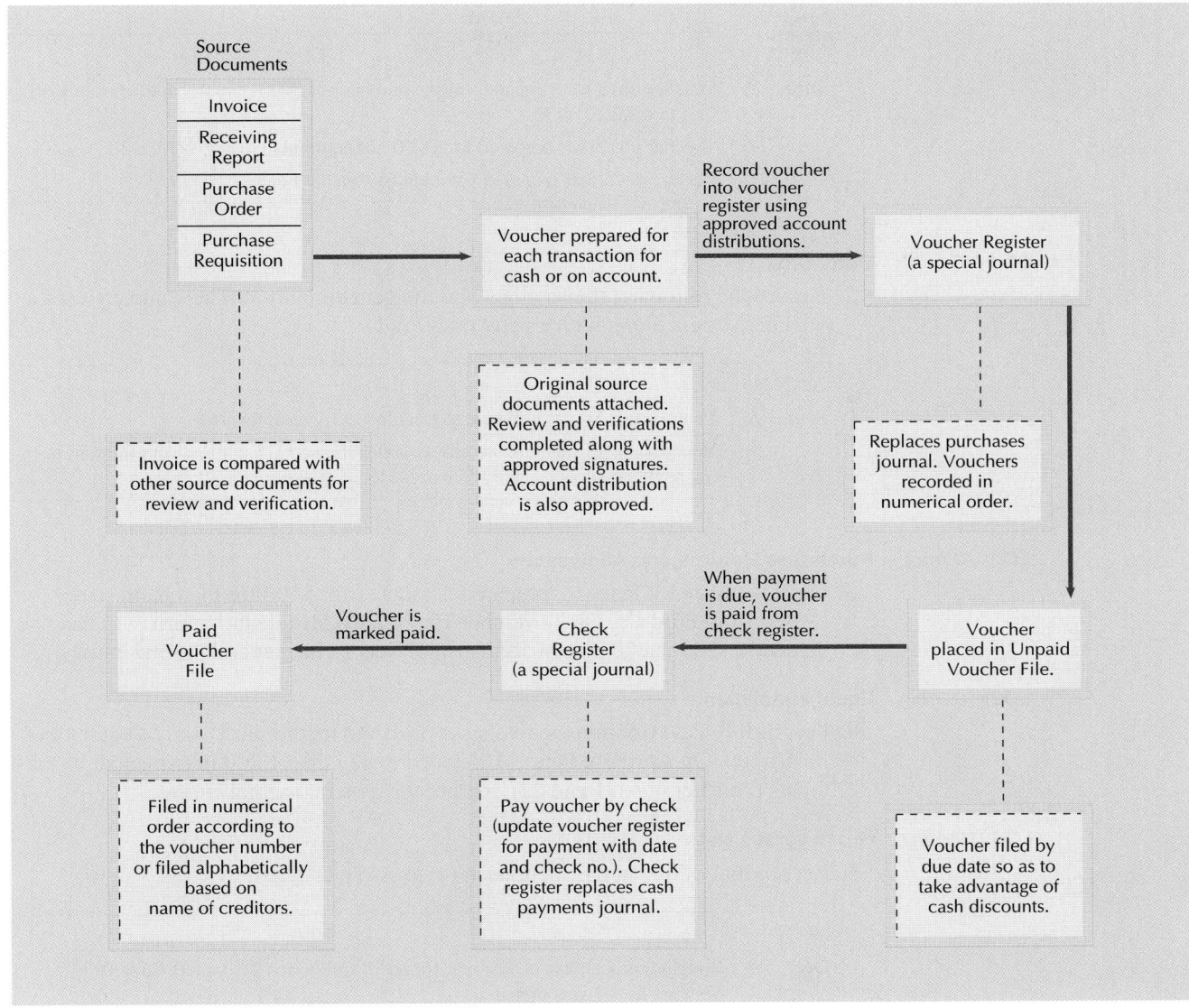

Equal Installments   *LO2 (10 min)*

4. On April 8, Pete Co. prepared voucher no. 18 to record purchases of equipment for $1,400. On April 16, Pete Co. decided to pay the $1,400 in two equal installments (voucher nos. 21 and 22). Record the general journal entries.

Gross versus Net   *LO3 (10 min)*

5. Record the following transactions at (a) gross and (b) net:

20XX

Dec.   8   Bought merchandise on account from Pill Co.; terms 2/10, n/30, $7,000. Voucher no. 31 was prepared.

20   Issued check no. 480 in payment of voucher no. 31.

SET B

LO1 (10 min)   **Journal Entries to Record and Pay Vouchers**

1. Record the following transactions in the general journal:

20XX		
June	9	Voucher no. 8 was prepared for the purchase of $900 of merchandise from Reel Co.; terms 2/10, n/30.
	12	Voucher no. 9 was prepared for $1,000 of equipment; terms 2/10, n/30.
	16	Check no. 15 was issued in payment of voucher no. 8.

LO1 (10 min)   **Petty Cash**

2. Record the following transactions into the general journal. The company uses a voucher system along with a petty cash fund.

20XX		
Sept.	9	Voucher no. 18 was prepared to establish petty cash for $90.
	28	Voucher no. 42 was prepared to replenish the petty cash fund from the following receipts: supplies, $15; delivery, $18.

LO2 (10 min)   **Purchases Returns and Allowances**

3. On November 15, Pete Co. prepared a voucher for $500 for merchandise purchased from Pool Co. On November 19, Pete Co. decided to return merchandise valued at $200 due to poor workmanship. Record the general journal entries.

LO2 (10 min)   **Equal Installments**

4. On April 8, Pete Co. prepared voucher no. 18 to record purchases of equipment for $1,200. On April 16, Pete Co. decided to pay the $1,200 in two equal installments (voucher nos. 21 and 22). Record the general journal entries.

LO3 (10 min)   **Gross versus Net**

5. Record the following transactions at (a) gross and (b) net:

20XX		
Dec.	8	Bought merchandise on account from Pill Co.; terms 2/10, n/30, $6,000. Voucher no. 31 was prepared.
	20	Issued check no. 480 in payment of voucher no. 31.

Exercises

LO1 (30 min)   **23-1.** Agnes Company, which is a medium-sized firm, uses a voucher system. Record each of the following entries in general journal form (explanations can be omitted):

20X9		
July	6	Voucher no. 50 was prepared for the purchase of $7,000 of merchandise from Loop Company; terms 2/10, n/30.
	9	Voucher no. 51 was prepared for the purchase of $4,000 of equipment; terms 2/10, n/30.
	15	Check no. 55 was issued in payment of voucher no. 51.
	16	Check no. 56 was issued in payment of voucher no. 50.

23-2. Dan Company uses a voucher system along with a petty cash fund. Record each of the following entries in general journal form (explanations can be omitted):   *LO1 (35 min)*

20X9

Aug. 10   Purchased $500 of merchandise from Glow Company; voucher no. 150 was prepared; terms 2/10, n/30.

     14   Voucher no. 151 was prepared to establish petty cash for $70.

     16   Issued check no. 60 in payment of voucher no. 150.

     17   Check was issued to pay voucher no. 151.

     28   Voucher no. 152 was prepared to replenish the petty cash fund from the following receipts: supplies, $17; delivery, $19.

23-3. On November 10, 20X9, a voucher for $1,000 for merchandise purchased from Gurn Company was prepared by Doll Corporation. On November 14, Doll decided to return the merchandise due to poor workmanship. The price of the merchandise was $600. Record the entries in general journal form for November 10 and 14 (explanations can be omitted).   *LO2 (20 min)*

23-4. On March 15, 20X9, Lori Company prepared voucher no. 89 to record the purchase of equipment for $900. On March 18, Lori Company decided to pay $900 in two equal installments. (Voucher nos. 90 and 91 were prepared.) Prepare the appropriate journal entries in general journal form for March 15 and 18.   *LO2 (20 min)*

23-5. Marvin Company records invoices at gross in its voucher system. From the following transactions, (a) record in general journal form the appropriate entries at gross and (b) record the entries as if Marvin Company recorded invoices at net.   *LO3 (20 min)*

20X9

Dec. 15   Bought merchandise on account from Levron Corporation; terms 2/10, n/30, $9,000. Voucher no. 300 was prepared.

     29   Issued check no. 600 in payment of voucher no. 300.

Group A Problems

23A-1. Fair Corporation uses a voucher system. Record the following transactions into the voucher register: *LO1 (30 min)*

20X9

June 8   Purchased office equipment from Tam Corporation, $900; voucher no. 300 was prepared.

     12   Established a petty cash fund of $70; voucher no. 301 was prepared.

     14   Purchased merchandise from Screen Corporation, $800; voucher no. 302 was prepared.

     15   Purchased office supplies from Longview Corp., $900; voucher no. 303 was prepared.

     29   Voucher no. 304 was prepared to replenish the petty cash fund based on the following receipts: supplies, $34; postage, $16.

> *Check Figure:*
> June 12
> Dr. Petty Cash (sundry) $70
> Cr. Vouchers Payable $70

23A-2. Skippy Corporation uses a voucher system. Record the following transactions into the voucher register and/or check the register as appropriate: *LO1 (30 min)*

20X9

July 5   Purchased merchandise for $2,000 from Dork Company; terms 2/10, n/30; voucher no. 280 was prepared authorizing payment on July 15.

     8   Purchased merchandise for $6,000 from Hornet Company; terms 2/10, n/30; voucher no. 281 was prepared authorizing payment on July 18.

(continued on next page)

15   Paid amount due Dork from voucher no. 280; check no. 91.

18   Paid amount due Hornet from voucher no. 281; check no. 92.

29   Voucher no. 282 was prepared for July rent to be paid to Loy Realty, $2,500.

30   Purchased office equipment for $2,900 from Lyle Company; voucher no. 283 was prepared.

30   Paid amount due Loy Realty from voucher no. 282; check no. 93.

LO1, 2 (45 min)   **23A-3.** Jona Corporation has been using a voucher system for several years. Prepare entries in the voucher register and check register for the following transactions:

20X8

Sept.   1   Purchased merchandise inventory from Ricardo Corporation for $6,000; terms 2/10, n/30; voucher no. 68 was prepared.

5   Purchased merchandise inventory from Ree Corporation for $7,000; terms 2/10, n/30; voucher no. 69 was prepared.

8   Issued check no. 75 to pay for voucher no. 69.

10   Issued check no. 76 to pay for voucher no. 68.

14   Purchased merchandise inventory from Langle Corporation for $9,000; terms 2/10, n/30; voucher no. 70 was prepared.

17   Returned $3,000 of the merchandise to Langle Corporation due to poor workmanship; voucher no. 71 was prepared to replace voucher no. 70.

20   Issued check no. 77 to pay for voucher 71.

LO1, 2 (60 min)   **23A-4.** The Swellon Company uses a voucher system. Record the following transactions:

20X9

Mar.   1   Voucher no. 200 was prepared for the purchase of $4,000 worth of merchandise inventory from Rolo Company; terms 2/10, n/30.

2   Voucher no. 201 was prepared for freight-in that was to be paid to Lance Company, $300.

3   Office supplies were purchased from Marge Company for $400; terms 2/10, n/30; voucher no. 202 was prepared.

8   Check no. 150 was issued in payment of voucher no. 200.

10   Purchased office equipment from Hal's Company for $10,000; payment is to be in two equal installments. Voucher nos. 203 and 204 were prepared to cover these payments.

12   Check no. 151 was issued to pay voucher no. 203.

12   Check no. 152 was issued to pay voucher no. 201.

18   Purchased $6,000 of merchandise from Lowe Corporation; terms 2/10, n/30; voucher no. 205 was prepared.

20   Purchased $3,000 of merchandise from Ken Company; terms 2/10, n/30; voucher no. 206 was prepared.

25   Check no. 153 was issued to pay voucher no. 205.

27   Returned $1,000 of merchandise bought from Ken Company; voucher no. 206 was canceled and voucher no. 207 was prepared.

29   Issued check no. 154 to pay voucher no. 207.

Group B Problems

23B-1. Fair Company uses a voucher system. Record the following transactions into the voucher register:

LO1 (30 min)

20X8

July 10   Purchased office equipment from Smooth Company, $1,600; voucher no. 400 was prepared.

       13   Established a petty cash fund of $60; voucher no. 401 was prepared.

       14   Purchased merchandise from Roy Corporation, $650; voucher no. 402 was prepared.

       15   Purchased office supplies from Kendall Corporation, $600; voucher no. 403 was prepared.

       29   Voucher no. 404 was prepared to replenish the petty cash fund based on the following receipts: supplies, $28; postage, $14.

Check Figure:
July 13
Dr. Petty Cash (sundry) $60
Cr. Vouchers Payable $60

23B-2. Caven Company uses a voucher system. Record the following transactions into the voucher register and/or check register as appropriate:

LO1 (30 min)

20X9

May 6   Purchased merchandise for $2,000 from Hall Company; terms 2/10, n/30; voucher no. 600 was prepared authorizing payment on May 14.

       8   Purchased merchandise for $8,000 from Ryan Company; terms 2/10, n/30; voucher no. 601 was prepared authorizing payment on May 17.

       14   Paid amount due Hall Company from voucher no. 600; check no. 300.

       17   Paid amount due Ryan Company from voucher no. 601; check no. 301.

       25   Voucher no. 602 was prepared for June rent to be paid to Paul Realty, $800.

       30   June rent was paid by check no. 302.

       30   Purchased office equipment for $3,000 from Kline Company; voucher no. 603 was prepared.

Check Figure:
May 17
Dr. Vouchers Payable $8,000
Cr. Purchases Discount $160
Cr. Cash $7,840

23B-3. Lava Company has been using a voucher system for several years. Prepare entries in the voucher register and check register for the following transactions:

LO1, 2 (45 min)

20X8

Nov. 1   Purchased merchandise inventory from Lester Corporation for $9,000; terms 2/10, n/30; voucher no. 52 was prepared.

       6   Purchased merchandise inventory from Jungle Corporation for $7,000; terms 2/10, n/30; voucher no. 53 was prepared.

       8   Issued check no. 50 to pay for voucher no. 53.

       10   Issued check no. 51 to pay for voucher no. 52.

       14   Purchased merchandise inventory from Horv Corporation for $11,000; terms 2/10, n/30; voucher no. 54 was prepared.

       17   Returned $2,000 of the merchandise to Horv Corporation due to poor workmanship; voucher no. 55 was prepared to replace voucher no. 54.

       19   Issued check no. 52 to pay for voucher no. 55.

Check Figure:
Nov. 8
Dr. Vouchers Payable $7,000
Cr. Purchases Discount $140
Cr. Cash $6,860

23B-4. Krown Corporation uses a voucher system. Record the following transactions:

LO1, 2 (60 min)

20X9

June 1   Voucher no. 100 was prepared for the purchase of $6,000 worth of merchandise inventory from Langley Corporation; terms 2/10, n/30.

(continued on next page)

2	Voucher no. 101 was prepared for freight-in that was to be paid to J. Kane Company, $400.
3	Office supplies were purchased from Harold Company for $600; terms 2/10, n/30; voucher no. 102 was prepared.
8	Check no. 150 was issued in payment of voucher no. 100.
10	Purchased office equipment from Lyon Company for $7,000; payment is to be in two equal installments. Vouchers nos. 103 and 104 were prepared to cover these payments.
12	Check no. 151 was issued to pay voucher no. 103.
12	Check no. 152 was issued to pay voucher no. 101.
18	Purchased $5,000 of merchandise from Von Company; terms 2/10, n/30; voucher no. 105 was prepared.
20	Purchased $5,000 of merchandise from Lallan Company; terms 2/10, n/30; voucher no. 106 was prepared.
25	Check no. 153 was issued to pay voucher 105.
26	Returned $200 of merchandise bought from Lallan Company; voucher no. 106 was canceled and voucher no. 107 was prepared.
27	Issued check no. 154 to pay voucher no. 107.

ON-THE-JOB TRAINING

LO1 (20 min) **T-1.** Mel Ring recently opened a pizza shop. Over lunch, a salesman told Mel that to control his operation he should set up a voucher system so that all bills would be paid on time and properly approved. Mel thinks that in 10 years he will probably franchise his pizza operation. As his accountant, do you think the voucher system is the best way to go? Why? Please respond in writing.

LO1 (20 min) **T-2.** Morris Company uses a voucher system. For the past two years the bookkeeper recorded installment purchases as a lump-sum payment in the voucher register. The bookkeeper thinks an unpaid voucher file is not needed because cash discounts are minimal compared with total dollar sales. When her supervisor is out to dinner, the bookkeeper will sign her name to the distribution accounts authorization. Her supervisor has told her not to worry, because she can adjust "any mistakes" later on.

After two weeks from the date a voucher is paid, the bookkeeper destroys all pertinent data about the transaction. May Weston, an accounting intern, is quite upset about what's going on at Morris Company. Her textbook theory is not being followed, but her supervisor told her that textbook principles are not always followed in the real world. Are May's concerns justified? State in writing your reasons.

FINANCIAL REPORT PROBLEM

LO1 (20 min) ### Reading the Kellogg's Annual Report

When you look at Appendix A, do you think Kellogg's uses a voucher system?

INTERNET PROJECT

Office Depot

Go to the Web and search: Annual Report Office Depot 2008.
Click on Investors Relations.
List out the latest news Office Depot is providing to its investors.
Order a free annual report.

24

Departmental Accounting

DID YOU KNOW? In shopping centers, Federated Department Stores (like Macy's) rent space for up to 20 years. Most leases require that the store pay real estate tax, maintenance fees, and sometimes even a percentage of sales. Visit *www.fds.com* to find more information about Federated Department Stores.

LEARNING OBJECTIVES

1. Preparing income statements focusing on gross profit by department.

2. Preparing income statements focusing on departmental net income.

3. Preparing income statements focusing on departmental contribution margin.

Many large companies like Macy's find it necessary to keep separate accounting records for their various departments so that management can see how efficient each department is and how each contributes to overall performance. This chapter focuses on various accounting and reporting aids that allow management to do so.

We use as our example Catlin's Department Store, which sells mainly clothing. The manager of the adult clothes department at the store is quite concerned about the department's performance; upper management is discussing the possibility of reducing the space of the adult department in favor of expanding the children's department.

Learning Unit 24-1 The Income Statement: Focus on Gross Profit by Department

LO1

Each department of Catlin's Department Store is a unit in which the manager has the responsibility for controlling and incurring certain costs as well as generating revenue. Each unit, or department, is known as a **profit center.** If a manager had the responsibility for controlling costs, but not for directly generating revenue, the unit would be called a **cost center** (an example is the office maintenance department at Catlin's).

Figure 24.1 shows the income statement for Catlin's Department Store. As you can see from this figure, the total gross profit of the company is $373,800 ($841,300 − $467,500), and the operating expenses are $170,000.

To break down the gross profit figure by department, a company must gather information about each department. It does so by setting up separate accounting records for each department, with separate accounts for Sales, Sales Returns and Allowances, Sales Discount, Merchandise Inventory, Purchases, Purchases Returns and Allowances, and Purchases Discount. Once this information is separated by department, we can calculate the gross profit of each department. The use of a computer makes it possible to record and gather information for many departments easily and quickly.

FIGURE 24.1
Income Statement for Catlin's Department Store

CATLIN'S DEPARTMENT STORE INCOME STATEMENT FOR YEAR ENDED DECEMBER 31, 20X8			
Revenue from Sales:			
Sales		$870 000 00	
Less: Sales Returns and Allowances	$14 700 00		
Sales Discount	14 000 00	28 700 00	
Net Sales			$841 300 00
Cost of Goods Sold:			
Merchandise Inventory, Jan. 1, 20X8		$143 000 00	
Purchases	$499 000 00		
Less: Purchases Returns and Allowances	15 400 00		
Purchases Discount	16 100 00	467 500 00	
Cost of Goods Available for Sale		610 500 00	
Less: Merchandise Inventory, Dec. 31, 20X8		143 000 00	
Cost of Goods Sold			$467 500 00
Gross Profit on Sales			373 800 00
Operating Expenses			170 000 00
Income Before Taxes			203 800 00
Income Tax Expense			89 520 00
Net Income			$114 280 00

Let's look at an example. Figure 24.2 shows how the sales journal of Catlin's Department Store includes a Sales account for the children's department and one for the adult department.

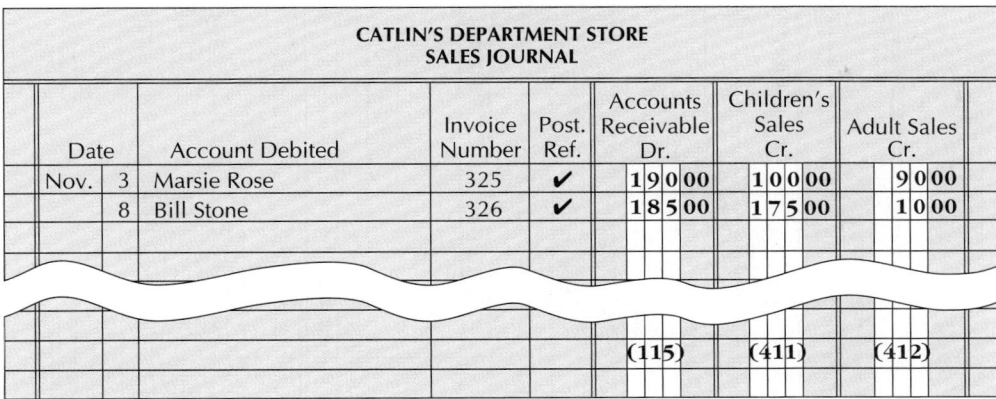

				Accounts Receivable Dr.	Children's Sales Cr.	Adult Sales Cr.	
	Date	Account Debited	Invoice Number	Post. Ref.			
Nov.	3	Marsie Rose	325	✔	1 9 0 00	1 0 0 00	9 0 00
	8	Bill Stone	326	✔	1 8 5 00	1 7 5 00	1 0 00
					(115)	(411)	(412)

FIGURE 24.2 Sales Journal of Catlin's Department Store

The income statement in Figure 24.3 on the following page shows the gross profit for each department and the combined totals. You would not see a balance sheet prepared in this way, broken down by department; only an income statement is prepared this way. Keep in mind that an income statement indicates how well a business or department is performing.

> Income statements can be broken down by departments; balance sheets are not.

LEARNING UNIT 24-1 REVIEW

AT THIS POINT you should be able to

- Explain the difference between a cost center and a profit center.
- Prepare an income statement focusing on gross profit by department.

Self-Review Quiz 24-1

Respond true or false to the following:

1. In a cost center a manager directly generates revenue.
2. Each department can have its own separate accounts for Sales, Sales Returns and Allowances, and so forth, to record information for the income statement.
3. A balance sheet is always separated by departments.

Solutions to Self-Review Quiz 24-1

1. False
2. True
3. False

Learning Unit 24-2 The Income Statement: Focus on Departmental Net Income

Departmental Income from Operations

So far we have looked at the way gross profit is accumulated by department. In this unit we look at how the $170,000 of operating expenses can be allocated by department if we want to extend departmental reporting beyond gross profit.

CATLIN'S DEPARTMENT STORE
INCOME STATEMENT SHOWING DEPARTMENTAL GROSS PROFIT
FOR YEAR ENDED DECEMBER 31, 20X8

	Children's		Adult		Total	
Revenue from Sales:						
Sales		$580 000 00		$290 000 00		$870 000 00
Less: Sales Returns and Allowances	$ 6 500 00		$ 8 200 00		$ 14 700 00	
Sales Discounts	8 000 00	14 500 00	6 000 00	14 200 00	14 000 00	28 700 00
Net Sales		$565 500 00		$275 800 00		$841 300 00
Cost of Goods Sold:						
Merchandise Inventory, Jan. 1, 20X8		75 000 00		$ 68 000 00		$143 000 00
Purchases	$289 000 00		$210 000 00		$499 000 00	
Less: Purchases Returns and Allowances	6 900 00		8 500 00		15 400 00	
Purchases Discounts	8 200 00	273 900 00	7 900 00	193 600 00	16 100 00	467 500 00
Cost of Goods Available for Sale		348 900 00		$261 600 00		$610 500 00
Less: Merchandise Inventory, Dec. 31, 20X8		79 000 00		64 000 00		143 000 00
Cost of Goods Sold		$269 900 00		$197 600 00		467 500 00
Gross Profit on Sales		$295 600 00		$ 78 200 00		$373 800 00
Operating Expenses						170 000 00
Income Before Taxes						203 800 00
Income Tax Expense						89 520 00
Net Income						$114 280 00

FIGURE 24.3 Income Statement with Gross Profit Broken Down by Department

The operating expenses of Catlin's Department Store that can be traced and identified **LO2**
directly to separate departments are called **direct expenses.** An example is the salaries of
the salespeople who work only for the children's department at Catlin's. The operating
expenses that cannot be identified with a specific department but are incurred on behalf of
the company are called **indirect expenses.** An example is the expense incurred in the
upkeep of the building in which Catlin's is located.

CATLIN'S DEPARTMENT STORE INCOME STATEMENT SHOWING DEPARTMENTAL INCOME BEFORE TAX FOR YEAR ENDED DECEMBER 31, 20X8	Children's	Adult	Totals
Net Sales	$565 500 00	$275 800 00	$841 300 00
Cost of Goods Sold	269 900 00	197 600 00	467 500 00
Gross Profit on Sales	$295 600 00	$ 78 200 00	$373 800 00
Operating Expenses:			
Sales Salaries	$ 25 000 00	$15 000 00	$ 40 000 00
Building Expense	12 000 00	4 000 00	16 000 00
Delivery Expense	6 000 00	4 000 00	10 000 00
Advertising Expense	9 000 00	5 000 00	14 000 00
Depreciation Expense	22 500 00	7 500 00	30 000 00
Administrative Expense	40 000 00	20 000 00	60 000 00
Total Operating Expenses	$114 500 00	$ 55 500 00	$170 000 00
Income Before Taxes	$181 100 00	$ 22 700 00	$203 800 00
Income Tax Expense			89 520 00
Net Income			$114 280 00

FIGURE 24.4 Operating Expenses Apportioned by Department

In Figure 24.4 we can see a sample of operating expenses that can now be apportioned
to the children's and adult departments. Note that the total is still $170,000. Now let's see
how these figures for operating expenses were calculated. Figure 24.5 is a summary of how
the expenses were apportioned. Following that is a detailed explanation. Use Figure 24.5
as a reference sheet as you read the explanation.

FIGURE 24.5 Direct and Indirect Operating Expenses by Department

	Children's		Adult		Total Operating Expense	
	Direct	Indirect	Direct	Indirect	Direct	Indirect
(1) Sales Salaries	$25,000.00		$15,000.00		$40,000.00	
(2) Building Expense		$12,000.00		$4,000.00		$16,000.00
(3) Delivery Expense	6,000.00		4,000.00		10,000.00	
(4) Advertising Expense	7,000.00	2,000.00	4,000.00	1,000.00	11,000.00	3,000.00
(5) Depreciation Expense		22,500.00		7,500.00		30,000.00
(6) Administrative Expense		40,000.00		20,000.00		60,000.00
	$38,000.00	$76,500.00	$23,000.00	$32,500.00	$61,000.00	$109,000.00
					$170,000	

1. Sales Salaries The payroll records of Catlin's show that salespeople in the children's department were paid $25,000 and salespeople in the adult department were paid $15,000. These expenses can be identified with specific departments, so they are considered direct expenses.

2. Building Expense The costs relating to the occupancy of Catlin's building are lumped into an account called Building Expense. Building Expense is an indirect expense, apportioned on the basis of square footage. Catlin's allocates the total cost of Building Expense of $16,000 on the basis of the number of square feet that each department occupies. Catlin's total space is 40,000 square feet, with the children's department occupying 30,000 square feet and the adult department 10,000 square feet. Building Expense is allocated to each department as follows:

Children's	Adult
$\dfrac{30{,}000 \text{ sqft}}{40{,}000 \text{ sqft}} = .75 = 75\%$	$\dfrac{10{,}000 \text{ ft}^2}{40{,}000 \text{ ft}^2} = .25 = 25\%$
$.75 \times \$16{,}000 = \$12{,}000$	$.25 \times \$16{,}000 = \$4{,}000$

Thus, of the $16,000 in Building Expense, the children's department is allocated $12,000 and the adult department $4,000.

3. Delivery Expense The children's department shipped 60% of all merchandise, and the adult department shipped 40% of the merchandise. The total cost of Delivery Expense is $10,000. Because the exact amount of Delivery Expense is traceable to each department, it is considered a direct expense. If the cost of delivery is *not* specifically traceable to each department, it is considered an indirect expense and can be charged to departments based on past delivery records. Delivery Expense is calculated as follows:

Children's	Adult
$.60 \times \$10{,}000 = \$6{,}000$	$.40 \times \$10{,}000 = \$4{,}000$

4. Advertising Expense Advertising Expense for Catlin's totaled $14,000. Of that total, $4,000 was spent on advertising adult clothes and $7,000 on advertising children's clothes. The remaining $3,000 ($14,000 − $11,000) was spent on advertising the store's image in general. Thus, this $3,000 is an indirect expense. How would you divide this expense by department? One common way is to apportion it based on gross sales of each department, as follows:

$$\begin{array}{rl} \text{Gross Sales:} & \$580{,}000 \quad \text{Children's} \\ & \underline{\quad 290{,}000} \quad \text{Adult} \\ & \$870{,}000 \quad \text{Total Gross Sales} \end{array}$$

Children's	Adult
$\dfrac{\$580{,}000}{\$870{,}000} \times \$3{,}000$	$\dfrac{\$290{,}000}{\$870{,}000} \times \$3{,}000$
$= \tfrac{2}{3} \times \$3{,}000 = \$2{,}000$	$= \tfrac{1}{3} \times \$3{,}000 = \$1{,}000$

Thus, of the $3,000 of indirect expenses, $2,000 is charged to the children's department and $1,000 to the adult department.

> Depreciation expense is an indirect expense.

5. Depreciation Expense Catlin's Department Store apportions depreciation on its building based on the square footage each department occupies. (Some companies apportion depreciation based on the average cost of the equipment in each department.) Catlin's has

40,000 square feet, of which the children's department takes up 30,000 (3/4) and the adult department takes up 10,000 (1/4). The amount of Depreciation Expense charged to each department is calculated as follows:

Children's	Adult
$\frac{3}{4} \times \$30{,}000 = \$22{,}500$	$\frac{1}{4} \times \$30{,}000 = \$7{,}500$

6. Administrative Expense Administrative expenses are incurred for the company as a whole and are not broken down by department; they are thus indirect expenses. In the case of Catlin's, it was decided that the Administrative Expense of $60,000 would be divided on the basis of each department's gross sales. We saw this method of allocation used in Advertising Expense. The calculation for indirect expenses charged to each department is as follows:

$580,000 Children's

$\underline{290{,}000}$ Adult

$\underline{\underline{\$870{,}000}}$ Total Gross Sales

Children's	Adult
$\dfrac{\$580{,}000}{\$870{,}000} = \frac{2}{3}$	$\dfrac{\$290{,}000}{\$870{,}000} = \frac{1}{3}$
$\frac{2}{3} \times \$60{,}000 = \$40{,}000$	$\frac{1}{3} \times \$60{,}000 = \$20{,}000$

Now take a moment to review Figure 24.4 to make sure you understand how we arrived at the total operating expenses of $170,000.

LEARNING UNIT 24-2 REVIEW

AT THIS POINT you should be able to

- Explain the difference between direct and indirect expenses.
- Explain how operating expenses are allocated to specific departments.
- Prepare, in proper form, an income statement showing departmental income before tax.

Self-Review Quiz 24-2

Given the following, apportion the rent expense on the basis of floor space:

	Dept. A	Dept. B	Total
Floor space	208,000	112,000	320,000
Rent expense			$ 30,800

Solution to Self-Review Quiz 24-2

Apportionment of rent expense:

Dept. A	Dept. B
$\dfrac{208{,}000}{320{,}000} \times \$30{,}800 = \$20{,}020$	$\dfrac{112{,}000}{320{,}000} \times \$30{,}800 = \$10{,}780$

LO3 # Learning Unit 24-3 The Income Statement Showing Department Contribution Margin

As shown in Figure 24.4 in Learning Unit 24-2, income before taxes for the children's department equaled $181,100 and the adult department showed $22,700. Some accountants think these figures are misleading, because the indirect expenses in Figure 24.5 were apportioned to the total operating expenses of each department. An alternative to this approach to indirect expense allocation is shown in Figure 24.6, which lists direct departmental expenses and the contribution each department makes to cover indirect expenses. This breakdown is called the **contribution margin,** which can also be defined as the gross profit of a department minus its direct expenses. This approach charges to a department only those expenses that are directly traceable to it. Note in Figure 24.6 that the children's department contributes $257,600 to cover indirect expenses and net income. This figure is quite different from the $181,100 listed in Figure 24.4.

FIGURE 24.6 Income Statement Showing Department Contribution Margin

CATLIN'S DEPARTMENT STORE INCOME STATEMENT SHOWING DEPARTMENTAL CONTRIBUTION MARGIN FOR YEAR ENDED DECEMBER 31, 20X8	Children's	Adult	Totals
Net Sales	$565 500 00	$275 800 00	$841 300 00
Cost of Goods Sold	269 900 00	197 600 00	467 500 00
Gross Profit on Sales	$295 600 00	$ 78 200 00	373 800 00
Direct Departmental Expenses			
Sales Salaries	$ 25 000 00	$ 15 000 00	$ 40 000 00
Advertising Expense	7 000 00	4 000 00	11 000 00
Delivery Expense	6 000 00	4 000 00	10 000 00
Total Direct Departmental Expenses	$ 38 000 00	$ 23 000 00	$ 61 000 00
Contribution Margin	$ 257 600 00	$ 55 200 00	$312 800 00
Indirect Departmental Expenses			
Building Expense			$ 16 000 00
Advertising Expense			3 000 00
Depreciation Expense			30 000 00
Administrative Expense			60 000 00
Total Indirect Expenses			$109 000 00
Income Before Taxes			$203 800 00
Income Tax Expense			89 520 00
Net Income			$114 280 00

> In this approach, indirect expenses are separated from direct expenses.

Supporters of this approach think indirect expenses are not controlled by the department manager and thus should not be used in evaluating departmental performance. Some accountants contend that even if a department is eliminated, the indirect expenses would not be decreased. For example, Catlin spends $3,000 in advertising that is basically aimed at advertising the store's overall image, and that expense would still remain if the adult department or the children's department were eliminated.

Determining whether certain departments at Catlin's should be expanded or reduced would involve investigation of the financial reports presented in the chapter along with topics such as the following:

1. The effect that dropping a department would have in terms of loss of its contribution margin. For example, would closing a jewelry department in a clothing store reduce the store's total administrative expenses?
2. The effect one department has in drawing customers to other departments. Do customers who come into the store to look at jewelry go on to look at dresses in another department?

3. Trends in the industry. Even though a certain department is not doing well, all the competing stores have such a department; the answer may be to cut down the size of the department rather than eliminate it.
4. Ability of suppliers to meet increasing demand for items. For example, it would not be a good idea to open a pastry shop in Catlin's until one had lined up a number of good, reliable suppliers.

We conclude this unit with an example that shows how eliminating a department that has a net loss may in fact cause an even greater loss in the overall net income for the company. The situation is as follows:

	Depts. A, B, C,	Dept. D Only	Totals for Depts. A–D	Totals if Dept. D Is Eliminated
Sales	$1,469,000	$130,000	$1,599,000	$1,469,000
Cost of Goods Sold	869,000	82,000	951,000	869,000
Gross Profit	600,000	48,000	648,000	600,000
Direct Expenses	340,000	31,000	371,000	340,000
Contribution Margin	260,000	17,000	277,000	260,000
Indirect Expenses	130,000	26,000	156,000	156,000
Net Income (Loss)	$ 130,000	$ (9,000)	$ 121,000	$ 104,000

Note that if Department D is eliminated, net income of the other departments is reduced by $17,000, from $121,000 to $104,000. This change is the result of losing the contribution margin of $17,000 from Department D.

LEARNING UNIT 24-3 REVIEW

AT THIS POINT you should be able to

- Explain why an income statement might report departmental contribution margin rather than listing all direct and indirect expenses under total operating expenses.
- Prepare an income statement showing the contribution margin.

Self-Review Quiz 24-3

Respond true or false to the following:

1. Allocating indirect expenses will never be subjective.
2. A direct expense is traceable to a respective department.
3. Direct expenses of a department in the contribution margin approach are combined with indirect expenses.
4. Eliminating one department could reduce sales of another department.
5. Contribution margin equals gross profit on sales plus direct department expenses.

Solutions to Self-Review Quiz 24-3

1. False
2. True
3. False
4. True
5. False

CHAPTER ASSIGNMENTS

SUMMARY OF KEY POINTS

LEARNING UNIT 24-1

1. A profit center means that a manager is responsible for controlling certain costs as well as generating revenues.
2. Separate accounts for Sales, Purchases, and so forth can be set up for each department so as to calculate departmental gross profit.
3. Income statements can be broken down by department; balance sheets are not.

LEARNING UNIT 24-2

1. Direct expenses can be directly identified with a specific department.
2. The method used to apportion indirect expenses to departments may vary from company to company; no single method is best in all cases.
3. One department's direct expense may be another department's indirect expense.
4. One way to apportion indirect expenses such as advertising expense or administrative expense by department is on the basis of each department's gross sales.

LEARNING UNIT 24-3

1. Indirect expenses are *not* combined with direct expenses when preparing an income statement showing departmental contribution margin.
2. Gross profit on sales minus direct departmental expenses equals contribution margin.

KEY TERMS

Contribution margin   A department's net profit, used to cover indirect expenses.

Cost center   A unit or department that incurs costs but does not generate revenues.

Direct expenses   Expenses that can be traced directly to a specific department.

Indirect expenses   Expenses that cannot be traced directly to one department.

Profit center   A unit or department that incurs costs and generates revenues.

BLUEPRINT: DEPARTMENTAL ACCOUNTING

		Dept. A	Dept. B	Total
Situation 1: Income statement showing departmental gross profit	Net Sales	1	2	3 (1 + 2)
	− Cost of Goods Sold	4	5	6 (4 + 5)
	= Gross Profit on Sales	7 (1 − 4)	8 (2 − 5)	9 (3 − 6)
	− Operating Expenses			10
	= Income Before Taxes			11 (9 − 10)
	− Income Tax Expense			12
	= Net Income			13 (11 − 12)

		Dept. A	Dept. B	Total
Situation 2: Income statement showing departmental income before tax	Net Sales	1	2	3 (1 + 2)
	Cost of Goods Sold	4	5	6 (4 + 5)
	Gross Profit on Sales	7 (1 − 4)	8 (2 − 5)	9 (3 − 6)
	Operating Expenses			
Direct and indirect expenses allocated →	Salaries Expense	10	11	12 (10 + 11)
	Delivery Expense	13	14	15 (13 + 14)
	Depreciation Expense	16	17	18 (16 + 17)
	Administrative Expense	19	20	21 (19 + 20)
	Total Operating Expenses	22 (10 + 13 + 16 + 19)	23 (11 + 14 + 17 + 20)	24 (12 + 15 + 18 + 21)
	Income Before Taxes	25 (7 − 22)	26 (8 − 23)	27 (9 − 24)
	Income Tax Expense			28
	Net Income			29 (27 − 28)

		Dept. A	Dept. B	Total
Situation 3: Income statement showing departmental contributions to indirect expenses	Net Sales	1	2	3 (1 + 2)
	Cost of Goods Sold	4	5	6 (4 + 5)
	Gross Profit on Sales	7 (1 − 4)	8 (2 − 5)	9 (3 − 6)
	Direct Departmental Expenses			
	Sales Salaries	10	11	12 (10 + 11)
	Advertising Expenses	13	14	15 (13 + 14)
	Delivery Expenses	16	17	18 (16 + 17)
	Total Direct Expenses	19 (10 + 13 + 16)	20 (11 + 14 + 17)	21 (12 + 15 + 18)
	Contribution to Indirect Expenses	22 (7 − 19)	23 (8 − 20)	24 (9 − 21)
	Indirect Departmental Expenses			
	Building Expense			25
	Advertising Expenses			26
	Depreciation Expenses			27
	Total Indirect Expenses			28 (25 + 26 + 27)
	Income Before Taxes			29 (24 − 28)
	Income Tax Expense			30
	Net Income			31 (29 − 30)

QUESTIONS, CLASSROOM DEMONSTRATION EXERCISES, EXERCISES, AND PROBLEMS

Discussion and Critical Thinking Questions/Ethical Case

1. What is the difference between a cost center and a profit center?

2. Explain how gross profit is calculated.

3. Special journals are not used in departmental accounting. Agree or disagree? Please explain.

4. Compare and contrast indirect expenses and direct expenses.

5. Explain how advertising expense could be both a direct cost and an indirect cost for a company.

6. Square footage is often used to allocate indirect costs to various departments within a company. Agree or disagree?

7. An income statement showing departmental income before tax does not list individual operating expenses for each department. Agree or disagree? Please explain.

8. Explain why a company might prepare an income statement showing each department's contribution margin.

9. Hernando Favor had been working in the bakery department of Long Company for four years when he was promoted to the accounting department. Since his promotion, sales in the bakery department slipped, and management is considering cutting the department in half. Hal Moore, who works in the bakery, will be laid off. Hernando thought about shifting some of the sales figures in his accounting records to the bakery department from other departments in order to save his friend Hal from losing his job. Hernando thinks no one will find out in the long run, because he knows the bakery can increase sales. Do you feel Hernando has clear justification for his actions? You make the call. Write down your recommendation to Hernando.

Classroom Demonstration Exercises

SET A

LO1 (10 min) **Appropriating Rent to Departments Based on Sales**

1. The cost of rent of $12,000 for Jean Co. is appropriated to each department based on sales. Given the following, assign the cost of rent to each department:

Rent	Toys Sales	Clothing Sales
$12,000	$20,000	$40,000

LO1 (10 min) **Appropriating Fire Insurance Based on Square Footage**

2. Calculate the assignment of fire insurance of $18,000 to each department based on square footage.

Indirect Expense	Basis of Assignment	Bakery	Grocery
Fire Insurance	4,000 ft^2 total	1,000 ft^2	3,000 ft^2

LO2 (15 min) **Calculating Net Income from Total Operating Expenses**

3. Given the following, calculate net income:

	Dept. 1	Dept. 2
Net Sales	$6,000	$8,000
Cost of Goods Sold	2,000	3,000
Operating Expenses		$1,800
Income Tax Expense, 40% rate		

Calculating Departmental Net Income

LO2 (20 min)

4. From the following, calculate departmental income before tax. Assume a tax rate of 30%.

	Dept. A	Dept. B
Net Sales	$4,000	$6,000
Cost of Goods Sold	2,000	2,000
Delivery Expense	600	800
Advertising Expense	500	600
Depreciation Expense	300	400

Calculating Contribution Margin

LO3 (20 min)

5. Calculate the contribution margin for each department and income before taxes, based on the following:

	Dept. A 1,000 ft^2	Dept. B 2,000 ft^2
Net Sales	$6,000	$11,000
Cost of Goods Sold	2,000	6,000
Sales Salaries	$ 900 (30% directly related to Dept. A and 70% related to Dept. B)	
Rent Expense	$ 500	
Advertising Expense	$1,000 ($800 directly related to Dept. A and $200 related to Dept. B)	

SET B

Appropriating Rent to Departments Based on Sales

LO1 (10 min)

1. The cost of rent of $6,000 for Moore Co. is appropriated to each department based on sales. Given the following, assign the cost of rent to each department:

Rent	Toys Sales	Clothing Sales
$6,000	$20,000	$40,000

Appropriating Fire Insurance Based on Square Footage

LO1 (10 min)

2. Calculate the assignment of fire insurance of $16,000 to each department based on square footage:

Indirect Expense	Basis of Assignment	Bakery	Grocery
Fire Insurance	4,000 ft^2 total	1,000 ft^2	3,000 ft^2

Calculating Net Income from Total Operating Expenses

LO2 (15 min)

3. Given the following, calculate net income:

	Dept. 1	Dept. 2	
Net Sales	$4,000	$6,000	
Cost of Goods Sold	1,000	2,000	
Operating Expenses			$2,500
Income Tax Expense, 40% rate			

LO2 (20 min) **Calculating Departmental Net Income**

4. From the following, calculate departmental income before tax. Assume a tax rate of 40%.

	Dept. A	Dept. B
Net Sales	$3,000	$4,000
Cost of Goods Sold	1,000	1,200
Delivery Expense	500	700
Advertising Expense	400	500
Depreciation Expense	200	300

LO3 (20 min) **Calculating Contribution Margin**

5. Calculate the contribution margin for each department and income before taxes, based on the following:

	Dept. A 1,000 ft²	Dept. B 2,000 ft²
Net Sales	$5,000	$10,000
Cost of Goods Sold	2,000	6,000
Sales Salaries	$ 800 (30% directly related to Dept. A and 70% related to Dept. B)	
Rent Expense	$ 400	
Advertising Expense	$ 900 ($400 directly related to Dept. A and $200 related to Dept. B)	

Exercises

LO1 (20 min) **24-1.** The cost of rent of $8,000 for Poller Company is appropriated to each department based on its sales. Given the following, assign the cost of rent to each department:

	Jewelry	Hardware	Automotive
Sales	$30,000	$50,000	$20,000

LO2 (20 min) **24-2.** Complete the assignment of fire insurance to each department.

Indirect Expense	Amount	Basis of Assignment	Candy Sales	Ice Cream Sales	Pizza Sales
Fire Insurance	$90,000	30,000 ft² total	18,000 ft² **a.**	7,500 ft² **b.**	4,500 ft² **c.**

LO2 (20 min) **24-3.** Given the following, calculate net income:

	Dept. 1	Dept. 2
Net Sales	$30,000	$40,000
Cost of Goods Sold	14,000	26,000
Operating Expenses		$16,000
Income Tax Expense, 30% rate		

24-4. From the following, calculate departmental income before tax. Assume a tax rate of 30%.   *LO2 (20 min)*

	Dept. A	Dept. B
Net Sales	$200,000	$250,000
Cost of Goods Sold	100,000	125,000
Delivery Expense	24,000	28,000
Advertising Expense	23,000	22,000
Depreciation Expense	25,000	24,000

24-5. Calculate the contribution margin for each department and income before taxes, based on the following: *LO3 (30 min)*

	Dept. A 10,000 ft²	Dept. B 20,000 ft²
Net Sales	$60,000	$90,000
Cost of Goods Sold	25,000	50,000
Sales Salaries	8,000 (40% directly related to Dept. A and 60% to Dept. B)	
Rent Expense	5,000	
Advertising Expense	18,000 ($3,000 directly related to Dept. A and $9,000 to Dept. B)	

Group A Problems

24A-1. From the following data, prepare in proper form an income statement showing departmental gross profit (assume a 25% tax rate) for Quick Stop for the year ended December 31, 20X9.   *LO1 (60 min)*

Check Figure:
Total Net Income $4,950

Cash	$12,000
Accounts Receivable	6,000
Allowance for Doubtful Accounts	1,500
Merchandise Inventory, January 1, 20X9, Grocery	7,000
Merchandise Inventory, January 1, 20X9, Pizza	5,000
Merchandise Inventory, December 31, 20X9, Grocery	19,000
Merchandise Inventory, December 31, 20X9, Pizza	7,000
Equipment	15,000
Accumulated Depreciation, Equipment	9,100
Accounts Payable	10,200
B. Smith, Capital	10,500
B. Smith, Withdrawals	3,100
Sales, Grocery	20,000
Sales, Pizza	18,000
Sales Returns and Allowances, Grocery	2,000
Sales Returns and Allowances, Pizza	3,000
Purchases, Grocery	22,400
Purchases, Pizza	14,500
Purchases Returns and Allowances, Grocery	800
Purchases Returns and Allowances, Pizza	400
Total Operating Expenses	4,700

LO2 (60 min) **24A-2.** Given the following information about the clothing and hardware departments of Sally Company, prepare a departmental expense allocation sheet showing expenses by department.

Check Figure:
Total Indirect Expenses $32,400

Account	Indirect Expenses	Direct Expenses	
		Clothing	Hardware
1. Rent Expense	$14,000		
2. Insurance Expense	7,000	$1,400	$2,600
3. Depreciation Expense		300	700
4. Advertising Expense	2,000		
5. Supplies Expense	3,000		
6. Salaries Expense	6,400		

Additional Facts

	Clothing	Hardware
Net sales	$70,000	$30,000
Cost of goods sold	50,000	18,000
Floor space	200 ft^2	500 ft^2

Allocation Basis

Rent and Insurance:	Floor space
Advertising and Supplies:	Net sales
Salaries:	Gross profit of clothing and hardware departments

LO2 (50 min) **24A-3.** From the following partial data, prepare an income statement showing departmental income before tax along with net income for Pete's Corporation for the year ended December 31, 20X9.

Net Sales, TVs	$60,000
Net Sales, Washers	30,000
Cost of Goods Sold, TVs	39,000
Cost of Goods Sold, Washers	18,000
Income tax rate 30%	
TV Dept., 5,000 sq. ft.	
Washers, 3,000 sq. ft.	

Check Figure:
Net Income $14,140

		Basis of Allocation
Sales Salary Expense	$4,500	Net sales
Building Expense	4,800	Square footage
Delivery Expense	2,700	Net sales
Depreciation Expense	800	Square footage

LO3 (60 min) **24A-4.** Educator Company has requested that you (1) assign indirect expenses to its jewelry and fur departments as appropriate and (2) prepare an income statement for November 20X9 showing departmental contribution margins along with net income. Assume a 30% tax rate.

	Jewelry (30,000 ft²)	Fur (10,000 ft²)	Indirect Cost
Net Sales	$280,000	$220,000	
Merchandise Inventory (Nov. 1)	50,000	70,000	
Merchandise Inventory (Nov. 30)	35,000	30,000	
Purchases	200,000	100,000	
Purchases Discount	10,000	20,000	
Salaries Expense	2,900	2,100	$10,000
Depreciation Expense	25,000	21,300	
Advertising Expense	1,000	2,000	20,000
Administrative Expense			32,000
Rent Expense			12,000

Check Figure:
Total Indirect Expenses $20,400

Salaries are based on net sales. All other indirect expenses are based on square footage.

Group B Problems

24B-1. From the following data, prepare in proper form an income statement showing departmental gross profit (assume a 25% tax rate) for Quick Stop for the year ended December 31, 20X9:

LO1 (60 min)

Cash	$13,100
Accounts Receivable	6,200
Allowance for Doubtful Accounts	2,400
Merchandise Inventory, January 1, 20X9, Cosmetics	8,000
Merchandise Inventory, January 1, 20X9, Jewelry	6,000
Merchandise Inventory, December 31, 20X9, Cosmetics	19,000
Merchandise Inventory, December 31, 20X9, Jewelry	8,000
Equipment	19,000
Accumulated Depreciation, Equipment	9,200
Accounts Payable	13,500
R. Glade, Capital	14,000
R. Glade, Withdrawals	5,000
Sales, Cosmetics	20,000
Sales, Jewelry	18,000
Sales Returns and Allowances, Cosmetics	2,000
Sales Returns and Allowances, Jewelry	1,500
Purchases, Cosmetics	24,800
Purchases, Jewelry	15,100
Purchases Returns and Allowances, Cosmetics	900
Purchases Returns and Allowances, Jewelry	500
Total Operating Expenses	5,500

Check Figure:
Net Income $2,625

24B-2. Given the following information about the toys and clothing departments of Avery Company, prepare a departmental expense allocation sheet showing expenses by department:

LO2 (60 min)

Account	Indirect Expenses	Direct Expenses	
		Toys	Clothing
1. Rent Expense	$15,000		
2. Insurance Expense	21,000	$1,900	$1,700

Check Figure:
Total Indirect Expenses $79,000

(continued on next page)

3. Depreciation Expense		1,000	700
4. Advertising Expense	3,000	
5. Supplies Expense	10,000	
6. Salaries Expense	30,000	

Additional Facts

	Toys	Clothing
Net sales	$20,000	$30,000
Cost of goods sold	10,000	20,000
Floor space	1,000 ft^2	2,000 ft^2

Allocation Basis

Rent and Insurance:	Floor space
Advertising and Supplies:	Net sales
Salaries:	Gross profit of toys and clothing departments

LO2 (50 min)   **24B-3.** From the following partial data, prepare an income statement showing departmental income before tax along with net income for Logan Corporation for the year ended December 31, 20X9:

Net Sales, Rugs (10,000 ft^2)	$180,000
Net Sales, Furniture (30,000 ft^2)	220,000
Cost of Goods Sold, Rugs	55,000
Cost of Goods Sold, Furniture	69,000
Income tax rate, 30%	

Check Figure:
Net Income $70,000

		Basis of Allocation
Sales Salary Expense	$60,000	Net Sales
Building Expense	20,000	Square footage
Delivery Expense	80,000	Net sales
Depreciation Expense	16,000	Square footage

LO3 (60 min)   **24B-4.** Lonestar Company requested that you (1) assign indirect expenses to its candy and grocery departments as appropriate, and (2) prepare an income statement for November 20X9 showing departmental contribution margins along with net income. Assume a 30% tax rate.

	Candy (20,000 ft^2)	Grocery (30,000 ft^2)	Indirect Cost
Net Sales	$18,000	$22,000	
Merchandise Inventory (November 1)	1,000	1,500	
Merchandise Inventory (November 30)	2,000	2,500	
Purchases	9,250	8,450	
Purchases Discount	250	450	
Salaries Expense	750	1,500	$2,500
Depreciation Expense	1,250	250	
Advertising Expense	250	1,500	
Administrative Expense			7,500
Rent Expense			2,000

Check Figure:
Total Indirect Expenses $7,075

Salaries are based on net sales. All other indirect expenses are based on square footage.

ON-THE-JOB TRAINING

T-1. Dot Jensen received the following memorandum: *LO1, 2, 3 (50 min)*

MEMO

To: Dot Jensen, Manager of Children's Clothing

From: Bill Barnes

Re: Annual evaluation

Based on the following data (attached), I am sorry to inform you that you will not be rehired at the end of your current contract. Your department's performance was far below the budgeted level we had projected for this period.

Dot is quite upset and thinks her evaluation is not justified. Analyze the data to see whether Dot's evaluation is indeed not justifiable. What additional factors might be considered? Please respond in writing.

Attachment: Annual Evaluation Data		
Clothing Sales		$320,000
Cost of Goods Sold		170,000
Gross Profit		$150,000
Operating Expenses:		
Hourly Wages	$75,000	
Manager's Salary	40,000	
Depreciation of Building	15,000	
Interest on Long-Term Bonds	12,000	
Payroll Taxes	16,000	
Total Operating Expenses		158,000
Departmental Loss		(8,000)

T-2. Moore Markets is considering the elimination of the Bakery Shop. Based on the following data, make your written recommendations to Jim Moore, president of Moore Markets.   *LO1, 2, 3 (50 min)*

	Produce	Dairy	Bakery
Sales	$60,000	$90,000	$82,000
Cost of Goods Sold	19,000	58,000	67,000
Gross Profit	$41,000	$32,000	$15,000
Direct Expenses	12,000	6,000	8,000
Indirect Expenses	6,000	12,000	4,000
Total Operating Expenses	18,000	18,000	12,000
Net Income Before Tax	$23,000	$14,000	$ 3,000

FINANCIAL REPORT PROBLEM

Reading the Kellogg's Annual Report   *LO1 (10 min)*

Go to Appendix A and locate note 14. Find the net sales figure for Latin America for 2006.

INTERNET PROJECT

Federated Department Stores

Go to the Web and search: Annual Report Federated Department Stores 2008.
Click on Investors Relations.
List out the latest news Federated Department Stores is providing to its investors.
Order a free annual report.

25

Manufacturing Accounting

DID YOU KNOW? In 2006 Revlon expensed research and development as it occurred. Revlon spent 24.4 million dollars in 2006. Visit *www.revlon.com* to find more information about Revlon.

LEARNING OBJECTIVES

1. Preparing a cost of goods manufacturing schedule.

2. Journalizing transactions recording the manufacturing process.

3. Preparing a worksheet for a manufacturing company.

Manufacturing accounting refers to the specialized accounting concepts and techniques that are required to record, report, and control the operations of a manufacturing company, like Revlon, properly. The financial accounting procedures discussed in the previous merchandising chapters are all still valid in a manufacturing firm, but they are supplemented by the manufacturing accounting to be presented in this chapter, including some new terms and techniques that were not considered or required in the accounting for merchandising operations.

Learning Unit 25-1 Cost of Goods Manufactured and the Income Statement

LO1

In a manufacturing company it is necessary to separate the manufacturing costs from all other selling and administrative expenses, because product costs, inventory costs, and even gross profit come from the manufacturing process. One way of thinking about it is to imagine manufacturing costs being incurred in one building and the other costs in another building as shown in Figure 25.1.

FIGURE 25.1

MANUFACTURING	ADMINISTRATIVE
Raw Material	Selling
Direct Labor	Administrative
Overhead	

All the costs incurred in the manufacturing building are manufacturing costs, including the managers' salaries, maintenance, all the labor, all materials, supplies, electricity, rent, and the depreciation of manufacturing property and machinery. In addition, it is necessary to allocate a portion of the accounting, personnel, purchasing, and data processing departments each month based on their contribution to manufacturing.

The administrative building would house top management, sales personnel, and other administrative personnel and their supplies and expenses.

Elements of Manufacturing Cost

Once we determine which costs are administrative and which are manufacturing, we can break the manufacturing costs into three elements: raw material, direct labor, and manufacturing overhead.

Raw material (or direct material) consists of all the items of material that will become a part of the product or will change the quality or characteristics of the product. For example, for a furniture manufacturer, the raw material includes lumber, metal parts, fabric, epoxy, finishing material, and even nuts and bolts. In a company that manufactures aluminum products, raw material includes the pure aluminum and the additives that are inserted to make the aluminum shiny or dull or rigid or flexible.

Direct labor includes the wages of those *personnel* whose efforts directly change the quality or characteristics of the products. In a furniture manufacturing company, the direct labor includes the person who saws the table top, the person who paints the furniture, the person who attaches the handles to the drawers, and so on. In that same company, however, the supervisor, the maintenance person, and the forklift driver are *not* direct labor.

Manufacturing overhead consists of all other manufacturing costs not included in raw material or direct labor. Manufacturing overhead includes many diverse items such as indirect labor, maintenance, engineering, manufacturing supervision, and supplies. Some of the most common items of manufacturing overhead are as follows:

- Maintenance wages and supplies
- Production supervision and expenses
- Depreciation expense of manufacturing assets
- Rent expense for buildings or machinery
- Electricity for manufacturing

- Insurance expense for manufacturing
- Indirect labor: material handlers
- Manufacturing clerical wages

Manufacturing Inventories

In a merchandise firm, one inventory is made up of goods for sale. A manufacturing firm tracks *three* major inventories: raw material, work-in-process, and finished goods. (In addition, other minor inventories are used for such things as maintenance supplies and operating supplies.)

The *raw material inventory* consists only of the cost of the items of raw material being held for production plus the freight cost to bring the material in. The acquisition of raw material is recorded as Purchases, the account reserved for the purchase of raw material.

The *work-in-process inventory* represents the cost of the products being processed (the step before becoming finished goods) and includes the raw material, direct labor, and the manufacturing overhead costs incurred at the time of the inventory.

The *finished goods inventory* consists of the manufacturing cost of the products that have been completed and are awaiting shipment to customers.

Cost of Goods Sold

To prepare an income statement for a manufacturing company, we first must figure the cost of goods sold. This section of the income statement for a manufacturing company is somewhat different from that of a merchandise company. The following diagram shows how cost of goods sold is calculated for a merchandise firm and for a manufacturing company.

LAYOUT TO CALCULATE COST OF GOODS SOLD

Merchandising Company	Manufacturing Company
Beginning Merchandise Inventory	Beginning Finished Goods Inventory
+ Net Purchases	+ Cost of Goods Manufactured
= Cost of Merchandise Available for Sale	= Cost of Goods Available for Sale
− Ending Merchandise Inventory	− Ending Finished Goods Inventory
= Cost of Goods Sold	= Cost of Goods Sold

As you can see in the diagram, the cost of goods manufactured replaces the purchases of the merchandise company statement. The purpose of the cost of goods sold section is to properly match the manufacturing costs with the sales, and for this reason it is necessary to include the beginning and ending finished goods inventories so as to calculate the cost. For example, the sales may have been for 500 units of product, whereas the company manufactured only 400 units this month. In this case there would be a 100-unit reduction in inventory. Thus, by adding the cost of goods manufactured to the beginning inventory and subtracting the ending inventory, the result will be the cost of 500 units of product. Similar reasoning is applied if the units manufactured for the month exceed the units sold.

The cost of goods manufactured is figured on a separate form or schedule. This statement is shown in Figure 25.2 on the following page. It is helpful to remember a few key points when preparing this figure:

1. Cost of raw materials equals beginning raw materials inventory plus purchases of inventory, less ending inventory of raw materials.
2. Total manufacturing costs incurred equal the following:
    Cost of Raw Material Used
    + Direct Labor
    + Factory Overhead
3. Cost of goods manufactured equals the following:
    Total Manufacturing Costs
    + Beginning Work-in-Process
    − Ending Work-in-Process

FIGURE 25.2 Statement of
Cost of Goods Manufactured

DUKE MANUFACTURING COMPANY STATEMENT OF COST OF GOODS MANUFACTURED FOR MONTH ENDED 6/30/X8			
Direct Materials:			
Raw Material Inventory, 6/1/X8		$ 5 000 00	
Plus: Net Purchases	55 000 00		
Less: Raw Material Inventory, 6/30/X8	8 000 00	47 000 00	
Raw Material Cost			$ 52 000 00
Direct Labor			90 000 00
Overhead:			
Factory Supervision	$ 37 000 00		
Maintenance Labor	15 000 00		
Electricity	6 000 00		
Maintenance Supplies	5 000 00		
Operating Supplies	3 000 00		
Depreciation of Machinery	4 000 00		
Total Overhead			70 000 00
Total Manufacturing Costs			212 000 00
+ Work-in-Process Inventory, 6/1/X8			7 000 00
− Work-in-Process Inventory, 6/30/X8			9 000 00
Total Cost of Goods Manufactured			$210 000 00

The first step in preparing the cost of goods manufactured is the calculation of the raw material cost for the month. If the accounting department has its records on a computer, the raw material cost may be readily available. If it is not, the cost must be calculated as shown by adding purchases to the beginning raw material inventory and then subtracting the ending inventory. The direct labor cost is usually a single figure found on the payroll or the labor distribution report. The overhead costs are then totaled and added to the raw material and direct labor to arrive at the total costs for the month. *The final step is to add the beginning work-in-process inventory and subtract the ending inventory.* Keep in mind that we subtract ending inventory because it is not part of the cost of goods manufactured (yet).

Let's see how this figure is then used in preparing the income statement, shown in Figure 25.3.

FIGURE 25.3 Income
Statement for a
Manufacturing Firm

DUKE MANUFACTURING COMPANY INCOME STATEMENT FOR MONTH ENDED 6/30/X8			
Sales			$400 000 00
Cost of Goods Sold:			
Finished Goods Inventory 6/1/X8		$ 25 000 00	
Plus: Cost of Goods Manufactured		210 000 00	
Cost of Goods Available for Sale		235 000 00	
Less: Finished Goods Inventory 6/30/X8		15 000 00	
Cost of Goods Sold			220 000 00
Gross Profit			180 000 00
Operating Expenses:			
Selling Expenses		$ 55 000 00	
Administrative Expense		65 000 00	120 000 00
Net Income (before taxes)			$ 60 000 00

LEARNING UNIT 25-1 REVIEW

AT THIS POINT you should be able to

- Define and explain the three elements of manufacturing costs: raw material, direct labor, and manufacturing overhead.
- Define and explain the three major inventories in a manufacturing company: raw material, work-in-process, and finished goods.
- Compare the cost of goods sold section on an income statement for a merchandising company with the cost of goods manufactured section for a manufacturing company.
- Prepare a cost of goods manufactured schedule.

Self-Review Quiz 25-1

Using the following accounts and amounts, prepare a separate statement of cost of goods manufactured and a cost of goods sold section of the income statement:

Finished Goods Inventory, June 1	$ 45,000
Depreciation of Machinery	15,000
Purchases (Net)	250,000
Maintenance Labor	15,000
Raw Material Inventory, June 1	15,000
Direct Labor	320,000
Work-in-Process Inventory, June 1	30,000
Factory Supervision Salaries	45,000
Finished Goods Inventory, June 30	60,000
Raw Material Inventory, June 30	20,000
Indirect Factory Labor	120,000
Work-in-Process Inventory, June 30	40,000
Factory Electricity Expense	15,000

Solution to Self-Review Quiz 25-1

Statement of Cost of Goods Manufactured		
Raw Material Inventory, June 1	$ 15,000	
Plus: Net Purchases	250,000	
Less: Raw Material Inventory, June 30	20,000	
Raw Material Cost		$245,000
Direct Labor		320,000
Overhead:		
Depreciation	$ 15,000	
Maintenance Labor	15,000	
Factory Supervision Salaries	45,000	
Indirect Labor	120,000	
Electricity Expense	15,000	210,000
Total Manufacturing Costs		$775,000
Plus: Work-in-Process Inventory, June 1		30,000
Less: Work-in-Process Inventory, June 30		40,000
Total Cost of Goods Manufactured		$765,000

(continued on next page)

Cost of Goods Sold	
Finished Goods Inventory, June 1	$ 45,000
Plus: Cost of Goods Manufactured	765,000
Cost of Goods Available for Sale	810,000
Less: Finished Goods Inventory, June 30	60,000
Cost of Goods Sold	$750,000

Learning Unit 25-2 The Flow of Manufacturing Costs

The Accumulation of Manufacturing Costs

As the raw material, direct labor, and overhead are charged into the manufacturing process, they must be recorded. The issuance of material from the warehouse, the assignment of labor to departments, and the movement of the products through the process must be provided to the cost accountants as the basis for journal entries.

Source Documents The required data are submitted to the cost accountants through various source documents. The timely receipt of legible documents is often a problem in some companies, and employees must be made aware of their importance.

Receiving reports are prepared by the receiving department to acknowledge receipt of all material and supplies from vendors. A typical receiving report is shown in Figure 25.4. The accounting copy becomes a part of the vendor payment voucher, along with the purchase order and the vendor invoice.

FIGURE 25.4 Receiving Report

RECEIVING REPORT			
Received from: Adams Company		Receiving Report No. _1031_ Date: 6/20/X8	
Quantity	Description	Unit Price	Total Price
50 Gals.	Paint	$6.50/Gal.	$325.00
Revilo Manufacturing Co. Inspected By _MS_ Received By _BJ_			

Material requisitions are the documents initiated by the manufacturing personnel, or other users, to request material from the inventory warehouse. The requisition (Fig. 25.5) is presented to the storekeeper as the materials are issued. Copies of the requisitions are kept in accounting as a basis for charging material to production.

FIGURE 25.5 Material Requisition

MATERIAL REQUISITION			
Department Finishing		Requisition No. _3648_ Date: 6/20/X8	
Quantity	Description	Unit Price	Total Price
8 Gals.	White Paint	$6.50	$52.00
Revilo Manufacturing Co. Inspected By _CY_ Received By _FU_			

A **clock card** is a card used by each hourly employee to clock in and out of the factory each day. A typical clock card is shown in Figure 25.6. The cards are collected each week

FIGURE 25.6 Clock Card

CLOCK CARD

Name: David Ross
Social Sec. No. 420-80-5178
Department: Cutting
Clock No. 1432

Day	In	Out	In	Out	Hours
Mon	7:58			4:03	8
Tue	7:57			4:01	8
Wed	8:00			4:02	8
Thu	7:59			5:02	9
Fri	7:57			4:03	8
Sat					
Sun					
				Total Hours	41

by the payroll department and become a basis for the payroll check and for charging labor to production.

Lot tickets, or move tickets, are documents that are written by departmental managers to reflect the movement of products, or parts of products, from one department to another. The department receiving the products must verify the quantity and quality of the products. These tickets become the basis for transferring costs between departments and to finished goods inventory. An example of a lot ticket is shown in Figure 25.7.

FIGURE 25.7 Lot Ticket

LOT TICKET

Date
Transferred from: Transferred to:
Assembling   Finishing

Quantity	Description
20 Tables	36" Oak
20 Tables	36" Pine

Received By ___MB___

A **labor distribution report** is a by-product of the payroll that has been allocated to the categories of direct labor, maintenance labor, and so forth. Based on this report, the cost accountants charge labor to the appropriate departments. An example of a typical labor distribution report is shown in Figure 25.8.

FIGURE 25.8 Labor Distribution Report

LABOR DISTRIBUTION REPORT
WEEK ENDING 9/10/X8

Employee	Department	Hours	Rate	Total
Direct Labor:				
James Amos	Cutting	42	$6.20	$260.40
Andrew Brown	Cutting	39	6.00	234.00
—				
Indirect Labor:				
Don Able	Cutting	40	7.20	288.00
Carl Baker	Cutting	40	7.50	300.00
—				

Bills of lading are documents that show the shipment of products to customers. The cost accounting copies of the bills become the basis for recording the transfer of the cost of the products from the finished goods inventory to the cost of goods sold. A typical bill of lading is shown in Figure 25.9 on the following page.

FIGURE 25.9 Bill of Lading

BILL OF LADING			
Shipper's No.			7/15/X8
Name of Customer __A.R. Owens__ Consigned to __Same__ Destination __Chicago__ State __Ill__ Route _____			

No. of Packages	Description	Weight	Class
60	Tables	3600	2

B.P. Smith Co. Atlanta, Georgia	__A.R.__ Agent

The Flow of Manufacturing Costs

To record and control manufacturing costs as the products move through the manufacturing process properly, it is necessary to establish the pattern of the flow of the costs. To do so, we use a flowchart.

> More explanations, along with an extra demonstration problem, follow the journal entries.

The Flowchart Figure 25.10 illustrates the movement of the material, labor, and overhead through the operation. Each step of the flow, from (a) to (h), is illustrated and is followed by an example of the journal entries and the source documents for each step. *Note that the journal entries reflect a debit to the destination and a credit to the source.*

FIGURE 25.10 Flow of Costs

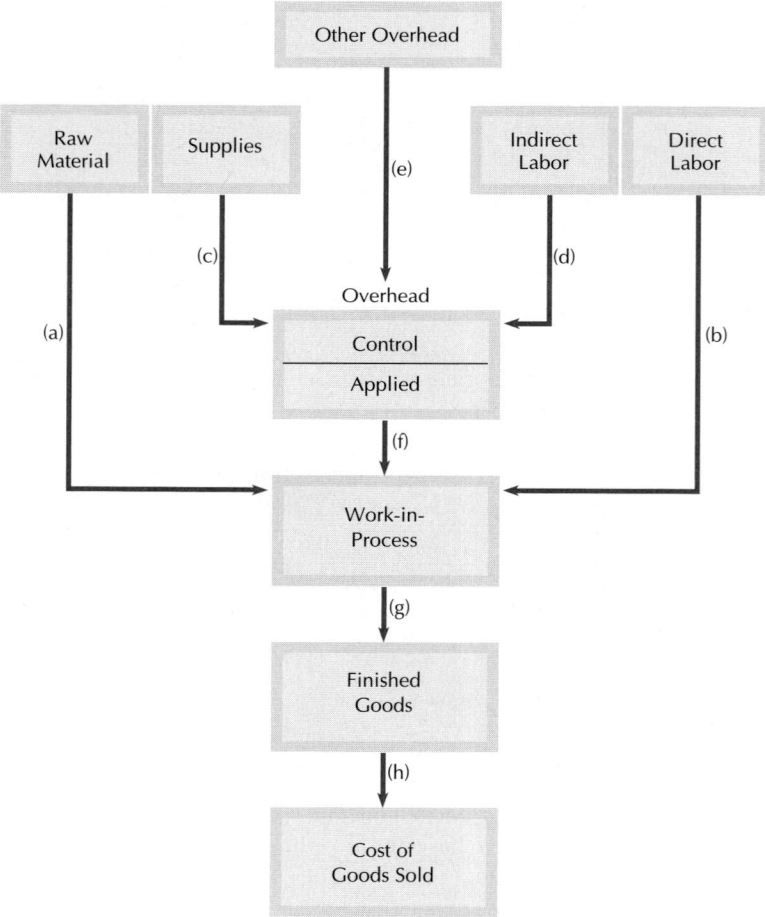

This process may seem overwhelming, so take the time to match each step in **LO2** Figure 25.10 with its corresponding journal entry in Figure 25.11. Remember that the debit is to the destination and the credit is to the source. See the Blueprint at the end of the chapter for samples involving T accounts.

FIGURE 25.11 Journal Entries

SOURCE DOCUMENTS

				Dr.	Cr.
Material requisitions	(a)	Work-in-Process Inventory		2 0 0 0 00	
		Raw Material Inventory			2 0 0 0 00
Labor distribution report	(b)	Work-in-Process Inventory		5 0 0 0 00	
		Payroll			5 0 0 0 00
Material requisitions	(c)	Overhead—Control		4 0 0 00	
		Supplies Inventory			4 0 0 00
Labor distribution report	(d)	Overhead—Control		1 0 0 0 00	
		Payroll			1 0 0 0 00
Various	(e)	Overhead—Control		1 0 0 0 00	
		Supervision Salaries			6 0 0 00
		Rent Expense			1 0 0 00
		Depreciation Expense			2 0 0 00
		Electricity Expense			1 0 0 00
None	(f)	Work-in-Process Inventory		25 0 0 0 00	
		Overhead—Applied			25 0 0 0 00
Lot tickets	(g)	Finished Goods Inventory		22 0 0 0 00	
		Work-in-Process Inventory			22 0 0 0 00
Bills of lading	(h)	Cost of Goods Sold		24 0 0 0 00	
		Finished Goods Inventory			24 0 0 0 00

Overhead Application As shown in the flow of cost journal entries (c), (d), and (e), the debit is to an account called Overhead—Control and in (f) the credit is to the account Overhead—Applied. It is desirable to maintain both these overhead accounts to avoid errors and confusion. Overhead—Control is used for the accumulation of all actual overhead costs as debits, and the Overhead—Applied is credited for the application of overhead to production.

It is necessary to apply overhead each week to determine the total costs for that week. Some overhead accounts, however, such as electricity, supervision, and depreciation, are not known until the end of the month. For this reason, an overhead rate must be established as a basis for applying the overhead. Several methods help to determine a rate, depending on the type of operation of the company.

The most common and practical methods are based on direct labor or machine hours. A rate can be developed from the annual budget of the overhead costs and the *direct labor dollars* (wages of those persons whose efforts *directly* affect the characteristics of the products manufactured) as follows:

Annual Overhead ÷ Annual Direct Labor Dollars

$$\$500,000 \div \$1,000,000 = 50\%$$

Based on this calculation, overhead can be applied to production each week or month at a rate of 50% of the direct labor cost charged to production. For example, if the direct labor this month is $20,000, overhead would be applied at $10,000, as shown in Figure 25.12.

FIGURE 25.12 Applying Overhead

Work-in-Process Inventory	10 0 0 0 0		
Overhead—Applied		10 0 0 0 0	

Another much-used rate is based on *direct labor hours*:

$$\text{Annual Overhead} \div \text{Annual Direct Labor Hours}$$
$$\$500,000 \quad \div \quad 200,000 \text{ Hours} \quad = \$2.50/\text{Hour}$$

In this case, the rate of $2.50 per direct labor hour would be applied as overhead. If direct labor hours this month were 2,000 hours, the applied overhead would be $5,000, as shown in Figure 25.13.

FIGURE 25.13 Applying Overhead by Direct Labor Hours

Work-in-Process Inventory	5 0 0 0 0		
Overhead—Applied		5 0 0 0 0	

Still another method that is convenient in some companies is based on *machine hours,* as follows:

$$\text{Annual Overhead} \div \text{Annual Machine Hours}$$
$$\$500,000 \quad \div 100,000 \text{ Machine Hours} = \$5.00/\text{Hour}$$

Using the $5.00 per machine hour rate, if the machine ran 3,000 hours, the overhead applied would be $15,000.

Demonstration Problem

To further illustrate the journal entries and overhead application, consider the following transactions and the resulting journal entries (Fig. 25.14) for the month of August:

a. Issued raw material from the storeroom costing $69,000.
b. Charged direct labor to production, $60,000.
c. Issued supplies from the storeroom costing $6,000.
d. Incurred indirect labor costs of $15,000.
e. Charged the following expenses to overhead: rent, $3,000; supervision, $12,000; depreciation, $4,000; electricity, $6,000.
f. Applied overhead at 85% of direct labor dollars.
g. Transferred completed products costing $200,000 to finished goods.
h. Sold products costing $208,000.

LEARNING UNIT 25-2 REVIEW

AT THIS POINT you should be able to

- List the six source documents covered in this unit and explain the function of each in the accounting process.
- List the steps of the flowchart showing the movement of raw materials through the manufacturing process.
- Explain the difference between Overhead—Control and Overhead—Applied.

Journal Entries

FIGURE 25.14 Manufacturing Transactions

		Debit	Credit
(a)	Work-in-Process Inventory	69 000 00	
	Raw Material Inventory		69 000 00
(b)	Work-in-Process Inventory	60 000 00	
	Payroll		60 000 00
(c)	Overhead—Control	6 000 00	
	Supplies Inventory		6 000 00
(d)	Overhead—Control	15 000 00	
	Payroll		15 000 00
(e)	Overhead—Control	25 000 00	
	Rent Expense		3 000 00
	Supervision Expense		12 000 00
	Depreciation Expense		4 000 00
	Electricity Expense		6 000 00
(f)	Work-in-Process Inventory	51 000 00	
	Overhead—Applied		51 000 00
(g)	Finished Goods Inventory	200 000 00	
	Work-in-Process Inventory		200 000 00
(h)	Cost of Goods Sold	208 000 00	
	Finished Goods Inventory		208 000 00

Self-Review Quiz 25-2

Prepare the general journal entries required to record the following transactions (omit explanations):

- **a.** Charged raw material to production, $6,000.
- **b.** Charged direct labor to production, $8,000.
- **c.** Issued operating supplies, $2,000.
- **d.** Charged indirect labor to production, $5,000.
- **e.** Incurred the following overhead: supervision, $4,500; rent, $1,000; depreciation, $500; electricity, $1,500; maintenance, $2,500.
- **f.** Applied overhead to production at 180% of direct labor dollars.
- **g.** Transferred products to finished goods, $9,000.
- **h.** Sold products costing $10,000.

Solution to Self-Review Quiz 25-2

FIGURE 25.15 Journalized Manufacturing Transactions

(a)	Work-in-Process		6 0 0 0 00	
	Raw Material			6 0 0 0 00
(b)	Work-in-Process		8 0 0 0 00	
	Payroll			8 0 0 0 00
(c)	Overhead—Control		2 0 0 0 00	
	Supplies Inventory			2 0 0 0 00
(d)	Overhead—Control		5 0 0 0 00	
	Payroll			5 0 0 0 00
(e)	Overhead—Control		10 0 0 0 00	
	Supervision			4 5 0 0 00
	Rent			1 0 0 0 00
	Depreciation			5 0 0 00
	Electricity			1 5 0 0 00
	Maintenance			2 5 0 0 00
(f)	Work-in-Process		14 4 0 0 00	
	Overhead—Applied			14 4 0 0 00
(g)	Finished Goods Inventory		9 0 0 0 00	
	Work-in-Process			9 0 0 0 00
(h)	Cost of Goods Sold		10 0 0 0 00	
	Finished Goods			10 0 0 0 00

LO3
Learning Unit 25-3 Worksheet for a Manufacturing Company

In past chapters we viewed worksheets for a service company as well as a merchandise company. We now examine and explain the preparation of a worksheet for a manufacturing company. Figure 25.16 shows a worksheet for Roe Corporation. We changed companies to provide you with more insight into other account titles used by different companies. The theory is the same. We then see how reports are prepared from the worksheet. Let's first look at some key points to remember when a worksheet is prepared. Keep in mind that the steps of the accounting cycle for a manufacturing company are the same as those used for a merchandise company.

Key Points to Look at on the Worksheet

Key points on the worksheet include the following:

> See number of key points circled on the worksheet (Fig. 25.16).

1. New set of columns for statement of cost of goods manufactured.
2. Beginning balances of raw materials inventory, $570, and work-in-process, $1,230, are listed in the debit column of statement of cost of goods manufactured. Ending balances of $960 and $1,590 are entered in the credit column.
3. Finished goods inventory is not listed on the statement of cost of goods manufactured. The beginning figure of finished goods, $750, is listed in the debit column of the income statement, whereas the ending balance of finished goods, $540, is listed in the credit column of the income statement and debit column of the balance sheet.
4. These expenses are not part of the cost of manufacturing and thus are not listed on the statement of cost of goods manufactured.

Account Titles	Trial Balance Dr.	Trial Balance Cr.	Adjustments Dr.	Adjustments Cr.	① Statement of Cost of Goods Manufactured Dr.	① Statement of Cost of Goods Manufactured Cr.	Income Statement Dr.	Income Statement Cr.	Balance Sheet Dr.	Balance Sheet Cr.
Cash	135000								135000	
Accounts Receivable	153000								153000	
Allowance for Doubtful Accounts		48000		(B)66000						114000
Raw Materials Inventory	57000				②57000	96000			②96000	
Work-in-Process Inventory	123000				②123000	159000			②159000	
Finished Goods Inventory	75000						③75000	54000	54000	
Factory Supplies	99000			(A)78000					21000	
Prepaid Factory Insurance	105000			(D)75000					30000	
Factory Machinery	648000								648000	
Accumulated Dep., Factory Mach.		120000		(C)84000						204000
Note Payable (due within 30 days)		225000								225000
Common Stock $10		225000								225000
Retained Earnings		180000								180000
Sales (Net)		2430000						2430000		
Raw Material Purchases (Net)	540000				540000					
Direct Labor	330000		(E)132000		462000					
Indirect Labor	102000		(E)48000		150000					
Heat, Light, and Power	174000				174000					
Machinery Repairs	45000				45000					
Rent Expense—Factory	180000				180000					
Selling Expense—Control	261000						261000			
Administrative Expenses (Control)	201000		(E)33000				234000			
	3228000	3228000								
Factory Supplies Expense			(A)78000		78000					
Bad Debts Expense			(B)66000				66000			
Dep. Expense—Factory Mach.			(C)84000		84000					
Factory Insurance Expense			(D)75000		75000					
Accrued Payroll Payable				(E)213000						213000
			516000	516000	1968000	255000				
Cost of Goods Manufactured						1713000 ④	1713000			
					1968000	1968000	2349000	2484000	1296000	1161000
Net Income							135000			135000
							2484000	2484000	1296000	1296000

FIGURE 25.16 Worksheet for a Manufacturing Company

Reports Prepared from the Worksheet

The following reports can be prepared from the worksheet.

Cost of Goods Manufactured

FIGURE 25.17 Statement of Cost of Goods Manufactured

ROE CORPORATION STATEMENT OF COST OF GOODS MANUFACTURED FOR YEAR ENDED DECEMBER 31, 20XX		
Direct Materials:		
Raw Materials Inventory (Beg.)	$ 5 7 0 00	
Raw Materials Purchased (Net)	5 4 0 0 00	
Cost of Available Raw Materials	5 9 7 0 00	
Less: Raw Materials Inventory (End.)	9 6 0 00	
Cost of Raw Materials Used		$ 5 0 1 0 00
Direct Labor		4 6 2 0 00
Factory Overhead:		
Indirect Labor	$ 1 5 0 0 00	
Heat, Light, and Power	1 7 4 0 00	
Rent Expense	1 8 0 0 00	
Machinery Repairs	4 5 0 00	
Factory Supplies Expense	7 8 0 00	
Deposit Expense, Factory Machinery	8 4 0 00	
Factory Insurance Expense	7 5 0 00	
Total Factory Overhead		$ 7 8 6 0 00
Total Manufacturing Cost Incurred		1 7 4 9 0 00
Plus: Work-in-Process (Beg.)		1 2 3 0 00
Less: Work-in-Process (End.)		1 5 9 0 00
Cost of Goods Manufactured*		$ 1 7 1 3 0 00

* This amount will go on the cost of goods sold section of the income statement, as shown in Figure 25.16.

The Income Statement Figure 25.18 is the income statement for Roe Corporation. Note how the $17,130 from the statement of cost of goods manufactured is listed below the beginning finished goods inventory. Note that the operating expenses, which were not part of the cost of the goods sold, are listed below gross profit. For example, Bad Debts

FIGURE 25.18 Income Statement

ROE CORPORATION INCOME STATEMENT FOR YEAR ENDED DECEMBER 31, 20XX		
Net Sales		$ 2 4 3 0 0 00
Cost of Goods Sold:		
Finished Goods Inventory (Beg.)	$ 7 5 0 00	
Cost of Goods Manufactured	1 7 1 3 0 00	
Cost of Goods Available for Sale	$ 1 7 8 8 0 00	
Less: Finished Goods Inventory (End.)	5 4 0 00	
Cost of Goods Sold:		$ 1 7 3 4 0 00
Gross Profit on Sales		$ 6 9 6 0 00
Operating Expenses:		
Selling Expense*	$ 3 2 7 0 00	
Administrative Expense	2 3 4 0 00	
Total Operating Expenses		$ 5 6 1 0 00
Net Income (before taxes)		$ 1 3 5 0 00

*Includes the $660 of bad debt expense.

Expense, a selling expense, had no part in the production of bean bag chairs for Roe. Remember that the cost of goods manufactured is not the same as the cost of goods sold.

The Balance Sheet Figure 25.19 is the completed balance sheet of Roe Corporation. The net income of $1,350 in Figure 25.18 helps update retained earnings in Figure 25.19. Note how under current assets the manufacturing company lists its raw materials and work-in-process as well as finished goods.

FIGURE 25.19 Balance Sheet

ROE CORPORATION BALANCE SHEET DECEMBER 31, 20XX			
Assets			
Current Assets:			
Cash			$ 1 3 5 0 00
Accounts Receivable	$ 1 5 3 0 00		
Less: Allowance for Doubtful Accounts	1 1 4 0 00	$ 3 9 0 00	
Inventories			
Raw Materials	$ 9 6 0 00		
Work-in-Process	1 5 9 0 00		
Finished Goods	5 4 0 00	$ 3 0 9 0 00	
Prepaid Expenses:			
Factory Supplies	$ 2 1 0 00		
Prepaid Factory Insurance	3 0 0 00	$ 5 1 0 00	
Total Current Assets		$ 5 3 4 0 00	
Plant and Equipment:			
Factory Machinery	$ 6 4 8 0 00		
Less: Accum. Depreciation, Factory Machinery	2 0 4 0 00	$ 4 4 4 0 00	
Total Assets		$ 9 7 8 0 00	
Liabilities and Stockholders' Equity			
Current Liabilities:			
Notes Payable	$ 2 2 5 0 00		
Accrued Payroll Payable	2 1 3 0 00	$ 4 3 8 0 00	
Stockholders' Equity			
Common Stock, $10 par 225 shares	$ 2 2 5 0 00		
Retained Earnings*	3 1 5 0 00	$ 5 4 0 0 00	
Total Liabilities and Stockholders' Equity		$ 9 7 8 0 00	

*Beginning Retained Earnings + Net Income = Retained Earnings

LEARNING UNIT 25-3 REVIEW

AT THIS POINT you should be able to

- Explain the key points to consider in a worksheet for a manufacturing company.
- From the worksheet, prepare a statement of cost of goods manufactured along with the income statement and balance sheet.

Self-Review Quiz 25-3

Respond true or false to the following:

1. The figure for cost of goods manufactured is always placed in the credit column of the income statement on the worksheet.
2. Finished goods are not listed in the statement of cost of goods manufactured.
3. All expenses are listed in the cost of goods manufactured.
4. The ending balances of raw materials inventory and work-in-process are entered in the debit columns of cost of goods manufactured.

Solutions to Self-Review Quiz 25-3

1. False   **2.** True   **3.** False   **4.** False

CHAPTER ASSIGNMENTS

SUMMARY OF KEY POINTS

LEARNING UNIT 25-1

1. Manufacturing costs are broken into raw materials, direct labor, and manufacturing overhead.
2. A manufacturing firm has three major inventories: raw materials, work-in-process, and finished goods.
3. Cost of goods manufactured is prepared first, before the income statement is completed.

LEARNING UNIT 25-2

1. When journal entries are prepared to record the movement of material, labor, and overhead through the operation of a company, each debit is the destination and each credit is the source.
2. Overhead may be applied based on direct labor hours, direct labor dollars, or machine hours.

LEARNING UNIT 25-3

1. The steps of the accounting cycle for a manufacturing company are the same as those used for a merchandise company.
2. The worksheet for a manufacturing company has columns for items used to calculate the statement of cost of goods manufactured. This figure is then updated on the income statement debit column of the worksheet.

KEY TERMS

Bill of lading   A formal document issued to the carrier of the finished product. It is the basis for charging the cost of goods sold.

Clock card   A card used by employees when clocking in and out of the factory; it becomes the basis for the payroll.

Direct labor   The wages of those persons whose efforts directly affect the quality or other characteristics of the products manufactured.

Labor distribution report   A report issued by the payroll department to categorize all the types of labor incurred during the week.

Lot ticket   A document prepared to show the movement of materials or products between departments. Also called *move ticket*.

Manufacturing overhead   All the manufacturing costs except raw material and direct labor.

Material requisition   A document used to order material or supplies from the storeroom that provides the basis for charging material into production.

Raw material   Material that is to be processed into a finished product or that changes the quality or characteristics of the product.

Receiving report   A document prepared by the receiving department to evidence the receipt of material or supplies that were ordered.

BLUEPRINT: MANUFACTURING ELEMENTS

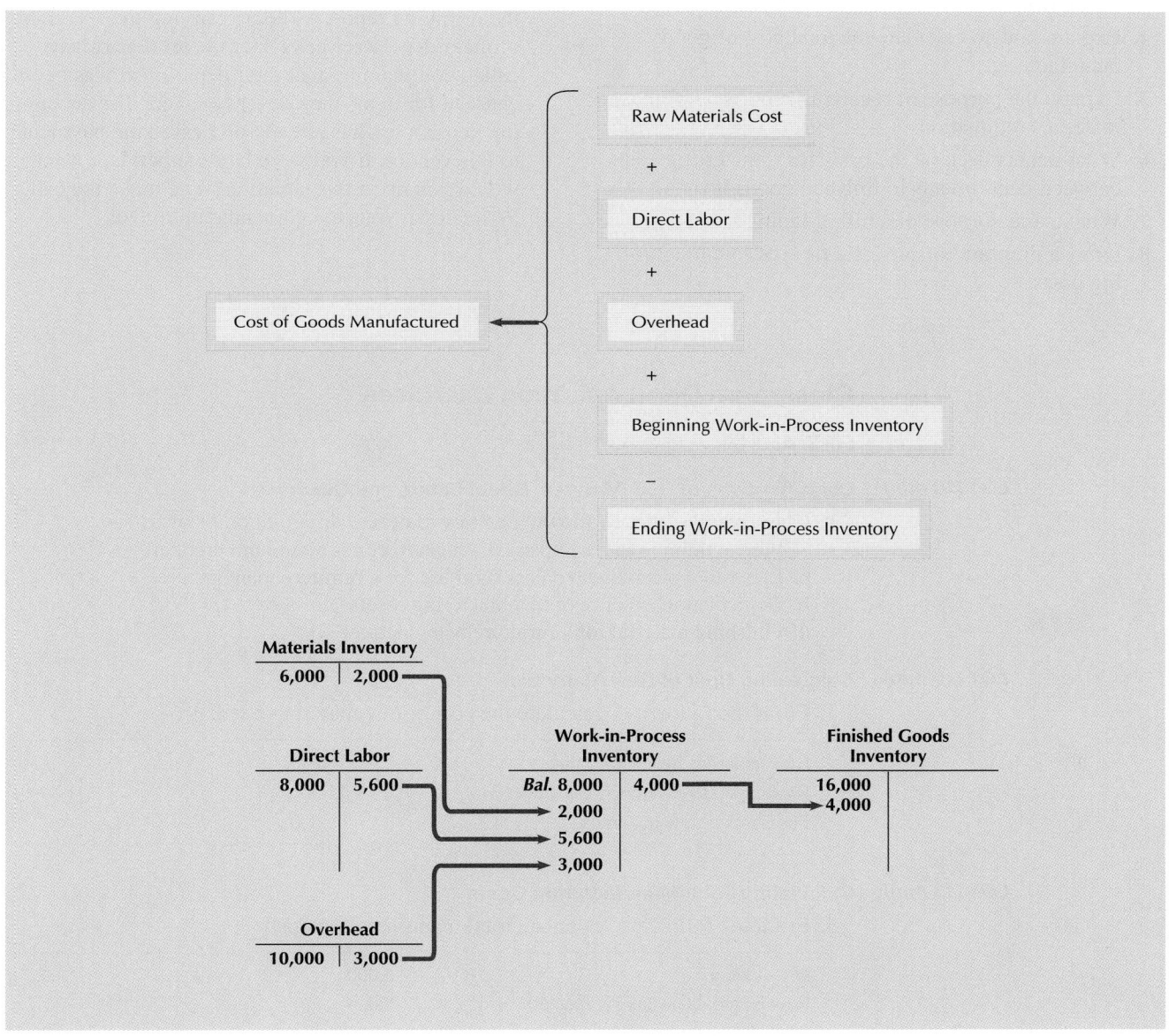

QUESTIONS, CLASSROOM DEMONSTRATION EXERCISES, EXERCISES, AND PROBLEMS

Discussion and Critical Thinking Questions/Ethical Case

1. Into what three elements can manufacturing costs be broken?

2. Direct labor includes the wages of those personnel whose efforts indirectly change the quality or characteristics of the product. Agree or disagree? Please explain.

3. What are the three major inventories of a manufacturing firm?

4. Explain how to calculate the total cost of goods manufactured.

5. Explain the purpose of receiving reports as well as materials requisitions.

6. What tickets become the basis for transferring costs between departments to finished goods inventory?

7. What is the purpose of a bill of lading?

8. Draw a diagram to show the flow of manufacturing costs.

9. Explain how overhead may be applied.

10. Compare and contrast the structure of a worksheet for a merchandise company and a manufacturing company.

11. Dot Lovet works in the receiving department of a leading publishing company. She has become good friends with many of the suppliers. At 4 P.M., Joe Andrews delivered a truckload of art supplies. Joe was in a hurry and asked Dot to accept the order. He promised that everything was there. Dot signed the receiving report without verifying the specifics of the order. Two weeks later the art department called complaining that their department was being charged for items they never received. The accounting department has already processed the payment to this vendor. If you were Dot's supervisor, what would you do in this situation? You make the call. Write down your recommendation to Dot.

Classroom Demonstration Exercises

SET A

LO1 (10 min) **Classifications of Raw Material, Direct Labor, and Overhead**

1. Classify each of the following as raw material, direct labor, or overhead:
   a. Pure aluminum in a company that manufactures aluminum products
   b. Labor of a person who paints furniture for a furniture manufacturer
   c. Depreciation expense of manufacturing assets
   d. Finishing material for a furniture manufacturer

LO1 (10 min) **Calculating Cost of Raw Materials**

2. From the following, calculate the cost of raw materials used:

Raw materials inventory, January 1	$ 6,000
Raw materials inventory, December 31	13,000
Purchases of raw materials	80,000

LO1 (15 min) **Calculating Total Manufacturing Costs**

3. From the following, calculate total manufacturing costs:

Direct labor	$ 8,000
Raw materials inventory, June 30	5,000
Raw materials purchases	16,000
Raw materials inventory, June 1	4,000
Overhead	6,000
Finished goods	9,000

Journal Entries to Record Manufacturing Costs

4. Journalize the following transactions: *LO2 (15 min)*
   a. Storeroom issued raw materials costing $6,000.
   b. Direct labor of $4,000 was charged to production.
   c. Supplies costing $3,000 were issued by the storeroom.
   d. Indirect labor cost of $6,000 was incurred.
   e. Rent of $1,000 and Depreciation of $500 were charged to overhead.

5. Identify where each title is placed on the worksheet.   *LO3 (10 min)*
   a. Raw materials purchases
   b. Ending finished goods inventory
   c. Ending raw materials inventory
   d. Sales

SET B

Classifications of Raw Material, Direct Labor, and Overhead   *LO1 (10 min)*

1. Classify each of the following as raw material, direct labor, or overhead:
   a. Finishing material for a furniture manufacturer
   b. Depreciation expense of manufacturing assets
   c. Labor of a person who paints furniture for a furniture manufacturer
   d. Pure aluminum in a company that manufactures aluminum products

Calculating Cost of Raw Materials   *LO1 (10 min)*

2. From the following, calculate the cost of raw materials used:

Raw materials inventory, January 1	$ 5,000
Raw materials inventory, December 31	12,000
Purchases of raw materials	70,000

Calculating Total Manufacturing Costs   *LO1 (15 min)*

3. From the following, calculate total manufacturing costs:

Direct labor	$ 7,000
Raw materials inventory, June 30	4,500
Raw materials purchases	15,000
Raw materials inventory, June 1	3,000
Overhead	4,000
Finished goods	8,000

Journal Entries to Record Manufacturing Costs

4. Journalize the following transactions: *LO2 (15 min)*
   a. Storeroom issued raw materials costing $5,000.
   b. Direct labor of $3,000 was charged to production.
   c. Supplies costing $2,000 were issued by the storeroom.
   d. Indirect labor cost of $4,000 was incurred.
   e. Rent of $1,000 and Depreciation of $400 were charged to overhead.

5. Identify where each title is placed on the worksheet.   *LO3 (10 min)*
   1. Cost of goods manufactured column
   2. Income statement column
   3. Balance sheet
      _____ a. Raw materials purchases
      _____ b. Ending finished goods inventory
      _____ c. Ending raw materials inventory
      _____ d. Sales

Exercises

LO1 (10 min) 25-1. Classify each of the following as raw material, direct labor, or overhead:

    a. The lumber in making furniture
    b. The insurance for a factory
    c. The wages of a forklift driver
    d. A manufacturing foreman's salary

LO1 (10 min) 25-2. From the following balances, calculate the cost of raw material used:

Raw materials inventory, January 1	$ 60,000
Raw materials inventory, December 31	90,000
Purchases of raw materials	800,000

LO1 (20 min) 25-3. From the following, calculate total manufacturing costs:

Direct labor	$ 80,000
Raw materials inventory, May 30	9,600
Raw materials purchases	70,000
Raw materials inventory, May 1	9,000
Overhead	75,000
Finished goods	120,000

LO2 (25 min) 25-4. From the following transactions, prepare the appropriate general journal entries for the month of May:

    a. Raw materials costing $75,000 were issued from the storeroom.
    b. Direct labor of $65,000 was charged to production.
    c. Supplies costing $7,000 were issued from the storeroom.
    d. Indirect labor costs of $18,000 were incurred.
    e. Rent of $3,000 and depreciation of $500 were charged to overhead.
    f. Eighty percent of the direct labor dollars used were applied to overhead.
    g. Completed products costing $70,000 were transferred to finished goods.
    h. Products costing $39,000 were sold.

LO3 (30 min) 25-5. **a.** In which columns on the worksheet would the following additional data be placed?

	Year-End Figures	Column
Raw materials	$34,000	
Goods-in-process	19,500	
Finished goods	30,000	

    b. In which columns would the beginning-of-year figures be placed?

Group A Problems

LO1 (30 min) 25A-1. An analysis of the accounts of Harwood Manufacturing reveals the following data for the month ended July 31, 20XX:

Inventories	Beginning	Ending
Raw materials	$18,000	$19,000
Work-in-process	13,000	17,000
Finished goods	15,000	14,000

Costs Incurred: Raw materials purchased, $130,000; direct labor, $130,000; manufacturing overhead, $52,000. These specific overheads included indirect labor, $20,000; factory insurance, $9,000; depreciation on machinery, $10,000; machinery repairs, $4,000; factory utilities, $6,000; and miscellaneous factory costs, $3,000.

Check Figure:
Total Cost of Goods
Manufactured $307,000

Instructions: Prepare a cost of goods manufactured statement.

25A-2. As the bookkeeper of Ace Manufacturing, you are to record the following transactions in the general journal for the month of November:

LO2 (50 min)

   a. Raw materials of $80,000 were issued from the storeroom.
   b. Charged $60,000 of direct labor to production.
   c. Supplies costing $7,000 were issued from the storeroom.
   d. Incurred indirect labor costs of $15,000.

Check Figure:
(d) Dr. Overhead Control $15,000
Cr. Payroll $15,000

   e. The following expenses were charged to overhead: rent, $3,000; supervision, $8,000; depreciation, $4,000; electricity, $6,500.
   f. Overhead was applied at 90% of direct labor dollars.
   g. Transferred completed products costing $160,000 to finished goods.
   h. Sold products costing $198,000.

25A-3. From the information in Figure 25.20, prepare a worksheet for Keep Corporation (assume no adjustments).

LO3 (60 min)

Year-End Figures	
Raw materials	$11,400
Goods-in-process	8,280
Finished goods	10,200

Check Figure:
Net Income $18,480

FIGURE 25.20 Trial Balance of Keep Corporation

	TRIAL BALANCE	
	Dr.	**Cr.**
Cash	6 2 4 0 00	
Raw Materials Inventory	8 8 8 0 00	
Work-in-Process Inventory	7 4 4 0 00	
Finished Goods Inventory	10 3 2 0 00	
Factory Supplies	3 2 4 0 00	
Prepaid Factory Supplies	3 6 0 00	
Desks	9 6 0 00	
Machinery	57 2 4 0 00	
Accumulated Depreciation, Machinery		8 2 8 0 00
Accounts Payable		3 1 2 0 00
Common Stock $10 Par		60 0 0 0 00
Retained Earnings		8 0 4 0 00
Sales		115 6 8 0 00
Raw Materials Purchases	38 4 0 0 00	
Direct Labor	22 3 2 0 00	
Indirect Labor	9 9 6 0 00	
Machinery Repairs	7 2 0 00	
Selling Expenses	14 7 6 0 00	
Administrative Expense	10 0 8 0 00	
Factory Supplies Expense	1 3 2 0 00	
Depreciation Expense, Machinery	2 8 8 0 00	
	195 1 2 0 00	195 1 2 0 00

Group B Problems

LO1 (30 min)   **25B-1.** An analysis of the accounts of Harwood Manufacturing reveals the following data for the month ended July 31, 20XX:

Inventories	Beginning	Ending
Raw materials	$16,000	$22,000
Work-in-process	12,000	16,000
Finished goods	16,000	14,000

Costs Incurred: Raw materials purchased, $130,000; direct labor, $90,000; manufacturing overhead, $39,000. These specific overheads included indirect labor, $9,600; factory insurance, $8,000; depreciation on machinery, $7,600; machinery repairs, $6,000; factory utilities, $6,300; and miscellaneous factory costs, $1,500.

Instructions: Prepare a cost of goods manufactured statement.

Check Figure:
Total Cost of Goods
Manufactured $249,000

LO2 (50 min)   **25B-2.** From the following transactions in May for Ace Manufacturing, record the appropriate general journal entries:
   a. Raw materials of $70,000 were issued from Ace's storeroom.
   b. Charged $75,000 of direct labor to production.
   c. Supplies of $4,000 were issued from the storeroom.
   d. Indirect labor costs were incurred for $20,000.
   e. The following expenses were charged to overhead: rent, $5,000; supervision, $9,000; depreciation, $6,200; electricity, $9,000.
   f. Overhead was applied at 80% of direct labor dollars.
   g. Completed products costing $180,000 were transferred to finished goods.
   h. Sold products costing $208,000.

Check Figure:
(d) Dr. Overhead Control $20,000
Cr. Payroll $20,000

LO3 (60 min)   **25B-3.** From the information in Figure 25.21, prepare a worksheet for Keep Corporation (assume no adjustments).

Year-End Figures	
Raw materials	$ 285
Goods-in-process	2,070
Finished goods	2,550

	TRIAL BALANCE	
	Dr.	Cr.
Cash	1 3 1 0 00	
Raw Materials Inventory	2 2 2 0 00	
Work-in-Process Inventory	1 8 6 0 00	
Finished Goods Inventory	2 5 8 0 00	
Factory Supplies	5 6 0 00	
Prepaid Factory Insurance	5 9 0 00	
Desks	2 4 0 00	
Machinery	14 3 1 0 00	
Accumulated Depreciation, Machinery		2 0 7 0 00
Accounts Payable		7 8 0 00
Common Stock $10 Par		15 0 0 0 00
Retained Earnings		2 0 1 0 00
Sales		28 9 2 0 00
Raw Materials Purchases	9 6 0 0 00	
Direct Labor	5 5 8 0 00	
Indirect Labor	2 4 9 0 00	
Machinery Repairs	1 8 0 00	
Selling Expenses	3 6 9 0 00	
Administrative Expense	2 5 2 0 00	
Factory Supplies Expense	3 3 0 00	
Depreciation Expense, Machinery	7 2 0 00	
	48 7 8 0 00	48 7 8 0 00

FIGURE 25.21 Trial Balance of Keep Corporation

Check Figure:
Net income $2,055

ON-THE-JOB TRAINING

LO1 (20 min)

T-1. Peter Roel had to leave the office on urgent business and asked you to close the costs to the manufacturing summary account. Please do so. Why do you think Peter forgot to close the accounts? Provide a written response.

MEMO

To: Peter Roel, Bookkeeper

From: M. V. Rooy, Vice President

Re: Closing Entries

I notice that you forgot to close the costs that appeared in the statement of cost of goods manufactured to the manufacturing summary account. Here is the data you need.

Raw Materials (Beg Inv.)	570
Raw Materials (Ending)	960
Completed Work-in-Process	1,220
Work-in-Process Current Inventory	1,590

LO1 (10 min) ## FINANCIAL REPORT PROBLEM

Reading the Kellogg's Annual Report

Go to Appendix A and find Note 15. What is the cost of finished goods and materials in process for 2006?

INTERNET PROJECT

Revlon

Go to the Web and search: Annual Report Revlon 2008.

Click on Investors Relations.

List out the latest news Revlon is providing to its investors.

Order a free annual report.

Appendix A
Kellogg Financial Report

Appendix A Kellogg Financial Report

Kellogg Company and Subsidiaries

Consolidated Statement of Earnings

(millions, except per share data)	2006	2005	2004
Net sales	**$10,906.7**	$10,177.2	$9,613.9
Cost of goods sold	**6,081.5**	5,611.6	5,298.7
Selling, general, and administrative expense	**3,059.4**	2,815.3	2,634.1
Operating profit	**$ 1,765.8**	$ 1,750.3	$1,681.1
Interest expense	**307.4**	300.3	308.6
Other income (expense), net	**13.2**	(24.9)	(6.6)
Earnings before income taxes	**$ 1,471.6**	$ 1,425.1	$1,365.9
Income taxes	**466.5**	444.7	475.3
Earnings (loss) from joint venture	**(1.0)**	—	—
Net earnings	**$ 1,004.1**	$ 980.4	$ 890.6
Per share amounts:			
Basic	**$ 2.53**	$ 2.38	$ 2.16
Diluted	**2.51**	2.36	2.14

Refer to Notes to Consolidated Financial Statements.

Consolidated Statement of Shareholders' Equity

(millions)	Common Stock Shares	Common Stock Amount	Capital in Excess of Par Value	Retained Earnings	Treasury Stock Shares	Treasury Stock Amount	Accumulated Other Comprehensive Income	Total Shareholders' Equity	Total Comprehensive Income
Balance, December 27, 2003	415.5	$103.8	$ 24.5	$2,247.7	5.8	$(203.6)	$ (729.2)	$1,443.2	$ 911.3
Common stock repurchases					7.3	(297.5)		(297.5)	
Net earnings				890.6				890.6	890.6
Dividends				(417.6)				(417.6)	
Other comprehensive income							289.3	289.3	289.3
Stock options exercised and other			(24.5)	(19.4)	(10.7)	393.1		349.2	
Balance, January 1, 2005	415.5	$103.8	$ —	$2,701.3	2.4	$(108.0)	$ (439.9)	$2,257.2	$1,179.9
Common stock repurchases					15.4	(664.2)		(664.2)	
Net earnings				980.4				980.4	980.4
Dividends				(435.2)				(435.2)	
Other comprehensive income							(136.2)	(136.2)	(136.2)
Stock options exercised and other	3.0	.8	58.9	19.6	(4.7)	202.4		281.7	
Balance, December 31, 2005	418.5	$104.6	$ 58.9	$3,266.1	13.1	$(569.8)	$ (576.1)	$2,283.7	$ 844.2
Revision (a)			101.4	(101.4)				—	
Common stock repurchases					14.9	(649.8)		(649.8)	
Net earnings				1,004.1				1,004.1	1,004.1
Dividends				(449.9)				(449.9)	
Other comprehensive income							121.8	121.8	121.8
Stock compensation			85.7					85.7	
Stock options exercised and other			46.3	(88.5)	(7.2)	307.5		265.3	
Impact of adoption of SFAS No. 158 (a)							(591.9)	(591.9)	
Balance, December 30, 2006	**418.5**	**$104.6**	**$292.3**	**$3,630.4**	**20.8**	**$(912.1)**	**$(1,046.2)**	**$2,069.0**	**$1,125.9**

Refer to Notes to Consolidated Financial Statements.
(a) Refer to Note 5 for further information on these items.

Kellogg Company and Subsidiaries

Consolidated Balance Sheet

(millions, except share data)	2006	2005
Current assets		
Cash and cash equivalents	$ **410.6**	$ 219.1
Accounts receivable, net	**944.8**	879.1
Inventories	**823.9**	717.0
Other current assets	**247.7**	381.3
Total current assets	$ **2,427.0**	$ 2,196.5
Property, net	**2,815.6**	2,648.4
Other assets	**5,471.4**	5,729.6
Total assets	**$10,714.0**	$10,574.5
Current liabilities		
Current maturities of long-term debt	$ **723.3**	$ 83.6
Notes payable	**1,268.0**	1,111.1
Accounts payable	**910.4**	883.3
Other current liabilities	**1,118.5**	1,084.8
Total current liabilities	$ **4,020.2**	$ 3,162.8
Long-term debt	**3,053.0**	3,702.6
Other liabilities	**1,571.8**	1,425.4
Shareholders' equity		
Common stock, $.25 per value, 1,000,000,000 shares authorized		
Issued: 418,515,339 shares in 2006 and 418,451,198 shares in 2005	**104.6**	104.6
Capital in excess of par value	**292.3**	58.9
Retained earnings	**3,630.4**	3,266.1
Treasury stock at cost:		
20,817,930 shares in 2006 and 13,121,446 shares in 2005	**(912.1)**	(569.8)
Accumulated other comprehensive income (loss)	**(1,046.2)**	(576.1)
Total shareholders' equity	$ **2,069.0**	$ 2,283.7
Total liabilities and shareholders' equity	**$10,714.0**	$10,574.5

Refer to Notes to Consolidated Financial Statements. In particular, refer to Note 15 for supplemental information on various balance sheet captions and Note 1 for details on the impact of adopting SFAS No. 158 "Employers' Accounting for Defined Benefit Pension and Other Postretirement Plans."

Kellogg Company and Subsidiaries

Consolidated Statement of Cash Flows

(millions)	2006	2005	2004
Operating activities			
Net earnings	**$1,004.1**	$ 980.4	$ 890.6
Adjustments to reconcile net earnings to operating cash flows:			
Depreciation and amortization	**352.7**	391.8	410.0
Deferred income taxes	**(43.7)**	(59.2)	57.7
Other (a)	**235.2**	199.3	104.5
Pension and other postretirement benefit plan contributions	**(99.3)**	(397.3)	(204.0)
Changes in operating assets and liabilities	**(38.5)**	28.3	(29.8)
Net cash provided by operating activities	**$1,410.5**	$1,143.3	$1,229.0
Investing activities			
Additions to properties	**$ (453.1)**	$ (374.2)	$ (278.6)
Acquisitions of businesses	**—**	(50.4)	—
Property disposals	**9.4**	9.8	7.9
Investment in joint venture and other	**(1.7)**	(.2)	.3
Net cash used in investing activities	**$ (445.4)**	$ (415.0)	$ (270.4)
Financing activities			
Net increase (reduction) of notes payable, with maturities less than or equal to 90 days	**$ (344.2)**	$ 360.2	$ 388.3
Issuances of notes payable, with maturities greater than 90 days	**1,065.4**	42.6	142.3
Reductions of notes payable, with maturities greater than 90 days	**(565.2)**	(42.3)	(141.7)
Issuances of long-term debt	**—**	647.3	7.0
Reductions of long-term debt	**(84.7)**	(1,041.3)	(682.2)
Issuances of common stock	**217.5**	221.7	291.8
Common stock repurchases	**(649.8)**	(664.2)	(297.5)
Cash dividends	**(449.9)**	(435.2)	(417.6)
Other	**21.9**	5.9	(6.7)
Net cash used in financing activities	**$ (789.0)**	$ (905.3)	$ (716.3)
Effect of exchange rate changes on cash	**15.4**	(21.3)	33.9
Increase (decrease) in cash and cash equivalents	**$ 191.5**	$ (198.3)	$ 276.2
Cash and cash equivalents at beginning of year	**219.1**	417.4	141.2
Cash and cash equivalents at end of year	**$ 410.6**	$ 219.1	$ 417.4

Refer to Notes to Consolidated Financial Statements.
(a) Consists principally of non-cash expense accruals for employee compensation and benefit obligations.

Note 1 Accounting Policies

Basis of Presentation

The consolidated financial statements include the accounts of Kellogg Company and its majority-owned subsidiaries. Intercompany balances and transactions are eliminated.

The Company's fiscal year normally ends on the Saturday closest to December 31 and as a result, a 53rd week is added approximately every sixth year. The Company's 2006 and 2005 fiscal years ended on December 30 and December 31, respectively. The Company's 2004 fiscal year ended on January 1, 2005, and included a 53rd week.

Cash and cash equivalents

Highly liquid temporary investments with original maturities of less than three months are considered to be cash equivalents. The carrying amount approximates fair value.

Accounts receivable

Accounts receivable consist principally of trade receivables, which are recorded at the invoiced amount, net of allowances for doubtful accounts and prompt payment discounts. Trade receivables generally do not bear interest. Terms and collection patterns vary around the world and by channel. In the United States, the Company generally has required payment for goods sold eleven or sixteen days subsequent to the date of invoice as 2% 10/net 11 or 1% 15/net 16, and days sales outstanding (DSO) has averaged approximately 19 days during the periods presented. The allowance for doubtful accounts represents management's estimate of the amount of probable credit losses in existing accounts receivable, as determined from a review of past due balances and other specific account data. Account balances are written off against the allowance when management determines the receivable is uncollectible. The Company does not have any off-balance sheet credit exposure related to its customers. Refer to Note 15 for an analysis of the Company's accounts receivable and allowance for doubtful account balances during the periods presented.

Inventories

Inventories are valued at the lower of cost (principally average) or market.

In November 2004, the Financial Accounting Standards Board (FASB) issued Statement of Financial Accounting Standard (SFAS) No. 151 "Inventory Costs" to converge U.S. GAAP principles with International Accounting Standards on inventory valuation. SFAS No. 151 clarifies that abnormal amounts of idle facility expense, freight, handling costs, and spoilage should be recognized as period charges, rather than as inventory value. This standard also provides that fixed production overheads should be allocated to units of production based on the normal capacity of production facilities, with excess overheads being recognized as period charges. The provisions of this standard are effective for inventory costs incurred during fiscal years beginning after June 15, 2005, with earlier application permitted. The Company adopted this standard at the beginning of its 2006 fiscal year. The Company's pre-existing accounting policy for inventory valuation was generally consistent with this guidance. Accordingly, the adoption of SFAS No. 151 did not have a significant impact on the Company's 2006 financial results.

Property

The Company's property consists mainly of plant and equipment used for manufacturing activities. These assets are recorded at cost and depreciated over estimated useful lives using straight-line methods for financial reporting and accelerated methods, where permitted, for tax reporting. Major property categories are depreciated over various periods as follows (in years): manufacturing machinery and equipment 5-20; computer and other office equipment 3-5; building components 15-30; building structures 50. Cost includes an amount of interest associated with significant capital projects. Plant and equipment are reviewed for impairment when conditions indicate that the carrying value may not be recoverable. Such conditions include an extended period of idleness or a plan of disposal. Assets to be abandoned at a future date are depreciated over the remaining period of use. Assets to be sold are written down to realizable value at the time the assets are being actively marketed for sale and the disposal is expected to occur within one year. As of year-end 2005 and 2006, the carrying value of assets held for sale was insignificant.

Goodwill and other intangible assets

The Company's intangible assets consist primarily of goodwill and major trademarks arising from the 2001 acquisition of Keebler Foods Company ("Keebler"). Management expects the Keebler trademarks, collectively, to contribute indefinitely to the cash flows of the Company. Accordingly, this asset has been classified as an "indefinite-lived" intangible pursuant to SFAS No. 142 "Goodwill and Other Intangible Assets." Under this standard, goodwill and indefinite-lived intangibles are not amortized, but are tested at least annually for impairment. Goodwill impairment testing first requires a comparison between the carrying value and fair value of a "reporting unit," which for the Company is generally equivalent to a North American product group or International country market. If carrying value exceeds fair value, goodwill is considered impaired and is reduced to the implied fair value. Impairment testing for non-amortized intangibles requires a comparison between the fair value and carrying value of the intangible asset. If carrying value exceeds fair value, the intangible is considered impaired and is reduced to fair value. The Company uses various market valuation techniques to determine the fair value of intangible assets and periodically engages third-party valuation consultants for this purpose. Refer to Note 2 for further information on goodwill and other intangible assets.

Revenue recognition and measurement

The Company recognizes sales upon delivery of its products to customers net of applicable provisions for discounts, returns, allowances, and various government withholding taxes. Methodologies for determining these provisions are dependent on local customer pricing and promotional practices, which range from contractually fixed percentage price reductions to reimbursement based on actual occurrence or performance. Where applicable, future reimbursements are estimated based on a combination of historical patterns and future expectations regarding specific in-market product performance. The Company classifies promotional payments to its customers, the cost of consumer coupons, and other cash redemption offers in net sales. The cost of promotional package inserts are recorded in cost of goods sold. Other types of consumer promotional expenditures are normally recorded in selling, general, and administrative (SGA) expense.

Advertising

The costs of advertising are generally expensed as incurred and are classified within SGA expense.

Research and development

The costs of research and development (R&D) are generally expensed as incurred and are classified within SGA expense. R&D includes expenditures for new product and process innovation, as well as significant technological improvements to existing products and processes. Total annual expenditures for R&D are disclosed in Note 15 and are principally comprised of internal salaries, wages, consulting, and supplies attributable to time spent on R&D activities. Other costs include depreciation and maintenance of research facilities and equipment, including assets at manufacturing locations that are temporarily engaged in pilot plant activities.

Stock compensation

The Company uses various equity-based compensation programs to provide long-term performance incentives for its global workforce. Refer to Note 8 for further information on these programs and the amount of compensation expense recognized during the periods presented.

In December 2004, the FASB issued SFAS No. 123(R) "Share-Based Payment," which generally requires public companies to measure the cost of employee services received in exchange for an award of equity instruments based on the grant-date fair value and to recognize this cost over the requisite service period. The Company adopted SFAS No. 123(R) as of the beginning of its 2006 fiscal year, using the modified prospective method. Accordingly, prior years were not restated, but 2006 results include compensation expense associated with unvested equitybased awards, which were granted prior to 2006.

Prior to adoption of SFAS No. 123(R), the Company used the intrinsic value method prescribed by Accounting Principles Board Opinion (APB) No. 25 "Accounting for Stock Issued to Employees" to account for its employee stock options and other stock-based compensation. Under this method, because the exercise price of stock options granted to employees and directors equaled the market price of the underlying stock on the date of the grant, no compensation expense was recognized. Expense attributable to other types of stock-based awards was generally recognized in the Company's reported results under APB No. 25.

Certain of the Company's equity-based compensation plans contain provisions that accelerate vesting of awards upon retirement, disability, or death of eligible employees and directors. Prior to adoption of SFAS No. 123(R), the Company generally recognized stock compensation expense over the stated vesting period of the award, with any unamortized expense recognized immediately if an acceleration event occurred. SFAS No. 123(R) specifies that a stock-based award is considered vested for expense attribution purposes when the employee's retention of the award is no longer contingent on providing subsequent service. Accordingly, beginning in 2006, the Company has prospectively revised its expense attribution method so that the related compensation cost is recognized immediately for awards granted to retirement-eligible individuals or over the period from the grant date to the date retirement eligibility is achieved, if less than the stated vesting period.

The Company classifies pre-tax stock compensation expense principally in SGA expense within its corporate operations. Expense attributable to awards of equity instruments is accrued in capital in excess of par value within the Consolidated Balance Sheet.

SFAS No. 123(R) also provides that any corporate income tax benefit realized upon exercise or vesting of an award in excess of that previously recognized in earnings (referred to as a "windfall tax benefit") will be presented in the Consolidated Statement of Cash Flows as a financing (rather than an operating) cash flow. Realized windfall tax benefits are credited to capital in excess of par value in the Consolidated Balance Sheet. Realized shortfall tax benefits (amounts which are less than that previously recognized in earnings) are first offset against the cumulative balance of windfall tax benefits, if any, and then charged directly to income tax expense. Under the transition rules for adopting SFAS No. 123(R) using the modified prospective method, the Company was permitted to calculate a cumulative memo balance of windfall tax benefits from post-1995 years for the purpose of accounting for future shortfall tax benefits. The Company completed such study prior to the first period of adoption and currently has sufficient cumulative memo windfall tax benefits to absorb arising shortfalls, such that earnings were not affected in 2006. Correspondingly, the Company includes the impact of pro forma deferred tax assets (i.e., the "as if" windfall or shortfall) for purposes of determining assumed proceeds in the treasury stock calculation of diluted earnings per share under SFAS No. 128 "Earnings Per Share."

Employee postretirement and postemployment benefits

The Company sponsors a number of U.S. and foreign plans to provide pension, health care, and other welfare benefits to retired employees, as well as salary continuance, severance, and long-term disability to former or inactive employees. Refer to Notes 9 and 10 for further information on these benefits and the amount of expense recognized during the periods presented.

In order to improve the reporting of pension and other postretirement benefit plans in the financial statements, in September 2006, the FASB issued SFAS No. 158 "Employers' Accounting for Defined Benefit Pension and Other Postretirement Plans," which is effective at the end of fiscal years ending after December 15, 2006. Prior periods are not restated. The standard generally requires company plan sponsors to measure the net over- or under-funded position of a defined postretirement benefit plan as of the sponsor's fiscal year end and to display that position as an asset or liability on the balance sheet. Any unrecognized prior service cost, experience gains/losses, or transition obligation are reported as a component of other comprehensive income, net of tax, in shareholders' equity. In contrast, under preexisting guidance, these unrecognized amounts were generally disclosed only in financial statement footnotes, often resulting in a disparity between plan balance sheet positions and the funded status. Furthermore, plan measurement dates could occur up to three months prior to year end.

The Company adopted SFAS No. 158 as of the end of its 2006 fiscal year. The Company had previously applied postretirement accounting concepts for purposes of recognizing its postemployment benefit obligations; accordingly, the adoption of SFAS No. 158 as of December 30, 2006, affected the balance sheet display of both the Company's postretirement and postemployment benefit obligations, as follows:

(millions)	Before application of SFAS No. 158 (a)	Adjustments	After application of SFAS No. 158
Other assets:			
Other intangibles — pension	$ 9.5	$ (9.5)	$ —
Pension	855.5	(502.9)	352.6
	$865.0	$(512.4)	$ 352.6
Total assets	$865.0	$(512.4)	$ 352.6
Other current liabilities:			
Pension, postretirement, and postemployment benefits	53.0	(34.2)	18.8
	$ 53.0	$ (34.2)	$ 18.8
Other liabilities:			
Pension, postretirement, and postemployment benefits (a)	287.2	412.6	699.8
Deferred income taxes (b)	(6.8)	(298.9)	(305.7)
	$280.4	$ 113.7	$ 394.1
Total liabilities	$333.4	$ 79.5	$ 412.9

Accumulated other comprehensive income (loss) (a)	$ (12.2)	$(591.9)	$(604.1)

(a) Includes additional minimum pension liability adjustment under pre-existing guidance of $28.5, which reduced accumulated other comprehensive income by $12.2 on an after-tax basis.

(b) Represents an asset component of deferred tax liabilities, which are presented on a net basis at the jurisdiction level.

The Company's net earnings, cash flow, liquidity, debt covenants, and plan funding requirements were not affected by this change in accounting principle. The Company has historically used its fiscal year end as the measurement date for its company-sponsored defined benefit plans.

Recently issued pronouncements

Uncertain tax positions

In July 2006, the FASB issued Interpretation No. 48 "Accounting for Uncertainty in Income Taxes" (FIN No. 48) to clarify what criteria must be met prior to recognition of the financial statement benefit, in accordance with FASB Statement No. 109, "Accounting for Income Taxes," of a position taken in a tax return. The provisions of the final interpretation apply broadly to all tax positions taken by an enterprise, including the decision not to report income in a tax return or the decision to classify a transaction as tax exempt. The prescribed approach is based on a two-step benefit recognition model. The first step is to evaluate the tax position for recognition by determining if the weight of available evidence indicates it is more likely than not, based on the technical merits and without consideration of detection risk, that the position will be sustained on audit, including resolution of related appeals or litigation processes, if any. The second step is to measure the appropriate amount of the benefit to recognize. The amount of benefit to recognize is measured as the largest amount of tax benefit that is greater than 50 percent likely of being ultimately realized upon settlement. The tax position must be derecognized when it is no longer more likely than not of being sustained. The interpretation also provides guidance on recognition and classification of related penalties and interest, classification of liabilities, and disclosures of unrecognized tax benefits. The change in net assets, if any, as a result of applying the provisions of this interpretation is considered a change in accounting principle with the cumulative effect of the change treated as an offsetting adjustment to the opening balance of retained earnings in the period of transition. The final interpretation is effective for the first annual period beginning after December 15, 2006, with earlier application encouraged.

The Company adopted FIN No. 48 as of the beginning of its 2007 fiscal year. Prior to adoption, the Company's pre-existing policy was to establish reserves for uncertain tax positions that reflected the probable outcome of known tax contingencies. As compared to the Company's historical approach, the application of FIN No. 48 resulted in a net decrease to accrued income tax and related interest liabilities of approximately $2 million, with an offsetting increase to retained earnings.

Interest recognized in accordance with FIN No. 48 may be classified in the financial statements as either income taxes or interest expense, based on the accounting policy election of the enterprise. Similarly, penalties may be classified as income taxes or another expense. The Company has historically classified income tax-related interest and penalties as interest expense and SGA expense, respectively, and will continue to do so under FIN No. 48.

Fair value

In September 2006, the FASB issued SFAS No. 157 "Fair Value Measurements" to provide enhanced guidance for using fair value to measure assets and liabilities. The standard also expands disclosure requirements for assets and liabilities measured at fair value, how fair value is determined, and the effect of fair value measurements on earnings. The standard applies whenever other authoritative literature requires (or permits) certain assets or liabilities to be measured at fair value, but does not expand the use of fair value. SFAS No. 157 is effective for financial statements issued for fiscal years beginning after November 15, 2007, and interim periods within those years. Early adoption is permitted. The Company plans to adopt SFAS No. 157 in the first quarter of its 2008 fiscal year. For the Company, balance sheet items carried at fair value consist primarily of derivatives and other financial instruments, assets held for sale, exit liabilities, and the trust asset component of net benefit plan obligations. Additionally, the Company uses fair value concepts to test various long-lived assets for impairment and to initially measure assets and liabilities acquired in a business combination. Management is currently evaluating the impact of adoption on how these assets and liabilities are currently measured.

Use of estimates

The preparation of financial statements in conformity with generally accepted accounting principles requires management to make estimates and assumptions that affect the reported amounts of assets and liabilities and disclosure of contingent assets and liabilities at the date of the financial statements and the reported amounts of revenues and expenses during the reporting period. Actual results could differ from those estimates.

Note 2 Acquisitions, Other Investments, and Intangibles

Acquisitions

In order to support the continued growth of its North American fruit snacks business, the Company completed two separate business acquisitions during 2005 for a total of approximately $50 million in cash, including related transaction costs. In June 2005, the Company acquired a fruit snacks manufacturing facility and related assets from Kraft Foods Inc. The facility is located in Chicago, Illinois and employs approximately 400 active hourly and salaried employees. In November 2005, the Company acquired substantially all of the assets and certain liabilities of a Washington State-based manufacturer of natural and organic fruit snacks. Assets, liabilities, and results of the acquired businesses have been included in the Company's consolidated financial statements since the respective dates of acquisition. The combined purchase price for both transactions was allocated to property ($22 million); goodwill and other indefinite-lived intangibles ($16 million); and inventory and other working capital ($12 million).

Joint venture arrangement

In early 2006, a subsidiary of the Company formed a joint venture with a third-party company domiciled in Turkey, for the purpose of selling co-branded products in the surrounding region. As of December 30, 2006, the Company had contributed approximately $3.5 million in cash for a 50% equity interest in this arrangement. The Turkish joint venture is reflected in the consolidated financial statements on the equity basis of accounting. Accordingly, the Company records its share of the earnings or loss from this arrangement as well as other direct transactions with or on behalf of the joint venture entity such as product sales and certain administrative expenses. Summary financial information for one hundred percent of the joint venture is as follows:

(millions)	2006
Net sales	$ 6.0
Gross profit	1.9
Net earnings (loss)	(1.9)
Current assets	5.9
Noncurrent assets	—
Current liabilities	1.3
Noncurrent liabilities	—

Goodwill and other intangible assets

For 2004, the Company recorded in selling, general, and administrative expense impairment losses of $10.4 million to write off the remaining carrying value of a $7.9 million contract-based intangible asset in North America and $2.5 million of goodwill in Latin America.

For the periods presented, the Company's intangible assets consisted of the following:

Intangible assets subject to amortization

(millions)	Gross carrying amount		Accumulated amortization	
	2006	2005	**2006**	2005
Trademarks	**$29.5**	$29.5	**$21.6**	$20.5
Other	**29.1**	29.1	**27.5**	27.1
Total	**$58.6**	$58.6	**$49.1**	$47.6

	2006	2005
Amortization expense (a)	**$1.5**	$1.5

(a) The currently estimated aggregate amortization expense for each of the four succeeding fiscal years is approximately $1.5 per year and $1.1 for the fifth succeeding fiscal year.

Intangible assets not subject to amortization

(millions)	Total carrying amount	
	2006	2005
Trademarks	**$1,410.2**	$1,410.2
Pension (a)	—	17.0
Total	**$1,410.2**	$1,427.2

(a) The Company adopted SFAS No. 158 "Employers' Accounting for Defined Benefit Pension and Other Postretirement Plans" as of the end of its 2006 fiscal year. The standard generally requires company plan sponsors to reflect the net over- or under-funded position of a defined postretirement benefit plan as an asset or liability on the balance sheet. Accordingly, the pension-related intangible included in the preceding table for 2005 was eliminated by the adoption of this standard. Refer to Note 1 for further information.

Changes in the carrying amount of goodwill

(millions)	United States	Europe	Latin America	Asia Pacific (a)	Consoli-dated
January 1, 2005	$3,443.3	—	—	$2.2	$3,445.5
Acquisitions	10.2	—	—	—	10.2
Other	(.3)	—	—	(.1)	(.4)
December 31, 2005	$3,453.2	—	—	$2.1	$3,455.3
Purchase accounting adjustments (b)	**(7.0)**	—	—	—	**(7.0)**
Other	(.1)	—	—	.1	—
December 30, 2006	**$3,446.1**	—	—	**$2.2**	**$3,448.3**

(a) Includes Australia and Asia.

(b) Relates principally to the recognition of an acquired tax benefit arising from the purchase of Keebler Foods Company in 2001.

Note 3 Cost-Reduction Initiatives

The Company views its continued spending on cost-reduction initiatives as part of its ongoing operating principles to reinvest earnings so as to provide greater reliability in meeting long-term growth targets. Initiatives undertaken must meet certain pay-back and internal rate of return (IRR) targets. Each cost-reduction initiative is normally one to three years in duration. Upon completion (or as each major stage is completed in the case of multi-year programs), the project begins to deliver cash savings and/or reduced depreciation, which is then used to fund new initiatives. To implement these programs, the Company has incurred various up-front costs, including asset write-offs, exit charges, and other project expenditures.

Cost summary

For 2006, the Company recorded total program-related charges of approximately $82 million, comprised of $20 million of asset write-offs, $30 million for severance and other exit costs, $9 million for other cash expenditures, $4 million for a multiemployer pension plan withdrawal liability, and $19 million for pension and other postretirement plan curtailment losses and special termination benefits. Approximately $74 million of the total 2006 charges were recorded in cost of goods sold within operating segment results, with approximately $8 million recorded in selling, general, and administrative (SGA) expense within corporate results. The Company's operating segments were impacted as follows (in millions): North America–$46; Europe–$28.

For 2005, the Company recorded total program-related charges of approximately $90 million, comprised of $16 million for a multiemployer pension plan withdrawal liability, $44 million of asset write-offs, $21 million for severance and other exit costs, and $9 million for other cash expenditures. All of the 2005 charges were recorded in cost of goods sold within the Company's North America operating segment.

For 2004, the Company recorded total program-related charges of approximately $109 million, comprised of $41 million in asset write-offs, $1 million for special pension termination benefits, $15 million in severance and other exit costs, and $52 million in other cash expenditures such as relocation and consulting. Approximately $46 million of the total 2004 charges were recorded in cost of goods sold, with approximately $63 million recorded in SGA expense. The 2004 charges impacted the Company's operating segments as follows (in millions): North America–$44; Europe–$65. Exit cost reserves were approximately $14 million at December 30, 2006, consisting principally of severance obligations associated with projects commenced in 2006, which are expected to be paid out in 2007. At December 31, 2005, exit cost reserves were approximately $13 million, primarily representing severance costs that were substantially paid out in 2006.

Specific initiatives

In September 2006, the Company approved a multi-year European manufacturing optimization plan to improve utilization of its facility in Manchester, England and to better align production in Europe. Based on forecasted foreign exchange rates, the Company currently expects to incur approximately $60 million in total up-front costs (including those already incurred in 2006), comprised of approximately 80% cash and 20% non-cash asset writeoffs, to complete this initiative. The cash portion of the total up-front costs results principally from management's plan to eliminate approximately 220 hourly and salaried positions from the Manchester facility by the end of 2008 through voluntary early retirement and severance programs. The pension trust funding requirements of these early retirements are expected to exceed the recognized benefit expense impact by approximately $10 million; most of this incremental funding occurred in 2006. During this period, certain manufacturing equipment will also be removed from service. For 2006, the Company incurred approximately $28 million of total up-front costs, including $9 million of pension plan curtailment losses and special termination benefits.

During 2006, the Company commenced several initiatives to enhance the productivity and efficiency of its U.S. cereal manufacturing network, primarily through technological and sourcing improvements in warehousing and packaging operations. In conjunction with these initiatives, the Company offered voluntary separation incentives, which resulted in the retirement of approximately 80 hourly employees by early 2007. During the fourth quarter of 2006, the Company incurred approximately $15 million of total up-front costs, comprised of approximately 20% asset write-offs and 80% cash costs, including $10 million of pension and other postretirement plan curtailment losses.

Also during 2006, the Company undertook an initiative to improve customer focus and selling efficiency within a particular Latin American market, leading to a shift from a third-party distributor to a direct sales force model. As a result of this initiative, the Company paid $8 million in cash during the fourth quarter of 2006 to exit the existing distribution arrangement.

To improve operational efficiency and better position its North American snacks business for future growth, during 2005, the Company undertook an initiative to consolidate U.S. bakery capacity, which was completed by the end of 2006. The project resulted in the closure and sale of the Company's Des Plaines, Illinois facility in late 2005 and closure of its Macon, Georgia facility in April 2006, with sale occurring in September 2006. These closures resulted in the elimination of over 700 hourly and salaried employee positions, through the combination of involuntary severance and attrition. Related to this initiative, the Company incurred up-front costs of approximately $80 million in 2005, comprised of approximately one-half asset write-offs and one-half cash costs, including $16 million for the present value of a projected multiemployer pension plan withdrawal liability associated with closure of the Macon facility. The Company incurred approximately $31 million in up-front costs for 2006, comprised of approximately one-third asset write-offs and two-thirds cash costs, including a $4 million increase in the Company's estimated pension plan withdrawal liability to $20 million. This increase was principally attributable to investment loss experienced during 2005 in conjunction with increased benefit levels for all participating employers. The final calculation of this liability is pending full-year 2007 employee hours attributable to the Company's remaining participation in this plan, and is therefore subject to adjustment in early 2008. The associated cash obligation is payable to the pension fund over a 20-year maximum period; management has not currently determined the actual period over which the payments will be made. Except for this pension plan withdrawal liability,

the Company's cash obligations attributable to this initiative were substantially paid out by year end 2006.

During 2004, the Company commenced an operational improvement initiative which resulted in the consolidation of veggie foods manufacturing at its Zanesville, Ohio facility and the closure and sale of its Worthington, Ohio facility by mid 2005. As a result of this closing, approximately 280 employee positions were eliminated through separation and attrition. Related to this initiative, the Company recognized approximately $20 million of up-front costs in 2004 and $10 million in 2005. For both years, the total amounts were comprised of approximately two-thirds asset writeoffs and one-third cash costs such as severance and removal, which were entirely paid out by the end of 2005.

During 2004, the Company's global rollout of its SAP information technology system resulted in accelerated depreciation of legacy software assets to be abandoned in 2005, as well as related consulting and other implementation expenses. Total incremental costs for 2004 were approximately $30 million. In close association with this SAP rollout, management undertook a major initiative to improve the organizational design and effectiveness of pan-European operations. Specific benefits of this initiative were expected to include improved marketing and promotional coordination across Europe, supply chain network savings, overhead cost reductions, and tax savings. To achieve these benefits, management implemented, at the beginning of 2005, a new European legal and operating structure headquartered in Ireland, with strengthened pan-European management authority and coordination. During 2004, the Company incurred various up-front costs, including relocation, severance, and consulting, of approximately $30 million. Additional relocation and other costs to complete this business transformation after 2004 have been insignificant.

In order to integrate it with the rest of our U.S. operations, during 2004, the Company completed the relocation of its U.S. snacks business unit from Elmhurst, Illinois (the former headquarters of Keebler Foods Company) to Battle Creek, Michigan. About one-third of the approximately 300 employees affected by this initiative accepted relocation or reassignment offers. The recruiting effort to fill the remaining open positions was substantially completed by year-end 2004. Attributable to this initiative, the Company incurred approximately $15 million in relocation, recruiting, and severance costs during 2004. Subject to achieving certain employment levels and other regulatory requirements, management expects to defray a significant portion of these up-front costs through various multi-year tax incentives, which began in 2005. The Elmhurst office building was sold in late 2004, and the net sales proceeds approximated carrying value.

Note 4 Other Income (Expense), Net

Other income (expense), net includes non-operating items such as interest income, charitable donations, and foreign exchange gains and losses. Net foreign exchange transaction losses for the periods presented were approximately (in millions): 2006–$2; 2005–$2; 2004–$15.

Other expense includes charges for contributions to the Kellogg's Corporate Citizenship Fund, a private trust established for charitable giving, as follows (in millions): 2006–$3; 2005–$16; 2004–$9. Other expense for 2005 also includes a charge of approximately $7 million to reduce the carrying value of a corporate commercial facility to estimated selling value. This facility was sold in August 2006.

Note 5 Equity

During the year ended December 30, 2006, the Company revised the classification of $101.4 million of prior net losses realized upon reissuance of treasury shares from capital in excess of par value to retained earnings on the Consolidated Balance Sheet. Such reissuances occurred in connection with employee and director stock option exercises and other share-based settlements. The revision did not have an effect on the Company's results of operations, total shareholders' equity, or cash flows.

Earnings per share

Basic net earnings per share is determined by dividing net earnings by the weighted-average number of common shares outstanding during the period. Diluted net earnings per share is similarly determined, except that the denominator is increased to include the number of additional common shares that would have been outstanding if all dilutive potential common shares had been issued. Dilutive potential common shares are comprised principally of employee stock options issued by the Company. Basic net earnings per share is reconciled to diluted net earnings per share in the following table. The total number of anti-dilutive potential common shares excluded from the reconciliation for each period was (in millions): 2006–.7; 2005–1.5; 2004–4.3.

(millions, except per share data)	Earnings	Average shares outstanding	Per share
2006			
Basic	**$1,004.1**	**397.0**	**$2.53**
Dilutive potential common shares	—	**3.4**	**(.02)**
Diluted	**$1,004.1**	**400.4**	**$2.51**
2005			
Basic	$ 980.4	412.0	$2.38
Dilutive potential common shares	—	3.6	(.02)
Diluted	$ 980.4	415.6	$2.36
2004			
Basic	$890.6	412.0	$2.16
Dilutive potential common shares	—	4.4	(.02)
Diluted	$890.6	416.4	$2.14

Stock transactions

The Company issues shares to employees and directors under various equity-based compensation and stock purchase programs, as further discussed in Note 8. The number of shares issued during the periods presented was (in millions): 2006–7.2; 2005–7.7; 2004–10.7. Additionally, during 2006, the Company established *Kellogg Direct™*, a direct stock purchase and dividend reinvestment plan for U.S. shareholders and issued less than .1 million shares for that purpose in 2006.

To offset these issuances and for general corporate purposes, the Company's Board of Directors has authorized management to repurchase specified amounts of the Company's common stock in each of the periods presented. In 2006, the Company spent $650 million to repurchase approximately 14.9 million shares. This activity consisted principally of a February 2006 private transaction with the W.K. Kellogg Foundation Trust to repurchase approximately 12.8 million shares for $550 million. In 2005, the Company spent $664 million to repurchase approximately 15.4 million shares. This activity consisted principally of a November 2005 private transaction with the W.K. Kellogg Foundation Trust to repurchase approximately 9.4 million shares for $400 million. In 2004, the Company spent $298 million to repurchase approximately 7.3 million shares.

On December 8, 2006, the Company's Board of Directors authorized a stock repurchase program of up to $650 million for 2007.

Comprehensive Income

Comprehensive income includes net earnings and all other changes in equity during a period except those resulting from investments by or distributions to shareholders. Other comprehensive income for the periods presented consists of foreign currency translation adjustments pursuant to SFAS No. 52 "Foreign Currency Translation," unrealized gains and losses on cash flow hedges pursuant to SFAS No. 133 "Accounting for Derivative Instruments and Hedging Activities," and minimum pension liability adjustments pursuant to SFAS No. 87 "Employers' Accounting for Pensions." Additionally, accumulated other comprehensive income at December 30, 2006, reflects the adoption of SFAS No. 158 "Employers' Accounting for Defined Benefit Pension and Other Postretirement Plans" as of the Company's 2006 fiscal year end. Refer to Note 1 for further information.

(millions)	Pretax amount	Tax (expense) benefit	After-tax amount
2006			
Net earnings			**$1,004.1**
Other comprehensive income:			
Foreign currency translation adjustments	**$ 10.0**	**$ —**	**10.0**
Cash flow hedges:			
Unrealized loss on cash flow hedges	**(12.6)**	**4.6**	**(8.0)**
Reclassification to net earnings	**11.9**	**(4.3)**	**7.6**
Minimum pension liability adjustments	**172.3**	**(60.1)**	**112.2**
	$ 181.6	**$(59.8)**	**121.8**
Total comprehensive income			**$1,125.9**
2005			
Net earnings			$ 980.4
Other comprehensive income:			
Foreign currency translation adjustments	$ (85.2)	$ —	(85.2)
Cash flow hedges:			
Unrealized loss on cash flow hedges	(3.7)	1.6	(2.1)
Reclassification to net earnings	26.4	(9.9)	16.5
Minimum pension liability adjustments	(102.7)	37.3	(65.4)
	$(165.2)	$ 29.0	(136.2)
Total comprehensive income			$ 844.2

2004			
Net earnings			$ 890.6
Other comprehensive income:			
Foreign currency translation adjustments	$ 71.7	$ —	71.7
Cash flow hedges:			
Unrealized loss on cash flow hedges	(10.2)	3.1	(7.1)
Reclassification to net earnings	19.3	(6.9)	12.4
Minimum pension liability adjustments	308.9	(96.6)	212.3
	$389.7	$(100.4)	289.3
Total comprehensive income			$1,179.9

Accumulated other comprehensive income (loss) at year end consisted of the following:

(millions)	2006	2005
Foreign currency translation adjustments	$ (409.5)	$(419.5)
Cash flow hedges — unrealized net loss	(32.6)	(32.2)
Minimum pension liability adjustments	—	(124.4)
Postretirement and postemployment benefits:		
Net experience loss	(540.5)	—
Prior service cost	(63.6)	—
Total accumulated other comprehensive income (loss)	$(1,046.2)	$(576.1)

Note 6 Leases and Other Commitments

The Company's leases are generally for equipment and warehouse space. Rent expense on all operating leases was (in millions): 2006–$122.8; 2005–$115.1; 2004–$107.4. Additionally, the Company is subject to a residual value guarantee on one operating lease of approximately $13 million which expires in July 2007. At December 30, 2006, the Company had not recorded any liability related to this residual value guarantee. During 2006 and 2005, the Company entered into approximately $2 million and $3 million, respectively, in capital lease agreements to finance the purchase of equipment. Similar transactions in 2004 were insignificant.

At December 30, 2006, future minimum annual lease commitments under noncancelable operating and capital leases were as follows:

(millions)	Operating leases	Capital leases
2007	$119.7	$ 2.1
2008	103.4	1.4
2009	85.9	1.3
2010	67.7	1.0
2011	49.8	.6
2012 and beyond	148.6	3.0
Total minimum payments	$575.1	$ 9.4
Amount representing interest		(1.6)
Obligations under capital leases		7.8
Obligations due within one year		(2.1)
Long-term obligations under capital leases		$ 5.7

One of the Company's subsidiaries is guarantor on loans to independent contractors for the purchase of DSD route franchises. At year-end 2006, there were total loans outstanding of $16.0 million to 517 franchisees. All loans are variable rate with a term of 10 years. Related to this arrangement, the Company has established with a financial institution a one-year renewable loan facility up to $17.0 million with a five-year term-out and servicing arrangement. The Company has the right to revoke and resell the route franchises in the event of default or any other breach of contract by franchisees. Revocations are infrequent. The Company's maximum potential future payments under these guarantees are limited to the outstanding loan principal balance plus unpaid interest. The estimated fair value of these guarantees is recorded in the Consolidated Balance Sheet and was insignificant for the periods presented.

The Company has provided various standard indemnifications in agreements to sell business assets and lease facilities over the past several years, related primarily to pre-existing tax, environmental, and employee benefit obligations. Certain of these indemnifications are limited by agreement in either amount and/or term and others are unlimited. The Company has also provided various "hold harmless" provisions within certain service type agreements. Because the Company is not currently aware of any actual exposures associated with these indemnifications, management is unable to estimate the maximum potential future payments to be made. At December 30, 2006, the Company had not recorded any liability related to these indemnifications.

Note 7 Debt

Notes payable at year-end consisted of commercial paper borrowings in the United States and to a lesser extent, bank loans and commercial paper of foreign subsidiaries at competitive market rates, as follows:

(dollars in millions)	2006		2005	
	Principal amount	Effective interest rate	Principal amount	Effective interest rate
U.S. commercial paper	$1,140.7	5.3%	$ 797.3	4.4%
Canadian commercial paper	87.5	4.4%	260.4	3.4%
Other	39.8		53.4	
	$1,268.0		$1,111.1	

Long-term debt at year end consisted primarily of issuances of fixed rate U.S. Dollar and floating rate Euro Notes, as follows:

(millions)	2006	2005
(a) 6.6% U.S. Dollar Notes due 2011	$1,496.2	$1,495.4
(a) 7.45% U.S. Dollar Debentures due 2031	1,087.8	1,087.3
(b) 4.49% U.S. Dollar Notes due 2006	—	75.0
(c) 2.875% U.S. Dollar Notes due 2008	464.6	464.6
(d) Guaranteed Floating Rate Euro Notes due 2007	722.1	650.6
Other	5.6	13.3
	3,776.3	3,786.2
Less current maturities	(723.3)	(83.6)
Balance at year-end	$3,053.0	$3,702.6

(a) In March 2001, the Company issued $4.6 billion of long-term debt instruments, primarily to finance the acquisition of Keebler Foods Company. The preceding table reflects the remaining principal amounts outstanding as of year-end 2006 and 2005. The effective interest rates on these Notes, reflecting issuance discount and swap settlement, were as follows: due 2011 – 7.08%; due 2031 – 7.62%. Initially, these instruments were privately placed, or sold outside the United States, in reliance on exemptions from registration under the Securities Act of 1933, as amended (the "1933 Act"). The Company then exchanged new debt securities for these initial debt instruments, with the new debt securities being substantially identical in all respects to the initial debt instruments, except for being registered under the 1933 Act. These debt securities contain standard events of default and covenants. The Notes due 2011 and the Debentures due 2031 may be redeemed in whole or in part by the Company at any time at prices determined under a formula (but not less than 100% of the principal amount plus unpaid interest to the redemption date).

(b) In November 2001, a subsidiary of the Company issued $375 million of five-year 4.49% fixed rate U.S. Dollar Notes to replace other maturing debt. These Notes were guaranteed by the Company and matured $75 million per year over the five-year term, with the final principal payment made in November 2006. These Notes, which were privately placed, contained standard warranties, events of default, and covenants. They also required the maintenance of a specified consolidated interest expense coverage ratio, and limited capital lease obligations and subsidiary debt. In conjunction with this issuance, the subsidiary of the Company entered into a $375 million notional US$/Pound Sterling currency swap, which effectively converted this debt into a 5.302% fixed rate Pound Sterling obligation for the duration of the five-year term.

(c) In June 2003, the Company issued $500 million of five-year 2.875% fixed rate U.S. Dollar Notes, using the proceeds from these Notes to replace maturing long-term debt. These Notes were issued under an existing shelf registration statement. The effective interest rate on these Notes, reflecting issuance discount and swap settlement, is 3.35%. The Notes contain customary covenants that limit the ability of the Company and its restricted subsidiaries (as defined) to incur certain liens or enter into certain sale and lease-back transactions. In December 2005, the Company redeemed $35.4 million of these Notes.

(d) In November 2005, a subsidiary of the Company (the "Borrower") issued Euro 550 million of Guaranteed Floating Rate Notes (the "Euro Notes") due May 2007. The Euro Notes were issued and sold in transactions outside the United States in reliance on exemptions from registration under the 1933 Act. The Euro Notes are guaranteed by the Company and bear interest at a rate of 0.12% per annum above three-month EURIBOR for each quarterly interest period. The Euro Notes contain customary covenants that limit the ability of the Company and its restricted subsidiaries (as defined) to incur certain liens or enter into certain sale and lease-back transactions. The Euro Notes were redeemable in whole or in part at par on interest payment dates or upon the occurrence of certain events in 2006 and 2007. In accordance with these terms, on January 31, 2007, the Borrower announced that it had exercised its right to call for early redemption all of the outstanding Euro Notes effective February 28, 2007, at a redemption price equal to the principal amount, plus accrued and unpaid interest through the redemption date.

At December 30, 2006, the Company had $2.2 billion of shortterm lines of credit, virtually all of which were unused and available for borrowing on an unsecured basis. These lines were comprised principally of an unsecured Five-Year Credit Agreement, which the Company entered into during November 2006 to replace an existing facility, which would have expired in 2009. The agreement allows the Company to borrow, on a revolving credit basis, up to $2.0 billion, to obtain letters of credit in an aggregate amount up to $75 million, and to provide a procedure for lenders to bid on short-term debt of the Company. The agreement contains customary covenants and warranties, including specified restrictions on indebtedness, liens, sale and leaseback transactions, and a specified interest coverage ratio. If an event of default occurs, then, to the extent permitted, the administrative agent may terminate the commitments under the credit facility, accelerate any outstanding loans, and demand the deposit of cash collateral equal to the lender's letter of credit exposure plus interest. The facility is available for general corporate purposes, including commercial paper back-up, although the

Company does not currently anticipate any usage under the facility.

Scheduled principal repayments on long-term debt are (in millions): 2007–$723.3; 2008–$466.1; 2009–$1.2; 2010 –$1.1; 2011–$1,500.5; 2012 and beyond–$1,100.2.

Interest paid was (in millions): 2006–$299; 2005–$295; 2004–$333. Interest expense capitalized as part of the construction cost of fixed assets was (in millions): 2006–$2.7; 2005–$1.2; 2004–$.9.

Subsequent events

As discussed in preceding subnote (d), on January 31, 2007, a subsidiary of the Company announced an early redemption, effective February 28, 2007, of Euro 550 million of Guaranteed Floating Rate Notes otherwise due May 2007. To partially refinance this redemption, the Company and two of its subsidiaries (the "Issuers") established a program under which the Issuers may issue euro-commercial paper notes up to a maximum aggregate amount outstanding at any time of $750 million or its equivalent in alternative currencies. The notes may have maturities ranging up to 364 days and will be senior unsecured obligations of the applicable Issuer. Notes issued by subsidiary Issuers will be guaranteed by the Company. The notes may be issued at a discount or may bear fixed or floating rate interest or a coupon calculated by reference to an index or formula.

In connection with these financing activities, the Company increased its short-term lines of credit from $2.2 billion at December 30, 2006 to approximately $2.6 billion, via a $400 million unsecured 364-Day Credit Agreement effective January 31, 2007. The 364-Day Agreement contains customary covenants, warranties, and restrictions similar to those described herein for the Five-Year Credit Agreement. The facility is available for general corporate purposes, including commercial paper back-up, although the Company does not currently anticipate any usage under the facility.

Note 8 Stock Compensation

The Company uses various equity-based compensation programs to provide long-term performance incentives for its global workforce. Currently, these incentives consist principally of stock options, and to a lesser extent, executive performance shares and restricted stock grants. The Company also sponsors a discounted stock purchase plan in the United States and matching-grant programs in several international locations. Additionally, the Company awards stock options and restricted stock to its outside directors. These awards are administered through several plans, as described within this Note.

The 2003 Long-Term Incentive Plan ("2003 Plan"), approved by shareholders in 2003, permits benefits to be awarded to employees and officers in the form of incentive and nonqualified stock options, performance units, restricted stock or restricted stock units, and stock appreciation rights. The 2003 Plan authorizes the issuance of a total of (a) 25 million shares plus (b) shares not issued under the 2001 Long-Term Incentive Plan, with no more than 5 million shares to be issued in satisfaction of performance units, performance based restricted shares and other awards (excluding stock options and stock appreciation rights), and with additional annual limitations on awards or payments to individual participants. At December 30, 2006, there were 15.0 million remaining authorized, but unissued, shares under the 2003 Plan. During the periods presented, specific awards and terms of those awards granted under the 2003 Plan are described in the following sections of this Note.

The Non-Employee Director Stock Plan ("Director Plan") was approved by shareholders in 2000 and allows each eligible non-employee director to receive 1,700 shares of the Company's common stock annually and annual grants of options to purchase 5,000 shares of the Company's common stock. At December 30, 2006, there were .4 million remaining authorized, but unissued, shares under this plan. Shares other than options are placed in the Kellogg Company Grantor Trust for Non-Employee Directors (the "Grantor Trust"). Under the terms of the Grantor Trust, shares are available to a director only upon termination of service on the Board. Under this plan, awards were as follows: 2006–50,000 options and 17,000 shares; 2005–55,000 options and 17,000 shares; 2004–55,000 options and 18,700 shares. Options granted to directors under this plan are included in the option activity tables within this Note.

The 2002 Employee Stock Purchase Plan was approved by shareholders in 2002 and permits eligible employees to purchase Company stock at a discounted price. This plan allows for a maximum of 2.5 million shares of Company stock to be issued at a purchase price equal to the lesser of 85% of the fair market value of the stock on the first or last day of the quarterly purchase period. Total purchases through this plan for any employee are limited to a fair market value of $25,000 during any calendar year. At December 30, 2006, there were 1.5 million remaining authorized, but unissued, shares under this plan. Shares were purchased by employees under this plan as follows (approximate number of shares): 2006–237,000; 2005–218,000; 2004–214,000. Options granted to employees to repurchase discounted stock under this plan are included in the option activity tables within this Note.

Additionally, during 2002, a foreign subsidiary of the Company established a stock purchase plan for its employees. Subject to limitations, employee contributions to this plan are matched 1:1 by the Company. Under this plan, shares were granted by the Company to match an approximately equal number of shares purchased by employees as follows (approximate number of shares): 2006–80,000; 2005–80,000; 2004–82,000.

The Executive Stock Purchase Plan was established in 2002 to encourage and enable certain eligible employees of the Company to acquire Company stock, and to align more closely the interests of those individuals and the Company's shareholders. This plan allows for a maximum of 500,000 shares of Company stock to be issued. At December 30, 2006, there were .5 million remaining authorized, but unissued, shares under this plan. Under this plan, shares were granted by the Company to executives in lieu of cash bonuses as follows (approximate number of shares): 2006–4,000; 2005–2,000; 2004–8,000.

For 2006, the Company used the fair value method prescribed by SFAS No. 123(R) "Share-Based Payment" to account for its equity-based compensation programs. Prior to 2006, the Company used the intrinsic value method prescribed by Accounting Principles Board Opinion (APB) No. 25 "Accounting for Stock Issued to Employees." Refer to Note 1 for further information on the Company's accounting policy for stock compensation.

For the year ended December 30, 2006, compensation expense for all types of equity-based programs and the related income tax benefit recognized was $95.7 million and $34.0 million, respectively. As a result of adopting SFAS No. 123(R) in 2006, the Company's reported pre-tax stock-based compensation expense for the year was $65.4 million higher (with net earnings and net earnings per share (basic and diluted) correspondingly lower by $42.4 million and $.11, respectively) than if it had continued to account for its equity-based programs under APB No. 25. Amounts for the prior years are presented in the following table in accordance with SFAS No. 123 "Accounting for Stock-Based Compensation" and related interpretations. Reported amounts consist principally of expense recognized for executive performance share and restricted stock awards; pro forma amounts are attributable primarily to stock option grants.

(millions, except per share data)	2005	2004
Stock-based compensation expense, pre-tax:		
As reported	$ 18.5	$ 17.5
Pro forma	$ 76.4	$ 64.1
Associated income tax benefit recognized:		
As reported	$ 6.7	$ 6.1
Pro forma	$ 27.7	$ 22.3
Stock-based compensation expense, net of tax:		
As reported	$ 11.8	$ 11.4
Pro forma	$ 48.7	$ 41.8
Net earnings:		
As reported	$980.4	$890.6
Pro forma	$943.5	$860.2
Basic net earnings per share:		
As reported	$ 2.38	$ 2.16
Pro forma	$ 2.29	$ 2.09
Diluted net earnings per share:		
As reported	$ 2.36	$ 2.14
Pro forma	$ 2.27	$ 2.07

As of December 30, 2006, total stock-based compensation cost related to nonvested awards not yet recognized was approximately $36 million and the weighted-average period over which this amount is expected to be recognized was approximately 1.4 years.

Cash flows realized upon exercise or vesting of stock-based awards in the periods presented are included in the following table. Within this table, the 2006 windfall tax benefit (amount realized in excess of that previously recognized in earnings) of $21.5 million represents the operating cash flow reduction (and financing cash flow increase) related to the Company's adoption of SFAS No. 123(R) in 2006. (Refer to Note 1 for further information on the Company's accounting policies regarding tax benefit windfalls and shortfalls.) Cash used by the Company to settle equity instruments granted under stock-based awards was insignificant.

(millions)	**2006**	2005	2004
Total cash received from option exercises and similar instruments	**$217.5**	$221.7	$291.8
Tax benefits realized upon exercise or vesting of stock-based awards:			
Windfall benefits classified as financing cash flow	**$ 21.5**	n/a	n/a
Other amounts classified as operating cash flow	**23.4**	40.3	38.6
Total	**$ 44.9**	$ 40.3	$ 38.6

Shares used to satisfy stock-based awards are normally issued out of treasury stock, although management is authorized to issue new shares to the extent permitted by respective plan provisions. Refer to Note 5 for information on shares issued during the periods presented to employees and directors under various long-term incentive plans and share repurchases under the Company's stock repurchase authorizations. The Company does not currently have a policy of repurchasing a specified number of shares issued under employee benefit programs during any particular time period.

Stock Options

During the periods presented, non-qualified stock options were granted to eligible employees under the 2003 Plan with exercise prices equal to the fair market value of the Company's stock on the grant date, a contractual term of ten years, and a two-year graded vesting period. Grants to outside directors under the Non-Employee Director Stock Plan included similar terms, but vested immediately. Additionally, "reload" options were awarded to eligible employees and directors to replace previously-owned

Company stock used by those individuals to pay the exercise price, including related employment taxes, of vested pre-2004 option awards containing this accelerated ownership feature. These reload options are immediately vested, with an expiration date which is the same as the original option grant.

Management estimates the fair value of each annual stock option award on the date of grant using a lattice-based option valuation model. Due to the already-vested status and short expected term of reload options, management uses a Black-Scholes model to value such awards. Composite assumptions, which are not materially different for each of the two models, are presented in the following table. Weighted-average values are disclosed for certain inputs which incorporate a range of assumptions. Expected volatilities are based principally on historical volatility of the Company's stock, and to a lesser extent, on implied volatilities from traded options on the Company's stock. For the lattice-based model, historical volatility corresponds to the contractual term of the options granted; whereas, for the Black-Scholes model, historical volatility corresponds to the expected term. The Company generally uses historical data to estimate option exercise and employee termination within the valuation models; separate groups of employees that have similar historical exercise behavior are considered separately for valuation purposes. The expected term of options granted (which is an input to the Black-Scholes model and an output from the lattice-based model) represents the period of time that options granted are expected to be outstanding; the weighted-average expected term for all employee groups is presented in the following table. The risk-free rate for periods within the contractual life of the options is based on the U.S. Treasury yield curve in effect at the time of grant.

Stock option valuation model assumptions for grants within the year ended:	2006	2005	2004
Weighted-average expected volatility	**17.94%**	22.00%	23.00%
Weighted-average expected term (years)	**3.21**	3.42	3.69
Weighted-average risk-free interest rate	**4.65%**	3.81%	2.73%
Dividend yield	**2.40%**	2.40%	2.60%
Weighed-average fair value of options granted	**$ 6.67**	$ 7.35	$ 6.39

A summary of option activity for the year ended December 30, 2006, is presented in the following table:

Employee and director stock options	Shares (millions)	Weighted-average exercise price	Weighted-average remaining contractual term (yrs.)	Aggregate intrinsic value (millions)
Outstanding, beginning of year	28.8	$38		
Granted	9.6	46		
Exercised	(10.9)	37		
Forfeitures	(.3)	43		
Expirations	(.2)	43		
Outstanding, end of year	27.0	$41	6.1	$243.0
Exercisable, end of year	19.9	$40	5.1	$199.0

Additionally, option activity for comparable prior-year periods is presented in the following table:

(millions, except per share data)	2005	2004
Outstanding, beginning of year	32.5	37.0
Granted	8.3	9.7
Exercised	(10.9)	(12.9)
Forfeitures and expirations	(1.1)	(1.3)
Outstanding, end of year	28.8	32.5
Exercisable, end of year	21.3	22.8
Weighted-average exercise price:		
Outstanding, beginning of year	$ 35	$ 33
Granted	44	40
Exercised	34	32
Forfeitures and expirations	41	41
Outstanding, end of year	$ 38	$ 35
Exercisable, end of year	$ 37	$ 35

The total intrinsic value of options exercised during the periods presented was (in millions): 2006–$114; 2005–$116; 2004–$119.

Other stock-based awards During the periods presented, other stock-based awards consisted principally of executive performance shares and restricted stock granted under the 2003 Plan.

In 2005 and 2006, the Company granted performance shares to a limited number of senior executive-level employees, which entitled these employees to receive a specified number of shares of the Company's common stock on the vesting date, provided cumulative three-year net sales growth targets were achieved. Subsequent to the adoption of SFAS No. 123(R), management has estimated the fair value of performance share awards based on the market price of the underlying stock on the date of grant, reduced by the present value of estimated dividends foregone during the performance period. The 2005 and 2006

target grants (as revised for non-vested forfeitures and other adjustments) currently correspond to approximately 275,000 and 260,000 shares, respectively; each with a grant-date fair value of approximately $41 per share. The actual number of shares issued on the vesting date could range from zero to 200% of target, depending on actual performance achieved. Based on the market price of the Company's common stock at year-end 2006, the maximum future value that could be awarded on the vesting date is (in millions): 2005 award–$27.5; 2006 award–$25.8. In addition to these performance share plans, a 2003 performance unit plan (payable in stock or cash under certain conditions) was settled at 74% of target in February 2006 for a total dollar equivalent of $2.9 million. The Company also periodically grants restricted stock and restricted stock units to eligible employees under the 2003 Plan. Restrictions with respect to sale or transferability generally lapse after three years and the grantee is normally entitled to receive shareholder dividends during the vesting period. Management estimates the fair value of restricted stock grants based on the market price of the underlying stock on the date of grant. A summary of restricted stock activity for the year ended December 30, 2006, is presented in the following table:

Employee restricted stock and restricted stock units	Shares (thousands)	Weighted-average grant-date fair value
Non-vested, beginning of year	447	$39
Granted	190	47
Vested	(176)	34
Forfeited	(27)	43
Non-vested, end of year	434	$45

Grants of restricted stock and restricted stock units for comparable prior-year periods were: 2005–141,000; 2004–140,000.

The total fair value of restricted stock and restricted stock units vesting in the periods presented was (in millions): 2006–$8; 2005–$4; 2004–$4.

Note 9 Pension Benefits

The Company sponsors a number of U.S. and foreign pension plans to provide retirement benefits for its employees. The majority of these plans are funded or unfunded defined benefit plans, although the Company does participate in a few multiemployer or other defined contribution plans for certain employee groups. Defined benefits for salaried employees are generally based on salary and years of service, while union employee benefits are generally a negotiated amount for each year of service. The Company uses its fiscal year end as the measurement date for its defined benefit plans.

Obligations and funded status

The aggregate change in projected benefit obligation, plan assets, and funded status is presented in the following tables. The Company adopted SFAS No. 158 "Employers'

Photo Credits